D0151280

Victorian Plays

Recent Titles in
Bibliographies and Indexes in the Performing Arts

Memorable Film Characters: An Index to Roles and Performers, 1915-1983
Susan Lieberman and Frances Cable, compilers

Stage Lives: A Bibliography and Index to Theatrical Biographies in English
George B. Bryan, compiler

The Federal Theatre Project: A Catalog-Calendar of Productions
Compiled by the Staff of the Fenwick Library, George Mason University

Victorian Plays

A Record of Significant Productions on the London Stage, 1837-1901

Compiled by DONALD MULLIN

Bibliographies and Indexes in the Performing Arts, Number 4

GREENWOOD PRESS
New York • Westport, Connecticut • London

Library of Congress Cataloging-in-Publication Data

Mullin, Donald C.
Victorian plays.

(Bibliographies and indexes in the performing arts,
ISSN 0742-6933 ; no. 4)
Bibliography: p.
Includes index.
1. Theater—England—London—History—19th century.
2. London (England)—Intellectual life—19th century.
I. Title. II. Series: Bibliographies and indexes in
the performing arts ; no. 4.
PN2596.L6M85 1987 792'.09421 86-25718
ISBN 0-313-24211-9 (lib. bdg. : alk. paper)

Library of Congress Catalog Card Number: 86-25718
ISBN: 0-313-24211-9
ISSN: 0742-6933

First published in 1987

Greenwood Press, Inc.
88 Post Road West, Westport, Connecticut 06881

Printed in the United States of America

The paper used in this book complies with the Permanent Paper Standard issued by the National Information Standards Organization (Z39.48-1984).

10 9 8 7 6 5 4 3 2 1

for

Patrick Carroll

CONTENTS

PREFACE

If all the information which is available concerning play-titles and cast-lists of the London theatre in the Victorian period were to be printed, the result would require perhaps ten or more volumes this size. In order to make a one-volume work possible it is necessary to accept certain restrictions and condensations. A partial work of this type can mislead the user if restrictions are not understood, but it can be a useful tool if the limitations are taken into account.

Play-titles, playwrights and cast lists are taken, for the most part, from original playbills with some filling-in provided from other sources when original playbills are not available. As a consequence there are numerous differences in spelling of titles and names from one listing to another. The printing of playbills appears to have been at best a casual business for the first two-thirds of the century, and reasonable accuracy in spelling of names can be assumed only for the last quarter of the century. In cases where the differences may appear obvious to the reader, no change has been made in transcription. Only those names which may be confusing have attention drawn to them by the addition of a following "[sic]."

Play-titles are limited to "legitimate" plays of recognized varieties: tragedies, comedies, and farces, or combinations of these; "comediettas" are listed as comedies. I do not include amateur performances, burlesques, travesties, sketches, operas, or operettas, in order to reduce the vast number of entertainments to reasonable size as well as to limit the listings to those of interest to students of drama. Under each listing it is the first performance within the Victorian era that is given, when possible, or another very close to it which includes the original cast. In order to economize space, subsequent performances of "runs" are not noted, but revivals in which performers of interest appeared are given in many instances. In particular, performances of the popular and regularly revived "Standard Plays" and plays by several of the greater playwrights are listed at length precisely to illustrate the types of parts taken by various players. Thus, while John Doe performing the part of "Pinchbeck" in Eliza's Escape may not mean much to the modern reader, his performance as "2nd Witch" in Macbeth may better illustrate his "line" of parts in a more informative manner.

While a listing of the titles of all dramatic pieces given in London during the period is not attempted, all the legitimate plays given in the most widely known source, The Stage Cyclopaedia: a Bibliography of Plays, compiled by Reginald Clarence for The Stage in 1909, have been included, with corrections made where more accurate data have been found. A few differences will be found between some items provided here and in Allardyce Nicholl's Alphabetical Catalogue of Plays, Volume Six of his monumental History of English Drama, 1660-1900, which arise from differences in original playbills.

Theatres are not listed in any regular order but rather are given chronologically from the first noted performance of the play under which each appears, with subsequent performances at the same theatre following. Thus, the first theatre listed after a play-title will be the first one at which the play was performed, while the second theatre is the second one, and so forth. In order to avoid unnecessary confusion and multiple listings of theatre-names, as well as to enable the student to follow through performances at a single theatre, all subsequent performances at a theatre follow after the first listing. The substance of this arrangement becomes apparent on examination of the listings after a play-title.

For much of the century many actors and actresses were listed only by surname, with the addition of "Mr.," "Mrs." or "Miss," as appropriate. It was usual for the senior member of the family--the first to appear on the stage--to be listed by surname alone, without initials or given-name. As others with the same surname appeared, distinguishing initials or given-names would be used by the late-comers or lesser figures. Thus, "Mr. Webster" is always Benjamin Webster, and all other members of the family are distinguished by initial or first-name. When possible it was preferred for actors and actresses to have a unique stage-name, one not carried by any other living performer. If the surname was shared by another, initials or first-names were given for later, junior, or lesser performers in order to distinguish them. As a surname was no longer used by a living performer it was then free to be taken by another—sometimes distinguished and sometimes not, a matter of some confusion to the modern scholar. For example, "Miss Vincent" was the identification employed by both Eliza Vincent and Annette Vincent, the latter following the former, with no indication on playbills of the moment when one career left off and the other began. Likewise, "Mr. Strickland" was used both by Robert Strickland and William Strickland, and the numerous individual male members of the Barnett and Barrett families frequently were referred to simply as "Mr." In cases where distinction is difficult to make I have taken the liberty of using my own judgement and am open to correction.

Where playbills list only surnames and the full name of the performer is certain or in little doubt, I have taken the liberty of adding the first name in order to make references easier for the reader to follow. Thus, "Mr. Webster" is not given and "Benjamin Webster" is substituted. This policy is general but not absolute, not being employed in the cases of a few performers who were and remain known by surname alone, such as Mme. Celeste, Mme. Vestris, and Mrs. Stirling. No other performers with those names appeared on the Victorian stage.

Cast lists always include all principal players when known. "Walking Ladies" and "Walking Gentlemen," or what we would now refer to as "bit-players," are omitted unless the cast-list is very short or unless the bit-player subsequently became a figure of interest or importance. Thus, the first appearances in bit parts of Ellen Terry and Marie Wilton, for example, are noted as exceptions to the general rule. As the majority of plays were written by male playwrights, and the Victorians being what they were, male parts far exceed female parts. In order to strike some reasonable balance I have therefore tended to include more female players, even if they were of lesser consequence, than male.

Even though the names of most minor male performers, and some minor female ones, are omitted, there are still a great number of actor and actress names included in this single volume. No pretense is made of listing all the persons who worked on the London stage during the period, but, with those provided, a large and useful array of personalities may be studied. Some scene-designers and other personnel also are given if listed on the original playbill but not otherwise, and names are as originally given.

In order to aid in condensation, character names are also abbreviated. In most cases, the male character last-name and the female character first-name are given, while titled and military characters have title or rank listed as well. This accords with the normal manner in which such characters would be identified in dialogue on stage. When two or more characters have the same surname, their first-names are also given in order to distinguish them.

Within the limits of this book it is not possible to provide an alphabetical list of players for ready reference, a lack which is as regretted as it is noticeable. A succeeding work, Victorian Performers: A Roster of Actors and Actresses on the London Stage, 1837-1901, is in preparation in order to satisfy what seems to me to be a need, and should be in press in 1988.

ABBREVIATIONS

a	act (as in 1a, 2a, etc.)
adap.	adapted
Adm.	Admiral
alt.	alternate
Amer.	American
D	Drama
C	Comedy
Capt.	Captain
CD	Comedy-Drama
Col.	Colonel
Com.	Commodore
D	Drama
Dan.	Danish
Dut.	Dutch
Elec.	Electrics
F	Farce
F	French (as in fr F)
FC	Farce-Comedy
Fr.	Father (religious)
fr	from
G	German
Gen.	General
Ital.	Italian
Jap.	Japanese
Lt.	Lieutenant
Maj.	Major
n.a.	not attributed
Norw.	Norwegian
P	Play
POW	Prince of Wales's Theatre
Pro	Prologue
prod.	producer (director)
Rus.	Russian
Sad. Wells	Sadler's Wells Theatre
Subt.	subtitled
T	Tragedy

THEATRES

Plays produced at the following theatres are listed in this book:

Adelphi
Alexandra
Alfred (Marylebone)
Alhambra
Aquarium (Imperial)
Astley's Amphitheatre
Athenaeum
Avenue
Britannia
City of London
Comedy
Court
Covent Garden
Criterion
Daly's
Drury Lane
Duke's (Holborn)
Duke of York's
Elephant and Castle
Folly (Charing Cross)
Gaiety
Gallery of Illustration
Garrick
Globe
Grand
Grecian (Grecian Saloon)
Haymarket
Her Majesty's
Holborn (Duke's)
Imperial
Lyceum
Lyric
Marylebone (Royal Alfred) (West London)
Matinée (St. George's Hall)
Mirror
Novelty
Olympic
Opera Comique
Park (Alexandra)
Pavilion
Prince of Wales's
Prince's
Princess's
Queen's
Royalty
Sadler's Wells
St. George's Hall (Matinée)
St. James's
Savoy
Shaftesbury
Standard
Strand
Surrey
Terry's
Toole's
Trafalgar Square (Duke of York's)
Vaudeville
Victoria
West London (Marylebone)
Wyndham's

ACKNOWLEDGMENTS

I wish to acknowledge with gratitude the support given to preparation of this book by the University of Guelph through award of a Donald Forster Fellowship.

INTRODUCTION

It is manifest that a one-volume work on a subject as large as this one is must be limited and partial. At present, there is no book in which one may find extensive information concerning plays and players on the London stage, 1837-1901, a lack as irritating as it is lamentable. A work of this kind, even condensed to fit into a single volume, may provide a reasonable amount of information of a kind normally required, and thus offer insights which might not otherwise be obtained.

Even from a limited work a large variety of things is available for discovery, and a few examples may suffice to illustrate this fact. The lack of success of Edwin Booth's later appearances on the London stage has frequently been attributed to the professional incompetence of his supporting casts, thus lessening the effect of this major American player. A cursory examination of this book will show that in each case, he was supported by players of wide experience and by some of considerable and long-applauded skill at a variety of theatres. In addition, some plays and some players beloved of critics and historians are shown to have obtained only a minor place in the stream of Victorian theatre, affecting few and effecting little. Some plays passed over entirely by students of the drama had an enormous and continuing success, while others considered of greater literary consequence had relatively little impact on theatre-going audiences, evidenced by a lack of revival. A growth of awareness in the "polite" audience concerning serious drama is usually given as characteristic of the end of the century, indicating both an elevation of taste and less of a preoccupation with "mere entertainment." Although this work does not proceed beyond the death of Victoria, it is apparent that the "popular" theatre remained popular and that the "serious" theatre was restricted to a few coterie playhouses, frequently given in only a few matinee performances. It took the new entertainment medium of film, a very few years later, to satisfy popular taste at a fraction of the cost, and to permanently change the course of play-going and production. Further, even Americans may be unaware how few seasons went by without some American actor of consequence appearing on the London stage, and occasionally there were several, perhaps giving to London audiences a generally greater and more continuing impression of American talent and dramatic standard than is usually noted. In addition, one may readily determine the method by which many Victorian dramatists acquired their theatrical skills merely by noting those who appeared as actors and actresses at various times in their careers. Some, indeed, managed both, maintaining success as playwrights and actors over a lifetime. It is, in fact, astonishing to note how many actors also wrote plays which were produced; the number of them seems to be greater than "literary" playwrights.

It will be noticed almost at once that minor theatres and the plays produced in them occupy a much larger share of space than the major ones, and, as a result, less well known players are listed more frequently than many a noted star; Henry Howe is mentioned about ten times as frequently as William Charles Macready, for example, just as the Olympic Theatre appears more frequently than Covent Garden Theatre. In the latter case it must be recalled that Covent Garden was converted into the Royal Italian Opera House in 1847, thus eliminating an historic playhouse from the list of dramatic theatres. The preponderance of minor theatre listings reflects the necessities of the time, when the lesser theatres, with fewer resources and with actors of lesser renown, were required to change their bills with considerably greater frequency than was necessary at the major houses in order to attract patrons. The listings of plays and players is greater as a consequence.

The appetite of a minor theatre for new plays was voracious, but from where were new plays obtained? Sometimes it was sufficient to re-title or rewrite a previously successful piece, and one may find in the following pages many familiar characters under unfamiliar play titles or a mixture of odd character names under a familiar title or variant. Plays could be stolen from competitors, as well, for it was common practice even in the eighteenth century to send a spy to a new play at a competing playhouse, and having him note down as accurately as possible all the dialogue spoken on the stage, thus providing a fair copy for his employer to use for his own purposes. The mistakes which arose from this practice are frequently amusing, as the copiest transcribed phonetically the names he heard spoken. Where copying could not supply the requirements, actors who had some literary capability were encouraged to write new pieces, although, more frequently than not, the majority of these were adaptations of familiar stories and types rather than entirely original works. Naturally the actor-playwright was principally interested in writing scenes that "worked" on the stage and which provided him or her with a juicy part as well as the manager with a script. Many a now-forgotten play served as excellent amusement for audiences of the time who looked upon the theatre then much as we look upon television today—as a diversion more than as an intellectual stimulant, even as superior intellectual quality was admired when it did appear. After all, first things first.

From almost the beginning of the Victorian period through to its end the French stage provided an unending source of new scripts, sometimes credited to their original playwrights but more often simply adapted to the English stage without any acknowledgement. Without the French vaudeville, in particular, to steal from, many a London manager would have lacked the quantity of fare necessary to keep his audiences amused. Even later in the century, when native dramatists of recognized literary quality once again began to emerge, the Continental stage was routinely plundered for new scripts in order to supply the ever-increasing number of playhouses—but later translations or adaptations were usually credited to their original authors.

It is interesting to note as well the changes in society reflected in the fare provided. For the more "polite" audiences, plays for most of the Victorian period were filled with titled characters, or at the least with monied middle-classes. For theatres whose patrons consisted mainly of local audiences of lesser station, dramas portraying the affairs of lesser persons were more popular. "Ordinary" persons, who were neither Irish, abused laborers, children, nor women (nor the peculiar French), are really only characteristic of the last quarter of the century, when "social conciousness" can be seen to intrude slowly into playhouses both high and low. For the English middle-class no other worlds seem to have existed except those of the upper-class, to envy and emulate, and the middle-class, to provide self-satisfaction.

The large number of short plays may puzzle the reader at first, as petit dramas hold little interest for modern audiences. It may be recalled that in the earlier part of the nineteenth century the bill-of-fare was a long one, and theatres tended to provide an evening of entertainment which would last from five to six hours. The "main piece," be it Shakespeare or a 5-act domestic drama, would be followed by shorter pieces, the fare growing more light in tone as the evening progressed. Thus, 2-act or 3-act farces were a staple. It was not until well after mid-century that the evening's bill shortened as the fashionable dinner-hour was put later. Then, the main-piece would require the major part of the evening, followed perhaps by the traditional farce or other entertainment. Later still, the late-comer from even later dinners had to be accommodated by pushing the main piece to last, providing short pieces, or "curtain-raisers," at the beginning of the evening rather than at the end. As a significant portion of theatre-goers returned to their suburbs by train, the evening's length was fixed by train schedules. For these reasons, one-act plays were important to the evenings's entertainment in a way unknown today, and it was not unusual for major playwrights to write them and major players to appear in them.

Even as one examines the large number of play-titles given, the condensed nature of this book must also be remembered. Together with the plays given here—the "legitimate" drama—there is an equal number of unlisted musical pieces, pantomimes, extravaganzas, operas, and operettas, as well as numerous entertaining "bits" of undetermined type.

In time one hopes to find a more extensive record of the kind offered here, which will provide for the nineteenth century what is now available for most of the eighteenth century: a complete listing cf all entertainments and of those who performed in them. The amount of available material is so great, however, that such a project can only be a life-time's work on the part of many persons. One awaits such a valuable reference with patience. Meanwhile, it is hoped that this stop-gap and admittedly limited work will serve some useful purpose.

PRODUCTION RECORD: PLAYS A-Z

A.S.S.// F 1a// J. M. Maddox// **Lyceum,** May 1853, with Frank Matthews as Hunter, William Suter as Smiggles, J.G. Rosiere as Adolphus, Mrs. Macnamara as Mrs. Hunter, Miss Wyndham as Sophia/ **Princess's,** Feb. 1861, with Frank Matthews as Hunter, Henry Saker as Sniggles, James Cathcart as Adolphus, Mrs. Weston as Mrs. Hunter, Rose Leclercq as Sophia.

ABBÉ VAUDREUIL; OR, THE COURT OF LOUIS XV// D// H. R. Addison// **Lyceum,** Mar. 1860, with Mme. Celeste as Abbé Vaudreuil, Frederick Villiers as Lt. Delcour, Miss Hudspeth as Marie de Rohan, Henry Butler as Louis XV, Mr. Palmer as Richelieu, Mr. Regan as de Beaumont, William S. Fredericks as Voltaire, J. H. White as Buffon, Kate Saville as Pompadour, Miss Holbroke as Marquise de Chevreuse, Miss Hunt as Mme. de Haussez/ Scenery by William Callcott.

ABD EL KADER, THE NAPOLEON OF THE DESERT; OR, THE SEIGE OF CONSTANTINE// D 3a// C. A. Somerset// **Sad. Wells,** Aug. 1842, with W. D. Broadfoot as Marshal Beaumont, Charles Fenton as Capt. Brissat, Henry Widdicomb as Lt. Sarron, Lionel Rayner as Corp. Bernard, Mr. Hillier as Abd el Kader, C. J. Smith as Hafer, Mr. Dry as Kalfas, Mr. Harwood as Bamboochi, John Herbert as Quabbo, Mrs. Hillier as Lady Beaumont, Mrs. Richard Barnett as Linetta, Mrs. Stickney as Felimah/ Scenery by T. Pitt & G. Smithyes Jr./ Machines by Mr. Cawdery/ Prod. by W. D. Broadfoot.

ABD EL KADER THE ARAB CHIEF; OR, THE WARRIOR OF ALGIERS// D// n.a.// **Victoria,** Feb. 1848, with John Dale as Said el Kalm, N. T. Hicks as Abd el Kader, Mr. Henderson as Mustapha, Mrs. George Lee as Si Haid, Mr. Lambe as Hamed, James Howard as Jocko, F. H. Henry as Abderrahman, Charles Morelli as Artaud, William Searle as Simkins, Mr. Fitzjames as Duke D'Aumale, T. H. Higgie as Col. St. Arnould, Mrs. N. T. Hicks as Adeline, Annette Vincent as Jacquette, Miss Burroughcliffe as Bidet/ Prod. by T. H. Higgie.

ABBOT OF ST. PAUL'S AND THE THIRTEENTH CHIME, THE; OR, THE SENTINEL AND THE HOUR// D 3a// n.a.// **Victoria,** July 1857, with Mr. Morrison as Sir Mark, Samuel Sawford as de Lancy, Mr. Henderson as Capt. Leslie, W. H. Pitt as Lisle, J. H. Rickards as Cyprian, Charles Rice as Peculate, Mrs. Robert Honner as Sybil, Miss Laporte as Maude, Mrs. Alfred Saville as Marian.

ABEL DRAKE// D 5a// Tom Taylor & John Saunders// **Princess's,** Jan. 1874, with David Fisher as Wolcombe, J. H. Barnes as Lancelot, John Clayton as Abel Drake, J. R. Crauford as Sgt. Leary, F. W. Irish as Job, Mrs. St. Henry as Mrs. Wolcombe, Mrs. C. H. Stephenson as Mrs. Giffard, Rose Coghlan as Barbara/ Scenery by Mr. Maugham.

ABELARD AND HELOISE// D 3a// J. B. Buckstone// **Victoria,** Sept. 1850, with E. F. Saville as Abelard, Henry Frazer as Fulbert, Mr. Lyon as Larenaudie, Mrs. E. F. Saville as Augustin, G. F. Forman as Maximilian, Robert Honner as Samson, Mr. Henderson as Gautier, Mrs. Robert Honner as Heloise, Eliza Terrey as Josette, Mrs. Cooke as Abbess/ **Olympic,** July 1852, with Charles Diddear as Fulbert, E. F. Edgar as Larenaudie, Isabel Adams as Augustin, Alfred Sanger as Barnaby, Henry Compton as Maximilian, E. Clifton as Samson, William Farren Jr. as Abelard, John Kinloch as Gautier, Charles Bender as Bernard, Mrs. Walter Lacy as Heloise, Mrs. Alfred Phillips as Jocette, Mrs. B. Bartlett as Beatrice.

ABOUT TOWN// C 3a// Arthur à Beckett// **Court,** May. 1873.

ABOVE AND BELOW// C 2a// Edward Stirling// **Lyceum,** July 1846, with Charles Diddear as Dorville, Alfred Wigan as St. Cloud, Mr. Bellingham as Thomas, John Kinloch as Notary, C. Bender as Herman, Drinkwater Meadows as Sans Souci, Miss Fairbrother as Cecile, Ellen Turner as Louise, Frank Matthews as Landré, Robert Keeley as Poisson, Henry Butler as Leonard, Ellen Daly as Lelot/ Scenery by P. Phillips & Mr. Hawthorn/ Machines by Mr. Stribley.

ABOVE AND BELOW// F 1a// n.a.// **Princess's,** Dec. 1847, with Henry Compton as Frank, Emma Stanley as Fanny.

ABOVE SUSPICION// D 3a// George Capel// **Sad. Wells,** Mar. 1884.

ABSENCE OF MIND; OR, WANTED, £5// C 1a// Adap. by William Poel fr G of August von Kotzebue// **Olympic,** July 1884.

ABSENT MAN, THE// C 1a// George Roberts// **Holborn,** 1870, with Arthur Wood, Annie Merton.

ABSENTEE, THE// C// W. Bayle Bernard// **Haymarket,** May 1844, with Mr. Tilbury as Sir Patrick, Henry Holl as Macarthy, Mr. Leonard as Lurgan, Julia Bennett as Norah, Miss Carre as Katy.

ABYSS OF THORNS, THE// D// Adolphe Faucquez// **Grecian,** June 1862, with George Clair as Abbe Francois, William James as Adolphe, J. H. Rickards as Jacques, Charles Mortimer as de Lisle, Jane Coveney as Suzanne, Jane Dawson as Mme. de Besanville, Miss Johnstone as Sophie, Ellen Hale as Julie, Amilie Conquest as Adelle.

ABYSSINIAN WAR, THE// D 2a// William Travers// **Britannia,** June 1868.

ACCUSING SPIRIT, THE; OR, THE THREE TRAVELLERS OF THE TYROL// D 3a// W. E. Suter// **Grecian,** Mar. 1860.

ACROBAT, THE// D 4a// (a vers. of Belphegor) Adap. by Wilson Barrett fr F of A. P. Dennery & Marc Fournier// **Olympic,** Apr. 1891, with Wilson Barrett as Belphegor, Winifred Emery as Madeline, Edie King as Henri, Pollie Smith as Jeannette, George Barrett as Flip Flap, Austin Melford as Duke de Montbazon, W. A. Elliott as Count de Blangy, H. Cooper Cliffe as Lavarennes, Horace Hodges as Viscount Hercule, Ambrose Manning as Viscount D'Arpignol, T. W. Percyval as Marquis de Courgemont, Edward Irwin as Gen. Pomtiere, Lily Hanbury as Mme. Catherine, Mrs. Henry Leigh as Mlle. de Vermandois, Alice Gambier as Therese/ Scenery by Walter Hann & Stafford Hill/ Music by Michael Connolly.

ACROSS HER PATH// Play 4a// Dram. by Annie Irish fr novel of Annie Swan// **Globe**, Jan. 1890, with Oscar Ayde as Sir Adrian, Henry Pagden as Leigh, George Arliss as Markham, George Belmore as Johnson, Josephine St. Ange as Lady Severne, T. Roma as Frances, Roma le Thiere as Lady Bassett, Mrs. E. H. Brooke as Elspeth, Annie Irish as Barbara/ Prod. by W. H. Vernon.

ACROSS THE CONTINENT// D Pro & 3a// James McCloskey// **Alfred**, July 1871.

ACTOR'S RETREAT, THE// F 1a// Andrew Halliday & William Brough// **Adelphi**, Aug. 1864.

ACTRESS BY DAYLIGHT, AN// Charles Reade// **St. James's**, Apr. 1871.

ACTRESS OF PADUA, THE// D 4a// Dram. by John Brougham fr F of Victor Hugo, Angelo.// **Haymarket**, May 1855, with Henry Howe as Malapiere, William Farren as Rodolpho, George Braid as Anafesto, Mr. Rogers as Omodei, Edwin Villiers as Taska, Miss Reynolds as Catarina, Charlotte Cushman as Tisbe/ **Sad. Wells**, Apr. 1856, with E. F. Edgar as Malapiere, Henry Vincent as Rodolfo, William Swanborough as Anafesto, George Cooke as Omodei, C. Kelsey as Taska, Charlotte Cushman as Tisbe, Miss Anderson as Catarina, Emma Barnett as Reginella, Julia Craven as Dafne.

ADA THE BETRAYED; OR, THE MURDER AT THE OLD SMITHY// D 3a// n.a.// **Victoria**, Aug. 1857, with S. Sawford as Learment, H. Dudley as Britton, J. H. Rickards as Gray, Charles Rice as Spikes, W. H. Pitt as Hartleton, Angelina Bathurst as Ada, Miss Laporte as Bridget, Mrs. E. F. Saville as Mad Maud.

ADAM BEDE// D 3a// Dram. by J. E. Carpenter fr novel of George Eliot// **Surrey**, Feb. 1862.

ADAM BUFF; OR, THE MAN WITHOUT A SHIRT// F 1a// E. L. Blanchard// **Surrey**, Mar. 1850.

ADELAIDE// Play 1a// Adap. fr G of Gustav Hein & Davis Bispham// **Matinee**, June 1898.

ADELGITHA; OR, THE CAVE OF THE SHRINE OF ST. HILDA// D// G. H. Lewis// **Sad. Wells**, Nov. 1837, with Mr. King as Emperor Michael, Mr. Wilkins as Guiscard, Mr. Scarbrow as Alciphron, Mr. Russell as Decetus, Mr. George as Rainulph, Mr. Pateman as Julian, C. H. Pitt as Lothair, Mr. Wilson as Tancred, Miss Williams as Adelgitha, Miss Vernon as Imma, Mrs. Worrell as Claudia.

ADELMORN THE OUTLAW// D// M. G. Lewis// **Sad. Wells**, Dec. 1843, with Mr. Dry as Emperor Sigismund, Henry Marston as Adelmorn, C.J. Bird as Count Ulrick, Mr. Coreno as Lodovick, Mr. Williams as Hugo, Miss Stephens as Herman, C. Fenton as Bruno, Caroline Rankley as Imogine, Mrs. Richard Barnett as Orelia, Miss Cooke as Reda.

ADMIRAL BENBOW// D 3a// n.a.// **Surrey**, Apr. 1838/ **Victoria**, Oct. 1854, with Alfred Saville as Adm. Benbow, Mr. Cohen as Capt. Wade, Mr. Hitchinson as Capt. Kirby, R. H. Kitchen as Capt. Hudson, Mr. Bradley as Lt. Galliot, N. T. Hicks as Ellinford, W. H. Pitt as Ismael, Mr. Morrison as Rollquid, F. H. Henry as Omai, Mrs. Henry Vining as Rosa, Miss Laporte as Cleopatra.

ADMIRAL GUINEA// Play 4a// W. H. Henley & R. L. Stevenson// **Avenue**, Nov. 1897, with William Mollison as Gaunt, Sydned Valentine as Pew, Robert Loraine as French, Dolores Drummond as Mrs. Drake, Cissie Loftus as Arethusa.

ADMIRAL SAM; OR, DEEDS OF OLD LONDON// D 3a// J. B. Johnstone// **Victoria**, Feb. 1848, with Mr. Henderson as Col. Walton, John Dale as Walton, F. H. Henry as Grayson, William Searle as Kitely, Mr. Fitzjames as Blake, Mr. Morelli as Butler, Mr. Forman as Brand, James W. Howard as Count Nobody, N. T. Hicks as Steady, Miss Burroughcliffe as Frank, Mrs. George Lee as Mabel, Mrs. N. T. Hicks as Bella, Mrs. Cooke as Babet.

ADMIRAL TOM, KING OF THE BUCCANNEERS// D// William Travers// **Britannia**, Sept. 1868.

ADOPTED CHILD, THE; OR, THE FISHERMAN OF MILFORD FERRY// D 2a// Samuel Birch// **Drury Lane**, May 1837, with Charles Diddear as Sir Bertram, Paul Bedford as Le Sage, George Bartley as Michael, Drinkwater Meadows as Record, A. Brindal as Spruce, F.H. Henry as Flint, Miss Marshall as Boy, Mrs. Humby as Lucy, Mrs. Charles Jones as Nell/ **Sad. Wells**, Mar. 1838, with Mr. Ranson as Sir Bertrand, Mr. James as Record, Mr. Gay as Le Sage, Mr. Nunn as Spruce, Miss Chartley as Adopted Child, Stephen Smith as Flint, David Osbaldiston as Michael, Miss Beresford as Clara, Miss Watkins as Nell, Eliza Pitt as Lucy, Miss Young as Jeanette/ **Princess's**, Aug. 1845, with Henry Lynne as Sir Bertram, F.C. Courtney as Le Sage, Mr. Granby as Record, J.W. Wallack as Michael, Augustus Harris as Spruce, James Ranoe as Flint, Miss E. Honner as Clara, Miss Sumers as Lucy, Mrs. John Brougham as Nell; Dec. 1852, with G. Everett as Sir Bertram, Mr. Graham as Le Sage, Drinkwater Meadows as Record, George Bartley as Michael, John Chester as Spruce, Mr. Terry as Flint, Kate Terry as Boy, Miss Daly as Clara, Miss Vivash as Jeannette, Carlotta Leclercq as Lucy, Mrs. W. Daly as Nelly.

ADOPTION// F 1a// Richard Butler ("Richard Henry") & H. Chance Newton// **Toole's**, May 1890, with Compton Coutts as Blockle, Reginald

Stockton as Theodosius, Alfred Balfour as Glumber, Cicely Richards as Barbara, Marie Illington as Constantia, Mary Jocelyn as Whisker.

ADRIENNE; OR, THE SECRET OF A LIFE// D 3a// H. T. Leslie// **Lyceum**, Nov. 1860, with George Vining as Eugene de Grassac, Henry Neville as Victor Savignie, Mr. Clifford as Hermann, John Rouse as Falloux, Frederick Villiers as Bertrand, James Johnstone as Scarotta, Henry Butler as Rochet, Mme. Celeste as Adrienne de Beaupré, Mrs. John Rouse as Mme. de Beaupré, Mrs. Keeley as Gianetta/ Scenery by William Callcott/ Music by George Loder/ Machines by Mr. Bare.

ADRIENNE LECOUVREUR// D 5a// Adap. fr F of Eugène Scribe & Ernest Legouvé// **Adelphi**, Aug. 1862, with J. L. Toole as Michonnet, John Billington as Maurice, John Sefton as Duke d'Aumont, David Fisher as Abbé Chazeuil, C. H. Stephenson as Quinalt, W. H. Eburne as Poisson, Avonia Jones as Adrienne, Mrs. Billington as Princess de Bouillon, Kate Bland as Mlle. Danozeville/ **Globe**, Feb. 1890, with Fred Terry as Maurice de Saxe, Gerald Maxwell as Prince de Bouillon, S. H. Basing as Abbé Chazeuil, H. A. Forde as Poisson, Walter Shaw as Quinault, Miss Vane as Princess de Bouillon, Miss J. Earle as Marquise de Sancerre, Violet Armbruster as Countess de Beauveau, Ellen Wallis as Adrienne, Adrienne Dairolles as Mlle. Jouvent.

ADRIENNE LECOUVREUR// D 5a// Adap. by Henry Herman fr F of Eugène Scribe & Ernest Legouvé, Adrienne Lecouvreur// **Court**, Nov. 1880, with Johnston Forbes Robertson, Helena Modjeska, Amy Roselle/ **Olympic**, 1882, with F. H. Macklin as Maurice de Saxe, F. Charles as Prince de Bouillon, Fred Terry as Abbe de Chazeuil, A. T. Hilton as Michonnet, R. Brennand as Poisson, P. C. Beverley as Quinnault, Helen Cresswell as Princess de Bouillon, Elinor Aickin as Duchess D'Aumont, Vane Featherston as Countess de Beauveau, Fanny Clarke as Marquise de Sancerre, Florence Worth as Mlle. Juvenot, Marie De Grey as Adrienne Lecouvreur/ **Lyceum**, Mar. 1885, with Henry Neville as Maurice de Saxe, Lewis Waller as Prince de Bouillon, E. B. Norman as Abbé de Chazeuil, William Farren Jr. as Michonnet, Henry Howe as Poisson, Lady Monckton as Princess de Bouillon, Florence West as Duchess d'Aumont, Kate Conroy as Marquise de Sancerre, Helena Modjeska as Adrienne/ **Her Majesty's**, July 1890/ **Royalty**, Apr. 1893, with Charles Charrington as Michonnet, Herbert Flemming as Maurice de Saxe, John Carter as Poisson, C. P. Little as Abbé de Chazeuil, Charles Rock as Prince de Bouillon, W. R. Staveley as Quinault, Janet Achurch as Adrienne, Florence Farr as Princess de Bouillon.

ADRIENNE LECOUVREUR; OR, THE REIGNING FAVORITE// D 3a// Adap. by John Oxenford fr F// **Olympic**, June 1851, with Charles Diddear as Prince de Bouilon, Henry Farren as Chauzeuil, William Farren Jr. as Count de Saxe, William Farren as Michonnet, Alfred Sanger as Quinalt, E. Clifton as Poisson, Mary Fielding as Princess de Bouillon, Mrs. Stirling as Adrienne, Mrs. B. Bartlett as Mme. Jouvenot, Isabel Adams as Mme. de Chateau-Neuf, Ellen Turner as Mme. de Belville/ **Sad. Wells**, Jan. 1869, with Mr. Furtado as Prince de Bouillon, Mr. Perry as Choiseul, J. H. Fitzpatrick as Count de Saxe, J. H. Loome as Michonnet, W. H. Abel as Guinault, Miss Hazlewood as Adrienne, Miss Fossete as Mme. Jouvenot, Miss Herbert as Mme. de Chateau-Neuf, Miss McErnest as Mme. de Belville.

ADRIFT ON THE WORLD// D// F. Bousfield// **Marylebone**, Nov. 1874.

ADVENTURE OF LADY URSULA, THE// C 4a// Anthony Hope// **Duke of York's**, Oct. 1898, with Herbert Waring as Sir George, George Raiemond as Rev. Blimboe, J. C. Buckstone as Lt. Devereux, J. W. Macdonald as Quilton, Percy Lyndal as Earl of Hassenden, Charles Fulton as Dent, Sam Sothern as Lt. Ward, Alfred E. Rayner as Capt. Clifford, Evelyn Millard as Lady Ursula, Agnes Miller as Dorothy, Florence Haydon as Mrs. Fenton/ Scenery by Bruce Smith.

ADVENTURER, THE; OR, THE FIEND'S MOUNTAIN// D 5a// n.a.// **Drury Lane**, Oct. 1856, with C. Verner as Monmouth, Arroche, and Hurricane, Barry Sullivan as de Croustillac, C. Vincent as Col. Rutter, Mr. Tilbury as Baron de Rupinell, A. Younge as Fr. Griffon, Mr. Carter as Capt. Daniel, R.H. Lingham as Count Chemerault, Miss Cleveland as Angela, Miss Florence as Marguerite.

ADVENTURER, THE; OR, PLOTS IN SPAIN// D// n.a.// **Surrey**, Apr. 1856.

ADVENTURER, THE; OR, THE FIEND'S MOUNTAIN// D 5a// **Drury Lane**, Oct. 1856.

ADVENTURERS, THE// C 3a// Adap. by Edward Rose fr F of Emile Augier, L'Aventurière// **Strand**, June 1892, with C. W. Somerset as Maj. Carew, Charles Myers as Armathwaite, Harry Eversfield as Archie, Arthur Elwood as Harold, Alice Aldercron as Cissy, Harriet Trench as Rosa, Claire Ivanova as Leila.

ADVENTURER'S DOOM, THE; OR, THE MURDER IN THE WILLOW MARSH// D 3a// A. Faucquez// **Grecian**, July 1862, with Henry Grant as Marquis de Foix, William James as Alfred, John Manning as Monaco, Thomas Mead as Jean Roux, Mrs. R. H. Lingham as Rose, Ellen Hale as Adele, Miss Wieland as Julie.

ADVENTURES OF A BILLET-DOUX// C 2a// C. J. Mathews// **Drury Lane**, Nov. 1860, with C. J. Mathews as Blunt, Mrs. C. J. Mathews as Catherine, Mrs. Frank Matthews as Mrs. Wagstaff.

ADVENTURES OF A GENTLEMAN, THE// D 3a// Edward Bulwer Lytton// **Olympic**, Oct. 1842, with Mr. Fitzjames as Sir Reginald, Mr. Halford as Pelham, Thomas Green as Tyrrel, Mr. Brookes as Hellebore, Charles Baker as Thornton, Mr. Ross as Sursingle, George Wild as Job, Mr. Rogers as Brumston Bess, Miss Fitzjames as Mrs. Glanville, Miss Arden as Lady Roseville, Lavinia Melville as Gertrude, Miss Lebatt as Letty/ Scenery by J. W. Beverly & Mr. Scott/ Music by Mr. Calcott.

ADVENTURES OF A LOVE LETTER, THE (also tit. Adventures of a Billet-Doux)// C 2a// adap. by C. J. Mathews fr F of Sardou, Les Pattes de Mouche// **Drury Lane,** Nov. 1860/ **Haymarket,** June 1861, with C. J. Mathews as Blunt, Henry Howe as Pencoolen, Mr. Rogers as Wagstaff, George Braid as Brown, William Clark as Clinton, Mr. Weathersby as William, Mrs. C. J. Mathews (Lizzie Davenport) as Catherine, Florence Haydon as Mrs. Pencoolen, Mrs. Poynter as Mrs. Wagstaff, Louise Leclercq as Emma.

ADVENTURES OF A NIGHT, THE// D 3a// Adap. by Meyrick Milton fr Span. of Calderon, Les Empenos de Seis Horas// **Strand,** July 1893, with Meyrick Milton as Don Caesar, W. H. Vernon as Don Pedro, Luigi Lablache as Don Carlos, Fuller Mellish as Don Octavio, May Whitty as Donna Bianca, Ada Ferrar as Donna Portia, Cicely Richards as Flora.

ADVENTURES OF FRITZ, OUR COUSIN-GERMAN// D 3a// Andrew Halliday// **Adelphi,** Jan. 1873, with Augustus Glover as Col. Crafton, Frank Roland as Grimm, J. K. Emmet as Fritz, Mr. Smithson as Sloper, Mr. Cooper as Julius, Robert Romer as Schneider, Miss Powell as Little Schneider, C. J. Smith as Judge, Miss Marston-Leigh as Katarina, Miss Hudspeth as Moppy.

ADVENTURES OF THE COUNT OF MONTE CRISTO, THE// D Pro & 3a// H. J. Smith// **Lyric,** Mar. 1899.

ADVERSITY// D// n.a.// **Grecian,** Mar. 1861, with Thomas Mead as Roland, William James as Basile, R. H. Lingham as de Berney, Alfred Rayner as Maltide, John Manning as Moise, Henry Grant as Antoine, Jane Coveney as Jacqueline, Miss Johnstone as Indeth, Lucreza Hill as Cosinne.

ADVICE GRATIS// F 1a// Charles Dance// **Olympic,** Sept. 1837, with William Farren as Oddbody, Mr. Stoker as Edmund, Mr. Wyman as Grimes, Frank Matthews as Eventide, Mrs. Orger as Mrs. Eventide/ **Cov. Garden,** Oct. 1839, with William Farren as Odbody, Frank Matthews as Eventide, Mr. Fitzjames as Edmund, Mr. Granby as Grimes, Miss Lee as Ellen, Mrs. Orger as Mrs. Eventide/ **Sad. Wells,** Mar. 1845, with A. Younge as Odbody, Mr. Williams as Eventide, Malone Raymond as Edmund, Mr. Coreno as Grimes, Mrs. Henry Marston as Mrs. Eventide, Fanny Huddart as Ellen/ **Globe,** Jan. 1882, with David Fisher as Odbody, C. Medwin as Eventide, L. Cantley as Edmund, Maria Harris as Mrs. Eventide, Miss Wilson as Ellen.

ADVICE TO HUSBANDS// C 1a// C. S. Lancaster// **Princess's,** Oct. 1845, with Mr. Granby as Gen. Leslie, James Vining as Trevor, Mrs. Stirling as Mrs. Trevor.

ADVOCATE AND HIS DAUGHTER, THE// Joseph Ebsworth// **Olympic,** Feb. 1852.

AESOP'S FABLES// FC 3a// J. P. Hurst// **Strand,** June 1889.

ATHELWOLD// D// W. H. Smith// **Drury Lane,** May 1843, with Helen Faucit, W. C. Macready, James Anderson, Samuel Phelps.

AFFAIR OF HONOR, THE// F 1a// C. Long// **Grecian,** Aug. 1845, with Mr. Collette as Bellerton, John Chester as Lt. Fitzroy, Frederick Robson as Prof. Lambson, Edmund Garden as Lionheart, Mrs. W. Watson as Mrs. Bellerton, Miss M. A. Crisp as Isabella.

AFRANCESADO; OR, SECRECY AND TRUTH// D 2a// T. J. Serle// **Cov. Garden,** Oct. 1837, with James Anderson as Duke de la Granja, Charles Diddear as Count Valcarlos, Mr. Waldron as Maj. D'Anville, George Bartley as Mora, Mr. Warde as Govarra, Drinkwater Meadows as Quesita, Mr. Leffler as Jolivet, George Bennett as Rodrigo, Miss Taylor as Maria, Eliza Vincent as Inesilla/ Music by A. Lee.

AFTER// Play 1a// J. S. Battams// **Vaudeville,** May 1887.

AFTER DARK; A TALE OF LONDON LIFE// D 4a// adap. by Dion Boucicault fr F of A. P. Dennery & E. P. Grangé, Les Oiseaux de Proie// **Princess's,** Aug. 1868, with J. G. Shore as Chumley, H. J. Montague as Sir George, Walter Lacy as Bellingham, George Vining as Old Tom, Dominick Murray as Morris, W. D. Gresham as Pointer, Mr. Cathcart as Bargee, John Maclean as Crumpets, Rose Leclercq as Eliza, Trissy Marston as Rose/ Scenery by F. Lloyds & Walter Hann/ Music by E. Audibert/ Machines by R. E. Warton/ **Globe,** July 1877, with John Ryder as Old Tom, John Billington as Chumley, H. H. Vincent as Medhurst, Edward Righton as Morris, W. J. Hill as Area Jack, Charles Harcourt as Bellingham, Emma Ritta as Rose Egerton, Lydia Foote as Eliza/ Scenery by G. Gordon & W. Harford/ **Adelphi,** Aug. 1877, with William Terriss as Sir George, J. G. Shore as Gordon, Howard Russell as Chandos, Henry Naylor as Pointer, Frederick Moreland as Crumpets, Edith Stuart as Eliza, Samuel Emery as Old Tom, J. C. Smith as the Colonel, Miss Hudspeth as Rose Egerton/ **Princess's,** Nov. 1891, with Henry Neville as Old Tom, W. L. Abingdon as Bellingham, W. E. Shine as Morris, S. H. Basing as Chumley, Henry Bedford as Area Jack, Fuller Mellish as Sir George, Ellaline Terriss as Rose, Beatrice Selwyn as Eliza/ Scenery by H. Norman, C. Grimani, G. Harcourt/ Gas by D. Jones.

AFTER DARKNESS, DAWN// D 1a// A. D. Dowty// **Toole's,** May 1882.

AFTER LONG YEARS// D 1a// Adap. by Sidney Grundy fr F of Eugene Scribe & M. Camille, Le Mauvais Sujet// **Folly,** 1879, with Mr. Shelton, Miss F. Delaval.

AFTER LONG YEARS// C 3a// Dram. by Arthur Law fr story of Mrs. Herbert Purvis// **Criterion**, Feb. 1887.

AFTER LONG YEARS// C 1a// Gerald Godfrey// **Pavilion**, Dec. 1889.

AFTER MANY DAYS// C 1a// Arthur Elwood// **Globe**, Mar. 1887, with Stewart Dawson as Jasper Clements, Wilfred Draycott as Ned Lloyd, W. Lestocq as Mole, Florence Haydon as Mrs. Clements, Blanche Horlock as Peggy.

AFTER THE BALL// C// F. K. Peile// **St. James's**, July 1885.

AFTER THE BALL// FC// Edward Ferris, Brander Matthews, & Neville Doone// **Globe**, 1901.

AGAINST THE TIDE// D// C. H. Hazlewood// **Britannia**, June 1879.

AGAINST THE TIDE// D 4a// F. A. Scudamore// **Surrey**, 1896.

AGATHA// Play 3a// Isaac Henderson// **Criterion**, 1892, with Herbert Waring as Col. da Vigno, Lewis Waller as Marchese Loreno, Laurence Cautley as Sebasti, Charles Fulton as Gen. Ricci, Charles Wyndham as Dow, Mary Moore as Gaeta, Olga Nethersole as Signora da Vigno, Rose Leclercq as Marchesa Faviola, Winifred Emery as Marchesa Loreno.

AGATHA; OR, THE LAWFUL WIFE// D Pro & 3a// Oswald Brand// **Sad. Wells**, 1892.

AGATHA TILDEN, MERCHANT AND SHIP-OWNER// D 4a// Edward Rose// **Haymarket**, Oct. 1892, with Lewis Waller as Ainsworth, Cyril Maude as Macfarlane, W. T. Lovell as Lord Cyprian, Frederick Everill as Evans, Edmund Maurice as Sondershausen, Rudge Harding as Christopherson, W. Cheesman as Thompson, Lillie Langtry as Agatha, Marie Linden as Winifred/ Scenery by Walter Johnstone/ Electrics by E. Wingfield Bowles.

AGED FORTY// C 1a// John Courtney// **Princess's**, 1844/ **Haymarket**, Aug. 1857, with Mr. Howe as Wilder, Edwin Villiers as Dapper, William Clark as Sam, "A Young Lady" as Lady Clifton, Miss Medex as Mary.

AGGRAVATING SAM// F 2a// Adap. by C. J. Mathews fr F// **Lyceum**, 1854, with C. J. Mathews/ **Drury Lane**, Dec. 1856, with C. J. Mathews as Muggins, Robert Roxby as Popplewig, Mr. Tilbury as Biffin, George Honey as Slowboy, Mr. Templeton as Peter, Miss M. Oliver as Clara, Miss Mason as Sophonisba, Mrs. Selby as Arabella/ **Olympic**, Aug. 1863, with Edward Atkins as Sam Naggles, William R. Belford as Popplewig, John Maclean as Biffin, Robert Soutar as Slowboy, Harwood Cooper as Peter, Lydia Foote as Clara, Mrs. Stephens as Arabella, Miss Raynham as Sophonisba.

AGNES// C// Adap. by Robert Buchanan fr F of Moliere, L'Ecole des Femmes// **Comedy**, Mar. 1885.

AGNES BERNAUE// D 2a// T. J. Serle// **Cov. Garden**, Apr. 1839, with T.J. Serle as Emperor Sigismund, Samuel Phelps as Duke Ernest, James Anderson as Prince Albert, Charles Diddear as Count Bornheim, W. H. Payne as Count Rodolph, Edward W. Elton as Herman, George Bennett as Maurice, Miss E. Phillips as Princess of Brunswick/ Music by G. A. Macfarren.

AGNES OF BAVARIA// Play 5a// Frederick Hawley// **Gaiety**, Oct. 1883.

AGNES ST. AUBIN// D 3a// Miss Pardoe// **Adelphi**, Feb. 1841, with Frederick Yates, Mr. Lyon, O. Smith, Mr. Morgan, John Sanders, George Maynard, J. Smith. Mr. Freeborn, Mrs. Yates, Mrs. Nailer, Mrs. Keeley.

AGNOLO DIORA// D 3a// J. A. Heraud// **Grecian**, Nov. 1859.

AGONY COLUMN, THE// F 1a// Tom Terriss// **Gaiety**, Feb. 1901.

AGREEABLE SURPRISE, THE// F// John O'Keefe// **Cov. Garden**, Nov. 1838, with George Bartley as Sir Felix, Mr. Leffler as Compton, Mr. Manvers as Eugene, Mr. Tilbury as Chicane, Edwin Yarnold as Thomas, Drinkwater Meadows as John, C. J. Smith as Cudden, John Collett as Stump, John Pritt Harley as Lingo, Mrs. W. Clifford as Mrs. Cheshire, Priscilla Horton as Cowslip, Mrs. Humby as Fringe, Miss Rainforth as Laura.

AIGLON, L'// D 6a// Trans. F of Edmond Rostand// **Her Majesty's**, June 1901.

AILEEN; OR, FOILED AT LAST// D 2a// J. P. Collins// **Grecian**, Apr. 1872.

ALABAMA, THE// Alt. by J. Maddison Morton fr H. M. Sloop "Spitfire."// **Drury Lane**, Mar. 1864.

ALABAMA, THE// Play 4a// Augustus Thomas// **Garrick**, Sept. 1895, with James Fernandez as Col. Preston, E. S. Willard as Harry Preston, Cecil Crofton as Lathrop Page, Basset Roe as Raymond Page, John Mason as Col. Moberley, W. T. Lovell as Armstrong, F. H. Tyler as Tucker, Agnes Miller as Carey, Marion Terry as Mrs. Page, Nannie Craddock as Atalanta, Keith Wakeman as Mrs. Stockton/ Scenery by Walter Hann.

ALADDIN// C 2a// n.a.// **Lyceum**, Aug. 1844.

ALAN'S WIFE// Play 3a// Dram. by Mrs. Hugh Bell fr story of Glin Ameen// **Terry's**, Apr. 1893, with James Welch as Warren, Mervyn Herapath as Col. Stewart, Elizabeth Robins as Jean, Mrs. E. H. Brooke as Mrs. Holroyd, Mrs. Edmund Phelps as Mrs. Ridley/ Prod. by J. T. Grein.

ALARCOS// T 5a// Benjamin Disraeli// **Astley's**, Aug. 1868, with Mr. Dannavalle as Manuel, Mr. Meade as Carlos, Brandon Ellis as Oran,

Brownlow Hill as Count of Leon, Paton Honey as Ferdinand, Walter Carle as Count of Sidonia, H. J. Broughton as Prior of Burgos, Charles Verner as Count Alarcos, Agnes Cameron as Solisa, Miss Marian as Countess Florimonde/ Scenery by Julian Hicks/ Music by William Corri/ Machines by Mr. Bartlet.

ALARMING SACRIFICE, AN// F// J. B. Buckstone// **Haymarket**, July 1849/ **Sad. Wells**, Oct. 1857, with Lewis Ball as Ticket, Charles Seyton as Pugwash, Mr. Walters as Skinner, Eliza Travers as Susan, Caroline Parkes as Miss Wadd, Bessie Heath as Miss Tidbit, Miss Anderson as Gimp, Miss Rawlings as Deborah/ **Drury Lane**, Jan. 1862, with Edward Atkins as Ticket, Frank Barsby as Pugwash, Mr. Hope as Skinner, Louise Keeley as Miss Sweetapple, Miss Stuart as Miss Wadd, Miss Bland as Miss Tibbit, Mrs. T. Dowton as Deborah/ **Olympic**, Aug. 1863, with Edward Atkins as Ticket, Henry Rivers as Pugwash, Harwood Cooper as Skinner, Louise Keeley as Susan, Florence Haydon as Miss Wadd, Miss Hayward as Miss Tidbit, Mrs. Stephens as Deborah.

ALBERT DE ROSEN// D 4a// Mrs. S. Lane// **Britannia**, Aug. 1875.

ALBUM, THE// F// T. H. Bayly// **St. James's**, Apr. 1838.

ALCESTIS// D// Adap. by Henry Spicer fr F of Hippolyte Lucas// **St. James's**, Jan. 1855, with Barry Sullivan as Admetus, W. Cooper as Pheres, Mr. Stuart as Hercules, Mr. Herbert as Adrastus, Henry Rivers as Oreus, Charlotte Vandenhoff as Alcestis, Miss Grey as The Pythia/ Music by Gluck, arr. by Henry R. Bishop.

ALCHEMIST OF MODENA, THE; OR, THE WRONGS OF LIFE// D// F. Charlton// **Britannia**, Nov. 1868.

ALDERMAN, THE// C 3a// Adap. by James Mortimer fr F of Théodore Barrière & M. Capendu, L'Heritage de M. Plumet// **Criterion**, 1886.

ALDERMAN'S GOWN, THE; OR, A TRIP TO PARIS// F 1a// Henry Abrahams// **Strand**, Oct. 1851.

ALDERSHOT WAGS, THE; OR, BLUNDER ON BLUNDER// F// n.a.// **Sad. Wells**, Aug. 1857, with Mr. Gladstone as Capt. Foreguard, R. Green as Sir John, Mr. Bailey as Lump, Mr. Hudspeth as Mactwolter, John Chester as Quotem, Kate Percy as Grace, Mary A. Victor as Lucy.

ALDGATE PUMP, THE// F// J. S. Faucit// **Sad. Wells**, June 1845, with Mr. Williams as Tontine, E. Morton as Rivers, C. Fenton as Stocks, Samuel Buckingham as Willis, Henry Scharf as Dive, Mr. Corrin as Swash, Miss Lebatt as Mary Ann, Miss Stephens as Sarah, Mrs. Henry Mellon as Seraphina, Georgiana Lebatt as Norah.

ALEXANDRA// Play 4a// Adap. fr G of Richard Voss// **Royalty**, Mar. 1893, with Herbert Flemming as Lord Knowlesford, Edmund Maurice as Owthwaite, Charles Rock as Dr. Howarth, Gilbert Trent as Rev. Bevan, Herman de Lange as Van Noorden, John Carter as Ash, Charles Charrington as Want, W. R. Staveley as Dicker, Janet Achurch as Alexandra, Mrs. Theodore Wright as Lady Knowlesford, Mabel Hardinge as Mrs. Bradley, Rose Nesbitt as Sara.

ALEXINA// D// J. Sheridan Knowles// **Strand**, May. 1866.

ALICE AUCKLAND; OR, THE HEART OF AN ENGLISH GIRL// D// Thomas Parry// **Victoria**, Oct. 1843, with William Seaman as Count Marsillon, John Dale as Hawkhurst, Charles Williams as St. Aulaire, Mr. Nantz as Count de Fleury, Mr. Paul as Babinette, John Gardner as Cobb, David Osbaldiston as Maj. Auckland, Charles Baker as Rougedragon, Mr. Hitchinson as Pierrepoint, Cecil Pitt as Lavigne, Mr. James as Thornton, Annette Vincent as Alice, Miss Saddler as Mlle. Myrtille, Mrs. Franklin as Elise, Miss Ridgway as Mme. Babinette, Mrs. Atkinson as Margaret/ Scenery by Roberts & Morelli/ Machines by Emmens & Moon/ Music by W. J. Hill.

ALICE DURAND; OR, THE MISSING BRACELETS// D// n.a.// **Victoria**, Oct. 1849, with Mr. Henderson as Sir George, John Neville Sr. as Durand, Mr. Bradshaw as Capt. Harman, J. T. Johnson as Darling, Mr. Morrison as Ernest, Mr. Humphreys as Manley, T. H. Higgie as Fitzdoodle, Mr. Forman as Duff, Henry Frazer as Old Ben, Mr. Hudspeth as Slick, James W. Howard as Slow, Annette Vincent as Alice, Mrs. George Lee as Emma, Miss Barrowcliffe as Kitty.

ALICE GREY, THE SUSPECTED ONE; OR, THE MORAL BRAND// D 3a// J. T. Haines// **Surrey**, Apr. 1839.

ALICE MAY// D// Edward Fitzball// **Surrey**, 1852.

ALICE WINGOLD// D// n.a.// **Astley's**, May 1862.

ALIENS// Play 1a// n.a.// **Lyric**, June 1889.

ALINE, THE ROSE OF KILLARNEY// D 3a// Edward Stirling// **Strand**, July 1853.

ALIVE AND MERRY// F 2a// Charles Dance// **Cov. Garden**, Oct. 1839, with William Farren as Perkins, C. J. Mathews as Saunders, George Bartley as Sharp, John Brougham as Day, Mrs. Orger as Penelope, Mrs. Humby as Bella.

ALIVE OR DEAD// D 4a// Robert Hall// **St. Geo. Hall**, May 1876.

ALIVE OR DEAD; OR, THE LOVER'S SIGNAL// D 3a// Dram. by Charles Webb fr G tale// **Sad. Wells**, Jan. 1844, with Mr. Dry as Baron Lutzlow, Henry Marston as Rudolph, Henry Hall as Sgt. Kutzenslitz, Charles Williams as Dr. Hanber, Mr. Coreno as Block, Charles Fenton as Bohlman, Caroline Rankley as Agnes, Miss Cooke as Gertrude, Mrs. Richard Barnett as Diana/ Scenery by F. Fenton/ Music by Walter Montgomery/ Prod. by Henry Marston.

ALL ABOUT LOVE AND JEALOUSY// C 5a// George Bolton// **Olympic**, Apr. 1846, with James Browne as Don Alvarez, Charles Boyce as Don Miguel, Joseph Cowell as Don Diego, Mr. Clifford as Don Alphonse, Thomas Manders as Ambrose, Robert Romer as Angelino, Miss Charles as Donna Violetta, Miss Bromley as Donna Helena, Mrs. Griffiths as Donna Louise, Miss Hamilton as Laura.

ALL ALIVE, OH!// F 3a// Adap. fr F of Alexandre Bisson & André Sylvane, Disparu// **Strand**, June 1897, with Arthur Bourchier as Green, Fred Thorne as Bordle, Gerald Biron as Sir George, Mark Kinghorne as Drake, Compton Coutts as Crebbin, Coventry Davies as Caratstein, Phyllis Broughton as Mrs. Bordle, Ada Sentance as Mrs. Crozier, May Palfrey as Myra, Helen Rous as Andromeda.

ALL AT COVENTRY; OR, LOVE AND LAUGH// F 2a// W.T. Moncrieffe// **Victoria**, 1842.

ALL BUT ONE// D// William Travers// **Britannia**, Feb. 1868.

ALL FOR GOLD// D 3a// Cherry Griffiths// **Britannia**, Sept 1878.

ALL FOR GOLD; OR, FIFTY MILLIONS OF MONEY// D 4a// Adap. by Francis Hopkins fr F of Eugène Sue, Le Juif Errant// **Surrey**, Feb. 1881.

ALL FOR HER// D 3a// J. Palgrave Simpson & Herman Merivale// **Mirror**, Oct 1875, with John Clayton, Rose Coghlan, Caroline Hill, Horace Wigan/ **St. James's**, Jan. 1876, with Mr. Crawford as Lord Edendale, George Robinson as Col. Damer, John Clayton as Trevor, Horace Wigan as Radford, Mr. Laurence as Lindsay, W. T. Richardson as Hamilton, Henry Leigh as Greystone, George Yarnold as Crake, Rose Coghlan as Lady Marsden, Caroline Hill as Mary/ **Princess's**, May 1876, with Mr. Elwood as Lord Edendale, Mr. Crauford as Col. Damer, John Clayton as Trevor, Horace Wigan as Radford, Mr. Lawrence as Lindsay, P. C. Beverley as Hamilton, George Yarnold as Crake, Rose Coghlan as Lady Marsden, Caroline Hill as Mary, Mrs. Lena St. Henry as Greystone/ **Grand**, May 1897.

ALL FOR MONEY// C 3a// Mlle. Guillon Le Thiere// **Haymarket**, July 1869, with G. Jordan as Mortimer, Henry Irving as Capt. Fitzhubert, W. H. Vernon as Lyle, Gaston Murray as Ashley, C. Swan as Rogers, Henry Naylor as Timmins, Amy Sedgwick as Ida, Maude Haydon as Margaret, Mrs. Stephens as Eglintina.

ALL FOR THE BEST// C// n.a.// **Princess's**, Nov. 1846, with Henry Compton as Walkinpop, Augustus Harris as Alfred, Stephen Smith as Parchment, Robert Honner as Isaac, Mrs. Fosbroke as Mrs. Raymond, Miss E. Honner as Clara.

ALL FOR THEM// C 1a// H. P. Lyste// **Folly**, Apr. 1876.

ALL IN A FOG// F// T. J. Williams// **Surrey**, Oct. 1869.

ALL IN THE DARK// D 2a// J. R. Planché// **Royalty**, Nov. 1861.

ALL IN THE WRONG// C 5a// A. Murphy// **Sad. Wells**, Apr. 1849, with Henry Marston as Sir John, Henry Mellon as Sir William, William Hoskins as Beverly, G. K. Dickinson as Belmont, Mr. Harrington as Blandford, Mr. Graham as Robert, Charles Fenton as Brush, Mr. Wilkins as William, Mrs. Henry Marston as Lady Restless, Miss Cooper as Belinda, Miss Huddart as Clarissa, Julia St. George as Tattle, Miss Murray as Tippet/ **Olympic**, (in 3a), June 1857, with Frederick Robson as Sir John Restless, Mr. Addison as Sir William, George Vining as Beverly, Gaston Murray as Bellmont, George Cooke as Blandford, Mrs. Stirling as Lady Restless, Miss Swanborough as Belinda, Beatrice Marston as Clarissa, Eleanor Bromley as Tattle.

ALL IS VANITY; OR, A CYNIC'S DEFEAT// C 1a// Alfred Thompson// **Haymarket**, Apr. 1879.

ALL LOST// D 1a// Tom Craven// **Sadler's Wells**, July 1883.

ALL THAT GLITTERS IS NOT GOLD [alt., All is not Gold that Glitters]// C 2a// Thomas & J. Maddison Morton// **Olympic**, Jan. 1851, with William H. Norton as Sir Arthur, William Farren as Jasper Plum, Leigh Murray as Stephen Plum, William Farren Jr. as Frederick Plum, Henry Compton as Twinkle, Mrs. B. Bartlett as Lady Leatherbridge, Louisa Howard as Lady Valeria, Mrs. Stirling as Martha Gibbs; Sept. 1851 supertitled as The Factory Girl with most of the same cast/ Scenery by W. Shalders/ **Grecian**, Apr. 1855, with Basil Potter as Lassell, Eaton O'Donnell as Jasper Plum, Richard Phillips as Stephen Plum, F. Charles as Frederick Plum, Henry Power as Harris, John Manning as Toby Twinkle, Miss Johnstone as Lady Leatherbridge, Maria Simpson as Lady Valeria, Jane Coveney as Martha/ **Sad. Wells**, Mar. 1859, with Charles Young as Twinkle, Charles Seyton as Frederick Plum, Samuel Emery as Stephen Plum, William R. Belford as Sir Arthur, J. W. Ray as Jasper Plum, Henry Butler as Sam, Annie Ness as Lady Valeria, Mrs. J. B. Hill as Lady Leatherbridge, Mrs. Charles Young as Martha/ **Princess's**, Mar. 1863, with Mr. Fitzjames as Jasper, Hermann Vezin as Stephen, Charles Seyton as Frederick, Alfred Wallace as Sir Arthur, George Belmore as Twinkle, Constance Aylmer as Martha, Mrs. Henry Marston as Lady Leatherbridge, Marian Jones as Lady Valeria/ **Astley's**, Nov. 1881, with Edward Fowler as Jasper Plum, E. N. Hallows as Stephen Plum, F. Owen as Frederick Plum, George Stretton as Sir Arthur, Mat Robson as Toby, Mrs. Henry Blandford as Lady Leatherbridge, Nellie Grahame as Lady Valeria, Marie Forde as Martha/ **Adelphi**, Dec. 1896, with Luigi Lablache as Sir Arthur, J. D. Beveridge as Jasper Plum, Charles Fulton as Stephen, Oscar Ayde as Frederick, Harry Nicholls as Toby,

Margaret Halstan as Lady Valeria, Kate Kearney as Lady Leatherbridge, Miss Vane Featherston as Martha Gibbs.

ALL THE COMFORTS OF HOME// F 3a// Adap. by William Gillette & H. C. Duckworth fr G, Ein Toller Einfall// **Globe**, Jan. 1891, with Frederick Glover as Pettibone, Stella Maris as Rosabella, Sybil Carlisle as Emily, Norman Forbes as Hastings, Ian Robertson as Dabney, Lily Linfield as Fifi, Harry Paulton as Bender, Fanny Coleman as Josephine, Mary Ansell as Evangeline/ Scenery by William Telbin.

ALLENDALE// FC 3a// Eden Phillpotts & G. B. Burgin// **Strand**, Feb. 1893.

ALLOW ME TO APOLOGISE// F 1a// J. P. Wooler// **Olympic**, Oct. 1850, with George Cooke as Pedigree, William H. Norton as Capt. Seymour, Henry Compton as Goth, Miss Adams as Fanny, Louisa Howard as Harriet, Isabel Adams as Mary, Ellen Turner as Kitty.

ALLOW ME TO EXPLAIN// F// W. S. Gilbert// **POW**, Nov. 1867.

ALMA; OR, THE DAUGHTER OF FIRE// D// n.a.// **Grecian**, Oct. 1851.

ALMA MATER; OR, A CURE FOR COQUETTES// C 3a// Dion Boucicault// **Haymarket**, Sept. 1842, with William Farren as Sir Samuel, Mr. Tilbury as Dr. Dactyl, Henry Howe as Venture, Malone Raymond as Maj. O'Gorman, Henry Holl as Wildfire, Mr. Vining as Gradus, Benjamin Webster as Pliant, Mr. Wilsone as Pluckt, J. Worrell as Longhorne, A. Brindal as Count Pavé, Julia Glover as Widow Venture, Miss Charles as Lily, Miss Carre as Sally/ Scenery by George Morris.

ALMINIA// D// n.a.// **Her Majesty's**, Apr. 1860.

ALMSHOUSE, THE// FC 3a// William Lockhart & Loring Fernie// **Parkhurst**, Dec. 1892.

ALONE// CD 3a// J. Palgrave Simpson & Herman Merivale// **Court**, Oct. 1873.

ALONE IN LONDON// D Pro & 4a// Robert Buchanan & Harriet Jay// **Olympic**, Nov. 1885, with Leonard Boyne as Biddlecomb, Amy Roselle as Annie, Mr. Chudleigh as Wood, Herbert Standing as Redcliffe, Mr. Tresahar as Spriggins, Harriet Jay as Gipsy Tom, Percy Bell as Jenkinson, Gilbert Farquhar as Burnaby, Clarence Hague as Walter, Grace Marsden as Ruth, Nellie Palmer as Liz, Dutton Somers as Johnson, Juliet Anderson as Mrs. Moloney/ Scenery by Perkins & Bruce Smith/ Music by J. Mallandaine & Mr. Bendix/ Machines by Mr. Collins/ Prod. by Robert Buchanan & Harriet Jay/ **Princess's**, Dec. 1891.

ALONE IN THE PIRATE'S LAIR// D// C. H. Hazlewood// **Britannia**, Sept. 1867.

ALONE IN THE WORLD; OR, HOME AND THE HOMELESS// D 4a// n.a.// **Grecian**, Sept. 1863, with Henry Grant as Lord Somerton, J. Jackson as Goodman, Thomas Mead as Hammersley, Henry Power as Zacary, F. Smithson as Potter, John Manning as Slanger, George Gillett as Patter, Miss Johnstone as Widow Hammersley, Marie Brewer as Adelaide, Mary A. Victor as Sophie, Ellen Hale as Catherine.

ALONE IN THE WORLD// D 4a// Prentiss Ingram// **Princess's**, Apr. 1892, with Theo Balfour as Marlowe, Fred Wright Jr. as Bolton, Maitland Marler as Bruce, Hamilton Reville as Sharpus, F. Weathersby as Snapper, Naomi Hope as Mrs. Shaeffer, Mrs. Frank Huntley as Mother Orsola.

ALONZO THE BRAVE AND THE FAIR IMOGINE// D 2a// T. J. Dibdin// **Victoria**, Mar. 1849, with Mr. Henderson as Philip, J. T. Johnson as Alonzo, John Dale as Addallak, Mr. Forman as Iago, Miss Mildenhall as Hypolita, James W. Howard as Marshall, Mrs. George Lee as Idlefonza, Miss Barrowcliffe as Marcella, Miss Richardson as Imogine.

ALPINE HOLD, THE// D// J. T. Haines// **Victoria**, June 1839.

ALWAYS INTENDED// C 1a// Horace Wigan// **Olympic**, Apr. 1865, with John Maclean as Muddle, E. F. Edgar as Charles, Horace Wigan as Project, Miss Sheridan as Mrs.Mowbray, Ada Harland as Mary/ **Lyceum**, Oct. 1888, with J. Burrows as Muddle, J. B. Booth as Constant, Joseph Frankau as Project, Maud White as Mary, Emma Sheridan as Mrs. Markwell, Helen Glidden as Jane.

ALWAYS READY// D 3a// E. R. Callender// **East London**, Oct. 1874.

AMAKOSA// D// Edward Fitzball// **Astley's**, Mar. 1853.

AMALDERAC, THE BLACK PIRATE// D// n.a.// **Pavilion**, Jan. 1840.

AMATEUR WIFE, AN// FC 3a// Ellen Lancaster Wallis// **Criterion**, Apr. 1897, with Sydney Harcourt as Barker, H. Athol Forde as Castelle, W. Graville Blake as Capt. Giffy, F. N. Lindo as Franks, Fewlass Llewellyn as Heavysides, Arnold Lucy as Lt. Younghusband, Lucy Roche as Miss Halliday, Henrietta Cowen as Mrs. Binny, Cicely Richards as Miss Smythe.

AMATEURS AND ACTORS// F 1a// R. B. Peake// **Victoria**, Oct. 1837, with Mr. Franks as Dulcet, Edward Hooper as Bustle, Mr. Roland as Berry, Benjamin Wrench as Wing, Mr. Loveday as Elderberry, William Davidge as Timkins, W. H. Oxberry as Muffincap, Miss Lee as Mary, Mrs. Frank Matthews as Mrs. Generil/ **Grecian**, June 1846, with John Collett as Elderberry, Edwin Dixon as Wing, Eaton O'Donnell as O. P. Bustle, Frederick Robson as Muffincap, Mrs. W. Watson as Mary Goneril, Miss Johnstone as Miss Hardacre/ **Olympic**, Nov. 1846, with Robert Romer as Elderberry, H. Lee as Bustle, Mr. Binge as Dulcet, J. Cowell as Wing, Mr. Wilkenson as Muffincap, Miss Harcourt as Mary Hardacre, Miss Ayres as Mary Generil.

AMAZONS, THE// C 3a// Arthur Wing Pinero// **Court**, Mar. 1893, with Fred Kerr as Barrington, W. G. Elliott as André, John Beauchamp as Minchin, Compton Coutts as Youatt, Weedon Grossmith as Earl Galfred, Rose Leclercq as Miriam, Ellaline Terriss as Lady Wilhelmina, Pattie Brown as Lady Thomasin, Lily Hanbury as Lady Noaline/ Scenery by T. Hall.

AMBASSADOR, THE// C 4a// Mrs. P. M. Craigie ("J. O. Hobbes")// **St. James's**, June 1898, with George Alexander as St. Orbyn, H. B. Irving as Sir William, H. V. Esmond as Beauvedere, Fred Terry as Maj. Lascelles, Arthur Royston as Sir Charles, Bertram Wallis as Lord Lavensthorpe, Sidney Hamilton as Lord Niton, Violet Vanbrugh as Lady Beauvedere, Fay Davis as Juliet, Winifred Dolan as Alice, Hilda Rivers as Lady Gwendoline/ Scenery by H. P. Hall & Walter Hann/ Machines by Mr. Cullen/ Electrics by Mr. Barbour.

AMBASSADOR'S LADY, THE// D// T. E. Wilks// **Strand**, Aug. 1843.

AMBER HEART, THE// D 3a// A. C. Calmour// **Lyceum**, June 1887, with Herbert Beerbohm Tree as Silvio, Henry Kemble as Geoffrey, E. S. Willard as Coranto, Cissy Grahame, Helen Forsyth, Ellen Terry as Ellaline; May 1888, with George Alexander as Silvio, Frank Tyars as Geoffry, Herman Vezin as Coranto, Ellen Terry as Ellaline/ Scenery by Hawes Craven/ Music by Hamilton Clarke.

AMBER WITCH, THE// D// n.a.// **City of London**, 1851.

AMBER WITCH, THE// D// Henry Saville// **Victoria**, 1862.

AMBITION// n.a.// **Surrey**, Sept. 1857.

AMBITION// D// n.a.// **Standard**, Mar. 1870.

AMBITION// C 3a// Leslie Fomm// **Globe**, Apr. 1899, with Jack Wilcox as Trevelyan, J. Norton Wilson as Worthington, George Holwood as Rowley, F. E. Wilkinson as Gilded Youth, Thea Lesbrooke as Constance, Alexes Leighton as Fanny, Mary Jocelyn as Hilda Vane, Vivian Vane as Miss Lorne, Nora Baird as Daisy/ Prod. by Lucy Rushton.

AMBITION'S SLAVE; OR, A GAME OF CHESS// D 3a// Joseph Fox// **Standard**, Mar. 1883.

AMBITIOUS MRS. MORESBY, THE// D 1a// Miss E. White// **Comedy**, Apr. 1898, with William Lugg as Moresby, George Temple as Wareham, Rupert Lister as Allanson, Beatrice Selwyn as Mrs. Moresby, Bella Graves as Jessie.

AMBROSE GWINNETT; OR, A SEASIDE STORY// D 3a// Douglas Jerrold// **Sad. Wells**, Mar. 1842, with Mr. Dry as Ambrose, Mr. Richardson as Gilbert, Mr. Lyon as Greyling, P. Williams as Collins, John Herbert as Label, Mr. Morton as George, Charles Fenton as Blackshore, Miss Richardson as Lucy, Mrs. Morgan as Mary, Mrs. Richard Barnett as Jenny/ **Grecian**, Sept. 1864, with William James as Ambrose Gwinett, J. B. Steele as Grayling, John Manning as Gilbert, W. Shirley as Collins, J. Jackson as Label, George Gillett as Mad George, Henry Grant as Blackthorn, Walter Holland as Ash, Jane Dawson as Lucy, Marie Brewer as Jenny, Louise Graham as Mary.

AMERICAN, THE// Play 3a// Joseph Derrick// **Alexandra**, June 1882.

AMERICAN, THE// Play 4a// Dram. by Henry James fr his novel// **Opera Comique**, Sept. 1891, with Edward Compton as Newman, Clarence Blakiston as Comte de Bellegarde, Young Stewart as Nioche, Sydney Paxton as Marquis de Bellegarde, C. M. Hallard as Lord Deepmore, Harrison Hunter as de Marignac, Adrienne Dairolles as as Mrs. Nioche, Louise Moodie as Mrs. Bread, Elizabeth Robins as Claire/ Scenery by Joseph Harker.

AMERICAN BRIDE, AN// C 4a// William Young & Maurice Noel// **Lyric**, May 1892, with Eric Lewis as Duke of St. Heliers, Arthur Elwood as Hilliard, Lewis Waller as Lord Dorrington, Charles Eaton as Stagg, Charles Fulton as Carston, E. Allan Aynesworth as East, Fred Kaye as McGuinis, Henrietta Lindley as Duchess of St. Heliers, Lilian Hingston as Lady Hilda, Ethel Norton as Violet, Janette Steer as Stella.

AMERICAN CITIZEN, AN// C 4a// Madeline Ryley// **Duke of York's**, June 1899, with Thomas Oberle as Barbury, Neil O'Brien as Sims, S. M. Hall as Lucas, Frank Mayne as Stroble, Clarence Handyside as Sir Humphrey, Nat. C. Goodwin as Cruger, H. V. Surrey as Bunn, Gertrude Elliott as Georgia, Yosabel Haskins as Lady Bunn, Estelle Mortimer as Carola, Maxine Elliott as Beatrice/ Prod. by Charles Frohman.

AMERICAN LADY, THE// C 3a// H. J. Byron// **Criterion**, Mar. 1874.

AMILIE; OR, THE QUEEN'S BOUQUET// D// n.a.// **Grecian**, Jan. 1856, with F. Charles as Linday, Richard Phillips as Lorin, Thomas Roberts as Chevalier, Mr. Hustleby as Dixmer, Henry Grant as Simon, Eaton O'Donnell as Gen. Sarterre, John Manning as Waggles, Jane Coveney as Amilie, Miss Johnstone as Mme. Tison, Harriet Coveney as Heloise.

AMONG THE BREAKERS// C 2a// John Brougham// **Strand**, July 1869/ **Adelphi**, Sept. 1874, with George Temple as Sir Thomas, Frederick Moreland as Eavesdrop, Frederick Dewar as Col. O'Gorman, Augustus Glover as Stagg, J. S. Clarke as Babbington Jones, Edith Stuart as Charlotte, Miss Hudspeth as Arabella, Fanny Morelli as Betty.

AMOS CLARK// D Pro & 4a// Watts Phillips// **Queen's**, Oct. 1872.

AMPLE APOLOGY, AN// F 1a// George Roberts// **Princess's**, Mar. 1865, with Charles Seyton as Clasper, F. Charles as Mawley, Dominick Murray as Spooner, Hetty Tracy as Mrs. Clasper.

AMY ARLINGTON; OR, MURDER IN THE OAK COPPICE// D// Douglas Steward// **Grecian,** May 1863, with W. Shirley as Mark, Henry Grant as George, Thomas Mead as Allerton, George Gillett as Popham, Henry Power as Tippets, Alfred Rayner as Grayling, John Manning as Simon, Mrs. Charles Dillon as Amy Arlington, Mary A. Victor as Emma, Miss Johnstone as Mrs. Potts.

AMY ROBSART// D 4a// Dram. by Andrew Halliday fr Sir Walter Scott's Kenilworth// **Drury Lane,** Sept. 1870, with J. B. Howard as Leicester, Mr. Douglas as Sussex, J. Neville as Hunsdon, Mr. Mead as Shrewsbury, F. Charles as Raleigh, Morton Tavares as Tressillian, T. C. King as Varney, Brittain Wright as Lambourne, Adelaide Neilson as Amy Robsart, Miss F. Addison as Queen Elizabeth, Rosina Vokes as Janet/ **Adelphi,** June 1879, with Henry Neville as Leicester, Robert Markby as Sussex, F. Charles as Raleigh, Hermann Vezin as Richard Varney, Edward Compton as Edmund Tressilian, Robert Pateman as Lambourne, Harriet Coveney as Flibbertigibbet, Bella Pateman as Queen Elizabeth, Adelaide Neilson as Amy Robsart, Clara Jecks as Janet/ Scenery by Julian Hicks/ Music by W. C. Levey/ Prod. by Charles Harris.

AMY ROBSART; OR, THE GOLDEN DAYS OF QUEEN BESS// D 3a// Charles Webb// **Grecian,** June 1854, with Richard Phillips as Leicester, Charles Horn as Tresillian, Mr. Hamilton as Goldthread, Basil Potter as Varney, Henry Grant as Foster, William Suter as Bully Mike, Eaton O'Donnell as Gosling, Jane Coveney as Amy Robsart, Ellen Crisp as Queen Elizabeth, Harriet Coveney as Janet.

AN OLD MASTER// C 1a// Henry Arthur Jones// **Princess's,** Nov. 1880, with C. W. Garthorne as Sir Rupert, Stanislaus Calhaem as Penrose, Mr. Darton as Simpson, Harriet Coveney as Penelope, Maud Milton as Sophie.

ANARCHIST TERROR, THE// D 4a// n.a.// **West London,** Oct. 1891.

ANARCHY; OR, PAUL KAUVAR// D 5a// Adap. by Steele Mackaye fr F./ **Elephant & Castle,** Apr. 1887.

ANATO, KING OF ASSYRIA// D// Play vers. of Verdi's Nabucco// **City of London,** 1850.

ANCESTRESS, THE; OR, THE DOOM OF BAROSTEIN// D 2a// Mark Lemon// **City of London,** May 1837.

ANCHOR OF HOPE, THE; OR, THE SEAMAN'S STAR// D 2a// Edward Stirling// **Surrey,** Apr. 1847/ **Astley's,** May 1864, with Mr. Denial as Dunmore, W. S. Gresham as Hargreave, W. Templeton as Mumps, J. F. Shaw as Crabtree, E. F. Edgar as Moses, Miss Aline as Emily, Fanny Clifford as Mary, Mrs. J. W. Simpson as Dame Wheatley.

ANCHOR'S WEIGHED, THE// D 3a// T. R. Taylor// **Standard,** May 1883.

ANDREA// C 4a// Adap. fr F of Victorien Sardou// **Opera Comique,** May 1875.

ANDREAS HOFER, THE "TELL" OF THE TYROL// D 3a// Edward Fitzball// **Victoria,** June 1842, with E. F. Saville as Hofer, William Seaman as Elric, Charles Williams as Gen. Bisson, John Dale as Donay, Mr. Morelli as Happinger, Mr. Griffith as Lt. Dittfort, John Gardner as Absolon, Mrs. George Lee as Marie, Miss Saddler as Josephine, Jane Coveney as Maulette, Mrs. Griffith as Mme. Rougegorge, Miss Edgar as Therese.

ANDROMACHE// D 3a// Gilbert Murray// **Garrick,** Feb. 1901.

ANDROMEDA// T 1a// Rose Seaton// **Vaudeville,** Mar. 1890, with Leonard Outram as Cleon, Josephine St. Ange as Nestrina, Mrs. Wyatt as Ismene, Rose Seaton as Andromeda.

ANDY BLAKE; OR, THE IRISH DIAMOND// CD 2a// Dion Boucicault// **Adelphi,** Feb. 1862.

ANGEL BOY, THE// C 1a// Walter Monck// **St. Geo. Hall,** June 1900.

ANGEL OF DARKNESS, THE// D// Adap. by George Conquest fr F/ **Grecian,** Oct. 1859, with Thomas Mead, Harriet Coveney.

ANGEL OF DEATH, THE// D 5a// Found. by George Conquest on W. E. Suter and T. H. Lacy's adap. fr F of Théodore Barrière & E. Plouvier./ **Grecian,** May 1861, with Thomas Mead as Dr. Meats, Alfred Rayner as Baron Mateaz, William James as Lantz, R. H. Lingham as Count Ruffack, Henry Grant as Braum, J. Jackson as Dr. Rauspack, Mrs. Charles Dillon as the Angel, Jane Coveney as Marguerite, Ellen Hall as Katherine, Lucreza Hill as Aga/ Scenery by C. Smithers/ Machines by J. Smithers/ Music by T. Derby/ Prod. by George Conquest/ **Surrey,** Sept. 1898.

ANGEL OF MIDNIGHT, THE// D 4a// Adap. by John Brougham fr F of Théodor Barriere & M. Plouvier// **Princess's,** Feb. 1862, with George Jordan as Werner, John Ryder as Col. Lambech, Basil Potter as Count de Stromberg, J. G. Shore as Karl de Stromberg, Henry Widdicomb as Dr. Von Blokk, Drinkwater Meadows as Beckmann, Mary Fielding as Katherine, Louisa Angel as Margaret, Marie Henderson as Agar, Alice Marriott as the Angel.

ANGEL OF THE ATTIC, THE// C 1a// Thomas Morton// **Princess's,** June 1843, with A. Walton as the Chevalier, Walter Lacy as Magnus, Emma Stanley as Mariette.

ANGEL OR DEVIL// D 1a// adap. by J. Stirling Coyne fr F, Une Femme qui deteste son Mari// **Lyceum,** Mar. 1857.

ANGELINE// C 1a// n.a.// **Olympic,** Mar. 1840, with Mr. Holl as Middleton, Mr. Brookes as Dr. Diaphram, Mr. Ross as Simkins, Mr. Turnour as Amore, Mrs. Stirling as Angeline, Mrs. Allcroft as Nanguette/ **Haymarket,** Aug. 1840, with John Webster as Middleton, Robert

Strickland as Dr. Diaphram, Mr. Mathews as Simkins, J. Worrell as Bruquere, O. Smith as Amere, Mrs. Stirling as Angeline, Miss Mattley as Nanguette/ **Princess's**, Mar. 1847, with Henry Hughes as Middleton, Mr. Granby as Dr. Diaphram, Sam Cowell as Simkins, Charles Fisher as Stranger, Stephen Smith as Amere, Mrs. Stirling as Angeline, Miss Marshall as Naguette.

ANGELS AND LUCIFERS; OR, COURTSHIP AND CONGREVES// F 1a// E. L. Blanchard// **Olympic**, Nov. 1841, with Mr. Brookes as Convex, Mr. Halford as Stanley, George Wild as Brimstone, Miss Arden as Miss Dormer, Miss Lebatt as Gingham/ **Sad. Wells**, Aug. 1843, with Mr. Brookes as Convex, George Wild as Brimstone, C. J. Bird as Stanley, Lavinia Melville as Caroline, Mrs. Richard Barnett as Sally/ **Astley's**, Aug. 1855, with J. W. Anson as Convex, C. Shaw as Stanley, George Wild as Brimstone, Fanny Williams as Sally Gingham.

ANGEL'S VISIT, AN; OR, THE TRIALS OF LOVE// D Pro & 2a// W. H. Abel// **East London**, Sept. 1870.

ANGELA TERESA// Play 3a// George Bancroft// **Comedy**, July 1897.

ANGELINA// Play 3a// Adap. by W. Cooper fr F of Alexandre Bisson, Une Mission Délicate// **Vaudeville**, May 1889.

ANGELINE DE LIS// D// J. T. Haines// **St. James's**, Sept. 1837.

ANGELO// T 4a// Adap. by Charles Reade fr F of Victor Hugo// **Olympic**, Aug. 1851, with Henry Farren as Malpieri, William Farren Jr. as Rodolfo, John Kinloch as Galesto, Mrs. Stirling as La Tisbe, Louisa Howard as Catarina/ Scenery by W. Shalders.

ANGELO AND THE ACTRESS OF PADUA// D 4a// Adap. by G. H. Davidson fr F of Victor Hugo, Angelo// **Haymarket**, 1855.

ANGLING IN TROUBLED WATERS// D 4a// Edward Towers// **Pavilion**, Oct. 1872.

ANIMAL MAGNETISM// F// Mrs. Inchbald// **Cov. Garden**, Oct. 1841, with Walter Lacy as Marquis de Lancy, William Farren as Doctor, John Pritt Harley as La Fleur, Drinkwater Meadows as Jeffrey, Miss Cooper as Constance, Mrs. Orger as Lisette/ **Sad. Wells**, Nov. 1845, with Mr. Morton as Marquis de Lancy, A. Younge as Doctor, Samuel Buckingham as Le Fleur, Miss Huddart as Constance, Miss Lebatt as Lisette.

ANNE BLAKE// Play 5a// Westland Marston// **Princess's**, Oct. 1852, with Mr. Addison as Sir Joshua, Charles Kean as Thorold, Walter Lacy as Llanisten, John Chester as Jillot, Mrs. Winstanley as Lady Toppington, Mrs. Charles Kean as Anne, Mrs. W. Daly as Mrs. Lloyd, Mrs. Saker as Davies/ **Standard**, May 1861/ **Sad. Wells**, Sept. 1866, with Mr. Sheppard as Sir Joshua, J. H. Slater as Thorold, L. Warner as Llaniston, J. W. Lawrence as Jillott, Mrs. J. F. Saville as Lady Toppington, Alice Marriott as Anne, Miss Leicester as Clara.

ANNE BOLEYN// D 5a// Tom Taylor// **Haymarket**, Feb. 1876, with Charles Harcourt as Henry VIII, Henry Howe as Surrey, Robert Dolman as Northumberland, Frederick Everill as Sir Thomas, Harold Kyrle as Percy, Arthur Cecil as Chapuis, Arthur Matthison as Wyatt, C. Allbrook as Norris, H. B. Conway as Weston, Adelaide Neilson as Anne Boleyn, Lucy Buckstone as Margaret, Blanche Henri as Joan, Emily Thorne as Maria de Rohas/ Scenery by John O'Conner, George Morris & T. Hall.

ANNE BOLEYN; OR, THE JESTER'S OATH// D 4a// Robert Dodson// **Victoria**, Mar. 1873.

ANNE MIE// D// Adap. by Clement Scott fr Dutch of Rosier Faassen// **POW**, Nov. 1880, with James Fernandez, Genevieve Ward, Mrs. Leigh Murray, Johnston Forbes Robertson, Annie Brunton.

ANNIE MONKSWORTH// William Seaman// **Britannia**, July 1859.

ANNIE TYRRELL// T. J. Serle// **Surrey**, Jan. 1852.

ANONYMOUS LETTER, THE// C 3a// Mark Ambient & Frank Latimer// **Lyric**, May 1891, with Lewis Waller as Sinclair, Eric Lewis as Credit, George Mudie as Sir Daniel, W. H. Vernon as Baron Goldschein, Annie Rose as Mrs. Sinclair, Florence West as Helen.

ANOTHER// FC 3a// Emily Hodson// **Vaudeville**, Dec. 1885.

ANOTHER MATINEE// C 1a// F. Castris// **Vaudeville**, June 1888.

ANOTHER PAIR OF SHOES// F 1a// Frederick Hay// **Globe**, Sept. 1875, with Julia Vokins, Henry Grafton, Henry Deane.

ANTIGONE// T// Trans. fr Gk of Sophocles// **Cov. Garden**, Jan. 1845, with George Vandenhoff as Creon, James Vining as Daemon, Mr. Archer as Tiresias, Mr. Hield as Phocian, Mr. Rae as Cleon, Charlotte Vandenhoff as Antigone, Mrs. James Cooke as Ismene, Mrs. W. Watson as Eurydice/ Scenery by John MacFarren/ Music by G. A. MacFarren/ Dances by Mr. Frampton.

ANTIGONE// T// Adap. by W. Bartholomew fr Gk of Sophocles// **Drury Lane**, May 1850, with Charlotte Vandenhoff as Antigone, George Vandenhoff as Creon, William Montague as Haemon, Mr. Cooper as Tiresias, Charles Fisher as Phocion, G. Everett as Cleon, John Parry as Chorus Speaker, Mrs. John Parry as Eurydice, Miss Phillips as Ismene.

ANTOINE THE SAVAGE; OR, THE ROCK OF CHARBONNIERE// D// Edward Fitzball// **Sad. Wells**, July 1843, with Henry Marston as St. Angeville, John Webster as Victor, C. J. Bird as Count Lenoir, R. H. Lingham as Rosenford, C. J. Smith as Antoine, James

Villiers as Von Franc, Caroline Rankley as Violetta, Mrs. Richard Barnett as Mary, Miss Cooke as Lantone.

ANTIPODES, THE// D 3a// Tom Taylor// **Holborn**, June 1857.

ANTOINETTE RIGAUD// C 3a// Trans. by Ernest Warren fr F of Raymond Deslandes// **St. James's**, Feb. 1886, with John Hare as Gen. de Prefond, J. H. Barnes as Rigaud, W. H. Kendal as de Tourvel, Herbert Waring as Sannoy, E. Hendrie as Bernardet, Robert Cathcart as Corp. Pierre, Mrs. W. H. Kendal as Antoinette, Linda Dietz as Marie, Miss Webster as Mme. Bernardet/ Scenery by W. Harford.

ANTONY AND CLEOPATRA// T// William Shakespeare// **Sad. Wells**, Oct. 1849, with Samuel Phelps as Marc Antony, G. K. Dickinson as Caesar, William Hoskins as Lepidus, Henry Marston as Pompeius, George Bennett as Enobarbus, Henry Mellon as Agrippa, Henry Rivers as Dolabella, Henry Nye as Clown, Isabela Glyn as Cleopatra, Miss Aldridge as Octavia, Miss T. Bassano as Charmian, Mrs. G. Smith as Iras/ Scenery by F. Fenton/ **Princess's**, May 1867, with Henry Loraine as Marc Antony, Henry Forrester as Caesar, Walter Joyce as Lepidus, E. F. Edgar as Pompeius, Charles Verner as Enobarbus, James Johnstone as Eros, Henry Mellon as Agrippa, W. R. Robins as Proculeius, Isabela Glyn as Cleopatra, Miss Page as Charmian, Miss Wood as Iras/ Scenery by T. Grieve & F. Lloyds/ Machines by R. Warton/ Music by Charles Hall; Nov. 1890 (arr. by Lewis Wingfield), with Charles Coghlan as Antony, F. Kemble Cooper as Caesar, P. C. Beverley as Lepidas, Kenneth Black as Pompeius, Arthur Stirling as Enobarbus, Frances Ivor as Octavia, Amy McNeil as Charmian, Miss F. Harwood as Iras, Lillie Langtry as Cleopatra/ Scenery by Bruce Smith, Harker, Banks & Perkins/ Music by Edward Jakobowski/ Machines by W. J. Cawdery/ Gas by Mr. Jones/ Lime-light by Mr. Kerr/ **Olympic**, May 1897, with Louis Calvert as Marc Antony, Alfred Kendrick as Caesar, Leonard Calvert as Lepidus, Frank Westerton as Pompeius, Carter Edwards as Enobarbus, Margaret Halstan as Octavia, Ada Mellon as Charmian, Marie Fauvet as Iris, Janet Achurch as Cleopatra/ Scenery by Hugh Freemantle & A. L. Grimshaw/ Music by Henry Watson/ Prod. by Louis Calvert/ **Lyceum**, Mar. 1900, with F. R. Benson as Mark Antony, H. R. Hignett as Octavius, G. Fitzgerald as Lepidus, Oscar Ashe as Pompeius, E. Lyall Swete as Enobarbus, E. Harcourt Williams as Dolabella, Henry Ainley as Agrippa, Mrs. F. R. Benson as Cleopatra, Helen Townsend as Octavia, Constance Robertson as Charmian, Lily Brayton as Iras/ Music by Michael Balling.

ANTONY AND CLEOPATRA// D 4a// Adap. by Andrew Halliday fr Shakespeare// **Drury Lane**, Sept. 1873, with James Anderson as Antony, Henry Sinclair as Caesar, John Ryder as Enobarbus, Howard Russell as Eros, Henry J. Byron as Lepidus, Robert Dolman as Agrippa, Mr. Manton as Diomedes, Joseph Morris as Clown, Augustus Glover as Mardian, Ellen Wallis as Cleopatra, Miss Hamilton as Octavia, Edith Stuart as Charmian, Miss Melville as Iras/ Scenery by William Beverley/ Music by W. C. Levey/ Machines by J. Turner/ Prod. by Andrew Halliday & F. B. Chatterton.

ANTONY AND CLEOPATRA; OR, HISTORY AND HER STORY// D// F. C. Burnand// **Haymarket**, Nov. 1866.

ANTONY AND CLEOPATRA// F 1a// Charles Selby// **Adelphi**, Dec. 1843, with Sarah Woolgar, Edward Knight.

ANXIOUS TIME, AN// F// Ellis Reynolds// **St. Geo. Hall**, Jan. 1889.

ANY PORT IN A STORM// J. H. Stocqueler// **Haymarket**, Dec. 1853.

ANYTHING FOR A CHANGE// C 1a// Shirley Brooks// **Lyceum**, June 1848, with John Pritt Harley as Honeyball, C. J. Mathews as Swoppington, Robert Honner as Census, Mrs. Leigh Murray as Mrs. Honeyball, Kathleen Fitzwilliam as Margaret/ **Sad. Wells**, Apr. 1855, with Robert Roxby as Honeyball, Frederic Robinson as Swopington, W. Templeton as Census, Frances Hughes as Mrs. Honeyball, Miss Martindale as Margaret, Emma Wadham as Eliza.

APOSTATE, THE; OR, THE MOORS IN SPAIN// D// R. L. Shiel// **Marylebone**, 1852, with McKean Buchanan, James Rogers, Mrs. Brougham.

APPEAL TO THE AUDIENCE, AN// F 1a// Albany Brown// **St. James's**, Dec. 1852.

APPEAL TO THE PUBLIC, AN// C// John Oxenford// **Haymarket**, July 1861, with C. J. Mathews as Rosemary, F. C. Courtney as Bilberry, Edwin Villiers as Blackberry, Mrs. Fitzwilliam as Mrs. James Bilberry, Eliza Weekes as Mrs. Jeremiah Bilberry, Mrs. Griffith as Mrs. Jinks.

APPEARANCES// C 2a// J. Palgrave Simpson// **Strand**, May 1860.

APPLE BLOSSOMS// C 3a// James Albery// **Vaudeville**, Sept. 1871.

APPLE PIE// n.a.// **Surrey**, Dec. 1866.

APRIL FOLLY// C 1a// Dram. by J. P. Hurst fr story of Beauchamp// **Olympic**, Apr. 1885, with Philip Beck as Featherly, W. Howell-Poole as Pybus, W. T. Elworthy as Ruggles, Gabrielle Goldney as Emily.

APRIL FOOL, AN// F 1a// Andrew Halliday & William Brough// **Drury Lane**, May 1864, with Henry M. Barrett as Oldbuck, Robert Roxby as Sparks, George Belmore as Poddles, G. Weston as Muffins, Lizzie Wilmore as Diana.

APRIL SHOWERS// C 3a// G. S. Bellamy & F. Romer// **Terry's**, Jan. 1889/ **Comedy**, Apr. 1890, with Nutcombe Gould as Lord Lacy, H. Reeves-Smith as Frank Lacy, Ells Dagnall as Clincher, Walter Everard as Charlie, Miss E. Brunton as Mrs. Lawrence, Maude Millett as Miss Lawrence, Annie Hughes as Miss Lacy.

ARAB OF THE DESERT, THE; OR, THE CALIPH ROBBER// D// n.a.// **Sad. Wells**, Jan. 1837, with N. T. Hicks as Caliph, C. H. Pitt as Hassan, John Ayliffe as Mesrour, Mr. Campbell as Chebib, Mr. Rogers as Cadi, Mr. Burton as Hazeb, Mr. Ennis as Mahoud, Miss Lebatt as Camira, Miss Williams as Darina/ **Astley's**, Feb. 1856.

ARABIAN NIGHTS, THE// F 3a// Dram. by Sidney Grundy fr G of G. von Moser, Haroun Alrachid// **Globe**, Nov. 1887, with Charles Hawtrey as Hummingtop, Frederick Glover as Omerod, W. Lestocq as Dobson, W. S. Penley as Gillibrand, Miss Vane Featherston as Mrs. Hummingtop, Carlotta Zerbini as Mrs. Gillibrand, Agnes Miller as Daisy Maitland, Lottie Venne as Rosa Columbier/ Prod. by F. Glover.

ARAJOON; OR, THE CONQUEST OF MYSORE// D 3a// J. Stirling Coyne// **Adelphi**, Oct. 1838, with William Cullenford, Mr. Lyon, John Webster, Arthur Wilkinson, Mr. Landsdowne, Frederick Yates, John Sanders, E. F. Saville, H. George, Mrs. Yates, Miss Cotterel.

ARCHIE LOVELL// D 4a// F. C. Burnand// **Royalty**, May 1874.

ARDEN OF FEVERSHAM// T 5a// George Lillo// **Sad. Wells**, Sept. 1852, with G. Mortimer as Lord Cheney, Mr. Knight as Mayor, Henry Marston as Arden, Mr. Wilkins as Franklin, Mr. Willis as Bradshaw, William R. Belford as Michael, Henry Mellon as Green, George Bennett as Mosby, Mrs. Ternan as Alice, Lizzie Mandelbert as Maria/ **St. Geo. Hall**, July 1897.

ARDEN OF FEVERSHAM// T 5a// Alt. by J. Hoadly fr orig. by George Lillo// **Sadler's Wells**, 1852.

ARE YOU A MASON?// FC 3a// Adap. fr G of C. Logenbrüder// **Shaftesbury**, Sept. 1901.

AREA BELLE, THE// F 1a// William Brough & Andrew Halliday// **Adelphi**, Mar. 1864, with J. L. Toole as Pitcher, Paul Bedford as Tosser, Mrs. Alfred Mellon as Penelope Ann; Mar. 1871, with J. L. Toole as Pitcher, Charles Wilmot as Tosser, Robert Romer as Chalks, Mrs. Alfred Mellon as Penelope Ann, Emma Barnett as Mrs. Croaker/ **Globe**, May 1880, with Charles Ashford as Pitcher, E. G. Osborn as Tosser, Clara Graham as Mrs. Croaker, Hilda Hilton as Penelope/ **Olympic** May 1888, with Harry Halley as Pitcher, J. G. East as Tosser, George Claremont as Chalks, Maude Graves as Mrs. Croaker, Rose Dearing as Penelope.

ARIADNE// D// n.a.// **Olympic**, Jan. 1850.

ARIANE// D 4a// Dram. by Richard Lee & authoress fr novel Wedlock// **Opera Comique**, Feb. 1888.

ARISTOCRATIC ALLIANCE, AN// C 3a// Adap. by Violet Greville fr F of Emile Augier & Jules Sandeau, Le Gendre de M. Poirier// **Criterion**, Mar. 1894, with Charles Wyndham as Gerald, Charles Groves as Potter, J. G. Taylor as Greenwood, Frank Worthing as Capt. Marchmont, Herman de Lange as Cordognac, Emily Fowler as Lady Winnifred, Annie Hughes as Rose, Mary Moore as Alice.

ARKWRIGHT'S WIFE, THE// D 3a// Tom Taylor & John Saunders// **Globe**, Nov. 1873, with Samuel Emery as Peter Hayes, Charles Kelly as Richard Arkwright, E. W. Garden as Lawson, J. H. Allen as Clayton, Helen Barry as Margaret Hayes, Maria Daly as Nancy, Miss Howard as Annie/ Music by T. Gough.

ARLINE; OR, THE FORTUNES AND VICISSITUDES OF A BOHEMIAN GIRL// C// W. Brough & R. B. Brough// **Haymarket**, Apr. 1851, with James Bland as Count Arnheim, Mrs. L. S. Buckingham as Count Florestine, Priscilla Horton as Thaddeus, J. B. Buckstone as Devilshoof, Miss Caulfield as child Arline, Annie Romer as adult Arline, Henry Bedford as Gipsy Queen, Mrs. Caulfield as Buda/ Scenery by George Morris & Mr. Conner/ Machines by F. Hesselton/ Music by T. German Reed.

ARMADA, THE; OR, A ROMANCE OF 1588// D 5a// Henry Hamilton & Augustus Harris// **Drury Lane**, Oct. 1888, with Winifred Emery as Sybil, Edith Bruce as Cicely, Ada Neilson as Elizabeth, Maud Milton as Fame, Kate James as Lola, Theresa Mayer as Martha, Leonard Boyne as Foster, Luigi Lablache as Don Alvarez, E. W. Gardiner as Don Guzman, A. Beaumont as Father Carey, Harry Nicholls as Blount/ Scenery by Ryan, Perkins, G. Hicks, & Kautsky/ Music by Walter Slaughter/ Machines by Mr. Farrell/ Prod. by Augustus Harris.

ARMAND; OR, THE PEER AND THE PEASANT// D 5a// Anna Cora Mowatt// **Marylebone**, June 1849/ **Drury Lane**, Feb. 1853.

ARMAND; OR, THE CHILD OF THE PUBLIC// D// n.a.// **Grecian**, June 1856, with F. Charles as Louis XV, Mr. Hustleby as Richelieu, Richard Phillips as Armand, Henry Grant as d'Antin, Eaton O'Donnell as Le Sage, Harriet Coveney, Jane Coveney, Miss Johnstone as Babette, Amelie Conquest.

ARMFULL OF BLISS// F 1a// W. Moncrieff// **Olympic**, Nov. 1843, with Mr. Brookes as Dr. Sassafras, John Webster as Squills, Mr. Salier as Hawblossom, Miss Hamilton as Hebe, Miss Lebatt as Henrietta, Mrs. Craven as Mrs. Blackthorn.

ARMOREL OF LYONESSE; OR, THE CLEVEREST MAN IN TOWN// Adap. by W. H. Browne & S. B. Lawrence fr novel of Besant// **Opera Comique**, Dec. 1890.

ARMOURER, THE// D// Robert Dodson// **Britannia**, Mar. 1876.

ARMS AND THE MAN// C 3a// George Bernard Shaw// **Avenue**, Apr. 1894, with James Welch

as Amiens, Basil Potter as Jaques, Richard Phillips as Orlando, Eaton O'Donnell as Adam, Mr. Smith as Charles, Mr. Hamilton as Oliver, John Manning as Touchstone, Mrs. Charles Montgomery as Rosalind, Miss Simpson as Celia, Miss Chapman as Phoebe, Harriet Coveney as Audrey; June 1863, with Alfred Rayner as Duke, Henry Grant as Duke Frederick, Thomas Mead as Jacques, Walter Holland as Oliver, William James as Orlando, W. Shirley as de Bois, John Manning as Touchstone, J. Jackson as Adam, George Gillett as Silvius, Henry Power as William, Mrs. Alfred Rayner as Rosalind, Jane Dawson as Celia, Marie Brewer as Phoebe, Mary A. Victor as Audrey/ **Royalty,** 1872/ **Gaiety,** Feb. 1875, with W. H. Kendal, Mrs. Kendal, Hermann Vezin, Arthur Cecil, John Maclean, Nellie Harris/ **St. James's,** Feb. 1878, with Dibdin Culver as Duke, F. Wood as Amiens, Henry Forrester as Jaques, Mr. Allerton as Duke Frederick, F. De Belleville as Le Beau, Mr. Allbrook as Charles, Mr. Holman as Oliver, Lin Rayne as Orlando, W. H. Stephens as Adam, J. D. Stoyle as Touchstone, Charles Steyne as Corin, Ada Cavendish as Rosalind, Miss Emmerson as Celia, Miss Gerard as Phoebe, Kate Rivers as Audrey; Jan. 1884, with Hermann Vezin, W. H. Kendal, John Hare, Mrs. Kendal, Linda Dietz; Jan. 1885, with J. F. Young as Exiled Duke, Mr. Denison as Duke Frederick, Joseph Tapley as Amiens, Hermann Vezin as Jaques, Brandon Thomas as 1st Lord, W. T. Lovell as 2nd Lord, E. Hamilton Bell as Le Beau, H. Vernon as Charles, Herbert Waring as Oliver, W. H. Kendal as Orlando, John Maclean as Adam, John Hare as Touchstone, Robert Cathcart as Corin, E. Hendrie as William, Mrs. W. H. Kendal as Rosalind, Linda Dietz as Celia, Miss Webster as Phoebe, Miss Lea as Audrey/ Scenery by W. Harford & Perkins/ Music by Alfred Cellier/ Feb. 1890, with Henry Arncliffe as Jaques, Laurence Cautley as Orlando, Charles Sugden as Touchstone, Charles Fulton as Duke, George Canninge as Duke Frederick, Ernest Lawford as Le Beau, Erskine Lewis as William, Amy McNeil as Celia, Marion Lea as Audrey, Beatrice Lamb as Phoebe, Lillie Langtry as Rosalind/ Scenery by Bruce Smith & William Perkins; Dec. 1896, with James Fernandez as Exiled Duke, C. Aubrey Smith as Duke Frederick, Bertram Wallis as Amiens, W. H. Vernon as Jaques, H. H. Vincent as 1st Lord, George Bancroft as 2nd Lord, Vincent Sternroyd as Le Beau, J. Wheeler as Charles, H. B. Irving as Oliver, George Alexander as Orlando, Henry Loraine as Adam, H. V. Esmond as Touchstone, William Day as Corin, Arthur Royston as Sylvius, George Hawtrey as William, Julie Opp as Hymen, Julia Neilson as Rosalind, Fay Davis as Celia, Ellis Jeffreys as Phoebe, Kate Phillips as Audrey/ Scenery by H. P. Hall, T. E. Ryan & Walter Hann/ Music by Edward German & Walter Slaughter/ **Imperial,** Feb. 1879, with Hermann Vezin, Lionel Brough, E. F. Edgar, Kyrle Bellew, William Farren Jr., Maria Litton, Helen Cresswell/ **Shaftesbury,** Oct. 1888/ **Lyceum,** July 1890, with Charles Wheatleigh as Duke, George Clarke as Jacques, Eugene Ormond as Oliver, John Drew as Orlando, Charles Fisher as Adam, James Lewis as Touchstone, Charles Leclercq as Corin, Edward Wilks as William, Kitty Cheatham as Hymen, Adelaide Prince as Celia, Edith Crane as Phoebe, Isabel Irving as Audrey, Ada Rehan as Rosalind/ Scenery by Amable, Bruce Smith, Henry Hoyt/ Music by Henry Widmer/ **Daly's,** Apr. 1894/ **Comedy,** Feb. 1901.

ASCOT// FC 2a// Percy Fendall// **Folies Dramatiques** (Novelty), Mar. 1883.

ASHES// D 3a// Edward Collins & Richard Saunders// **POW,** Nov. 1894, with Charles Glenney as Denning, Philip Cunningham as Sir. Everett, Oswald Yorke as Dr. Courtney, Stuart Champion as Broadleigh, Richard Saunders as Fairfax, Lawrance d'Orsay as Capt. Fawsett, Lucy Wilson as Muriel, Gwynne Herbert as Comtesse de St. Maur, Robertha Erskine as Mrs. Ponsonby, Alice de Winton as Lady Constance.

ASHORE AND AFLOAT// D 3a// C. H. Hazlewood// **Surrey,** Feb. 1864.

ASK NO QUESTIONS// C 2a// Charles Selby// **Olympic,** Oct. 1838, with Charles Selby as Count de Commas, James Vining as Theodore, William Farren as Matthias, W. H. Oxberry as Gimblet, Mrs. Orger as Baroness de Serigny, Miss Lee as Celine, Agnes Taylor as Mrs. Gimblet/ Scenery by William Telbin & Mr. Cuthbert/ **Cov. Garden,** Oct. 1839, with Mr. Selby as Count de Cesanne, James Vining as Theodore, William Farren as Matthias, Drinkwater Meadows as Gimblet, Mrs. Orger as Baroness de Serigny, Miss Lee as Cecile, Agnes Taylor as Mme. Gimblet/ **Sad. Wells,** Oct. 1851, with Charles Wheatleigh as Count de Cesanne, Mr. Graham as Theodore, Henry M. Barrett as Mathias, Mr. Wilkins as Martinet, Henry Mellon as Pettitverre, Frederick Younge as Gimblet, Charles Mortimer as Francois, Mrs. Henry Marston as Baroness de Serigar, Eliza Travers as Mme. Gimblet, Lucy Rafter as Coline.

ASMODEUS, THE DEVIL ON TWO STICKS// C// n.a.// **Adelphi,** Apr. 1859.

ASMODEUS, THE LITTLE DEMON; OR, THE ——'S SHARE// C 2a// Adap. by Thomas Archer fr F of Eugène Scribe, Part du Diable// **Surrey,** June 1843/ **Grecian,** Nov. 1868, with Henry Grant as Ferdinand, Samuel Perfitt as Fra Antonio, J. Jackson as as Vargos, W. Shirley as Medora, William James as Don Rafael, Lizzie Mandelbert as Carlo, Alice Denvil as Casilda.

ASMODEUS; OR, THE KING AND THE MINSTREL// C 2a// n.a.// **Sad. Wells,** May 1868, with Mrs. Henry Powell as Carlos, W. Chamberlain as Raphael, Mr. Walton as Varges, Mr. Hammond as King Ferdinand, Miss Landon as Queen Isabella, Marie Willis as Casilda.

ASSIGNATION, THE; OR, WHAT WILL MY WIFE SAY?// C 2a// G. A. à Beckett// **St. James's,** Nov. 1837, with John Pritt Harley as Dubois, Mr. Forester as de Belmont, Mr. Hollingsworth as Count di Ferro, Mr. Sidney [Alfred Wigan] as Giovanni, Miss Allison as

Florentina, Mrs. Penson as Carlina, Mme. Sala as Mme. Dubois.

AT A HEALTH RESORT// F 1a// H. M. Paull// **Comedy**, June 1893, with Gerald Maxwell as Macdona, Thomas Kingston as Tellier, Gwynne Herbert as Sadie, Helen Lambert as Lady Barrymore, Violet Thornycroft as Clara.

AT BAY// D pro & 4a// Ina Cassilis & Charles Lander// **Novelty**, Apr. 1896, with William Felton as Dudley, Augustin Symonds as Gray, W. M. Franks as Watson, George Abel as Hackett, Watty Brunton Sr. as Darrell, Pemberton Beach as Philip, Daisy England as Lucy, Katie Parry as Alice, Ina Cassilis as Mrs. Hackett.

ATAR GULL// Play// George Almer// **Royalty**, Nov. 1861.

ATCHI// C 1a// J. Maddison Morton// **POW**, Sept. 1868.

ATHALIE// T 5a// Trans. by J. C. Knight fr F of Jean Racine// **Drury Lane**, Aug. 1855.

ATHELSTANE// n.a.// **City of London**, June 1854.

ATHELWOLD// T 5a// William Smith// **Drury Lane**, May 1843, with W. C. Macready, Helen Faucit.

ATHENIAN CAPTIVE, THE// T// Serjeant Talfourd// **Cov. Garden**, 1838/ **Haymarket**, Aug. 1838, with Mr. Waldron as Creon, Edmund Glover as Hyllus, Charles Perkins as Iphitus, J. W. Gough as Calchas, W. C. Macready as Thoas, Mr. Hemming as Pentheus, J. Worrell as Lycus, Mary Warner as Ismene, Agnes Taylor as Creusa/ Scenery by G. Morris.

ATONEMENT, THE// D Pro & 3a// Dram. by William Muskerry fr Victor Hugo's Les Miserables// **Victoria**, Aug. 1872/ **Sadler's Wells** (in 4a), Sept. 1872.

ATROCIOUS CRIMINAL, AN// F 1a// J. Palgrave Simpson// **Olympic**, Mar. 1867, with John Clayton as Flickerdorf, Harwood Cooper as Hahnenkamm, Jerrold Reeves as Bock, Mrs. Stephens as Cunigunda, Ellen Farren as Lisa.

ATTIC ANGEL, THE; OR, A NIGHT OF TERROR// D// n.a.// **Sad. Wells**, June 1857, with Mrs. Robert Honner as Mariette, Frederick Morton as De Courcey, E. F. Saville as Le Grange, G. Pennett as Antoine.

ATTIC DRAMA, AN// Frederick James// **Garrick**, Apr. 1898, with George Raiemond as Pimblett, Albert Rayner as Lindsay, Maud Abbott as Nellie.

ATTIC STORY, AN// F 1a// J. Maddison Morton// **Drury Lane**, May 1842, with Charles Selby as Capt. Carbine, William Bennett as Carney, Charles Hudson as Sloper, Robert Keeley as Poddy, Mrs. Selby as Mrs. Carbine, Mrs. Charles Jones as Mrs. Carney, Mrs. Keeley as Mrs. Poddy.

AULD ACQUAINTANCE// C 1a// Joseph Dilley// **St. Geo. Hall**, Mar 1878.

AULD LANG SYNE// C 1a// Basil Hood// **POW**, Nov. 1892, with Harry Grattan as Boothroyd, Graham Wentworth as Fellowes, Maud Hobson as Marion, Lilian Heath as Lucy.

AULD ROBIN GREY// n.a.// **Drury Lane**, Apr. 1858.

AULD ROBIN GREY// D 1a// Adap. by George Roy fr F/ **Imperial**, Sept. 1883.

AUNT CHARLOTTE'S MAID// F 1a// J. Maddison Morton// **Adelphi**, 1858/ **Princess's**, Nov. 1882, with Neville Doone as Sparkins, Frank Huntley as Maj. Volley, W. H. Elliott as Pivot, Mrs. Huntley as Mrs. Puddifoot, Miss Woodsworth as Fanny, Amy Singleton as Matilda.

AUNT JACK// F 3a// R. R. Lumley// **Court**, July 1889; May 1891, with George Siddons as Brue, H. Reeves-Smith as Cornish, Seymour Hicks as Col. Tavenor, Gerald Maxwell as Lord St. John, Percy Brough as Joseph, Edward Righton as Juffin, Susie Vaughan as Mrs. Vanstreek, Ethel Matthews as Mildred, Mrs. John Wood as Joan.

AUNT'S ADVICE// C 1a// E. G. Southern// **Haymarket**, Dec. 1861.

AUNTIE// F 3a// H. J. Byron// **Toole's**, Mar. 1882, with J. L. Toole, John Billington, Winifred Emery, Emily Thorne.

AURAMANIA; OR, DIAMOND'S DAUGHTER// D Pro & 4a// Johana Pritchard// **Alfred**, Sept. 1871.

AURORA FLOYD// D 4a// Dram. by C. S. Cheltnam fr novel of Miss Braddon// **Princess's**, Mar. 1863, with John Collett as Floyd, Alfred Wallace as Bulstrode, Hermann Vezin as Mellish, Robert Roxby as Conyers, George Belmore as Hargreaves, Charles Seyton as Harrison, Amy Sedgwick as Aurora, Maria Henderson as Lucy, Mrs. Simpson as Mrs. Powell.

AURORA FLOYD, THE BANKER'S DAUGHTER// D 4a// Adap. by Benjamin Webster fr novel of Miss Braddon// **Adelphi**, Mar. 1863, with Richard Phillips as Conyers, Benjamin Webster as as Hargreaves, L. J. Sefton as Bulstrode, John Billington as Mellish, Avonia Jones as Aurora Floyd, Mrs. Billington as Mrs. Powell.

AURORA FLOYD// D 3a// Adap. by W. E. Suter fr novel of Miss Braddon// **Queen's**, Apr. 1863.

AURORA FLOYD// D 3a// Adap. by J. B. Ashley & Cyril Melton fr novel of Miss Braddon// **Imperial**, Aug. 1885.

AURORA FLOYD; OR, THE DARK DUEL IN THE WOOD// D 3a// dram. by C. H.

Hazlewood fr novel of Miss Braddon// **Britannia**, Apr. 1863.

AURORA FLOYD; OR, THE DARK DEED IN THE WOOD// D// dram. fr novel of Miss Braddon// **Lyceum**, July 1871, with E. H. Brink as John Mellish, J. R. Spackman as Floyd, George Barton as Conyers, E. T. Clinton as Bullstrode, A. D. Holman as Harrison, William Davidge Jr. as Steeve Hargrave, James Jones as Wilson, Blanche Bradshaw as Aurora Floyd, Belle Sidney as Mrs. Powell.

AUSTERLITZ; OR, THE SOLDIER'S PRIDE (see also, Battle of Austerlitz)// D 3a// J. T. Haines// **Queen's**, 1845.

AUSTRALIA; OR, THE BUSHRANGERS// D 5a// W. A. and A. G. Stanley// **Grecian**, Apr. 1881.

AUTUMN MANOEUVRES// F 1a// W. R. Stow// **Vaudeville**, Oct. 1871/ **Adelphi**, Mar. 1872, with Mr. Ashley as Truffles, A. C. Lilly as Sparks, Stanislaus Calhaem as Sneaker, Lotti Wilmot as Miss Spanker, Mrs. Addie as Miss Trimmer, Maud Howard as Laura, Mrs. Alfred Mellon as Joanna.

AVALANCHE, THE; OR, THE TRIALS OF THE HEART// D 3a// Augustus Harris// **Surrey**, Oct. 1854.

AVENGER AND HIS THREE DOGS, THE// D// n.a.// **Grecian**, June 1862, with J. Jackson as Kreutzner, John Manning as Puffendorf, John Hayes as Martin, Walter Holland as Fritz, C. Phillips as Andrew and Arnold Wolfe, Ellen Hale as Louise, Mary A. Victor as Justine.

AWAKENING, THE// Play 4a// C. Haddon Chambers// **St. James's**, Feb. 1901, with H. B. Irving.

AWAKENING, THE// C 3a// Arthur Benham// **Garrick**, Oct. 1892, with Herbert Waring as as Peyton, Sant Matthews as Harley, E. Allan Aynesworth as Nicholson, Leonard Calvert as Mason, Arthur Elwood as Darbishire, Vane Featrherston as Lady Gertrude, Nina Boucicault as Archie, Estelle Burney as Helen/ Scenery by William Harford.

AWAY WITH MELANCHOLY// F 1a// J. Maddison Morton// **Princess's**, Mar. 1854, with David Fisher as Brown, Drinkwater Meadows as Trimmer, Henry Saker as David, Miss Murray as Mrs. Maynard, Maria Daly as Kitty, Miss Clifford as Dainty/ **Haymarket**, Apr. 1863, with E. A. Sothern as Brown, Mr. Rogers as Trimmer, William Clark as David, Lucreza Hill as Mrs. Maynard, Mrs. Edward Fitzwilliam as Kitty, Miss Coleman as Dainty.

AZAEL, THE PRODIGAL SON// D 3a// Adap. by Edward Fitzball fr F of Eugène Scribe & Esprit Auber, L'Enfant Prodigue// **Grecian**, Apr. 1855, with Basil Potter, Henry Grant, Richard Phillips, Thomas Roberts, Eaton O'Donnell, Jane Coveney, Ellen Crisp, Harriet Coveney/ **Victoria**, Mar. 1859, with J. H. Rickards as Reuben, W. H. Pitt as Azael, S. Sawford as Amenophis, Mr. Carter as Bucharis, John Bradshaw as Nemroud, James Howard as Amblefaddle, George Pearce as Leo, Miss Barrowcliffe as as Aron, Angelina Bathurst as Jephtele, Miss Honey as Nefte, Miss Edgar as Palmea, Miss Laporte as Messeque, Mrs. F. Lauri as Lia/ Limelight by Mr. Cox/ **Sad. Wells**, Sept. 1867, with Henry Loraine as Reuben, Alice Marriott as Azael, J. L. Warner as Amenophis, Harry Chester as Bucharis, A. J. Wilkinson as Theophas, Grace Edgar as Spirit, Miss Leigh as Jepthele, Marie Henderson as Lia, Miss Fitzgerald as Palmea/ Scenery by William Gowrie, W. Broadfoot & Horace Norman/ Lime-lights and illusions by Thomas Robbins.

*

B.B.// F 1a// F. C. Burnand & Montagu Williams// **Olympic**, Mar. 1860, with Frederick Robson as Bobbin, George Cooke as Greenfield, Horace Wigan as Rattles, Harwood Cooper as Joe, Mrs. Stephens as Mrs. Puncheon, Mrs. W. S. Emden as Dorothy/ **Adelphi**, Jan. 1898, with Howard Russell as Squire Greenfield, W. St. John as Bob Rattles, Arthur Bawtree as Joe, A. G. Poulton as Bobbin, Miss Crofton as Mrs. Puncheon, Alice Beet as Dorothy.

BABES IN THE WOOD, THE// C 3a// Tom Taylor// **Haymarket**, Nov. 1860, with W. H. Chippendale as Earl of Lazenby, William Farren as Rushton, Henry Compton as Slidell, Edwin Villiers as Loosestrife, J. B. Buckstone as Beetle, William Clark as Todd, Thomas Coe as Peacock, Amy Sedgwick as Lady Blanche, Mrs. Wilkins as Mrs. Beetle, Eliza Weekes as Trotter/ Scenery by Mr. O'Conner/ Machines by Oliver Wales.

BABY; OR, A SLIGHT MISTAKE// FC 3a// Walton Hook// **Vaudeville**, June 1888.

BACCARAT; OR, THE KNAVE OF HEARTS// D Pro & 2a// W. E. Suter// **Sad. Wells**, Mar. 1865, with George Melville as Fipport, Thomas Mead as Roussell, John Mordaunt as Ventur, T. B. Bennett as Count de Chomery, William Ellerton as Grignon, Walter Joyce as Henri, Walter Lacy as Tonio, Alice Marriott as Baccarat, Mrs. Stevenson as Mme. Fipport, Lizzie Harrison as Fanchette, Lizzie Willmore as Cerise, Ethel Somers as Tulipe, Ellen Beaufort as Violanti.

BACHELOR OF ARTS, A// C 2a// Pelham Hardwick// **Lyceum**, Nov. 1853/ **Drury Lane**, Dec. 1855, with C. J. Mathews as Jasper, A. Younge as Wylie, C. Vincent as Thornton, W. Templeton as Adolphus, E. F. Edgar as Adderly, Emma Wadham as Mrs. Thornton, Fanny Hughes as Emma/ **Sad. Wells**, Apr. 1855, with Frederic Robinson as Jasper, Frank Matthews as Wylie, Mr. Williams as Thornton, Gaston Murray as Adderly, W. Templeton as Adolphus, Mr. Swan as Matthew, Miss Wadham as Mrs. Thornton, Frances Hughes as Emma.

BACHELORS' BUTTONS// F 1a// Edward Stirling// **Strand**, May 1837/ **Olympic**, May 1842, with Mr. Turnour as Wilton, Mr. Fitzjames as Masterton, Mr. Ross as Samson, F. B. Conway as Tom, Mr. Brown as Dick, Miss Mitchell in 4 char. parts, Miss Granby as Mary/ **Sad. Wells**, Aug. 1844, with Mr. Williams as Wilton, Mr. Sharpe as Masterton, G. F. Forman as Sam, Mr. Evain as Dick, Mr. Franks as Tom, Kate Howard as Emily, Georgiana Lebatt as Mary, Miss Morelli as Betty; Oct. 1865, with Samuel Perfitt as Wilton, E. H. Brooke as Masterton, John Rouse as Sampson, Clara St. Casse in 3 char. parts, Miss Rogers as Betty.

BACHELOR'S ROMANCE, A// C 4a// Martha Morton// **Gaiety**, Sept. 1897/ **Globe**, Jan. 1898, with John Hare as David Holmes, Frederick Kerr as Gerald Holmes, Gilbert Hare as Beggs, Frank Gillmore as Savage, Charles Cherry as Reynolds, James Leigh as Mulberry, May Harvey as Helen le Grand, Mona Oram as Harriet, Susie Vaughan as Miss Clementina, Nellie Thorne as Sylvia/ Scenery by W. Harford.

BACHELOR'S VOW, THE// F 1a// Mrs. Alfred Phillips// **Olympic**, June 1852, with George Cooke as Middleton, E. F. Edgar as Nugent, Isabel Adams as Rose, Mrs. Alfred Phillips as Mrs. O'Neil and Biddy O'Conner.

BACHELOR'S WIFE, THE// C 2a// F. Watson// **Drury Lane**, Oct. 1860, with C. J. Mathews as Rigby, Robert Roxby as Maywood, Edwin Dixon as Jackson, Frederic Robinson as Watkins, Mrs. C. J. Mathews as Mrs. Honeydew, Miss Arden as Mrs. Maywood, Miss Palmer as Mrs. Stranger.

BACHELORS// C// Adap. by Robert Buchanan & Hermann Vezin fr G// **Haymarket**, Sept. 1884, with Stewart Dawson as Marrable, H. B. Conway as Lovelace, Charles Brookfield as Bromley, Edmund Maurice as Dr. West, Charles Coote as Potts, Kate Munroe as Mrs. Loseby, Ruth Francis as Emmeline, Mary A. Victor as Mrs. Moody, Julia Gwynne as Sophia, Mary Marden as Susan.

BACHELORS' HALL// F// G. L. Gordon// **Opera Comique**, Apr. 1887.

BACHELOR'S WIVES// F 3a// Fred Bousfield// **Strand**, Dec. 1886.

BACK IN FIVE MINUTES// F 1a// H. T. Johnson// **Strand**, Apr. 1891, with Sydney Barraclough as Robinson, William Lugg as Roe, Robert Nainby as Prosser, Georgie Esmond as Mary, Lilian Millward as Theresa.

BACKING THE FAVOURITE// F// G. L. Gordon// **Opera Comique**, Aug. 1875.

BAD BOYS// C 3a// Adap. by Clement Scott fr F, Clara Soleil// **Comedy**, Apr. 1885, with C. D. Marius, Arthur Roberts, Edward Rose, Violet Cameron.

BAD PENNY, A// F 1a// W. Lestocq// **Vaudeville**, June 1882, with Walter Howe, W. Lestocq, Clara Calvert.

BAFFLED; OR, PARMA VIOLETS// D 4a// n.a.// **Standard**, Sept. 1881.

BAFFLED CRIME, A// D 4a// C. W. McCabe// **Novelty**, Nov. 1896.

BAG OF GOLD, THE// D 2a// J. Hillyard// **Olympic**, June 1852, with William Farren Jr. as Mortimer, Charles Diddear as Thornton, William Hoskins as Clark, E. Clifton as Dawson, W. Shalders as Shilling, George Cooke as Dixon, Mrs. Walter Lacy as Florence, Isabel Adams as Mrs. Weston, Mrs. B. Bartlett as Mrs. Dixon, Ellen Turner as Kate.

BAILIFF, THE// C 1a// F. W. Broughton// **Royalty**, May 1890, with Robert Medlicott as Grattan, Henry Arncliffe as Frank, Walter McEwen as Daniel, Mary Kinsley as Minnie/ **Toole's**, July 1890.

BALACLAVA// D 3a// J. B. Johnstone// **Standard**, June 1878.

BALANCE OF COMFORT, THE// C 1a// W. Bayle Bernard// **Haymarket**, Nov. 1854, with Henry Howe as Torrington, Mr. Rogers as Pollard, W. H. Clark as Sheepshanks, Miss Reynolds as Mrs. Torrington, Miss Grantham as Miss Pollard, Ellen Chaplin as Mary/ **Lyceum**, May 1885, with George Alexander as Torrington, Mr. Harbury as Pollard, Mr. Carter as Sheepshanks, Mr. Harvey as Bates, Miss F. Harwood as Emily Pollard, Rose Leclercq as Mrs. Torrington.

BALLA-GO-FAUGH// D 3a// Edward Towers// **Pavilion**, Nov. 1880.

BALLAD-MONGER, THE// Play 1a// Adap. by Walter Besant & W. H. Pollock fr F of Thèodore de Banville, Gringoire// **Haymarket**, Sept. 1887, with C. H. Brookfield as Louis XI, Herbert Beerbohm Tree as Gringoire, Charles Allan as Oliver, Stewart Dawson as Simon, Marion Terry as Loyse, Esther Hayland as Nicole/ Scenery by Walter Johnstone.

BALLET GIRL'S REVENGE, THE// D// Frederick Marchant & Rose Mortimer// **Grecian**, Sept. 1865, with J. B. Steele as Count Lerno, J. Jackson as Mortimer, C. Arnold as Flathers, Frederick Marchant as Halliday, Henry Grant as Booth, John Manning as Grabbe, Lizzie Mandlebert as Rose, Mary A. Victor as Sukey, Mrs. J. W. Simpson as Mrs. Halliday, Marie Brewer as Clara.

BALLINASLOE BOY, THE// D 2a// C. H. Hazlewood// **Britannia**, June 1867.

BALLOON, THE// FC 3a// J. H. Darnley & G. M. Fenn// **Terry's**, Nov. 1888/ **Strand**, Feb. 1889.

BAMBOOZLING// F 1a// T. E. Wilks// **Sad. Wells**, May 1845, with A. Young as Sir Marmaduke, Samuel Buckingham as Capt. Bamboozle, Mr. Raymond as Tiverton, Mr. Bologna as Sims, Mrs. Henry Marston as Lady

Meadows, Miss Lebatt as Emily, Georgiana Lebatt as Sophy/ **Olympic**, Nov. 1845, with Charles Boyce as Capt. Pendennis, Mr. Turnour as Meadows, Mr. Jones as Dolly, Mr. Darcie as Tiverton, Mrs. Griffiths as Lady Meadows, Miss Hamilton as Emily, Miss Beauchamp as Sophy/ **Princess's**, 1863, with Mr. Fitzjames as Sir Marmaduke, Walter Montgomery as Capt. Frank, Robert Cathcart as Sam, Mr. Munroe as Tiverton, Mrs. J. W. Simpson as Lady Marmaduke, Miss Frazer as Sophy.

BANDIT KING, THE// D// n.a.// **Adelphi**, June 1867, with Brandon Ellis, C. Britton, W. Robinson, Mr. Adlard, Mr. Percy, R. Power, Bella Richardson, Eliza Rudd, Mrs. G. James.

BANDIT KING, THE// D 5a & 3 tabl.// n.a.// **Pavilion**, Dec. 1895.

BANDIT MERCHANT, THE; OR, THE DUMB GIRL OF GENOA// D// John Farrell// **Sad. Wells**, Mar. 1841, with Mr. Elvin as Count Corvenio, Mr. Williams as Tristram, Mr. Smart as Moco, Mr. Dry as Cerenza, Mr. Jefferini as Strapado, J. W. Collier as Desperetta, Mrs. J. W. Collier as Julietta.

BANDIT'S SON, THE; OR, THE BOY OF CORSICA// D// n.a.// **Sad. Wells**, June 1838, with Mr. Harwood as Capt. Xavier, J. W. Collier as Corp. Garboni, Mr. Dry as Marvina, Miss Pincott as Fortunato, C. J. Smith as Manfrina, Mr. Mellor as Strozzi, Miss Cooke as Gennetta.

BANISHED FROM HOME// D 3a// J. C. Griffiths// **Britannia**, May 1875.

BANK ROBBERY, THE// D// Forbes Dawson// **Strand**, Jan. 1896.

BANTRY BAY// Play 1a// Stephen Bond// **Surrey**, Dec. 1897.

BARBARA// Play 1a// Jerome K. Jerome// **Globe**, Apr. 1886, with Cissy Grahame as Barbara, Miss C. Mayne as Lilie, A. G. Andrews as Norton, Norman Bent as Finnicane.

BARBER AND THE BRAVO, THE; OR, THE PRINCESS WITH THE RAVEN LOCKS// F// Isabella Vernier// **Surrey**, Oct. 1846.

BARBER BRAVO, THE// n.a.// **Princess's**, 1846.

BARBER'S SECRET, THE; OR, THE INVENTOR OF POWDER// F 1a// Thomas Archer// **Grecian**, Oct. 1846, with Eaton O'Donnell as Hector, Frederick Robson as Formoso, John Collett as Tagliarini, Miss Merion as Duchess Norino, Mary A. Crisp as Floretta.

BARGEMAN OF THE THAMES, THE// D 2a// T. Mead// **Grecian**, Sept. 1866, with George Gillett as Lord George, J. Jackson as Adm. Goodboy, Alfred Rayner as Halstead, Henry Power as Daw, John Manning as Latherem, Mrs. Atkinson as Lady Greenwood, Lizzie Mandelbert as Rosalie, Miss Dearlove as Dame Halstead, Mary A. Victor as Selina.

BARKARK JOHNSON; OR, THE BLIND WITNESS// D 1a// Wybert Reeve// **Surrey**, Apr. 1844.

BARNABY RUDGE// D 3a// Dram. by Charles Selby & Charles Melville fr novel of Charles Dickens// **Eng. Opera House** (Lyceum), June 1841.

BARNABY RUDGE; OR, THE MURDER OF THE WARREN// D// Dram. by C. Z. Barnett fr novel of Charles Dickens// **Sad. Wells**, (n.d.), with Mr. Dry as Haredale, Henry Marston as Chester, Mr. Elvin as Edward, Robert Honner as Stranger, Mrs. Robert Honner as Barnaby, Mr. Williams as Varden, John Herbert as Tappertit, Mr. Aldridge as John Willet, J. W. Collier as Joe Willet, George Ellis as Hugh, Miss Richardson as Mrs. Rudge, Miss Hicks as Emma, Miss Cooke as Mrs. Varden, Mrs. Richard Barnett as Miggs, Mrs. Morgan as Dolly.

BARNABY RUDGE// D 3a// Dram. fr novel of Charles Dickens// **Adelphi**, Jan. 1842.

BARNABY RUDGE// D 3a// Dram. by Watts Phillips & Mr. Vining fr novel of Charles Dickens// **Princess's**, Nov. 1866.

BARNABY RUDGE// D 4a// n.a.// **Marylebone**, Nov. 1876.

BARNABY RUDGE; OR, MURDER AT THE WARREN// D// Dram. fr novel of Charles Dickens// **Grecian**, Nov. 1863, with Henry Grant as Haredale, William James as Chester, George Gillett as Edward Chester, J. Jackson as Gabriel, W. Shirley as Willett, Henry Power as Joe, John Manning as Simon Tappertit, Thomas Mead as Stranger, Mrs. Charles Dillon as Barnaby Rudge, Marie Brewer as Emma, Ellen Crisp as Mrs. Varden, Laura Conquest as Dolly Varden, Mary A. Victor as Miggs, Jane Dawson as Mrs. Rudge.

BARNARD THE VICTIM PATRIOT; OR, THE DOUBLE FRATRICIDE// D 3a// n.a.// **Victoria**, Oct. 1846, with E. Edwards as Barnard Donay, C. J. Bird as Pierre Donay, William Searle as Bardin, G. F. Forman as Butler, F. Wilton as Perlet, Alfred Raymond as Mouncey, James Ranoe as Valtone, Mr. Hitchinson as Brissolt, Mr. Fitzjames as Garnaret, J. Howard as Latrobe, Miss Backhous as Philippe, Mrs. George Lee as Mme. Donay, Mrs. Henry Vining as Mariette, Mrs. Cooke as Mme. Jervoise, Mrs. Andrews as Mme. St. Val.

BARNES OF NEW YORK// D// Dram. by Hal Collier-Edwards fr novel of A. C. Gunter// **Marylebone**, June 1888.

BARNEY THE BARON// F 1a// Samuel Lover// **Sad. Wells**, July 1858, with Barney Williams as O'Toole, Walter Vernon as Bloomenthal, John Vollaire as Bluffenwig, Alfred Tapping as Karl, Mrs. John Billington as Lady Matilda, Kate Kelly as Edith, Miss Ferguson as Emma; Nov. 1879, with Edmund Lyons as O'Toole, Nelson Wheatcroft as Capt. Harlstein, Mr. Fosbrooke as Max, Arthur Redwood as Katzleig,

Miss Gordon as Lady Marguerite, Miss Montague as Christine/ **Drury Lane**, Feb. 1859, with Barney Williams as O'Toole, Henry Butler as Bloomenthal, Mr. Tilbury as Bluffenwig, Stephen Artaud as Karl, Miss Wilmington as Lady Matilda, Miss Simpson as Edith/ **Adelphi**, 1881, with Shiel Barry as Barney, J. A. Rosier as Augustus, Harry Proctor as Karl, T. A. Palmer as Bluffenberg, Maud Howard as Lady Margaret, Clara Jecks as Edith.

BARONET, THE; OR, FEMALE SOCIETY// C 2a// n.a.// **Cov. Garden**, Mar. 1840, with C. J. Mathews as Sir Frederick, Mrs. Walter Lacy (Miss Taylor) as Emily, Miss Lee as Mary, Mrs. Charles Jones as Miss Mistletoe, Mrs. Tayleure as Mrs. Whimperly, Mrs. Macnamara as Mrs. Ruffle, Mrs. Emden as Mrs. Spigot, Mrs. Humby as Mitts.

BARON'S WAGER, THE// C 1a// Charles Young// **Avenue**, Oct. 1897, with Sydney Warden as Baron de Geraudot, Edith Ostlere as Clothilde.

BARRACK ROOM, THE// C 2a// T. H. Bayley// **Olympic**, Feb. 1837, with Frank Matthews as Marquis de Cruzac, James Vining as Col. Ferrier, Charles Selby as Capt. Valmont, James Bland as Bernard, Mme. Vestris as Clarisse/ **Haymarket**, June 1838, with Robert Strickland as Marquis de Crusac, C. J. Mathews as Bernard, Mr. Hemming as Col. Ferrier, Mr. Hutchings as Capt. Valmont, Mme. Vestris as Clarisse/ **Princess's**, June 1846, with Mr. Granby as Marquis de Cruzac, James Vining as Col. Ferrier, A. Walton as Bernard, Charles Fisher as Capt. Valmont, Mme. Vestris as Clarisse.

BARRINGTON THE PICKPOCKET; OR, ADVENTURES OF THE IRISH DICK TURPIN// D 2a// n.a.// **Victoria**, July 1848, with Mr. Henderson as Viscount Loftly, T. H. Higgie as Sir Alexander, J. T. Johnson as Waldron, John Bradshaw as Price, G. F. Forman as Martin, F. H. Henry as Brown, Walter Searle as Mahone, J. Howard as Withers, Mrs. George Lee as Fiera, Miss Sharpe as Molly, Mrs. Cooke as Mrs. O'Doozle.

BARREN LAND// Play 4a// Henry Byatt & William Magnay// **Olympic**, Apr. 1888 (in 3 acts).

BARRICADE, THE// D// Pro & 4a// Adap. by Clarence Holt fr F of Victor Hugo, Les Miserables// **Duke's**, Sept. 1878.

BARRINGTONS, THE// D 4a// S. J. Fitzgerald & J. H. Merrifield// **Novelty**, Mar. 1884.

BARRISTER, THE// FC 3a// George Fenn & J. H. Darnley// **Comedy**, Sept. 1887/ **Royalty**, May 1890, with Fred Mervin as Maxwell, Lawrance d'Orsay as Capt. Walker, Robert Medlicott as Maj. Drayton, Fred Emney as Price, Fred Burton as Sgt. Crisp, Walter McEwen as Roderick, Susie Vaughan as Miss Foster, Alice Yorke as Mrs. Maxwell, Mary Kingsley as Ellen, Delia Carlyle as Kittie.

BARTONMERE TOWERS// C 3a// Rutland Barrington// **Savoy**, Feb. 1893, with Cyril Maude as Sir Richard, Yorke Stephens as Cope, William Herbert as Farquhar, Philip Cunningham as Maurice, Frank Lacy as Moline, Rutland Barrington as Sir James, Charles Fulton as Dr. Farquhar, Rosina Brandram as Mrs. Johnson, Lily Hanbury as Mary, Helen Leyton as Gertie, Emily Cross as Lady Hanbury.

BARWISE'S BOOK// C 2a// H. T. Craven// **Haymarket**, Apr. 1870, with E. A. Sothern as Mulcraft, W. H. Kendal as Vere, J. B. Buckstone as Cuckfield, W. H. Chippendale as Bogate, Henry Compton as Laglot, Mrs. Frank Matthews as Mrs. Mulcraft, Agnes Robertson as Ellen, Fanny Gwynne as Kate/ Scenery by John O'Conner/ Music by G. A. Schmuck.

BASE IMPOSTER, THE// F// Adap. by Horace Wigan fr F, Le Contre Bass// **Olympic**, Dec. 1859, with George Cooke as Capt. Cottenham, Harwood Cooper as Robinson, Horace Wigan as Beleuil, Henry Rivers as Peter, Miss Stevens as Mrs. Smith, Miss Cottrell as Mary.

BASHFUL IRISHMAN, THE// F// Mark Lemon// **Haymarket**, Apr. 1843, with Mr. Tilbury as Quakely, Henry Howe as Capt. Pester, T. F. Mathews as Scoremore, Mr. Leonard as O'Gallagher, Mrs. Stanley as Mrs. Quakely, Miss C. Conner as Emmeline.

BASTILE, THE// D 1a// n.a.// **Haymarket**, Dec. 1842, with Henry Holl as Louis XIV, Henry Howe as Conde, Mr. Gough as Verney, Mr. Tilbury as de Retez, A. Brindal as Joly, J. Worrell as Cinq Mars, Benjamin Webster as Fricandeau, Miss Charles as Duchess de Montbazon, Mme. Celeste as Ninon.

BATHING// F 1a// James Bruton// **Olympic**, May 1842, with Mr. Brookes as Pepperpod, Charles Baker as Beauchamp, Mr. Rogers as Charles, Mr. Ross as Stokes, George Wild as Finch, Mrs. Granby as Mrs. Pepperpod, Miss Arden as Jane, Miss Bartlett as Julia/ **Astley's**, Apr. 1859, with Mr. Lloyd as Pepperpod, John Herbert as John Beauchamp, J. T. Anderson as Charles Beauchamp, J. W. Anson as Finch, Mrs. William Dowton as Mrs. Pepperpod.

BATTLE OF AUSTERLITZ, THE; OR, THE SOLDIER'S BRIDE// D 3a// Adap. by J. T. Haines fr F of Eugene Scribe & M. Amant, La Conscript// **Sad. Wells**, Apr. 1841, with Mr. Turnour as Napoleon, Mr. Chudleigh as Count Las Casas, Mr. Jones as Gen. Latour,, Mr. Aldridge as Capt. Monville, Mr. Heyling as Col. Montdidier, Charles Fenton as Retard, Mr. Hance as Ambrose, Henry Marston as Le Clercq, F. B. Conway as St. Louis, Mr. Hamilton as Dumont, J. W. Collier as Lovaine, Mr. Lewis as Gaspar, Mrs. Robert Honner as Louise, Mrs. Richard Barnett as Jeannette, Miss Cooke as Dame Lodine/ **Victoria**, Aug. 1846, with F. Wilton as Col. Le Froi, G. W. Walton as Capt. Roue, G. F. Forman as Pontoon, E. G. Burton as Index, William Seaman as St. Louis, Alfred Raymond as Merlet, Mr. Archer as Marcel, J. Howard as Graspeau, Mrs. Henry Vining as Constance, Lydia Pearce as Merial, Mrs. Cooke as Dame Canteen.

BATTLE OF LIFE, THE// D 3a// Dram. by Albert Smith fr novel of Charles Dickens// **Lyceum**, Dec. 1846, with Frank Matthews as Jeddler, Frederick Vining as Wardon, Drinkwater Meadows as Snitchey, Henry J. Turner as Craggs, Robert Keeley as Britain, Ellen Daly as Grace, Mrs. Woollidge as Mrs. Snitchey, Mrs. Keeley as Clemency/ Scenery by P. Phillips.

BATTLE OF LIFE, THE// D 3a// Dram. by Edward Stirling fr novel of Charles Dickens// **Surrey**, Jan. 1847.

BATTLE OF LIFE, THE// D 3a// Dram. fr novel of Charles Dickens// **Astley's**, Mar. 1867, with W. H. Stephens as Dr. Jeddler, James Fernandez as Alfred, W. T. Richardson as Warden, Mr. Arthur as Snitchey, Edward Atkins as Britain, Edith Stuart as Marion, Nelly Clifton as Grace, Ellen Thirlwall as Clemency, Mrs. Caulfield as Mrs. Snitchey.

BATTLE OF LIFE, THE// D 3a// Dram. by Charles Dickens, Jr., fr novel of his father// **Gaiety**, Dec. 1873.

BATTLE OF LIFE, THE// D// Adap. fr F, Le Pailasse// **Surrey**, 1851/ **Olympic**, Apr. 1891/ **Standard**, May 1893.

BATTLE OF SEDGEMOOR, THE// D 3a// George Almar// **Pavilion**, Feb. 1837.

BATTLE OF THE HEART, THE// D 4a// J. H. Wilkins// **Duke's**, Mar. 1880, with Clarence Holt, Fanny Brough.

BATTLE OF WATERLOO, THE// D 3a// J. H. Amherst// **Astley's**, May 1869.

BATTLE OF WATERLOO AND THE CONQUESTS OF QUATRE BRAS AND LIGNY, THE// D 3a// n.a.// **Sad. Wells**, June 1842, with Mr. Dry as Wellington, Mr. Crowther as Lord Hill, Basil Baker as Prince of Orange, Mr. Boswell as Marquis of Anglesea, Mr. Hicken as Duke of Brunswick, Mr. Stickney as Gen. Pictor, Mr. Lyon as Corp. Standfast, Mr. Frederick as Thompson, Mrs. Richard Barnett as Mary, John Herbert as Molly Maloney, Mr. Gomersal as Napoleon, Henry Widdicomb as Ney, W. D. Broadfoot as Gen. Dushame, P. Williams as Maladroit, Miss Richardson as Phedora, Mrs. Hildebrand as Mathilde, Mrs. Stickney as Marinette, Mrs. Morgan as Rose/ Scenery by T. Pitt.

BAUBLE SHOP, THE// Play 4a// Henry Arthur Jones// **Criterion**, Jan. 1893, with Charles Wyndham as Viscount Clivebrook, C. W. Somerset as Earl of Sarum, E. Allan Aynesworth as Cheviot, Frank Atherley as Sir John, William Blakeley as Bussey, Sydney Valentine as Stoach, Frank Worthing as Ireson, Fanny Enson as Lady Kate, Louise Moddie as Lady Bellenden, Ellis Jeffreys as Gussy, Mary Moore as Jessie/ Scenery by W. T. Hemsley.

BAVARIAN GIRL, THE; OR, THE BLACK HELMET// D 4a// W. E. Suter// **Sad. Wells**, Nov. 1869, with J. G. Rosiere as Duke Adrien, Edmund Phelps as Alexis, T. W. Ford as Count Everard, Thomas Goodwin as Count Bertrand, Mr. Howard as Raymond, Charles Blythe as Capt. Bloomfield, Mr. Lacy as Brioni, Richard Edgar as Frivola, Julia Summers as Princess Octavia, Mrs. E. F. Edgar as Agatha, Margaret Eburne as Isoliene, Miss Bennett as Constance.

BEAR HUNTERS, THE// D// J. B. Buckstone// **Victoria**, Mar. 1854, with N. T. Hicks as Caribert, T. E. Mills as Estevan, Mr. Henderson as Claude, Watty Brunton as Lizier, R. H. Kitchen as Andrea, F. H. Henry as Felix, John Bradshaw as Larone, Mr. Hudspeth as Bluebell, Mrs. Henry Vining as Aline, Miss Laporte as Jeannette, Miss Lebatt as Catrine, Mrs. Manders as Mme. Manette.

BEARD AND MOUSTACH MOVEMENT, THE// F 1a// W. E. Suter// **Grecian**, May 1854, with Richard Phillips as Fitzgig, Eaton O'Donnell as Piggy, Henry Power as Plug, Agnes De Warde as Julia, Miss Johnstone as Mrs. Boniface, Harriet Coveney as Sally.

BEATA// D 3a// Adap. by Austin Fryers fr Norw. of Henrik Ibsen, Rosmersholm// **Globe**, Apr. 1892, with Frances Ivor as Beata, Estelle Burney as Rebecca West, Susie Vaughan as Helseth, Henry Vernon as Rector Kroll, George Hughes as Mortensgard, Robert Soutar as Dr. West, Leonard Outram as Rosmer/ Prod. by Leonard Outram/ Scenery by Richard Durant.

BEAU AUSTIN// C 4a// W. E. Henley & R. L. Stevenson// **Haymarket**, Nov. 1900, with Herbert Beerbohm Tree as Austin, Charles Brookfield as Menteith, Fred Terry as Fenwick, Edmund Maurice as Musgrave, Rose Leclercq as Evalina, Mrs. Tree as Dorothy.

BEAU BRUMMEL, THE KING OF CALAIS// D 2a// M. W. B. Jerrold// **Lyceum**, Apr. 1859.

BEAUTIFUL FOR EVER// F// G. F. Hodgson// **Surrey**, Oct. 1868.

BEAUTY AND THE BEAST// F// John Oxenford// **Drury Lane**, Dec. 1863, with G. F. Neville as Higgins, G. Weston as Figgins, George Spencer as Wiggins, Henry M. Barrett as Wadding, Mr. Addison as Stubbs, Mrs. Edmund Falconer as Mrs. Stubbs, Rose Leclercq as Hetty, Miss Seymour as Anne.

BEAUTY OF GHENT, THE// D 3a// n.a.// **Grecian**, Aug. 1845, with Henry Horncastle as Marquis de San Lucar, Mr. Campbell as Cesarius, Harry Chester as Bustamente, Edwin Dixon as Benedict, Frederick Robson as Zephinos, Annette Mears as Beatrice, Miss Johnstone as Agnes, Mary A. Crisp as Julia/ Scenery by Mr. Muir/ Music by Mr. Harroway.

BEAUTY OR THE BEAST// F 1a// John Oxenford// **Drury Lane**, Nov. 1863.

BEAUX' STRATAGEM, THE// C 5a// George Farquhar// **Haymarket**, May 1842, with Henry Holl as Archer, Henry Howe as Aimwell, Robert Strickland as Sullen, Benjamin Webster as

Scrub, Malone Raymond as Foigard, Henry Wallack as Gibbet, Mrs. Stanley as Lady Bountiful, Miss Charles as Dorinda, Louisa Nisbett as Mrs. Sullen, Mrs. Malone Raymond as Cherry; Jan. 1856, with William Farren as Aimwell, Leighton Walter as Freeman, Henry Howe as Archer, W. H. Chippendale as Sullen, George Braid as Foigard, Mr. Rogers as Boniface, Edwin Villiers as Gibbet, J. B. Buckstone as Scrub, Mrs. Poynter as Lady Bountiful, Miss Swanborough as Dorinda, Miss Reynolds as Mrs. Sullen, Bella Copeland as Cherry/ **Imperial**, Aug. 1879, with E. F. Edgar, William Farren, Jr., Kyrle Bellew, Lionel Brough, Mrs. Stirling, Carlotta Addison.

BED OF ROSES, A// C 1a// Henry Arthur Jones// **Globe**, Jan. 1882, with A. Wood, Arthur Dacre, Miss Goldney, Miss Meredith/ **St. James's**, Feb. 1886, with Charles Brookfield as Peter Vellacott, W. T. Lovell as Charles Vellacott, Herbert Waring as Dalyson, E. Hendrie as Basker, Miss Webster as Dora, Annie Rose as Amy.

BEDROOM WINDOW, THE// F 1a// Edward Stirling// **Olympic**, Mar. 1848, with H. J. Turner as Baron de Reisbach, John Kinloch as Wenzel, Lysander Thompson as Kalt, Miss Bromley as Clara, Miss F. Hamilton as Bertha.

BECKET// D 5a// Alfred Tennyson// **Lyceum**, Feb. 1893, with Henry Irving as Becket, William Terriss as Henry II, Mr. Bond as King Louis, Mr. Lacy as Bishop Foliot, A. Beaumont as Roger, Mr. Cushing as Hereford, Frank Cooper as Fitzurse, Ian Robertson as John of Oxford, Genevieve Ward as Eleanore of Aquitaine, Ellen Terry as Rosamund/ Scenery by William Telbin & Hawes Craven/ Music by C. Villiers Stanford.

BEFORE THE MAST// D 4a// F. W. Broughton// **Olympic**, Mar. 1884, with C. W. Somerset as Capt. Watson, Philip Beck as Harold Watson, T. P. Haynes as Prout, C. H. Stephenson as Blount, T. J. Merridew as Rev. Weston, Miss E. J. Clayton as Teddie, Agnes Thomas as Ethel, Nellie Bouverie as Nellie, Mrs. C. H. Stephenson as Mrs. Watson/ Scenery by George Harcourt/ Music by Walter Slaughter.

BEGGAR'S PETITION, THE; OR, A FATHER'S LOVE AND MOTHER'S CARE// D 3a// G. D. Pitt// **Victoria**, Nov. 1848, with J. Howard as Squire Grandly, Mr. Henderson as Edgar, Mr. Shepperd as Brightwell, J. T. Johnson as Brace, John Dale as Darkly, G. F. Forman as Links, Mr. Hawkins as Bacon, Miss Richardson as Matilda, Annette Vincent as Jane, Miss Barrowcliffe as Polly, Mrs. Sharpe as Mrs. Massey, T. H. Higgie as Sir William, John Bradshaw as Haulyard, Mrs. George Lee as Lady Carmine.

BEGGAR ON HORSEBACK, A// C 5a// R. Sullivan// **Haymarket**, Mar. 1846, with Mr. Tilbury as Sir John, Henry Holl as Ernest, Charles Hudson as Waldgrave, Benjamin Webster as Foxall, William Farren as Morecraft, T. F. Mathews as Baggs, James Bland as Schneidermann, William Clark as Spavin, Henry Widdicomb as Jolt, A. Brindal as Thomas, Mrs. Julia Glover as Lady Coverdale, Julia Bennett as Selina, Mrs. Seymour as Emmeline/ Scenery by George Morris.

BEGGING LETTER, THE// D 3a// Mark Lemon// **Drury Lane**, Dec. 1853, with George Bennett as Sir Arthur, Frederick Belton as Reginald, John Kinloch as Sir Hugh, A. Younge as Thistledown, Henry Lee as Bramble, Mr. Morgan as Richard, A. Walton as Black Joe, Mrs. E. Lewis as Lady Alicia, Mrs. Vickery as Mad Bess, Miss Featherstone as Julie.

BEGINNING AND THE END, THE// D 4a// Maria Lacy// **Haymarket**, Oct. 1855.

BEGUM'S DIAMONDS, THE// C 3a// J. P. Hurst// **Avenue**, Jan. 1889.

BEHIND A MASK// C 3a// Bernard Dixon & Arthur Wood// **Royalty**, Mar. 1871.

BEHIND THE SCENES// C 3a// Adap. by G. P. Hawtrey & Felix Morris fr The First Night, a transl. fr F, Le Père de la Debutante// **Comedy**, July 1896, with Cosmo Stuart as Cardew, Felix Morris as Talma, W. F. Hawtrey as Schreiber, Ernest Cosham as Huggett, Frederick Volpé as Duncan, Frank Lacy as Bennett, Alice Beet as Miss Pettigrew, Gertrude Henriquez as Miss Hamilton, Sarah Brooke as Miss Dufard.

BEHIND TIME// F 1a// Benjamin Webster, Jr.// **Adelphi**, Dec. 1865.

BEL DEMONIO// D 4a// dram by John Brougham fr Stendahl, L'Abbaye de Castro// **Lyceum**, Oct. 1863, with George Jordan as Count Campireali, F. Charles as Fabio, John Brougham as Cardinal Montalto, Samuel Emery as Ranuccio, Charles Fechter as Angelo, Kate Terry as Lena, Miss Elsworthy as Countess Campireali/ Scenery by Mr. Gates/ Music by W. H. Montgomery.

BELFORD CASTLE; OR, THE SCOTTISH GOLD MINE// C 3a // Joseph Lunn// **Haymarket**, June 1841, with Robert Maywood as Muckle, Frederick Vining as Mortimer, Henry Wallack as Earl of Belford, George Bennett as Stapleton, Robert Strickland as Sterling, John Webster as Murray, Henry Howe as Oswald, Mrs. Stirling as Lady Grace, Priscilla Horton as Emily, Mrs. Stanley as Dorcas.

BELL RINGER, THE; OR, THE SPIRIT OF THE CHIMES// D 4a// Sutton Vane & Arthur Shirley// **Grand**, July 1898.

BELL-RINGER OF NOTRE DAME, THE; OR, THE HUNCHBACK'S LOVE// D 3a// Adap. by W. H. Abel fr novel of Victor Hugo// **East London**, July 1871.

BELL-RINGER OF ST. PAUL'S AND HIS DAUGHTER, THE; OR, THE HUNTSMAN AND THE SPY// **Sad. Wells**, Feb. 1839 with Mr. Cathcart as John, Robert Honner as Fairfax, J. W. Collier as Macray, Mr. Dry as Russell, Mrs. Robert Honner as Madeline, Mr. Harwood as Lord Ludlow, Mr. Phillips as Grey, Benjamin Conquest as Skim, Miss Pincott as Barbara, Mr. Elvin as Charles II// Scenery by Fenwick & Smithyes/ Music by Mr. Herbert/ Machines by B. Sloman.

BELLA'S BIRTHDAY// F// C. H. Stephenson// **Princess's**, Jan. 1873.

BELLAMONDE; OR, THE KING'S AVENGER// D Pro & 3a// Edward Towers// **Pavilion**, Nov. 1879.

BELLE BELAIR// Play 4a// Ralph Lumley// **Avenue**, May 1897, with Weedon Grossmith as Pigeon, Gilbert Farquhar as Sir Barnaby, John Beauchamp as Tracey, John Martin Harvey as Strange, H. Athol Forde as Jessop, Louise Moodie as Lady Bullingham, Irene Vanbrugh as Vivian, Emily Fitzroy as Lady Poltower, Mrs. John Wood as Mrs. Belair.

BELLE RUSSE, LA// D 4a// David Belasco// **Pavilion**, Apr. 1886.

BELLE SAUVAGE, LA// F// John Brougham// **St. James's**, Jan. 1870, with Mrs. John Wood as Pocahontas, Miss H. Everard as Krosascanbe, Sally Turner as Dimundi, Bessie Lovell as Dahlinduk, Mark Smith as Powhatan, A. W. Young as Count Rolff, Lionel Brough as John Smith, James Bradley as Lt. Brown, George Grainger as Opodildoc/ Scenery by Grieve, Caltoo, & J. Galt/ Music by W. H. Montgomery.

BELLE VUE// D 3a// R. Quittenden// **Victoria**, Apr. 1877.

BELLE'S STRATAGEM, THE// C 3a// Hannah Cowley// **Drury Lane**, May 1838, with Mr. Cooper as Doricourt, William Dowton as Hardy, J. S. Balls as Flutter, Gerard King as Sir George, Mr. Baker as Saville, H. Cooke as Villiers, A. Brindal as Courtall, Mrs. Ternan as Letitia, Mrs. Lovell as Mrs. Racket, Miss Fitzwalter as Lady Francis, Miss Barnett as Kitty, Miss Somerville as Miss Ogle; Dec. 1851, with James Anderson as Doricourt, Mr. Cooper as Touchwood, Miss Fitzpatrick as Letitia Hardy// **Cov. Garden**, May 1840, with Mr. Cooper as Touchwood, James Anderson as Doricourt, William Farren as Hardy, C. J. Mathews as Flutter, James Vining as Saville, Mr. Fitzjames as Villars, Thomas Green as Courtall,Alfred Wigan as Trifle, C. J. Smith as Sir Toby, Mme. Vestris as Letitia, Ellen Tree as Lady Frances, Louisa Nisbett as Mrs. Rackett, Mrs. Brougham as Miss Ogle, Miss Lee as Kitty/ **Sad. Wells**, Nov. 1841, with Mr. Dry as Touchwood, Mr. Tidd as Doricourt, Mr. Williams as Hardy, Henry Marston as Flutter, Mr. Elvin as Saville, George Ellis as Villers, Mr. Morton as Courtall, Charles Fenton as Silvertongue, Mrs. Tidd as Letitia Hardy, Mrs. Richard Barnett as Lady Frances, Miss Richardson as Mrs. Racket, Miss Cooke as Miss Ogle, Mrs. Morgan as Kitty; Aug. 1849, with George Bennett as Touchwood, A. Younge as Hardy, Henry Marston as Doricourt, William Hoskins as Flutter, Frank Graham as Saville, Henry Mellon as Villers, G. K. Dickinson as Courtall, Miss Fitzpatrick as Letitia Hardy, Mrs. Henry Marston as Mrs. Rackett, Miss T. Bassano as Lady Frances, Mrs. G. Smith as Miss Ogle, Mrs. Graham as Kitty/ Scenery by F. Fenton/ **Haymarket**, Nov. 1843, with Henry Holl as Doricourt, Mr. Stuart as Sir George, Robert Strickland as Hardy, Benjamin Webster as Flutter, J. Worrell as Villers, Henry Howe as Saville, A. Brindal as Courtall, Louisa Nisbett as Letitia Hardy, Mrs. Julia Glover as Mrs. Racket, Julia Bennett as Lady Frances, Miss Conner as Miss Ogle, Miss Kendall as Kitty; Nov. 1858, with Henry Howe as Doricourt, W. H. Chippendale as Hardy, George Braid as Sir George, C. J. Mathews as Flutter, Edwin Villiers as Saville, J. Worrell as Villiers, Mrs. C. J. Mathews as Letitia, Mrs. Wilkins as Mr. Rackett, Mrs. Buckingham White as Lady Touchwood, Miss Fitzinman as Miss Ogle/ **Princess's**, June 1846, with John Ryder as Sir George, Mr. Wallack as Doricourt, Mr. Granby as Hardy, C. J. Mathews as Flutter, Charles Fisher as Saville, Augustus Harris as Courtall, Mr. Wynn as Villars, Mme. Vestris as Letitia Hardy, Mrs. Henry Hughes as Lady Frances, Mrs. Stirling as Mrs. Rackett, Miss E. Honner as Miss Ogle, Miss Taylor as Kitty/ **St. James's**, Oct. 1866, with Henry Irving/ **Lyceum**, June 1876, with Henry Irving, Isabel Bateman, Lucy Buckstone; Apr. 1881 (in 3a), with Henry Irving as Doricourt, Henry Howe as Hardy, William Terriss as Flutter, Arthur Wing Pinero as Saville, Mr. Elwood as Villiers, Frank Tyars as Courtall, A. Beaumont as Touchwood, Sophie Young as Mrs. Rackett, Ellen Terry as Letitia Hardy/ Scenery by Hawes Craven & W. Cuthbert/ Gas by Mr. Biggs/ Music by Hamilton Clarke.

BELLES OF THE KITCHEN, THE// F// n.a.// **Adelphi**, 1875.

BELLING THE CAT// C 1a// Martin Becher// **St. Geo. Hall**, Nov. 1886.

BELLS, THE// D 3a// Adap. by Leopold Lewis fr F of Erckmann-Chatrian, Le Juif Polonais// **Lyceum**, Nov. 1871, with Henry Irving as Mathias, Frank Hall as Walter, F. W. Irish as Hans, Herbert Crellin as Christian, Edward Dyas as Dr. Zimmer, Georgina Pauncefort as Catherine, Fanny Heywood as Annette, Ellen Mayne as Sozel/ Scenery by Hawes Craven & H. Cuthbert/ Music by M. E. Singla/ Machines by H. Jones/ Prod. by H. L. Bateman; June 1879, with Henry Irving, Arthur Wing Pinero, Alma Murray; Apr. 1890, with Henry Irving as Mathias, Henry Howe as Walter, Sam Johnson as Hans, William Haviland as Christian, John Martin Harvey as Zimmer, Georgina Pauncefort as Catherine, Kate Phillips as Sozel.

BELLS IN THE STORM, THE// D// C. H. Hazlewood// **Sadler's Wells**, Feb. 1874.

BELLS OF FATE// D 5a// Edward Darbey// **Sadler's Wells**, Nov. 1891.

BELLS OF HASLEMERE, THE// D 4a// Henry Pettitt & Sidney Grundy// **Adelphi**, July 1887, with William Terriss as Frank Beresford, J. D. Beveridge as Silkstone, Charles Cartwright as Capt. Vere, Sidney Hayes as Brookfield, John Beauchamp as Thorndyke, E. W. Garden as Armstrong, Jessie Miss Millward as Evelyn, Annie Irish as Mary Northcote, Clara Jecks as Dorothy, J. H. Darnley as Salem, R. Courtneidge as Desmond, Helen Forsyth as Norah/ Scenery by William Telbin, W. Perkins, & Bruce Smith/ Music by Henry Sprake/ Machines by Benjamin Burns/ Prod. by William Sidney.

BELOW LONDON BRIDGE// D 4a// Richard Dowling// **Novelty**, Apr. 1896, with W. Felton as Jeaters, Augustin Symonds as Crane, Frank Stanvill as Sherwin, W. Adams as Natchbrook, Ethel Fennar as Edith, Mrs. Gordon Gray as Mrs. Orr, Ina Cassilis as Widow Natchbrook.

BELPHEGOR THE MOUNTEBANK; OR, THE PRIDE OF BIRTH// D 3a// Adap. by Benjamin Webster fr F of A. P. D'Ennery & M. Fourier, Le Pallasse// **Adelphi**, Jan. 1851, with Henry Hughes as de Montbazon, Charles Boyce as St. Cyr, Paul Bedford as de Montroulade, O. Smith as de Rolac, Benjamin Webster as Belphegor, Edward Wright as Ajax, J. Worrell as Puffieres, William Cullenford as Grein, Ellen Chaplin as Henri, Mme. Celeste as Madeliene, Sarah Woolgar as Nina, Emma Harding as Mlle. de Basbleu, Mrs. Woolidge as Mme. de Ventadour; Oct. 1856, with Charles Dillon/ **Grecian**, Oct. 1861, with William James as Belphegor, Laura Conquest as Henri, Henry Grant as Lavareannes, George Conquest as Fanfaronade, Jane Dawson as Madeline, R. H. Lingham as Viscount Hercule, J. Jackson as the Duke de Montbason, Mary A. Victor as Zephryina, Miss Johnstone as Mlle. Vermandois.

BELPHEGOR THE MOUNTEBANK; OR, THE PRIDE OF BIRTH (also subt. Woman's Constancy)// Trans. by Charles Webb fr F of Marc Fournier & A. P. Dennery, La Pailasse// **Sad. Wells**, Apr. 1856, with Charles Dillon as Belphegor, Rose Edouin as Henri, James Rogers as Fanfaronade, Henry M. Barrett as Duke de Montbazon, E. F. Edgar as Lavarennes, C. Cooke as Viscount Hercule, C. Kelsey as Count de Blangy, Mr. Swanborough as Viscount d'Arpignol, Mrs. Charles Dillon as Madeline, Miss Cuthbert as Zepherina, Mrs. B. Bartlett as Mlle. Vermandois, Miss Sidney as Mlle. Caroline; Apr. 1866, with Thomas Swinbourne as Belphegor, Miss Hudspeth as Henri, George Belmore as Fanfaronade, William McIntyre as Lavrennes, Ada Dyas as Madeline, William H. Barrett as Duke de Montbazon, Charles Warner as Viscount Hercule, Mr. Holland as Count de Blangy, Frank Barsby as Viscount D'Arpignol, Mrs. Poynter as Mlle. Vermandois, Lizzie Wilmore as Zephyrina, Marie Willis as Mme. Catherine/ **Lyceum**, Sept. 1856, with Charles Dillon as Belphegor, Mrs. Dillon as Madeline, Maria Wilton as Henri, Miss C. Howard as Jeannette, J. L. Toole as Fanfaronade, William H. Barrett as Duke de Montbazon, J. G. Shore as Viscount Hercule, Mr. De Burt as Count de Blangy, Mr. Clifton as Marquis de Courgemont, Mr. Swanborough as Viscount d'Arpignol, Mr. Clifford as Duperron, Mrs. Tannett as Mlle. Vermandois, Harriet Gordon as Zepherina, Miss Morrell as Mme. Catherine/ Scenery by Tannett & Holding/ **Sad. Wells**, Apr. 1866.

BELPHEGOR; OR, THE MOUNTEBANK AND HIS WIFE// D 4a// Adap. by John Courtney fr F of A. P. D'Ennery & M. Fournier, Le Pallasse// **Surrey**, Jan. 1851.

BELPHEGOR; OR, THE MOUNTEBANK AND HIS WIFE// D 3a// Adap. by Thomas Higgie & T. H. Lacy fr F of A. P. D'Ennery & M. Fournier, Le Pallasse// **Victoria**, Jan. 1851.

BEN BOLT// D 2a// J. B. Johnstone// **Surrey**, Mar. 1854.

BEN LIEL, THE SON OF THE NIGHT// D// H. Young// **City of London**, May 1857/ **Victoria**, June 1857, with Mr. Henderson as Count Vertoni, Frederick Byefield as Count Manfrone, W. H. Pitt as Duke of Scylia and Ben Liel, J. H. Rickards as Anniello, Charles Rice as Quarrago, Alfred Saville as Viceroy, Samuel Sawford as Hypolito, Henry Dudley as Antonato, Mrs. Henry Vining as Volante, Mrs. H. Wallis as Christobel, Julia Seaman as Emmeline, Mrs. J. H. Rickards as Illia, Emily Thorne as Leoni/ Scenery by James Gates & Robert Mildenhall/ Machines by Wood & Foster/ Music by Mr. Mingaye/ Prod. by J. Johnson Towers.

BEN-MY-CHREE, THE// D 5a// Dram. by Hall Caine & Wilson Barrett from novel of Hall Caine, The Deemster// **Princess's**, May 1888, with Wilson Barrett as Mylrea, Mary Eastlake as Myra, Charles Fulton as Ewan, Austin Melford as Thorkell, John Maclean as Gilcrist, H. Cooper-Cliffe as Harcourt, George Barrett as Fayle, W. A. Elliott as Quilleash, S. Murray Carson as Teare, Lillie Belmore as Kitty, Mrs. Hudson Kirby as Kerry, Harietta Polini as Liza, Alice Belmore as Nancy/ Scenery by Walter Hann/ Music by Michael Connolly.

BEN THE BOATSWAIN; OR, SAILORS, SWEETHEARTS & THE PIRATES OF SICILY// D 3a// T. E. Wilks// **Surrey**, Aug. 1839/ **Victoria**, Feb. 1850, with John Dale as Somerton, Mr. Henderson as Sir Arthur, Mrs. Humphreys as Sir Archibald, Mrs. George Lee as Edwin/ **Drury Lane**, Aug. 1858, with F. Charles as Capt. Acton, Mr. Hartley as Lt. Berkley, H. Weston as Atherlone, Mrs. Robert Honner as Edwin, John Douglas as Ben, William Smith as Dabbleton, John Dale as Sir Arthur, Henry Butler as Somerton, Miss E. Dowton as Rose, Mrs. T. Dowton as Dame Oatfield, Miss R. Young as Margery, Miss Westleigh as Palmyra/ **Sad. Wells**, Sept. 1865, with John Gardiner as Sir Arthur, W. Wallace as Sommerton, Mr. Manderville as Capt. Acton, Adelaide Downing as Gage, Miss Jonson as Vincent, George Pearce as Redriff, John Mordaunt as Hens, James Elphinstone as Ben, George Lewis as Dabbleton, Henry Reeves as Stokes, Miss E. Jones as Rose, Marie Jones as Palmyra, Mrs. Jones as Margery.

BENEATH THE STARS// D 5a// Brandon Ellis// **Surrey**, Oct. 1900.

**BENEATH THE SURFACE; OR, THE LOSS

OF THE EURYDICE// D 4a// Mortimer Murdoch// **Grecian**, June 1873/ **Marylebone**, June 1878.

BENEFIT OF THE DOUBT, THE// C 3a// Arthur Wing Pinero// **Comedy**, Oct. 1895, with Aubrey Fitzgerald as Emtage, Cyril Maude as Sir Fletcher, Ernest Cosham as Rev. Cloys, J. G. Graham as Fraser, Leonard Boyne as Allingham, J. W. Pigott as Shafto, Stuart Champion as Elphick, Henrietta Lindley as Mrs. Emptage, Esmé Beringer as Justina, Winifred Emery as Theophila, Rose Leclercq as Mrs. Cloys, Lily Hanbury as Olive, Eva Williams as Mrs. Twelves/ Scenery by Walter Johnstone & Walter Hann.

BENEVOLENT JEW, THE// F 1a// Thomas Dibden// **Grecian**, Sept. 1861, with Henry Grant as Bromley, John Manning as Dr. Specific, J. Jackson as Abednego, William James as Changeable, George Gillett as Charles, Henry Power as William, Lucreza Hill as Mrs. Changeable, Ellen Hale as Emily, Mary A. Victor as Betty.

BENGAL TIGER, THE// F 1a// Charles Dance// **Olympic**, Dec. 1837, with William Farren as Pagoda, Charles Selby as Henderson, Mr. Stoker as Arthur, Robert Keeley as David, Miss M. A. Crisp as Charlotte, Mrs. Orger as Miss Yellowleaf; Jan. 1854, with Alfred Wigan as Pagoda, Mr. Leslie as Henderson, Mr. Vincent as Onslow, Frederick Robson as David, Mrs. Alfred Wigan as Miss Yellowleaf, Miss Marston as Charlotte/ **Cov. Garden**, Oct. 1839, with William Farren as Pagoda, Charles Selby as Henderson, Mr. Fitzjames as Onslow, Robert Keeley as David, Miss Lee as Charlotte, Mrs. Orger as Miss Yellowleaf/ **Sad. Wells**, Apr. 1847, with A. Younge as Pagoda, E. Morton as Henderson, William Branson as Onslow, Henry Scharf as David/ **Princess's**, June 1852, with Alfred Wigan as Pagoda, G. Everett as Henderson, Charles Wheatleigh as Onslow, Drinkwater Meadows as David, Mrs. Alfred Wigan as Miss Yellowleaf, Miss Vivash as Charlotte; June 1870/ **Adelphi**, Mar. 1858, with Alfred Wigan, Mrs. Wigan/ **St. James's**, Oct. 1861, with Alfred Wigan as Pagoda, Henry Ashley as Henderson, F. Charles as Onslow, Frank Matthews as David, Nelly Moore as Charlotte, Mrs. Alfred Wigan as Miss Yellowleaf/ **Haymarket**, July 1863, with Alfred Wigan as Sir Paul, Walter Gordon as Henderson, Mr. Weathersby as Onslow, Henry Compton as David, Mrs. Alfred Wigan as Miss Yellowleaf, Henrietta Lindley as Charlotte.

BENNETTS, THE// Play 4a// Adap. by Rosina Filippi fr novel of Jane Austin, Pride and Prejudice// **Court**, Mar. 1901.

BERTHA GRAY, THE PAUPER CHILD; OR, THE DEATH FETCH// D// Mrs. H. Young// **Victoria**, Nov. 1854, with F. H. Henry as Geddes, W. H. Pitt as Sir Richard, Alfred Saville as Muttleby, Mr. Morrison as Pomfret, J. Howard as Witchet, Mr. Gates as Gray, C. H. Stephenson as Jem, Mrs. Henry Vining as Bertha, Mrs. Manders as Mrs. Messeter, Mrs. Andrews as Mrs. Pomfret, Miss Dansor as Janet, Miss Laporte as Dolly, Miss M. A. Young as Sarah.

BERTRAM; OR, THE CASTLE OF ST. ALDOBRAND// T 5a// R. C. Maturin// **Cov. Garden**, Mar. 1837, with John Webster as St. Aldobrand, George Bennett as Prior, Thomas Hamblin as Bertram, Helen Faucit as Imogine, Miss Lee as Clotilda, Miss Nicholson as Teresa/ **Sad. Wells**, Jan. 1840, with Mr. Dry as Prior, Mr. Elvin as St. Aldobran, Mr. Denvil as Bertram, Mrs. Robert Honner as Imogine; May 1847, with Samuel Phelps as Bertram, Henry Marston as St. Aldobrand, George Bennett as Prior, Laura Addison as Imogine, Miss Huddart as Clotilde, Miss Stephens as Teresa/ **Drury Lane**, 1861.

BESS// Play 3a// Mrs. Oscar Berringer// **St. James's**, June 1893.

BESS OF THE BELL; OR, THE LOVE STORY// D// T. G. Blake// **Astley's**, Feb. 1850, with Mr. Johnson as Adam Thorne, Mr. Crowther as Job Granby, N. T. Hicks as Hyland, Thomas Barry as Wheedle, Miss Ely Loveday as Bess.

BESSIE// D 1a// E. H. Brooke// **Royalty**, May 1878.

BEST MAN, THE// F 3a// Robert Lumley// **Toole's**, Mar. 1894, with John Billington as Sir Lovel, J. L. Toole as Puttow, C. M. Lowne as Skifford, E. A. Coventry as Brewer, George Shelton as Minch, Charles Brunton as Williams, Beatrice Lambb as Mrs. Mont Aubyn, Florence Fordyce as Brenda, Cora Poole as Ada, Alice Kingsley as Nina, Eliza Johnstone as Sarah/ Scenery by Joseph Harker.

BEST MAN WINS, THE// F 1a// Mark Melford// **Novelty**, Jan. 1890, with Mark Melford as Perks, James Woodbridge as Jopper, Raymond Capp as Kairns, Mrs. Mark Melford as Carlotta.

BEST PEOPLE, THE// C 4a// Mrs. Fairfax// **Globe**, July 1890, with H. Percival as Capt. Lester, Tom Squire as Skinner, Compton Coutts as Mummery, W. S. Buist as Mawler, Sophie Larkin as Lady Diana, Adrienne Dairolles as Signora Parrini, Exxes Dane as Edith, Rhoda Larkin as Lucy.

BEST WAY, THE// C 1a// Horace Wigan// **Olympic**, Sept. 1866, with John Clayton as Speed, Horace Wigan as Tonic, Mrs. St. Henry as Mrs. Mowbray, Louisa Moore as Alice.

BETRAYED BY A KISS// C 1a// H. A. Saintsbury// **Opera Comique**, May 1891, with Leonard Outram as Tremont, H. A. Saintsbury as de Vernois, J. G. Taylor as Licard, Marie de Valge as Comtesse de Cardillac, Loie Fuller as Gabrielle, Maud Digby as Adele, Mrs. Campbell Bradley as Cerise.

BETROTHAL, THE// Play 5a// G. H. Boker// **Drury Lane**, Sept. 1853, with Mr. Evans as Marquis di Tiburazzi, Frederick Belton as Jaranio, E. L. Davenport as Salvatore, G. V. Brooke as Marsio, E. F. Edgar as Rogo, A. Younge as Pulti, Mr. Hustleby as Carlo, Miss Anderton as Constanzi, Miss Featherstone as Filippa, Mrs. Belton as Marchioness di Tiburzzi.

BETSY// C 3a// Adap. by F. C. Burnand fr F of Maurice Henniquin & Emile de Najac// **Criterion**, Aug. 1879, with W. J. Hill, Lytton Sothern, Alfred Maltby, Mary Rorke; Aug. 1892, with William Blakeley as Birkett, George Giddens as Talbot, Sydney Valentine as Manus, David James as Dawson, Welton Dale as Adolphus, Fanny Robertson as Mrs. Birkett, Jenny Rogers as Betsy, Ellis Jeffreys as Mme. Polenta/ Dec. 1896.

BETSY BAKER; OR, TOO ATTENTIVE BY HALF// F 1a// J. Maddison Morton// **Princess's**, Nov. 1850, with Robert Keeley as Mouser, James Vining as Crummy, Miss Murray as Mrs. Mouser, Mrs. Keeley as Betsy/ **Adelphi**, Apr. 1853, with Robert Keeley as Mouser, John Parselle as Crummy, Fanny Maskell as Mrs. Mouser, Mrs. Keeley as Betsy; June 1883, with Harry Proctor as Mouser, C. W. Somerset as Crummy, Harriet Coveney as Mrs. Mouser, Clara Jecks as Betsy/ **Sad. Wells**, Sept. 1856, with Lewis Ball as Mouser, William Belford as Crummy, Caroline Parkes as Mrs. Mouser, Eliza Travers as Betsy/ **Drury Lane**, Mar. 1857, with Robert Keeley as Mouser, C. Vincent as Crummy, Miss Cleveland as Mrs. Mouser, Mrs. Keeley as Betsy/ **Grecian**, Oct. 1857, with William Shuter as Crummy, George Conquest as Mouser, Ellen Hale as Mrs. Mouser, Harriet Coveney as Betsy; Sept. 1861, with George Gillett, George Conquest, Ellen Hale, Mary A. Victor/ **Gaiety**, July 1880, with J. L. Toole, Mrs. Keeley, Amy Roselle/ **Olympic**, Jan. 1883, with W. E. Blatchley as Mouser, Philip Beck as Crummy, Kate Lee as Betsy, Janet Achurch as Mrs. Mouser.

BETSY'S FOUND// F 1a// n.a.// **Grecian**, Nov. 1856, with John Manning as Brown, George Conquest as Waggledy, Henry Power as Tilt Spoon, Henry Grant as Mr. Spoon, Harriet Coveney as Betsy.

BETTER HALF, THE// C 1a// T. J. Williams// **Strand**, June 1865.

BETTER LATE THAN NEVER// D 4a// H. R. Beverley// **Grecian**, Oct. 1865, with Dacre Baldie as Kingsley as as Will Wild, W. Shirley as Lord Heatherford, J. H. Steele as Stanton, William James as Halstead, George Conquest as Socks, Laura Conquest as Joe, Alice Denvil as Grace, Mrs Dearlove as Mary, Mary A. Victor as Nelly, Henry Grant as Clopton.

BETTER LATE THAN NEVER// C 2a// F. C. Burnand// **Royalty**, June 1874.

BETTER LIFE, THE// D 4a// Arthur Shirley & Sutton Vane// **Adelphi**, Feb. 1900.

BETTER POLICY, THE// C 1a// Henry Here// **Coronet**, July 1900.

BETTING BOY'S CAREER, THE: FROM HIS HOME TO THE HULKS// D// C. S. James & J. B. Johnstone// **Victoria**, Sept. 1854, with J. T. Johnson as Goodwood, W. H. Pitt as Reynard, F. H. Henry as Blackall, Mr. Morrison as Ben, Mr. Hitchinson as Sly, Mr. Bradley as Haddy, J. Hicks as Nail, Alfred Saville as Bob, Charles Rice as Dough, Mrs. Henry Vining as Mrs. Goodwood, Miss Dansor as Susan, Miss Laporte as Sally, Mrs. Manders as Nanny, Mr. Harwood as Fat Lady.

BETTY MARTIN// F 1a// Adap. by Augustus Harris fr F of Mme. Girardin, Le Chapeau de l'Horioger// **Adelphi**, Mar. 1855/ **Olympic**, Aug. 1867, with George Vincent as Maj. Mohawk, John Clayton as Singleton, Harwood Cooper as Mainspring, Charles Cowdery as Buttons, Ellen Farren as Betty Martin, Maria Harris as Miss Bobbins; Aug. 1878, with Henry Andrews as Maj. Mohawk, H. Bennett as Singleton, A. Thorne as Mainspring, Polly Hunter as Buttons, Miss M. Ancoyle as Mrs. Mohawk, Fanny Wallis as Bobbin, Charlotte Saunders as Betty Martin/ **Victoria**, Sept. 1871, with Robert Soutar as Major Mohawk, George Carter as Singleton, A. Stilt as Mainspring, Miss Platt as Buttons, Ellen Farren as Betty Martin, Annie Bentley as Julia, Miss Ewell as Bobbins/ **Globe**, July 1876, with Henry Andrews as Maj. Mohawk, H. Bennett as Mainspring, Miss P. Lemmon as Mrs. Mohawk, C. A. Cowdery as Singleton, Miss L. Vere as Miss Bobbin, Charlotte Saunders as Betty Martin.

BETWEEN THE DANCES// Play 1a// H. T. Johnson// **Comedy**, Mar. 1898.

BEULAH SPA, THE// C 1a// Charles Dance// **Olympic**, Apr. 1837, with James Vining as Beauchamp, John Brougham as Capt. Kildare, Frank Matthews as Batchelor, W. H. Oxberry as Templeton, J. W. Collier as Hector, Mr. Wyman as James, Mr. Kerridge as Leander, Mr. Hitchenson as Richard, Mary A. Crisp as Caroline, Mrs. Macnamara as Mrs. Templeton, Mrs. Fitzwalter as Grace/ **Victoria**, June 1837, with James Vining as Beauchamp, James Bland as Capt. Kildare, Frank Mathews [sic] as Batchelor, W. H. Oxberry as Magnus Templeton, Mr. Kerridge as Hector Templeton, G. Crisp as James, Mr. Hichinson as Richard, Priscilla Horton as Caroline, Mrs. Macnamara as Mrs. Templeton, Miss Fitzwalter as Grace, Mrs. Frank Mathews [sic] as Parker/ **Eng. Opera House** (Lyceum), June 1837, with James Vining as Beauchamp, John Brougham as Capt. Kildare, Frank Matthews as Batchelor, W. H. Oxberry as Templeton, Mme. Vestris as Caroline, Mrs. Macnamara as Mrs. Templeton, Miss Fitzwaller as Grace.

BEWARE OF MAN TRAPS// C// A. Younge// **Sad. Wells**, Mar. 1851, with Mr. Williams as Todd, Frederick Younge as Giles, Charles Wheatleigh as Thornhill, A. Younge as Ray, Mrs. Archbold as Mrs. Todd, Lucy Rafter as Caroline, Eliza Travers as Mrs. Nightingale, Mrs. Graham as Mrs. O'Lundy.

BEYOND HUMAN POWER// D 2a// Trans. by Jessie Muir fr Norw. of Bjornstjerne Bjornson// **Royalty**, Nov. 1901.

BEYOND THE BREAKERS// D 4a// Sutton Vane// **Grand**, Oct. 1893.

BIANCA CONTARINI; OR, THE DOGE'S DAUGHTER AND THE PIRATE'S OATH// D 4a// Thomas Greenwood// **Sad. Wells**, Apr. 1840, with Henry Marston as Pisani, Mr. Elvin as Micheli, Mr. Aldridge as Priuli, Mr. Priorson as Pietro, George Burt as Ludovico, Mrs. Robert Honner as Bianca, Miss Cooke as Genova, Mrs. J. F. Saville as Zoe, Mr. Dry as Anagnosti, X as The Seawolf/ Scenery by F. Fenton/ Machines by B. Sloman/ Music by Mr. Collins/ Prod. by R. Honner.

BIB AND TUCKER// C 2a// n.a.// **Gaiety**, Aug. 1873.

BIDDY O'NEILL; OR, A DAUGHTER OF ERIN// D 2a// W. H. Pitt// **Britannia**, Mar. 1869.

BIG FORTUNE, A// D 4a// William Bourne// **Surrey**, July 1891.

BILIOUS ATTACK, A// F 1a// Arthur Wood// **Sadler's Wells**, Apr. 1872.

BILLING AND COOING// C 2a// John Oxenford// **Royalty**, Jan. 1855.

BILLY DOO// F 1a// C. M. Rae// **Globe**, Apr. 1874.

BINKS THE BAGMAN// F 1a// J. Stirling Coyne// **Adelphi**, Apr. 1843/ **Sad Wells**, June 1854, with J. W. Collier, Henry M. Barrett as Robinson, Edward Wright as Binks, Miss Lavine, Miss Rawlings as Mary, Caroline Parkes.

BIRD IN THE HAND WORTH TWO IN THE BUSH, A// Play 2a// Frederick Phillips// **Surrey**, Jan. 1857/ **Globe**, Sept. 1878, with James Fernandez as Praiseworthy, J. R. Crauford as Prodigal, George Grainger as Maj. Stormont, Shiel Barry as Sharke, Emma Chambers as Mme. Prodigal, Fanny Enson as Ellen.

BIRD OF PARADISE// F// Adap. by Alfred Thompson fr F// **Gaiety**, June 1869.

BIRD OF PASSAGE// F 1a// Benjamin Webster// **Haymarket**, Sept. 1849.

BIRDS IN THEIR LITTLE NESTS AGREE// F 1a// C. M. Rae// **Haymarket**, Nov. 1876.

BIRDS OF ARISTOPHANES, THE// C 1a// J. R. Planché// **Haymarket**, Apr. 1846.

BIRTHDAY, THE// C 1a// George Bancroft// **Court**, Dec. 1894, with William Day as Leslie, Wilfred Draycott as Wakefield, W. H. Quinton as Hubbard, Dora de Winton as Ruth.

BIRTHPLACE OF PODGERS, THE// F 1a// John Hollingshead// **Lyceum**, Mar. 1858/ **Adelphi**, Jan. 1859, with J. L. Toole/ **St. James's**, Feb. 1864, with J. L. Toole as Cranky, W. Chamberlain as Maresnest, Henry Ashley as Earlybird, H. J. Montague as Lexicon, Miss Dalton as Amelia, Mrs. Stoker as Penelope, Fanny Josephs as Mrs. Cranky/ **Lyceum**, July 1881, with J. L. Toole as Cranky, G. Shelton as Maresnest, Henry Westland as Earlybird, E. W. Garden as Lexicon, John Billington as Podgers, Effie Liston as Amelia, Eliza Johnstone as Mrs. Cranky, Emily Thorne as Penelope/ **Drury Lane**, May 1883, with J. L. Toole as Cranky, G. Shelton as Maresnest, Henry Westland as Earlybird, Lewis Waller as Ledwin, Walter Brunton as Podgers, Ely Kempster as Amelia, Bella Wallis as Penelope, Eliza Johnstone as Mrs. Cranky.

BISHOP'S CANDLESTICKS, THE// D 1a// Adap. by Norman McKinnel fr portion of Victor Hugo's Les Miserables// **Duke of York's**, Aug. 1901.

BISHOP'S EYE, THE// Play 3a// Clotilde Graves// **Vaudeville**, Feb. 1900.

BIT OF HUMAN NATURE, A// D 1a// Mrs. George Corbett// **Terry's**, June 1899, with Charles Wilson as Thorne, Wylie Thompson as Heriot, Leah Hedingham as Marjorie, Lilian Corbett as Erica.

BIT OF OLD CHELSEA, A// Play 1a// Mrs. Oscar Berringer// **Court**, Feb. 1897/ **St. James's**, May 1897, with Edmund Maurice as Hillier, C. M. Hallard as McDonnell, E. W. Tarver as Dixon, Annie Hughes as Alexandra/ **Royalty**, Oct. 1897/ **Avenue**, Jan. 1898.

BITTER COLD// D 2a// n.a.// **Marylebone**, Jan. 1868.

BITTER LESSON, A// Play 1a// J. R. Burnland & Alec Weatherly// **Lyric**, May 1896.

BITTER RECKONING; OR, A ROVER FROM MANY LANDS// D 3a// C. H. Hazlewood// **Britannia**, June 1871.

BITTER WRONG, A; OR, A WIFE IN ENGLAND AND NO WIFE IN FRANCE// D 5a// George Lander & John Douglass// **Standard**, Apr. 1884.

BLACK AND WHITE// D 3a// Wilkie Collins & Charles Fechter// **Adelphi**, Mar. 1869, with Charles Fechter as Maurice de Layrac, Arthur Stirling as Westcraft, Edward Atkins as Michaelmas, George Belmore as Plato, Richard Phillips as Wolf, Carlotta Leclercq as Miss Milburn, Miss Lennox Grey as Mrs. Penfold, Mrs. Leigh Murray as Ruth/ Scenery by Hawes Craven/ Machines by Mr. Charker/ Gas by G. Bastard/ Music by Edwin Ellis.

BLACK BOOK, THE// D 3a// J. Palgrave Simpson// **Drury Lane**, Feb. 1857, with A. Younge as Baron Stolzenbeck, C. Vincent as Count Strubel, Mr. Tilbury as Baron Kaseworm, C. J. Mathews as Wolf, R. H. Lingham as Caspar, George Honey as Zitterchenkel, Miss Cleveland as Countess Strubel, Miss M. Oliver as Mina, Mrs. Selby as Dame Aspen.

BLACK BROTHERHOOD, THE; OR, THE OLD RUINS OF THE CASTLE OF ZASTROZZI// D// C. Z. Barnett// **Victoria**, Oct. 1846, with

James Ranoe as Capt. Groff, A. Raymond as Ochler, C. J. Bird as Vandenstitchell, E. G. Burton as Nix, Mr. Fitzjames as Hornberg, Walter Searle as Gahn, F. H. Henry as Ferrand, F. Wilton as Bertrand, Mrs. Henry Vining as Lestelle, Mrs. Cooke as Widow Vanderstitchell, Miss Edgar as Annette.

BLACK BUT COMELY// D// Dram. by Stephanie Forrester fr story by Whyte-Melville// **Gaiety**, Sept. 1882.

BLACK CAESAR; OR, THE FATAL THICKET// D// C. I. Dibdin// **Sad. Wells**, Oct. 1841, with Mr. Aldridge as Sir Francis, Mr. Moreton as Bertrand, Charles Montgomery as Caesar, J. W. Collier as Jib, Mrs. Richard Barnett as Phoebe.

BLACK CAT, THE// Play 3a// John Todhunter// **Opera Comique**, Dec. 1893.

BLACK DIAMONDS; OR, THE LIGHTS AND SHADOWS OF PIT LIFE// D 5a// L. S. Denbigh & Fenton Mackay// **Surrey**, July 1892.

BLACK DOCTOR, THE// D 5a// Trans. by T. V. Bridgman fr F of Anicet-Bourgeois & P. F. Dumanoir, Le Medecin Noir// **City of London**, Nov. 1846/ **Lyceum**, Nov. 1856, with Charles Dillon, Mrs. Dillon, Sarah Woolgar, J. L. Toole/ **Sad. Wells**, May 1863, with Charles Harcourt as St. Luce, J. F. Warden as Fabian, Mr. Wilson as Leon, F. Shephard as Christian, Mr. Bartolo as Dominique, Charles Bender as Jean, Mrs. Hudson Kirby as Pauline, Kate Harrod as Countess Aurelia, Miss Austin as Lia, G. W. Broughton as Andre, Mrs. William Dowton as Marchioness.

BLACK DOCTOR, THE; OR, THE FATED LOVERS OF BOURBON// Adap. by Thomas Archer fr F of Anicet-Bourgeois & P. F. Dumanoir, Le Medecin Noir// **Victoria**, Nov. 1846, with C. J. Bird as St. Luce, E. Edwards as Fabian, G. F. Forman as Briquet, J. Howard as Jaques, F. Wilton as Grimaud, F. H. Henry as Christian, Annette Vincent as as Pauline, Miss Greville as Lia, Mrs. Cooke as Lizetta, Lydia Pearce as Suzanne, Mrs. Richard Barnett as Mlle. Aurelia.

BLACK DOCTOR, THE// D// n.a.// **Grecian**, Aug. 1861, with R. H. Lingham as St. Luce, John Manning as Briquet, Henry Power as Fils, Thomas Mead as Fabian, William James as Andre, Ellen Hale as Countess Amelia, Jane Coveney as Madeline, Miss Johnstone as Marchionesse.

BLACK DOMINO, THE; OR, THE MASKED BALL// D 3a// Adap. by T. E. Wilks fr F of Eugène Scribe, Le Domino Noir// **Olympic**, Jan. 1838, with Mme. Vestris as Black Domino, C. J. Mathews as Julio, Charles Selby as Gomez, William Vining as Elsenheim, Mr. Wyman as Gregorio, Mrs. Macnamara as Dorothea, Miss Lee as Olivia, Mary A. Crisp as Teresa/ **Sad. Wells**, Feb. 1838, with Mr. Forester as Don Sylvio, J. Worrell as de Maranisa, Mr. Campbell as Comte de Sal Voisy, Mr. Rogers as Gil Perez, Mr. Ranson as Andreas, Mr. Scarbrow as Rolando, Annette Vincent as Black Domino, Miss Beresford as Cecile, Miss Watkins as Beatrice, Mrs. Weston as Jacintha, Miss Chartley as Rosolia, Eliza Pitt as Sulpicia/ Scenery by Mr. Battie/ Music by W. Montgomery/ **Victoria**, Oct. 1841, with William Seaman as Juliano, J. Howard as Sal Voissy, David Osbaldiston as Don Sylvio, John Gardner as Gil, Charles Williams as Father Andreas, Mr. Scarbrow as Rolando, Mr. Hitchinson as di Vincio, Mr. Franklin as de Vane, E. F. Edgar as Perez, Annette Vincent as Black Domino, Maid of Arragon, and as Sister Angela, Mrs. George Lee as Cecile, Miss Clifford as Rosolia, Mrs. Howard as Beatrice, Mrs. Seaman as Sulpicia, Mrs. Garthwaite as Dame Jacintha/ Scenery by Telbin & Hawthorn/ Machines by Mr. Moulds/ **Grecian**, Dec. 1846, with Charles Horn as Don Sylvio, Edwin Dixon as Julano, Mr. Campbell as Comte de Savoisy, John Collett as Padre Andreas, Mr. Baldwin as Gil, Annette Mears as Black Domino, Miss Brunton as Cecile, Miss Johnstone as Beatrice, Miss Merion as Jacintha/ Music by Mr. Isaacson.

BLACK DOMINO, THE// D 3a// Adap. fr F of Eugène Scribe, Le Domino Noir// **Victoria**, Nov. 1850, with Mr. Henderson as Juliano, J. Howard as Comte de Sal Volsey, David Osbaldiston as Don Sylvio, G. F. Forman as Perez, J. Neville as Father Andreas, Mr. Humphreys as Rolando, Annette Vincent as Maid of Arragon and as Sister Angela, Mrs. George Lee as Cecile, Miss Mildenhall as Rosolia, Georgiana Lebatt as Beatrice, Miss Edgar as Sulpicia, Mrs. Cooke as Dame Jacintha.

BLACK DOMINO, THE// D 5a// G. R. Sims & Robert Buchanan// **Adelphi**, Apr. 1893, with Charles Glenney as Lord Dashwood, W. L. Abingdon as Capt. Greville, G. W. Cockburn as Pierre Berton, Welton Dale as Chase, T. B. Thalberg as Dr. Maitland, John Le Hay as Maj. O'Flaherty, C. M. Hallard as Vavasour, R. C. Stuart as Drewcourt, Arthur Williams as Honeybun, Evelyn Millard as Mildred Vavasour, Mrs. Patrick Campbell as Clarice/ Scenery by Bruce Smith & Walter Johnstone/ Music by Henry Sprake.

BLACK DOUGLASS, THE; OR, THE DEATH OF THE PARRICIDE// D 3a// n.a.// **Victoria**, Aug. 1850, with John Ryder as Douglass, Henry Frazer as Duval, J. Neville as Peduzzi, Mr. Henderson as Moreton, J. T. Johnson as de Courcy, John Bradshaw as Kettrell, G. F. Forman as Jemmy, J. Howard as Forster, Amelia Mercer as Helen, Georgiana Lebatt as Eliza, Mrs. George Lee as Julia,, Miss Barrowcliffe as Jenny.

BLACK EAGLE, THE; OR, THE CAPTAIN'S NOT A-MISS (see, The Captain is Not a Miss).

BLACK EYED SUSAN; OR, ALL IN THE DOWNS// D 2a// Douglas Jerrold// **Drury Lane**, Jan. 1837, with Mr. Gann as William, Charles Diddear as Crosstree, Drinkwater Meadows as Gnatbrain, Mr. Wilson as Peter, Basil Baker as Admiral, J. C. Hughes as Twig, Agnes Taylor as Susan, Mrs. Humby as Dolly/ **Cov. Garden**, Feb. 1837, with Mr. Tompson as Admiral, John Webster as Capt. Crosstree, Mr. Tilbury as Doggrass, Charles Bender as Hatchet, E. Harris as Seaweed, T. P. Cooke as William, Mr. Collins as Blue Peter, Benjamin Webster as Gnatbrain, Mr. Ross as Twig, Annette Vincent as Susan, Miss Nicholson as Dolly/ **Sad. Wells**, Feb. 1837, with Gerard King as Admiral, C. H. Pitt as Capt. Crosstree, John Ayliffe as Doggrass, Mr. Campbell as William, Mr. Rogers as Gnatbrain, Thomas Lee as Twig, Mr. Scarbrow as Blue Peter, H. George as Hatchet, Miss Williams as Susan, Miss Julian as Dolly; Dec. 1838, with T. P. Cooke as William; June 1854, with Henry M. Barrett as Admiral, F. Charles as Capt. Crosstree, J. W. Collier as Gnatbrain, Mr. James as Lt. Pyke, C. Poynter as Doggrass, E. L. Davenport as William, A. Judd as Twig, Fanny Vining as Susan, Miss Lavine as Dolly; July 1864, with Edmund Phelps as William, Kate Stonor as Susan, Minnie Davis as Dolly, T. B. Bennett as Doggrass, Mr. Williams as Gnatbrain, G. Clementson as Capt. Crosstree, T. Maynard as Twig, Charles Mowbray as Quid; Dec. 1867, with Alice Marriott as Susan, Grace Edgar as Dolly, Henry Loraine as William, Walter Searle as Gnatbrain, Harry Chester as Doggrass, George Fisher as Twig, Mr. Hamilton as Admiral, Mr. Murray as Capt. Crosstree; May 1868, with Adah Isaacs Menken as William, Harry Rignold as Admiral, Mr. Walton as Doggrass, Mr. Campbell as Capt. Crosstree, M. Robson as Gnatbrain, Mr. Anderson as Twig, Miss Landon as Susan, Marie Willis as Dolly, Rita Percy as Blue Peter/ **Haymarket**, Oct. 1837, with T. P. Cooke as William, J. W. Gough as Admiral, Mr. Hemming as Capt. Crosstree, Mr. Hutchings as Lt. Pike, Mr. Strickland as Doggrass, Mr. Collins as Blue Peter, J. B. Buckstone as Gnatbrain, J. T. Haines as Hatchet, T. F. Mathews as Twig, Mrs. Waylett as Susan, Mrs. Humby as Dolly; Feb. 1851, with E. L. Davenport as William, Mr. Rogers as Admiral, John Parselle as Crosstree, George Braid as Lt. Pike, Mr. Lambert as Doggrass, J. B. Buckstone as Gnatbrain, Henry Bedford as Twig, Amelia Vining as Susan, Mrs. Caulfield as Dolly; Aug. 1857, with T. P. Cooke as William, Edwin Villiers as Capt. Crosstree, George Braid as Lt. Pike, W. H. Chippendale as Doggrass, Mr. Rogers as Admiral, Mr. Clark as Twig, J. B. Buckstone as Gnatbrain, Miss Lavine as Blue Peter, Miss M. Oliver as Susan, Mrs. Edward Fitzwilliam as Dolly/ **Victoria**, Dec. 1838, with T. P. Cooke as William, Charles Melville as Crosstree, Mr. Scriven as Raker, Gerard King as Hatchet, Mr. Johnson as Doggrass, Mr. Vining as Admiral, John Parry as Twigg, W. J. Hammond as Gnatbrain, J. B. Hill as Blue Peter, Lavinia Melville as Susan, Mrs. Melville as Dolly/ **Olympic**, Dec. 1851, with Charles Diddear as Admiral, John Kinloch as Capt. Crosstree, Mr. Harris as Lt. Pike, Henry Farren as William, George Cooke as Doggrass, Henry Compton as Gnatbrain, E. Clifton as Twig, Mrs. Lingham as Susan, Mrs. Alfred Phillips as Dolly/ **Princess's**, May 1853, with Mr. Graham as Admiral, G. Everett as Capt. Crosstree, Hermann Vezin as Lt. Pike, Drinkwater Meadows as Doggrass, Edward Wright as Gnatbrain, Henry Saker as Twig, Mr. Terry as Hatchett, T. P. Cooke as William, John Collett as Raker, Miss Murray as Susan, Mrs. Walter Lacy as Dolly/ **Grecian**, Apr. 1856, with Eaton O'Donnell as Admiral, F. Charles as Capt. Crosstree, Professor Anderson as William, Harriet Coveney as Blue Peter, John Manning as Gnatbrain, Henry Power as Jacob Twig, Henry Grant as Doggrass, Mrs. Robert Honner as Susan, Constance Stanley as Molly; June 1863, with J. Jackson, Henry Grant, George Gillett, William James, John Manning, B. Summersby, Mrs. Charles Dillon, Ellen Jerman/ **Astley's**, July 1865, with Adah Isaacs Menken as William, Basil Potter as Admiral, T. J. Anderson as Crosstree, W. S. Gresham as Hatchet, Edward Atkins as Gnatbrain, J. Johnson as Doggrass, Harry Crouest as Twig, Vernon Rigby as Blue Peter, Josephine Fiddes as Susan, Minnie Sidney as Dolly/ **Adelphi**, Dec. 1896, with William Terriss as William, Charles Fulton as Crosstree, Oscar Ayde as Hatchett, H. Trant Fischer as Baker, J. D. Beveridge as Doggrass, Luigi Lablache as Admiral, Cyril Melton as Twig, Harry Nicholls as Gnatbrain, Charles Fisher as Blue Peter, Jessie Millward as Susan, Miss Vane Featherston as Dolly/ Prod. by Fred Latham.

BLACK FLAG, THE; OR, ESCAPED FROM PORTLAND// D 4a// Henry Pettitt// **Grecian**, May 1879/ **Sad. Wells**, Sept. 1882, with M. Mortimer as Owen Glyndon, George Stretton as John Glyndon, E. N. Hallows as Harry Glyndon, Mat Robson as Lazarus, F. Owen as Scarum, J. E. Kellerd as Capt. Handyside, G. Irwin as Seaton, H. Gregory as Hawthorn, Marie Forde as Ned, Alice Denvil as Ruth, Helen Grahame as Naomi, Lizzie Lilly as Topsy/ Scenery by W. T. Hemsley/ **Olympic**, Mar. 1892.

BLACK FOREST, THE; OR, THE BANDIT HOST// D// n.a.// **Sad. Wells**, July 1839, with Mr. Cathcart as Frederick the Great, John Webster as Adelbert, Mr. Aldridge as De Reiner, Benjamin Conquest as Van Groat, J. W. Collier as Cartouche, Mr. Dry as Moresko, Miss Pincott as Rosalie, Miss Cooke as Martha.

BLACK HEARTS; OR, THE KING OF DARKNESS// D 3a// Edward Towers// **East London**, May 1868.

BLACK MAIL// D 4a// Watts Phillips// **Grecian**, Oct. 1880.

BLACK MAIL// CD 3a// G. H. Roque & H. R. Dabbs// **Criterion**, Oct. 1888.

BLACK MASK, THE; OR, THE RECLUSE OF THE ABBEY RUIN// D// n.a.// **Sad. Wells**, Oct. 1837, with Mr. Campbell as Morton, Gerard King as Woodburn, Thomas Lee as Cold, C. H. Pitt as Black Mask, Mr. George as Lt. Lawton, Mr. Russell as Blount, Mr. Wilkins as Mad Mark, Miss Williams as Grace, Miss Vernon as Madge.

BLACK PRINCE, THE// C 3a// Adap. by H. B. Farnie & Charles Lecocq fr F of Labiche & A. C. Delacour// **St. James's**, 1874, with Mme. Selina Dolaro as Sybil, Nellie Bromley as Flossie, Inez D'Aquilar as Gab, Linda Verner as Bab, Belle Britain as Mary, John Hall as Dr. Maresnest, John Rouse as Old Cobb, C. W. Norton as Fluchsec, Emily Duncan as Lord Skyraker, Mr. Belleville as Mash, H. Clifford as Ringtail, Walter Vernon as Cactus/ Scenery by Grieve & Son.

BLACK ROVER, THE; OR, THE BLOODHOUND AND THE SHARK// D 3a// Thomas Greenwood// **Sad. Wells**, Nov. 1841, with Henry Marston as Morton, Mr. Elvin as Capt. Martingale, Charles [?] Williams as Sir William, Robert Honner as Starboard, John Herbert as Belvedere, Mr. Dry as Francisco, J. W. Collier as Teddy, Mr. Aldridge as Herman, Charles Fenton as Dunbreaks, Mrs. Robert Honner as X, Mrs. Richard Barnett as Miriam, Miss Richardson as Widow Morton, Miss Cooke as Lisette, Mrs. J. W. Collier as Pacquita/ Scenery by F. Fenton, Music by Isaac Collins/ Machines by Mr. Cawdery/ Prod. by R. Honner.

BLACK SENTINEL, THE; OR, THE COURT JESTER// C// n.a.// **Sad. Wells**, Aug. 1843, with Charles [?] Williams as Skinflint, Mr. Coreno as Pops, C. J. Bird as Capt. Hector, Mr. Lamb as Holdfast, Mr. Franks as Gripe, Miss Cooke as Mrs. Smith, Lavinia Melville as Miss Smith, J. Dunn as Jim Crow.

BLACK SHEEP// C 3a// J. Stirling Coyne// **Haymarket**, Apr. 1861, with Henry Howe as Lester, Mr. Rogers as Mortmain, J. B. Buckstone as Bunny, Edwin Villiers as Hardpace, George Braid as Smithers, Henry Compton as Shotter, Mrs. Charles Young as Ethel, Mrs. Wilkins as Lady Barbican, Mrs. Griffiths as Mrs. Todhunter, Mrs. Poynter as Mrs. Lester/ Scenery by John O'Conner & George Morris.

BLACK SHEEP// D 3a// Dram. by J. Palgrave Simpson & Edmund Yates fr novel of Yates// **Olympic**, Apr. 1868.

BLACK TOWER OF LONDON, THE; OR, A FOSTER-BROTHER'S REVENGE// D// Cecil Pitt// **Britannia**, Sept. 1869.

BLACK TULIP, THE// Play 5a// Dram. by Sidney Grundy fr F of Alexandre Dumas, La Tulipe Noire// **Haymarket**, Oct. 1899, with Frederick Harrison as William of Orange, Will Dennis as de Witt, Cyril Maude as van Baerle, Mark Kinghorne as Boxtel, F. H. Tyler as van Systens, Samuel Johnson as van Spennen, Sidney Valentine as Gryphus, Clarence Blakiston as Capt. van Deken, Winifred Emery as Rosa, Mrs. E. H. Brooke as Zug/ Music by Frederick Corder.

BLACK VAMPIRE, THE// D 5a// C. A. Clarke & Harry Spiers// **Britannia**, Sept. 1900.

BLACKBIRDING// D// C. H. Hazlewood// **Britannia**, Sept. 1873.

BLACKMAILERS, THE// D 4a// John Grey & Andre Raffalovich// **POW**, June 1894.

BLACKSMITH OF GHENT, THE; OR, THE CRAFTSMEN OF FLANDERS// D 3a// John Courtney// **Victoria**, June 1848, with David Osbaldiston as Charles V of Spain, T. H. Higgie as Count Albert, J. T. Johnson as Sir Gaston, Mr. Hitchinson as Marquis de Leyra, E. Edwards as Schertell, John Bradshaw as Gropper, Mr. Henderson as Marnix, G. F. Forman as Fritterman, J. Howard as Fronsperg, F. H. Henry as Laultzberg, Mrs. George Lee as Lady Blanche, Annette Vincent as Alice, Miss Burroughcliffe as Abigail, Mrs. Cooke as Marion, Miss Young as Annette.

BLACKSMITH'S DAUGHTER, THE// C 1a// Arnold Goldsworthy & E. B. Norman// **Opera Comique**, Oct. 1888.

BLANCHE AND BLANCHETTE// D 2a// Adap. fr F// **Grecian**, Mar. 1854, with Henry Grant as Roquebert, Charles Horn as Anatole, Basil Potter as Glauchet, Harriet Coveney as Blanche, Jane Coveney as Blanchette, Miss Johnstone as Marchionesse d'Aubervilles.

BLANCHE DE VALMY// D 2a// W. Bayle Bernard// **Princess's**, July 1844, with Mr. Granby as Col. Chatillon, A. Walton as Franval, Walter Lacy as St. Hilare, W. H. Oxberry as Roux, Robert Honner as Phillipe, Mr. Chichely as Capt., Eugenie Prosper as Blanche, Miss Noel as Justine.

BLANCHE OF JERSEY (also titled Blanche Heriot)// D 2a// R. B. Peake// **Engl. Opera House** (Lyceum), Aug. 1837, with Mr. Baker as La Croix, A. Brindal as D'Harancourt, William Bennett as Bethune, S. Jones as Tronchet, Charles Diddear as Crussol, Henry Compton as Jachére, Priscilla Horton as Blanche, Mme. Simon as Barbara/ Scenery by Mr. Pitt/ Music by John Barnett.

BLANCHE WESTGARTH; OR, THE NEMISIS OF CRIME// D 3a// Templeton Lucas// **Grecian**, Mar. 1871.

BLANCHETTE// Play 3a// Adap. by J. T. Grein & M. L. Churchhill fr F of Eugène Brieux// **Court**, May 1901.

BLEAK HOUSE// D// Dram. by George Lander fr novel of Charles Dickens// **Pavilion**, Mar. 1876.

BLEEDING NUN, THE; OR, THE TRAVELLERS BENIGHTED (also tit. Bleeding Nun of Lindenberg, or the Robbers of the Black Forest)// D// n.a.// **Victoria**, May 1838, with John Parry as Don Raymond, William Davidge as Don Felix, Mr. Maddocks as Robert, Gerard King as Baptiste, Mr. Vale as Theodore, Mr. Varnby as Conrad, Mr. Johnstone as Claude, H. Lewis as Jaques, Mr. Harwood as Marco, Miss Richardson as Marguerite, Miss Wilson as Agnes, Mrs. Loveday as Beatrice, Miss Edgar as Spirit of the Bleeding Nun/ **Grecian**, Dec. 1863, with William James as Don Raymond, John Manning as Theodore, W. Shirley as Don Felix, Henry Power as Conrad, Walter Holland as Marco, J. Jackson as Baptiste, J. B. Steele as Robert, Mrs. Charles Dillon as Agnes, Ellen Crisp as Ursula, Jane Dawson as Marguerite, Marie Brewer as The Bleeding Nun.

BLETCHINGTON HOUSE// D 3a// H. T. Craven// **City of London**, Apr. 1846.

BLIGHTED BEING, A// F 1a// Adap. by Tom Taylor fr F, Une Existence Décolorée// **Olympic**, Oct. 1854, with Mr. Leslie as Spanker, Harwood Cooper as Cummings, Mr. Danvers as O'Rafferty, Frederick Robson as Job Wort, Ellen Turner as Susan/ **Sad. Wells**, Aug. 1855, with Mr. Leslie as Spanker, Harwood Cooper as Cumming, Mr. Danvers as O'Rafferty, Frederick Robson as Job Wort, Miss Marston as Susan/ **Globe**, Feb. 1876, with E. W. Royce as Job Wort, Mr. Tritton as Ned Spanker, E. G. Osborne as O'Rafferty, Linda Verner as Susan.

BLIGHTED WILLOW, THE; OR, THE SHEPHERD HEIR// D 2a// n.a.// **Sad. Wells**, Oct. 1839, with Mr. Dry as Lord Derwent, Mr. Cathcart as Sir Wilfred, Henry Hall as Shock, J. W. Collier as Rooney, Mr. Williams as Gerard, Mr. Elvin as Walter, Mr. Aldridge as Gervais, W. D. Broadfoot as Seneschal, Mrs. J. F. Saville as Lady Matilda, Miss Richardson as Alice.

BLIND BOY, THE; OR, THE HEIR OF STANISLAUS// D 2a// J. Kenney// **Sad. Wells**, June 1839, with Mr. Aldridge as King Stanislaus, Mr. Dry as Prince Rudolph, Mr. Jefferini as Kalig, Mr. Williams as Oberto, Charles Montgomery as Starrow, Mr. Conquest as Molino, Mrs. Robert Honner as Edmund, Mrs. J. F. Saville as Elvina/ **Grecian**, Feb. 1845, with John Collett as King Stanislaus, Annette Mears as Edmond, Edwin Dixon as Rodolph, Edmund Garden as Starow, Harry Chester as Kalig, Frederick Robson as Molino, Miss Johnstone as Elvina.

BLIND GIRL'S FORTUNE, THE// D (A vers. of The Two Orphans)// n.a.// **East London**, Nov. 1874.

BLIND JUSTICE// D Pro & 3a// E. C. Bertrand// **Standard**, Apr. 1887.

BLIND MARRIAGE, A// Play 4a// Francis Francis// **Criterion**, Aug. 1896, with Herbert Standing as Hurd, Herbert Waring as Lord Langdale, Charles Fulton as Spencer, Henry Esmond as Talbot, Arnold Lucy as Gussy, Carlotta Addison as Mrs. Saville, Eva Moore as Miss Saville, Kate Rorke as Linda.

BLIND ORPHAN, THE; OR, THE DOGS OF RAVENSDALE// D// n.a.// **Sad. Wells**, Apr. 1837, with Mr. Ede as Mowbray, N. T. Hicks as Michael, John Ayliffe as Spoonbill, Mr. Rogers as Sigismund, Miss Beresford as Theodore, Miss Lebatt as Flora, Mrs. Rogers as Alicia.

BLIND SINGER, THE// D 3a// George Dabbs// **Comedy**, Apr. 1898, with C. F. Collings as Prince Cipriani, Arthur Wood as Dr. Glover, Thomas Kingston as Vere Glover, Herman de Lange as Vendome, Neville Doone as Marquis Carramba, Cecil York as Klaus, Julian Cross as Brand, Mrs. Bennett as Salvadora, Madge McIntosh as Ida.

BLIND SISTER, THE// D 4a// Paul Meritt & George Conquest// **Grecian**, Oct. 1874.

BLIND WITNESS, THE// D// n.a.// **Grecian**, Sept. 1866, with Mr. Richards as Johnson, Samuel Perfitt as Parry, J. Jackson as Ronald, John Manning as Dennis, Lizzy Mandelbert as Phillis, Mary A. Victor as Sally.

BLINDFOLD// C 1a// Robert Soutar// **Gaiety**, May 1882.

BLOBB'S HOLIDAY// F// Charles Crozier// **Marylebone**, Apr. 1892.

BLOODHOUNDS, THE; OR, THE ORPHAN'S GRAVE// D// n.a.// **Victoria**, Aug. 1850, with J. Howard as Master Mintlove, Henry Frazer as Lamberte, E. F. Taylor as Rippon, Mr. Cony as Dick, J. T. Johnson as Gayton, Mr. Humphries as Webb, Mr. Hudspeth as Snipe, Dog Hector and Dog Neptune as Bloodhounds, Amelia Mercer as Ady, Mrs. George Lee as Madeline, Miss Mildenhall as Grace.

BLOOMER COSTUME, THE; OR, THE FIGURE OF FUN// F// Edward Stirling// **Strand**, Sept. 1851.

BLOOMERISM; OR, THE FOLLIES OF THE DAY// F// J. H. Nightingale & Charles Millward// **Adelphi**, Oct. 1851.

BLOT ON THE 'SCUTCHEON, THE// D 3a// Robert Browning// **Drury Lane**, Feb. 1843, with Samuel Phelps as Lord Tresham, James Anderson as Earl Mertoun, Charles Hudson as Austin, George Bennett as Gerard, Henry Mellon as Andrew, Charles Selby as Arthur, Helen Faucit as Mildred, Mrs. Stirling as Gwendolen/ **Sad. Wells**, Nov. 1848, with Samuel Phelps as Lord Tresham, Mr. Hoskins as Austin, G. H. Dickinson as Earl Merionn, Mr. Graham as Gerard, Mr. Harrington as Ralph, Charles Fenton as Frank, Mr. Knight as Richard, Mr. Stilt as Walter, Miss Cooper as Mildred, Miss Huddart as Gwendolin/ Scenery by F. Fenton & Mr. Brunning/ **Olympic**, Mar. 1888.

BLOW FOR BLOW// D Pro & 3a// H. J. Byron// **Grecian**, Aug. 1869, with Lizzie Mandelbert as Mildred, Mary A. Victor as Kitty, Henry Grant as Josiah, Thomas Mead as Drummond, George Conquest as Spraggs, William James as Linden, Samuel Perfitt as Bolder, Alice Denvil as Lady Ethel, Mrs. Atkinson as Mrs. Moulsey/ **Adelphi**, Mar. 1870, with Mr. Stuart as Josiah, Harwood Cooper as Boulder, Arthur Stirling as Drummond, H. J. Byron as Spraggs, J. D. Beveridge as Sir Harry, C. H. Stephenson as Dr. Grace, Maria Harris as Lady Ethel, Teresa Furtado as Petherick and as Craddock, Eliza Johnstone as Wobbler/ **Holborn**, Sept. 1868.

BLOW IN THE DARK, THE// C 1a// Thompson Townsend// **Surrey**, 1855.

BLOWER JONES// F 1a// n.a.// **Sadler's Wells**, Feb. 1881.

BLUE BEARD; OR, FEMALE CURIOSITY// D// George Colman the younger// **Drury Lane**,

Feb. 1837, with Mr. Mathews as Abomelique, Mr. Wilson as Selim, George Bartley as Ibrahim, John Duruset as Shacabac, Robert Honner as Hassan, Miss Betts as Fatima, Mrs. East as Irene, Mrs. Humby as Beda/ **Sad. Wells**, July 1840, with Mr. Dry as Abomelique, Mr. Williams as Ibrahim, J. B. Hill as Selim, Henry Hall as Shacabac, Mrs. Morgan as Fatima, Mrs. Richard Barnett as Irene, Mrs. J. F. Saville as Beda/ Scenery by F. Fenton/ Music by Michael Kelly/ Machines by B. Sloman/ **Cov. Garden**, Jan. 1843, with Charles Diddear as Abomelique, Mr. Granby as Ibrahim, Mr. Travers as Selim, John Pritt Harley as Shacabac, Mr. Moore as Hassan, Miss Betts as Fatima, Miss Collett as Irene, Miss Poole as Beda.

BLUE BELLS OF SCOTLAND, THE// CD 5a// Dram. by Robert Buchanan fr his own story, A Child of Nature// **Novelty**, Sept. 1887.

BLUE BOAR, THE// F 3a// L. N. Parker & Murray Carson// **Terry's**, Mar. 1895, with Edward Terry as Honeydew, Harcourt Beatty as Strawthwaite, George Belmore as The Griffin, Leslie Kenyon as Boots, Fanny Brough as Dr. Prendergast, Alexis Leighton as Mrs. Pounder, Madge McIntosh as Millicent.

BLUE DEVILS, THE// F 1a// George Colman the younger// **Haymarket**, May 1839, with O. Smith as Megrim, Mr. Strickland as Demisou, Mr. Green as Bailiff, J. B. Buckstone as James, Mrs. Fitzwilliam as Annette; June 1869, with Henry Howe as Megrin, Mr. Rogers as Dennison, J. B. Buckstone Jr. as James, Fanny Wright as Annette/ **Victoria**, June 1840, with J. T. Haines as Megrim, Edward Burton as Demisou, Mr. Howard as James, Mrs. Howard as Annette/ **Sad. Wells**, July 1842, with Mr. Lyon as Megrim, John Herbert as James, P. Williams as Demisou, Mrs. Richard Barnett as Annette/ **Grecian**, Jan. 1855, with Richard Phillips as Megrim, Eaton O'Donnell as Demisou, John Manning as James, Harriet Coveney as Annette/ .

BLUE DWARF, THE; OR, MYSTERY, LOVE AND CRIME// D// Dram. by Frederick Marchant fr a pop. tale// **Sad. Wells**, Aug. 1866, with Philip Hannan as Blakesley, T. B. Bennett as Carabosse, G. F. Warde as Sir Edgar, J. F. Young as Sapathwa, Walter Roberts as Leopold, W. H. Schofield as Lord Charles, Watty Brunton as Mudlark, Miss Neville as Lilian, Mrs. Philip Hannan as Lucy, Julia Summers as Mary, Annette Vincent as Marian, Etty Brandon as Pauline.

BLUE-EYED WITCH, THE; OR, NOT A FRIEND IN THE WORLD// D 3a// C. H. Hazlewood// **Britannia**, June 1869.

BLUE JACKETS, THE; OR, HER MAJESTY'S SERVICE// F// Edward Stirling// **Adelphi**, Oct. 1838, with Frank Matthews, Mr. Saville, John Sanders, O. Smith, William Cullenford, Mrs. Honey, Mrs. Keeley, Miss O'Neil/ **Grecian**, Oct. 1853, with Eaton O'Donnell as Admiral Trunnion, Mr. Roberts as Herbert, Richard Phillips as Binnacle, Edwin Dixon as Chaser, Henry Power as Jacko, Mary A. Crisp as Fanny, Harriet Coveney as Betsy/ **Sad. Wells**, Mar. 1864, with T. B. Bennett as Adm. Trunnion, E. H. Brooke as Herbert, George Fisher as Binnacle, D. Perfitt as Chaser, W. Clifton as Jacko, Lizzie Harrison as Fanny, Eliza Hamilton as Betsy.

BLUE-LEGGED LADY, THE// F// W. J. Hill// **Court**, Mar. 1874.

BLUE OR GREEN// C 1a// Mrs. Hugh Bell// **Comedy**, Mar. 1896, with Carlotta Addison as Sophie, Beatrice Herford as Betsinda.

BLUE RIBBONS// F 3a// Walter Browne & J. E. Soden// **Gaiety**, May 1887.

BLUEJACKETS; OR, HER MAJESTY'S SERVICE// F 1a// Edward Stirling// **Adelphi**, Oct. 1838.

BLUESKIN (see also Early Days of Blueskin)// D// Frederick Marchant// **Grecian**, Dec. 1867, with J. Jackson, Samuel Perfitt, W. Shirley, Henry Grant, Charles Mortimer, William James, John Manning, Alice Denvil, Mrs. Atkinson, Mary A. Victor, Mrs. Dearlove.

BLUNDERS// C 1a// n.a.// **Opera Comique**, Apr. 1898, with George Temple as Sir Henry, Thomas Kingston as Wilding, F. G. Nettleford as Capt. Strong, Phyllis Manners as Martha, Cissie Neil as Henrietta.

BOARD AND RESIDENCE// F 1a// Conway Edwards// **Globe**, Oct. 1870, with Shafto Robertson as Fitzfaddle, Henry Rignold as Beard, Rowley Cathcart as Tootles, Emily Burns as Matilda Mildew, Isabelle Armour as Maria Mildew, Clara Weston as Smart.

BOARDING SCHOOL, THE// F 1a// W. Bayle Bernard// **Haymarket**, Sept. 1841, with Benjamin Webster as Lt. Varley, Mr. J. W. Gough as Maj. Marsden, John Webster as Capt. Harcourt, Frederick Vining as Kavanagh, David Rees as James, Mrs. W. Clifford as Mrs. Grosdenap, Mrs. Frank Matthews as Miss Biggs, Mrs. Stirling as Caroline, Miss Charles as Julia, Priscilla Horton as Mary, Miss Partridge as Ellen; Mar. 1860, with William Cullenford as Maj. Marsden, Edwin Villiers as Lt. Varley, William Farren as Capt. Harcourt, George Braid as Kavanagh, J. Worrell as Sgt. Saunders, Mr. Clark as Holly, Mrs. Poynter as Mrs. Grosdenap, Mrs. Griffiths as Miss Biggs, Mrs. Edward Fitzwilliam as Miss Blythe, Maria Ternan as Miss Manvers, Eliza Weekes as Miss Mite/ **St. James's** Nov. 1861, with George Vining as Capt. Harcourt, F. Charles as Kavanagh, Frederick Dewar as Lt. Varley, Mr. Terry as Maj. Marsden, R. Cockrill as Holly, George Belmore as James, Miss Rainforth as Mrs. Grosdenap, Miss Herbert as Caroline, Kate Terry as Mary Mite, Nelly Moore as Julia, Mrs. Frank Matthews as Miss Biggs/ Scenery by F. Lloyds & Walter Hann.

BOATMAN OF THE SHANNON, THE// D 3a// Edward Towers// **Pavilion**, Feb. 1877.

BOATSWAIN'S WHISTLE, THE; OR, THE RAVEN'S GAP// D// n.a.// **Sad. Wells**, Feb. 1840, with Mr. Williams as Anchor, Robert

Honner as Cable, Mr. Stilt as Binnacle, Mr. Dry as Gimbolt, Mr. Aldridge as Mainmast, Charles Montgomery as Porpoise, J. W. Collier as Noggin, Henry Hall as Hatband, Mrs. Robert Honner as Mary, Mrs. J. F. Saville as Fanny, Miss Cooke as Mrs. Noggin, Mrs. Morgan as Sally/ Scenery by F. Fenton & G. Smithyes/ Machines by B. Sloman/ Music by Mr. Herbert.

BOB// C 3a// Frederick Marsden// **Novelty,** Dec. 1888/ **Strand,** Feb. 1889.

BOB BRADSHAW'S DREAM// Play 1a// B. W. Thomas// **Strand,** May 1899.

BOB BRETTON; OR, THE DEAD SHOT OF THE WOODS// D// n.a.// **Victoria,** July 1877.

BOB LUMLEY'S SECRET; OR, THE DARK DEEDS OF BLUEGATE FIELDS// D 2a// Cecil & William Pitt// **Britannia,** Dec. 1869.

BOB SHORT// F 1a// Mark Lemon// **Haymarket,** Jan. 1841, with John Webster as Short, David Rees as Tot, Robert Strickland as Dipwick, J. W. Gough as Hoyle, Priscilla Horton as Esther, Mrs. Stanley as Mrs. Ticknot, Mrs. Frank Matthews as Betty/ **Sad. Wells,** Oct. 1848, with Mr. Williams as Dipwick, Mr. Hoskins as Bob Short, Henry Scharf as Tot, Mr. Knight as Hoyle, Fanny Huddart as Esther, Miss Stephens as Mrs. Ticknot.

BOGIE// Play 3a// H. V. Esmond// **St. James's,** Sept. 1895, with H. V. Esmond as Uncle Archie, Frederick Everill as Gradden, Mr. Elliot as Maclachlan, Phillip Cunningham as Tiddy, Gaston Mervale as Emens, W. R. Staveley as Kennedy, Ethel Matthews as Marion, Eva Moore as Fairy, Pattie Bell as Miss Minden.

BOHEMIA AND BELGRAVIA// C 3a// Arthur O'Neill// **Royalty,** June 1872.

BOHEMIAN, A// Play 4a// L. N. Parker// **Globe,** Feb. 1892, with Frederick Everill as Rev. Bellairs, Murray Carson as Capt. Bellairs, E. Allan Aynesworth as Rev. Disney, Lewis Waller as Brooke, T. W. Percyval as Clifford, Florence West as Olga, Maude Millett as Sibyl/ Scenery by Walter Hann & Durant/ Prod. by W. Lestocq.

BOHEMIANS, THE; OR, THE ROGUES OF PARIS// D 3a// Adap. by Edward Stirling fr F of Eugène Sué, Mystères de Paris// **Adelphi,** Nov. 1843, with George Maynard as Montorgeuil, R. Hughes as Leonard, Mr. Lyon as Charles Didier, Mr. Freeborn as Franconier, Mr. Wright as Criquet Bagnolet, Stephen Smith as Chalumeau, Mr. Williamson as Pierre, O. Smith as Creve Coeur, Mrs. Frederick Yates as Louise, Mrs. Frank Matthews as Madame Papclard/ Scenery by Pitt and Finley/ Dances by Mr. Frampton/ Music by G. H. Rodwell/ Machinery by Mr. Cooper/ Prod. by Edward Stirling.

BOHEMIANS, THE; OR, THE THIEVES OF PARIS// D// Adap. fr F of Eugène Sué, Mystères de Paris// **City of London,** Nov. 1843.

BOHEMIANS OF PARIS, THE; OR, THE MYSTERIES OF CRIME// D 3a// Adap. by C. Z. Barnett fr F of Eugène Sué, Mystères de Paris// **Surrey,** Nov. 1843.

BOILING WATER// FC 3a// Julian Cross// **Comedy,** July 1885.

BOLD STROKE FOR A HUSBAND, A// C// Hannah Cowley// **Sad. Wells,** May 1850 (in 3a), with Henry Marston as Don Julio, G. K. Dickinson as Don Carlos, A. Younge as Don Caesar, William Hoskins as Don Vincentio, William Belford as Don Garcia, Mr. Williams as Gaspar, Miss Fitzpatrick as Olivia, Miss T. Bassano as Victoria, Mrs. Graham as Laura, Miss Johnstone as Marcella, Miss A. Brown as Minetta, Fanny Morelli as Inis.

BOMBASTES FURIOSO// F 1a// W. B. Rhodes// **Princess's,** Apr. 1848, with Sam Cowell as King Artaxominous, J. Neville as Fusbos, Henry Compton as Furioso, Emma Stanley as Distaffina; Nov. 1852, with John Pritt Harley as Artaxominous, Mr. Addison as Fusbos, Edward Wright as Bombastes/ **Astley's,** Sept. 1856, with W. Anson as Artaximines, Mr. Jackson as Fusbos, W. Gomersal as General Bombastes, Julia Weston as Distaffina/ **Olympic,** Sept. 1863, with Robert Soutar as Artxominous, Horace Wigan as Fusbos, F. B. Conway as Bombastes, Miss Hughes as Distaffina.

BONA FIDE TRAVELLERS, THE// F 1a// William Brough// **Adelphi,** Oct. 1854/ **Sad. Wells,** June 1855, with Mrs. Keeley as Jemima, George Fisher, James Rogers as Joe, Henry M. Barrett as O'Gripper, Robert Soutar as Simkins, Mr. Shepperd as Sims, C. Kelsy as Bolter, Miss Macarthy as Mary, Miss Nash as Jane, Miss Lane as Susan.

BONDAGE// Play 4a// Adap. fr F of Pierre d'Abry// **Opera Comique,** Mar. 1883, with Charles Kelly, George Alexander, William Farren Jr., Nelly Bromley, Mabel Hardinge.

BONNET BUILDER'S TEA PARTY, THE// F// Arthur Moore// **Sad. Wells,** Oct. 1867, with J. W. Lawrence as Winchcomb, John W. White as Sniffkins, R. H. Edgar as Whiffles, Walter Searle as Wobbler, Mrs. Walton as Mrs. Puddicomb, Grace Edgar as Seraphina, Miss Lawrence as Rosa, Mary Henderson as Isabella.

BONNIE DUNDEE// D// Edmund Falconer// **Drury Lane,** Mar. 1863, with Edmund Phelps as Graham, Henry Sinclair as Glenlyon, G. F. Neville as Lochiel, N. M. Barrett as McIan, J. Graham as Campbell, Henry Loraine as McDonald, Henry Haigh as Allan, George Spencer as Jonas, Mrs. D. P. Bowers as Helen.

BONNIE DUNDEE// Play 5a// Laurence Irving// **Adelphi,** Mar. 1900.

BONNIE FISHWIFE, A// C 1a// Charles Selby// **Sad. Wells** Dec. 1880, with Nelson Wheatcroft as Sir Hiccory, Walter Brooks as Heartycheer, Edmund Lyons as Gaiters, Miss M. Bell as Miss Thistledown and as Maggie.

BONNIE PRINCE CHARLIE// D// J. B.

Buckstone// **East London**, July 1868.

BOOK OF FATE, THE; OR, A TAILOR'S DREAM// D// n.a.// **Victoria**, Aug. 1843, with John Gardner as Tidlitz, Mr. Howard as Gabello, Mr. James as Dottledorf, Mr. Wilton as Balidor, F. H. Henry as Carl, Cecil Pitt as Paul, Miss Hicks as Mariette, Miss Vaughan as Bridget, Miss Ridgeway as Marcellina, Miss Saddler as Rosa.

BOOK THE THIRD, CHAPTER THE FIRST// C 1a// Adap. fr F of Eugène Pierron & Adolphe Laferrière// **Court**, June 1875/ **Lyceum**, Apr. 1879, with Mr. Teesdale as Leslie, Mr. Elwood as Arundel, Mr. Russell as Joseph, Eleanor Bufton as Lucy Arundel.

BOOKMAKER, THE// C 3a// J. W. Pigott// **Terry's**, 1889/ **Gaiety**, Aug. 1890.

BOOM OF BIG BEN, THE// D 4a// Adap. by Arthur Shirley fr F of A. Fantanes, Le Porteur aux Halles// **Pavilion**, Nov. 1901/ **Princes's**, Dec. 1901.

BOOT ON THE RIGHT LEG, THE// F// n.a.// **Olympic**, Oct. 1871.

BOOTBLACK, THE// D Pro & 4a// Arthur Jefferson// **West London**, July 1898.

BOOTLE'S BABY// C 4a// Adap. by Hugh Moss fr story of J. S. Winter// **Globe**, May 1888, with Edmund Maurice as Capt. Ferrers, C. W. Garthorne as Capt. Lucy, Charles Sugden as Capt. Gilchrist, Gilbert Farquhar as Dr. Blantyre, C. Montague as Lt. Gray, Charles Collette as Saunders, Forbes Dawson as Lt. Miles, Henrietta Lindley as Mrs. Smith, Rose Evelyn as Humpty Dumpty, Minnie Terry as Mignon, Edith Woodworth as Helen Grace/ Scenery by W. T. Hemsley/ Music by Walter Slaughter/ **Garrick**, Feb. 1900.

BOOTS AT THE HOLLY TREE INN; OR, THE INFANT ELOPEMENT TO GRETNA GREEN// F 1a// Dram. by Benjamin Webster fr story of Charles Dickens// **Adelphi**, Feb. 1856.

BOOTS AT THE SWAN, THE// F 1a// Charles Selby// **Strand**, July 1842/ **Lyceum**, Sept. 1846, with Henry Butler as Higgins, Frederick Vining as Friskly, J. W. Collier as Pippin, Robert Keeley as Jacob Earwig, Ellen Daly as Cecilia, Miss Hicks as Emily, Mrs. Alfred Wigan as Sally/ **Olympic**, Aug. 1853, with John Kinloch as Higgins, Henry Marston as Friskly, E. Clifton as Pippins, Frederick Robson as Jacob Earwig, Harriet Gordon as Cecilia, Isabel Adams as Emily, Ellen Turner as Sally, Miss S. Pitt as Betty; Dec. 1876, with Dibdin Culver as Higgins, Mr. Flockton as Friskly, T. G. Warren as Pippin, W. J. Hill as Jacob Earwig, Miss Gerard as Cecilia, Miss Beaumont as Emily, Amy Crawford as Sally/ **Grecian**, Mar. 1854, with Charles Horn as Higgins, Richard Phillips as Friskly, Thomas Roberts as Pippin, Mr. Copping as Earwig, Jane Coveney as Cecilia, Harriet Coveney as Sally, Agnes De Warde as Emily, Ellen Crisp as Polly/ **Sad. Wells**, July 1863, with Walter Joyce as Friskly, T. T. Pugh as Higgins, C. Lester as Pippin, G. A. Palmer as Jacob Earwig, Miss Lavine as Cecilia, Georgina Vyze as Emily, Bessie Heath as Sally/ **Vaudeville**, 1870, with Henry Irving.

BORDER MARRIAGE, A// CD 1a// Adap. by W. J. Sorrel fr F, Un Mariage à l'Arquebus// **Adelphi**, Nov. 1856.

BORDER MARRIAGE, A// CD 1a// Adap. by H. T. Craven fr F, Un Mariage à l'Arquebus// **St. James's**, Jan. 1860.

BORGIA RING, THE; A LEGEND OF STONEHENGE// D 2a// A. R. Slous// **Adelphi**, Jan. 1859, with Benjamin Webster as Piers, John Billington as Langley, Charles Selby as Hiram, C. J. Smith as Hilary, Edmund Garden as Sir Arthur, W. H. Eburne as Col. Thornton, Mr. Manley as Capt. Steele, Paul Bedford as Maximus, J. L. Toole as Tim Weazle, Mrs. Alfred Mellon (Sarah Woolgar) as Mabel, Mrs. Billington as Eleanore, Kate Kelly as Lucy, Mary Keeley as Cecily.

BORN TO GOOD LUCK; OR, THE IRISHMAN'S FORTUNE (also titled, Born to be Lucky; or, the Fortune of an Irishman)// F 2a// Tyrone Power// **Haymarket**, Aug. 1837, with Robert Strickland as Count Malfi, E. F. Saville as Count Manfredi, Charles Selby as Coradino, Tyrone Power as O'Rafferty, E. Harris as Rufo, Mrs. Tayleure as Countess Molinga, Miss E. Honner as Margaretta, Eliza Vincent as Nina; Sept. 1850, with Charles Hudson as O'Rafferty, Mr. Lambert as Count Malfi, Charles Boyce as Manfredi, Mr. Caulfield as Coradino, C. J. Smith as Rufo, Mr. Waye as Pedro, Mrs. Laws as Countess Melinga, Mrs. Caulfield as Margarita, Sarah Woolgar as Nina/ **Sad. Wells**, Aug. 1837, with Mr. Griffiths as Count Benini, Gerard King as Count Caliari, Mr. Jones as Albertini, Thomas Lee as O'Rafferty, Mr. Scarbrow as Lupo, H. George as Malvoglio, Mrs. Harris as Countess Viteria, Lavinia Melville as Genette; June 1854, with C. Poynter as Count Malfi, Samuel Perfitt as Count Manfredi, F. Charles as Coradine, George Robson as O'Rafferty, Miss Rawlings as Countess Rolinga, Lizzie Mandelbert as Marguerita, Miss Lavine as Nina/ **Cov. Garden**, Feb. 1838, with Robert Strickland as Count Malfi, Charles Diddear as Count Manfredi, Mr. Roberts as Coradino, W. H. Payne as Rufo, C. J. Smith as Carlo, Tyrone Power as O'Rafferty, Edwin Yarnold as Pedro, Mrs. Griffith as Countess Molinga, Mrs. Serle as Margaretta, Priscilla Horton as Nina/ **Grecian**, Nov. 1844, with Mr. Campbell as Count Malfi, Harry Chester as Manfredi, Mr. Melvin as Conradini, Mr. Hodson as Paudreen, Miss Merion as Countess, Mary A. Crisp as Nina, Miss Johnstone as Margueritte/ **Victoria**, May 1854, with Alfred Saville as Count Malfi, F. H. Henry as Count Manfredi, Mr. Henderson as Coradine, George Hodson as O'Rafferty, Mrs. Manders as Countess Melinga, Miss Laporte as Nina, Miss Dansor as Marguerite/ **Adelphi**, July 1856, with Charles Selby as Count Malfi, John Parselle as Count Manfredi, J. G. Shore as Florenzi, Barney Williams as O'Rafferty, Mrs. Chatterley as Countess Molinga, Mary Keeley as Nina/

Princess's, May 1864, with Henry Mellon as Count Malfi, Joseph Robins as Count Manfredi, Mr. Brooke as Count Coradine, Dominick Murray as O'Rafferty, Mrs. Henry Marston as Countess Malinga, Emma Barnett as Margaretta, Helen Howard as Nina.

BOROUGH POLITICS// D 2a// Westland Marston// **Haymarket**, June 1846, with Benjamin Webster as Thompson, Mr. Tilbury as Dr. Neville, Henry Howe as Frank, J. B. Buckstone as Florid, A. Brindal as Sweetlip, Mrs. Julia Glover as Mrs. Thompson, Mrs. Stanley as Mrs. Neville, Mrs. Edwin Yarnold as Pansy.

BORROWED LOVER, THE// F 1a// n.a.// **Lyceum**, July 1871, with Maggie Harold as Gertrude, Belle Sidney as Ernestine, William Davidge Jr. as Peter Spyke, E. T. Clinton as Suggle, E. M. Bellew as Capt. Amesford.

BORROWED PLUMES// F 1a// G. A. Maltby// **Sad. Wells**, Sept. 1866, with E. Shepherd as Bibbins, J. Collier as Rattleton, John Rouse as Mizzle, Miss Leigh as Violet, Grace Edgar as Emma/ **Drury Lane**, Oct. 1868, with Mr. Barrett as Bibbins, Alfred Nelson as Tattleton, John Rouse as Mizzle, Kate Harfleur as Violet, Miss Hudspeth as Emma/ **Adelphi**, Apr. 1885, with M. Bentley as Bibbins, T. Fulljames as Tattleton, Ernest Travers as Mizzle, May Harlowe as Violet, Harriet Coveney as Emma.

BORROWING A HUSBAND; OR, SLEEPING OUT// C 1a// W. T. Moncrieff// **Princess's**, 1843; Oct. 1862, with Mr. Cathcart as Sir Vivian, Henry Widdicomb as Buckthorn, Mr. Moreland as Alec, Mr. Raymond as Frisby, Miss Fielding as Dame Partington, Maria Harris as Pamela/ **Sad. Wells**, Oct. 1845, with Samuel Buckingham as Sir Vivian, Henry Scharf as Gilbert, Charles Fenton as Alec, E. Morton as Frisby, Miss Lebatt as Pamela, Mrs. Henry Marston as Dame Partington/ **Grecian**, Nov. 1857, with Henry Grant as Sir Vivian, George Conquest as Gilbert, Henry Power as Alec, Richard Phillips as Frisby, Miss Johnstone as Dame Partington, Harriet Coveney as Pamela/ **Haymarket**, Apr. 1863, with Henry Howe as Sir Vivian, Henry Compton as Buckthorne, Mr. Clark as Alec, Thomas Coe as Tristey, Mrs. Griffith as Dame Partington, Miss Harris as Pamela.

BOTH SIDES OF THE WORLD// D Pro & 3a// Mr. Bailey// **Elephant & Castle**, May 1882.

BOTHERATION; OR, A TEN YEARS' BLUNDER// F// W. C. Oulton// **Sad. Wells**, Oct. 1841, with George Ellis as Varnish, Mr. Elvin as Hopeful, Mr. Aldridge as Dr. Wisepate, Mr. Richardson as Robert, Thomas Lee as O'Blarney, Mrs. Richard Barnett as Mrs. Varnish, Miss Cooke as Mrs. Wisepate/ **Grecian**, Mar. 1845, with Harry Chester as Hopeful, Edwin Dixon as Varnish, Mr. Baldwin as Wisepate, Mr. Kerridge as Robert, Edmund Garden as Thady O'Blarney, Miss Merion as Lady Apes, Miss Johnstone as Mrs. Varnish, Mary A. Crisp as Rose.

BOTTLE, THE// D 2a// T. P. Taylor// **City of London**, Oct.1847/ **Victoria**, May 1856, with Alfred Saville as Milford, R. H. Lingham as Alfred, W. H. Pitt as John, Mr. Henderson as Lushington, J. Howard as Old Dan, Mr. Warlow as Moke, John Bradshaw as Flunkey, H. Hudspeth as Basil, Watty Brunton as Patterclap, F. H. Henry as Clapatter, Mrs. Henry Vining as Mary, Julia Seaman as Selina, Mrs. Manders as Mrs. Moneygrub.

BOTTLE IMP, THE// D 2a// R. B. Peake// **Drury Lane**, May 1838, with Henry Frazer as Albert, Henry Compton as Willibald, Charles Perkins as Nicola, Mr. Baker as Waldeck, A. Brindal as Conrade, R. McIan as Imp, Miss Poole as Marcella, Miss H. Cawse as Phillippa, Miss Fitzwalter as Lucretia/ **Olympic**, Apr. 1851, with John Kinloch as Albert, Henry Compton as Willibald, Charles Diddear as Nicola, Charles Bender as Waldeck, W. Shalders as Shadrack, Mr. Geoffrey as Montorio, H. Lee as the Bottle Imp, Miss Adams as Marcelia, Isabel Adams as Lucretia, Ellen Turner as Philippa.

BOTTLE OF SMOKE// n.a.// **Adelphi**, May 1856.

BOUDOIR GALLANT, THE; OR, THE ASSIGNATION, THE INTERVIEW, AND THE PROBLEM// C 1a// n.a.// **Sad. Wells**, Sept. 1837, with C. H. Pitt as Belmour, Lavinia Melville as Harriet, Miss Williams as Mrs. Belmour, Mrs. Harris as Rose.

BOULD SOGER BOY, THE// F 1a// Edward Stirling// **Olympic**, Nov. 1848, with C. Bender as Sir George, W. H. Norton as Power, Mr. Hammersley as Capt. O'Slasher, Mr. Neale as Trevanion, Mr. Sidney as Courton, Redmond Ryan as Kildare, Charles Hale as Prettyman, H. J. Turner as William, Miss Murray as Miss Dashwood, Mrs. C. A. Tellet as Jenny/ **Strand**, Nov. 1851.

BOULOGNE// C 3a// Adap. by F. C. Burnand fr F of Maurice Henniquin & Albert Millaud// **Gaiety**, Apr. 1879, with Edward Terry, William Elton, Ellen Farren.

BOUNCE// F 3a// Arthur Maltby// **Opera Comique**, Oct. 1876.

BOUND 'PRENTICE TO A WATERMAN// D// A. V. Campbell// **Grecian**, Sept. 1861, with J. Cobden, J. Jackson, George Gillett, James Marsh, W. Addison, Alfred Rayner, Mrs. Charles Dillon, Miss Johnstone, Ellen Hale.

BOUND TO SUCCEED; OR, A LEAF FROM THE CAPTAIN'S LOGBOOK// D// George Conquest & Henry Pettitt// **Grecian**, Oct. 1877.

BOUND TO THE WHEEL// n.a.// **Pavilion**, Apr. 1866.

BOUQUET; OR, THE LANGUAGE OF FLOWERS// D 3a// Edward Towers// **East London**, Oct. 1870.

BOW BELLS// D// n.a.// **City of London**, May 1863, with J. F. Young.

BOW BELLS// C 3a// H. J. Byron// **Royalty**, Oct. 1880, with Edward Righton, Kate Lawler.

BOW OF ORANGE RIBBON, THE// Play 4a// Frank Cooper & Henry Jardine// **Daly's**, Aug. 1897.

BOWL'D OUT; OR, A BIT OF BRUMMAGEM// F 1a// H. T. Craven// **Princess's**, July 1860, with Henry Widdicomb as Yearner, Henry Saker as Quorms, Mr. Cathcart as Arlington, Mr. Collett as Kidman, Mrs. Weston as Mrs. Brefton, Carlotta Leclercq as Sarah, Rose Leclercq as Marian.

BOX AND COX// F 1a// J. Maddison Morton// **Lyceum**, Nov. 1847, with J. B. Buckstone as Box, John Pritt Harley as Cox, Mrs. Macnamara as Mrs. Bouncer/ **Haymarket**, Dec. 1849, with J. B. Buckstone as Box, Robert Keeley as Cox, Mrs. Stanley as Mrs. Bouncer/ **Sad. Wells**, July 1854, with Robert Roxby as Box, C. Swan as Cox, Mrs. Foote as Mrs. Bouncer/ **Astley's**, Apr. 1861, with J. B. Buckstone as Box, Lewis Ball as Cox, Mrs. Griffiths as Mrs. Bouncer/ **Olympic**, Feb. 1866, with J. B. Buckstone as Box, Henry Compton as Cox, Mrs. Stephens as Mrs. Bouncer/ **POW**, Dec. 1867, with John Hare as Box, George Honey as Cox, Mrs. Leigh Murray as Mrs. Bouncer/ **Globe**, June 1873, with Henry Compton as Cox, E. W. Garden as Box, Louisa Manders as Mrs. Bouncer.

BOX AND COX, MARRIED AND SETTLED// F 1a// J. Stirling Coyne// **Haymarket**, Oct. 1852, with J. B. Buckstone as Box, Robert Keeley as Cox, Thomas Coe as Gent., Mrs. Caulfield as Mrs. Box, Mrs. L. S. Buckingham as Mrs. Cox, Mrs. Selby as Mrs. Bouncer.

BOX LOBBY CHALLENGE, THE// C 5a// Adap. by W. R. Walkes fr orig. of Richard Cumberland// **Royalty**, June 1894, with H. A. Saintsbury as Capt. Waterland, E. Lawford as Crotchet, Douglas Gordon as Grampus, Edgar Skeet as Fulsome, Fred Grove as Squire Robert, A. Ferrand as Old Crotchet, Katherine Stewart as Lady Jane, Lizzie Henderson as Diana, Lilian Revele as Letitia, Mary Besslie as Theodosia.

BOY KING, THE; OR, PETITE PECCADILLOS// C// Adap. fr F// **Adelphi**, Aug. 1845, with J. Worrell as Richelieu, William Cullenford as Dubois, Mr. Lindon as Duke de Pompadour, Maud Taylor as Marie Leczinska, Miss Vernon as Mlle. de Mailly, Mme. Celeste as Louis XV, Sarah Woolgar as Duke de Lauzun, Ellen Chaplin as Duke de Roquelaure/ Scenery by Pitt & Johnstone/ Machinery by Mr. Cooper.

BOYS TOGETHER// D 4a// C. Haddon Chambers & J. Comyns Carr// **Adelphi**, Aug. 1896, with William Terriss as Frank Villars, W. L. Abingdon as Hugo, C. W. Somerset as Earl of Harpenden, J. D. Beveridge as Tom Wrake, Harry Nicolls as Viscount Ayot, Luigi Lablache as Hassan, Oscar Ayde as Col. Lannock, James Lindsay as Cholmondeley, Jessie Millward as Ethel, Alice Kingsley as Lady Ayot, Kate Kearney as Mrs. Babbage, Miss Nesbitt as Mariam/ Scenery by W. Harford, W. Perkins, Bruce Smith, & Walter Hann/ Music by John Crook/ Prod. by Fred Latham.

BOYS WILL BE BOYS// C 1a// Joseph Mackay// **Opera Comique**, July 1889/ **Strand**, July 1894, with Richard Purdon as Wapshot, Forbes Dawson as Cholmondely, Robert Nainby as Alick, Georgie Esmond as Evelina.

BOZ; OR, THE PICKWICK CLUB// D// Adap. fr Charles Dickens// **Sad. Wells**, Aug. 1837, with Mr. Campbell as Pickwick, Mr. Ennis as Tupman, Mr. Spilling as Winkle, Mr. George as Snodgrass, C. H. Pitt as Alfred Jingle, Gerard King as Rakely, C. J. Smith as Joe, Mr. Rogers as Sam Weller, Thomas Lee as Weller Sr., Mr. Williams as Fiskin, Lavinia Melville as Emily, Mrs. Harris as Rachel, Mrs. Worrell as Isabella, Mrs. Rogers as Mrs. Hunter.

BRACEY; OR, THE PHANTOM ROBBER AND THE ROUNDHEAD'S DAUGHTER// D// T. G. Blake// **Sad. Wells**, June 1841, with George Ellis as Lt. Wharton, Mr. Elvin as Benson, Mr. Dry as Phillips, Henry Marston as Bracey, Mr. Stilt as Sgt. McAllister, Mr. Aldridge as Jefferies, J. W. Collier as Jacob, Mrs. Robert Honner as Joan, Mrs. Richard Barnett as Grace/ Scenery by F. Fenton, G. Smithyes Jr., & Mr. Daniels/ Music by Isaac Collins/ Machines by B. Sloman.

BRAG// CD 5a// W. G. Wills (see Ellen).

BRAND// D 1a// The 4th act of Henrik Ibsen's play, trans. fr Norw. by C. H. Hereford// **Opera Comique**, June 1893.

BRANDED// D 5a// Richard Lee// **Princess's**, Apr. 1881, with Henry Neville as Lacroix/ Ferron, Frank Archer as Col. St. Cyr, William Redmund as Corp. Paul, J. S. Hewitt as Sgt. Verjuiceau, John Beauchamp as Leseque, Henry Evans as Krantz, John Gardiner as Mouche, W. Chamberlain as Grenier, F. Charles as Laurelle, Caroline Hill as Lina, Maud Milton as Corinne, Mrs. Huntley as Hagar, Mrs. Lyons as Mme. Verjuiceau/ Scenery by Charles Brooke/ Music by Michael Connolly/ Machines by Mr. Warton/ Gas by David Jones/ Lime-light by Messrs. Kerr/ Prod. by Harry Jackson.

BRANDED RACE// D// n.a.// **Surrey**, Sept. 1858.

BRANTINGHAME HALL// D 4a// W. S. Gilbert// **St. James's**, Nov. 1888, with Mrs. Gaston Murray as Lady Saxmundham, Miss Norreys as Mabel, Julia Neilson as Ruth, Nutcombe Gould as Lord Saxmundham, William Herbert as Arthur Redmayne, Duncan Fleet as Alaric Redmayne, Norman Forbes as Rev. Ross, Gilbert Trent as Parfit, Lewis Waller as Crampton, Rutland Barrington as Thursby/ Scenery by Walter Johnstone, Julian Hicks, & Henry Emden.

BRAS DE FER// D 2a// E. Manuel// **Britannia**, May 1875.

BRASS// CD 5a// G. F. Rowe// **Haymarket**, Aug. 1877, with F. H. Macklin as Wyvern, William Hargreaves as Adm. Hawker, H. R. Teesdale as Masham, R. H. Astley as Tom, Henry Howe as Armstrong, David Fisher Jr. as Tibbets, Harold Kyrle as Balance, G. F. Rowe as Stray, Emily Thorne as Mrs. Masham, Maria Harris, Blanche Henri as Mary, Violet Orme as Sybil.

BRAVADO// C// Adap. by Mrs. T. S. Smale fr F// **Strand**, July 1889.

BRAVE AS A LION// C// J. T. Douglass// **Standard**, Mar. 1872.

BRAVE COWARD, A// Play 3a// J. S. Blythe// **Strand**, Dec. 1886, with John Beauchamp, Bassett Roe, Alma Murray, Annie Hughes.

BRAVE HEARTS// D 2a// Adap. by Arthur Matthison fr F of Bumanoir & Lafargue, Le Gentilhomme Pauvre// **Criterion**, Jan. 1881, with Herbert Beerbohm Tree, William Blakeley, Mrs. Alfred Mellon, Mary Rorke.

BRAVIN'S BROW// n.a.// **Marylebone**, June 1863.

BRAVING THE STORM// F 1a// Adelaide Woodruffe// **Drury Lane**, Feb. 1871/ **Sadler's Wells**, Oct. 1871.

BREACH OF PROMISE, A// C 2a// T. W. Robertson// **Globe**, Apr. 1869, with David Fisher as Pentlecopp, John Clarke as Phillip, E. Marshall as Croople, Henry Andrews as Fullawords, J. Paulo as David, Rose Behrend as Clementina, Maggie Brennan as Honor.

BREACH OF PROMISE, A// C 1a// Mabel Freund-Lloyd// **Opera Comique**, Dec. 1891, with Orlando Barnett as Greythorpe, Graham Wentworth as Capt. Heriot, Mary Mordaunt as Linolia, Alice Maitland as Winifred, Eleanor Bufton as Mrs. Grimley.

BREACH OF PROMISE OF MARRIAGE, THE// C 2a// Adap. fr F of Eugène Scribe, La Chaine// **Adelphi**, Feb. 1842, with Frederick Yates, Arthur Wilkinson, Mr. Lyon, Edward Wright, Ellen Chaplin, Mrs. Yates.

BREADWINNER, THE// Play 3a// A. C. Calmour// **Avenue**, Mar. 1892, with Frederick Everill as Dr. Digby, Lewis Waller as Chancellor, C. W. Carthorne as Sir George, Arthur Elwood as Philip, Alma Murray as Freda, Laura Linden as Clari, Mrs. G. Canninge as Mrs. Digby, Olga Brandon as Mrs. Armadale.

BREAK BUT NOT BEND// D 3a// C. H. Hazlewood// **Britannia**, Oct. 1867.

BREAKERS AHEAD; OR, A SEAMAN'S LOG// D 3a// J. T. Haines// **Victoria**, Apr. 1837; Sept. 1846, with Mr. Fitzjames as Macartney, Alfred Raymond as Campbell, Mr. Archer as Capt. Oakum, Miss Fielding as Wayward, Mr. Florrington as Maydew, C. J. Bird as Layland, G. F. Forman as Blowcoal, T. H. Higgie as Fromage, J. Howard as Pert, Walter Searle as Graham, Eliza Vincent as Amy, Lydia Pearce as Joan, Miss Edgar as Chico, Miss Greville as Wang.

BREAKING A BUTTERFLY// Play 3a// Adap. by Henry Arthur Jones and Henry Hermann fr Norw. of Henrik Ibsen, A Doll's House// **Prince's**, Mar. 1884, with Kyrle Bellew, Herbert Beerbohm Tree, John Maclean, G. W. Anson, Miss Lingard, Helen Mathews, Mrs. Leigh Murray.

BREEZY MORNING, A// C 1a// Eden Philpotts// **Comedy**, Dec. 1891, with Sam Sothern as Goldie, Florance Fordyce as Mrs. Goldie.

BREWING A BRUIN// F// Louis Gee// **Britannia**, June 1873.

BRIAN BOROIHME; OR, THE MAID OF ERIN// D 3a// Adap. by Sheridan Knowles fr D. O'Mara// **Cov. Garden**, Apr. 1837, with Sheridan Knowles as Brian, John Pritchard as Moore, John Webster as O'Donohue, Benjamin Webster as Roderick, Mr. Tilbury as Terence, Helen Faucit as Erina, Eliza Vincent as Hene, George Bennett as Tormagnus, John Vandenhoff as Voltimer, Mr. Harris as Udislaus, Mrs. W. West as Elgitha/ Scenery by Mr. Marshall/ Music by Mr. Rodwell/ Machines by Mr. Sloman/ Prod. by Mr. Webster.

BRIARS AND BLOSSOMS// D 3a// C. H. Hazlewood// **Britannia**, Dec. 1873.

BRIDAL, THE// D 5a// Adap. by J. Sheridan Knowles fr Beaumont & Fletcher, The Maid's Tragedy// **Haymarket**, June 1837, with J. T. Haines as Arcanes, W. C. Macready as Melantius, E. W. Elton as Amintor, E. F. Saville as Lysippus, John Webster as Diphilus, Charles Selby as Calianax, J. Worrell as Cleon, Mr. Harris as Strato, Fanny Huddart as Evadne, Agnes Taylor as Aspatia, Miss E. Phillips as Antiphila, Mrs. Humby as Dula/ **Cov. Garden**, Oct. 1837, with George Bennett as Arcanes, W. C. Macready as Melantius, James Anderson as Amintor, Charles Diddear as Calianax, Mr. Roberts as Lysippus, John Pritchard as Diphilus, Mr. Tilbury as Archas, W. H. Payne as Cleon, Mr. Harris as Strato, Fanny Huddart as Evadne, Agnes Taylor as Aspatia, Miss E. Phillips as Antiphila, Mrs. East as Cleanthe, Miss Garrick as Olympias, Eliza Vincent as Dula/ **Sad. Wells**, Aug. 1844, with George Bennett as Arcanes, Henry Marston as Amintor, Samuel Phelps as Melantius, John Webster as Dephilus, E. Morton as Hysippus, Charles Fenton as Cleon, Mr. Knight as Calianax, Mrs. Mary Warner as Evadne, Miss Cooper as Aspatia, Georgiana Lebatt as Dela, Fanny Huddart as Antiphlia/ **Princess's**, June 1847, with John Ryder as Arcanes, William Creswick as Amintor, W. C. Macready as Melantius, John Webster as Lysippus, Augustus Harris as Diphilus, Mr. Tyrrell as Cleon, Charles Fisher as Calianax, Robert Honner as Archas, Mrs. Mary Warner as Evadne, Mrs. Stirling as Aspatia, Mrs. H. Hughes as Antiphila, Miss Rourke as Cleanthe, Miss Laporte as Olympus, Miss E. Honner as Dula/ Grecian , May 1855, with Henry Grant, Thomas Roberts as Lysippus, Richard Phillips as Amintor, Basil Potter as Melantius, F.

Charles, Eaton O'Donnell as Calianax, Jane Coveney, Maria Simpson as Antiphila, Mrs. Charles Montgomery as Aspatia/ **Standard** , June 1859, with Hermann Vezin.

BRIDAL EVE, THE; OR, THE DICER'S DOOM// D// n.a.// **Sad. Wells**, May 1840, with Mr. Dry as de Courville, Mr. Elvin as Hypolite, Henry Marston as Capt. Delmar, Henry Hall as Mixture, Mr. Aldridge as Chienne, Mr. Richardson as Cheval, Mrs. Robert Honner as Elitha, Mrs. Richard Barnett as Gigotte/ Scenery by F. Fenton & G. Smithyes Jr./ Machines by B. Sloman/ Music by Isaac Collins/ prod. by R. Honner.

BRIDAL EVE, THE// D// W. T. Townsend// **Sad. Wells**, May 1863, with Mr. Warren as Sir Mark, N. Griffiths as Col. Wilmot, Charles Harcourt as Lord Philip, Mr. Barton as Capt. Musgrave, H. Josephs as Sergeant, J. F. Warden as Hargrave, Lewis Ball as Stock, Mrs. W. Dowton as Lady Wilmot, Mrs. Hudson Kirby as Mabel, Bessie Heath as Maud, Emily Dowton as Tippet.

BRIDAL OF BEATRIZ, THE// Adap. fr G of Gotthold Lessing, Emilia Galotti// **Surrey**, Oct. 1859, with William Creswick, Sarah Thorne, Edith Heraud.

BRIDAL PHANTOM, THE: OR, THE SECRET OF LIFE// D 4a// George Conquest// **Grecian**, May 1863, with Thomas Mead as Herman, William James as de Mansdorf, John Manning as Krabbau, J. Jackson as Dr. Strauss, Henry Grant as Meatheas, Mrs. Charles Dillon as Olivia, Mary A. Victor as Baptista, Marie Brewer as Grutchen/ Scenery by C. Smithers/ Music by S. Edroff/ Gas by Mr. Dimes/ Machines by Mr. Smither Sr./ Prod. by George Conquest.

BRIDAL TOUR, A// C 3a// Dion Boucicault// **Haymarket**, Aug. 1880, with Mrs. Canninge as Mrs. Tarbox, Miss Gerard as Fanny, Mrs. John Wood as Virginia, Mrs. Alfred Mellon as Miss Sniffe, Winnifred Emery as Rosalie, Edith Bruce as Josephine, Harry Beckett as Persimmons, H. B. Conway as Meek, Henry Howe as Auldjo, J. G. Grahame as Walter/ Scenery by Walter Hann.

BRIDAL WREATH, THE// D 2a// C. H. Hazlewood// **City of London**, 1861.

BRIDE OF ALBI, THE; OR, THE OLD DRAW WELL// D// C. Harding// **Grecian**, Aug. 1861, with Alfred Rayner as Castagnari, Walter Holland as Deleblonde, R. H. Lingham as Durvilliers, John Manning as Lelonette, Miss Johnstone as Mme. Leblanc, Jane Coveney as Mme. Delporte, Lucreza Hill as Janet, Ellen Hale as Antoinette.

BRIDE OF ALDGATE, THE; OR, THE REPROBATE KNIGHT// D 3a// n.a.// **Victoria** Sept. 1843, with Mr. Shepherd as Fitzarnold, Charles Baker as Neave, William Seaman as Sir Mark, Charles Williams as Scribe, John Gardner as Pittikin, Mr. Dale as Winter, Annette Vincent as Alice, Miss Ridgway as Maud, Mrs. Franklin as Drusilla, Miss Saddler as Miss Huntley.

BRIDE OF BOW, THE: OR, THE TOWER OF LONDON// D 2a// J. Bosworth// **Grecian**, Feb. 1855, with Henry Grant as Musgrave, Richard Phillips as Philip, Thomas Roberts, F. Charles as Charles II, Basil Potter as Morvandale, Henry Power as Delastri, Jane Coveney as Margaret.

BRIDE OF LAMMERMOOR, THE// D 4a// Dram. by J. W. Calcraft fr novel of Sir Walter Scott// **Marylebone**, 1848.

BRIDE OF LAMMERMOOR, THE// D// Dram. fr novel of Sir Walter Scott// n.a.// **Sad. Wells**, June 1854, with C. Poynter as Sir William, Samuel Perfitt as Col. Ashton, Lizzie Mandelbert as Henry, E. L. Davenport as Edgar, James Worrell as Wayston, F. Charles as Capt. Craigengelt, J. B. Johnstone as Lockhart, Mr. Barrett as Balderstone, Mrs. Barrett as Lady Ashton, Fanny Vining as Lucy, Miss James as Marion, Miss Howard as Dame Lightbody.

BRIDE OF LAMMERMOOR, THE; OR, "I BIDE MY TIME"// D// Dram. fr novel of Sir Walter Scott// **Grecian**, Sept. 1861, with Henry Grant as Sir William, George Gillett as Col. Ashton, Henry Power as Henry Ashton, C. J. Bird as Edgar, Walter Holland as Capt. Craigengelt, Mr. Costello as Randolph, William James as Hayston, Mrs. Charles Dillon as Lucy Ashton, Jane Coveney as Lady Ashton, Lucreza Hill as Mysle.

BRIDE OF LAMMERMOOR, THE; OR, THE MERMAID'S WELL// D 3a// Dram. fr novel of Sir Walter Scott// **Sad. Wells**, Jan. 1842, with Mr. Dry as Sir William, Mr. Aldridge as Col. Ashton, G. Maskell as Henry, Mr. Norton as Edgar, Mr. Elvin as Hayston, John Herbert as Capt. Craigengelt, Mr. Williams as Balderstone, Miss Richardson as Lady Ashton, Mrs. Robert Honner as Lucy, Mrs. Morgan as Dame Lightbody, Miss Hicks as Marion/ Scenery by F. Fenton & G. Smithyes Jr./ Music by Isaac Collins/ Machines by Mr. Cawdery.

BRIDE OF LOVE, THE// Play 4a// Robert Buchanan// **Adelphi**, May 1890, with Ada Cavendish as Aphrodite, Clara Jecks as Eridon, Marie Fraser as Erotion, Lionel Rignold as Zephyros, T. B. Thalberg as Eros, Alfred Brydone as Methonos, Bassett Roe as Lycas, Leonard Outram as Atlantos, Ada Ferrar as Creusa, Harriet Jay as Psyche/ Scenery by F. G. Fenton/ Music by Walter Slaughter.

BRIDE OF LUDGATE, THE// D// Douglas Jerrold// **Sad. Wells**, Aug. 1838, with Mr. Cathcart as Charles II, C. Montague as Sedley, Dibdin Pitt as Shekel, Benjamin Conquest as Doeskin, J. W. Collier as Mouse, Miss Richardson as Melissa, Miss Pincott as Ruth; Mar. 1851, with Henry Marston as Charles II, Charles Wheatleigh as Sedley, Mr. Graham as Mapleton, A. Younge as Shekel, Frederick Younge as Doeskin, George Bennett as Capt. Mouth, Sarah Lyons as Melissa, Eliza Travers as Ruth/ **Grecian**, Mar. 1856, with Richard Phillips as Charles II, Thomas Roberts as Charles

Sedley, Eaton O'Donnell as Shekel, John Manning as Doeskin, Mr. Hustleby as Mapleton, Henry Grant as Capt. Mouth, Jane Coveney as Lissa, Harriet Coveney as Ruth.

BRIDE OF MESSINA, THE// D 5a// J. Sheridan Knowles// **Cov. Garden**, Sept. 1840, with Mr. Moore as de Procida, James Anderson as Fernando, Mr. Cooper as Guiscardo, W. H. Payne as Martini, Mr. Hemming as Andrea, Mr. Binge as Cario, C. J. Smith as Stefano, Charles Diddear as Governor, James Vining as Louis, A. Brindal as Martel, James Bland as Ambrose, Alfred Wigan as Le Clerc, Ellen Tree as Isoline, Miss Fitzjames as Margueritte/ Scenery by Grieve, T. Grieve & W. Grieve/ Music by Robert Hughes & J. H. Tully.

BRIDE OF THE PROSCRIBED, THE; OR, THE WIDOW'S NUPTIALS// D// Adap. fr F// **Sad. Wells**, Mar. 1840, with Mr. Dry as The Proscribed, Mr. Elvin as Arthur, Mr. Aldridge as Lucien, Robert Honner as Dubourg, Henry Hall as Nimbis, Mrs. Robert Honner as Louise, Mrs. J. F. Saville as Marchioness de Mellisens, Miss Cooke as Ursule/ Scenery by F. Fenton/ Music by Mr. Herbert, Machines by B. Sloman/ prod. by R. Honner.

BRIDE OF THE WAVE, THE// D 3a// William Travers// **East London**, Oct. 1867.

BRIDE, WIFE, AND WIDOW// D 3a// Charles Webb// **Grecian**, July 1854, with Richard Phillips as Monmouth, Henry Grant as Atherley, Eaton O'Donnell as Sir Edward, William Suter as John Say, Basil Potter as Kirk, Thomas Roberts as Stone, Ellen Crisp as Mrs. Atherley, Jane Coveney as Marian, Harriet Coveney as Sally Stubbs.

BRIDE'S DEATH SLEEP, THE// D 3a// C. H. Hazlewood// **City of London**, July 1868.

BRIDE'S JOURNEY, THE; OR, THE ESCAPES OF ADELAIDE OF DRESDEN// D 2a// John Courtney// **Victoria**, Apr. 1846, with James Ranoe as De Gaston, Alfred Raymond as Lockroy, Walter Searle as Mazoulo, J. Howard as Karl, Mr. Wilton as Bertholde, E. G. Burton as Patoche, F. H. Henry as Gaspard, Mr. Hitchinson as Paolo, Annette Vincent as Adelaide, Mrs. George Lee as Claudine, Mrs. Andrews as Mme. Lachette, Eliza Terrey as Ninetta, Miss Jefferson as Nina/ Prod. by T. H. Higgie.

BRIDGE OF KEHL, THE; OR, THE MINER OF THE MOUNTAIN// D// T. G. Blake// **Sad. Wells**, June 1841, with Mr. Williams as Gervais, Henry Marston as Eugene, Mr. Dry as Valence, Mr. Elvin as Albert, Mr. Aldridge as Darville, Robert Honner as Van Glotzen, Mr. Richardson as Michael, J. W. Collier as Phillipots, Mrs. Robert Honner as Madelon, Miss Richardson as Isabel/ Scenery by F. Fenton & G. Smithyes Jr./ Music by Isaac Collins/ Machines by B. Sloman.

BRIDGE OF NOTRE DAME, THE; OR, THE PARRICIDE'S CURSE// D 3a// E. N. Hudson// **Surrey**, Apr. 1847.

BRIDGET O'BRIEN, ESQUIRE// FC 2a// Fred Lyster & J. F. Sheridan// **Opera Comique**, Oct. 1887.

BRIDADIER, THE// C 1a// T. H. Reynoldson// **Princess's**, Jan. 1845, with James Wallack as Brasdefer, Mr. Granby as Col. d'Amancy, Mr. Compton as Pomade, F. H. Henry as Capt. Gaston, James Ranoe as Sgt., Miss E. Honner as Constance, Emma Stanley as Louise.

BRIGAND, THE// D 2a// Adap. by J. R. Planché fr F// **Drury Lane**, June 1838, with F. Cooke as Prince Bianchi, Mr. Brindal as Theodore, Mr. Baker as Albert, Mr. Cooper as Massaroni, Mr. Hughes as Fabio, Henry Compton as Nicolo, S. Jones as Rubaldo, Miss Fitzwalter as Ottavia, Mme. Simon as Marie/ **Sad. Wells**, Apr. 1839, with Mr. Williams as Prince Bianchi, Mr. Dry as Albert, Mr. Elvin as Theodore, J. W. Collier as Nicolo, Mr. Broadfoot as Fabio, John Webster as Massaroni, Charles Montgomery as Rubalo, Miss Pincott as Ottavia, Miss Richardson as Maria/ **Haymarket**, Sept. 1840, with Mr. Waldron as Prince Bianchi, Henry Howe as Albert, John Webster as Theodore, T. F. Mathews as Nicolo, James Wallack as Massaroni, Mr. Gallot as Rubaldo, Mrs. Edwin Yarnold as Ottavia, Miss Charles as Maria; Mar. 1849, with Mr. Rogers as Prince Bianchi, Henry Vandenhoff as Albert, Henry Howe as Theodore, Mr. Tilbury as Nicolo, Mr. Clark as Fabio, James Wallack as Massaroni, James Bland as Rubaldo, Mr. Caulfield as Spoleto, Mr. Santer as Carlotti, Mrs. L. S. Buckingham as Ottavia, Priscilla Horton as Maria/ Music of T. Cooke/ **Princess's**, Aug. 1845, with Mr. Lynne as Prince Bianchi, Leigh Murray as Albert, Walter Lacy as Theodore, Mr. Granby as Nicolo, Robert Honner as Fabio, James Wallack as Massaroni, James Ranoe as Rubaldo, Florence Grey as Ottavia, Mrs. Brougham as Maria/ **Grecian**, Mar. 1845, with Harry Chester as Massaroni, Mr. Campbell as Prince Bianchi, Mr. Baldwin as Rubaldo, John Collett as Albert, Edwin Dixon as Theodore, Frederick Robson as Nicolo, Annette Mears as Maria, Mary A. Crisp as Ottavia/ **Surrey**, Feb. 1867.

BRIGAND AND HIS BANKER, THE// C// Adap. by Tom Taylor fr F of Edmond About, Le Roi des Montagnes// **Lyceum**, Oct. 1860, with Mrs. Keeley, Mme. Celeste.

BRIGAND CHIEF, THE// D// n.a.// **Astley's**, June 1870, with T. B. Bennett as Matteo, James Francis as Alezzio, Walter Holland as Sampeiro, Clingan Jones as Nicolo, Emily Levettez as Cortunio, Miss Wallace as Guiseppa.

BRIGAND OF ANCONA, THE// D// n.a.// **Astley's**, Mar. 1849, with Mr. Crowther as Marquis del Picchini, Mr. Bedford as Fabian, Mr. Johnson as Nicole, T. Fredericks as the Brigand, Ellen Daly as Marinette, Rosa Henry as Zalitta.

BRIGAND OF EBOLI, THE; OR, THE LAST DEED OF GARBONI// D// n.a.// **Victoria**, Aug. 1850, with Henry Frazer as Garboni, Mr. Hitchinson as di Nuavo, John Bradshaw as Brignoli, G. F. Forman as Masetti, Mr. Henderson as Luigi, Miss Barrowcliffe as Lissa, Georgiana Lebatt as Inez, Mrs. Cooke as Gianetta.

BRIGANDS IN THE BUD// C 2a// T. Mildenhall// **Olympic**, Jan. 1849, with Charles Bender as Baron Stolberg, H. J. Turner as Baron Bornholm, John Kinloch as Slokens, Mr. Norton as Bruno, Harwood Cooper as Carlo, Charles Hale as Peterkin, Henry Compton as Count Toddlebeg, Mrs. Stirling as Ulric, Miss Acosta as Amelia, Miss Spiller as Lauretta, Mrs. H. J. Turner as Dame Stormold.

BRIGAND'S SECRET, THE// n.a.// **Britannia**, Oct. 1858.

BRIGHT BEAM AT LAST, A// D// G. H. Macdermott// **Britannia**, Sept. 1872.

BRIGHT FUTURE, THE// D 4a// Sefton Parry// **Grand**, Aug. 1883.

BRIGHTER DAYS IN STORE// D 2a// Edward Towers// **City of London**, Nov. 1867.

BRIGHTON// C 4a// Adap. by F. A Marshall fr Bronson Howard's Saratoga/ **Court**, May 1874/ **St. James's**, 1875, with George De Vere as Carter, E. A. Russell as Fred Carter, W. J. Hill as Vanderpump, Edgar Bruce as Benedict, Charles Wyndham as Sackett, Clifford Cooper as Sir Louis, Charles Steyne as Drake, Miss Litton as Effie, Edith Challis as Mrs. Alston, Mrs. Clifford Cooper as Mrs. Vanderpump, Miss Murielle as Virginia, Rose Egan as Mrs. Carter/ Scenery by Walter Hann/ **Haymarket**, June 1875, with same cast/ **Olympic**, Jan. 1880, with Charles Wyndham as Sackett, J. G. Grahame as Benedict, Edward Righton as Vanderpump, David Fisher Jr. as Sir Louis, F. Charles as Drake, John Maclean as Carter, W. S. Penley as Frederick, Rose Saker as Effie, Gwynne Williams as Virginia, Edith Bruce as Mrs. Alston, Miss Amalia as Mrs. Carter, Mrs. Leigh as Mrs. Vanderpump/ **Criterion**, Oct. 1881.

BRISTOL DIAMONDS// F 1a// John Oxenford// **St. James's**, Aug. 1862, with Frank Matthews as Kerr Mudgeon, Garstin Belmore as Symes, F. Charles as Rigsby, Mrs. Frank Matthews as Mrs. Mudgeon, Caroline Carson as Mrs. Symes.

BRITISH BORN// D Pro & 3a// Paul Meritt & Henry Pettitt// **Grecian**, Oct. 1872.

BRITISH BULLDOGS, THE; OR, ENGLAND'S SONS OF THE SEA// D 2a// J. B. Johnstone// **Victoria**, Dec. 1853, with Mr. Morrison as Jacqueline, T. E. Mills as Col. Renard, Mr. Hitchinson as De Lancy, F. H. Henry as Le Grand, N. T. Hicks as Bobstay, John Bradshaw as Bowling, J. Howard as Grandeur, Miss Dansor as Julietta, Miss Laporte.

BRITISH LEGION, THE// C// T. H. Bayly// **Haymarket**, July 1838, with Thomas Green as Col. Davenport, James Worrell as Capt. Ranger, D. W. King as Harcourt, W. H. Oxberry as Timothy, Mrs. Honey as Maria, Miss Williams as Louisa, Mrs. Frank Matthews as Susan/ **St. James's**, Feb. 1839, with George Ellis as Col. Davenport, Alfred Wigan as Capt. Ranger, Mr. Hughes as Tim, D. W. King as Harcourt, Mrs. Hooper as Maria, Miss Williams as Louisa, Jane Mordaunt as Barbara, Mrs. Frank Matthews as Susan.

BRIXTON BURGLARY, THE// F 3a// F. W. Sidney// **Terry's**, Dec. 1898, with James Welch as Pontifex, Frank Curzon as Sharples, J. H. Barnes as Green, Ferdinand Gottschalk as James, Victor Widdicombe as K.1001, Violet Trelawney as Millicent, Geraldine Wrangham as Jessie.

BROAD ARROW, THE// D 5a// Gerald Holcroft// **Standard**, Sept. 1885.

BROAD ROAD, THE// Play 3a// Robert Marshall// **Terry's**, Nov. 1898, with Arthur Bromley-Davenport as Lord Garderoy, W. L. Abingdon as Arnold, John Martin Harvey as as Dufrene, Gilbert Farquhar as as Dean, Arthur Holmes-Gore as Dr. Albrey, Ida Molesworth as Mrs. Arnold, Lena Ashwell as Cecilia, Rome Le Thière as Lady Rawstone, Laura Baradell as Effie, Helen Rous as Harriet/ Scenery by Walter Hann.

BROKEN CHAIN, THE; OR, THE LADY OF NUREMBERG// D// n.a.// **Surrey**, Oct. 1838.

BROKEN FAITH: A DOMESTIC STORY// D 2a// n.a.// **Grecian**, July 1855, with Richard Phillps as Villiers, F. Charles as Daunton, Basil Potter as Forester, Henry Grant as Maj. Kyte, Thomas Roberts as Danvers, Eaton O'Donnell as Ownright, Henry Power as Feeble, Jane Coveney as Helen, Harriet Coveney as Polly.

BROKEN FETTERS// Play 1a// Charles Thursby// **Matinée**, July 1897.

BROKEN HALO, A// Play 1a// Charles Thursby// **Globe**, Mar. 1900, with Oswald Yorke as Florio, Edward Ferris as Father Pietro, Warren Smith as Lupo, Beverly Sitgreaves as Berta/ Music by Haydn Waud/ Prod. by Guy Waller.

BROKEN HEARTED CLUB, THE// C// J. Stirling Coyne// **Haymarket**, Jan. 1868, with George Braid as Maj. McCool, Walter Gordon as Pleydell, Mr. Weathersby as Flexor, Henry Vincent as Chomley, Mrs. W. H. Chippendale as Mrs. Lovebird, Ione Burke as Cissy, Miss Dalton as Camilla, Fanny Wright as Araminta, Miss Coleman as Ida, Miss Matthews as Louisa.

BROKEN HEARTS// C 3a// W. S. Gilbert// **Court**, Dec. 1875, with Miss Hollinshead, Mrs. Kendal, W. H. Kendal, G. W. Anson.

BROKEN HOME, THE; OR, THE MECHANIC'S DAUGHTER// D 3a// J. H. Wilkins// **Victoria**, July 1848, with John Bradshaw as Marquis de Boileau, J. Howard as Garnaud, J. T. Johnson as Stephen, E. Edwards as La Fourbe, G. F. Forman as Roulouse, Mr. Hitchinson as Dubourg, Walter Searle as Sanglette, George Hawkins as de Courci, F. H. Henry as Devigne, Mrs. George Lee as Marchioness de Boileau, Miss Atkins as Nina, Miss Burroughcliffe as Victorine/ Prod. by T. H. Higgie.

BROKEN OATH, THE; OR, THE WORD OF HONOR AND THE FATHER'S CURSE// D// Thomas Greenwood// **Sad. Wells**, Aug. 1840, with Henry Marston as Goldsmith, Mr. Elvin as Forrester, J. W. Collier as Goodheart, Mr. Dry as Norris, Charles Fenton as Sneakwell, Mr. Priorson as Bluff, Mr. Williams as Van Heysen, Mrs. Robert Honnor as Helen, Miss Cooke as Diana/ Scenery by F. Fenton/ Music by Isaac Collins, Machines by B. Sloman/ Prod. by R. Honner.

BROKEN PROMISE, THE; OR, A SISTER'S HONOUR AND A BROTHER'S DUTY// D 2a// n.a.// **Victoria**, Apr. 1842, with Mr. James as Gen. Morin, William Seaman as Amedee, Annette Vincent as Josephe, J. Howard as Bizot, Charles Morelli as Hillaire, John Gardner as Boyravet, Mrs. George Lee as Mme. Morin, Mrs. Griffith as Dame Munier, Miss Coveney as Eloise.

BROKEN SIXPENCE, A// C 1a// Mrs. G. Thompson & Kate Sinclair// **Toole's**, Jan. 1890, with C. Wilson as Grant, C. M. Lowne as Hammond, Effie Liston as Molly, Irene Vanbrugh as Kitty, Mary Brough as Jane.

BROKEN SWORD, THE; OR, THE DUMB BOY OF THE TORRENT (also subt., The Torrent of the Valley)// D// William Dimond// **Victoria**, May 1838, with Mr. Archer as Estevan, Mr. Maddocks as Col. Rigolio, John Parry as Claudio, Mr. Loveday as Capt. Zavier, William Davidge as Baron, Mr. Vale as Pablo, Mrs. John Parry as Myrtillo, Mrs. Corry as Rosara, Mrs. Badderley as Stella/ Scenery by J. C. James/ **Sad. Wells**, Aug. 1841, with Mr. Aldridge as The Baron, Mr. Williams as Capt. Xavior, Henry Marston as Estevan, J. W. Collier as Pablo, Mr. Elvin as Claudio, Mr. Dry as Col. Rigolo, Mrs. J. W. Collier as Myrtillo, Miss Richardson as Rosina, Mrs. Richard Barnett as Stella, Mrs. Morgan as Jacintha.

BROKEN TIES// C 2a// Adap. & Alt. by J. Palgrave Simpson fr Ital. of Mario Uchard, La Fiammina// **Olympic**, June 1872, with T. N. Wenman as Lord Castletowers, J. S. Wood as Sir John, W. H. Vernon as Randal, Henry Sinclair as Lionel Warner, Frank Harvey as Herbert Warner, Mlle. Beatrice as La Silvia, Mrs. Parker as Lady Richmond, Miss Blake as Lucy, Miss Chapman as Mrs. Sherwood.

BROKEN TOYS// D 2a// John Daly// **Sad. Wells**, Nov. 1850, with A. Younge as Winter, Henry Mellon as Colddrawn, Mr. Williams as Proper, William Hoskins as Dauntless, Charles Wheatleigh as Homestead, Frederick Younge as Corks, Eliza Travers as Katherine, Lucy Rafter as Mrs. Dauntless, Mrs. Archbold as Mrs. Proper/ **Grecian**, Aug. 1857, with Mr. Barrett as Abel Winter, Richard Phillips as Dauntless, Basil Potter as Homstead, Henry Grant as Coldrawn, Eaton O'Donnell as Proper, John Manning as Corks, Jane Coveney as

BROKEN VOW, THE// D 5a// Dion Boucicault & J. V. Bridgeman// **Olympic**, Feb. 1851, with Henry Farren as Hugo, Ellen Turner as Beppo, Leigh Murray as Adrien, William Farren as Cardinal Montaldo, W. H. Norton as Count Colonna, William Farren Jr. as Fabio, Mrs. Leigh Murray as Countess, Louisa Howard as Bianca, Charles Bender as Matteo, Isabel Adams as Agnes and as Monique, William Shalders as Pietro, Miss E. Shalders as Maria, Miss Rawlings as Abbess, John Kinloch as Count Colount de Castro/ Scenery by W. Shalders & Mr. Batty/ Music by J. Barnard.

BROKEN VOWS; OR, LOVE'S CONFLICTS// D 4a// Edward Towers// **East London**, Feb. 1871.

BROTHER BEN// F 1a// J. Maddison Morton// **Cov. Garden**, Dec 1840, with George Bartley as Com. Cutlass, C. J. Mathews as Bowles, John Pritt Harley as Snuffleton, Mrs. Brougham as Mrs. Cutlass, Miss Lee as Mrs. Bowles, Mrs. Charles Jones as Dorothy/ **Sad. Wells**, Aug. 1853, with Mr. Barrett as Com. Cutlass, Lewis Ball as Snuffleton, William Hoskins as Bowles, Miss Portman as Mrs. Cutlass, Miss Younge as Mrs. Bowles, Mrs. Henry Marston as Dorothy.

BROTHER BILL AND ME// F 1a// W. E. Suter// **Grecian**, Sept. 1866, with J. Jackson as Archibald, George Gillett as Simon, Henry Grant as William, George Conquest as Benjamin, Mrs. Atkinson as Mrs. Noodle, Harriet Western as Wilhelmina, Mary A. Victor as Martha/ **Adelphi**, Mar. 1883, with E. R. Fitzdavis as Noodle, Harwood Cooper as Squib, Arthur Redwood as Wm. Wiggles, Harry Proctor as Benj. Wiggles, Harriet Coveney as Seraphina, Julia Roselle as Wilhelmina, Clara Jecks as Martha.

BROTHER FOR BROTHER// D 3a// Dram. by Arthur Shirley fr F of Alexandre Dumas, Les Frères Corses// **Pavilion**, Aug. 1899.

BROTHER OFFICERS// C 3a// Leo Trevor// **Garrick**, Oct. 1898.

BROTHER SAM// C// John Oxenford, E. A. Sothern, & J. B. Buckstone// **Haymarket**, May 1865, with E. A. Sothern as Slingsby, J. B. Buckstone as Rumbelow, Henry Compton as Trimbush, Mr. Butler as Peter, Miss Snowdon as Mrs. Trimbush, Nelly More as Alice, Miss Lewin as Marie/ Scenery by John O'Conner & George Morris/ Gas by Mr. Hope/ Machines by Oliver Wales.

BROTHER'S REVENGE, THE; OR, THE ROSE OF IRELAND AND THE FAIRIES OF O'DONAGHUE'S LAKES// D// n.a.// **Victoria**, Mar. 1854, with Alfred Saville as Col. Merrythought, Mr. Henderson as Lord Castletree, T. E. Mills as Slinky, N. T. Hicks as O'Barry, F. H. Henry as Hull, John Hudspeth as O'Kelly, John Bradshaw as Mandrake, J. Howard as Tatters, Mrs. Henry Vining as Kate, Miss Laporte as Nelly, Mrs. Manders as Mother Grinders, Miss Edgar as Kathleen, Miss Dansor as Sabrina, R. H. Kitchen as Mountain Dew/ Scenery by

Mr. Hawthorn/ Machines by Mr. Wood/ Music by Mr. Mingaye/ Prod. by J. T. Johnson.

BROTHER'S SACRIFICE, THE; OR, SELF-ACCUSATION// D// Mark Lemon// **Sad. Wells**, Feb. 1841, with Mr. Aldridge as Kindly, Mr. Elvin as Howard, Mr. Dry as Dawson, J. W. Collier as Raby, Henry Marston as Brandon, Robert Honner as Darvill, Mrs. Robert Honner as Mary, Mrs. Richard Barnett as Patty/ Scenery by F. Fenton/ Music by Isaac Collins/ Machines by B. Sloman/ Prod. by R. Honner.

BROTHER TOM; OR, MY DEAR RELATIONS// F// adap. fr F by J. B. Buckstone// **Haymarket**, Oct. 1839, with William Strickland as Tom, O. Smith as Capt. Jack, Mr. Hemming as Edmund, J. B. Buckstone as Slyboots, Mrs. W. Clifford as Mrs. Silvertongue, Eliza Travers as Sophia, Mrs. Gallot as Mrs. Tiplady.

BROTHERS// C 3a// Charles Coghlan// **Court**, Nov. 1876, with John Hare, H. B. Conway, Ellen Terry, Miss Hollingshead, G. W. Anson.

BROTHERS, THE// Play 1a// Henry Byatt// **Vaudeville**, Mar. 1887/ **Olympic**, Feb. 1888/ **Haymarket**, Mar. 1892, with Laurence Cautley as Richard, W. L. Abingdon as William, Annie Hill as Kitty.

BROTHERS; OR, A PLUNGE IN THE DARK// D 4a// Olive Lipthwaite// **Marylebone**, Nov. 1885.

BROTHERS; OR, THE WOLF AND THE LAMB// D// n.a.// **St. James's**, Apr. 1838, with Mrs. Stirling as Gossamer and as Edward, W. H. Oxberry as Tassel, Mr. Hart as Johnson, Miss Stuart as Lady Eversley, Mrs. Frank Mathews as Trimmer, Jane Mordaunt as Rose.

BROUGHT TO BOOK// CD 1a// G. H. Macdermott & Henry Pettitt// **Britannia**, May 1876.

BROUGHT TO JUSTICE// D// Henry Pettitt & Paul Meritt// **Surrey**, Mar. 1880.

BROUGHT TOGETHER// C 1a// Fred Mouillot// **Elephant & Castle**, Oct. 1894.

BROWN, JONES, & ROBINSON: A LEGEND OF THE HACKNEY ROAD// F// n.a.// **Cov. Garden**, Sept. 1838, with Mr. Tilbury as Brown, James Vining as Benjamin, George Bartley as Jones, John Pritt Harley as Smith, Miss E. Phillips as Jemima, Mrs. Griffith as Selina, Mrs. W. Clifford as Miss Robinson, Mrs. Humby as Cleopatra.

BROWN THE MARTYR// F 1a// Templeton Lucas// **Court**, Jan 1872, with W. J. Hill, W. Bedford.

BRUTUS; OR, THE FALL OF TARQUIN// T 5a// John Howard Payne// **Drury Lane**, Feb. 1837, with Edwin Forrest as Brutus, Mr. Cooper as Titus, Charles Diddear as Tarquin, Mr. Hooper as Aruns, Mr. Warde as Collatinus, A. Brindal as Claudius, Mr. Baker as Valerius, Mr. Mathews as Lucretius, F. H. Henry as Horatius, W. R. Blake as Celius, Fanny Huddart as Tullia, Agnes Taylor as Tarquinia, Mrs. Hooper as Lucretia, Mrs. W. Clifford as Priestess, Mrs. East as Vestal, Miss Lee as Lavinia; Jan. 1854, with G. V. Brooke as Brutus, George Bennett as Tarquin, John Kinloch as Aruns, Mr. Morgan as Collatinus, Henry Lee as Claudius, E. Walton as Corunna, Fred Belton as Titus, Mr. Pearson as Valerius, Mrs. Vickery as Tullia, Fanny Cathcart as Tarquinia, Mrs. Lewis as Lucretia, Miss Johnson as Lavinia/ Scenery by Nichols, Aglio & Cooper/ Machines by Mr. Tucker/ Music by G. Hayward/ Prod. by Edward Stirling/ **Sad. Wells**, Apr. 1837, with J. B. Booth as Brutus, C. H. Pitt as Tarquin, C. J. Smith as Arius, Mr. Lee as Claudius, D. W. King as Valerius, N. T. Hicks as Titus, Mr. Campbell as Collatinus, Miss Williams as Tullia, Lavinia Melville as Lucretia, Miss Lebatt as Lavinia, Miss Beresford as Tarquinia/ Scenery by Mr. Mildenhall; Apr. 1846, with Samuel Phelps as Brutus, Henry Marston as Titus, E. Morton as Tarquin, Mr. Warde as Aruns, Charles Fenton as Claudius, George Bennett as Collatinus, Henry Mellon as Lucretius, Mrs. Mary Warner as Tullia, Miss Cooper as Tarquinia, Mrs. Henry Marston as Priestess/ Scenery by F. Fenton & Mr. Finlay; Sept. 1859, with Samuel Phelps as Brutus, Frederic Robinson as Titus, T. C. Harris as Tarquin, W. R. Belford as Aruns, Charles Seyton as Claudius, J. W. Ray as Valerius, Miss Atkinson as Tullia, Bessie Heath as Tarquinia, Miss Phillips as Lucretia, Caroline Parkes as Lavinia/ **Olympic**, Apr. 1848, with G. V. Brooke as Brutus, Henry Hall as Titus, E. Morton as Tarquin, John Kinloch as Aruns, Mr. Lawrence as Claudius, Mr. Archer as Collatinus, H. Lee as Valerius, George Almar as Lucretius, E. Marie Duret as Tullia, Miss May as Tarquinia/ **Sadler's Wells**, Sept. 1859, with Samuel Phelps, Miss Atkinson.

BUBBLE AND SQUEEK// F// Frederick Hay// **Vaudeville**, May 1871.

BUBBLE REPUTATION, A// FC 3a// James Witling & John Douglass// **Standard**, Apr. 1885.

BUBBLES// C 1a// Charles Fawcett// **Gaiety**, Oct. 1881, with Charles Fawcett, J. J. Dallas, Bella Howard.

BUBBLES OF THE DAY// C 5a// Douglas Jerrold// **Cov. Garden**, Feb. 1842, with William Farren as Lord Skindeep, John Pritt Harley as Sir Phenix, C. J. Mathews as Capt. Smoke, Frank Matthews as Brown, James Vining as Chatham Brown, Walter Lacy as Melon, George Bartley as Spreadweasel, Drinkwater Meadows as Shark, Mr. Hemming as Waller, Alfred Wigan as Miffin, Louisa Nisbett as Pamela, Mrs. Walter Lacy as Florentia, Mrs. W. West as Mrs. Quarto, Mrs. Orger as Guinea/ Scenery by Grieve, T. Grieve & W. Grieve/ **Haymarket**, June 1842, with William Farren as Lord Skindeep, Henry Holl as Melon, Henry Howe as Brown, J. W. Gough as Brown Sr., Benjamin Webster as Capt. Smoke, William Strickland as Spreadweasel, Mr. Tilbury as Shark, Benjamin Wrench as Sir Phoenix, Mr. Clark as Miffin, Henry Widdicomb as Kimbo, Miss Charles as Florentia, Louisa Nisbett as Pamela, Mrs.

W. Clifford as Mrs. Quarto, Mrs. Malone Raymond as Guinea.

BUCKINGHAM// D 4a// W. G. Wills// **Olympic**, Nov. 1875, with William Creswick as Oliver Cromwell, Henry Neville as Buckingham, F. Haywell as Fairfax, Mr. Vollaire as Col. Hip-and-Thigh, Mr. Westall as White, Mr. Crichton as Landlord, Fanny Enson as Lady Mary, Miss Goliere as Lady Elizabeth, Nellie Phillips as Jane/ Scenery by Julian Hicks, Music by J. Mallandaine.

BUCKSTONE'S ADVENTURE WITH A POLISH PRINCESS// F 1a// G. H. Lewis ("Slingsby Lawrence")// **Haymarket**, July 1855.

BUD AND BLOSSOM// Play 1a// Lady Colin Campbell// **Terry's**, June 1893, with Herbert Waring as Elder, Frederick Thorne as Vanbrugh, Charles Rock as Charlie, Stewart Dawson as Bill, Gilbert Trent as George, Esmé Beringer as Mrs. Gayworthy, Mary Jocelyn as Madge, Annie Hughes as Nelly.

BUFFALO BILL// D 4a// George Roberts// **Elephant & Castle**, May 1887.

BUFFALO GIRLS, THE; OR THE FEMALE SERENADERS// F// Edward Stirling// **Surrey**, Apr. 1847.

BUGLE CALL, THE// Play 1a// L. N. Parker & Addison Bright// **Haymarket**, Nov. 1899, with Graham Browne as Lt. Steuart, Clarence Blakiston as Stern, O. G. Oughterson as Bates, Mrs. E. H. Brooke as Lady Kinnordie, Marie Linden as Mrs. Denbigh, Sybil Carlisle as Millicent/ Scenery by Walter Hann.

BULL BY THE HORNS, THE// F 3a// H. J. Byron// **Gaiety**, Aug. 1876.

BULL IN A CHINA SHOP, A// C 2a// C. J. Mathews// **Haymarket**, Nov. 1863, with Henry Compton as Tipthorpe, C. J. Mathews as Bagshot, Walter Gordon as Flitter, Mr. Clark as Piper, Mr. Rogers as Brownjohn, Henrietta Lindley as Emily, Fanny Wright as Lucy, Mrs. Edward Fitzwilliam as Susan, Caroline Hill as Arabella.

BUNCH OF BERRIES, THE// F// E. L. Blanchard// **Adelphi**, May 1875.

BUNCH OF VIOLETS, A// Play 4a// Adap. by Sidney Grundy fr F of Octave Feuillet, Montjoye// **Haymarket**, Apr. 1894, with Herbert Beerbohm Tree as Sir Philip, Nutcombe Gould as Viscount Mount-Sorrell, C. M. Hallard as Inglis, Lionel Brough as Murgatroyd, G. W. Anson as Schwartz, Holman Clark as Harker, Lily Hanbury as Lady Marchant, Audrey Ford as Violet, Mrs. Beerbohm Tree as Mrs. Murgatroyd/ Scenery by Walter Hann.

BUNGALOW, THE// FC 3a// Adap. by Fred Horner fr F of Eugène Medina, La Garçonnière// **POW**, Jan. 1889.

BUNKUM MILLER// C// n.a.// **Haymarket**, Feb. 1864.

BURGLAR AND THE JUDGE, THE// F 1a// F. C. Phillips & C. H. Brookfield// **Haymarket**, Nov. 1892/ **Court**, Jan. 1893.

BURGLARS// FC 3a// Mark Melford// **Avenue**, Apr. 1895.

BURGOMASTER'S DAUGHTER, THE// D// n.a.// **Marylebone**, May 1863.

BURIED TALENT, A// Play 3a// L. N. Parker// **Vaudeville**, June 1890/ **Comedy**, May 1892.

BURLINGTON ARCADE, THE// C// Charles Dance// **Olympic**, Jan. 1839, with Robert Keeley as Wigton, Thomas Green as Ready, John Brougham as O'Slack, James Bland as Longstaff, Mrs. Macnamara as A. Cloud, Mrs. Orger as Clementina.

BURNING FOREST, THE// D// n.a.// **Sad. Wells**, Apr. 1843, with C. J. Bird as Ferdinand, Mr. Lambe as Werther, E. Morton as Wolfender, Mr. Williams as Kaunitz, Mr. Franks as Dangerfeldt, Mr. Aldridge as Schampt, Robert Romer as Moritz, Miss Richardson as Amelia, Lavinia Melville as Maria, Mrs. Richard Barnett as Laura.

BUSH KING, THE// D 4a// W. J. Lincoln/ **Surrey**, Nov. 1893.

BUSYBODY, THE// C 3a// Adap. by Susannah Centlivre fr Dryden's Sir Martin Marall// **Haymarket**, July 1844, with Henry Holl as Sir George, William Farren as Sir Francis, A. Brindal as Charles, William Strickland as Sir Jealous, C. J. Mathews as Marplot, James Worrell as Whisper, Mme. Vestris as Miranda, Miss Lee as Isabinda, Miss Carre as Scentwell, Mrs. Humby as Patch; **Haymarket**, July 1855; Jan. 1859, with J. B. Buckstone, Miss Reynolds/ **Princess's**, June 1846, with Mr. Granby as Sir Francis, Robert Roxby as Sir George, Charles Fisher as Charles, A. Walton as Sir Jealous, Augustus Harris as Whisper, C. J. Mathews as Marplot, Mrs. Henry Hughes as Miranda, Miss E. Honner as Isabinda, Miss Somers as Patch/ **Sad. Wells**, Oct. 1849, with Henry Marston as Sir George, A. Younge as Sir Francis, Mr. Williams as Sir Jealous, G. K. Dickinson as Charles, Charles Fenton as Whisper, Miss Fitzpatrick as Miranda, Miss T. Bassano as Isabinda, Mrs. Henry Marston as Patch, Mrs. Graham as Scentwell/ **Drury Lane**, Nov. 1856, with A. Younge as Sir Francis, Mr. Tilbury as Sir Jealous, Robert Roxby as Sir George, C. Vincent as Charles, C. J. Mathews as Marplot, Mr. Templeton as Whisper, C. Walton as John, Miss M. Oliver as Miranda, Miss Bulmer as Isabinda, Miss E. Wadham as Patch, Miss Barnes as Scentwell/ **Grecian**, Nov. 1856, with Henry Grant as Sir Jealous, Mr. Hustleby as Sir George, Richard Phillips, C. Kelsey as Charles, Eaton O'Donnell as Sir Francis, Jane Coveney as Miranda, Ellen Hale as Isabinda.

BUT HOWEVER—// F 1a// Henry Mayhew & Henry Baylis// **Haymarket**, Oct. 1838, with Robert Strickland as Standwell, Mr. Hemming as Cashmere, Benjamin Wrench as Chizzler, as Cashmere, Benjamin Wrench as Chizzler, Miss Williams as Julia, Mrs. Frank Matthews as Mrs. Juniper/ **Sad. Wells**, Feb. 1847, with William Hoskins as Chizzler, E. Morton as Cashmere, Mr. Williams as Standwell, Mr. Knight as Prowl, Charles Fenton as Gaby, Miss Stephens as Mrs. Juniper, Fanny Huddart as Julia.

BUTCHER VERSUS BAKER; OR, THE MARCH OF INTELLECT// F 1a// Francis Talfourd// **Olympic**, June 1852, with George Cooke as Bounce, William Shalders as Jollifat, Henry Compton as Crumbs, Alfred Sanger as Joseph, Ellen Turner as Maggy, Mrs. Alfred Phillips as Kitty.

BUTCHER'S DOG OF GHENT, THE; OR, THE VISION OF THE HEATH// D// n.a.// **Victoria**, June 1850, with Mr. Cony as Black Martin, Mr. Taylor as Andrew & Arnold Wolfe, John Bradshaw as Kreutzner, Mr. Henderson as Fritz, J. Howard as Karl, Mrs. George Lee as Louise, Miss Barrowcliffe as Justine.

BUTLER, THE// C 3a// Mr. & Mrs. Herman Merivale// **Toole's**, Dec. 1886, with J. L. Toole as Trot, John Billington as Sir John, Emily Thorne as Lady Tracey, Violet Vanbrugh as Alice, Kate Phillips as Lady Anne.

BUTTERFLY FEVER// C 3a// Adap. by James Mortimer fr La Papillione// **Criterion**, May 1881, with Charles Wyndham, George Giddens, Rose Saker, Mary Eastlake.

BUTTERMILK VOLUNTEERS// n.a.// **Adelphi**, May 1850.

BY AND BY// C 4a// n.a.// **St. Geo. Hall**, Feb. 1896.

BY COMMAND OF THE CZAR// D// Robert Glover & C. M. Hermann// **Victoria**, Nov. 1877.

BY COMMAND OF THE KING// D// Edward Towers// **Pavilion**, Nov. 1871.

BY ROYAL COMMAND// CD 3a// Edward Stirling// **Lyceum**, Aug. 1856.

BY SPECIAL REQUEST// C 1a// J. M. Watson// **Strand**, Feb. 1887.

BY THE SEA// F// n.a.// **Strand**, Apr. 1872/ **Haymarket**, Oct. 1877, with Henry Howe as Doddles, Harry Crouch as Merryspouse, Mr. Weathersby as Bermondsey, Harold Kyrle as Vincent, Henry Rivers as Dan, Maria Harris as Lucinda, Fanny Morelli as Mrs. St. Lush.

BY THIS TOKEN// C 1a// J. K. Angus// **Sadler's Wells**, May 1884.

BYEWAYS// C 1a// G. S. Payne// **Comedy**, Mar. 1897.

BYGONES// C 1a// Arthur Wing Pinero// **Lyceum**, Sept. 1880, with Mr. Elwood as Granshawe, Mr. Carter as Rev. Horncastle, Arthur Wing Pinero as Prof. Mazzoni, Miss Moreley as Bella, Alma Murray as Ruby; May 1895, with Ben Webster as Curzon Gramshawe, Mr. Haviland as Giles Horncastle, Sidney Valentine as Prof. Mazzoni, Alisa Craig as Bella, Annie Hughes as Ruby.

*

CANARY, THE// C 3a// Constance Fletcher ("George Fleming")// **POW**, Nov. 1899, with E. W. Garden as Temple-Martin, Yorke Stephens as Glendenning, Gerald du Maurier as Burlingham, Harley Graville Barker as Bailey, Arthur Bromley-Davenport as Scott, Mrs. Patrick Campbell as Mrs. Temple-Martin, Elinor Molyneux as Mrs. Twigge, Rosina Filippi as Mrs. Glendenning, Pattie Bell as Mrs. Jones/ Scenery by Walter Hann.

CANDIDA// Play 3a// George Bernard Shaw// **Strand**, July 1900.

CANDIDATE, THE// C 3a// Adap. by J. H. McCarthy fr F of Alexandre Bisson, Le Député de Bombignac// **Criterion**, Dec. 1884, with Charles Wyndham, Alfred Maltby, Fanny Coleman, Kate Rorke, Rose Saker; May 1894/ **Royalty**, Mar. 1888.

CANONBURY HOUSE; OR, THE CHRONICLES OF SOUTHWARK// D// n.a.// **Victoria**, Dec. 1860, with W. H. Pitt as Earl of Northampton, W. Harmer as Brandon, J. H. Rickards as Foster, John Bradshaw as Brandwell, Mr. Henderson as Arden, Mr. Anderson as Maynard, George Pearce as Amyntus, George Yarnold as Pinkletop, Mrs. E. F. Saville as Queen Elizabeth, Mrs. Charles Boyce as Marguerite, Lydia Pearce as Maude, Miss Edgar as Ann.

CANTAB, THE// F 1a// T. W. Robertson// **Strand**, Feb. 1861.

CAPE MAIL, THE// D 1a// Adap. by Clement Scott fr F// **St. James's**, Oct. 1881, with Mr. Mackintosh as Quicke, Mr. Brandon as Marsden, Robert Cathcart as Bartle, Mrs. Gaston Murray as Mrs. Preston, Jessie Millward as Mary, Mrs. W. H. Kendal as Mrs. Frank Preston/ Scenery by W. Harford/ **Court**, May 1894/ **Vaudeville**, Oct. 1897.

CAPERS AND CORONETS// C 1a// Morris Barnett// **Eng. Opera House** (Lyceum), June 1837, with Morris Barnett as Marquis de Grandville, Miss Lee as Frank Rivera, Mr. Collier as James, Mr. Hollingsworth as Vellum, Mrs. Knight as Lady Meriton, Miss Murray as Mlle. Flore.

CAPITAL AND LABOUR// D 4a// W. S. Patmore & H. B. Moss// **Pavilion**, Mar. 1899.

CAPITAL MATCH, A// F 1a// J. Maddison Morton// **Haymarket**, Nov. 1852, with Henry

Howe as Capt. Tempest, Robert Keeley as Sunnyside, Mrs. Leigh Murray as Mrs. Singleton, Rosa Bennett as Rosamond.

CAPITOLA; OR, THE MASKED MOTHER AND THE HIDDEN HAND// D 3a// C. H. Hazlewood// **City of London**, 1860.

CAPRICE// Play 4a// H. P. Taylor, rev. by F. W. Broughton// **Globe**, Oct. 1889, with J. G. Grahame as Jack Henderson, John Maclean as Mr. Henderson, Fuller Mellish as Woodthorpe, Aubrey Boucicault as Wally Henderson, T. J. Herndon as Baxter, Alfred Maltby as Potts, Nellie Lindgard as Jake, Marie Lindon as Edith, Susie Vaughan as Emma/ Scenery by Mr. Wood/ Music by W. Corri Jr.

CAPRICE, A// Play 1a// Trans. by J. H. McCarthy fr F of Alfred de Musset// **Victoria**, May 1892/ **Garrick**, Nov. 1892.

CAPTAIN BIRCHELL'S LUCK// Play 3a// Alt. by L. N. Parker fr his play, Chris// **Vaudeville**, Mar. 1892/ **Terry's**, Oct. 1899, with Scott Buist as Capt. Birchell, John Beauchamp as Featherstone, Fred Wright as Hervey, Arthur Holes-Gore as Branksome, Evelyn Weedon as Christine, Beatrice Day as Mrs. Hervey, Mabel Archdall as Mary.

CAPTAIN CHARLOTTE// F 2a// Adap. by Edward Stirling fr F// **Adelphi**, Mar. 1843, with George Maynard, John Sanders, Edward Wright, A. J. Wilkinson, Miss Faucit, Mrs. Henry Beverly, Kate Howard/ **Sad. Wells**, Aug. 1844, with E. Morton as St. Leon, Mr. Williams as Count Bellaflor, Mr. Sharpe as Juan, G. F. Forman as Prince Bambinelli, Fanny Huddart as Duchess Marie, Mrs. Henry Marston as Countess Bellaflore, Kate Howard as Charlotte/ **Olympic**, Nov. 1845, with Walter Lacy as Bambinelli, Charles Boyce as St. Leon, Mr. Turnour as Count Bellaflor, Mr. Laurence as Sylvie, Mr. Cockrill as Joan, Mr. Edwards as Gianni, Mr. Richardson as Sebastian, Lavinia Melville as Duchess Maria, Miss Treble as Countess Bellaflor, Kate Howard as Charlotte.

CAPTAIN CUTTLE// C// Adap. fr novel of Charles Dickens, Martin Chuzzlewit// **Gaiety**, Nov. 1880, with W. J. Florence.

CAPTAIN IS NOT A MISS, THE// F 1a// T. E. Wilks// **Sad. Wells**, (under title of Black Eagle), June 1841, with Mr. Laws as Capt. Daring, Henry Widdicomb as Stock, Mr. Elliott as Landlord, Mr. Lawrence as Gen. Stormwell, Mr. Harwood as Halbert, Ellen Daly as Emily, Mrs. Harwood as Fanny, Mrs. Campbell as Mary/ **Grecian**, Mar. 1847, with John Collett as Gen. Stormwell, Edwin Dixon as Capt. Daring, Frederick Robson as John Stock, Eaton O'Donnell as Halbert, Mary A. Crisp as Emily, Annette Mears as Fanny/ **Victoria**, Oct. 1847, with Walter Searle as Capt. Stormwell, T. H. Higgie as Capt. Daring, G. F. Forman as Stock, J. Howard as Tuhley, F. H. Henry as Halbert, Mrs. George Lee as Emily, Miss Burroughcliffe as Fanny, Mrs. N. T. Hicks as Mary/ **Astley's**, Mar. 1859, with J. W. Anson as Gen. Stormwell, J. T. Anderson as Capt. Baring, James Francis as Stock, J. Smith as Tunley, Miss Dowton as Emily, Julia Weston as Fanny.

CAPTAIN JOHN LUCK; OR, THE GOLDEN TRADER OF HULL// D// J. B. Johnstone// **Victoria**, Sept. 1850, with J. Neville as Sir Edward, Mr. Henderson as Wallingford, J. T. Johnson as Captain John, Mr. Morrison as Donalton, John Bradshaw as Father Martin, Henry Frazer as Armistead, John Hudspeth as Titmouse, J. Howard as Foxey, Mrs. George Lee as Alice, Georgiana Lebatt as Agatha, Amelia Mercer as Monica.

CAPTAIN JOHN LUCK// D// n.a.// **Victoria**, May 1856, with Alfred Saville as Sir Edward, Mr. Henderson as Willingford, W. H. Pitt as Capt. John, Mr. Morrison as Donaldson, R. H. Lingham as Armistead, John Bradshaw as Martin, Julia Seaman as Alice, Mrs. Warlow as Agatha, Mrs. Henry Vining as Monica.

CAPTAIN OF THE VULTURE, THE; OR, WHICH IS WHICH?// D 3a// Dram. fr novel of Mrs. Braddon// **Grecian**, Nov. 1863, with Thomas Mead as George Duke, William James as Duke and as Markham, John Manning as Packer, J. B. Steele as Masterson, Walter Holland as Capt. Fanny, George Gillett as Ringwood, Henry Grant as Surley, Mrs. Charles Dillon as Millicent, Ellen Crisp as Sarah, Mary A. Victor as Mary, Isabella Conquest as Shanty.

CAPTAIN OF THE WATCH, THE// F 1a// J. R. Planché// **Cov. Garden**, Feb. 1841, with C. J. Mathews as Viscount de Ligny, George Bartley as Baron Vanderpotter, James Vining as de Courtray, Mrs. Walter Lacy as Kristina, Mrs. Humby as Katryn/ **Lyceum**, July 1848, with C. J. Mathews as de Ligny, Mr. Granby as Vanderpotter, Robert Roxby as de Courtray, Louisa Howard as Kristina, Miss Marshall as Katryn; Dec. 1881, with William Terriss as Viscount de Ligny, Mr. Andrews as de Courtray, Mr. Carter as Vanderpotter, Louisa Payne as Kristina, Helen Matthews as Katryn/ Scenery by Hawes Craven/ Music by J. Meredith Ball/ **Drury Lane**, Dec. 1856, with C. J. Mathews as Viscount de Ligny, A. Younge as Baron Vanderpotter, Robert Roxby as de Courtray, Miss M. Oliver as Kristina, Miss Mason as Katryn/ **Haymarket**, Apr. 1869, with E. A. Sothern as Viscount de Ligny, W. H. Chippendale as Baron Vanderpotter, Henry Vincent as de Courtray, Ada Cavendish as Kristina, Caroline Hill as Katrya/ Scenery by John O'Conner & George Morris.

CAPTAIN PRO. TEM. (alt. title, Captain Query)// C// Mark Lemon// **Victoria**, June 1840, with Edward Burton as Yellowton, Mr. Courtney as Capt. Vincent, Thomas Lee as O'Ridley, Mr. Howard as Johnson, Mr. Hitchinson as Touchit, Mrs. Hicks as Emily, Mrs. Howard as Betty, Mrs. France as Mrs. Donoughhou/ **Sad. Wells**, Apr. 1841, with George Ellis as Capt. Vincent, Thomas Lee as O'Reilly, Mr. Williams as Yellowton, Mr. Lewis as John, Mr. Richardson as James, Mrs. Richard Barnett as Betty, Miss Cooke as Mrs. O'Donoghue, Miss Hicks as Emily.

CAPTAIN SABRETACHE OR, THE BARBER OF THE REGIMENT// F// A. Z. Barnett// **Grecian**, Sept. 1847, with Eaton O'Donnell as Col. Desmarais, John Webster as Eustache, Mr. Griffiths as Brigadier, Frederick Robson as Pierotin, Ada Harcourt as Clemence, Mme. Leclercq as Mariette.

CAPTAIN STEVENS// F// Charles Selby// **Sad. Wells**, Mar. 1845, with Charles Morelli as Col. Rochfort, E. Morton as Capt. Stevens, John Webster as Splashton, G. F. Forman as Stag, Mr. Coreno as Timkins, Mr. Evain as Podger, Charles Fenton as Felton, Fanny Huddart as Miss Rochfort, Miss Lebatt as Blonde, Miss Morelli as Betty.

CAPTAIN SWIFT// Play 4a// C. Haddon Chambers// **Haymarket**, Oct. 1888, with Herbert Beerbohm Tree as Wilding, Henry Kemble as Seabrook, Fuller Mellish as Harry, F. H. Macklin as Gardiner, Charles Brookfield as Marshall, Charles Allan as Ryan, Lady Monckton as Mrs. Seabrook, Rose Leclercq as Lady Staunton, Angela Cudmore as Mabel, Mrs. Tree as Stella/ Scenery by Walter Johnstone.

CARACTACUS// T 5a// Alt. by J. R. Planché fr Beaumont & Fletcher, Bonduca// **Drury Lane**, Nov. 1837, with Mr. Baker as Caesar, Mr. King as Scapula, Mr. Cooper as Posthumus, A. Brindal as Junius, J. S. Balls as Petilus, Mr. Harris as Demetrius, John Duruset as Regulus, H. Cooke as Drusius, S. Jones as Sempronius, Henry Butler as Caractacus, a "Young Gentleman" as Hengo, Mr. Howell as Nennius, Mrs. Lovell as Guideria, Miss Charles as Bonvica, W. Templeton as Druid, Mr. Giubilei as Bard, Miss Romer as Druidess/ Scenery by Grieve, T. Grieve & W. Grieve/ Music by M. W. Balfe/ Machines by Mr. Nall.

CARACTACUS// D// Found. on T of Mason// **Sad. Wells**, Nov. 1837, with Mr. Wilkins as Caractacus, C. H. Pitt as Elidurus, Mr. Ede as Vellinus, Mr. King as Didus, Mr. Gay as Collywobble, Mr. Ennis as Arnold, Mr. Rogers as Poeus, Miss Williams as Evelina, Miss Vernon as Bridget, Mr. Campbell as Modred, H. George as Mador, Mr. Pateman as Volpias, Mr. Scarbrow as Amadeas/ Scenery by Mr. Mildenhall/ Machines by Mr. Copping/ Prod. by B. S. Fairbrother.

CARBONARI, THE; OR, THE BRIDE OF PARMA// D 2a// Adap. fr F of Eugène Scribe// **Princess's**, Feb. 1845, with Mr. Fitzjames as Marquis Palarcini, Augustus Harris as del Dongo, Henry Compton as Pepito, Mrs. Stirling as Rebecca, Emma Stanley as Gianina.

CARD CASE, THE// F 1a// H. T. Craven// **Grecian**, July 1846, with Mr. Campbell as Maj. Pepperley, Edwin Dixon as Hector, Frederick Robson as Poppy, Eaton O'Donnell as O'Flinn, Mrs. W. Watson as Diana, Mary A. Crisp as Ribbon.

CARDINAL, THE// D 4a// L. N. Parker// **Comedy**, Oct. 1901.

CARDINAL'S DAUGHTER, THE// D// n.a.// **Marylebone**, Sept. 1852.

CARLINE, THE FEMALE BRIGAND// D 2a// Edward Stirling// **Pavilion**, Jan. 1837.

CARLO LEONI// D// n.a.// **Britannia**, Mar. 1859.

CARMELITES, THE; OR, THE CONVENT BELLES// F// Edward Fitzball// **Sad. Wells**, Mar. 1837, with Mr. Campbell as Count de Courley, Mr. Tilbury as Beaudeau, Benjamin Webster as Capt. Brissac, C. H. Pitt as Capt. Ernest, Mr. Rogers as Pichard, Miss Lebatt as Marie, Eliza Lee as Louise, Mrs. Harris as Superior, Mrs. Macnamara as Opportune, Mrs. Rogers as Genevieve, Miss Julian as Ursula.

CARMEN// D// Dram. by Henry Hamilton fr F of Prosper Merimée// **Gaiety**, June 1896.

CARMENCITA, LA// D 1a// Dram. by Louis Cohen fr F of Prosper Merimée// **Coronet**, Dec. 1900.

CARMILHAN; OR, THE DROWNED CREW// D// Edward Fitzball// **Sad. Wells**, June 1843, with C. J. Smith as Carmilhan, Henry Marston as Spiel, C. J. Bird as Petis, Mr. Williams as Sharkshead, Mr. Aldridge as Heist, Caroline Rankley as Uda, Mrs. Richard Barnett as Norna/ Scenery by F. Fenton/ Machines by Mr. Cawdery/ Music by Walter Montgomery.

CARNAC SAHIB// Play 4a// Henry Arthur Jones// **Her Majesty's**, Apr. 1899, with Herbert Beerbohm Tree as Col. Carnac, Lewis Waller as Col. Syrette, F. Percival Stevens as Gen. Scrivener, Frank Mills as Maj. Kynaston, J. D. Beveridge as Maj. Radnage, Herbert Ross as Rev. Hobbs, J. Fisher White as Ford, Gerald du Maurier as Lt. Barton, Scott Craven as Lt. Lovatt, Eva Moore as Ellice, Marie Harris as May, Marie Brierly as Mrs. Carmichael, Grace Otway as Mrs. Remington, Lillian Moubrey as Mrs. Whitmore, Rose Dupre as Madge, Mrs. Brown Potter as Olive/ Scenery by Walter Hann, William Telbin & Joseph Harker.

CAROONA// D 4a// Eileen Ray// **St. Geo. Hall**, Apr. 1899.

CARPENTER OF ROUEN, THE; OR, THE MASSACRE OF ST. BARTHOLOMEW// D 4a// J. S. Jones// **Drury Lane**, Mar. 1853/ **Victoria**, Aug. 1853, with T. E. Mills as Duke de Sangbigne, F. H. Henry as Lourney, N. T. Hicks as Marteau, Thomas Green as Maroine, Alfred Raymond as Bellard, John Hudspeth as La Nyppe, J. Howard as Grander, Phoebe Johnson as Pierre, Mrs. Henry Vining as Madelon, Miss Laporte as Julie, Mrs. Manders as Mme. Grander/ **Sad. Wells**, May 1869, with Mr. Perry as Duke De Saubigne, Frederick Maynard as Bellard, Charles Horsman as Marteau, Mr. Weston as la Lieppe, Mr. Young as Lournay, Mr. Bisson as Grander, Miss N. Horsman as Madelon, Mrs. E. F. Edgar as Mme. Grander, Miss R. Vacy as Julie, Miss Gilbert as Cecile.

CARPENTERS OF LAMBETH, THE; OR, THE BRIDE OF THE THAMES// D// n.a.// **Victoria**,

Oct. 1847, with John Dale as Maitland, N. T. Hicks as Charles Martin, Alfred Raymond as Robert Martin, J. Howard as Old Barnard, T. H. Higgie as Winter, G. F. Forman as Starling, F. H. Henry as Gregson, Annette Vincent as Marian, Mrs. N. T. Hicks as Mary, Miss Burroughcliffe as Fanny, Mrs. Andrews as Mrs. Potts, Mrs. Cooke as Mrs. Stubbs.

CARRIER AND HIS DOG, THE// D// n.a.// **Victoria**, May 1854, with Mr. Henderson as Villars, Alfred Saville as Old Michael, N. T. Hicks as Morris, J. Howard as Canvass, John Hudspeth as Rocket, Edwin Blanchard as Toby Flint, Dog Hector as Dog Trusty, Mrs. Henry Vining as Caroline, Mrs. Manders as Alice, Miss Sutton as Dame Dewlap, Miss Laporte as Chloe.

CARRIER OF LONDON, THE// D// n.a.// **Strand**, Jan. 1855.

CARTE DE VISITE// F 1a// Montagu Williams & F. C. Burnand// **St. James's**, June 1863, with S. Johnson as Winkin, Mr. Western as Ranger, Mr. Trafford as Dusoleil, Adeline Cottrell as Mrs. Winkin, Ada Dyas as Mrs. Montgomery, Miss Nisbett as Betsy.

CARTHUSIANA// Play 1a// B. C. Stephenson// **Haymarket**, June 1899, with Johnston Forbes Robertson as Peyton, Frederick Kerr as Capt. Travers, William Young as Baldock, Sybil Carlisle as Rose, O. E. Thomas as Prior, Alan Mackinnon as Sutton, Charles Allan as Scourge, B. C. Stephenson as Lord Suffolk, Cyril Maude as Peyton, C. Aubrey Smith as Col. Newcome, Muriel Beaumont as Rose.

CARTOUCHE, THE FRENCH HOUSEBREAKER (also subt., The French Jack Sheppard)// D// n.a.// **Victoria**, Mar. 1862, with W. H. Pitt as Cartouche, W. Harmer as Count D'Aubrani, Mr. Henderson as Marquis de Grandelieu, Walter Fredericks as Cariol, Mr. Hitchinson as Traville, Mr. Wood as Antoine, George Yarnold as Gribichon, J. Howard as Bobilet, Miss M. Foster as Louise, Helen Love as Eugene/ **Sad. Wells**, Sept. 1865, with Mr. Wallace as Count D'Aubrani, H. Reeves as Marquis De Grandelieu, Mr. Gardiner as Cariol, Mr. Johnson as Traville, T. Marks as Antoine, J. Russell as Bobilet and as Gribichon, C. Moorhouse as Cartouche, Mary Fielding as Louise, Nelly Jones as Eugene, Mrs. Wallace as Mme. Bobilot.

CASE FOR EVICTION, A// C 1a// S. Theyre Smith// **St. James's**, Dec. 1883, with George Alexander as Frank, Linda Dietz as Dora, May Whitty as Mary.

CASE OF CONSCIENCE, A// F 1a// John Oxenford// **Princess's**, Nov. 1857, with David Fisher as Clamber, G. Everett as Miles, F. Cooke as Kidd, Mr. Raymond as Stokes, Rose Leclercq as Lucretia, Miss Murray as Sarah.

CASE OF PICKLES, A// F// G. C. Baddeley// **Royalty**, May 1871.

CASE OF REBELLIOUS SUSAN, THE// C 3a// Henry Arthur Jones// **Criterion**, Oct. 1894, with Charles Wyndham as Sir Richard, Henry Kemble as Admiral Darby, C. P. Little as Harabin, Frederick Kerr as Pybus, Ben Webster as Edensor, Fanny Coleman as Lady Darby, Gertrude Kingston as Mrs. Quesnel, Nine Boucicault as Elaine, Mary Moore as Lady Susan/ **Wyndham's**, May 1901.

CASH VERSUS CUPID// C 1a// n.a.// **Princess's**, Mar. 1862, with J. G. Shore as Hartley, Henry Widdicomb as Newington Butts, Maria Harris as Nelly, Helen Howard as Tilly, Mrs. Weston as Mrs. Debar/ **Olympic**, Apr. 1869, with Henry Vaughan as Hartley, J. G. Taylor as Butts, Mrs. Caulfield as Mrs. Debar, Maria Harris as Tilly, Nelly Harris as Bella.

CASKET OF JEWELS, THE// D 3a// n.a.// **Drury Lane**, Feb. 1853.

CASPER THE DOOMED; OR, THE VICTIM OF THE VAULT// D 3a// Adap. fr F// **Victoria**, Nov. 1841, with Mr. Cullen as Count of Ranspach, William Seaman as Vorhne, John Dale as Schwartz, Mr. Wilton as Oln, John Gardner as Blaise, E. F. Saville as Casper Hauser, Mr. Paul as Pompe, Mrs. George Lee as Baroness of Hapsburg.

CASSILDA// D// n.a.// **Surrey**, July 1862.

CASSIOPE// n.a.// **Alexandra**, Aug. 1866.

CAST ADRIFT// D 4a// R. Palgrave & Fred Gover// **Sadler's Wells**, Apr. 1882/ **Olympic**, Feb. 1884, with H. H. Vincent as Markham, C. W. Somerset as Silas, Philip Beck as Hinchcliffe, Fuller Mellish as Aylmer, Austin Melford as Appleyard, E. Hendrie as Halcomb, Rowland Buckstone as Edwards, Alma Murray as Ethel, Laura Lindon as Lucy, Maud Cathcart as Jenny.

CAST ASIDE; OR, LOVING NOT WISELY BUT TOO WELL// D// C. H. Hazlewood// **Britannia**, Oct. 1871.

CAST ON THE MERCY OF THE WORLD// D// C. H. Hazlewood// **Britannia**, Oct. 1862.

CASTAWAY, THE// D// C. H. Hazlewood// **Britannia**, Mar. 1866.

CASTAWAYS, THE// C 1a// S. Theyre Smith// **St. James's**, June 1885, with W. H. Kendal as Juan, Mrs. W. H. Kendal as Lilian/ Scenery by W. Harford.

CASTE// C 3a// T. W. Robertson// **POW**, Apr. 1867, with Squire Bancroft, Mrs. Bancroft, George Honey, John Hare, Sophia Larkin; Jan. 1879, with Squire Bancroft, John Clayton, George Honey, Arthur Cecil, Amy Roselle, Mrs. Bancroft/ **Haymarket**, Jan. 1883, with H. B. Conway as D'Alroy, Squire Bancroft as Capt. Hawtree, David James as Eccles, Charles Brookfield as Gerridge, Henry Vernon as Dixon, Mrs. Stirling as Marquise de St. Maur, Miss Gerard as Esther, Mrs. Bancroft as Polly Eccles/ Scenery by Walter Hann & Mr. Johnstone/ **Lyceum**, Oct. 1896, with Frank Gillmore as D'Alroy, Frederick Kerr as Hawtree,

John Hare as Eccles, Gilbert Hare as Gerridge, Susie Vaughan as Marquise De St. Maur, Mona Oram as Esther, May Harvey as Polly/ Scenery by W. Harford/ **Garrick**, Feb. 1897/ **Court**, June 1897/ **Globe**, Mar. 1899.

CASTING THE BOOMERANG// C 4a// Adap. by Augustin Daly fr G of Franz von Schönthan, Schwabenstreich// **Toole's**, July 1884/ **Lyceum**, June 1890, with John Drew as Corliss, James Lewis as Bargiss, George Clarke as Hollyhock, Charles Wheatleigh as Postman, Charles Leclercq as Prof. Gasleigh, Mrs. G. H. Gilbert as Hypatia, Adelaide Prince as Dora, Ada Rehan as Floss.

CASTLE OF LIMBURG, THE// D// n.a.// **Sad. Wells**, Nov. 1842, with Henry Marston as Delaval, J. W. Collier as O'Clogerty, P. Williams as Baron de Limburg, Caroline Rankley as Lady Clara.

CASTLE OF OTRANTO, THE// D// Adap. fr novel of Horace Walpole// **Haymarket**, Apr. 1848, with Robert Keeley as Manfred, James Bland as Marquis Vincenza, Priscilla Horton as Theodore, Mr. Caulfield as Odonto, Mrs. W. Clifford as Hippolita, Miss Reynolds as Isabella, Mrs. Caulfield as Matilda/ Scenery by P. Phillips & George Morris/ Machines by Mr. Hesslcton/ Music by T. German Reed.

CASTLE OF ST. ALMO, THE// D 3a// Thomas Archer// **Victoria**, May 1850, with J. Neville as Marquis of St. Almo, Mr. Humphreys as Don Ferdinand, J. T. Johnson as Capt. Beauclerk, Mr. Henderson as Capt. Morton, John Bradshaw as Willis, J. Howard as Ludigno, John Hudspeth as Pedro, Mr. Morrison as Clewline, R. H. Kitchen as di Palermo, Mrs. George Lee as Leonora, Mrs. Humphreys as Sister Beatrice, Miss Barrowcliffe as Theresa, Mrs. Cooke as Agnesta, Miss Mildenhall as Milanette.

CASTLE SPECTRE, THE; OR, OSMOND'S DREAM AND THE SLAVE'S REVENGE// D 5a// M. G. Lewis// **Drury Lane**, Apr. 1837, with Mr. Cooper as Earl Osmond, Mr. Mathews as Earl Reginald, A. Brindal as Earl Percy, Drinkwater Meadows as Motley, George Bartley as Father Philip, Mr. Diddear as Kenric, Mr. Warde as Hassan, Fanny Huddart as Angela, Mrs. W. Clifford as The Spectre, Mrs. Charles Jones as Alice/ **Sad. Wells**, May 1840, with Henry Marston as Osmond, Mr. Aldridge as Reginald, Mr. Elvin as Percy, Mr. Williams as Philip, J. W. Collier as Motley, J. B. Hill as Kenric, Mrs. Robert Honner as Angela, Miss Cooke as Alice, Miss Richardson as Evelina; Jan. 1863, with Henry Forrester as Osmond, Mr. Stalman as Reginald, Henry Dalton as Percy, James Johnstone as Philip, Lewis Ball as Motley, Alfred Montague as Kenric, Sophie Miles as Angela, Mrs. William Dowton as Alice, Miss Edgar as Evelina/ **Grecian**, Dec. 1862 with Thomas Mead as Earl Osmond, George Gillett as Percy, J. Jackson as Reginald, Alfred Rayner as Father Phillip, Henry Grant as Hassan, Walter Holland as Kenric, Henry Power as Motley, Jane Dawson as Angela, Marie Brewer as Evilina, Miss Johnston as Alice/ **Gaiety**, May 1880, with J. D. Beveridge, J. B. Johnstone, Louise Willes.

CASTLES IN THE AIR// C 1a// C. M. Rae// **Vaudeville**, Dec. 1879, with Henry Howe, Kate Bishop.

CASTRUCCIO; OR, THE DEFORMED// D// Edgar Newbound// **Britannia**, July 1878.

CASUAL ACQUAINTANCE, A// Play Pro & 3a// J. F. Cooke// **Trafalgar**, May 1893, with Edmund Maurice as Thorton, W. L. Abingdon as Marsden, Ernest Percy as The American, C. M. Hallerd as Ralph, Stewart Dawson as Dunsford, W. T. Lovell as Wilde, Mrs Conyers d'Arcy as Lady Garston, Mrs. B. M. de Solla as Mrs. Harcourt, Constance Abbott as Miss Briggs, Mrs. Edmund Phelps as Mrs. Dunsford.

CASUAL WARD, THE// D// C. H. Hazelwood// **Marylebone**, Feb. 1866/ **Sad. Wells**, Sept. 1866, with G. P. Jaques as Graspleigh, Philip Hannan as Glover, Walter Roberts as Wilson, Watty Brunton as Tibbets, Miss George as Clara.

CAT AND THE CHERUB, THE// Adap. by C. B. Fernald fr Chinese// **Lyric**, Oct. 1897.

CATARACT OF THE GANGES, THE; OR, THE WARHORSE OF GUZERAT (also subt., The Bramin of Guzzerat)// D// W. T. Moncrieff// **Cov. Garden**, May 1837, with John Dale as Saheb, John Pritchard as Mokarra, Mr. Thompson as Ackbar, John Webster as Iran, Mr. Harris as Mordaunt, Benjamin Webster as Robinson, Mr. Tilbury as Mokajee, Mrs. Sarah Garrick as Matali, Miss Nicholson as Ubra, Miss Lacy as Dessa, Miss Lee as Zamine/ Scenery by Mr. Marshall/ **Sad. Wells**, Oct. 1843, with Mr. Williams as Emperor Ackbar, C. J. Smith as Rajah Saheb, Henry Marston as Mokarra, R. H. Lingham as Iran, C. J. Bird as Mordaunt, W. H. Williams as Robinson, Mrs. Stickney as Princess Dessa, Miss Cooke as Matali, Mrs. Richard Barnett as Ubra, Mrs. J. W. Collier as Zobeide, Caroline Rankley as Zaninc/ Scenery by F. Fenton/ Machines by Mr. Cawdery/ Music by W. Montgomery/ Prod. by Henry Marston.

CATCH A WEAZEL// F 1a// J. Maddison Morton// **Strand**, Mar. 1862.

CATCHING AN HEIRESS// F 1a// Charles Selby// **Sad. Wells**, Mar. 1845, with John Webster as Capt. Poodle, E. Morton as Capt. Killingly, Charles Morelli as Gayton, Mr. Sharpe as Stubby, G. F. Forman as Tom Twig, Miss Lebatt as Caroline, Georgiana Lebatt as Sally/ **Olympic**, Feb. 1850, with F. B. Conway as Capt. Poodle, Fred Belton as Capt. Killingly, Mr. Morrison as Gayton, John Reeve as Twigg; Apr. 1853, with W. Morgan as Capt. Poodle, John Kinloch as Capt. Killingly, Charles Bender as Gayton, Frederick Robson as Twig, E. Clifton as Stubby, Harriet Gordon as Caroline and as Fip, Ellen Turner as Sally and as Jessamy.

CATHERINE// D 1a// Cecil Fitzroy// **Novelty**, Mar. 1897.

CATHERINE HOWARD// D 3a// Adap. by W. D. Suter fr F of Alexandre Dumas// **Grecian**,

Sept. 1863, with Alfred Rayner as Henry VIII, J. Jackson as Cranmer, Thomas Mead as Duke of Ethelwold, George Gillett as Sussex, Mr. Howard as Sir John, F. Smithson as Fleming, W. Shirley as Norfolk, Jane Dawson as Catherine, Ellen Hale as Princess Marguerite.

CATHERINE OF RUSSIA; OR, THE CHILD OF THE STORM// D// John Courtney// **Victoria**, Sept. 1850, with David Osbaldiston as Peter I, Henry Frazer as Gen. Scheremtief, Mr. Richards as Sgt. Hetzenoff, John Neville as Skovronski, G. F. Forman as Radutzypadutzky, Annette Vincent as Catherine, Mrs. Cooke as Mme. Alexiana, Georgiana Lebatt as Carline, Miss Mildenhall as Zettea/ Prod. by T. Higgie.

CATO// T// Joseph Addison// **Cov. Garden**, Nov. 1838, with Mr. Vandenhoff as Cato, E. W. Elton as Porcius, Samuel Phelps as Marcus, James Anderson as Juba, George Bennett as Sempronius, Mr. Warde as Syphax, Charles Diddear as Lucius, Mr. Waldron as Decius, W. H. Payne as Junius, C. J. Smith as Titus, Charlotte Vandenhoff as Marcia, Mrs. Mary Warner as Lucia.

CATSPAW, THE// C 5a// Douglas Jerrold// **Haymarket**, May 1850, with Henry Howe as Capt. Burgonet, Robert Keeley as Snowball, James Wallack as Petgoose, Charles Selby as Audley, J. B. Buckstone as Appleface, Mr. Tilbury as Dust, Benjamin Webster as Coolcard, Miss Reynolds as Mrs. Peachdown, Mrs. L. S. Buckingham as Cassandra, Mrs. Keeley as Rosemary/ Scenery by Mr. Johnstone & George Morris/ Machines by F. Heselton.

CATSPAW, THE// Play 3a// John Tresahar// **Terry's**, July 1889.

CATTLE STEALERS, THE// D 2a// n.a.// **Grecian**, May 1855, with Edwin Blanchard as McNeil, Drovers Dogs by Hector and Bruin, Thomas Roberts as Saunders, Henry Grant as Lisle, Richard Phillips as Leslie, John Manning as Maclain, Emma Lonsdale as Miss Campbell, Harriet Coveney as Jennie, Miss Johnstone as Maggie.

CAUGHT// C 3a// Adap. by Stanislaus Calhaem// **Comedy**, June 1886.

CAUGHT AT LAST// D// Nelson Lee// **City of London**, Apr. 1884.

CAUGHT AT LAST// C// Adap. by Lady Cadogan fr F of Armand des Roseux, La Souris// **Comedy**, June 1886/ **Avenue**, Oct. 1889.

CAUGHT AT LAST; OR, A CHANGE IN THE WIND// C// n.a.// **St. James's**, Dec. 1873.

CAUGHT BY THE CUFF// F 1a// Frederick Hay// **Victoria**, Sept. 1865.

CAUGHT IN A TRAP// C 2a// Benjamin Webster// **Haymarket**, Nov. 1843, with Benjamin Webster as Marquis D'Arblay, Henry Holl as Count de Merville, J. B. Buckstone as Goguenard, Louisa Nisbett as Countess de Merville, Julia Bennett as Rose, Miss Mattley as Fanchette, Miss C. Conner as Babette/ Scenery by George Morris.

CAUGHT IN A TRAP// C 3a// Henry Holl// **Princess's**, Feb. 1860.

CAUGHT IN HIS OWN TRAP// C 1a// Mrs. Alfred Phillips// **Olympic**, Oct. 1851, with William Farren as Vraimont, John Kinloch as Francois, William Shalders as Jonas, Mrs. Alfred Phillips as Mme. Vonderbushell, Ellen Turner as Agatha.

CAUGHT IN THE TOILS// D Pro & 3a// Dram. by John Brougham fr novel of Mrs. Braddon// **St. James's**, Oct. 1865, with Mr. Belton as Lowther, F. Charles as Lt. Lowther, Edward Dyas as Hillary, Frank Matthews as Grunderson, Walter Lacy as Tredethlyn, Miss A. Colinson as Maud, Louisa Herbert as Julia, Miss Wentworth as Susan, Mrs. Frank Matthews as Polly, Eleanor Bufton as Rosa.

CAUGHT NAPPING// F// n.a.// **Cov. Garden**, Oct. 1841, with Frank Matthews as Gen. Griffin, A. Brindal as Capt. Griffin, Mr. Hemming as Kildare, W. H. Oxberry as Duster, John Brougham as Oregan, Miss Lee as Harriet, Mrs. Humby as Kitty, Mrs. Tayleure as Mrs. Leary.

CAUGHT ON A LINE// C// n.a.// **Strand**, Mar. 1862.

CAUGHT OUT// C// Adap. by Florence Bright fr G of Pfahl, Die Kunstreiterin// **St. Geo. Hall**, July 1888.

CAUSE AND EFFECT// D// n.a.// **Surrey**, Feb. 1860.

CAVALIER, THE// D// D. C. Whitehead// **Sad. Wells**, Aug. 1840, with J. B. Hill as Lord Morton, Mr. Elvin as Beauchamp, Mr. Dry as Maynard, E. W. Elton as Hargrave, Mrs. J. F. Saville as Mrs. Maynard, Miss Richardson as Mme. De Grave, Mrs. Robert Honner as Mrs. Hargrave; Sept. 1850, with George Bennett as Hargrave, Charles Wheatleigh as Lord Moreton, Henry Mellon as Beauchamp, Frank Graham as Maynard, Eliza Travers as Mrs. Hargrave, Miss Marston as Mrs. Maynard, Mrs. Archbold as Mme. Le Grave/ Scenery by F. Fenton; Mar. 1868, with Charles Dillon as Hargrave, Mr. Hamilton as Lord Morton, Gratton Murray as Maynard, J. L. Warner as Beauchamp, Walter Lacy as Hubert, Alice Marriott as Margaret, Miss Leigh as Mistress Maynard, Mrs. Walton as Mme. de Grace.

CAVALLERIA RUSTICANA// D 1a// Adap. fr Ital. of Giovanni Verga// **Lyric**, May 1893.

CEAN MILLE FAIL, THE// D Pro & 3a// Mortimer Murdoch// **East London**, Dec. 1877.

CELESTE; OR, THE EMPEROR'S VICTIM// D 2a// n.a.// **Sad. Wells**, Oct. 1839, with Mr. Elvin as Napoleon, Mr. Cathcart as D'Armannon, J. W. Collier as Taffy, Mr. Aldridge as Duroche, Charles Montgomery as Picard, Mrs. Robert Honner as Celeste, Miss Pincott as Pauline,

Miss Lovell as Empress Josephine.

CENCI, THE// T 5a// Percy Shelley// **Grand,** May 1886, with Alma Murray, Maude Brennan, Hermann Vezin.

CENSUS, THE// F 1a// Andrew Halliday & William Brough// **Adelphi,** Apr. 1861, with J. L. Toole as Familias, Miss Laidlaw as Rose, W. H. Eburne as Albert, Robert Romer as Taturs, Kate Kelly as Jenny.

CERISE & CO// FC 3a// Mrs. Musgrave// **POW,** Apr. 1890, with F. H. Kerr as Vanderbone, Eric Lewis as Styleman, H. H. Morell as Lord Perfect, Gilbert Trent as Flutter, John Le Hay as Barlow, Myra Kemble as Lady Kilkenny, Emily Thorne as Mrs. Vanderbone, Lottie Venne as Virginia, Josephine St. Ange as Miss Blunt, Sylvia Grey as Miss Prettyman, Ettie Williams as Miss Sweet.

CHAIN OF EVENTS, A// D 8a// G. H. Lewis ("Slingsby Lawrence") & C. J. Mathews// **Lyceum,** Apr. 1852, with C. J. Mathews as Gaspard, Frank Matthews as Père Bonneau, Robert Roxby as Le Fort, Fred Belton as Michel, Henry Horncastle as Marquis de Melcy, Basil Baker as Baptiste, Henry Butler as Cabri, Lydia Foote as Edouard, Mme. Vestris as Marie Bonneau, Laura Keene as Thérèse, Mrs. Frank Matthews as Madeleine, Julia St. George as Javette, Mrs. Charles Horn as Mme. de St. Prie, Mrs. Macnamara as Countess de Melcy, Miss M. Oliver as Louisa/ Scenery by W. Beverly/ Music by J. H. Tully/ Machines by H. Sloman.

CHAIN OF GUILT, THE; OR, THE INN OF THE HEATH// D// A. V. Campbell// **Sad. Wells,** Jan. 1837, with Mr. Rogers as Dibbs, Mr. Campbell as Morris, N. T. Hicks as Will, C. H. Pitt as Clare, Mr. Ray as Edmund, Mr. Scarbrow as Lt. Durnford, Miss Williams as Margaret, Miss Lebatt as Ellen, Mrs. Harris as Harriet.

CHAINED TO THE OAR// D 4a// H. J. Byron// **Gaiety,** May 1883.

CHALK AND CHEESE// C 1a// Ellie Norwood// **Terry's,** June 1892, with Eille Norwood as Raymond, Ethel Norton as Sybil/ **Vaudeville,** Nov. 1899.

CHALLENGE AT SEA, THE; OR, THE BATTLE BETWEEN THE CHESAPEAKE AND THE SHANNON// D 3a// n.a.// **Victoria,** Mar. 1846, with F. Wilton as Capt. Broke, Mr. Randall as Lt. Sinclair, Mr. Edgar as Capt. Lawrence, E. F. Saville as Harford, J. T. Johnson as Lt. Castleton, T. Fredericks as Stanmore, Mr. James as Twist, F. H. Henry as O'Snannon, Mr. Hitchinson as Tackle, John Dale as Peter, Miss Jefferson as Tabitha, Eliza Terrey as Harriett, Miss Richardson as Mary.

CHAMBER OF HORRORS, THE// F// n.a.// **Sad. Wells,** Nov. 1847, with A. Younge as Tramper, William Hoskins as Honeysuckle, Charles Fenton as Walkup, Mr. Franks as Sgt. Bounceable, Julia St. George as Kitty.

CHAMBER PRACTICE// F 1a// Charles Selby// **Olympic,** Feb. 1851, with W. H. Norton as Beamish, William Farren Jr. as Flarehault, Henry Compton as Chucks, Charles Bender as Jacobs, Mrs. B. Bartlett as Miss Eyesinglass, Isabel Adams as Miss Flarehault.

CHAMELEON, THE; OR, THE ART OF PLEASING// C// William Brough// **Drury Lane,** Apr. 1853.

CHANDOS; OR, THE JESTER WHO TURNED TRAITOR// D 5a// Adap. by Hartbury Brooklyn fr novel of Ouida// **Adelphi,** Sept. 1882.

CHANGE ALLEY// C 5a// L. N. Parker & Murray Carson// **Garrick,** Apr. 1899, with Fred Terry as Heartright, J. H. Barnes as Father O'Nimble, J. A. Welch as Parchment, John Beauchamp as Sir Withering, Robert Loraine as Spurway, Eric Lewis as Sir Barely, John Billington as Dr. Moody, F. Hamilton Knight as Goldworm, Charles Goodhart as Fallowfield, Frank Emery as Mole, Mrs. Lewis Waller as Vesta, Geraldine Olliffe as Mme. Moody, Hall Caine as Mistress Belleville, Lillah McCarthy as Mistress Delancy, Lizzie Scobie as Mme. Fallowfield, Jessie Ferrar as Araminta, Julia Neilson as Celia, Mrs. H. B. Tree as Prologue/ Scenery by Leolyn Hart.

CHANGE FOR A SOVEREIGN// F// Horace Wigan// **Strand,** Mar. 1861.

CHANGE FOR A SOVEREIGN// C 2a// J. U. Spellon// **Grecian,** July 1855, with F. Charles as Louis XV, Basil Potter as Richelieu, Richard Phillips as de Bobinet, John Manning as Passe Partout, Eaton O'Donnell as Duroset, Jane Coveney as Mlle. de Bellchase, Miss Johnstone as Mme. Vassan.

CHANGE OF NAME// F// Arthur Moore// **Sadler's Wells,** Sept. 1867.

CHANGE OF SYSTEM, A// C 1a// Howard Paul// **St. James's,** Apr. 1860.

CHANGED HEART, THE// D// Adap. fr F, Le Comtesse de Noailles// **Surrey,** Jan. 1860.

CHANGES// D 3a// H. Proctor// **St. Geo. Hall,** Oct. 1876.

CHANGES// C 3a// John Aylmer// **Toole's,** Apr. 1890, with Adolphus Ellis as Sir Timothy, Reginald Stockton as Hewitt, E. H. Patterson as Flimsleigh, John Aylmer as Maj. Jungle, Walter Arnould as Migley, Josephine St. Ange as Mrs. Croker, Alice Yorke as Lady Una, Mary Collette as Ethel.

CHANGES AND CHANCES// D 2a// n.a.// **Avenue,** Mar. 1891, with James Nelson as Harrison, Acton Bond as Vernon, A. Ellis as Harbinger, S. H. Basing as Dodson, Julia Seaman as Mrs. Harbinger, Beatrice Adair as Rachel.

CHAOS IS COME AGAIN// F 1a// J. Maddison Morton// **Cov. Garden,** Nov. 1838, with George Bartley as Col. Chaos, James Vining as Bounce, Drinkwater Meadows as Tottenham, John Ayliffe as Blazes, Miss Charles as Harriet/ **Sad. Wells**, July 1844, with Mr. Williams as Col. Chaos, Charles Morelli as Tottenham, Charles Hudson as Jack Bounce, Georgiana Lebatt as Harriet.

CHAPTER OF ACCIDENTS, A// F 1a// J. T. Douglass// **Standard**, Sept. 1870/ **Olympic**, July 1871, with William Blakeley as Hill, C. H. Peveril as Henry, E. W. Garden as St. Pauls, Miss Wood as Mrs. Hill, Miss Venner as Matilda.

CHARCOAL BURNER, THE; OR, THE DROPPING WELL OF KNARESBOROUGH// D 2a// George Almar// **Victoria**, May 1838, with Mr. Loveday as Harrington, William Davidge as Mathew Esdaile, Mr. Archer as Arden, Mr. Forester as Edmund Esdaile, Mr. Johnstone as Brown, John Parry as Cole, Mr. Scriven as Jones, Miss Richardson as Edith, Mrs. Loveday as Barbara; Apr. 1854, with Alfred Saville as Harrington, T. E. Mills as Mathew Eskdale, Mr. Henderson as Edmund Eskdale, N. T. Hicks as Arden, John Bradshaw as Brown, Charles Hudspeth as Verdict, J. Howard as Cole, Mrs. Henry Vining as Edith, Miss Laporte as Barbara, Georgiana Lebatt as Cecilia, Mrs. Manders as Mother Grumble.

CHARITABLE MAN, THE// F// Henry Barry// **Novelty**, Feb. 1887.

CHARITY; OR, "MY LORD WELCOME"// D 2a// Dram. by C. H. Hazlewood fr F of Victor Hugo, Les Misérables// **Sad. Wells**, Nov. 1862, with James Johnstone as Meriel, Lewis Ball as Grongilion, Charles Crook as Mathias, Henry Forrester as Valjean, Catherine Lucette as Little Jarvis, Charles Lloyds as Lebarre, Alfred Montague as Sgt. Galliard, Mrs. William Dowton as Mme. Meriel, Emily Dowton as Lucille.

CHARITY// Play 4a// W. S. Gilbert// **Haymarket**, Jan. 1874, with W. H. Chippendale as Dr. Athelney, Henry Howe as Smailey, W. H. Kendal as Fred, Mr. Teesdale as Ted, J. B. Buckstone as Partington, Mr. Clark as Cripps, Madge Robertson (Mrs. Kendal) as Mrs. Van Brugh, Amy Roselle as Eve, Sarah Woolgar (Mrs. Mellon) as Ruth/ Scenery by John O'Conner & George Morris/ Machines by Oliver Wales.

CHARITY'S LOVE// D 3a// John Wilkins// **City of London**, Mar. 1854/ **Sad. Wells** June 1854, with F. Charles, C. Poynter, J. Worrell, E. L. Davenport as Capt. Algernon, Mr. Barrett as Fustian, J. B. Johnstone as Advocate, Fanny Vining as Charity, Emily Norton as Floribel.

CHARLATAN, THE// Play 4a// Robert Buchanan// **Haymarket**, Jan. 1894, with Herbert Beerbohm Tree as Woodville, Nutcombe Gould as Earl of Wanborough, Fred Terry as Lord Dewsbury, Frederick Kerr as Darrell, Charles Allan as Darnley, Holman Clark as Marrables, Lily Hanbury as Lady Carlotta, Mrs. E. H. Brooke as Mrs. Darnley, Irene Vanbrugh as Olive, Gertrude Kingston as Mme. Obnoskin, Mrs. Beerbohm Tree as Isabel/ Scenery by Walter Hann.

CHARLEMAGNE// D 2a// n.a.// **Drury Lane**, Oct. 1838, with Mr. King as Charlemagne, Mr. Baker as Roland, A. Brindal as Ganalon, Mr. Mathews as Oliver, Mr. Jones as Bertram, F. Sutton as Ogier, Gerard King as Renaud, Henry Wallack as Marsila, Mr. Ducrow as Hamet, Henry Compton as Andrel/ Scenery by Grieve, T. Grieve & W. Grieve/ Music by Mr. Eliason & Mr. Stansbury/ Machines by Mr. Nall/ Prod. by Mr. Ducrow.

CHARLES I// D 4a// W. G. Wills// **Lyceum**, Sept. 1872, with Henry Irving as Charles I, George Belmore as Cromwell, Mr. Addison as Marquis of Huntley, E. F. Edgar as Lord Moray, Robert Markby as Ireton, Georgina Pauncefort as Lady Eleanor, Isabel Bateman as Queen Henrietta Maria/ Scenery by Hawes Craven & Cuthbert; May 1879, with Henry Irving, Arthur Wing Pinero, Georgina Pauncefort, Ellen Terry.

CHARLES I AND II// T// Gerald & Guy Du Maurier// **Court**, Oct. 1901.

CHARLES KING// C 2a// n.a.// **Olympic**, Mar. 1851, with Henry Farren as Charles II, W. H. Norton as Rochester, E. Clifton as Audley, John Kinloch as Sedley, William Farren Jr. as Charles King, Leigh Murray as Van Pousten, Ellen Turner as Walter, Isabel Adams as Guido, Mrs. Stirling as Mimi, Louisa Howard as Nell Gwynne/ Scenery by W. Shalders.

CHARLES II// C 1a// Gilbert à Beckett// **Sad. Wells**, May 1847, with Henry Marston as Charles II, William Hoskins as Rochester, A. Younge as Capt. Copp, Julia St. George as Edward, Fanny Huddart as Lady Clara, Julia Wallack as Mary/ **Lyceum**, May 1877, with E. H. Brooke as King Charles, R. C. Lyons as Rochester, W. L. Branscombe as Edward, Mrs. Louther as Lady Clara, Miss Claire as Mary.

CHARLES II; OR, THE MERRY MONARCH (add'l subt. and the Fair Maid of Wapping)// D 2a// John Howard Payne// **Sad. Wells**, Apr. 1838, with J. Worrell as Charles II, Mr. Forester as Rochester, Mr. Campbell as Capt. Copp, Miss Beresford as Lady Clara, Eliza Vincent as Mary/ **Cov. Garden**, Dec. 1838, with James Anderson as Charles II, James Vining as Rochester, George Bartley as Capt. Copp, Mr. Manvers as Edward, Miss Charles as Lady Clara, Miss Rainforth as Mary/ **Victoria**, Mar. 1844, with David Osbaldiston as Charles II, Mr. Nantz as Rochester, William Seaman as Edward, Mr. James as Capt. Copp, Miss Arden as Lady Clara, Annette Vincent as Mary/ **Grecian**, July 1845, with Harry Chester as Charles II, Edwin Dixon as Rochester, Mr. Campbell as Capt. Copp, Annette Mears as Edward, Miss Hebbard as Lady Clara, Mary A. Crisp as Mary/ **Princess's**, Nov. 1852, with Walter Lacy as Charles II, James Vining as Rochester, George Bartley as Capt. Copp, Miss Murray as Lady Clara, Carlotta Leclercq as Mary.

CHARLES XII; OR, THE SIEGE OF STRALSUND (also subt., The Battle of Stralsund)// D// J. R. Planché// **Cov. Garden**, Jan. 1837, with William Farren as Charles XII of Sweden, Henry

Wallack as Brock, George Bennett as Maj. Vanberg, John Webster as Gustavus, Benjamin Webster as Muddlewerk, John Collett as Officer, J. Smith as Duckert, Eliza Vincent as Endiga, Miss Lee as Ulrica; Dec. 1841, with William Farren as Charles XII, George Bartley as Brock, John Pritt Harley as Muddlewerk, Mr. Cooper as Maj. Vanberg, James Vining as de Mervelt, Alfred Wigan as Col. Reichel, Mme. Vestris as Eudiga, Miss Cooper as Ulrica/ **Sad. Wells,** May 1839, with Mr. Cathcart as Charles XII of Sweden, Mr. Williams as Brock, Mr. Conquest as Muddlewerk, Mr. Elvin as Merveldt, W. D. Broadfoot as Gen. Duckert, Mr. Dry as Maj. Vanberg, Miss Pincott as Eudiga, Mrs. J. F. Saville as Ulrica; July 1845, with A. Younge as Charles XII of Sweden, Edward Knight as Duckert, Samuel Buckingham as Mervelt, George Bennett as Maj. Vanberg, Fanny Huddart as Ulrica, Miss Lebatt as Eudiga/ **Haymarket,** July 1848, with William Farren as Charles XII, J. W. Gough as Gen. Duckert, George Braid as Col. Reichel, Henry Vandenhoff as de Mervelt, Henry Howe as Maj. Vanberg, Benjamin Webster as Brock, Mr. Tilbury as Muddlework, Miss Fortescue as Ulrica, Miss Reynolds as Eudiga; July 1863, with Alfred Wigan as Charles XII, George Braid as Col. Reichel, Henry Howe as Maj. Vanberg, Walter Gordon as Gustavus, J. B. Buckstone as Brock, Henry Compton as Muddlework, Louisa Angel as Ulrica, Louise Keeley as Udiga/ **Lyceum,** Feb. 1850, with C. J. Mathews as Charles XII, Frank Matthews as Brock, John Pritt Harley as Muddlewerk, Mr. Bellingham as Reichel, John Parselle as de Mervelt, Miss Kenworthy as Ulrica, Julia St. George as Eudiga.

CHARLES O'MALLEY, THE IRISH DRAGOON// D 3a// Found. on story of Harry Lorrequer// **Olympic,** Apr. 1840, with Mr. Halford as Charles O'Malley, Mr. Mulford as Godfrey O'Malley, Mr. Brookes as Maj. Considine, Charles Baker as Gen. Dashwood, Mr. Freeborn as Sir Harry, Mr. Turnour as Dr. Mooney, Mr. Stoker as Capt. Power, Thomas Parry as Frank Webber, Thomas Lee as Mikey Free, Mrs. T. W. Edmonds as Lucy Dashwood, Miss Hamilton as Mary/ Scenery by Mr. Wilson/ Machines by Mr. Hagley, Music by Mr. Arthur.

CHARLEY'S AUNT// F 3a// Brandon Thomas// **Royalty,** Dec. 1892/ transf. to **Globe,** Jan. 1893, with Ernest Hendrie as Spettigue, Walter Everard as Col. Chesney, H. Reeves Smith as Jack Chesney, Harry Farmer as Wykeham, W. S. Penley as Lord Babberley, Cecil Thornbury as Brassett, Ada Branson as Donna Lucia, Audrey Ford as Amy, Beatrice Ferrer as Kitty, Emily Cudmore as Ela.

CHARLOTTE CORDAY// D 4a// H. Kyrle Bellew// **Adelphi,** Jan. 1898, with Kyrle Bellew as Marat, Luigi Lablache as de Corday d'Armont, Fred Everill as Abbé, Henry Vibart as Lux, W. T. Lovell as David, A. G. Poulton as Potin, H. A. Saintsbury as de la Garde, Betty Macdonald as Rose de Corday, Olive Stettith as Simmone, Mabel Hackney as Marianne, Miss Stirling as Mme. Richard, Mrs. Brown Potter as Charlotte Corday/ Music by John Crook.

CHARLOTTE HANWELL; OR, CRIME AND SORROW// D 3a// Edward Fitzball// **Sad. Wells,** Jan. 1842, with Mr. Norton as Capt. Arkhurst, Mr. Dry as Hanwell, John Herbert as Popkins, P. Williams as Cummins, Charles Fenton as Paddy, Mr. Richardson as Phelim, Mrs. Robert Honner as Charlotte, Miss Cooke as Mrs. Grimfagin, Miss Pitt as Sally.

CHARM, THE// C 1a// Walter Besant & W. H. Pollock// **St. Geo. Hall,** July 1884.

CHARMING MRS. GAYTHORNE, THE// C 3a// C. S. Cheltham// **Criterion,** Apr. 1894, with C. W. Somerset as Earl Pinckbeck, Yorke Stephens as Lord Groomsbury, Frank MacRae as Sir Rupert, A. E. Mason as Fairmain, Harley Granville Barker as Brightwell, Essex Dane as Lord Oakfield, Di Travers as Gabrielle, Mary Jocelyn as Augustine, Mrs. Ivy Dacre as Mrs. Gaythorne.

CHARMING PAIR, A// F 1a// T. J. Williams// **Princess's,** May 1863, with Robert Roxby as Splicer, Mr. Fitzjames as Maj. Bouncer, George Belmore as Smythe, Mr. Cockrill as Bob, Mrs. Henry Marston as Sophonisba, Marian Jones as Clementina, Maria Henderson as Susan; Aug. 1868, with Charles Harcourt as Splicer, Dan Leeson as Maj. Bouncer, Mr. Holston as Smythe, Robert Cathcart as Bob, Mrs. Addie as Sophonisba, Emma Barnett as Mrs. Bouncer, Miss Kemp as Susan.

CHARMING POLLY, THE// D 2a// J. T. Haines// **Surrey,** June 1838.

CHARMING WIDOW, A// C 1a// John Oxenford// **Lyceum,** Mar. 1854.

CHARMING WOMAN, THE// C 3a// Adap. by Horace Wigan fr F// **Olympic,** June 1861, with George Cooke as Sir Mulberry, Frederic Robinson as Ardent, Horace Wigan as Symptom, Walter Gordon as Bitterbliss, Henry Rivers as Pickings, Amy Sedgwick as Mrs. Bloomly, Mrs. Stephens as Mrs. Bitterbliss, Miss Cottrell as Julia.

CHARMS// CD 4a// C. L. Young// **Queen's,** July 1871.

CHASTE SALUTE, THE// n.a.// **Olympic,** Oct. 1838.

CHATEAU OF VALENZA, THE// D 3a// n.a.// **Olympic,** July 1851, with George Cooke as Marquis Salviate, Alfred Sanger as Constable, W. H. Norton as Galeas, William Farren Jr. as Lucio, Henry Farren as Rapello, Charles Diddear as Jacopo, William Shalders as Piombo, Louisa Howard as Violetta, Ellen Turner as Gianetta.

CHECK TO THE KING; OR, THE QUEEN'S FIRST MOVE// D 2a// n.a.// **Sad. Wells,** Feb. 1846, with Miss Cooper as Christian of Denmark, A. Younge as Duke of Oldenburg, E. Morton as Sweburg, Henry Marston as Count Eric, Mrs. Henry Marston as Duchess of Oldenburg, Miss Lebatt as Marguerite/ Scenery by F. Fenton & Mr. Finlay.

CHEVALIER DE ST. GEORGE// D 2a// Adap. by T. W. Robertson fr F// **Princess's**, May 1845, with J. W. Wallack as Chevalier de St. George, Mr. Hield as Baron de Tourval, Mr. Granby as De Boulogne, James Ranoe as De Moliere, W. H. Oxberry as Jujube, F. C. Courtney as Platon, F. H. Henry as Joseph, Robert Honner as Exempt, Mrs. Stirling as Countess, Miss E. Honner as Fanchette, Miss Mott as Lolo/ Scenery by William Beverley, Mr. Nichols, & Mr. Aglio/ Music by C. Horn/ **Victoria**, Nov. 1853, with T. E. Mills as Boulogne, Fred Moreland as Baron de Tourval, F. H. Henry as Capt. Morliere, Watty Brunton as La Ducie, T. J. Johnson as St. George, Mr. Hitchinson as Antoine, J. Howard as Platon, R. H. Kitchen as Larole, Julian Hicks as Saubigny, Alfred Saville as Frapeau, Mrs. Henry Vining as Countess de Presle, Miss Sutton as Mme. de Grendier, Miss Edgar as Mme. de Morville.

CHATTERBOX, THE// C 1a// Blanchard Jerrold// **St. James's**, Dec. 1859, with A. Denial as Poundes, Mr. Barrett as Joe Pense, Mr. Frazier as George Pense, J. H. Reeves as Dayley, Mr. Craxford as de Servette, Mrs. Manders as Mrs. Poundes, Nelly Moore as Clarissa, Mrs. Frank Matthews as Miss Tingleng, Eliza Arden as Emily, Miss Murray as Fritters.

CHATTERTON// Play 1a// Henry Arthur Jones & Henry Herman// **Princess's**, May 1884, with Wilson Barrett as Chatterton, George Barrett as Boaden, Emmeline Ormsby as Lady Mary, Mary Dickens as Cecilia/ **Drury Lane**, June 1884, with same cast/ **Lyceum**, Jan. 1888, with Wilson Barrett as Chatterton, George Barrett as Nat Boaden, Alice Cooke as Mrs. Angel, Lily Belmore as Cecilia, Alice Belmore as Lady Mary.

CHEAP EXCURSION, A// F 1a// Edward Stirling// **Strand**, May 1851/ **Victoria**, Feb. 1852, with G. F. Forman as Snobbs, Watty Brunton as Ragged-and-Tough, J. Howard as Popps, Mr. Morrison as Joe, F. H. Henry as Billy, Miss Laporte as Mrs. Snobbs, Georgiana Lebatt as Jane, Mrs. Manders as Maud.

CHEAP JACK; OR, LOVED AND DECEIVED// D 3a// Edward Towers// **Pavilion**, Apr. 1874.

CHECKMATE// C 2a// Andrew Halliday// **Royalty**, July 1869.

CHEER, BOYS, CHEER// D 4a// Augustus Harris, Cecil Raleigh, & Henry Hamilton// **Drury Lane**, Sept. 1895, with Fanny Brough as Lady Hilyard, Pattie Browne as Kitty, Fannie Ward as Mrs. Cholmondley, Eleanor Calhoun as Blanche, Henry Neville as Marquis of Chepstone, Sidney Howard as Lord Archibald, Hamilton Revelle as Hilyard, Charles Dalton as Fitzdavis, Lionel Rignold as Meikstein, William Rignold as Rev. Nugent/ Scenery by Robert Caney, Mr. Schweitzer, & Joseph Harker/ Machines by E. A. Taylor/ Prod. by Augustus Harris/ Music by J. M. Glover/ Transf. to **Olympic**, Dec. 1895.

CHERRY BOUNCE// F 1a// R. J. Raymond// **Sad. Wells**, Nov. 1843, with Mr. Williams as Oldrents, J. B. Hill as Gammon, W. H. Williams as Gregory, Robert Romer as Springe, Miss Cooke as Mrs. Homespun/ **Astley's**, May 1849, with Mr. Johnson as Oldrents, Mr. Adrian as Gregory, Stephen Smith as Gammon, Mr. Crowther as Spinage, Helen Lane as Mrs. Homespun.

CHERRY HALL// Play 3a// Forbes Dawson// **Avenue**, June 1894, with Charles Glenney as Trevor, J. A. Rosier as Lord Baynton, W. L. Abingdon as Lord Elgar, Gilbert Trent as Dr. Taylor, Lawrance d'Orsay as Walter Stockson, Compton Coutts as Jock Stockson, Mrs. Bennett as Lady Baynton, Ettie Williams as Miss Metcalf, Marjorie Christmas as Mrs. Taylor, Dora Baston as Mabel.

CHESTERFIELD THINSKIN// F 1a// J. M. Maddox// **Princess's**, July 1853, with John Pritt Harley as Thinskin, Mr. Addison as Brangle, John Chester as Redthorn, Drinkwater Meadows as Burr, J. Collins as John, Miss Vivash as Miss Brangle.

CHEVALIER ST. GEORGE, THE// D 3a// Adap. fr F of Duveyrier ("Melesville") & Roger de Beauvoir// **Princess's**, May 1845, with J. W. Wallack, Mrs. Stirling/ **Surrey**, Nov. 1859, with Edith Heraud, Mr. Shepherd.

CHILD OF THE REGIMENT; OR, THE DAUGHTER OF A THOUSAND FATHERS// D// Dram. vers. of Donizetti's Figlia del Regimento// **Victoria**, Aug. 1857, with W. H. Pitt as Sgt. Bombard, Charles Rice as Felix, J. Howard as Hurtenstone, Mr. Morrison as Jose, Mrs. J. H. Rickards as Duchess of Crankenthorp, Miss Bailey as Lisetta, Clara St. Casse as Georgette, Julia Seaman as Marie, Mrs. Alfred Saville as Susanne.

CHILD OF THE SUN, THE// D 3a// John Brougham// **Astley's**, Oct. 1865, with Adah Isaacs Menken in 4 char. parts, J. Elphinstone as Don Pedro, Basil Potter as Don Fernande and as Fray Renito, T. J. Anderson as Roderigues, Edward Atkins as Coon, Edmund Garden as California Pat, W. M. Terrott as Diego, Mrs. St. Henry as Senora Orviedo, Kate Carson as Juanita, J. B. Johnstone as Kanisko/ Scenery by Charles & William Brew/ Music by J. H. Tully & W. H. Montgomery/ Machines by Mr. Lanham/ Prod, by Mr. Friend.

CHILD OF THE WRECK, THE// D 2a// J. R. Planché// **Drury Lane**, Oct. 1837, with Mr. Cooper as Hartmann, A. Brindal as Albert, Mlle. [sic] Celeste as Maurice, William Bennett as Greindel, R. McIan as Frantz, Robert Honner as Christopher, Mrs. Charles Jones as Mme. Tremens, Miss Fitzwalter as Sophia/ Scenery by Grieve, T. Grieve & W. Grieve/ Music by T. Cooke/ **Haymarket**, July 1838, with Charles Perkins as Hartman, Edmund Glover as Albert, Mlle. [sic] Celeste as Maurice, Robert Strickland as Greindel, Benjamin Webster as Frautz, Mrs. W. Clifford as Mme. Tremens, Miss Cooper as Sophia/ **Adelphi**, Feb. 1853, with Samuel Emery as Hartman, John Parselle as Albert, Mme. Celeste as Maurice, William Cullenford as Girondel, Mrs. Keeley as Frantz, Miss Keeley as Sophia, Mrs. Laws as Mme. Tremens/ **Lyceum**, Feb. 1859/ **Sad. Wells**, May 1863, with James Johnstone as Hartman, Mr. Britten as Albert, William Worboys as Frantz, J. W. Collier as Grummel, Mme. Celeste as Maurice, Mr. Stalman as Christopher, Miss Rawlings as Mme. Fremens, Kate Lemmon as Sophie.

CHILD STEALER, THE// D Pro & 3a// Adap. by W. E. Suter fr F// **Grecian**, June 1866, with Charles Mortimer as Chesterton, Samuel Perfitt as Seymore, J. Jackson as Poynter, Alfred Rayner as Simpson, Henry Grant as Rutherford, Lizzie Mandlebert as Jane, William James as Lt. Weston, John Manning as Nibbs, George Gillett as Arthur, Harriet Western as Lady Marian, Mary A. Victor as Miss Touchemup.

CHILDREN IN THE WOOD, THE// D// n.a.// **Sad. Wells**, Apr. 1837, with Mr. Campbell as Walter, H. George as Lord Alford, Mr. King as Lord Roland, John Ayliffe as Apathy, Mr. Ede as Oliver, Thomas Lee as Gabriel, Miss Williams as Lady Alford, Mrs. Harris as Dame, Lavinia Melville as Josephine/ **Haymarket**, Dec. 1840, with George Bennett as Sir Rowland, Henry Howe as Lord Alford, James Wallack as Walter, Robert Strickland as Apathy, O. Smith as Oliver, W. H. Oxberry as Gabriel, Priscilla Horton as Josephine, Miss Grove as Lady Helen, Mrs. Stanley as Winifred/ **Drury Lane**, Feb. 1850, with Thomas Barry as Sir Rowland, Mr. Frazer as Lord Alford, Samuel Emery as Walter, Mr. Manderson as Oliver, William Davidge as Apathy, W. H. Angel as Gabriel, Clara Tellett as Josephine, Miss Morant as Lady Helen, Mrs. Griffith as Winifred.

CHILDREN OF THE CASTLE, THE// D 3a// Edward Fitzball// **Marylebone**, Nov. 1857.

CHILDREN OF THE GHETTO// D 4a// Israel Zangwill// **Adelphi**, Dec. 1899, with Wilton MacKaye as Shemuel, Robert Edeson as Brandon, William Norris as Melchitsedek, Adolphe Lestina as Ansell, Morris Wright as Wolf, Gus Frankel as Guedalyah, Emil Hoch as Birnbaum, Frank Cornell as Phillips, Ada Curry as Becky, Louise Muldener as Mrs. Jacobs, Ada Dwyer as Malka, Laura Almonsino as Milly, Ellen Burg as Leah, Mrs. B. M. de Solla as Beggar Woman/ Scenery by Gates & Morange/ Music by William Furst.

CHILI WIDOW, THE// C 3a// Adap. by Arthur Bourchier & Alfred Sutro fr F of Alexandre Bisson & Fabrice Carré, M. le Directeur// **Royalty**, Sept. 1895, with Arthur Bourchier as Sir Reginald, Cosmo Stuart as Lavender, William Blakeley as Crabbe, Welton Dale as Martindale, Frank Lindo as Crawley, Charles Troode as Fielding, Ernest Hendrie as O'Dwyer, Sophie Larkin as Mrs. Jeffries, Violet Vanbrugh as Gladys, Kate Phillips as Honor, Irene Vanbrugh as Dulcie/ Scenery by W. Hemsley.

CHIMES, THE// D 4a// Dram. by Mark Lemon & Gilbert à Beckett fr story of Charles Dickens// **Adelphi**, Dec. 1844.

CHIMES, THE// D 4a// Dram. by Edward Stirling fr story of Charles Dickens// **Lyceum**, Jan. 1845.

CHIMNEY CORNER, THE// D 2a// H. T. Craven// **Olympic**, Feb. 1861, with Horace Wigan as Old Probity, Frederick Robson as Peter Probity, Walter Gordon as John Probity, Gaston Murray as Chetty, Harwood Cooper as Sifter, Mrs. Leigh Murray as Mrs. Probity, Miss Hughes as Grace/ **St. James's**, Feb. 1868, with Mr. Evans as Old Probity, H. T. Craven as Peter Probity, Mr. Stretton as John Probity, Thomas Bridgeford as Sifter, Miss Marion as Grace, Sophie Larkin as Patty.

CHIMNEY PIECE, THE// F 1a// G. H. Rodwell// **Cov. Garden**, Feb. 1837, with William Farren as Muddlebrain, John Webster as Frederick, Benjamin Webster as Shuffle, Mr. Tilbury as Horn, Miss Pelham as Lucretia, Miss Nicholson as Mary/ **Sad. Wells**, June 1837, with Mr. Tilbury as Muddlebrain, C. H. Pitt as Frederick, Benjamin Conquest as Shuffle, Mr. Griffiths as Horn, Lavinia Melville as Lucretia, Mrs. Harris as Mary.

CHINESE ROMANCE, A// C// F. L. Horne// **Sad. Wells**, Oct. 1862, with C. Lloyds as Moneygrub, Alfred Montague as Octavius, Mr. Fisher as Maj. Baldhead, Thomas Mowbray as Capt. Wary, Charles Crook as Flexible, James Johnstone as Tackle, Miss Clements as Florence, Emily Dowton as Susan, Mrs. William Dowton as Mrs. Olderaft.

CHIP OF THE OLD BLOCK, THE// C 1a// E. P. Knight// **Victoria**, Apr. 1838, with Mr. Loveday as Sir Arthur, Mr. Harwood as Capt. Single, W. H. Oxberry as Fairland, William Davidge as Andrew, Alfred Rayner as Chip, Mrs. Loveday as Lady Evergreen, Miss Lee as Emma, Mrs. Frank Matthews as Rose, Miss Wilson as Jane.

CHISELLING// F 1a// James Albery & Joseph Dilley// **Vaudeville**, Aug. 1870/ **Gaiety**, May 1886.

CHIVALRY// Play 4a// Richard Lee// **Globe**, Sept. 1873, with Charles Harcourt as Charles Hantayne, H. J. Montague as Philip, Samuel Emery as Bayard, George Vincent as Col. Kirke, E. W. Garden as Mallock, J. H. Allen as Trenchard, Frank Selby as Luttrell, Carlotta Addison as Lillian Avenant, Louisa Manders as Dame Thorne/ Scenery by Gordon, Callcott, & Harford/ Music by Richard Lee & T. Gough.

CHOPS OF THE CHANNEL, THE// F 1a// Frederick Hay// **Strand**, July 1869.

CHOPSTICKS AND SPIKINS// F 1a// Paul Meritt// **Grecian**, Sept. 1873// **Gaiety**, May 1883.

CHRISTENING, THE// F// J. B. Buckstone// **Haymarket**, Feb. 1850, with J. B. Buckstone as Twiddy, Mr. Tilbury as Grum, Henry Vandenhoff as Wharton, A. Brindal as Pilbury, Mrs. Keeley as Dolly, Mrs. W. Clifford as Mrs. Carney, Mrs. Stanley as Mrs. Motherton, Mrs. Caulfield as Mrs. Pilbury.

CHRISTIAN, THE// D Pro & 4a// Hall Caine// **Duke of York's,** Oct. 1899, with Herbert Waring as Storm, Charles Groves as Wealthy, Ben Webster as Drake, Percy Lyndal as Bro. Paul, Charles Fulton as Father Lamplugh, E. Allan Aynesworth as Lord Robert, George Raiemond as Quayle, J. C. Buckstone as Lorimer, J. W. MacDonald as Lord Storm, Evelyn Millard as Glory, Lilly Caine as Polly, Janet Evelyn as Nelly, Ethel Henry as Letty, Lizzie Scobie as Mrs. Callender, Maude Sinclair as Aggie/ Scenery by E. Banks & B. Hicks.

CHRISTINA// D 4a// Percy Lynwood & Mark Ambient// **POW,** Apr. 1887/ **Olympic,** Mar. 1888, with E. S. Willard as Count Freund, Frank Archer as Beltravers, R. S. Boleyn as Prince Koroskoff, Yorke Stephens as Capt. Arden, E. Smedley Yates as O'Sullivan, E. M. Robson as George, Frank Rodney as Alexis, Alma Murray as Princess Christina, Rose Leclercq as Mme. Morozoff, Adrienne Dairolles as Cherubine, Helen Leyton as Hortense/ Scenery by Julian Hicks, Walter Hann & E. G. Banks/ Limelight by Mr. Kerr/ Prod. by E. S. Willard.

CHRISTINE; OR, THE POISONERS OF PARIS// D// n.a.// **Sad. Wells,** Mar. 1842, with Mr. Dry as de la Reynie, E. Morton as De Bussy, Mr. Lyon as Beauvillars, John Herbert as Eucroe, Charles Fenton as Destinelli, Mrs. Robert Honner as Louise, Miss Richardson as Christine, Mrs. Henry Marston as Catherine/ Scenery by F. Fenton, G. Smithyes Jr., & Mr. Daniels/ Machines by Mr. Cawdrey, Music by Isaac Collins/ Prod. by R. Honner.

CHRISTMAS DINNER, A// C 1a// Adap. by Tom Taylor fr F, Je Dine Chez ma Mére/ **Olympic,** Apr. 1860, with Walter Gordon as Lord Beaudésert, Frederick Vining as Sir Peregrine, Horace Wigan as Hogarth, Miss Seymour as Pompey, Henry Rivers as Casserolle, Mrs. Stirling as Peg Woffington, Mrs. W. S. Emden as Patchett.

CHRISTMAS EVE// F 1a/ C. S. Cheltenam// **St. James's,** Apr. 1871, with Lionel Brough as Brown, Harry Cox as Smythe, Julian Crosse as O'Barlock.

CHRISTMAS EVE; OR, THE DUEL IN THE SNOW// D 3a// Edward Fitzball// **Drury Lane,** Mar. 1860, with Samuel Emery as Sir Charles, Robert Roxby as Capt. Dartford, Mr. Douglas as Moncton, Mr. Warren as Eustache, Mrs. Dowton as Emily, Miss E. Howard as Gimp.

CHRONONHOTONTHOLOGOS// Mock T 1a// Harrey Carey// **Gaiety,** Nov. 1880.

CHURCH AND STAGE// D 5a// G. W. Reynolds// **Avenue,** Apr. 1888.

CHURCH AND STAGE// Play 1a// Malcolm Watson// **Criterion,** Dec. 1900.

CHURCHWARDEN, THE// F 3a// Trans. by C. Ogden & H. Cassell fr G of Rudolph Kneisel, & adap. to Engl. stage by Edward Terry// **Olympic,** Dec. 1886, with Edward Terry as Chuffy, T. C. Valentine as Gaddam, Alfred Bishop as Bearder, John Clulow as Bilton, J. G. Taylor as Alfred, Maria Jones as Amelia, Clara Cowper as Kate, Miss S. Stanhope as Amanda, Lottie Harcourt as Jane/ **Terry's,** Oct. 1887.

CIGARETTE-MAKER'S ROMANCE, A// Play 3a// Dram. by Charles Hannon fr novel of Marion Crawford// **Court,** Feb. 1901/ **Apollo,** May 1901.

CINDERELLA// D 3a// Edward Towers// **Pavilion,** June 1881.

CINQ MARS// D// Alwyne Maude & Maurice Minton// **Olympic,** Jan. 1883.

CIRCASSIAN, THE// Adap. by F. W. Broughton fr F of Emile Blavet & Fabrice Carré, Le Voyage au Caucase// **Criterion,** Nov. 1887.

CIRCUMSTANCES ALTER CASES// C 1a// I. G. Asher// **Gaiety,** June 1889.

CITY MADAM, THE// C// Adap. fr orig. of Philip Massinger// **Sad. Wells,** Oct. 1844, with George Bennett as Sir John, Samuel Phelps as Luke Frugal, A. Younge as Sir Maurice, John Webster as Edmund, Henry Marston as Plenty, Edward Knight as Hoyst, Mr. Williams as Holdfast, Mrs. Mary Warner as Lady Frugal, Miss Huddart as Ann, Miss Cooper as Mary, Miss Lebatt as Millicent, Georgiana Lebatt as Mistress Charmer/ Scenery by F. Fenton/ Machines by Mr. Cawdery.

CIVIL WAR// D 4a// Adap. by Herman Merivale fr F of Albert Delpit, Mademoiselle de Bressier// **Gaiety,** June 1887.

CIVILIZATION// D 5a// Founded by J. A. Wilkens on Le Huron & Voltaire's L'Ingénu// **City of London,** Nov. 1852/ **Strand,** Jan. 1853/ **Drury Lane,** Apr. 1853/ **Marylebone,** Oct. 1857.

CLAIMANT, THE; OR, THE LOST ONE FOUND// D// H. P. Grattan// **Surrey,** Apr. 1872.

CLAIMANTS// D 1a// Adap. by Herman Vezin fr G of August von Kotzebue & Schneider// **Matinée,** Nov. 1898.

CLAM// D 3a// C. H. Ross// **Surrey,** Apr. 1870/ **Grecian,** July 1870, with Samuel Perfitt as Capt. Weatherwell, Walter Holland as Hartley, William James as Warrington, Miss Dearlove as Mrs. Warrington, Miss Gerrish as Carrie, J. Jackson as Webb, G. H. MacDermott as Swift, John Manning as Doubledick, Lizzie Mandelbert as Clam, Alice Denvil as Nelly/ Scenery by Mr. Messender.

CLANDESTINE MARRIAGE, THE// C 5a// David Garrick & George Colman the elder// **Cov. Garden,** Jan. 1837, with William Farren as Lord Ogleby, John Webster as Sir John, Mr. Tilbury as Stirling, John Pritchard as Lovewell, Benjamin Webster as Canton, Henry Wallack as Brush, Eliza Vincent as Fanny, Miss Pelham as Miss Stirling, Mrs. Julia Glover as Mrs. Heidelberg, Miss Lee as Betty/

Haymarket, June 1837, with William Farren as Ogleby, Robert Strickland as Sterling, John Webster as Sir John, J. T. Haines as Lovewell, Benjamin Webster as Canton, J. W. Gough as Sgt. Flower, J. Worrell as Truman, T. F. Mathews as Traverse, Mrs. Julia Glover as Mrs. Heidelberg, Mrs. W. Clifford as Miss Sterling, Eliza Vincent as Fanny/ **Strand**, Nov. 1849, with Mrs. Julia Glover, Mrs. Stirling, William Farren/ **Olympic**, Sept. 1853, with William Farren as Lord Ogleby, F. Charles as Melvil, George Cooke as Sterling, William Farren Jr. as Lovewell, E. Clifton as Sgt. Flower, Alfred Sanger as Traverse, John Kinloch as Canton, William Shalders as Brush, Mrs. Alfred Phillips as Mrs. Heidelberg, Harriet Gordon as Miss Sterling, Isabel Adams as Betty, Sarah Lyons as Fanny/ **Sad. Wells**, Nov. 1857, with Samuel Phelps as Lord Ogleby, Henry Marston as Melvil, Frederic Robinson as Lovewell, J. W. Ray as Sterling, Mr. Williams as Canton, William Belford as Brush, Miss Fitzpatrick as Miss Sterling, Mrs. Charles Young as Fanny, Mrs. Henry Marston as Mrs. Heidelberg, Eliza Travers as Betty/ **Gaiety**, Apr. 1874, with Samuel Phelps, Hermann Vezin, Charles Harcourt, Robert Soutar, Mrs. Leigh, John Maclean.

CLANRONALD: THE USURPER OF GLENCAIRN// D 2a// n.a.// **Victoria**, June 1850, with Mr. Henderson as Clanronald, Miss Vaul as Adelbert, J. T. Johnson as Matthew, J. Neville as Andrew, John Hudspeth as Sandy, Amelia Mercer as Adela, Georgiana Lebatt as Marian, Mrs. Cooke as Mause.

CLARA VERE DE VERE// Play 4a// Dram. by Campbell Rae-Brown fr Tennyson// **POW**, June 1888.

CLARENCE CLEVEDON, HIS STRUGGLES FOR LIFE OR DEATH// D 3a// Edward Stirling// **Victoria**, Apr. 1849.

CLARI; OR, THE MAID OF MILAN// John Howard Payne & J. R. Planché// **Sad. Wells**, May 1840, with Mr. Elvin as Duke Vivaldi, Henry Marston as Rolamo, J. B. Hill as Jocoso, Edmund Garden as Claudio, Mr. Aldridge as Nicolo, Mr. Richardson as Gironio, J. W. Collier as Nimpedo, Mrs. Robert Honner as Clari, Miss Richardson as Fidalma, Mrs. J. F. Saville as Ninetta/ **Grecian**, Mar. 1844, with Edwin Dixon as Duke Vivaldi, Edmund Garden as Jocose, Mr. Campbell as Rolamo, Frederick Robson as Nimpedo, Mr. Baldwin as Geronio, Henry Bedford as Nicolo, Marian Taylor as Clari, Annette Mears as Vespina, Mary A. Crisp as Nisetta, G. Norman as Pelgrine, John Collett as Nobleman.

CLARICE; OR, ONLY A WOMAN// D Pro & 4a// Walter Browne & Frank Roberts// **Strand**, Nov. 1886.

CLARISSA// D 4a// Dram. by Robert Buchanan fr novel of Richardson// **Vaudeville**, Feb. 1890, with Thomas Horne as Belford, T. B. Thal berg as Lovelace, Cyril Maude as Solmes, Oswald Yorke as Capt. Harlowe, Fred Grove as Sir Harry, Frank Gillmore as Aubrey, Fred Thorne as Capt. Macshane, Winifred Emery as Clarissa, Mary Collette as Jenny, Coralie Owen as Mrs. Osborne, Lily Hanbury as Sally/ Scenery by Walter Hann, William Perkins & W. T. Hemsley.

CLARISSA HARLOWE// D 3a// Dram. by T. H. Lacy & George Courtney fr novel of Richardson// **Princess's**, Nov. 1846, with John Ryder as Harlowe, Mr. Paulo as Anthony, Charles Fisher as James, Mrs. Fosbroke as Mrs. Harlowe, Mrs. Henry Hughes as Arabella, Mrs. Stirling as Clarissa, James Vining as Lovelace, Henry Hughes as Macdonald, Miss Marshall as Mary, Miss Somers as Mrs. Smith.

CLARISSE; OR, THE MERCHANT'S DAUGHTER// D// Adap. by Edward Stirling fr F, Le Canal Saint-Martin// **Adelphi**, Sept. 1845, with O. Smith as Laroche, J. Worrell as Armand, Benjamin Webster as Martial, James Munyard as John Cabot, Edward Wright as Barbillon, Paul Bedford as Galon, William Cullenford as Martin, Mr. Freeborn as Joseph, Mme. Celeste as Clarisse, Sarah Woolgar as Milanie/ Scenery by Pitt & Johnstone/ Machinery by Mr. Cooper/ Music by Alfred Mellon.

CLAUDE DUVAL// F 1a// T. P. Taylor// **City of London**, May 1842.

CLAUDE DUVAL THE HIGHWAYMAN OF HOLLOWAY; OR, WOMAN, WINE, THE GAMING TABLE, AND THE ROAD// D 3a// W. Moncrieff// **Sad. Wells**, Apr. 1843, with E. Morton as Charles II, Mr. Lambe as Lord Talbot, Mr. Beale as Lord Chesterfield, G. Norman as Capt. Ogle, John Herbert as Jacques, Mr. Starmer as Sir Charles, Mr. Williams as Dr. Van Opal, Mr. Collins as Claude, Mr. Aldridge as Jervis, Robert Romer as Maj. Clancy, J. B. Hill as Lovelocks, Miss M. Lee as Queen Catherine, Helen Lane as Estelle, Miss M. S. Taylor as Aurelia, Miss Richardson as Duchess, Mrs. Richard Barnett as Nelly, Mrs. Andrews as Mme. La Trappe/ Scenery by F. Fenton/ Machines by Mr. Cawdery, Music by Mr. Hudson/ Prod. by Mr. Collins.

CLAUDE DUVAL, THE LADIES' HIGHWAYMAN; OR, THE HUNCHBACK OF THE SANCTUARY// D// J. T. Haines// **Victoria**, June 1857, with Mr. Morrison as Sir Stephen, Mr. Henderson as Col. Shelton, W. H. Pitt as Seldon, George Pearce as Col. Braddock, Frederick Byefield as Capt. Errall, H. Dudley as Neverright, J. H. Rickards as Duval, S. Sawford as Maj. Clancy, J. Howard as Ellgood, Charles Rice as Scraggs, Julia Seaman as Mabel, Mrs. J. H. Rickards as Lady Araminta, Miss Laporte as Meg, Mrs. Alfred Saville as Poll/ Prod. by J. Johnson Towers.

CLAUDIAN// Play Pro & 3a// Henry Herman & W. G. Wills// **Princess's**, Dec. 1883, with Wilson Barrett as Claudian, E. S. Willard as Clement, Frank Cooper as Theorus, Frank Huntley as Zosimus, Neville Doone as Volpas, C. Fulton as Symachus, Emmeline Ormsby as Serena, Clifford Cooper as Alcares, George Barrett as Belos, Helen Vincent as Edessa, Nellie Palmer as Clia, Mrs. Huntley as Galena, Mary Eastlake as Almida/ Scenery by Walter

Hann, Stafford Hill & William Telbin/ Music by Edward Jones/ Prod. by Wilson Barrett.

CLEAN YOUR BOOTS// F 1a// J. Bruton// **Surrey**, May 1858/ **Astley's** Nov. 1859, with S. Johnson as Old Comfit, George Belmore as Puppy, Mr. Jones as Dob, Mrs. William Dowton as Mrs. Comfit, Miss E. Dowton as Emily, Julia Weston as Becky.

CLEFT STICK, A// C 3a// John Oxenford// **Olympic**, Nov. 1865, with Horace Wigan as Fix, Frederick Younge as Tackleback, Mr. Andrews as Daffodil, Mr. Franks as Bankes, Charles Cowdery as Jackson, Mrs. Stephens as Mrs. Strombelow, Miss Beauclerc as Mrs. Fix, Mrs. St. Henry as Sibylla, Ellen Farren as Phoebe, Ada Harland as Fatima.

CLEMENTINA// F// Edward Moncrieffe// **Surrey**, Sept. 1892.

CLEOPATRA// FC 3a// Adap. by Arthur Shirley fr F, Les Amours de Cléopatre// **Shaftesbury**, June 1891, with Harry Paulton as Rawkins, Fred Mervin as Vane, W. S. Buist as Lupton, Algernon Newark as Jelks, Herman de Lange as Mowler, E. Stirling as Landlord, Lilian Hingston as Milly, Maud Milton as Cleopatra.

CLERICAL ERROR, A// C 1a// Henry Arthur Jones// **Court**, Oct. 1879/ **Drury Lane**, May 1883, with Wilson Barrett as Capel, E. S. Willard as Dick, George Barrett as Perry, Mary Eastlake as Minnie/ **Olympic**, Dec. 1890, with W. A. Elliott as Rev. Capel, T. W. Percyval as Richard, Lily Hanbury as Minnie, Austin Melford as Perry.

CLERK OF ISLINGTON, THE (see also, My Fellow Clerk)// F// John Oxenford// **Sad. Wells**, May 1840, with Mr. Williams as Hooker, Henry Marston as Tactic, J. W. Collier as Victim, Mr. Richardson as Fag, Miss Cooke as Mrs. Dobson, Mrs. J. F. Saville as Fanny, Mrs. Richard Barnett as Juliet.

CLEVER ALICE// FC 3a// Adap. by Brandon Thomas fr G of Adolf Willbrandt// **Royalty**, Apr. 1893, with Janet Achurch.

CLEVER SIR JACOB// C 1a// P. Toft & Percival Graves// **Gaiety**, Dec. 1873/ **Globe**, May 1874, with Lionel Brough as Sir Jacob Fluff, V. Robinson as George Wentworth, George Temple as Capt. Sterling, J. H. Allen as Wentworth, Maria Harris as Ida Wentworth, Miss T. Lavis as Mrs. Rumbold.

CLIMBING BOY, THE// D// R. B. Peake// **Victoria**, Mar. 1838, with Mr. Loveday as Strawberry, John Parry as Sir Gilbert, William Davidge as Buzzard, Mr. Salter as Slinker, Rebecca Isaacs as The Climbing Boy, W. H. Oxberry as Jack Rag, Mrs. Loveday as Prudence, Mrs. Frank Matthews as Rebecca, Miss Lee as Rosalie/ **Olympic**, Mar. 1844, with Mr. Brookes as Strawberry, Thomas Green as Sir Gilbert, Mr. Turnour as Buzzard, Miss Goodwin as the Climbing Boy, George Wild as Ragg, Mr. Thornton as Mordaunt, Mr. Scott as Courtroll, Mrs. Sarah Garrick as Miss Prudence, Lavinia Melville as Rosalie, Miss Lebatt as Rebecca.

CLIO// Play 5a// Bartley Campbell// **Elephant & Castle**, Aug. 1885.

CLITO// T 5a// Sidney Grundy & Wilson Barrett// **Princess's**, May 1886, with Wilson Barrett as Clito, Mary Eastlake as Helle, E. S. Willard as Glaucias, Charles Hudson as Critias, Austin Melford as Theramenes, J. H. Clynds as Xenocles, Charles Fulton as Dares, S. M. Carson as Atys, W. A. Elliott as Corax, Carrie Coote as Irene, Eva Wilson as Chloe/ Scenery by William Telbin, Stafford Hall & Walter Hann/ Music by Edward Jones/ Prod. by Wilson Barrett.

CLOAK AND THE BONNET, THE// C 1a// n.a.// **Engl. Opera House** (Lyceum), Aug. 1841, with Robert Maywood as Jemmie Laidlaw, Charles Selby as Woodford, Augustus Harris as Aylmer, Miss Fitzwalter as Ann, Mrs. Harris as Mary.

CLOCK ON THE STAIRS, THE// D 1a// C. H. Hazlewood// **Britannia**, Feb. 1862.

CLOCKMAKER'S HAT, THE// F 1a// T. W. Robertson// **Olympic**, Jan. 1860, with George Cooke as Col. Capstick, F. Charles as Christopher, Charles Bender as Fubbs, Harwood Cooper as Duplex, Miss Herbert as Mrs. Capstick, Mrs. Stephens as Jemima, Mrs. W. S. Emden as Sally/ **Princess's**, Apr. 1887, with E. Gurney as Col. Capstick, Hudson Howard as Christopher, Mr. Shaw as Fubbs, A. Holles as Duplex, Miss Beckett as Mrs. Capstick, Miss Lyndhurst as Jemima, Miss Hampton as Sally.

CLOSE SHAVE, A// F// T. W. Speight// **Haymarket**, Aug. 1884, with Henry Kemble as Chirrup, Mr. Morgan as Larkin, Stewart Dawson as Bangle, Mr. Moynham as Wiggins, James Francis as Duffle, Maude Williamson as Mrs. Chirrup, Augusta Wilton as Bella.

CLOUD AND SUNSHINE; OR, LOVE'S REVENGE// D 4a// James Anderson// **Drury Lane**, Feb. 1858, with Robert Roxby as Marquis de Marcilly, John Kinloch as Count de Roqueteuille, Mr. Carter as de Lusignan, R. H. Lingham as Richelieu, James Anderson as both Dunois twins, A. Younge as Leslie, Miss Elsworthy as Diana, Mrs. Selby as Countess Dunois.

CLOUD OF LIFE// n.a.// **Grecian**, May 1859.

CLOUDS AND SUNSHINE IN A LIFE, THE// D 3a// Adolphe Faucquez// **Sad. Wells**, Sept. 1862, with Henry Forrester as James Clark, W. H. Stephens as Richard Clark, E. F. Edgar as Charlton, Charles Crook as Sam, Sophie Miles as Sophia, Emily Dowton as Lucy, Alfred Montague as Alfred, Lewis Ball as Crayon, Fanny Rivers as Clara, Mr. Regan as Wormly.

CLOVEN FOOT, THE// Dram. by Frederick Mouillot & Janet Steer fr novel of Miss Braddon// **Pavilion**, June 1890/ **Grand**, June

1891.

CLUB BABY, THE// FC 3a// Lawrence Sterner & Edward Knoblauch// **Avenue**, Apr. 1898.

CLYTIE// D 5a// J. P. Hatton// **Olympic**, Jan. 1876, with F. H. Macklin as Mayfield, Alfred Nelson as Ransforth, John Vollaire as Waller, Mr. Odell as Cuffing, Mr. Haywell as Holland, Mr. Winstanley as Horton, Henrietta Hodson as Mary, Louisa Howard as Mrs. Wilding, Annie Taylor as Sarah, Ellen Cowle as Madge/ Scenery by Julian Hicks,

COAL AND COKE// F// Charles Harding & W. H. Swanborough// **Strand**, Jan. 1868.

COAL MINE, THE// D// J. B. Buckstone// **Pavilion**, Mar. 1867.

COALS OF FIRE, THE// CD 3a// H. T. Craven// **Court**, Nov. 1871.

COAT OF MANY COLOURS, A// C 4a// Maude Ryley// **West London**, July 1897.

COBBLER'S DAUGHTER, THE// D 4a// Mrs. S. Lane// **Britannia**, Mar. 1878.

COBWEBS// C 3a// Charles Wills// **Vaudeville**, Mar. 1880.

COERCION// FC 3a// W. H. Denney & Thomas Burnside// **Gaiety**, Nov. 1886.

COEUR DE LION; OR, THE MAID OF JUDAH// D// Charles Cooke// **Victoria**, Sept. 1876.

COINER'S DREAM, THE// D 1a// Cecil Noel// **Standard**, July 1899.

COLLABORATORS, THE// F 1a// C. Haddon Chambers// **Vaudeville**, Jan. 1892.

COLLABORATORS, THE// F 1a// Lord Kilmarnock// **Matinée**, July 1897.

COLLEEN BAWN, THE; OR, THE BRIDES OF GARYOWEN// D 3a// Dram. by Dion Boucicault fr novel of Gerald Griffin, The Collegians// **Adelphi**, Oct. 1860, with Agnes Robertson (Mrs. Dion Boucicault) as Ely O'Conner, Mrs. Alfred Mellon (Sarah Woolgar) as Anne, Mrs. John Billington as Mrs. Cregan, Mrs. Chatterley as Sheelah, Lydia Foote as Darcie, Dion Boucicault as Myles-na-Coppaleen, John Billington as Cregan, Edmund Falconer as Danny Mann, David Fisher as Kyrle Daly, C. J. Smith as Corrigan, C. H. Stephenson as Father Tom, J. G. Warde as Hyland, Robert Romer as O'More/ **Astley's**, Dec. 1861, with Marian Lacey as Eily O'Conner, Caroline Carson as Ann Chute, Angelina Bathurst as Mrs. Cregan, D. W. Larson as Miles Na' Coppaleen, William McIntyre as Cregan, Charles James as Corrigan, Robert Lees as O'More, William Searle as Danny Man, Charles Mortimer as Daly/ Scenery by M. Comperte/ Music by Thomas Baker/ Machines by J. Mathews/ Prod. by Wm. Searle/ **Drury Lane**, Oct. 1862, with Charles Vandenhoff as Cregan, H. Harrell as Daly, Dion Boucicault as Myles na Coppaleen, Walter Searle as Danny Mann, William Holston as Corrigan, Dan Leeson as Father Tom, Mr. Denial as O'Moore, H. Morris as Creigh, Mme. Celeste as Mrs. Cregan, Sarah Stevens as Eily, Miss Latimer as Anne, Mrs. Chatterley as Sheelah, Miss Lennox as Ducie/ **Princess's**, Nov. 1867; Jan. 1896.

COLOMBA, THE CORSICAN SISTER// D 3a// Dram. fr F tale of Prosper Mérimée// **Adelphi**, Jan. 1847, with Mr. Lambert as Col. Neville, Henry Howe as Antonio Della Rebbia, Charles Selby as M. Dudevant, William Cullenford as Barricini, Paul Bedford as Brandolaccio, O. Smith as Castriconi, Mme. Celeste as Colomba, Sarah Woolgar as Chilina, Mrs. Yates as Lydia Neville/ Scenery by Pitt & Johnstone/ Music by Alfred Mellon/ Machinery by Mr. Cooper.

COLOMBE'S BIRTHDAY// Play 5a// Robert Browning// **Haymarket**, Apr. 1853, with Henry Howe as Prince Berthold, Mr. Rogers as Melchior, Barry Sullivan as Valence, William Farren as Guibert, Henry Corri as Gaucelme, George Braid as Maufroy, Mr. Tilbury as Clugny, Henry Vincent as Adolf, Helen Faucit as Colombe, Amelia Vining as Sabyne/ Scenery by George Morris & Mr. O'Conner.

COLOMBO, THE CORSICAN SISTERS// D// Dram. fr novel of Gerald Griffin, The Collegians// **Adelphi**, Dec. 1846/ **Sad. Wells**, Oct. 1868, with Miss Hazelwood as Eily, Miss Hill as Anne, Mrs. Howe as Mrs. Cregan, Miss Weston as Shelah, Miss Herbert as Kathleen, Miss Falkland as Ducie, Mr. Newbound as Cregan, W. H. Abel as Daly, Mr. Matthews as Creagh, Mr. Lacey as O'Moore, J. H. Loome as Father Tom, J. H. Fitzpatrick as Miles Na-Coppaleen/ Scenery by T. Evans.

COLONEL, THE// C 3a// Adap. by F. C. Burnand fr F of J. F. Bayard, Le Mari a la Champagne// **POW**, Feb. 1881, with Charles Coghlan, James Fernandez, Mrs. Leigh Murray, Amy Roselle, Myra Holme.

COLONEL BLOOD; OR, THE ROBBERY AT THE TOWER OF LONDON// D 3a// n.a.// **Victoria**, Aug. 1846, with Mr. Archer as Col. Blood, William Seaman as Langdale, J. Howard as Botts, G. F. Forman as Scrape, Mr. Geary as Jump, Mr. Franklin as Harrold, Mrs. Henry Vining as Catherine,, Lydia Pearce as Jenny, Mrs. Cooke as Margery, G. W. Walton as Buckingham, Alfred Raymond as Amule, Mr. Fitzjames as Shaftesbury, Mr. Hitchinson as Gresham, F. Wilton as Edwards.

COLONEL CROMWELL// D 4a// Dram. by Arthur Paterson & Charles Cartwright fr novel, Cromwell's Own// **Globe**, Oct. 1900, with Charles Goodheart as Lord Willoughby, Richard Boleyn as Col. Fairweather, Arthur Rodney as Col. Strickland, George Shelton as Sanctify Jordan, Charles Cartwright as Cromwell, Edith Cartwright as Betty Cromwell, Florence Wade as Esther, Suzanne Sheldon as Rachael.

COLONEL NEWCOME// Play 4a// Adap. by Michael Morton fr novel of Thackeray// **Terry's**,

Apr. 1901.

COLONEL SELLERS// C 5a// Dram. fr novel of Mark Twain// **Gaiety**, July 1880, with John T. Raymond, Katherine Rogers.

COLONEL'S BELLE, THE; OR, THE NON-MARRIABLES// C 2a// R. M. White// **Princess's**, May 1846, with James Vining as Count de Ruse, Leigh Murray as Maj. Vidette, Robert Roxby as Capt. Fanfaron, Emma Stanley as Mabelle, Florence Grey as Laurette, Mrs. Fosbroke as Mme. Fanfaron.

COLORADO BEETLE, THE// F// W. Minto// **Princess's**, Oct. 1877.

COLOUR SERGEANT, THE// D 1a// Brandon Thomas// **Princess's**, Feb. 1885, with John Dewhurst as William Honor, Charles Fulton as Henry Honor, H. Bernage as Tucker, George Barrett as Atkins, Mary Dickens as Nelly/ **Lyceum**, Nov. 1899, with J. Carter-Edwards as William Honour, Edward Irwin as Harry Honour, Horace Hodges as Bob Atkins, Paul Belmore as Charlie Tucker, Lillian McCarthy as Nellie/ **Olympic**, Jan. 1891, with W. A. Elliott as Honour, Edward Irwin as Harry, Austin Melford as Atkins, H. Hodges as Tucker, Lily Hanbury as Nellie.

COME HERE; OR, THE DEBUTANTE'S TEST// Play 1a// Augustin Daly// **Haymarket**, May 1876.

COMEDY AND TRAGEDY// D 5a// W. S. Gilbert// **Lyceum**, Feb. 1884, with J. H. Barnes as Duc d'Orléans, George Alexander as D'Aulnay, E. F. Edgar as Dr. Choquart, E. T. March as Abbé Dubois, Frank Griffin as De Grancy, Arthur Lewis as De la Ferté, Eileen O'Reilly as Pauline, Mary Anderson as Clarice/ Scenery by Hawes Craven/ Prod. by W. S. Gilbert/ **Haymarket**, Apr. 1890, with Nutcombe Gould as Duc d'Orleans, Fred Terry as D'Aulnay, Charles Allan as Chequart, Mr. Leith as Abbé Dubois, Mr. Warden as De Grancy, Robb Harwood as De la Ferte, Miss Aylward as Pauline, Julia Neilson as Clarice.

COMEDY OF ERRORS, A// C// William Shakespeare// **Sad. Wells**, Nov. 1855, with Mr. Lunt as Solinus, Henry M. Barrett as Aegeon, Henry Marston as Antipholus of Ephesus, Frederic Robinson as Antopholus of Syracuse, Lewis Ball as Dromio of Ephesus, Charles Fenton as Dromio of Syracuse, Walter Lacy as Balthazar, T. C. Harris as Angelo, Miss Rawlings as Emilia, Margaret Eburne as Adriana, Eliza Travers as Luciana/ **Princess's**, Feb. 1864, with W. R. Robins as Solinius, Henry Mellon as Aegeon, John Nelson as Antipholus of Ephesus, George Vining as Antipholus of Syracuse, Henry Webb as Dromio of Ephesus, Charles Webb as Dromio of Syracuse, Mr. Tapping as Balthazar, Charles Seyton as Angelo, Robert Cathcart as Dr. Pinch, Miss Stafford as Emilia, Caroline Carson as Adriana/ **Drury Lane**, Sept. 1866, with James Johnstone as Duke, Henry Sinclair as Antipholus of Ephesus, Frank Barsby as Antipholus of Syracuse, Henry Webb as Dromio of Ephesus, C. Webb as Dromio of Syracuse, Thomas Mead as Aegeon, E. Clifton as Pinch, Frederick Morton as Balthasor, George Spencer as Angelo, J. B. Johnstone as Merchant, Mrs. Henry Vandenhoff as Emilia, Isabel Adams as Adriana/ **Strand**, Jan. 1883, with J. S. Clarke, Henry Paulton, G. L. Gordon, Henrietta Lindley, Blanche Thompson.

COMEDY OF SIGHS, A// C 4a// John Todhunter// **Avenue**, Mar. 1894, with Bernard Gould as Sir Geoffrey, Yorke Stephens as Maj. Chillingworth, James Welch as Rev. Greenwell, Florence Farr as Lady Brandon, Vane Featherston as Mrs. Chillingworth, Enid Erle as Lucy/ Scenery by W. T. Hemsley.

COMFORTABLE LODGINGS// F// R. B. Peake// **Sad. Wells**, May 1851, with Mr. Williams as Capt. Benassas, Henry Mellon as Babillard, Charles Wheatleigh as Dorville, A. Younge as Sir Hippington, Frederick Younge as Rigmarole, Augustus Harris as Roue, Clara Rarcourt as Antoinette, Mrs. Henry Mellon as Mme. Pelagie.

COMFORTABLE SERVICE// F// T. H. Bayley// **Haymarket**, Oct. 1854, with Mr. Tilbury as Adm. Brown, Edward Wright as Simon, William Cullenford as Masterton, Thomas Coe as Cork, George Braid as Tierbouchon, Mrs. Poynter as Mrs. Alldove, Ellen Chaplin as Mary, Miss E. Woulds as Mrs. Jam.

COMICAL COUNTESS, A// F 1a// William Brough// **Lyceum**, Nov. 1854/ **Drury Lane**, Dec. 1855/ **Haymarket**, Apr. 1857, with William Farren as De Vilbrac, Mr. Rogers as Baron de Bergonce, Miss Talbot as Countess De L'Espalier/ **Olympic**, Mar. 1867, with Mr. Addison as The Baron, C. J. Mathews as The Chevalier, Mrs. C. J. Mathews as The Countess.

COMING HOME// D 3a// G. R. Walker// **Globe**, July 1873.

COMMISSION, A// C 1a// Weedon Grossmith// **Terry's**, June 1891/ Trans. to **Court**, Dec. 1891/ **St. James's**, May 1897, with Wilfred Draycott as Marshall, Brandon Thomas as Gloucester, Weedon Grossmith as Shaw, Lily Hanbury as Mrs. Hemmersley, May Palfrey as Parker.

COMMITTED FOR TRIAL// F 2a// F. L. Tomline// **Globe**, Jan. 1874.

COMMITTED FOR TRIAL// D 4a// Edward Towers// **East London**, Nov. 1878.

COMMON SENSE; OR, THE SLAVES OF MAMMON// D 4a// Edward Towers// **Pavilion**, May 1878.

COMPLETE CHANGE, A// F// Burnand McDonald// **St. Geo. Hall**, Jan. 1896.

COMPROMISING CASE, A// C 1a// Adap. by Mrs. T. E. Smale fr F, Le Porte Cigar// **Haymarket**, May 1888.

COMPROMISING COAT, THE// C 1a// J. T. Grein & C. W. Jarvis// **Globe**, June 1892, with Walter Everard as Thornton, Hilda Abinger as Lucy, Douglas Gordon as Fairfield, Einna Cullum as Fanny.

COMRADES: AN ANECDOTE OF THE SPANISH WAR// D 1a// n.a.// **Adelphi**, Mar. 1848, with William Cullenford as Marquis Santiago, Charles Boyce as Capt. Belancour, James Munyard as Don Domingo, C. J. Smith as Guzzleman, Redmond Ryan as Corney Casey, Emma Harding as Juanna.

COMRADES// C 3a// Brandon Thomas & B. C. Stephenson// **Court**, Feb. 1882, with John Clayton, Charles Coghlan, Arthur Cecil.

CONFEDERACY, THE// C// John Vanbrugh// **Haymarket**, June 1848, with Mr. Tilbury as Gripe, William Farren as Moneytrap, Alfred Wigan as Dick, Benjamin Webster as Brass, J. W. Gough as Clip, William Clark as Jessamin, Mrs. Nisbett as Clarissa, Mrs. Seymour as Araminta, Mrs. Julia Bennett as Corinna, Mrs. Keeley as Flippanta, Julia Glover as Mrs. Amlet, Mrs. Stanley as Mrs. Cloggit.

CONFEDERATES// D 1a// Henry Woodville// **Globe**, Jan. 1893, with Cecil Thornbury as Amos Hansen, Wilton Heriot as Dick Burton, Henry Farmer as Harry Leigh, Gordon Tomkins as Sgt. Doughty, Mabel Lane as Nora.

CONFIDENCE// C// Adap. by Dion Boucicault fr F// **Haymarket**, May 1848, with Mr. Rogers as Congreve, Benjamin Webster as Gresham, Henry Howe as St. Leger, Henry Vandenhoff as Williams, Miss Reynolds as Mrs. Gresham, Mrs. L. S. Buckingham as Mrs. Congreve.

CONFIDENCE// D 3a// R. F. Cantwell// **Britannia**, Oct. 1872.

CONFIDENTIAL CLERK, THE// FC 3a// Adap. by Sidney Wittman & Shedden Wilson fr G. of G. von Moser, Der Leibrenter// **Gaiety**, June 1886.

CONFOUNDED FOREIGNERS// F 1a// J. H. Reynolds// **Haymarket**, Jan. 1838, with Tyrone Power as Lt. O'Phelan, Robert Strickland as Western, Mr. Ranger as La Folie, Mrs. Humby as Martha, Mrs. Tayleure as Katty, Mrs. Nisbett as Rose; Oct. 1848, with Mr. Tilbury as Western, Charles Hudson as Lt. O'Phelan, Alfred Wigan as La Folie, Mrs. Stanley as Martha, Mrs. L. S. Buckingham as Rose, Mrs. Humby as Katty.

CONFUSION// FC 3a// Joseph Derrick// **Vaudeville**, May 1883, with Philip Day, Charles Groves, Fred Thorne, Sophie Larkin, Kate Bishop; May 1891/ **Drury Lane**, June 1884, with Henry Neville as Mumpleford, Charles Groves as Blizzard, E. B. Norman as Sunbery, Frederick Thorne as James, Sophie Larkin as Lucretia, Winifred Emery as Rose, Gabrielle Goldney as Violet, Kate Phillips as Maria.

CONGRESS AT PARIS, A// F// Edward Rose// **Olympic**, July 1878.

CONJUGAL LESSON, A// C 1a// Henry Danvers// **Olympic**, July 1856, with Frederick Robson as Lullaby, Mrs. Stirling as Mrs. Lullaby.

CONQUEROR'S STEED, "KARABAGH;" OR, THE PROPHET OF THE CAUCASUS// D// n.a.// **Sad. Wells**, Aug. 1842, with Mr. Dry as Khan Chaybyn, W. D. Broadfoot as Mansour, Mr. Richardson as Napsi, John Herbert as Jumbo, Mrs. Richard Barnett as Nina, Alfred Rayner as Demetrius, P. Williams as Marco, Mr. Crowther as Jaco, Mrs. Adams as Ianthe, Henry Hall as Potemkin, Charles Fenton as Stanislaus/ Scenery by T. Pitt & G. Smithyes Jr./ Prod. by W. D. Broadfoot.

CONQUERING GAME, THE// W. Bayle Bernard// **Olympic**, Nov. 1837, with William Farren as Charles XII, James Vining as Count Fritterling, James Bland as Maj. Rapp, Charles Selby as Von Lieben, Mrs. Macnamara as Baroness Ormsdoff, Mme. Vestris as Catherine.

CONQUERORS, THE// D 4a// Paul M. Potter// **St. James's**, Apr. 1898, with George Alexander as Von Rodeck, W. H. Vernon as Gen. Von Brandenberg, J. D. Beveridge as Maj. Wolfshagen, H. V. Esmond as Capt. Korner, Robert Loraine as Lt. Berent, Bertram Wallis as Lt. Heiberg, Fred Terry as Hugo, H. H. Vincent as Dagobert, H. B. Irving as Baudin, Julia Neilson as Yvonne, Fay Davis as Babiole, Constance Collier as Jeanne, Mary A. Victor as Poulette/ Scenery by H. P. Hall, William Hann & W. Telbin/ Music by W. Robins.

CONRAD AND LIZETTE; OR, LIFE ON THE MISSISSIPPI// Play 4a// n.a.// **Duke's**, Mar. 1880.

CONSCIENCE// D 4a// Edward Lytton// **Vaudeville**, July 1888.

CONSCIENCE MONEY// CD 3a// H. J. Byron// **Haymarket**, Sept. 1878, with H. J. Byron, William Terriss, John Pateman, Bella Pateman, Henry Howe.

CONSCRIPT OF LYONS, THE// F 1a// James Barber// **Astley's**, Aug. 1851, with Stephen Smith as Sgt. Francis, Arthur Stirling as Augustus, Mr. Stickney as Sub-Prefect, Thomas Barry as Bloquet, Mrs. Beacham as Adele.

CONSPIRITOR IN SPITE OF HIMSELF, A// D 2a// H. C. Coape// **Olympic**, Feb. 1852, with George Cooke as Col. Cecil, William Farren Jr. as Hastings, William H. Norton as Ogilvie, William Farren as Inkhorn, Henry Compton as Von Block, Louisa Howard as Bertha, Mrs. B. Bartlett as Margaret.

CONSTANCE FRERE// Play Pro & 3a// Herbert Gough & Morris Edwards// **Vaudeville**, June 1887.

CONTEMPT OF COURT// C 3a// Dion Boucicault// **Marylebone**, Oct. 1879.

CONTESTED ELECTION, THE// C 3a// Tom Taylor// **Haymarket**, July 1859, with C. J. Mathews as Dodgson, William Farren as Wapshott, Henry Compton as Honeybun, J. B. Buckstone as Peckover, Mr. Rogers as Topper, William Cullenford as Crawley, J. Worrell as Copperthwaite, Mrs. C. J. Mathews (Lizzie Davenport) as Mrs. Honeybun, Fanny Wright as Clara/ Scenery by Mr. O'Conner & George Morris/ Machines by Oliver Wales.

CONVENT BELLES// C// Edward Fitzball// **Olympic**, 1841.

CONVERT, THE// D 4a// Trans. by Constance Garnett fr Rus. of Sergius Stepniak// **Avenue**, June 1898, with Laurence Irving as Murinov, Charles Charrington as Count Mentrirov, Herbert Swears as Volkov, Clifton Tabor as Norov, W. L. Belmore as Gorlov, Mrs. Theodore Wright as Mme. Murinov, Margaret Halstan as Katia, Suzanne Sheldon as Mme. Gorlov, Marguerite Roche as Akoulina.

CONVICT, THE// D// n.a.// **City of London**, Nov. 1838.

CONVICT, THE; OR, THE BRANDED FELON OF ST. ARNE// D 2a// n.a.// **Victoria**, Nov. 1842, with Mr. James as Gervaise, John Dale as L'Ambair, E. F. Saville as Count de Valcour, William Seaman as Antoine, Charles Williams as Morville, Mr. Cullen as Duval, John Gardner as Clorin, Mrs. George Lee as Christine, Miss Martin as Pauline, Mrs. Griffith as Mme. de Montford, Miss Edgar as Rosette.

CONVICT, THE; OR, HUNTED TO DEATH// D Pro & 4a// C. H. Stephenson// **Pavilion**, Feb. 1868.

CONVICT'S WIFE, THE// CD 3a// n.a.// **Grand**, May 1890.

COOL AS A CUCUMBER// F 1a// W. B. Jerrold// **Lyceum**, Mar 1851, with C. J. Mathews as Plumper, Basil Baker as Barkins, Mr. Bellingham as Frederick Barkins, Fanny Baker as Jessy, Miss Martindale as Mary/ **St. James's**, Feb. 1864, with Walton Chamberlaine as Old Barkins, H. J. Montague as Frederick, C. J. Mathews as Plumper, Miss Dalton as Jenny, Miss Percival as Wiggins/ **Sad. Wells**, Dec. 1866, with Edward Hastings as Plumper, Miss Norton as Wiggins, Amy Florence as Jessie/ **Gaiety**, Nov. 1872/ **Olympic**, Aug. 1874, with W. H. Vernon as Plumper, A. Hilton as Old Barkins, L. F. Lewis as Frederick Barkins, Annie Taylor as Wiggins, Miss Pearce as Jessie.

COOPERATIVE MOVEMENT, A// F// Harry Lemon// **Haymarket**, Apr. 1868, with W. H. Kendal as Jones, Henry Compton as Gillingham, Mrs. Chippendale as Anna, Marie Dalton as Lucy.

COQUETTE, THE// Play 3a// Adap. by T. Mead fr F// **Haymarket**, July 1867, with W. H. Kendal as de Augustus, Henry Howe as Alexandre, Walter Gordon as Alphonse, Mr. Weathersby as De Grenoir, H. Vincent as Edouard, Henry Compton as Baptiste, Amy Sedgwick as Countess de Raincourt, Miss Matthews as Clari.

CORA// D Pro & 3a// Adap. by W. S. Wills & Frank Marshall fr F of Adolphe Belot, L'Article 47// **Globe**, Feb. 1877, with James Fernandez as du Hamel, Edmund Leathes as Mazillier, David Fisher Jr. as Potain, Mrs. Hermann Vezin as Cora de Lille, W. H. Stephens as Comte de Rives, J. D. Beveridge as Dr. Combes/ Scenery by Bruce Smith.

CORA; OR, THE SLAVES OF THE SOUTH// D 3a// George Conquest// **Grecian**, June 1865, with J. B. Steele as Poynings, J. Jackson as M'Cutun, David Jones as Marble, Henry Grant as Hyltofts, Dan Leeson as Neb, Mrs. J. W. Simpson as Mrs. Lorymer, Lizzie Mandelbert as Cora.

CORALIE// Play 4a// Adap. by G. W. Godfrey fr F of Albert Delpit, Le Fils de Coralie// **St. James's**, May 1881, with T. N. Wenman as Sir Jonas, John Clayton as Kelson-Derrick, John Hare as Critchell, W. H. Kendal as Capt. Mainwaring, Wilfred Draycott as Polwhele, Mr. Brandon as Bates, Mrs. Gaston Murray as Miss Meryon, Miss Cowle as Mrs. Prattleton, Winnifred Emery as Mabel, Mrs. W. H. Kendal as Mrs. Travers/ Scenery by T. Harford.

CORINNE// D 4a// Robert Buchanan// **Lyceum**, June 1876, with Henry Forrester as Raoul Recamier, Charles Warner as Victor de Beauvoir, Thomas Mead as Archbishop of Paris, Johnston Forbes Robertson as Abbe de Larose, Edward Atkins as Marat, H. Moxon as Father Doré, Evan Gordon as d'Artois, Mrs. Fairfax as Corinne, Amy Lionel as Clarisse, Mrs. Edward Fitzwilliam as Vicomtesse de Laverne.

CORINNE// D// Dram. fr novel of Mrs. Otto von Booth// **Standard**, May 1885.

CORIOLANUS// T// William Shakespeare// **Cov. Garden**, Mar. 1837, with John Pritchard as Aufidius, John Webster as Volusius, Mr. Thomas as Sextus, D. W. King as Lucius, Thomas Hamblin as Coriolanus, George Bennett as Cominius, Mr. Tilbury as Menenius, J. Worrell as Fulvius, Mr. Bender as Appius, Mrs. W. West as Volumna, Eliza Vincent as Virginia, Miss Lee as Valeria; Sept. 1838, with John Vandenhoff, Samuel Phelps, Mrs. Mary Warner, Charlotte Vandenhoff/ **Victoria**, Oct. 1842, with William Seaman as Aufidius, C. J. Bird as Volsius, Mr. Millington as Sextus, Mr. Graham as Coriolanus, John Dale as Cominius, Julia Seaman as Young Marcius, Mr. James as Agrippa, Mr. Ayres as Appius, Mr. Aldridge as Velutus, F. H. Henry as Brutus, Mrs. W. West as Volumna, Miss Hamilton as Virgilia, Miss Garrick as Veleria/ **Marylebone**, 1843, with Charles Dillon/ **Sadler's Wells**, Sept. 1848, with Samuel Phelps as Coriolanus, Edward Knight as Lartius, George Bennett as Cominius, A. Younge as Agrippa, Henry Mellon as Velutus, Frank Graham as Brutus, Henry Marston as Aufidius, Isabela Glyn as Volumna, Miss Cooper as Virgilia, Mrs. Henry Marston as Valeria, Miss Morelli as Servilia/ Scenery by F. Fenton & A. Finlay/ **Drury Lane**, Jan. 1851, with James Anderson as Coriolanus, Mr. Cathcart as Cominius, Samuel Emery as Menenius, J. Neville as Brutus, Mr. Beckett as Appius, J. W. Ray as Velutus, Mr. Cooper as Aufidius, H. T. Craven as Volusius, Henry Butler as Sextus, Mrs. Weston as Volumna, Fanny Vining as Virgilia, Mrs. Barrett as Valeria,

Mrs. Bisson as Servilia/ **Lyceum**, Apr. 1901, with Henry Irving, J. H. Barnes, Laurence Irving, Ellen Terry, Mabel Hackney.

CORISANDE// Play 4a// Charles Hoyte// **Comedy**, Mar. 1890, with Leonard Boyne, Cyril Maude, Alfred Bishop, Olga Brandon, Beatrice Lamb, Agnes Thomas.

CORK LEG, THE; OR, THE LADY OF MUNSTER// F 1a// n.a.// **Sad. Wells**, Apr. 1842, with Mr. Williams as Sir Lawrence, John Webster as Charles, John Herbert as Sam, Mrs. H. P. Grattan as Kate, Mrs. Richard Barnett as Susan.

CORNEY RHUE// D// Barry Conner// **Britannia**, Aug. 1879.

CORNISH MINERS, THE// D// R. B. Peake// **Victoria**, Nov. 1837, with Mr. Loveday as Kenyan, Thomas Green as Stephen, Mr. Franks as Trevallion, W. H. Oxberry as Redruth, L. Smith as Michael, Mr. Salter as Githian, Benjamin Wrench as Sal Ammoniac, Mrs. Hooper as Anne, Mrs. Griffith as Dame Oswald, Mrs. Loveday as Dame Kenyan.

CORONER, THE// D Pro & 4a// J. W. Hemming & Cyril Harrison// **Elephant & Castle**, Aug. 1889; **Novelty**, Mar. 1897, with Jack Haddon as Grey, Mr. Thompson as Goodman, William Luff as Mike, Mr. Jackson as Redford, Robert Smith as Corbin, Reginald Eyre as Reginald Corbin, Bernard Copping as Harding, Cecil Hill as Jebb, Harry Danby as Seal, Newman Maurice as Dicky, Geraldine Grey as Maude, Lucy Murray as Molly.

CORPORAL, THE; OR, BROTHERS IN ARMS// C 2a// C. Long// **Grecian**, May 1845, with John Collett as Col. Mander, Edwin Dixon as Capt. Serrier, Harry Chester as Lt. Valcour, Mary A. Crisp as Julia, Miss Johnstone as Miss Millson, Miss E. Mears as Eliza.

CORPORAL SHAKO// F// Frederick Hay// **Surrey**, June 1879.

CORPORAL'S WEDDING, THE; OR, A KISS FROM THE BRIDE// F 1a// J. Maddison Morton// **Adelphi**, Jan. 1845.

CORRUPT PRACTICES// C 2a// Frank Marshall// **Lyceum**, Jan. 1870, with Charles Coghlan as Sir Victor, George Vincent as Durant, G. F. Neville as Jekyll, F. Stainforth as Lord Henry, Louisa Thorne as Mary, Miss L. Wilson as Lady Avenly, Susan Rignold as Bertha/ Scenery by W. Brew/ Prod. by F. A. Marshall.

CORSAIR, THE; OR, THE GREEK PIRATE OF THE GULF// D// n.a.// **Victoria**, May 1859, with W. H. Pitt as Conrad, Frederick Byefield as Alexis, Mr. Carter as Demetrius, Mr. Henderson as Anselmo, Mr. Hitchinson as Rinaldo, George Yarnold as Pedrillo, Mary Fielding as Medero, Miss Laporte as Iolama, Mrs. E. F. Saville as Gulnare.

CORSAIR'S REVENGE, THE// D 2a// H. P. Grattan// **Victoria**, Mar. 1843.

CORSICAN BROTHERS, THE// D 3a// Adap. by Dion Boucicault fr F of E. P. Grangé & Xavier de Montépin, derived fr Les Frères Corses of Alexandre Dumas// **Princess's**, Feb. 1852, with Charles Kean as Fabien and Louis dei Franchi, Alfred Wigan as Chateau-Renaud, James Vining as Montgiron, Charles Wheatleigh as Martelli, George Everett as Meynard, John Ryder as Orlando, Drinkwater Meadows as Colonna, Miss Phillips as Mme. dei Franchi, Miss Murray as Emilie, Miss Robertson as Marie, Carlotta Leclercq as Coralie; Dec. 1860 in a rev. vers. by Charles Fechter, with Charles Fechter as Fabien and Louis dei Franchi, Augustus Harris as Chateau-Renaud, J. G. Shore as Baron de Montgiron, Robert Cathcart as Baron Martelli, Mr. Raymond as Meynard, Mrs. Weston as Mme. dei Franchi, Miss Murray as Emilie, Rose Leclercq as Folichone; June 1876, with John Clayton as Fabien and Louis dei Franchi, J. H. Barnes as Chateau-Renaud, J. R. Crauford as Meynard, A. Elwood as de Montgiron, P. C. Beverley as Martelli, George Yarnold as Orlando, F. W. Irish as Colonna, Mr. Dormar as Beauchamp, J. B. Johnstone as Verner, Mrs. St. Henry as Mme. dei Franchi, Caroline Hill as Emilie, Miss C. Brabant/ **Marylebone**, Mar. 1852/ **Surrey**, 1852/ **Queen's**, 1852/ **Grecian**, 1852; June 1868, with Thomas Mead as Fabien and Louis dei Franchi, William James as Renaud, George Gillett as Maynard, Samuel Perfitt as de Montgiron, Henry Grant as Orlando, John Manning as Colonna, Lizzie Mandelbert as Emilie, Miss De Lacie as Coralie, Mary A. Victor as Estelle/ **City of London**, 1852/ **Standard**, 1852/ Adap. by Mr. Fletcher/ **Princess's**, Dec. 1860; Jan. 1861, with Charles Fechter/ **Sad. Wells**, Nov. 1865, with J. C. Cowper as Fabien and Louis dei Franchi, E. F. Edgar as Chateau Reynaud, Gratton Murray as Reynard, Samuel Perfitt as Montgiron, John Rouse as Orlando, Richard Norman as Colonna, Mr. Martindale as Giordano, Miss M. A. Bellair as Emillie, Mrs. E. F. Edgar as Mme. dei Franchi, Miss Rogers as Marie, Miss Leigh as Estelle, Miss Barker as Corrella, Miss Graham as Celeste/ **Drury Lane**, Mar. 1877, with Henry Sinclair as Louis and Fabian dei Franchi, Howard Russell as Chateau Renaud, R. Dolman as Meynard, Charles Fenton as de Mongiron, Percy Bell as Martelli, Mr. Douglas as Beauchamps, James Johnstone as Judge, Frederick Hughes as Colonna, J. B. Johnson as Tomasso, Miss Murielle as Emilie, Cicely Nott as Mme. dei Franchi, Clara Jecks as Rosette/ **Lyceum**, Sept. 1880, with Henry Irving as Fabien and Louis dei Franchi, William Terriss as Chateau-Renaud, Mr. Elwood as Baron de Montgiron, Arthur Wing Pinero as Meynard, John Ryder as Orlando, Drinkwater Meadows as Colonna, Georgina Pauncefort as Savilla dei Franchi, Miss Fowler as Émilie de Lesparre, Alma Murray as Marie/ Scenery by Hawes Craven, W. Cuthbert & H. Cuthbert/ Music by Hamilton Clarke/ Machines by Mr. Mather; May 1891/ **Novelty**, Aug. 1880.

CORSICAN BROTHERS, THE; OR, THE FATAL DUEL// D 3a// Adap. by George Almar fr F// **Victoria**, June 1857, with J. H. Rickards as Fabian and Louis dei Franchi, W. H. Pitt as Renaud, Mr. Morrison as Giordarno, Frederick Byefield as Montgiron, J. Howard as Orlandi, Mr. Hitchinson as Judge, Mr. Henderson as Meynard, Charles Rice as Colonna, Mrs. J. H. Rickards as Mme. dei Franchi, Mrs. Henry Vining as Emilie, Miss Laporte as Marie, Julia Seaman as Coralia.

CORSICAN BROTHERS, THE; OR, THE VOW OF VENGEANCE// D 3a// Adap. fr F of Alexandre Dumas// **Sad. Wells,** May 1854, with Henry Farren as Fabien and Louis, George Vining as Chateau Renaud, Oliver Summers as Meynard, James Worrell as de Montgiron, F. Charles as Martelli, Mr. Palmer as Beauchamp, Mr. Barrett as Orlando, George Yarnold as Colonna, Mrs. Barnett as Mme. dei Franchi, Miss Castleton as Emilie, Miss Lavine as Marie.

COTTAGER'S DAUGHTER, THE; OR, THE MURDER OF THE RUIN// D// Mr. Upshere// **Victoria,** Jan. 1838, with Mr. Wilkins as Capt. Smithe, W. H. Oxberry as Jeremy, Mr. Salter as Puggy, Mr. Loveday as Ralph, William Davidge as Wilmot, Mrs. Hooper as Jane, Miss Richardson as Fanny, Miss Wilson as Miss Buckram.

COTTON KING, THE// D 4a// Sutton Vane// **Adelphi,** Mar. 1894.

COUNSEL FOR THE DEFENCE// Play 5a// n.a.// **Opera Comique,** Sept. 1895.

COUNSEL'S OPINION// Play 1a// Frederick Bingham// **Her Majesty's,** May 1898, with W. H. Denny as Sir John, Frank Barclay as Morgan, Master Field-Fisher as Maximilian, Majorie Field-Fisher as Mrs. Lovelace.

COUNT OF LUGARTO, THE (see Serpent on the Hearth).

COUNT TEZMA// Play 3a// A. N. Homer// **Comedy,** Apr. 1901.

COUNTERFEITS// F 1a// n.a.// **Grecian,** Mar. 1844, with John Collett as Grub, Frederick Robson as Styling, Mr. Kerridge as Charles, G. Norman as Tom, Mary A. Crisp in 4 char. parts.

COUNTESS, THE; OR, THE CASTLE OF CRONSTADT// D 3a// n.a.// **Victoria,** Oct. 1857, with Frederick Byefield as Rickman, H. Dudley as Count of Cronstadt, W. H. Pitt as Leopold, J. H. Rickards as Herman, S. Sawford as Hans, George Yarnold as Max, F. H. Henry as Fritz, Mrs. E. F. Saville as Albertina, Miss Laporte as Bertha, Mrs. Vickery as Countess of Cronstadt.

COUNTESS AND THE DANCER, THE// Adap. by Charles Reade fr F of Victorien Sardou, Andrea// **Olympic,** Feb. 1886, with William Herbert as Count Nyrode, Edward Price as Baron Kaulbars, Cecil Crofton as Frederic, A. Wood as Kraft, Fred Irving as Fritz, A. T. Hilton as Benjamin, Etelka Borry as Olga, Edith Bruce as Stella, Miss A. Herbert as Josepha, Nelly Daly as Sylvine.

COUNTESS D'ARGENTINE; OR, THE PAGE'S REVENGE// C 2a// Alfred Stalman// **Sad. Wells,** Oct. 1862, with W. H. Stephens as Col. Bellegarde, Henry Forrester as Lt. Montescan, C. Lloyds as Jacques, Alfred Montague as Le Fleur, Sophie Miles as Adolphe, Emily Dowton as Lisette, Catherine Lucette as the Countess.

COUNTESS GUCKI, THE// C 3a// Adap. by Augustin Daly fr G of Franz von Schönthan// **Comedy,** July 1896, with James Lewis as Counsellor von Mittersteig, Edwin Stevens as Gen. Suvatscheff, Charles Richmond as von Neuhoff, Sidney Shepherd as Wensel, William Haseltine as Baumann, Mrs. G. H. Gilbert as Clementina, Helma Nelson as Lilli, Mabel Gillman as Rosa, Ada Rehan as Countess Hermana.

COUNTRY GIRL, THE// C 3a// A rev. by David Garrick of William Wycherly's The Country Wife// **Haymarket,** Aug. 1840, with William Strickland as Moody, John Webster as Harcourt, Walter Lacy as Sparkish, Henry Howe as Belville, Mrs. Fitzwilliam as Peggy, Miss Charles as Alithea, Mrs. Frank Matthews as Lucy/ **Terry's,** June 1898.

COUNTRY SQUIRE, THE; OR, TWO DAYS AT THE HALL// C 2a// Charles Dance// **Cov. Garden,** Jan. 1837, with William Farren as Broadlands, John Webster as Selwood, John Pritchard as George, Benjamin Webster as Sparrow, J. Smith as Richard, John Collett as Samuel, Eliza Vincent as Fanny, Miss Lee as Sophy, Mrs. Julia Glover as Temperence, Miss Nicholson as Alice/ **Olympic,** Sept. 1837, with William Farren as Broadlands, C. J. Mathews as Horace Selwood, James Vining as George Selwood, Mr. Wyman as Sparrow, Mme. Vestris as Fanny, Mrs. Orger as Temperance/ Scenery by W. Marshall; Sept. 1851 with William Farren as Broadlands, William Farren Jr. as George Selwood, Henry Farren as Horace Selwood, E. Clifton as Sparrow, Mrs. Alfred Phillips as Mrs. Temperence, Louisa Howard as Fanny, Isabel Adams as Sophia, Ellen Turner as Alice/ **Sad. Wells,** Mar. 1859, with J. W. Ray as Broadlands, W. R. Belford as Horace Selwood, Charles Seyton as George Selwood, Mr. Williams as Sparrow, Caroline Parkes as Sophy, Miss A. Ness as Fanny, Mrs. Henry Marston as Temperence, Mrs. J. B. Hill as Alice.

COUNTY, THE// Play 4a// Estelle Burney & Arthur Benham// **Terry's,** June 1892, with Herbert Waring as Duke of Allonby, Henry Esmond as Rawdon, Herbert Ross as Soames, Alfred Courtenay as Col. Sumner, W. L. Abingdon as Price, Annie Hughes as Lady Cynthia, Henrietta Cowen as Lucy, Estelle Burney as Mrs. Price, Mrs. Herbert Waring as Mrs. Soames/ Scenery by T. W. Hall.

COUNTY COUNCILLOR, THE// FC 3a// H. Graham// **Strand,** Nov. 1892/ **Trafalgar,** Feb. 1893.

COUNTY FAIR, THE// D 4a// Charles Bernard// **Princess's,** June 1897.

COUPE GORGE, LA; OR, THE BLACK INN ON THE HEATH// D// Adap. fr F// **Astley's**, Dec. 1851, with John Dale as de Mirande, Thomas Barry as Jacques, Mr. Maddocks as Martin, Mr. Chaddock as Jerome, Mr. Johnson as Chase, Mr. Stickney as Joseph, Mrs. Beacham as Marie, Miss Barnett as Cathline, Clara Tellett as Emmaline.

COURAGE; THE STORY OF A BIG DIAMOND// D 4a// Henry Gascoigne// **Marylebone**, Oct. 1886.

COURIER OF LYONS, THE; OR, THE ATTACK UPON THE POST MAIL// D 4a// Adap. by Charles Reade fr F of Moreau, Siraudin & A. C. Delacour// **Standard**, 1851/ **Princess's**, June 1854, with Mr. Graham as Jerome Lesurgues, John Cathcart as Didier, James Vining as Dorval, David Fisher as Courriol, Mr. Addison as Choppard, Henry Saker as Foulnard, Charles Kean as Dubosc and Joseph Lesurgues, Mr. Terry as Lambert, Kate Terry as Joliquet, Carlotta Leclercq as Julie, Caroline Heath as Jeannette/ Scenery by Walter Gordon & F. Lloyds/ **Victoria**, July 1854, with T. E. Mills as Jerome Lesurques, E. F. Saville as Joseph and Pierre Lesurques, Henry Frazer as Rosiere, Alfred Saville as Dumaine, Charles Rice as Choppard, J. Howard as Popinet, Mr. Henderson as Fleury, Miss Dansor as Julia, Mrs. Henry Vining as Madelaine, Miss Sutton as Elise/ Music by Mr. Mingaye/ Prod. by J. T. Johnson/ **Grecian**, July 1854, with Basil Potter as Jerome Lesurgues, Richard Phillips as Joseph Lesurgues and Dubosc, Thomas Roberts as Didier, Henry Grant as Dauberton, Eaton O'Donnell as Choppard, Charles Horn as Courriol, William Suter as Fournard, Harriet Coveney as Julie, Jane Coveney as Jeanne/ **Adelphi**, July 1854, with O. Smith as Jerome Lesurques, Leigh Murray as Joseph Leserques, John Parselle as Daubenton, C. J. Smith as Lambert, Charles Selby as Courriol, Paul Bedford as Choppard, Leigh Murray as Dubosc, James Rogers as Joliquet, Mrs. Leigh Murray as Jeanne, Fanny Maskell as Julie/ **Sad. Wells**, Mar. 1856 (in 3a), with Mr. Cooke as Daubenton, Mr. Williams as Jerome Lesurques, Leigh Murray as Joseph Lesurques and Dubosc, Mr. Swanborough as Didier, C. Kelsey as Lambert, Mr. Barrett as Choppard, E. F. Edgar as Couriol, Charles Swan as Foulnard, Miss M. Oliver as Julie, Jenny Marston as Jeanne/ **St. James's**, 1859/ **Gaiety**, July 1870.

COURIER OF THE CZAR, THE// D 4a// Hugh Marston// **Standard**, May 1877.

COURSE OF TRUE LOVE, THE// C 1a// n.a.// **Sad. Wells**, July 1857, with Mr. Gladstone as Don Carlos, John Chester as Sancho, E. Clifton as Lopez, Kate May as Leonora, Mary A. Victor as Jacintha.

COURT AND CAMP// D 3a// Paul Meurice & George Vining// **Princess's**, May 1863, with George Vining as Bibi, Charles Verner as Conte Salviata, Gaston Murray as Duke de Maurepas, Henry Marston as Marchall Saxe, George Belmore as Ramponneau, J. P. Warde as Angelus, Amy Sedgwick as Countess Du Barri, Louise Laidlaw as Diane, Lydia Thompson as Guillemette/ Scenery by F. Lloyds/ Machines by Mr. Garnett/ Music by C. Hall.

COURT AND CITY// C 5a// Adap. by R. B. Peake fr scenes in Richard Steele's Tender Husband and Mrs. Francis Sheridan's Discovery// **Cov. Garden**, Nov. 1841, with William Farren as Sir Paladin, C. J. Mathews as Sir Harry, George Bartley as Sir Hector, Mr. Cooper as Winnington, John Pritt Harley as Rumbush, Frank Matthews as Bearbinder, Alfred Wigan as Lionel, Mme. Vestris as Lady Whiffle, Mrs. W. West as Lady Dangerfield, Miss Cooper as Louisa, Louisa Nisbett as Mrs. Charmington, Mrs. Tayleure as Mrs. Bearbinder, Miss Charlton as Miss Covertly, Mrs. Walter Lacy as Barbara.

COURT BEAUTIES, THE// C// J. R. Planché// **Lyceum**, Oct. 1848, with Charles Selby as Charles II, C. J. Mathews as Buckingham, Robert Roxby as Hewit, Frank Matthews as Hunks, Mr. Granby as Lely, Louisa Howard as Miss Lawson, Miss Marshall as Tiffany.

COURT CARDS// CD 2a// Adap. by J. Palgrave Simpson fr F of Eugène Scribe, La Frileuse// **Olympic**, Nov. 1861.

COURT CAVE, THE; OR, THE PRINCE, THE PILGRIM, AND THE PETRONEL// D// n.a.// **Sad. Wells**, Mar. 1841, with E. F. Saville as James IV, Mr. Aldridge as Sir David, Mr. Williams as Colville the Elder, George Ellis as Colville the Younger, Mr. Elvin as Winton, J. W. Collier as Laidlaw, Miss Richardson as Edith, Mr. Stilt as MacShane, Charles Fenton as Robart/ Scenery by F. Fenton/ Music by Isaac Collins/ Machines by B. Sloman/ Prod. by R. Honner.

COURT DISTURBER, THE// F 1a// Adap. by W. J. Lucas fr F, Deux Heures du Matin// **Grecian**, Oct. 1845, with Frederick Robson as Jenkinson, Harry Chester as Fitzarlington.

COURT FAVOR; OR, PRIVATE AND CONFIDENTIAL// C 2a// J. R. Planché// **Sad. Wells**, Aug. 1847, with J. T. Johnson as Duke of Albemarle, A. Younge as Sir Andrew, Henry Marston as Capt. Kilkenny, Charles Fenton as Sir Charles, Mrs. Henry Marston as Lady Plumbercourt, Miss Cooper as Lucy/ **Haymarket**, Aug. 1855, with Henry Howe as Duke of Albemarle, W. H. Chippendale as Sir Andrew, J. B. Buckstone as Brown, George Braid as Col. Kilkenny, William Cullenford as Dr. Oracle, Mr. Weathersby as Sir Charles, Mrs. Poynter as Lady Flambercourt, Blanche Fane as Lucy, Miss Grantham as Lady Hinton/ **Strand**, Aug. 1858/ **Princess's**, Dec. 1862, with Henry Marston as Duke of Albemarle, Mr. Fitzjames as Sir Andrew, George Vining as Brown, Robert Cathcart as Col. Kilkenny, John Collett as Dr. Oracle, Mr. Brooke as Sir Charles, Marie Wilton as Lucy, Mrs. Henry Marston as Lady Flambercourt, Marie Henderson as Lady Hinton.

COURT FOOL, THE; OR, THE JESTER'S REVENGE (also subt. The Jester's Vengeance)// D// n.a.// **Grecian**, Sept. 1863, with William James as Francis I, F. Smithson as Marquis Landry, Mr. Howard as de Pienne, Alfred Rayner as Tribulet, Mr. Shirley as as St. Vallier, Mr. Hayes as de Montmorency, Henry Power as de Cosse, Walter Holland as Marot, J. Jackson as Saltabadil, Mrs. Charles Dillon as Blanche, Marie Brewer as Countess de Cosse, Mary A. Victor as Madelone, Miss Johnstone as Dame Berarde.

COURT FOOL THE; OR, A KING'S AMUSEMENT// TD 3a// W. E. Burton// **Sadler's Wells,** May 1840.

COURT GALLANTS// C// Adap. by Charles Selby fr F// **Royalty,** Aug. 1863.

COURT JESTER, THE; OR, A QUESTION OF FINANCE// C// C. J. Mathews// **Sad. Wells,** Feb. 1841, with Henry Marston as Grand Duke of Ferrara, Mr. Dry as Marquis Castelli, Mr. Elvin as Count Marini, Mr. Williams as Bambino, Mrs. Robert Honner as Paulina, Miss Cooke as Susannah.

COURT OF HONOUR, A// Play 3a// John Lart & Charles Dickenson// **Royalty,** May 1887.

COURT OF OLD FRITZ, THE// C 1a// J. F. Smith// **Olympic,** Dec. 1838, with William Farren as Frederick the Great and as Voltaire, James Vining as Harlstein, Mr. Granby as Hertzberg, Charles Selby as Leopold, James Bland as Katzleig, Mrs. Franks as Countess Bertha.

COURT OF SPAIN, THE; OR, THE QUEEN OF A DAY// D// Thompson Townsend// **Sad. Wells,** May 1839, with Mr. Elvin as Don Luis, Mr. Phillips as Don Diego, John Webster as Don Pedro, Mr. Conquest as Filippo, Mr. Cathcart as Don Ruy, Mr. Aldridge as Don Juan, Mr. Dry as Gonsalvez, J. W. Collier as Sancho, Charles Montgomery as Don Alonzo, Mrs. Robert Honner as Beatrice, Mrs. J. F. Saville as Juanna, Miss Pincott as Inez, Miss Wallis as Blanche/ Scenery by Mr. Fenwick & G. Smithyes Jr./ Music by Mr. Herbert/ Machines by B. Sloman.

COURT SCANDAL, A// C 3a// Adap. by Aubrey Boucicault & Osmond Shillingford fr F of J. F. Bayard & P. F. Dumanoir, Les Armes de Richelieu// **Court,** Jan. 1899, with Seymour Hicks as Richelieu, E. Allan Aynesworth as de Matignon, Brandon Thomas as Baron de Bellechasse, J. D. Beveridge as Abbé, Webb Darley as Michelin, Miriam Clements as Duchess de Bourgogne, Roma le Thiére as Duchess de Noailles, Dorothea Baird as Duchess de Richelieu, Ethel Matthews as Cesarine, Florence Wood as Baronne de Bellechasse/ Scenery by Walter Hann/ Transf. to **Garrick,** May 1899.

COURT, THE PRISON, AND THE SCAFFOLD, THE// D// R. Bell// **Britannia,** Nov. 1874.

COURTSHIP AND CONGREVES// F// E. L. Blanchard// **Drury Lane,** Mar. 1856, with Mr. Tilbury as Convex, J. Worrell as Stanley, George Wild as Brimstone, Isabel Adams as Caroline, Fanny Williams as Sally.

COURTSHIP; OR, THE THREE CASKETS// C 3a// H. J. Byron// **Court,** Oct. 1879, with Charles Coghlan, Wilson Barrett, Amy Roselle, Mrs. Leigh Murray.

COURTSHIP OF MORRICE BUCKLER, THE// Play 4a// Adap. by A. E. Mason & Isabel Bateman fr novel of Mason// **Grand,** Dec. 1897.

COURTYARD JESTER, THE; OR, THE BLACK SENTINEL// C// n.a.// **Sad. Wells,** Feb. 1838, with J. Worrell as Capt. Hector, Mr. James as Skinflint, Mr. Rogers as Pop, Mr. Dunn as Jim Crow, Mr. George as Tap, Mr. Nunn as Brainless, Mrs. Weston as Mrs. Smith, Miss Beresford as Ellen.

COUSIN CHERRY// C 1a// Henry Spicer// **Olympic,** Mar. 1849, with John Kinloch as Earl of Mandeville, William H. Norton as Thomas Primrose, Charles Bender as Jacob Primrose, Mrs. Stirling as Cherry, Mrs. Leigh Murray as Elinor/ **Globe,** Apr. 1876, with Vyner Robinson as Charles, Kate Rivers as Cherry, H. Sainsbury as Primrose, Blanche Hayes as Elinore.

COUSIN DICK// C 1a// Val Prinsep// **St. James's,** Dec. 1881, with Kate Bishop as Constance, Jessie Millward as Florence, Wilfred Draycott as Richard.

COUSIN FROM AUSTRALIA, THE// FC 3a// Sidney Blackburn// **Opera Comique,** Apr. 1898, with Dalton Summers as Foglight, Thomas Kingston as Liner, Willis Searle as Perks, Ells Dagnall as Kirschman, C. A. Russell as Offitt, Kate Osbourne as Mrs. O'Flaherty, Lizzie Collier as Seraphin, Phyllis Manners as Miss Howard.

COUSIN JACK// C 3a// Adap. by Hermann Vezin fr G of Roderick Benedix// **Opera Comique,** Nov. 1891, with Hermann Vezin as Jack, George Foss as Dunn, Gerald Gurney as Frank Dunn, Alfred Courtenay as Sharpe, Beatrice Lamb as May, Elsie Chester as Daisy.

COUSIN JOHNNY// C 3a// J. F. Nisbet & C. M. Rae// **Strand,** July 1885, with J. S. Clarke, Eleanor Bufton, Lucy Buckstone.

COUSIN LAMBKIN// F// J. Maddison Morton// **Cov. Garden,** Oct. 1842, with George Bartley as Mulberry, Walter Lacy as Capt. Bantam, John Pritt Harley as Dr. Lambkin, W. H. Payne as Clutchem, Miss Cooper as Mrs. Bantam, Miss Lee as Rose, Mrs. Humby as Dainty/ **Sad. Wells,** Oct. 1856, with J. W. Ray as Mulberry, William Belford as Capt. Rantam, Lewis Ball as Lambkin, Mr. Meagreson as Clutchem, Jenny Marston as Mrs. Rantam, Caroline Parkes as Rose, Eliza Travers as Dainty.

COUSIN PETER// C 1a// T. E. Wilks// **Olympic,** Oct. 1841, with Mr. Fitzjames as Marquis de la Foix, Mr. Ross as Nicholas, Mr. Halford as Gibelon, Mrs. Waylett as Cecile, Miss Bartlett as Marguerite/ **Sad. Wells,** Sept. 1845, with Samuel Buckingham as Marquis de la Foix, Henry Scharf as Nicholas, E. Morton as Gibelon, Miss Lebatt as Cecile, Georgiana Lebatt as

Marguerite.

COUSIN TOM// C 1a// George Roberts// **Princess's,** June 1863, with Mr. Fitzjames as Lothbury, George Belmore as Cosway, Mr. Cathcart as Vane, Miss M. Oliver as Lucy, Maria Henderson as Susan.

COUSINS ONCE REMOVED// C 1a// A. M. Heathcote// **Terry's,** Apr. 1901.

COWARDLY FOE, A// Play 1a// Wynne Miller// **Criterion,** July 1892.

COWBOY AND THE LADY, THE// C 3a// Clyde Fitch// **Duke of York's,** June 1899.

COZY COUPLE, A (also supertitled An Eipsode in the Life of)// F 1a// G. H. Lewis ("Slingsby Lawrence")// **Lyceum,** Apr. 1854/ **Sad. Wells,** Apr. 1855, with Frank Matthews as Dormouse, Mrs. Frank Matthews as Mrs. Dormouse, Gaston Murray as Russelton, Miss Martindale as Mary/ **St. James's,** Oct. 1861, with Frank Matthews as Dormouse, George Vining as Russleton, Mrs. Frank Matthews as Mrs. Dormouse, Miss Tunbridge as Mary.

CRAMOND BRIG, THE; OR, THE GUDE MAN O' BALLANGEICH (see also, King and the Miller)// C 2a// Dram. by W. H. Murray fr novel of Sir Walter Scott, Miller of Mansfield// **Drury Lane,** July 1837/ **Sad. Wells,** Aug. 1838, with John Webster as James I, Mr. Williams as Howieson, Mr. Dry as Lord Birke, Mr. Phillips as Lord Malcolm, Mr. Mellor as Maxwell, J. W. Collier as Grime, C. Montague as Armstrong, Mr. Priorson as Donald, Miss E. Honnor as Marian, Miss Cooke as Tibbie, Mrs. Harwood as Maggie/ **Eng. Opera House** (Lyceum), Sept. 1838, with Mr. Frazer as King James, R. McIan as Howison, Mr. Halford as Maxwell, Mrs. Searle as Marian, Mme. Simon as Tibbie, Lavinia Melville as Maggie/ **Cov. Garden,** Feb. 1845 (as F 1a), with Mr. Hield as James IV [sic], J. C. Bird as Maxwell, George Braid as Birkie, Mr. Bass as Howieson, Mr. Butler as Elcho, Mr. Lee as Glencairn, Mrs. Griffiths as Jessie, Miss Love as Maggie, Miss L. Lyons as Marion/ **Surrey,** Apr. 1850/ **Duke's,** Apr. 1878.

CRAZED// F 1a// Charles Morton// **Globe,** Mar. 1876, with W. J. Hill as Brown, E. Perrini as Smith, Miss E. Wiber as Sally; Mar. 1887, with W. J. Hill as Brown, W. Lestocq as Smith, Hettie Gray as Sally.

CREMORNE// FC 3a// T. A. Palmer// **Strand,** Nov. 1876.

CREOLE, THE; OR, LOVE'S FETTERS// D 3a// Charles W. Brooks// **Lyceum,** Apr. 1847.

CREOLE, THE; OR, THE POISONED PEARL// D 4a// n.a.// **Grecian,** May 1862, with Thomas Mead as Brigand, William James as Morland, Henry Grant as de Lafare, F. Smithson as de Launay, John Manning as Frizzle, Henry Power as Raoul, Mr. Howard as Fabian, Mr. Jackson as Gaspard, Mrs. Charles Dillon as Clarisse, Mary A. Victor as Julie, Ellen Hale as Marie, Miss Johnstone as Mrs. Merryweather.

CRICHTON OF CLUNY AND CATHERINE DE MEDICIS// D 3a// T. E. Wilks// **Victoria,** Nov. 1842, with John Dale as Henry III of France, Mr. Chapino as de Joyeuse, Mr. Hitchinson as D'Epernon, William Seaman as di Gonzago, Mr. Scarbrow as Henry of Navarre, C. Williams as de Nevers, Mr. Cullen as Caravaja, Mr. James as D'Amboise, E. F. Saville as Crichton, John Gardner as Chicot, Mrs. George Lee as Catherine de Medicis, Miss Martin as Ginevra, Miss Saddler as Esclairmonde.

CRICKET MATCH, THE// F// James Anderson// **Drury Lane,** Apr. 1850, with William Davidge as Smith, Mr. Rafter as Lt. Lovemore, Robert Romer as Hopeful, Stephen Artaud as Brush, Samuel Emery as Andrew, S. Jones as Shot, Mrs. Winstanley as Sarah, Lucy Rafter as Sophia, Clara Tellett as Patty, Annie Lonsdale as Sally.

CRICKET ON THE HEARTH, THE// D 3a// Dram. by Albert Smith fr novel of Charles Dickens// **Lyceum,** Dec. 1845, with Samuel Emery as Peerybingle, Mr. Meadows as Tackleton, Robert Keeley as Caleb Plummer, Frederick Vining as Stranger, Mrs. Keeley as Mrs. Peerybingle, Mary Keeley as Bertha, Louisa Howard as May, Miss Turner as Miss Slowboy.

CRICKET ON THE HEARTH, THE// D// Adap. fr novel of Charles Dickens// **Princess's,** Mar. 1860, with John Ryder as Perrybingle, Drinkwater Meadows as Tackleton, Frank Matthews as Caleb Plummer, Mr. Cathcart as Stranger, Carlotta Leclercq as Mrs. Perrybingle, Miss Clifford as Bertha, Rose Leclercq as May, Mrs. Collier as Mrs. Fielding, Miss Wadham as Tilly Slowboy, Miss Laidlaw as Cricket.

CRICKET ON THE HEARTH, THE: A FAIRY TALE OF HOME// D 2a// Dram. by Edward Stirling fr novel of Charles Dickens// **Adelphi,** Dec. 1845; Jan. 1846, with O. Smith as John Peerybingle, Mr. Lambert as Caleb Plummer, William Cullenford as Tackleton, Charles Selby as Edward, Mrs. Fitzwilliam as Dot, Sarah Woolgar as Bertha, Edward Wright as Tilly Slowboy, Ellen Chaplin as the Fairy/ **Haymarket,** Jan. 1846, with Benjamin Webster as Peerybingle, Mr. Tilbury as Tackleton, William Farren as Caleb Plummer, Henry Holl as Stranger, Miss Fortescue as Dot, Mrs. Seymour as Bertha, Mrs. W. Clifford as Mrs. Fielding, Miss Telbin as May, J. B. Buckstone as Tilly Slowboy, Mrs. L. S. Buckingham as The Presence/ Scenery by George Morris/ Music by T. German Reed.

CRICKET ON THE HEARTH, THE: A FAIRY TALE OF HOME// D 2a// Dram. by Thomas Archer fr novel of Charles Dickens// **Princess's,** Jan. 1846, with John Ryder as Peerybingle, F. C. Courtney as Tackleton, Henry Compton as Caleb Plummer, Leigh Murray as Stranger, Mrs. Stirling as Mrs. Peerybingle, Miss Marshall as Bertha, Miss Brentnall as May, Mrs. Fosbroke as Mrs. Fielding, Miss Somers as Tilly Slowboy/ Scenery by William Beverley, Mr. Nicholls,

& Mr. Grey/ Machines by Mr. Breckell/ **Grecian**, Jan. 1846, with Edwin Dixon as Peerybingle, Mr. Campbell as Tackleton, Mr. Baldwin as Caleb Plummer, Edmund Garden as Stranger, Annette Mears as Mrs. Peerybingle, Mary A. Crisp as Bertha, Frederick Robson as Tilly Slowboy, Mrs. W. Watson as Mrs. Fielding, Miss E. Cushnie as Cricket.

CRICKET ON THE HEARTH, THE// Dram. by W. T. Townsend fr novel of Charles Dickens// **City of London**, Jan. 1846.

CRIES OF LONDON, THE; OR, THE TREASURE TROVE// C// W. E. Suter// **Grecian**, June 1865, with Henry Grant as Chizzelm, George Gillett as Percival, Walter Holland as Ginspinner, W. Shirley as Jacob Green, William James as Billy Green, J. Jackson as Old Cotton, John Manning as Tom Cotton, Louise Graham as Mrs. Chizzelm, Mary A. Victor as Mary Ann.

CRIME; OR, THE BLACK HEART// D// L. G. Kean// **Victoria**, Aug. 1877.

CRIME AND CHRISTENING// F// Richard Butler & H. C. Newton ("Richard Henry")// **Opera Comique**, Mar. 1891, with E. Banstock as Prowle, J. Ettinson as Gribble, S. Hill as Algernon, Linda Verner as Mrs. Townley, Ethel Blenheim as Mrs. Prowle, Katie Seymour as Lucinda.

CRIME AND JUSTICE; OR, THE SHADOW OF THE SCAFFOLD// D 5a// Burford Delannoy & Norman Harvey// **Sadler's Wells**, Dec. 1892.

CRIME AND REPENTANCE// D 2a// Edward Towers// **Grecian**, June 1864, with J. B. Steele as Reardon, William James as Glanville, W. Shirley as Pulltrap, Walter Holland as Edwards, John Manning as Sponge, Henry Grant as Snare, Henry Power as Weazel, Mrs. Charles Dillon as Mary, Marie Brewer as Susan.

CRIMELESS CRIMINAL, A// F 1a// Martin Becher// **Strand**, Apr. 1874, with William Terriss, Fanny Hughes.

CRIMES OF PARIS, THE// D 6a// Paul Meritt & George Conquest// **Surrey**, Oct. 1883.

CRIMINAL COUPLE, A// F// Frank Herbert// **Princess's**, June 1871, with Mr. Barrett as Pyefinch, Charles Seyton as Featherwhite, Bernard Cullen as O'Cator, Miss Lennox Grey as Mrs. Featherwhite.

CRIMINAL JUDGE, A; OR, THE LIGHT OF TRUTH// D Pro & 4a// Arthur Shirley & Benjamin Landeck// **Pavilion**, Nov. 1900.

CRIMSON CROSS, THE// D 4a// Clement Scott ("Savile Rowe") & E. Manuel// **Adelphi**, Feb. 1878, with Charles Flockton as Charles VI, Hermann Vezin as Count D'Armagnac, Johnston Forbes Robertson as Chevalier de Boisredon, Henry Neville as Perrinet, Robert Markby as Hugonnet, Harwood Cooper as Duchastel, Robert Pateman as Bornibus, Clara Jecks as Gontran, Adelaide Neilson as Queen Isabel, Harriet Coveney as Mme. Bornibus.

CRIMSON ROCK, THE// D 3a// Julian Cross// **Pavilion**, May 1879.

CRINOLINE// F 1a// Robert Brough// **Olympic**, Dec. 1856, with Frederick Robson as Coobiddy, George Vining as Capt. Le Brown, Harwood Cooper as Liptrot, Mr. Danvers as Grimes, Miss Maskell as Mrs. Coobiddy, Miss Marston as Bella, Miss Stevens as Miss Tite, James Rogers as Nancy.

CRISIS, THE// Adap. by James Albery fr F of Emile Augier, Les Fourchambault// **Haymarket**, Dec. 1878, with Henry Howe as Denham, William Terriss as Fawley Denham, David Fisher Jr. as Lord Whitehead, Charles Kelly as Goring, Mrs. John Wood as Mrs. Denham, Lucy Buckstone as Blanche, Louise Moodie as Mrs. Goring, Mary Eastlake as Haidee.

CRITIC, THE; OR, A TRAGEDY REHEARSED// F 3a// Richard Brinsley Sheridan// **Cov. Garden**, Nov. 1840, with William Farren as Sir Fretful, C. J. Mathews as Puff, Mr. Cooper as Sneer, Mr. Hemming as Dangle, Mrs. Brougham as Mrs. Dangle, John Pritt Harley as Whiskerandos, James Bland as Leicester, Drinkwater Meadows as Raleigh, Frank Matthews as Governor, Mrs. Orger as Tilburnia, Mrs. Charles Jones as Confidante/ **Haymarket**, May 1843, with C. J. Mathews as Puff, Mr. Stuart as Sneer, Mr. Tilbury as Dangle, William Farren as Sir Fretful, Mr. Gallot as Prompter, Mrs. Stanley as Mrs. Dangle, J. W. Gough as Burleigh, William Strickland as Governor, James Bland as Leicester, William Clark as Raleigh, J. B. Buckstone as Whiskerandos, Mrs. Humby as Tilburnia, Miss Mattley as Confidante; Nov. 1858, with C. J. Mathews as Puff and Sir Fretful, Edwin Villiers as Dangle, George Braid as Sneer, Miss Fitzinman as Mrs. Dangle, F. C. Courtney as Burleigh, William Cullenford as Governor, Thomas Coe as Leicester, J. Worrell as Raleigh, Henry Compton as Wiskerandos, Mrs. C. J. Mathews as Tilburnia, Mrs. Griffiths as Confidante; Jan. 1892, with Charles Hawtrey as Dangle, Charles Hudson as Sneer, Mr. Wigley as Under Prompter, Henry Neville as Puff, Arthur Cecil as Burleigh, Fred Leslie as Governor, Robb Harwood as Leicester, Henry Kemble as Raleigh, George Barrett as Whiskerandos, Mrs. E. H. Brooke as Confidante, Kate Phillips as Tilburnia/ **Sad. Wells**, Feb. 1845, with A. Young as Sir Fretful, John Webster as Puff, George Bennett as Sneer, E. Morton as Dangle, Frank Graham as Leicester, Mr. Coreno as Raleigh, Charles Fenton as Sir Christopher, Charles Williams as Governor, Miss Lebatt as Tilburnia, Mrs. Henry Marston as Confidante, Georgiana Lebatt as Niece/ **Princess's**, June 1846, with C. J. Mathews as Sir Fretful and as Puff, John Ryder as Sneer, Robert Roxby as Dangle, Robert Honner as Prompter, Miss E. Honner as Mrs. Dangle, Henry Compton as Whiskerandos, W. H. Oxberry as Leicester, Augustus Harris as Sir Walter Raleigh, Mr. Wynn as Sir Christopher, A. Walton as Governor, Emma Stanley as Tilburnia, Miss Somers as Confidante; June 1852, with James Vining as Sneer, Mr. Addison as Sir Fretful, Mr. Edmonds as Prompter, Alfred Wigan as

Puff, Charles Wheatleigh as Dangle, Miss Murray as Mrs. Dangle, John Chester as Leicester, William Graham as Governor, Drinkwater Meadows as Raleigh, George Everett as Sir Christopher, John Pritt Harley as Whiskerandos, Mrs. W. Daly as Confidante, Mrs. Alfred Wigan as Tilburnia/ **Lyceum**, Oct. 1848, with C. J. Mathews as Sir Fretful, Charles Selby as Puff, John Parselle as Dangle, Mrs. Charles Horn as Mrs. Dangle, John Pritt Harley as Whiskerandos, Robert Roxby as Leicester, Drinkwater Meadows as Raleigh, Mr. Bellingham as Sir Christopher, Frank Matthews as Governor, Mrs. Yates as Tilburnia, Mrs. Macnamara as Confidante/ **Drury Lane**, Oct. 1855, with C. J. Mathews as Sir Fretful and Puff, Mr. Stuart as Sneer, C. Vincent as Dangle, Emma Wadham as Mrs. Dangle, Robert Roxby as Whiskerandos, C. Swan as Leicester, W. Templeton as Raleigh, A. Younge as Governor, Mrs. Frank Matthews as Tilburnia, Mrs. Selby as Confidante/ **Globe**, May 1871, with H. J. Montague, Charles Neville, J. H. Barnes, Henry Compton, Carlotta Addison/ **Gaiety**, Oct. 1872; Aug. 1883/ **St. James's**, Feb. 1880, with Charles Harcourt, G. W. Anson, John Maclean, Edward Terry, Emily Duncan, Miss E. Farren.

CROCK OF GOLD, THE; OR, MURDER AT THE HALL// D 2a// Dram. by Edward Fitzball fr story of M. F. Tupper// **City of London**, May 1848/ **Astley's**, June 1849, with Mr. Silvain as Sir John, Bruce Norton as Simon, Mr. Johnson as Justice Sharp, Mr. Crowther as Roger Acton, Stephen Smith as Burke, Henry Bedford as Jonathan, Mrs. Beacham as Mrs. Quarles, Rosa Henry as Grace, Helen Lane as Sarah.

CROMWELL// D 5a// A. B. Richards// **Queen's**, Dec. 1872.

CROMWELL; OR, THE CONSPIRACY// D// Adap. by Frederick Phillips fr F of Victor Hugo// **Surrey**, Feb. 1859.

CROOKED MILE, A// Play 3a// Clara Lemore// **Vaudeville**, Apr. 1888.

CROSS-BOW LETTER, THE; OR, THE MILLER OF WHETSTONE// D// T. E. Wilks// **Victoria**, June 1854, with Mr. Henderson as Lovell, Mr. Morrison as Leslie, Mr. Green as Basnet, Mr. Hitchinson as Lancelot, James W. Howard as Carraway, Charles Rice as Goodfellow, Miss Laporte as Cyprian, Annette Vincent as Kate, Miss Dansor as Duchess of Exeter.

CROSS OF DEATH, THE; OR, THE DOG WITNESS// D// n.a.// **Victoria**, Aug. 1850, with Mr. Henderson as Munoz, J. Neville as Gen. Morier, Mr. Hitchinson as Capt. Lenoir, Henry Frazer as Carvallho, E. F. Taylor as Monville, G. F. Forman as Maggot, Mr. Cony as Cabroni, John Bradshaw as Blarney, Dog Hector, Amelia Mercer as Adeline, Miss Barrowcliffe as Violante.

CROSS OF GOLD, THE; OR, A WOMAN'S LOVE AND A SOLDIER'S HONOUR// D// Adap. fr F// **Sad. Wells**, June 1857, with Frederick Morton as Eugene, James Johnstone as Sgt. Carronade, G. B. Bigwood as Brant, Mrs. Robert Honner as Madeline, Mary A. Victor as Jocette.

CROSS OF HONOUR, THE// D 5a// Adap. by Arthur Shirley & Maurice Gally fr F of Léopold Stapleaux, Le Couçon// **Royalty**, July 1892.

CROSS OF THE DEAD, THE; OR, THE BLACK BROTHERHOOD OF WERSTENSFIELD// D 2a// n.a.// **Victoria**, Aug. 1843, with F. Wilton as Capt. Groff, Charles Williams as Ochler, William Seaman as Vanderstitchell, John Gardner as Nix, F. H. Henry as Hornberg, Mr. Hitchinson as Helman, John Dale as Gaen, Annette Vincent as Lestelle, Miss Ridgeway as Widow Vanderstichell, Miss Saddler as Annette, Mrs. Franklin as Cecile.

CROSS PURPOSES// C// Adap. by J. Parselle fr F// **Strand**, Mar. 1865.

CROSSBOW LETTER, THE// C// T. E. Wilks// **Victoria**, Feb. 1848, with T. H. Higgie as Lovyll, Mr. Henderson as Leslie, Walter Searle as Bonnet, Mr. Hitchinson as Lancelot, Miss Burroughcliffe as Cyprian, Mrs. N. T. Hicks as Duchess of Exeter, Annette Vincent as Kate.

CROSSROADS OF LIFE, THE; OR, THE SCAMPS OF LONDON// D 3a// Adap. fr F of Eugène Sue, Mystères de Paris// **Sad. Wells**, Nov. 1843, with Henry Marston as Deverex, Robert Romer as Dorrington, C. J. Bird as Frank Danvers, Mr. Melvin as Herbert Danvers, P. Williams as Shabner, W. H. Williams as Yorkney, C. J. Smith as Fogg, Mr. Coreno as Brindle, Charles Fenton as Smith, Caroline Rankley as Louisa, Mrs. Richard Barnett as Charlotte, Miss Stephens as Miss Dorrington/ Scenery by F. Fenton/ Prod. by Henry Marston/ **Grecian**, Nov. 1862, with Alfred Rayner as Deverley, W. Shirley as Dorrington, J. Jackson as Shabner, William James as Frank Danvers, John Manning as Yorkney, Thomas Mead as Herbert Danvers, George Conquest as Tom Fog, Henry Power as Brindle, Henry Grant as Onion, Mrs. Charles Dillon as Louisa, Mary A. Victor as Charlotte, Marie Brewer as Miss Dorrington.

CROTCHETS// F// Frederick Hay// **Strand**, June 1876.

CROWN OF THORNS, A// D 4a// Gilbert Elliott// **Olympic**, Oct. 1896, with Gilbert Elliott as Count Vauthier, Dudley Clinton as Lefrane, William Felton as Baron Holstein, John Ottaway as Froude, Harry Paulton as Picot, Louis Ford as Abbé, Charles Holmes as Officer, Mrs. Walter Edwin as Countess Vauthier, Alice de Winton as Salonara, Georgie Wright as Ninette, Millicent Marsden as Marie, Emily Edwin as Mother Bagnolet, Agnes Hewitt as Princess Mathilde.

CROWN PRINCE, THE; OR, THE BUCKLE OF BRILLIANTS// D 2a// T. E. Wilks// **Sadler's Wells**, July 1838, with Robert Honner as Prince Augustus, Mr. Harwood as Count Alvitz, C. Montague as Baron Ritzberg, Mr. Day as Count Hermann, Mr. Mellor as Count Rossult, Mr.

Hitchinson as Col. Rausten, Mrs. J. F. Saville as Lady Anne, Miss Lee as Lady Gouche, C. J. Smith as Roderic, John Webster as Frederick, Dibdin Pitt as Storke, Miss E. Honner as Katherine, Mrs. Weston as Dame Barbara, Miss Cooke as Dame Gertrude/ Prod. by R. Honner/ **Grecian**, Sept. 1847, with Richard Phillips as Prince Albert, Edwin Dixon as Count Herman, Mr. Manley as Count Renault, Mr. Hamilton as Col. Roustan, John Webster as Frederick, Miss Merion as Dame Barbara, Ellen Crisp as Dame Gertrude, Annette Mears as Catherine, Ada Harcourt as Carina.

CRUEL CITY, THE; OR, LONDON BY NIGHT// D 4a// Gertrude Warden & Wilton Jones// **Surrey**, Oct. 1896/ **Novelty**, May 1897, with Jack Haddon as Geoffrey Darrell, Bernard Copping as Stanley Darrell, Reginald Eyre as Gascoigne, F. J. Beresford as Brown, Charles Cameron as Fawley, Ernest Nelson as Hartmann, Horace Lownds as Dr. Whiteley, Cecil Hill as Banks, Geraldine Montrose as Lulu, Margaret Marshall as Auntie Baxter, Lucy Murray as Sarah, Isa Bellington as May.

CRUEL KINDNESS, THE// Play 5a// Catherine Crowe// **Haymarket**, June 1853, with Henry Howe as Duke of Urbino, Barry Sullivan as Guilio, William Farren as Carlo, Mr. Rogers as Lorenzo, Mr. Tilbury as Lanzi, Henry Vincent as Antonio, Thomas Coe as Ribaldo, J. B. Buckstone as Hans Wurz, Miss Reynolds as Florentia, Mrs. Fitzwilliam as Gretchen, Mrs. L. S. Buckingham as Viola, Ellen Chaplin as Lisa, Miss E. Romer as Brigida/ Scenery by Charles Marshall, George Morris & John O'Conner/ Machines by James Frow.

CRUEL TO BE KIND// C 1a// T. J. Williams & Augustus Harris// **Princess's**, Mar. 1860, with Augustus Harris as Brown, Frank Matthews as Blackstone, Carlotta Leclercq as Mrs. Trelawney, Mrs. Weston as Miss Sacharissa, Rose Leclercq as Lucy, Mrs. J. W. Collier as Petty/ **Drury Lane**, July 1860, with same cast.

CRUSADERS, THE// D// Joseph Ebsworth// **Marylebone**, Nov. 1849.

CRUSADERS, THE// D 3a// Henry Arthur Jones// **Avenue**, Nov. 1891, with Arthur Cecil as Lord Burnham, Yorke Stephens as Rusper, Lewis Waller as Ingerfield, Weedon Grossmith as Palsam, Henry Kemble as Burge-Jawle, Sant Matthews as Figg, E. Allan Aynesworth as Rev. Portal, Winifred Emery as Cynthia, Lady Monckton as Mrs. Campion-Blake, Ettie Williams as Lady Gloire, Therèse Mayer as Victorine, Olga Brandon as Una/ Scenery by Walter Hann.

CRUSHED TRAGEDIAN, THE// C 5a// adap. fr H. J. Byron's The Prompter's Box// **Haymarket**, May 1878, with E. A. Sothern as Fitzaltamont, Henry Howe as Bristowe, G. F. De Vere as Glendenning, H. B. Conway as Ernest, George Holland as Capt. Rackett, Harry Crouch as Mandeville, Frederick Everill as Gadsby, Marion Terry as Florence, Mrs. G. F. De Vere as Miss Mountcashel, Emily Thorne as Mrs. Galpin, Jenny Ashley as Reynolds.

CRUTCH AND TOOTHPICK// C 3a// Adap. by G. R. Sims// **Royalty**, Apr. 1879, with Edgar Bruce, W. S. Penley, Lytton Sothern, Rose Cullen/ **Gaiety**, Nov. 1879.

CRYPTOIDSYMPHONOSTOMATA// F 1a// Charles Collette// **Globe**, Apr. 1876, with Charles Collette as Plantagenet Smith, Arthur Wing Pinero as Toddleposh, Miss A. Anderson as Polly.

CRYSTAL-GAZER, THE// C 1a// Leopold Montague// **Coronet**, June 1899.

CRYSTAL GLOBE, THE// D 5a// Adap. by Sutton Vane fr F of Xavier De Montépin & Jules Dornay, La Joueuse D'Orgue// **Princess's**, Jan. 1899, with Lawrence Irving as Petrovski, Arthur Playfair as Picard, John Saunders as Richard Bernier, Oscar Adye as Robert Bernier, Frank Dyall as Capt. Savan, Fred Lane as Daniel Savan, Oswald Yorke as Henri Savan, Charles Garry as Grivot, Lennox Pawle as Roc, H. Athol Forde as Poisson, Bella Pateman as Veronique, Ethel Hope as Mme. Felix, Groegie Esmond as Marie, Edith Bottomley as Catherine, Dora De Winton as Judith, Lena Ashwell as Claire/ Scenery by J. M. Davis, Cecil Hicks, Henry Brooke & W. T. Hemsley/ Music by T. Harrow/ Electrics by Niblett & Sutherland/ Prod. by E. B. Norman.

CUCKOO, THE// C 1a// Walter Helmore// **Criterion**, Oct. 1887.

CUCKOO, THE// C 3a// Adap. by C. H. Brookfield fr F of Henri Meilhac, Décoré// **Avenue**, Mar. 1899, with Charles Hawtrey as Farrant, Lyston Lyle as Col. Gower, Arthur Williams as Penfold, Frederick Volpé as Sir Robert, Charles Stevens as Colefax, Frank Curzon as Pratt, Hugh Goring as Hewson, Fanny Ward as Guinevere, Constance Collier as Lady Alexandra, Vane Featherston as Leggatt.

CUFFS AND KISSES// F 1a// Adap. by Thomas Archer fr F// **Sad. Wells**, Aug. 1846, with E. Morton as Duke de Bassompiere, Henry Scharf as Grillon, Charles Fenton as Paul, Mr. Maskell as Jaques, Mrs. Brougham as Marchioness de Lanroy, Miss St. George as Julie, Miss Maskell as Priscille/ **Grecian**, May 1847, with Mr. Manley as Duke de Bassompierre, Frederick Robson as Grillon, Mr. Griffiths as Haymaker, Miss Merion as Marchionesse, Mary A. Crisp as Julie.

CULPRIT, THE// F 1a// T. H. Bayly// **St. James's**, Jan. 1838, with John Pritt Harley as Capt. Hussey, John Gardner as Bob, Mrs. Stirling as Mrs. Hussey, Mme. Sala as Miss Wyndham, Julia Smith as Bridget/ **Haymarket**, June 1840, with John Webster as Capt. Hussey, J. B. Buckstone as Bob, Miss Charles as Mrs. Hussey, Mrs. Frank Matthews as Bridget, Mme. Sala as Miss Wyndham/ **Sad. Wells**, Oct. 1848, with William Hoskins as Capt. Hussey, Mr. Williams as Bob, Miss Cooper as Mrs. Hussey, Mrs. Henry Marston as Miss Wyndham, Miss Stephens as Bridget.

CULPRITS// F 3a// Arthur Law// **Terry's**, Mar. 1891, with Edward Terry as Maj. Rackshaw, Fred Kaye as Sir Joseph, Walter Everard as Fanlight, Henry Esmond as Pendlecoop, Herman de Lange as Count Octave, Robert Soutar as Burton, Sophie Larkin as Lady Pendlecoop, Elinore Leyshon as Mary, Alice Yorke as Countess, Eva Moore as Gwendoline, Susie Vaughan as Mrs. Rackshaw.

CULTURE// C 3a// Adap. by Sebastian and Frank Evans fr F of Edouard Pailleron, Le Monde où l'on s'Ennuie// **Gaiety**, May 1885.

CUP, THE// T 2a// Alfred Tennyson// **Lyceum**, Jan. 1881, with Henry Irving as Synorix, William Terriss as Sinnatus, Georgina Pauncefort as Phoebe, Ellen Terry as Camma, Frank Tyars as Antonius, Mr. Hudson as Publius/ Scenery by William Telbin, Hawes Craven & W. Cuthbert/ Music by Hamilton Clarke.

CUP OF TEA, A// C 1a// n.a.// **Princess's**, Feb. 1869/ **Olympic**, May 1872, with Frank Harvey as Sir Charles, Henry Andrews as Scroggins, H. Bennett as Joseph, Eva Hamilton as Lady Clara; July 1881 (as The Cup of Tea), with David Gaunt as Sir Charles, Henry Andrews as Scroggins, H. Bennett as Josephs, Rose Murray as Lady Clara/ **Haymarket**, Sept. 1874, with Frank Harvey as Sir Charles, Henry Andrews as Scroggins, H. Bennett as Joseph, Annie La Fontaine as Lady Clara/ **Gaiety**, Mar. 1883/ **Sad. Wells**, Apr. 1883, with F. Tannehill Jr. as Sir Charles, Richard Waldon as Scroggins, George Richard as Joseph, Lizzie Kelsey as Lady Seymour.

CUPBOARD LOVE// F 1a// Frederick Hay// **Vaudeville**, Apr. 1870.

CUPBOARD LOVE// F 3a// H. V. Esmond// **Court**, Dec. 1898, with Herbert Standing as Sir Gifford, Seymour Hicks as Cruttendan, Dion Boucicault as Cadge, Kenneth Douglas as Silman, Aubrey Fitzgerald as Kertchley, C. P. Little as Jenkyn, George Hawtrey as Griffiths, Cyril Vernon as Grant, May Whitty as Rosamond, Sybil Carlisle as Eva, Nina Boucicault as Baby, Grace Dudley as Jessie, Marianne Caldwell as Lady Carter, Mary A. Victor as Miss Benstead/ Scenery by William Perkins/ Prod. by Dion G. Boucicault.

CUPID IN CAMP// C 2a// G. C. Vernon// **Criterion**, May 1882, with A. M. Denison, William Blakeley, Lytton Sothern, Mary Rorke, Rose Saker.

CUPID IN WAITING// C 3a// Blanchard Jerrold// **Royalty**, June 1871.

CUPID'S DIPLOMACY// C// n.a.// **Drury Lane**, Jan. 1840, with Mrs. Stirling as Louis XV, Mr. Archer as Leckzinska, William Bennett as Stockman, Miss Montague as Princess Marie, Mrs. Selby as Ulrica.

CUPID'S LADDER// D 2a// Leicester Buckingham// **St. James's**, Oct. 1859.

CUPID'S MESSENGER// Play 1a// Alfred C. Calmour// **Novelty**, July 1884/ **Vaudeville**, 1885.

CUPS AND SAUCERS// F// Adap. by George Grossmith fr F, La Ceramique// **Opera Comique**, Aug. 1878.

CURE FOR LOVE, A// C 2a// Thomas Parry// **Haymarket**, Nov. 1842, with William Farren as Trimmer, J. B. Buckstone as Sadgrove, Henry Howe as Markworth, Mr. Tilbury as Staples, Henry Widdicomb as Switch, Mrs. Malone Raymond as Mrs. Trimmer, Mrs. W. Clifford as Mrs. Browne, Mrs. Frank Matthews as Mrs. Tubbs, Miss C. Conner as Cecilia; Nov. 1853, with W. H. Chippendale as Trimmer, J. B. Buckstone as Sadgrove, Edwin Villiers as Markworth, William Cullenford as Staple, William Clark as Switch, Ellen Chaplin as Mrs. Trimmer, Mrs. Stanley as Mrs. Brown, Mrs. Poynter as Miss Bitterton, Miss W. Woulds as Mrs. Tubbs, Amelia Vining as Cecilia/ Scenery by George Morris & John O'Conner; July 1870, with J. B. Buckstone as Sadgrove, Frederick Everill as Trimmer, Walter Gordon as Markworth, P. White as Staple, William Clark as Switch, Mrs. Edward Fitzwilliam as Mrs. Trimmer, Mrs. Chippendale as Mrs. Brown, Miss Lewin as Mrs. Tubbs, Mrs. Laws as Miss Bitterton, Fanny Wright as Jeanette/ **Sad. Wells**, June 1855, with J. B. Buckstone as Sadgrove, Mr. Barrett as Trimmer, Edwin Villiers as Markwell, William Cullenford as Staple, Robert Soutar as Switch, C. Kelsy as William, Ellen Chaplin as Mrs. Trimmer, Mrs. Barrett as Miss Bitterton, Mrs. Griffiths as Mrs. Brown, Miss Macarthy as Mrs. Tubbs.

CURE FOR THE FIDGETS, A// F 1a// T. J. Williams// **Surrey**, Sept. 1867/ **Gaiety**, Sept. 1876.

CURE FOR THE GOUT, A// F// H. A. Major// **Sad. Wells**, June 1860, with F. A. Chart as Sir George, Mr. Boyden as Col. Medway, H. A. Major as Quicksett, Miss Graham as Emily, Emily Vining as Rose.

CURE FOR THE HEARTACHE, A// C// Thomas Morton// **Sad. Wells**, Mar. 1841, with George Ellis as Sir Hubert, Mr. Elvin as Stanley, Mr. Dry as Vortex, J. S. Balls as Young Rapid, Mr. Williams as Old Rapid, Robert Honner as Frank Oatland, Mr. Aldridge as Farmer Oatland, Mrs. J. F. Saville as Ellen, Miss Richardson as Miss Vortex, Mrs. Robert Honner as Jessy; Dec. 1848 (in 3a), with Henry Mellon as Sir Hubert, Frank Graham as Stanley, Mr. Williams as Vortex, William Hoskins as Young Rapid, A. Younge as Old Rapid, Henry Scharf as Oatland, Mr. Gladstone as Bronze, Fanny Huddart as Ellen, Mrs. Henry Marston as Miss Vortex, Miss Garthwaite as Jessy/ **Haymarket**, Dec. 1841, with David Rees as Old Rapid, Frederick Vining as Young Rapid, Henry Wallack as Sir Hubert, Henry Howe as Young Stanley, William Strickland as Vortex, Benjamin Webster as Frank Oatland, Mr. Gallot as Farmer Oatland, J. W. Gough as Heartley, Miss Charles as Ellen, Mrs. W. Clifford as Miss Vortex, Priscilla Horton as Jessy/ **Grecian**, Oct. 1847 (in 3a), with John Collett as Sir Hubert, Edwin Dixon as Charles,

Mr. Baldwin as Vortex, John Webster as Young Rapid, Eaton O'Donnell as Old Rapid, Frederick Robson as Frank Oatland, Miss Leclercq as Ellen, Annette Mears as Miss Vortex, Ada Harcourt as Jessy/ **Marylebone**, Oct. 1853 (in 5a), with J. W. Wallack, Henry Vandenhoff/ **Drury Lane**, Mar. 1857 (in 3a), with Mr. Carter as Sir Hubert, Charles Vincent as Charles, Mr. Tilbury as Vortex, Robert Keeley as Old Rapid, C. J. Mathews as Young Rapid, Mrs. Keeley as Oatland, W. Templeton as Bronze, Mrs. Frank Matthews as Miss Vortex, Miss Cleveland as Ellen, Miss M. Oliver as Jessy/ **Royalty**, Sept. 1872.

CURIOSITIES OF LITERATURE, THE// F// Dion Boucicault// **Haymarket**, Sept. 1842, with Mr. Tilbury as Sir Terence, A. Brindal as Maj. Blunt, Benjamin Webster as Dibbs, William Clark as Chicane, J. Worrell as Finesse, Mrs. Stanley as Lady Pension, Miss Stanley as Jenny, Miss C. Conner as Emily, Miss Carre as Mrs. Biggs.

CURIOUS CASE, A// C 2a// T. H. Reynoldson// **Princess's**, Oct. 1846, with James Vining as Aubrey, C. J. Mathews as Twiggleton, Charles Fisher as Stanton, Robert Honner as Edward, Mrs. Stirling as Mrs. Aubrey/ **Drury Lane**, Mar. 1857, with Charles Vincent as Aubrey, Walter Gordon as Stanton, C. J. Mathews as Twiggleton, W. Templeton as Edward, Miss M. Oliver as Mrs. Aubrey.

CURIOSITY; OR, THE DOOMED ENTOMBED// F 1a// Joseph Clarence// **Astley's**, Mar. 1849, with Mr. Johnson as Barnaby, Henry Bedford as Capt. Dashon, Joseph Clarence as Bob Short, Mr. Mathews as Eben. Short, Mrs. Beacham as Mrs. Barnaby, Miss Henry as Marian, Ellen Daly as Susan.

CURIOSITY// FC 3a// Joseph Derrick// **Vaudeville**, Sept. 1886, with Edward Righton, Sophie Larkin, Kate James.

CURIOUS CASE, A// C 2a// T. H. Reynoldson// **Princess's**, 1846/ **Lyceum**, Feb. 1850, with C. J. Mathews as Twiggleton, Robert Roxby as Aubrey, John Parselle as Stanton, Robert Honner as Edward, Miss H. Gilbert as Mrs. Aubrey/ **Gaiety**, Oct. 1872.

CURLING IRONS AND CAPERS// F 1a// W. E. Suter// **Grecian**, Nov. 1869, with J. Jackson as Col. Capsicum, George Gillett as Addlenob, Henry Grant as Twizzle, Samuel Perfitt as Formost, George Conquest as Fitzmagig, Alice Denvil as Mrs. Capsicum, Miss Dearlove as Camilla, Mary A. Victor as Betsy.

CURRENT CASH// D Pro & 4a// C. A. Clarke & N. Shields// **Surrey**, July 1887.

CURSE OF INTEMPERENCE, THE; OR, THE DRUNKARD'S WARNING// D 2a// H. P. Grattan// **Sad. Wells**, Oct. 1842, with Mr. Aldridge as Spiggot, Mr. Dry as Springe, C. J. Bird as Wheatear, Henry Marston as Redburn, John Herbert as Fungus, Mr. Richardson as Weazle, Caroline Rankley as Ellen, Mrs. Richard Barnett as Susan/ Scenery by F. Fenton/ Machines by Mr. Cawdery/ Music by Isaac Collins/ Prod. by Henry Marston.

CURSE OF ST. VALLIER, THE; OR, THE JESTER'S DAUGHTER// D 3a// Adap. fr F// **Sad. Wells**, May 1840, with Mr. Dry as Francis I, Mr. Houghburt as Marquis Landry, J. W. Collier as Viscount de Pienne, Mr. Stilt as Marquis de Montmorency, Henry Marston as Triboulet, Mr. Williams as Count de St. Vallier, Mr. Aldridge as Count de Copé, Mrs. Robert Honner as Lady Florine, Mme. Louise as Countess de Copé, Miss Cooke as Mme. Berarde, Mrs. Richard Barnett as Madelonne/ Scenery by F. Fenton & G. Smithyes Jr./ Music by Isaac Collins/ Machines by B. Sloman/ Prod. by R. Honner.

CUSHLA-MA-CREE// D 3a// John Levey// **Marylebone**, Oct. 1873.

CUSTOM HOUSE, THE// FC 3a// L. A. D. Montague// **Vaudeville**, Mar. 1892, with Cecil Crofton as Crabb, John Clulow as Young, Howard Sturge as Cotfield, Ells Dagnall as Chalker, Lillie Belmore as Mrs. Young, Charlotte Morland as Tryphena, Lilian Daily as Miss Montrevor, Emily Dowton as Mrs. Brimblecombe/ Scenery by W. T. Hemsley/ Prod. by George Belmore.

CUT AND COME AGAIN// F 1a// Robert Soutar// **Olympic**, Aug. 1879, with Clifford Cooper as Stuckuppington, Luigi Lablache as Merrydash, Frank Wood as Coldscran, Miss A. Bruce as Veiled Lady, Miss Coleridge as Muffled Lady.

CUT FOR PARTNERS// F 1a// James Bruton// **Princess's**, Apr. 1845.

CUT OFF WITH A SHILLING// C 1a// S. Theyre Smith// **POW**, April 1871.

CUTLET FOR TWO, A// F// n.a.// **Princess's**, Dec. 1848, with W. H. Oxberry as Cutlet, Mr. Wynn as Pomp, George Honey as Meddlemake, Miss Kenworthy as Lady Narcissa, Mrs. Selby as Mrs. Pomp, Emma Stanley as Patty.

CYCLING// C 1a// Albert Chevalier// **Strand**, July 1888.

CYMBELINE, KING OF BRITAIN// D// William Shakespeare// **Cov. Garden**, May 1837, with John Dale as Cymbeline, John Webster as Guiderius, J. Worrell as Arviragus, Benjamin Webster as Cloten, George Bennett as Bellarius, John Pritchard as Pisanio, W. C. Macready as Posthumus, E. W. Elton as Iachimo, Mr. Thompson as Lucius, Mr. Harris as Philario, Helen Faucit as Imogen, Mrs. W. West as Queen, Miss Nicholson as Helen/ **Drury Lane**, Feb. 1843, with John Ryder as Cymbeline, Henry Compton as Cloten, James Anderson as Posthumus, Samuel Phelps as Bellarius, Charles Hudson as Guiderius, Mr. Allen as Arviragus, Miss Ellis as Queen, Helen Faucit as Imogen, Miss Fairbrother as Helen, W. C. Macready as Iachimo, W. H. Bland as Philario, George Bennett as Lucius; Oct. 1864, with Samuel Phelps as Posthumous, William Creswick as Iachimo, Henry Marston as Bellarius, Edmund

Phelps as Passanio, Walter Lacy as Cloten, Alfred Rayner as Cymbeline, G. F. Neville as Guiderius, Mr. Meagerson [sic] as Lucius, Miss Atkinson as Queen, Helen Faucit as Imogen, Miss Green as Helen/ **Sad. Wells**, Aug. 1847, with Henry Mellon as Cymbeline, Henry Scharf as Cloten, Samuel Phelps as Posthumus, George Bennett as Delarius, William Hoskins as Guiderius, J. T. Johnson as Arviragus, Frank Graham as Philario, Henry Marston as Iachimo, Mr. Williams as Cornelius, Mrs. Henry Marston as Queen, Laura Addison as Imogen, Miss Morelli as Helen/ Scenery by F. Fenton & A. Finlay/ **Lyceum**, Sept. 1896 (arr. by Henry Irving), with F. H. Macklin as Cymbeline, Norman Forbes as Cloten, Frank Cooper as Posthumus, Frederic Robinson as Belarius, Ben Webster as Guiderius, Gordon Craig as Arviragus, Frank Tyars as Pisanio, Genevieve Ward as the Queen, Mrs. Tyars as Helen, Ellen Terry as Imogen, Henry Irving as Iachimo, Fuller Mellish as Philario/ Scenery by Hawes Craven & J. Harker/ Music by Hamilton Clarke.

CYNIC, THE// C 4a// Dram. fr the Faust legend by Hermann Merivale// **Globe**, Jan. 1882, with Herman Vezin as Count Lestrange, Arthur Dacre as Guy Faucit, David Fisher Sr. as Lord Rosherville, Henry Hamilton as Gosling, Philip Beck as Capt. Fairfield, Marie Litton as Daisy Brent, Louise Willes as Lady Luscombe, Miss Meredith as Carrie.

CYNTHIA'S SACRIFICE// D 1a// Edwin Drew// **St. Geo. Hall**, Apr. 1893.

CYRANO DE BERGERAC// Play 5a// Edmond Rostand// **Lyceum**, July, 1898/ **Adelphi**, June, 1899/ **Wyndham's**, Apr. 1900.

CYRENE// D 3a// Alfred C. Calmour// **Avenue**, June 1890.

CYRIL WOODBINE; OR, THE OLD ELM GROVE// D// n.a.// **Sad. Wells**, Apr. 1837, with C. H. Pitt as Cyril, Mr. Campbell as Yamou, C. J. Smith as Blackburn, Thomas Lee as Ned, Mr. Rogers as Spiggot, Mr. Scarbrow as Heartless, Mrs. Harris as Mrs. Mansell, Miss Beresford as Jane, Miss Melville as Madge, Miss Rogers as Susan.

CYRIL'S SUCCESS// C 3a// H. J. Byron// **Globe**, Nov. 1868, with Charles Warner as Viscount Glycerine, W. H. Vernon as Cuthbert, David Fisher as Maj. Treherne, Maggie Brennan as Titeboy, John Clarke as Pincher, John Newbound as Fitzpelham, Henry Andrews as Grimley, Mary Henrade as Mrs. Cuthbert, Mrs. Stephens as Miss Grannett, Miss Hughes as Mrs. Bliss/ Scenery by T. W. Hall; Oct. 1872, with Carlotta Addison/ **Folly**, Jan. 1880, with E. D. Ward, H. J. Byron, Effie Liston/ **Criterion**, Jan. 1890, with David James as Pincher, Leonard Boyne as Cuthbert, Arthur Elwood as Maj. Treherne, Henry Saker as Grimley, Olga Brandon as Mrs. Cuthbert.

CZAR AND THE KING, THE; OR, THE FORTRESS AND THE MILL// D 2a// n.a.// **Sad. Wells**, May 1839, with Mr. Cathcart as Charles XII of Sweden, Mr. Aldridge as Ronchild, Mr. Elvin as Col. Eugene, George Ellis as Count Hoorn, John Webster as Peter the Great, Mr. Dry as Col. Drazenki, J. W. Collier as Coraski, Charles Montgomery as Sgt. Hinck, Miss Richardson as Floreski, Miss Cooke as Briska, Miss Pincott as Pauliska.

*

DADDY GREY// D 3a// Andrew Halliday// **Lyceum**, Dec. 1868, with W. E. Mills as Daddy Gray, J. Daniels as Peter Bell, Charles Sennett as Harry, J. L. Warner as Travers, Mr. Siddons as Jinks, H. C. Bond as Grudge, Lady Don as Kitty, Mrs. Morgan as Mrs. Bell, Miss E. Forde as Jessie/ **Royalty**, Feb. 1868, with Carlotta Leclercq.

DADDY HARDACRE// D 2a// Adap. by J. Palgrave Simpson fr F, La Fille de l'Avare// **Olympic**, Mar. 1857, with Frederick Robson as Hardacre, George Vining as Clinton, George Cooke as Jobling, Mr. Leslie as Adolpheus, Miss Hughes as Esther, Miss Stevens as Mary.

DAGGER, THE! THE CROSS!: OR, THE GIBBET OF MONTFAUCON// D 4a// Brownlow Hill// **Grecian**, Oct. 1867, with Henry Grant as Charles of France, Charles Mortimer as Dartagnole, George Gillett as Marcel, William James as Leciere, John Manning as Roba, Samuel Perfitt as Tonmal, J. Jackson as Leclerc, Alice Denvil as Queen Isabella, Miss Martineau as Marie, Mary A. Victor as Julie.

DAGGERS DRAWN// C 1a// Pryce Seaton// **Strand**, Jan. 1891, with William Lugg as Sir George, Sydney Barraclough as Capt. Grantley, Ruth Rutland as Mrs. Deering, Georgie Esmond as Alice, Lillian Milward as Ford.

DAISY// C 2a// E. Manuel// **Britannia**, Oct. 1878.

DAISY FARM// D 4a// H. J. Byron// **Olympic**, May 1871, with George Belmore as Armstrong, Charles Warner as Burridge, William Blakeley as Cole, E. W. Garden as Warriner, H. J. Byron as Craven, Edgar Newbound as Dobson, Miss Hughes as Bridget, Mrs. W. H. Liston as Cribbage, Marie O'Berne as Kate, Miss Alma as Jane/ Scenery by John Johnson/ Music by G. Barnard/ Machines by T. Drummond/ Prod. by Mrs. W. H. Liston/ **Gaiety**, Oct. 1879, with John Maclean, H. J. Byron, Louise Willes.

DAISY'S ESCAPE// C 1a// Arthur Wing Pinero// **Lyceum**, Nov. 1879, with Arthur Wing Pinero as Augustus Caddel, Frank Cooper as Tom Rossiter, Mr. Ganthony as Bullamore, Alfred Tapping as Tulk, Clifford Cooper as Maj. Mullet, Miss Harwood as Molly, Myra Holme as Daisy.

DALRYMPLE VERSUS TUBBS// F 1a// n.a.// **Astley's**, Apr. 1854, with J. W. Anson as Tubbs, Mr. Lloyd as Ferret, W. T. Simpson as the stranger, Mrs. Dowton as Mrs. Dalrymple.

DAME AUX CAMELIAS, LA// D 5a// Adap. fr F of Alexandre Dumas fils// **Lyceum**, 1858.

DAME DE ST. TROPEZ, LA; OR, THE POISONER// D 3a// Adap. by James Barber fr F of Anicet Bourgeoise & A. P. Dennery// **Olympic**, Mar. 1845, with Henry Craven as Arnold, Mr. Waldron as George, Mr. Binge as D'Arbel, W. D. Broadfoot as Antoine, Mr. Turnour as Langlois, Mr. Jeffries as Jerome, F. Burton as Gerfaut, Mr. Darcie as Brasfort, Miss Davenport as Hortense, Kate Howard as Pauline, Mrs. Cooke as Toinette.

DAMON AND PYTHIAS; OR, THE TYRANT OF SYRACUSE// T 5a// John Banim & R. L. Shiel// **Victoria**, Nov. 1841, with John Dale as Dionysius, Mr. Cullen as Philistius, David Osbaldiston as Damon, Charles Williams as Damocles, William Seaman as Procles, E. F. Saville as Pythias, Annette Vincent as Calanthe, Mrs. George Lee as Hermion, Mrs. Seaman as Arria; July 1846, with Hudson Kirby as Damon, Mark Howard as Pythias, George Gray as Dyonisius, F. Wilton as Procles, Mrs. George Lee as Hermion, Miss Fielding as Gallanthe/ **Princess's**, Mar. 1845, with Edwin Forrest as Damon, Mr. Graham as Pythias, Mr. Archer as Dionysius, James Ranoe as Damocles, Mr. Fitzjames as Procles, F. C. Courtney as Philistius, Augustus Harris as Lucullus, Mrs. Stirling as Calanthe, Mrs. Brougham as Hermion, Mrs. W. Watson as Arria/ **Marylebone**, Feb. 1846, with J. R. Scott/ **Sad. Wells**, Dec. 1846, with Samuel Phelps as Damon, William Creswick as Pythias, George Bennett as Dionysius, E. Morton as Procles, Frank Graham as Lucullus, Henry Mellon as Philisthus, Charles Williams as Nicius, William Branson as Damocles, Laura Addison as Calanthe, Miss Cooper as Hermion, Mrs. Henry Marston as Arria/ Scenery by F. Fenton & Mr. Finlay/ **Standard**, Oct. 1859, with Joseph Proctor/ **Surrey**, Feb. 1860/ **Grecian**, Nov. 1864, with David Jones as Damon, William James as Pythias, J. B. Steele as Dionysius, Henry Grant as Procles, J. Jackson as Philistius, W. Shirley as Damocles, Walter Holland as Lucullus, Lizzle Mandlebert as Calanthe, Mrs. Alfred Rayner as Hermion, Marie Brewer as Arris.

DAMON AND PYTHIAS// F 1a// J. B. Buckstone// **Grecian**, Mar. 1845, with John Chester as Damon, Frederick Robson as Pythias, John Collett as Timepiece, Edmund Garden as Billy, Mary A. Crisp as Mrs. Stokes, Miss Johnstone as Jane.

DAN, THE OUTLAW// D 3a// Jessie Robertson// **Novelty**, May 1892.

DANCING BARBER, THE// C// Charles Selby// **Adelphi**, Jan. 1838/ **St. James's**, 1874, with Clifford Cooper as Twaddle, Mr. Vincent as Fitzfrolic, Mr. Russell as Flitterly, Charles Steyne as Mincington, George De Vere as Snapley, E. W. Royce as Fitzfrizzle, Miss Murielle as Lady Flitterly, Rose Egan as Mrs. Snapley.

DANCING GIRL, THE// Play 4a// Henry Arthur Jones// **Haymarket**, Jan. 1891, with Herbert Beerbohm Tree as Duke of Guisebury, Frederick Kerr as Slingsby, Mr. Batson as Cheevers, James Fernandez as Ives, Fred Terry as Christinson, Charles Allan as Crake, Robb Harwood as Goldspink, Charles Hudson as Capt. Leddra, Rose Leclercq as Lady Bawtry, Adelaide Gunn as Lady Brislington, Julia Neilson as Drusilla, Blanche Horlock as Faith, Miss Ayrtoun as Mrs. Christinson, Mrs. E. H. Brooke as Mrs. Leddra/ Scenery by Walter Hann & Walter Johnstone/ Lighting by Verity.

DANCING MASTER, THE// C 1a// Max Pemberton & Milton Wellings// **Opera Comique**, Oct. 1889/ **Criterion**, Feb. 1894, with Charles Thursby as Winward, Arthur Bromley-Davenport as Lord George, Irene Vanbrugh as Marjorie.

DANDOLO; OR, THE LAST OF THE DOGES// F 1a// Edward Stirling// **City of London**, Jan. 1838.

DANDY DICK// F 3a// Arthur Wing Pinero// **Court**, Jan. 1887/ **Toole's**, Sept. 1887.

DANGEROUS FRIEND, A// C 4a// Adap. by John Oxenford fr F of Octave Feuillet, La Tentation// **Haymarket**, Oct. 1866, with Henry Howe as Sir Lancelot, Walter Gordon as Sir Charles, C. J. Mathews as Handiman, Mr. Weathersby as Winthrop, W. H. Kendal as Mandeville, Mrs. C. J. Mathews as Marian, Mrs. Laws as Lady Livingston, Mrs. Chippendale as Mrs. Everbloom, Caroline Hill as Mrs. Winthrop, Nelly Moore as Amelia/ Scenery by John O'Conner & George Morris/ Machines by Oliver Wales/ Gas by Mr. Hope.

DANGEROUS GAME, A// D Pro & 3a// Randal Roberts// **Grand**, Apr. 1885/ **Olympic**, May 1885, with Randal Roberts as Picquet, J. H. Clynds as Clancey, Arthur Ellwood as de Vero, Henry Alleyne as Charleton, Blanche Garnier as Mrs. Bristowe, Florence Wade as Kate, Mrs. B. M. de Solla as Mme. Picquet.

DANGEROUS RUFFIAN, A// C 1a// W. D. Howells// **Avenue**, Nov. 1895, with William Hawtrey as Roberts, J. L. MacKay as Campbell, William Wyes as Bemis, E. Hatfield as Bemis Jr., Evelyn Harrison as Mrs. Crashaw, Florence Harrington as Mrs. Roberts.

DANGERS OF LONDON, THE// D 4a// F. A. Scudamore// **Surrey**, June 1890.

DANISCHEFFS, THE; OR, MARRIED BY FORCE// CD 3a// Adap by Lord Newry fr F of Alexandre Dumas & Pierre Newsky// **St. James's**, June 1876; Jan. 1877, with Charles Warner as Count Danischeff, George Darrell as Prince Valanoff, F. H. Macklin as Paulovitch, Hermann Vezin as de Taldi, Clifford Cooper as Zakaroff, Alfred Parry as Father André, John Clayton as Osip, Mr. Winstanley as Ivan, Fanny Addison as Countess Danischeff, Mrs. John Wood as Princess Lydia, Edith Challis as Baroness Dozène, Lydia Foote as Anna, Marie Daly as Anffisa/ Music by George Richardson.

DANITES, THE// D 5a// Joaquin Miller// **Sadler's Wells**, Apr. 1880, with G. B. Waldron, McKee Rankin, E. M. Holland, Mrs. McKee Rankin/ **Globe**, June 1880, with M. V. Lingham as Bill Hickman, George Waldron as Carter, McKee Rankin as McGee, W. E. Sheridan as Godfrey, E. M. Holland as Wise, Henry Lee as Grosvenor, Charles Morton as Stubbs, J. G. Peakes as Jake, Mrs. McKee Rankin as Nancy Williams, Isabel Waldron as Hulda Brown, Eva Randolph as Sally, Emma Marble as Henrietta.

DAN'L DRUCE, BLACKSMITH// D 3a// W. S. Gilbert// **Haymarket**, Sept. 1876, with Henry Howe as Sir Jasper, Hermann Vezin as Dan'l, Mr. Odell as Haines, Johnston Forbes Robertson as Wynyard, George Braid as Marple, Mr. Weathersby as Ripley, Marion Terry as Dorothy/ Scenery by John O'Conner, T. Hall & George Morris/ **Court**, Mar. 1884, with John Clayton, Hermann Vezin, Charles Hawtrey, Miss Fortescue/ **POW**, Feb. 1894, with William Rignold as Sir Jasper, William Mollison as Dan'l, Sydney Valentine as Haines, Fuller Mellish as Winyard, Julian Cross as Marple, F. W. Permain as Ripley, Nancy McIntosh as Dorothy.

DARBY AND JOAN// Play 1a// Bellingham & Best// **Terry's**, Feb. 1888.

DARE-DEVIL DICK, THE HIGHWAYMAN AND HOUSEBREAKER// D 3a// n.a.// **Victoria**, May 1850, with Henry Frazer as Sir Mark, J. T. Johnson as Dick Turpin, Mr. Henderson as Fielder, Mr. Humphreys as Tom King, James Howard as Slider, John Bradshaw as Redwood, J. Neville as Lawrence, John Hudspeth as Green, Amelia Mercer as Susan, Mrs. George Lee as Patty,, Miss Mildenhall as Lucy.

DARK CLOUD, THE// D 2a// George Rose ("Arthur Sketchley")// **St. James's**, Jan. 1863, with Mr. Josephs as Sir Marmaduke, Mr. Western as Granville, Arthur Stirling as Austin, Frank Matthews as Dr. McTab, Mr. Trafford as John, Richard Norman as Richard, Adeline Cottrell as Lady Granville, Ada Dyas as Caroline, Mrs. Frank Matthews as Mrs. McTab, Miss Nisbett as Susan.

DARK CONTINENT, THE// D 5a// Frederick Mouillot & H. H. Morell// **Grand**, Oct. 1892.

DARK DAYS// Play 5a// Adap. by J. Comyns Carr & Hugh Conway fr Conway's novel// **Haymarket**, Sept. 1885, with Herbert Beerbohm Tree as Sir Mervyn, Robert Pateman as Evans, Charles Sugden as Pentland, Edmund Maurice as Adams, Forbes Dawson as Gilling, Basil West as Drummond, Maurice Barrymore as Dr. North, Lydia Foote as Mrs. North, Helen Forsyth as Ethel, Alice Lingard as Phillippa/ Scenery by Walter Johnstone, Mr. Telbin & Mr. Perkins/ Machines by Oliver Wales/ Limelight by Mr. Kerr.

DARK DAYS IN A CUPBOARD// C 1a// J. Stirling Coyne// **Adelphi**, Dec. 1864.

DARK DEEDS// F// n.a.// **Lyceum**, 1839.

DARK DEEDS// D 4a// Dram. by Mrs. Fairburn fr Miss Braddon's novel, The Trail of the Serpent// **Philharmonic**, Mar. 1882.

DARK HOUR, THE// D Pro & 4a// Daisy St. Aubin// **St. Geo. Hall**, Apr. 1885.

DARK NIGHT'S BRIDAL, A// C 1a// Dram. by Robert Buchanan fr story of R. L. Stevenson// **Vaudeville**, Apr. 1887.

DARK NIGHT'S WORK, A// D 3a// Adap. by Dion Boucicault fr F of Eugène Scribe// **Princess's**, Mar. 1870, with Emma Barnett as The Queen, William Rignold as Philip, Robert Romer as Mendoza, Herbert Crellin as Hannel, George Belmore as Pablo, Rose Leclercq as Paquita/ Scenery by F. Lloyds & Walter Hann.

DARK SECRET, A; A TALE OF THE THAMES VALLEY// D Pro & 4a// Dram. by J. Douglass & J. Willing Jr fr story of Sheridan Le Fanu, Uncle Silas// **Standard**, Oct. 1886/ **Princess's**, Nov. 1895, with Robert Pateman as Jonas Norton, Arthur Widdicomb as James Norton, E. Rochelle as Stephen, G. Leslie as Raines, Frank Harding as Loates, George Harker as Brooke, George Yates as Hardacre, Charles Baldwin as Slim, Lesly Thompson as Thomas, Agnes Hewitt as May, Amy Steinberg as Mme. La Fontaine, Ida Millais as Nelly, Alice Vitu as Lady Allcash, Harriet Clifton as Madge/ Scenery by Cecil Hicks, W. T. Hemsley & J. Johnstone/ Electrics by J. T. Niblett.

DARK SHADOWS AND SUNSHINE OF LIFE, THE// D// n.a.// **Victoria**, Apr. 1857.

DARK SIDE OF THE GREAT METROPOLIS, THE// D 3a// William Travers// **Britannia**, May 1868.

DASH FOR FREEDOM, A// D 5a// George Roy// **Olympic**, Nov. 1884.

DAUGHTER OF EVE// D 1a// Adap. by William McCullough fr Lady Audley's Secret// **South London**, May 1893.

DAUGHTER OF ISHMAEL, A// D 4a// W. J. Patmore// **Surrey**, Mar. 1897.

DAUGHTER OF THE PEOPLE, THE// D 5a// Adap. by Frank Harvey fr F// **Grand**, June 1891.

DAUGHTER OF THE REGIMENT, THE// D 2a// Adap by Edward Fitzball fr F, La Fille du Regiment// **Drury Lane**, Nov. 1843.

DAUGHTER OF THE STARS, THE// D 2a// Shirley Brooks// **Strand**, Aug. 1850/ **Olympic**, Sept. 1850, with William Farren as Hawkstone, George Cooke as Crawley, William Farren Jr. as Lt. Dalton, Mrs. B. Bartlett as Mrs. Mountcataract, Mrs. Stirling as Miriam.

DAUGHTER TO MARRY, A// C// J. R. Planché// **Sad. Wells**, Dec. 1844, with Charles

Williams as Dobbs, A. Younge as Rumble, E. Morton as Vivid, Mr. Coreno as Sam, Mrs. Henry Marston as Mrs. Dobbs, Jane Mordaunt as Mary/ **Haymarket**, Apr. 1860, with William Farren as Vivid, William Cullenford as Dobbs, Mr. Rogers as Rumble, William Clark as Sam, Mrs. Poynter as Mrs. Dobbs, Eliza Weekes as Mary.

DAUGHTER'S HONOUR, A// D 4a// Benjamin Landeck & Arthur Shirley// **Surrey**, Dec. 1894.

DAUGHTER'S SACRIFICE, A// Play 1a// Neville Doone// **Globe**, May 1888.

DAUGHTER'S SECRET, A// D 2a// George Peel// **Britannia**, Feb. 1874.

DAUGHTERS OF BABYLON, THE// Play 4a// Wilson Barrett// **Lyric**, Feb. 1897, with Alfred Brydone as Zoar, Wilson Barrett as Lemuel, Frank McLeay as Jediah, Charles Hudson as Sabaal, Edward Irwin as Ahira, James Barber as Arad, George Wensleydale as Hezron, Reginald Dance as Adoram, Horace Hodges as Elymas, Stafford Smith as Elkanus, Ambrose Manning as Alorus, Percy Foster as Mananihim, Charles Derwood as Gazabar, George Bernage as Parnach, Norman Jefferies as Secheni, Lily Hanbury as Elcia, Constance Collier as Meraioth, Daisy Belmore as Sarepta, Henrietta Polini as Melkina, Alice Gambier as Ibleanna, Marie Towning as Genetho, Helen Bancroft as Naomi, Maud Jeffries as Elna, Rose Pendennis as Cozbi/ Scenery by Walter Hann, William Telbin & T. E. Ryan/ Music by Edward Jones/ Electrics by T. J. Digby.

DAVID// Play 4a// L. N. Parker & Murray Carson// **Garrick**, Nov. 1892.

DAVID COPPERFIELD// Play 3a [retitled Born With a Caul]// **Strand**, Oct. 1850/ **Surrey**, [another vers.], Nov. 1850/ another vers. **Standard**, Nov. 1850.

DAVID COPPERFIELD// D 2a// Amer. vers. of novel of Charles Dickens// **Grecian**, Oct. 1870.

DAVID GARRICK// C 3a// Adap. by T. W. Robertson fr F, Sullivan// **Haymarket**, Apr. 1864, with Mr. Chippendale as Ingot, E. A. Sothern as Garrick, J. B. Buckstone as Chivy, Mr. Rogers as Smith, Thomas Coe as Brown, William Clark as Jones, Mr. James as Thomas, Mr. Weathersby as George, Nelly Moore as Ada, Miss Snowdon as Mrs. Smith, Mrs. Edward Fitzwilliam as Araminta; Mar. 1879/ **Criterion**, Nov. 1886, with Charles Wyndham, David James, William Blakeley, Emily Miller, Miss F. Paget; Mar. 1890, with Charles Wyndham as Garrick, George Giddens as Chivey, William Blakeley as Smith, Sydney Valentine as Brown, Stanley Hewson as Jones, William Farren as Ingot, Ffolliott Paget as Mrs. Smith, Emily Miller as Araminta, Mary Moore as Ada/ Scenery by Bruce Smith/ **Princess's**, June 1890, with Kyrle Bellew as Garrick, J. Musgrave as Gresham, Thomas Bolton as Rumbelow, A. G. Poulton as Sowerberry, Wilson Forbes as Simpkins, Madge Herrick as Selina, Helen Kinnaird as Mrs. Rumbelow, Mrs. Potter as Violet/ **Wyndham's**, Feb. 1900.

DAVY CROCKETT// D 5a// Frank Murdoch// **Olympic**, Aug. 1879, with Frank Mayo as Davy Crocket, Clifford Cooper as Maj. Royston, Mr. Meade as Oscar Crampton, Luigi Lablache as Neil Crampton, Alfred Phillips as Younkers, Frank Wood as Big Dan, Mr. Bullen as Briggs, Mr. Jackson as Quickwitch, Mr. Hatton as Parson Ainsworth, Maria Davis as Dame Crockett, Emma Ritta as Eleanore, Katie Neville as Little Sal/ Scenery by John Brunton.

DAWN// D 4a// George Thomas & Frank Oswald// **Vaudeville**, June 1887.

DAWN OF HOPE, THE// D Pro & 4a// Clarence Burnette & Herbert Cooper// **Novelty**, Jan. 1896, with Herbert Cooper as Bravo, William Passmore as Marquis de Rennes, G. Arrandale as Marchmont, James Mathewson as O'Gorman, Victor Mason as Bobbin, H. C. Johnson as Jake, H. Maule as Travers, J. Holland as Fichu, Rose Maitland as Kitty, Frances Drew as Little Meg, Mrs. E. Powers as Granny, Gladys Gaunt as Margaret.

DAY AFTER THE FAIR, THE// F 2a// C. A. Somerset// **Sad. Wells**, Apr. 1843, with Charles Williams as Fidget, Mr. Starmer as Sterling, Robert Romer as Clod, John Herbert in 6 char. roles, Mrs. Richard Barnett in 3 char. roles/ **Grecian**, July 1845, with John Collett as Old Fidget, Mr. Griffith as Sterling, Frederick Robson in 6 parts, Edmund Garden as Clod, Annette Mears in 3 parts/ **Astley's**, Apr. 1850, with Mr. Johnson as Old Fidget, Arthur Stirling as Mr. Sterling, Thomas Barry in 5 character parts, Mr. Crowther as Adam, Lydia Pearce as Folly/ **Victoria**, Aug. 1854, with Alfred Saville as Old Fidget, Mr. Henderson as Stirling, Charles Rice in 6 character parts, James Howard as Clod, Miss Laporte in 3 character parts/ **Princess's**, Dec. 1876 (in vers. arr. by Henry Jackson), with Mr. Ford as Fidget, Mr. Pedley as Clod, Fannie Leslie in 4 character parts, Harry Jackson in 5 character parts.

DAY AFTER THE WEDDING, THE// F 1a// M. T. Kemble// **Cov. Garden**, Apr. 1837, with John Pritchard as Freelove, John Webster as Lord Rivers, Mr. Tilbury as James, Mr. Collett as John, Helen Faucit as Lady Freelove, Mrs. Sarah Garrick as Mrs. Davies/ **Victoria**, Jan. 1838, with Edward Hooper as Col. Freelove, John Parry as Lord Rivers, William Davidge as James/ **Sad. Wells**, Mar. 1842, with John Webster as Col. Freelove, E. Morton as Lord Rivers, Mr. Aldridge as James, Mrs. Robert Honner as Lady Charlotte, Miss Cooke as Mrs. Davis/ **Astley's**, Nov. 1851, with John Chester as Col. Freelove, Mr. Johnson as Lord Rivers, Miss Barrett as Lady Elizabeth, Mrs. Beacham as Mrs. James/ **Princess's**, June 1853, with Walter Lacy as Col. Freelove, George Everett as Lord Rivers, Henry Saker as James, Mrs. Walter Lacy as Lady Elizabeth, Mrs. W. Daly as Mrs. Davies/ **Lyceum**, Oct. 1865, with Charles Horsman as Col. Freelove, William McIntyre as Lord Rivers, John Collett as Davis, Mrs. Charles Horsman as Lady Elizabeth, Mrs. George

Lee as Mrs. Davis.

DAY AT AN INN, A// F 1a// Taken fr Killing No Murder, by Theodore Hook// **Lyceum**, May 1838/ **Sad. Wells**, Mar. 1839, with Dibdin Pitt as Sir Walter, Mr. Elvin as Bradford, W. D. Broadfoot as Tap, Mr. Wild in 4 character parts, Mrs. J. F. Saville as Fanny/ **Drury Lane**, Mar. 1855.

DAY AT DOVER, A// D 2a// n.a.// **Princess's**, May 1848, with Charles Fisher as Count Carvalho, F. B. Conway as Richard, Henry Compton as Sadgrove, Anna Thillon as Henriette, Mrs. Selby as Lady Dunderhead, Miss Villars as Louisa, Miss Somers as Rosa/ Scenery by Brunning & Grey.

DAY DREAMS// Play 1a// Herbert Swears// **Opera Comique**, July 1895, with Dennis Eadie as Sir Wilfred, A. G. Brown as Capt. Danford, Martin Cahill as Morton, Lena Heinekey as Lady Ormond, Marie Towle as Hester.

DAY IN PARIS, A// C// Charles Selby// **St. James's**, Jan. 1838, with Mr. Sidney [Alfred Wigan] as Wyndham, Mr. Wright as Sam, Mrs. Stirling in 5 char. parts, Mrs. Harris as Jane/ **Sad. Wells**, Mar. 1861, with Charles Seyton as Wyndham, Lewis Ball as Sam, Mrs. Charles Young in 5 char. parts, Caroline Parkes as Jane.

DAY OF RECKONING, A// D 3a// J. R. Planché// **Lyceum**, Dec. 1850, with C. J. Mathews as Count d'Arental, Robert Roxby as Boquillard, Henry Butler as de Barville, Henry Horncastle as Fauvel, George Vining as Claude Moreau, Frank Matthews as Graboulot, Mr. Harcourt as Germain, Mr. Bellingham as Pyrene, Mme. Vestris as Countess d'Arental, Mrs. Charles Horn as Pernette, Mrs. Macnamara as Mme. Cavalon/ **Grecian**, Jan. 1855, with Basil Potter as D'Arental, F. Charles as Bouguillard, Richard Phillips as Moreau, Percy Corri as Barville, Henry Grant as Fauvel, Eaton O'Donnell as Graboulot, Jane Coveney as Countess D'Arental, Harriet Coveney as Pernette, Miss Johnstone as Mme. Cavalon, Ellen Crisp as Mme. Ango/ **Adelphi**, June 1868, with C. J. Mathews as D'Arental, W. H. Eburne as Bouquillard, Henry Ashley as de Burville, John Billington as Moreau, Carlotta Leclercq as Miss D'Arental, Emily Pitt as Pernette.

DAY OF RECKONING, THE// D 4a// Beatrice Isaacson// **Surrey**, Dec. 1900.

DAY WELL SPENT, A// F 1a// John Oxenford// **Victoria**, June 1837, with G. Crisp as Cotton, Benjamin Wrench as Bolt, W. H. Oxberry as Mizzle, John Parry as Cutaway, Mr. Macdonald as Newgate, Mr. Stuart as Prig, Miss M. A. Crisp as Harriet, Mrs. Macnamara as Mrs. Stichely, Mrs. Frank Mathews as Miss Brown, Miss Richardson as Mrs. Chargely, Miss C. Crisp as Bridget/ **Haymarket**, Oct. 1838, with William Strickland as Cotton, Benjamin Wrench as Bolt, J. B. Buckstone as Mizzle, Mr. Hemming as Cutaway, T. F. Mathews as Newgate, Miss Gallot as Harriet, Mrs. Gallot as Mrs. Stichley, Mrs. Frank Matthews as Miss Brown, Mrs. Danson as Mrs. Chargely/ **Princess's**, Jan. 1844, with Mr. Granby as Cotton, Walter Lacy as Bolt, W. H. Oxberry as Mizzle, Mr. Fitzjames as Cutaway, Augustus Harris as Newgate, T. Hill as Prig, Mme. Sala as Mrs. Stichly, Miss Noel as Miss Brown, Miss E. Honner as Miss Cotton, Miss Somers as Mrs. Chargable/ **Grecian**, Mar. 1857, with Eaton O'Donnell as Cotton, John Manning as Mizzle, C. Kelsey as Cutaway, Henry Power as Newgate, Mr. Coleman as Prig, Miss Chapman as Harriet, Ellen Crisp as Mrs. Stichly, Miss Johnstone as Miss Brown.

DAY WILL COME, A// D 4a// W. J. MacKay// **Sad. Wells**, Jan. 1893.

DAY'S FISHING, A// F 1a// J. Maddison Morton// **Adelphi**, Mar. 1869, with George Belmore as Waggs, C. J. Smith as Jellicoe, C. H. Stephenson as Robbins, Robert Romer as Cumming, W. H. Eburne as Sharp, Miss Lennox Grey as Julia, Miss Turtle as Charlotte, Mrs. H. Lewis as Mrs. Compass, Mrs. Leigh Murray as Phoebe.

DAY'S TRAINING, A// C// n.a.// **St. James's**, Mar. 1839, with Mr. Brookes as Adm. Whimsey, Robert Roxby as Lord Dangerly, W. H. Angell as Bounce, George Ellis as Nicknack, James Bland as Buckle, Mrs. Cooke as Lady Whimsey, Mrs. J. Bland as Arethusa, Miss Williams as Lady Fashionoille, Miss Fortesque as Patty.

DAYBREAK// D Pro & 4a// James Willing// **Standard**, Sept. 1894.

DAYS OF CROMWELL, THE// D 5a// **West London**, Nov. 1896.

DAYS TO COME, THE// D 4a// Forbes Dawson// **Elephant & Castle**, May 1893.

DE CROISSEY; OR, THE ORPHANS OF OLIVAL// D// n.a.// **Sad. Wells**, Oct. 1841, with Henry Marston as Count de Croissey, Mr. Dry as Roland, Mr. Elvin as Gregorie, Charles Williams as Hubert, John Herbert as Lubin, Mrs. Robert Honner as Paul, Mrs. Richard Barnett as Justin, Miss Richardson as The Baroness, Miss Cooke as Marceline, Mrs. Morgan as Louise.

DEACON, THE// C 2a// Henry Arthur Jones// **Shaftesbury**, Aug. 1890, with E. S. Willard as Boothroyd, Charles Fulton as Dempster, Annie Hill as Rosa, Mrs. F. H. Macklin as Mrs. Bolingbroke.

DEACON BRODIE; OR, THE DOUBLE LIFE// D 4a// R. L. Stevenson & W. E. Henley// **Prince's**, July 1884.

DEAD BEAT// D 5a// George Conquest & George Corner// **Surrey**, Oct. 1885.

DEAD BOXER, THE// D// n.a.// **Albion**, Sept. 1875.

DEAD CALM, A; OR, THE FISHER'S STORY// D 2a// J. Douglass Jr// **Standard**, Aug. 1868.

DEAD DUCHESS// D// n.a.// **Britannia**, Mar. 1856.

DEAD HEART, THE// D Pro & 5a// Watts Phillips// **Adelphi**, Nov. 1859, with John Billington as Count St. Valerie, David Fisher as Abbé Latour, Benjamin Webster as Robert Landry, Mr. Stuart as Jacques, Paul Bedford as Reboul, W. H. Eburne as Michel, J. L. Toole as Toupet, C. J. Smith as Jocrisse, Mrs. Alfred Mellon (Sarah Woolgar) as Catherine, Kate Kelly as Cerisette/ **Marylebone**, Apr. 1862/ **Lyceum**, Sept. 1889, with Henry Irving, Squire Bancroft, Gordon Craig, Arthur Stirling, Edward Righton, Kate Phillips, Ellen Terry.

DEAD LETTER, A// D 1a// W. A. Brabner// **Opera Comique**, Sept. 1891, with Lewis Ball as Somers, Sydney Paxton as Chadwick, Harrison Hunter as Armstrong, Evelyn McNay as Polly.

DEAD LETTER, THE; OR, SECOND SIGHT// D Pro & 3a// Walter Roberts// **Marylebone**, Dec. 1873.

DEAD MAN'S GOLD, A; OR, THE HISTORY OF A CRIME// D 5a// George Conquest & Henry Spry// **Surrey**, Nov. 1887.

DEAD OF NIGHT// D// n.a.// **Novelty**, Apr. 1897.

DEAD OR ALIVE// D 3a// Tom Taylor// **Queen's**, July 1872.

DEAD RECKONING, THE; OR, PRESSED FOR THE NAVY// D// C. H. Hazlewood// **Britannia**, Aug. 1868.

DEAD SECRET, THE// D Pro & 3a// Dram. by E. W. Bramwell fr novel of Wilkie Collins// **Lyceum**, Aug. 1877, with Kate Bateman as Sarah Leeson, Mrs. St. John as Mme. Treverton, Miss Ewell as Mrs. Pentreath, Eva Morley as Susan, W. Branscombe as James, Virginia Francis as Rosamond, H. Jenner as Leonard, Clifford Cooper as Andrew, Arthur Wing Pinero as Shrowle, Edmund Lyons as Buschmann/ Scenery by Hawes Craven/ Music by Robert Stoepel.

DEAD SHOT, THE// F 1a// J. B. Buckstone// **Sad. Wells**, Aug. 1843, with Mr. Conquest as Timid, Charles Williams as Capt. Cannon, Mr. Bird as Frederick, Mr. Corenon as Wiseman, Mrs. Richard Barnett as Chatter, Miss Martin as Louisa/ **Haymarket**, July 1845, with Mr. Tilbury as Capt. Conner, J. B. Buckstone as Timid, A. Brindal as Wiseman, Henry Howe as Thornton, Julia Bennett as Louise, Miss Carre as Chatter/ **St. James's**, Dec. 1859, with H. Cockrill as Timid, A. Denial as Capt. Cannon, Mr. Brazier as Thornton, Mr. Robins as Wiseman, H. Reeves as Williams, Eliza Arden as Louisa Lovetrick, Miss Evans as Chatter/ **Astley's**, June 1864, with Lucy Rushton as Louisa Lovetrick, Miss Burton as Chatter, Mr. Norman as Capt. Cannon, J. F. Shaw as Timid, Henry Frazer as Wiseman, Fitzroy Wallace as Frederick/ **Olympic**, Sept. 1866, with John Maclean as Capt. Cannon, Edward Atkins as Timid, Robert Soutar as Wiseman, Walter Joyce as Thornton, Emily Miller as Louisa Lovetrick, Ellen Farren as Chatter/ **Adelphi**, Jan. 1889, with Howard Russell as Cannon, Eardley Turner as Timid, James East as Wiseman, Wallace Erskine as Thornton, Georgie Esmond as Louisa, Adrienne Dairolles as Chatter.

DEAD TAKE IN, A// F 2a// Adap. by Alfred Wigan fr F// **Olympic**, 1850, with George Cooke as Col. Ferville, Alfred Wigan as Capt. Darcourt, Fred Belton as Dumesail, Henry Compton as Poulet, Mr. Morrison as Lefevre, Mrs. Parker as Mme. de Lagmy, Miss M. Oliver as Clara.

DEAD TO THE WORLD// D 4a// George Conquest & Henry Pettitt// **Grecian**, July 1875.

DEAD WITHOUT A NAME// D// n.a.// **Olympic**, Feb. 1853.

DEADLY REPORTS// C 1a// J. Palgrave Simpson// **Olympic**, Oct. 1857, with Mr. Addison as Maj. Mortar, Mr. Leslie as Simperton, Walter Gordon as Smith, George Cooke as Beakhead, Miss Swanborough as Mrs. Ratclyffe, Miss Wyndham as Barbara.

DEADLY SAMPSON// D// W. M. Akhurst & James Twigg// **Pavilion**, Sept. 1876.

DEADMAN'S POINT; OR, THE LIGHTHOUSE ON THE CARN RUTH// D 4a// F. C. Burnand// **Adelphi**, Feb. 1871.

DEADWOOD DICK// D 5a// Paul Korell// **Pavilion**, Mar. 1894.

DEAF AND DUMB; OR, THE ORPHAN PROTECTED// D 5a// Thomas Holcroft// **Haymarket**, Oct. 1841, with Mlle. [sic] Celeste as Julio, Henry Wallack as Darlemont, Frederick Vining as St. Alme, John Webster as Franval, James Wallack as De L'Epee, George Bennett as Dupre, William Strickland as Dominique, Mrs. Stanley as Mme. Franval, Priscilla Horton as Marianne.

DEAF AS A POST// F 1a// John Poole// **Drury Lane**, Jan. 1837, with Mr. Cooper as Capt. Templeton, Drinkwater Meadows as Sappy, F. Cooke as Old Walton, Mr. Hughes as Crupper, Mr. Richardson as Gallop, Mrs. East as Sophia, Miss Lee as Amy, Miss Somerville as Mrs. Plumply, Mrs. C. Jones as Sally/ **Cov. Garden**, Oct. 1842, with Mr. Cooper as Capt. Templeton, Mr. Granby as Old Walton, Mr. Kerridge as Gallop, John Collett as Crupper, John Pritt Harley as Sappy, Miss Lee as Amy, Miss Lane as Sophia, Mrs. Tayleure as Mrs. Plumpley, Mrs. Orger as Sally/ **Princess's**, Nov. 1852, with Drinkwater Meadows as Old Walton, Edward Wright as Sappy, James Vining as Capt. Templeton, Henry Saker as Crupper, F. Cooke as Gallop, Jenny Marston as Sophy, Miss Desborough as Amy, Mrs. W. Daly as Mrs. Plumpty, Miss Marshall as Sally/ **Olympic**, July 1866, with A. Vivian as Walton, Thomas Thorne as Sappy, William Belford as Capt. Templeton, Harwood Cooper as Crupper, Miss Schavey as Sophie, Miss Wilson as Amy, Ellen

Farren as Sally; Apr. 1881, with Gray Dolby as Capt. Templeton, Henri Crisp as Walton, Percy Compton as Sappy, L. Grahame as Crupper, Mr. Wycher as Gallop, Miss C. Steele as Amy, Miss F. Leyton as Sophie, Mrs. C. Humphreys as Mrs. Plumply, Florence Smithers as Sally.

DEAL BOATMAN, THE// D 2a// F. C. Burnand// **Drury Lane**, Sept. 1863, with Mr. Barrett as Sir John, F. Charles as Leslie, Mr. Warde as Prescott, George Belmore as Vance, G. Wiston as Bramber, T. Mathews as Bucket, Mrs. Edmund Falconer as Mrs. Bridget, Rose Leclercq as Mary/ **Sad. Wells**, Apr. 1866, with Mr. Neilson as Sir John, Charles Warner as Leslie, Walter Holland as Prescott, George Belmore as Vance, A. Bishop as Bramber, Mrs. Poynter as Mrs. Bridgett, Fanny Gwynne as Mary/ **Adelphi**, Nov. 1877, with James Johnstone as Sir John, Luigi Lablache as Edward, Howard Russell as George, Samuel Emery as Jacob, Alma Murray as Mary Vance.

DEAN'S DAUGHTER, THE// Play 4a// Dram. by Sidney Grundy & F. C. Phillips, fr Phillips's novel// **St. James's**, Oct. 1888, with Caroline Hill as Mrs. Fortesque, Olga Nethersole as Miriam, Adrienne Dairolles as Elise, Mary Barton as Mrs. Peel, Emily Cross as Lady Ashwell, John Beauchamp as Sir Henry, Edward Sass as Prince Balanikoff, Lewis Waller as Sabine, Allan Aynesworth as Lord Ashwell, Rutland Barrington as Rev. St. Aubyn/ Scenery by Walter Johnstone & Julian Hicks.

DEAR FRIENDS// C 1a// Mary Righton// **Vaudeville**, July 1890, with Annie Howard as Violet, Sylvia Southgate as Daisy.

DEAREST ELIZABETH// F// John Oxenford// **Haymarket**, Jan. 1848, with Robert Keeley as Lax, Mr. Rogers as Winch, William Clark as Humphrey, Mrs. L. S. Buckingham as Mrs. Lax, Mrs. Caulfield as Mrs. Winch, Mrs. Keeley as Betsy.

DEAREST MAMA// C 1a// Adap. by Walter Gordon fr F, La Belle-mére et Le Gendre// **Olympic**, May 1860, with George Vining as Croker, Walter Gordon as Clinton, Mr. Addison as Browser, Harwood Cooper as Jones, Mrs. Leigh Murray as Mrs. Fussell, Miss Cottrell as Edith, Miss Herbert as Mrs. Honeywood; Nov. 1866, with George Vincent as Croker, J. Reeves as Clinton, Mr. Addison as Browser, Harwood Cooper as Jones, Mrs. Stephens as Mrs. Fussell, Miss E. Wilson as Edith, Miss Sheridan as Mrs. Honeywood; June 1883, with Hamilton Knight as Clinton, F. Staunton as Croker, W. E. Blatchley as Browser, Mrs. Leigh Murray as Mrs. Fussell, Janet Achurch as Edith, Katie Lee as Mrs. Honeywood/ **Criterion**, Oct. 1890.

DEATH BY THE LAW// D// Edward Towers// **Pavilion**, Aug. 1876.

DEATH DOOM; OR, A SOLDIER'S HONOUR// D 3a// n.a.// **Victoria**, June 1843, with John Dale as De Mondal, C. Williams as Pietro, David Osbaldiston as Leandio, E. F. Saville as Andreas, Mr. Glindon as Annelo, William Seaman as Allessio, John Gardner as Semitone, William James as Jeronimo, Miss Ridgeway as Ursula, Annette Vincent as Theresina, Mrs. George Lee as Constanza, Miss Saddler as Annette/ Scenery by Morelli & Glindon/ Music by W. J. Hill/ Machines by Emmens & Moon.

DEATH OF CAPTAIN COOK, THE; OR, THE ISLANDERS OF OTAHEITE// D 3a// J. S. Faucit// **Victoria**, Sept. 1854, with T. E. Mills as Capt. Cook, Mr. Henderson as Lt. King, Miss Laporte as Harry, N. T. Hicks as Barnacle, Alfred Saville as Terreeboe, John Bradshaw as Koah, Mrs. Henry Vining as Karrabeca, Phoebe Johnson as Madeboo.

DEATH OMEN, THE; OR, THE WIZARD TREE// D 4a// Dram. by Thomas Greenwood fr novel of Harrison Ainsworth, Rookwood// **Sad. Wells**, Feb. 1840, with Mr. Elvin as Sir Ranulph, J. W. Collier as Coates, Mr. Dry as Bradley, Mr. Denvil as Luke, Robert Honner as Dick Turpin, Charles Montgomery as Rust, Mr. Aldridge as Poynder, Henry Hall as Tyrconnell, Miss Richardson as Lady Rookwood, Mrs. J. F. Saville as Eleanor, Mrs. Morgan as Agnes, Mr. Aldridge as Balthazar, Mr. Williams as Barbara Lovel, Mrs. Robert Honner as Sybila/ Scenery by F. Fenton/ Music by Mr. Herbert/ Machines by B. Sloman/ Prod. by R. Honner.

DEATH OR GLORY// D 5a// John Mill// **Britannia**, Oct. 1896.

DEATH TRAP, THE; OR, A CATSPAW// D 4a// J. Redding Ware// **Grecian**, June 1870.

DEATH WARRANT, THE; OR, A RACE FOR LIFE// D// H. P. Grattan// **Grecian**, Oct. 1879.

DEBORAH; OR, THE JEWISH MAIDEN'S WRONG// D 3a// a vers. of Leah the Forsaken by Charles Cheltnam// **Victoria**, July 1864.

DEBORAH// Play 5a// Langdon Mitchell// **Avenue**, Feb. 1892, with Charles Fulton as Leviq St. Michael, Bernard Gould as Bastien St. Michael, Austin Melford as Crawford, Rudge Harding as Marshall, Richard Boleyn as Dupre, Beatrice Lamb as Helen, Henrietta Cowen as Mrs. St. Michael, Annie Webster as Camille, Marion Lea as Deborah, Elizabeth Robins as Prologue.

DEBORAH; OR, THE JEWESS OUTCAST (a vers of Mosenthal's Leah the Forsaken)/ D 4a// Adap. by George Conquest fr G.// **Grecian**, Feb. 1864, with J. Jackson as Lorenz, William James as Joseph, J. B. Steele as Nathan, Henry Grant as Hantz, Mrs. Charles Dillon as Hanna, John Manning as Rosenta, W. Shirley as Abraham, Edith Heraud as Deborah, Marie Brewer as Sarah/ Scenery by C. Smithers/ Prod. by George Conquest.

DEBT// FC 2a// E. A. De Pass// **Gaiety**, Nov. 1872.

DEBT OF HONOUR, A// Play 1a// C. P. Colnaghi// **Opera Comique**, Dec. 1891, with Charles Fulton as Col. Desmond, A. Courtenay as Sir Hubert, Ben Webster as Aubrey, Mrs. F. Copleston as Lady Hazeldean, Marie Linden as Sylvia.

DEBT OF HONOUR, A// Play 5a// Sidney Grundy// **St. James's**, Sept. 1900, with George Alexander as Carlyon, W. H. Vernon as Holroyd, H. V. Esmond as Antrobus, Marsh Allen as Graham, H. H. Vincent as Rev. Baxter, Julie Opp as Isabel, Fay Davis as Gipsy, Marguerite Aubert as Yvette/ Scenery by William Telbin & Walter Hall.

DECEIVERS EVER// FC 2a// Malcolm Salaman// **Strand**, Nov. 1883.

DECOY, THE// CD 3a// Frederick Eastwood// **Gaiety**, Apr. 1883.

DEED OF DARKNESS, A; OR, THE ASSASSIN OF VERONA// D 2a// n.a.// **Victoria**, May 1848, with John Bradshaw as Gen. Mirandeau, Mr. Henderson as Cerville, J. T. Johnson as Landonne, E. Edwards as Renardette, J. Howard as Martois, T. H. Higgie as Boncour, G. F. Forman as Jacques, Mrs. George Lee as Agnese, Miss Burroughcliffe as Colinette.

DEED WITHOUT A NAME, A// F// Robert Soutar// **Olympic**, Feb. 1853, with George Cooke as Muddlebuppy, Henry Compton as A Mysterious Individual, E. Clifton as Thomas, Mrs. B. Bartlett as Mrs. Muddlebuppy, Ellen Turner as Sarah Jane.

DEEDS AND DOINGS OF THE DARK HOUSE, THE; OR, SIMPLE BESS OF BILLINGSGATE// D 3a// n.a.// **Victoria**, Sept. 1841, with Mr. Wilton as Elford, William Seaman as Charles, Mr. Cullen as Edgar, John Dale as Bradburn, Mr. Paul as Hoppy Bob, Mr. Howard as Dipthong, John Gardner as Dabbs, C. Williams as Ben, Mrs. G. Lee as Bess, Mrs. Garthwaite as Anne, Miss Howard as Drusilla.

DEEDS, NOT WORDS// D 2a// J. Courtney// **Surrey**, Jan. 1855.

DEEDS OF DREADFUL NOTE// D 1a// Adap. by Dubois fr F of De Rosier// **Adelphi**, 1842.

DEEMSTER, THE// D 5a// Dram. by Hall Caine & Wilson Barrett fr novel of Caine// **Lyceum**, Nov. 1899, with Wilson Barrett as Dan Mylrea, Edward Irwin as Ewan Mylrea, J. Carter-Edwards as Gilchrist Mylrea, D. McCarthy as Thorkell Mylrea, T. Wigney Percyval as Harcourt, Ambrose Manning as Fayle, Paul Belmore as Curphney, Maud Jeffries as Mona, Daisy Belmore as Kitty, Rose Pendennis as Liza/ Scenery by Walter Hann/ Music by Michael Connolley.

DEER SLAYERS, THE; OR, THE FREE ARCHERS OF THE NEW FOREST// D// W. & C. Pitt// **Britannia**, Dec, 1870.

DEERFOOT// F 3a// F. C. Burnand// **Olympic**, Dec. 1861.

DEFENDER OF THE FAITH, THE// D 4a// Charles Darrell// **Standard**, May 1898.

DEGENERATES, THE// C 4a// Sidney Grundy// **Haymarket**, Sept. 1899, with Lily Hanbury as Lady Samaurez, Lottie Venne as Mrs. Bennett-Boldero, Dorothy Drake as Lady Stornoway, Charles Hawtrey as Duke of Orme, Leslie Kenyon as de Lorano, Harcourt Beatty as Hentsch, Ferdinand Gottschalk as Mosenthal, George Grossmith Jr. as Stornoway, Edmund Maurice as Sir William, Lillie Langtry as Mrs. Trevelyan, Lily Grundy as Una/ **Garrick**, Oct. 1899.

DELIA HARDING// Play 3a// Adap. by J. Comyns Carr fr F of Victorien Sardou// **Comedy**, Apr. 1895, with Cyril Maude as Sir Arthur, Fred Terry as Studley, W. Mackintosh as French, Gilbert Farquhar as Ormsby, Lyston Lyle as Lumley, Rose Leclercq as Lady Carstairs, Dorothy Dorr as Mrs. Venables, Eva Williams as Mrs. Jay, Mrs. E. H. Brooke as Janet, Marion Terry as Delia/ Scenery by Walter Johnstone.

DELICATE ATTENTIONS// C 2a// John Poole// **St. James's**, Feb. 1837, with Robert Strickland as Gingerly, Mr. Hollingsworth as Damper, Mr. Saville as Hobnill, Mr. Sidney as Tapelace, Mme. Sala as Mrs. Bustle, Miss Allison as Betsy, Mrs. Penon as Jenny, Miss Walpole as Mrs. Fubsworth, Miss Stuart as Mrs. Waddelove.

DELICATE GROUND; OR, PARIS IN 1793// C// Charles Dance// **Lyceum**, Nov. 1849, with C. J. Mathews, Mme. Vestris/ **Drury Lane**, Dec. 1853, with Mr. Grahn as Sangfroid, Henry Lee as Grandier, Miss Grahn as Pauline/ **Sad. Wells**, Apr. 1855, with Frederic Robinson as Sangfroid, Robert Roxby as de Grandier, Miss M. Oliver as Pauline/ **Olympic**, July 1856, with Alfred Wigan as Sangfroid, Mr. Leslie as Alphonse, Mrs. Stirling as Pauline/ **Princess's**, Oct. 1862, with George Vining as Sangfroid, Robert Roxby as de Grandier, Miss M. Oliver as Pauline/ **Astley's**, Oct. 1866, with Walter Joyce as Sangfroid, W. Ryder as De Grandier, Maud Shelley as Pauline/ **Globe**, Jan. 1870, with Walter Lacy as Sangfroid, W. H. Vernon as de Grandier, Ada Cavendish as Pauline/ **Adelphi**, June 1882, with Walter Joyce as Sang Froid, E. H. Brooke as Alphonse, Ellen Meyrick as Pauline; Mar. 1890, with Arthur Dacre as Sangfroid, Heinrich Varna as Grandier, Amy Roselle as Pauline/ **Criterion**, Apr. 1890/ **Terry's**, Jan. 1897.

DELILAH; OR, MARRIED FOR HATE// D Pro & 3a// Adap. by James Willing fr novel of Ouida, Held in Bondage// **Olympic**, Oct. 1880, with William Redmund as Tempest, Arthur Dacre as Lord Tinsley, John Beauchamp as Maj. Bond, Ernest Wilmore as Hazleton, Amy Steinberg as Miss Trevelyan and as Delilah, Bella Cuthbert as Lady Greytown, Fanny Addison as Lady Tempest, W. Vincent as Robinson, Charles Harrison as Lord Castleton, Ada Murray as Lady Wyndham, Fanny Thorne as May, Leonard Boyne, Arthur Dacre, Amy Steinberg, Stella Brereton/ **Sad. Wells**, Sept. 1892.

DEMON BRACELETS, THE; OR, THE MYSTIC CYPRESS TREE// D// C. H. Hazlewood// **Britannia**, Aug. 1869.

DEMON DARRELL// D 5a// Ina Cassilis & Frank Morland// **Britannia**, June 1898.

DEMON DWARF, THE// Play// n.a.// **Victoria**, Jan. 1839.

DEMON GIFT, THE; OR, THE VISIONS OF THE FUTURE// D 2a// John Brougham & Mark Lemon// **Eng. Opera House** (Lyceum), July 1840, with Mr. Baker as Count Ulric, Mr. Fitzjames as Ernest, Mr. Turnour as Wiezleback, Henry Compton as Dullwitz, Stephen Smith as Mephistophiles, John Sanders as Astaroth, Miss Cooper as Lady Ida, Mme. Simon as Frau Wiesleback, Miss Bartlett as Jienswille, Miss R. Romer as Kristine, Miss Smithson as Bertha/ Music by J. H. Tully/ Scenery by Mr. Pitt/ Machines by Mr. Stribley/ **Olympic**, Apr. 1841; Sept. 1851, with John Kinloch as Count Ulric, Charles Bender as Weizelbock, Henry Farren as Ernest, Henry Compton as Dullwitz, Mr. Mason as Fritz, E. Clifton as Knibb, Mr. Norton as Mephistophiles, Mr. Tanner as Astaroth, Miss Fielding as Lady Ida, Mrs. Alfred Phillips as Frau Wiezelbock, Isabel Adams as Jeansville, Ellen Turner as Kristine.

DEMON KNIGHT, THE; OR, THE DOOM KISS// D// n.a.// **Sad. Wells**, Mar. 1837, with C. J. Smith as Prince Gheranzi, Mr. King as Count Rodolpho, N. T. Hicks as Almanza, C. H. Pitt as Vincentio, Mr. Ennis as Vampo, Mr. Rogers as Launcelot, Thomas Lee as Snick, Miss Beresford as Lady Isabel, Mrs. Harris as Dame, Miss Williams as Enchantress, Lavinia Melville as Flora/ Scenery by Mildenhall/ Music by Mr. Nicholson/ Machines by Mr. Copping.

DEMON LOVER, THE// C 2a// John Brougham// **Royalty**, Oct. 1864.

DEMON MUSICIAN, THE; OR, THE GOBLIN'S GIFT// D// Adap. fr G// **Sad. Wells**, Sept. 1839, with Mr. Cathcart as Ursenstein, Miss Hicks as Albert, Mr. Conquest as Jocopo, J. W. Collier as Krantz, Mr. Aldridge as Kreutzer, W. D. Broadfoot as Chamberlain, Mr. De Burt as Duke, Robert Honner as Demon, Mrs. Robert Honner as Madeline/ Scenery by F. Fenton & G. Smithyes Jr./ Music by Mr. Herbert/ Machines by B. Sloman/ Prod. by R. Honner.

DEMON OF DARKNESS, THE// D// n.a.// **Victoria**, Apr. 1865/ **Grecian**, Dec. 1867, with Thomas Mead as Headley, Charles Mortimer as Backinson, J. Jackson as Vandergraeef, Samuel Perfitt as ----, Henry Power as Melchoir, George Gillett as Maj. Clare, Lizzie Mandelbert as Madeline, William James as Wilfred, Miss De Lacie as Rose.

DENHAMS, THE// C 4a// Adap. by James Albery// **Court**, Feb. 1885, with Edward Price, H. B. Conway, Arthur Cecil, John Clayton, Mrs. John Wood, Lydia Foote, Marion Terry.

DENNIS; OR, THE GIBBIT LAW OF HALIFAX// D 2a// F. C. Nantz// **Sad. Wells**, Aug. 1840, with Mr. Aldridge as Sir William, Mr. Dry as Colbeck, Mr. Houghburt as Varley, Mr. Williams as Lacy, Mr. Elvin as Dennis, Henry Marston as Gibbit Jack, Henry Hall as Matchlove, Miss Richardson as Marion, Mrs. Richard Barnett as Prudence/ Scenery by F. Fenton/ Music by Isaac Collins/ Machines by B. Sloman/ prod. by R. Honner.

DENOUNCED; OR, FAITHFUL TO THE END// D// Henry Gascoigne & Frank Jefferson// **Elephant and Castle**, Aug. 1883.

DEOCH AU DUR'ASS// D 3a// R. Dodson// **Britannia**, Oct. 1877.

DEPUTY, THE// FC 3a// J. M. Campbell// **Criterion**, May 1888.

DEPUTY REGISTRAR, THE// FC 3a// Ralph Lumley & Horace Ledger// **Criterion**, Dec. 1888.

DEPUTY SHERIFF, THE; OR, DAN'L BARTLETT// D 4a// **Elephant & Castle**, Oct. 1892.

DER FREISCHUTZ; OR, THE SEVEN CHARMED BULLETS// D// Dram. fr opera of Weber// **Grecian**, Dec. 1866, with W. Shirley as Duke of Snider, Charles Mortimer as Casper, Henry Grant as Rolla, Samuel Perfitt as Bertram, George Gillett as Rodolph, John Manning as Killian, J. Jackson as Zamiel, Mrs. Atkinson as Bianca, Alice Denvil as Agnes, Emma Victor as Ann.

DERBY DAY, THE// D// Nelson Lee// **Pavilion**, Feb. 1867.

DERBY WINNER, THE// D 4a// Augustus Harris, Cecil Raleigh, & Henry Hamilton// **Drury Lane**, Sept. 1894, with Mrs. John Wood as Duchess of Milford, Beatrice Lamb as Countess of Desborough, Louise Moodie as Mrs. Donelly, Pattie Browne as Annette, Alma Stanley as Vivien, Hetty Dene as Mary, Archur Bourchier as Earl of Desborough, Evelyn Hughes as Harold, James East as Col. Donelly, Charles Cartwright as Maj. Mostyn, Maurice Drew as Langford.

DESERTED MILL, THE; OR, THE SOLDIER'S WIDOW// D// Edward Fitzball// **Astley's**, Mar. 1850, with Mr. Johnson as Pierre, Mr. Crowther as Edouard, N. T. Hicks as Theodore, Thomas Barry as Paul, Mrs. Jackson as Lisette, Mrs. Moreton Brookes as Jacqueline.

DESERTER, THE (see Dominique The Deserter)

DESPERATE DEED, A// D 3a// Burford Delaunoy// **Sad. Wells**, Feb. 1893.

DESPERATE GAME, A// C 1a// J. Maddison Morton// **Adelphi**, Apr. 1853, with Leigh Murray as Capt. Ratcliffe, Robert Keeley as Percy, James Rogers as David, Sarah Woolgar as Mrs. Somerton, Mrs. Laws as Peggy.

DESPERATE MAN, A; OR, AT ANY COST// C 4a// Anson Pond// **Strand**, May 1891.

DESTINY// D 4a// Edward Towers// **East London**, Feb. 1869.

DESTINY// D 3a// George Conquest// **Grecian**,

Jan. 1861, with Henry Grant as James III, R. H. Lingham as Charles, William James as Ramsey, John Manning as Macfer, Alfred Rayner as Duke Robert, Thomas Mead as Hattrick, Lucreza Hill as Henrietta, Harriet Coveney as Betty, Jane Coveney as Catherine.

DESTROYER, THE; OR, JOCRISSE THE BANDIT// D// n.a.// **Sad. Wells**, Aug. 1842, with P. Williams as Guampino, C. J. Bird as Bernardo, C. J. Smith as Roselli, John Herbert as Jocrisse, Mr. Aldridge as Griffino, Mr. Dry as Antonio, Miss Pitt as Amanda.

DESTRUCTION OF THE BASTILLE, THE// D 2a// Benjamin & F. Webster// **Adelphi**, 1844.

DETECTIVE, THE// Play// C. H. Hazlewood// **Victoria**, July 1863.

DETECTIVE, THE// D 4a// Clement Scott & E. Manuel// **Mirror**, May 1875.

DEVIL AND DR. FAUSTIS, THE// D 3a// Leman Rede// **Olympic**, June 1851, with Henry Farren as Faustus, E. Clifton as Schaeffer, Charles Diddear as Mark, Miss Fielding as The Devil, W. Shalders as Fiend, Mrs. B. Bartlett as Mary, Miss Adams as Fanny, Ellen Turner as Jeanette, Isabel Adams as Bridget, Miss E. Shalders as Martha/ Scenery by W. Shalders & Mr. Batty/ Machines by J. Matthews/ Music by J. Barnard.

DEVIL AND THE DESERTER, THE (a vers. of Dominique the Deserter)// D// n.a.// **Grecian**, Sept. 1868, with Henry Grant as Col. La Lache, George Gillett as D'Arvil, George Conquest as Dominique, Charles Mortimer as ——, Samuel Perfitt as Gaspard, Alice Denvil as Blanche, Mary A. Victor as Jeanette, Mrs. Atkinson as Mme. Dominique.

DEVIL AT THE ELBOW, THE; OR, TWO MOTHERS TO ONE CHILD// D// C. H. Hazlewood// **Britannia**, Aug. 1874.

DEVIL CARESFOOT// Play 4a// Adap. by C. Haddon Chambers & J. Stanley Little fr Rider Haggard's novel, Dawn// **Vaudeville**, July 1887/ **Strand**, Aug. 1887/ **Comedy**, Aug. 1887

DEVIL IN PARIS, THE; OR, THE SIGHTLESS BRIDE// D// Adap. fr F// **Sad. Wells**, Sept. 1865, with J. B. Howe as Dr. Moncardo, John Gardner as Marcel, John Russell as Peloti, George Pearce as Jerome, Mr. Lindsey as Gervais, Mrs. Moreton Brookes as Baroness de Clercy, Mary Fielding as Julia.

DEVIL OF MARSEILLES, THE; OR, THE SPIRIT OF AVARICE// D// R. B. Peake// **Adelphi**, 1846, with William Cullenford as Brissao, Mr. Lambert as Tremblonque, Charles Boyce as Dr. Launay, O. Smith as Cranon, Edward Wright as de L'Oye, Charles Perkins as Aveira, C. J. Smith as Maquas, James Munyard as Africanus, Paul Bedford as Capt. Beausobre, Mme. Celeste as Clementine, Sarah Woolgar as Jacqueline/ Scenery by Pitt & Johnstone/ Music by Alfred Mellon/ Machinery by Mr. Cooper.

DEVIL OF PARIS, THE// D// n.a.// **Sad. Wells**, Jan. 1863, with Henry Forrester as Dr. Moncarde, E. F. Edgar as Marcel, C. Lloyds as Jerome, Lewis Ball as Petoit, Alfred Montague as David, Sophie Miles as Baroness de Clercy, Emily Dowton as Blanche, Catherine Lucette as Julie.

DEVIL'S GAP, THE; OR, TIME TELLS TALES// D 3a// George Conquest// **Grecian**, Oct. 1862, with Thomas Mead as George Clayton and as Alfred Clayton, Henry Grant as Bowes, F. Smithson as Lewis, George Conquest as Phinings, Walter Holland as Capt. Boden, Jane Dawson as Sarah, William James as Rigby, Mrs. Charles Dillon as Mary, Marie Brewer as Alice.

DEVIL'S IN IT, THE// D 3a// Adap. by T. E. Wilks fr F of Eugène Scribe// **Princess's**, Aug. 1845, with Mr. Lynne as Grand Duke, Walter Lacy as Holstein, Henry Compton as Bunne, James Ranoe as Baron Gompertz, Augustus Harris as Count Melstein, Emma Stanley as Rollo, Mrs. Brougham as Grand Duchess, Miss E. Honner as Felicia.

DEVIL'S IN THE ROOM, THE// F 1a// W. T. Moncrieff// **Sad. Wells**, Apr. 1840, with Mr. Elvin as Lovell, Mr. Moreton as Manton, Mr. Stilt as Stammerer, Henry Hall as O'Shaughnessy, Miss Pincott as Mrs. Lovell, Mrs. J. F. Saville as Eliza/ **Grecian**, Mar. 1854, with Charles Horn as Duprez, Thomas Roberts as Rivers, Charles Rice as Barnaby, Jane Coveney as Mrs. Duprez, Harriet Coveney as Charlotte.

DEVIL'S LUCK; OR, THE MAN SHE LOVED// D 5a// Lily Tinsley & George Conquest// **Surrey**, Sept. 1885.

DEVIL'S MINE, THE// D 4a// Fred Darcy// **Pavilion**, July 1894.

DEVIL'S MOUNT, THE; OR, THE FEMALE BLUEBEARD// D 2a// Adap. fr F by Thomas Higgie// **Queen's**, May 1847.

DEVOTION// D 3a// F. G. Cheatham// **Sad. Wells**, Mar. 1870, with James Johnstone as Raymond, David Evans as Morgan, Edmund Phelps as Gifford, Mr. Howard as Pilgrim, Richard Edgar as Zacariah, T. W. Ford as Jardine, Mr. Hudson as Dawson, Edgar Newbound as Crawshay, Alice Marriott as Ruth, Florence Gerald as Cassandra, Miss Wilson as Honora, Miss Cheatham as Rosalie, Miss Rogers as Bella, Mrs. Jones as Mrs. Banker, Miss Fitzgerald as Mrs. Hodson.

DEVOTION// Play 4a// Adap. by Dion Boucicault Jr. fr F of Lockroy & Badon, Un Duet Sous Richelieu// **Court**, May 1884, with John Clayton, H. B. Conway, Dion Boucicault Jr., Ada Cavendish, Lottie Venne.

DEVOTION; OR, A PRICELESS WIFE// D Pro & 3a// Adap. by Mrs. S. Lane fr F// **Britannia**, Mar. 1881.

DIAMOND CUT DIAMOND// F// n.a.// **Sad.**

Wells, Apr. 1856, with W. Williams as Heartly, Mr. Swanborough as Capt. Seymour, C. Kelsey as Capt. Howard, Mr. Moore as Clay, James Rogers as Trap, George Webster as Trick, Miss Stuart as Charlotte.

DIAMOND DEANE// Play 4a// Henry Dam// **Vaudeville**, Mar. 1891, with Thomas Thorne as Rev. Grant, H. B. Conway as Henry Dennison, W. Scott Buist as Robert Dennison, Lawrance d'Orsay as Lord Sheldon, J. S. Blythe as Murray, Fred Thorne as Johnson, Dorothy Dorr as Mary, Mrs. Canninge as Mrs. Maclane, Jessie Milward as Miss Young/ Scenery by Mr. Maple & W. T. Hemsley.

DIAMOND GANG, THE// D 4a// Edward Darbey// **Surrey**, July 1893.

DIAMOND NECKLACE, THE; OR, THE FOUR GUARDSMEN// D// Adap. fr F of Alexandre Dumas// **Victoria**, Mar. 1873, with C. T. Burleigh as D'Artagnan, Walter Lacy as Louis XIII, Henry Dudley as Richelieu, Mr. Selby as Buckingham, Mr. Prescott as de Rochfort, Mr. Hamilton as De Treville, F. Shepherd as Athos,, J. Hudspeth as Porthos, H. C. Sidney as Aramis, G. Roberts as Boniface, Miss Lee as Seadrift, Miss M. Henderson as Anne of Austria, Mrs. Stephenson as Lady de Winter.

DIAMOND QUEEN, THE// FC 3a// Albert Edwards// **St. Geo. Hall**, Aug. 1889.

DIAMONDS AND HEARTS// C 3a// Adap. by Gilbert à Beckett// **Haymarket**, Mar. 1867, with Henry Howe as Sir Charles, W. H. Chippendale as Welbourne, William Farren as Frank, William Clark as Pennybrass, William James as Stiltsworth, Ione Burke as Lady Claverton, Nelly Moore as Maud, Miss Sidney as Cherry, Miss Matthews as Mrs. Clinton/ Scenery by John O'Conner & George Morris/ Machines by Oliver Wales.

DIANE// Play 5a// Adap. by James Mortimer fr F of Alexandre Dumas fils, Diane de Lys// **Toole's**, Sept. 1882, with Hermann Vezin, Fanny Davenport.

DICE OF DEATH, THE; OR, A LEGEND OF THE HARTZ MOUNTAINS// D 3a// John Oxenford// **Victoria**, Jan. 1838, with Mr. Wilkins as Winter, Catln Barnard as Spiegleberg, W. H. Oxberry as Presto, John Parry as Mephistophiles, Mr. Loveday as Keiwitz, Miss E. Lee as Louisa, Mrs. Frank Matthews as Theresa, Mr. Phillips as Frau Schnapps/ **Sad. Wells**, Jan. 1838, with Mr. Campbell as Winter, Mr. Forester as Spiegelberg, Mr. Rogers as Presto, Mr. Rumball as Mephistophiles, Mr. James as Baron Keinwitz, Mr. Nunn as Schwartz, Eliza Vincent as Louisa, Miss Watkins as Theresa, Mrs. Weston as Frau Schnapps, Miss Chartley as Rosa, Miss Pitt as Matilde.

DICK AND HIS DOUBLE// F 1a// Thomas Archer// **Olympic**, Oct. 1845, with James Browne as Dick, Mr. Dean as Quaver, Mr. Turnour as Mr. Brown, Kate Howard as Isabella/ **Grecian**, Nov. 1845, with Frederick Robson as Dick Doubleton, John Collett as Brown, John Chester as Quaver, Mary A. Crisp as Isabel, Annette Mears as Isabella/ **Sad. Wells**, Feb. 1846, with E. Morton as Dick Doubleton, Charles Williams as Brown, R. H. Lingham as Quaver, Fanny Huddart as Isabel, Miss Lebatt as Isabella, Miss Stephens as Jane, Georgiana Lebatt as Mary, Miss Morelli as Fanny.

DICK SHERIDAN// C 4a// Robert Buchanan// **Comedy**, Feb. 1894, with H. B. Irving as R. B. Sheridan, Brandon Thomas as O'Leary, Cyril Maude as Lord Dazzleton, Lewis Waller as Capt. Matthews, Sidney Brough as Sir Harry, Edmund Maurice as Mr. Linley, Will Dennis as David Garrick, F. M. Paget as Wade, Miss Vane as Lady Miller, Lena Ashwell as Lady Pamela, Miss Radclyffe as Lady Shuttleworth, Constance Brietzcke as Mrs. Elliott, Ettie Williams as Miss Copeland, Winifred Emery as Elizabeth/ Scenery by Walter Hann.

DICK TURPIN; OR, THE KNIGHT OF THE ROAD// D// W. E. Suter// **Sad. Wells**, Sept. 1866, with J. Baker as Watson, Phillip Hannan as Whimsey, Walter Roberts as Turpin, G. P. Jaques as King, Watty Brunton as Fitzfoozle, Miss Neville as Mary, Julia Summers as Simkins.

DICK VENABLES// D 4a// Arthur Law// **Shaftesbury**, Apr. 1890, with E. S. Willard as Venables, Alfred Bishop as Jellicoe, Arthur Ewlood as Capt. Lankester, E. W. Garden as Paganstecher, Henry Esmond as Kirby, Royston Keith as Clifford, Mrs. George Canninge as Lady Harriet, Annie Rose as Helen, Annie Hill as Wilson, Olga Brandon as Mrs. Lisle/ Scenery by Walter Hann/ Prod. by E. S. Willard.

DICK WILDER// Play 4a// Mrs. H. Musgrave// **Vaudeville**, June 1891, with Fred Thorne as Sir Harry, Lawrance d'Orsay as St. Maur, H. B. Conway as Wilder, Dorothy Dorr as Molly, Adrienne Dairolles as Barbara/ Scenery by W. T. Hemsley.

DID I DREAM IT?// F 1a// J. P. Wooler// **Strand**, Nov. 1860.

DID YOU EVER SEND YOUR WIFE TO CAMBERWELL?// F 1a// J. Stirling Coyne// **Adelphi**, Mar. 1846/ **Haymarket**, July 1848, with Edward Wright as Honeybun, O. Smith as Crank, Emma Harding as Mrs. Honeybun, Mrs. Frank Matthews as Mrs. Crank, Mrs. Laws as Mrs. Jewel/ **Sad. Wells**, May 1854, with Edward Wright as Honeybun, Mr. Webb as Crank, Miss Levine as Mrs. Honeybun, Miss Rawlings as Mrs. Jewel, Mrs. Barrett as Mrs. Crank.

DIMITY'S DILEMMA// F 1a// Malcolm Salaman// **Gaiety**, Feb. 1887.

DINNER FOR NOTHING// F 1a// Charles Cheltman// **POW**, Oct. 1865.

DINNER FOR TWO// C 1a// R. C. Carton// **Trafalgar Sq.**, Mar. 1893, with Yorke Stephens as Kidbrook, Cyril Maude as Maj. Powneby, J. Willis as Achille.

DINORAH UNDER DIFFICULTIES// F 1a// William Brough// **Adelphi**, Nov. 1859, with

J. L. Toole as Topsawyer, C. J. Smith as Snuffles, W. H. Eburne as Sharp, Kate Kelly as Creechy, Paul Bedford as Growler, Lydia Foote as Nix, Robert Romer as Chowker.

DIPLOMACY// Play 5a// Adap. by Clement Scott & B. C. Stephenson fr F of Victorien Sardou, Dora// **POW**, Jan. 1878, with W. H. Kendal, Mrs. Kendal, Mr. Clayton, Mrs. Bancroft, Arthur Cecil, Squire Bancroft, Roma Le Thière/ **Haymarket**, Nov. 1884, with Squire Bancroft as Henry Beauclerc, Johnston Forbes Robertson as Julian Beauclerc, Mr. Elliot as Fairfax, Maurice Barrymore as Count Orloff, Mr. York as Markham, Charles Eaton as Antoine, Mrs. Bancroft as Lady Henry, Roma Le Thière as Marquise de Rio-Zarès, Mrs. Bernard Beere as Countess Zicka, Miss Calhoun as Dora/ Scenery by Mr. Telbin & Walter Johnstone/ **Garrick**, Feb. 1893, with Mrs. Bancroft, Johnston Forbes Robertson, Kate Rorke, Olga Nethersole, Squire Bancroft, Arthur Cecil, Gilbert Hare, John Hare.

DIPLOMATIC THEFT, A// D 1a// Havelock Ettrick// **Garrick**, July 1901.

DIRECTOR, THE// F 3a// Harry Greenbank// **Terry's**, May 1891, with Edward Terry as Sudds, Henry Esmond as Augustus, E. M. Robson as Jonquil, Robert Ganthony as Chiffins, Philip Cunningham as Ashford, Mrs. Charles Calvert as Caroline, Alice Maitland as Dolly, Rose Dearing as Gertie, Sophie Larkin as Rebecca.

DISCARDED SON, THE// D 3a// Trans. by Benjamin Webster fr F, Le Fils de Famille// **Adelphi**, Oct. 1853, with Charles Selby as Col. Fermain, Leigh Murray as Blondel, John Parselle as Roland, Paul Bedford as Schnapps, Robert Keeley as Dux, Mrs. Keeley as Mme. Lefort, Sarah Woolgar as Adeline, Fanny Maskell as Mme. Petitverre/ Scenery by Pitt & Turner.

DISOWNED, THE; OR, HELEN OF THE HURST// D 3a// Thomas Parry// **Adelphi**, Mar. 1851, with William Cullenford as Sir Ralph, Charles Boyce as Frank, C. J. Smith as Col. Waseley, J. Worrell as Capt. Crediton, Mme. Celeste as Leonard, Edward Wright as The Lurcher, George Honey as Widgeon, Samuel Emery as Ironstone, Paul Bedford as Peter, Emma Harding as Kate, Laura Honey as Adèle, Sarah Woolgar as Helen/ Scenery by Pitt & Turner/ Music by Alfred Mellon/ Machinery by Mr. Cooper.

DIVIDED DUTY// CD 1a// Silvanus Daunsey// **Globe**, Mar. 1891.

DIVIDED HOUSE, THE// F 1a// n.a.// **Grecian**, Mar. 1856, with Richard Phillips as Benjamin Bibbs, John Manning as Barnaby Bibbs, Eaton O'Donnell as Grumpy, Thomas Roberts as Peter Parker, Jane Coveney as Mrs. Benj. Bibbs, Harriet Coveney as Snarley, Miss Johnstone as Mrs. Barn. Bibbs.

DIVIDED WAY, THE// Play 3a// H. V. Esmond// **St. James's**, Nov. 1895, with W. H. Vernon as Gen. Humeden, George Alexander as Gaunt Humeden, Allan Aynesworth as Jack Humeden, Herbert Waring as Grist, H. H. Vincent as Dr. Macgrath, E. M. Robson as Swendal, Frank Dyall as Kelly, Violet Lyster as Phyllis, Evelyn Millard as Lois/ Scenery by H. P. Hall/ Music by Walter Slaughter.

DIVORCE// FC 3a// Adap. by Robert Reece fr F of Victorien Sardou, Divorçons// **Vaudeville**, Jan. 1881, with John Maclean, J. G. Grahame, Kate Bishop, Marie Illington, Cecily Richards.

DIVORCED// D 4a// Reginald Rutter// **Imperial**, May 1898.

DOBSON AND CO.; OR, MY TURN NEXT// F 1a// J. Stirling Coyne// **Adelphi**, Oct. 1842.

DOCTOR, THE// F 3a// Adap. by F. C. Burnand fr F of Ferrier & Bocage, La Doctoresse// **Globe**, May 1887, with W. S. Penley as Blossom, Henry Kemble as Count di Remo, Stewart Dawson as Prof. Kenrick, A. G. Andrews as Bertie Cameron, W. J. Hill as Bigge, Norman Bent as Chevalier O'Leari, Graham Wentworth as Thizzledon, Fanny Enson as Angelina, Rose Dearing as Signora Leari, Grace Arnold as Lady Thizzledon, Blanche Horlock as Edith, Miss Vane Featherston as Maggie, Cissy Grahame as Elizabeth.

DR. AND MRS. NEILL// Play 3a// Clotilde Graves// **Grand**, Sept. 1895.

DR. BELGRAFF// Play// Charles Klein// **Vaudeville**, Oct. 1896.

DR. BILL// FC 3a// Adap. by Hamilton Aïdé fr F of Albert Carré, Le Docteur Jo-Jo// **Avenue**, Feb. 1890, with Fred Terry as Dr. Brown, Ben Webster as Webster, George Capel as Horton, Harry Grattan as Baggs, Elizabeth Robins as Louisa, Carlotta Leclercq as Mrs. Firmin, Marie Linden as Ellen, Fanny Brough as Mrs. Horton/ **Court**, Dec. 1894.

DOCTOR DAVY// C// Adap. by James Albery fr F// **Lyceum**, June 1866/ **Opera Comique**, 1886.

DOCTOR DILWORTH// F 1a// John Oxenford// **Olympic**, Apr. 1839, with William Farren as Dilworth, Robert Keeley as Syntax, John Brougham as O'Laughlin, Mr. Granby as Paddington, Mrs. Orger as Mrs. Dilworth, Miss Murray as Zee/ **Cov. Garden**, Oct. 1839, with William Farren as Dilworth, Robert Keeley as Syntax, John Brougham as O'Loughlin, Mr. Granby as Paddington, Mrs. Orger as Mrs. Dilworth, Mrs. Brougham as Zoe/ **Sad. Wells**, Mar. 1847, with A. Younge as Dr. Dilworth, Mr. Williams as Paddington, Charles Fenton as O'Laughlin, Henry Scharf as Syntax, Mrs. Henry Marston as Mrs. Dilworth, Miss Stephens as Zoe/ **Haymarket**, Apr. 1853, with W. H. Chippendale as Dilworth, Henry Corri as O'Loughlin, Henry Compton as Syntax, William Clark as Paddington, Mrs. Poynter as Mrs. Dilworth, Ellen Chaplin as Zoe.

DOCTOR DORA// C 1a// F. W. Broughton & Henry Pettitt// **Garrick**, Apr. 1881, with Horatio Saker, Bessie Harrison, Florence

Harrison.

DR. FAUSTUS'S TRAGICAL HISTORY// T 5a// Christopher Marlowe// **St. Geo. Hall**, July 1896.

DOCTOR IN SPITE OF HIMSELF, THE// C 3a// Gerald Dixon// **Globe**, June 1877.

DR. JEKYLL AND MR. HYDE// D 4a// Dram. by T. Russell Sullivan fr story by R. L. Stevenson// **Lyceum**, Aug. 1888, with Richard Mansfield as Dr. Jekyll and Mr. Hyde, Mr. Harkins as Dr. Lanyon, John Sullivan as Gabriel Utterson, Mr. Holland as Gen. Carew, Mr. Burrows as Poole, Mr. Crompton as Inspector Newcome, Miss Sheridan as Rebecca Moor, Beatrice Cameron as Agnes Carew.

DR. JEKYLL AND MR. HYDE// Play 4a// Dram. by Daniel Bandmann fr story by R. L. Stevenson// **Opera Comique**, Aug. 1888.

DOCTOR'S BOY, THE// F// Roland Grant// **Surrey**, Jan. 1877.

DOCTOR'S BROUGHAM, THE// F// E. Manuel// **Strand**, Oct. 1875.

DOCTOR'S DILEMMA, THE// C 3a// Douglas M. Ford// **St. Geo. Hall**, May 1901.

DODGE FOR A DINNER, A// F 1a// T. A. Palmer// **Strand**, Dec. 1872.

DOES HE LOVE ME?// C 3a// Edmund Falconer// **Haymarket**, Oct. 1860, with Henry Howe as Mowbray, Edwin Villiers as Leigh, J. B. Buckstone as Dubble, W. H. Chippendale as Vandeleur, J. Worrell as Purvey, Amy Sedgwick as Miss Vandeleur, Florence Haydon as Miss Melrose, Mrs. Wilkins as Mrs. Comfort/ Scenery by John O'Conner/ Machines by Oliver Wales.

DOG OF MONTARGIS, THE (see, Forest of Bondi, The)

DOGE OF VENICE, THE// D 4a// Adap. by W. Bayle Bernard partly fr Lord Byron's Marino Faliero & partly fr Casimir De la Vigne's Marino// **Drury Lane**, Nov. 1867, with Samuel Phelps as Faliero, Edmund Phelps as Fernando, Mr. Barrett as Leoni, Henry Sinclair as Steno, James Johnstone as Benentendi, J. C. Cowper as Bertuccio, Charles Warner as Calendaro, William McIntyre as Stozzi, Mr. Moreland as Beppo, C. Webb as Andrea, Charles Harcourt as Bertram, Mrs. Hermann Vezin as Angiolina, Miss Grattan as Mariana.

DOGS OF ST. BERNARD, THE// D// Clement Scott// **Mirror**, Aug. 1875.

DOING BANTING// F 1a// William Brough & Andrew Halliday// **Adelphi**, Oct. 1864/ **Haymarket**, Dec. 1864, with Harry Cox as Prof. Pankey, Edwin Shepherd as Podge, Alfred Sanger as Dollop, Henry Westland as Dr. Lavender, Mrs. Bishop as Mrs. Podge, Ellen Leigh as Patty.

DOING FOR THE BEST// D 2a// Rophino Lacy// **Sad. Wells**, Nov. 1861, with Mr. Williams as Parchment, Samuel Phelps as Stubbs, Charles Seyton as Harry, Charles Fenton as Thomas, Lewis Ball as Hawkins, Mrs. Barrett as Betsy, Miss Hudspeth as Jane, Ada Dyas as Emily.

DOING MY UNCLE// F 1a// Rophino Lacy// **Surrey**, Sept. 1866.

DOING THE HANSOM// F 1a// Augustus Harris// **Lyceum**, Nov. 1866.

DOING THE SHAH// F// Nugent Robinson// **Globe**, July 1873.

DOLL'S HOUSE, A// D 3a// Trans. by William Archer fr Norw. of Henrik Ibsen// **Novelty**, June 1889/ **Terry's**, Jan. 1891, with C. Forbes Drummond as Helmer, William Herbert as Rank, Charles Fulton as Krogstad, Elizabeth Robins as Mrs. Linden, Marie Fraser as Nora/ **Criterion**, June 1891/ **Globe**, May 1897.

DOLLARS AND SENSE// C 3a// Adap. by Augustin Daly fr G// **Toole's**, Aug. 1884/ **Daly's**, Sept. 1893, with James Lewis as Lamb, George Clarke as Hemmarsly, Arthur Bourchier as Latimer, William Owen as Tremont, Charles Leclercq as Col. Briggs, Sidney Herbert as Griggles, Ada Rehan as Phronic, Mrs. G. H. Gilbert as Saphira, Lucie Celeste as Sybilia, Florence Conron as Hope, Frances Ross as Mrs. Tremont, Adelaide Stirling as Jane/ Scenery by T. E. Ryan/ Prod. by Augustin Daly.

DOLLY VARDEN// D 4a// Murray Wood// **Astley's**, Apr. 1878, with H. S. Granville as Mr. Chester, F. Bathurst as Edward Chester, Edward Chamberlaine as Haredale, R. H. Lingham as The Stranger, Emilie Blackwood as Barnaby Rudge, S. Reid as Varden, Frank Cates as Joe, J. W. Robertson as Maypole, Miss B. Marlborough as Mrs. Rudge, Fanny Wright as Mrs. Varden, Virginia Blackwood as Miggs and as Dolly Varden/ **Surrey**, Oct. 1872.

DOLORES// D// Mrs. S. Lane// **Britannia**, Apr. 1874.

DOMESTIC BLISS// C// n.a.// **Princess's**, May 1848, with Mr. Cooper as Goodliman, James Vining as Snap, Mr. Howard as Gadbee, Mrs. Stirling as Adela, Miss Villars as Rhoda.

DOMESTIC ECONOMY// F 1a// Mark Lemon/ **Adelphi**, Nov. 1849; Jan. 1856, with Edward Wright as Grumly, Miss Stoker as Joey, Mr. Henry as Sgt. Brown, Miss Wyndham as Mrs. Grumly, Kate Kelly as Mrs. Shackles/ **Haymarket**, Aug. 1850, with Edward Wright as Grumley, C. J. Smith as Sgt. Brown, Mrs. Frank Matthews as Mrs. Grumley, Ellen Chaplin as Mrs. Shackles, Mrs. Laws as Mrs. Nagley/ **Sad. Wells**, Aug. 1869, with Edward Atkins as Grumly, Mr. Skinner as Brown, Miss Stoker as Joe, Mrs. Lewis as Mrs. Grumly, Mrs. Stoker as Mrs. Snugsby, Emily Turtle as Mrs. Shackles/ **Toole's**, Jan. 1890, with J. L. Toole as Grumley, C. Wilson as Sgt. Tom, Charles Brunton as

Nix, Eliza Johnstone as Mrs. Grumley, Jenny Donald as Mrs. Shackles, Mary Brough as Mrs. Knagley.

DOMESTIC HERCULES, A// F 1a// Martin Becher// **Drury Lane**, Sept. 1870.

DOMINIQUE THE DESERTER; OR, THE GENTLEMAN IN BLACK (also titled The Deserter)// C 1a// W. H. Murray// **Sad. Wells**, July 1844, with E. Morton as Duverne, Charles Fenton as D'Auville, Edward Knight as Le Lache, G. F. Forman as Dominique, Mr. Sharpe as Gaspard, Mrs. Henry Marston as Genevieve, Georgiana Lebatt as Lady Blanche, Miss Lebatt as Jeannette; Oct. 1864, with Charles Horsman as Duverne, W. S. Foote as D'Anville, W. H. Drayton as Col. Le Lache, Walter Lacy as Morvillier, William Ellerton as Dominique, T. Sidney as Gaspard, Nelly Boyce as Lady Blanche, Mrs. Charles Horsman as Jeannette, Mrs. Stevenson as Genevieve, Maggie Campbell as Lucette/ **Victoria**, Aug. 1846, with E. Forman as Dominique, William Seaman as Duvergne, James Ranoe as La Roche, Alfred Raymond as Danville, Miss Fielding as Lady Blanche, Mrs. Cooke as Genevieve, Lydia Pearce as Janette, Miss Backhous as Susette/ **Astley's**, Dec. 1859, with George Belmore as Dominique, Mr. Ennis as Duverne, Alfred Raymond as La Luché, Mr. Leach as Morvillier, Mr. Ellis as Count D'Anville, Emily Dowton as Lady Blanche, Mrs. W. Dowton as Genevieve, Julia Weston as Julia/ **Princess's**, Aug. 1873, with Charles Fenton as Count D'Anville, Mr. Harrington as Duverne, B. Egan as de Lache, L. Clarke as Morvillier, Stanislaus Calhaem as Dominique, Mr. Hardorf as Gaspard, Miss Lynd as Lady Blanche, Miss Cowper as Jeannette, Miss Everard as Genevieve, Miss Grace as Susette.

DON, THE// C 3a// Adap. by Mr. & Mrs. Herman Merivale fr G// **Toole's**, Mar. 1888; Jan. 1890, with J. L. Toole as Millikin, John Billington as Pappendick, George Shelton, C. M. Lowne, Charles Brunton, Henry Westland, Effie Liston as Mrs. Sparkle, Florence Henry as Dora, Eliza Johnstone, Mary Brough, Irene Vanbrugh.

DON CAESAR DE BAZAN// D 3a// Adap. by Gilbert à Beckett & Mark Lemon fr F of M. Dumanois & A. P. Dennery// **Princess's**, Oct. 1844, with A. Walton as Charles II of Spain, Mr. Fitzjames as Don Jose, James Wallack as Don Caesar, Mr. Granby as Marquis di Rotondo, Miss Marshall as Lazarilla, Thomas Hill as Lopez, Mrs. Stirling as Maritana, Mrs. Fosbroke as Countess di Rotondo/ Scenery by Nicholls & Agilo/ Music by W. L. Phillips; Feb. 1861, with J. G. Shore as Charles II of Spain, Basil Potter as Don Jose, Charles Fechter as Don Caesar, Frank Matthews as Marquis de Rotondo, Maria Harris as Lazarillo, Carlotta Leclercq as Maritana, Mrs. Weston as Countess de Rotondo/ **Haymarket**, Jan. 1849, with Henry Howe as Charles II of Spain, Mr. Rogers as Don Jose, James Wallack as Don Caesar, Mr. Tilbury as Marquis di Rotondo, Priscilla Horton as Lazarillo, Mr. Ennis as Lopez, Mr. A. Brindal as Pedro, Julia Bennett as Maritana, Mrs. Stanley as Countess di Rotondo.

DON CAESAR DE BAZAN// D 3a// Adap by Dion Boucicault & Benjamin Webster fr F of M. Dumanois & A. P. Dennery// **Adelphi**, Oct. 1844.

DON CAESAR DE BAZAN// D 3a// Adap. fr F of M. Dumanois & A. P. Dennery// **Marylebone**, Apr. 1846, with Charles Dillon/ **Olympic**, Mar. 1850, with F. B. Conway as Charles II of Spain, James Johnstone as Don Jose, E. L. Davenport as Don Caesar, George Cooke as Marquis di Rotondo, Louisa Marshall as Lazarillo, Mr. Greene as Lopez, Mr. Macklin as Judge, Fanny Vining as Maritana, Mrs. Parker as Marchioness di Rotondo; May 1852, with John Kinloch as Charles II of Spain, F. H. Edgar as Don Jose, Henry Farren as Don Caesar, George Cooke as Marquis Pompioso, Alfred Sanger as Dan Manuel, Miss Fielding as Lazarillo, Louisa Howard as Maritana, Mrs. B. Bartlett as Countess Pompioso.

DON CESAR OF BAZAN// D 3a// Adap. by Thomas Archer fr F of M. Dumanois & A. P. Dennery// **Grecian**, Nov. 1844, with Edwin Dixon as King Charles, Mr. Campbell as Don Jose, John Chester as Don Cesar, Mr. Baldwin as Montefior, Annette Mears as Maritana, Miss Merion as Marchionesse of Montifior/ Scenery by Mr. Muir/ Music by Mr. Isaacson; Aug. 1856, with Richard Phillips as Don Caesar, F. Charles as Charles II, Mr. Hustleby as Don Jose, Eaton O'Donnell as Marquis de Montifore, Miss Johnstone as Marchioness, Jane Coveney as Maritana; Mar. 1862 (in adap. by Thomas Mead), with R. H. Lingham, Alfred Rayner, Thomas Mead, Harriet Coveney, Jane Coveney/ **Sad. Wells**, May 1856, with E. F. Edgar as Charles II of Spain, Charles Dillon as Don Caesar, William Morgan as Don Jose, Mr. Barrett as Marquis de Montefiori, Miss Cuthbert as Lazarillo, Mrs. Charles Dillon as Maritana, Mrs. B. Bartlett as Marchioness de Montefiori; Nov. 1865 (in adap. by Charles Webb), with E. H. Brooke as King of Spain, Richard Norman as Don Jose, J. C. Cowper as Don Caesar, James Johnstone as Marquis de Rotunda, Minnie Davis as Lazarillo, Miss M. A. Bellair as Maritana, Mrs. E. F. Edgar as Marchioness de Rotunda.

DON JOHN OF SEVILLE// D 4a// Edgardo Colonna// **Elephant & Castle**, Sept. 1876.

DON JUAN'S LAST WAGER// Play 4a// Adap. by Mrs. Cunningham Grahame fr Sp of José Zorilla// **POW**, Feb. 1900.

DON QUIXOTE// D 1a// Dram. by W. G. Wills fr an episode in Sp of Cervantes// **Lyceum**, May 1895, with Henry Irving as Don Quixote, S. Johnson as Sancho Panza, Mr. Haviland as Father Perez, Frank Archer as Pedro, Miss De Silva as Antonia, Maud Milton as Maria, Mrs. Lacy as Dulcina/ Scenery by Hawes Craven/ Machines by Mr. Fillery.

DON QUIXOTE, JR// C 1a// J. C. Goodwin & John Howson// **Globe**, July 1879, with John Howson as Nestor, L. Vincent as Meredith, Maggie Duggan as Henrietta, Clara Grahame as Julia.

DONAGH, THE// D 3a// George Rowe// **Grand**, Apr. 1884.

DONE ON BOTH SIDES// F 1a// J. Maddison Morton// **Lyceum**, Mar. 1847, with C. J. Mathews as Brownjohn, Frank Matthews as Whiffles, J. B. Buckstone as Phibbs, Mrs. Charles Jones as Mrs. Whiffles, Louisa Marshall as Lydia/ **St. James's**, Oct. 1861, with Frank Matthews as Whiffles, George Vining as Brownjohn, J. Robins as Phibbs, Mrs. Frank Matthews as Mrs. Wiffles, Nelly Moore as Lydia/ **Haymarket**, Oct. 1889, with Mr. Hargreaves as Whiffles, Charles Collette as Brownjohn, Charles Allan as Phibbs, Miss Morland as Mrs. Whiffles, Miss Aylward as Lydia.

DONELLAN// D 4a// P. R. Innes// **Strand**, June 1889.

DONNA DIANA// C 4a// Adap. by Westland Marston fr G vers. of Augustin Moreto's El Desden con El Desden// **Princess's**, Jan. 1864, with E. Hooper as Don Diego, Hermann Vezin as Don Caesar, Henry Forrester as Don Luis, David Fisher as Don Gaston, George Vining as Perin, Mrs. Hermann Vezin (late Mrs. Charles Young) as Donna Diana, Caroline Carson as Donna Laura, Emma Barnett as Donna Fenisa, Rebecca Powell as Floretta/ Music by Charles Hill/ **POW**, Nov. 1896.

DON'T BE FRIGHTENED// F 2a// J. Maddison Morton// **Cov. Garden**, Nov. 1839, with George Bartley as Sir Timothy, C. J. Mathews as Maj. Rocket, John Pritt Harley as Brown, Drinkwater Meadows as Humphrey, Miss Lee as Maria, Mrs. Humby as Mrs. Dainty.

DON'T JUDGE BY APPEARANCES// F 1a// J. Maddison Morton// **Princess's**, Oct. 1855, with Mr. Cooper as Maj. Pepper, George Everett as Topham, Drinkwater Meadows as Plump, Carlotta Leclercq as Diana, Miss Eglinton as Angelina.

DON'T LEND YOUR UMBRELLA// C 2a// Leicester Buckingham// **Strand**, Jan. 1857.

DONZELLA, THE HEROINE OF CASTILE; OR, THE MONK AND THE ASSASSINS (also titled, Donzella's Oath; or, The Colonel, The Monk, and the Assassins)// D// Adap. fr F// **Victoria**, Apr. 1847, with C. J. Bird as Col. Beauville, Mr. Fitzjames as Capt. Linois, Mr. Hitchinson as Capt. Fomard, John Dale as Father Anthony, John Gardner as Geppo, Annette Vincent as Donzella, Mrs. Cooke as Dame Delcaro.

DOO, BROWN, & CO// F 3a// C. M. Rae// **Vaudeville**, Mar. 1886, with Thomas Thorne, E. M. Robson, Sophie Larkin, Helen Forsyth.

DOOMED BRIDGE, THE// D// n.a.// **Victoria**, Mar. 1856.

DORA// D 3a// Dram. by Charles Reade fr poem of Alfred Tennyson// **Adelphi**, June 1867, with Henry Neville as Farmer Allan, Henry Ashley as William, John Billington as Luke, Mr. Paulo as Jem, Kate Terry as Dora, Miss Hughes as Mary/ Machinery by G. Bastard/ Music by Edwin Ellis/ Machines by Mr. Charker/ Prod. by R. Phillips; Jan. 1883.

DORA INGRAM// D 4a// Mortimer Murdock// **Pavilion**, Feb. 1885.

DORA MAYFIELD; OR, LOVE THE LEVELER// D 1a// Edgar Newbound// **Britannia**, Feb. 1878.

DORA'S DEVICE// C 2a// Robert Reece// **Royalty**, Jan. 1871.

DOROTHY GRAY// D 5a// J. F. Nesbit// **Princess's**, Apr. 1888.

DOROTHY VERNON// D 5a// J. W. Boulding// **Savoy**, Oct. 1892, with Ian Robertson as Sir George, Lawrance d'Orsay as Thomas Stanley, Orlando Barnett as Edward Stanley, Henry Bedford as Shaw, Arthur Wood as Dawson, Philip Cunningham as Manners, Mrs. Edmund Phelps as Luce, Geraldine St. Maur as Cecily, Marion Lind as Margaret, Sydney Phelps as Dorothy.

DOROTHY'S STRATAGEM// C 2a// James Mortimer// **Criterion**, Dec. 1876.

DOT// D// Dram. by Dion Boucicault fr Charles Dickens, Cricket on the Hearth// **Adelphi**, Apr. 1862/ **Sad. Wells**, Apr. 1866, with Kate Bishop as Oberon, Hetty Tracey as Titania, Miss F. Morris as Puck, Miss Ella as Ariel, Ada Harland as Cricket, Ada Dyas as Dot, Rosine Power as May, Miss Hudspeth as Bertha, Lizzie Wilmore as Tilly Slowboy, Mrs. Poynter as Mrs. Fielding, Thomas Swinbourne as Peerybingle, George Belmore as Caleb Plummer, Charles Warner as Ned, William McIntyre as Tackleton/ Scenery by John Johnson/ **Queen's**, Jan. 1869/ **Folly**, Sept. 1880, with J. L. Toole, Lilian Cavalier.

DOTHEBOYS HALL// D 3a// Dram. by J. Daly Besemeres fr Charles Dickens's Nicholas Nickleby// **Court**, Dec. 1871.

DOUBLE-BEDDED ROOM, THE// F 1a// J. Maddison Morton// **Haymarket**, June 1843, with William Farren as Pipes, William Strickland as Maj. Minus, T. F. Mathews as Spigot, Mrs. Julia Glover as Mrs. Lomax, Mrs. Humby as Nancy.

DOUBLE DOSE, A// F// Arthur Shirley// **Surrey**, Mar. 1890.

DOUBLE DUMMY// F 1a// N. H. Harrington & Edmund Yates// **Lyceum**, Mar. 1858.

DOUBLE EVENT, THE// D 4a// Edward Towers// **East London**, Apr. 1871.

DOUBLE-FACED PEOPLE// C 3a// John Courtney// **Haymarket**, Feb. 1857, with W. H. Chippendale as Vacile, William Farren as Medley, J. B. Buckstone as Scrummel, Henry Compton as Gloss, George Braid as Scripp, Edwin Villiers as Pike, Mr. Rogers as Moneybee, William Cullenford as Wrangle, Mrs. Edward Fitzwilliam as Emily, Miss Reynolds as Fanny,

Mrs. Poynter as Mrs. Wrangle.

DOUBLE GALLANT, THE; OR, THE SICK LADY'S CURE// C// Colly Cibber// **Cov. Garden**, Mar. 1839, with William Farren as Sir Solomon, C. J. Mathews as Atall, George Vandenhoff as Careless, James Vining as Clerimont, Frank Matthews as Wilful, Mr. Granby as Sir Harry, Charles Selby as Capt. Strutt, Alfred Wigan as Saunter, Mrs. Walter Lacy (Agnes Taylor) as Lady Dainty, Mrs. Nisbett as Lady Sadlife, Mme. Vestris as Clarinda, Mrs. Brougham as Sylvia, Mrs. Orger as Wishwell, Mrs. Humby as Situp/ **Haymarket**, Mar. 1848, with William Farren as Sir Solomon, Henry Howe as Clerimont, Henry Vandenhoff as Careless, Benjamin Webster as Atall, Mr. Tilbury as Old Wilful, Mr. Rogers as Sir Harry, A. Brindal as Capt. Strut, James Bland as Sir Squabble, William Clark as Supple, J. W. Gough as Dr. Bolus, Mr. Caulfield as Saunter, Julia Bennett as Lady Dainty, Mrs. Nisbett as Lady Sadlife, Miss Fortescue as Clarinda, Mrs. L. S. Buckingham as Sylvia, Mrs. Caulfield as Situp, Mrs. Humby as Wishwell.

DOUBLE LIFE, A// D 4a// n.a.// **Marylebone**, Dec. 1876.

DOUBLE MARRIAGE, THE// D 2a// Beaumont & Fletcher// **Marylebone**, Apr. 1848, with Mrs. Mary Warner, Fanny Vining, Charlotte Saunders, T. H. Lacy, James Johnstone, George Vining/ **Adelphi**, Mar. 1863.

DOUBLE ROSE, THE// Play 5a// J. W. Boulding// **Adelphi**, June 1882, with William Rignold, A. C. Hatton, Louise Neville, Sophie Eyre.

DOUBT// D 4a// J. Stanley Little// **Strand**, June 1889.

DOUBTFUL VICTORY, A// C // John Oxenford// **Olympic**, Apr. 1858, with George Vining as Col. Clive, Walter Gordon as Cleveland, Mrs. Stirling as Mrs. Flowerdale, Miss Hughes as Violet.

DOUGLAS: OR, THE NOBLE SHEPHERD// T 5a// John Home// **Sad. Wells**, May 1837, with N. T. Hicks as Douglas, D. W. King as Old Norval, Mr. Campbell as Glenalvon, C. H. Pitt as Lord Randolph, Miss Williams as Lady Randolph, Mrs. Harris as Anne; Dec. 1841, with Mr. Elvin as Lord Randolph, Mr. Dry as Glenalvon, Mr. Williams as Old Norval, Mrs. Robert Honner as Young Norval, Miss Richardson as Lady Randolph, Miss Cooke as Anna; May 1850, with Henry Mellon as Lord Randolph, George Bennett as Glenalvon, G. K. Dickinson as Young Norval, Frank Graham as Old Norval, Isabela Glyn as Lady Randolph, Miss T. Bassano as Anna/ **Victoria**, Jan. 1838, with Mr. Cobham Jr. as Young Norval, John Parry as Lord Randolph, Mr. Wilkins as Glenalvon, Mr. Loveday as Old Norval, Miss Richardson as Lady Randolph, Miss Lee as Anne.

DOULOUREUX, LA// C 4a// Louise Maurice Donnay// **Lyric**, June 1897.

DOVE AND THE SERPENT, THE// n.a.// **City of London**, Mar. 1859.

DOVE-COT, THE// C 3a// Adap. by Charles Brookfield fr F of Bisson & Leclercq, Jalouse// **Duke of York's**, Feb. 1898, with Seymour Hicks as Allward, Charles Sugden as Bamford, William Wyes as Mellish, Laurence Caird as Sir Barrington, Charles France as Brindle, James Welch as Elisha, Ellis Jeffries as Eva, Sybil Carlisle as Clara, Leonora Braham as Juanita, Kate Kearney as Bridget, Dorothea Desmond as Elaine, Carlotta Addison as Mrs. Brindal/ Scenery by Walter Hann & W. T. Hemsley.

DOVES IN A CAGE// C 2a// Douglas Jerrold// **Drury Lane**, Feb. 1855.

DOWAGER, THE// C 1a// Adap. by Charles Mathews fr F, Le Chateau de Ma Mère// **Haymarket**, Dec. 1842, with C. J. Mathews as Lyndsay, Henry Holl as Chasemore, A. Brindal as Beauchamp, Mme. Vestris as Countess of Tresilian, Miss Charles as Lady Bloom, Miss C. Conner as Margaret/ **Olympic**, July 1861, with Frederic Robinson as Lord Alfred, Walter Gordon as Sir Frederick, Gaston Murray as Beauchamp, Amy Sedgwick as Countess of Tresilian, Miss Marston as Lady Bloomer, Miss Cottrell as Margaret/ **Olympic**, Jan. 1881, with Leonard Boyne as Lord Alfred, Mr. Pery as Sir Frederick, Mr. De Lange as Beauchamp, Mr. Weathersby as Richard, Caroline Hill as Countess of Tressilian, Rose Roberts as Lady Bloomer, Doreen O'Brien as Margaret.

DOWN AMONG THE COALS// F// W. A. Vicars// **Court**, Nov. 1873.

DOWN IN A BALLOON// F 1a// John Oxenford// **Adelphi**, July 1871, with C. H. Stephenson as Serene, Henry Ashley as Mountjoy, A. C. Lilly as Meteor, Mrs. Addie as Mrs. Serene, Maud Howard as Mrs. Meteor, Miss Lovell as Fedora/ **Princess's**, Mar. 1872, with Mr. Moreland as Serene, Henry Ashley as Mountjoy, Charles Seyton as Meteor, Mrs. R. Power as Mrs. Serene, Miss Leigh as Mrs. Meteor, Jenny Lovell as Fedora.

DRAGON KNIGHT, THE; OR, THE QUEEN OF BEAUTY// D 2a// Dram. by Edward Stirling fr H. Ainsworth's Crichton// **Adelphi**, Nov. 1839.

DRAPERY QUESTION, THE; OR, WHO'S FOR INDIA?// C 1a// Charles Selby// **Adelphi**, Oct. 1857.

DRAWING ROOMS, SECOND FLOOR AND ATTICS// F 1a// J. Maddison Morton// **Princess's**, Mar. 1864, with David Fisher as Brown, Henry Mellon as Bunny, Charles Seyton as Cockletop, Henry Forrester as Capt. Hardaport, Robert Cathcart as Sharp, Emma Barnett as Caroline, Rebecca Powell as Arabella, Helen Howard as Phoebe.

DRAWN FOR THE MILITIA (see also, Conscript of Lyons)// F 1a// Thomas Blake// **Grecian**, May 1846, with Edwin Dixon as Capt. Gorgon, Mr. Manley as Domville, Frederick Robson as Billy Small, Eaton. O'Donnell as O'Knobbs, Mrs. W. Watson as Widow Small, Mary A. Crisp as Sally.

DREAM AT SEA, THE// D 3a// J. B. Buckstone// **Sad. Wells**, July 1839, with Mr. Cathcart as Lynwood, Robert Honner as Black Ralph, Mr. Dry as Trevanion, Arthur Wilkinson as Croker, Mr. Conquest as Tinkle, Mr. Elvin as Penderell, Mrs. J. F. Saville as Anne, Miss Pincott as Biddy, Miss Cooke as Margaret; Apr. 1854, with George Vining as Lynwood, C. Poynter as Sir John, F. Charles as Penderell, Henry Farren as Black Ralph, Mr. Barrett as Croaker, William Suter as Tinkle, Lizzie Mandelbert as Anne, Miss Marshall as Biddy, Miss Rawlings as Margaret/ **Olympic**, Mar. 1850, with H. Lee as Trevanion, John Kinloch as Penderell, F. B. Conway as Lynwood, James Johnstone as Black Ralph, George Cooke as Croaker, Henry Compton as Tinkle, Jane Coveney as Anne, Mrs. Seymour as Biddy, Mrs. Parker as Margaret/ **Adelphi**, Jan. 1875, with Howard Russell as Trevanion, A. C. Lilly as Richard, James Fernandez as Launce, William McIntyre as Black Ralph, Augustus Glover as Alley, James Fawn as Tommy, Edith Stuart as Anne, Miss Hudspeth as Biddy, Miss E. Phillips as Margaret/ Scenery by F. Lloyds/ Music by Edwin Ellis.

DREAM FACES// Play 1a// Wynn Miller// **Terry's**, Nov. 1888/ **Garrick**, Feb. 1890.

DREAM OF FATE, THE; OR, SARAH THE JEWESS// D 2a// C. Z. Barnett// **Sadler's Wells**, Aug. 1838, with Mr. Cathcart as Stolberg, John Webster as Clissold, Benjamin Conquest as Trinkalles, Robert Honner as Cardinham, Mrs. Robert Honner as Sarah, Miss Pincott as Rebecca, Mr. Mellor as Pierre.

DREAM OF LOVE// C 2a// John Oxenford// **Opera Comique**, Oct. 1872.

DREAM OF LIFE, A// D 3a// n.a.// **Grecian**, Mar. 1861, with Alfred Rayner as Henry Bertram, Mr. Smithson as Lawyer, Jane Coveney as Grace, R. H. Lingham as Sir George, G. Harding as Billy, Henry Power as Gregory, Walter Holland as Jack, Jane Coveney as Grace, Harriet Coveney as Susan.

DREAM OF THE FUTURE, A// C 3a// Charles Dance// **Olympic**, Nov. 1837, with C. J. Mathews as Mildmay, James Vining as Lovelock, Frank Matthews as Harbottle, John Brougham as Patrick, Mr. Hughes as Richard, Mme. Vestris as Honoria, Miss Crisp as Mrs. Seagreen/ **Haymarket**, June 1838, with C. J. Mathews as Mildmay, Benjamin Webster as Capt. Lovelock, Robert Strickland as Harbottle, John Brougham as Patrick, Mme. Vestris as Honoria, Miss Cooper as Georgiana, Mrs. Orger as Watson; Mar. 1853, with Leigh Murray as Capt. Lovelock, Henry Howe as Mildmay, Mr. Lambert as Harbottle, Henry Bedford as Patrick, Mrs. Stirling as Honoria, Mrs. Leigh Murray as Georgiana, Amelia Vining as Watson, Mrs. Selby as Mrs. Seagreen, Miss A. Woulds as Old Lady.

DREAM SPECTRE, THE; OR, THE LEGEND OF THE SLEEPER'S SHRIFT// D 3a// T. E. Wilks// **Victoria**, July 1842, with William Seaman as Robert, Mr. Hitchinson as Delaville, E. F. Saville as Spritsail, John Gardner as Watts, Charles Morelli as Van Doene, Mr. Paul as Hooler. Mr. Cullen as Grey, James Howard as Sibsey, Annette Vincent as Ruth, Mrs. Griffiths as Dame Cowley, Mrs. George Lee as Syrea, Mrs. Seaman as Betsy.

DREAMER, THE// C// T. H. Reynoldson// **Princess's**, Mar. 1846, with C. J. Mathews as Lord Dormer, James Vining as Count de Florville, Mr. Wynn as Col. Sheldrake, Augustus Harris as Sedley, W. H. Oxberry as Gage, Mrs. Stirling as Lady Clara.

DREAMS// D 5a// T. W. Robertson// **Gaiety**, Mar. 1869.

DRED// D// F. Phillips & John Coleman// **Surrey**, Oct. 1856.

DRED; A TALE OF THE DISMAL SWAMP// D 2a// Dram. by W. E. Suter fr novel of Harriet Beecher Stowe// **Queen's**, Oct. 1856/ **Victoria**, Oct. 1856, with Frederick Byefield as Clayton, Mr. Hitchinson as Yekyl, W. Richards as Judge Oliver, John Bradshaw as Gordon, George Pearce as Hannabal, John Warlow as Jem, W. H. Pitt as Dred, N. T. Hicks as Harry, James Howard as Old Hundred, T. E. Mills as Uncle Tiff, Charles Rice as Tomtit, J. F. Donald as Cripps, Mr. Henderson as Frank, Jane Dawson as Nina, Mrs. Henry Vining as Milly, Mrs. Warlow as Aunt Nesbitt, Miss Laporte as Livy, Julia Seaman as Polly, Mrs. Alfred Saville as Old Rose/ Scenery by R. Mildenhall & Mr. Fenhowlet/ Machines by W. Woods/ Music by Mr. Mingaye/ Prod. by J. Johnson Towers.

DRED; OR, A TALE OF THE DISMAL SWAMP// D 2a// Dram. by H. Young fr novel of Harriet Beecher Stowe// **Astley's**, Nov. 1856, with Mark Howard as Tom Gordon, W. Cooke Jr. as Harry Gordon, J. W. Anson as Old Tiff, James Holloway as Dred, J. Smith as Cripps, H. Reeves as Clayton, W. Vokes as Jekyl, J. Craddock as Dexter, Mrs. J. W. Anson as Nina, Mrs. Jackson as Cora, Mrs. Thorne as Anne, Mrs. W. Dowton as Aunt Nesbit, Julia Weston as Lisette/ Scenery by T. Thompson & Thorne/ Machines by E. Pryce/ Music by G. Phillips/ Horses trained by Wm. Cooke/ **Grecian**, Apr. 1864, with Frederick Marchant as Dred, William James as Gordon, John Manning as Cute, Walter Holland as Jekyl, J. Jackson as Uncle Tiff, J. B. Steele as Tom Gordon, Henry Grant as Clayton, W. Shirley as Cripps, Jane Dawson as Cora, Marie Brewer as Ninna, Louisa Graham as Mrs. Cripps, Miss Smithers as Fanny.

DRESS COAT, THE// F// Frank Green// **Strand**, June 1876.

DRINK// D 5a// Adap. by Charles Reade fr F of Busnach & Gastineau, L'Assommoir// **Princess's**, June 1879, with Charles Warner as Coupeau, William Redmund as Lantier, William Rignold as Gouget, John Beauchamp as Poisson, T. P. Haynes as Bottes, C. Wilford as Bibi, A. Murray as Sali, William Strickland as Colombe, Amy Roselle as Gervaise, Fannie Leslie as Phoebe, Ada Murray as Virginie, Kate Barry as Nana/ Scenery by Julian Hicks/ Music by Mr. Mallandaine/ Machines by R. Warton/ Gas by D. Jones/ Lime-light by Mr. Kerr/ Prod. by Charles Reade/ **Adelphi**, (in 7a), Aug. 1882, with Charles Warner as Coupeau, Cyril Searle as Gouget, Philip Beck as Lantier, Harry Proctor as Poisson, F. Thorne as Mes Bottes, Harwood Cooper as Bibi, Blanche Henri as Gervaise, Fannie Leslie as Phoebe, Ada Neilson as Virginie, Julia Roselle as Juliette, Miss E. Heffer as Delphine/ **Drury Lane**, Mar 1884, with Charles Warner as Coupeau, Charles Glenney as Lantier, Edward Gurney as Gouget, Julian Cross as Poisson, William Morgan as Bottes, Alfred Phillips as Bibi, Mr. Staunton as Sali, Reginald Cox as Colombe, Herbert Terris as Jacques, Ronald Power as Adolphe, Jessie Millward as Gervais, Katie James as Phoebe, Ada Neilson as Virginia, Mrs. Billington as Mme. Rouge, Alice Kingsley as Juliet, Lily Brooking as Delphine/ Prod. by Augustus Harris/ **Princess's**, July 1896/ **Adelphi**, Dec. 1899.

DRIVEN FROM HOME// D 3a// G. H. Macdermott// **Grecian**, July 1871/ **Pavilion**, (in 4a), June 1886.

DROWNED MAN'S LEGACY, THE// D 3a// William Seaman// **Britannia**, Sept. 1872.

DRUID'S OAK, THE// n.a.// **Victoria**, June 1851.

DRUNKARD'S CHILDREN, THE// D 2a// J. B. Johnstone// **Pavilion**, July 1848.

DRUNKARD'S CHILDREN, THE// D// John Courtney// **Victoria**, July 1848, with G. F. Forman as Fuzzle, Walter Searle as Hawkeseye, J. T. Johnson as Milford, Annette Vincent as Barbara, James Howard as Basil Milford, Miss Edgar as Fanny, Miss Burroughcliffe as Bright, Miss De Vere as Flirt, Mrs. George Lee as Whistle/ Scenery by Mildenhall & Macdonald/ Prod. by Mr. Osbaldiston & T. H. Higgie.

DRUNKARD'S GLASS, THE// D 1a// Thomas Morton// **Lyceum**, Apr. 1845.

DU BARRY// Play// David Belasco// **Elephant & Castle**, Dec. 1901.

DUBLIN BAY// C// T. W. Robertson// **Folly**, Dec. 1875.

DUCHESS DE LA VALLIERE, THE// D 5a// Edward Bulwer-Lytton// **Cov. Garden**, Jan. 1837, with John Vandenhoff as Louis XIV, William Farren as Duke de Lauzun, John Pritchard as Count de Grammont, W. C. Macready as Marquis de Bragelone, Benjamin Webster as Marquis de Montespan, Mr. Tilbury as Bertrand, Miss Pelham as Mme. de Montespan, Mrs. W. West as Mme. de la Valliere, Helen Faucit as Duchess de la Valliere, Miss Partridge as Queen, Mrs. Sarah Garrick as Abbess/ Scenery by Marshall/ Prod. by Henry Wallack.

DUCHESS ELEANOUR// Play 5a// H. F. Chorley// **Haymarket**, Mar. 1854, with William Farren as Duke of Ferrara, H. Corri as Count Raphael, Henry Howe as Count Abelard, Edwin Villiers as Count Leonard, George Vandenhoff as The Incognito, Mr. Rogers as Bellotto, Charlotte Cushman as Duchess Eleanour, Mrs. L. S. Buckingham as Violet/ Scenery by W. Callcott, George Morris & Mr. O'Conner.

DUCHESS OF BAYSWATER & CO., THE// C 1a// A. M. Heathcote// **Haymarket**, Mar. 1889, with Charles Brookfield as Duke of Bayswater, Charles Allan as Sir Jeremy, Edmund Maurice as Stubs, Rose Leclercq as Dowager Duchess, Miss Aylward as Kathleen.

DUCHESS OF COOLGARDIE, THE// D 5a// Euston Leigh & Cyril Clare// **Drury Lane**, Sept. 1896, with Charles Glenney as Big Ben, J. L. Shine as Hooligan, Laurence Cautley as Sailor Jack, Edward O'Neill as Bill, C. M. Lowne as Dick, Oswald Yorke as Airy, Claud Llewellyn as Vannicker, Watty Brunton Jr. as Jerry, Hermann Vezin as Macdonald, Hilda Spong as Sybil, Laura Johnson as Wallaroo, Laura Linden as Kathleen, Edith Jordan as Nellie.

DUCHESS OF GUISE, THE// D 3a// Adap. fr. F of Alexandre Dumas// **Olympic**, Apr. 1845, with Mr. Denvil as Duc de Guise, F. Burton as Henry III, Robert Roxby as St. Megrin, Henry Mellon as Ruggeiri, Henry Bedford as Joyeuse, Mr. Darcie as D'Epernon, Mr. Turnour as St. Luc, H. T. Craven as George, Miss Davenport as Duchess of Guise, Mrs. Griffith as Mme. de Cosse, Kate Howard as Catherine de Medicis, Miss Fielding as Marie.

DUCHESS OF MALFI, THE// Adap. by R. H. Horne fr John Webster// **Sad. Wells**, Nov. 1850, with Samuel Phelps as Ferdinand, Frank Graham as Cragiani, Henry Mellon as Malateste, Mr. Waller as Antonio, Charles Wheatleigh as Delio, George Bennett as Bosola, Charles Fenton as Silvio, Isabela Glyn as Duchess, Mrs. Archbold as Guiseppa, Mrs. Graham as Cariola; Jan. 1864, with David Jones as Ferdinand, Edmund Phelps as Antonio, E. H. Brooke as Grasiani, A. Baildon as Delio, T. B. Bennett as Malateste, T. Robinson as Castruccio, George Vining as Silvio, W. D. Gresham as Bosola, Alice Marriott as Marina, Mrs. H. Wallis as Guiseppa, Maggie Grainger as Cariola/ **Standard**, May 1859, with Isabel Glyn/ **Sad. Wells**, 1864/ **Standard**, Apr. 1868.

DUCHESS OF MALFI, THE// D// Adap. by William Poel fr John Webster// **Opera Comique**, Nov. 1892, with Murray Carson as Bosola, Sydney Barraclough as Ferdinand, Basset Roe as Cardinal, F. Rawson Buckley as Antonio, Frank Westerton as Delio, G. H. Kersley as Castruccio, Rex Shirley as Roderigo, C. W. Perkins as Silvio, Hall Caine as Cariola, Alice de Winton as Julia, Mary Rorke as Duchess/ Scenery by F. Taylor/Machines by R. Warton/ Limelight by H. Parnell/Prod. by William Poel.

DUCHESS OR NOTHING// C 1a// Adap. by

Walter Gordon fr F, La Marquise de Carabas// **Olympic**, July 1860, with Walter Gordon as Prince de Conti, Mr. Addison as Duke de Boissec, George Cooke as Chev. de Beauminet, F. Charles as Lucien, Mrs. Stephens as Mlle. de Beauminet, Mrs. Stirling as Suzanne.

DUCK HUNTING// F 1a// J. Stirling Coyne// **Haymarket**, Nov. 1862, with William Farren as Tom, Henry Howe as Capt. Turvey, Henry Compton as Pybus, Mrs. Wilkins as Mrs. Pybus, Caroline Hill as Lizzie.

DUEL, THE; OR, MY TWO NEPHEWS// C// R. B. Peake// **Olympic**, Dec. 1837, with William Farren as Oldencourt, Robert Keeley as Rumflit, Charles Mathews as Buoyant, James Vining as Skylark, Frank Matthews as Silverhead, Mr. Stoker as Lt. Buoyant, John Brougham as O'Manley, Miss Lee as Harriet, Miss Goward as Mrs. Barbottle, Miss Brookes as Rebecca.

DUEL IN THE DARK, A// F 1a// J. Stirling Coyne// **Haymarket**, Jan. 1852, with J. B. Buckstone as Greenfinch, Mrs. Fitzwilliam as Mrs. Greenfinch, Mrs. Caulfield as Betsy.

DUEL IN THE SNOW, THE; OR, CHRISTMAS EVE// D 3a// Edward Fitzball// **Sad. Wells**, June 1862, with James Johnstone as Sir Charles, Henry Forrester as Capt. Dartford, Lewis Ball as Titmouse, Mr. Harris as Monckton, Charles Bender as Eustache, Mrs. W. Dowton as Lady Andry, Miss M. Percy as Emily, Emily Dowton as Gimp.

DUGALD THE DROVER; OR, THE CATTLE STEALER AND THE ROVER'S DOG// D// n.a.// **Sad. Wells**, Nov. 1842, with Mr. Blanchard as Leslie, Mr. Cony as McNeil, C. J. Bird as Lisle, John Herbert as McClair, Charles Fenton as Lt. Greville, Mr. Lambe as Saunders, Caroline Rankley as Jessie, Mrs. Richard Barnett as Maggie/ Scenery by F. Fenton/ Machines by Mr. Cowdery/ Music by Isaac Collins.

DUKE IN DIFFICULTIES, A// C 3a// Tom Taylor// **Haymarket**, Mar. 1861, with Henry Howe as Grand Duke, Edwin Villiers as Landgrave, Mr. Rogers as Dampfnoodle, George Braid as Wetterhahn, J. B. Buckstone as De la Rampe, Henry Compton as Bellecour, Florence Haydon as Princess Wilhelmina, Mrs. Wilkins as Baroness Dampfnoodle, Mrs. Poynter as Mlle. Griffinheim, Mrs. Stirling as La Joconde, Fanny Stirling as Colombe, Fanny Wright as Mlle. Roucoule, Miss Addington as Mlle. Girouette/ Scenery by John O'Conner & George Morris/ Machines by Oliver Wales/ Music by D. Spillane.

DUKE OF SHOREDITCH, THE; OR, THE HUMOURS OF ADAM ALLEYNE AND HIS MERRY WIFE JOAN// C// n.a.// **Victoria**, Apr. 1842, with John Dale as Henry VIII, Charles Williams as Lord Raby, William Seaman as Lord Ribbesdale, Mr. Griffiths as Lord Lovewell, James Howard as Bell, John Gardner as Alleyne, Mr. James as Cotsby, Mr. Hitchinson as Vantree, Miss Coveney as Joan, Mrs. George Lee as Catharine, Mrs. Griffith as Dame Cotsby.

DUKE OF SWINDLETON, THE// FC 3a// William Burnside// **Opera Comique**, June 1885.

DUKE'S BOAST, THE// Play 3a// Adap. by H. Osborne Buckle fr F of Alexandre Dumas, Mdlle. de Belle Isle// **Avenue**, Mar. 1889.

DUKE'S DEVICE, THE: "I'm Here"// A re-title of Duke's Motto (see below)// **Olympic**, Sept. 1876, with Henry Neville as Lagardere, Charles Flockton as Philippe d'Orleans, Frank Archer as Prince de Gonzague, Frederick Cameron as Duke de Nevers, Trevor Glyndon as Chaverny, Dibdin Culver as Aesop, Robert Pateman as Carrigue, W. J. Hill as Peyrolles, Amy Crawfored as Blanche de Caylus, Miss Carlisle as Blanche as Nevers, Camille Dubois as Pepita/ Machines by Mr. Collins/ Lime Light by Mr.Sabin/ Gas by Mr. Hinckley.

DUKE'S DOUBLE, THE// F 1a// n.a.// **Astley's**, Nov. 1857, with J. W. Anson as Ramire, W. Cooke Jr. as Angeli, J. T. Anderson as Guzman, Mr. Regas as Courtois, Julia Weston as Lisette, Miss Dowton as Inez, Mrs. W. Dowton as Senora Vitulos.

DUKE'S MOTTO, THE// D 3a// Adap. by John Brougham fr F of Anicet Bourgeois & Paul Féval, Le Bossu// **Lyceum**, Apr. 1863, with George Jordan as Prince de Gonzageres, John Brougham as Carrickfergus, Henry Widdicomb as Pegrolies, J. G. Shore as Orleans, F. Charles as the Duke de Novera, Edmund Garden as the Patriarch, Charles Fechter as Henri de Lagardere, Carlotta Leclercq as Sillah, Kate Terry as Blanche de Nevers, Miss Elsworthy as the Duchess de Novera/ Scenery by Gates, Cuthbert, & David/ Music by W. Montgomery.

DUKE'S WAGER, THE// Adap. by A. R. Slous fr F of Alexandre Dumas, Mlle. de Belle Isle (also titled Duke's Boast [see above])// **Princess's**, June 1851, with Alfred Wigan as Richelieu, Mr. Wynne as Duke D'Aumont, F. Cooke as Count D'Auvray, George Everett as Chamillac, Charles Kean as St. Mars, Miss Vivash as Philippe, Mrs. Winstanley as Marchioness de Prie, Mrs. Charles Kean as Lestelle, Mrs. Alfred Wigan as Mariette/ Scenery by Walter Gordon & F. Lloyds.

DULVERY DOTTY// F 1a// Mrs. Adams Acton// **Terry's**, June 1894, with George Belmore as Sandbird, E. H. Kelly as Joshua Sandbird, Huntley Wright as Westbrook, Jessie Danvers as Mrs. Sandbird, Blanche Barnette as Polly, Lizzie Ruggles as Vera.

DUMB BELLE, THE// C 1a// W. Bayle Bernard// **Lyceum**, 1874, with H. B. Conway as Vivian, John Carter as Manvers, J. D. Beveridge as O'Smirk, Miss St. Ange as Eliza, Miss Hampden as Mary.

DUMB DRIVER, THE// D 2a// T. G. Blake// **Astley's**, Mar. 1849, with Henry Bedford as Charles Lafond, Mr. Johnson as Duvergne, T. Fredericks as Bertrand, W. H. Harvey as Michael, Mr. Attwood as Phillipe, Rosa Henry as Adele, Ellen Daly as Jeanette.

DUMB GIRL OF GENOA, THE; OR, ANTONIO THE ROBBER// D 2a// John Farrell// **Sad. Wells**, Mar. 1842 (as Dumb Girl of the Inn), with Mr. Dry as Count Corvenio, Mr. Williams as Justin, John Herbert as Moco, Mr. Norton as Cirenzo, J. W. Collier as Strapado, Charles Fenton as Desperetto, Miss Richardson as Julietta/ **Victoria**, Aug. 1857, with John Dale as Justin, Mr. Henderson as Count Corvenio, James Howard as Moco, Watty Brunton as Jaspero, S. Sawford as Antonio, F. H. Henry as Desperetto, Tom Blanchard as Strapado, Mlle. Theodore as Juliette.

DUMB GUIDE OF THE TYROL, THE// D 2a// T. G. Blake// **Adelphi**, Oct. 1837.

DUMB BOY OF MANCHESTER, THE// D// n.a.// **Sad. Wells**, Mar. 1842, with G. Wieland as Tom, John Webster as Wilton, E. Morton as Palmerston, John Herbert as Welter, Mrs. Robert Honner as Jane, Miss Richardson as Mme. Phillipine, Mrs. Richard Barnett as Patty.

DUMB MAN OF MANCHESTER, THE; OR, THE FELON HEIR// D 3a// B. F. Rayner// **Sad. Wells**, Mar. 1838, with J. Worrell as Palmerstone, Mr. Ranson as Judge, Mr. Campbell as Wilton, T. Ellar as Tom, Mr. Rogers as Welter, Miss Watkins as Jane, Mrs. Weston as Mme. Phillipine, Miss Beresford as Patty; Feb. 1866, with R. H. Kitchen as Tom, E. H. Brooke as Edward, Richard Norman as Lord Chief Justice, John Rouse as Welter, Mr. Ewing as Cobler, Mr. Murray as Palmerstone, Miss M. A. Bellair as Jane, Mrs. E. F. Edgar as Mrs. Wilton, Minnie Davis as Patty/ **Astley's**, May 1838 (in 2a), with Mr. Dillon as Lord Chief Justice, Mr. Elliott as Edward Wilton, Andrew Ducrow as Tom, Charles Williams as Palmerston, Henry Widdicomb as Welter, Mrs. Gomersal as Mrs. Wilton, Miss Julian as Patty/ **Adelphi**, Oct. 1837/ **Grecian**, Mar. 1861, with R. H. Lingham as Edward Wilton, R. H. Kitchen as Tom, Walter Holland as Palmerston, John Manning as Crispin, Mr. Smithson as Lord Chief Justice, Miss Johnstone as Mrs. Wilton, Jane Coveney as Jane, Harriet Coveney as Patty/ **Victoria**, Mar. 1864, with Brownlow Hill as Wilton, W. Stretton as Palmerston, George Yarnold as Welter, J. B. Johnstone as Lord Chief Justice, J. Mathews as Ferret, W. Gray as Shackle, R. Marchant as Waxend, R. H. Kitchen as Dumb Man, Adelaide Bowring as Jane, Mrs. W. Daly as Mrs. Wilton, Ellen Farren as Milk Maid.

DUMB RECRUIT, THE; OR, THE CONSCRIPT OF TOURNAY// D// n.a.// **Sad. Wells**, June 1841, with Mr. Aldridge as Gaspard, Mr. Stilt as Capt. Dupré, Mr. Frampton as Henri, Mr. Priorson as Sgt. Grenade, Charles Fenton as Robert, Mrs. J. W. Collier as Pauline, Miss Bown as Sophia, Miss Waite as Rosalie, Miss Lancaster as Louise/ Scenery by F. Fenton & G. Smithyes/ Prod. by Mr. Frampton.

DUMB SAILOR BOY, THE; OR, THE DOGS OF THE FERRY// D// n.a.// **Victoria**, June 1854, with Mr. Morrison as Count Latilla, Edwin Blanchard as Truelove, Mr. Green as Lt. Morton, Alfred Saville as Old Stubbs, J. Howard as Brickdust, Miss Dansor as Mariette, Mrs. Manders as Mrs. Stubbs, Miss Laporte as Susan, Dog Hector as Dog Neptune.

DUMB SAVOYARD AND HIS MONKEY, THE// D 1a// C. P. Thompson// **Drury Lane**, June 1838, with Mr. Baker as Count Maldechini, Miss Marshall as Florio, R. McIan as Sturmwald, William Bennett as Vatchvell, Miss Ballin as Pipino, Mr. Wieland as Marmazette, Charles Fenton as Spielsburgh, F. Cooke as Leopoldstadt, Mrs. Lovell as Countess Celestina, Mme. Simon as Teresa/ **Sad. Wells**, Sept. 1838, with Mr. Dry as Count Maldechini, C. Montague as Pepino, W. D. Broadfoot as Sturmwald, Dibdin Pitt as Vatchvell, Miss O. Hicks as Florio, Mr. Mellor as Leopoldstadt, Mr. Harwood as Russenstein, J. W. Collier as Monkey, Miss Richardson as Countess Maldechini, Miss Cooke as Terese/ **Victoria**, Feb. 1841, with Mr. Howell as Pepino, Mr. Blanchard as Marmozette, Mr. Cony as Sturmwald, Charles Bender as Vatchfull, Mr. Courtney as Count Maldachini, Mr. Reynolds as Leopoldstadt, Miss B. Kemble as Countess Maldachini, Mrs. France as Gertrude.

DURING HER MAJESTY'S PLEASURE// D 3a// George Conquest & Henry Pettitt// **Grecian**, May 1877.

DUSKIE// Play 1a// Mrs. G. Thompson & Kate Sinclair// **St. Geo. Hall**, May 1893.

DUST// FC 3a// Adap. by Sidney Grundy fr F of Eugène Labiche & A. C. Delacour// **Royalty**, Nov. 1881, with G. W. Anson, J. G. Taylor, Richard Mansfield, Lydia Thompson, Harriet Coveney.

DUST IN THE EYES// C 1a// n.a.// **Haymarket**, Mar. 1879, with Harry Crouch as Chariton, David Fisher Jr. as Wrigby, Mr. Weathersby as John, Blanche Henri as Louisa, Miss Harrison as Mrs. Wrigby, Emily Thorne as Martha.

DUSTMAN'S BELLE, THE// C 2a// Charles Dance// **Lyceum**, June 1846, with Robert Keeley, Frederick Vining, Drinkwater Meadows, Charles Diddear, Mrs. Keeley, Miss Villars.

DUTCH METAL; OR, DOING FOR THE BEST// C 2a// Rophino Lacy// **Globe**, Oct. 1880, with Harry Paulton as Dick Stubbs, J. Vivian as Harry, Charles Ashford as Hawkins, N. Marchant as Parchment, Maria Davis as Betsy Stubbs, Clara Graham as Jane, Kate Aubrey as Emily.

DUTY// C 4a// Adap. by James Albery fr F of Victorien Sardou, Les Bourgeois de Pont Arcy// **POW**, Sept. 1879, with H. B. Conway, Johnston Forbes Robertson, David Fisher Jr., Mrs. Hermann Vezin, Mrs. John Wood, Marion Terry.

DUX REDUX; OR, A FOREST TANGLE// Play 3a// James Rhoades// **Novelty**, Jan. 1887.

DYING FOR A KISS// D 2a// n.a.// **Princess's**, July 1847, with Mr. Granby as Don Fernando, John Webster as Don Felix, Henry Compton as Zarillo, Robert Honner as President, Miss Taylor as Juan, Mme. Vestris as Queen, Emma

Stanley as Paquita/ Scenery by William Beverly.

DYING FOR LOVE// F 1a// J. Maddison Morton// **Princess's**, July 1858, with Drinkwater Meadows as Dr. Mangle, George Everett as Capt. Fickleton, David Fisher as Thornton, Miss Heath as Mrs. Mangle, Miss Murray as Mrs. Lorimer.

DYING GIFT, THE; OR, THE PRECIPICE OF DEATH// D// F. L. Phillips// **Grecian**, Nov. 1863, with Thomas Mead as Martelli, William James as Francisco, Henry Grant as Marco, Walter Holland as Antonia, J. Jackson as Bartolo, George Gillett as Ricardo, W. Shirley as Nicoli, John Manning as Pietro, Jane Dawson as Selia, Mary A. Victor as Annette.

DYING TO LIVE// F 1a// n.a.// **Astley's**, Mar. 1859, with J. W. Anson as Whimsey, J. T. Anderson as Hopeful, James Francis as Spouter, Mrs. W. Dowton as Emma Everbloom, Miss Dowton as Mrs. Hopeful, Julia Weston as Jenny.

*

EAGLE JOE// D 4a// Henry Herman// **Princess's**, Dec. 1892, with William Day as Rothenschlag, Dan Fitzgerald as O'Laney, Rollo Balmain as McCloskey, Leonard Outram as Spencer, Alfred Bucklaw as Gregory, Arthur Lyle as Bob, Charles Carlile as Richardson, Maurice Drew as John, Andrew Davidson as de la Fere, Dorothy Harwood as Gamin, Mary Griffith as Nelly, Miss C. de Yonson as Lisa.

EARL OF POVERTY, THE; OR, THE OLD WOODEN HOUSE OF LONDON WALL// D 2a// George Almer// **Surrey**, Feb. 1838.

EARL'S HOUSEKEEPER, THE// D// William Seaman// **Britannia**, Apr. 1872.

EARLY CLOSING; OR, A NIGHT AT THE CASINO// F// A. B. Reach & Herbert Hamilton// **Princess's**, July 1847, with Mr. Granby as Linenhall, Samuel Cowell as Shandygaff, Henry Compton as Velvetpall, John Webster as Kidds, Mr. Wynn as Drabbs, Mr. Bologna as Buffs, Augustus Harris as Rowdedowa, Mrs. Fosbroke as Mrs. Linenhall, Emma Stanley as Jemima.

EARLY DAYS OF BLUESKIN, THE; OR, NEWGATE IN 1780// D// n.a.// **Grecian**, Dec. 1862, with William James as Fitzhazard, Walter Holland as Wilton, J. Jackson as Shuttleworth, Alfred Rayner as Blackburn, W. Shirley as Robson, Mr. Groves as Sgt. Bruff, Miss Johnstone as Lady Hanton, Mrs. Charles Dillon as as Emily, John Manning as Blueskin.

EARLY IMPRESSIONS// C 1a// n.a.// **Globe**, Aug. 1875, with George Warde as Maurice, H. Bennett as Samuel, Miss B. Edwards as Mrs. Lavington, C. A. Cowdery as Charles Herbert, Kate Elliston as Alice.

EARNEST APPEAL, AN// F// Frederick Hay// **Strand**, May 1875.

EAST LYNNE// D 4a// Dram. by John Oxenford fr novel of Mrs. Henry Wood// **Lyceum**, May 1867, with Mr. Waters as Earl Mount Severn, Fred Hastings as Capt. Levison, Jones Finch as Carlyle, John Saunders as Justice Hare, E. A. Creamer as Richard Hare, C. S. Lester as Dill, Avonia Jones as Lady Isabel and Mme. Vine, Sara Lewis as Cornelia, Annie Willmott as Barbara, Mrs. Henry Courte as Mrs. Hare/ **Sad. Wells**, May 1869, with Frederick Maynard as Carlyle, Charles Horsman as Capt. Levison, Richard Edgar as Dill, J. H. Loome as Hare, Knox Furtado as Richard, Mr. Richards as Mount Severn, Miss Douglass as Barbara, Miss Vasey as Joyce, Mrs. E. F. Edgar as Cornelia, Miss Horsman as Wilson, Susan Denin as Mme. Vine/ **Globe**, Oct. 1875, with Henry Grafton as Earl Mount Severn, Lin Rayne as Capt. Levison, P. Everard as Justice Hare, Henry Deane as Richard Hare, Frederick Mitchell as Lawyer Dill, Polly Hunter as Willie Carlyle, Ada Ward as Lady Isabel and as Mme. Vine, Nelly Harris as Barbara Hare/ **Standard**, May 1878/ **Olympic**, 1879; Dec. 1898 (in vers. by Wilson Barrett & Miss Heath), with L. Cory Thomas as Carlyle, H. Trant Fischer as Mountsevern, Ernest Montefiore as Levison, Ernest Percy as Justice Hare, Lees Squier as Richard Hare, Thomas Young as Dill, Edmund Campbell as Bullock, Ethel Hardacre as Barbara, Sophy Shenton as Cornelia, Lucy Collenson as Joyce, Mabel Manisty as Lady Isabel and as Mme. Vine/ **Astley's**, Oct.1879/ **Adelphi**, Dec. 1879, with E. H. Brooke as Archibald Carlyle, James Fernandez as Sir. Francis, Robert Pateman as Lord Mt. Severn, Harwood Cooper as Justice Hare, Bella Pateman as Lady Isabel and as Madame Vine, Emily Duncan as Barbara Hare, Harriet Coveney as Miss Carlyle, Clara Jecks as Joyce/ **Royalty**, Oct. 1891/ **Princess's**, Mar. 1896/ **Opera Comique**, Apr. 1897.

EAST LYNNE// D// Dram. by Harry St. Maur// **Haymarket**, Sept. 1881, with Harry St. Maur as Capt. Leverson, Stewart Dawson as Lord Mount Severn, Morton Selten as Carlyle, Lytton Grey as Hare, Eugene Stepan as Bullock, James Fawcett as Deil, T. H. Friend as Justice Hare, Kate Grattan as Little Willie, Florence Wade as Barbara, Emily Thorne as Cornelia, Rosalie Taylor as Wilson, Nelly Palmer as Suzanne, Ada Ward as Lady Isabelle and Mme. Vine.

EAST LYNNE; OR, THE DIVORCED WIFE// D 3a// George Conquest// **Grecian**, Apr. 1866, with William James as Carlyle, Charles Mortimer as Levison, J. Jackson as Dill, George Gillett as Hare, Henry Power as Jones, Lizzie Mandlebert as Lady Isabel, Harriet Western as Barbara, Mrs. Atkinson as Mrs. Corny, Mrs. Dearlove as Joyce.

EASY SHAVING// F// F. C. Burnand & Montagu Williams// **Haymarket**, June 1863, with Walter Gordon as Lusle, Henry Compton as Dibble, Mr. Rogers as Morton, Louise Keeley as Ninette,

Fanny Wright as Adela; Mar. 1874, with Walter Gordon as Lysle, Mr. Clark as Dibble, Mr. Rogers as Morton, Fanny Wright (Mrs. Osborne) as Ninette, Helen Massey as Adela.

EBONY CASKET, THE; OR, MABEL'S TWO BIRTHDAYS// D 4a// T. W. Speight// **Gaiety**, Nov. 1872.

ECARTE// C 4a// Lord Newry// **Globe**, Dec. 1870.

ECHO// C 3a// Arthur Heathcote// **Trafalgar Sq.**, Apr. 1893, with G. K. Paley as Jamblin, A. Hamilton Revelle as Hugh, Roy Horniman as Drake, Howard Sturge as Coventry, Arthur Heathcote as Pargather, A. F. Olphert as Strangeways, Mrs. Edmund Phelps as Mrs. Jamblin, Lizzie Webster as Celia, Annie Webster as Hester, Agnes Hill as Donna Ramona.

ECHO OF WESTMINSTER BRIDGE, THE// D// n.a.// **Victoria**, Feb. 1838, with William Davidge as Old Smeltum, Mr. Wilkins as Bushell, Mr. Salter as Nicks, W. H. Oxberry as Timkins, Mr. Harwood as Scoutwell, Miss Richardson as Martha, Mrs. Frank Matthews as Dolly.

ECHOES OF THE NIGHT// D 4a// H. P. Grattan & Joseph Eldred// **Pavilion**, July 1884.

EDDA// D// Edward Fitzball// **Surrey**, n.d.

EDDYSTONE ELF, THE; OR, THE FIEND OF THE LIGHTHOUSE (also subt. The Lighthouse Keepers - a tale of 1703)// D 2a// G. D. Pitt// **Sad. Wells**, Sept. 1837, with Gerard King as Traverson, C. H. Pitt as Clifton, Mr. Rogers as Partlet, Mr. Griffith as Capt. Brilliant, Mr. Campbell as Mat/ **Victoria**, May 1842, with C. Williams as Traverson, William Seaman as Clifton, Mr. Griffith as Capt. Brilliant, Mr. Paul as Mat, John Gardner as Partlett, John Dale as The Elf, Mrs. George Lee as Lucy.

EDITHA'S BURGLAR// Play 1a// Adap. by Edwin Cleary fr story of Mrs. Frances Burnett// **Princess's**, Oct. 1887.

EDUCATION// C// Thomas Morton// **Haymarket**, Apr. 1841, with Samuel Phelps as Count Villars, George Bennett as Templeton, Robert Strickland as Sir Guy, John Webster as Vincent, W. H. Oxberry as Suckling, Henry Wallack as Damper, Frederick Vining as Aspic, Benjamin Webster as George, Mrs. Stirling as Mrs. Templeton, Miss Charles as Rosine, Priscilla Horton as Ellen, Mrs. W. Clifford as Dame Broadcast.

EFFIE AND JEANIE DEANS// D// George Hamilton// **Albion**, Oct. 1877/ **Marylebone**, Aug. 1879.

EFFIE DEANS, THE LILY OF ST. LEONARDS// D// Dram. by Shepherd fr Sir Walter Scott's The Heart of Midlothian// **Surrey**, Feb. 1863.

EGYPTIAN, THE// Play 5a// J. H. Wilkins// **City of London**, Apr. 1853.

EIDERDOWN QUILT, THE// FC 3a// Tom Wotton// **Terry's**, Dec. 1896, with Herman de Lange as de Bologna, Nicol Pentland as Sir John, Arthur Playfair as Capt. Bernard, A. E. Matthews as Dick, Frederick Volpé as Mumforth, Audrey Ford as Sybil, Ethel Matthews as Lucy, Spencer Brunton as Rosamund, Fanny Brough as Patricia/ Scenery by Leolyn Hart.

EIGHT POUNDS REWARD// F// Adap. by John Oxenford fr F// **Olympic**, 1855.

EILEEN OGE; OR, DARK'S THE HOUR BEFORE THE DAWN// D 4a// Edmund Falconer// **Princess's**, June 1871, with George Jordan as Loftus, Mr. Moreland as Moriarty, J. G. Shore as O'Donnell, Mr. Barrett as Mahoney, Mr. Clifford as Maclean, Edmund Falconer as O'Farrell, Charles Seyton as Thomas, Robert Romer as McCann, Rose Leclercq as Eileen, Edith Stuart as Norah, Mrs. R. Power as Mrs. O'Donnell, Miss Hudspeth as Bridget/ Scenery by F. Lloyds/ Music by W. C. Levey/ Machines by R. E. Wharton/ Prod. by Benjamin Webster.

EL HYDER; OR, THE CHIEF OF THE GHAUT MOUNTAINS// D// William Barrymore// **Sad. Wells**, Dec. 1837, with Gerard King as Abaulerim, Mr. Morrison as Nilauf, S. Palmer as El Hyder, Mr. Ede as Hafnez, Mr. Campbell as Mizen, Lavinia Melville as Clifton, Mr. Rogers as Hafiz, Miss O. Hicks as Prince Chereddin, Miss Williams as Princess Zada, Miss Pitt as Nina, Miss Vernon as Orissa./ **Victoria**, Mar. 1843, with John Dale as El Hyder, C. Williams as Hamet, Mr. James as Abensallah, E. F. Saville as Mizen, Mr. Wilton as Hafez, Mr. Hitchinson as Nilauf, William Seaman as Ichander, Miss Wilton as Chereddin, Miss Martin as Harry, Mrs. George Lee as Zaida, Miss Saddler as Nina.

ELAINE// Play 1a// Royston Keith// **Strand**, May 1898, with Royston Keith as Steele, Mrs. Edmund Phelps as Mrs. Gwyn, Lily Erratt as Muriel, Kittie Grattan as Elaine.

ELDER BROTHER, THE; OR, LOVE AT FIRST SIGHT// C// Adap. fr John Fletcher// **Drury Lane**, Mar. 1850, with Charles Diddear as Lord Lewis, Samuel Emery as Miramount, William Davidge as Brisac, James Anderson as Charles, William Montague as Eustace, John Parry as Egremont, Henry Frazer as Cowsy, Basil Baker as Andrew, Charlotte Vandenhoff as Angellina, Annie Lonsdale as Sylvia, Miss Morant as Lilly.

ELDER MISS BLOSSOM, THE// C 3a// Ernest Hendrie & Metcalfe Wood// **St. James's**, Sept. 1898, with W. H. Kendal as Quick, Charles Groves as Blossom, Frank Fenton as Twentyman, Rudge Harding as Rev. Leacroft, Rodney Edgcumbe as Jones, Nellie Campbell as Sophia, Mrs. Charles Sennett as Mrs. Wells, Mrs. W. H. Kendal as Dorothy/ Scenery by William Harford.

ELEANOR'S VICTORY// D 4a// Dram. by John Oxenford fr novel of Mrs. Braddon// **St. James's**, May 1865, with Arthur Stirling as Thornton, Frank Matthews as Maj. Lennard, James Johnstone as Vane, Frederic Robinson as Bourdon, H. J. Montague as Darrell, Gaston Murray as Monkton, Louisa Herbert as Eleanore, Mrs. Frank Matthews as Mrs. Lennard, Miss Weber as Laura/ Scenery by Mr. Grieve.

ELECTRIC SPARK, THE// C 1a// Adap. by Elizabeth Bessie fr F of Pailleron, L'Etincelle// **Olympic**, May 1889/ **Trafalgar Sq.**, Sept. 1894, with Graham Wentworth as Capt. Norreys, Blanche Ripley as Lady Treherne, Delia Carlyle as Geraldine.

ELECTRIC TELEGRAPH, THE; OR, THE FAST MAN IN A FIX// F 1a// C. A. Somerset// **Grecian**, June 1855, with Eaton O'Donnell as Brown, Mr. Melvin as Steady, Richard Phillips as Rapid, John Manning as Telegraph, F. Charles as Sinclair, Miss Johnstone as Arabella the Elder, Harriet Coveney as Tibby Tattle, Mrs. C. Montgomery as Arabella the Younger/ **Astley's**, Oct. 1858, with Mr. Lloyd as Brown, Richard Phillips as Rapid, Mr. Francis as Telegraph, Mr. Regan as Steady, Mr. Alexander as Sinclair, Mrs. W. Dowton as Miss Arabella the Elder, Miss Dowton as Miss Arabella the Younger, Julia Weston as Tibby.

ELEVENTH HOUR, THE// Ronald Macdonald & H. A. Saintsbury// **Olympic**, July 1896.

ELF OF THE EDDYSTONE LIGHTHOUSE, THE// D// n.a.// **Sad. Wells**, July 1843, with C. J. Bird as Trevanian, Mr. Moreton as Clifton, Mr. Williams as Capt. Brilliant, C. J. Smith as The Elf, Mr. Coreno as Partlett, Henry Marston as Metrical, R. H. Lingham as Grapnell, Caroline Rankley as Lucy.

ELFINELLA; OR, HOME FROM FAIRYLAND// C 4a// Ross Neil// **Princess's**, June 1878, with Caroline Heath, Charles Warner, Mr. Rignold.

ELIGIBLE BACHELOR, AN// C 1a// n.a.// Strand, Dec. 1871.

ELIXIR OF LIFE, THE// D 3a// George Conquest// **Grecian**, Sept. 1873.

ELIXIR OF YOUTH, THE// FC 3a// Adap. by G. R. Sims & Leonard Merrick fr G of Hirschberger & Kraatz// **Vaudeville**, Sept. 1899, with George Giddens as Greedslade, Fred Eastman as Maroldi, Frank Atherley as Newlyn, Oswald Yorke as Featherley, George Arliss as Jeffrey, Edward Ferris as Wingrove, Henry Doughty as Capt. O'Dowd, Florence Wood as Mrs. Jeffrey, Juliette Nesville as Suzette, Millie Legarde as Mena, Helen Palgrave as Mrs. Greenslade, Lucie Milner as Florrie, Ellis Jeffreys as Cora/ Scenery by William Harford.

ELIZA FENNING// D 2a// n.a.// **Victoria**, Aug. 1857, with John Dale as Apsley, J. H. Rickards as Arthur, S. Sawford as Fenning, Mr. Henderson as Harland, W. H. Pitt as Layzel, James Howard as Redpole, Charles Rice as Hammernail, H. Dudley as Gaston, Mrs. J. H. Rickards as Mrs. Apsley and Mme. de Caterane, Mrs. E. F. Saville as Eliza, Miss Laporte as Nancy.

ELIZABETH, QUEEN OF ENGLAND// D 5a// Trans. fr Ital. of Giacometti// **Lyceum**, Dec. 1869/ **Drury Lane**, July 1882, with J. H. Barnes as Essex, Arthur Matthison as Burleigh, A. C. Lilly as Effingham, Walter Avondale as Mendoza, Harry Nicholls as Davison, Arthur Dacre as Bacon, T. Nye as Drake, Augustus Cook as James VI, Sophie Eyre as Lady Howard, Madge Carr as Lady Burleigh, Agnes Thomas as Marie, Adelaide Ristori as Queen Elizabeth.

ELLA ROSENBERG; OR, THE FUGITIVE OF MOLWITZ// D 2a// James Kenney// **Sad. Wells**, June 1840, with Mr. Elvin as The Elector, Mr. Dry as Col. Mountfort, Henry Marston as Rosenberg, J. W. Collier as Flutterman, Mr. Williams as Storm, Mrs. Robert Honner as Ella, Mrs. Richard Barnett as Christina, Miss Cooke as Mrs. Flutterman; July 1862, with A. Baildon as The Elector, James Johnstone as Col. Mountfort, Henry Forrester as Rosenberg, Ersser Jones as Storm, Lewis Ball as Flutterman, Miss M. Percy as Ella, Emily Dowton as Christina, Mrs. W. Dowton as Mrs. Flutterman/ **Grecian**, Feb. 1845, with Edwin Dixon as De Mountfort, John Collett as the Elector, Mr. Campbell as Storm, John Chester as Rosenberg, Annette Mears as Ella Rosenberg, Miss Merion as Mrs. Flutterman, Miss Johnstone as Christine.

ELLEN; OR, LOVE'S CUNNING// C 5a// W. G. Wills// **Haymarket**, Apr. 1879, with Henry Howe as McCail, William Terris as North, Charles Kelly as Pye, G. W. Anson as Plaque, Norman Forbes as Andrew, Mr. Weathersby as Maj. Dale, Florence Terry as Ellen, Blanche Henri as Lady Breezy, Emily Thorne as Dame Ester, Miss Abington as Jeannie, Mrs. Edward Osborne as Mrs. Stubbs, Miss E. Harrison as Mrs. Brock, Julia Roselle as Mrs. Freer/ Rev. by author & perf. at **Haymarket**, June 1879 as Brag.

ELLIE BRANDON; OR, REVENGE AND LOVE// D// Morton Price// **City of London**, Apr. 1868.

ELOPEMENTS IN HIGH LIFE// C 5a// Robert Sullivan// **Haymarket**, Apr. 1853, with W. H. Chippendale as Lord Betterton, Barry Sullivan as Travers, Henry Howe as Singlehart, William Farren as Perfect, J. B. Buckstone as Tulip, Henry Compton as Gapt. Gawk, Mrs. Fitzwilliam as Lady Betterton, Miss Reynolds as Mrs. Lovelock, Mrs. L. S. Buckingham as Sybilla, Louisa Howard as Katherine, Mrs. Caulfield as Betsy/ Scenery by George Morris & John O'Conner.

ELSA DENE// D 4a// A. C. Calmour// **Strand**, Oct. 1886, with J. D. Beveridge, Lewis Waller, Agnes Hewitt, Lucy Buckstone.

ELSIE// D 1a// Frederick Broughton// **Globe**, Sept. 1883.

ELSIE'S RIVAL// Play 1a// Dora V. Greet// **Strand**, May 1888.

EMBASSY, THE// D 3a// Adap. fr F by J. R. Planché// **Cov. Garden**, Mar. 1841, with Mr. Moore as Duke de Nevers, James Anderson as Viscount de Rohan, A. Brindal as Solignac, W. H. Payne as de Valois, Alfred Wigan as Lamont, Ellen Tree as Baroness du Pont, Mme. Vestris as Mme. de Brissac, Mr. Hemming as Count Lasky, Miss Fairbrother as Queen Marguerite.

EMERALD QUEEN, THE// D// William Travers// **Britannia**, July 1870.

EMIGRANT'S DAUGHTER, THE// D 1a// R. J. Raymond// **Engl. Opera House** (Lyceum), 1838.

EMIGRANT'S PROGRESS, THE// n.a.// **City of London**, Oct. 1852.

EMIGRÉ'S DAUGHTER, THE// D 2a// W. Bayle Bernard// **Adelphi**, July 1850, with Mr. Hughes as De Sombreuil, Charles Boyce as St. Ambert, O. Smith as Babouf, Edward Wright as Ronlade, William Cullenford as Quiral, Sarah Woolgar as Aline, Kathleen Fitzwilliam as Mme. Roulade/ Scenery by Mr. Pitt/ Music by Alfred Mellon/

EMILY// D 4a// George Hamilton// **Albion**, Apr. 1870.

EMPTY STOCKING, AN// Play 1a// F. Wright Jr.// **Strand**, Dec. 1898, with Herbert Sleath as Author, Marie Wright as Daughter.

EN VOYAGE// C// Lewis Coen// **Vaudeville**, Dec. 1883.

ENCHANTED HORSE, THE// A. Smith & Tom Taylor// **Lyceum**, Dec. 1845.

END OF A DAY, THE// Play 1a// Herbert Barnett// **Royalty**, Dec. 1891, with H. A. Saintsbury as Rev. Thornton, Kenneth Rivington as Carlyon, Thomas Terriss as Fielding, Violet Thornycroft as Evelyn.

ENEMIES// CD 5a// Adap. by Charles Coghlan fr F of Georges Ohnet, La Grande Marnière// **POW**, Jan. 1886, with Henry Kemble, James Fernandez, Charles Coghlan, Robert Pateman, Lillie Langtry, Miss A. Hardinge.

ENEMY OF THE PEOPLE, AN// D 5a// Adap. fr Norw. of Henrik Ibsen// **Haymarket**, June 1893, with Herbert Beerbohm Tree as Dr. Stockman, Charles Allan as Peter Stockman, Lionel Brough as Kiil, James Welch as Hovstad, Holman Clark as Billing, E. M. Robson as Aslaksen, Mr. Revelle as Capt. Horster, Mrs. Theodore Wright as Mrs. Stockman, Lily Hanbury as Petra.

ENEMY'S CAMP, THE// D 4a// Herbert Leonard// **Pavilion**, Mar. 1894.

ENGAGED// FC 3a// W. S. Gilbert// **Haymarket**, Oct. 1877, with George Honey as Hill, Harold Kyrle as Belvawney, Henry Howe as Symperson, Mr. Weathersby as Maj. McGillicuddy, Marion Terry as Belinda, Lucy Buckstone as Minnie, Emily Thorne as Mrs. Macfarlane, Julia Stewart as Maggie/ Scenery by John O'Conner; Feb. 1886, with Herbert Beerbohm Tree as Cheviot Hill, Maurice Barrymore as Belvawney, Mr. Mackintosh as Symperson, Charles Brookfield as Macalister, Ulick Winter as Maj. McGillicuddy, Mrs. Beerbohm Tree as Belinda, Augusta Wilton as Minnie, Mrs. E. H. Brooke as Mrs. Macfarlane/ **Court**, Nov. 1881, with H. J. Byron, Kyrle Bellew, Marion Terry, Carlotta Addison.

ENGINEER, THE// D// n.a.// **Victoria**, Mar. 1863.

ENGLAND HO!; OR, THE BUCCANEERS OF THE ARCTIC REGIONS// D// n.a.// **Marylebone**, July 1878.

ENGLAND IN THE DAYS OF CHARLES THE SECOND// D 4a// Dram. by W. G. Wills fr novel of Sir Walter Scott, Peveril of the Peak// **Drury Lane**, Sept. 1877, with Samuel Emery as Maj. Bridgenorth, James Fernandez as Edward Christian, E. F. Edgar as William Christian, William Terriss as Peveril, Mr. Pennington as Charles II, Augustus Glover as Buckingham, Henry Collard as Hudson, Richard Norman as Cutram, R. H. Lingham as Col. Blood, Mr. Brockley as Ormond, Mr. Douglas as Colesby, Miss Leighton as Countess of Derby, Alma Murray as Alice, Miss Willes as Fenella, Miss D'Arcy as Lady Griselda, Rhoda Clare as Duchess of Portsmouth, Sarah Bassett as Duchess of Cleveland/ Scenery by William Beverley/ Machines by J. Tucker/ Music by Karl Meyder/ Prod. by Edward Stirling.

ENGLAND'S ADMIRAL; OR, OUR BLUE JACKETS ON THE BLACK SEA// D 2a// J. B. Johnstone// **Victoria**, June 1854, with T. E. Mills as Adm. Sir Charles, Mr. Bradley as Second Admiral, Henry Frazer as Oakheart, N. T. Hicks as Toprail, James Howard as Cheekhead, Mr. Brunton as Spooner, Mr. Morrison as Haulyard, Alfred Saville as Romanoff, Mr. Henderson as Rubanzoff, Miss Dansor as Emily, Miss Laporte as Betty, Mrs. Henry Vining as Selina.

ENGLISH ETIQUETTE// F 2a// John Oxenford// **Olympic**, Nov. 1840/ **Sad. Wells**, Sept. 1842, with J. S. Balls as Hibbs, Mr. Turnour as Sir George, Mr. Dean as Bloomington, Charles Hill as Townsend, Mrs. Henry Marston as Agatha, Miss Hicks as Charlotte, Mrs. Naylor as Peggy/ **Princess's**, Apr. 1843, with F. Williams as Sir George, J. S. Balls as Hibbs, Morris Barnett as Townsend, Mr. Roberts as Bloomington, Mr. Chicheley as Takem, Mr. Turner as Richard, Mr. Graham as Doublerap, Mme. Sala as Agatha, Miss Noel as Isabella, Miss Wilkenson as Charlotte, Miss E. Honner as Peggy/ **Eng. Opera House** (Lyceum), Apr. 1843, with John Ayliffe as Sir George, J. S. Balls as Handel Hibbs, F. H. Henry as Townsend, Mr. Young as Bloomington, Mr. Griffith as Scroggins, Mrs. Griffith as Agatha, Miss Bartlett as Isabella, Miss Atkins as Charlotte.

ENGLISH GENTLEMAN, AN; OR, THE SQUIRE'S LAST SHILLING// CD 4a// H. J. Byron// **Haymarket**, May 1871, with E. A. Sothern as Cuckles, Edward Arnott as Gresham, Henry Howe as Brandon, W. H. Chippendale as Grindrod, George Braid as Clinch, Mr. Rogers as Buller, Edward Osborne as Hodges, Mrs. Chippendale as Lady Logwood, Caroline Hill as Malvina, Amy Roselle as Polly, Fanny Gwynne as Rachel/ Scenery by John O'Conner & George Morris/ Machines by Oliver Wales/ **Gaiety,** Oct. 1879, with H. J. Byron, William Elton, Louise Willes.

ENGLISH NELL// C 4a// Dram. by Anthony Hope & Edward Rose fr novel Simeon Dale// **POW**, Aug. 1900.

ENGLISH ROSE, THE// D 4a// G. R. Sims & Robert Buchanan// **Adelphi**, Aug. 1890, with Bassett Roe as Kingston, J. D. Beveridge as Ballyveeney, Leonard Boyne as Harry O'Malley, T. B. Thalberg as Father O'Mailley, W. L. Abingdon as Capt. Macdonell, Lionel Rignold as Dickenson, Charles Dalton as O'Mara, J. L. Shine as O'Reilly, Kate James as Patsie, Olga Brandon as Ethel Kingston, Mary Rorke as Bridget, Clara Jecks as Louisa/ Scenery by Bruce Smith, Philip Goatcher, & W. Perkins/ Music by Henry Sprake/ Prod. by William Sidney.

ENGLISHMAN'S HOUSE IS HIS CASTLE, AN// F 1a// J. Maddison Morton// **Princess's**, May 1857, with John Pritt Harley as Pocock, Frank Barsby as Capt. Connaught, Henry Saker as Dr. Bang, George Everett as Briggs, Eleanor Bufton as Mrs. Bang, Kate Terry as Virginia, Miss Murray as Mary.

ENGLISHMEN IN INDIA// D// William Dimond// **Drury Lane**, Nov. 1839, with William Dowton as Sir Mathew, John Duruset as Count Glorieux, George Bennett as Col. Oswald, Mr. Morley as Capt. Dorrington, Mr. Frazer as Capt. Tancred, W. J. Hammond as Tom Tape, Mrs. Selby as Lady Scraggs, Mrs. Stirling as Sally, Miss Betts as Guinare, Miss Daly as Poplin.

ENGLISHWOMAN, AN// D 5a// St. Aubyn Miller// **Novelty**, Aug. 1896, with Oswald True as Capt. Earlsworthy, Bernard Copping as Maj. Gordon, Jack Haddon as Chatsworth, Harold Child as Rev. Evergreen, Percy Murray as Mayne, Arthur Elton as Lord Henry, Newman Maurice as Pipkins, Henry Bertram as Sgt. Davidson, Charles Sutton as Rudge, Daisy Cook as May, Thea Lesbrooke as Grace, Winifred Wood as Rose, V. St. Lawrence as Sylvia.

ENLISTED// D 4a// Frederick Harcourt// **Sadler's Wells**, Feb. 1891.

ENSNARED// D 3a// Adap. by Walter Frith fr F, Le Drame de la Rue de la Paix// **Gaiety**, Mar. 1883.

ENTRANCES AND EXITS// D Pro & 3a// George Spencer// **East London**, Apr. 1868.

ENTRAPPED// D 2a// Edgar Newbound// **Britannia**, July 1880.

ERIC, THE PHANTOM; OR, THE ACCUSING SPIRIT// D 3a// W. E. Suter// **Grecian**, Mar. 1870, with Henry Grant as President, W. Shirley as Gen. Fellman, Thomas Mead as Eric, George Gillett as Rodolphe, William James as Georges, John Manning as Joachim, Lizzie Mandelbert as Amelie, Mary A. Victor as Baptista.

ERIC'S GOOD ANGEL// Play 1a// Frank Bird & Cecil Crofton// **Elephant & Castle**, July 1894.

ERIN-GO-BRAGH; OR, THE WREN BOYS OF KERRY// D// C. H. Hazlewood// **Britannia**, Apr. 1870.

ERIN-GO-BRAGH; OR, THE MILESIAN TRUST IN LUCK// D// W. J. Travis// **Victoria**, May 1873.

ERNEST MALTRAVERS// D 3a// Rose Medina// **Britannia**, Sept. 1874.

ERNESTINE// D 2a// Adap. by T. W. Robertson fr F of Dennery & Clément// **Princess's**, Apr. 1846, with Mr. Cooper as de Champeurville, James Wallack as Frederick, Leigh Murray as d'Aspremont, Miss May as Juliette, Emma Stanley as Marie, Mrs. Fosbroke as Agatha, Mrs. Stirling as Ernestine; Dec. 1860, with Basil Potter as de Champeurville, J. G. Shore as Frederick, Robert Cathcart as Charles, Miss Heath as Ernestine, Carlotta Leclercq as Marie, Miss Murray as Juliette, Mrs. Weston as Agatha/ **Haymarket**, July 1849, with Mr. Cooper as Viscount de Champeurville, James Wallack as Frederick, Henry Vandenhoff as d'Aspremont, Miss Reynolds as Ernestine, Mrs. Keeley as Marie, Miss Chalmers as Juliette, Mrs. Stanley as Agatha.

ERNESTINE AND GEORGETTE; OR, A LOVER LENT// F 1a// C. Long// **Grecian**, Nov. 1846, with Mr. Manley as Baron Rudhen, Eaton O'Donnell as Dumont, Frederick Robson as Katkin, Mr. Kerridge as André, Carlotta Leclercq as Ernestine, Mary A. Crisp as Georgette.

ESCAPED; OR, THRICE MARRIED// D 4a// William Travers// **East London**, June 1870.

ESCAPED FROM PORTLAND// D Pro & 3a// Adap. fr F// **Princess's**, Oct. 1869.

ESMERALDA, THE GYPSEY GIRL OF NOTRE DAME// D 3a// Dram. fr novel of Victor Hugo// **Sad. Wells**, Mar. 1838, with Mr. Campbell as Quasimodo, Mr. Ranson as Frolio, Mr. Forester as Capt. Phoebus, J. Worrell as Capt. Ernest, Mr. Rogers as Gringoire, Stephen Smith as Clopin, Mr. Williams as Executioner, Mr. Scarbrow as Audrey, Eliza Vincent as Esmeralda, Miss Watkins as Gudule, Miss Beresford as Mahiette, Miss Chartley as Fleur de Lys, Mrs. Weston as Julie.

ESMERALDA; OR, THE HUNCHBACK OF NOTRE DAME// D 3a// Dram. fr novel of Victor Hugo// **Olympic**, May 1852, with Charles Diddear as Claude, Mr. Edgar as Capt. Phoebus, John Kinloch as Capt. Ernest, George Cooke as Clopin, Henry Compton as Gringoire, Henry Farren as Quasimodo, Louisa Howard as Esmeralda, Miss Fielding as Sr. Gudule, Ellen Turner as Mahiette, Isabel Adams as Mme. Gondelaurier, Miss Smalders as Fleur de Lys, Charles Bender as Goucon.

ESMERALDA; OR, THE DEFORMED OF NOTRE DAME// D 3a// Dram. by Edward Fitzball fr novel of Victor Hugo// **Grecian**, May 1846, with Edwin Dixon as Frollo, Mr. Manley as Capt. Phoebus, Mr. Melvin as Capt. Ernest, Frederick Robson as Gringoire, Mr. Campbell as Quasimodo, Eaton O'Donnell as Clopin, Mme. Leclercq as Esmeralda, Miss M. A. Crisp as Sister Gelude, Mrs. W. Watson as Coucou, Jane Trafford as Fleur-de-Lys.

ESMERALDA AND THE HUNCHBACK OF NOTRE DAME// D 4a// Adap. by Charles Jefferys fr F of Battisté// **Drury Lane**, June 1856.

ESMERALDA, LA; OR, THE HUNCHBACK OF NOTRE DAME// Adap. fr F of Victor Hugo// **Olympic**, Feb. 1845, with C. Howard as Trullo, Mr. Mestayer as Capt. Phoebus, R. Johns as Quasimodo, Mr. Dunn as Clopin, Mr. Robinson as Gringoire, Mr. Harrison as Ernest, Mrs. G. Jones as Esmeralda, Mrs. Henry as Godule, Mrs. Mestayer as Julie, Miss Fitzjames as Fleur de Lys.

ESMONDS OF VIRGINIA, THE// Play 4a// Cazauran// **Royalty**, May 1886.

ESPERANZA; OR, THE STRANGER IN BLACK// D 3a// George Conquest// **Grecian**, May 1864, with Henry Grant as Morosini, J. Jackson as the Doge, Thomas Mead as Esperanza, J. B. Steele as Annibal, William James as Duc Caesar, John Manning as Pasquino, Jane Dawson as Bianca, Mary A. Victor as Peplia/ Scenery by Jones, Messender, Mason & Hall/ Machines by Mr. Smithers Sr./ Prod. by George Conquest.

ESTELLE DUMAS; OR, LOVE AND WAR// D 2a// Adap. fr F// **Sad. Wells**, Apr. 1842, with Mr. Lyon as Capt. Fremont, E. Morton as Garlois, Mr. Aldridge as Lambert, Mr. Dry as Le Mare, John Herbert as Jacque, Mrs. Robert Honner as Estelle, Mrs. Richard Barnett as Lucille, Mrs. Phillips as Madeline/ Scenery by G. Smithyes Jr./ Music by Isaac Collins/ Machines by Mr. Cawdery/ prod. by R. Honner.

ESTHER SANDREZ// Play 3a// Adap. by Sidney Grundy fr F of Adolphe Belot, Femme de Glace// **POW**, June 1889/ **St. James's**, May 1890, with Charles Sugden as Vandelle, Arthur Bourchier as Deschampes, Frederick Everill as Fourcanade, H. De Lange as Boisgommeux, Erskine Lewis as Justin, Mrs. Charles Calvert as Mme. Fourcanade, Marion Lea as Henriette, Carrie Benton as Clarisse, Lena Meyers as Berthe, Lillie Langtry as Esther/ Scenery by W. Perkins & Bruce Smith.

ESTRANGED// CD 3a// H. Williamson// **Globe**, Aug. 1881, with Richard Purdon, Charles Groves, Ada Lester, Clara Thompson.

ETHEL; OR, ONLY A LIFE// D// n.a.// **Adelphi**, Oct. 1866.

ETHEL'S REVENGE// Play 4a// Dram. by Walter Stephens fr Ouida's novel, Strathmore// **Court**, Sept. 1876.

ETHEL'S TEST// C 2a// H. W. Williamson// **Strand**, Mar. 1883.

ETIQUETTE; OR, A WIFE FOR A BLUNDER// C// Tyrone Power// **Haymarket**, Sept. 1837, with Robert Strickland as Sir. P. Langley, J. W. Gough as Gen. Forrester, Tyrone Power as O'More, Charles Selby as Capt. Langley, Benjamin Webster as Bob, T. F. Mathews as Precise, Miss Allison as Louisa, Miss E. Phillips as Emma, Mrs. Humby as Bell.

ETOILE DU NORD, L'// D// n.a.// **Drury Lane**, Mar 1855, with Henri Drayton as Michaeloff, Mr. Williams as Skavronski, Mr. Bowler as Danilowitz, Mr. Leffler as Gritzembo, Jenny Baur as Catherine, Mrs. Henri Drayton as Prascovia, Miss E. Arden as Ekimonia, Miss Johnson as Nathalie.

ETON BOY, THE// F 1a// Edward Morton// **Drury Lane**, Oct. 1842, with William Bennett as Col. Curry, C. J. Mathews as Capt. Popham, Robert Keeley as Dabster, Mrs. Stirling as Fanny, Mrs. Selby as Sally/ **Olympic**, Sept. 1848, with H. J. Turner as Col. Curry, Leigh Murray as Capt. Popham, Henry Compton as Dabster, Mrs. Stirling as Fanny, Mrs. Leigh Murray as Sally.

ETRANGÈRE, L'// D// Adap. fr F of Alexandre Dumas// **Haymarket**, June 1876, with Hermann Vezin as Duc de Septmonts, Charles Harcourt as Clarkson, Henry Howe as Mauriceau, Clifford Cooper as Rémonin, H. B. Conway as Gérard, Harold Kyrle as Bernecourt, Henrietta Hodson as Catherine, Helen Barry as Mrs. Clarkson, Emily Thorne as Marquise de Rumières, Blanche Henri as Mme. D'Arnelines, Maria Harris as Mme. Calmeron.

EUGENE ARAM// D// W. T. Moncrieff// **Sad. Wells**, June 1837, with N. T. Hicks as Aram, Mr. Campbell as Houseman, Mr. Tilbury as Rowland Lester, C. H. Pitt as Walter Lester, Benjamin Conquest as Corp. Bunting, Mr. Rogers as Peter, Mr. Griffiths as Courtland, Mrs. W. West as Madeline, Lavinia Melville as Elinor, Mrs. Harris as Bess, Mrs. Andrews as Dame Darkmans.

EUGENE ARAM// D 3a// W. G. Wills// **Lyceum**, Apr. 1873, with Henry Irving as Eugene Aram, J. Carter as Parson Meadows, E. F. Edgar as Houseman, Willa Brown as Joey, Isabel Bateman as Ruth Meadows.

EUGENE ARAM// D// A. Fancquez// **Standard**, July 1879.

EUGENIA CLAIRCILLE; OR, THE NEW FOUND HOME// D 3a// Tom Parry// **Adelphi**, Sept. 1846, with Charles Boyce as Langrol, William Cullenford as Rugleigh, Mr. Lambert as Buzzard, Paul Bedford as Toffey, Henry Howe as Biceps, O. Smith as Matlock, Mme. Celeste as Eugenia, Mrs. Frank Matthews as Mrs. Toffey/ Scenery by Pitt & Johnstone/ Music by Alfred Mellon/ Machinery by Mr. Cooper.

EUGENIE// Play 1a// Dion Boucicault// **D.L**, Jan. 1855.

EUNICE; OR, LOVE AND DUTY// D 4a// Edward Towers// **Pavilion**, Nov. 1882.

EUSTACHE BAUDIN// D 3a// John Courtney// **Surrey**, Jan 1854.

EVADNE; OR, THE HALL OF STATUES// T 3a// R. L. Shiel// **Sad. Wells**, Nov. 1840, with J. B. Hill as King of Naples, Mr. Dry as Ludovico, Mr. Elvin as Viceato, Henry Marston as Colonna, Mr. Aldridge as Spalatro, Mrs. Robert Honner as Evadne, Miss Richardson as Olivia; May 1851, with Henry Mellon as King of Naples, George Bennett as Ludovico, Henry Marston as Colonna, G. K. Dickinson as Vicentio, Mr. Wilkins as Spaltro, Miss Goddars as Evadne, Mrs. Graham as Olivia/ **Grecian**, Dec. 1854, with Henry Grant as King of Naples, Basil Potter as Ludovico, Richard Phillips as Colonna, Thomas Roberts as Spalatro, Jane Coveney as Evadne, Miss Simpson as Olivia.

EVE// D 3a// Benjamin Webster Jr.// **Adelphi**, May 1869.

EVE OF MARRIAGE, THE// D 4a// Arthur Shirley & Benjamin Landeck// **Elephant & Castle**, July 1899.

EVENING SHADOWS// CD 3a// Cyril Bowen// **Aquarium**, Aug. 1878.

EVERGREEN// C 2a// Adap. by W. H. Pollock fr F of Jaime & Bayard, Le Reveil du Lion// **Haymarket**, Aug. 1884, with Charles Brookfield as De Fonblanche, Edmund Maurice as Ernest, H. B. Conway as Maulcon, H. Reeves as D'Arcy, Mr. Leonard as Rouvière, Mary A. Victor as Charlotte, Julia Gwynne as Léonie, Maud Williamson as Mme. de Miravel, Jenny Lefevre as Baronne Cabrion.

EVERSLEIGH HOUSE// D 2a// Edgar Newbound// **Britannia**, Mar. 1879.

EVERY DAY OCCURENCES// C 2a// Horton Rhys// **Sad. Wells**, May 1862, with Catherine Lucette in 4 char. parts, Horton Rhys in 3 char. parts, Charles Crook in 2 char. parts.

EVERY MAN FOR HIMSELF// D 5a// May Holt// **Pavilion**, Oct. 1885.

EVERY MAN IN HIS HUMOUR// C 5a// Ben Jonson// **Haymarket**, July 1838, with W. C. Macready as Kitely, J. W. Gough as Old Knowell, Edmund Glover as Young Knowell, Mr. Hemming as Wellbred, Mr. Hill as Master Stephen, J. B. Buckstone as Matthew, T. F. Mathews as Clement, Charles Perkins as Downright, Benjamin Webster as Capt. Bobadil, Robert Strickland as Brainworm, Agnes Taylor as Dame Kitely, Miss Gallot as Bridget.

EVERYBODY'S FRIEND (see also, Widow Hunt)// C 3a// J. Stirling Coyne// **Haymarket**, Apr. 1859, with C. J. Mathews as Featherley, Henry Compton as Icebrook, J. B. Buckstone as Wellington de Boots, Mrs. C. J. Mathews as Mrs. Featherley, Mrs. Wilkins as Mrs. de Boots, Miss Reynolds as Mrs. Swandown, Fanny Wright as Fanny/ Scenery by Mr. O'Conner & George Morris/ Machines by Oliver Wales/ **Olympic**, May 1865, with Henry Neville as Featherley, Robert Soutar as Icebrook, Charles Walcot as Major Wellington de Boots, Lydia Foote as Mrs. Featherley, Mrs. Leigh Murray as Mrs. de Boots, Kate Terry as Mrs. Swandown.

EVERYBODY'S HUSBAND// F// Richard Ryan// **Sad. Wells**, Dec. 1846, with William Hoskins as Twisselton, Henry Scharf as Busbury, Frank Graham as Figgins, Mr. Williams as Spriggins, Mrs. Henry Marston as Mrs. Pimpernel, Fanny Huddart as Miss Thompson, Fanny Morelli as Miss Tomkins, Miss Stephens as Miss Twisselton, Miss Warde as Fanny.

EVERYONE HAS HIS FAULT// C 5a// Mrs. Inchbald// **Drury Lane**, Dec. 1841, with Samuel Phelps as Lord Norland, Charles Hudson as Sir Robert, Henry Compton as Solus, W. C. Macready as Harmony, Robert Keeley as Placid, James Anderson as Capt. Irwin, Mr. Waldron as Hammond, Mrs. Mary Warner as Lady Eleanor, Mrs. Keeley as Mrs. Placid, Mrs. C. Jones as Miss Spinster/ **Sad. Wells**, May 1845, with Samuel Buckingham as Sir Robert, Henry Mellon as Lord Norland, Henry Scharf as Flacid, Mr. Coreno as Solus, Henry Marston as Irwin, A. Younge as Harmony, Mrs. Mary Warner as Lady Elinor, Miss Cooper as Miss Woburn, Mrs. Henry Marston as Miss Spinster, Miss Lebatt as Mrs. Placid/ **Haymarket**, Dec. 1850, with Mr. Stuart as Lord Norland, E. L. Davenport as Sir Robert, J. B. Buckstone as Solus, Mr. Lambert as Harmony, Henry Howe as Placid, Mr. Cooper as Irwin, Mrs. Mary Warner as Lady Elinor, Priscilla Horton as Mrs. Placid, Mrs. Stanley as Miss Spinster, Miss Reynolds as Miss Woodburn/ **Princess's**, Nov. 1855, with Mr. Cooper as Lord Norland, Walter Lacy as Sir Robert, John Pritt Harley as Solus, Frank Matthews as Harmony, David Fisher as Placid, John Ryder as Irwin, Kate Terry as Edward, Mrs. Charles Kean as Lady Eleanor, Miss Murray as Mrs. Placid, Mrs. W. Daly as Miss Spinster, Miss Heath as Miss Woodburn.

EVICTION, THE// D 3a// Hubert O'Grady// **Standard**, Aug. 1880/ **Olympic**, Aug. 1880, with Walter Roberts as Lord Hardman, P. C. Beverley as Downey, Lin Rayne as Chessman, Charles Frew as Rooney, Gus Reynolds as Rody, Hubert O'Grady as Dermot, J. P. Domican as Father Mike, Maude Thornton as Lady Eveleen, Mrs. O'Grady as Molly/ Scenery by W. T. Hemsley.

EVIL EYE, THE// D 2a// R. B. Peake// **Eng. Opera House** (Lyceum), Sept. 1838, with Mr. Baker as Mavroyeni, A. Brindal as Demetrius, Mr. Howell as Basilius, Henry Compton as Kiebala, Mr. Halford as Andrea, Lavinia Melville as Helena, Miss Poole as Phrosina/ Scenery by Mr. Pitt/ Music by G. H. Rodwell.

EVIL GENIUS, THE// C 3a// W. Bayle Bernard// **Haymarket**, Mar. 1856, with W. H. Chippendale as Cooley, J. B. Buckstone as Ripstone, William Farren as Walmsley, Edwin Villiers as Barton, Mr. Rogers as Docket, Henry Compton as Withers, Miss Reynolds as Lady Aurora, Mrs. Poynter as Mrs. Montgomery, Ada Swanborough as Clara/ Scenery by William Callcott, George Morris & John O'Conner/ Machines by Oliver Wales.

EVIL GENIUS, THE// D 5a// Adap. by Wilkie Collins fr his novel// **Vaudeville**, Oct. 1885.

EVIL HANDS AND HONEST HEARTS// D// n.a.// **Britannia**, Mar. 1864.

EXCHANGE NO ROBBERY; OR, WHO'S FATHER TO ME? (alt. subt., Who's to Father Me)// C 3a// Theodore Hook// **Olympic**, Sept. 1853, with George Cooke as Sir Christopher, John Kinloch as Sir Lennox, F. Charles as Capt. Littleworth, Charles Bender as Swipes, Frederick Robson as Sam Swipes, E. Clifton as Lamotte, Mr. Marchant as Potts, Sarah Lyons as Lady Cranbery, Isabel Adams as Mrs. Melrose, Mrs. B. Bartlett as Mrs. Swipes, Ellen Turner as Lapelle/ **Sad. Wells**, June 1854, with Mr. Barrett as Sir Christopher, James Worrell as Sir Lennox, F. Charles as Capt. Littleworth, C. Poynter as Swipes, Edward Wright as Sam Swipes, J. W. Collier as Lamotte, Miss Lavine as Lady Cranberry, Miss S. Elsworthy as Miss Melrose, Mrs. Barrett as Mrs. Swipes.

EXCURSION TRAIN, THE// FC 3a// Adap. by Juston McCarthy & W. Yardley fr F of Hennequin, Mortier, & St. Albin, Le Train de Plaisir// **Opera Comique**, Apr. 1885, with David Jones, W. Lestocq, Cicely Richards, Lucy Buckstone.

EXILE, THE// D 3a// J. Holmes Grover// **Elephant & Castle**, Aug. 1879.

EXILE, THE; OR, THE DESARTS [sic] **OF SIBERIA**// D// n.a.// **Sad. Wells**, June 1837, with Gerard King as Count Ulrick, J. Dunn as Count Colmar, Mr. Griffiths as Vermack, Mr. Tilbury as Governor, Benjamin Conquest as Servitz, Mrs. W. West as Alexina, Miss Williams as Empress, Miss Land as Catherine.

EXILE OF MESSINA, THE; OR, WHO'S THE MURDERER?// D 3a// Adap. by T. G. Blake fr F// **Victoria**, July 1848, with Mr. Henderson as Count di Tor, E. Edwards as Count Ferrara, John Bradshaw as di Vinci, J. T. Johnson as Julio, Walter Searle as Romaldi, G. F. Forman as Pourrit, Mrs. George Lee as Mme. Laurent, Miss Atkins as Marie, Miss Burroughcliffe as Elize, Miss Young as Gianetta, Miss Andrews as Cicely.

EXILES OF ERIN, THE; OR, ST. ABE AND HIS SEVEN WIVES (see Mormons).

EXPIATION// D Pro & 3a// E. Manuel// **Britannia**, June 1876.

EXTORTED OATH, THE: OR, THE CHATEAU OF THE FOREST// D 3a// n.a.// **Sad. Wells**, Apr. 1842, with Mr. Lyon as Count di Selvista, Mr. Aldridge as Marquis of Castello, Mr. Moreton as Ferdinand, Mr. Dry as Lorenzo, John Herbert as Paolo, Miss Richardson as Countess of Salvista, Mrs. Richard Barnett as Zarlina.

EXTRAORDINARY BEHAVIOUR OF MRS. JALLOWBY, THE// FC 3a// Clive Brooke// **Novelty**, Dec. 1896, with J. Norton-Wilson as Gen. Jallowby, Cecil Compton as Wibbler, Graham Wentworth as Beale, Clive Brooke as Arthur Jallowby, Isabel Grey as Mrs. Jallowby, May Rosine as Charlotte, Eleanor Lane as Estelle.

EXTREMES; OR, MEN OF THE DAY// C 3a// Edmund Falconer// **Lyceum**, Aug. 1858, with Mr. Fitzjames as Sir Lionel, J. G. Shore as Adolphus, Mr. Barrett as Dr. Playfair, Edmund Garden as Mr. Cunningham, Leigh Murray, Samuel Emery, Kate Saxon, Mrs. Weston/ **City of London**, 1859/ **Princess's**, Mar. 1860, with Harcourt Bland as Sir Lionel, J. G. Shore as Adolphus, Drinkwater Meadows as Playfair, Edmund Garden as Cunningham, Robert Cathcart as Digby, Henry Saker as James, George Melville as Hawthorn, Henry Widdicomb as Wildbriar, Mrs. Watson as Mrs. Vavasour, Mrs. Charles Young as Lucy, Mrs. Weston as Mrs. Wildbriar, Louise Keeley as Jenny, Rose Leclercq as Euphemia; Feb. 1881, with H. Templeton as Sir Lionel, J. C. Buckstone as Adolphus, Philip Beck as Hawthorne, W. E. Lane as Cunningham, Henry Leigh as Dr. Playfair, Fred Terry as Digby, Mr. Fosbrooke as Wildbriar, Miss Huntley as Mrs. Vavasour, Miss Measor as Jenny, Miss Chapman as Euphemia, Mrs. Chippendale as Mrs. Wildbriar/ **Drury Lane**, Mar. 1862, with Henry Sinclair as Sir Lionel, G. Weston as Adolphus, Mr. Barrett as Playfair, Mr. Neville as Cunningham, Mr. Warde as Digby, Henry Loraine as Hawthorne, Stanislaus Calhaem as Wildbriar, J. Rogers as James, Mrs. D. P. Bowers as Lucy, Mrs. Edmund Falconer as Mrs. Wildbriar, Mrs. Stephenson as Mrs. Vavasour, Miss C. Weston as Jenny, Miss L. Laidlaw as Euphemia.

EXTREMES MEET// C 1a// Kate Field// **St. James's**, Mar. 1877, with F. H. Macklin as Capt. Howard, Kate Field as Maude, Maria Daly as Mme. Bienville, Ada Morgan as Lina.

*

FABIAN; OR, THE MÉSALLIANCE// F 4a// n.a.// **Lyceum**, Nov. 1856, with Charles Dillon as Fabian, Mr. McLien as de St. Luce, E. Clifton as d'Auberville, George Burt as de la Frenage, Mr. Francis as St. Croix, J. G. Shore as André, Mrs. Charles Dillon as Pauline, Mrs. Weston as Marchionesse de la Reyserie, Miss Morrelli as Mme. de Montigny/ Scenery by E. Tannett & Holding/ Music by W. H. Montgomery/ Machines by H. Sloman.

FACE TO FACE// D 4a// Thomas Archer// **Marylebone**, May 1877.

FACES IN THE FIRE// C 3a// Leicester Buckingham// **St. James's**, Feb. 1865, with

C. J. Mathews as Vane, Arthur Stirling as Hargrave, Frederic Robinson as Glanvil, H. J. Montague as Verner, Mrs. C. J. Mathews as Mrs. Hargrave, Louisa Herbert as Mrs. Glanvil.

FACING THE MUSIC// FC 3a// J. H. Darnley// **Strand**, Feb. 1900.

FACTORY BOY, THE; OR, THE LOVE SACRIFICE// D 3a// J. T. Haines// **Surrey**, June 1840.

FACTORY GIRL, THE; OR, ALL THAT GLITTERS IS NOT GOLD (see also All That Glitters Is Not Gold)// D// J. Maddison Morton// **Princess's**, May 1881, with Henry Neville as Stephen Plum, John Beauchamp as Jasper Plum, H. C. Sydney as Frederick Plum, Harry Jackson as Twinkle, Mr. Bolyen as Sir Arthur, Hilda Hilton as Martha, Maud Milton as Lady Valeria, Mrs. D. Lyons as Lady Leatherbridge.

FACTORY LADS, THE; OR, THE WORKMAN'S SATURDAY NIGHT// D 2a// n.a.// **Victoria**, Apr. 1846, with Alfred Raymond as Westwood, T. Fredericks as Allen, James Ranoe as Wilson, Roberts Tindall as Hatfield, Mr. Franklin as Smith, E. F. Saville as Rushton, E. G. Burton as Wagstaff, Mrs. Gecrge Lee as Jane, Mrs. Backhous as Mary, Miss Jefferson as Dame Wagstaff, Eliza Terrey as Nelly.

FACTORY STRIKE, THE; OR, WANT, CRIME AND RETRIBUTION// D 3a// G. F. Taylor// **Victoria**, May 1838, with Mr. Loveday as Ashfield, Mr. Maddocks as Warner, Mr. Archer as Harris, Mr. Harwood as Snipe, Mr. Williams as Moseley, Mr. Johnstone as Brown, Mr. Vale as Guzzle, Miss Richardson as Mary Warner, Mrs. Loveday as Lucy, Charles Montague as Capt. Ashfield, William Davidge as Beeswing.

FADED FLOWERS// Play 1a// Arthur à Beckett// **Haymarket**, Apr. 1872/ **Garrick**, Jan. 1895.

FAINT HEART NEVER WON FAIR LADY// C 1a// J. R. Planché// **Olympic**, Feb. 1839, with Miss Lee as Charles II of Spain, James Bland as Marquess de Santa Cruz, C. J. Mathews as Ruy Gomez, Mme. Vestris as Duchess de Terrenueva, Mrs. Macnamara as Donna Leonora/ Scenery by William Telbin & Mr. Cuthbert; Nov. 1850 with Louisa Howard as Charles II of Spain, W. H. Norton as Santa Cruz, Alfred Sanger as Guzman, Henry Farren as Ruy Gomez, Mrs. Leigh Murray as Duchess de Terrenova. Mrs. B. Bartlett as Donna Leonora/ **Cov. Garden**, Oct. 1839, with Miss Lee as Charles II of Spain, James Bland as Marquis de Santa Cruz, C. J. Mathews as Ruy Gomez, Robert Honner as Guzman, Mr. Kerridge as Lopez, Mr. Ireland as Pedro, Mme. Vestris as Duchess de Torrenueva, Mrs. Macnamara as Donna Leonora; **Olympic**, Nov. 1874, with Henry Neville as Ruy Gomez, Annie Taylor as Charles II of Spain, John Vollaire as Santa Cruz, Mr. Westall as Guzman, Mr. Calvert as Lopez, Mrs. Stephens as Donna Leonora, Miss Fowler as Duchess de Terrenueva/ **Haymarket**, Apr. 1843, with Miss Lee as Charles II of Spain, C. J. Mathews as Ruy Gomez, James Bland as Santa Cruz, Mme. Vestris as Duchess de Torreneva, Mrs. W. Clifford as Donna Leonora/ **Sad. Wells**, Mar. 1848, with Miss Marsh as Charles II of Spain, Henry Mellon as Santa Cruz, William Hoskins as Gomez, Edward Knight as Guzman, Mr. Wilkins as Lopez, Mr. Franks as Pedro, Miss Cooper as Duchess de Torreneueva, Mrs. W. Watson as Donna Leonora/ **Drury Lane**, Apr. 1853; Dec. 1874, with Henry Neville as Ruy Gomez, Annie Taylor as Charles II of Spain, John Vollaire as Santa Cruz, Mr. Westall as Guzman, Mr. Calvert as Lopez, Mr. Leighton as Pedro, Mrs. Stephens as Donna Leonora, Miss Fowler as Duchess de Torreneueva/ **Grecian**, Aug. 1857, with Emma Wilton as Charles II of Spain, Eaton O'Donnell as San Cruz, Harry Hill as Ruy Gomez, Jane Coveney as Duchess de Torrenueuva, Miss Johnstone as Donna Leonora/ **Princess's**, Dec. 1862, with Marie Henderson as Charles II of Spain, Mr. Melton as Gomez, G. Dickeson as Santa Cruz, John Collett as Guzman, Mr. Clements as Lopez, Marian Jones as Duchess de Terranueva, Mrs. Sims as Donna Leonora; Nov. 1875, with Mabel Hayes as Charles II of Spain, E. Shepherd as Santa Cruz, Osmond Tearle as Ruy Gomez, T. W. Thorne as Guzman, J. B. Johnstone as Lopez, Mr. Fotheringham as Pedro, Miss Gainsborough as Duchess de Torreneva, Mrs. J. B. Howard as Donna Leonora.

FAINT HEART WHICH DID WIN A FAIR LADY// C 1a// J. P. Wooler// **Strand**, Feb. 1863.

FAIR CIRCASSIAN, THE; OR, THE CHEVALIER, THE COUNT, AND THE ITALIAN// D 2a// C. H. Hazlewood// **Britannia**, Nov. 1872.

FAIR ENCOUNTER, A// C 1a// Adap. by Charles Rae fr F of Octave Gastineau, Les Souliers de Bal// **Haymarket**, Apr. 1877, with Ella Dietz as Lady Clara, Kathleen Irwin as Celia/ **Globe**, Nov. 1882, with Alexes Leighton as Lady Clara, Maggie Hunt as Mrs. Grenville.

FAIR EXCHANGE, A// C 1a// Adap. by Montagu Williams fr F// **Olympic**, Aug. 1860, with Walter Gordon as Earl of Dudley, Horace Wigan as Dubkins, Henry Rivers as Stubble, Miss Herbert as Lady Vane, Miss Seymour as Jenny, Louise Keeley as Mabel Gray.

FAIR MAID OF TOTTENHAM COURT, THE; OR, THE CHARCOAL BURNER OF CHARING// D// n.a.// **Sad. Wells**, Oct. 1840, with Mr. Dry as Baron Lovel, J. W. Collier as Friskey, Mr. Aldridge as Goodright, Mr. Williams as Fin, J. B. Hill as Snap, Mr. Stilt as Bagshot, Charles Fenton as Barnett, Henry Marston as Gilbert, Mr. X as Arnold, Mrs. Robert Honner as Emily, Mrs. Richard Barnett as Bridget/ Scenery by F. Fenton/ Music by Isaac Collins/ Machines by B. Sloman/ Prod. by R. Honner.

FAIR PRETENDER, A// C 2a// J. Palgrave Simpson// **POW**, May 1865.

FAIR SINNER, A// Play 5a// G. W. Appleton// **Gaiety**, Mar. 1885.

FAIR WORDS AND FOUL DEEDS// D 3a//

William Travers// **East London**, July 1868.

FAIRLEIGH'S BIRTHRIGHT// D 3a// George Peel// **Britannia**, Aug. 1878.

FAIRLY FOILED// D 4a// Oswald Allan// **Grecian**, May 1871.

FAIRY CIRCLE, THE; OR, CON O'CAROLAN'S DREAM// D// H. P. Grattan// **Adelphi**, July 1857, with Barney Williams as Con, Charles Selby as Philip, John Billington as Robert, Edmund Garden as General Travers, James Bland as Moore, Mary Keeley as King cf the Fairies, Mrs. Barney Williams as Moleshee/ **Sad. Wells**, July 1858, with Barney Williams as O'Carolan, Bruce Norton as Philip, Henry Sinclair as O'Neil, Mr. Butler as Gen. Travers, James Bland as Mocre, Mrs. Billington as King of the Fairies, Kate Kelly as Ellen, Mrs. Barney Williams as Moleshee.

FAIRY TALE, A// C 2a// George Colman the elder & David Garrick// **Princess's**, May 1848, with James Vining as Rafaello, Charles Fisher as Malvoglio, F. B. Conway as Ascanio, Mr. Norton as Spadillo, Mrs. Stirling as Marchioness Vilani, Emma Stanley as Zina.

FAIRY'S FATHER, A// C 1a// C. S. Cheltnam// **Olympic**, Feb. 1862, with Frederick Robson as Milford, Walter Gordon as Henslow, Florence Haydon as Susan, Mrs. Stephens as Mrs. Dunstable.

FAITH; OR, EDDICATION AND RIGHTS// C 3a// John Lart// **Gaiety**, Aug. 1884.

FAITH AND FALSEHOOD; OR, THE LIFE OF A BUSH-RANGER// D// W. L. Rede// **Sad. Wells**, July 1838, with John Webster as Sir Charles, C. J. Smith as Pereau, C. Montague as Capt. Garton, Mr. James as Lt. Gorget, Mr. Harwood as Benjamin, W. L. Rede as Graves, Benjamin Conquest as Dobbs, Mrs. Robert Honner as Jane, Miss Pincott as Arabella, Mrs. J. F. Saville as Louise, Mrs. Weston as Mrs. Slammerkeys.

FAITH, HOPE, AND CHARITY; OR, CHANCE AND CHANGE// D 3a// E. L. Blanchard// **Surrey**, July 1845.

FAITH UNDER PERIL// D// H. Abel// **Pavilion**, Aug. 1873.

FAITHFUL HEART, THE; OR, THE LOVE THAT NEVER DIES// D 4a// R. Palgrave// **Astley's**, Aug. 1881, with G. Stretton as Vanstone, E. Fowler as Wilmott, E. N. Hallows as Trenfield, Mat Robson as Sparrow, E. Hughnott as Dr. Sampson, G. Hardynge as Fred, S. J. A. Fitzgerald as Parker, Marie Forde as Bessie, Jennie Vernon as Kitty, Nellie Grahame as Mary, Mrs. H. Blandford as Lady Trevalyon, Frances Flemming as Lady Agnes/ Scenery by Gordon Harford, Mark Barraud, & Frank Paul/ Machines by R. Gilbert/ Music by George Chapman/ Gas by Mr. Pepper.

FAITHFUL JAMES// FC 1a// B. C. Stephenson// **Court**, July 1892, with Brandon Thomas as Adm. Vincent, Wilfred Draycott as Duncan, C. P. Little as Melville, Weedon Grossmith as James, Sybil Grey as Mrs. Melville, Ellaline Terriss as Mrs. Duncan.

FAITHFUL UNTO DEATH// D// Edgar Newbound// **Britannia**, Mar. 1876.

FAITHLESS WIFE, THE// D 4a// Mrs. S. Lane// **Britannia**, Apr. 1876.

FALCON, THE// Play 1a// Dram. by Alfred Tennyson fr story of Boccaccio// **St. James's**, Dec. 1879, with W. H. Kendal as Count Federigo, Mr. Denny as Filippo, Mrs. Kendal as Lady Giovanna, Mrs. Gaston Murray as Elizabetta/ Scenery by Gordon & Harford.

FALL OF THE AVALANCHE, THE; OR, THE MOUNTAIN HOME// D pro & 3a// George Conquest and W. E. Suter// **Grecian**, Feb. 1865, with James Jackson as Duc de Chateau Gontier, J. B. Steele as Dubois, David Jones as Maurice, William James as Eugene, Mrs. Alfred Rayner as Countess Gontier, Marie Brewer as Leonide, Lizzie Mandlebert as Paurette, Mary A. Victor as Hortensia/ Scenery by Mr. Messender/ Music by W. Edroff/ Prod. by George Conquest.

FALLEN AMONG THIEVES// D Pro & 4a// W. E. Morton// **Elephant & Castle**, Mar. 1888.

FALLEN AMONG THIEVES// D 5a// Frank Harvey// **Grand**, Sept. 1890.

FALLS OF CLYDE, THE// D 2a// George Soane// **Sad. Wells**, July 1838, with Robert Honner as Kenmure, Mr. Dry as Gen. Worthington, Mr. Williams as Enfield, John Webster as Edward, Mr. Cathcart as Malcolm, Dibdin Pitt as Donald, C. J. Smith as Lindley, Charles Montague as Evan, Mrs. Weston as Dame Enfield, Mrs. Robert Honner as Ellen/ **Victoria**, Dec. 1838, with Gerard King as Gen. Wilford, Mr. Melville as Kenmure, Mr. Johnstone as Enfield, Mr. Forester as Edward, William Vining as Donald, N. T. Hicks as Malcolm, J. B. Hill as Lindley, Charles Montague as Dernclough, Miss Darion as Mrs. Enfield, Mrs. John Parry as Ellen, Mrs. Worrell as Janet, Mrs. J. B. Hill as Jessey.

FALSE AND TRUE; OR, MARRIAGE A LOTTERY// D 1a// n.a.// **Grecian**, Sept. 1863, with T. Mead as Merrington, William James as Carlingford, James Jackson as Quisby, Jane Dawson as Mrs. Merrington, Miss Smithers as Annie, Mary A. Victor as Mrs. Quisby.

FALSE ACCUSATION, THE; OR, WHILE THERE'S LIFE THERE'S HOPE// D// Frank Fuller// **Marylebone**, May 1875.

FALSE AND TRUE; OR, MARRIAGE A LOTTERY// D 1a// Charles Dance (as Marriage a Lottery)// **Grecian**, Aug. 1863, with Thomas Mead, William James, James Jackson, Jane Dawson, Miss Smithers, Mary A. Victor.

FALSE COLOURS// C// G. F. Pass// **Royalty**, Oct. 1881, with E. Sothern, John Benn, Mellie

Younge.

FALSE COLOURS; OR, THE FREE TRADER// D 2a// Edward Fitzball// **Cov. Garden**, Mar. 1837, with Mr. Harris as Capt. Mordaunt, Mr. Tilbury as Langford, T. P. Cooke as Paul, John Pritchard as Hawkset, Benjamin Webster as Mike, Eliza Vincent as Phoebe.

FALSE CONCLUSIONS// D 2a// Adap. by C. Long fr F// **Grecian**, Jan. 1845, with John Chester as Sir Henry, Edwin Dixon as Sir Walter, Mr. Melvin as Vapor, Mr. Campbell as Rookson, Annette Mears as Mary, Miss Merion as Mrs. Mortmain.

FALSE EVIDENCE// D 4a// Wynne Miller// **Pavilion**, Sept. 1891.

FALSE FRIEND, THE; OR, THE ASSASSIN OF THE ROCKS// D// J. C. Cross// **Victoria**, Mar. 1838, with John Parry as Horatio, Mr. Loveday as Zubeck, William Davidge as Fitzhugh, Mr. Phillips as Rapine, Mr. King as Mandeville, Mrs. Loveday as Julia, Mrs. Frank Matthews as Alice, Miss Wilson as Widow Wantly.

FALSE HANDS AND FAITHFUL HEARTS// D Pro & 3a// Edward Towers// **City of London**, Apr. 1867.

FALSE LIGHTS// D 4a// T. B. Bannister// **Marylebone**, Nov. 1886/ **Pavilion**, Aug. 1887.

FALSE MR. POPE, THE// C 2a// R. B. Peake// **Haymarket**, Oct. 1845, with Charles Hudson as Lacey, Henry Howe as Capt. Breval, J. B. Buckstone as Redwing, Mr. Tilbury as Concanon, J. W. Gough as Rector, Miss Telbin as Mrs. Breval, Julia Bennett as Jenny, Mrs. Edwin Yarnold as Mrs. Lacey, Miss Carre as Mrs. Nibblecomb.

FALSE PRIDE// C 4a// May Holt// **Vaudeville**, May 1884.

FALSE SHAME (also titled White Feather)// D 3a// Frank Marshall// **Globe**, Nov. 1872, with Mr. Poynter as Earl Dashington, H. J. Montague as Arthur, E. W. Garden as Col. Howard, Charles Neville as Lt. Grey, John Billington as Bragleigh, Rose Massey as Magdalen, Maria Harris as Mary, Carlotta Addison as Constance, Sophie Larkin as Mrs. Howard/ Scenery by A. Callcott & Walter Hann/ Music by J. T. Haynes/ **Royalty**, June 1880, with Charles Sugden, H. M. Pitt, Maude Brennan, Kate Lawler.

FALSELY ACCUSED// D 4a// J. C. Griffiths// **Britannia**, Aug. 1876.

FALSELY ACCUSED// D 4a// Rita Carlyle// **Pavilion**, July 1897.

FAME// C 3a// Charles Rae// **Haymarket**, Apr. 1877, with J. B. Buckstone as Sir Percy, Walter Gordon as Lord Tarleton, William Herbert as Courtenay, Henry Howe as Lyttleton, Harold Kyrle as Tracy, Mr. Clark as Raffles, Annie Lafontaine as Miss Rolles, Maria Harris as Flossie, Miss E. Harrison as Susan, Marion Terry as Rose/ Scenery by John O'Conner.

FAMILIAR FRIEND, A// F 1a// Mark Lemon// **Olympic**, Feb. 1840.

FAMILIES SUPPLIED// F 1a// Ernest Cuthbert// **Adelphi**, Aug. 1882, with Philip Beck as Fred, Harry Proctor as Old Rogers, Miss G. Warden as Mrs. Meadows, Miss E. Heffer as Arabella.

FAMILY FAILING, A// F 1a// John Oxenford// **Haymarket**, Nov. 1856, with J. B. Buckstone as Lord Gawkey, W. H. Chippendale as Sir Samson, Henry Howe as Sir Folliot, Blanche Fane as Clorinda/ Scenery by John O'Conner.

FAMILY FOOL, THE// C 3a// Mark Melford// **Vaudeville**, June 1885.

FAMILY HONOUR// C 3a// Frank Marshall// **Aquarium**, May 1878.

FAMILY JARS// F 1a// Joseph Lunn// **Haymarket**, May 1841, with Robert Strickland as Peter Porcelain, Mr. Caulfield as Benedict Porcelain, David Rees as Delph, W. H. Oxberry as Diggory, Miss Mattley as Emily, Mrs. Frank Matthews as Liddy/ **Drury Lane**, Mar. 1850, with Thomas Barry as Peter Porcelain, George Everett as Benedict Porcelain, Basil Baker as Delph, Stephen Artaud as Diggory, G. Watson as Joe, Miss Morant as Emily, Miss Baker as Liddy/ **Sad. Wells**, May 1856, with Walter Williams, Mr. Swanborough as Benedict, Mr. Barrett as Delph, James Rogers as Diggory, Emma Barnett as Emily, Miss Cuthbert as Liddy/ **Grecian**, Oct. 1856, with Henry Grant as Mr. Porcelain, William Shuter as Benedict, Eaton O'Donnell as Delph, Henry Power as Diggory, Ellen Hale as Emily, Harriet Coveney as Liddy/ **Globe**, Sept. 1873, with E. W. Garden as Mr. Porcelain, Frank Selby as Benedict, Henry Compton as Delph, E. W. Garden as Diggory, Nelly Harris as Emily, Maria Harris as Liddy/ **Olympic**, Nov. 1875, with Mr. Graeme as Porcelain, Mr. Westall as Benedict, John Vollaire as Delph, Mr. Crichton as Diggory, Miss Hazleton as Emily, Annie Taylor as Liddy/ **Adelphi**, Feb. 1886, with Howard Russell as Porcelain, T. Fulljames as Benedict, E. Dagnall as Delph, Ernest Travers as Diggory, Jenny Rogers as Emily, Lizzie Nelson as Liddy.

FAMILY MATTER, A// C 3a// C. G. Compton & A. G. Hockley// **Garrick**, June 1894, with Charles Groves as Rev. Consibee, C. M. Hallard as Gilbert, Alfred Bucklaw as Rev. Richardson, W. Granville as Lord Leslie, Howard Sturge as Sir George, Mary Rorke as Lady Consibee, Winifred Fraser as Dulcie, Ellis Jeffries as Jean.

FAMILY PICTURE, A// D 2a// Charles Webb// **Grecian**, May 1855, with Richard Phillips as Clermont, F. Charles as Viscount Davason, Henry Grant as Dr. Mohr, John Manning as Blaincau, Jane Coveney as Mme. Clermont, Harriet Coveney as Victorine.

FAMILY PICTURES// F 1a// Edward Stirling// **Marylebone**, Mar. 1849.

FAMILY PRIDE (see also Poor Gentleman)// D 2a// Adap. by Gaston Murray fr F, Le Pauvre Gentilhomme// **Sad. Wells**, May 1862, with Morton Price as Marquis de St. Hilaire, Ersser Jones as Rigollet, A. Baildon as Adolphe, C. Lloyds as Vandeleur, James Johnstone as Martel, Lewis Ball as Pipon, Mrs. W. Dowton as Mme. Botibol, Miss Clements as Justine, Catherine Lucette as Leonie.

FAMILY RELATIONS// F// n.a.// **Sad. Wells**, Dec. 1850, with A. Younge as Merrett, Charles Fenton as Suckling, Mr. Wilkins as Frampton, Charles Wheatleigh as Hector, Mr. Williams as Stag, Frederick Younge as Foster, Mrs. Graham as Mrs. Merrett, Mrs. Archbold as Mrs. Frampton, Miss Glyndon as Lydia, Lucy Rafter as Miss Frampton, Miss Morelli as Susan, Eliza Travers as Dolly.

FAMILY SECRET, THE// C 3a// Edmund Falconer// **Haymarket**, May 1860, with William Farren as Lord Avonmore, Edwin Villiers as Travers, Henry Howe as Col. O'Donnell, Mr. Rogers as Woodside, W. H. Chippendale as Butterworth, J. B. Buckstone as Frederick, James Worrell as Bellowes, Mrs. Buckingham White as Lady Francis, Amy Sedgwick as Una, Mrs. Wilkins as Mrs. Butterworth, Miss Addington as Mlle. St. Valerie/ Scenery by John O'Conner & George Morris/ Machines by Oliver Wales.

FAMILY TIES// C 3a// F. C. Burnand// **Strand**, Sept. 1877.

FAMILY TREASON; OR, TRUTH MAY BE BLAMED, BUT NEVER BE SHAMED// D// n.a.// **Grecian**, Sept. 1861, with Thomas Mead as Ferdinand, Henry Grant as Julio, Alfred Rayner as Gaston, William James as de Marcy, Mr. Jackson as Pomponella, John Manning as Babillard, Jane Coveney as Leoni, Lucreza Hill as Cephese.

FAMINE, THE// Play Pro & 4a// Hubert O'Grady// **Grand**, June 1886.

FAN-FAN THE TULIP; OR, A SOLDIER'S FORTUNE// D 2a// Adap. by W. E. Suter fr F of Paul Meurice// Perf. as Court and Camp at the **Princess's**, May 1863.

FANATIC, THE// C 4a// John Day// **Strand**, Oct. 1897, with Edmund Gurney as Isaiah Baxter, Charles Troode as Wilfred Baxter, H. Nye Chart as Fanshaw, J. Graham as Stirling, Lesly Thomson as Sir Barbour, Stuart Champion as Flagg, Florence Fordyce as Mrs. Baxter, Beatrix Mervyn as Janet, Lena Benson as Susan, Kate Phillips as Matilda.

FANCHETTE; OR, THE WILL-O'-THE-WISP// D 4a// Adap. by Mrs. Bateman fr G dram. of novel of Georges Sand, Die Grille// **Lyceum**, Sept. 1871, with Isabel Bateman as Fanchette, Georgina Pauncefort as Mother Fadet, Mrs. F. B. Egan as Mme. Barbeau, Marion Hill as Madelon, Mr. Addison as Father Barbeau, Henry Irving as Landry Barbeau, George Belmore as Sylvinet Barbeau, John Collett as Father Caillaud, John Royston as Etienne, W. L. Branscombe as Pierre/ Music by Edward Silas.

FANCHONETTE; OR, THE CRICKET// D 5a// Adap. fr G dram. of novel of Georges Sand, Die Grille// **Standard**, Sept. 1871.

FANNETTE; OR, UP IN THE DARK// D 1a// J. B. Johnstone// **Pavilion**, Oct. 1868.

FANNY// F 3a// G. R. Sims & Cecil Raleigh// **Strand**, Apr. 1895, with J. L. Shine as O'Brien, William Day as Bixley, Owen Harris as Kellaway, T. P. Haynes as Saunders, Osmond Shillingford as Gregory, George Blackmore as Tapping, Robb Harwood as Barnes, Lydia Cowell as Flo, May Whitty as Grace, Alma Stanley as Paquita/ Scenery by W. P. Warren.

FANNY IN A FIX// F// n.a.// **Sad. Wells**, Apr. 1865, with W. S. Foote as Sydenham, John Mordaunt as Culverin, William Ellerton as Barney, Ethel Somers as Mrs. Trevor, Mrs. Stevenson as Mrs. Culverin, Lizzie Willmore as Fanny.

FANNY LEAR// n.a.// **Royalty**, Oct. 1885.

FANNY'S FLIRTATIONS// F// Wynne Miller & Philip Howard// **Pavilion**, July 1887.

FANTASTICKS, THE// C 3a// Adap by Constance Fletcher ("George Fleming") fr F of Edmond Rostand, Les Romanesques// **Royalty**, May 1900.

FAR AWAY WHERE ANGELS DWELL// D 3a// C. H. Hazlewood// **Britannia**, Oct. 1869.

FAR FROM THE MADDING CROWD// D 3a// Adap by Thomas Hardy & Comyns Carr fr Hardy's novel// **Globe**, Apr. 1882, with Charles Kelly as Oak, J. H. Barnes as Troy, A. Wood as Poorgrass, H. E. Russell as Coggan, C. Medwin as Moon, Maggie Hunt as Fanny, Alexes Leighton as Lydia, Mrs. Bernard Beere as Bathsheba.

FAR OFF; OR, THE ROYAL VISIT TO EDINBURGH// D// W. T. Moncrieff// **Sad. Wells**, Sept. 1842, with Mr. Aldridge as Butts, C. J. Bird as Scampur, Mr. Richardson as Goahead, Charles Fenton as Floatlight.

FARM BY THE SEA, THE// D 1a// Adap. by Frederick Wedmore fr F of André Theuriet, Jean-Marie// **Vaudeville**, May 1889.

FARM OF STERWICK, THE; OR, THE SIGNAL FIRE// D// n.a.// **Sad. Wells**, Oct. 1841, with Henry Marston as Col. Walstein, Mr. Elvin as Capt. Albert, Mr. Aldridge as Bernard, J., W. Collier as Cokaski, John Herbert as Walter, Mr. Richardson as Guidee, Charles Fenton as Blonski, Mrs. Robert Honner as Ulrica, Miss Cooke as Driska, Mrs. Morgan as Paulina, Mr. Dry as Count Cronstadt, E. Morton as Col. Langstorff.

FARMER'S STORY, THE// D 3a// W. Bayle Bernard// **Victoria**, Sept. 1837, with Mr. Green as Lockwood, John Parry as Mortlake, William Davidge as Baggs, Mr. Marwood as Ryland, Benjamin Wrench as Bristles, W. H. Oxberry as Rut, Mrs. Hooper as Mary, Miss Lewis as Peggy/ **Olympic**, Nov. 1850, with Leigh Murray as Lockwood, William Farren Jr. as Mortlake, Mr. Norton as Ryland, Henry Compton as Bristles, George Cooke as Baggs, Charles Bender as Vails, Mrs. Stirling as Mary Lockwood, Ellen Turner as Tippet.

FASCINATING FELLOWS// F 1a// T. A. Palmer// **Olympic**, May 1876, with Mr. Vollaire as Capt. Boyeant, Mr. Hallows as Jack, Mr. Darley as Deane, Lytton Sothern as Gay, Miss Hazleton as Lycy, Miss Beaumont as Fanny, Maud Branscombe as Jane.

FASCINATING INDIVIDUAL, A; OR, TOO AGREEABLE BY HALF// F 1a// Henry Danvers// **Olympic**, June 1856, with Samuel Emery as Walton, Frederick Robson as Fitz-Mortimer, Gaston Murray as Capt. Thompson, Mr. Danvers as Francis, Miss Marston as Julia, Miss Castleton as Mrs. Thornton.

FASCINATION// C 3a// Robert Buchanan & Harriet Jay// **Novelty**, Oct. 1887/ **Vaudeville**, Jan. 1888.

FASHION; OR, LIFE IN NEW YORK// C// Anna Cora Mowatt// **Olympic**, Jan. 1850.

FASHIONABLE ARRIVALS// C 2a// Mark Lemon// **Cov. Garden**, Oct. 1840, with William Farren as Sir Thomas, James Vining as Capt. Maitland, John Brougham as O'Brian, A. Brindal as Fondleton, W. H. Payne as Daniel, George Bartley as Sureman, C. J. Mathews as Nix, Mme. Vestris as Mrs. Maitland, Miss Cooper as Mrs. O'Brian, Mrs. Humby as Mrs. Mode, Agnes Taylor as Mrs. Fondleton, Miss Lee as Mrs. Jones/ **Olympic**, Mar. 1859, with Mr. Addison as Sir Thomas, George Cooke as Sureman, Walter Gordon as Capt. Maitland, F. Charles as Fondleton, Horace Wigan as O'Brian, George Vining as Nix, Harwood Cooper as Daniel, Miss Wyndham as Mrs. Maitland, Miss Cottrell as Mrs. Fondleton, Miss Hughes as Mrs. O'Brian, Mrs. W. S. Emden as Mrs. Mode.

FAST ASLEEP// C 3a// Adap. by C. H. Abbott fr story of W. S. Gilbert, Wide Awake// **Criterion**, Mar. 1892, with John Beauchamp as Maj. Blister, T. G. Warren as Hereward, Gilbert Trent as Hatley-Hylo, William Wyes as John Blister, E. Hardrie as James Blister, George Giddens as Pointer, Mrs. Edmund Phelps as Mrs. Blister, Mary Ansell as Sophia, Kate Phillips as Mrs. Harkaway, Helen Lambert as Jane.

FAST COACH, THE// F 1a// C. J. Claridge & Robert Soutar// **Olympic**, June 1851, with George Cooke as Whiffleblinks, John Kinloch as Phastley, Henry Compton as Boldt, Isabel Adams as Laura, Mrs. Alfred Phillips as Mary, Miss Rawlings as Mrs. Gubbige/ **Olympic**, Apr. 1869, with Harwood Cooper as Whiffleblinks, Henry Vaughan as Phastley, J. G. Taylor as Bolt, Nelly Harris as Laura, Miss Schavey as Mary/ **Gaiety**, Sept. 1873.

FAST FAMILY, THE// C 4a// Adap by Benjamin Webster Jr. fr F of Victorien Sardou, La Famille Benoiton// **Adelphi**, May 1866, with Henry Ashley as Champrosé, Richard Phillips as Benoiton, Paul Bedford as Formichel, J. L. Toole as Prudent, John Billington as Didier, Teresa Furtado as Ploydore, W. H. Eburne as Francois, Nelly Smith as Fanfan, Mrs. Alfred Mellon (Sarah Woolgar) as Clotilde, Henrietta Simms as Blanche, Miss A. Seaman as Rose, Mrs. H. Lewis as Adolphine/ Scenery by Mr. Herberte/ Machines by Mr. Charker.

FAST FRIEND, A// F// Frank Herbert// **Olympic**, July 1877.

FAST LIFE, A// D 4a// Hubert O'Grady// **Imperial**, Oct. 1898.

FAST MAIL, THE// Play 4a// Lincoln J. Carter// **Grand**, June 1892.

FATAL BEAUTY// D Pro & 4a// Gylbert Fisher// **Sadler's Wells**, Apr. 1892.

FATAL CARD, THE// D 5a// C. Haddon Chambers & B. C. Stephenson// **Adelphi**, Sept. 1894, with William Terriss as Gerald Austin, Murray Carson as Marrable, Harry Nicholls as Burgess, Charles Fulton as A. K. Austin, W. L. Abingdon as Dixon, Richard Purdon as O'Flynn, Cory Thomas as Smith, Herbert Budd as Curtis, Caleb Porter as Webster, William Strickland as Winnigan, Jessie Millward as Margaret, Laura Linden as Cecile, Sophie Larkin as Penelope/ Scenery by Joseph Harker, T. W. Hall & Bruce Smith.

FATAL CROWN, A// Play 4a// Brandon Ellis & J. Bell// **Pavilion**, July 1901.

FATAL DOWERY, THE// D// Philip Massinger// **Sad. Wells**, Aug. 1845, with George Bennett as Rochfort, Henry Mellon as Novall, Mr. Warde as Ducroy, Henry Marston as Charlois, Charles Fenton as Lucan, Samuel Buckingham as Young Novall, Samuel Phelps as Moment, E. Morton as Beaumont, Frank Graham as Charmi, Miss Cooper as Beaumelle, Miss Lebatt as Bellapert, Miss Huddart as Florimel/ Scenery by F. Fenton & Mr. Finlay.

FATAL LETTER, THE; OR, THE MIDNIGHT REVELATION// D 3a// W. E. Suter// **East London**, May 1868.

FATAL MARRIAGE, THE// D Pro & 3a// Edward Towers// **East London**, Sept. 1870.

FATAL MAY MORN, THE; OR, THE LILY OF THE VALLEY// D// T. P. Taylor// **Sad. Wells**, May 1837, with Mr. Campbell as Redburn, N. T. Hicks as Wildheath, C. H. Pitt as Oakleigh, Mr. King as Graham, Mr. Rogers as Sharpwit, H. George as Hobnail, C. J. Smith as Ralph, Miss Beresford as Emma, Lavinia Melville as Jenny.

FATAL RAVINE, THE; OR, THE BEAR HUNTERS OF THE PYRENEES// D// n.a.// **Sad. Wells**, Aug. 1838, with Mr. Cobham as Caribert, Mr. Cathcart as Estevan, John Webster as Claude, Richard Phillips as Felix, Charles Montague as Lizier, Mr. Priorson as Perez, Mr. Hitchinson as Andrea, Mr. Stilt as Dumas,

Mr. Dry as Larole, Benjamin Conquest as Muskito, Dibdin Pitt as Mornard, J. W. Collier as Nicolon, Mr. Harwood as Guilloteaux, Miss Richardson as Aline, Miss Pincott as Jeannette, Mrs. J. F. Saville as Catrine, Miss Cooke as Mme. Manetti, Miss Walton as Iniz.

FATAL SECRET, THE; OR, WHY DID I LISTEN?// C 2a// n.a.// **St. James's**, Mar. 1838, with John Pritt Harley as Blaball, John Webster as Templeman, Mr. Halford as Lovedale, Mr. Hollingsworth as Credit, Miss Smith as Emma, Julia Smith as Lucy, Miss Stuart as Kitty.

FATAL SNOWSTORM, THE// D 2a// William Barrymore// **Victoria**, Aug. 1853, with Mr. Hitchinson as Gen. Mercandorff, T. E. Mills as Count Ostroff, Alfred Raymond as Count Romanoff, Mr. Richards as Yermitz, Mr. Morrison as Michael, James Howard as Brandt, Julian Hicks as Sturmwald, F. H. Henry as Ivanoff, Mr. Hudspeth as Peteroff, Miss Vaul as Alexis, Miss Clinton as Countess Lowina, Mrs. Manders as Dame Laudalin.

FATAL VISION, THE; OR, THE OSTLER'S DREAM// D 1a// Alfred Rayner// **Grecian**, July 1862, with Alfred Rayner as Isaac, William James as Wilfred, George Gillett as Joseph, W. Shirley as Frothwell, Henry Grant as The Guest, F. Smithson as Birchwood, John Manning as Cobbs, Marie Brewer as Nelly, Jane Dawson as Rebecca, Miss Johnstone as Hester.

FATALITY// F 1a// Caroline Boaden// **Olympic**, Jan. 1847, with George Maynard, Mr. Binge, Mr. Wilkenson, Mrs. R. Gordon, Miss Hamilton.

FATE; OR, DRIVEN FROM HOME// D// Bartley Campbell// **Gaiety**, Aug. 1884.

FATE AND FORTUNE; OR, THE JUNIOR PARTNER// D 4a// James Blood// **Princess's**, July 1891, with Henry Pagden as Glendon, Basset Roe as Ralph, Henry Dana as Halmshaw, W. L. Abingdon as Kopain, Frank Wood as Tranter, W. Cheesman as Woollett, T. F. Doyle as Blister, Stephen Caffrey as Marklow, John East as Swadler, Henry Bedford as Swagg, May Whitty as Grace, Sally Turner as Mrs. Tranter, May Protheroe as Mrs. Prowse, Grace Muriel as Madge, Cicely Richards as Matilda/ Scenery by Potts, Durant, Groome & Robson.

FATE OF A COQUETTE, THE (a vers. of Camille)// D// n.a.// **Sad. Wells**, June 1863, with Frank Huntley as Armand, James Johnstone as Duval, W. Worboys as Rient, George Maynard as de Varville, Wallace Britton as Gustave, Helen Western as The Coquette, Bessie Heath as Prudence, Caroline Collier as Nichette, Miss L. Collier as Nanine, Emma Leslie as Olympe.

FATE OF CALAS, THE// D 3a// Thomas Dibdin// **Sad. Wells**, Sept. 1839, with Mr. Dry as Calas, Mr. Elvin as Antoine, Mr. Cathcart as Edward, Robert Honner as Ambroise, Mr. Aldridge as Capitoul, W. D. Broadfoot as Gilbert, Mr. Williams as Jacob, Benjamin Conquest as Laurence, Mrs. J. F. Saville as Pauline, Miss Pincott as Jeanette, Miss Richardson as Mme. Calas.

FATE OF EUGENE ARAM, THE (see Eugene Aram)

FATE OF THE FALLEN, THE// D 4a// Thomas Hill// **Elephant & Castle**, Aug. 1901.

FATES AND FURIES// D 6a// G. B. Densmore// **Surrey**, Oct. 1877.

FATHER AND DAUGHTER; OR, SMILES AND TEARS// D 3a// W. T. Moncrieff// **Victoria**, May 1859, with J. H. Rickards as Fitzarden, W. H. Pitt as Capt. Alvanley, Mr. Henderson as Goodall, Mr. Carter as Rattleton, George Yarnold as Bachelor, James Howard as Michaelmas, Mary Fielding as Agnes, Miss Laporte as Merrel, Miss Donaldson as Emily.

FATHER AND SON; OR, THE ROCK OF CHARBONNIERE// D 2a// Edward Fitzball// **Sad. Wells**, Aug. 1841, with Henry Marston as Count St. Angeville, Mr. Elvin as Victor, George Ellis as Marquis Lenoir, Mr. Aldridge as Capt. Rosenford, Mr. Dry as Antoine, James Villiers as Vonfranc, Miss Richardson as Violette, Mrs. Richard Barnett as Amy, Miss Cooke as Mme. Lantone.

FATHER BUONAPARTE// Play 3a// C. W. Hudson// **Olympic**, Mar. 1891.

FATHER SATAN// D 5a// Harry Spiers// **Britannia**, June 1896.

FATHER'S OATH, THE// D 4a// Frederick Gould// **Surrey**, May 1893.

FATHERLAND// D 5a// Henry Labouchere// **Queen's**, Jan. 1878.

FATHOMS DEEP// D// John Cleve// **Sadler's Wells**, Mar. 1883.

FAUST// T Pro & 5a// Adap. by W. Bayle Bernard fr G of Goethe// **Drury Lane**, Oct. 1865, with Edmund Phelps as Faust, W. Harrison as Valentine, Charles Warner as Frosch, Mr. Fitzjames as Brander, Charles Harcourt as Siebel, Frank Barsby as Wagner, E. Morton as Hans, J. B. Johnstone as Jacob, Mrs. Hermann Vezin as Margaret, Mrs. Henry Vandenhoff as Martha, Adelaide Golier as Elsie, Miss F. Bennett as Katren, Samuel Phelps as Mephistopheles, James Johnstone as Earth, Charles Seyton as Syxorax, William McIntyre as Baubo, George Spencer as Tegel, Lizzie Grosvenor as Sybil/ Scenery by William Beverley/ Music by J. H. Tully/ Prod. by Edward Stirling.

FAUST// T// Adap. by W. G. Wills fr G of Goethe// **Lyceum**, Dec. 1885, with H. B. Conway as Faust, George Alexander as Valentine, Frank Tyars as Brander, Mrs. Stirling as Martha, Henry Howe as Burgomaster, Ellen Terry as Margaret, Henry Irving as Mephistopheles/ **Sadler's Wells**, Feb. 1886.

FAUST; OR, THE DEMON OF THE DRACHENFELS// D 2a// H. P. Grattan// **Sadler's Wells**,

Sept. 1842, with Mr. Lyon as Faust, Henry Marston as Mephistophiles, Mr. Dry as Albert, John Herbert as Petreus, Mr. Aldridge as Caspar, Caroline Rankley as Marguerite, Mrs. Richard Barnett as Hanehen/ Scenery by T. Pitt, G. Smithyes Jr. & Mr. Daniels/ Machines by Mr. Cawdery/ Music by **Isaac** Collins/ Prod. by Henry Marston; June 1857, with Mr. Lyon as Faust, G. B. Bigwood as Petreus, George Cooke as Rodolph, G. Pennett as Eric, E. B. Gaston as Mephistophiles, John Mordaunt as Albert, Mr. Edwin as Caspar, Mary A. Victor as Hancheon, Amelia Wright as Spirit, Mrs. Robert Honner as Margurite [sic]/ **Grecian**, Apr. 1867, with William James as Faust, Alfred Rayner as Mephisophiles, J. Jackson as Albert, John Manning as Petrous, Henry Grant as Rodolph, W. Shirley as Eric, Samuel Perfitt as Caspar, Lizzie Mandelbert as Marguerite, Mary A. Victor as Hanaben.

FAUST; OR, THE FATE OF MARGARET// Play 4a// Adap. by W. Bayle Bernard fr G of Goethe// **Drury Lane**, Oct. 1866.

FAUST AND MARGARET// D// Adap. by Brian Daly & C. W. Somerset fr G of Goethe// **West London**, Feb. 1899.

FAUST AND MARGUERITE// D 3a// Adap. by Mrs. Denvil fr F of Michel Carré// **Princess's**, Apr. 1854, with David Fisher as Faust, Charles Kean as Mephistopheles, John Cathcart as Valentine, Alfred Raymond as Brander, Henry Saker as Seibel, Kate Terry as Karl, Carlotta Leclercq as Marguerite, Mrs. Winstanley as Dame Martha/ Scenery by Walter Gordon & F. Lloyds/ Music by J. L. Hatton/ **Grecian**, Aug. 1854, with Richard Phillips as Faust, William Suter as Michel, Charles Horn as Valentine, Basil Potter as Mephistopheles, Jane Coveney as Marguerite, Miss Johnstone as Martha, Miss Chapman as Madeliene, Harriet Coveney as Helene, Agnes De Warde as Ernestiene/ Scenery by Mr. Jones/ Machines by Mr. Smithers/ Gas by Mr. Dimes/ Music by T. Berry/ Prod by R. Phillips.

FAUSTINE// D 3a// Charles L. Young// **Olympic**, June 1880, with William Magnay as Comte de Beauvais, Charles Myers as Prince Tolstoi, C. P. Colnaghl as Sir Claude, John Maclean as Dr. Serlupi, Charles Young as Baron de Meridor, Mrs. G. Wrottesley as Lady Belville, Mrs. King as Mathilde, Lady Monckton as Faustine.

FAUSTINE'S LOVE// D Pro & 3a// Dram. by Walter Stanhope fr novel of Rita// **Strand**, June 1889.

FAVETTE// C 1a// Adap. by John Tresahar fr story of Ouida// **Vaudeville**, Jan. 1885.

FAVORITE, THE// D 4a// by "Riada"// **Elephant & Castle**, Mar. 1899.

FAVORITE OF FORTUNE, THE// C 4a// Westland Marston// **Haymarket**, Apr. 1866, with E. A. Sothern as Annerley, J. B. Buckstone as Sutherland, Mr. Rogers as Maj. Price, W. H. Chippendale as Bromley, Mrs. Chippendale as Mrs. Lorrington, Kate Saville as Hester, Nelly Moore as Lucy, Mrs. Edward Fitzwilliam as Mrs. Witherby, Lucreza Hill as Euphemia, Henrietta Lindley as Camilla/ Scenery by John O'Conner & George Morris/ Machines by Oliver Wales.

FAVOURITE OF THE KING, THE// Play 4a// F. S. Boas & Jocelyn Brandon// **Comedy**, Mar. 1890, with Thomas Lewen as Francis, Royce Carleton as Villiers, Basset Roe as Lambe, J. R. Crauford as Felton, Allen Beaumont as Sir Roger, Lawrance d'Orsay as Barton, Dorothy Dene as Helen, Annie Rose as Lady Katherine, Mrs. C. L. Carson as Cecilia, Louise Moodie as Lady Villiers.

FAY O' THE FERN, THE// F// Robert Legge// **Comedy**, Mar. 1893, with Ben Greet as Benedoct, Stratton Rodney as Shalspere, F. Topham as Maj. Auger, Willis Searle as Hammersmith, Constance Hellyer as Huon, Mrs. Tom Wilson as Tib, Hilda Rivers as Augusta, Florence Tanner as Daisy, Marie Wilson as Elfia.

FAZIO; OR, THE ITALIAN WIFE (also subt., Italian Wife's Revenge)// T 5a// H. H. Milman// **Sad. Wells**, Mar. 1840, with Mr. Dry as Duke, Mr. Aldridge as Gonsalvo, Mr. Morgan as Aurio, Henry Marston as Fazio, Robert Honner as Bartolo, A. Walton as Dandolo, Mr. Moreton as Philario, J. W. Collier as Falodio, Mrs. Robert Honner as Bianca, Mrs. J. F. Saville as Marchesa of Aldebella, Mrs. Morgan as Clara; Sept. 1866, with J. H. Slater as Fazio, J. L. Warner as Duke, Richard Norman as Bartolo, James Edwin as Gonsalvo, Walter Lacy as Aurio, Mr. Williams as Falsetto, J. W. Lawrence as Theodore, Alice Marriott as Bianca, Miss Nason as Countess Aldabella, Miss Fitzgerald as Clara/ **Princess's**, Feb. 1845, with Frank Graham as Fazio, A. Walton as Duke of Florence, Mr. Fitzjames as Philario, Augustus Harris as Falsetto, W. H. Oxberry as Bartolo, James Ranoe as Gonsalvi, Charlotte Cushman as Bianca, Mrs. John Brougham as Marchesa Aldabella, Miss Somers as Clara/ **Drury Lane**, Mar. 1850, with Charles Fisher as Duke, Thomas Barry as Gonsalvo, F. H. Henry as Aurio, Mr. Cooper as Fazio, William Davidge as Bartolo, Henry Frazer as Philario, George Everett as Falsetto, John Parry as Dandolo, Miss Phillips as Aldabella, Laura Addison as Bianca, Miss Niel as Clara; Dec. 1851 with Isabella Glyn as Bianca/ **Adelphi**, Mar. 1865/ **Lyceum**, Jan. 1877 (in 4 acts), with A. Beaumont as Duke of Florence, E. H. Brooke as Giraldi Fazio, Thomas Mead as Bartolo, P. C. Lyons as Philario, Mr. Carton as Falsetto, Mr. Stuart as Theodore, Georgina Pauncefort as Marchesa Aldabella, Kate Bateman as Bianca/ Scenery by Hawes Craven/ Music by Robert Stoepel/ **Strand**, July 1890.

FEAR OF ROBERT CLIVE, THE// Play 1a// Sarah Grand & Haldane McFall// **Lyceum**, July 1896.

FEARFUL FOG, A// F// Frederick Hay// **Vaudeville**, Apr. 1871.

FEARFUL TRAGEDY IN THE SEVEN DIALS//

F 1a// Charles Selby// **Adelphi**, May 1857, with Edward Wright as Slumpington, Paul Bedford as Mulligatawney, Frank Hall as Twigley, C. J. Smith as Weazle, Mrs. Garden as Mrs. Slumpington.

FEATHERBRAIN// C 3a// Adap. by James Albery fr F of Théodore Barrière & M. Goudinet, Tête de Linotte// **Criterion**, June 1884, with William Blakeley, Rose Saker, Marie Jansen, Miss E. Vining.

FEDORA// D 4a// Adap. by Herman Merivale fr F of Victorien Sardou// **Haymarket**, May 1883, with Charles Coghlan as Ipanoff, Squire Bancroft as De Siriex, Mr. Carne as Boroff, Mr. Smedley as Rouvel, H. Fitzpatrick as Vernet, Mr. Elliot as Loreck, Charles Brookfield as Gretch, Mr. Francis as Lasinski, Frederick Everill as Tchileff, Julia Gwynne as Dmitri, Stewart Dawson as Kirill, Mrs. Bernard Beere as Fedora, Mrs. Bancroft as Countess Olga, Miss Herbert as Baroness Ockar, Miss Merrill as Mme. de Tournis/ Scenery by Walter Johnstone; June 1895, with Herbert Beerbohm Tree as Count Ipanoff, Nutcombe Gould as de Siriex, Berte Thomas as Boroff, C. M. Hallard as Rouvel, Gayer Mackay as Vernet, Edward Ferris as Laroche, Edmund Maurice as Loreck, Holman Clark as Gretch, Charles Allan as Lasinski, Mrs. Patrick Campbell as Fedora, Mrs. Bancroft as Countess Olga, Hilda Hanbury as Baroness Ockar/ Dir. by Squire Bancroft.

FELON'S BOND, THE// D 3a// W. E. Suter// **Queen's**, Sept. 1859/ **Grecian**, Apr. 1866, with J. Jackson as Darlington, William James as Gerald, Samuel Perfitt as Dr. Wilton, Charles Mortimer as Marini, Alfred Rayner as Grayland, John Manning as Johnson, Henry Grant as Devulshbard, George Gillett as Wallingford, Mrs. Atkinson as Mrs. Montford, Lizzie Mandlebert as Emily, Mary A. Victor as Mrs. Millington.

FELON'S DEATH, THE// D// n.a.// **Victoria**, June 1854, with N. T. Hicks as Leslie, Edwin Blanchard as Macneil, James Howard as Maclain, Mrs. Henry Vining as Jessie, Miss Laporte as Maggie, Dogs Hector and Bruin.

FEMALE FORGER, THE; OR, THE FIRST STEP IN GUILT// D 3a// G. D. Pitt// **Victoria**, May 1843, with Mr. James as Cheerly, William Seaman as Lt. Cheerly, Mr. Glindon as Darlington, Mr. Paul as Old Jack, John Gardner as John ap Jack, John Dale as Lyon, George Maynard as Craunstoun, C. Williams as Dick, Annette Vincent as Ellen, Miss Ridgeway as Dame Burton, Miss Saddler as Fanny.

FEMALE IAGO, A// F// W. H. Goldsmith// **Royalty**, July 1873.

FEMALE PIRATE, THE; OR, THE LIONESS OF THE SEA// D// Douglas Stewart// **Victoria**, Oct. 1870.

FENIAN, THE// D 4a// Hubert O'Grady// **Standard**, Sept. 1889.

FENNEL// Play 1a// Adap. by Jerome K. Jerome fr F of François Coppée, Le Luthier de Crémone// **Novelty**, Mar. 1888.

FERDINANDO// F// Walter Parke// **Grand**, Nov. 1886.

FERNANDE// D 4a// Adap. by Sutherland Edwards fr F of Victorien Sardou// **St. James's**, Oct. 1870, with Mrs. Hermann Vezin as Clotilde, Mrs. John Wood as Georgette, Fanny Brough as Fernande, Sophie Larkin as Mme. Seneschal, Sallie Turner as Therese, William Farren Jr. as Pomerol, Dan Leeson as Roqueville, Lionel Brough as Jarbi, Lin Rayne as Des Arcis, Gaston Murray as Bracassin, Charles Otley as Frederic/ Scenery by Hann & Roberts/ Music by King Hall/ **Court**, Sept. 1879, with Charles Coghlan, Wilson Barrett, Caroline Heath (Mrs. Wilson Barrett), Amy Roselle, Mrs. Leigh Murray.

FETCHES, THE// F// Edmund Falconer// **Lyceum**, Aug. 1861.

FETTERED FREEDOM// D 3a// Milner Kenney & C. H. Stephenson// **Vaudeville**, Sept. 1887.

FETTERED LIVES// D 5a// Harold Whyte// **Britannia**, July 1893/ **Novelty**, May 1896, with William Felton as Meredith, Leonard Shepherd as Hazleton, George Abel as Goodman, E. Beasley as Denam, Helena Head as Madge, Kate Brunton as Nelly, V. St. Lawrence as May.

FEUDAL TIMES// T 5a// James White// **Sad. Wells**, Feb. 1847, with Henry Marston as James III, Samuel Phelps as Cochrane, George Bennett as Douglas, William Hoskins as Lennox, Frank Graham as Gairlies, Edward Knight as Lord Grey, Mr. Branson as Lord Drummond, Mr. Fitzgerald as Lord Seaton, Henry Mellon as Bishop of Dunkeld, Miss Cooper as Queen Margaret, Laura Addison as Margaret, Mrs. Henry Marston as Lady Drummond/

FIAT OF THE GODS, THE// Play 1a// Adap. by Leonard Outram fr F of M. Sonnet, Le Gladiateur// **Avenue**, Aug. 1891/ **Globe**, Apr. 1892.

FIBS// C 3a// Welborn Tylar// **Toole's**, June 1882.

FIELD OF FORTY FOOTSTEPS, THE; OR, THE BROKEN CONTRACT AND THE BROTHER'S DUEL// D 3a// Dram. by William Farren fr tale by Miss Porter// **Sad. Wells**, Mar. 1842, with Master Maskell as Duke Henry, John Webster as Sir Arthur, E. Morton as Matchlowe, Mr. Aldridge as Sir Nicholas, J. W. Collier as Pipkin, John Herbert as Barebones, Miss Cooke as Lady Vere, Mrs. Robert Honner as Frances, Mrs. Richard Barnett as Rose, Mrs. Morgan as Mabel/ **Victoria**, Sept. 1854, with Phoebe Johnson as Henry of Gloucester, N. T. Hicks as Sir Arthur, W. H. Pitt as Matchlowe, Alfred Saville as Sir Nicholas, Mr. Morrison as Fairfax, F. H. Henry as Hearnshaw, Charles Rice as Barebones, Mr. Hitchinson as Fearnought, Miss Dansor as Lady Vere, Mrs. Henry Vining as Frances, Miss Laporte as Rose, Mrs. Manders as Mabel.

FIELD OF THE CLOTH OF GOLD, THE; OR, HENRY THE EIGHTH AND FRANCIS THE FIRST// D 3a// Shafto Scott// **Astley's**, Apr. 1869.

FIEND OF THE FLEET, THE; OR, LONDON LABOUR AND LONDON POOR// D// n.a.// **Victoria**, Aug. 1854, with Alfred Saville as Sir Charles, Mr. Green as Capt. Benson, E. F. Saville as Robert Wild, Mr. Henderson as Pink, T. E. Mills as Bertholdy, N. T. Hicks as Mildew, Charles Rice as Medler, Mrs. Henry Vining as Ellen, Phoebe Johnson as Mary, Mrs. Manders as Molly, Miss Laporte as Biddy.

FIEND OF THE VOLCANO, THE; OR, THE ERUPTION OF VESUVIUS// D// n.a.// **Sad. Wells**, Aug. 1837, with N. T. Hicks as Alphonso, H. George as Cascarilios, C. H. Pitt as di Crece, Mr. King as Octavio, Mr. Griffith as Pomposo, Thomas Lee as Argos, C. J. Smith as Florentine, Miss Williams as Leonora, Lavinia Melville as Belinda/ Scenery by Mr. Mildenhall/ Music by Mr. Nicholson/ Machines by Mr. Copping.

FIEND ON THE HEARTH, THE; OR, THE OLD MILL OF ST. DENIS// D// n.a.// **Sad. Wells**, Aug. 1866, with Walter Roberts as Darville, Philip Hannan as Montgerand, F. Watts as Edward, Watty Brunton as Snipe, George Skinner as Jaques, Miss Neville as Leoni, Annette Vincent as Louise, Julia Summers as Mariette.

FIERY ORDEAL// D// n.a.// **Britannia**, Jan. 1862.

FIESCO; OR, THE REVOLT OF GENOA// D 5a// Adap. by J. R. Planché fr G of Friedrich Schiller// **Drury Lane**, Feb. 1850, with Mr. Cooper as Andrea Doria, Charles Fisher as Prince Doria, William Montague as Marquis de Calcagno, James Anderson as Fiesco, Mr. Cathcart as Count Lomellino, Mr. Frazer as Count Secco, Mr. Vandenhoff as Verrina, Charles Diddear as Zenturioni, Mrs. Ternan as Julia, Laura Addison as Leonora, Miss Neil as Bertha, Florence Grey as Arabella/ Scenery by Brunning, Jones, Wilson & C. Adams/ Machines by W. Adams.

FIFTEEN YEARS OF LABOUR LOST// F 1a// Dram. by J. H. Amherst fr F of M. A. Gautier, Nature et Philosophie// **St. James's**, Oct. 1867, with G. W. Blake as Phillipe, Mr. Williams as Anselme, Eleanore Bufton as Lubin, Ada Cavendish as Elisa, Sophie Larkin as Gertrude.

FIFTY YEARS AFTER// D Pro & 3a// Adap. by Z. Topelius fr Swed., Efter Femtis Ar// **St. Geo. Hall**, Feb. 1888.

FIGHT FOR HONOUR, A// D 5a// Frank Harvey// **Surrey**, June 1892.

FIGHT FOR LIFE, A// D 4a// F. A. Scudamore// **Surrey**, July 1895.

FIGHT WITH FATE, A// D 4a// n.a.// **Surrey**, Sept. 1864.

FIGHTING BY PROXY// F 1a// James Kenny// **Princess's**, Oct. 1847, with Henry Compton as Flinch, Samuel Cowell as Allsop, F. B. Conway as Clairmont, James Vining as Minus, J. Neville as Stilton, Mrs. Selby as Mrs. Stilton, Miss Capel as Sophia.

FIGHTING FIFTH, THE// D 5a// George Conquest Sr. & Herbert Leonard// **Surrey**, Oct. 1900.

FIGHTING FORTUNE// D 4a// F. C. Scudamore// **Marylebone**, July 1882.

FIGHTING FIFTY-FIRST, THE// C 3a// C. H. Hazlewood// **Britannia**, Sept. 1876.

FIGURE OF FUN; OR, THE BLOOMER COSTUME// F 1a// Edward Stirling// **Strand**, Sept. 1851.

FIN MACCOUL// CD 3a// Dion Boucicault// **Elephant & Castle**, Feb. 1887.

FINE FEATHERS// CD Pro & 3a// H. J. Byron// **Globe**, Apr. 1873.

FINESSE; OR, SPY AND COUNTERSPY// C 3a// Countess of Giffard// **Haymarket**, May 1863, with W. H. Chippendale as Baron Freitenhorsen, Alfred Wigan as Bertrand, George Braid as St. Clair, Walter Gordon as Count Filippi, Henry Howe as Capt. Mortimer, J. B. Buckstone as Poppleton, William Farren as d'Artigny, Mrs. Wilkins as Baroness Freitenhorsen, Louisa Angel as Laura, Mrs. Alfred Wigan as Mrs. Bobbin, Fanny Wright as Caterina.

FIRE DAMP; OR, MURDER IN THE MINE// D// n.a.// **Sad. Wells**, Nov. 1842, with Mr. Dry as Kennedy, Mr. Aldridge as Pardoe, C. J. Bird as Morris, Mr. Franks as Thorne, Mr. Grammani as Bissell, Mr. Williams as Old Morris, Charles Fenton as Brooks, John Herbert as Lamb, J. W. Collier as Walter, Mrs. Henry Marston as Dame Morris, Miss Morelli as Susan, Caroline Rankley as Ellen, Mrs. Richard Barnett as Sybil/ Scenery by F. Fenton, G. Smithyes Jr., & Mr. Daniel/ Machines by Mr. Cawdery/ Music by Isaac Collins/ Prod. by Henry Marston/ **Victoria**, Aug. 1846, with William Seaman as Kennedy, Alfred Raymond as Morris, Mr. Hitchinson as Thorne, Mr. Franklin as Bissell, F. Wilton as Old Morris, Mr. Fitzjames as Brooks, E. G. Burton as Lamb, Walter Searle as Walter, Lydia Pearce as Sybil, Mrs. Cooke as Dame Morris, Mrs. Henry Vining as Ellen, Miss Fielding as Susan.

FIRE EATER, THE// F 1a// Charles Selby// **Olympic**, June 1851, with John Kinloch as Col. Marchmont, Mr. Mason as Maj. Belton, Charles Bender as Longchalk, Henry Compton as Gosling, William Shalders as Fusee, Ellen Turner as Grace.

FIREFLY// D Pro & 3a// Dram. by Edith Sandford fr story of Ouida, Under Two Flags// **Surrey**, May 1869/ **Britannia**, May 1870.

FIREMAN OF NEW YORK, THE// D 2a// n.a.// **Grecian**, Sept. 1865, with William James as

Jerome, J. Jackson as Wealthy, Walter Holland as Stubbe, Henry Grant as Moornington, Dan Leeson as Blubber, John Manning as Press, Lizzie Mandlebert as Alice, Mrs. J. W. Simpson as Mrs. Waddletongue, Marie Brewer as Lucretia.

FIRESIDE HAMLET, A// TF// J. Comyns Carr// **Prince's**, Nov. 1884.

FIREWORKS// FC 3a// F. C. Philips & Percy Fendall// **Vaudeville**, June 1893, with Alfred Maltby as Rev. Needham, W. T. Lovell as Fraser, Eric Lewis as Grindley, William Wyes as Tuffet, Lottie Venne as Ada, Gertrude Kingston as Mrs. Fraser, Ethel Mathews as Mrs. Grindley.

FIRM AS AN OAK; OR, ENGLAND'S PRIDE// D// George Peel// **Britannia**, June 1873.

FIRST AFFECTIONS// C 1a// J. Palgrave Simpson// **St. James's**, Feb. 1860, with H. T. Craven as Capt. Egerton, George Spencer as Elliot, Mr. Lever as Twangely, H. Reeves as Motus, F. Craxford as Thomas, Miss Wyndham as Mrs. Meriton, Nelly Moore as Matilda, Alice Evans as Mary.

FIRST AND SECOND FLOOR// F// n.a.// **Haymarket**, July 1857, with J. B. Buckstone as Tripkin, Mr. Rogers as Fizakerley, Miss Talbot as Mrs. Nankeen, Mrs. Edward Fitzwilliam as Mrs. Fizakerley, Marie Wilton as Kitty.

FIRST BORN, THE// Play 2a// Francis Powers// **Globe**, Nov. 1897, with May Buckley as Loey Tsing, Nellie Cummins as Cho Pow, Carrie Powers as Chan Lee, George Osbourne as Dr. Pow Len, Francis Powers as Chan Wang, J. H. Benrimo as Hop Kee, Harry Spear as Chum Woe, John Armstrong as Kwa Kee, Venie Wells as Chan Toy/ Prod. by Charles Frohman.

FIRST CRIME// D// n.a.// **City of London**, Oct. 1856.

FIRST FAVOURITE, THE// D 1a// C. H. Hazlewood// **Britannia**, Oct. 1873.

FIRST FLOOR, THE// C// James Cobb// **Cov. Garden**, Nov. 1840, with William Farren as Whimsey, C. J. Mathews as Young Whimsey, James Vining as Monford, John Pritt Harley as Tartlett, Drinkwater Meadows as Furnish, Mrs. Charles Jones as Mrs. Pattypan, Miss Cooper as Charlotte, Mrs. Humby as Nancy/ **Sad. Wells**, July 1845, with A. Younge as Old Whimsey, Samuel Buckingham as Young Whimsey, E. Morton as Monford, Mr. Corrie as Tartlett, Mr. Williams as Furnish, Charles Fenton as Simon, Mr. Bologna as Frank, Edward Knight as Strap, Mrs. Henry Marston as Mrs. Pattypan, Miss Huddart as Charlotte, Georgiana Lebatt as Nancy.

FIRST IN THE FIELD// C 1a// Adap. by C. M. Rae fr F of Henri Meilhac, Suzanne et les Deux Viellards// **Globe**, May 1882/ **Haymarket**, May 1883, with Alfred Bishop as Gen. Dennistoun, Charles Brookfield as William, Mr. Carne as Lionel, Miss Tilbury as Beatrice.

FIRST LOVE; OR, THE WIDOWED BRIDE// D 3a// W. E. Suter// **Grecian**, June 1863, with Alfred Rayner as Count de Lambert, William James as Albert, Thomas Mead as Eustache, George Conquest as Tittinet, Henry Grant as Taquet, John Manning as Moonie, Miss Johnstone as Mme. de Lambert, Jane Dawson as Camille, Mary A. Victor as Jacquinette.

FIRST MATE// C 2a// Richard Henry// **Gaiety**, Dec. 1888.

FIRST NIGHT, THE// C 1a// Adap. by Alfred Wigan fr F, Le Père de la Débutante// **Princess's**, Oct. 1849; Aug. 1860, with Augustus Harris as Dufard, T. H. Higgie as Fitzdangle, Robert Cathcart as Parnassus, John Collett as Vamp, Mr. Garden as Flat, Rose Leclercq as Arabella, Maria Harris as Emilie/ **Olympic**, Jan. 1854, with Alfred Wigan as Dufard, Mr. Leslie as Manager, Mr. Lindon as Stage Manager, Harwood Cooper as Author, Mr. Vincent as Fitzurse, Priscilla Horton as Rose, Miss Wyndham as Arabella; Mar. 1883, with Herbert Beerbohm Tree as Dufard, T. C. Bindloss as Flutter, Mr. Staunton as Author, A. Darvell as Prompter, W. E. Blatchley as Manager, H. Knight as Alonzo, Lucy Buckstone as Emilie, Kate Lee as Arabella/ **Sad. Wells**, Aug. 1855, with Alfred Wigan as Dufard, Mr. Leslie as Manager, Mr. Franks as Stage Manager, Harwood Cooper as Author, Mr. Danvers as Fitzurse, Julia St. George as Rose, Emily Ormonde as Arabella/ **Gaiety**, Feb. 1870/ **Drury Lane**, July 1872/ **Folly**, July 1879/ **Comedy**, Oct. 1887/ **Haymarket**, May 1887, with Charles Brookfield as Fitzdangle, Edward Righton as Parnassus, Henry Kemble as Vamp, Henry Ashley as Flat, Herbert Beerbohm Tree as Dufard, Charles Allan as Alonzo, Kate Rorke as Emilie, Gertrude Kingston as Arabella/ **Her Majesty's**, May 1899.

FIRST OF MAY, THE// F 1a// Alfred Younge// **Sadler's Wells**, Oct. 1849, with A. Younge as Snolts, William Hoskins as Vermillien, Henry Mellon as Macaw, Mrs. Henry Marston as Mrs. Snolts, Mrs. G. Smith as Mrs. Bustle, Miss Johnson as Fanny, Julia St. George as Jenny.

FIRST PRINTER, THE// D 3a// Charles Reade & Tom Taylor// **Princess's**, Mar. 1856, with Frank Matthews as Persyn, Charles Kean as Costar, John Ryder as John of Gutenberg, Henry Mellon as Otto, John Cathcart as Floris, George Everett as Vanderbeke, David Fisher as Reineke, Miss Murray as Jacqueline, Miss Heath as Margaret, Miss Eglinton as Gertrude, Mrs. W. Daly as Katryn/ Scenery by Walter Gordon & F. Lloyds.

FISH OUT OF WATER, THE// F 1a// Joseph Lunn// **Haymarket**, Aug. 1840, with Mr. Waldron as Sir George, Robert Strickland as Gayfare, John Webster as Charles, David Rees as Savoury, Eliza Travers as Ellen, Miss Mattley as Lucy; Sept. 1860, with William Cullenford as Gayfare, Mr. Rogers as Sir George, Henry Compton as Savoury, Edwin Villiers as Charles, Miss Henrade as Ellen, Miss Addington as Lucy; Dec. 1872, with Mr. Rogers as Sir George, Frederick Everill as Savoury, Walter Gordon as Charles, George Braid as Steward, Edward Osborne as Gayfare, Miss E. Harrison as Ellen, Miss Mathews as Lucy/ **Sad. Wells**, Nov. 1866, with J. W. Lawrence as Sir George, John Rouse as Sam Savoury, J. Collier as Gayfair, Richard Norman as Alderman, Fanny Leicester as Ellen, Miss Mansfield as Lucy/ **Lyceum**, Oct. 1874, with Henry Compton as Savory, H. B. Conway as Gayfare, John Carter as Alderman Gayfare, A. Beaumont as Sir George, Miss St. Ange as Ellen, Miss Hampden as Lucy.

FISHERMAN OF THE FERRY, THE; OR, THE CASTLE OF GLENCAIRN (see Warlock of the Glen).

FISHERMAN'S DAUGHTER, THE// D 2a// Charles Garvice// **Royalty**, Dec. 1881.

FITS AND STARTS// F 2a// Wilton Jones & Walter Browne// **Gaiety**, May 1885.

FITZSMYTHE, OF FITZSMYTHE HALL// F 1a// J. Maddison Morton// **Haymarket**, June 1860, with J. B. Buckstone as Fitzsmythe, William Farren as Tottenham, Mr. Rogers as Gregory, Mrs. Wilkins as Mrs. Fitzsmythe, Miss Henrade as Penelope/ **Drury Lane**, July 1860, with J. B. Buckstone as Fitzsmythe, William Farren Jr. as Tottenham, Mr. Rogers as Gregory, Mrs. Wilkins as Mrs. Fitzsmythe, Miss Henrade as Penelope/ **Sad. Wells**, May 1863, with W. Worboys as Fitzsmythe, J. W. Collier as Gregory, T. T. Pugh as Tottenham, Miss Rawlings as Mrs. Fitzsmythe, Isa Russell as Penelope.

FIVE HUNDRED POUNDS REWARD// Adap by Alfred Wigan fr F, Le Capitaine de Voleurs// **Lyceum**, 1845.

FIVE POUNDS REWARD// F 1a// John Oxenford// **Olympic**, Dec. 1855.

FLAG, THE; OR, THE BATTLEFIELD// D 3a// **Surrey**, Nov. 1870.

FLASH OF LIGHTNING, A// D 4a// Murdoch & Daly// **Grecian**, Nov. 1870.

FLATS// FC 4a// Adap. by G. R. Sims fr F, Les Locataires de Monsieur Blondeau// **Criterion**, July 1881, with W. J. Hill, Alfred Maltby, William Blakeley, Mrs. Alfred Mellon, Dora Vivian.

FLIGHT// Play 4a// Walter Frith// **Terry's**, Feb. 1893, with H. B. Conway as Amherst, Murray Carson as Sargent, Edward Terry as Marley, H. V. Esmond as Carr, W. T. Lovell as Tanfield, T. W. Percyval as Gascoigne, Harry Eversfield as Lord Bond, May Whitty as Mrs. Amherst, Annie Hill as Blanche, Helen Forsyth as Sylvia/ Scenery by W. T. Hemsley.

FLIGHT FOR LIFE// D// n.a.// **Surrey**, July 1895.

FLAP, FLAP, FLOP// F// Adap by Paul Meritt fr F// **Surrey**, Sept. 1882.

FLIP FLAP FOOTMAN// F 1a// R. B. Peake// **Adelphi**, Oct. 1840, with Arthur Wilkinson, Henry Hall, Mr. Wieland, John Sanders, J. F. Smith, Mrs. Keeley/ **Haymarket**, Aug. 1844, with Mr. Granby as Faddle, Augustus Harris as Philomel, Mr. Chicheley as Livid, Mr. Green as Old Saunders, Mr. Ennis as Cornelius, Mr. Wieland as Cork, Miss Brooks as Prudence.

FLIRTATION// C 3a// F. Romer & G. S. Bellamy// **Globe**, June 1878, with W. P. Grainger as General Leith, Edward Righton as Maj. Shoreshot, B. D'Arley as Jack Rollope, William Bourne as Archie, Isabel Clifton as Mrs. Brayley, Blanche Stammers as Cissy Morley.

FLITTING DAY, THE; OR, THE TRIALS OF AN ENGLISH FARMER// D 3a// n.a.// **Victoria**, June 1846, with T. Fredericks as Sir Charles, James Ranoe as Lord Follyscourt, Alfred Raymond as Col. Thorn, James Howard as Capt. Torrington, T. H. Higgie as Nettlewig, E. F. Saville as John Rockley, Walter Searle as Benjamin Rockley, Roberts Tindall as Johnson, E. G. Burton as Munns, Annette Vincent as Jane, Mrs. George Lee as Mrs. Rockley, Mrs. Andrews as Tabitha, Miss Jefferson as Mrs. Strype, Eliza Terrey as Biddy.

FLORENTINES, THE// D 5a// E. L. Berwick// **Sad. Wells**, June 1845, with Henry Marston as Duke Lorenzo, E. Morton as Vassali, Samuel Phelps as Fernando, Mrs. Mary Warner as The Duchess, Miss Cooper, Miss Huddart, Mrs. Henry Marston.

FLO'S FIRST FROLIC// F// n.a.// **Princess's**, May 1868.

FLOATING A COMPANY// C 1a// Julian Cross// **Royalty**, June 1894, with Hurdman Lucas as Capt. Caruthers, Henrietta Cross as Rosalind.

FLOATING BEACON, THE; OR, THE WILD WOMAN OF THE WRECK// D 2a// Edward Fitzball// **Victoria**, Apr. 1838, with Mr. Loveday as Weinstadt, John Parry as Junk, Charles Montague as Frederick, Mr. Wilkins as Angerstaff, Miss Richardson as Mariette, Miss Lee as Christine/ **Sad. Wells**, Dec. 1843, with Mr. Dry as Angerstoff, Mr. Williams as Weignstadt, W. H. Williams as Jack Junk, C. J. Bird as Frederick, Charles Fenton as Ormoloff, Caroline Rankley as Mariette, Mrs. Richard Barnett as Christine.

FLOATING KINGDOM, THE; OR, THE LAST VOYAGE OF CAPTAIN COOK// D// J. S. Faucit// **Sad. Wells**, Jan. 1838, with Mr. Ranson as Capt. Cook, Mr. Forester as Malcolm, Mr. Scarbrow as Hallaway, Mr. Campbell as Wattman, Mr. James as Terrecabeo, S. Smith as Koah, Mr. Nunn as Pareea, Miss Watkins as Karrabeea/ Scenery by Mr. Battie/ Music by W. Montgomery/ Machines by Mr. Copping.

FLORENTINE WOOING, A// C 4a// Clotilde Graves// **Avenue**, July 1898.

FLORENTINES, THE// n.a.// **Sadler's Wells**, June 1845.

FLOWER GIRL, THE; OR, THE CONVICT

MARQUIS// D 3a// T. Townsend// **Sad. Wells**, Dec. 1862, with James Johnstone as Le Beau, C. Lloyds as Antoine, William Creswick as Cranon, E. F. Edgar as Barennes, Alfred Montague as Lansay, Lewis Ball as Baptiste, Sophie Miles as Madelon, Mrs. W. Dowton as Mme. Legarde, Emily Dowton as Jeannette/ **Surrey**, 1858; Nov. 1867/ **City of London**, July 1865, with William Creswick.

FLOWER MAKERS AND HEART BREAKERS: A TALE OF TRIAL AND TEMPTATION// D 3a// C. H. Hazlewood// **Grecian**, Nov. 1869, with J. Jackson as Dacre, William James as Reginald, Charles Mortimer as Durand, John Manning as Batter, Samuel Perfitt as Falcon, Henry Power as James, George Gillett as Wharton, Henry Grant as Barkins, Mrs. Atkinson as Mme. Fauchon, Mary A. Victor as Bobbin, Lizzie Mandelbert as Lizzie, Alice Denvil as Mrs. Daroc, Mrs. Dearlove as Grace.

FLOWERS OF THE FOREST, THE: A GIPSY STORY// D 3a// J. B. Buckstone// **Adelphi**, Mar. 1847, with C. J. Smith as Capt. Lorrock, Charles Boyce as Alfred, James Worrell as Leybourne, Mr. Freeborn as Headborough, Emma Harding as Lady Agnes, O. Smith as Ishmael, Mme. Celeste as Cynthia, Sarah Woolgar as Lemuel, Paul Bedford as The Kinchin, Mrs. Fitzwilliam as Starlight Bess; Aug. 1859, with J. L. Toole, Kate Kelly, Mrs. Billington/ **Haymarket**, Aug. 1848, with C. J. Smith as Capt. Lavrock, Charles Boyce as Alfred, James Worrell as Leybourne, Mr. Morgan as Linton, Mr. Aldridge as Mayfield, Edward Wright as Cheap John, Emma Harding as Lady Agnes, Miss M. Taylor as Abigail, Miss Taylor as Winifred, O. Smith as Ishmael, Mr. Glennaire as Pharos, Mme. Celeste as Cynthia, Sarah Woolgar as Lemuel, Paul Bedford as The Kinchin/ Scenery by Pitt & Johnstone/ Music by E. Fitzwilliam & Alfred Mellon/ **Marylebone**, Nov. 1848, with J. B. Buckstone, Mrs. Fitzwilliam/ **Astley's**, Mar. 1867, with W. Arthur as Capt. Lavrock, W. T. Richardson as Alfred, W. Corri as Leyborne, E. Atkins as Cheap John, Miss Marion as Lady Agnes, Nelly Clifton as Abigale, James Fernandez as Ishmael, Annie Richardson as Cynthia, Edith Stuart as Lemuel, W. H. Stephens as the Kinchin, Ellen Thirlwall as Starlight Bess, Mrs. Caulfield as Hagar/ **Grecian**, Dec. 1866, with Henry Grant as Capt. Lavrock, William James as Alfred, John Manning as Cheap John, Henry Power as Headborough, Samuel Perfitt as Gilbert, Emma Victor as Abigail, Charles Mortimer as Ishmael, W. Shirley as Pharos, Alice Denvil as Cynthia, Lizzie Mandelbert as Lemuel, J. Jackson as The Kinchin, Mrs. Atkinson as Hager, Mary A. Victor as Bess/ **Sad. Wells**, Oct. 1868, with L. Smythe as Capt. Lorrock, Mr. Newbound as Alfred, Richard Edgar as Cheap John, Mr. Jefferson as Mayfield, Mr. Foxcroft as Leybourn, Miss Hill as Lady Agnes, Miss Falkland as as Abigail, Miss Herbert as Winifred, Miss Hazlewood as Cynthia, J. H. Fitzpatrick as Ishmael, W. H. Abel as Pharoah, Mr. Lacey as Lemuel, J. H. Loome as The Kinchen, Mrs. G. Howe as Hagar, Miss Seymour as Elpsy, Miss Williams as Starlight Bess.

FLY AND THE WEB, THE// C 2a// Adolphus Troughton// **Strand**, Feb. 1866.

FLYING COLOURS; OR, CROSSING THE FRONTIER// C 2a// H. C. Coape// Adelphi, May 1847, with Benjamin Webster as Capt. Sans-souci, Mr. Lambert as Duke de Sombreuse, Charles Selby as Col. Amadou, Sarah Woolgar as Margaret, Mme. Celeste as Helene de Montéreau, Ellen Chaplin as Justine/ Scenery by Pitt & Johnstone.

FLYING DUTCHMAN, THE// D// n.a.// **Grecian**, Mar. 1861, with J. Jackson as Capt. Peppercoal, Henry Power as Smutta, R. H. Lingham as Lt. Mowbray, Mr. Smithson as Rockalda, Alfred Rayner as Vanderdecken, John Manning as Von Brummel, William James as Toby, Henry Grant as Tom, Jane Coveney as Lestelle, Harriet Coveney as Lucy.

FLYING DUTCHMAN, THE; OR, THE PHANTOM SHIP// C 3a// Edward Fitzball// **Sad. Wells**, Mar. 1838, with Mr. James as Peppercoal, James Worrell as Lt. Mowbray, Stephen Smith as Willis, Mr. Gay as Von Swigs, Mr. Rogers as Von Bummell, Mr. Forrester as Toby Varnish, Mr. Campbell as Vanderdecken, Mr. George as Rockalda, Miss Beresford as Lestelle, Miss Chartley as Lucy/ **Victoria**, Oct. 1841, with Mr. James as Peppercoal, C. Williams as Mowbray, John Gardner as Von Bummell, William Seaman as Toby Varnish, Mr. Wilton as Willis, John Dale as Vanderdecken, James Howard as Smutta, Charles Morelli as Von Swiggs, Mr. Cullen as Rockalda, Mrs. George Lee as Lestelle, Mrs. Howard as Lucy; Nov. 1853, with Alfred Saville as Capt. Peppercoal, Mr. Moreland as Mowbray, John Hudspeth as Von Bummell, T. E. Mills as Toby Varnish, N. T. Hicks as Vanderdecken, F. H. Henry as Willis, Mr. Morrison as Von Swiggs, Mr. Hitchinson as Rockalda, Miss Dansor as Lestelle, Miss Laporte as Lucy/ **Adelphi**, July 1856, with Charles Selby as Capt. Peppercoal, J. G. Shore as Lt. Mowbray, Edward Wright as Von Bummel, Benjamin Webster as Toby Varnish, Mr. Moreland as Von Swiggs, Mme. Celeste as Vanderdecken, Mary Keeley as Lestelle, James Bland as Rockalda, Kate Kelly as Lucy.

FLYING FROM JUSTICE// D 4a// Mark Melford// **Sadler's Wells**, June 1891.

FLYING SCUD, THE; OR, A FOUR-LEGGED FORTUNE// D 4a// Dion Boucicault// **Grecian**, May 1868, with Charles Mortimer as Capt. Goodge, Henry Grant as Col. Mulligan, J. Jackson as Mo Davis, Samuel Perfitt as Chouser, W. Shirley as Quail, Lizzie Mandelbert as Lord Woodbie, George Conquest as Gosling, William James as Meredith, Mary A. Victor as as Buckskin, Alice Denvil as Julia, Miss De Lacie as Katey/ **Adelphi**, Aug. 1868, with John Billington as Meredith, Henry Ashley as Capt. Goodge, J. G. Taylor as Davis, C. H. Stephenson as Col. Mulligan, George Belmore as Gosling, Charlotte Saunders as Bob Buckskin, Maria Harris as Woodbie/ **Olympic**, Aug. 1871, with George Belmore as Gosling, A. D. Holman as Goodge, Edgar W. Garden as Capt. Mulligan,

John Russell as Davis, Mr. Davis as Chowser, E. Newbound as Quail, Mr. Hollman as Woodbie, Charles Warner as Meredith, E. Garden Jr. as Buckskin, Miss Alma as Ned, Miss Beckett as Dickey, Miss Davis as Sam, Miss Stevens as Harry, Miss Sutherland as Julia, Nelly Harris as Katey.

FLYING VISIT, A// C 1a// Mrs. W. Greet// **Criterion**, Nov. 1889/ **Princess's**, July 1894, with Roland Atwood, Kate Bealby.

FOGGED// F 1a// n.a.// **Drury Lane**, Aug. 1882, with John Morris in 7 char. parts, J. Elmore as Twibbletop, Augustus Cook as Jumbles, Miss Delphine as May.

FOGGERTY'S FAIRY// C 3a// W. S. Gilbert// **Criterion**, Dec. 1881, with Charles Wyndham, William Blakeley, Alfred Maltby, Rose Saker, Mary Rorke, Kate Rorke, Mrs. Alfred Mellon, Mrs. John Wood.

FOILED// D 3a// Warwick Buckland// **St. Geo. Hall**, Oct. 1890.

FOILED// D 1a// J. R. Alberton// **Globe**, Oct. 1891, with P. Barton as Richlee, Charles Barrett as Verance, Norman Clark as Downie, Lilian Lewis as Pollie, Winifred Elliott as Mabel.

FOILED BY FATE// D 4a// J. Darlison// **West London**, Oct. 1900.

FOLLE FARINE// D// Adap. by Walter Avondale fr novel of Ouida// **Sadler's Wells**, Oct. 1884.

FOLLIES OF A NIGHT, THE// C// Adap. by Thomas Holcroft fr F of Beaumarchais// **Haymarket**, May 1844, with Henry Holl as Duke de Chartres, Mr. Caulfield as Brassic, William Strickland as Duggerdraft, C. J. Mathews as Palliot, Mme. Vestris as Duchess de Chartres, Miss Lee as Mlle. Duval/ **Sad. Wells**, Mar. 1850, with Henry Marston as Count Almaviva, Mr. Dolman as Pedro, Miss Fitzpatrick as Hannibal, William Hoskins as Figaro, Henry Nye as Antonio, Mrs. Brougham as Countess Almaviva, Teresa Bassano as Susanna.

FOLLIES OF A NIGHT, THE// C 2a// Adap. by J. R. Planché fr F of Beaumarchais// **Drury Lane**, Oct. 1842, with Charles Hudson as Duke de Chartres, Mr. Roberts as Count de Brissac, Henry Compton as Druggendraft, C. J. Mathews as Palliot, Mme. Vestris as Duchess de Chartres, Miss Turpin as Mlle. Duval/ **Princess's**, Mar. 1846, with James Vining as Duke de Chartres, Augustus Harris as Count de Brissac, Henry Compton as Dr. Druggendraft, C. J. Mathews as Palliot, Mme. Vestris as Duchess de Chartres, Miss E. Honner as Mlle. Duval/ **Olympic**, 1846, with Charles Walcot, Frank Chanfrau/ **Lyceum**, Oct. 1849, with Robert Roxby as Duke de Chartres, Frank Matthews as Dr. Druggendraft, C. J. Mathews as Pierre Palliot, Mme. Vestris as Duchess de Chartres, Mrs. Julia Glover as Mlle. Duval/ **Grecian**, May 1855, with Basil Potter as Duke de Chartres, Thomas Roberts as Count de Brissac, Eaton O'Donnell as Dr. Druggendraft, Richard Phillips as Palliot, Jane Coveney as Duchess of Chartres, Maria Simpson as Mlle. Duval/ **Sad. Wells**, Nov. 1855, with William Belford as Duke de Cartres, Mr. Haywell as de Brissac, Mr. Barrett as Dr. Druggendraft, Frederic Robinson as Palliot, Mr. Righton as Antoine, Eliza Travers as Duchess de Chartres, Caroline Parkes as Mlle. Duval.

FOLLIES OF THE DAY, THE; OR, FAST LIFE// D 4a// H. P. Grattan & Joseph Eldred// **Pavilion**, July 1883.

FOLLY// C 2a// n.a.// **Sad. Wells**, Apr. 1862, with James Johnstone as Col. Strictly, A. Baildon as Fairly, Henry Forrester as Sir Robert, Miss H. Percy as Julia, Emily Dowton as Agnes, Miss Heath as Letty.

FOLLY OF AGE, A// C 1a// Arthur Ingram// **Opera Comique**, Nov. 1894, with Hurdman Lucas as Dick Ardingley, C. Medwin as Richard Ardingley, Zilla Nanson as Violet, Beatrice Summers as Kate.

FOOL AND HIS MONEY, A// C 3a// H. J. Byron// **Globe**, July 1878, with Edward Righton as Vandeleur, G. H. Grainger as Pentland, J. L. Toole as "Chawles", W. Herbert as Ransome, Henry Westland as Milligan, Ellen Meyrick as Kate, Eliza Johnstone as Mary/ Scenery by John Johnstone.

FOOL OF THE FAMILY, THE// C 3a// Fergus Hume// **Duke of York's**, Jan. 1896, with Robert Pateman as Col. Cardington, Charles Cartwright as Grison, H. B. Irving as Lambert, Wilfred Forster as Saville, Lyston Lyle as Marlin, Gertrude Kingston as Rose, Lena Ashwell as Kitty, Marie Lyons as Tilly/ Scenery by W. T. Hemsley & Bruce Smith/ Limelight by Mr. Digby.

FOOL'S MATE// C 1a// F. W. Broughton// **Toole's**, Dec. 1889/ **Avenue**, Feb. 1890, with Fred Terry as Earl of Somerdale, Nutcombe Gould as Egerton, Mary Kingsley as Mary, Gracie Murielle as Dorothy.

FOOL'S PARADISE, A// Play 3a// Sidney Grundy// **Gaiety**, Feb. 1889/ **Garrick**, Jan. 1892, with John Hare, Kate Rorke, Olga Nethersole, H. B. Irving, Gilbert Hare/ **Coronet**, Mar. 1901.

FOOL'S REVENGE, THE// D 3a// Tom Taylor/ **Sad. Wells**, Oct. 1859, with Henry Marston as Manfredi, Mr. Meagreson as Malatesta, Samuel Phelps as Bertuccio, Frederic Robinson as Serafino, William Belford as Torelli, Charles Seyton as Ascolti, T. C. Harris as Ordolaffi, Caroline Hill as Ascanio, Caroline Parkes as Ginevra, Miss Atkinson as Francesca, Miss Heath as Fiordelisa, Mrs. Henry Marston as Brigitta/ Scenery by Charles James; Oct. 1869, with Samuel Phelps as Bertuccio, James Johnstone as Malatesta, J. G. Rosiere as Galeotto, Edmund Phelps as dell' Aquilla, Edgar Newbound as Torelli, Mr. Howard as Ascolti, T. W. Ford as Ordelaffi, Miss Gerald as Ginevra, Miss Fitzgerald as Francesca, Margaret Eburne as Fiordelisa, Mrs. E. F. Edgar as Brigitta/ **Princess's**, Apr. 1860, with John Ryder as Manfredi, Mr. Graham as Malatesta, Samuel

Phelps as Bertuccio, J. G. Shore as Dell'Aquila, Frederick Villiers as Torelli, Robert Cathcart as Ordelaffi, Edmund Garden as Ascolti, Miss B. Adams as Ginevra, Miss Atkinson as Francesca, Mrs. Weston as Brigitta, Caroline Heath as Fiordelisa; Dec. 1880, with Edwin Booth as Bertuccio, William Redmund as Manfredi, John Beauchamp as Malatesta, F. Charles as Torelli, P. C. Beverley as Ordelaffi, C. W. Garthorne as Ascolti, Charles Cartwright as dell'Aquila, John Gardiner as Ascanio, Violet Temple as Ginevra, Mrs. Hermann Vezin as Francesca, Miss Gerard as Fiordelisa, Mrs. Lyons as Brigitta/ **Queen's**, Dec. 1869/ **Adelphi**, June 1882, with Edwin Booth as Bertuccio, Samuel Fisher as Manfredi, Edward Price as Malatesta, Robert Pateman as Torelli, J. G. Shore as Ordelaffi, Eben. Plympton as Dell'Aquila, Miss Leslie Bell as Ginevra, Ellen Meyrick as Francesca, Bella Pateman as Fiordellsa.

FOOL'S TRICK, A// F// Adelene Votieri// **St. Geo. Hall**, June 1891.

FOOTBALL KING, THE// D 4a// George Gray// **Elephant & Castle**, July 1896.

FOOTMARKS IN THE SNOW// D 3a// Edward Towers// **City of London**, Oct. 1867.

FOR A CHILD'S SAKE// D 4a// Henry Herman & Montague Turner// **Surrey**, Dec. 1899.

FOR A LIFE// D 4a// Adap. by J. J. M'Closkey fr novel of Marcus Clarke, His Natural Life// **Surrey**, May 1889.

FOR AULD LANG SYNE// D 4a// Seymour Hicks & Frederick Latham// **Lyceum**, Oct. 1900, with Leonard Boyne as Earl of Fellsdale, Basset Roe as Lord Estcourt, William Mollison as Bird, J. H. Barnes as Gale, W. L. Abingdon as Capt. Carey, Fanny Brough as Daisy, Irene Rooke as Mary, Lily Hanbury as Dawn.

FOR BONNIE PRINCE CHARLIE// D 4a// Joseph Clarke// **Shaftesbury**, Jan. 1897.

FOR CHARITY'S SAKE// CD 1a// C. S. Fawcett// **Comedy**, Jan. 1891, with William Wyes as Nubbles, W. F. Hawtrey as Catterpole, Wilfred Draycott as Esher, Charles Milton as Jones, Lydia Cowell as Charity/ **Strand**, Feb. 1894.

FOR CLAUDIA'S SAKE// C 3a// Mabel Freund-Lloyd// **Vaudeville**, July 1891, with H. A. Saintsbury as Sir Lionel, Acton Bond as Lord Vivian, Alfred Cross as Capt. Charteris, Leo Leather as Stonewall, Foster Courtenay as Gardener, Edith Jordan as Sylvia, Ida Logan as Claudia, Laura Laughton as Lady Charteris, Mabel Freund-Lloyd as Mrs. Simmons.

FOR DEAR LIFE// D 4a// William Muskerry// **Victoria**, June 1873.

FOR ENGLAND// D 5a// Sutton Vane// **Pavilion**, May 1893.

FOR ENGLAND'S SAKE// D 4a// Dram. by Henrietta Lindley fr novel of Robert Cromie// **Haymarket**, Aug. 1889.

FOR EVER// D 7a// Paul Meritt & George Conquest// **Surrey**, Oct. 1882, with A. C. Hatton, Algernon Sims, George Conquest, Bella Titheradge, Alice Raynor.

FOR FAMILY FAME; OR, THE SEA AND ITS DEAD// D Pro & 3a// Bernard McDonald// **Royalty**, Mar. 1895.

FOR GOOD OR EVIL// Play 3a// Mrs. A. J. Macdonnell// **Royalty**, June 1894.

FOR HER CHILD'S SAKE// D 1a// Charles Young// **Terry's**, Mar. 1890, with Oscar Ayde as Ormonde, A. Ellis as Marsham, James Nelson as Verschoyle, Miss M. A. Giffard as Edith, Helen Leyton as Geraldine.

FOR HER SAKE// D 1a// E. B. Aveling ("Alec Nelson")// **Olympic**, June 1888.

FOR HONOUR'S SAKE// D 3a// C. H. Hazlewood// **Britannia**, Oct. 1873.

FOR KING AND COUNTRY// D// Edmund Leathes// **Gaiety**, May 1883.

FOR LIFE THROUGH THICK AND THIN// D 2a// J. G. Taylor// **Alexandra**, Mar. 1868.

FOR LOVE OF PRIM// Play 1a// Eden Philpotts// **Court**, Jan. 1899.

FOR LOVE OR MONEY// C 3a// Andrew Halliday// **Vaudeville**, Apr. 1870.

FOR OLD LOVE'S SAKE// CD 3a// Stanley Rogers & H. Kimm// **Royalty**, May 1886.

FOR OLD VIRGINIA// Play 1a// Henry Herman// **Grand**, June 1891.

FOR SALE// D 3a// John Douglass Jr.// **Standard**, Feb. 1869.

FOR THE CROWN// Play 4a// Adap. by John Davidson fr F of François Coppée, Pour La Couronne// **Lyceum**, Feb. 1890, with Ian Robertson as King Stephen, Charles Dalton as Prince Michael, Johnston Forbes Robertson as Brancomir, W. Macintosh as Ibrahim, Frank Gillmore as Lazare, Winifred Emery as Bazilde, Sarah Brooke as Anna, Mrs. Patrick Campbell as Militza/ Scenery by Walter Hann, Joseph Harker, Hawes Craven & T. E. Ryan/ Music comp. by Carl Armbruster.

FOR THE CZAR// T 1a// Percival Sykes// **Strand**, Nov. 1896.

FOR THE HONOUR OF THE FAMILY// CD 3a// Adap. fr F of Emile Augier, Mariage d'Olympe// **Comedy**, June 1897.

FOR THE KING// D 4a// Walter Howard & Sidney Pease// **Elephant & Castle**, Feb. 1900.

FOR THE SAKE OF A WOMAN// D 4a// W. J. Patmore// **Pavilion**, Sept. 1900.

FORBIDDEN FRUIT// D 4a// Adap. by F. M. Abbotts fr F of Emile Augier, Paul Forester// **Lyceum**, Nov. 1869, with Brandon Ellis as Michael Jocelyn, Mr. Allerton as Hugh Jocelyn, Charles Coghlan as Frederick, Beatrix Shirley as Ida Tyrone, Isabelle Armour as Constance.

FORBIDDEN FRUIT// C 3a// Adap. by Dion Boucicault fr F of Emile Augier, Paul Forester// **Adelphi**, July 1880, with J. G. Taylor as Serjeant Buster, Robert Pateman as Cato Dove, E. H. Brooke as Derringer, Harwood Cooper as Podd, Harry Proctor as Swallbach, Bella Pateman as Mrs. Dove, Helen Barry as Arabella, Marie Williams as Zulu/ **Vaudeville**, May 1883.

FORCED FROM HOME// D 4a// W. G. Wills// **Duke's**, Feb. 1880, with A. C. Calmour, J. B. Johnstone, May Holt, Fanny Brough.

FORCED MARRIAGE, THE; OR, THE RETURN FROM SIBERIA// D 2a// Mrs. T. P. Cooke// **Surrey**, Dec. 1842.

FOREIGN AFFAIRS; OR, THE COURT OF QUEEN ANNE// C 2a// Benjamin Webster// **Haymarket**, Aug. 1841, with Mlle. [sic] Celeste as Count St. Louis, Robert Strickland as Fitzstoutz, Benjamin Webster as Courtall, Miss Charles as Lady Grace, Mrs. W. Clifford as Marchioness of Dumbarton, Priscilla Horton as Lady Bell, Mrs. Stirling as Baroness Fitzstoutz.

FOREIGN AIRS AND NATIVE GRACES// C// W. Moncrieff// **Haymarket**, July 1839, with Robert Strickland as Oldcourt, Benjamin Webster as Alfred, J. B. Buckstone as Buckland, Mrs. Fitzwilliam in 4 char. parts, Mrs. Frank Matthews as Fanny/ Music by Mr. Blewitt.

FOREIGN POLICY// Play 1a// Arthur Conan Doyle// **Terry's**, June 1893, with Charles Charrington as Foreign Secretary, Edmund Maurice as Sir William, Herbert Waring as Prime Minister, Janet Achurch as Lady Clara, Esmé Beringer as Miss Ida.

FOREMAN OF THE WORKS, THE// D 4a// Dram. by George Fenn fr his novel The Parson o' Dumford// **Standard**, Mar. 1886.

FOREST KEEPER, THE// D 2a// Henry Holl// **Drury Lane**, Feb. 1860, with Charles Dillon as Reynold, Henry Mellon as Duchamp, Robert Roxby as Justin, Miss Page as Louise, Miss Howard as Mariette, Mr. Tilbury as Picardo, Fanny Thirwell as Annette.

FOREST OF BONDY, THE; OR, THE DOG OF MONTARGIS// D 3a// William Barrymore// **Sad. Wells**, Dec. 1838, with Mr. Dry as Col. Gontram, Dibdin Pitt as Seneschal, Mr. Cathcart as Lt. Macaire, Mr. Conquest as Bertand, Mr. Coney as Lt. Landry, Mr. Blanchard Jr. as Capt. Didier, Dog Carlo as Dog Hector, Robert Honner as Dumb Boy, Miss Cooke as Dame Gertrude, Mrs. Robert Honner as Ursula/ **Victoria**, Jan. 1840, with Mr. Cony as Landry, Mr. Blanchard as Capt. Aubry, Mr. Hicks as Lt. Macaire, Mr. King as Col. Gontram, Edward Burton as Seneschal, Mr. Manders as Bertrand, Miss Stoker as the Dumb Boy, Mrs. Howard as Ursula, Mrs. France as Gertrude/ **Olympic**, Feb. 1847 (prod. under reverse title, The Dog of Montargis; or, The Forest of Bondy), with Henry Butler as Col. Gontram, Mr. Turnour as Seneschal, Mr. Blanchard as Capt. Aubri, Mr. Cony as Lt. Landry, Mr. Morland as Lt. Macaire, J. W. Collier as Bertrand, Dog Hector as Dragon, Mrs. Griffiths as Dame Gertrude, Mrs. Boyce as Ursula/ **Grecian**, Apr. 1853, with Edwin Dixon as Seneschal, Eaton O'Donnell as Col. Gontram, Charles Horn as Col. Aubri, Richard Phillips as Lt. Landry, Basil Potter as Lt. Macaire, Jane Coveney as Ursula, Harriet Coveney as Eloi, Miss Johnstone as Gertrude, Dog Hector as Dog Dragon.

FOREST OF REMIVAL, THE// D// n.a.// **Sad. Wells**, Aug. 1838, with James Villiers as Samuel, John Webster as Charles, Mr. Conquest as Thomas, J. W. Collier as Durand, Charles Montague as Colon, Dibdin Pitt as Prynce, Richard Phillips as Conde, Miss Richardson as Annette, Miss Cooke as Mme. Simon, Miss Pincott as Ephine.

FOREST ROSE AND THE YANKEE PLOUGH-BOY, THE// C 2a// Samuel Woodworth// **Adelphi**, Oct. 1851, with Josh Silsbee as Jonathan Plough-Boy, James Worrell as Bellamy, Mr. Caulfield as Blandford, William Cullenford as Miller, George Honey as William, Sarah Woolgar as Harriet, Ellen Chaplin as Sally Forest.

FORESTERS, THE// D 3a// T. J. Serle// **Cov. Garden**, Oct. 1838, with John Vandenhoff as Karlstein, Mr. Frazer as Adolphus, James Anderson as Leopold, Mr. Warde as Count Hassenfeldt, George Bennett as Maj. Bortheim, John Pritt Harley as Buzzendorf, George Bartley as Dalner, Charles Diddear as Everard, Mr. Waldron as Luke, Mrs. Mary Warner as Mme. Karlstein, Miss Rainforth as Viola, Priscilla Horton as Beatrix/ Music by E. J. Loder.

FORESTERS, ROBIN HOOD AND MAID MARION, THE// D 4a// Alfred Tennyson// **Lyceum**, Mar. 1892/ **Daly's**, Oct. 1893.

FORGER, THE; OR, GOOD AND EVIL// D 4a// n.a.// **Elephant & Castle**, Nov. 1886.

FORGER'S VOW, THE; OR, SIDI BAROSSA, THE BEDOUIN CHIEF OF JARRA// D 3a// G. D. Pitt// **Victoria**, Apr. 1847, with James Howard as Capt. Hallington, Mr. Hitchinson as Lt. Murray, N. T. Hicks as Henry Melrose and as Abdallah, F. H. Henry as Hamed, John Gardner as Phelps, Alfred Raymond as Edwin Melrose, John Dale as Sidi Barossa, Mr. Franklin as Ben Aly, J. B. Johnstone as Mohamed, Annette Vincent as Adelaide, Julia Johnstone as Matilda, Lydia Pearce as Ziska, Mrs. Cooke as Mrs. Mump.

FORGET AND FORGIVE; OR, LOVE ME, LEAVE ME NOT// D 4a// Dram. by George Conquest partly fr story of Pierce Egan// **Grecian**, Apr. 1861, with Alfred Rayner as Dick Stoney, George Conquest as Gull, Walter Holland as

Fairland, William James as Moreland, Mrs. Charles Dillon as Adele, George Gillett as Anderson, Thomas Mead as Lake, Jane Coveney as Edith.

FORGET-ME-NOT// D 3a// Herman Merivale & F. C. Grove// **Lyceum**, Aug. 1879, with Johnston Forbes Robertson as Sir Horace Welby, Stanislaus Calhaem as Prince Malleotti, Frank Tyars as Barrato, Genevieve Ward as Stephanie, Louise Willes as Alice Verney, Mrs. Leigh Murray as Mrs. Foley, Eily Paton as Rose/ Scenery by Hawes Craven/ Music by Hamilton Clarke; Mar. 1888 with W. H. Vernon as Sir Horace Welby, C. W. Somerset as Prince Malcotti, Leonard Outram as Barrato, Dorothy Dene as Alice Verney, Genevieve Ward as Stephanie/ **POW**, Feb. 1880, with John Clayton, Genevieve Ward, Kate Pattison, Mrs. Leigh Murray/ **Olympic**, Jan. 1883, with W. H. Vernon as Sir Horace Welby, David Fisher as Prince Malleotti, Philip Beck as Barrato, Lucy Buckstone as Alive Verney, Mrs. Leigh Murray as Mrs. Foley, Genevieve Ward as Stéphanie/ **Avenue**, May 1892.

FORGIVE AND FORGET// C 1a// n.a.// **Olympic**, Oct. 1838.

FORGIVEN// C 4a// James Albery// **Globe**, Mar. 1872, with Charles Flockton as Lord Dart, Charles Neville as Orleigh Dart, David Fisher as Fallow, E. W. Garden as Pole, Henry Compton as Cudlipp, H. J. Montague as Redruth, Louisa Moore as Lady Maude, Nelly Harris as Laura, Carlotta Addison as Rose/ Scenery by Hawes Craven, Dayes, & Cany/ Music by J. T. Haynes.

FORGIVENESS// C 4a// J. Comyns Carr// **St. James's**, Dec. 1891, with Nutcombe Gould as Sir Edward, Arthur Bourchier as Earle, H. H. Vincent as Rev. Muir, E. W. Gardiner as Tommy, Fred Everill as Tansworth, H. De Lange as Plack, George Alexander as Hamilton, Dolores Drummond as Mrs. Badger, Laura Graves as Lucy, Fanny Coleman as Miss Menkin, Marion Terry as Nina/ Scenery by H. P. Hall & W. Hann.

FORLORN HOPE, THE// D 3a// C. H. Hazlewood// **Britannia**, May 1871.

FORMOSA; OR, THE RAILROAD TO RUIN// D 4a// Dion Boucicault// **Drury Lane**, Aug. 1869, with Mr. Barrett as Doremus, Mr. Offord as Talbot, Mr. Woodfield as Merivale, J. A. Meade as Sadler, Mr. Wood as Bancroft, Mr. O'Neil as Harvey, Percy Corri as Burbage, J. B. Howard as Burroughs, Miss M. Brennan as Earl of Eden, Henry Irving as Kerr, David Fisher as Major Jorum, John Rouse as Boker, Britan [sic] Wright as Sanders, F. Charles as Spooner, Mrs. Billington as Mrs. Boker, Katherine Rogers as Jenny, Miss Macdonald as Edith, Miss Dalton as Nelly, Miss M. Elsworthy as Comtess de Vaurian, Miss Hudspeth as Mrs. Dudley/ Scenery by William Beverley/ Music by W. C. Levey; May 1891, with Charles Glenney as Burroughs, Katie James as Lord Eden, Mark Quinton as Kerr, Austin Melford as Maj. Jorum, Walter Russell as Doremous, Julian Cross as Boker, Harry Nicholls as Saunders, Cecil Crofton as Spooner, Ronald Power as Byfield, Jessie Millward as Jenny, Mrs. John Billington as Mrs. Boker, Mary Ansell as Nelly/ **Princess's**, Feb. 1870, with Richard Phillips as Dr. Doremus, Alfred Tapping as Sir John, Mr. Thomas as Merivale, Mr. Travers as Sadler, Mr. Chapman as Bancroft, C. Walters as Harvey, William Rignold as Burroughs, Miss E. Brennan as Earl of Eden, Lin Rayne as Kerr, Henry Ashley as Maj. Jorum, John Rouse as Boker, J. G. Taylor as Sanders, F. Charles as Spooner, W. H. Eburne as Dudley, Dan Leeson as Welch, Katherine Rogers as Formosa, Mrs. Billington as Mrs. Boker, Emma Barnett as Edith, Miss Lennox Grey as Nelly/ Scenery by F. Lloyds & Walter Hann/ **Adelphi**, Nov. 1877, with James Johnstone as Dr. Doremus, J. G. Shore as Kerr, Henry Sinclair as Jorum, Samuel Emery as Boker, Clara Jecks as Earl of Eden, Mrs. Billington as Mrs. Boker, Alma Murray as Edith, Miss Hudspeth as Nelly/ Scenery by Stafford Hall/ **Drury Lane**, May 1891.

FORSAKEN: AN EVERYDAY STORY// D// Frederick Marchant// **Victoria**, Mar. 1869.

FORTRESS, THE// F// H. Stocqueler// **Olympic**, Feb. 1848, with William Davidge as Maj. Snapperman, E. Morton as Leopold, Mr. Buxton as Kugel, Miss Walcott as Amelia, Miss Bromley as Minna.

FORTUNE'S FROLIC// F 1a// J. T. Allingham// **Victoria**, Mar. 1838, with R. Rayner as Roughhead, Mr. Loveday as Snacks, John Parry as Rattle, Mr. Phillips as John, William Davidge as Franks, Miss Wilson as Nancy, Mrs. Frank Matthews as Dolly, Mrs. Loveday as Margery/ **Olympic**, Mar. 1848, with Lysander Thompson as Roughhead, H. J. Turner as Old Snacks, John Kinloch as Rattle, Miss F. Matthews as Nancy, Miss F. Hamilton as Dolly, Mrs. H. Lee as Margery/ **Sad. Wells**, June 1863, with W. Worboys as Roughhead, J. W. Collier as Snacks, Mr. Britten as Frank, George Maynard as Rattle, Charles Crook as Clown, Emma Leslie as Nancy, Bessie Heath as Margery, Caroline Collier as Dolly.

FORTUNE'S FROLIC// F 1a// J. T. Allingham// **Grecian**, Feb. 1852, with Mr. Lindon as Robin, Eaton O'Donnell as Snacks, Edwin Dixon as Frank, Charles Horn as Ratree, Miss Morgan as Nancy, Miss Johnstone as Margery.

FORTUNE OF WAR, THE// Play 1a// Cosmo Hamilton// **Criterion**, May 1896, with W. L. Abingdon as Harcourt, Lottie Venne as Finette, Dorothy Wood as Lucille.

FORTUNES AND CHANCE OF WAR, THE; OR, THE GYPSEY HORSE STEALER// D 3a// n.a.// **Victoria**, Mar. 1849, with T. H. Higgie as Col. Manly, Mr. Henderson as Capt. Lindsay, Mr. Leake as Capt. Stanley, F. H. Henry as Old Joe, John Bradshaw as Mizen, J. T. Johnson as Marsden, G. F. Forman as Wildfire, Mr. Hitchinson as Trusty, James Howard as Slimp, Annette Vincent as Mary, Miss Barrowcliffe as Peggy.

FORTUNES OF SMIKE, THE; OR, A SEQUEL TO NICHOLAS NICKLEBY// D 2a// Edward Stirling// **Adelphi**, Mar. 1840.

FORTY AND FIFTY// F 1a// T. H. Bayly// **Olympic**, Mar. 1837, with John Liston as Lillywhite, James Vining as Altamont, Mr. Wyman as Peter, Miss Crawford as Clementina, Miss Goward as Jessy, Mrs. Orger as Mrs. Lillywhite; July 1848, with A. Younge as Lilywhite, Henry Butler as Altamont, Mr. Lawrence as Peter, Mrs. Gilbert as Mrs. Lilywhite/ **Victoria**, Sept. 1837, with Frank Matthews as Lilywhite, William Davidge as Peter, James Vining as Altamount, Mrs. Frank Matthews as Mrs. Lilywhite, Miss Crisp as Clemtina/ **Princess's**, May 1843, with Frank Matthews as Lilywhite, T. H. Higgie as Altamount, Robert Honnor as Peter, Mrs. Frank Matthews as Mrs. Lilywhite, Miss E. Honnor as Clementina, Miss Wilkenson as Jenny/ **Sad. Wells**, Aug. 1846, with A. Younge as Lilywhite, E. Morton as Altamont, Frank Graham as Peter, Mrs. Henry Marston as Mrs. Lilywhite, Miss Stephens as Clementina, Miss St. George as Jessy/ **Lyceum**, Dec. 1850, with Frank Matthews as Lilywhite, Mr. Clifford as Altamont, Mr. Simmonds as Peter, Mrs. Frank Matthews as Mrs. Lilywhite, Miss Kenworth as Clementina, Miss Martindale as Jessy/ **St. James's**, Oct. 1876, with Clifford Cooper as Lilywhite, George Darrell as Fitzwhite, Mr. Bauer as Peter, Miss Lavis as Mrs. Lilywhite, Miss Oscar Byrne as Clementina.

FORTY THIEVES, THE// D// George Conquest// **Cov. Garden**, Mar. 1837, with Mr. Thompson as Cassim, Mr. Tilbury as Ali Baba, John Webster as Ganem, Benjamin Webster as Mustapha, Mr. Beckett as Selim, J. Smith as Aleph, Miss Lee as Zelie, Miss Nicholson as Zaide, Mrs. Sarah Garrick as Cogia, Eliza Vincent as Morgiana, Mr. Harris as Abdallah, John Pritchard as Hassarac, James Worrell as Yuseph, R. McIan as Orcobrand, Robert Honner as Fraud/ **Sad. Wells**, Sept. 1839, with Mr. Dry as Ali Baba, W. D. Broadfoot as Cassion Baba, Mr. Elvin as Ganem, Mr. Conquest as Mustapha, Charles Montgomery as Abdallah, Mr. Aldridge as Orcobrand, Mrs. J. F. Saville as Cogia, Miss Cooke as Zaide, Miss Norman as Zelie, Miss Pincott as Morgiana/ **Grecian**, Nov. 1863, with James Jackson as Ali Baba, George Gillett as Ganim, Ben Summersby as Mustapha, W. Shirley as Cassim, Henry Grant as Abdalla, J. B. Steele as Hasarac, Miss K. Cornish as Cogian, Marie Brewer as Zadie, Mary A. Victor as Morgiana.

FORTY WINKS// C 1a// George Roberts// **St. James's**, June 1862, with George Vining as Poppyfield, Miss Herbert as Mrs. Honiton.

FOSTER SISTERS; OR, THE VILLAGE ORPHAN// D 2a// n.a.// **Grecian**, May 1855, with F. Charles as Viscount de Normes, Basil Potter as Count d'Avrigny, Richard Phillips as Eugene, Mrs. Charles Montgomery as Mlle. de Query, Harriet Coveney as Annette Perrot, Jane Coveney, Miss Johnstone as Mme. Marguerite.

FOUND// D 4a// Frederick Hawley ("Fred Haywell")// **Gaiety**, Nov. 1883.

FOUND AT SEA// D// n.a.// **Victoria**, Apr. 1863.

FOUND BRUMMY// F 1a// Alfred Maltby// **Princess's**, Sept. 1874.

FOUND DEAD IN THE STREET// D Pro & 2a// W. R. Waldron// **Grecian**, Apr. 1873/ **Marylebone**, Apr. 1882.

FOUND DROWNED; OR, OUR MUTUAL FRIEND// D 4a// Dram. by G. F. Rowe fr Charles Dickens's Our Mutual Friend// **Opera Comique**, Dec. 1870.

FOUND DYING; OR, THE OLD WATCHMAN'S SECRET (alt. title, Found Dying in the Streets; or, a Will Made in a Snowdrift on the Flyleaf of a Rake's Diary)// D 3a// Matthew Wardhaugh// **Elephant & Castle**, May 1877.

FOUND IN A FOUR-WHEELER!// F// T. J. Williams// **New Royalty**, Apr. 1866.

FOUNDED ON FACTS// F 1a// J. P. Wooler// **Olympic**, Aug. 1848, with A. Younge as Capt. Harwood, Henry Compton as Skeptic, Henry Butler as Lt. Oakly, Mrs. Leigh Murray as Mrs. Skeptic, Miss Murray as Helen/ **Sad. Wells**, Apr. 1849, with Mr. Williams as Capt. Harwood, William Belford as Lt. Oakley, A. Younge as Skeptic, Miss Huddart as Mrs. Skeptic, Miss Murray as Helen/ **Grecian**, June 1857, with Richard Phillips as Lt. Oakly, Eaton O'Donnell as Capt. Harwood, Mr. Smithson as George, John Manning as Skeptic, Jane Coveney as Mrs. Skeptic, Harriet Coveney as Helen.

FOUNDERED FORTUNE, A// D Pro & 4a// W. E. Morton// **Elephant & Castle**, Dec. 1890.

FOUNDLING, THE// F 3a// William Lestocq & E. M. Robson// **Terry's**, Aug. 1894, with Charles Groves as Maj. Cotton, Sidney Brough as Pennell, Huntley Wright as Hucklebridge, Oswald Yorke as Stanton, George Warde as Sir Nicholas, Ellis Jeffreys as Alice, Susie Vaughan as Mrs. Cotton, Fanny Erris as Sophie, Minnie Clifford as Miss Ussher, Emmeline Orford as Maybud/ Scenery by Bruce Smith/ Prod. by Edward Terry.

FOUNDLING OF FORTUNE, THE; OR, NEXT OF KIN// D Pro & 3a// F. G. Cheatham// **Victoria**, Apr. 1867.

FOUNDLING OF THE FOREST, THE// D// William Dimond// **Sad. Wells**, Sept. 1842, with Mr. Lyon as Valmont, Mr. Lynne as Longueville, C. J. Bird as Florian, John Herbert as Le Clair, C. J. Smith as Bertrand, P. Williams as Gaspard, Charles Fenton as Sanguino, Caroline Rankley as Geraldine, Mrs. Richard Barnett as Rosabelle, Mrs. Henry Marston as Monica, Miss Richardson as Eugenia.

FOUNDLINGS, THE// C 5a// Adap. by J. B. Buckstone fr F// **Haymarket**, June 1852, with John Parselle as Lord Moonshyne, Leigh Murray as Greatrakes, Henry Howe as Jackson, J. B. Buckstone as Dixon, Mr. Lambert as Dr. Juniper, Robert Keeley as Moleskin, George Braid as Lucas, Mr. Edwards as James, Mrs. L. S. Buckingham as Lady Emily, Mrs. Leigh Murray as Mrs. Armitage, Amelia Vining as Esther, Mrs. Fitzwilliam as Pamela, Mrs. Stanley as Mrs. Keys, Miss E. Woulds as Mrs. Grubb.

FOUNDLINGS, THE; OR, THE OCEAN OF LIFE// D 7a// Adap by Leopold Lewis fr F, La Dame de la Halle// **Sad. Wells**, Oct. 1881, with Edward Price as Cassade, William McIntyre as Leonard, A. C. Lilly as Dumont, Eric Dering as Marquis de Savannes, Harry Proctor as Jean-Marie, Fredrick Moreland as Baptiste, E. Emery as Capt. Volney, J. E. Mortimer as Bontemps, Fuller Mellish as Caboche, Rose Leclercq as Celestine, Maud Howard as Javotte, Annie Merton as Genevieve, Amy Fanchette as Countess de Savannes/ Scenery by John Johnson/ Music by John Barnard/ Prod. by F. B. Chatterton.

FOUR COUSINS, THE// C 2a// Augustus Mayhew & Sutherland Edwards// **Globe**, May 1871, with Fred Dewar as Dr. Flam, William Worboys as Samuel Scudder, Dan Leeson as Hobson, Isabella Armour as Julia, Emily Burns as Mrs. Brooms.

FOUR LITTLE GIRLS// F 3a// Walter Craven// **Criterion**, July 1897, with James Welch as Muggeridge, J. H. Barnes as Raddlestone, William Blakeley as Tyndal, Richard Lambart as Dick, Kenneth Douglas as Percy, Mary A. Victor as Mrs. Humbleton, Emily Miller as Mrs. Middleage, Sydney Fairbrother as Charlotte.

FOUR MOWBRAYS, THE// C 1a// n.a.// **Drury Lane**, Feb. 1854/ **Olympic**, Aug. 1866, with John Maclean as Old Wilton, Edward Atkins as Primrose, Walter Joyce as Charles Mobray, Ellen Farren as Peggy, Master Percy Roselle as Marmaduke, Hector, Gobbleton, and Foppington Mobray.

FOUR SISTERS, THE; OR, WOMAN'S WORTH AND WOMAN'S WRONGS// F 1a// W. Bayle Bernard// **Eng. Opera House** (Lyceum), Apr. 1843, with John Ayliffe as Mr. Merton, J. S. Balls as Beauchamp, John Courtney as Sam Snaffle, Mrs. Waylett in 4 parts, Mrs. Harris as Susan.

FOUR STAGES OF LIFE, THE// D 4a// John Vollaire// **Surrey**, Apr. 1862.

FOURTEEN DAYS// C 3a// Adap. by H. J. Byron fr F of P. E. Gondinet & Alexandre Bisson// **Criterion**, Mar. 1882, with Charles Wyndham, William Blakeley, Lytton Sothern, Mary Rorke, Kate Rorke.

FOX AND GOOSE// F 1a// n.a.// **Princess's**, 1878, with T. P. Haynes as Tom, T. W. Thorne as Capt. Rambleton, Mr. Murray as Varnish, Fanny Lee as Ellen.

FOX AND THE WOLF, THE// F 1a// n.a.// **Sad. Wells**, Aug. 1837, with N. T. Hicks as Rambleton, C. H. Pitt as Varnish, Mr. Rogers as Tom, Lavinia Melville as Ellen.

FOX CHASE, THE// C 5a// Dion Boucicault// **St. James's**, May 1864.

FOX VERSUS GOOSE// FC// William Brough & J. D. Stockton// **Strand**, May 1869.

FRA ANGELO// Play 5a// W. C. Russell// **Haymarket**, Aug. 1865.

FRANCE IN 1792// C 1a// n.a.// **Grecian**, Oct. 1855, with Richard Phillips as Legrange, Basil Potter as Count de Beauvilliers, Mr. Smithson as Gerard, Jane Coveney as Marietta.

FRANCESCA, A DREAM OF VENICE// D 5a// Edmund Falconer// **Lyceum**, Mar. 1858, with Mrs. Charles Young, Edmund Falconer, Gaston Murray.

FRANCESCA DA RIMINI// D Pro & 4a// F. Marion Crawford// **Shaftesbury**, Oct. 1901.

FRANCILLON// C 3a// Adap. fr F of Alexandre Dumas fils// **Duke of York's**, Sept. 1897.

FRANK HEARTWELL; OR, THE HIDDEN TREASURE OF THE OLD MANOR HOUSE// D 3a// T. P. Taylor// **Victoria**, Apr. 1850, with Henry Dudley as Brady, Mr. Leake as Lt. Heartwell, J. T. Johnson as Frank Heartwell, J. Neville as Shaft, Mr. Henderson as Shipkins, James Howard as Wendever, John Bradshaw as Brailsford, John Hudspeth as Bratts, Mr. Hitchinson as Hoggs, Mrs. Cooke as Mrs. Heartwell, Miss Mildenhall as Helen, Mrs. George Lee as Margaret, Miss Barrowcliffe as Sally.

FRANK MARKHAM; OR, THE BRIDAL CURSE// D// n.a.// **Sad. Wells**, Mar. 1837, with Mr. Ede as Fitz Eustace, Mr. King as Grey, C. H. Pitt as Albert, John Ayliffe as Quickpace, Mr. Rogers as Backstitch, Mr. Campbell as Markham, H. George as Anselm, C. J. Smith as Clement, Mr. Scarbrow as Mallison, Miss Beresford as Marian, Miss Lebatt as Jessy.

FRANKENSTEIN; OR, THE MAN AND THE MONSTER// D 2a// Dram. by H. M. Milner fr Mrs. Shelly's novel and fr F, Le Magician et la Monstre// **Lyceum**, 1839, with Mr. Norman/ **Sadler's Wells**, Nov. 1843, with C. J. Bird as Prince Piombino, Henry Marston as Frankenstein, Mr. Coreno as Strutt, Mr. Williams as Ritzburg, Robert Romer as Quadro, C. J. Smith as The Monster, Miss Stephens as Rosaura, Caroline Rankley as Emmeline, Mrs. Richard Barnett as Lisetta.

FRANKLIN THE CONVICT; OR, THE WORLD'S WAYS AND LIFE AS IT IS// D// T. G. Blake// **Victoria**, Sept. 1854, with Mr. Morrison as Eugene Neville, W. H. Pitt as Nugent Neville, N. T. Hicks as Franklin, F. H. Henry as Morgan, R. H. Kitchen as Dalton, James Howard as Twitch, Alfred Saville as Somers, Charles Rice as Lily, Miss Dansor as Lady Walmsly, Mrs. Henry Vining as Martha, Miss Laporte as Patty.

FRAUD AND ITS VICTIMS// D 4a// J. Stirling Coyne// **Surrey**, Mar. 1857.

FREAKS AND FOLLIES// F 2a// G. H. Rodwell// **Eng. Opera House** (Lyceum), July 1839, with William Cullenford as Sir William, Mr. Horton as Ned, Mr. Turnour as Dr. Growl, Mr. Burnett as Capt. Rowland, Miss Goward as Ellen.

FRED FROLIC: HIS LIFE AND ADVENTURES// C// C. Pitt// **Britannia**, June 1868.

FREDA// Play 3a// Bernard Bussy & W. T. Blackmore// **Strand**, July 1887.

FREDERICK THE GREAT// D// n.a.// **Victoria**, July 1850, with Mr. Neville as Frederick the Great, J. Howard as Phelps, Mrs. George Lee as Mme. Ritzberg, Miss Mildenhall as Caroline, Mrs. Cooke as Lisbeth, Miss Barrowcliffe as Mrs. Phelps.

FREE AND EASY// F// S. J. Arnold// **Cov. Garden**, Nov. 1841, with C. J. Mathews as Sir John, George Bartley as Courtly, John Pritt Harley as Michael, W. H. Payne as Richard, Mr. Kerridge as Ralph, Miss Dowton as Peter, Rebecca Isaacs as Rose, Miss Cooper as Mrs. Courtly, Miss Murray as Eugenia, Mrs. Orger as Gertrude.

FREE LABOUR; OR, PUT YOURSELF IN HIS PLACE// D 4a// Charles Reade// **Adelphi**, May 1870.

FREE LANCE, THE// D 3a// Charles Horsman// **Astley's**, Oct. 1869, with W. D. Gresham as Marchese Sforza, Henry Drayton as Count of Lagruno, Edmund Coles as del Sarto, Clarence Holt as Ludovico Carini, E. F. Edgar as Parco, E. St. Albyn as Jacopo, Henry Dudley as Leaga, Hardy Pritchard as Baldini, Rosetta Vacey as Marcia, May Holt as Marchesa Margaretta, Georgina Pauncefort as Bianci Grazzi/ Scenery by Thomas Millar/ Machines by Mr. Lanham/ Gas by Mr. Pepper.

FREE PARDON, THE// D 4a// F. C. Philips & Leonard Merrick// **Olympic**, Jan. 1897, with W. L. Abington as Washington, Harrison Hunter as Eric Annesley, Courtnay Thorpe as Col. Annesley, George Cockburn as Sgt. Twentyman, Edward O'Niell as Julian, A. T. Hilton as Pennyquick, Lesley Thomson as Bunter, Esme Beringer as Ethel, Cicely Richards as Peggy/ Scenery by C. Durant/ Music by Carlile Vernon/ Prod. by John Douglass.

FREEDOM// D 4a// George Rowe & Augustus Harris// **Drury Lane**, Aug. 1883, with Augustus Harris as Gascoigne, James Fernandez as Araf Bey, Henry George as Sadyk, E. F. Edgar as Loring, J. H. Manley as Duncan, Harry Jackson as Blompet, Harry Nicholls as Hassan, George Rowe as Slingsby, Sophie Eyre as Suleima, Miss Bromley as Constance, Mary A. Victor as Lady Betty, Fanny Enson as Amaranthe, Lydia Foote as Zaydee, Alice Denvil as Alfa/ Scenery by William Beverley & Henry Emden/ Machines by Mr. White/ Music by Oscar Barrett/ Prod. by Augustus Harris.

FREEMASON, THE; OR, THE SECRET OF THE LODGE ROOM// D 2a// J. P. Hart// **Queen's**, June 1839.

FREISCHUTZ, DER (see Der Freischutz)

FRENCH EXHIBITION, THE; OR, THE NOODLES IN PARIS// F// Frederick Hay// **Strand**, Apr. 1867.

FRENCH GIRL'S LOVE, A// D// C. H. Hazlewood// **Britannia**, Feb. 1872.

FRENCH IN ALGIERS, THE// n.a.// **Astley's**, Apr. 1857.

FRENCH POLISH// F 1a// Joseph Lunn// **Olympic**, Feb. 1849, with Mr. Baker as Reynolds, Mr. Ross as Simon, Morris Barnett as Courmonde, Mr. Beckett as Spot, Miss Fitzwalter as Mrs. Reynolds, Miss M. A. Atkinson as Louisa.

FRENCH REFUGEE, THE// C 2a// Mrs. S. C. Hall// **St. James's**, Feb. 1837, with Morris Barnett as St. Pierre, Edmund Saville as Hamilton, Mr. Gardner as Jacob, Mme. Sala as Lady Alice, Miss Allison as Louise, Julia Smith as Madge.

FRENCH SPY, THE; OR, THE SIEGE OF CONSTANTINA// D 3a// J. T. Haines// **Adelphi**, Dec, 1837/ **Haymarket**, July 1841, with J. W. Gough as Gen. Bourmont, John Webster as Col. de Courcy, Henry Howe as Capt. Didier, Robert Strickland as Sgt. Dubourg, W. H. Oxberry as Bernard, Mrs. Stanley as Mme. Dubourg, Miss Grove as Marie, Mlle. [sic] Celeste in 3 char. parts, Henry Wallack as Hussein, James Worrell as Murad, George Bennett as Mohammed/ Scenery by George Morris/ **Sad. Wells**, June 1863, with Helen Western in 3 char. parts, J. W. Collier as Bourmont, George Maynard as de Courcy, Wallace Britton as Capt. Didier, James Johnstone as Sgt. Dubourg, W. Worboys as Bernard, Frank Huntley as Hassin Pasha, G. Pierce as Mohammed, Charles Crook as Murad, Mr. Routledge as Osmin, Bessie Heath as Mme. Dubourg, Emma Leslie as Marie.

FRETFUL PORCUPINE, A// F// Adap. by Leicester Buckingham// **Adelphi**, Apr. 1867.

FRIEND IN NEED, A// C 2a// Sidney French & William Sorrell// **St. James's**, Apr. 1860, with Mr. Robins as Bedford, Frederic Robinson as Hastings, William Belford as Sparkley, George Spencer as Leslie, Charles Young as Wannop, R. Cockrill as Fennell, Miss Murray as Ada, Nelly Moore as Fannie, Cecilia Ranoe as Liza/ **Sad. Wells**, 1860, with James Johnstone as Bedford, Charles Seyton as Hastings, William Belford as Sparkley, George Spencer as Leslie, W. Templeton as Warmup, F. Dixon as Fennell, Miss Murray as Ada, Fanny Hughes as Fanny, Caroline Parkes as Liza.

FRIEND OF THE PEOPLE, THE// D 5a// Mary Rowsell & H. A. Saintsbury// **Haymarket**, Feb. 1898.

FRIEND WAGGLES// F 1a// J. Maddison Morton// **Strand**, Apr. 1850/ **Drury Lane**, July

1850/ **Olympic**, Oct. 1850, with George Cooke as Jollyboy, Henry Compton as Waggles, William Shalders as Dr. Sasafras, Ellen Turner as Mrs. Sasafras, Mrs. B. Bartlett as Mrs. Prettyman, Isabel Adams as Mrs. Waggles/ **Sad Wells**, Nov. 1856, with J. W. Ray as Jollyboy, Lewis Ball as Waggles, William Belford as Sasafras, Mr. Williams as Plump, Mrs. Henry Marston as Mrs. Prettyman, Eliza Travers as Mrs. Sasafras, Caroline Parkes as Mrs. Waggles/ **Globe**, Dec. 1871, with Charles Flockton as Jollyboy, Henry Compton as Waggles, E. W. Garden as Sassafras, Louisa Manders as Mrs. Prettyman, Maria Harris as Mrs. Sassafras.

FRIENDS AND NEIGHBORS// C// T. H. Bayly// **St. James's**, Feb. 1839, with William Dowton as Catermole, T. F. Mathews as Perfect, Alfred Wigan as Mortimer, Mr. Canning as William, Mrs. Cooke as Mrs. Catermole, Mrs. Julia Glover as Miss Peeps.

FRIENDS OR FOES// C 4a// Adap. by Horace Wigan fr F/ **St. James's**, Mar. 1862, with George Vining as Union, Frederick Dewar as Dr. Bland, Frank Matthews as Yielding, W. H. Stephens as Meanley, F. Charles as Fervid, Mr. Terry as Borrowell, George Belmore as Capt. Donoghue, J. Robins as Chimeinwell, Miss Herbert as Mrs. Union, Mrs. Frank Matthews as Mrs. Meanley, Nelly Moore as Amy, Elizabeth Romer as Gimp.

FRIENDSHIP; OR, GOLDING'S DEBT// D 3a// Robert Reece// **Alexandra**, May 1873.

FRIENDSHIP, LOVE, AND TRUTH// D 3a// Henry Leslie// **Surrey**, Mar. 1868.

FRIENDSHIP, LOVE, AND TRUTH; OR, THE GRAND MASTER's DAUGHTER// D 3a// n.a.// **Olympic**, May 1845, with Mr. Bass as Marton, Mr. Grafton as George Marton, Walter Grisdale as Brand, Mr. Hollingsworth as Harry Marton, Mr. Wilson as Shaw, W. Gomersal as Sammy, Amalie Mercer as Mary, Miss M. A. Egan as Nancy.

FRIGHTENED TO DEATH// F 1a// W. C. Oulton// **Olympic**, Oct. 1845, with J. Browne as the Phantom, Mr. Turnour as Sir Joshua, Mr. Dean as Carleton, Mr. Lawrence as Col. Bluff, Miss Beauchamp as Corinthia, Miss Stoker as Emily, Miss Hamilton as Patty.

FRIGHTFUL ACCIDENT, A// n.a.// **Strand**, Mar. 1860.

FRILLED PETTICOATS// CD 2a// Lewis Lyne// **Gaiety**, Oct. 1871.

FRINGE OF SOCIETY, THE// Play 4a// Adap. by Charles Wyndham & J. Moore fr F of Alexandre Dumas fils, Le Demi Monde// **Criterion**, Apr. 1892, with Charles Wyndham as Sir Charles, E. H. Vanderfelt as Cuthbert, William Blakeley as Poynder, Cyril Maude as Duke of Mayfair, Frank Atherley as Phillips, Mary Moore as Marion, Carlotta Addison as Lady Carslow, Ellis Jeffreys as Mrs. Poynder, Lille Langtry as Mrs. Eve-Allen.

FRITZ, OUR COUSIN GERMAN// (see Adventures of...).

FRITZ, THE OUTLAW; OR, THE WIFE OF TWO HUSBANDS// n.a.// **Pavilion**, Dec. 1838.

FROG// CD 3a// E. B. Aveling ["Alec Nelson"]// **Royalty**, Oct. 1893, with Edmund Gurney as Rogg, Alfred Bucklaw as Deville, Fred Grove as Graham, Douglas Gordon as Arthur, Mrs. Theodore Wright as Mrs. Rogg, Nancy Noel as Susan, Miss E. B. Sheridan as Mary, Annie Rose (Mrs. Horace Neville) as Alice.

FROG HE WOULD A WOOING GO// C// n.a.// **Marylebone**, Dec. 1875.

FROLICSOME FANNY// F 3a// A. C. Calmour// **Gaiety**, Nov. 1897, with Arthur Williams as Hazzard, L. MacKinder as Erskine, Edmund Gurney as Trench, E. H. Kelly as Lord Craven, Robert Nainby as Marrydew, Emily Thorne as Caroline, Nina Boucicault as Muriel, Rose Dearing as Zamora, Sophie Larkin as Penelope.

FROM BENEATH THE DEEP// D Pro & 3a// W. H. Abel// **Pavilion**, Feb. 1876.

FROM GRAVE TO GAY// C 3a// Adap. by Benjamin Webster, Jr// **Olympic**, Dec. 1867, with Mr. Addison as Colburn, C. J. Mathews as Wise, Henry Ashley as Armitage, Horace Wigan as Tattenham, Mrs. Stirling as Lady Driver Kidd, Louisa Moore as Constance.

FROM GULF TO GULF// Play Pro & 4a// Henry John Smith// **Avenue**, Nov. 1892, with Graham Wentworth as Earl of Montreal, T. B. Thalberg as Falkland, Wilfred Winton as Sir Francis, R. Lambert as Sir Henry, H. Wenman as Sir Percy, G. H. Kersley as Lord Fenwicke, Julian Cross as Tracy, Arthur Wood as Stanly, Davies Webster as Eveline, Kate Calton as Lady St. Claire, Miss F. Leclercq as Lady Marchmont, Henrietta Cross as Nora.

FROM LIFE TO DEATH// D 4a// n.a.// **St. Geo. Hall**, May. 1875.

FROM SHADOW TO SUNSHINE// D 4a// Lilian Revell & Hawley Francks// **Elephant & Castle**, July 1901.

FROM STEM TO STERN// D// Frederick Hay// **Surrey**, Apr. 1876.

FROM VILLAGE TO COURT// C 2a// J. Maddison Morton// **Princess's**, June 1854, with John Pritt Harley as Baron Von Grosenbach, John Cathcart as Capt. Manheim, F. Cooke as Lt. Schwabb, David Fisher as Krootz, Miss Murray as Countess Bertha, Bessie Heath as Rose, Miss Vivash as Jenny/ Scenery by Walter Gordon & F. Lloyds.

FROST OF YOUTH, THE// D// John Wilkins// **City of London**, 1856.

FROU FROU// C 5a// Adap. by Sutherland Edwards fr F of Henri Meilhac & Ludovic Halèvy// **Olympic**, Apr. 1870.

FROU FROU// C 5a// Adap. by J. Comyns Carr fr F of Henri Meilhac & Ludovic Halevy// **Princess's**, May 1870; June 1881, with G. W. Anson as Brigard, Wilson Barrett as de Sartorys, Johnston Forbes Robertson as Comte de Valrèas, Edward Price as Baron de Cambri, Norman Forbes as Pitou, Eugenie Edwards as Zanetto, Helena Modjeska as Gilberte, Ada Ward as Louise, Miss M. A. Giffard as Baronne de Cambri, Dora Vivian as Pauline/ **Globe**, July 1876, with T. N. Wenman as Brigard, J. Carter-Edwards as de Sartorys, Frank Harvey as de Valreas, C. A. Cowdery as Baron de Cambri, H. Andrews as Pitou, H. Bennett as Jean, Mlle. Beatrice as Gilberte, Bessie Edwards as Louise, Miss P. Lemmon as Baroness de Cambri, Miss Louie Vere as Pauline.

FROU FROU (also subt. **Fashion and Passion**)// D 5a// Adap. by Benjamin Webster Jr. fr F of Henri Meilhac & M. Halevy// **St. James's**, May 1870, with Mlle. Marie Beatrice as Gilberte, Mary Henrade as Louise, Sophie Larkin as Baroness De Cambri, Miss Turner as Pauline, Miss Lovell as Suzanne, William Farren Jr. as Brigard, Barton Hill as De Sartorys, J. G. Shore as De Valreas, Gaston Murray as Pitou/ Scenery by Walter Hann, Grieve, & J. Galt/ **Haymarket**, Sept. 1874, with T. N. Wenman as Brigard, James Carter-Edwards as de Sartoris, Frank Harvey as Count de Valreas, Mr. Cowdry as Baron de Cambri, Henry Andrews as Pitou, H. Bennett as Jean, Mlle. Marie Beatrice as Gilberte, Miss B. Edwards as Louise, Miss P. Chapman as Baroness de Cambri, Miss Nelly Lingham as Pauline, Ida Courtney as Governess.

FROU FROU// Adap. fr F of Henri Meilhac & Ludovic Halèvy// **St. James's**, July 1890, with Arthur Bourchier as Brigard, Fred Terry as Comte de Valreas, Gilbert Farquhar as Baron de Cambri, Forbes Dawson as Pitou, Charles Milton as Vincent, Henry Neville as Sartorys, Fanny Brough as Baronne de Cambri, Gertrude Kingston as Louise, Edith Chester as Pauline, Mrs. Charles Kettlewell as Gilberte/ **Comedy**, Mar. 1894.

FROZEN DEEP, THE// D 3a// Wilkie Collins// **Olympic**, Oct. 1866, with Harwood Cooper as Capt. Helding, Horace Wigan as Lt. Crayford, H. J. Montague as Aldersley, Henry Neville as Wardour, John Clayton as St. Steventon, Dominick Murray as Want, Lydia Foote as Clara, Mrs. St. Henry as Lucy, Miss Alliston as Rose, Miss Sheridan as Mrs. Steventon/ Scenery by Hawes Craven/ Machines by Mr. Cooper/ Music by J. H. Tully/ Prod. by Horace Wigan.

FROZEN STREAM, THE; OR, THE DEAD WITNESS// D 3a// Alfred Coates// **Britannia**, Mar. 1872.

FUGITIVE, THE// D 4a// Tom Craven// **Surrey**, June 1888.

FUGITIVES, THE// D// n.a.// **Grecian**, Nov. 1858.

FUHRMANN HENSCHEL// D 4a// Adap. fr G of Gerhardt Hauptmann// **Comedy**, Oct. 1900.

FULL PARTICULARS OF THAT AFFAIR AT FINCHLEY, THE// n.a.// **Strand**, Oct. 1861.

FUN IN A FOG// F 1a// n.a.// **Drury Lane**, Oct. 1872, with Fred Vokes as Postelthwaite, W. F. Vokes as Dan, Victoria Vokes as Columbia, Jessie Vokes as Ella, Rosina Vokes as Janet/ **Imperial**, 1878.

FUNNIBONE'S FIX// F 1a// Arthur Williams// **Surrey**, Mar. 1880.

*

GABRIEL'S TRUST// D 1a// Alfred Calmour// **Vaudeville**, July 1891, with Arthur Calmour as Stroud, Philip Cunningham as Field, H. Nelson as Rhodes, Alice Bruce as Mary, Florence Haydon as Janet.

GABRIELLE// D 4a// Sidney Hodges// **Gaiety**, Mar. 1884.

GABRIELLI; OR, THE BEQUEATHED HEART// D 2a// R. B. Peake// **Adelphi**, Nov. 1847, with Mr. Boyce as O'Carrol, James Worrell as Maj. Dunmore, Paul Bedford as di Mincio, Mr. Lambert as Capt. Charmigny, C. J. Smith as Finisterra, Edward Wright as Bob Bit, Mme. Celeste as Gabrielli/ Scenery by Pitt & Johnstone/ Music by Alfred Mellon.

GABRIELLE DE BELLISLE; OR, THE LIBERTINE'S WAGER LOST// D 2a// Adap. fr F// **Sad. Wells**, Nov. 1840, with Henry Marston as Richelieu, J. B. Hill as Duke D'Aumont, Mr. Williams as D'Auvray, Mr. Elvin as D'Aubigny, J. W. Collier as Manchin, Mrs. Robert Honner as Gabrielle, Miss Richardson as Marchioness Du Prie, Mrs. Richard Barnett as Mariette.

GAFFER JARGE// C 1a// Alicia Ramsay// **Comedy**, Jan. 1896, with Cyril Maude as Jarge, Clarence Blakiston as Master, J. Byron as Benson, Alice Mansfield as Mrs. Jones, Jessica Black as Susie.

GAIN// D 3a// Henry Sargent// **Elephant & Castle**, June 1880.

GALANTEE SHOW, THE; OR, MR. PEPPERCORN AT HOME// Douglas Jerrold// **Strand**, 1837.

GALE BREEZELY; A TALE OF A TAR// D 2a// J. B. Johnstone// **Victoria**, June 1850, with James Howard as Allsorts, Mr. Humphreys as Bazil, J. T. Johnson as Breezly, John Bradshaw as Tritton, John Hudspeth as Robert, Mrs.

Cooke as Rachel, Mrs. George Lee as Morna, Miss Barrowcliffe as Sally/ **Grecian**, Mar. 1861, with James Jackson as Allsorts, Mr. Smithson as Valentine, Thomas Mead as Gale Breezeley, John Manning as Robert, R. H. Lingham as Diedrick, Henry Grant as Ironbrace, Miss Johnstone as Rachael, Harriet Coveney as Sally, Jane Coveney as Morna; Dec. 1869, with James Jackson, W. Shirley, William James, John Manning, Charles Mortimer, Henry Grant, Samuel Perfitt, Mrs. Atkinson, Alice Denvil, Mary A. Victor.

GALLEY SLAVE, THE// CD 5a// Bartley Campbell// **Grand**, Feb. 1886.

GALLEY SLAVES OF TOULON, THE; OR, THE HIDDEN TREASURE OF THE OCEAN (also subtitled, Hidden Treasure of the Cross)// D 3a// T. E. Wilks// **Victoria**, June 1841, with John Dale as De Lavigne, Mr. Wilton as Bourgignon, Mr. Franklin as Rodil, James Howard as Jacquelon, Charles Williams as Fontaine, Mr. Hitchinson as de Bisse, E. F. Saville as Lapelle, Mr. Paul as Blois, Miss Clifford as Annette, Miss Hawthorn as Isabelle, Miss Brooks as Violette, David Osbaldiston as de Valere, William Seaman as Dubois, Mr. Gardner as Bouquet, Miss G. Lee as Leonora/ Prod. by E. F. Saville.

GALWAY GO BRAGH; OR, LOVE, FUN, AND FIGHTING// Play// Adap. by Edmund Falconer fr C. Lever's Charles O'Malley// **Drury Lane**, Nov. 1865.

GAMBLER, THE// Play 3a// J. W. Boulding// **Royalty**, Dec. 1891, with Leonard Outram as Capt. Dudley, John Carter as Gen. Dudley, Richard Saunders as Montrose, Cecil Thornbury as Fraser, Hamilton Hine as Blackley, Hugh Fleming as Wildman, Howard Thompson as Darnley Miss de Naucaze as Maud, Octavia Kenmore as Kathleen, Mrs. Bennett as Victoria.

GAMBLER'S FATE, THE; OR, THE DESOLATE HUT OF THE RED MOUNTAIN// D// H. M. Milner// **Sad. Wells**, Apr. 1842, with P. Williams as Germaine, Mr. Dry as Dumont, Mr. Aldridge as Lindorf, Mr. Lyon as Albert, John Webster as Malcour, E. Morton as Bertrand, Mr. Lambe as Martin, Charles Fenton as Capt. Desterre, Robert Honner as Henry, John Herbert as Balaam, Miss Richardson as Julia, Mrs. Morgan as Mme. Belcour, Mrs. Richard Barnett as Mrs. Balaam.

GAMBLER'S LIFE IN LONDON, THE// D// A. Campbell// **Sad. Wells**, Oct. 1837, with Mr. Griffith as Old Wildflower, C. H. Pitt as Young Wildflower, Mr. King as Shark, S. Palmer as Hazardous, Mr. Wilkins as Rook, Mr. Rogers as Clover, Mr. Ennis as Oatlands, Miss Williams as Mrs. Shark, Miss Vernon as Emma, Mrs. Worrel as Mme. Coquet, Mrs. Rogers as Dame Wildflower, Miss Young as Peggy.

GAME AND GAME// F// E. L. Blanchard// **Sad. Wells**, Sept. 1844, with Mr. Williams as Sir Benjamin, E. Morton as Velium, Mr. Collins as Murphy, T. H. Higgie as Clayton, Mr. Coreno as Diggs, Miss Lebatt as Fanny, Miss Huddart as Lydia, Miss Morelli as Molly.

GAME AND GAME; OR, WHO'S THE WINNER// F 1a// E. L. Blanchard// **Olympic**, Nov. 1843, with Mr. Brookes as Sir Benjamin, James Ranoe as Clayton, Mr. Green as Vellum, Mr. Rogers as Diggs, Mr. Collins as Murphy, Georgiana Lebatt as Lydia, Miss Hamilton as Fanny.

GAME OF LIFE// D// n.a.// **Surrey**, Nov. 1863.

GAME OF LIFE, THE// D Pro & 3a// W. Howell Poole// **Grand**, Dec. 1887.

GAME OF LIFE AND DEATH, THE// D// n.a.// **City of London**, Dec. 1856.

GAME OF LOVE, THE// C 1a// Gilbert Dale// **Strand**, May 1900.

GAME OF ROMPS, A// F 1a// J. Maddison Morton// **Princess's**, Mar. 1855, with John Pritt Harley as Dr. Rhododendrum, Maria Daly as Julian, John Chester as Jolivet, Mrs. Winstanley as The Marchioness, Maria Ternan as Violet, Carlotta Leclercq as Isabelle, Miss Heath as Blanche, Miss Murray as Jeannette.

GAME OF SPECULATION, THE// C 3a// Dram. by George Henry Lewis ("Slingsby Lawrence") fr F of Honore de Balzac// **Lyceum**, Oct. 1851, with C. J. Mathews as Affable Hawk, Robert Roxby as Harry Lester, Frank Matthews as Earthworm, Basil Baker as Prospectum, William Suter as Grossmark, Henry Horncastle as Hardcore, Henry Butler as Noble, W. H. Oxberry as Thomas, Mrs. Charles Horn as Mrs. Hawk, Miss M. Oliver as Julia, Miss Grove as Dimity/ **Drury Lane**, Nov. 1855, with C. J. Mathews as Affable Hawk, Robert Roxby as Sir Harry, C. Vincent as Hardcore, Mr. Swan as Grossmark, Mr. Tilbury as Prospectus, A. Younge as Earthworm, Mrs. Selby as Mrs. Hawk, Miss M. Oliver as Julia, Miss Wadham as Mrs. Dimity, Miss De Vere as Mrs. Mason/ **Gaiety**, 1872/ **Opera Comique**, May 1877.

GAMECOCK OF THE WILDERNESS, THE// D 2a// Adap. by Leman Rede// **Olympic**, with Mr. Mellon as Col. Mereville, Mr. Binge as Roderick, F. Burton as Dorrington, Henry Bedford as Jonas, Mr. Turnour as Dodger, Mr. Marble as Samson Hardhead, H. T. Craven as Magistrate, Miss Fielding as Clara, Mrs. Griffith as Mabel, Kate Howard as Nance Butler.

GAMESTER, THE// T 5a// Edward Moore// **Drury Lane**, Jan. 1842, with W. C. Macready as Beverley, James Anderson as Lewson, E. W. Elton as Jarvis, George Bennett as Bates, Samuel Phelps as Stukeley, Mrs. Mary Warner as Mrs. Beverley, Miss Ellis as Charlotte, Miss Turpin as Lucy; Dec. 1849, with James Anderson as Beverley, Charles Fisher as Lewson, Mr. Cooper as Stukely, Charles Diddear as Jarvis, William Montague as Dawson, Laura Addison as Mrs. Beverley, Miss Phillips as Charlotte, Miss Foster as Lucy/ **Haymarket**, Apr. 1842, with Charles Kean as Beverley, Mr. Stuart as Stukeley, Henry Holl as Lewson, Robert

Strickland as Jarvis, Henry Howe as Bates, Mrs. Charles Kean (Ellen Tree) as Mrs. Beverley, Mrs. Edwin Yarnold as Charlotte; Nov. 1848, with Charles Kean as Beverley, William Creswick as Stukeley, Henry Howe as Lewson, Mr. Rogers as Jarvis, Mr. Caulfield as Bates, Henry Vandenhoff as Dawson, Mrs. Charles Kean as Mrs. Beverley, Mrs. L. S. Buckingham as Charlotte, Miss Woulds as Lucy/ **Sad. Wells,** Feb. 1844, with Henry Marston as Beverley, C. J. Bird as Lewson, Richard Younge as Stukely, Mr. Williams as Jarvis, Charles Fenton as Bates, Caroline Rankley as Mrs. Beverley, Mrs. Richard Barnett as Charlotte, Miss Stephens as Lucy; Mar. 1867, with J. H. Slater as Beverley, J. L. Warner as Stukeley, J. Collier as Lewson, Richard Norman as Jarvis, Alice Marriott as Mrs. Beverley, Mrs. J. W. Lawrence as Charlotte/ **Princess's,** Dec. 1847, with Mr. Cooper as Beverley, John Ryder as Stukely, F. B. Conway as Lewson, Charles Fisher as Bates, John Gilbert as Jarvis, Emmeline Montague as Mrs. Beverley, Susan Cushman as Charlotte, Miss Somers as Betty; July 1851, with Charles Kean as Beverley, James Vining as Lewson, Charles Fisher as Stukeley, Mr. Addison as Jarvis, F. Cooke as Bates, George Everett as Dawson, Mrs. Charles Kean as Mrs. Beverley, Miss Phillips as Charlotte, Miss Daly as Lucy.

GAMMON// C 3a// Adap. by James Mortimer fr F of Eugène Labiche & M. Martin, La Poudre aux Yeux// **Vaudeville,** July 1882, with J. F. Young, John Maclean, Gabrielle Goldney, Lydia Cowell.

GARCIA; OR, THE NOBLE ERROR// T 5a// F. G. Tomlins// **Sadler's Wells,** Dec. 1849, with Samuel Phelps as Garcia, Henry Marston as Marquis de Pacheco, G. K. Dickinson as Don Manuel, William Hoskins as Count D'Aguilar, Mr. Wilkins as Diego, Frank Graham as Xerife, Henry Mellon as Morilla, Isabela Glyn as Countess de Vyera, Miss T. Bassano as Camilla/ Scenery by F. Fenton.

GARDEN PARTY, THE// C 1a// J. Maddison Morton// **Haymarket,** Aug. 1877, with W. J. Hill as Jodkinson, Harold Kyrle as Chaffy, David Fisher Jr. as Dallington, Henry Rivers as Ching-Chang, Mr. Weathersby as Plotter, W. Hargreaves as Tomkins, Emily Thorne as Mrs. Jodkinson, Maria Harris as Nancy.

GARIBALDI// D// Tom Taylor// **Astley's,** Oct. 1859.

GARIBALDI EXCURSIONISTS, THE// F// H. J. Byron// **Princess's,** Nov. 1860.

GARRICK; OR, ONLY AN ACTOR// C 3a// William Muskerry// **Strand,** Aug. 1886, with Edward Compton, Virginia Bateman.

GARRICK FEVER, THE// F 1a// J. R. Planché// **Olympic,** Apr. 1839, with John Brougham as Maj. Derrydown, Thomas Green as Hardup, Mr. Wyman as Undertone, Mr. O'Connell as Pumpwell, Robert Keeley as Gig, Mrs. Macnamara as Lady O'Leary, Miss Jackson as Mrs. Hardup, Agnes Taylor as Polly, Miss Goward as Kitty/ **Lyceum,** Oct. 1849, with Henry Hall as Maj. Derry Down, John Pritt Harley as Hardup, W. H. Oxberry as Decimus Gig, F. Cooke as Undertone, George Burt as Dresser, Robert Honner as Pumpwell, Mr. De Courcy as Polonius, Mrs. Macnamara as Lady O'Leary, Miss Marshall as Polly/ **Olympic,** June 1855, with Samuel Emery as Hardup, J. H. White as Undertone, H. Danvers as Maj. Derrydown, Frederick Robson as Gingle, Mr. Franks as Pumpwell, Mrs. Fitzallan as Lady O'Leary, Fanny Ternan as Polly, Miss Stevens as Mrs. Hardup.

GARRYOWEN; OR, THE BELLES OF THE SHANNON// D 4a// John Levey// **Victoria,** May 1877.

GASCON, THE; OR, LOVE AND LOYALTY// D 5a// Adap. by William Muskerry fr F of Théodore Barrière & L. Davye// **Olympic,** Feb. 1876, with Henry Neville as Chev. de Puycadere, Mr. Haywell as Ruthven, Mr. Darley as Dumburgh, W. H. Fisher as Chastelard, Albert Bernard as Thomassin, Mr. Bartlett as Jacquemot, George Neville as Lord Maxwell, Frederick Vollaire as Marquis D'Altemarre, Lytton Sothern as Lord Henry Darnley, Miss Rousby as Marie Stuart, Fanny Josephs as Mary Carmichael, Mrs. Stephens as Dame Brigetta, Miss Hazleton as Mme. Miriam/ Scenery by Julian Hicks/ Music by J. Mallandaine/ Machines by Mr. Collins/ Lime Light by Mr. Sabin.

GASMAN, THE; OR, FIGHT AGAINST FATE// D 3a// Henry Bradford// **Oriental,** Apr. 1873.

GASPARDO THE GONDOLIER// D 3a// George Almar// **Surrey,** July 1838.

GASTON DUBARRY; OR, A NIGHT IN LA BERTAUDIERE// D 2a// n.a.// **Olympic,** Jan. 1847, with Mr. Binge as Philippe, Mr. Darcie as Colbert, James Johnstone as Ru, George Maynard as Gaston Dubarry, Mr. Turnour as Manchon, Mr. Fortesque as St. Angive, Miss Charles as Mme. de Guai, Mrs. R. Gordon as Casilda.

GAUNTLET, A// Play 3a// Adap. by George Hawtrey fr Osman Edwards's trans. fr Norw. of Björnsterne Björnson// **Royalty,** Jan. 1894, with W. A. Elliot as Riis, George Hawtrey as Christensen, Gaston Mervale as Alf, Alfred Bucklaw as Hoff, Herbert George as Peter, Louise Moodie as Mrs. Riis, Katherine Stewart as Mrs. Christensen, Eileen Munro as Marie, Cornelie Charles as Frederike, Florence Munro as Kamma, Kate Graves as Hanna, Frances Burleigh as Else, Maud Clifford as Olga, Edith Maitland as Ortrude, Annie Rose as Svava.

GAY CITY, THE; OR, A SCENE AT THE SIEGE// F// n.a.// **Royalty,** June 1871.

GAY DECEIVER, A// FC 3a// James Mortimer// **Royalty,** Feb. 1879.

GAY GROCER OF THREE WIVES, THE// D// n.a.// **Grecian,** Feb. 1846, with Charles Horn as Count de Lasco, Mr. Campbell as

Lascari, T. W. Edmonds as Pepito, Edmund Garden as Carlo, Frederick Robson as Godivet, Mary A. Crisp as Countess de Lasco, Annette Mears as Nisida, Mrs. W. Watson as Mme. Godivet.

GAY HUSBAND, A// D 3a// Adap. by Allerton fr F of Octave Feuillet// **Criterion**, June 1886.

GAY LORD QUEX, THE// C 4a// Arthur Wing Pinero// **Globe**, Apr. 1899, with Dawson Milward as Quex, Gilbert Hare as Frayne, Richard Lambert as Bastling, C. M. Hallard as Pollitt, Fanny Coleman as Julia, Mona Oram as Mrs. Eden, Mabel Terry Lewis as Muriel, Irene Vanbrugh as Sophy Fullgarney.

GAY LOTHARIO, THE// C 1a// Alfred Calmour// **St. James's**, Jan. 1891, with George Alexander as Sir Harry, Ben Webster as Sparks, Maude Millet as Amalida, Laura Graves as Letty.

GAY WIDOW, A// F 3a// Adap. by F. C. Burnand fr F of Victorien Sardou & R. Deslandes, Belle Maman// **Court**, Oct. 1894, with Charles Hawtrey as Dudley, Edward Righton as Rutherford, Gilbert Hare as Bruce, H. N. Chart as Dunford, E. H. Kelly as Anstruther, Wilfred Draycot as Vicomte de Barsac, Fred Thorne as Col. Mumby, Compton Coutts as Dodd, Will Dennis as Bentham, Robb Harwood as Count Caramanti, Fred Vaughan as Uncle Popley, Aubrey Fitzgerald as Walworth Mumby, Eva Moore as Nellie, Mrs. Charles Maltby as Mrs. Pipwidge, Mabel Hardinge as Adelisa, Violet Ray as Countess Caramanti, Lottie Venne as Mrs. Marbrook.

GAY WIDOWER, A// C 3a// Adap. by Sylvain Mayer fr G of Laufs & Kneisel// **Vaudeville**, Mar. 1892, with Cecil Ramsey as Penfold, Alfred Cross as Liston, Thomas Kingston as Harding, Norman V. Norman as Capt. Languish, Nicol Pentland as Fellowes, C. W. Garthorne as Baldwin, Mary Mordaunt as Kate, Louise Peach as Mabel, Alice Maitland as Ethel, Ina Goldsmith as Sophie, Mrs. Beaumont Nelson as Mrs. Grist.

GEMEA// D Pro & 3a// Edgar Newbound// **Britannia**, Mar. 1880.

GENEVA CROSS, THE// D 4a// George Rowe// **Adelphi**, Oct. 1874, with William McIntyre as Pierre le Brun, Augustus Glover as Mathieu, Henry Sinclair as de Bourg, Stanislaus Calhaem as Cornichet, Frederick Moreland as Pontrame, Henry Russell as The Unknown, Edward Butler as Raba, James Fernandez as Spadassin, Harwood Cooper as Antoine, Marie Henderson as Gabrielle, Edith Stuart as Martago, Mrs. Gaston Murray as Mlle. Cassandre, Miss Hudspeth as Fraizette/ Scenery by F. Lloyds/ Music by Edwin Ellis/ Machines by E. Charker.

GENEVIEVE// D// Adap. fr F, Les Orphellines de Valneige// **Lyceum**, Jan. 1859, with Mme. Celeste, Samuel Emery, Marian Keeley.

GENEVIEVE, A STORY OF THE FRENCH REVOLUTION (also subt. The Reign of Terror)// D// Adap. fr F of Alexandre Dumas & August Maquet, Le Chevalier de la Maison Rouge// **Adelphi**, June 1853/ **Astley's**, May 1880, with E. N. Hallows as Linday, F. Terriss as Lorin, W. D. Gresham as Gen. Santerre, T. C. Valentine as Dixmer, F. Owen as de Salvoisy, Mat Robson as Simon, May Rimboult as the Dauphin, Emily Forde as Marie Antoinette, Josephine St. Ange as Genevieve, Lottie Russell as Heloise.

GENEVIEVE; OR, THE LOST WIFE// D Pro & 2a// George Conquest// **Grecian**, Apr. 1872.

GENEVIEVE, THE LOST STAR// D, Pro & 2a// George Conquest// **Grecian**, Apr. 1855, with Basil Potter as Luidgi, Henry Grant as Gen. Roger, John Manning as Honest Peter, Richard Phillips as Vernet, Jane Coveney as Genevieve, Eaton O'Donnell as Count D'Arezzo, Eaton O'Donnell as Morel, F. Charles as Col. Roger, Henry Power as Simon, Maria Simpson as Josephine/ Prod. by H. Phillips.

GENEVIEVE DE BRABANT; OR, THE HALL OF TORTURE// D// n.a.// **Sad. Wells**, Apr. 1839, with Mr. Cathcart as Duke Henri, J. W. Collier as Oliver, Mr. Williams as Vender, Benjamin Conquest as Gobemouche, Mr. Dry as Count Hainhault, Charles Montgomery as Robert, Mrs. Robert Honner as Genevieve, Mrs. J. F. Saville as Marguerite/ Scenery by Mr. Fenwick & G. Smithers/ Machines by B. Sloman/ Music by Mr. Herbert.

GENEVRA THE SCOURGED ONE; OR, THE CONVICT OF MUNICH// D 3a// n.a.// **Victoria**, Aug. 1846, with Mr. Archer as St. Firmin, William Seaman as Ernest, James Ranoe as Delauney, Walter Searle as La Roche, Mrs. Henry Vining as Baroness Feldberg, Lydia Pearce as Adele, Miss Fielding as Rose.

GENIUS, THE// C// n.a.// **Haymarket**, Sept. 1863, with W. H. Chippendale as Cooley, J. B. Buckstone as Ripstone, William Farren as Walmsley, Mr. Rogers as Docket, Walter Gordon as Barton, Henry Compton as Withers, Mrs. Edward Fitzwilliam as Lady Aurora, Mrs. Dowton as Mrs. Montgomery, Caroline Hill as Clara.

GENIUS, THE// C 1a// H. W. Williamson// **Globe**, Jan. 1881, with Charles Ashford as Smallstock, Frederick Clifton as Crib, A. H. Forrest as Joseph, Maria Davis as Mrs. Smallstock.

GENTLE IVY// Play 4a// W. E. Clery ("Austin Fryers")// **Strand**, May 1894, with Alfred Cross as Lord Hartland, Stanley Pringle as Plowden, H. A. Saintsbury as Lord Ruislip, Rowland Atwood as Bucklaw, Leonard Calvert as Polwyl, Orlando Barnett as Trefelyn, Miss Valli as Ernie, Susie Vaughan as Mrs. Polwyl, Mrs. Theodore Wright as Countess of Elgin, Rose Nesbitt as Lady Gwendoline, Kate Bealby as Lady Adelaide, Charlotte Morland as Mrs. Trefelyn, Mrs. Gordon-Ascher as Miss Trefelyn, Frances Ivor as Ivy.

GENTLEMAN IN BLACK, THE// C 1a// Mark Lemon// **Olympic**, Mar. 1840, with Richard

Jones as Punctilio, George Wild as Forage, Mr. Ross as Dan, Mrs. Anderson.

GENTLEMAN IN BLACK, THE (also titled or subt. Dominique the Deserter, or, The Devil and the Deserter)// C// n.a.// **Sad. Wells,** June 1857, with George Cooke as Count D'Anville, G. Pennett as Morvillier, John Mordaunt as De Lache, G. B. Bigwood as Dominique, E. B. Gaston as Duverne, Mr. Edwin as Gaspard, Emma Barnett as Lady Blanche, Miss M. A. Murry as Jeanette, Mrs. J. Gates as Genevieve/ **Olympic,** Sept. 1866, with Edward Atkins as Dominique, Charles Horsman as Duverne, T. B. Bennett as La Lache, Henry Reeves as Count D'Auville, Henry Rivers as Gaspard, Miss Wilson as Lady Blanche, Mrs. Poynter as Genevieve, Ellen Farren as Jeannette.

GENTLEMAN IN DIFFICULTIES, A// C 1a// T. H. Bayly// **Olympic,** May 1837, with Frank Matthews as Crisp, John Brougham as Simmonds, John Liston as Sedley, Mrs. Macnamara as Mrs Crisp, Miss Fitzwalter as Mrs. Sedley, Mrs. Orger as Piminy/ **St. James's,** Nov. 1837, with Mr. Brookes as Crisp, Mr. Wright as Sedley, Mr. Sidney as Simmons, Mrs. Penson as Mrs. Crisp, Annette Mears as Mrs. Sedley, Mrs. Stirling as Piminy.

GENTLEMAN JACK// D 5a// Charles Vincent & William Brady// **Sad. Wells,** Sept. 1849, with Mr. Williams as Crisp, Henry Nye as Sedley, William Belford as Simmons, Mrs. G. Smith as Mrs. Crisp, Miss T. Bassano as Mrs. Sedley, Miss Johnson as Mrs. Simmons, Julia St. George as Piminy/ **Drury Lane,** Apr. 1891, with James J. Corbett as Jack, William Brady as Royden, Ben Hendricks as Halliday, Cuyler Hastings as George, John Donaldson as Houston, Jay Wilson as Southgate, John McVey as Splash, Georgie Esmond as Alice, Sadie McDonald as Polly, Robertha Erskine as Mrs. Royden, Florrie West as Tottie.

GENTLEMAN JOE// D// T. E. Wilks// **Sad. Wells,** Sept. 1838, with John Webster as Joe, J. W. Collier as Bill, Mr. Dry as Darking, Charles Montague as Merton, Dibdin Pitt as Van Trapp, Benjamin Conquest as Boss, Miss E. Honnor as Florence, Mrs. J. F. Saville as Ellen, Miss Cooke as Mrs. Mayfly.

GENTLEMAN OPPOSITE, THE// C// n.a.// **Lyceum,** July 1854.

GENTLEMAN WHIP, THE// C 1a// H. M. Paull// **Terry's,** Feb. 1894, with Frederick Volpé as Brown, Sydney Warden as Slade, J. R. Hatfield as Ellicott, George Robinson as Dixon, Helena Dacre as Lady Jane, Esmé Beringer as Mabel.

GEORGE BARNWELL; OR, THE LONDON MERCHANT// T 5a// George Lillo// **Sad. Wells,** May 1837, with N. T. Hicks as Barnwell, C. H. Pitt as Truman, Mr. King as Thorogood, Mr. Ede as Uncle, Thomas Lee as Blunt, Miss Williams as Milwood, Miss Beresford as Maria, Lavinia Melville as Lucy/ **Cov. Garden,** May 1837, with John Webster as Barnwell, Mr. Thompson as Thorogood, Mr. Tilbury as Old Barnwell, John Pritchard as Trueman, Mr. Ross as Blunt, Mrs. W. West as Millwood, Miss Lee as Maria, Miss Nicholson as Lucy/ **Gaiety,** Apr. 1880/ **Olympic,** May 1880, with John Maclean as Thorowgood, J. B. Buckstone as Uncle, J. R. Crauford as Barnwell, C. Fawcett as Trueman, Mr. Alwin as Blunt, Louise Willes as Millwood, Miss Wadman as Lucy, Miss Louis as Maria.

GEORGE DARVILLE// D 5a// Dion Boucicault// **Adelphi,** June 1857, with Benjamin Webster as George Darville, Edward Wright as Jonas, John Billington as Edgar, Edmund Garden as Grant, James Bland as Richards, C. J. Smith as Dr. Roberts, Paul Bedford as Union Jack, Mme. Celeste as Marion, Miss Wyndham as Patty/ Scenery by Pitt & Brew/ Machines by T. Bartlett.

GERALDINE; OR, THE MASTER PASSION// D// Mrs. H. L. Bateman// **Adelphi,** June 1865.

GERMANS AND FRENCH; OR, INCIDENTS IN THE WAR OF 1870-1// D// John Douglas Jr// **Standard,** Mar. 1871.

GERTRUDE'S CHERRIES// C 2a// Douglas Jerrold// **Cov. Garden,** Sept. 1842, with George Bartley as Willoughby, Walter Lacy as Vincent, Charles Diddear as Gilbert, John Pritt Harley as Halcyon, Drinkwater Meadows as Crossbone, Alfred Wigan as Blague, Miss Cooper as Angelica, Mrs. Humby as Mrs. Crossbone, Mrs. Walter Lacy as Gertrude.

GERTRUDE'S MONEY BOX// C// Harry Lemon// **Sad. Wells,** Jan. 1869, with J. H. Loome as Teddington, Henry Perry as Burton, Mr. Jefferson as Quirk, Mr. Furtado as Fenley, Maude Dudley as Gertrude, Mrs. Howe as Mrs. Warder.

GHETTO, THE// D 3a// Adap. by C. B. Fernald fr Dutch of H. Heijerman Jr.// **Comedy,** Sept. 1899, with Kyrle Bellew as Rafael, George Titherage as Sachel, J. D. Beveridge as Haezer, Frederick Volpé as Aaron, Gilbert Yorke as Samson, Arthur Wonter as Daniel, James Craig as Isaiah, John Keats as Joseph, Mrs. Charles Calvert as Esther, Constance Collier as Rebecca, Mrs. Brown Potter as Rosa/ Scenery by E. G. Banks/ Electrics by Mr. Digby.

GHOST HUNTER, THE; OR, THE COLLEEN DHAS// D 3a// George Conquest// **Grecian,** Mar. 1862, with Henry Grant as Randal, William James as Morris, Thomas Mead as William, Alfred Rayner as Joe, Jane Dawson as Rose, Ellen Hale as Patty, Lucreza Hill as Aileen, Miss Johnstone as Mrs. Brady.

GHOST IN SPITE OF HIMSELF, A// F// n.a.// **Princess's,** July 1868, with Brandon Ellis as Nicodemus, W. D. Gresham as Aldwinkle, Frank Crellin as Capt. Vauntington, Dominick Murray as Dickery, Robert Cathcart as Paul, Miss Keep as Georgiana, Emma Barnett as Lavinia.

GHOST STORY, THE// Play 2a// T. J. Searle// **Marylebone,** Oct. 1863.

GHOSTS// D 3a// Trans. by William Archer

fr Norw. of Henrik Ibsen// **Royalty**, Mar. 1891, with Mrs. Theodore Wright, Leonard Outram, Sidney Howard, Edith Kenward, Frank Lindo.

GIANT OF THE DESERT AND THE DEMON DWARF, THE// D// Lemon Rede// **Olympic**, Mar. 1843, with Charles Baker as Jacopo Sforza, Mr. Barrett as Leonato Sforza, Sign. Nano as Daimonion, Mr. Fitzjames as Tormichelle, Thomas Green as Baptiste, Mr. Bologna as Guiseppe, Mr. Freeman as the Giant, Lavinia Melville as Lady Isabelle, Miss Lebatt as Festina.

GIANT OF THE MOUNTAINS, THE// Frederick Marchant// **Britannia**, Dec. 1869.

GIL BLAS; OR, THE BOY OF SANTILLANE// D 3a// n.a.// **Victoria**, Oct. 1837, with Mrs. Hooper as Gil Blas, Mr. Loveday as Perez, William Davidge as Don Martin, Mr. Roland as Alvarez, Edward Hooper as Corenole, Mr. Green as Capt. Rolande, John Parry as Despardo, W. H. Oxberry as Domingo, Miss E. Lee as Donna Meusia, Mrs. Griffith as Leonardo, Mrs. Loveday as Brunetta.

GILDED FOOL, A// C 4a// H. G. Carleton// **Shaftesbury**, Feb. 1900.

GILDEROY THE BONNY BOY// D// W. H. Murray// **Sad. Wells**, Sept. 1840, with Henry Marston as Gilderoy, Mr. Dry as Logan, George Burt as Col. Havoc, Mr. Elvin as Capt. Manly, J. B. Hill as Stephen, Mr. Williams as Howie, J. W. Collier as Cloutem, Mr. Richardson as McNab'em, Charles Fenton as Fitzwalter, Miss Richardson as Jessy; Apr. 1857, with Mr. Stuart as Gilderoy, John Chester as Muir, R. H. Lingham as Logan, George Burt as Sgt. Musketoon, Charles Seyton as Duncartym Mr. Warren as McTavish, Marianne Jackson as Lillian, Mrs. Hill as Mrs. McTavish, Miss Evans as Peggy.

GILESO SCROGGINI// Play// Mark Lemon// **Olympic**, 1841.

GIN// D// Adap fr F novel of Emile Zola, Assommoire// **Victoria**, Mar. 1880.

GIN AND WATER; OR, MAN'S FRIEND AND FOE// D 3a// H. Young// **Victoria**, Jan. 1854, with N. T. Hicks as Lambert Ruble, T. E. Mills as Richard Ruble, Alfred Saville as Mason, Mr. Henderson as Lemoure, Watty Brunton as George Ruble, John Bradshaw as Bundle, James Howard as Little Will, John Hudspeth as Goldfinch, F. H. Henry as Jenkins, Mrs. Henry Vining as Harriet, Miss Dansor as Sarah, Miss Laporte as Betty, Georgiana Lebatt as Mrs. Goldfinch, Phoebe Johnson as Nancy, Miss Humpreys as Amelia, Miss Vaul as Emma/ Prod. by J. T. Johnson.

GIOCONDA// T 4a// Trans by Winifred Mayo fr Ital of Gabriel d'Annunzio// **Lyceum**, May 1900.

GIPSY EARL, THE// D 4a// G. R. Sims// **Adelphi**, Aug. 1898, with Fred Terry as Pharoah, George Hippisley as Lord Trevannion, Edmund Maurice as Sir Jasper, Creagh Henry as Silas, Harry Nicholls as 'Lijah, G. W. Hawtrey as Dr. Verner, Julia Neilson as Naomi, Miss Keith Wakeman as Alice, May Ronaldson as Birdie, Inez Soleyz as Kitty, Madge Girdlestone as Lady. St. Ives, Alice Marriott as Granny/ Scenery by W. Harford & Bruce Smith/ Prod. by Fred Latham.

GIPSY FARMER, THE; OR, JACK AND JACK'S BROTHER// D 2a// J. B. Johnstone// **Surrey**, Mar. 1849/ **Grecian**, Dec. 1863, with J. Jackson as Caleb, J. B. Steele as Hatfield, E. Howard as Mark, Walter Holland as Matthew, William James as Alfred, Thomas Mead as Jack, John Manning as Joe, Henry Grant as Abel, Jane Dawson as Marian, Marie Brewer as Marguerite, Mary A. Victor as Mary.

GIPSY KING, THE// D 3a// J. Bosworth// **Queen's**, May 1837/ **Grecian**, Mar. 1861, with Alfred Rayner as St. Maur, Thomas Mead as Zerico, William James as De Briancourt, Harriet Coveney as Caraxa, Mr. Jackson as Maurice, John Manning as Justin, Henry Power as Saunders, Jane Coveney as Marguerite, Ellen Hale as Angelique, Lucreza Hill as Clotilde.

GIPSY OF MILAN, THE; OR, THE TENANT OF THE TOMB// D// n.a.// **Sad. Wells**, Jan. 1844, with Mr. Dry as Marquis Salviati, C. J. Bird as Andreas di Monzani, Henry Marston as Lucio di Monzani, C. J. Smith as Rapallo, Mr. Williams as Di Rizzi, Mr. Coreno as Jocopo, Caroline Rankley as Helena, Mrs. Richard Barnett as Miriana/ Scenery by F. Fenton/ Music by W. Montgomery/ Prod. by Henry Marston.

GIPSY QUEEN, THE// Play 1a// n.a.// **West London**, June 1893.

GIPSY'S ROMANCE// n.a.// **Victoria**, Nov. 1852.

GIPSY'S VENGEANCE, THE// D 4a// Adap. to play vers by Charles Jeffreys of Verdi's Il Trovatore// **Drury Lane**, Mar. 1856.

GIRALDA; OR, THE INVISIBLE HUSBAND// C 3a// Adap. by Hy Welstead fr F of Eugène Scribe// **Olympic**, Sept. 1850, with William Farren Jr. as Don Philip, George Cooke as Don Japhet, Leigh Murray as Don Manuel, Henry Compton as Piquillo, Mrs. Leigh Murray as Princess Ysabel, Mrs. Stirling as Giralda, Miss Adams as Pepita, Isabel Adams as Rita/ Scenery by W. Shalders & R. Mildenhall/ Music by J. Barnard/ Machines by Mr. Matthews/ Gas by J. Palmer/ **Astley's**, Nov. 1859, with Mr. Ennis as Philip III, Mr. S. Johnson as Don Raphael, Richard Phillips as Don Roderick, Emily Dowton as Urban, George Belmore as Antonia, Mrs. W. Dowton as Queen Catherine, Kate Carson as Adeline, Mrs. Clifton as Lucette/ **Sad. Wells**, Oct. 1863, with Edmund Phelps as King, David Jones as Don Manuel, George Fisher as Gil Perez, T. B. Bennett as Dan Japhet, George Vining as Tailor, Mrs. H. Wallis as Queen, Lizzie Mandelbert as Giralda, Mrs. Barnett as Amina/ **Lyceum**, Sept. 1876.

GIRALDA; OR, THE MILLER'S WIFE// D 3a//

Adap. by Benjamin Webster fr F of Eugène Scribe// **Haymarket**, Sept. 1850, with Henry Hughes as Philip, Paul Bedford as Don Japhet, Charles Boyce as Dan Manuel, Edward Wright as Gil, Emma Harding as Grand Duchess, Kathleen Fitzwilliam as Giralda/ Scenery by Pitt & Turner/ Machines by Mr. Cooper/ **Adelphi**, Oct. 1850, with same cast.

GIRALDA; OR, WHO'S MY HUSBAND?// C 3a// Adap. by George Conquest fr F of Eugène Scribe// **Grecian**, Dec. 1855, with F. Charles as King Philip, Eaton O'Donnell as Don Japhet, Richard Phillips as Don Manuel, John Manning as Gill Perez, Ellen Crisp as Queen of Spain, Jane Coveney as Giralda.

GIRL I LEFT BEHIND ME, THE// C// John Oxenford// **Olympic**, Nov. 1863, with E. F. Edgar as Capt. Fortesque, Henry Andrews as Brownson, Henry Rivers as Piano Tuner, Miss Sheridan as Mrs. Maltravers, Mrs. Harwood Cooper as Miss Mims, Miss Harland as Amy.

GIRL I LEFT BEHIND ME, THE// D 4a// David Belasco & Franklyn Fyles// **Sad. Wells**, Jan. 1893/ **Adelphi**, Apr. 1895, with F. H. Macklin as Gen. Kennion, Charles Fulton as Maj. Burleigh, William Terriss as Lt. Hawkesworth, W. L. Abingdon as Lt. Parlow, E. W. Gardiner as Penwick, George Cockburn as Pvt. Jones, Julian Cross as Landru, Richard Purdon as McGlynn, Edwin Rorke as Jackson, Dora Barton as Dick, Jessie Millward as Kate, Hope Dudley as Lucy, Mary Allestree as Fawn/ Scenery by Joseph Harker & Bruce Smith.

GIRL OF MY HEART, THE; OR, JACK ASHORE// D 4a// Herbert Leonard// **Surrey**, Dec. 1896.

GIRL'S FREAK, A// FC 2a// Lilian Feltheimer & Kate Dixey// **St. Geo. Hall**, Feb. 1899.

GIRLS, THE// C 3a// H. J. Byron// **Vaudeville**, Apr. 1879, with Henry Howe, Sophie Larkin, William Farren Jr., Mr. James.

GIRLS AND BOYS: A NURSERY TALE// C 3a// Arthur Wing Pinero// **Toole's**, Nov. 1882, with J. L. Toole, John Billington, Melly Lyons, Myra Holme.

GIRLS OF THE PERIOD, THE// C// F. C. Burnand// **Drury Lane**, Mar. 1869, with F. Charles as Brown, John Rouse as Robinson, Henry Barrett as Dr. Mentor, Harriet Coveney as Mrs. Brown, Miss M. O'Berne as Mrs. Circe, Kate Harfleur as Calypso.

GIRONDIST, THE// n.a.// **City of London**, Aug. 1854.

GISIPPUS// D 5a// Gerald Griffin// **Drury Lane**, Feb. 1842, with James Anderson as Titus, W. C. Macready as Gisippus, J. Graham as Medon, Edward Elton as Pheax, Charles Hudson as Chremes, George Bennett as Lycias, Miss E. Phillips as Norban, William Bennett as Davus, Helen Faucit as Sophronia, Miss Turpin as Hero/ Music by T. Cooke.

GITANA, LA// D Pro & 3a// Edward Towers// **Pavilion**, Apr. 1876.

GITANILLA, THE; OR THE CHILDREN OF THE ZINCALI// D 3a// J. Crawford Wilson// **Surrey**, Oct. 1860.

GIVE A DOG A BAD NAME// D 2a// G. H. Lewis ("Slingsby Lawrence")// **Lyceum**, Apr. 1854/ **Adelphi**, Nov. 1876, with Brittain Wright as Mr. Goldsworthy, J. G. Shore as George Balfour, Samuel Emery as Tom Balfour, William Terriss as Capt. Chamleigh, C. J. Smith as Johnson, Rose Coghlan as Alice, Cicely Nott as Clarissa, Miss E. Phillips as Dora.

GIVE ME MY WIFE// F 1a// W. E. Suter// **Grecian**, June 1859.

GLAD TIDINGS// D Pro & 5a// J. T. Douglas ("James Willing") & Frank Stamforth// **Standard**, Aug. 1883.

GLADIATOR, THE// T 5a// James Montgomery Bird// **Drury Lane**, May 1875.

GLADYS; OR, THE GOLDEN KEY// C 3a// Arthur Law// **Strand**, Dec. 1886/ **Avenue**, Aug. 1888.

GLASHEN GLORIA; OR, THE LOVER'S WELL// D 3a// Robert Dodson// **Pavilion**, Sept. 1885.

GLASS OF FASHION, THE// C 4a// Sidney Grundy & G. R. Sims// **Globe**, Sept. 1883, with H. J. Lethcourt as Col. Trevanion, Herbert Beerbohm Tree as Prince Borowski, J. L. Shine as Macadam, Charles Smily as Stanhope, E. W. Gardiner as Jenkyn, Alice Lingard as Mrs. Trevanion, Carlotta Leclercq as Lady Coombe, Lottie Venne as Peg O'Reilly/ Scenery by Spong & Perkins/ Music by Alois Brousil.

GLASS OF WATER, A; OR, GREAT EVENTS FROM TRIFLING CAUSES SPRING// C 2a// Adap. by W. E. Suter fr F of Eugène Scribe, Verre d'Eau// **Queen's**, May 1863.

GLEN OF WILLOWS, THE; OR, THE FRATRICIDE AND THE TREACHEROUS PLOT// D// James Bruton// **Sad. Wells**, Sept. 1837, with Mr. Wilkins as Dietrich, Mr. Campbell as Claude, C. J. Smith as Hanns, C. H. Pitt as Carl, Mr. Rogers as Piggywiggy, Thomas Lee as Tapps, Miss Williams as Agnes, Lavinia Melville as Linda.

GLENCOE; OR, THE FATE OF THE MACDONALDS// T 5a// Sergeant Talfourd// **Haymarket**, May 1840, with Benjamin Webster as Mac Vich Ian, John Webster as John Macdonald, Priscilla Horton as Alaster, W. C. Macready as Halbert Macdonald, Henry Howe as Henry Macdonald, Mr. Waldron as Kenneth, Mrs. Mary Warner as Lady Macdonald, Samuel Phelps as Capt. Campbell, Walter Lacy as Lindsay, James Worrell as Drummond, Helen Faucit as Helen/ Scenery by Charles Marshall & G. Morris.

GLIN GATH; OR, THE MAN IN THE CLEFT// D 4a// Paul Meritt// **Grecian**, Apr. 1872.

GLITTER// C 2a// Gilbert à Beckett// **St. James's**, Dec. 1868.

GLORIANA// C 3a// Adap. by James Mortimer fr F of M. Chivot & Alfred Duru, Le Truc d'Arthur (derived from Marivaux)// **Globe**, Nov. 1891, with Harry Paulton as Chadwick, Forbes Dawson as Jocelyn, T. W. Percyval as Evitoff, W. Lestocq as Spinks, Florence West as Mrs. Lovering, Georgie Esmond as Jessie.

GO STRAIGHT; OR, HONEST HEARTS// D// Leonard Outram// **Globe**, Aug. 1894.

GO TO BED TOM// F 1a// Thomas Morton// **Olympic**, Nov. 1852, with George Cooke as Cockletop, Henry Compton as Tom Smith, W. Shalders as O'Lugger, Mrs. B. Bartlett as Mrs. Smith, Ellen Turner as Sally.

GO TO PUTNEY; OR, A STORY OF THE BOAT RACE// F// Harry Lemon// **Adelphi**, Apr. 1868.

GODOLPHINS, THE// n.a.// **Surrey**, Apr. 1860.

GODPAPA// FC 3a// F. C. Philips & Charles Brookfield// **Comedy**, Oct. 1891, with Charles Hawtrey as Reginald,James Nelson as Sir George, William Wyes as Pygmalion, W. F. Hawtrey as Craven, Charles Brookfield as Bunbury, Annie Irish as Mrs. St. Germain, Vane Featherston as Mrs. Craven, Lottie Venne as Mary, Violet Armbruster as Violet, Helem Lambert as Trixie.

GOGGIN'S GINGHAM// C// n.a.// **Strand**, May 1863.

GOING IT! ANOTHER LESSON TO FATHERS// FC 3a// J. Maddison Morton & W. A. Vicars// **Toole's**, Dec. 1885.

GOING THE PACE// D 4a// Arthur Shirley & Benjamin Landeck// **Pavilion**, Oct. 1898/ **Princess's**, Aug. 1899, with Ernest Leicester as Mervyn, Walner Gregory as Parici, Charles Dodsworth as Swanson, Edmund Gurney as O'Rafferty, C. F. Collings as Margrave, H. Landeck as Nathan, Lionel Rignold as Bowyer, Beatrix May as Alice, Essex Dane as Lucy, Marie Illington as Anna, Olga Andree as Electrina.

GOING TO THE BAD// C 2a// Tom Taylor// **Olympic**, June 1858, with Frederick Robson as Peter Potts, George Vining as Hardingham, Frederick Vining as Gen. Dashwood, Mr. Addison as Maj. Steel, George Cooke as Marks, Gaston Murray as Rushout, Horace Wigan as Smythers, Miss Wyndham as Lucy, Miss Herbert as Miss Dashwood, Mrs. Stephens as Mrs. Polkinghorn, Miss Evans as Miss Fullalove.

GOING TO THE DERBY// F 1a// J. Maddison Morton// **Adelphi**, May 1848, with Edward Wright as Jeremiah Twiddle, Paul Bedford as Chucks, Charles Munyard as Sam, Sarah Woolgar as Mrs. Twiddle, Mrs. Frank Matthews as Mrs. Chucks; June 1867, with John Clarke as Jeremiah Twiddle, J. G. Taylor as Chucks, W. H. Eburne as Nobble, C. H. Stephenson as Sam, Mrs. Billington as Mrs. Twiddle, Miss A. Seaman as Mrs. Chucks, Mrs. H. Lewis as Mrs. Plummy/ **Haymarket**, Aug. 1848, with same Adelphi company.

GOING TO THE DOGS// F 1a// William Brough & Andrew Halliday// **Drury Lane**, Mar. 1865, with George Belmore as Fidge, George Spencer as Trotter, Mr. Warde as Capt. Lightfoot, Thomas Matthews as Boodle, Helen Howard as Mrs. Fidge, Mrs. C. Melville as Miss Dibbs, Miss Seymour as Mary.

GOLD// D 5a// Charles Reade// **Drury Lane**, Jan. 1853, with E. L. Davenport as Sandford, Mr. Moorhouse as William, Mr. Hughes as Winchester, Edward Stirling as Levi, Henry Wallace as Robinson, H. Lee as Meadows, Charles Selby as Crawley, Fanny Vining as Susan, Miss St. Clare as Sarah, Mrs. Griffiths as Mary.

GOLD CRAZE// Play 4a// Brandon Thomas// **Princess's**, Nov. 1889.

GOLD FIEND, THE; OR, THE DEMON GAMESTER// D 3a// W. Thompson Townsend// **Queen's**, May 1850.

GOLD GUITAR, THE; OR, THE BOHEMIAN PROPHECY// D 3a// T. E. Wilks// **Victoria**, Aug. 1843, with William Seaman as Duke of Braganza, Mr. James as Don Roque, C. Williams as Don Alonzo, Mr. Morelli as Don Pedro, Mr. Wilton as Marquis de la Puebla, John Dale as Don Zunigo, E. F. Saville as Felix, John Gardner as Coco, Mrs. Atkinson as Leanthe, Miss Ridgeway as Dorothé, Miss Saddler as Georgette, Miss Hicks as Inéz/ **City of London**, Sept. 1851.

GOLD IS NOTHING - HAPPINESS IS ALL// D// John Levey// **East London**, Nov. 1869.

GOLD MINE, A// D 3a// G. H. Jessop & Brander Matthews// **Gaiety**, July 1890, with Nat. C. Goodwin as Wolcott, William Farren as Sir Everard, Harry Eversfield as Foxwood, Eric Thorne as Wilson, Frank Wood as Krebs, Charles Glenney as Riordan, Kate Forsyth as Mrs. Meredith, Jenny McNulty as Una, Carlotta Leclercq as Mrs. Vandervas.

GOLD MINE, THE; OR, THE MILLER OF GRENOBLE// D 2a// Edward Stirling// **Drury Lane**, 1854.

GOLD SEEKERS, THE; OR, THE DYING GIFT// D// n.a.// **Victoria**, 1838.

GOLD SEEKERS, THE; OR, THE OUTCASTS OF ANZASCA (also titled, The Goldseekers of Anzasca)// D// H. P. Grattan// **Sad. Wells**, July 1839, with Mr. Cathcart as Martelli, John Webster as Francisco, Charles Montgomery as Marco, Mr. Dry as Antonio, W. D. Broadfoot as Bartole, Mr. Elvin as Ricardo, Mr. Aldridge as Nicolo, Benjamin Conquest as Pietro, Mrs. Robert Honner as Leila, Miss Pincott as Annette/ Scenery by F. Fenton// Music by Mr. Herbert/ Machines by B. Sloman.

GOLD, THE IDOL OF MEN'S SOULS; OR, THE THREE BROTHERS OF FRANKFORT// D// n.a.// **Grecian**, Dec. 1865, with Dacre Baldie as Alto, Mr. Dacey as Albert, Mr. Don as Goetz, Charles Mortimer as The Baron, Henry Grant as The Count, Walter Holland as The Colonel, E. Howard as Mira, William James as Franz, Henry Power as Polyte, Mrs. R. Atkinson as Sara, Marie Brewer as Noemie, Mary A. Victor as Batailleur, Louise Heron as Gertrude.

GOLDEN BAND, THE// D 4a// Henry Herman & Freeman Wills// **Olympic**, June 1887.

GOLDEN CALF, THE// C 3a// Douglas Jerrold// **Grecian**, July 1856, with Richard Phillips as Mounteney, Eaton O'Donnell as Chrystal, Henry Grant as Pinchbeck, Mr. Hustleby as Lord Tares, F. Charles as Echo, John Manning as Rags, Henry Power as Owley, Jane Coveney as Mrs. Mounteney, Ellen Hale as Clara, Miss Johnstone as Mrs. Pinchbeck, Ellen Crisp as Mrs. Heartsease.

GOLDEN CALF, THE; OR, DOLLARS AND DIMES// Pro & 3a// George Coveney// **Standard**, June 1883.

GOLDEN CASK, THE// D// n.a.// **Sadler's Wells**, Dec. 1866.

GOLDEN CHANCE, THE// D 6a// St. Aubin Miller// **Standard**, Aug. 1892.

GOLDEN DAGGERS, THE// D 5a// Adap. fr F by Charles Fechter & Edmund Yates// **Princess's**, Apr. 1862, with George Jordan as Sir Percival, Basil Potter as Duke de Rivas, Charles Fechter as Lester, J. G. Shore as Towah, Henry Widdicomb as Duckett, Mr. Garden as Old Jack, Robert Cathcart as Trevor, Mrs. Weston as Lady Mansfield, Carlotta Leclercq as Ellen, Miss Elsworthy as Duchess de Rivas/ Scenery by Gates, Cuthbert, & W. Telbin/ Machines by Mr. Sloman/ Music by W. H. Montgomery.

GOLDEN DUSTMAN, THE// D 4a// Adap. by H. B. Farnie fr novel of Charles Dickens, Our Mutual Friend// **Sad. Wells**, June 1866, with Thomas Swinbourne as Harmon, Mr. Barrett as Boffin, George Belmore as Wegg, Frank Barsby as Wrayburn, Alfred Bishop as Lightwood, Charles Warner as Headstone, William McIntyre as Riderhood, Walter Holland as Radfoot, Ada Dyas as Lizzie, Mrs. Poynter as Mrs. Wilfer, Fanny Gwynne as Bella, Ada Harland as Lavvy, Mrs. Bishop as Mrs. Boffin/ Scenery by John Johnson/ Music by John Barnard/ **Astley's**, Oct. 1866, with James Fernandez as Headstone, W. H. Stephens as Boffin, Edward Atkins as Wegg, W. T. Richardson as Wrayburn, Walter Joyce as Harmon, T. C. Harris as Riderhood, W. Arthur as Radfoot, Fanny Gwynne as Lizzie, Nelly Nisbett as Bella, Nelly Burton as Lavvy, Mrs. Caulfield as Mrs. Boffin/ Scenery by Julian Hicks/ Music by J. Barnard/ Machines by Mr. Lanham.

GOLDEN FARMER, THE; OR, THE LAST CRIME// D 2a// Benjamin Webster// **Victoria**, Mar. 1843, with Charles Williams as Lord Fitzallan, E. F. Saville as The Golden Farmer, William Seaman as Harvey, John Dale as Old Mobb, John Gardner as Hammer, Mr. Paul as Twitcher, Mrs. George Lee as Elizabeth, Miss Wilton as Louisa, Mrs. Griffith as Mrs. Hammer, Miss Saddler as Mary/ **Astley's**, 1867.

GOLDEN FRUIT// D 4a// Henry Pettitt// **East London**, July 1873.

GOLDEN GOBLIN, THE// D 4a// Frank Marryat// **Marylebone**, July 1888.

GOLDEN LADDER, THE// D 5a// George Sims & Wilson Barrett// **Globe**, Dec. 1887, with Wilson Barrett as Rev. Frank Thornhill, Mary Eastlake as Lillian Grant, Edith King as Lillie, George Barrett as Peckaby, Austin Melford as Severn, Harwood Cooper Cliffe as Peranza, Charles Hudson as Dixon, Charles Fulton as Grant, W. A. Elliott as Learoyd, Horace Hodges as Brunning, E. Cathcart as Inspector, Mrs. Henry Leigh as Mrs. Peckaby, Alice Belmore as Mrs. Freyne, Lillie Belmore as Mrs. Strickley, Phoebe Carlo as Victoria/ Scenery by William Telbin, Bruce Smith, & Walter Hann/ Music by M. Michael Connolly.

GOLDEN PLOUGH, THE// D 4a// Paul Meritt// **Adelphi**, Aug. 1877, with John Billington as Sir Francis, William Terriss as Rev. Preston, Frederick Moreland as Joshua, Samuel Emery as Jerry, J. G. Shore as Thomas, William McIntyre as Alfred, Henry Vaughan as Jim, Ernest Travers as Joe, Louise Willes as Grace, Alma Murray as May, Miss Hudspeth as Helen/ Scenery by Stafford Hall.

GOLDEN PROSPECT, THE; OR, A FORLORN HOPE// D 4a// Rev. & Alt. by J. J. Dowling & J. C. Stewart fr orig. of Katherine Rund// **Pavilion**, June 1891.

GOLDEN WEDDING, A// C// Sidney Valentine & Cyril Maude// **Haymarket**, June 1898.

GOLDFISH, THE// Play 3a// Trans. by A. T. de Mattos fr Dut. of W. G. van Nouhuys// **Opera Comique**, July 1892, with W. L. Abingdon as Herman Koorders, Philip Cunningham as Frans Koorders, Edward Lennox as Van Rompel, William Bonney as Joosten, Rex Shirley as Fransen, Jessie Millward as Marie, Maud Milton as Greta, Mrs. Edmund Phelps as Mrs. van Borsden, Charlotte Morland as Stijntje, Ada Branson as Doortje.

GOMBEEN'S GOLD, THE// D 5a// n.a.// **Sadler's Wells**, Mar. 1891.

GONDOLIER, THE; OR, THE THREE BANISHED MEN// D pro & 2a// n.a.// **Sad. Wells**, July 1857, with Watkins Young as Viconti, R. Green as Riccardo, Alfred Rayner as Sforza, Mr. Myon as Gaspardo, Charles Seyton as Raphael, Mrs. E. F. Saville as Catarina, Mr. Gladstone as Count Contarini, G. Shore as Francisco, John Chester as Brabantio, Kate May as Lady Blanche, Mary A. Victor as Rosalie.

GONE TO TEXAS// F 1a// John Oxenford// **Princess's**, Apr. 1845, with Walter Lacy as Swellington, Mr. Granby as Mildmay, Augustus Harris as Rapture, Mrs. Brougham as Mrs. Swellington, Miss Somers as Betty/ **Olympic**, Nov. 1845, with Walter Lacy as Swellington, Mr. Binge as Rapture, Robert Romer as Mildmay, Mrs. Lacy as Mrs. Swellington, Miss Harvey as Betty.

GONZAGA: A TALE OF FLORENCE// T 5a// Henry Solly// **St. Geo. Hall**, Apr. 1877.

GOOD AS GOLD// C 1a// Adap. by Charles Coghlan fr F// **Lyceum**, Dec. 1869.

GOOD AS GOLD; OR, A FRIEND IN NEED WHEN OTHERS FAIL// D 3a// C. H. Hazlewood// **Britannia**, Sept. 1869.

GOOD BUSINESS// C 1a// R. K. Hervey// **Novelty**, Dec. 1887/ **Lyceum**, Jan. 1888, with Arthur Williams, J. Le Hay, Forbes Dawson, Maria Jones.

GOOD-BYE// Play 1a// Seymore Hicks// **Court**, Nov. 1893, with William Herbert as Winter, Seymour Hicks as Lt. Winter, Wilfred Draycott as Strangeways, Ellaline Terriss as Mary.

GOOD-BYE// Play 1a// Henry Johnson// **Strand**, May 1896, with C. M. Lowne as Lt. Tibbets, J. A. Bentham as Lt. Melrose, Richard Blunt as Crosby, Francis Hawley as Kitson, Mary Allestree as Florence, Florence Forster as Hetty.

GOOD FOR NOTHING// F 1a// J. B. Buckstone// **Haymarket**, Feb. 1851, with J. B. Buckstone as Dibbles, Henry Howe as Collier, John Parselle as Charley, Mrs. Fitzwilliam as Nan; June 1885, with Henry Kemble as Dibbles, Charles Brookfield as Collier, Edmund Maurice as Charley, Mr. Elliot as Simpson, Mrs. Bancroft as Nan/ **Sad. Wells**, Apr. 1857, with Sarah Woolgar as Nan, John Chester as Dibbles, R. H. Lingham as Collier, Charles Seyton as Charley, Mr. Baily as Simpson; May 1869, with Rosetta Vacy as Nan, Richard Edgar as Dibbles/ **Adelphi**, Jan. 1859, with J. L. Toole as Dibbles, Mrs. Alfred Mellon (Sarah Woolgar) as Nan/ **Lyceum**, May 1859, with Charles Young as Dibbles, William Belford as Harry, F. Charles as Charley, Marie Wilton as Nan/ **Princess's**, Mar. 1860, with J. L. Toole as Dibbles, J. G. Shore as Harry, Robert Cathcart as Charley, Louise Keeley as Nan/ **Olympic**, Sept. 1865, with Mrs. Alfred Mellon (Sarah Woolgar)/ **Olympic**, Oct. 1877, with Robert Pateman as Tom Dibbles, Johnston Forbes Robertson as Collier, T. G. Warren as Charley, George Peyton as Young Simpson/ **Haymarket**, Dec. 1889.

GOOD FOR NOTHING// F// Edmund Yates & N. H. Harrington// **Adelphi**, Dec. 1858.

GOOD FOR NOTHING// F 1a// n.a.// **Globe**, Nov. 1868, with Clara Thorne as Nell, Charles Warner as Dormer, John Newbound as Johnstone, E. Marshall as Bibbles, Henry Andrews as Simpson.

GOOD FORTUNE// C 3a// Adap. by Charles Coghlan fr F of Octave Feuillet// **St. James's**, Dec. 1880, with W. H. Kendal as Denis, John Clayton as Sir George, Wilfred Draycott as Bolger, T. N. Wenman as Ward, Mr. Brandon as Dr. Chester, Mr. Mackintosh as Gilbert, Mrs. Stephens as Lady Banks, Mrs. Gaston Murray as Mrs. Ransome, Mrs. W. H. Kendal as Isabel, Linda Dietz as Miss Somers, Miss B. Buckstone as Jenny/ Scenery by Gordon & Harford.

GOOD GRACIOUS!// C// George Hawtrey// **Court**, Jan. 1885.

GOOD HEARTS// n.a.// **Surrey**, Nov. 1858.

GOOD INTENTIONS// C// n.a.// **Sad. Wells**, Aug. 1849, with A. Younge as Sweetpea, Mr. Williams as Grab, William Hoskins as Rushington, Charles Fenton as Peter, Mrs. Henry Marston as Mrs. Snaps, Fanny Marsh as Amelia.

GOOD NAME, A// F 1a// J. H. Stocqueler// **Lyceum**, May 1845, with Frank Matthews as Goodman, Mr. Stanton as Walker, Charles Bender as Pennywick, Drinkwater Meadows as Joe, Miss Dawson as Emily, Mrs. Woollidge as Mrs. Weasel.

GOOD-NATURED MAN, THE// C 5a// Oliver Goldsmith// **Sad. Wells**, Dec. 1850, with Henry Mellon as Sir William, Henry Marston as Honeywood, A. Younge as Croaker, William Hoskins as Lofty, Mr. Williams as Jarvis, Charles Wheatleigh as Leontine, Frederick Younge as Muggins, Sarah Lyons as Miss Richland, Miss Marston as Olivia, Mrs. Archbold as Mrs. Croaker, Miss Glindon as Garnet/ **Gaiety**, Feb. 1881/ **Vaudeville**, Nov. 1886.

GOOD NEWS// D 3a// H. J. Byron// **Gaiety**, Aug. 1872.

GOOD NIGHT'S REST, A; OR, TWO IN THE MORNING// F 1a// Mrs. C. Gore// **Strand**, July 1839/ **Olympic**, Jan 1846, with James Browne as Snobbington, Walter Lacy as Stranger.

GOOD OLD TIMES, THE// D 4a// Hall Caine & Wilson Barrett// **Princess's**, Feb. 1889, with Wilson Barrett as Langley, Mary Eastlake as Mary, Lewis Waller as Grainger, S. M. Carson as Parson Langley, Austin Melford as Barton, Charles Hudson as Braithwaite, George Barrett as Joe, Robert Pateman as Spot, Harwood Cooper Cliffe as Moore, T. W. Percyval as Col. Wayne, Miss Webster as Lucy, Lily Belmore as Biddy, Miss A. Cooke as Martha, Miss A. Gambier as Sally/ Scenery by Walter Hann/ Music by Michael Connolly.

GOOD RUN FOR IT, A// F 1a// T. V. Bridgeman// **Sad. Wells**, Feb. 1854, with J. W. Ray as Kickshaw, Mr. Barrett as O'Mulligataway, Lewis Ball as Slickem, Miss Portman as Mrs. Kickshaw, Eliza Travers as Jemima.

GOOSE WITH THE GOLDEN EGGS, THE// F 1a// Augustus Mayhew & Sutherland Edwards//

Strand, Sept. 1859/ **Olympic,** Sept. 1866, with C. Murray as Turby, Robert Soutar as Flickster, Henry Reeves as Benser, Mrs. Williams as Mrs. Turby, Miss E. Wilson as Clara/ **Adelphi,** Nov. 1875, with John Clarke as Turby, James Fawn as Hickster, W. Everard as Bouser, Mrs. Charlton as Mrs. Turby, Miss E. Phillips as Clara/ **Haymarket,** June 1875, with E. W. Royce as Turby, Charles Steyne as Flickster, E. A. Russell as Bouser, Mrs. Clifford Cooper as Mrs. Turby, Rose Egan as Miss Turby/ **St. James's,** June 1885, with Mr. Mackintosh as Turby, E. Hendrie as Flickster, T. W. Lovell as Bouser, Mrs. Paget as Mrs. Turby, Miss Webster as Clara, May Whitty as Mary.

GOSSIP// C 2a// Adap. by Augustus Harris & T. J. Williams fr F// **Princess's,** Nov. 1859, with Mrs. Charles Young.

GOSSIP// C 4a// Clyde Fitch & Leo Dietrichstein// **Grand,** June 1895/ **Comedy,** Feb. 1896, with Leonard Boyne as Count Marcy, Herbert Standing as Stanford, J. W. Piggott as Barry, E. Cosham as Dr. Robbins, Stuart Chamption as Berney, Eleanor Calhoun as Mrs. Stanford, Annette Skirving as Miriam, Clara Daniels as Mrs. Cummings, Esmé Beringer as Clara, Lillie Langtry as Mrs. Barry/ Scenery by Walter Johnstone.

GOTOBED TOM!// F 1a// Thomas Morton// **Olympic,** Nov. 1852.

GOTZEN// D 4a// Henri Blau// **St. Geo. Hall,** Mar. 1901.

GOVERNESS, THE// D Pro & 4a// Adap. by Adolphe Belot fr Miss Multon// **Olympic,** Oct. 1886.

GOVERNOR'S WIFE, THE; OR, MATRIMONIAL SPECULATIONS// C 2a// T. Mildenhall// **Olympic,** Sept. 1848, with W. H. Norton as The Governor, Samuel Emery as Capt. Holystone, Frederick Vining as Lt. Trevor, H. J. Turner as Short, Harwood Cooper as Neb, Clara Wynne as Mrs. Somerdown, Mrs. C. A. Tellet as Letty/ **Sad. Wells,** Apr. 1847, with R. H. Lingham as The Governor, Charles Fenton as Capt. Holystone, J. G. Shore as Lt. Trevor, Robert Keeley as Short, Mrs. Keeley as Letty, Marianne Jackson as Miss Somerdown/ **Drury Lane,** Dec. 1861, with Henry Mellon as The Governor, Edward Atkins as Short, Mr. Tilbury as Capt. Holystone, H. Farrell as Lt. Trevor, Frank Barsby as Neb, Miss E. Arden as Miss Somerdown, Louise Keeley as Letty.

GRACE HUNTLEY// D// Henry Holl// **Sad. Wells,** Mar. 1839, with Mr. Cathcart as Huntley, Dibdin Pitt as Darnley, Mr. Dry as Smith, Benjamin Conquest as Simon, Mr. Harwood as Giles, Mrs. Robert Honner as Grace, Mrs. Harwood as Peggy, W. D. Broadfoot as Justice, Mr. Phillips as Lambert, J. W. Collier as Cracks.

GRANDFATHER WHITEHEAD// Adap. by Mark Lemon fr F// **Haymarket,** Sept. 1842, with Mr. Tilbury as Drayton, William Farren as Whitehead, Mr. Stuart as Langley, William Strickland as Driver, Benjamin Webster as Lincoln, William Clark as Snap, Mrs. Edwin Yarnold as Louisa, Mrs. Stanley as Susan.

GRANDFATHER'S CLOCK// D 3a// C. E. Bertrand// **Pavilion,** Aug. 1879.

GRANDFATHER'S CLOCK// F// Joseph Barron// **Sad. Wells,** Dec. 1883.

GRANDFATHER'S SECRET// D 1a// n.a.// **Surrey,** June 1885.

GRANDMOTHER GRIZZLE// C// J. B. Buckstone// **Haymarket,** Sept. 1851, with Mr. Lambert as Sir Oliver, John Parselle as Pinchbecke, A. Brindal as Sidney, J. B. Buckstone as Fuddle, Mrs. Fitzwilliam as Mrs. Pinchbecke, Amelia Vining as Polly, Mrs. L. S. Buckingham as Cicely, Mrs. Caulfield as Betsey.

GRANDSIRE, THE// Play 3a// Adap. by Archer Woodhouse fr F of Jean Richepin, Le Flibustier// **Terry's,** May 1880/ **Avenue,** May 1890.

GRANNA WAILE AND THE BRIDAL EVE// D// J. Archer// **East London,** Dec. 1874.

GRAPE GIRL OF MADRID, THE; OR, THE MAN, THE SPIRIT, AND THE MORAL// D// n.a.// **Victoria,** June 1858, with W. H. Pitt as de Morisco, James Elphinstone as Paul, George Pearce as Perez, Mr. Henderson as Manuel, James Howard as Corp. Plunge, Henry Dudley as Braganza, Mr. Morrison as Julien, F. H. Henry as Fernando, George Yarnold as Sancho, S. Sawford as O'Splash, Jane Dawson as Maremma, Julia Seaman as Constanza, Mrs. Alfred Saville as Beatrix.

GRASSHOPPER, THE// D 3a// Adap. by Benjamin Webster Jr. fr F novel of Georges Sand// **Olympic,** Aug. 1867, with Horace Wigan as Old Barbeau, John Clayton as Landry Barbeau, Dominick Murray as Beaucadet, Harwood Cooper as Aldemine, Ada Webb as Fanchon, Emma Webb as Mère Fadet, Miss Sheridan as Madelon/ Scenery by Hawes Craven/ Music by Edwin Ellis/ Prod. by Horace Wigan.

GRASSHOPPER, THE// CD 3a// Adap. by John Hollingshead fr F novel of Georges Sand// **Gaiety,** Dec. 1877.

GRATITUDE; OR, A BATTLE FOR GOLD// D 3a// W. H. Pitt// **Britannia,** June 1869.

GRAVEN IMAGE, THE; OR, THE ARTIST OF ROME// D 3a// T. Cheatham// **Grecian,** Mar. 1862, with Thomas Mead as Florio, Henry Grant as Count Raphael, Alfred Rayner as Father Barnabas, John Manning as Poppolo, Mrs. Charles Dillon as Angela, Jane Dawson as Ursula, Mary A. Victor as Nathalle.

GRAY LADY OF FERNLEA, THE// D// C. H. Hazlewood// **Britannia,** Sept. 1867.

GRAY LADYE OF FERNLEA, THE// D// Edward Towers// **City of London,** Aug. 1867.

GREAT CATCH, A// C 3a// Hamilton Aïdé// **Olympic,** Mar. 1883, with W. H. Vernon as

Sir Martin, David Fisher as Lord de Motteville, F. Staunton as Sir George, Herbert Beerbohm Tree as Lord Boodle, T. C. Bindloss as Anson, Mrs. Leigh Murray as Lady de Motteville, Lucy Buckstone as Bertha, Janet Achurch as Lady Stanmore, Katie Lee as Miss Beaumont, Genevieve Ward as Mrs. de Motteville.

GREAT CITY, THE// D 4a// Andrew Halliday// **Drury Lane**, June 1867, with Charles Warner as Lord Churchmouse, Frederick Morton as Dawlish, Mr. Fitzjames as Maj. O'Gab, Charles Harcourt as Carrington, Frederick Villiers as Mendez, J. C. Cowper as Blount, William McIntyre as Mogg, John Rouse as Jenkinson, Joseph Irving as Jack, J. B. Johnstone as Bos/ Scenery by William Beverley/ Music by J. H. Tully/ Gas by J. Hinkley/ Prod. by Edward Stirling/ **Grecian**, Dec. 1867 (in 3a), with W. Shirley as Lord Churchmouse, Samuel Perfitt as Dawlish, Henry Grant as Maj. O'Gab, George Gillett as Carrington, J. Jackson as Mendez, William James as Blount, Alfred Rayner as Mogg, John Manning as Jenkinson, George Conquest as Ragged Jack, Lizzie Mandelbert as Edith, Alice Denvil as Mrs. Mauvray, Mrs. Atkinson as Aunt Judith/ Scenery by Mr. Messender/ Music by J. H. Tully/ Prod. by George Conquest/ **Surrey**, Nov. 1869.

GREAT DEMONSTRATION, THE// F 1a// Israel Zangwill// **Royalty**, Sept. 1892, with Frank Lindo as Howard, R. H. Douglass as Boggles, Lizzie Ruggles as Mary.

GREAT DIAMOND ROBBERY, THE// D Pro & 4a// W. R. Waldron & Burford Delannoy// **Sadler's Wells**, Oct. 1892.

GREAT DIAMOND ROBBERY, THE// D 4a// E. M. Elfriend & A. C. Wheeler// **Pavilion**, May 1898.

GREAT DIVORCE CASE, THE// C 3a// Clement Scott ("John Doe") & J. C. Ponsonby ("Richard Roe")// **Criterion**, Apr. 1876.

GREAT EXPECTATIONS// D Pro & 3a// Dram. by W. S. Gilbert fr Charles Dickens// **Court**, May 1871.

GREAT FELICIDAD, THE// C 3a// H. M. Paull// **Gaiety**, Mar. 1887.

GREAT METROPOLIS, THE// D 5a// Rewr. by William Terriss & Henry Neville fr orig. of Lester Teale & George Jessop// **Princess's**, Feb. 1892.

GREAT MILLIONAIRE, THE// D 5a// Cecil Raleigh// **Drury Lane**, Sept. 1901.

GREAT PINK PEARL, THE// Play 3a// R. C. Carton & Cecil Raleigh// **Olympic**, May 1885, with C. D. Marius, Hamilton Bell, Gabrielle Goldney, Clara Jecks.

GREAT RUBY, THE// D 4a// Cecil Raleigh & Henry Hamilton// **Drury Lane**, Sept. 1898, with Mrs. John Wood as Lady Garnett, Mrs. Raleigh as Countess Charkoff, Bella Pateman as Mrs. Elsmere, Miss Hoffman as Brenda, Marie Rignold as Moya, Mabel Lowe as Kathleen, Lillian Menelly as Louisa, Birdie Sutherland as Flossie, Augusta Walters as Millie, Mary Brough as Jane, Robert Loraine as Prince Wadia, C. M. Lowne as Viscount Montyghal, J. B. Gordon as Sir John, Dawson Milward as Capt. Dalrymple, Robert Pateman as Longman/ Scenery by W. Perkins, Mr. McLeery, Bruce Smith & R. Caney/ Music by J. M. Glover/ Machines by E. Taylor/ Prod. by Arthur Collins.

GREAT RUSSIAN BEAR, THE; OR, ANOTHER RETREAT FROM MOSCOW// D// Thomas Morton// **Strand**, Oct. 1859, with Maria Simpson, Marie Wilton.

GREAT SENSATION, A// F 1a// Smyth Lee// **Sad. Wells**, May 1862, with Henry Forrester as Dunner, A. Baildon as Jones, C. Lloyds as Prancer, Charles Crook as Tottle, Miss M. Percy as Mrs. Dunner, Emily Dowton as Fanny, Mrs. Ersser Jones as Mrs. Prancer, Bessie Heath as Sarah.

GREAT STRIKE, THE// D// n.a.// **Pavilion**, Oct. 1866.

GREAT TEMPTATION, THE// F// n.a.// **East London**, May 1874.

GREAT UNKNOWN, THE// C 3a// Adap. by Augustin Daly fr G of Franz von Schönthan & Gustav Kadelberg, Die Berümpte Frau// **Lyceum**, Aug. 1890, with James Lewis as Jeremiah Jarraway, John Drew as Ned Dreemer, Frederick Bond as O'Donnell, Eugene Ormond as Tom Prowde, Will Sampson as Patrick, Ada Rehan as Etna, Isabel Irving as Pansy, May Silvie as Mrs. Jarraway, Mrs. G. H. Gilbert as Aunt Penelope, Edith Crane as Shirley.

GREAT UNPAID, THE// C 3a// Adap. by Fred Horner fr F of Alexandre Bisson, Le Famille Pont-Biquet// Comedy, May 1893, with W. H. Vernon as Clements, Cyril Maude as Knight-Williams, H. V. Esmond as Watts, E. W. Gardiner as Somerset, Herman de Lange as Bouillabaisse, Frank Wood as Wurzel, Wilfred Shine as Pettifer, Mary A. Victor as Mrs. Knight-Williams, Annie Hill as Eva, Beatrice Ferrar as Grace, Mary Rorke as Mrs. Clements.

GREAT WORLD OF LONDON, THE// D 4a// George Lander & Walter Melville// **Standard**, Oct. 1898.

GREATEST OF THESE—, THE// D 4a// Sidney Grundy// **Garrick**, June 1896.

GREED OF GOLD// D 4a// H. R. Silva// **Surrey**, July 1896.

GREEK CAPTIVE, THE; OR, INGOMAR THE BARBARIAN (see Ingomar)

GREEK SOPRANO, THE// C 1a// n.a.// **Strand**, Sept. 1897.

GREEN BUSHES, THE; OR, A HUNDRED YEARS AGO// D 3a// J. B. Buckstone// **Adelphi**, Jan. 1845, with Charles Selby as O'Kennedy, Charles Hudson as George, O. Smith as Murtogh,

John Sanders as Kelly, Mrs. Yates as Geraldine, Mrs. Fitzwilliam as Nelly, Mme. Celeste as Miami, Paul Bedford as Jack Gong/ Music by Alfred Mellon/ Scenery by Pitt & Johnstone/ Machinery by Mr. Cooper; Dec. 1880, with Henry Neville, Robert Pateman, Bella Pateman, Mrs. Bernard Beere, Lydia Foote; Apr. 1890/ **Haymarket**, July 1848, with Charles Boyce as O'Kennedy, Redmond Ryan as George, O. Smith as Murtogh, John Sanders as Kelly, Mrs. Yates as Geraldine, Sarah Woolgar as Nelly, James Worrell as Capt. Dartois, Edward Wright as Grinnidge, Paul Bedford as Gong, Mme. Celeste as Miami, Mrs. Worrell as Tigertail/ **Sad. Wells**, May 1855, with E. F. Edgar as O'Kennedy, Frederick Moreland as George, Henry Butler as Murtogh, Robert Soutar as Kelly, Miss Cleveland as Geraldine, Kate Kelly as Nelly, C. Kelsey as Capt. Dartois, W. Shalders as Grinnage, George Cooke as Jack Gong/ Music by Edward Fitzwilliam & Alfred Mellon; June 1858, with John Billington as O'Kennedy, Frederick Moreland as George, Edmund Garden as Murtogh, Miss Arden as Geraldine, Mary Keeley as Melly, Mr. Henry as Dartois, Charles Selby as Grinnidge, Paul Bedford as Gong, Mme. Celeste as Miami, Miss Laidlaw as Tigertail, Robert Romer as Dennis; Sept. 1872, with George Warde as O'Kennedy, Henry Sidney as George, J. G. Rainbow as Murtoch, James Fawn as Grinnidge, Henry Leigh as Gong, Clavering Power as Dartois, Marie Henderson as Mme. St. Aubert and Miami, Mrs. C. T. Burleigh as Geraldine, Mrs. Hudspeth as Nelly, Eliza Rainbow as Meg, Miss H. Farren as Tigertail.

GREEN-EYED MONSTER, THE// C 1a// J. R. Planché// **Haymarket**, June 1839, with William Farren as Baron Speyenhausen, Mr. Hemming as Col. Arnsdorf, Walter Lacy as Marcus, J. B. Buckstone as Krout, Mrs. Danson as Lady Speyenhausen, Miss Travers as Amelia, Mrs. Fitzwilliam as Luise; Nov. 1850, with Mr. Lambert as Baron Speyenhausen, John Parselle as Col. Arnsdorf, Charles Selby as Marcus, Henry Bedford as Krout, Mrs. Stanley as Lady Speyenhausen, Amelia Vining as Amelia, Priscilla Horton as Luise/ **Sad. Wells**, Apr. 1848, with A. Younge as Baron Speyenhausen, J. T. Johnson as Count Arnsdorf, William Hoskins as Marcas, Henry Scharf as Kraut, Mrs. Henry Marston as Baroness Speyenhausen, Miss Cooper as Amelia, Julia St. George as Louise/ **Olympic**, Aug. 1856, with Frederick Robson as Baron Speyenhausen, Gaston Murray as Col. Arnsdorf, George Vining as Marcus, Mr. Danvers as Kraut, Miss Castleton as Mady Speyenhausen, Miss Bromley as Amelia, Fanny Ternan as Luise.

GREEN HILLS OF THE FAR WEST, THE// D// John Wilkins// **City of London**, 1861/ **Grecian**, Dec. 1866, with Samuel Perfitt as Wentworth, Henry Grant as Col. Dart, Charles Mortimer as Marston, George Gillett as Walter, William James as Gilbert, Alfred Rayner as Bob, John Manning as Scrubbs, Henry Power as Calix, Mrs. Dearlove as Madeline, Lizzie Mandelbert as Azenie, Alice Denvil as Alice, Mary A. Victor as Dolly.

GREEN HILLS OF TYROL, THE// D// T. P. Taylor// **Sad. Wells**, Sept. 1837, with Mr. Wilkins as Arnold, C. H. Pitt as Walter, Mr. Griffiths as Conrad, Thomas Lee as Blueskin, Mr. Scarbrow as Lichenstein, Mr. King as Duval, Mr. Campbell as Balz, Lavinia Melville as Marie, Miss Williams as Ella, Miss Vernon as Rose.

GREEN LANES OF ENGLAND, THE// D 4a// George Conquest & Henry Pettitt// **Grecian**, Aug. 1878.

GREEN RIDERS, THE; OR, IVAN DE BASSENVELT// D 3a// n.a.// **Grecian**, Feb. 1855, with Henry Grant as Duke Angelo, F. Charles as Ferdinand, Richard Phillips as Ivan, Basil Potter as Malothen, John Manning as Charley Huntem, Henry Power as Maurice, Jane Coveney as Madeline, Miss Johnstone as Widow Justine, Harriet Coveney as Patty.

GREENWICH PENSIONER, THE// CD 2a// C. S. Cheltnam// **Adelphi**, July 1869.

GRELLEY'S MONEY// D 4a// Eric Ross// **Marylebone**, Aug. 1887.

GRETCHEN// D 4a// Adap. by W. S. Gilbert fr Goethe's <u>Faust</u>// **Olympic**, Mar. 1879, with H. B. Conway as Faustus, John Billington as Gottfried, Frank Archer as Mephisto, Mr. Vollaire as Anselm, J. A. Rosier as Domenic, Mrs. Bernard Beere as Lisa, Miss Folkard as Barbara, Marion Terry as Gretchen/ Scenery by Gordon, Lloyd, & W. Hann/ Prod. by G. S. Gilbert.

GRETNA GREEN// F// Samuel Beazley// **Haymarket**, Sept. 1838, with Robert Strickland as Tomkins, Mr. Hemming as Lord Lovel, T. F. Mathews as Larder, Benjamin Wrench as Jenkins, Miss Gallot as Emily, Mrs. Fitzwilliam as Betty/ **Cov. Garden**, June 1840, with Mr. Fitzjames as Lord Lovel, William Bennett as Tomkins, W. H. Oxberry as Larder, Benjamin Wrench as Jenkins, Miss Kelly as Betty, Miss Lee as Emily.

GREY DOUBLET, THE// F 1a// Mark Lemon// **Eng. Opera House** (Lyceum), Aug. 1838, with Mr. Baker as Charles II, Mr. Burnett as St. Clair, Mr. Halfourd as Digby, Henry Compton as Simon Bung, Lavinia Melville as Catherine.

GREY MARE, THE// FC 3a// G. R. Sims & Cecil Raleigh (drawn in part fr G of Roderik Benedix, <u>Das Lügen</u>)// **Comedy**, Jan. 1892, with Charles Hawtrey as John Maxwell, Eric Lewis as David Maxwell, James Nelson as Count de Chevrelle, William Wyes as Collins, Ernest Cosham as Stubbs, Gerard Gurney as Algernon, W. F. Hawtrey as Beswick, Charles Brookfield as Col. Gravacahn, Annie Irish as Julia, Adrienne Dairolles as Marie, Violet Armbruster as Hélène, Lottie Venne as Kate.

GREY PARROT, THE// Play 1a// W. W. Jacobs & Charles Rock// **Strand**, Nov. 1899, with Charles Rock as Gannet, George Shelton as Hobson, Wilton Heriot as Rogers, Cybel Wynne as Mrs. Gannet, Robertha Erskine as Mrs. Rogers.

GRIERSON'S WAY// Play 4a// H. V. Esmond// **Haymarket**, Feb. 1899, with George Titheradge as Grierson, J. H. Barnes as Capt. Ball, Fred Terry as Capt. Murray, H. V. Esmond as Keen, Pattie Bell as Miss Anne, Lena Ashwell as Pamela.

GRIF// D 4a// Adap. by W. Lestocq fr novel of L. Farjeon// **Surrey**, Oct. 1891.

GRIFFITH MURDOCH// Play 4a// Montague Spier// **St. Geo. Hall**, Mar. 1893.

GRIMALDI; OR, THE LIFE OF AN ACTRESS// D 5a// Dion Boucicault// **Adelphi**, Mar. 1862.

GRIMSHAW, BAGSHAW, AND BRADSHAW// F 1a// J. Maddison Morton// **Haymarket**, July 1851, with J. B. Buckstone as Grimshaw, Henry Bedford as Bagshaw, A. Brindal as Bradshaw, Charles Selby as Towzer, Mrs. L. S. Buckingham as Fanny, Amelia Vining as Emily.

GRINGOIRE// Play 1a// Adap. by W. G. Wills fr F of Théodore de Banville// **Prince's**, June 1885, with Richard Mansfield, Dorothy Dene/ **Globe**, Jan. 1891, with Ian Robertson as Louis XI, Norman Forbes as Gringoire, George Bernage as Fourniez, H. De Lange as Olivier, Mary Ansell as Louise, Adrienne Dairolles as Susan/ Scenery by W. Harford/ Costumes by Edwin Abbey/ Music by C. J. Hargitt.

GRINGOIRE// Play 1a// Adap. by B. C. Stephenson fr F of Théodore de Banville// **Haymarket**, June 1899, with Charles Allan as Louis XI, Alan Mackinnon as Gringoire, A. J. Tassell as le Dain, J. Brabourn as Fournier, W. R. Stephenson as Archer, Lily Hanbury as Loyse, Hilda Hanbury as Dame Nicole.

GRIP OF IRON, THE// D 4a// Adap. by Arthur Shirley fr F of Adolphe Belot, Les Etrangleurs de Paris// **Surrey**, Oct. 1887/ **Princess's**, June 1896, with Fred Powell as Jagon, James Thompson as de Ribas, Charles East as Blanchard, Arthur Godfrey as de Coucon, Wilfred Carr as de Belfort, Charles Girdlestone as De Baudin, Florence Nelson as Sophie, Frances Ruttledge as Marie, Cissie Liston as Babette, Florence Townsend as Zelie.

GRIP OF STEEL, THE// D 4a// Arthur Shirley & Benjamin Landeck// **Surrey**, Dec. 1892.

GRISELDA; OR, THE PATIENT WIFE// D 4a// Mrs. M. E. Braddon// **Princess's**, Nov. 1873, with William Rignold as Gualtiero, Wybert Rousby as Cosmo, Mr. Bruton as Paolo, John Clarke as Beppo, Mr. Egan as Envoy, Stanislaus Calhaem as Lelio, Mrs. Rousby as Griselda, Miss Everard as Anna, Miss Kemp as Anita/ Scenery by Frederick Fenton & Mr. Emden/ Gas by Mr. Cooper/ Lime-light by Mr. Cox/ Music by John Barnard/ Prod. by Alfred Nelson.

GRIST TO THE MILL// C 2a// J. R. Planché// **Haymarket**, Feb. 1844, with Henry Holl as Prince de Conti, C. J. Mathews as Marquis de Richeville, William Strickland as Merluchet, Henry Howe as Dumont, Mrs. W. Clifford as Mme. de Merluchet, Mme. Vestris as Francine.

GROVES OF BLARNEY, THE// D 3a// Mrs. S. G. Hall// **Adelphi**, Apr. 1838.

GUARDIAN ANGEL, A// C 1a// John Oxenford & Joseph Hatton// **St. James's**, Oct. 1874, with John Rouse as Trumble, C. W. Norton as Stubbs, Walter Vernon as Wise, Louise Howard as Mrs. Trumble, Bessie Hollingshead as Lucy, Inez D'Aquilar as Mrs. Stubbs, J. L. Hall as Fidget.

GUARDIAN ANGEL, THE// F// C. W. Brooks// **Haymarket**, Oct. 1849, with Henry Howe as Capt. Myrtle, Mr. Tilbury as Cranky, Henry Vandenhoff as Lazytongs, Robert Keeley as Dulcimer, Mrs. L. S. Buckingham as Mrs. Myrtle, Emma Harding as Kate, Mrs. Keeley as Moggy.

GUARDIANS OFF THEIR GUARD, THE// C 2a// Adap. fr Susanna Centlivre's A Bold Stroke for a Wife// **Olympic**, Feb. 1840, with Mr. Butler as Col. Feignwell, Morris Barnett as Modelove, Mr. Brookes as Perriwinkle, Richard Jones as Prim, Mr. Halford as Freeman, Mr. Baker as Tradelove, George Wild as Simon Pure, Miss Fitzwalter as Anne, Mrs. Sarah Garrick as Mrs. Pure, Miss Stephens as Betty.

GUDGEONS// C 3a// Murray Carson ("Thornton Clark") & L. N. Parker// **Terry's**, Nov. 1893, with Murray Carson as Hooper, Charles Fulton as Harrison, W. T. Lovell as Ffolliott, Richard Blunt as Gover, James Welch as Smith, Herbert Waring as Treherne, Charlotte Morland as Bundy, Sybil Carlisle as Persis, Janette Steer as Mrs. Treherne/ Scenery by Richard Durant.

GUERILLA CHIEF, THE; OR, THE LAST OF HIS NAME// D 2a// J. S. Balls// **Sad. Wells** Jan. 1841, with Mr. Elvin as Capt. Damien, Charles Fenton as Lt. Davrieux, Mr. Priorson as Perez, Mr. Dry as Losquez, J. S. Balls as Ronquillo, Mr. Stilt as Marten, Mr. Aldridge as Don Sosa, Mr. Williams as Michael, Mrs. Richard Barnett as Clara, Miss Richardson as Mary, Miss Cooke as Gianetta/ Scenery by F. Fenton/ Music by Isaac Collins/ Machines by B. Sloman/ Prod. by R. Honner.

GUERILLAS, THE; OR, THE STORMING OF ST. SEBASTIAN// D 2a// n.a.// **Victoria**, Feb. 1850, with Mr. Carter as Col. Debois, S. Sawford as Capt. Charleville, Frederick Byefield as Dubois, J. H. Rickards as Moreno, John Bradshaw as Diaz, George Pearce as Sebastian, F. H. Henry as Fernandez, I. Cohen as Cadorina, Angelina Bathurst as Julietta, Miss Barrowcliffe as Marguerite, Miss Laporte as Rosetta.

GUIDING STAR, THE; OR, THE ADVENTURER'S BRIDE// D 3a// W. E. Suter// **East London**, Feb. 1868.

GUILTY GOVERNESS AND THE DOWNEY DOCTOR, THE// C// n.a.// **Folly**, May 1876.

GUILTY MAN, THE// D 4a// St. Aubyn Miller// **Britannia**, July 1900.

GUILTY MOTHER, A// D 5a// Benjamin

Landeck// **Pavilion**, Apr. 1894.

GUILY MOTHER, THE// D// A. Faucquez// **Grecian**, June 1862, with Thomas Mead as Francois, Alfred Rayner as Jacques, Walter Holland as Hubert, F. Smithson as Maitland, Mr. Howard as Riz, Henry Power as Benolt, Helen Love as Mme. Veril, Kate Verner as Blanche, Ellen Hale as Marie, Mary A. Victor as Ninette/ **Sad. Wells**, Sept. 1862, with Henry Forrester as Francois, Henry Frazer as Jacques, Mr. Regan as Hubert, N. Harrison as Maitland, Charles Bender as Riz, Charles Crook as Benolt, John Dale as Capt. Brauelbas, Harry Dalton as Antonio, Julia Seaman as Mme. Veril, Louise Stuart as Blanche, Bessie Heath as Marie, Emily Dowton as Ninette.

GUILTY OR NOT GUILTY// D// Charles Hilder// **Grecian**, July 1882.

GUILTY SHADOWS// CD Pro & 4a// Emile de Witt// **Imperial**, Feb. 1885.

GUINEA GOLD; OR, LIGHTS AND SHADOWS OF LONDON LIFE// D 4a// H. J. Byron// **Princess's**, Sept. 1877, with Charles Warner as John Rawlinson, William Rignold as Richard Rawlinson, Harry Jackson as Tweezer, W. H. Stephens as Larch, T. P. Haynes as Sprottler, Fannie Leslie as Rob, G. H. Rogers as Ruffler, B. Bentley as Eaglet, T. W. Thorne as Golland, Lydia Foote as Guinea, Marie Illington as Polly, Mrs. R. Power as Mrs. Medlicott, Nellie Palmer as Mrs. O'Flanagan/ Scenery by Julian Hicks/ Machines by Mr. Wharton/ Gas by Mr. Jones/ Lime-light by Mr. Kerr/ Music by W. C. Levey/ Prod. by Henry Jackson.

GUINEA STAMP, THE// D// n.a.// **Globe**, Mar. 1875.

GUINEA STAMP, THE// Play 1a// Cyril Hallward// **Comedy**, Apr. 1896.

GUNPOWDER PLOT, A// F 1a// Sidney Hodges// **Olympic**, May 1873, with J. K. Murray as Maj. Buffles, C. H. Peveril as Fielder, Mr. Graeme as Sam, Elise Melville as Mrs. Simkin, Miss C. Brabant as Bella, Miss Griffiths as Susan.

GUV'NOR, THE// FC 3a// Adap. by Robert Reece ("E. G. Lankester") fr G// **Vaudeville**, June 1880, with John Maclean, Thomas Thorne, Marie Illington, Cicely Richards; Jan. 1893.

GUY DOMVILLE// Play 3a// Henry James// **St. James's**, Jan. 1895, with George Alexander as Domville, W. G. Elliott as Lord Devenish, Herbert Waring as Humber, H. V. Esmond as Round, Marion Terry as Mrs. Peverel, Mrs. Edward Saker as Mrs. Domville, Evelyn Millard as Mary, Irene Vanbrugh as Fanny/ Scenery by H. P. Hall.

GUY FAWKES; OR, THE GUNPOWDER CONSPIRACY OF 1605// D// n.a.// **Sad. Wells**, Nov. 1840, with Mr. Williams as James I, Mr. Houghburt as Salisbury, Charles Fenton as Suffolk, Mr. Elvin as Mounteagle, J. W. Collier as Collywobble, Mrs. Richard Barnett as Lady Alice, Miss Richardson as Eleanor, Henry Marston as Tresham, Mr. Aldridge as Digby, J. B. Hill as Piercy, Mr. Dry as Catesby, Robert Honner as Faux.

GUY MANNERING; OR, THE GIPSY'S PROPHECY// D// Dram. by J. R. Planché fr novel of Sir Walter Scott//**St. James's**, Jan. 1837, with Mr. Saville as Col. Mannering, John Braham as Henry Bertram, John Pritt Harley as Sampson, G. Stansbury as Dinmont, Mr. Hollingsworth as Mucklethrift, Mr. Daly as Hatteraick, Robert Strickland as Glossin, Mr. Leffler as Gabriel, Miss C. Booth as Franco, Julia Smith as Julia, Miss Rainforth as Lucy, Miss Allison as Flora, Mme. Sala as Meg Merrilies/ **Drury Lane**, May 1837, with Charles Diddear as Col. Mannering, Mr. Wilson as Henry Bertram, Mr. Shuter as Glossin, Drinkwater Meadows as Sampson, Mr. Hughes as Mucklethrift, Mr. Howell as Sgt. McCraw, S. Jones as Gabriel, Mr. Mears as Sebastian, Mr. Henry as Crabtree, Miss Betts as Lucy, Miss Romer as Julia, Mrs. Humby as Flora, Mrs. C. Jones as Mrs. McCandlish, Mrs. W. Clifford as Meg Merrilies; Apr. 1850, with Charles Fisher as Col. Mannering, Mr. Rafter as Henry Bertram, Basil Baker as Sampson, Samuel Emery as Dinmont, Mr. Frazer as Hatteraick, Thomas Barry as Mucklethrift, John Parry as Glossin, Lucy Rafter as Julia, Miss E. Nelson as Lucy, Mrs. Griffiths as Mrs. McCandlish, Mrs. Ternan as Meg Merrilies, Miss Morant as Flora/ **Sad. Wells**, June 1837, with John Pritchard as Col. Mannering, N. T. Hicks as Hatteraick, Mr. Manvers as Bertram, Mr. Ennis as Glossin, Mr. Griffiths as Mucklethrift, A. Dawson as Dinmont, Mr. Tilbury as Sampson, C. J. Smith as Sebastian, Mrs. W. West as Meg Merilies [sic], Lavinia Melville as Julia, Miss Land as Lucy, Mrs. Rogers as Flora; Apr. 1856, with Mr. Swanborough as Col. Mannering, Charles Ford as Bertram, Charles Swan as Sampson, E. F. Edgar as Hatteraick, Mr. Barrett as Dinmont, C. Kelsey as Glossin, Walter Williams as Mucklethrift, Charlotte Cushman as Meg Merrilies, Miss M. Oliver as Lucy, Harriet Gordon as Julia, Miss Cuthbert as Flora, Mrs. B. Bartlett as Mrs. McCandlish/ **Engl. Opera House** (Lyceum), Sept. 1837, with Mr. Frazer as Henry Bertram, A. Brindal as Col. Mannering, William Bennett as Gilbert, Mr. Turnour as Mucklethrift, Henry Compton as Sampson, R. McIan as Dinmont, Mr. Baker as Dirk, Mr. Ransford as Gabriel, Miss Rainforth as Lucy, Priscilla Horton as Julia Mannering, Mme. Simon as Meg Merrilies.

GUY MANNERING; OR, THE GIPSY'S PROPHECY// D// Dram. by Robert Reece fr novel of Sir Walter Scott// **Cov. Garden**, Nov. 1837, with James Anderson as Col. Mannering, Mr. Wilson as Bertram, Drinkwater Meadows as Sampson, Edwin Ransford as Dinmont, W. H. Howard Payne as Hatteraick, Mr. Tilbury as Glossin, John Ayliffe as Mucklethrift, Miss Shirreff as Lucy, Priscilla Horton as Julia, Mrs. Sarah Garrick as Mrs. McCandlish; Feb. 1843, with Mr. Cooper as Col. Mannering, Mr. Travers as Bertram, John Pritt Harley as Sampson, George Horncastle as Dinmont, W. H. Payne as Hatteraick, Frank

Matthews as Glossin, Mr. Granby as Mucklethrift, Alfred Wigan as Sebastian, Miss Rainforth as Lucy, Miss Betts as Julia, Mrs. Humby as Flora, Mrs. Tayleure as Mrs. McCandlish, Mrs. Stanley as Meg Merrilles [sic]/ **Princess's**, June 1845, with Mr. Archer as Col. Mannering, Mr. Allen as Bertram, Henry Compton as Sampson, Mr. Granby as Glossin, Mr. Walton as Dinmont, James Ranoe as Hatterick, Emma Stanley as Julia, Helen Condell as Lucy, Mrs. Fosbroke as Mrs. McCandlish, Charlotte Cushman as Meg Merrilies/ **Haymarket**, July 1846, with Mr. Caulfield as Bertram, A. Brindal as Col. Mannering, Benjamin Webster as Dinmont, William Farren as Sampson, Henry Howe as Hatteraick, James Bland as Gabriel, Mr. Tilbury as Glossin, T. F. Mathews as Mucklethrift, Priscilla Horton as Julia, Mrs. L. S. Buckingham as Lucy, Charlotte Cushman as Meg Merrilies, Miss Carre as Flora, Mrs. Stanley as Mrs. McCandlish/ **Victoria**, Oct. 1854 (in 2a), with Mr. Holloway as Col. Mannering, James Howard as Bertram, S. Howard as Sampson, R. McGowan as Dinmont, Mr. Byers as Hatteraick, Mr. Mayson as Sebastian, F. Howson as Gabriel, Sarah Flower as Julia, Mrs. Guerin as Lucy, Mrs. Branscombe as Flora, Mrs. Chester as Meg Merrilies/ **Adelphi**, May 1858, with John Billington as Col. Mannering, Fourness Rolfe as Henry Bertram, Edward Wright as Sampson, Benjamin Webster as Dandie Dinmont, Paul Bedford as Gabriel, C. J. Smith as Dirk, Charles Selby as Gilbert, Edmund Garden as Bailie, James Bland as Sebastian, Mme. Celeste as Meg Merrilies, Miss Roden as Julia, Mary Keeley as Lucy, Marie Wilton as Flora, Mrs. Chatterley as Mrs. McCandlish; June 1877, with Charles Harcourt as Col. Mannering, Samuel Emery as Dinmont, Wilford Morgan as Henry Bertram, Lionel Brough as Dominie Sampson, James Fernandez as Dirk, William McIntyre as Gilbert, Harwood Cooper as Jock, Mrs. Arthur Stirling as Meg Merrilies, Mrs. Manders as Mrs. McCandlish, Annie Taylor as Flora, Rachel Sanger as Julia Mannering, Lucy Franklein as Lucy/ **Astley's**, Mar. 1859, with Mr. Herbert as Col. Mannering, J. T. Anderson as Glossen, J. Smith as Mucklethrift, J. Francis as Jabos, J. W. Anson as Sampson, W. H. Eburne as Henry Bertram, Richard Phillips as Dinmont, Paul Bedford as Gabriel, Rebecca Isaacs as Julia Mannering, Julia Weston as Flora, Mrs. Dowton as Meg Merrilies; Apr. 1866, with Henry Haigh, Charles Lyall, W. Templeton, George Honey, E. Garden, Mr. Everard, Basil Potter, Aynsley Cooke, Mme. Haigh-Dyer, Minnie Sidney, Nelly Nesbitt, Mrs. H. Harper.

GUY MANNERING; OR, THE GIPSEY'S PROPHECY// D// Dram. by Daniel Terry fr novel of Sir Walter Scott// **Haymarket**, Feb. 1854, with William Farren as Col. Mannering, Elliott Galer as Bertram, Henry Compton as Sampson, Mr. Rogers as Dinmont, Henry Howe as Hatteraick, William Clark as Mucklethrift, William Cullenford as Glossin, Mrs. L. S. Buckingham as Julia, Julia Harland as Lucy, Charlotte Cushman as Meg Merrilies, Ellen Chaplin as Flora, Mrs. Stanley as Mrs. McCandlish/ Scenery by W. Callcott, George Morris & Mr. O'Conner/ Machines by James Frow.

GWYNNETH OF PLINLIMMON; OR, THE WELCH [sic] **GIRL'S STORY**// D 3a// G. D. Pitt// **Victoria**, Aug. 1848, with T. H. Higgie as Col. Grenville, E. Edwards as Maj. Lindford, Mr. Hawkins as Williams, J. T. Johnson as Llewellyn, Mr. Hitchinson as Capt. Selby, Mr. Henderson as Sgt. Dash, James Howard as Ap-Reece, G. F. Forman as Tattle, John Bradshaw as Conroy, F. H. Henry as Frill, Annette Vincent as Gwynneth, Mrs. George Lee as Ellen, Miss Young as Lady Lindford, Mrs. Cooke as Winnifred/ Prod. by T. H. Higgie.

GWYNNETH VAUGHAN// D 2a// Mark Lemon// **Olympic**, Apr. 1840, with Mr. Baker as Williams, Henry Holl as Pritchard, Mr. Halford as Johns, George Wild as Hugh Morgan, Mr. Brookes as Morgan Morgan, Mr. Turnour as Farmer Vaughan, Mrs. Stirling as Gwynneth Vaughan, Mrs. Sarah Garrick as Dame Williams, Miss M. A. Atkinson as Lyddy/ Music by L. Phillips/ Scenery by Mr. Wilson/ **Sad. Wells**, Jan. 1841, with Henry Marston as Williams, Mr. Elvin as Pritchard, Charles Fenton as Johns, J. W. Collier as Hugh Morgan, Robert Honner as Morgan Morgan, Mr. Aldridge as Vaughan, Mrs. Robert Honner as Gwynneth, Mrs. Richard Barnett as Lyddy, Mrs. Morgan as Betsy, Miss Cooke as Dame Williams/ **Princess's**, July 1844, with Mr. Fitzjames as Williams, T. H. Higgie as Pritchard, Augustus Harris as Johns, W. H. Oxberry as Hugh Morgan, Mr. Walton as Morgan Morgan, Mr. Chichely as Vaughan, T. Hill as David, Mrs. Stirling as Gwynneth, Miss Somers as Betsy, Mme. Sala as Dame Williams/ **Drury Lane**, Dec. 1853, with Frederick Belton as Williams, Mr. Morgan as Pritchard, Mr. Walton as Johns, George Wild as Hugh, A. Younge as Morgan Morgan, Mrs. Lewis as Gwynneth, Miss Featherstone as Lyddy, Miss S. Lewis as Betsy, Mrs. Selby as Dame Williams.

GYPSEY [sic] **KING, THE; OR, THE PERILOUS PASS OF THE CATARACT**// D// n.a.// **Sad. Wells**, July 1837, with C. H. Pitt as Count de Briancourt, Mr. Campbell as Count St. Mauer, C. J. Smith as Mauleon, Benjamin Conquest as Justin, N. T. Hicks as Zeruco, Mr. Manvers as Zedeka, Miss Williams as Countess Marguerite, Mrs. Rogers as Angelique, Mrs. Harris as Clotilde.

*

HAG OF THE NIGHT, THE; OR, THE EVE OF HOLLOW MASS (see <u>Night Hag</u>).

HAGAR THE OUTCAST JEWESS// D// n.a.// (a vers. of <u>Leah</u>)// **Britannia**, July 1869.

HAG'S PROPHECY, THE; OR, A NIGHT IN A CHURCHYARD// D// n.a.// **Victoria**, Aug. 1854, with N. T. Hicks as Claremont, Mr. Henderson as Wetheral, T. E. Mills as Wildbird, James Howard as Grayling, Mr. Morrison as Moncton, Charles Rice as Rumsbanks, Alfred Saville as Foggyskull, Miss Vaul as Tommy, Miss Dansor as Rose, Mrs. Henry Vining as The Hag, Miss Laporte as Judith, Mrs. Manders as Sophonisba.

HAL O' THE WYND// D 4a// Leonard Rae// **Standard**, Sept. 1874.

HAL THE HIGHWAYMAN// Play 1a// H. M. Paull// **Vaudeville**, Dec. 1894, with T. Kingston as Hal, Frederick Volpé as Sir James, Arthur Helmore as Danby, J. L. MacKay as Tim, Esmé Beringer as Celia, Helena Dacre as Kitty.

HALF CASTE, THE; OR, THE POISONED PEARL// D 3a// Adap. by T. W. Robertson fr F// **Surrey**, Sept. 1856.

HALF MAST HIGH// D 4a// Tom Craven// **Pavilion**, Apr. 1893.

HALF SEAS OVER// D// Mrs. Mark Kendal// **St. Geo. Hall**, June 1882.

HALF-WAY HOUSE, THE// C 3a// G. R. Sims// **Vaudeville**, Oct. 1881.

HALVEI THE UNKNOWN; OR, THE DOOM AT MIDNIGHT// D 3a// T. E. Wilks// **Sad. Wells**, June 1843, with C. J. Bird as D'Arville, John Webster as St. Claire, Henry Marston as Halvei, John Herbert as Joginot, Mr. Coreno as Moret, Caroline Rankley as Clara, Mrs. Richard Barnett as Mme. D'Arville, Miss Stephens as Octavie/ Scenery by F. Fenton/ Machines by Mr. Cawdery/ Music by W. Montgomery/ Prod. by Henry Marston/ **City of London**, Sept. 1848.

HALVES// Play Pro & 3a// Arthur Conan Doyle// **Garrick**, June 1899, with James Welch as Dawson, George Shelton as John, Charles Troode as Slater, Fitzroy Morgan as Sir Charles, Frank Emery as Mayfield, Gerald Biron as Henderson, Brandon Thomas as Robert Dawson, Geraldine Olliffe as Mrs. William Dawson, Ross Selwick as Lady Early, Mrs. Charles Maltby as Mrs. Dawson, Nellie Thorne as Mary.

HAMILTON OF BOTHWELLHAUGH// D// A. R. Slous// **Sad. Wells**, Oct. 1855, with Frederic Robinson as Stuart, Samuel Phelps as Hamilton, William Belford as Eustace, Mr. Barrett as Ballenden, Henry Marston as Baliol, C. Seaton as Lorn, T. C. Harris as Sackville, Margaret Eburne as Margaret.

HAMLET, PRINCE OF DENMARK// T// William Shakespeare// **Cov. Garden**, Jan. 1837, with W. C. Macready as Hamlet, William Farren as Polonius, Mr. Thompson as Claudius, George Bennett as Ghost, John Webster as Laertes, Henry Wallack as Horatio, Benjamin Webster as 1st Gravedigger, Charles Bender as Rosencrantz, Mr. Roberts as Guildenstern, Mr. Harris as 1st Actor, Mrs. W. West as Gertrude, Miss Turpin as Ophelia/ **Sad. Wells**, Apr. 1837, with J. B. Booth as Hamlet, Mr. King as Claudius, John Ayliffe as Polonius, C. H. Pitt as Laertes, C. J. Smith as Horatio, H. George as Rosencrantz, Mr. Ede as 1st Player, Mr. Bishop as Guildenstern, N. T. Hicks as Ghost, Mr. Rogers as 1st Gravedigger, Miss Williams as Gertrude, Miss Melville as Ophelia; Nov. 1837, with Mrs. W. West as Hamlet; Mar. 1840, with Mr. Dry as Claudius, Mr. Williams as Polonius, Henry Marston as Hamlet, Robert Honner as Laertes, Mr. Aldridge as Horatio, Mr. Moreton as Rosencrantz, J. W. Collier as Guildenstern and as Osrick, Henry Hall as 1st Gravedigger, Mr. Broadfoot as 1st Actor, Miss Richardson as Gertrude, Mrs. J. F. Saville as Ophelia; July 1844, with George Bennett as Claudius, Samuel Phelps as Hamlet, A. Younge as Polonius, John Webster as Laertes, E. Morton as Horatio, Mr. Sharpe as Rosencrantz, Charles Fenton as Guildenstern, Henry Marston as Ghost, Edward Knight as 1st Player, G. F. Forman as 1st Gravedigger, Mrs. Mary Warner as Gertrude, Georgiana Lebatt as Ophelia/ **Haymarket**, June 1837, with W. C. Macready as Hamlet, J. T. Haines as Claudius, Robert Strickland as Polonius, John Webster as Laertes, Mr. Saville as Horatio, Frederick Vining as Osrick, Charles Selby as Rosencrantz, James Worrell as Guildenstern, Mr. Gallot as 1st Actor, Benjamin Webster as 1st Gravedigger, Mr. Elton as Ghost, Fanny Huddart as Gertrude, Eliza Vincent as Ophelia; June 1839, with Charles Kean as Hamlet, Charles Perkins as Claudius, Robert Strickland as Polonius, Mr. Hemming as Horatio, Walter Lacy as Laertes, James Worrell as Guildenstern, Mr. Caulfield as Rosencrantz, Mr. Gallot as 1st Actor, J. B. Buckstone as 1st Gravedigger, Mr. Cooper as Ghost, Miss Pelham as Gertrude, Agnes Taylor as Ophelia; Aug. 1844, with James Anderson as Hamlet, Henry Howe as Claudius, Robert Strickland as Polonius, Henry Holl as Laertes, A. Brindal as Horatio, Mr. Caulfield as Rosencrantz, James Worrell as Guildenstern, James Bland as 1st Actor, Mr. Tilbury as 1st Gravedigger, Mr. Stuart as Ghost, Mrs. W. Clifford as Gertrude, Priscilla Horton as Ophelia; Jan. 1849, with Mr. Rogers as Claudius, Charles Kean as Hamlet, Mr. Tilbury as Polonius, Henry Howe as Horatio, Henry Holl as Laertes, Mr. Caulfield as Rosencrantz, George Braid as Guildenstern, William Creswick as Ghost, Robert Keeley as 1st Gravedigger, James Bland as 1st Actor, Mrs. Mary Warner as Gertrude, Mrs. Charles Kean as Ophelia; Mar. 1851, with Mr. Rogers as Claudius, J. William Wallack as Hamlet, Mr. Lambert as Polonius, Henry Howe as Horatio, John Parselle as Laertes, Mr. Caulfield as Rosencrantz, George Braid as Guildenstern, Mr. Stuart as Ghost, J. B. Buckstone as 1st Gravedigger, James Bland as 1st Actor, Laura Addison as Gertrude, Priscilla Horton as Ophelia; Feb. 1851, with Barry Sullivan as Hamlet, Mrs. Henry Vining as Gertrude; Oct. 1853, with Mr. Rogers as Claudius, George Vandenhoff as Hamlet, W. H. Chippendale as Polonius, Edwin Villiers as Laertes, William Farren as Horatio, Mr. Weathersby as Rosencrantz, George Braid as Guildenstern, Henry Compton as 1st Gravedigger, William Cullenford as 1st Actor,

Henry Howe as Ghost, Mrs. L. S. Buckingham as Gertrude, Louisa Howard as Ophelia; Jan. 1892, with F. H. Macklin as Claudius, Herbert Beerbohm Tree as Hamlet, Henry Kemble as Polonius, Arthur Dacre as Horatio, Fred Terry as Laertes, Mr. Hallard as Rosencrantz, Mr. Caravoglia as Guildenstern, James Fernandez as Ghost, George Barrett as 1st Gravedigger, Charles Hudson as 1st Actor, Rose Leclercq as Gertrude, Mrs. Beerbohm Tree as Ophelia/ Scenery by W. Telbin, Walter Hann & Walter Johnston/ Music by George Henschel/ Electrics by E. Wingfield Bowles/ **St. James's**, Dec. 1837, with Edward Otway as Hamlet, Mr. Ranson as Claudius, Mr. Brookes as Polonius, Mr. Jones as Horatio, Mr. Sidney as Rosencrantz, Mr. Burnett as Guildenstern, Mr. Hart as 1st Actor, Mr. Hollingsworth as Ghost, Mme. Sala as Gertrude, Miss Allison as Ophelia/ **Drury Lane**, Jan. 1838, with Mr. Baker as Claudius, Charles Kean as Hamlet, William Dowton as Polonius, Mr. King as Laertes, H. Cooke as Horatio, F. Cooke as Rosencrantz, Mr. Duruset as Guildenstern, R. Mclan as 1st Actor, Henry Compton as 1st Gravedigger, Mr. Cooper as Ghost, Mrs. Ternan as Gertrude, Miss Romer as Ophelia; Jan. 1843, with George Bennett as Claudius, W. C. Macready as Hamlet, Henry Compton as Polonius, Mr. Elton as Laertes, Mr. Graham as Horatio, Mr. Lynne as Guildenstern, Charles Selby as Rosencrantz, Mr. Waldron as 1st Actor, Robert Keeley as 1st Gravedigger, Samuel Phelps as Ghost, Mrs. Mary Warner as Gertrude, Priscilla Horton as Ophelia; Feb. 1844, with Charles Diddear as Claudius, Charles Kean as Hamlet, Drinkwater Meadows as Polonius, William West as Laertes, Charles Selby as Horatio, W. H. Payne as Rosencrantz, Henry Horncastle as Guildenstern, George Horncastle as 1st Actor, John Pritt Harley as 1st Gravedigger, Mr. Cooper as Ghost, Mrs. Mary Warner as Gertrude, Miss Romer as Ophelia; July 1852, with C. Gilbert as Claudius, Frederick Belton as Laertes, Mr. Tilbury as Polonius, Henry Mellon as Horatio, E. Morton as Rosencrantz, Mr. Percival as Guildenstern, McKean Buchanan as Hamlet, Edward Knight as 1st Actor, William Suter as 1st Gravedigger, Mr. Stuart as Ghost, Mrs. Ternan as Gertrude, Miss Huddart as Ophelia; Feb. 1861, with Charles Kean as Hamlet, William Belford as Claudius, Mr. Lambert as Polonius, George Everett as Horatio, J. F. Cathcart as Laertes, Mr. Farrell as Rosencrantz, George Spencer as Guildenstern, Mr. McLein as Ghost, Mr. Tilbury as 1st Gravedigger, Henry Mellon as 1st Player, Mrs. Charles Kean as Gertrude, Miss Chapman as Ophelia, Miss N. Chapman as Actress; Mar. 1869, with T. C. King as Hamlet, James Johnstone as Claudius, John Ryder as Ghost, Mr. Barrett as Polonius, Wilson Barrett as Laertes, Mr. Seymour as Horatio, F. Charles as Rosencrantz, W. C. Temple as Guildenstern, John Rouse as 1st Gravedigger, Mr. O'Neill as 1st Actor, Mrs. Henry Vandenhoff as Gertrude, Caroline Heath as Ophelia; Dec. 1878, with Daniel Bandmann as Hamlet, Howard Russell as Claudius, Mr. Shepherd as Polonius, Edmund Leathes as Laertes, Leonard Outram as Horatio, John Sergeant as Rosencrantz, W. Dempsey as Guildenstern, R. Dolman as 1st Player, F. Huntley as 1st Gravedigger, Stanley Garland as Ghost, Miss E. Clifton as Gertrude, Miss Wallis as Ophelia/ **Victoria**, July 1842, with Mr. James as Polonius, C. Williams as Horatio, Mr. Howard as Osric, William Seaman as Laertes, John Dale as Claudius, E. F. Saville as Hamlet, David Osbaldiston as Ghost, E. F. Edgar as Rosencrantz, Mr. Cullen as Guildenstern, Mr. Gardner as 1st Gravedigger, Mrs. George Lee as Gertrude, Annette Vincent as Ophelia/ Scenery by Telbin, Morelli & Lancaster; Sept. 1844, with John Dale as Claudius, Mr. Otway as Hamlet, Mr. James as Polonius, T. H. Lacy as Laertes, William Seaman as Horatio, James Howard as Osric, Mr. Binge as Rosencrantz, Mr. Hitchinson as Guildenstern, David Osbaldiston as Ghost, Mr. Aldridge as 1st Player, J. Herbert as 1st Gravedigger, Mrs. W. West as Gertrude/ **Victoria**, Aug. 1853, with John Bradshaw as Claudius, James Howard as Polonius, N. T. Hicks as Hamlet, Alfred Raymond as Laertes, Mr. Richards as Horatio, F. H. Henry as Rosencrantz, Mr. Hitchinson as Guildenstern, Mr. Morrison as 1st Player, Mr. Hudspeth as 1st Gravedigger, T. E. Mills as Ghost, Mrs. Henry Vining as Gertrude, Georgiana Lebatt as Ophelia/ **Princess's**, Oct. 1845, with John Ryder as Claudius, W. C. Macready as Hamlet, Mr. Granby as Polonius, Leigh Murray as Laertes, Charles Fisher as Horatio, Mr. Wynn as Rosencrantz, F. C. Courtney as Guildenstern, A. Walton as 1st Actor, Henry Compton as 1st Gravedigger, Mr. Cooper as Ghost, Mrs. Ternan (late Miss Jarman) as Gertrude, Emma Stanley as Ophelia; Sept. 1850, with John Ryder as Claudius, Charles Kean as Hamlet, Mr. Addison as Polonius, James Vining as Horatio, Fredrick Belton as Laertes, John Cathcart as Rosencrantz, George Everett as Guildenstern, Alfred Wigan as Osric, Charles Fisher as Ghost, John Pritt Harley as 1st Gravedigger, Frederick Cooke as First Player, Miss Phillips as Gertrude, Mrs. Charles Kean as Ophelia/ Scenery by T. Grieve; Oct. 1859, with Frank Graham as Claudius, George Melville as Hamlet, Drinkwater Meadows as Polonius, Harcourt Bland as Laertes, J. G. Shore as Horatio, Robert Cathcart as Rosencrantz, Mr. Dawson as Guildenstern, Henry Irving as Osric, John Ryder as Ghost, Henry Widdicomb as 1st Gravedigger, Mr. Garden as 1st Player, Mrs. Weston as Gertrude, Carlotta Leclercq as Ophelia; May 1861, with John Ryder as Claudius, Charles Fechter as Hamlet, Drinkwater Meadows as Polonius, Hermann Vezin as Laertes, J. G. Shore as Horatio, Basil Potter as Ghost, Alfred Raymond as 1st Player, Henry Widdicomb as 1st Gravedigger, Robert Cathcart as Rosencrantz, Frederick Moreland as Guildenstern, Miss Welsworthy as Gertrude, Caroline Heath as Ophelia; June 1866, with Thomas Mead as Claudius, Charles Kean as Hamlet, John Vollaire as Polonius, George Everett as Horatio, J. F. Cathcart as Laertes, George Spencer as Rosencrantz, W. R. Robins as Guildenstern, Basil Potter as Ghost, Dominick Murray as 1st Gravedigger, Charles Seyton as 1st Player, Mrs. Charles Kean as Gertrude, Miss Chapman as Ophelia; July 1868, with Basil Potter as Claudius, Charles Allerton as Hamlet, Dan Leeson as Polonius, J. G. Shore as Horatio,

Mr. Herwyn as Laertes, Mr. Manley as Rosencrantz, Mr. Newbound as Guildenstern, Brandon Ellis as Ghost, Dominick Murray as 1st Gravedigger, Mr. Maclean as 1st Player, Miss Elsworthy as Gertrude, Emily Cross as Ophelia; Nov. 1880, with Edwin Booth as Hamlet, Thomas Swinbourne as Claudius, William Farren as Polonius, John Ryder as Ghost, Edmund Leathes as Laertes, John Beauchamp as Horatio, C. W. Garthorne as Guildenstern, P. C. Beverley as Rosencrantz, J. A. Rosier as 1st Actor, Stanislaus Calhaem as 1st Gravedigger, Miss Gerard as Ophelia, Mrs. Hermann Vezin as Gertrude/ Scenery by Charles Brooke/ Machines by Mr. Warton/ Gas by Mr. Jones/ Lime-light by Mr. Kerr/ Prod. by Harry Jackson; Oct. 1884, with Wilson Barrett as Hamlet, Mary Eastlake as Ophelia, E. S. Willard as Claudius, John Dewhurst as Ghost, Clifford Cooper as Polonius, J. R. Crauford as Horatio, Frank Cooper as Laertes, Walter Speakman as 1st Actor, G. R. Foss as Rosencrantz, Charles Fulton as Guildenstern, George Barrett as 1st Gravedigger, Margaret Leighton as Gertrude/ Scenery by William Beverley, W. L. Telbin, Stafford Hall & Walter Hann/ Music by Edward Jones/ Prod. by Wilson Barrett/ **Olympic**, Mar. 1847, with George Bolton as Hamlet, Mr. Johnstone as Claudius, Mr. Butler as Horatio, Mr. Robertson as Laertes, Mr. Turnour as Polonius, Mr. Darcie as Rosencrantz, Mr. Fortesque as Guildenstern, Robert Romer as 1st Gravedigger, George Maynard as Ghost, Mrs. R. Gordon as Gertrude, Mrs. Boyce as Ophelia; Mar. 1848, with Mr. Archer as Claudius, G. V. Brooke as Hamlet, Henry Holl as Laertes, H. Lee as Horatio, William Davidge as Polonius, Mr. Conquest as 1st Gravedigger, Mr. Darcie as Rosencrantz, J. Binge as Guildenstern, Mr. Stuart as Ghost, Mrs. Brougham as Gertrude, Miss May as Ophelia; Sept. 1866, with Alice Marriott as Hamlet, Walter Roberts as Claudius, John Maclean as Polonius, Walter Joyce as Laertes, Mr. Dalton as Horatio, Charles Horsman as Ghost, Mr. Reeves as Rosencrantz, Mr. Berne as Guildenstern, T. B. Bennett as 1st Actor, Edward Atkins as 1st Gravedigger, Mrs. Saville as Gertrude, Emma Barnett as Ophelia; Apr. 1891, with Wilson Barrett as Hamlet, Austin Melford as Claudius, H. Cooper Cliffe as Laertes, R. Miller Rext as Horatio, W. A. Elliott as Ghost, Stafford Smith as Polonius, A E. Field as Rosencrantz, George Barrett as 1st Gravedigger, Louise Moodie as Gertrude, Winifred Emery as Ophelia; May 1897, with Frank Dyall as Claudius, Nutcombe Gould as Hamlet, Ben Greet as Polonius, George Foss as Laertes, Alfred Kendrick as Horatio, E. H. Brooke as Rosencrantz, Roland Atwood as Guildenstern, Arthur Wood as 1st Gravedigger, W. R. Staveley as 1st Player, Courtnay Thorpe as Ghost, Mary Allestree as Gertrude, Lily Hanbury as Ophelia/ **Standard**, Mar. 1859, with McKean Buchanan; Mar. 1859, with Henry Marston/ **Surrey**, Nov. 1859, with William Creswick, Edith Heraud/ **Adelphi**, Aug. 1863, with Mrs. Ada Dyas as Hamlet, C. Vernon as Ghost, George F. Sinclair as Claudius, W. H. Sharpe as Laertes, Mr. Levison as Horatio, W. Champion as Polonius, Mrs. W. H. Dentith as Gertrude, Marie Sinclair as Ophelia; June 1868, with Henry Neville, Miss St. Henry, Carlotta Leclercq, George Belmore, Mr. Neville; Feb. 1873, with Howard Russell as Claudius, Daniel Bandmann as Hamlet, H. Dalton as Laertes, C. H. Fenton as Horatio, F. Charles as Osric, R. Dolman as 1st Actor, John Clarke as 1st Gravedigger, William McIntyre as Ghost, E. Shepherd as Polonius, J. Sargent as Rosencrantz, Ernest Travers as Guildenstern, Roma Le Thiere as Gertrude, Mrs. Bandmann as Ophelia/ **Lyceum**, May 1864, with Charles Fechter as Hamlet, Kate Terry as Ophelia, Samuel Emery, John Brougham, G. F. Neville; 1867, with Charles Fechter as Hamlet, Samuel Emery as Claudius, Frank Matthews as Polonius, John Ryder as Ghost, W. H. Kendal as Laertes, Stanislaus Calhaem as 1st Gravedigger, Henry Mellon as 1st Player, Miss Elsworthy as Gertrude, Carlotta Leclercq as Ophelia; Oct. 1874, with Henry Irving as Hamlet, Thomas Swinbourne as Claudius, W. H. Chippendale as Polonius, Edmund Leathes as Laertes, G. F. Neville as Horatio, Thomas Mead as Ghost, H. B. Conway as Osric, Henry Compton as 1st Gravedigger, Georgiana Pauncefort as Gertrude, Isabel Bateman as Ophelia; Dec. 1878, with Henry Irving as Hamlet, W. H. Chippendale, Kyrle Bellew, Arthur Wing Pinero, Georgiana Pauncefort, Ellen Terry; Oct. 1894, with Henry Irving, Thomas Swinbourne, W. H. Chippendale, Edmund Leathes, George Neville, T. Mead [sic], H. B. Conway, J. D. Beveridge, Henry Compton, Georgina Pauncefort, Isabel Bateman; Sept. 1897, with H. Cooper Cliffe as Claudius, Johnston Forbes Robertson as Hamlet, Harrison Hunter as Horatio, J. H. Barnes as Polonius, Bernard Gould as Laertes, Ian Robertson as Ghost, Grahame Browne as Rosencrantz, Frank Dyall as Guildenstern, James Hearn as First Player, John Martin Harvey as Osric, Miss Granville as Gertrude, Mrs. Patrick Campbell as Ophelia/ Scenery by Hawes Craven/ Music by Hamilton Clarke & Carl Armbruster; Dec. 1899, with Wilson Barrett/ **Astley's**, Aug. 1864, with W. L. Percival as Claudius, Edward Atkins as Polonius, W. J. Grove as Laertes, F. Barclay as Horatio, T. Reid as Ghost, W. T. Mead as 1st Gravedigger, Edgar Chalmers as Hamlet, Miss Grosvenor as Gertrude, Marian Chalmers as Ophelia/ Scenery by W. Maugham; May 1865, with Alice Marriott as Hamlet, Mr. Frazer as Claudius, W. D. Gresham as Laertes, Mr. Stanley as Horatio, Mr. Johnson as Polonius, Basil Potter as Ghost, Mrs. Poynter as Gertrude, Miss Fiddes as Ophelia/ **Grecian**, Oct. 1866, with Henry Grant as Claudius, J. Jackson as Polonius, David Jones as Hamlet, Charles Mortimer as Ghost, William James as Laertes, Samuel Perfitt as Horatio, Mr. Goodin as Rosencrantz, E. Howard as Guildenstern, John Manning as 1st Gravedigger, Jane Coveney as Gertrude, Lizzie Mandelbert as Ophelia/ **Globe**, Mar. 1890, with F. R. Benson as Hamlet, Charles Cartwright as Claudius, George Black as Polonius, Herbert Ross as Laertes, Otho Stuart as Horatio, Arthur Grenville as Rosencrantz, G. M. Howard as Guildenstern, G. R. Weir as 1st Gravedigger, Alfred Brydone as 1st Actor, Stephen Phillips as Ghost, Ada Ferrar as Gertrude, Mrs. F. R. Benson as Ophelia/ Scenery by W. T. Hemsley/ **Her Majesty's**, Aug. 1897, with Herbert Beerbohm

Tree/ **Comedy**, Mar. 1901, with F. R. Benson.

HAND IN GLOVE; OR, PAGE THIRTEEN OF THE BLACK BOOK// D 3a// George Conquest & Paul Meritt// **Grecian**, May 1874.

HAND AND HEART// Play 1a// W. Yardley & H. P. Stephens// **Gaiety**, May 1886.

HAND IN HAND// CD 4a// Edward Darbey// **Surrey**, Mar. 1890/ **Novelty**, Oct. 1890, with Edwin Fergusson as Edgar Hartington, H. B. Clair as Herbert Harrington, Charles Lerigo as Drummond, Charles Daley as Ward, Brian McCullough as Barton, Nellie Nelson as Polly, Julia Listelle as Elsie, Ada Douglas as Grace.

HAND OF JUSTICE, THE// D 4a// Max Goldberg// **Sad. Wells**, Sept. 1891/ **West London**, Dec. 1901.

HAND OF PROVIDENCE, THE// D 4a// T. Gideon Warren// **Surrey**, Aug. 1897.

HANDFAST// Play Pro & 3a// Henry Hamilton & Mark Quinton// **POW**, Dec. 1887/ **Shaftesbury**, May. 1891.

HANDS ACROSS THE SEA// D 5a// Henry Pettitt// **Princess's**, Nov. 1888, with Henry Neville as Dudley, Robert Pateman as de Lussac, E. W. Garden as Basset, W. L. Abingdon as Stillwood, Julian Cross as Melford, Edmund Gurney as Capt. Land, H. H. Morell as Hickory, Edmund Grace as Joseph Stillwood, Mary Rorke as Lilian, Miss Webster as Lucy, Ina Barnard as Mme. Vallerie, Miss Vizetelly as Polly/ Scenery by Bruce Smith, Julian Hicks & R. C. Durant/ Prod. by Robert Pateman & Henry Pettitt.

HANDSEL PENNY// C 1a// Charles Selby// **Olympic**, June 1844, with Mr. France as Rigot, John Simpson as Temeraire, Charles Selby as Chaumiere, Mr. Turnour as Volage, Mr. Scott as Babolin, Mrs. Selby as Albertine, Miss Bartlett as Claudine.

HANDSOME APOLOGY, A// C// Andrew Longmuir// **POW**, July 1888.

HANDSOME HUSBAND, A// C 1a// Mrs. J. R. Planché// **Cov. Garden**, Nov. 1839, with C. J. Mathews as Wyndham, James Vining as Fitzherbert, Mr. Kerridge as Stephen, Mme. Vestris as Mrs. Wyndham, Mrs. Macnamara as Mrs. Twisden, Miss Lee as Mrs. Melford/ **Haymarket**, Nov. 1842, with C. J. Mathews as Wyndham, Henry Holl as Fitzherbert, William Clark as Stephen, Mme. Vestris as Mrs. Wyndham, Miss Charles as Mrs. Melford, Mrs. W. Clifford as Mrs. Twisden; Nov. 1858, with C. J. Mathews as Fitzherbert, Henry Compton as Wyndham, Mrs. C. J. Mathews as Mrs. Wyndham, Miss Fitzinman as Mrs. Melford, Mrs. Poynter as Mrs. Twisden/ **Sad. Wells**, Sept. 1846, with William Hoskins as Wyndham, E. Morton as Fitzherbert, Charles Fenton as Stephen, Miss Cooper as Mrs. Wyndham, Mrs. Henry Marston as Mrs. Twisden, Miss Stephens as Mrs. Melford/ **Lyceum**, Dec. 1850, with C. J. Mathews as Mr. Wyndham, George Vining as Fitzherbert, Mr. Charles as Stephen, Miss M. Oliver as Mrs. Wyndham, Mrs. Charles Horn as Mrs. Melford./ **Strand**, Nov. 1895.

HANDSOME IS THAT HANDSOME DOES// C 4a// C. J. Ribton-Turner// **Vaudeville**, June 1888.

HANDSOME IS THAT HANDSOME DOES; A STORY OF THE LAKE COUNTRY// CD 4a// Tom Taylor// **Olympic**, Sept. 1870.

HANDSOME JACK, THE HIGHWAYMAN// n.a.// **Marylebone**, Aug. 1862.

HANDY ANDY// C 1a// W. R. Floyd// **Lyceum**, Nov. 1860, with T. Lyon as Squire Egan, Henry Butler as Edward O'Conner, Frederick Villiers as Dick Dawson, James Johnstone as Tom Murphy, Mr. Forrester as Furlong, John Drew Sr. as Handy Andy, Miss Neville as Mrs. Egan, Maria Ternan as Fanny Dawson, Mrs. John Rouse as Nance, Fanny Hudspeth as Oonah/ Scenery by William Callcott/ Music by George Loder.

HANGED MAN, THE// D 3a// George Conquest// **Grecian**, Sept. 1862, with William James as Dartigues, George Gillett as Cirrac, Henry Grant as Moretto, W. Shirley as President, Jane Dawson as Diana, Mary A. Victor as Lucille, George Conquest as Christol, Mr. Jackson as Latremblade, F. Smithson as Duvernale, Mrs. Charles Dillon as Suzanne, Marie Brewer as Casilda.

HANGED MAN, THE; OR, THE ADVENTURESS// D 3a// n.a.// **Victoria**, Apr. 1866, with C. West as President Montbazon, Henry Forrester as Dennier, J. C. Levey as Cevenes, Frederick Thomas as Cospetto, Mr. Butler as Robin, Mrs. J. F. Young as Diana, Miss Musgrave as Mme. Montbazon, Miss Wright as Lucille, W. D. Gresham as Dr. Fabian, George Yarnold as Le Blanc, Mr. Mandeville as Devance, R. Marchant as Robinette, Maria Daly as Susanne, Emilie De Vigne as Sister Annette.

HANS VON STEIN; OR, THE ROBBER KNIGHT// D 2a// Edward Fitzball// **Marylebone**, Aug. 1851.

HAPPIEST DAY OF MY LIFE, THE// F 2a// J. B. Buckstone// **Cov. Garden**, Apr. 1837, with Benjamin Webster as Gillman, Mr. Tilbury as Dudley, John Pritchard as Frederick, John Webster as Charles, Mr. Ray as Jones, James Worrell as John, John Collett as Thomas, Mrs. Julia Glover as Mrs. Dudley, Eliza Vincent as Sophia, Miss Lee as Mary, Mrs. Sarah Garrick as Mrs. Grimsley/ **Haymarket**, June 1837, with Benjamin Webster as Gillman, Robert Strickland as Dudley, John Webster as Charles, Mr. Saville as Vincent, James Worrell as John, Mrs. Julia Glover as Mrs. Dudley, Mrs. Humby as Sophy, Miss E. Phillips as Mary, Miss Tayleure as Mrs. Grimley; June 1861, with Henry Compton as Gillman, William Cullenford as Dudley, George Braid as Vincent, Edwin Villiers as Charles, Mr. Hill as Jones, James Worrell as John, Mrs. Wilkins as Mrs.

Dudley, Eliza Weekes as Sophia, Miss Henrade as Mary, Miss S. Henrade as Jane/ **Sad. Wells,** Nov. 1841, with John Herbert as Gillman, Mr. Williams as Dudley, Mr. Elvin as Charles, Mr. Aldridge as Vincent, Mr. Archer as Jones, Charles Fenton as Thomas, Miss Cooke as Mrs. Dudley, Mrs. Richard Barnett as Sophie, Miss Hicks as Mary, Mrs. Morgan as Mrs. Grimsby, Miss Melville as Jane; Mar. 1854, with Lewis Ball as Gilman, Mr. Josephs as Dudley, T. C. Harris as Vincent, William Belford as Charles, Mr. Scholey as Jones, Mr. Frost as Smith, Miss Portman as Sophia, Mrs. Henry Marston as Mrs. Dudley, Miss Wyatt as Mary, Miss F. Younge as Mrs. Grimley/ **Grecian,** July 1845, with Frederick Robson as Gillman, F. Ede as Dudley, Edwin Dixon as Charles, Harry Chester as Vincent, Mrs. W. Watson as Mrs. Dudley, Annette Mears as Sophia, Mary A. Crisp as Mary; Nov. 1862, with H. Cavendish as Gillman, J. Jackson as Dudley, Walter Holland as Vincent, George Burton as Charles, Marie Brewer as Mrs. Dudley, Mary A. Victor as Sophia, Ellen Hale as Mary, Miss Johnstone as Mrs. Grinsley/ **Olympic,** May 1854, with Frederick Robson as Gillman, J. H. White as Dudley, Mr. Leslie as Charles, Mr. Vincent as Frederick, Mr. Franks as Jones, Mrs. Chatterley as Mrs. Dudley, Priscilla Horton (Mrs. T. G. Reed) as Sophia, Miss Marston as Mary, Miss Stevens as Mrs. Grimsley.

HAPPIEST MAN ALIVE, THE// C 1a// W. Bayle Bernard// **Olympic,** Mar. 1840, with Frederick Vining as Euston, Mr. Halford as Fusser, Mr. Ross as Frank, Mr. Turnour as Drax, Miss Conner as Ellen.

HAPPINESS AT HOME// D// C. H. Hazlewood// **Britannia,** May 1871.

HAPPY CRUISE, A// C// Ernest Cuthbert// **Vaudeville,** Nov. 1873.

HAPPY DAY, A// F// Richard Butler & H. Chance Newton ("Richard Henry")// **Gaiety,** Oct. 1886, with Arthur Williams, Harriet Coveney, Florence Beale.

HAPPY FAMILY, A// D 5a// Adap. by Benjamin Thompson fr G of August Kotzebue// **Lyceum,** Mar. 1848, with Mme. Vestris, C. J. Mathews, Mrs. Stirling, J. B. Buckstone, John Pritt Harley, Frank Matthews, Louisa Howard, Mrs. Fitzwilliam.

HAPPY-GO-LUCKY// D// Frederick Hazleton// **Marylebone,** July 1875.

HAPPY-GO-LUCKY// Play 3a// T. E. Pemberton// **Globe,** June 1884.

HAPPY HYPOCRITE, THE// Play 1a// Max Beerbohm// **Royalty,** Dec. 1900.

HAPPY LIFE, THE// C 3a// L. N. Parker// **Duke of York's,** Dec. 1897/ **Terry's,** Nov. 1899.

HAPPY MAN, THE// F 1a// Samuel Lover// **Olympic,** May 1842, with Mr. Rogers as Rusty, Mr. Boyd as Foxy, Walter Searle as Ski Hi, Edward Atkins as Rhun Phaster, Mr. Harold as Paddy Murphy, Mrs. Harold as Ko Ket, Mrs. Watson as Singh Smahl/ **Haymarket,** May 1843, with James Bland as Ram Rusti, William Strickland as Foxi-Fum, J. W. Gough as Ski-Hi, William Clark as Run-Phaster, Mr. Leonard as Paddy Murphey, Miss Lee as Ko-Ket, Miss Kendall as Sing-Smahl/ **Cov. Garden,** Oct. 1843, with Mr. Hamilton as Paddy Murphy, Mr. Attwood as Rusti, Edwin Yarnold as Foxi-Fum, Mr. Ridgway as Ski-Hi, Mr. Ross as Run-Phaster, Jane Mordaunt as Ko-Ket, Miss Grove as Sing-Smahl/ **Princess's,** Sept. 1870, with C. F. Marshall as Rusti, John Vollaire as Foxi Fum, Alfred Tapping as Ski Hi, Shiel Barry as Paddy Murphy, Ernest Travers as Phaster, Miss Merton as Ko Ket, Miss J. Lovell as Sing Smahl.

HAPPY MEDIUM, A// F 1a// T. E. Pemberton// **Haymarket,** Nov. 1875, with Frederick Everill as Bullett, Minnie Walton as Maisey, Mr. Weathersby as Aylwood, Charles Warner as Wildsmith, Mrs. Edward Fitzwilliam as Mrs. Bullett, Maria Harris as Fanny.

HAPPY NOOK, A// D 3a// Adap. by Alice Greeven & J. T. Grein fr G of Sudermann, Das Glück in Winkel// **Court,** June 1901.

HAPPY PAIR, A// C 1a// S. Theyre Smith// **St. James's,** Mar. 1868, with William Farren as Honeyton, Louisa Herbert as Mrs. Honeyton/ **Adelphi,** Mar. 1871, with Caroline Duvernay as Mrs. Honeyton, John Billington as Honeyton/ **Lyceum,** July 1872, with Charles Warner as Mr. Honeyton, Virginia Francis as Mrs. Honeyton/ **Drury Lane,** Dec. 1848, with Edmund Leathes as Honeyton, Agnes Thomas as Mrs. Honeyton.

HAPPY RETURN, THE// C 1a// Arthur Law// **Court,** Jan. 1883.

HAPPY RETURNS// FC 3a// Adap. by Fred Horner fr F of Paul Ferrier, L'Article 231// **Vaudeville,** Mar. 1892, with Thomas Thorne as Sir Robert, Cyril Maude as Diprose, Charles Fawcett as Hemsley, Bill Edwards as Ra-Ka-Too, C. W. Somerset as Farquhar, Charles Dodsworth as Doyle, Oswald Yorke as Wilson, Dorothy Dorr as Mrs. Hemsley, Ella Banister as Mrs. Beauchamp.

HAPPY THOUGHT, A// Play 1a// H. Tripp Edgar// **Strand,** Jan. 1895, with H. Tripp Edgar as Wentworth, Edgar Stevens as Jack, Dudley Cloraine as Woodpeck, Frank Stather as Stranger, Kate Ruskin as Kitty.

HARBOUR LIGHTS, THE// D 5a// G. R. Sims & Henry Pettitt// **Adelphi,** Dec. 1885, with William Terriss as Lt. David Kingsley, J. D. Beveridge as Nicholas Morland, Percy Lyndal as Frank Morland, John Maclean as Capt. Nelson, Howard Russell as Capt. Hardy, Duncan Campbell as Helstone, E. W. Garden as Dossiter, T. Fulljames as Drake, Jessie Millward as Dora, Mary Rorke as Lina, Clara Jecks as Peggy, Maude Brennan as Mrs. Helstone/ Scenery by Bruce Smith, W.

Johnstone, & W. Perkins/ Music by Henry Sprake/ Machines by Benjamin Burns.

HARBOUR MASTER'S SECRET, THE; OR, THE WRECK OF THE GOLDEN EAGLE// D// n.a.// **Britannia**, Dec. 1868.

HARD CASE, A// FC 3a// W. Carleton Dawe// **Terry's**, Oct. 1893, with Laurence Cautley as Meakham, H. N. Chart as Sir Frederick, Fred Thorne as Trencher, Willie Drew as Lord Dasham, Albert Bernard as Hicks, Sophie Larkin as Mrs. Trencher, Jennie Rogers as Belle, Eva Moore as Kate.

HARD HEARTS// D 5a// A. J. Charleson & Charles Wilmot// **Grand**, Apr. 1886.

HARD HIT// Play 4a// Henry Arthur Jones// **Haymarket**, Jan. 1887, with Frank Archer as Baldwun, E. S. Willard as Saxon, Herbert Beerbohm Tree as Cudlip, Arthur Dacre as Geoffrey, C. Dodsworth as Bratby, Henry Kemble as Maj. Fysh, Ulick Winter as Frobisher, Compton Coutts as Nangle, P. Ben Greet as Jeffcoat, Marion Terry as Bertha, Mary Rorke as Mrs. Ashbee, Lydia Cowell as Cherry/ Scenery by Walter Johnstone.

HARD LINES// D// Charles Dickenson// **St. Geo. Hall**, Mar. 1887.

HARD STRUGGLE, A// D 1a// Westland Marston// **Lyceum**, Feb. 1858, with Charles Dillon, Mrs. Dillon.

HARD TIMES// D// Dram. by F. F. Cooper fr novel of Charles Dickens// **Grecian**, Sept. 1854, with Henry Grant as Gradgrind, Eaton O'Donnell as Bounderby, Basil Potter as Harthouse, Richard Phillips as Blackpool, William Suter as Bitzer, Miss Morgan as Mrs. Gradgrind, Miss Johnstone as Sparsit, Jane Coveney as Rachel, Harriet Coveney as Miss Gradgrind, Ellen Crisp as Mrs. Pegler.

HARD UP// CD 2a// Edward Righton// **Strand**, Oct. 1883.

HARMONIOUS DISCORDS// C// n.a.// **Opera Comique**, Mar. 1873.

HARMONY// D 1a// Henry Arthur Jones// **Strand**, June 1884/ **Royalty**, Sept. 1895, with Mark Kinghorne as Kinsman, Arthur Armstrong as Seaton, Charles Troode as Muggins, Ettie Williams as Jenny.

HAROLD HAWK; OR, THE CONVICT'S VENGEANCE// D 2a// Charles Selby// **Surrey**, Sept. 1858.

HARP OF ALTENBURG, THE; OR, LEONORA'S GRAVE// D// n.a.// **Grecian**, Mar. 1857, with William Shuter as Altenburg, Mr. Hustleby as Ludolph, C. Kelsey as Claude, Henry Grant as Herman, Richard Phillips as Albert, Eaton O'Donnell as Conrade, John Manning as Peter, Jane Coveney as Leonora, Harriet Coveney as Janette.

HARRY OF ENGLAND, OR, THE TRUMPETER'S HORSE AND THE CONQUEST OF HARFLEUR// D 3a// Thomas Greenwood// **Sad. Wells**, May 1842, with Mr. Lyon as Henry V, Mr. Dry as Charles of Valois, Mr. Stickney as Dauphin, Henry Widdicomb as Orleans, Mr. Adams as Constable of France, Mr. Cottrell as Bourainault, Mr. Johnson as Braguemont, Mr. Williams as Mortimer, Mr. King as Erpingham, Mrs. Adams as Queen Isabel, Mrs. Stickney as Katherine, Mrs. Morgan as Rose, Miss Richardson as Eglantine, Mrs. Richard Barnett as Mabel/ Scenery by T. Pitt/ Music by Isaac Collins/ Prod. by R. Honner.

HARVEST// Play Pro & 3a// Henry Hamilton// **Princess's**, Sept. 1886, with Arthur Dacre as Musgrave, Brandon Thomas as Capt. Tressider, W. H. Denny as Hamish, Amy Roselle as Brenda, C. H. Hawtrey as Brooke, Yorke Stephens as Marston, Fanny Brough as Nora, Miss A. Measor as Lettice, Carlotta Addison as Miss Macleod, Amy Roselle as Mrs. Marston.

HARVEST HOME// D 3a// Tom Parry// **Adelphi**, Mar. 1848, with Henry Hughes as Cecil Derwent, Mr. Lambert as Reves, Edward Wright as Popjoy, Charles Munyard as Trubbs, Paul Bedford as Peeps, O. Smith as Kestrel, William Cullenford as Brough, Mme. Celeste as Amy, Sarah Woolgar as Mary, Mrs. Frank Matthews as Mrs. Peeps/ Scenery by Pitt and Johnstone/ Music by Alfred Mellon/ **Haymarket**, Aug. 1848, with same cast/ **Sad. Wells**, May 1855, with Edward Wright as Popjoy, E. F. Edgar as Kestral, George Fisher as Reves, C. Kelsy as Brough, Henry Butler as Derwent, Frederick Moreland as Marsdale, Mr. Blyth as Smith, Mr. Marchant as Swift, Mr. Barrett as Peeps, Mr. Sheppard as Trackwell, Miss Markham as Amy, Kate Kelly as Mary, Miss Florence as Mrs. Peeps, Mrs. Leman Rede as Martha/ **Grecian**, Aug. 1867, with William James as Derwent, Charles Mortimer as Reves, Henry Grant as Brough, George Gillett as Maridale, Alfred Rayner as Kestrel, John Manning as Popjoy, Henry Power as Trubbs, James Howard as Smith, J. Jackson as Peape, W. Shirley as Swift, Lizzie Mandelbert as Amy, Alice Denvil as May, Mrs. Atkinson as Mrs. Peape, Miss De Lacie as Martha.

HARVEST HOME// D// Benjamin Webster// **Astley's**, 1867.

HARVEST QUEEN, THE// D 2a// n.a.// **Grecian**, Jan. 1854, with Eaton O'Donnell as Sir Griffyth, Basil Potter as Wyllyams, Charles Horn as Beaumaris, Richard Phillips as Glendwyr, Percy Corri as Thomas, Henry Grant as Jerome, Charles Rice as ap Morgan, Henry Power as Jenkin, Jane Coveney as Eva, Harriet Coveney as Peggy, Miss Johnstone as Leoline.

HARVEST STORM, THE// D 1a// C. H. Hazlewood// **Britannia**, June 1862.

HASKA// D 3a// Henry Spicer// **Drury Lane**, Mar. 1877, with William Creswick as Count Stourdza, James Johnstone as Count Karoly,

Mr. Douglas as Palfy, Percy Bell as Domoko, Mr. Evans as Zichy, G. Weston as Micklos, Frank Tyars as Yan, R. Dolman as Josef, Miss Leighton as Haska, Cicely Nott as Espa, Clara Jecks as Maria/ Scenery by William Beverley/ Music by Karl Meyder.

HASTE// C 3a// Charles Wood// **St. Geo. Hall**, Jan. 1879.

HASTY CONCLUSION, A// F 1a// n.a.// **Olympic**, Apr. 1838, with C. J. Mathews as Abbé Le Bon, William Farren as Martelle, James Bland as Carl, Mme. Vestris as Marie.

HASTY CONCLUSIONS// C 2a// Mrs. J. R. Planché// **Lyceum**, Apr. 1844, with Charles Diddear as Gen. Mowbray, Frank Matthews as Hartley, Frederick Vining as Hartley, H. T. Craven as Sydney, Samuel Emery as Andrew, Miss Fairbrother as Gertrude, Mrs. Keeley as Nancy.

HATE'S ASSIGNATION; OR, THE DOUBLE AMBUSCADE// D// n.a.// **Grecian**, Sept. 1863, with Henry Grant as Henrico, Alfred Rayner as Duke D'Aquila, T. Mead as Paulo, William James as Lugi, W. Holland as Count Castelli, J. Jackson as Tomaso, Laura Conquest as Ernesto, Jane Dawson as Tercalna, Mrs. Charles Dillon as Francesca, Miss Johnstone as Signora Cossi.

HAUNTED FOR EVER// D 2a// J. B. Howe// **Britannia**, Feb. 1880.

HAUNTED HEATH, THE// F 1a// n.a.// **Victoria**, July 1857, with J. Howard as Quake, John Hudspeth as Simon, W. H. Pitt as Capt. Bolding, Mr. Henderson as Weatherleigh, Mr. Brunton as Smart, Phoebe Towers as Lucretia, Miss Laporte as Sophia, Miss Bailey as Rose.

HAUNTED HOUSES; OR, LABYRINTHS OF LIFE, A STORY OF LONDON AND THE BUSH// D Pro & 4a// H. J. Byron// **Princess's**, Apr. 1872, with James Johnstone as Geoffrey Mardyke, J. C. Cowper as Blake, John Billington as Guy Mardyke, J. Clarke as Morris, Howard Russell as Capt. Banger, Stanislaus Calhaem as Guinea, William Terriss as Coburn, Bernard Cullen as O'Flaherty, Rose Leclercq as Alice, Miss Hudspeth as Mary/ Scenery by F. Lloyds/ Music by W. C. Levey.

HAUNTED INN, THE// F 1a// R. B. Peake// **Sad. Wells**, Apr. 1840, with Mr. Williams as Sir Tompkin, Mr. Elvin as Capt. Levant, J. W. Collier as Corp. Trot, Charles Montgomery as Bluff, W. D. Broadfoot as Gristle, Henry Hall as Tadpole, Mrs. J. F. Saville as Angelica, Miss Cooke as Mrs. Gristle, Miss Pincott as Jenny/ **Olympic**, Nov. 1841, with Mr. Fitzjames as Capt. Levant, George Wild as Corp. Trot, Mr. Thompson as Sir Tomkyn, Mr. Brookes as Gristle, Mr. Turnour as Tadpole, Mr. Green as Etiquette, Mr. Searle as Bluff, Miss Fitzjames as Angelica, Mrs. Granby as Mrs. Gristle/ **Haymarket**, July 1869, with P. White as Sir Tomkyn, Mr. Kendal as Capt. Levant, Henry Compton as Corp. Trot, Mr. Rogers as Gristle, J. B. Buckstone Jr. as Tadpole, George Braid as Etiquette, Miss Harrison as Angelica, Mrs. Laws as Mrs. Gristle, Fanny Wright as Jenny.

HAUNTED LIVES// D 5a// J. Wilton Jones// **Olympic**, May. 1884, with J. B. Durham as Squire Edenbridge, Philip Beck as Frank Edenbridge, Royce Carlton as Capt. Edenbridge, Harry Courtaine as Count Orloff, Sydney Sarl as Branston, Charles Ashford as Stokes, C. W. Somerset as Duval, Fuller Mellish as Maxwell, Ernest Hendrie as Thwaites, Katie Barry as Martha, Alma Murray as Ruth, Rose Leclercq as Countess Zilinska, Laura Linden as Gwenny.

HAUNTED MAN, THE// D// n.a.// **Adelphi**, 1849.

HAVEN OF CONTENT, THE// Play 4a// Malcolm Watson// **Garrick**, Nov. 1896, with Ernest Leicester as Northcote, Julius Knight as Lord Solcroft, John Beauchamp as Fenton, A. E. George as Vulliamy, R. E. Warton as Cheadley, Lesly Thomson as Saunders, Miss Granville as Lady Jane, Haidee Wright as Chris.

HAWAIA: OR, THE BURNING GULF// D// n.a.// **Alhambra**, Dec. 1880.

HAZARD OF THE DIE// D// Douglas Jerrold// **Sad. Wells**, Nov. 1838, with Mr. Cathcart as David Devigne, John Lee as Charles Devigne, Dibdin Pitt as St. Ange, Robert Honner as Kalmer, J. W. Collier as Caniche, Benjamin Conquest as Gryps, Mr. Dry as Binko, Miss Richardson as Mme. Devigne, Mrs. J. F. Saville as Violette.

HAZEL KIRKE// D 4a// Steele Mackaye// **Vaudeville**, June 1886, with James Fernandez, J. D. Beveridge, Maria Davis, Fanny Brough, Jessie Millward.

HE LIES LIKE TRUTH// F 1a// F. Kimton// **Haymarket**, Dec. 1845, with Mr. Howe as Sir Charles, Mr. Tilbury as Truepenny, Henry Holl as Rattler, T. F. Mathews as Clincher, Mrs. L. S. Buckingham as Harriet, Priscilla Horton as Priscilla/ **Olympic**, Mar. 1874, with Mr. Estcourt as Sir Charles, Charles Neville as Rattler, John Vollaire as Truepenny, G. W. Anson as Clincher, Elsie Pearce as Harriet, Annie Taylor as Priscilla/ **Haymarket**, Jan. 1878, with Mr. Weathersby as Sir Charles, Harry Crouch as Rattler, Frederick Everill as Truepenny, David Fisher Jr. as Clincher, Lucy Buckstone as Harriet, Maria Harris as Priscilla.

HE WOULD BE A SAILOR; OR, BREAKERS AHEAD// D 2a// C. H. Hazlewood// **Britannia**, Mar. 1868.

HE WOULD BE AN ACTOR// F 1a// C. J. Mathews// **Olympic**, Jan. 1837, with W. Vining as Currant, Mr. Selby as Sinclair, Mr. Wyman as Morgan, W. H. Oxberry as Dicky Darling, C. J. Mathews as Motley, Mrs. Orger as Becky/ **Eng. Opera House** (Lyceum), June 1837, with C. J. Mathews as Motley, W. H. Oxberry as Darling, Charles Selby as Sinclair, William Vining as Currant, Mrs. Orger as Becky/ **Haymarket**, June 1838, with C. J. Mathews as Motley, J. W. Gough as Currant, James Worrell as Sinclair, J. B. Buckstone as Dicky Darling, T. F. Mathews as Morgan, Mrs. Orger as Becky/ **Cov. Garden**, June 1837, with same cast/ **Princess's**, Mar. 1846, with C. J. Mathews as Motley, Mr. Granby as Morgan, W. H. Oxberry as Dickey Darling, Stephen Smith as Currant, Augustus Harris as Sinclair, Emma Stanley as Becky.

HE'S A LUNATIC// F// Herman Merivale ("Felix Dale")/ **Princess's**, Feb. 1871, with John Clayton as Hare, C. F. Marshall as Trotter, Ernest Travers as Ruggles, Miss Lennox Grey as Arabella, Miss Seymour as Matter/ **Lyceum**, Sept. 1873, with John Clayton as March Hare, J. Carter as Trotter, Mr. Harwood as Ruggles, Roma Le Thière as Arabella, Miss Seymour as Hatter.

HEAD OF ROMULUS, THE// C 1a// Adap. by Sidney Grundy fr F of Eugène Scribe// **St. James's**, May 1900, with H. H. Vincent as Turnbull, W. H. Vernon as Barnstaple, Roland Cunningham as Harold, Susie Vaughan as Mrs. Turnbull, Lily Grundy as Dolly, Amy Betteley as Jane.

HEAD OF THE FAMILY, THE// C 1a// Adap. by W. S. Emden fr F, Le Moulin à Paroles// **Olympic**, Nov. 1859, with Horace Wigan as Hackle, Walter Gordon as Edgar, Henry Rivers as Gregory, Mrs. Stirling as Charity, Miss Cottrell as Prudence.

HEADLESS HORSEMAN, THE; OR, THE RIDE OF DEATH// D 2a// Adap. by C. H. Hazlewood fr novel of Mayne Reid// **Britannia**, 1865.

HEADLESS MAN, THE// C 3a// Adap. by F. C. Burnand fr F// **Criterion**, July 1889; Dec. 1893, with Charles Wyndham as Hedley, William Blakeley as Bletchingly, J. G. Taylor as Bracebridge, Frank Atherley as Otway, Frank Worthing as Harcourt, Sydney Valentine as Nupley, Ellis Jeffreys as Mrs. Torrington, Miss F. Frances as Mrs. Bletchingly, Ethel Matthews as Mrs. Hedley, May Blayney as Lydia.

HEADS OR TAILS// C 1a// J. Palgrave Simpson// **Olympic**, June 1854, with Samuel Emery as Wrangleworth, Alfred Wigan as Dycaster, Frederick Robson as Quaile, Miss Marston as Rosamond, Mrs. Alfred Wigan as Winifred.

THE HEADSMAN// D 1a// Albert Smith// **Olympic**, Jan. 1849, with William Norton as Count of Flanders, Edward Stirling as Vander, Leigh Murray as Gerard, Henry Compton as Franz, Miss De Burgh as Bertha, Mrs. H. J. Turner as Margaret/ Scenery by Roberts & J. Roberts.

HEADSMAN'S AXE, THE; OR, QUEEN, CROWN, AND COUNTRY// D 3a// G. H. Macdermott// **Grecian**, Oct. 1870.

HEART; OR, THE LIBERTINE'S LESSON// D 2a// n.a.// **Victoria**, June 1848, with James Howard as Barton, J. T. Johnson as Selden, Mr. Henderson as Murray, G. F. Forman as Snacks, Mr. Hitchinson as Stapleton, Annette Vincent as Laura, Mrs. George Lee as Ellen, Julia Seaman as Fanny, Miss Burroughcliffe as Polly.

HEART OF A BROTHER, THE// D 2a// n.a.// **Britannia**, May 1871.

HEART OF A HERO, THE// D 4a// Lingford Carson// **Pavilion**, July 1900.

HEART OF AN IRISHMAN, THE// D 3a// n.a.// **Grecian**, Apr. 1846, with Mr. Campbell as Peery Carroll, Edwin Dixon as Michael, John Collett as Hunkstone, Eaton O'Donnell as Danny Scallion, T. W. Edmonds as Hamilton, Mr. Manley as Stranger, Mary A. Crisp as Winifred, Miss Johnstone as Biddy.

HEART OF GOLD, A// D 3a// Douglas Jerrold// **Princess's**, Oct. 1854, with John Ryder as Dymond, John Cathcart as Thanet, Mr. Addison as Nutbrown, David Fisher as Michaelmas, Henry Saker as Weevil, Drinkwater Meadows as Towberry, F. Cooke as Knacks, Miss Heath as Maude, Miss Murray as Molly, Mrs. W. Daly as Widow Peacock.

HEART OF HEARTS// Play 3a// Henry Arthur Jones// **Vaudeville**, Nov. 1887.

HEART OF LONDON, THE; OR, VICE AND ITS VICTIMS// D 3a// W. T. Moncrieff// **Sad. Wells**, Aug. 1857, with George Clair as Fitzhazard, Charles Seyton as Wilton, Watkins Young as Shuttleworth, Alfred Rayner as Blackburn, R. Green as Robson, Mr. Gladstone as Capt. Belton, Mrs. J. B. Johnstone as Lady Hauton, Mary A. Victor as Emily.

HEART OF MARYLAND, THE// D 4a// David Belasco// **Elephant & Castle**, Sept. 1895/ **Adelphi**, Apr. 1898, with Harry Harwood as Gen. Kendrick, Maurice Barrymore as Col. Alan Kendrick, Edward Morgan as Col. Thorpe, Frank Mills as Lt. Telfair, Odell Williams as Sgt. Blount, Henry Weaver Jr. as Tom Boone, Helen Tracy as Mrs. Gordon, Mrs. Leslie Carter as Maryland Calvert, Helen Macbeth as Phoebe/ Scenery by Ernest Albert & Richard Marston/ Music by John Crook/ Prod. by Charles Frohman.

HEART OF MIDLOTHIAN, THE// D 3a// Adap. by Charles Dibdin fr novel of Sir Walter Scott// **Sad. Wells**, July 1843, with John Webster as Duke of Argyle, Henry Marston as Staunton, Mr. Starmer as Deans, C. J. Bird as Butler, Mr. Lambe as Saddletree, Mr. Williams as Archibald, C. J. Smith as Ratcliffe, John Herbert as The Laird, Caroline Rankley as Jeannie Deans, Miss Lane as Queen, Miss Pitt as Lady Suffolk, Mrs. Richard Barnett as Effie Deans, Mrs. Fitzwilliam as Madge Wildfire, Miss Cooke as Margery, Mrs. Andrews as Mrs. Balchristie, Miss Melville as Sally; Apr. 1856, with C. Cooke as Duke of Argyle, E. F. Edgar as Staunton, Walter Williams as David, C. Kelsey as Saddletree, Mr. Swanborough as Butler, Mr. Wareham as Ratcliffe, Miss Sidney as Caroline, Jenny Marston as Jeanie, Miss Craven as Effie, Harriet Gordon as Madge, Mrs. B. Bartlett as Margery, Emma Barnett as Mrs. Balchristie.

HEART OF MIDLOTHIAN; OR, THE LILY OF ST. LEONARD'S// D// Adap. fr novel of Sir Walter Scott// **Sad. Wells**, Nov. 1838, with Robert Honner as Duke of Argyle, J. Lee as Staunton, Mr. Williams as Dumbiedikes, Dibdin Pitt as Deans, Mr. Elvin as Butler, Mr. Broadfoot as Saddletree, C. Montague as Ratcliffe, J. W. Collier as Archibald, Mrs. J. F. Saville as Queen Caroline, Miss Thompson as Lady Suffolk, Mrs. Robert Honner as Jeanie, Mrs. Harwood as Mrs. Saddletree, Miss E. Honner as Effie Deans, Miss Richardson as Madge.

HEART OF MIDLOTHIAN; OR, THE SISTERS JEANIE AND EFFIE// D// Dram. fr novel of Sir Walter Scott// **Grecian**, Nov. 1862, with William James as Duke of Argyle, Thomas Mead as Staunton, Alfred Rayner as Fairbrother, Henry Grant as David Deans, J. Jackson as Laird of Dumbiedikes, John Manning as Black Frank, George Gillett as Butler, Walter Holland as Ratcliffe, Marie Brewer as Queen Caroline, Jane Dawson as Jeanie Deans, Mrs. Charles Dillon as Effie Deans, Mrs. Alfred Rayner as Margery, Miss Johnstone as Mrs. Balchristie, Mary A. Victor as Magdalen.

HEART OF THE WORLD, THE// Play// Westland Marston// **Haymarket**, Oct. 1847.

HEART'S DELIGHT// D 4a// Dram. by Andrew Halliday fr novel of Charles Dickens, Dombey and Son// **Globe**, Dec. 1873.

HEART STRINGS AND FIDDLE STRINGS// F// David Fisher// **Princess's**, Nov. 1865, with Robert Cathcart as John Thompson, Charles Seyton as Tom Thompson, David Fisher as Smith, Hetty Tracy as Kate, Emma Barnett as Ellen.

HEART THAT CAN FEEL FOR ANOTHER, THE// D// William Rogers// **Sad. Wells**, June 1837, with Mr. Campell as Somerton, C. H. Pitt as Greenville, Mr. Griffiths as Old Stanley, Mr. King as Gray, Mr. Rogers as Doleful, N. T. Hicks as Gilbert, H. George as Blind Fiddler, Mr. Pateman as Lame Fiddler, Mrs. Harris as Mabel, Miss Williams as Agnes, Lavinia Melville as Dolly.

HEART'S ORDEAL// D// n.a.// **City of London**, Aug. 1863.

HEART'S VICTORY, THE// D 2a// Thomas Mead// **Grecian**, Mar. 1861, with R. H. Lingham as de Renneville, William James as Victor, Thomas Mead as Marcel, Jane Coveney as Madeline, Lucreza Hill as Henriette/ **Sad. Wells**, Mar. 1865, with T. Mead as Marselle, Walter Joyce as de Rennerville, W. S. Foote as Victor, Milford Byrne as Julian, Mrs. Stevenson as Countess de Cherval, Ellen Beaufort as Lucille.

HEARTLESS// Play Pro & 3a// Dram. by Marion Webb fr novel of Ouida, Puck// **Olympic**, Apr. 1885.

HEARTS ARE TRUMPS// D 3a// Mark Lemon// **Olympic**, Aug. 1851, with William Farren as Gray, Henry Farren as Capt. Wagstaff, William Farren Jr. as Wilmot, Henry Compton as Martin, George Cooke as Goad, Mr. Clifton as Trotter, Mrs. Stirling as Miss Gray, Mrs. B. Bartlett as Mrs. Miller, Mrs. Alfred Phillips as Susan.

HEARTS ARE TRUMPS// D 4a// Cecil Raleigh// **Drury Lane**, Sept. 1899, with Violet Vanbrugh as Lady Winifred, Dora Barton as Dora, Mary Brough as Jane, Vane Featherston as Countess of Fairfield, Louise Moodie as Lady Dovedale, Dolores Drummond as Mrs. Angerstein, Beatrice Ferrar as Maude, Birdie Sutherland as Mrs. Bailey, John Tresahar as Earl of Burford, Cooper Cliffe as Rev. Thorold, William Devereux as Gillespie, Michael Brough as Wain/ Scenery by W. Perkins, Mr. McLeery, Bruce Smith & R. Caney/ Music by J. M. Glover/ Prod. by Arthur Collins.

HEARTSEASE// D 4a// Adap. by James Mortimer fr F of Alexandre Dumas fils, La Dame aux Camélias// **Princess's**, June 1875, with Bruton Robins as Sir Stephen, William Rignold as Herbert, W. S. Parkes as Capt. Bloodgood, P. C. Beverley as Triss, W. Vincent as as Leighton, C. Northcote as Dr. Hicks, Helen Barry as Constance, Cicely Nott as Mrs. Ponsonby, Miss Carlisle as Kitty, Alma Murray as Amy, Jenny Lovell as Dolly; June 1881, with Johnston Forbes Robertson as Armand, Edward Price as M. Duval, Brian Darley as Comte de Varville, G. W. Anson as Rieux, Norman Forbes as Gustave, Neville Doone as Doctor, Helena Modjeska as Constance, Miss M. A. Giffard as Mme. Prudence, Dora Vivian as Nichette, May Burney as Olympe/ **Court**, May 1880, with Arthur Dacre, Edward Price, Helena Modjeska/ **Olympic**, Jan. 1892.

HEATHER FIELD, THE// Play 3a// Eduard Martyn// **Terry's**, June 1899, with Ben Webster as Ussher, Marsh Allen as Tyrrell, Marcus St. John as Lord Shrule, Trevor Lowe as Dowling, J. E. Wilkinson as Roche, Thomas Kingston as Carden Tyrrell, May Whitty as Grace, Adelina Baird as Lady Shrule.

HEATHER FLOWER, THE; OR, SNAPDRAGON THE HIGHWAYMAN, AND THE MYSTERIES OF GRASSDALE MANOR// D 4a// Thomas Mead// **Grecian**, Mar. 1862, with Thomas Mead as Snapdragon, Alfred Rayner as Fertherfew, Mr. Jackson as Goodenough, Henry Grant as Foster, John Manning as Blaze, Henry Power as Squirts, Mr. Costello as Thompson, R. H. Lingham as Horsefall, William James as Sedley, Mrs. Charles Dillon as Amy, Jane Dawson as Isa, Mary A. Victor as Mrs. Prynne, Miss Johnstone as Mrs. Goodenough.

HEAVY FATHERS// F// B. H. Hilton// **Folly**, Apr. 1879, with Harry Nicholls, Minnie Marshall.

HEBREW, THE// D// n.a.// **City of London**, Feb. 1852.

HEDDA GABLER// Play 4a// Trans. by Edmund Gosse & William Archer fr Norw. of Henrik Ibsen// **Vaudeville**, Apr. 1891, with Charles Sugden as Brack, W. Scott Buist as Tesman,

Arthur Elwood as Lovborg, Marion Lea as Mrs. Elvsted, Henrietta Cowen as Juliana, Elizabeth Robins as Hedda/ **St. Geo. Hall**, Nov. 1901.

HEDGE CARPENTER, THE// D// C. H. Hazlewood// **Britannia**, Feb. 1870.

HEIR AT LAW, THE// C 5a// George Colman the younger// **Haymarket**, Aug. 1837, with William Farren as Daniel Dowlas, Frederick Vining as Dick Dowlas, Benjamin Webster as Dr. Pangloss, J. B. Buckstone as Zekiel Homespun, Charles Selby as Moreland, J. T. Haines as Stedfast, Mrs. Julia Glover as Deborah, Miss E. Phillips as Caroline, Mrs. Fitzwilliam as Cicely; Sept. 1866, with W. H. Chippendale as Daniel, William Farren as Dick Dowlas, Henry Compton as Dr. Pangloss, Walter Gordon as Morland, Mr. Rogers as Stedfast, J. B. Buckstone as Zekiel Homespun, George Braid as Kenrick, Mrs. Chippendale as Deborah, Lucreza Hill as Caroline, Nelly Moore as Cicely; Sept. 1873, with John S. Clarke as Pangloss, George Belmore as Homespun, Harry Crouch as Dick Dowlas, S. Hargreaves as Daniel Dowlas, Charles Wilmot as Kenrick, George Temple as Moreland, E. L. Branscombe as Steadfast, Emily Thorne as Deborah, Eleanor Bufton as Cicely, Linda Dietz as Caroline; Sept. 1879, with John S. Clarke, H. B. Conway, Charles Harcourt, John Ryder, Linda Dietz, Emily Thorne/ **Sad. Wells**, Mar 1842, with Mr. Williams as Daniel Dowlas, E. F. Saville as Dick Dowlas, John Herbert as Dr. Pangloss, E. Morton as Morland, Mr. Robson as Stedfast, Robert Honner as Homespun, Mrs. Robert Honner as Cecily Homespun, Miss Cooke as Deborah, Mrs. Richard Barnett as Caroline; May 1850, with A. Younge as Lord Duberly, G. K. Dickinson as Dick Dowlas, Henry Nye as Dr. Pangloss, William Belford as Morland, Frank Graham as Stedfast, Henry Mellon as Kenrick, William Hoskins as Zekiel Homespun, Mrs. Brougham as Lady Duberly, Miss Fitzpatrick as Cicely, Miss T. Bassano as Caroline/ **Olympic**, Feb. 1848, with William Davidge as Daniel Dowlass and Lord Duberly, Henry Holl as Dick Dowlas, Lysander Thompson as Homespun, Mr. Conquest as Dr. Pangloss, Mr. Archer as Steadfast, Miss Hamilton as Cecily, Lucreza Hill as Caroline, Mrs. H. Lee as Lady Duberly; Mar. 1851, with William Farren as Daniel Dowlas and Baron Duberly, Henry Farren as Dick Dowlas, Henry Compton as Dr. Pangloss, William Farren Jr. as Morland, Charles Diddear as Stedfast, William Shalders as Zekiel Homespun, Mrs. B. Bartlett as Deborah, Miss Adams as Caroline, Mrs. Stirling as Cicely Homespun; Feb. 1880, with John S. Clarke as Dr. Pangloss, Charles Harcourt as Homespun, Mr. Carton as Dick Dowlas, John Maclean as Daniel Dowlas, Mr. Weathersby as Kenrick, John Ryder as Steadfast, F. Charles as Morland, Mr. Thornton as John, Edith Bruce as Cicely, Mrs. Leigh as Deborah, Gwynne Williams as Caroline/ **Princess's**, Nov. 1855, with Frank Matthews as Dowlass and Duberly, Walter Lacy as Dick Dowlas, John Pritt Harley as Dr. Pangloss, John Cathcart as Morland, Frank Graham as Stedfast, Drinkwater Meadows as Zekiel Homespun, Henry Mellon as Kenrick, Mrs. Winstanley as Deborah, Miss Desborough as Caroline, Carlotta Leclercq as Cecily/ **Strand**, Feb. 1870.

HEIR OF MOWBRAY, THE; OR, THE GYPSEY SON// D 3a// W. L. Rede// **Sad. Wells**, Nov. 1838, with J. Lee as Greyling, Mr. Dry as Lee, Robert Honner as Wallett, Mr. Williams as Lowther, Dibdin Pitt as Dotter, Mr. Broadfoot as Campbell, Benjamin Conquest as Jack, J. W. Collier as Kumyyum, Mr. Mellor as Morrison, C. Montague as Gipsey Jack, Mrs. Robert Honner as Amy, Mrs. J. F. Saville as Rose, Miss Richardson as Kate, Miss Pincott as Maud, Miss Cooke as Sara.

HEIRESS, THE// D// Dion Boucicault// **Cov. Garden**, Feb. 1842.

HEIRS OF RABOURDIN, THE// Trans. by A. Teixeira de Mattos fr F of Emile Zola, Les Héritiers de Rabourdin// **Opera Comique**, Feb. 1894, with James Welch as Rabourdin, Harding Cox as Chapuzot, C. H. Hallard as Dominique, Gouglas Gordon as Le Doux, Charles Goodhart as Dr. Morgue, F. N. Connell as Isaac, Mrs. Arthur Ayres as Vaussard, Mrs. Lois Royd as Fiquet, Lena Dene as Eugenie, Mary Jocelyn as Charlotte.

HELD ASUNDER// D 4a// Malcolm Watson// **POW**, Apr. 1888.

HELD AT BAY; OR, THE EXILED MOTHER// D// n.a.// **Marylebone**, Sept. 1879.

HELD BY THE ENEMY// D 5a// William Gillette// **Princess's**, Apr. 1887, with Charles Warner as Col. Prescott, Charles Overton as Gen. Stamburg, E. W. Gardiner as Lt. Hayne, Stanislaus Calhaem as Uncle Rufus, Yorke Stephens as Bean, William Rignold as Fielding, Edmund Gurney as Col. McPherson, E. W. Thomas as Capt. Woodford, Mrs. Canninge as Euphemia, Annie Hughes as Susan, Alma Murray as Rachel/ **Vaudeville**, July 1887.

HELD IN TERROR// D 4a// Frank Dix// **Imperial**, Aug. 1898.

HELEN DOUGLAS// D 5a// n.a.// **Haymarket**, July 1870.

HELEN'S BABIES// F// Garnet Walch// **Gaiety**, Sept. 1878.

HELOISE AND ABELARD// D 4a// Adap. fr F of Anicet Bourgeois & Francis Cornu// **Sad. Wells**, May 1837, with N. T. Hicks as Abelard, Mr. King as Fulbert, Mr. Ede as Bernard, C. H. Pitt as Gautier, Mr. Campbell as Larenodi, J. Dunn as Barnaby, C. J. Smith as Elias, Mr. Griffiths as Galluchet, Miss Williams as Heloise, Lavinia Melville as Jossetta/ Scenery by Mr. Mildenhall/ Machines by Mr. Copping/ Music by Mr. Nicholson.

HELPING A FRIEND// FC 3a// W. H. Denny// **Strand**, May 1899, with H. O. Clarey as Benjamin Dimbleby, Frank Hollins as Gilbert Dimbleby, Windham Guise as Prabbles, Lawrance d'Orsay as Nesbitt, W. H. Denny as Smithers, Susie Vaughan as Mrs. Benj. Dimbleby, Clara Nicholls as Mrs. Prabbles, Ada Marius as Florrie.

HELPING HANDS// D 2a// Tom Taylor// **Adelphi**, June 1855.

HEMLOCK DRAUGHT, THE// D 2a// John Oxenford// **Olympic**, Jan. 1849, with Leigh Murray as Clinias, John Kinloch as Cleon, William Norton as Paris, Mrs. Stirling as Hippolita/ Scenery by Roberts & J. Roberts.

HEN AND CHICKENS; OR, A SIGN OF AFFECTION// C 2a// Benjamin Webster Jr.// **Olympic**, Feb. 1868, with Henry Ashley as Casby, C. H. Stephenson as Sawderley, Mr. Stanley as Tom, George Vincent as James, Mrs. Stirling as Mrs. Sawderley, Louisa Moore as Angelina, Miss Schavey as Prinks/ **Globe**, July 1875, with John Billington as Casby, J. Jackson as Sawderley, P. Meynall as Tom Sawderley, A. D. Anderson as James, Mrs. Billington as Mrs. Soft Sawderley, Miss E. Meyrick as Mrs. Casby.

HENRI THE WITLESS; OR, LIFE'S CLOUD AND SUNSHINE// D 3a// W. E. Suter// **Grecian**, June 1854, with Henry Grant as President, Basil Potter as Vernuil, Richard Phillips as D'Harcourt, Eaton O'Donnell as Dr. Roger, Charles Horn as Hercule, Jane Coveney as Genevieve, Harriet Coveney as Julie, Miss Johnstone as Countess D'Harcourt, Ellen Crisp as Mme. de Serun.

HENRIETTA, THE// C 4a// Bronson Howard// **Elephant & Castle**, Sept. 1887/ **Avenue**, Mar. 1891.

HENRIETTE; OR, A TIMELY WARNING// D 3a// George Conquest// **Grecian**, Mar. 1856, with Richard Phillips as Albert, Mr. Hustleby as Derville, Eaton O'Donnell as Bernard, Henry Grant as Stranger, John Manning as Stepinford, F. Charles as Raymond, William Shuter as Baron Chaurigny, Ellen Crisp as Duchess of Royan, Miss Chapman as Marie, Jane Coveney as Henriette, Miss Johnstone as Tronguette.

HENRY III// D// n.a.// **Drury Lane**, 1893.

HENRY IV, Part I// C// William Shakespeare// **Drury Lane**, Nov. 1839, with Mr. Archer as Henry IV, Henry Marston as Prince of Wales, J. W. Ray as Westmoreland, Mr. Baker as Worcester, George Cooke as Northumberland, Mr. Elton as Hotspur, Mr. Melville as Douglas, Mr. Roberts as Vernon, James H. Hackett as Falstaff, Mr. Duruset as Blunt, John Lee as Poins, Edwin Yarnold as Bardolph, Mrs. Ashton as Lady Percy, Mrs. Selby as Dame Quickly; Dec. 1850, with Mr. Cooper as Henry IV, James Anderson as Prince of Wales, Julia Bleaden as Prince John, John Cathcart as Worcester, J. Neville as Northumberland, George Vandenhoff as Hotspur, Mr. Harris as Douglas, Mr. Simpson as Blount, William West as Vernon, Mr. Barratt as Falstaff, H. T. Craven as Poins, Robert Romer as Gadshill, Mr. Bisson as Peto, S. Jones as Bardolph, Fanny Vining as Lady Percy, Mrs. Parker as Hostess; May 1864, with John Ryder as Henry IV, Walter Lacy as Prince of Wales, J. Neville Sr. as Henry Percy, Samuel Phelps as Falstaff, Walter Montgomery as Hotspur, Robert Roxby as Poins, George Belmore as Francis, Henry Vandenhoff as Mortimer, Mr. Barrett as Thomas Percy, Mr. Fitzjames as Westmoreland, George Spencer as Blunt, Alfred Rayner as Glendower, Edmund Phelps as Vernon, W. Ellerton as Bardolph, Mr. Warde as Gadshill, Rose Leclercq as Lady Percy, Edith Wynne as Lady Mortimer, Mrs. C. Melville as Mrs. Quickly/ Scenery by William Beverley/ **Cov. Garden**, Feb. 1845, with Mr. Archer as Henry IV, James Vining as Prince of Wales, Miss Beauchamp as Lancaster, Mr. Hollingsworth as Westmorland, Mr. Rae as Worcester, Mr. Lee as Northumberland, George Braid as Vernon, Henry Betty as Hotspur, J. C. Bird as Blount, Mr. Hann as Douglas, James H. Hackett as Falstaff, Mr. Hield as Poins, Mr. Rogers as Bardolph, Mrs. J. Cooke as Lady Percy, Mrs. Griffiths as Mrs. Quickly/ **Princess's**, Dec. 1850, with Mr. King as Henry IV, Frederick Belton as Prince Henry, Miss Daly as Prince John, Charles Fisher as Westmorland, George Everett as Blunt, John Ryder as Worcester, Mr. Wynn as Northumberland, Charles Kean as Hotspur, F. Cooke as Douglas, John Cathcart as Vernon, George Bartley as Falstaff, James Vining as Poins, Mr. Addison as Bardolph, Mrs. Charles Kean as Lady Percy, Mrs. Keeley as Hostess/ **Grecian**, Sept. 1856, with Henry Grant as King Henry, Richard Phillips as Prince of Wales, Miss Chapman as Lancaster, Mr. Hustleby as Hotspur, Eaton O'Donnell as Worcester, William Shuter as Poins, Mr. Barrett as Falstaff, Henry Power as Bardolph, Jane Coveney as Mrs. Quickly, George Conquest as Glendower, Miss Johnstone as Hostess/ **Astley's**, (in 3a) Mar. 1857, with Mark Howard as King Henry, W. Cooke Jr. as Prince Hal, C. Bradbury as Lancaster, Mr. Campbell as Worcester, T. Cooke as Northumberland, J. T. Anderson as Douglas, H. Hemmings as Vernon, James Holloway as Hotspur, J. W. Anson as Falstaff, Henry Reeves as Poins, Mrs. J. W. Anson as Lady Percy, Mrs. W. Dowton as Hostess/ Scenery by T. Thompson & Thorne/ Machines by E. Pryce/ Music by G. Phillips/ Horses trained by Wm. Cooke/ **Olympic**, May 1879 (in 4a), with George Leicester as King Henry, J. H. Barnes as Prince of Wales, J. A. Rosier as Hotspur, Mr. Chamberlain as Blunt, Mr. Germon as Lancaster, R. Craufurd as Poins, Henry Murray as Falstaff, Mr. Hargreaves as Bardolph, Charlotte Saunders as Mistress Quickly/ **Haymarket**, June 1896, with Herbert Beerbohm Tree as Falstaff, William Mollison as Henry IV, Herbert Ross as Prince of Wales, Berte Thomas as Lancaster, Mr. Romaine as Westmoreland, Fred Everill as Thomas Percy, Charles Allan as Northumberland, Lewis Waller as Hotspur, C. M. Hallard as Mortimer, F. Percival Stevens as Blunt, Alfred Wigley as Poins, Holman Clark as Glendower, Henry Vibart as Douglas, Lionel Brough as Bardolph, Lesly Thompson as Gadshill, Mrs. Beerbohm Tree as Lady Percy, Marion Evans as Lady Mortimer, Kate Phillips as Mrs. Quickly/ Scenery by Walter Johnstone, Mr. Freemantle & Walter Hann/ Music by Raymond Roze/ Prod. by H. B. Tree & Louis Calvert/ **Lyceum**, Mar. 1890, with Henry Irving.

HENRY IV, Part II// CD// William Shakespeare// **Drury Lane**, May 1843, with W. C. Macready, James Anderson, Samuel Phelps/ **Sad. Wells**, Apr. 1853, with Samuel Phelps as Henry IV and as Shallow, Frederic Robinson as Prince of Wales, Mr. Clinton as Lancaster, Lizzie Mandelbert as Prince Humphrey, Miss F. Younge as Clarence, Mr. Robins as Chief Justice, T. C. Harris as Westmorland, Henry Mellon as York, G. Bassil as Mowbray, Mr. Barrett as Falstaff, Mr. Williams as Bardolph, Mr. Wilkins as Pistol, William Belford as Poins, Lewis Ball as Davy, Mrs. Henry Marston as Mrs. Quickly, Mrs Dixon as Doll Tearsheet.

HENRY V// D// William Shakespeare// **Cov. Garden**, Nov. 1837, with W. C. Macready as Henry V, Miss Fairbrother as Gloucester, Henry Howe as Bedford, Mr. Warde as Exeter, Mr. Roberts as Westmoreland, George Bennett as Canterbury, Mr. Paulo as Ely, Edwin Yarnold as Cambridge, C. J. Smith as Scroop, W. H. Payne as Grey, Mr. Tilbury as Erpingham, James Anderson as Gower, Drinkwater Meadows as Fluellen, John Ayliffe as Nym, W. J. Hammond as Pistol, Mr. Macarthy as Bardolph, Mrs. Sarah Garrick as Mrs. Quickly, Mr. Waldron as Charles VI, Mr. Vining as Dauphin, John Pritchard as Burgundy, Mrs. W. Clifford as Queen Isabel, Priscilla Horton as Katherine; June 1839, with W. C. Macready, John Pritt Harley, John Vandenhoff, Mrs. Mary Warner, Samuel Phelps/ **Sad. Wells**, Nov. 1852, with Henry Marston as Chorus, Samuel Phelps as Henry V, Henry Mellon as Exeter, Mr. Lacy as Ely, Lewis Ball as Finellen [sic], Mr. Willis as Gower, Charles Fenton as Nym, Edward Knight as Bardolph, George Bennett as Pístol, Mrs. Henry Marston as Mrs. Quickly, Frederic Robinson as Dauphin, C. Moorhouse as Burgundy, Mrs. Barrett as Queen Isabel, Miss T. Bassano as Katherine/ Scenery by F. Fenton/ Music by W. Montgomery/ Machines by Mr. Cawdery/ **Princess's**, Mar. 1859, with Charles Kean as Henry V, Mr. Daly as Bedford, Miss Daly as Gloucester, Mr. Cooper as Exeter, Mr. Flemming as York, Mr. Warren as Warwick, Henry Mellon as Canterbury, F. Cooke as Ely, Frank Graham as Erpingham, George Everett as Gower, Drinkwater Meadows as Fluellen, Frank Matthews as Pistol, Henry Saker as Bardolph, John Cathcart as Dauphin, Mr. Rolleston as Burgundy, Alfred Raymond as Constable of France, Miss Murray as Queen Isabel, Miss Chapman as Katherine, Mrs. W. Daly as Mrs. Quickly/ Scenery by Grieve & Telbin, Music by Mr. Isaacson, Machines by G. Hodsdon/ **Queen's**, Sept. 1876, with Samuel Phelps, Mr. Coleman, John Ryder, Margaret Leighton/ **Lyceum**, Feb. 1900, with F. R. Benson as Henry V, H. H. Ainley as Gloster, Sinclair Neil as Bedford, E. A. Warburton as Canterbury, Arthur Whitby as Ely, O. Tidman as Scroop, Harcourt Williams as Sir Thomas Grey, Oscar Ashe as Pistol, H. Asheton Tonge as Bardolph, Alfred Brydone as Charles VI of France, A. Vezin as Orleans, G. Fitzgerald as Constable of France, Mrs. F. R. Benson as Katherine, Miss Denvil as Hostess; Jan. 1901, with Lewis Waller as Henry V, Gerald Gurney as Gloster, Arthur Soames as Bedford, William Dunlop as York, George Warde as Canterbury, Arthur Lewis as Ely, Gordon Bailey as Scroop, George Hayward as Sir Thomas Grey, Alexander Calvert as Gower, E. M. Robson as Fluellen, Charles Goodhart as Bardolph, William Mollison as Pistol, Basset Roe as Charles VI, Frank Dyall as Mountjoy, William Devereux as Constable of France, Sarah Brooke as Katherine, Kate Phillips as Hostess, Lily Hanbury as Chorus.

HENRY V; OR, THE BATTLE OF AGINCOURT// D// Arr. by George Rignold fr Charles Calvert's vers. of Shakespeare// **Drury Lane**, Nov. 1879, with George Rignold as Henry V, Brabrook Henderson as Chorus, L. Arthur as Glo'ster, H. Raven as Bedford, C. H. Stephenson as Exeter, Mr. Standish as York, J. K. Keane as Salisbury, James Wheeler as Westmoreland, Mr. Thorpe as Warwick, John Ryder as Canterbury, Mr. Hall as Ely, Mr. Holland as Scroop, A. H. Warren as Gower, Stanislaus Calhaem as Fluellen, Walter Grisdale as Nym, Robert Mansell as Bardolph, Mr. Odell as Pistol, Frank Barsby as Philip of France, W. Robertson as Burgundy, Charles Harcourt as Montjoy, Dora Vivian as Katherine, Ida Beaumont as Queen Isabel, Miss Marlborough as Mrs. Quickly.

HENRY VIII// D// William Shakespeare// **Cov. Garden**, May 1837, with Mr. Vandenhoff as Henry VIII, W. C. Macready as Wolsey, Sheridan Knowles as Buckingham, John Dale as Cromwell, George Bennett as Surrey, John Pritchard as Cranmer, John Webster as Norfolk, Benjamin Webster as Sands, Mr. Tilbury as Winchester, Mr. Thompson as Campeius, Helen Faucit as Katherine, Eliza Vincent as Anne Bullen, Mrs. Julia Glover as Lady Denny, Miss Partridge as Duchess of Norfolk/ **Sad. Wells**, Apr. 1845, with George Bennett as Henry VIII, Samuel Phelps as Wolsey, Mr. Rae as Compeius, Henry Marston as Buckingham, A. Younge as Sands, Edward Knight as Suffolk, Mr. Sievier as Norfolk, E. Morton as Surrey, Charles Morelli as Gardener, Charles Fenton as Guilford, Mr. Sharpe as Lovel, Mrs. Mary Warner as Catherine, Miss Huddart as Anne Boleyn, Mrs. Henry Marston as Lady Deney/ **Princess's**, Oct. 1847, with Mr. Cooper as Henry VIII, W. C. Macready as Cardinal Wolsey, Mr. Wynn as Campeius, John Gilbert as Cranmer, John Ryder as Buckingham, Charles Fisher as Norfolk, Mr. Howard as Suffolk, F. B. Conway as Surrey, Henry Compton as Sands, James Vining as Cromwell, Charlotte Cushman as Queen Katherine, Susan Cushman as Anne Boleyn, Mrs. Selby as Lady Denny, Miss A. Romer as Patience; May 1855, with Walter Lacy as Henry VIII, Charles Kean as Cardinal Wolsey, F. Cooke as Cardinal Campeius, Frank Graham as Cranmer, James Vining as Norfolk, John Ryder as Buckingham, Henry Mellon as Suffolk, George Everett as Surrey, David Fisher as Lord Chamberlain, Drinkwater Meadows as Gardiner, Mr. Addison as Lord Sands, John Cathcart as Cromwell, Mrs. Charles Kean as Queen Katherine, Caroline Heath as Anne Boleyn, Maria Daly as Patience/ Scenery under dir. of Mr. Grieve/ Machines by G. Hodsdon/ Music by J. L. Hatton/ Aug. 1862, with Basil Potter as Henry VIII, Charles Kean as Wolsey, Mr. Cathcart as Cardinal Campeius, Edmund

Garden as Norfolk, Alfred Raymond as Suffolk, George Jordan as Buckingham, George Everett as Surrey, Drinkwater Meadows as Lord Sands, J. F. Cathcart as Cromwell, Mrs. Charles Kean as Queen Katherine, Miss Chapman as Anne Boleyn, Miss N. Chapman as Patience/ Scenery by J. Gates, H. Cuthbert, & Dayes/ Machines by Mr. Sloman/ **Haymarket**, Dec. 1850, with Mr. Cooper as Henry VIII, W. C. Macready as Wolsey, Mr. Rogers as Campeius, Mr. Caulfield as Capucius, William Cullenford as Cranmer, E. L. Davenport as Buckingham, John Parselle as Norfolk, Charles Selby as Suffolk, Mr. Stuart as Surrey, Mr. Lambert as Sands, Mrs. Mary Warner as Queen Katharine, Mrs. Stanley as Lady Denny, Miss Reynolds as Anne Boleyn, Priscilla Horton as Patience/ **Drury Lane**, Jan. 1865, with Walter Lacy as Henry VIII, Samuel Phelps as Cardinal Wolsey, George Spencer as Campeius, Alfred Rayner as Norfolk, Henry Marston as Buckingham, Mr. Harris as Suffolk, Henry Sinclair as Surrey, Miss Atkinson as Catherine, Rose Leclercq as Anne Bullen, Mrs. Vandenhoff as Lady Denny/ **Gaiety**, Nov. 1875 (in 3a), with Samuel Phelps, John Clayton, Charles Harcourt/ **Aquarium**, Feb. 1878, with Samuel Phelps, William Rignold, Charles Warner, Norman Forbes, Louise Moodie, Edith Challis/ **Lyceum**, June 1892, with William Terriss as Henry VIII, Henry Irving as Wolsey, Arthur Stirling as Cranmer, Johnston Forbes Robertson as Buckingham, Frank Tyars as Suffolk, Clarence Hague as Surrey, Alfred Bishop as Lord Chamberlain, Gilbert Farquhar as Lord Sands, Gordon Craig as Cromwell, Henry Howe as Griffith, Ellen Terry as Queen Katherine, Violet Vanbrugh as Anne Bullen, Roma Le Thiere as Old Lady, Georgina Pauncefort as Patience/ Scenery by J. Harker & Hawes Craven/ Music by Edward German/ Machines by Mr. Fillery.

HENRY DUNBAR; OR, THE OUTCAST// D 4a// Dram. by Tom Taylor fr novel of Miss Braddon// **Olympic**, Dec. 1865, with Henry Neville as Henry Dunbar, H. J. Montague as Austin, H. G. Clifford as Lovell, Robert Soutar as Carter, George Vincent as The Major, Harwood Cooper as Jerrame, Henry Rivers as Hartogg, S. H. Williams as Baldersby, Kate Terry as Margaret, Ellen Leigh as Laura, Ellen Farren as Mary Madden/ Scenery by Hawes Craven/ Prod. by Horace Wigan; Nov. 1877, with Henry Neville as Dunbar, Johnston Forbes Robertson as Austin, Mr. Warren as Lovell, Robert Pateman as Carter, G. W. Anson as The Major, J. W. Hill as Jerrams, Mr. Harmond as Hartogg, Mr. Bauer as Balderby, Miss Gerard as Mary, Ellen Meyrick as Laure, Bella Pateman as Margaret/ **Adelphi**, 1897.

HENWITCHERS, THE// C 1a// Percy Fitzgerald// **Haymarket**, Jan. 1879, with Henry Howe as Henwitcher, Mr. Weathersby as Focus, Emily Thorne as Mrs. Henwitcher, Julia Roselle as Mrs. Jenkinson.

HER ADVOCATE// Play 3a// Walter Frith// **Duke of York's**, Sept. 1895.

HER COUSIN FRANK// F// George Capel// **Surrey**, June 1879.

HER DEAREST FOE// CD 4a// Adap. by Henrietta Lindley fr novel of Mrs. Alexander// **Criterion**, May. 1894, with Frank Worthing as Sir Hugh, Frank Atherley as Maj. Upton, Acton Bond as Ford, A. H. Revelle as Reid, Sydney Valentine as Trapes, Charles Allan as Slade, Dolores Drummond as Lady Styles, Annie Webster as Amy, Henrietta Lindley as Mrs. Travers.

HER FATHER// D 3a// Dram. by J. T. Douglas & Edward Rose fr Span. of José Echegaré, Conflicto Entre dos Deberes// **Vaudeville**, May 1899.

HER FATHER'S FRIEND// Play 3a// H. A. Rudal// **Savoy**, June 1896, with George Cockburn as Marquis de Tournac, Sydney Paxton as Dermont, Harrison Hunter as Maurice, H. A. Saintsbury as Père Jerome, Charles Dodsworth as Jacques, George Riddell as Gen. Hansberger, Clarence Fitzclarence as Camille, Kate Turner as Rosette, Italia Conti as Aline.

HER FATHER'S SIN// D 4a// n.a.// **Strand**, July 1889.

HER GUARDIAN// C// J. R. Brown// **Royalty**, Mar. 1895, with J. R. Hatfield as Davenant, Douglas Hamilton as Martineau, Ida Heron as Violet, Kitty Leslie as Miss Morant.

HER LADYSHIP// Play 3a// Dram. by George Manville fr his own novel, The Master of the Ceremonies// **Strand**, Mar. 1889.

HER NEW DRESSMAKER// C// W. R. Walkes// **St. Geo. Hall**, May 1895.

HER OATH// D 5a// Mrs. Harry Wilde// **Princess's**, Nov. 1891.

HER OWN ENEMY// D// Dram. fr novel of Florence Marryat// **Gaiety**, Mar. 1884.

HER OWN RIVAL// C// Fred Broughton & Boyle Lawrence// **Opera Comique**, Apr. 1889.

HER OWN WITNESS// Play 3a// G. H. Dabbs// **Criterion**, Nov. 1889.

HER TRUE COLOURS// C// W. A. Brabner// **Avenue**, June 1892.

HER TRUSTEE// D 4a// James Blood// **Vaudeville**, Mar. 1887.

HER WEDDING DAY// D 4a// E. T. de Banzie// **Surrey**, May 1899.

HER WORLD AGAINST A LIE// D Pro & 3a// Dram. by Florence Marryat & George Neville fr novel of same name// **Adelphi**, Feb. 1881, with T. P. Haynes as Mr. Bond, E. H. Brooke as William Moray, W. McIntyre as James Moray, Gertrude Norman as Delia, Florence Marryat as Mrs. Horton, Dora Lingraff as Mrs. Moray, Eugenie Vernie as Mrs. Trimmings, Mr. Miller as Baron Saxe, E. B. Norman as Le Blois, Frank Hibbert as Angus Moray, Nelson Wheatcroft as Simon, Annie Beaumont as Patsey.

HERCULES, KING OF CLUBS (also titled, The Statue Gallery)// F 1a// F. F. Cooper// **Sad. Wells,** July 1837, with H. B. Roberts as Capt. Darling, W. J. Hammond as Tim, Mr. Griffiths as Granite, Mr. Ennis as Fuzby, J. Dunn as Tommy, Mr. Scarbrow as Harry, Mrs. Harris as Mrs. Ramsbottom, Lavinia Melville as Lavinnia; Nov. 1841, with Mr. Elvin as Capt. Darling, John Herbert as Tim and Hercules, Mr. Williams as Granite, Mr. Aldridge as Fuzby, Miss Cooke as Mrs. Ramsbottom, Mrs. Richard Barnett as Lavinia/ **Victoria,** Aug. 1850, with J. Neville as Granite, Mr. Henderson as Capt. Darling, Mr. Morrison as Fusby, G. F. Forman as Tim, J. Howard as Tommy, Georgiana Lebatt as Lavinia, Mrs. Cooke as Mrs. Ramsbottom/ **Astley's,** May 1851, with Arthur Stirling as Capt. Darling, Thomas Barry as Tim, Mr. Johnson as Granite, Mr. Danaville as Fuzby, Mrs. Moreton Brookes as Mrs. Ramsbottom, Miss Fenton as Lavinia/ **Grecian,** Mar. 1854, with T. Roberts as Capt. Dashing, Eaton O'Donnell as Granite, Charles Rice as Tim, Edwin Dixon as Fusby, Henry Power as Tommy, Miss Johnstone as Mrs. Ramsbottom, Agnes De Warde as Lavinia.

HERMINE// Play 1a// Charles Thomas// **Court,** Sept. 1888.

HERNE THE HUNTER; OR, THE WIZARD OAK// D// n.a.// **Victoria,** Mar. 1859, with John Bradshaw as Henry VIII, J. H. Rickards as Herne, Mr. Wilson as Surrey, Mr. Henderson as Wiltshire, Frederick Byefield as Wyat, George Yarnold as Somers, Samuel Sawford as Cardinal Wolsey, James Howard as Patch, George Pearce as Fytton, Angelina Bathurst as Catherine, Miss Honey as Mabel, Mary Fielding as Anne Boleyn, Miss F. Lauri as Jane Seymour.

HERO OF JERUSALEM, THE// D 4a// Sigmund Fineman// **Standard,** June 1896.

HERO OF ROMANCE, A// D Pro & 5a// Westland Marston// **Haymarket,** Mar. 1868, with E. A. Sothern as Marquis de Tourville, J. B. Buckstone as Dr. Lafitte, Henry Compton as De Vaudray, W. H. Chippendale as Dumont, Henry Vincent as De Lille, William Clark as Antoine, P. White as Jourdain, Mr. Rogers as Michel, Mrs. Chippendale as Mme. Dumont, Miss Robertson as Blanche, Ione Burke as Mlle. Busigny, Mrs. Edward Fitzwilliam as Mme. Bocage, Mrs. Laws as Ursule, Alice Daubiny as Ninon/ Scenery by John O'Conner, George Morris, Mr. Barraud, & Mr. Maltby/ Machines by Oliver Wales.

HEROD// Play 3a// Stephen Philips// **Her Majesty's,** Oct. 1900.

HEROES// C 3a// Conway Edwardes// **Aquarium,** Jan. 1877.

HERTFORD// D 3a// Frederick Eastwood// **Royalty,** Mar. 1880.

HESTER'S MYSTERY// C 1a// Arthur Wing Pinero// **Folly,** June 1880/ **Toole's,** Jan. 1891, with Henry Westland as Silverdale, C. M. Lowne as Royle, George Shelton as Joel, Effie Liston as Nance, Irene Vanbrugh as Hester.

HIDDEN HAND, THE// D 4a// Tom Taylor// **Olympic,** Nov. 1863, with Henry Neville as Lord Penarvon, H. Coghlan as Sir Caradoc, John Maclean as Caerleon, George Vincent as Madoc, Harwood Cooper as Price, Kate Terry as Lady Penarvon, Louise Moore as Muriel, Mrs. Bowring as Lady Gryffydd, Lydia Foote as Enid, Miss Farren as Gwynnedd/ Scenery by Hawes Craven & Walford Grieve/ Music by J. H. Tully/ Machines by Mr. Chapman.

HIDDEN LIGHT// D Pro & 3a// George Conquest// **Grecian,** Feb. 1861, with Thomas Mead as John the Hunter, Alfred Rayner as Maxwell, Walter Holland as Lord Richmond, John Manning as Timothy, Ellen Chapman as Amy, Jane Coveney as Clara, George Gillett as Charles II, R. H. Lingham as Bedford, William James as Albinus, Lucreza Hill as Kate.

HIDDEN HAND, THE// D 4a// Adap. by Tom Taylor fr F of A. P. D'Ennery & Charles Edmond, L'Aieule// **Olympic,** Nov. 1864, with Ellen Terry.

HIDDEN TREASURE, THE// D 3a// Tom Parry & John Oxenford// **Adelphi,** Nov. 1871.

HIDDEN WORTH// Play Pro & 3a// Dram. by Horace Sedger fr novel of Florence Marryat, Phyllida// **POW,** Nov. 1886.

HIDE AND SEEK// F 1a// n.a.// **Drury Lane,** June 1838, with Basil Baker as Mordaunt, John Duruset as Merton, Robert Keeley as Moses, Mrs. Ellen Ternan as Mrs. Mordaunt, Miss Fitzwalter as Charlotte.

HIDE AND SEEK// F 1a// n.a.// **Adelphi,** Mar. 1874, with Augustus Glover, Mr. Thorn, Bernard Cullen, Maud Howard, Miss E. Phillips.

HIGH LIFE BELOW STAIRS// F 2a// James Townley// **Sad. Wells,** Feb. 1837, with William Rogers as Lovel, Thomas King as Freeman, Thomas Lee as Sir Harry, Mr. Hallford as Duke, Mr. Scarbrow as Tom, Mr. Ray as Philip, Mr. Moore as Kingston, Miss Williams as Lady Bab, Mrs. Harris as Lady Charlotte, Miss Julian as Kitty, Miss Hambleton as Cook; July 1844, with Henry Marston as Lovel, Mr. Binge as Freeman, Mr. Williams as Phillip, Charles Hudson as Duke, G. F. Forman as Sir Harry, Georgiana Lebatt as Kitty/ **Cov. Garden,** Apr. 1838, with James Anderson as Lovel, Henry Howe as Freeman, Mr. Vining as Duke's Servant, John Pritt Harley as Sir Harry's Servant, Mr. Tilbury as Philip, W. H. Payne as Robert, John Ayliffe as Tom, Charles Bender as Kingston, Mrs. Humby as Mrs. Kitty, Mrs. Barrett as Chloe, Mrs. Sarah Garrick as Cook/ **Victoria,** Mar. 1843, with E. F. Saville as Duke, John Gardner as Sir Harry, C. Williams as Freeman, Miss Martin as Kitty, Mrs. George Lee as Lady Charlotte, Mrs. Grifffith as Lady Bab, Mrs. Franklin as Cook/ **Princess's,** Jan. 1845, with Henry Compton as Lovell, Mr. Fitzjames as Freeman, Walter Lacy as Duke, W. H. Oxberry as Sir Harry, Mr. Granby as Philip, Robert Honner as Thomas, Emma Stanley as Mrs. Kitty, Miss E. Honner as Lady Bab, Mrs. Fosbroke as Lady Charlotte, Miss Somer as

Cook/ **Grecian**, Sept. 1863, with William James, Walter Holland, W. Shirley, James Jackson, Henry Power, Mary A. Victor, George Gillett, John Manning,, Marie Brewer, Miss Johnstone/ **Olympic**, Apr. 1865, with Horace Wigan as Lovell, Charles Coghlan as Freeman, George Vincent as Duke, Robert Soutar as Sir Harry, Harwood Cooper as Tom, Miss Sheridan as Lady Bab, Mrs. Leigh Murray as Lady Charlotte, Miss Farren as Kitty, Mrs. Stephens as Cook/ **St. James's**, Mar. 1868, with Mr. Blake as Lovel, Mr. Stretton as Freeman, Mr. Evans as Philip, Eleanor Bufton as Kitty, Miss Jones as Cook/ **Lyceum**, July 1879, with Kyrle Bellew as Lovel, Mr. Beaumont as Freeman, Mr. Lowther as Robert, Arthur Wing Pinero as Philip, Frank Tyars as Tom, W. Branscombe as Kingston, Miss Bufton as Kitty, Alma Murray as Maid/ **Terry's**, Jan. 1895.

HIGHLAND CATERAN, THE// D// W. H. Murray// **Eng. Opera House** (Lyceum), Sept. 1837, with A. Brindal as Macdonald of Barisdale, S. Jones as Gen. Baillie, Mr. Heath as Capt. Monkton, Mr. Baker as Sgt. Musquetoon, William Bennett as McTavish, Priscilla Horton as Lilias, Mme. Simon as Mrs. McTavish.

HIGHLAND FLING, A// F 1a// Joseph Dilley// **Vaudeville**, Jan. 1879.

HIGHLAND LEGACY, A// Play 1a// Brandon Thomas// **Strand**, Nov. 1888.

HIGHLY IMPROBABLE// F// W. S. Gilbert// **New Royalty**, Dec. 1867.

HIGHWAYMAN, THE// F 1a// J. Maddison Morton// **Cov. Garden**, Jan. 1843, with George Bartley as Jollyboy, John Pritt Harley as Smiley, Alfred Wigan as Col. Rocket, James Vining as Capt. Pump, Drinkwater Meadows as Tadcaster, W. H. Payne as Grab, Miss Lee as Phoebe, Mrs. Humby as Kitty, Mrs. Emden as Sally.

HIGHWAYMAN'S HOLIDAY, THE// F 1a// W. E. Suter// **Queen's**, Sept. 1863.

HIGHWAYS AND BYEWAYS OF LIFE// D Pro & 3a// W. E. Suter// **Grecian**, Apr. 1861, with Thomas Mead as Sorel, John Manning as Smigely, Henry Grant as Sluford, Alfred Rayner as Huntley, William James as Algernon, Jane Coveney as Martha, Lucreza Hill as Florinda, Henry Power as Swigsly, Harriet Coveney as Jerry, Miss Johnstone as Mrs. Thompson.

HIGHWAYS AND BYWAYS// C// n.a.// **Cov. Garden**, Apr. 1837, with John Pritchard as Stapleton, Benjamin Webster as Stubble, John Collett as James, Charles Bender as Robert, Mr. Beckett as John, Mrs. Julia Glover as Susan, Miss Lee as Eliza, Mrs. Sarah Garrick as Miss Primly.

HILDA// Play 3a// n.a.// **Princess's**, May 1892, with Julian Cross as Sydney, Arthur Wood as Gilbert, Foster Courtenay as Dundas, Kate Bealby as Daisy, Marie Linden as Hilda.

HILDA, THE MISER'S DAUGHTER// D 3a// Dram. by Andrew Halliday fr novel of Harrison Ainsworth// **Adelphi**, May 1872, with James Fernandez as Scarve, Brittain Wright as Post, A. C. Lilly as Randulph, C. H. Stephenson as Abel, William McIntyre as Frewin, Henry Ashley as Puckeridge, Harwood Cooper as Diggs, F. Stainforth as Linstock, Miss Furtado as Hilda, Mrs. Alfred Mellon as Thomasine/ Scenery by F. Lloyds & Maugham/ Music by Edwin Ellis/ Machines by Edward Charker/ Prod. by Benj. Webster.

HILDA'S INHERITANCE; OR, LIVINGSTONE'S SIN// D 4a// William Muskerry// **New Pavilion**, Oct. 1871.

HIS EIGHTIETH BIRTHDAY// C// Scott Craven// **Grand**, Mar. 1901.

HIS EXCELLENCY// C 1a// Charles W. Mathews// **Haymarket**, July 1860/ **Drury Lane**, Oct. 1860, with Mr. Tilbury as Count de Rosda, Mr. Farrell as de Rougemont, C. J. Mathews as La Rose, Miss Clyde as Isabella, Mrs. C. J. Mathews as Teresina.

HIS EXCELLENCY THE GOVERNOR// F 3a// Robert Marshall// **Court**, June 1898, with Paul Arthur as Capt. Carew, E. Allan Aynesworth as Sir Montague, Arthur Bromley-Davenport as Carlton, Dion G. Boucicault as Baverstock, James Erskine as Capt. Rivers, R. Purdon as Maj. Kildare, Fanny Coleman as Mrs. Bolingbroke, Nellie Thorne as Ethel, Irene Vanbrugh as Stella/ Scenery by William Harford.

HIS FIRST CHAMPAGNE// F 2a// W. L. Rede// **Grecian**, July 1844, with Mr. Campbell as Morton, Henry Horncastle as Capt. Smith, Frederick Robson as Watt, Henry Frazer as Craven, Edmund Garden as Terence, Miss Merion as Mrs. Morton, Mary A. Crisp as Miss Morton, Annette Mears as Mary/ **Haymarket**, Aug. 1851, with James Bland as Morton, George Braid as Capt. Smith, Leigh Murray as Craven, Henry Bedford as Watt, Mrs. Stanley as Mrs. Morton, Mrs. L. S. Buckingham as Miss Bygrove, Amelia Vining as Emily, Mrs. Caulfield as Mary/ **Sad. Wells**, Mar. 1856, with Mr. Swanborough as Capt. Smith, Leigh Murray as Craven, W. Williams as Morton, Charles Swan as Watt, C. Kelsey as Connelly, Mrs. B. Barrett as Mrs. Morton, Miss E. Barnett as Miss Morton, Miss Craven as Miss Bygrove, Miss Cuthbert as Mary/ **Drury Lane**, Jan. 1858, with Mr. Tilbury as Morton, Leigh Murray as Craven, James Worrell as Capt. Smith, Mrs. Selby as Mrs. Morton, Miss Carson as Miss Morton, Miss K. Carson as Miss Bygrove, Emma Wadham as Mary.

HIS FIRST PECCADILLO// F 1a// n.a.// **Princess's**, Dec. 1848, with W. H. Oxberry as Jenkin, Henry Horncastle as Sadboy, Charles Fisher as Capt. Furbish, Miss Norman as Clara, Miss Rourke as Rosanna.

HIS HIGHNESS// FC 3a// Brandon Hurst// **Opera Comique**, Feb. 1894.

HIS LAST LEGS// F 2a// W. Bayle Bernard// **Haymarket**, Oct. 1839, with Tyrone Power as O'Callaghan, Robert Strickland as Rivers, Walter Lacy as Charles, J. W. Gough as Dr. Banks, Mrs. W. Clifford as Mrs. Montague, Eliza Travers as Julia, Mrs. Gallot as Mrs. Banks, Miss Gallot as Betty; June 1848, with Charles Hudson as O'Callaghan, Mr. Tilbury as Rivers, Henry Vandenhoff as Charles, J. W. Gough as Dr. Banks, William Clark as John, Mrs. W. Clifford as Mrs. Montague, Miss E. Messent as Julia, Miss Woulds as Mrs. Banks, Miss Carre as Betty/ **Cov. Garden**, Oct. 1839, with Tyrone Power/ **Princess's**, Feb. 1867, with Charles Verner as O'Callaghan, C. H. Fenton as Charles, Henry Mellon as Rivers, W. R. Robins as Dr. Hanks, Mrs. Buckingham White as Mrs. Montague, Miss Wentworth as Julia.

HIS LAST STAKE// D 1a// J. P. Webster// **Princess's**, Apr. 1888.

HIS LAST VICTORY// D 2a// Watts Phillips// **St. James's**, June 1862, with George Vining as Lacroix, F. Charles as de Fauconville, Frederick Dewar as Doucet, Henry Ashley as Kopp, W. H. Stephens as Molasse, George Belmore as Sgt. Pons, Miss Herbert as Countess Beauregard, Ellen Turner as Julie, Isabel Adams as Mme. Molasse, Lillie Lonsdale as Fichu.

HIS LITTLE DODGE// C 3a// Adap. by J. H. McCarthy fr F of Georges Feydeau & Maurice Henniquin// **Royalty**, Oct. 1896, with Fred Terry as Sir Hercules, Weedon Grossmith as Hobb, Alfred Maltby as Petlow, Frank Dyall as Grice, Ellis Jeffreys as Lady Miranda, Leila Repton as Candy/ Scenery by Frank Giles.

HIS MAJESTY'S MUSKETEERS// Play 5a// Adap. by Frederick Carl fr F of Alexandre Dumas// **St. Geo. Hall**, May 1899.

HIS NEW FRENCH COOK// C// n.a.// **St. Geo. Hall**, Feb. 1899.

HIS NOVICE// F 1a// Henry Spicer// **D. Lane**, Dec. 1878.

HIS OWN ENEMY// C 1a// A. Meadow// **Haymarket**, Mar. 1873, with W. H. Kendal, Madge Robertson (Mrs. Kendal).

HIS OWN GUEST// C 3a// Arthur Ayres & P. Blake// **Opera Comique**, May. 1883.

HIS RELATIONS// FC 3a// H. A. Saintsbury// **Avenue**, May 1896, with Walter McEwan as Gen. Faraday, H. A. Saintsbury as Fitz-Coolington, J. F. Soutar as Lake, W. Cheesman as Pinker, Frank Wood as Barlings, Graham Price as Morgan, Florence Fordyce as Gertie, Audrey Ford as Rose, Marianne Caldwell as Jennings, Dorothy Chesney as Jenny.

HIS ROMANCE// C 4a// Adap. by Mayrick Milton fr Michael Klapp's Rosenkrantz and Guildenstern// **Olympic**, Feb. 1888.

HIS SECOND WIFE// Play 3a// Vivian Hope// **Avenue**, June 1892, with Frank Gillmore as Eversleigh, E. M. Robson as Selby, Tripp Edgar as Harry, Charles Fawcett as Craig, Alice de Winton as Mrs. Eversleigh, Kate Ruskin as Edith, Florence Hayden as Miss Primley.

HIS TOAST// C// A. M. Heathcote// **Court**, July 1889.

HIS WIFE// Play 5a// Adap. by Henry Arthur Jones fr novel, A Prodigal Daughter// **Sad. Wells**, Apr. 1881, with Isabel Bateman, E. H. Brooke, J. D. Beveridge, William Younge, Laura Lindon, Kate Pattison.

HIS WIFE'S PICTURE// Play 1a// Ernest Cosham// **Avenue**, May 1900.

HIS WIVES// FC 3a// T. G. Warren// **Strand**, May 1888.

HIS WIVES// Ellis Cleveland// **Avenue**, Nov. 1894.

HIT HIM: HE HAS NO FRIENDS// F 1a// Edmund Yates & N. H. Harrington// **Strand**, Sept. 1860.

HOBBS, DOBBS, AND STUBBS// F 1a// Benjamin Webster// **Haymarket**, Apr. 1840, with Benjamin Webster as Hobbs, Robert Strickland as Dobbs, O. Smith as Stubbs, John Webster as Valentine, W. H. Oxberry as Jeremiah, Mrs. W. Clifford as Mrs. Hobbs, Mrs. Frank Matthews as Mrs. Dobbs, Miss Charles as Mrs. Stubbs, Eliza Travers as Rose.

HOBBY HORSE, THE// C 3a// Arthur Wing Pinero// **St. James's**, Oct. 1886, with Herbert Waring as Rev. Brice, John Hare as Jermyn, C. W. Somerset as Pinching, Mr. Mackintosh as Shattock, E. Hendrie as Pews, W. M. Cathcart as Lyman, Fuller Mellish as Clark, Mrs. W. H. Kendal as Mrs. Jermyn, Mrs. Gaston Murray as Mrs. Porcher, Miss B. Tree as Miss Moxon, Miss Webster as Bertha/ Scenery by W. Harford/ **Court**, May 1897.

HOGMANAY; OR, NEW YEAR'S EVE// C 1a// Frederick Sidney// **St. Geo. Hall**, June 1898/ **Globe**, Aug. 1898, with Wilfred Shine as McLachlan, Stephen Vincent as Scarsdale, Watty Brunton Jr. as Manners, Muriel Ashwynne as Margaret.

HOLD YOUR TONGUE// C 1a// J. R. Planché// **Lyceum**, Mar. 1849, with C. J. Mathews as Lord Lurewell, Charles Selby as Ryder, John Parselle as Vernon, Mr. Kerridge as Thomas, Mme. Vestris as Mrs. Lovejoy, Miss H. Gilbert as Lady Ryder.

HOLE IN THE WALL, A// F 1a// John Poole// **Victoria**, July 1854, with Henry Frazer as Dupre, Charles Rice as Thomas, Miss Laporte as Mme. Dupre, Miss Sutton as Angelica.

HOLLY BUSH HALL; OR, THE TRACK IN THE SNOW// D 2a// Dram. by W. E. Suter// **Queen's**, Feb. 1860/ **Grecian**,July 1866, with Charles Mortimer as Sir Ernest, Henry Power as Edward Millward, E. Howard as Gen. Willis, W. Shirley as Maj. Bell, George Gillett as Charles

Acton, Alfred Rayner as Mark Acton, John Manning as Potts, Henry Grant as Jafed, Harriet Western as Lady Millward, Mrs. Atkinson as Dame Acton, Mary A. Victor as Winnifred, Lizzie Mandlebert as Meda.

HOLLY TREE INN// Play 1a// Dram. by Mrs. Oscar Beringer fr Charles Dickens// **Terry's**, Jan. 1891, with Ernest Hendrie as Cobbs, H. Reeves Smith as Capt. Walmers, Fred Baxter as Tom, Mrs. E. H. Brooke as Mrs. Cobbs, Minnie Terry as Norah, Mary Collette as Betty, Vera Beringer as Harry.

HOLSTEIN HUSSAR, THE; OR, THE GRENADIER GUARD// D// G. D. Pitt// **Sad. Wells**, Jan. 1838, with Mr. Forrester as Cologne, Mr. Nunn as Capt. Almarine, Mr. James as Brehl, Mr. Campbell as Bluffendorf, Mr. Ede as Sgt. Mack, S. Smith as Shutz, Mr. Williams as Corp. Zug, Mr. Rogers as Olmutz, Mrs. Weston as Githa, Miss Chartley as Claribel, Eliza Vincent as Minna/ Scenery by Mr. Battie/ Music by W. Montgomery/ **Victoria**, Apr. 1842, with William Seaman as Cologne, C. Williams as Capt. Almarine, Mr. James as Brehl, Mr. Howard as Bluffenhorf, Mr. Hitchinson as Sgt. Mack, Mr. Paul as Shutz, Miss Saddler as Claribel, Mrs. Griffiths as Githa, Miss Coveney as Minna.

HOME// C 3a// Adap. by T. W. Robertson fr F of Emile Augier, L'Aventurière// **Haymarket**, Jan. 1869, with W. H. Chippendale as Dorrison, E. A. Sothern as Col. White, Henry Compton as Capt. Mountraffe, Robert Astley as Thompson, Ada Cavendish as Mrs. Pinchbeck, Ione Burke as Lucy, Caroline Hill as Dora/ Scenery by John O'Conner/ Machines by Oliver Wales/ Gas by F. Hope/ **St. James's**, Sept. 1881, with T. N. Wenman as Dorrison, W. H. Kendal as Col. White, John Hare as Capt. Mountraffe, T. W. Robertson as Thompson, Kate Bishop as Dora, Maud Cathcart as Lucy, Mrs. W. H. Kendal as Mrs. Pinchbeck.

HOME; OR, A FATHER'S LOVE// D// n.a.// **Victoria**, Feb. 1880.

HOME AGAIN// D// Hugh Marston// **Standard**, Mar. 1877.

HOME AGAIN; OR, THE LIEUTENANT'S DAUGHTERS// D 3a// Edward Fitzball// **Lyceum**, Nov. 1844.

HOME COMING, THE// Play 1a// Ernest Cosham// **Comedy**, July 1892, with Robb Harwood as Travers, Harold Constable as Drydon, Sam Sothern as Harding, Alice Yorke as Mrs. Musgrave, Nina Boucicault as Stella, Florance Farr as Martha.

HOME FEUD, THE// D 3a// Walter Frith// **Comedy**, Feb. 1890, with Stewart Dawson as Joliffe, Nutcombe Gould as Capt. Hargreaves, William Herbert as George Beilby, W. S. Buist as John Beilby, Wilfred Draycott as Horace, Gertrude Kingston as Louise, May Whitty as Helen, Eva Moore as Alice.

HOME FOR A HOLIDAY// C 1a// Adap. by Walter Gordon fr F// **Olympic**, Nov. 1860, with Frederic Robinson as Sir Wylde, Walter Gordon as Evelyn, Horace Wigan as Naggleton, Harwood Cooper as Simms, Louise Keeley as Anabel.

HOME FOR HOME// C// Richard Lee// **Vaudeville**, Aug. 1869.

HOME IN THE HEART, THE; OR, LIFE'S PILOT// D 3a// George Conquest// **Grecian**, July 1861, with Thomas Mead as Beaujolais, Henry Grant as Count de Varennes, Walter Holland as de Seligny, Alfred Rayner as Raoul, William James as Lucien, George Conquest as Perlinpepin, Jane Coveney as Countess de Varennes, Mrs. Charles Dillon as Helene.

HOME ONCE MORE; OR, A FALSE ACCUSATION// D 4a// A. L. Crauford// **Britannia**, Apr. 1885.

HOME RULE// D 3a// E. F. Brady// **Elephant & Castle**, Mar. 1880.

HOME RULE, A FIRESIDE STORY// C 1a// J. G. Taylor// **Olympic**, Dec. 1886, with J. G. Taylor as Bowles, William Calvert as Veal, John Clulow as Lanyard, Maria Jones as Nancy, Miss C. Stanhope as Mary.

HOME SECRETARY, THE// Play 3a// R. C. Carton// **Criterion**, May 1895, with Charles Wyndham as Trendel, Alfred Bishop as Haylett, David James as Lord Blayver, Sydney Brough as Frank Trendel, Charles Brookfield as Capt. Chesnall, Herman de Lange as Thorpe-Didsbury, Lewis Waller as Lecaile, Julia Neilson as Rhoda, Dolores Drummond as Lady Clotilda, Maud Millett as Esme, Mary Moore as Mrs. Thorpe-Didsbury/ Scenery by Walter Hann & Mr. Johnson.

HOME SPUN// D// A. C. Calmour// **Novelty**, Nov. 1884.

HOME, SWEET HOME// D 4a// B. L. Farjeon// **Olympic**, June 1876, with Henry Neville as Fielding, W. J. Hill as Sparrow, Mr. Graeme as Jim Naldret, George Neville as George Naldret, T. A. Palmer as Million, Lytton Sothern as Fred Million, Mr. Haywell as Fairly, Mr. Winstanley as Staples, John Vollaire as Bill, Mrs. Stephens as Mrs. Naldret, Carlotta Addison as Jane, Fanny Josephs as Bessie, Annie Taylor as Mrs. Simpson, Miss Beaumont as Mrs. Allen, Alice Drew as Alice/ Scenery by Julian Hicks/ Music by J. Mallandaine/ Machines by Mr. Collins/ Lime Light by Mr. Sabin.

HOME, SWEET HOME// FC 3a// Herbert Swears// **St. Geo. Hall**, Mar. 1895.

HOME TRUTHS// D 3a// Adap. by T. H. Reynoldson fr F of Emile Augier, Gabrielle// **Princess's**, Dec. 1859, with George Melville as Vaughan, J. G. Shore as Beaumont, Frank Matthews as Saffron, Mrs. Charles Young as Mrs. Vaughan, Miss E. Lavenu as Alice, Carlotta Leclercq as Mrs. Saffron.

HOME WRECK, THE// D 3a// Dram. by Stirling

& Dennis Coyne fr Tennyson's Enoch Arden// **Surrey**, Feb. 1869.

HOMESTEAD STORY, A// C 1a// n.a.// **Princess's**, June 1861, with John Ryder as Holly, J. G. Shore as Sam, Maria Harris as Mary.

HONEST JOHN// D// C. H. Hazlewood// **Britannia**, July 1875.

HONEST LABOUR; OR, THE SHIFTING SCENES OF A WORKMAN'S LIFE// D 3a// Frederick Marchant// **Britannia**, Aug. 1870.

HONEST MAN, AN// D 1a// Henry Pettitt// **Surrey**, Nov. 1878.

HONEST MAN'S FORTUNE, THE// D// Adap. by R. H. Horne fr Beaumont & Fletcher// **Sad. Wells**, Mar. 1848, with Henry Marston as Duke of Orleans, G. K. Dickinson as Earl of Amiens, Samuel Phelps as Montague, William Hoskins as Longueville, Julia St. George as Veramour, Henry Mellon as Laverdine, George Bennett as La Pocp, A. Younge as Malicorn, Miss Cooper as Lamira, Miss Huddart as Duchess of Orleans, Miss Murray as Paulette.

HONEST THIEVES// F 1a// T. Knight// **Drury Lane**, Feb. 1839, with Mr. Baker as Col. Careless, A. Brindal as Capt. Manly, Mr. Harris as Storey, Charles Fenton as Day, John Duruset as Abel, Henry Compton as Obadiah, Mr. Sloan as Teague, Mrs. Charles Jones as Mrs. Day, Miss Fitzwalter as Arabella, Miss Poole as Ruth/ **Sad. Wells**, Apr. 1840, with Mr. Fitzjames as Capt. Carless, Mr. Williams as Justice Day, Thomas Lee as Teague, J. W. Collier as Abel, J. B. Hill as Capt. Manly, William Smith as Obadiah, Mrs. J. F. Saville as Ruth, Miss Cooke as Mrs. Day, Mrs. Morgan as Arabella/ **Haymarket**, Aug. 1842, with Robert Strickland as Obadiah, Henry Widdicomb as Abel, James Worrell as Col. Careless, A. Brindal as Capt. Manly, G. W. Gough as Story, Malone Raymond as Teague, Mr. Tilbury as Day, Mrs. Malone Raymond as Ruth, Miss C. Conner as Arabella, Mrs. Frank Matthews as Mrs. Day/ **Grecian**, Dec. 1844, with Harry Chester as Col. Careless, Edwin Dixon as Capt. Manly, Mr. Melvin as Lt. Story, John Collett as Justice Day, Frederick Robson as Obadiah, Mr. Hodson as Teague, Mary A. Crisp as Ruth, Miss Johnstone as Arabella, Miss Merion as Mrs. Day.

HONESTY; OR, THE WAGER BY BATTLE// D 5a// Henry Spicer// **Cov. Garden**, Jan. 1845, with Mr. Archer as Sir Philip, Mr. Butler as Lord Seyle, George Vandenhoff as Trafford, Mr. Rae as Pembroke, George Braid as Gisborne, James Vining as Gage, Miss Fitzjames as Cyril, Mr. Rogers as Deverill, Mr. Bass as Fairfax, Miss Vandenhoff as Lady Julia, Mrs. Brougham as Infelice, Mrs. Cooke as Mable, Mrs. Matthews as Alice/ Scenery by John MacFarren/ Machines by Mr. Sloman/ Prod. by Edward Stirling/ **Olympic**, Mar. 1848, with Mr. Archer as Sir Phillip, Mr. Stuart as Trafford, H. Lee as Pembroke, Mr. Fitzgerald as Lord Seyle, Mr. Mazzoni as Mordaunt, Henry Holl as Gage, Susan Kenneth as Cyril, Charles Perkins as Deverell, William Davidge as Fairfax, E. Marie Duret as Julia, Miss May as Infelice.

HONESTY - A COTTAGE FLOWER// Play 1a// Margaret Young// **Avenue**, Nov. 1897, with S. A. Cookson as Wentworth, Ridgewood Barrie as Tom, Kate Rorke as Clorinda, Una Cockerell as Lucy.

HONEYMOON, THE: OR, HOW TO RULE A WIFE// C 5a// John Tobin// **Sad. Wells**, June 1837, with C. H. Pitt as Montalban, N. T. Hicks as Rolando, Mr. Griffiths as Balthazar, John Pritchard as Duke Aranza, Mr. Conquest as Jaquez, Mr. Tilbury as Lampedo, Mrs. W. West as Juliana, Lavinia Melville as Volante, Miss Williams as Zamora; Apr. 1842, with Mr. Lyon as Duke Aranza, John Webster as Rolando, Mr. Moreton as Count Montalban, P. Williams as Balthazar, Mr. Williams as Lampedo, John Herbert as Mock Duke, Mrs. Robert Honner as Juliana, Mrs. Tidd as Volante, Mrs. Richard Barnett as Zamora; Dec. 1846, with William Creswick as Duke Aranza, E. Morton as Montalban, William Hoskins as Rolando, Henry Mellon as Balthazar, Mr. Williams as Lampedo, Mr. Branson as Campillo, A. Younge as Jacques, Henry Scharf as Lopez, Laura Addison as Juliana, Miss Cooper as Volante, Fanny Huddart as Zamora, Mrs. Henry Marston as Hostess; Mar. 1869, with C. Harley as Duke Aranza, Mr. Prescott as Capt. Rolando, Mr. Rendell as Count Montalban, J. Charles as Jacques, T. J. Howard as Balthazar, Harry Seed as Lopez, Gertrude Reynolds as Juliana,, Ellen Macdonald as Volante, Clara Stuart as Zamora/ **Victoria**, Dec. 1841, with David Osbaldiston as Duke Aranza, John Gardner as Jacquez, Mr. Paul as Lampedo, Mr. Howard as Lopez, E. F. Saville as Rolando, Annette Vincent as Juliana, Mrs. George Lee as Volante, Mrs. Howard as Zamora, Mrs. Garthwaite as Hostess/ **Lyceum**, Feb. 1844, with Mr. Wentworth as Duke Aranza, Mr. Hemming as Count Montalban, Harvey Tuckett as Rolando, Mr. Harrington as Balthazar, Mr. Turner as Lampedo, Robert Keeley as Jaques, Edwin Yarnold as Lopez, Miss Angell as Juliana, Mrs. Seymore as Volante, Jane Mordaunt as Zamora/ Scenery by Mr. Marshall/ **Grecian**, Oct. 1844, with Mr. Campbell as Duke Aranza, Harry Chester as Rolando, Edwin Dixon as Count Montalban, John Collett as Balthazar, Edmund Garden as Lampedo, Frederick Robson as Jaques, Mrs. Chester as Juliana, Annette Mears as Volante, Mary A. Crisp as Zamora; Sept. 1861, with Thomas Mead as Duke Aranza, Henry Power as Montalban, Henry Sinclair as Rolando, John Manning as Jacques, Jane Dawson as Juliana, Mrs. Charles Dillon as Volante, Ellen Hale as Zamora/ **Princess's**, May 1845, with J. W. Wallack as Duke Aranza, Leigh Murray as Montalban, Walter Lacy as Rolando, Mr. Granby as Balthazar, Henry Compton as Jaques, F. C. Courtney as Lampedo, W. H. Oxberry as Lopez, Charlotte Cushman as Juliana, Mrs. Stirling as Volante, Emma Stanley as Zamora, Mrs. Fosbroke as Hostess; July 1851 (in 3a), with Charles Kean as Duke of Aranza, Frederick Belton as Montalban, Alfred Wigan as Rolando, F. Cooke as Balthazar, Drinkwater Meadows as Lopez, John Pritt

Harley as Jaquez, Mrs. Charles Kean as Juliana, Miss Robertson as Volante, Mary Keeley as Zamora/ **Marylebone**, Feb. 1848, with Anna Cora Mowatt, E. L. Davenport, Fanny Vining/ **Olympic**, Sept. 1848, with Leigh Murray as Duke Aranza, Henry Butler as Montalban, Frederick Vining as Rolando, Charles Bender as Balthazar, Henry Compton as Jacques, Mrs. Stirling as Juliana, Mrs. C. A. Tellet as Volante, Mrs. Leigh Murray as Zamora/ **Haymarket**, Dec. 1848, with Charles Kean as Duke Aranza, Henry Vandenhoff as Count Montalban, Benjamin Webster as Rolando, Mr. Tilbury as Balthazar, Robert Keeley as Jaquez, William Clark as Lopez, Mrs. Charles Kean as Juliana, Julia Bennett as Volante, Mrs. L. S. Buckingham as Zamora/ **Drury Lane**, Mar. 1853, with E. L. Davenport as Duke Aranza, Henry Wallack as Rolando, Mr. Moorhouse as Count Montalban, Mr. White as Balthazar, Henry Lee as Lampedo, Charles Selby as Jaques, Edwin Yarnold as Lopez, James Lickfold as Campello, Fanny Vining as The Duchess, Mrs. Lewis as Volante, Mrs. Griffith as Hostess, Emma Feist as Zamora.

HONEYMOON// n.a.// **Haymarket**, Mar. 1859, with Amy Sedgwick.

HONEYMOON IN ECLIPSE, THE// Dram. by George Moore fr story, Ugly Barrington// **St. Geo. Hall**, Apr. 1888.

HONEYMOON TRAGEDY, A// C 1a// Mrs. W. K. Clifford// **Comedy**, Mar. 1896, with Acton Bond as Count Del Mezzio, Mrs. Herbert Waring as Countess Del Mezzio.

HONOUR// Play 4a// Adap. by Maurice Barrymore fr F of Leon Battu & Mauirgue, L'Honour de la Maison// **Court**, Sept. 1881.

HONOUR; OR, ONE REDEEMING SPARK// D 3a// John Levey// **Grecian**, Sept. 1871.

HONOUR AMONG THIEVES// D 3a// Edward Towers// **Pavilion**, Aug. 1877.

HONOUR BEFORE TITLES// D// Charles Reade// **St. James's**, Nov. 1854, with Mr. Stuart as Count de la Tourangeraie, Mr. Moreland as Gaston, Henry Rivers as Jerome, J. L. Toole as Pailleux, John Herbert as Pervenche, George Burt as Colibert, Mrs. Stanley as the Countess, Mrs. Seymour as Madeleine, Miss Clifford as Aurelie.

HONOUR BEFORE WEALTH; OR, THE ROMANCE OF A POOR YOUNG MAN// D 4a// Adap. by Pierpont Edwards & Lester Wallack fr F of Octave Feuillet// **Queen's**, Mar. 1861.

HONOUR BRIGHT// D 4a// Ronald Grahame, E. T. Bauzie & Cecil Harringay// **West London**, Mar. 1898.

HONOUR BRIGHT; OR, A STORY OF THE STAGE// D Pro & 3a// Edward Towers & W. Paolo// **East London**, Apr. 1870.

HONOUR OF THE HOUSE, THE// D 5a// H. Lewis// **Pavilion**, July 1895.

HONOUR THY FATHER// Play 4a// C. A. Clarke & H. R. Silva// **Imperial**, Sept. 1898.

HONOURABLE HERBERT, THE// Play 4a// C. Haddon Chambers// **Vaudeville**, Dec. 1891, with Thomas Thorne as Brady, Arthur Elwood as Tenby, Sydney Brough as Doring, Charles Dodsworth as Lavender, A. Vane Tempest as Amner, Dorothy Dorr as Mrs. Doring, Mary Collette as Dorcas, Gertrude Warden as Lady Highfield, Ella Banister as Florrie.

HONOURABLE MEMBER, AN// CD 3a// A. W. Gattie// **Court**, July 1896, with G. W. Anson as Ditherby, W. Scott Buist as Heron, George Bernage as Hubbock, James Welch as Beamer, Graham Browne as Williams, Thomas Courtice as Davies, Mrs. Edmund Phelps as Mrs. Ditherby, Mrs. A. R. McIntosh as Mrs. Hubbock, Madge McIntosh as Margery.

HONOURS// D// Fawney Vane// **Grecian**, Oct. 1879.

HONOUR'S PRICE// D 5a// Mortimer Murdoch// **Marylebone**, July 1885.

HOODED BRIDEGROOM, THE// F 2a// n.a.// **Sad. Wells**, July 1841, with Mr. Williams as Duke of Ribera, J. S. Balls as Don Alphonso, Mr. Elvin as Don Fernando, Miss Cooke as Sylvia, Mrs. Morgan as Isabella, Mrs. Richard Barnett as Marguerita.

HOODMAN BLIND// D 4a// Henry Arthur Jones & Wilson Barrett// **Princess's**, Aug. 1885, with Wilson Barrett as Yeulett, Mary Eastlake as Nance, E. S. Willard as Lezzard, Clifford Cooper as Kridge, Charles Fulton as Lendon, George Barrett as Chibbles, George Walton as Qoadling, Charles Hudson as Lattiker, Miss L. Garth as Polly, Mrs. Huntley as Granny, Alice Cooke as Mrs. Beevor, Mrs. Beckett as Mrs. Chawner/ Scenery by Walter Hann & T. E. Ryan.

HOOK AND EYE// C// Ellie Norwood// **Opera Comique**, Nov. 1891, with Young Stewart as Gedling, Clarence Blakiston as Fairleigh, Harrison Hunter as Selbourne, Evelyn McNay as Sylvia.

HOOP OF GOLD, THE// D 3a// Mortimer Murdoch// **Pavilion**, Mar. 1878.

HOP-PICKERS, THE// D 3a// Thomas Parry [?]// **Adelphi**, Apr. 1849, with Mr. Lambert as Gen. Raynham, Charles Boyce as Herbert Raynham, Edward Wright as Wriggle, Paul Bedford as Tray, Henry Hughes as Gaveling, O. Smith as Callum, William Cullenford as Enmore, Mme. Celeste as Vivien, Sarah Woolgar as Hester, Mrs. Frank Matthews as Letty, Ellen Chaplin as Crotchet/ Scenery by Pitt & Johnstone/ Music by Alfred Mellon/ Machinery by Mr. Cooper.

HOP-PICKERS AND GIPSIES; OR, THE LOST DAUGHTER// D 3a// C. H. Hazlewood// **Britannia**, May 1869.

HOPE// D 4a// Arthur Law// **Standard**, Oct. 1882.

HOPE OF THE FAMILY, THE// C 3a// J. Stirling Coyne// **Haymarket**, Dec. 1853, with Mr. Rogers as Sir William, W. H. Chippendale as Duckweed, Henry Compton as Dr. Penguin, J. B. Buckstone as Wadd, Henry Corri as Peckover, William Farren as Brown, Edwin Villiers as Flourish, George Braid as Maj. O'Reilly, Mrs. L. S. Buckingham as Selina, Mrs. Poynter as Mrs. Peckover, Mrs. Fitzwilliam as Penny, Ellen Grey as Alice, Mrs. Stanley as Mrs. Lobjoit.

HOPELESS PASSION, A// C 1a// J. Maddison Morton// **Strand**, Sept. 1851.

HORNET'S NEST, A// C// G. L. Gordon// **Opera Comique**, Jan. 1876.

HORNET'S NEST, THE// C 4a// H. J. Byron// **Haymarket**, June 1878, with E. A. Sothern as Spoonbill, Frederick Everill as Gen. Bloss, David Fisher Jr. as Bingham, G. F. De Vere as Dollop, George Holland as Drone, Henry Rivers as Bulbs, Henry Howe as Marks, Henry Crouch as Tipper, Amy Roselle as Carry, Emily Thorne as Mrs. Mandrake, Fanny Morelli as Mrs. McTab, Julia Roselle as Jane.

HORNSEY CARRIER, THE; OR, THE FATAL SHOT// D 2a// n.a.// **Sad. Wells**, Feb. 1838, with Mr. James as Adm. Vanguard, Mr. Rogers as Proudsides, Mr. Campbell as the Hornsey Carrier, James Worrell as Danvers, Mr. Williams as Hartley, S. Smith as David, Mr. Gay as Church, Miss Watkins as Margaret, Miss Beresford as Patience.

HORRIBLE MURDER AT HOXTON, THE// F 1a// George Conquest// **Grecian**, Sept. 1861, with George Conquest as Squeakem, John Manning as Glummy, George Gillett as Longford, Henry Power as James, Lucreza Hill as Rose.

HORSE STEALER, THE// D 3a// n.a.// **Astley's**, Dec. 1876, with John Paley as Will Land, G. N. Wallace as Luff, B. Robins as Catchpole, Alfred Raymond as Pegs, A. Lauraine as Pip, R. Bruton as Chittenden, J. H. Manley as Barry, Adelaide Stoneham as the Horse Stealer, Mrs. G. N. Wallace as Dame Catchpole, Miss F. M. Ryan as Sally, Rose Carew as Mrs. Palmer/ Scenery by Dayes & Caney/ Prod. by George Sanger.

HOT AND COLD// F 1a// Thomas Dibdin// **Princess's**, Feb. 1850, with J. W. Ray as Narcissus, Mr. Stacey as Marston, G. W. Forman as Satterthwaite, Miss Somers as Mrs. Plumbago, Miss Saunders as Fanny, Miss Bennett as Dorothy.

HOT WATER// FC 3a// Adap. by H. B. Farnie fr F of Henri Meilhac & Léon Halévy, La Boule// **Criterion**, Nov. 1876; Aug. 1894.

HOTEL CHARGES; OR, HOW TO COOK A BIFFIN// F 1a// Charles Selby// **Adelphi**, Oct. 1853.

HOUP LA!// C// T. G. Warren// **Comedy**, Aug. 1891.

HOUR AT RUGBY JUNCTION, AN// C 1a// Adap. by Frank Harvey fr F// **Haymarket**, Sept. 1874, with Frank Harvey as Hastie, H. Bennett as Baggs, Nelly Lingham as Charlotte, Isa Courtney [sic] as Jemima.

HOUR LA! TRA-LA-LA!// C// Adap. by H. M. Dunstan fr G// **Royalty**, May 1886.

HOUSE DOG, THE// F 1a// Thomas Higgie// **Grecian**, May 1855, with Eaton O'Donnell as Clinkscales, F. Charles as Capt. Hazard, T. Roberts as Doo, John Manning as Dust, Harriet Coveney as Betty, Miss Johnstone as Melpomene, Miss Morgan as Cecilia.

HOUSE IN THE VALLEY, THE// D 3a// George Conquest// **Grecian**, Mar. 1862, with Mr. Jackson as Gen. Mountford, Henry Grant as Harding, Thomas Mead as Reapwell, Alfred Rayner as Sir Joseph, George Conquest as Thistlethorn, William James as George, Jane Dawson as Louise, Lucreza Hill as Lucille, Ellen Hale as Mary.

HOUSE OF DARNLEY, THE// C 5a// Edward Bulwer-Lytton; 5th a. by Charles Coghlan// **Court**, Oct. 1877, with Robert Cathcart, John Hare, Ellen Terry, Amy Roselle, Charles Kelly.

HOUSE OF MYSTERY, A// D 4a// Frank Harvey// **Imperial**, May 1898.

HOUSE ON THE BRIDGE OF NOTRE DAME, THE// D 3a// Adap. by Rophino Lacy fr F of Théodore Barrière & Henri de Kock// **Lyceum**, Feb. 1861, with James Johnstone as Count de Forquerolles, George Vining as Chevalier de Forquerolles, Mme. Celeste as Ernest and Zambaro, Mr. Fredericks as Count de Tulle, Henry Forrester as Beauvais, John Rouse as Achille, Frederick Villiers as Rigobart, Miss Rawlings as Countess de Forquerolles, Maria Ternan as Adeline, Kate Saville as Melanie, Lydia Thompson as Colette, Miss Hudspeth as Susanne/ Scenery by William Callcott/ Music by George Loder/ Machines by Mr. Bare/ **Sad. Wells**, Apr. 1863, with J. W. Collier as Count de Forquerolles, Charles Maynard as Chevalier de Forquerolles, Mme. Celeste as Ernest and Zambaro, Mr. Britten as Adolphe, Mr. Stalman as Mahy, James Johnstone as Rigobart, Miss Rawlings as Countess de Forquerolles, Emma Leslie as Adeline, Kate Lemmon as Melanie, Miss Mason as Colette, Ida Russelle as Susanne/ **Princess's**, May 1869, with W. D. Gresham as Count de Forquerolles, G. F. Neville as Chevalier de Forquerolles, C. H. Fenton as Beauvais, Alfred Tapping as Mahy, Dominick Murray as Pettiso, Mme. Celeste as Ernest and Zambara, William Rignold as Rigobert, Helen Paget as Countess de Forquerolles, Miss Litton as Adeline, Emma Barnett as Melanie, Louisa Moore as Colette, Miss Kemp as Suzanne, Mrs. Addie as Madeleine.

HOUSE ON THE BRIDGE OF NOTRE DAME, THE// D 3a// Adap. by C. H. Hazlewood fr F of Théodore Barrière & Henri de Kock//

Marylebone, Apr. 1861.

HOUSE ON THE MARSH, THE// D 4a// Dram. by Florence Warden fr her novel// **Standard**, June 1885.

HOUSE? OR THE HOME? THE// C 2a// Adap. by Tom Taylor fr F of Octave Feuillet, Peril dans le Demeure// **Adelphi**, May 1859, with Charles Selby as Gen. Witherington, John Billington as Frederick, Alfred Wigan as Horace, Mrs. Alfred Wigan as Mrs. Wardour, Henrietta Simms as Lady Helen, Miss Laidlaw as Hopwood.

HOUSE OUT OF WINDOWS, A// F 1a// William Brough// **Lyceum**, Oct. 1852, with Robert Roxby as Paul Potter, Basil Baker as Closecard, Mrs. Macnamara as Miss Webb, Miss Martindale as Julia.

HOUSE-BOAT, THE// C// H. W. Williamson// **POW**, Nov. 1886.

HOUSEBREAKER, THE// FC 3a// Stanley Rogers// **Elephant & Castle**, July 1893.

HOUSEHOLD FAIRY, THE// C 1a// Francis Talfourd// **Olympic**, Aug. 1863, with Henry Neville as Julian, Miss Hughes as Katherine.

HOUSEKEEPER, THE; OR, THE WHITE ROSE// C 2a// Douglas Jerrold// **Haymarket**, June 1837, with Frederick Vining as Maynard, John Webster as Purple, Benjamin Webster as Father Oliver, Mr. Ross as Box, E. F. Saville as Laval, Mr. Gallot as Daguere, Mr. Harris as Layer, T. F. Mathews as Bin, Mrs. Nisbett as Felicia, Mrs. Humby as Sophy, Mrs. Taylcure as Widow Duckling; Feb. 1849, with Charles Kean as Maynard, Alfred Wigan as Purple, Benjamin Webster as Oliver, Robert Keeley as Box, George Braid as Daguerre, Mr. Caulfield as Laval, William Clark as Bin, Mrs. Charles Kean as Felicia, Mrs. Humby as Sophy, Mrs. W. Clifford as Widow Duckling/ **Grecian**, Apr. 1856, with Richard Phillips as Maynard, F. Charles as Purple, John Manning as Box, Eaton O'Donnell as Father Oliver, Henry Grant as Daquerre, Jane Coveney as Celicia, Harriet Coveney as Hawes, Miss Johnstone as Widow Duckling/ **Royalty**, 1872.

HOW LONDON LIVES// D 5a// Adap. by Martyn Field & Arthur Shirley fr F of Paul Andry, Max Maurey, & Georges Jubin, Le Camelot// **Princess's**, Dec. 1897, with Charles Warner as Ferrers, Charles Garry as Sir George, Oscar Ayde as Grainger, Stephen Ewart as Lt. Maxwell, Herbert Vyvyan as Tigser, F. Walford as Crumpets, J. H. Bishop as Microbe, Alfred Phillips as Benson, Geraldine Olliffe as Lady Ferrers, Mary Duggan as Molly, Blanche Stanley as Mrs. Delaney, Millicent Barr as Maud, Kate Tyndall as Gladys.

HOW SHE LOVES HIM// C 5a// Dion Boucicault// **POW**, Dec. 1867, with John Hare.

HOW STOUT YOU'RE GETTING!// F 1a// J. Maddison Morton// **Princess's**, July 1855, with David Fisher as Plummy, Mr. Raymond as Dr. Dulcet, George Everett as George, Henry Saker as Slide, Miss Murray as Mrs. Plummy, Miss Clifford as Margery.

HOW TIME FLIES; OR, THINGS THAT HAPPEN EVERY HOUR// D// James Elphenstone// **Victoria**, Apr. 1869.

HOW TO DIE FOR LOVE// F 1a// n.a.// **Sad. Wells**, Sept. 1841, with Henry Marston, Mr. Williams, John Herbert, J. W. Collier, Miss Richardson, Mrs. Richard Barnett, Miss Cooke/ **Haymarket**, Feb. 1870, with Mr. Rogers as Heartley, Mr. Kendal as Capt. Seymour, Walter Gordon as Capt. Howard, Henry Compton as Trap, Mr. Clark as Trick, Mr. Johnson as Clay, Kathleen Ryan as Charlotte.

HOW TO GET A WIFE// C 3a// n.a.// **Grecian**, Aug. 1856, with F. Charles, William Shuter as Sir C. Freeman, Henry Grant as Sullen, Richard Phillips as Archer, Eaton O'Donnell, Henry Power as Boniface, Mr. Hustleby as Gibbett, Miss Johnstone as Lady Bountiful, Jane Coveney as Mrs Sullen, Harriet Coveney as Cherry.

HOW TO MAKE HOME HAPPY// F 1a// William Brough// **Lyceum**, Nov. 1853/ **Haymarket**, July 1859, with C. J. Mathews as Dabchick, Mr. Rogers as Tuffins, Edwin Villiers as Frederick, Mr. Weathersby as Peter, Mrs. C. J. Mathews (Lizzie Davenport) as Mrs. Dabchick, Maria Ternan as Emily.

HOW TO PAY THE RENT// F// Tyrone Power// **Haymarket**, Apr. 1840, with Tyrone Power as Rattler, Mr. Green as Star-the-Glaze, G. W. Gough as Blowhard, Mr. Clark as Shooter, Mr. Caulfield as Billy, Robert Strickland as Miller, Mrs. W. Clifford as Mrs. Conscience, Mrs. Frank Matthews as Kitty, Miss Grove as Betty/ **Sad. Wells**, June 1844, with Charles Hudson as Rattler, Mr. Williams as Miller, Mr. Sharp as Billy, Frank Graham as Blowhard, Mrs. Henry Marston as Mrs. Priscience, Georgiana Lebatt as Kitty, Fanny Morelli as Betty.

HOW TO SETTLE ACCOUNTS WITH YOUR LAUNDRESS// F 1a// J. Stirling Coyne// **Adelphi**, July 1847, with Edward Wright as Widgetts, Charles Munyard as Brown, Emma Harding as Cheri Bounce, Sarah Woolgar as Mary White/ **Haymarket**, Aug. 1848, with Edward Wright as Widgetts, Charles Munyard as Brown, Redmond Ryan as Twill, Sarah Woolgar as Mary, Emma Harding as Mlle. Bounce.

HOW WE SPENT CHRISTMAS DAY IN '69// D// Harry Pitt// **Surrey**, Jan. 1870.

HOW WILL THEY GET OUT OF IT?// C 3a// Arthur Sketchley// **St. James's**, Aug. 1864.

HOW'S YOUR UNCLE? OR, THE LADIES OF THE COURT// F 1a// T. E. Wilkes// **Adelphi**, Dec. 1855, with Edward Wright as Wiggs, Paul Bedford as Tomkins, C. J. Smith as Docket, Mrs. Garden as Lydia, Mary Keeley as Sally, Kate Kelly as Mary/ **Victoria**, July 1848, with G. F. Forman as Wiggs, James Howard as Tomkins, Mrs. George Lee as Mary, Miss

Burroughcliffe as Sally, Miss Sharpe as Jane, Mrs. Cooke as Lydia, Miss Edgar as Emily.

HOWARD HOWARD// C// Alfred Arthur// **St. Geo. Hall**, Nov. 1888.

HOWLETT'S HAUNT; OR, THE FIRESIDE STORY// D// W. T. Moncrieff// **Sad. Wells**, Sept. 1841, with Mr. Williams as Felton, Mr. Elvin as Rushton, Mr. Dry as Darrell, Henry Marston as Richard, John Herbert as Huxtable, J. W. Collier as Martlett, Mr. Aldridge as Capt. Crafter, Miss Richardson as Letitia, Mrs. Richard Barnett as Mabel.

HUBBY// FC 1a// H. A. Sherburn// **Shaftesbury**, May 1891, with Fred Mervin as Maj. O'Braggerty, Walter Everard as Hopscotch, Fawdon Vokes as Bobbins, Victoria Vokes as Mrs. O'Braggerty, Lillian Hingston as Mrs. Hopscotch, Annie Fawdon as Mrs. Cattermole.

HUBERT, THE BOWYER'S SON// D// Douglas Stewart// **Victoria**, Feb. 1874.

HUE AND CRY, THE// D 4a// Arthur Shirley & Benjamin Landeck// **Pavilion**, Apr. 1897.

HUE AND DYE// F 1a// Frederick Hay// **Strand**, Jan. 1869.

HUGO BAMBINO; OR, THE COURT JESTER// C// n.a.// **Olympic**, Oct. 1837, with James Vining as Grand Duke of Ferrara, Charles Selby as Marquis Castelli, James Bland as Marini, William Farren as Hugo Bambino, Mrs. Macnamara as Susanna, Mme. Vestris as Pauline.

HUGO DE MAURAVERT; OR, THE WOLF OF FRANCE AND THE RING OF FATE// Pro & 3a// n.a.// **Victoria**, July 1850, with J. Neville as Count de Mauravert, John Ryder as Hugo, Henry Frazer as Reney, G. F. Forman as de Blay, James Howard as Cantillon, Mr. Henderson as Count de Teligny, Mr. Humphries as Duke de Guise, Mr. Richards as Cardinal Lauraine, Amelia Mercer as Catherine de Medicis, Mrs. George Lee as Bona, Miss Barrowcliffe as Ninon, Georgiana Lebatt as Jaconet.

HUGUENOT CAPTAIN, THE// D 3a// Watts Phillips// **Princess's**, July 1866, with J. G. Shore as de Savigny, Mr. Meagreson as Lemours, George Spencer as Chateauvieux, Mr. Wallbank as Beaujeu, George Vining as Pardillian, W. R. Robins as Pare, George Honey as Locust, James Cathcart as Mousqueton, Henry Mellon as Tappa, Charles Seyton as Ismael, Mrs. Stirling as Duchess Jeanne, Miss Neilson as Gabrielle, Augusta Thompson as Juanita/ Scenery by F. Lloyds, Walter Hann, A. Lloyds/ Music by J. L. Hatton & Charles Hall/ Machines by Mr. Warton/ Prod. by George Vining.

HUGUENOT LOVER, THE// C 4a// Max Pemberton & James McArthur// **Globe**, May 1901.

HUGUENOTS, THE; OR, THE MASK, THE SURGEON, ETC// D// J. B. Howe// **Surrey**, June 1873.

HUMAN NATURE// C// Adap. by Augustus Harris & T.J. Williams// **Olympic**, July 1867.

HUMAN NATURE// D 5a// Henry Pettitt & Augustus Harris// **Drury Lane**, Sept. 1885, with Henry Neville as Capt. Temple, Edmund Leathes as Hawker, J. G. Grahame as De Vigne, J. H. Clynds as Mardyke, R. C. Lyons as Rev. Lukwarm, Harry Nicholls as Spofkins, Frederick Thorne as Lambkin, Henry Elmore as Stone, Arthur Yates as Col. Brandon, Maud Fisher as Frank, Katie Barry as Dick, Isabel Bateman as Nellie, Emmeline Ormsby as Cora, Marie Illington as Madge, Lizzie Claremont as Mrs. Lambkin/ Scenery by Henry Emden/ Music by Oscar Barrett.

HUMAN SPORT, A// D 1a// W. E. Cleary ("Austin Fryers")// **Globe**, May 1895, with Philip Cunningham as Groves, Wilton Heriot as Foudriant, James Welch as Old Nip, Katherine Glover as Minnie, Mrs. Theodore Wright as Mrs. Chessle.

HUMANITY; OR, LIFE FOR LIFE// D 4a// Charles Locksley// **Astley's**, Oct. 1881, with Frank Paul as Dennis O'Dowd, E. N. Hallows as Phelim O'Dowd, E. Fowler as Michael, George Stretton as Richard, Mat Robson as Flaherty, G. Hardynge as Reardon, Marie Forde as Kate, Nellie Grahame as Mary, Mrs. H. Blandford as Widow Mulvaney/ Scenery by Frank Paul/ Machines by Mr. Gilbert/ Music by W. H. Brinkworth.

HUMANITY; OR, A PASSAGE IN THE LIFE OF GRACE DARLING// D 4a// Hugh Marston & Leonard Rae// **Standard**, Apr. 1882.

HUMBUG// C 2a// Adap. by F. C. Burnand partly fr F, Les Faux Bonshommes// **Royalty**, Dec. 1867.

HUNCHBACK, THE// D 5a// Sheridan Knowles// **Haymarket**, Apr. 1838, with Sheridan Knowles as Master Walter, Edmund Glover as Sir Thomas, Benjamin Webster as Tinsel, Mr. Hutchings as Wilford, Mr. Hemming as Modus, J. W. Gough as Heartwell, James Worrell as Gaylove, T. F. Mathews as Thomas, J. B. Buckstone as Fathom, Miss Elphinstone as Julia, Mrs. Fitzwilliam as Helen; Aug. 1841, with James Wallack as Master Walter, Henry Howe as Sir Thomas, Benjamin Webster as Tinsel, Mr. Vining as Modus, Mr. Caulfield as Wilford, J. W. Gough as Heartwell, James Worrell as Gaylove, W. H. Oxberry as Fathom, Helen Faucit as Julia, Mrs. Stirling as Helen; July 1851, with Walter Lacy as Tinsel, Leigh Murray as Sir Thomas, J. William Wallack as Master Walter, Benjamin Webster as Modus, J. B. Buckstone as Fathom, John Parselle as Wilford, George Braid as Gaylove, Laura Addison as Julia, Mrs. Walter Lacy as Helen; Feb. 1860, with Henry Howe as Master Walter, William Farren as Sir Thomas, Edwin Villiers as Tinsel, J. B. Buckstone as Modus, George Braid as Wilford, William Cullenford as Heartwell, Henry Compton as Fathom, F. C. Courtney as Gaylove, Amy Sedgwick as Julia, Miss Swanborough as Helen; Mar. 1878, with Henry

Howe as Master Walter, H. B. Conway as Sir Thomas, Harold Kyrle as Tinsel, Henry Crouch as Wilford, Charles Harcourt as Modus, A. Allbrook as Heartwell, Mr. Weathersby as Gaylove, E. Everill as Fathom, Adelaide Neilson as Julia, Henrietta Hodson as Helen/ **Cov. Garden**, Oct. 1838, with Mr. Warde as Master Walter, James Anderson as Sir Thomas, Henry Howe as Tinsel, Mr. Roberts as Wilford, Edwin Yarnold as Gaylove, Mr. Vining as Modus, Charles Diddear as Heartwell, Drinkwater Meadows as Fathom, Mr. Tilbury as Thomas, Helen Faucit as Julia, Charlotte Vandenhoff as Helen; Feb. 1840, with Mr. Cooper as Master Walter, James Anderson as Sir Thomas, Thomas Green as Tinsel, Mr. Fitzjames as Wilford, Alfred Wigan as Gaylove, Drinkwater Meadows as Fathom, Ellen Tree as Julia, Mrs. Walter Lacy (Miss Taylor) as Helen/ **Sad. Wells**, Mar. 1839, with Mr. Cathcart as Master Walter, Mr. Lyon as Sir Thomas, John Webster as Modus, J. W. Collier as Tinsel, Mr. Dry as Heartwell, Mr. Elvin as Wilford, Richard Phillips as Gaylove, Mr. Conquest as Fathom, W. D. Broadfoot as Thomas, Mrs. Robert Honner as Julia, Miss Pincott as Helen; July 1846, with William Creswick as Master Walter, Henry Marston as Sir Thomas, William Hoskins as Modus, E. Morton as Tinsel, Mr. Branson as Wilford, Henry Scharf as Fathom, Charles Fenton as Gaylove, Mr. Williams as Thomas, Henry Mellon as Heartwell, Edward Knight as Holdwell, Mrs. Pollock as Julia, Miss Cooper as Helen; Sept. 1866, with L. Warner as Master Walter, J. H. Slater as Sir Thomas, W. Cameron as Modus, Mr. Edwin as Tinsel, Richard Norman as Heartwell, Mr. Murray as Wilford, John Rouse as Fathom, Mr. Byrne as Gaylove, J. W. Lawrence as Stephen, Alice Marriott as Julia, Louisa Periera as Helen; Nov. 1879, with Charles Kelly as Master Walter, Walter Bentley as Sir Thomas, F. W. Wyndham as Modus, Robert Lyons as Tinsel, Mr. Redwood as Heartwell, Mr. Wheatcroft as Wilford, Mr. Gurney as Gaylove, Mr. Fosbrooke as Fathom, Isabel Bateman as Julia, Virginia Francis as Helen/ **Princess's**, Apr. 1845, with James Wallack as Master Walter, Leigh Murray as Sir Thomas, Walter Lacy as Tinsel, Mr. Hield as Wilford, Henry Compton as Modus, Mr. Archer as Heartwell, Augustus Harris as Gaylove, W. H. Oxberry as Fathom, James Ranoe as Thomas, Robert Honner as Stephen, Charlotte Cushman as Julia, Mrs. Stirling as Helen; Mar. 1848, with Mr. Cooper as Master Walter, F. B. Conway as Sir Thomas, James Vining as Tinsel, Charles Fisher as Wilford, Henry Compton as Modus, W. H. Norton as Heartwell, Augustus Harris as Gaylove, S. Cowell as Fathom, Mrs Butler (Fanny Kemble) as Julia, Emmeline Montague as Helen; Apr. 1847, with William Creswick as Master Walter, John Webster as Sir Thomas, Charles Fisher as Wilford, Henry Compton as Modus, John Ryder as Heartwell, Augustus Harris as Gaylove, S. Cowell as Fathom, Mrs. Butler (Fanny Kemble) as Julia, Mrs. Stirling as Helen; Apr. 1861, with John Ryder as Master Walter, Hermann Vezin as Sir Thomas, T. H. Higgie as Tinsel, J. G. Shore as Modus, Mr. Cathcart as Wilford, Mr. Raymond as Gaylove, John Collett as Holdwell, Edmund Garden as Heartwell, Drinkwater Meadows as Fathom, Miss Heath as Julia, Carlotta Leclercq as Helen; Oct. 1862 with Henry Marston as Master Walter, Hermann Vezin as Sir Thomas, Robert Roxby as Modus, J. G. Shore as Tinsel, Mr. Cathcart as Wilford, George Belmore as Fathom, Charles Seyton as Gaylove, Amy Sedgwick as Julia, Miss M. Oliver as Helen/ **Olympic**, May 1845, with Mr. Bass as Master Walter, Walter Grisdale as Sir Thomas, Mr. Grafton as Tinsel, Mr. Roarke as Modus, R. Manley as Wilford, Mr. Hollingsworth as Heartwell, Mr. Jones as Gaylove, Mr. Turnour as Thomas, Mr. Gomersal as Fathom, Amelia Mercer as Julia, Miss M. A. Egan as Helen; Oct. 1846, with Henry West Betty as Master Walter, Walter Lacy as Tinsel, Leigh Murray as Sir Thomas, John Howard as Modus, Mr. Clifford as Master Wilford, Mr. Wilkenson as Fathom, Thomas Archer as Heartwell, Spencer Ford as Gaylove, Mrs. R. Gordon as Julia, Mrs. Walter Lacy as Helen; June 1866, with Henry Neville as Master Walter, H. J. Montague as Sir Thomas, Robert Soutar as Tinsel, W. M. Terrott as Master Wilford, Horace Wigan as Modus, Harwood Cooper as Heartwell, H. Vincent as Gaylove, Edward Atkins as Fathom, Mr. Andrews as Thomas, Henry Rivers as Stephen, Kate Terry as Julia, Ellen Terry as Helen/ **Grecian**, Apr. 1853, with Mr. Roberts as Earl Rocheale, Charles Horn as Tinsel, Mr. Campbell as Master Walter, Richard Phillips as Sir Thomas, Basil Potter as Modus, Edwin Dixon as Heartwell, Charles Rice as Fathom, Jane Coveney as Julia, Harriet Coveney as Helen; Aug. 1857, with Charles Harcourt as Tinsell, Richard Phillips as Clifford, John Manning as Modus, Henry Grant as Heartwell, Basil Potter as Master Walter, William Shuter as Master Wilford, Edwin Yarnold as Fathom, Margaret Eburne as Julia, Eliza Johnstone as Helen/ **Astley's**, Oct. 1866, with John Ryder as Master Walter, Walter Joyce as Lord Tinsel, Mr. Dugarde as Master Wilford, W. Ryder as Modus, A. Denial as Heartwell, Henry Vandenhoff as Sir Thomas, George Webster as Gaylove, W. Arthur as Fathom, Sophie Young as Julia, Maud Shelley as Helen/ **Adelphi**, Aug. 1867, with Mr. Stuart as Master Walter, Henry Neville as Sir Thomas, Henry Ashley as Tinsel, W. H. Eburne as Master Wilford, John Billington as Modus, C. H. Stephenson as Master Heartwell, John Clarke as Fathom, Kate Terry as Julia, Ellen Terry as Helen; Mar. 1879, with Henry Neville & Hermann Vezin alt. as Master Walter and Sir Thomas, Charles Flockton as Tinsel, Charles Harcourt as Modus, Robert Pateman as Fathom, F. Charles as Master Wilford, Harwood Cooper as Stephen, Adelaide Neilson as Julia, Lydia Foote as Helen/ Scenery by Julian Hicks; Mar. 1890, with Julian Cross as Master Walter, Luigi Lablache as Sir Thomas, A. Rodney as Tinsel, R. de Fonblanque as Rochdale, Ben Greet as Modus, Mrs. Patrick Campbell as Helen/ **Lyceum**, Feb. 1885, with Arthur Stirling as Master Walter, William Terriss as Sir Thomas, Arthur Lewis as Lord Tinsel, J. Anderson as Master Wilford, Herbert Standing as Modus, George Warde as Heartwell, R. De Cordova as Gaylove, Bella Pateman as Helen, Mary Anderson as Julia/ Scenery by Hawes Craven, W. Perkins & Bruce Smith.

HUNCHBACK OF LAMBYTHE, THE; OR, EVA THE BETRAYED// D 3a// n.a.// **Victoria,** Dec. 1853, with Mr. Green as Thorneley the Elder, Mr. Henderson as Thorneley the Younger, N. T. Hicks as More, T. E. Mills as Wilbert, John Bradshaw as Bellisle, John Hudspeth as John, James Howard as Lambkins, Mr. Morrison as Fenwicke, Mrs. Henry Vining as Eva, Miss Dansor as Katherine, Miss Laporte as Lucie, Miss Mildenhall as Blanche.

HUNDRED THOUSAND POUNDS, A// D 3a// H. J. Byron// **POW,** May. 1866, with John Hare.

HUNT FOR A HUSBAND, A// F 1a// Adap. by J. P. Wooler fr F// **Strand,** Mar. 1864.

HUNTED DOWN; OR, THE TWO LIVES OF MARY LEIGH// D 3a// Dion Boucicault// **St. James's,** Nov. 1866, with Walter Lacy as John Leigh, Louisa Herbert as Mary Leigh, [Roma] Guillon Le Thière as Lady Glencarrig, Mrs. Frank Matthews as Mrs. Jones, Ada Dyas as Clara, Henry Irving as Rawdon Scudamore/ Scenery by John Gray/ Music by Mr. Van Hamme/ **Globe,** Dec. 1876, with J. D. Beveridge as John Leigh, Edgar Bruce as Rawdon Scudamore, Louise Willes as Mary Leigh, Miss Ges Smythe as Lady Glencarrig, Louisa Howard as Fanny, Mrs. Charles Pitt as Mrs. Bolton Jones.

HUNTED TO DEATH// D// Harwood Cooper// **Victoria,** Oct. 1867.

HUNTER OF THE ALPS, THE// D 2a// William Dimond// **Drury Lane,** Mar. 1837, with Mr. Cooper as Felix, Mr. Warde as Rosalvi, Mr. Henry as Juan, Miss Marshall as Florio, Mr. Hughes as Jeronymo, Mr. Bedford as Baptista, Mr. Mears as Mareo, Charles Fenton as Pietro, Mrs. W. Clifford as Helena, Miss Poole as Genevieve/ **Sad. Wells,** Feb. 1841, with Henry Marston as Felix, Mr. Dry as Rosvali, Mr. Williams as Jeronyno, Mr. Priorson as Juan, Mr. Aldridge as Baptiste, Miss Richardson as Helina, Mrs. Richard Barnett as Genivive [sic], Mrs. Morgan as Claudine, Miss Louise as Ninette; Apr. 1857, with T. Lyon as Felix, R. H. Lingham as Rosvali, Mr. Warren as Jeronymo, Charles Seyton as Juan, Marianne Jackson as Helena, Mary A. Victor as Genevieve, Miss E. Collins as Claudine/ **Grecian,** Mar. 1844, with Henry Frazer as Felix, Mr. Campbell as Rosalvi, G. Norman as Jeronymo, Mr. Kerridge as Juan, Mr. Baldwin as Baptista, John Collett as Marco, Miss Merion as Helina, Annette Mears as Genevieve, Mary A. Crisp as Claudine.

HUNTING A TURTLE// F 1a// Charles Selby// **Sad. Wells,** Apr. 1845, with E. Morton as Turtle, Mr. Coreno as Smatter, John Webster as Levison, G. F. Forman as Dandelion, Miss Lebatt as Mrs. Turtle/ **Grecian,** Mar. 1856, with F. Charles as Turtle, Richard Phillips as Levison, Henry Power as Smatter, John Manning as Dandelion, Jane Coveney as Mrs. Turtle.

HURLY BURLY, THE; OR, NUMBER SEVEN TWENTY EIGHT// FC 3a// Adap. by Herman Hendricks fr G of Franz von Schöthan, Schwabenstreich// **Globe,** June 1884.

HUSBAND AND WIFE// FC 3a// F. C. Philips & Percy Fendall// **Criterion,** Apr. 1891, with George Giddens as Greenthorne, William Blakeley as Smith, James Nelson as Stepit, Sydney Valentine as Insp. Thickhead, Stanley Hewston as Softdown, Laura Linden as Mrs. Springfield, Carlotta Addison as Mrs. Greenthorne, Mary A. Victor as Mrs. Smith, Ellaline Terriss as Mrs. Softdown, Annie Hill as Mrs. Delamere, Edith Kenward as Mary.

HUSBAND AT SIGHT, A// F 2a// J. B. Buckstone// **Sad. Wells,** May 1839, with J. Webster as Louisburg, Mr. Conquest as Gundershoff, Mr. Williams as Parchwitz, Mr. Phillips as Leonard, Mr. Priorson as Carl, Miss Cooke as Baroness Louisburg, Miss Pincott as Catherine, Mrs. J. F. Saville as Augusta; July 1845, with Samuel Buckingham as Louisburg, Mr. Corrie as Gundershoff, Mr. Williams as Parchwitz, Frank Graham as Carl, Mr. Raymond as Leonard, Edward Knight as George, Mrs. Henry Marston as Baroness, Miss Lebatt as Catherine, Miss Cooper as Augusta/ **Grecian,** May 1847, with Mr. Phillips as Louisburg, Frederick Robson as Gundershoff, Eaton O'Donnell as Parchwitz, Miss Merion as Baroness Louisburg, Mary A. Crisp as Augusta, Annette Mears as Catherine.

HUSBAND OF AN HOUR, A// D 2a// Edmund Falconer// **Haymarket,** June 1857, with William Farren as Marquis de Crevecoeur, Mr. Clark as La Fleur, J. B. Buckstone as Robert and Lord Thornley, Mr. Rogers as Le Clerc, Henry Compton as Rouge and Jenkins, Miss Reynolds as Julie, Mrs. Poynter as Countess de Clairville, Mrs. Edward Fitzwilliam as Fanchette, Edwin Villiers as Count D'Aubigny, L. Walter as Vicomte de la Bruyere, George Braid as Duke de Rohan, Ellen Sabine as Louise/ Scenery by William Callcott, George Morris & John O'Conner/ Machines by Oliver Wales.

HUSBAND IN CLOVER, A// F 1a// Henry Merivale// **Lyceum,** Dec. 1873, with John Clayton as Horace, Virginia Francis as Lydia/ **Adelphi,** Nov. 1879, with Fanny Brough as Lydia, R. S. Boleyn as Horace.

HUSBAND OF MY HEART, THE// CD 2a// Charles Selby// **Haymarket,** Oct. 1850, with Henry Howe as Duke de Fronsac, Charles Selby as Viscount de Belletulippe, J. B. Buckstone as Brioche, George Braid as Dubois, Miss Reynolds as Duchess de Fronsac, Mrs. Fitzwilliam as Eugenie, Mrs. Stanley as Mme. Coquillarde.

HUSBAND OF MY WIFE, THE// C 2a// n.a.// **Lyceum,** May 1849, with Charles Selby as King of Spain, C. J. Mathews as Don Fernando, Frank Matthews as Don Philip, John Pritt Harley as Don Juan, Miss O'Conner as Queen of Spain, Miss H. Gilbert as Inez/ Scenery by W. Beverly & Mr. Grey.

HUSBAND ON TRIAL, A// F 1a// W. E. Suter// **Grecian,** Oct. 1853, with Richard Phillips as Whittaker, Charles Rice as Flueflake, Miss

Johnstone as Mrs. Green, Harriet Coveney as Jane Wiggins.

HUSBAND TO ORDER, A// C 2a// Adap. by J. Maddison Morton fr F, Un Mariage sous l'Empire// **Olympic**, Oct. 1859, with Horace Wigan as Baron de Beaupré, George Vining as Marceau, Walter Gordon as Latour, George Cooke as Phillipeau, Miss Wyndham as Josephine, Miss Hughes as Elise, Mrs. W. S. Emden as Mme. Phillipeau; Mar. 1863, with Horace Wigan as Baron de Beaupré, Henry Neville as Marceau, Walter Gordon as Latour, George Vincent as Phillipeau, Kate Saville as Josephine, Miss Hughes as Elise, Mrs. W. S. Emden as Mme. Phillipeau.

HUSBAND'S HUMILIATION, A// C 1a// Annie Hughes// **Criterion**, June 1896, with Edmund Maurice as Wldfire, Herbert Ross as Blcillus, Annie Hughes as Mrs. Wildfire.

HUSBANDS REJOICE; OR, SERVE HIM RIGHT// C 2a// n.a.// **Sad. Wells**, Apr. 1855, with Frank Matthews as Shuttleworth, Frederic Robinson as Bellamy, Robert Roxby as Greenfinch, C. Swan as Hobbs, Miss Martindale as Mrs. Shuttleworth, Miss M. Oliver as Julia, Mrs. Frank Matthews as Mrs. Smith.

HUSBAND'S SECRET, THE// F 1a// n.a.// **Globe**, July 1877, with Miss Fulton, Miss Warden, Mr. Vincent, Mr. Bradbury.

HUSBAND'S VENGEANCE, A// D// n.a.// **Marylebone**, Nov. 1857.

HUSBANDS AND WIVES// F 1a// Isaac Pocock// **Victoria**, Nov. 1837, with Benjamin Wrench as Capt. Pickall, Mr. Loveday as Sir Peregrine, Edward Hooper as Capt. Wingham, W. H. Oxberry as Crab, Mr. Salter as Clover, Mr. Harwood as Nab, Miss Richardson as Lady Peery, Miss Lee as Eliza, Mrs. Frank Matthews as Dame Briarly, Mrs. Loveday as Mary, Mrs. Hooper as Rose.

HUSH MONEY// F 2a// Charles Dance// **Olympic**, June, 1854, with Frederick Robson as Touchwood, J. H. White as Snuggle, Mr. Vincent as White, Henry Rivers as Stock, Samuel Emery as Tiller, Miss Dormer as Lydia, Miss Stevens as Mrs. Crab, Mrs. Alfred Wigan as Sally; Sept. 1858.

HUSH MONEY// D 4a// Herbert Keith// **Terry's**, June 1892, with Yorke Stephens as Sinclair, W. L. Abingdon as Marshall, John Beauchamp as Rev. Joy, J. R. Crauford as Chester, Orlando Barnett as Walton, Cicely Richards as Mrs. Westgarth, Mary Mordaunt as Amy, Edith Gordon as Evelyn.

HUT OF THE HEATH, THE; OR, LOVE AND DUTY// D// n.a.// **Sad. Wells**, Sept. 1839, with Mr. Williams as Bertrand, Mr. Elvin as Eugene, Mr. Aldridge as Dennis, Mr. Phillips as Jacques, J. W. Collier as Pierre, Mr. Dry as Baptiste, Robert Honner as Francois, Mrs. Robert Honner as Mariette, Miss Pincott as Estelle; Oct. 1842 (as Hut On the Heath), with P. Williams as Bernard, C. J. Bird as Eugene, Mr. Aldridge as Dennis, Charles Fenton as Jacques, Mr. Richardson as Pierre, J. W. Collier as François, Mr. Dry as Baptiste, Caroline Rankley as Mariette, Mrs. Richard Barnett as Estelle.

HUT OF THE RED MOUNTAIN, THE; OR, THIRTY YEARS OF A GAMBLER'S LIFE// D 3a// H. M. Milner// **Victoria**, June 1846, with Walter Searle as Dorance, E. F. Saville as Augustus, T. Fredericks as Warner, Roberts Tindell as Dermont, Alfred Raymond as d'Haricourt, Mrs. George Lee as Amelia, Miss Jefferson as Louise/ **Sad. Wells**, Feb. 1863, with James Johnstone as Derance, Henry Forrester as Henry, E. F. Edgar as Warner, C. Lloyd as Dermond, A. Montague as d'Hericourt, Sophia Miles as Amelia, Miss Ashton as Louisa, Charles Bender as Valentine, Mr. Dalton as Albert, Lewis Ball as Birman, Bessie Heath as Mme. Birman, Emily Dowton as Augusta.

HYPATIA// D 4a// Dram. by Stuart Ogilvie fr novel by Kingsley// **Haymarket**, Jan. 1893, with James Fernandez as Cyril, Mr. Foss as Arsenius, Charles Hudson as Peter, Mr. Garry as James, Fred Terry as Philammon, Lewis Waller as Orestes, Herbert Beerbohm Tree as Isaachar, James Welch as Kalisthenes, Henry Kemble as Theon, A. Wigley as Hazael, Holman Clark as Kaliphronos, Olga Brandon as Ruth, Charlotte Morland as Barea, Marion Grey as Suana, Constance Carew as Leda, Henrietta Leverett as Nerea, Ethel Johnson as Thymele, Julia Neilson as Hypatia/ Scenery by T. Hall, Walter Johnstone, Walter Hann & J. Harker/ Music by Hubert Parry.

HYPOCRITE, THE// C 5a// Isaac Bickerstaff's alt. of Cibber's Nonjuror, an adap. of Moliere's Tartuffe// **Drury Lane**, May 1837, with Mr. Mathews as Sir John, Mr. Cooper as Col. Lambert, George Bartley as Cantwell, Drinkwater Meadows as Mawworm, Mr. Hooper as Darnley, A. Brindal as Seyward, Mrs. Charles Jones as Old Lady Lambert, Mrs. Hooper as Miss Lambert, Miss Taylor as Charlotte, Mrs. East as Betty; Jan 1850, with Charles Diddear as Sir John, Basil Baker as Cantwell, Frederick Vining as Col. Lambert, Charles Fisher as Darnley, William Montague as Seyward, Stephen Artaud as Mawworm, Mrs. Winstanley as Old Lady Lambert, Fanny Huddart as Young Lady Lambert, Louisa Nisbett as Charlotte, Miss Foster as Betty/ **Cov. Garden**, Apr. 1838, with much of same cast/ **Princess's**, May 1847, with John Ryder as Sir John, James Vining as Col. Lambert, John Webster as Darnley, Mr. Granby as Cantwell, Charles Fisher as Siward, Henry Compton as Mawworm, Mrs. Fosbroke as Old Lady Lambert, Mrs. H. Hughes as Lady Lambert, Mrs. Stirling as Charlotte, Miss Laporte as Betty/ **Haymarket**, Apr. 1848, with Mr. Tilbury as Sir John, William Farren as Cantwell, Henry Farren as Col. Lambert, Henry Howe as Darnley, Robert Keeley as Mawworm, Henry Vandenhoff as Seward, Mrs. Julia Glover as Old Lady Lambert, Mrs. Seymour as Young Lady Lambert, Mrs. Nisbett as Charlotte, Miss Woulds as Betty/ **Sad. Wells**, June 1848, with Henry Mellon as Sir John,

Henry Marston as Col. Lambert, A. Younge as Cantwell, Henry Scharf as Mawworm, E. Morton as Darnley, James Howard as Seyward, Mr. Wilkins as Tipstaff, Mrs. Henry Marston as Old Lady Lambert, Miss Marsh as Lady Lambert, Miss Cooper as Charlotte, Fanny Morelli as Betty; Oct. 1858, with Samuel Phelps, Mrs. Charles Young, Charles Young, Mrs. Henry Marston, Miss Atkinson, Henry Marston/ **Grecian**, Jan. 1854, with Henry Grant as Sir John, Eaton O'Donnell as Cantwell, Richard Phillips as Col. Lambert, Charles Horn as Darnley, Charles Rice as Mawworm, Harriet Coveney as Charlotte, Miss Johnstone as Old Lady Lambert, Jane Coveney as Lady Lambert.

*

I AND MY DOUBLE// F// John Oxenford// **Victoria**, Oct. 1837, with Benjamin Wrench as Rocket, W. H. Oxberry as Puff, William Davidge as Scutcheon, John Parry as Dial, Miss E. Lee as Lydia, Miss Richardson as Miss Satanet, Mrs. Frank Matthews as Miss Brown.

I COULDN'T HELP IT// F 1a// John Oxenford// **Lyceum**, Apr. 1862.

I.O.U.; OR, THE WAY OF THE WICKED// D// J. Holmes Grover// **Elephant & Castle**, June 1879.

I'LL SEE YOU RIGHT// C// J. R. Crauford// **Gaiety**, Nov. 1882.

I'LL TELL YOUR WIFE// F 1a// N. S. Webster// **Adelphi**, Mar. 1855, with Leigh Murray, Robert Keeley, Mrs. Stoker.

I'LL WRITE TO BROWNE// F// n.a.// **Olympic**, Feb. 1859, with Lewis Ball, George Vining, Mrs. Leigh Murray.

I'LL WRITE TO THE TIMES// C 1a// J. P. Wooler// **Sad. Wells**, Oct. 1856, with Mr. Haywell as Sir Harry, William Belford as Huntly, J. W. Ray as Block, Jenny Marston as Maria, Caroline Parkes as Mrs. Huntly.

I'M NOT MYSELF AT ALL// F// C. A. Maltby// **Drury Lane**, Dec. 1869.

I'VE EATEN MY FRIEND// F 1a// John Bridgeman// **Olympic**, Sept. 1851.

I'VE WRITTEN TO BROWNE; OR, A NEEDLESS STRATAGEM// C 1a// T. J. Williams// **Olympic**, Feb. 1859, with Lewis Ball as Dotts, George Vining as Browne, Walter Gordon as Hetherington, Mrs. Leigh Murray as Mrs. Walsingham, Miss Cottrell as Laura.

ICEBOUND; OR, THE EXILES OF FORTUNE// D 4a// Frederick Cooke// **Pavilion**, July 1893.

ICI ON PARLE FRANCAIS; OR, FRENCH BEFORE BREAKFAST// F 1a// T. J. Williams// **Adelphi**, May 1859, with Charles Selby as Major Regulus, John Billington as Dubois, J. L. Toole as Mr. Spriggins, Miss Laidlaw as Angelina, Mrs. Billington as Julia, Kate Kelly as Anna/ **Globe**, Mar. 1874, with Lionel Brough as Maj. Rattan, Arthur Cecil as Victor Dubois, J. L. Toole as Spriggins, Nelly Harris as Angelina, Maria Harris as Jula, Eliza Johnstone as Anna; Jan. 1878, with Henry Westland as Rattan, Charles Collett as Dubois, J. L. Toole as Spriggins, Miss Hewitt as Mrs. Rattan, Miss Vivian as Angelina, Eliza Johnstone as Anna Maria, Isabel Clifton as Mrs. Spriggins/ **Toole's**, Jan. 1890, with J. L. Toole as Spriggins, Henry Westland as Maj. Rattan, C. M. Lowne as Dubois, Cora Poole as Mrs. Rattan, Effie Liston as Mrs. Spriggins, Irene Vanbrugh as Angelina, Eliza Johnstone as Anna.

I'LL NOT HAVE A WIFE; OR, MUTUAL OBJECTIONS// F// Charles Selby// **Sad. Wells**, June 1838, with Mr. Williams as Tweezer, John Webster as Trivet, Mr. Conquest as Wigler, Miss E. Honner as Miss Marchmont, Miss Pincott as Clipper.

IDALIA; OR, THE ADVENTURESS// D 3a// Dram. by George Roberts fr novel of Ouida// **St. James's**, Apr. 1867, with Charles Wyndham as Stoneleigh, Henry Irving as Count Falcon, F. Charles as Vane, J. D. Stoyle as Vitelle, Gaston Murray as Baron Lintz, Henry Rivers as Batz, Louisa Herbert as Idalia, Mrs. Frank Matthews as Mme. Paravent, Kate Kearney as Cerise.

IDEAL HUSBAND, AN// Play 5a// Oscar Wilde// **Haymarket**, Jan. 1895, with Alfred Bishop as Earl of Caversham, Charles Hawtrey as Lord Goring, Lewis Waller as Chiltern, Cosmo Stuart as de Nanjac, Henry Stanford as Montford, C. H. Brookfield as Phipps, Julia Neilson as Lady Chiltern, Fanny Brough as Lady Markby, Vane Featherston as Lady Basildon, Helen Forsyth as Mrs. Marchmont, Maude Millett as Mabel, Florence West as Mrs. Cheveley/ Scenery by Walter Hann & Mr. Harford.

IDIOT OF THE MOUNTAIN, THE// D 3a// Adap. by W. E. Suter fr F of Eugène Grangé & L. Thiboust// **Surrey**, Sept. 1861/ **Grecian**, Feb. 1862, with Henry Grant as Purcel, Mr. Jackson as Father Simon, Alfred Rayner as Caussade, R. H. Lingham as Paul, John Manning as Bandier, William James as Ravel, Thomas Mead as Claude, Jane Dawson as Jeanne, Mary A. Victor as Marie, Miss Johnstone as Mme. Flavel, Ellen Hale as Neomie/ Music by B. Isaacson.

IDIOT WITNESS, THE; OR, THE SOLITARY OF THE HEATH (also subt., A Tale of Blood)// D 2a// J. T. Haines// **Sad. Wells**, Aug. 1840, with Mr. Dry as Arnaud, Mr. Elvin as Robert, J. B. Hill as Gerthold, Alfred Rayner as Gilbert, Mr. Houghburt as Sussex, Mr. Williams as Tugscull, Mrs. Richard Barnett as Arlington, Miss Cooke as Dame Tugscull, Mrs. J. F. Saville as Janet.

IDLE APPRENTICE, THE; OR, THE TWO ROADS OF LIFE// D 5a// Frederick Marchant// **City of London**, June 1865/ **Grecian**, July 1865, with J. Jackson as Plainworthy, Henry Grant as Sir Barton, George Gillett as Lord Bernard, J. B. Steele as Barker, Dan Leeson as Blue Joe, Walter Holland as Rivers, Frederick Marchant as Young Idle, Marie Brewer as Mrs. Idle, Mrs. J. W. Simpson as Mrs. Plainworthy, Lizzie Mandlebert as Lilly.

IDLER, THE// Play 4a// C. Haddon Chambers// **St. James's**, Feb. 1891, with George Alexander as Cross, Herbert Waring as Sir John, John Mason as Strong, Nutcombe Gould as Gen. Merryweather, Alfred Holles as Bennett, Marion Terry as Lady Harding, Lady Monckton as Mrs. Cross, Gertrude Kingston as Mrs. Glynn-Stanmore, Maude Millett as Kate/ Scenery by Walter Hann, Walter Johnstone & Joseph Harker/ Music by Walter Slaughter.

IDOL, THE// C 3a// Adap. by Charles Wyndham fr F of Henri Meilhac & Ludovic Halèvy, La Veuve// **Folly**, Sept. 1878, with Mary Eastlake, Lionel Brough.

IDOL'S BIRTHDAY, THE// C// John Oxenford// **Olympic**, Nov. 1838, with James Vining as Lord Frippery, Robert Honner as Brag, Mr. Granby as Acid, Charles Selby as Downright, John Brougham as Crambe, W. H. Oxberry as Mark, Mrs. Nisbett as Clarinda, Mrs. Franks as Prudence, Miss Goward as Lady Snarl/ Scenery by William Telbin & Mr. Cuthbert.

IDOLS OF THE HEART// Play 1a//Janette Steer// **Grand**, June 1891/ **Criterion**,July 1892.

IDYLL OF SEVEN DIALS, AN// Rosina Filippi// **POW**, May 1899.

IDYLL OF THE CLOSING CENTURY, AN// Play 1a// Estelle Burney// **Lyceum**, Nov. 1896.

IF I HAD A THOUSAND A YEAR!// F 1a// J. Maddison Morton// **Olympic**, Oct. 1867 (in 2a), with C. J. Mathews as Green, Horace Wigan as Chaffington, Henry Farrell as Chesterton, Mrs. St. Henry as Mrs. Green, Louisa Moore as Julia.

IF THE CAP FITS// C 1a// N. H. Harrington & Edmund Yates// **Princess's**, June 1859, with Walter Lacy as Capt. Lynch, George Everett as Lt. Dalrymple, Frank Matthews as Dr. Flapperton, Ellen Terry as Tom, Mr. Daly as Jacob, Miss Murray as Mrs. Ellerton, Eleanor Bufton as Merton, Miss J. Lovell as Sally.

ILLUSION// Play 3a// Pierre Leclercq// **Strand**, July 1890, with W. H. Vernon as Lullworth, Fuller Mellish as Slawson, Lawrance d'Orsay as Earl of Bramber, Ivan Watson as Count de Buci, Henry Arncliffe as Joseph Revellin, Fred Grove as Arterberry, Cecil Ramsey as Bob, Lewis Waller as John Revellin, Rose Leclercq as Blanche, Florence Bright as Matilda, Marion Lea as Una.

ILLUSTRIOUS STRANGER, THE; OR, MARRIED AND BURIED// F 1a// J. Kenney & J. Millingen// **Drury Lane**, Nov. 1838, with Mr. Baker as Aboulifar, Mr. Franks as Arzan, Mr. Hughes as Alibajou, A. Brindal as Gimbo, Henry Compton as Bowbell, Miss Somerville as Irza, Miss Fitzwalter as Fatima/ **Sad. Wells**, Oct. 1839, with Mr. Aldridge as Aboulifar, Mr. Elvin as Azan, W. D. Broadfoot as Alibajou, Henry Hall as Bowbell, Mrs. J. F. Saville as Izra, Miss Pincott as Fatima/ **Victoria**, Sept. 1854, with Alfred Saville as Aboulifar, W. H. Pitt as Prince Azan, Charles Rice as Bowbell, James Howard as Gimbo/ **St. James's**, with Mr. Sidney as Aboulifar, Mr. Halford as Azae, Mr. Hollingsworth as Alibajou, John Pritt Harley as Bowbell, John Gardner as Gimbo, Miss C. Crisp as Irza, Priscilla Horton as Fatima/ **Grecian**, Apr. 1844, with John Collett as Aboulifar, Edwin Dixon as Alibajou, Edmund Garden as Gimbo, Frederick Robson as Benjamin Bowbell, Marian Taylor as Irza, Annette Mears as Fatima/ **Adelphi**, Nov. 1880, with H. Proctor as King Aboulifar, E. B. Norman as Azan, Harwood Cooper as Alibajon, J. G. Taylor as Bowbell, Robert Pateman as Gimbo, Clara Jecks as Fatima, Miss Vane as Irza.

IMPEACHED// D// Miss H. L. Walford// **Gal. of Illust.**, May 1873.

IMPERIAL GUARD, THE// D// C. H. Hazlewood// **Britannia**, Sept. 1872.

IMPORTANCE OF BEING EARNEST, THE// C 3a// Oscar Wilde// **St. James's**, Feb. 1895, with George Alexander as Jack, Allan Aynesworth as Algernon, H. H. Vincent as Rev. Chasuble, Frank Dyall as Merriman, F. Kinsey Peile as Lane, Rose Leclercq as Lady Bracknell, Irene Vanbrugh as Gwendolen, Violet Lyster as Cicely, Mrs. George Canninge as Miss Prism/ Scenery by H. P. Hall & Walter Hann/ **Coronet**, Dec. 1901.

IMPRUDENCE// C 3a// Arthur Wing Pinero// **Folly**, July 1881.

IMPUDENT PUPPY, AN// C 2a// L. S. Buckingham// **Drury Lane**, Nov. 1855, with C. J. Mathews as Nimble, C. Vincent as Paragon, A. Younge as Maj. Firebrace, C. Swan as Sir Felix, James Worrell as Dobbs, Miss Talbot as Lady Olivia, Fanny Hughes as Emma, Miss De Vere as Mrs. Dobbs, Emma Wadham as Maria.

IMPULSE// Play 5a// Adap. by B. C. Stephenson fr F, La Maison du Mari// **St. James's**, Dec. 1882, with Mrs. W. H. Kendal as Mrs. Beresford, Linda Dietz as Mrs. Macdonald, Mrs. Gaston Murray as Miss Kilmore, Miss Cowle as Mrs. Birkett, Mr. Beaumont as Sir Henry, T. N. Wenman as Col. Macdonald, Arthur Dacre as de Riel, Mr. Brandon as Graham/ Scenery by W. Harford.

IN A DAY// D 3a// Augusta Webster// **Terry's**, May 1890.

IN A FOG// C// F. Kinsey Peile// **POW**, Jan. 1901.

IN A LOCKET// Play 3a// Harry & Edward Paulton// **Strand**, Sept. 1895, with Clinton Baddeley as Gen. Greville, Harold Child as Garnet Greville, Laurence Cautley as Mallock, W. Scott Buist as Bonner, Frank Wood as Marler, James Welch as Comyns, Harry Paulton as Simpkin, Annie Hill as Judith, Gladys Evelyn as Elaine, Julia Warden as Susan, Amy Elstob as Marian, Alice de Winton as Cicely/ Scenery by E. G. Banks.

IN A WOMAN'S GRIP// D 4a// Fred Melville// **Standard**, Oct. 1901.

IN AN ATTIC// C 1a// Wilton Jones// **St. James's**, Mar. 1895/ **Trafalgar**, July 1895.

IN AND OUT OF PLACE// F// Julia Daly// **Princess's**, Mar. 1872, with Frederick Moreland as Etiquette, Fred Hughes as Clod, Julia Daly in 6 character parts.

IN AND OUT OF SERVICE// C// J. T. Douglass// **Standard**, Oct. 1869.

IN BLACK AND WHITE// D 4a// E. C. Bertrand// **Pavilion**, Sept. 1880.

IN CHANCERY// C 3a// Arthur Wing Pinero// **Gaiety**, Dec. 1884/ **Terry's**, Nov. 1890.

IN DANGER// D 3a// W. Lestocq & Henry Creswell// **Vaudeville**, Nov. 1887.

IN DAYS OF OLD// D 4a// Edward Rose// **St. James's**, Apr. 1899, with F. Rawson Buckley as Henry VI, H. B. Irving as Sir Ulick, Kenneth Douglas as Odo, George Alexander as Beddart, Basset Roe as Sir Piers, Arthur Royston as Earl of Wynnesley, Sidney Brough as Lord Harry, Alexander Calvert as de Sproughton, H. V. Esmond as Haygarth, H. H. Vincent as Old Stokes, Violet Vanbrugh as Margaret of Anjou, Esmé Beringer as Lady Agatha, Kate Sergeantson as Lady Eve, Fay Davis as Lilian/ Scenery by William Telbin/ Music by William Robins/ Machines by Mr. Cullen/ Electrics by Mr. Barbour.

IN DUTY BOUND// D 4a// J. Mortimer Murdoch// **Pavilion**, Aug. 1878/ **Sadler's Wells**, Aug. 1882.

IN FACE OF THE FOE// D 4a// n.a.// **Marylebone**, July 1892.

IN FETTERS// Play 1a// J. P. Hurst// **Strand**, Nov. 1885.

IN FOR A DIG; OR, LIFE IN THE DIGGINGS// D 1a// Hugo Vamp// **Astley's**, Apr. 1853, with J. W. Anson as Gustavus, Dominick Murray as Josephus, Harry Munro as Charles, Mrs. Anson as Peggy, Mrs. George Lee as Clementina, Mrs. Simpson as Letitia, Mrs. Dowton as Mrs. Bagshaw.

IN HIS POWER// D 3a// Mark Quinton// **Olympic**, Jan. 1885, with Kyrle Bellew as Graham, J. G. Grahame as Dr. Cameron, Edward Rose as Walker, Mark Quinton as René, Charles Cartwright as Scara, Lizzie Claremont as Mrs. Walker, Ada Cavendish as Marie.

IN HONOUR BOUND// C 1a// Loosely adap. by Sidney Grundy fr F of Eugène Scribe, Une Chaine// **POW**, Sept. 1880.

IN LIFE OR DEATH// D 4a// Adap. by E. A. Elton fr novel of Charles Gibbon, For the King// **Olympic**, Mar. 1885, with Charles Glenney as Sir Robert, J. R. Crauford as Col. Bland, Arthur Wood as Dr. Brodie, Walter Everard as Capt. Lisle, F. A. Peton as Earl of Killairn, Stephen Caffrey as Sgt. O'Brien, J. B. Ashley as Gen. Hope, Adeline Montague as Florence, Bella Pateman as Lady Eleanore.

IN LOVE// C 1a// n.a.// **Terry's**, May 1890, with Edward Lennox as Falcon, Fred Tyrrell as Capt. Findlay, Henry Belding as Dr. Barton, Irene Rickards as Amabel, Lena Greville as Bessie.

IN MARY'S COTTAGE// Play 1a// Charles Beckwith// **Terry's**, Dec. 1896, with Sydney Brough as Grantley, Charles Terric as Bassett, Mrs. Campbell Bradley as Mrs. Purritt, Dora Barton as Jane.

IN OLD KENTUCKY// D 4a// Adap. by Montague Turner fr Amer. orig. of C. T. Dazey// **Pavilion**, June 1898/ **Princess's**, Nov. 1899, with Frank Lacy as Harley, Alfred Bankes as Col. Beauchamp, William Clayton as Lindsay, Clarence Hague as Lorey, Maude Grendon as Cloe, Lena Flowerdew as Barbara, Cicely Richards as Alethea, Lileth Leyton as Madge.

IN OLDEN DAYS// C 1a// Agatha & Archibald Hodgson// **Vaudeville**, June 1890.

IN POSSESSION// F 1a// Martin Becher// **Drury Lane**, Dec. 1871.

IN SIGHT OF ST. PAUL'S// D 5a// Sutton Vane// **Princess's**, Aug. 1896, with Story Gofton as Chichester, Ernest Leicester as Tom, George Hippisley as Harry, Austin Melford as Gridston, Walter Howard as Burnsides, Lyston Lyle as Fletcher, Miss Keith Wakeman as Cynthia, Alice Yorke as Beatrice, Flora Wills as Countess Fellstar, Mary Bates as Mrs. March, Lily Gordon as Lady Snow, Sydney Fairbrother as Gracie, Kate Tyndall as Aileen/ Scenery by Conrad Trischler, Cecil Hicks & J. Johnstone.

IN SPITE OF ALL// Play 3a// Edna Lyall// **Comedy**, Feb. 1900.

IN SPITE OF SOCIETY// Play 1a// Charles Dickenson // **Duke of York's**, Nov. 1898, with Gerald Lawrence as Fraser, F. J. Nettlefold as Winstanley, Arthur Burne as Rev. White, May Warley as Cora, Vane Featherston as Lady Duncan.

IN STRICT CONFIDENCE// C 1a// Paul Heriot// **Comedy**, Oct. 1893, with W. T. Lovell as Bittersweet, J. Byron as Edgways, Lena Ashwell as Amelia.

IN THE CAUSE OF CHARITY// C 1a// Leo Trevor// **St. Geo. Hall**, Feb. 1900.

IN THE CORRIDOR// C 1a// Rudolph Dircks// **Court**, May 1889.

IN THE DAYS OF THE DUKE// D Pro & 4a// C. Haddon Chambers & J. Comyns Carr// **Adelphi**, Sept. 1897, with William Terriss as Col. Aylmer, Charles Cartwright as Capt. Lanson, Henry Vibart as Capt. Maine, J. D. Beveridge as O'Hara, Harry Nicholls as Sgt. Blunder, Charles Fulton as Col. Wellesley, Marion Terry as Mrs. Aylmer, Eily Desmond as Mrs. Maine, Miss Millward as Dorothy Maine, Millicent Barr as Mrs. Clinton, Miss Vane Featherston as Mrs. Blunder/ Scenery by William Harford & Joseph Harker/ Music by John Crook/ Prod. by Fred Latham.

IN THE EYES OF THE WORLD// Play 1a// A. C. Wood// **Globe**, Mar. 1894, with H. Reeves Smith as Carlton, Harry Farmer as Lord Wilfred, Cecil Thornbury as Parr, E. H. Wynne as Wilks, Mabel Lane as Lady Mabel.

IN THE GOLDEN DAYS// Play 4a// Adap. by Edwin Gilbert fr novel of Edna Lyall// **St. Geo. Hall**, June 1897.

IN THE MOONLIGHT// D 4a// Rev. by Mark Melford fr his Nightingale// **Surrey**, Oct. 1893.

IN THE OLD TIME// Play 4a// Walter Frith// **St. James's**, May. 1888.

IN THE ORCHARD// C 1a// G. R. Walker// **Folly**, Feb. 1880.

IN THE QUEEN'S NAME// D Pro & 3a// William Trevor & John Delille// **Sadler's Wells**, Dec. 1890.

IN THE RANKS// D 5a// G. R. Sims & Henry Pettitt// **Adelphi**, Oct. 1883, with Charles Warner as Ned Drayton, John Ryder as Col. Wynter, J. D. Beveridge as Gideon, W. Herbert as Capt. Holcroft, J. G. Shore as Herrick, E. W. Garden as Joe, Isabel Bateman as Ruth, Mary Rorke as Barbara, Harriet Coveney as Mrs. Timmins, Maggie Watson as Polly/ Scenery by Walter Hann, Thomas Hall, & Bruce Smith/ Music by Henry Sprake/ Prod. by Charles Harris/ **Princess's**, May 1900, with Charles Warner as Drayton, C. H. Hewetson as Blake, Alfred Harding as Col. Wynter, Randolph Read as Capt. Holcroft, Christopher Walker as Herrick, James Chippendale as Buzzard, Ernest Owttrimm as Belton, Ethel Gerard as Barbara, Mrs. Henry Leigh as Mrs. Buzzard, Mrs. Lyons as Mrs. Timmins, Ida Thompson as Polly, Grace Warner as Ruth.

IN THE SEASON// Play 1a// Langdon Mitchell// **Strand**, Feb. 1895, with Herbert Waring as Sir Harry, Arthur Roylston as Fairburne, Miss Elliott Page as Sybil.

IN THE SHADOW OF NIGHT// D 4a// James Willard// **Britannia**, Dec. 1898.

IN THE SOUP// FC 3a// Ralph Lumley// **Strand**, Aug. 1900.

IN THREE VOLUMES// F 1a// Taylor Bilkins// **Strand**, Feb. 1871.

IN THREE VOLUMES// C 1a// Arthur Law// **POW**, Jan. 1893, with Philip Cunningham as Lobb, Day Ford as Kate, Jessie Moore as Mrs. Tyrrell.

IN TWO MINDS// Play 1a// Arthur Heathcote// **Garrick**, June 1894, with Annie Webster as Lady Margaret, Agnes Hill as Parkins.

INCENDIARIES, THE// D// n.a.// **Britannia**, Aug. 1859.

INCHAVOGUE// D 4a// W. B. Cahill// **East London**, Apr. 1873.

INCHCAPE BELL, THE; OR, THE DUMB SAILOR BOY OF THE ROCKS// D// Edward Fitzball// **Sad. Wells**, Apr. 1837, with Mr. King as Sir John, C. J. Smith as Taffrail, Mr. Campbell as Hattock, N. T. Hicks as Ruthven, Mrs. Worrell as The Dumb Boy, Miss Lebatt as Amelia/ **Victoria**, May 1838, with William Davidge as Sir John, Charles Montague as Capt. Taffrail, Mr. Maddocks as Hattock, Mr. King as Ruthven, H. Lewis as the Dumb Boy, John Parry as Seabreeze, Miss Williamson as Amelia, Mrs. Loveday as Mrs. Tapps, Mrs. Vale as Becky.

INCOGNITO// Play 3a// Hamilton Aïdé// **Haymarket**, Jan. 1888.

INCONSTANT, THE; OR, THE WAY TO WIN HIM// C 5a// George Farquhar// **Haymarket**, Sept. 1856, with W. H. Chippendale as Old Mirabel, James Murdoch as Young Mirabel, William Farren as Duretete, Edwin Villiers as Dugard, Mr. Clark as Petit, Mrs. Edward Fitzwilliam as Orinia, Miss Talbot as Bisarre, Miss Coe as Lamerce.

INDIA IN 1857// D// n.a.// **Surrey**, Nov. 1857.

INDIAN GIRL, THE// D 2a// n.a.// **Drury Lane**, Oct. 1837, with Mr. Cooper as Maj. Goffe, H. Cooke as Capt. Bradford, Mr. King as Reuben, J. S. Balls as Cloudesley, R. McIan as Conanchet, Mlle. [sic] Celeste as Narramattah, Mrs. Ternan as Rose/ Scenery by Grieve, T. Grieve & W. Grieve/ Music by Mr. Eliason.

INDIAN QUEEN, THE; OR, A HOME IN THE MOUNTAINS// D 5a// Matthew Wardhaugh// **Victoria**, Dec. 1877.

INDUSTRY AND INDOLENCE; OR, THE ORPHAN'S LEGACY// D 3a// Dram. by Edward Stirling fr F// **Adelphi**, Apr. 1846, with Charles Perkins as M. Delamare, Henry Howe as Etienne, Charles Selby as Marcel, Edward Wright as Sansonet, Paul Bedford as St. Amour, George Braid as Francois, O. Smith as Rollin, Sarah Woolgar as Batifole, Ellen Chaplin as Agathe, Mme. Celeste as Cecile.

INFANTICIDE; OR, THE PRECIPICE OF BRISSAC// D// J . M. Maddox// **Victoria**, May 1850, with Mr. Henderson as de Francheville, John Bradshaw as St. Mars, J. T. Johnson as Picard, J. Neville as Father Lambert, James

Howard as Slap, Mrs. George Lee as Mme. Catherine, Annette Vincent as Louise, Miss Barrowcliffe as Marianne, Miss Mildenhall as Annette/ Scenery by Mr. Mildenhall/ Music by Mr. Barrowcliffe.

INFATUATION// D 4a// Adap. by Charles Young fr F of M. Dinot & Ernest Legouvé// **Haymarket**, May 1879.

INFATUATION; A TALE OF THE FRENCH EMPIRE// D 5a// James Kenney// **Princess's**, May 1845, with Henry Wallack as Duke de Bracciano, Mr. Hield as Col. St. Ange, Walter Lacy as Gobert, Leigh Murray as Lindorff, James Wallack as Laroche, Mr. Granby as Dauphin, James Ranoe as Glapisson, Charlotte Cushman as Duchess de Bracciano, Mrs. Brougham as Countess de Chateau-Vieux, Miss E. Honner as Justine/ Scenery by William Beverley, Mr. Nichols & Mr. Aglio.

INGOMAR THE BARBARIAN; OR, THE SON OF THE WILDERNESS// D 5a// Aadp. by Maria Lovell fr G// **Drury Lane**, June 1851, with J. Neville as Timark, J. W. Ray as Polydor, Mr. Cooper as Myron, S. Jones as Amyntas, G. Watson as Elpenor, Mr. Williams as Neocles, Mr. Barrett as Lyron, James Anderson as Ingomar, H. T. Craven as Alastor, Mr. Manley as Trinobantes, W. West as Ambivar, Mrs. Weston as Actea, Mrs. Barrett as Theano, Miss Vandenhoff as Parthenia/ **Sad. Wells**, Oct. 1851 (as Ingomar), with Henry Mellon as Timarch, J. W. Ray as Polydor, George Bennett as Myron, Mr. Barrett as Lykon, Samuel Phelps as Ingomar, Frank Graham as Alastor, Charles Fenton as Trinobantes, Charles Wheatleigh as Novio, Mrs. Henry Marston as Actea, Fanny Vining as Parthenia, Mrs. Graham as Theano/ Scenery by A. Finley; June 1854, with E. L. Davenport as Ingomar, Fanny Vining as Parthenia; Dec. 1867, with R. Norman as Myron, Harry Chester as Ploydor, Mr. Lawrence as Elphenor, J. H. White as Amyntos and Trinobantes, George Fisher as Lykon, Alice Marriott as Parthenia, Mrs. Walton as Actea, Miss Fitzgerald as Theano, Henry Loraine as Ingomar, Mr. Hamilton as Alastor, Walter Lacy as Ambivar/ **Victoria**, June 1857, with Alfred Saville as Polydor, Henry Dudley as Myron, S. Sawford as Timarch, Mr. Henderson as Elphenor, James Howard as Lykon, Sarah Thorne as Parthenia, Mrs. Wallis as Actea, Charles Pitt as Ingomar, Frederick Byefield as Alaster, George Pearce as Ambivor/ **Lyceum**, Sept. 1883, with J. H. Barnes as Ingomar, J. A. Rosier as Alastor, Joseph Anderson as Ambivar, J. G. Taylor as Polydor, W. H. Stephens as Myron, Mrs. Arthur Stirling as Actea, Mary Anderson as Parthenia/ Scenery by Hawes Craven, E. Ryan, Spong & Perkins/ Music by Andrew Levey/ Prod. by W. H. Vernon.

INGULPH// D 1a// Edgar Newbound// **Britannia**, Dec. 1879.

INHERITANCE, THE// Play 3a// Cecil Raleigh// **Comedy**, May 1889.

INJURED INNOCENCE// F 1a// George Conquest// **Grecian**, July 1861, with Mr. Jackson as Heartall, George Conquest as Traddles, Henry Grant as Snapanarley, Mr. Costello as Splutter, Henry Power as Galpin, Ellen Hale as Celina.

INNISFALLEN; OR, THE MAN IN THE GAP// D 3a// Edmund Falconer// **Lyceum**, Sept. 1870.

INNKEEPER OF ABBYVILLE, THE// D 2a// Edward Fitzball// **Victoria**, Oct. 1854, with F. H. Henry as Marquis Romane, E. F. Saville as Idenberg, Mr. Morrison as Voilaire, Alfred Saville as Clausen, N. T. Hicks as Ozzrand, W. H. Pitt as Dyrkile, Charles Rice as Zyrtille, Miss Dansor as Lady Emma,, Mrs. Henry Vining as Louise.

INNKEEPER'S DAUGHTER, THE; OR, MARY THE MAID OF THE INN (also subt. The Bough of Yew)// D 2a// George Soane// **Sad. Wells**, Aug. 1838, with Mr. Williams as Langley, Mr. Dry as Monkton, W. D. Broadfoot as Frankland, Dibdin Pitt as Harrop, John Webster as Richard, J. W. Collier as Tricksey, Robert Honner as Ketzlar, Mr. Mellor as Wentworth, C. Montague as William, Mrs. Robert Honner as Mary, Miss Cooke as Marian/ **Victoria**, Apr. 1842, with William James as Langley, William Seaman as Monkton, John Dale as Harrop, Mr. Griffith as Frankland, Mr. Franklin as Edward, E. F. Saville as Richard, Robert Honner as Ketzler, C. Williams as William, Mr. Howard as Tricksey, Mrs. Robert Honner as Mary, Mrs. Griffith as Marian/ **Drury Lane**, Feb. 1851.

INNOCENT; OR, LIFE IN DEATH// D Pro & 4a// Murray Wood// **Surrey**, Apr. 1873.

INNOCENT ABROAD, AN// F 3a// W. Stokes Craven// **Terry's**, Jan. 1895, with Edward Terry as Pilkington, Leslie Kenyon as Dick, Harcourt Beatty as Summerville, Jack Thompson as Dr. Hanson, Ernest Hendrie as Bouncer, George Belmore as Dennis, Robert Soutar as Knowles, Kate Mills as Mrs. Pilkington, Eily Desmond as Lilly, Madge McIntosh as Cissy, Jessie Danvers as Rose/ Scenery by Bruce Smith & Mr. Story & Mr. Warren.

INTEMPERANCE; OR, A DRUNKARD'S SIN// D 4a// Fred Hazleton// **Elephant & Castle**, July 1879.

INTERLUDE, AN// Play 1a// Mrs. W. K. Clifford & Walter Pollock// **Terry's**, June 1893, with Herbert Waring as Lord Vereker, Janet Achurch as Miss Renton.

INTERRUPTED HONEYMOON, AN// C 3a// F. Kinsey Peile// **Avenue**, Sept. 1899, with Arthur Holmes-Gore as Sir Charles, Sam Sothern as Benyon, Arthur Elwood as Gordon, Gerald de Maurier as Trevor, Sarah Brooke as Violet, Mrs. George Canninge as Rachel, Bella Pateman as Georgina, Clara Denman as Agatha, Charlotte Granville as Mrs. Gordon/ Scenery by E. G. Banks.

INTERVIEW, THE// C // T. G. Warren// **Garrick**, Nov. 1895.

INTRIGUE; OR, THE WOLF AND THE FOX

(also subt., The Bath Road)// F 1a// John Poole// **Sad. Wells**, Apr. 1837, with N. T. Hicks as Capt. Rambleton, C. H. Pitt as Varnish, Mr. Rogers as Tom, Lavinia Melville as Ellen; Oct. 1844, with Henry Marston as Varnish, E. Morton as Capt. Rambleton, Mr. Coreno as Tom, Miss Lebatt as Ellen/ **Victoria**, July 1848, with T. H. Higgie as Rambleton, Mr. Henderson as Varnish, G. F. Forman as Tom, Miss Burroughcliffe as Ellen.

INTRUDER, THE// D 1a// Adap. fr F of Maurice Maeterlinck// **Haymarket**, Jan. 1892, with Herbert Beerbohm Tree as Grandfather, James Fernandez as Uncle, F. H. Macklin as Father, Mrs. Beerbohm Tree as 1st Daughter, Blanche Horlock as 2nd Daughter, Miss Thompson as 3rd Daughter.

INUNDATION, THE; OR, THE MISER OF THE HILL FORT// D 3a// Thomas Archer// **City of London**, Apr. 1847.

INVINCIBLES, THE// C// Thomas Morton// **Cov. Garden**, Feb. 1839, with Robert Strickland as Gen. Verdun, Mr. Tilbury as Dorval, Mr. Manvers as Capt. Florville, George Bartley as Brusque, Thomas Lee as O'Slash, Mr. Meadows as Tactique, Mr. Roberts as Frivole, Miss P. Horton as Juliette, Miss Charles as Victoire.

INVISIBLE WITNESS, THE; OR, THE GAMESTER'S DOOM// D 3a// T. J. Dibdin// **Sad. Wells**, July 1839, with Mr. Dry as Chev. Bonval, J. Webster as Albert, Mr. Cathcart as Venoni, Mr. Elvin as Armand, Mr. Phillips as Michelin, Mr. Aldridge as Jerome, Mr. Stilt as Brigadier, Miss Richardson as Ernestine, Miss Hicks as Amelia, Miss Cooke as Magdalen/ Scenery by F. Fenton & G. Smithyes Jr./ Music by Mr. Herbert/ Machines by B. Sloman.

IOLANTHE// Play 1a// Dram. by W. G. Wills fr poem of Henrik Herz, King René's Daughter// **Lyceum**, May 1880, with Henry Irving as Count Tristan, J. H. Barnes as King René, F. Cooper as Sir Goeffrey, Norman Forbes as Sir Almeric, Thomas Mead as Edn Jahia, Georgina Pauncefort as Martha, Ellen Terry as Iolanthe.

ION// T// Serjeant Talfourd// **Cov. Garden**, Apr. 1837, with Mr. Vandenhoff as Adrastus, John Webster as Ctesiphon, James Worrell as Cassander, W. C. Macready as Ion, Mr. Thompson as Medon, George Bennett as Phocion, John Pritchard as Agenor, Mr. Tilbury as Cleon, Mr. Harris as Timocles, Helen Faucit as Clemanthe/ **Haymarket**, June 1837, with W. C. Macready as Ion, Mr. Elton as Adrastus, Frederick Vining as Ctestiphon, Mr. Saville as Cassander, Charles Selby as Medon, John Webster as Phocion, Miss E. Phillips as Irus, Miss Allison as Clemanthe; Sept. 1839, with Ellen Tree as Ion, Mr. Cooper as Adrastus, Walter Lacy as Ctesiphon, Mr. Hemming as Cassander, James Worrell as Medon, Samuel Phelps as Phocion, Mrs. Walter Lacy (Miss Taylor) as Clemanthe, Miss Partridge as Abra; Feb. 1846, with Mr. Stuart as Adrastus, Charlotte Cushman as Ion, Charles Hudson as Ctesiphon, A. Brindal as Cassander, James Worrell as Medon, Henry Holl as Phocion, Charles Perkins as Agenor, J. W. Gough as Cleon, James Bland as Timocles, Miss Telbin as Irus, Susan Cushman as Clementhe, Miss A. Woulds as Abra/ Scenery by George Morris/ **Surrey**, Nov. 1846, with Charlotte & Susan Cushman/ **Sad. Wells**, Dec. 1846, with Samuel Phelps as Adrastus, William Creswick as Ion, Henry Mellon as Agenor, Frank Graham as Medea, Edward Knight as Cleon, Mr. Stilt as Timocles, William Hoskins as Ctesiphon, E. Morton as Phocion, Mr. Branson as Cassander, Miss Cooper as Clemanthe/ **Drury Lane**, Feb. 1850.

IRELAND AS IT IS; OR, THE MIDDLEMAN// D 3a// J. H. Amherst// **Adelphi**, Aug. 1856, with Barney Williams as Pat, Edmund Garden as Dan, John Parsello as Neil, Mr. Moreland as Conor, J. G. Shore as Mons. Voyage, James Bland as Magistrate, Charles Selby as Stone, Mrs. Barney Williams as Judy, Kate Kelly as Florence.

IRELAND AS IT WAS; OR, THE MIDDLEMAN// D 3a// J. H. Amherst// **Sad. Wells**, July 1858, with Barney Williams as Pat, John Vollaire as O'Carolan, Henry Sinclair as Neil, Alfred Tapping as O'Flaherty, Walter Vernon as Voyage, James Bland as Magistrate, C. J. Smith as Slang, Bruce Norton as Stone, Mrs. Barney Williams as Judy, Kate Kelly as Honor, Miss Ferguson as Florence/ **Standard**, Apr. 1859, with Mr. & Mrs. Barney Williams.

IRIS// D 5a// Arthur Wing Pinero// **Garrick**, Sept. 1901.

IRISH AMBASSADOR, THE// C 2a// James Kenney// **Haymarket**, Aug. 1837, with J. T. Haines as Grand Duke, Charles Selby as Prince Rodolph, Robert Strickland as Count Morenos, T. F. Mathews as Baron Lowincraft, Tyrone Power as Sir Patrick, Mrs. Nisbett as Lady Emily, Miss Taylor as Isabella; Sept. 1854, with William Cullenford as Grand Duke, Henry Howe as Prince Rudolph, W. H. Chippendale as Count Morenos, Mr. Rogers as Baron Lowencraft, Charles Hudson as Sir Patrick, George Braid as Olmutz, Mrs. L. S. Buckingham as Lady Emily, Miss Reynolds as Isabella/ **Cov. Garden**, Jan. 1838, with Tyrone Power as Sir Patrick, Charles Diddear as Grand Duke, James Anderson as Prince Rodolphe, George Bartley as Count Morenos, Robert Strickland as Baron Lowencraft, John Ayliffe as Olmutz, Ellen Clifford as Lady Emily, Miss Taylor as Isabella/ **Princess's**, Aug. 1845, with Mr. Archer as Grand Duke, Leigh Murray as Prince Rodolph, Mr. Granby as Count Morenos, James Ranoe as Baron Lowencroft, Mr. Collins as Sir Patrick, Mrs. Brougham as Lady Emily, Emma Stanley as Isabella.

IRISH ASSURANCE AND YANKEE MODESTY// C 2a// Mrs. Barney Williams// **Adelphi**, Aug. 1856, with Barney Williams as Pat, Edmund Garden as Buffer, J. G. Shore as Charles, Charles Selby as Clifton, Mrs. Barney Williams as Nancy, Mary Keeley as Susan.

IRISH ATTORNEY, THE; OR, GALWAY

PRACTICE IN 1770// F 2a// W. Bayle Bernard// **Haymarket**, May 1840, with Tyrone Power as O'Hara, J. W. Gough as Wylie, W. H. Oxberry as Hawk, Mr. Clark as Saunders, James Worrell as Charlcote, Eliza Travers as Miss Charlcote, Miss Mattley as Sally/ **Sad. Wells**, June 1854, with Mr. Barrington as O'Hara, G. Harrison as Hawk, Mr. Barrett as Wylie, James Worrell as Charlcote, A. Judd as Saunders, Samuel Perfitt as Fielding, Lizzie Mandelbert as Miss Charlcote, Julia Lavine as Sally.

IRISH DOCTOR, THE; OR, THE DUMB LADY CURED// F 1a// Adap. by G. Wood fr F of Molière, Le Medecin Malgre Lui// **Queen's**, Nov. 1844.

IRISH EMIGRANT, THE// D 2a// John Brougham// **Princess's**, Feb. 1862, with W. J. Florence as O'Bryan, Basil Potter as Bobolink, Robert Cathcart as Travers, John Collett as Granite, Mr. Raymond as Sterling, Rose Leclercq as Polly, Marie Henderson as Mary, Mrs. Weston as Mrs. Grimgriskin/ **Sad. Wells**, Nov. 1864, with Charles Horsman as Bobolink, Gardiner Coyne as O'Brien, W. S. Foote as Travers, William Artaud as Sterling, T. B. Bennett as Granite, Mrs. Charles Horsman as Polly, Mrs. Stevenson as Mrs. Grimgriskin, Ellen Beaufort as Mary.

IRISH EMIGRANT, THE; OR, THE HEART OF A SON OF OLD ERIN// D 2a// n.a.// **Victoria**, May 1854, with T. E. Mills as Michael Connell, Alfred Saville as Pierce Connell, George Hodson as O'Brien, James Howard as Hunkstone, Mr. Henderson as Stranger, Mr. Morrison as Dorgan, Mrs. Henry Vining as Winifred, Miss Laporte as Biddy, Phoebe Johnson as Edith.

IRISH FOOTMAN, THE; OR, TWO TO ONE// F// Arthur Clements// **Sad. Wells**, Dec. 1872.

IRISH GENTLEMAN, AN// Play 3a// D. C. Murray & J. L. Shine// **Globe**, June 1897, with J. L. Shine as Dorsay, H. Reeves Smith as Dillon, J. B. Gordon as MacQuarrie, Richard Purdon as Kelly, T. Kingston as Lord Avon, J. L. MacKay as Doyle, Howard Russell as Horsley, Eva Moore as Ellaleen, Mrs. George Canninge as Mrs. Dunrayne, Lilian Menelly as Constance, Kate Kearney as Katty.

IRISH HEIRESS, THE// C 5a// Dion Boucicault// **Cov. Garden**, Feb. 1842, with William Farren as Lord William, George Vandenhoff as Sir William, C. J. Mathews as Ardent, John Pritt Harley as Maj. Fuss, Mr. Cooper as Supple, Alfred Wigan as Lenoir, Louisa Nisbett as Lady Daventry, Mrs. Orger as Mrs. Comfort, Mme. Vestris as Miss Merrion/ Scenery by Grieve, T. Grieve & W. Grieve.

IRISH HERCULES, THE KING OF CLUBS, THE// F 1a// n.a.// **Grecian**, Dec. 1845, with Harry Chester as Capt. Darling, John Collett as Granite, Mr. Campbell as Fuzby, George Hodson as Tim, Frederick Robson as Tommy, Mrs. W. Watson as Mrs. Ramsbottom, Miss M. A. Crisp as Lavinia.

IRISH HEIRESS, THE// C 5a// Dion Boucicault// **Cov. Garden**, Feb. 1842.

IRISH LIFE// D 4a// Auguste Creamer & L. Downey// **Sadler's Wells**, Nov. 1890.

IRISH LION, THE// F 1a// J. B. Buckstone// **Haymarket**, June 1838, with Robert Strickland as Squabbs, J. W. Gough as Puffy, Mr. Hutchings as Wadd, Tyrone Power as More, James Worrell as Capt. Dixon, Mr. Kerridge as Slim, Mr. Green as Yawkins, T. F. Mathews as Long, Mrs. Fitzwilliam as Mrs. Fitzgig, Mrs. Gallot as Mrs. Crummy, Miss Beresford as Miss Echo/ **Sad. Wells**, Mar. 1842, with John Brougham as Moore, Mr. Williams as Squabbs, Mr. Aldridge as Puffy, Mr. Archer as Wadd, E. Morton as Capt. Dixon, Mrs. Brougham as Cerulea, Miss Cooke as Mrs. Crummy, Mrs. Morgan as Miss Echo.

IRISH POST, THE// C 2a// J. R. Planché// **Haymarket**, Mar. 1846, with James Bland as Capiscomb, Mr. Tilbury as Lane, Mr. Carle as George, Charles Hudson as O'Grady, Mrs. L. S. Buckingham as Mrs. Capiscomb, Miss Woulds as Mary, Mrs. Humby as Mrs. Lump/ **Adelphi**, May 1849, with Mr. Lambert as Bartholomew Lane, James Worrell as George Lane, Charles Hudson as his nephew, William Cullenford as the Sheriff, Mrs. Frank Matthews as Mrs. Lump, Emma Harding as Mrs. Capsicomb.

IRISH TIGER, THE// F 1a// J. Maddison Morton// **Haymarket**, Apr. 1846.

IRISH TUTOR, THE; OR, THE NEW LIGHTS// C 1a// Adap. by Richard Butler fr F// **Cov. Garden**, Apr. 1837, with Mr. Tilbury as Flail, John Webster as Charles, Mr. Thompson as Tillwell, Mr. Macarthy as O'Rourke, Miss Lee as Rosa, Miss Nicholson as Mary/ **Haymarket**, July 1837, with Mr. Daly as O'Toole, Robert Strickland as Flail, John Webster as Charles, J. W. Gough as Tilwell, Miss E. Phillips as Rosa, Miss Wrighten as Mary/ **Sad. Wells**, Oct. 1837, with Thomas Lee as O'Rourke, C. H. Pitt as Charles, Mr. Ennis as Tilden, Mr. Scarbrow as Beadle, Lavinia Melville as Mary, Miss Vernon as Rose; June 1855, with Mr. Barrett as O'Toole, Mr. Lacey as Tilwell, George Fisher as Dr. Flail, Mr. Kelsy as Charles, Miss Lamb as Rosa, Miss Lavine as Mary/ **Olympic**, Oct. 1848, with Charles Bender as Tilwell, William Norton as Charles, H. J. Turner as Flail, Redmond Ryan as Dr. O'Toole, Josephine St. George as Rosa, Mrs. C. A. Tellet as Mary; Sept. 1866, with Master Percy Roselle as Dr. O'Toole, T. B. Bennett as Flail, Henry Rivers as Tillwell, Mr. Dalton as Tidwell, Amy Roselle as Mary, Miss Scavey as Rose/ Adelphi, May 1872, with Robert Romer as Tillwell, A. C. Lilly as Charles, Harwood Cooper as Dr. Flail, C. H. Stephenson as Terry, Lotti Wilmot as Rose, Maud Howard as Mary.

IRISH WIDOW, THE// C 2a// David Garrick// **Sad. Wells**, Aug. 1840, with Mr. Dry as O'Male, Mr. Williams as Whittle, Mr. Elvin as Nophen, J. B. Hill as Bates, Mr. Aldridge as Kicksy, J. W. Collier as Thomas, Mrs. Robert Honner as Widow Brady.

IRISH WIFE, THE// C 2a// n.a.// **Victoria**, Mar. 1838, with W. H. Oxberry, John Parry, Mr. Loveday, William Davidge, Mr. Phillips, Mrs. Charles Jones, Miss Poole.

IRISHMAN, THE// D 5a// J. W. Whitbread// **Elephant & Castle**, Nov. 1889.

IRISHMAN IN LONDON, THE// F 1a// n.a.// **Grecian**, Dec. 1844, with Mr. Melvin as Capt. Seymore, Edmund Garden as Collooney, Frederick Robson as Cymon, George Hodson as Murtoch Delaney, Mary A. Crisp as Louisa.

IRISHMAN'S HEART, AN; OR, A KISS O' THE BLARNEY// C// John Levey// **Britannia**, Sept. 1879.

IRMA; OR, THE SPIRIT OF THE RHINE// D// n.a.// **Sad. Wells**, Feb. 1843, with Henry Howe as Huntley, John Herbert as Shufflekrantz, Mr. Aldridge as Shyysel, Mrs. George Honey as Irma, Mrs. Henry Marston as Mme. Piffel, Mrs. Richard Barnett as Roschen.

IRON ARM, THE// D// n.a.// **Surrey**, Apr. 1857.

IRON CHEST, THE// D 4a// George Colman the younger// **Haymarket**, Sept. 1837, with Samuel Phelps as Mortimer, Robert Strickland as Capt. Fitzharding, Frederick Vining as Wilford, William Farren as Winterton, J. T. Haines as Rawbold, Benjamin Webster as Sampson, Mr. Saville as Armstrong, Mr. Gallot as Orson, Mr. Hart as Walter, Miss E. Phillips as Helen, Mrs. Humby as Blanche, Mrs. W. Clifford as Judith, Mrs. Gallot as Dame Rawbold, Mrs. Fitzwilliam as Barbara; July 1843, with Charles Kean as Mortimer, Robert Strickland as Fitzharding, Henry Holl as Wilford, William Farren as Winterton, Henry Howe as Rawbold, J. B. Buckstone as Sampson, Mrs. Mary Warner as Helen, Miss Lee as Blanche, Mrs. Worrell as Dame Rawbold, Julia Bennett as Barbara, Mrs. Stanley as Judith/ **Sad. Wells**, Apr. 1838, with David Osbaldiston as Sir Edward Mortimer, Mr. Campbell as Fitzharding, Mr. James as Winterton, Charles Pitt as Wilford, Mr. Ranson as Rawbold, Mr. Ede as Armstrong, Miss Watkins as Helen, Miss Beresford as Blanche, Miss Chartley as Barbara, Mrs. Weston as Judith; Apr. 1845, with Samuel Phelps as Sir Edward, Henry Marston as Fitzharding, John Webster as Wilford, A. Younge as Winterton, E. Morton as Armstrong, Mr. Rae as Rawbold, G. F. Forman as Sampson, George Bennett as Orson, Fanny Huddart as Lady Helen, Miss Lebatt as Blanche, Georgiana Lebatt as Barbara, Mrs. Henry Marston as Judith/ **Drury Lane**, June 1838, with Charles Kean as Sir Edward, Henry Cooke as Fitzharding, A. Brindal as Wilford, William Dowton as Winterton, Mr. Cooper as Rawbold, Henry Compton as Samson, R. McIan as Orson, Mrs. Ternan as Lady Helen, Mrs. Anderson as Blanche, Miss Forde as Barbara, Mrs. Lovell as Judith, Mme. Simon as Dame Rawbold/ **Olympic**, May 1848, with George Bennett as Sir Edward Mortimer, Mr. Butler as Fitzharding, Henry Holl as Wilford, William Davidge as Winterton, Henry Mellon as Gilbert Rawbold, Mr. Attwood as Samson Rawbold, Lysander Thompson as Orson, Mrs. Beverley as Lady Helen, Miss F. Hamilton as Blanche, Mrs. Bromley as Barbara, Mrs. Parker as Judith/ **Princes's**, Jan. 1852, with Charles Kean as Sir Edward, Mr. Addison as Capt. Fitzharding, John Cathcart as Wilford, Drinkwater Meadows as Winterton, John Ryder as Rawbold, John Pritt Harley as Samson, Charles Fisher as Orson, Mrs. Frankland as Helen, Miss Murray as Blanch, Mary Keeley as Barbara/ **Grecian**, Mar. 1854, with H. Somerville as Sir Edward Mortimer, Richard Phillips as Willford, Basil Potter as Old Rawbold, Henry Grant as Fitzharding, Charles Rice as Samson Rawbold, Charles Horn as Armstrong, Eaton O'Donnell as Adam, Jane Coveney as Lady Helen, Harriet Coveney as Blanche, Agnes De Warde as Barbara, Ellen Crisp as Judith/ **Lyceum**, Sept. 1879, with Henry Irving as Sir Edward Mortimer, J. H. Barnes as Capt. Fitzharding, Norman Forbes as Wilford, J. Carter as Winterton, Thomas Mead as Rawbold, S. Johnson as Samson Rawbold, Mr. Branscombe as Peter, Florence Terry as Lady Helen, Myra Holme as Blanche, Alma Murray as Barbara, Georgina Pauncefort as Judith.

IRON CLASP, THE; OR, THE GITANA GIRL// D 2a// Thompson Townsend// **Grecian**, June 1863, with Thomas Mead as Cardan, Adolphe Beronaut, the Muleteer and as De Melchon, John Manning as Snow, Walter Holland as Adolphe, J. Jackson as Johan, W. Shirley as as Lerchaus, Henry Power as Peppo, Henry Grant as Capt. Rohan, Jane Dawson as Satina, Miss Johnstone as as Mme. Mellain, Marie Brewer as Alice, Mary A. Victor as Ninon.

IRON HANDS// D 4a// Harry Pitt// **Grecian**, Oct. 1874.

IRON OF DEATH, THE; OR, THE DOG WITNESS// D// n.a.// **Victoria**, Mar. 1849, with F. H. Henry as Lord Mountaina, Mr. Henderson as Capt. Stanley, Mr. Hitchinson as Moreland, Mr. Harrison as Francisco, Mr. Leake as Tweedle, James Howard as Nowit, Mr. Franklin as Todgher, Mr. Clifford as Hewyn, Mrs. Cooke as Mrs. Tweedle, Miss Mildenhall as Mary, Dog Hector as Dog Neptune.

IRON STATUE, THE// D// n.a.// **Victoria**, 1868.

IRONMASTER, THE// Play 4a// Adap. by Arthur Wing Pinero fr F of Georges Ohnet, Le Maître de Forges// **St. James's**, Mar. 1884, with Mr. Henley as Duc de Bligny, George Alexander as Octave, Herbert Waring as Baron de Prefont, W. H. Kendal as Derblay, Mr. Brandon as de Pontac, J. F. Young as Moulinet, John Maclean as Béchelin, A. Knight as Dr. Servan, Robert Cathcart as Old Gobert, Mrs. Gaston Murray as Marquise de Beaupré, Linda Dietz as Baronne de Préfont, Mrs. W. H. Kendal as Claire, Miss Vane as Athénaïss/ Scenery by W. Harford/ Prod. by John Hare/ **Avenue**, Mar. 1893.

IS HE JEALOUS?// C 1a// Samuel Beazely Jr.// **Sad. Wells**, Mar. 1837, with John Pritchard as Belmour, Miss Williams as Mrs. Belmour,

Miss Lee as Harriet/ **Victoria**, Mar. 1838, with Edward Hooper as Belmour, Miss Desborough as Harriet, Miss Lee as Mrs. Belmour, Mrs. Frank Matthews as Rose/ **Drury Lane**, May 1843, with Charles Hudson as Belmour, Mrs. Mary Warner as Mrs. Belmour, Louisa Nisbett as Harriet, Mrs, Keeley as Rose/ **St. James's**, Jan. 1868, with G. W. Blake as Belmour, Eleanor Bufton as Harriet, Ada Cavendish as Mrs. Belmour, Kate Kearney as Rose.

IS LIFE WORTH LIVING?// D 4a// F. A. Scudamore// **Surrey**, July 1888.

IS SHE GUILTY?// D// A. Faucquez// **Britannia**, June 1877.

IS SHE HIS WIFE? OR, SOMETHING SINGULAR// Charles Dickens// **St. James's**, Mar. 1837.

ISABEL BERTRAND; OR, THE WINE DRINKERS OF PARIS// D 3a// n.a.// **Victoria**, Aug. 1846, with Mr. Fitzjames as Count de Bussieres, William Seaman as Henri de Bussieres, Mr. Archer as di Marranos, James Howard as Barthele, G. W. Walton as Bertrand, Walter Searle as Remy, G. F. Forman as Pierre, F. Wilton as Grosmeme, James Ranoe as Guillaume, Miss Fielding as Adelaide, Mrs. Cooke as Catherine, Lydia Pearce as Marguerite/ Scenery by Mr. Mildenhall/ Machines by Woods & Foster/ Music by W. J. Hill.

ISABELLA; OR, A FATAL MARRIAGE// D 5a// Alt. by David Garrick fr Southerne// **Sad. Wells**, Sept. 1845, with George Bennett as Don Carlos, Henry Marston as Biron, Henry Mellon as Count Baldwin, Samuel Buckingham as Villeroy, Charles Fenton as Maurice, R. H. Lingham as Egmont, Mr. Warde as Belford, Henry Scharf as Sampson, Mrs. Mary Warner as Isabella, Mrs. Henry Marston as Nurse/ **Marylebone**, Mar. 1848, with Mrs. Mary Warner, George Vining, James Johnstone.

ISABELLE; OR, A WOMAN'S LIFE// D 3a// J. B. Buckstone// **Olympic**, Aug. 1852, with William Farren Jr. as Eugene, E. F. Edgar as Scipio, William Shalders as Andrew, Charles Bender as Michael, Mr. Clifton as Philippe, Mrs. Walter Lacy as Isabelle, Mrs. Alfred Phillips as Sophie, Henry Compton as Bajazet, Ellen Turner as Marie, Isabel Adams as Vincent.

ISALDA// Play 1a// Fred Horner// **Toole's**, Feb. 1890, with Bassett Roe as Don Antonio, Matthew Brodie as Comte Henri, Reginald Stockton as Oedro, Vane Featherston as Isalda/ Scenery by Lill Hart.

ISLE OF ST. TROPEZ, THE// D 4a// Montague Williams & F. C. Burnand// **St. James's**, Dec. 1860, with Alfred Wigan as Desart, Samuel Emery as Launay, Frederick Dewar as Darville, Mr. Terry as Gerfaut, George Belmore as Dumery, James Dawson as Louis, Miss Herbert as Amelie, Miss King as Estelle, Mrs. Buckingham White as Margot.

ISLINGTON; OR, LIFE IN THE STREETS [a vers. of Streets of London]// D Pro & 4a// W. R. Osman// **Sad. Wells**, May 1867, with John Bellair as Capt. Weathergale, Basil Potter as Ferrett, Walter Searle as Chizzler, Henry Crouch as Inglestone, Frank Barsby as Arthur, J. Robins as Puffybun, Mrs. J. Russell as Mrs. Weathergale, Fanny Gwynne as Fanny, Nelly Burton as Louise, Miss A. Evans as Mrs. Puffybun/ Scenery by John Johnson/ Machines by Mr. Caudery [sic], Prod. by Basil Potter.

ISOLINE OF BAVARIA// D 4a// W. E. Suter// **Sadler's Wells**, Nov. 1869.

IT IS BETTER LATE THAN NEVER// D 3a// Henry Beverley// **Grecian**, Oct. 1865, with Dacre Baldie, W. Shirley, J. B. Steele, William James, George Conquest, Laura Conquest, Alice Denvil, Mrs. Dearlove, Miss M. A. Victor.

IT NEVER RAINS BUT IT POURS// F// n.a.// **Grecian**, Dec. 1863, with J. Jackson as Redsage, H. A. Major as Impulse, John Manning as Jeremiah, Ellen Crisp as Miss Redsage, Marie Brewer as Flora.

ITALIAN BOY, THE// D// n.a.// **Sad. Wells**, Aug. 1839, with Mr. Dry as Adm. Fluke, Mr. Elvin as Woodbourn, Mr. Williams as Yarn, Mr. Wieland as Patrick, John Webster as Aufant, W. D. Broadfoot as Dominico, J. W. Collier as Stock, Miss Pincott as Estelle, Miss Cooke as Miss Fluke, Miss Norman as Hannah.

ITALIAN LOVER, THE; OR, THE PLEDGE, THE PICTURE, AND THE WITNESS// D 3a// F. L. Phillips// **Grecian**, Nov. 1863, with Walter Holland as Bragelone, Henry Grant as Lord Durazzo, Thomas Mead as Montevole, William James as Claudio, J. Jackson as Babinetto, J. B. Steele as Maletoal, John Manning as Harry Pym, Mrs. Charles Dillon as Julia, Marie Brewer as Olympia, Ellen Crisp as Mother Pym, Mary A. Victor as Zelinda.

ITALIAN TRAITOR, THE// T// R. L. Shiel// **Grecian**, May 1863, with Henry Grant as the King, W. S. Addison as Ludovico, Fawcett Bethson as Columna, William James as Vincentio, Walter Holland as Spalatro, Jane Dawson as Evadne, Ellen Hale as Olivia.

IT'S NEVER TOO LATE TO MEND// D 4a// Dram. by George Conquest fr novel of Charles Reade// **Victoria**, Mar. 1859, with W. H. Pitt as George Fielding, Frederick Byefield as William Fielding, S. Sawford as Meadows, J. H. Rickards as Levi, George Yarnold as Crawley, Mr. Henderson as Merton, Mrs. F. Lauri as Josephs, J. Johnson Towers as Robinson, Mary Fielding as Susan, Miss Laporte as Polly, John Bradshaw as Hawes, F. H. Henry as Abner, James Howard as Jackey/ **Grecian**, Mar. 1861, with Alfred Rayner as Meadows, R. H. Lingham as George, George Gillett as William, William James as Tom, Thomas Mead as Isaac, Laura Conquest as Josepha, George Conquest as Peter, Henry Grant as Hawes, Jane Coveney as Susan/ **Sad. Wells**, Apr. 1861, with Charles Seyton as George, George Sidney as William, T. C. Harris as Meadows, Mr. Barrett as Levi, Lewis Ball as Crawley, Eliza Josephs as Josephs, Henry Sinclair as Robinson, Margaret Eburne as Susan/ **Princess's**, Dec. 1865, with Alfred Tapping as Winchester, George Melville as George Fielding, Gaston Murray as William Fielding, Henry Mellon as Merton, Frederick Villiers as Meadows, George Vining as Robinson, J. G. Shore as Rev. Eden, Thomas Mead as Levi, Dominick Murray as Crawley, Charles Seyton as Hawes, Louisa Moore as Josepha, Stanislaus Calhaem as Jarky, Katherine Rodgers as Susan/ Scenery by F. Lloyds, Walter Hann, A. Lloyds & Mr. Parry/ Music by Charles Hall/ Machines by Mr. Warton/ Prod. by George Vining; Dec. 1878, with Charles Warner as Robinson, F. De Belleville as William Fielding, A. Murray as Winchester, Alfred Nelson as Merton, Howard Russell as Meadows, William Redmund as Rev. Eden, John Cowper as Levi, F. W. Irish as Crawley, John Beauchamp as Hawes, Maud Milton as Josephs, Stanislaus Calhaem as Jacky, Henry Sinclair as George Fielding, Miss T. Stewart as Mary, Rose Leclercq as Susan/ Scenery by Julian Hicks & George Gordon/ Machines by Mr. Warton/ Gas by Mr. Jones/ Lime-light by Mr. Kerr/ Music by Charles Hall/ Prod. by Charles Reade/ **Grecian**, June 1868, with Charles Mortimer, John Gardiner, George Gillett, William James, Thomas Mead, Miss De Lacie, George Conquest, Henry Grant, Lizzie Mandelbert/ **Princess's**, Jan. 1879, with Charles Warner, Rose Leclercq/ **Adelphi**, Sept. 1881, with Charles Warner as Tom Robinson, F. W. Irish as Crawley, E. H. Brooke as George Fielding, W. H. Perrette as William Fielding, James Fernandez as Isaac, Howard Russell as Meadows, Clara Jecks as Josephs, Stanislaus Calhaem as Jacky, Miss Gerard as Susan/ **Drury Lane**, July 1885, with Charles Warner, Isabel Bateman; Apr. 1891.

IT'S NEVER TOO LATE TO REPENT// D// G. Lewis// **Britannia**, Aug. 1875.

'TWAS I// F// John Howard Payne// **Haymarket**, May 1859, with Edwin Villiers as Delorme, Mr. Clark as Marcel, F. C. Courtney as Mayor, Mrs. Coe as Marchioness de Merville, Mrs. Poynter as Mme. Mag, Mrs. Edward Fitzwilliam as Georgette, Fanny Wright as Juliette.

IVAN DANILOFF; OR, THE SLEDGE DRIVER// D// Mrs. J. R. Planché// **Sad. Wells**, Apr. 1844, with Alfred Raymond as Emperor Paul, C. J. Smith as Grand Duke, Mr. Williams as Count Saltikoff, Henry Marston as Daniloff, Charles Fenton as Count Ronski, Caroline Rankley as Catherine, Mrs. Henry Marston as Fedora/ Scenery by F. Fenton/ Machines by Mr. Cowdery, Music by W. Montgomery/ Prod. by Henry Marston.

IVAN SAFERI// D// n.a.// **Surrey**, Apr. 1854.

IVANHOE// D 3a// n.a.// Dram. fr novel of Sir Walter Scott// **Victoria**, May 1854, with N. T. Hicks as Ivanhoe, Mr. Henderson as Unknown Knight, Mr. Green as Sir Brian, R. H. Kitchen as Athelstane, Mr. Hitchinson as Prince John, T. E. Mills as Isaac of York, Mr. Morrison as Robin Hood, Alfred Saville as Friar Tuck, F. H. Henry as Cedric, Miss Dansor as Rowena, Mrs. Manders as Ulrica, Mrs. Henry Vining as Rebecca, Miss Laporte as Elgiva.

IVANHOE; OR, THE JEW'S DAUGHTER (also subt., The Jew of York)// D// n.a.// **Sad. Wells**, Apr. 1837, with Mr. Morrison as Prince John, N. T. Hicks as Pilgrim, Mr. Bishop as Aymer, Mr. Ede as Beaumenoir, Mr. King as Cedric, C. J. Smith as Unknown Knight, C. H. Pitt as Guilbert, John Ayliffe as Friar Tuck, Mr. Cobham as Isaac, Miss Lebatt as Rowena, Miss Williams as Rebecca, Miss Beresford as Ulrica, Mrs. Rogers as Elgiva.

IVANHOE; OR, THE KNIGHT TEMPLAR// D// Dram. fr novel of Sir Walter Scott// **Cov. Garden**, Feb. 1837, with George Bennett as Rotherwood, Benjamin Webster as Wamba, Mr. Collins as Robin Hood, Mr. Ransford as Friar Tuck, R. McIan as Allan-a-Dale, Miss Land as Rowena, Mrs. W. West as Ulrica, John Pritchard as Ivanhoe, John Webster as de Bois Guilbert, Mr. Vandenhoff as Sir Reginald, Charles Bender as de Bracy, Mr. Tilbury as Sir Lucas, Henry Wallack as Isaac, Eliza Vincent as Rebecca.

IVY// C 3a// Mark Melford// **Royalty**, Apr. 1887.

IVY HALL// D 4a// Adap. by John Oxenford// **Princess's**, Sept. 1859, with Harcourt Bland as Sir Gilbert, Henry Widdicomb as Sir Bugle, Frank Matthews as Trusty, Drinkwater Meadows as Capt. Hawkesworth, Henry Irving as Johnson, J. W. Collier as Evergreen, Mrs. Newbery as Mrs. Hawkesworth, Mrs. Weston as Mrs. Grumbleton, Kate Saville as Camilla, Mrs. Charles Young as Amoret/ Scenery by T. Grieve & W. Telbin.

*

J.P., THE// FC 3a// Fenton Mackay// **Opera Comique**, Mar. 1897/ **Strand**, Apr. 1898, with Charles Fawcett as Vivian, Percy Marshall as Noel, Laurence Caird as Maj. Bombard, Alfred Webb as Robert, Lionel Rignold as Montague, Florence Lloyd as Flo, Amy Farrell as Kate, Marie Daltra as Mrs. Loveboy, Kittie Grattan as Suzette, Daisy Atherton as Amy, Maud Sandford as Rose/ Scenery by R. Rider.

JACK// C 4a// Mrs. Harry Beckett// **Royalty**, June 1886, with Eben Plympton, Carlotta Leclercq.

JACK AND JILL// C 1a// Trans. by "Marcus" fr F// **Britannia**, May. 1882.

JACK BRAG// F 2a// Gilbert à Beckett// **St. James's**, May 1837, with John Pritt Harley as Jack Brag, Mr. Halford as Rushton, Mr. Burnett as Sir Charles, Mr. Sidney as Lord Tom, Miss C. Crisp as Blanche, Priscilla Horton as Mrs. Dallington, Mme. Sala as Mrs. Brag.

JACK BY THE HEDGE// D// Dram. fr tale in Penny Miscellany// **Grecian**, Aug. 1867, with J. Jackson as Martin, Charles Mortimer as Algernon, Samuel Perfitt as Langley, William James as Walter, John Manning as Chizler, Henry Power as Pighead, George Conquest as Jack, Lizzie Mandelbert as Marian, Alice Denvil as Lucy, Mary A. Victor as Patty.

JACK IN A BOX// C 1a// J. Palgrave Simpson// **St. James's**, June 1866.

JACK IN THE BOX// D 4a// Edward Towers// **Pavilion**, Nov. 1881.

JACK IN THE GREEN; OR, HINTS ON ETIQUETTE// F// Mark Lemon// **Adelphi**, May 1850, with Charles Boyce as Durham, Paul Bedford as White, John Sanders as Fluey, Mr. Lindon as John, Edward Wright as Bryanstone, Emma Harding as Miss Durham, Mrs. Laws as Mrs. White, Ellen Chaplin as Emma/ **Haymarket**, Aug. 1850, with same cast.

JACK IN THE WATER; OR, THE LADDER OF LIFE// C 3a// W. L. Rede// **Olympic**, May 1842, with Mr. Fitzjames as Lorrington, Mr. Halford as Fragile, Mr. Ross as Didapper, Walter Searle as Duffey, Mr. Green as Jauney, Mr. Turnour as Quilluit, Mr. Brookes as Joe Hatch, Miss Arden as Clara, Miss Plowman as Jane, Miss Granby as Sarah, George Wild as Jack, C. Baker as Loftus, Miss Lebatt as Betty/ Scenery by Mr. Pitt/ Music by Mr. Callcott/ Machines by Mr. Hagley/ **Sad. Wells**, July 1843, with Henry Marston as Lorrington, John Webster as Fragile, Mr. Coreno as Didapper, Mr. Moreton as Dick, R. H. Lingham as Janney, Mr. Williams as Quillett, Mr. Brookes as Joe Hatch, George Wild as Jack, Miss Lane as Clara, Miss Stephens as Jane, Miss Melville as Sarah, Mr. Bird as Loftus, Caroline Rankley as Emily/ Scenery by F. Fenton/ Music by Mr. Calcott/ Machines by Mr. Cawdery/ Prod. by George Wild.

JACK JUNK// F 1a// n.a.// **Astley's**, Aug. 1850, with Mr. Johnson as Capt. Bertram, Mr. Lawrence as M. Bertram, Arthur Stirling as Harry, S. Smith as Jack Junk, Mr. Crowther as Caplas, Mrs. Beacham as Emma, Mrs. Moreton Brookes as Mrs. Moral.

JACK KETCH; OR, A LEAF FROM TYBURN TREE// D// George Almar// **Sad. Wells**, Sept. 1841, with Robert Honner as Ketch, George Almar as George, Mr. Dry as Sir Gregory, Mr. Elvin as Lawson, Mr. Aldridge as Lord Egerton, Charles Fenton as Digby, Mr. Williams as Barabas, John Herbert as Bluster, J. W. Collier as Sir Titus, Mrs. Robert Honner as Barbara, Mrs. Richard Barnett as Calista/ Scenery by F. Fenton/ Music by Isaac Collins/ Prod. by R. Honner.

JACK LONG OF TEXAS; OR, THE SHOT IN THE EYE// D// n.a.// **Victoria**, Apr. 1847, with John Dale as Gibbs, N. T. Hicks as Jack Long, John Gardner as Small, James Howard as Hector, J. B. Johnstone as Jones, Walter Searle as Capt. Hinch, C. J. Bird as White, Annette Vincent as May, Mrs. N. T. Hicks as Dinah/ **Grecian**, July 1865, with Charles Morton as Jack Long, H. R. Power as Small, Henry Grant as Hiach, W. Shirley as Gibbs, Marie Brewer as May, Miss E. Churchill as Dinah.

JACK OF ALL TRADES// C 2a// Adap. fr F.// **Olympic**, Oct. 1861, with Henry Neville as Toby Crank, J. W. Ray as Stapleton, Walter Gordon as Heartall, Horace Wigan as Crank, Harwood Cooper as Jacob, Florence Haydon as Violet, Mrs. Stephens as Mrs. Comely.

JACK O' BOTH SIDES// F 1a// Adap. fr F// **Princess's**, Oct. 1845, with Robert Honner as Lathem, W. H. Oxberry as Tweedle, Augustus Harris as Timkins, Miss E. Honner as Mary, Emma Stanley as Mary Anne, Miss Taylor as Caroline, Louisa Marshall as Eliza.

JACK O' LANTERN// D// C. H. Hazlewood// **Britannia**, June 1867.

JACK O'LANTERN; OR, THE CHILDREN OF THE DEEP// D// n.a.// **Victoria**, May 1843, with Mr. James as Don Alonzo, Mr. Hitchinson as Capt. Cavagos, Miss Saddler as Louis, John Gardner as Crumbs, E. F. Saville as Bowin, John Dale as Raoul, C. Williams as Davillo, J. W. Collier as Felix, Mrs. George Lee as Donna Geraldine, Miss Martin as Inez.

JACK O' THE HEDGE// D 2a// W. E. Suter// **Queen's**, Nov. 1862.

JACK RANN; OR, THE KNAVES OF KNAVE'S ACRE// D 2a// T. E. Wilks// **Victoria**, Aug. 1843, with William Seaman as Grantley, Mr. James as Millhurst, Mr. Hitchinson as Briggs, John Gardner as Pattypan, E. F. Saville as Jack Rann, Mr. Paul, as Mordaunt, Mr. Howard as Daunton, C. Williams as Davis, Mrs. Atkinson as Rosalie, Miss Saddler as Phyllis, Miss Ridgeway as Elizabeth.

JACK ROBINSON AND HIS MONKEY; OR, THE DESOLATE ISLAND// D 2a// C. P. Thompson// **Victoria**, Jan. 1845, with Mr. Cony as Jack, Mr. Johnson as Recrerio, Walter Searle as Muley, Mr. Henry as Drago, Mr. Edgar as Sebastian, Mr. Hitchinson as Fernando, Miss Jefferson as Emeline, Miss Treble as Isadore, Mr. Blanchard as Monkey/ **Grecian**, Sept. 1861, with William James as Jack Robinson, George Gillett as Capt. Rimero, Mr. Costello as Tomaso, F. Smithson as Sebastian, R. Cobden as Muley, Ellen Hale as Emmeline, Lucreza Hill as Isadore.

JACK SHEPPARD// D// Dram. by W. T. Moncrieff fr novel of Harrison Ainsworth// **Victoria**, Oct. 1839; Sept. 1842, with Mr. Cullen as Sir Rowland, Mr. James as Kneebone, John Gardner as Wood, John Dale as Jonathan Wild, E. F. Saville as Jack Sheppard, William Seaman as Darrell, Mrs. Griffith as Mrs. Wood, Mrs. George Lee as Mrs. Sheppard.

JACK SHEPPARD (see also, The Life and Death of Jack Sheppard)// D// Dram. fr novel of Harrison Ainsworth// **Grecian**, Aug. 1855, with Eaton O'Donnell as Wood, Basil Potter as Trenchard, Harriet Coveney as Jack Sheppard, Percy Corri as Blueskin, Mr. Melvin as Kettleby, Richard Phillips as Jonathan Wild, Mrs. C. Montgomery as Darrell (as child), F. Charles as Darrell (as adult), Henry Grant as Arnold, Ellen Crisp as Lady Aliva, Miss Johnstone as Mrs. Wood, Jane Coveney as Mrs. Sheppard.

JACK SHEPPARD// D 4a// Joseph Hatton// **Pavilion**, Apr. 1898.

JACK SHEPPARD; OR, THE HOUSEBREAKER OF THE LAST CENTURY// D 4a// Dram. by J. B. Buckstone fr novel of Harrison Ainsworth// **Adelphi**, Oct. 1839, with George Maynard, Mr. Freeborn, J. F. Saville, Mr. Lyon, Mr. Wilkinson, Harry Beverly, Frederick Yates, Mrs. Keeley, William Cullenford, Paul Bedford, E. H. Butler, John Sanders, Mrs. Fosbroke, Miss E. Honner, Mrs. Nailer/ **Haymarket**, Sept. 1852, with John Parselle as Sir Rowland, Mr. Freeborn as Sir James, Samuel Emery as Jonathan Wild, Mr. Waye as Gay, James Worrell as Hogarth, O. Smith as Wood, William Cullenford as Kneebone, C. J. Smith as Mendez, Mrs. Keeley as Jack Sheppard, Paul Bedford as Blueskin, Ellen Chaplin as Darrell, Mrs. Woolidge as Mrs. Wood, Laura Honey as Winifred, Miss Penson as Sally/ Scenery by T. Pitt & Mr. Turner/ Machines by Mr. Cooper.

JACK SHEPPARD; OR, THE HOUSEBREAKER OF THE LAST CENTURY// D 5a// Dram. by Thomas Greenwood fr novel of Harrison Ainsworth// **Sad. Wells**, Oct. 1839, with Mr. Williams as Wood, Edwin Villiers as Sir Cecil, Mr. Dry as Sir Rowland, W. D. Broadfoot as Darrell, Henry Hall as Jonathan Wild, C. Montgomery as Blueskin, Mr. Aldridge as Kattleby, Miss Richardson as Mrs. Sheppard, Mrs. J. F. Saville as Lady Aliva, Robert Honner as Sheppard, J. W. Collier as Kneebone, Miss Cooke as Mrs. Wood, Mrs. Morgan as Winifred/ Scenery by F. Fenton/ Music by Mr. Herbert/ Machines by B. Sloman/ Prod. by R. Honner.

JACK STEDFAST; OR, WRECK AND RESCUE// D 3a// Cecil Pitt// **Britannia**, Aug. 1869.

JACK TAR// D 5a// Arthur Shirley & Benjamin Landeck// **Pavilion**, Oct. 1896.

JACK'S DELIGHT// F 1a// T. J. Williams// **Strand**, Nov. 1862.

JACK'S THE LAD; OR, THE PRIDE OF THE NAVY// D// n.a.// **Sad. Wells**, Dec. 1837, with Mr. Wilkins as Redbelt, Mr. King as Sternhold, Mr. Gay as Capias, Mr. Campbell as Jack Spry, Mr. Ennis as Nipperkin, Mr. Rogers as Jeremiah, Mr. Scarbrow as Backstay, Miss Vernon as Nancy, Lavinia Melville as Polly.

JACKAL, THE// C 3a// Adap. by Alec Nelson fr F// **Strand**, Nov. 1889.

JACKS AND JILLS// C 3a// James Albery// **Vaudeville**, May 1880, with Henry Howe, W. H. Vernon, John Maclean, Cicely Richards, Sophie Larkin.

JACOBITE, THE// C 2a// J. R. Planché// **Haymarket**, June 1847; Nov. 1849, with Mr. Stuart as Sir Richard, Henry Howe as Maj. Murray, J. B. Buckstone as Duck, Mrs. L. S. Buckingham as Lady Somerford, Mrs. Stanley as Widow Pottle, Mrs. Caulfield as Patty/ **Sad. Wells**, Nov. 1853, with Mr. Lunt as Sir Richard, William Belford as Maj. Murray, Lewis Hall as Duck, Miss Hickson as Lady Sommerford, Mrs. Henry Marston as Widow Pottle, Eliza Travers as Patty.

JACQUES STROP; OR, A FEW MORE PASSAGES IN THE LIFE OF THE RENOWNED AND ILLUSTRIOUS ROBERT MACAIRE// D 3a// Charles Selby// **Strand**, Sept. 1838/ **Grecian**, Apr. 1856, with Mr. Melvin as Dumont, Henry Power as Pierre, Richard Phillips as Robert Macaire, F. Charles as Charles, Henry Grant as Duval, John Manning as Jacques Strop, Eaton O'Donnell as Ganache, Jane Coveney as Louise, Miss Chapman as Clementine, Ellen Crisp as Marie, Miss Johnstone as Mme. Ganache.

JAMES OF SCOTLAND; OR, THE GUDEMAN O' BALLANGEICH// C// n.a.// **Sad. Wells**, Oct. 1863, with Edmund Phelps as James V, Mr. Hastings as Birkie, George Fisher as Howieson, T. Robinson as Maxwell, Miss Rogers as Lindsay, Mr. Routledge as Grimes, George Vining as Muller, Mrs. H. Wallis as Jabos, Maggie Grainger as Marion.

JAMES VI; OR, THE GOWRIE PLOT// T 5a// James White// **Sad. Wells**, Mar. 1852, with Samuel Phelps as James VI, Henry Marston as Earl of Gowrie, Frederic Robinson as Ruthven, George Bennett as Bailrig, Henry Mellon as Ramsey, Mr. Barrett as Ayliffe, Eliza Travers as Anne of Denmark, Miss Goddard as Countess Gowrie, Miss E. Feist as Lady Beatrix, Miss Cooper as Catherine/ Scenery by F. Fenton.

JANE// FC 3a// Harry Nicholls & William Lestocq// **Comedy**, Dec. 1890, with Charles Brookfield as William, Henry Kemble as Kershaw, E. M. Robson as Pixton, Charles Hawtrey as Shakleton, Ethel Matthews as Lucy, Miss Ewell as Mrs. Chadwick, Ada Murray as Mrs. Pixton, Lottie Venne as Jane/ **Terry's**, Dec. 1899.

JANE BRIGHTWELL; OR, THE OLD WITCH OF STONEHENGE// D// n.a.// **Grecian**, Sept. 1862, with W. Shirley as Magistrate, F. Smithson as Grampus, John Manning as Links, Thomas Mead as Brightwell, Alfred Rayner as Darkly, Walter Holland as Grantly, Henry Grant as Edgar, James Howard as Pettifold, Henry Power as Spriggs, George Gillett as Markwell, Miss Johnstone as Matilda, Mary A. Victor as Laura, Jane Dawson as Jane Brightwell, J. Jackson as the Witch.

JANE EYRE// D 2a// n.a.// **Surrey**, Nov. 1867.

JANE EYRE// D 4a// Adap. by W. G. Wills fr novel of Charlotte Brontë// **Globe**, Dec. 1882, with Mrs. Bernard Beere as Jane Eyre, Carlotta Leclercq as Lady Ingram, Kate Bishop as Blanche Ingram, Maggie Hunt as Mary Ingram,

Nelly Jordan as Miss Beechey, Alexes Leighton as Mrs. Fairfax, Charles Kelly as Rochester, A. M. Denison as Lors Desmond, H. E. Russell as Rev. Prior, H. H. Cameron as Nat Lee/ Scenery by Perkins, Spong, & Banks/ Music by Hamilton Clarke.

JANE LOMAX// D// n.a.// **Adelphi**, Feb. 1839.

JANE PAUL; OR, THE VICTIM OF UNMERITED PERSECUTION// D 3a// Edward Fitzball// **Victoria**, June 1842, with John Dale as Necker, E. F. Saville as Paul, William Seaman as Tuliptree, John Gardner as Brown, Harriet Coveney as Charles, Mr. Paul as Jack, C. Pitt as Straitlegs, Mr. Howard as Sammy, C. Williams as Snatch, Annette Vincent as Jane, Jane Coveney as Martha, Mrs. Griffith as Nerissa, Mrs. George Lee as Ruth, Mrs. Seaman as Mary, Miss Saddler as Poll/ Scenery invented by Mr. Osbaldiston & painted by Fenton & Morelli/ Machines by Emmens, Wood & Foster/ Music by W. J. Hill/ Prod. by E. F. Saville.

JANE SHORE// T 5a// Nicholas Rowe// **Cov. Garden**, Jan. 1837, with George Bennett as Glo'ster, John Webster as Ratcliffe, Mr. Roberts as Catesby, W. C. Macready as Hastings, George Vandenhoff as Dumont, John Pritchard as Belmour, John Collett as Porter, Charles Bender as Derby, Helen Faucit as Jane Shore, Mrs. W. West as Alicia/ **Drury Lane**, Apr. 1837, with Mr. Mathews as Glo'ster, Mr. Cooper as Hastings, F. Cooke as Ratcliffe, Mr. Henry as Catesby, Mr. Mears as Derby, Mr. Warde as Dumont, A. Brindal as Belmour, Miss Taylor as Jane Shore, Miss Huddart as Alicia/ **Sad. Wells**, May 1837, with Mr. King as Glo'ster, Mr., Griffiths as Belmour, N. T. Hicks as Hastings, C. H. Pitt as Dumont, C. J. Smith as Catesby, Mr. Scarbrow as Ratcliffe, Mr. Bishop as Derby, Miss Williams as Alice, Helen Townley as Jane Shore; Apr. 1840, with Mr. Archer as Glo'ster, Mr. Elton as Hastings, Henry Marston as Dumont, Mr. Elvin as Belmour, Mrs. Robert Honner as Jane Shore, Miss Richardson as Alicia; Mar. 1846, with Samuel Phelps as Lord Hastings, George Bennett as Glo'ster, Henry Mellon as Belmour, Henry Marston as Dumont, E. Morton as Catesby, Miss Cooper as Jane Shore, Mrs. Mary Warner as Alicia/ **Cov. Garden**, Dec. 1837, with W. C. Macready, Samuel Phelps, George Bennett, Helen Faucit, Miss Huddart/ **Princess's**, Dec. 1847, with John Ryder as Gloucester, Mr. Cooper as Hastings, F. B. Conway as Dumont, Charles Fisher as Belmour, Mr. Bowtall as Buckingham, Mr. Palmer as Derby, Mr. Wynn as Ratcliff, William Norton as Catesby, Emmeline Montague as Jane Shore, Susan Cushman as Alicia.

JANE SHORE// D 5a// W. G. Wills// **Princess's**, Sept. 1876, with James Fernandez as Gloucester, Edward Price as Shore, B. Bentley as Catesby, A. Revelle as Grist, J. W. Ford as Coote, Caroline Heath as Jane Shore, Mrs. Alfred Mellon as Queen Elizabeth, Mary Brunell as Lady Coote/ Scenery by F. Lloyds/ Music by W. C. Levey.

JANE SHORE// Play 4a// J. W. Boulding & R. Palgrave// **Grand**, Mar. 1886.

JANET PRIDE// D 5a// Dion Boucicault & Benjamin Webster// **Adelphi**, Feb. 1855, with Benjamin Webster as Pride, Charles Selby as Leonard, Mr. Woolgar as Dr. Robert, Mme. Celeste as Janet Pride, Robert Romer as Sgt. Grey, Robert Keeley as Dicky, Mary Keeley as Minnie/ Scenery by Pitt & Turner/ Music by Alfred Mellon/ Machines by T. Bartlett; Aug. 1881 (in Pro. & 3a), with Charles Warner as Pride, James Fernandez as Bernard, F. Campbell as Dr. Robert, H. Proctor as Black Jack, Howard Russell as Sgt. Grey, F. W. Irish as Trotter, E. J. Henley as George Heriot, Miss Gerard as Janet Pride, Clara Jecks as Minnie/ Scenery by William Beverly/ **Sad. Wells**, June 1858, with Benjamin Webster as Richard Pride, Charles Selby as Bernard, Mr. Henry as Dr. Robert, Paul Bedford as Black Jack, Mme. Celeste as Janet Pride, Robert Romer as Sgt. Grey, Mr. Moreland as Trotter, Edmund Garden as Heriot, Mr. Thompson as Rook, Mr. Fredericks as George Heriot, Walter Vernon as Counsel, Mary Keeley as Minnie, Mrs. Stoker as Nancy/ **Princess's**, July 1874, with Benjamin Webster as Richard Pride, Frank Barsby as Bernard, C. J. Smith as Dr. Roberts, William McIntyre as Black Jack, Mrs. Alfred Mellon as Jane Pride, George Belmore as Trotter, Thomas Stuart as Heriot, P. C. Beverley as George, Miss G. Claire as Minnie, Mrs. Stoker as Nancy.

JANET'S RUSE// C// n.a.// **Royalty**, 1872.

JAPHET IN SEARCH OF A FATHER// D 3a// G. D. Pitt// **Victoria** Sept. 1845, with T. H. Higgie as Dr. Cophagus, E. F. Saville as Japhet, John Herbert as Oldmixon, E. Edwards as Melchior, Mr. Franklin as Bishop, Miss Richardson as Nathaile, Miss Backhouse as Fleta, Miss Young as Lady Maelstram, Miss Jefferson as Mrs. McShane, Eliza Terrey as Kathleen, Mrs. George Lee as Mrs. Cophagus, Miss Edgar as Susannah.

JARED SWOOL; OR, THE IDIOT OF THE ONE-TREE LANE// D 3a// E. R. Lancaster// **Victoria**, Oct. 1856, with W. H. Pitt as Dunmorton, Mr. Henderson as Lincoln, T. E. Mills as Jared, Frederick Byefield as Michael, George Pearce as Darkdo, F. H. Henry as Cellersprite, James Howard as Hush, Jane Dawson as Rosalie, Mrs. Warlow as Lady Grace, Miss Laporte as Dorothy.

JARVIS, THE HONEST MAN: A TALE OF THE TIMES OF JUDGE JEFFRIES// D// G. D. Pitt// **Victoria**, June 1854, with Alfred Saville as Sir Thomas, T. E. Mills as Jarvis, Mr. Henderson as Palmer, Henry Frazer as Valpone, Charles Rice as Blom, Mr. Green as Dragon, Mrs. Henry Vining as Cordelia, Mrs. Manders as Margaret.

JASPER'S REVENGE// Play 1a// Wynne Miller// **Shaftesbury**, June 1891.

JEALOUS IN HONOUR// Play 4a// Basil Broke// **Garrick**, Apr. 1893, with Bernard Gould as Prince Newski, Sant Matthews as Col. Strange,

Edmund Maurice as Count von Bohrer, Gilbert Hare as Comte de Cerny, W. T. Lovell as Ferrers, Sydney Brough as Nugent, Mrs. Edmund Phelps as Mrs. Strange, Helen Luck as Alice, Kate Rorke as Countess Helen/ Scenery by William Harford.

JEALOUS MISTAKE, A// Play 1a// S. J. Adair Fitzgerald// **Globe**, Apr. 1899, with Edmund Gwenn as John Tadgers, Alfred Phillips as Smithers, Charles Kenney as Tupper, Vivian Vane as Jane, Mary Jocelyn as Mary.

JEALOUS WIFE, THE// C 5a// Dram. by George Colman the elder fr Fielding's Tom Jones// **Haymarket**, Aug. 1837, with W. C. Macready as Oakley, William Farren as Russet, William Strickland as Maj. Oakley, Frederick Vining as Trinket, J. B. Buckstone as Sir Harry, Mr. Daly as O'Cutter, Charles Selby as Charles, Miss Huddart as Mrs. Oakley, Mrs. W. Clifford as Lady Freelove, Mrs. Gallot as Toilette, Eliza Vincent as Harriet; July 1840, with W. C. Macready, Benjamin Webster, Tyrone Power, Walter Lacy, Mrs. Julia Glover/ **Sad. Wells**, Nov. 1841, with Henry Marston as Oakley, Mr. Dry as Maj. Oakley, Mr. Elvin as Charles, Mr. Williams as Russet, J. W. Collier as O'Cutter, George Ellis as Trinket, John Herbert as Beagle, Charles Fenton as Paris, Mr. Archer as William, Mrs. Henry Marston as Mrs. Oakley, Miss Richardson as Lady Freelove; Sept. 1866, with J. H. Slater as Mr. Oakley, E. Shepherd as Maj. Oakley, Walter Holland as Charles, John Rouse as Beagle, J. Collier as Trinket, R. Norman as Russett, Alice Marriott as Mrs. Oakley, Mrs. J. F. Saville as Lady Freelove, Miss Mansfield as Toilet/ **Princess's**, Mar. 1848, with Mr. Cooper as Pakly, J. Neville as Maj. Oakly, F. B. Conway as Charles, Charles Fisher as Trinket, Henry Compton as Sir Harry, Mr. Wynn as Capt. O'Cutter, John Gilbert as Russet, Mrs. Barrett as Mrs, Oakly, Mrs. Selby as Lady Freelove, Mrs. H. Hughes as Harriet, Miss Somers as Toilet; Jan. 1856 (in 3a), with Mr. Cooper as Maj. Oakly, Charles Kean as Oakly, John Cathcart as Charles Oakly, Walter Lacy as Trinket, Frank Matthews as Russet, John Pritt Harley as Beagle, Mrs. Winstanley as Lady Freelove, Mrs. Charles Kean as Mrs. Oakly, Caroline Heath as Harriet, Miss Clifford as Toilet; June 1866, with Charles Kean as Oakley, George Everett as Maj. Oakley, J. F. Cathcart as Charles Oakley, J. G. Shore as Trinket, Mrs. Charles Kean as Mrs. Oakley, Miss Chapman as Harriet, Mrs. Henry Marston as Lady Freelove, Miss Stoner as Toilet/ **Olympic**, Dec. 1855, with Alfred Wigan as Oakley, Samuel Emery as Maj. Oakley, George Vining as Lord Trinket, Mr. Leslie as Charles, Mr. Danvers as Sir Harry, J. H. White as Russet, Mrs. Stirling as Mrs. Oakley, Miss Castleton as Lady Freelove, Miss Marston as Harriet, Miss Bromley as Toilet/ **Grecian**, Feb. 1856, with Richard Phillips as Oakly, Henry Grant as Maj. Oakly, F. Charles as Charles, Mr. Hustleby as Trinket, Eaton O'Donnell as Russet, John Manning as Beagle, Jane Coveney as Mrs. Oakly, Miss Johnstone as Lady Freelove, Mrs. C. Montgomery as Harriet, Ellen Hale as Toilet/ **St. James's**, June 1867, with Frank Matthews as Maj. Oakley, F. Charles as Charles, Edward Dyas as Russet, Walter Lacy as Trinket, Thomas Bridgeford as Sir Harry, Arthur Brown as John, Louisa Herbert as Mrs. Oakley, Eleanor Bufton as Lady Freelove, Ada Cavendish as Harriet, Kate Kearney as Tellet [sic]/ **Strand**, July 1892.

JEALOUSY// C 2a// Charles Shannon & Mrs. F. S. Shannon// **Cov. Garden**, Oct. 1838, with Mr. Vandenhoff as Col. Neville, James Anderson as Hartley, Drinkwater Meadows as Sir Harry, Henry Howe as Louis, Mrs. Mary Warner as Mrs. Neville, Miss Charles as Caroline, Mrs. East as Lappet.

JEALOUSY// D 4a// Adap. by Charles Reade fr F of Victorien Sardou, Andrea// **Olympic**, Apr. 1878, with Henry Neville as Count Beudoz, W. Younge as Frederic, A. Elwood as Baron Kaulben, G. Harmond as Benjamin, Charles Flockton as Kraft, J. G. Bauer as Wilmer, George Yarnold as Fritz, Sophie Young as Olga, Miss Gerard as Stella, Miss Cranstoun as Sylvine, Clara May as Josepha/ Scenery by W. Hann.

JEALOUSY AND MYSTERY// F// n.a.// **Sad. Wells**, Aug. 1857, with Watkins Young as Dupuis, Mr. Gladstone as Valere, John Chester as Thomas, Kate Percy as Cecile, Miss Heath as Angelica.

JEAMES// C 3a// F. C. Burnand// **Gaiety**, Aug. 1878.

JEAN; OU, LA REPUBLIQUE// D 4a// Adap. fr F// **Sad. Wells**, Oct. 1882, with E. N. Hallows as Jean, M. Mortimer as Count de Breval, George Stretton as de Ferras, F. Owen as Lucien, Mat Robson as Le Franc, J. Lawson as Diogenes, Mr. Edwardes as Guiliume, H. Gregory as Jerome, W. Williams as Michel, Helen Grahame as Henriette, Lizzie Lilly as Virginia, Miss M. Blandford as Genevieve, Marie Forde as Pauline/ Scenery by W. T. Hemsley.

JEANIE DEANS; OR, THE SISTERS OF ST. LEONARD'S// D 4a// Dram. by C. H. Hazlewood fr Sir Walter Scott, Heart of Midlothian// **Sad. Wells**, Jan. 1867, with R. Norman as David, John Rouse as Dumbie, J. H. Slater as Stanton, J. Collier as Duke of Argyle, Mr. Murray as Butler, J. W. Lawrence as Sharpitlaw, Mr. Hamilton as Ratcliffe, Mr. Edwin as Frank, Walter Lacy as Tyburn, J. L. Warner as Fairbrother, Miss Fitzgerald as Queen Caroline, Miss Leigh as Effie, Alice Marriott as Jeanie, Mrs. J. F. Saville as Margery, Louise Pereira as Madge/ Scenery by W. Gowrie/ Music by B. Isaacson/ Prod. by Alice Marriott.

JEANNETTE AND JEANNOT; OR, THE CONSCRIPT'S BRIDE// D 2a// John Courtney// **Victoria**, May 1848, with Mr. Henderson as de Valberg, James Howard as Gigot, G. F. Forman as Jennot, Mr. Hawkins as Capt. Larmateau, Mr. Hitchinson as Pomponet, Mrs. George Lee as Adelaide, Annette Vincent as Jeannette, Mrs. Cooke as Mme. Glaniere, Miss Burroughcliffe as Carline/ Music by W. J. Hill.

JEANNETTE'S WEDDING// C 1a// Leicester Buckingham & Augustus Harris// **Princess's**, Oct. 1861, with Henry Widdicomb as Jean, Miss Lavenu as Pierre, John Collett as Jerome, Maria Harris as Jeannette.

JEANNIE DEANS; OR, THE HEART OF MID-LOTHIAN// Play// Dram. fr novel of Sir Walter Scott// **Princess's**, Mar. 1868.

JEANNE DUBARRY// D 3a// Henry Herman// **Charing Cross**, May 1875, with Miss Lynd.

JEDBURY JUNIOR// C 3a// Madeleine Ryley// **Terry's**, Feb. 1896, with Frederick Kerr as Jedbury Jr., John Beauchamp as Christopher Jedbury, J. L. MacKay as Maj. Hedway, Arthur Playfair as Bellaby, G. E. Bellamy as Glibb, Edward Beecher as Simpson, Gilbert Farquhar as Whimper, Emily Cross as Mrs. Jedbury, Elsie Chester as Mrs. Glibb, Eva Moore as Nellie, Maud Millett as Dora/ Scenery by Harry Potts/ Prod by Edward Terry/ **Globe**, Dec. 1896.

JENKINSES, THE; OR, BOARDED AND DONE FOR// F 2a// J. R. Planché// **Lyceum**, Dec. 1852, with Frank Matthews as Carraway, Robert Roxby as John Jenkins, Henry Butler as Gingham, Lydia Foote as Master Jenkins, Mrs. Frank Matthews as Mrs. Jenkins, Fanny Baker as Georgiana Jenkins, Mrs. Macnamara as Martha.

JENNY FOSTER, THE SAILOR'S CHILD; OR, THE WINTER ROBIN// D 2a// C. H. Hazlewood// **Britannia**, Oct. 1855.

JENSON FAMILY, THE// C 4a// Trans. by May Morrison fr play by Edward Höyer// **Criterion**, Apr. 1901.

JEREMIAH CLIP AND THE WIDOW'S VICTIM// F// n.a.// **Victoria**, June 1857, with Frederick Byefield as Twitter, Richard Thorne Jr. as Podge, G. W. Simms as Jeremiah, Tinsel, and as Strappado, Julia Seaman as Mrs. Rattleton, Mrs. J. M. Rickards as Mrs. Twitter, Emily Thorne as Jane.

JERRY AND A SUNBEAM// Play 1a// Cosmo Hamilton// **Strand**, Sept. 1898, with F. W. Leonard as Corbet, Daisy Atherton as May.

JERRY BUILDER, THE// FC 3a// Mark Melford// **Grand**, June 1894, with Willie Edouin as Grubb, Cecil Paget as Lord Cumberland, Ernest Hendrie as Joseph Baxter, Robert Nainby as George, Herbert Ross as Arthur Baxter, Douglas Gordon as Rodney, E. M. Sillward as Pollard, Susie Vaughan as Mrs. Pollard, Helen Conway as Lucy, May Edouin as Mattie, Edith Hilton as Lady Cumberland, Emily Dowton as Mrs. Billows.

JERRY BUNDLER// C 1a// W. W. Jacobs & Charles Rock// **St. James's**, June 1899, with E. Holman Clarke as Penfold, Holmes Gore as Malcolm, Cyril Maude as Hirst, Frank Gilmore as Somers, Charles Hallard as Dr. Leek.

JESS// D 4a// Adap. by Eweretta Lawrence & J. J. Bisgood fr novel of H. Rider Haggard// **Adelphi**, Mar. 1890, with J. D. Beveridge as Croft, T. B. Thalberg as Neil, Charles Dalton as Muller, Julian Cross as Coetzee, John Clulow as Carolus, Gilbert Yorke as Jan, Josephine St. Ange as Mrs. Neville, Helen Forsyth as Bessie, Eweretta Lawrence as Jess/ **Surrey**, Dec. 1890.

JESSAMY'S COURTSHIP// F 1a// C. H. Hazlewood// **Adelphi**, Aug. 1879, with E. J. George as Adolphus, Harwood Cooper as Firedrake, Harriet Coveney as Priscilla, Maria Harris as Araminta, Clara Jecks as Perkins.

JESSIE ASHTON// D// William Sawyer// **Surrey**, Dec. 1862.

JESSIE FARLEIGH// D// n.a.// **City of London**, Feb. 1863.

JESSIE GRAY// D 3a// Robert Brough & J. V. Bridgman// **Adelphi**, 1850, with Henry Hughes as Sir Richard, Charles Boyce as Philip, C. J. Smith as Capt. Wyndham, O. Smith as Dr. Gray, George Honey as Jukes, Paul Bedford as Prof. Chester, Mme. Celeste as Jessie Gray, Kathleen Fitzwilliam as Lizzy, Laura Honey as Tippet.

JESSIE TYRRELL// D// n.a.// **Victoria**, Mar. 1866.

JESSY CAMPBELL; OR, THE LOVER'S LAST VISIT// D// n.a.// **Sad. Wells**, Aug. 1840, with Mr. Williams as Campbell, J. W. Collier as McFluke, Mr. Elvin as Barnside, J. B. Hill as Lee, Mr. Priorson as McFillibag, Mrs. Robert Honner as Jessy, Miss Cooke as Dame Campbell, Miss Richardson as Matty.

JESSY VERE; OR, THE RETURN OF THE WANDERER (also, Jessie Vere)// D 2a// C. H. Hazlewood// **Victoria**, May 1856, with J. F. Donald as Vere, R. H. Lingham as Arthur Fanshawe, Mr. Henderson as Sigismund Fanshawe, W. H. Pitt as Thorne, Mr. Warlow as Chirrup, John Bradshaw as Nightingale, F. H. Henry as Wheatly, Mr. Morrison as Giles, Mr. Mellish as Buttercup, Jane Dawson as Jessie, Julia Seaman as Emily, Miss Bailey as Phoebe, Miss Laporte as Polly/ Scenery by Mr. Mildenhall/ Machines by Wood & Foster/ **Britannia**, Feb. 1866.

JEST, THE// Play 3a// Murray Carson & Louis Parker// **Criterion**, Nov. 1898.

JEW AND THE DOCTOR, THE// F// T. J. Dibdin// **Drury Lane**, Oct. 1839, with William Dowton as Abednego, J. W. Ray as Dr. Specific, John Lee as Changeable, William Bennett as Bromley, Mr. Roberts as Charles, Edwin Yarnold as William, Mrs. Ashton as Mrs. Changeable, Miss Cooper as Emily, Miss Barnett as Betty.

JEW OF CADIZ, THE// C// Adap. fr Cumberland// **Sad. Wells**, Sept. 1839, with Mr. Aldridge as Sir Stephen, Mr. Elvin as Frederick, Mr. Dry as Ratcliffe, W. D. Broadfoot as Saunders, James Villiers as Sheva, Mr. Starmer as Jabal, Miss Richardson as Mrs.

Ratcliffe, Mrs. J. F. Saville as Mrs. Goodison, Miss Cooke as Dorcas, Mrs. Robert Honner as Eliza.

JEW OF CONSTANTINE, THE; OR, THE VEILED VICTIM// D// n.a.// **Victoria**, June 1851, with E. Laws as Joseph, J. T. Johnson as Capt. D'Arville, John Silver as St. Aubin, Mr. Raymond as Taleb, John Bradshaw as Benasen, F. H. Henry as Haroun, G. F. Forman as Nobbles, James Howard as Beebee, Mrs. Hudson Kirby as Naomi, Mrs. George Lee as Kadiga, Mrs. Manders as Ruth, Georgiana Lebatt as Fifine/ Scenery by Mr. Hawthorn/ Machines by Wood & Foster/ Music by Mr. Barrowcliffe/ Prod. by T. H. Higgie.

JEW OF LUBECK, THE; OR, THE FATHER AND THE PRODIGAL SON// D// H. M. Milner// **Sad. Wells**, Jan. 1843, with Mr. Aldridge as Prince Ferdinand, C. J. Bird as Donamar, Mr. Dry as Magliano, Henry Marston as The Jew, Charles Fenton as Stefano, Mr. Williams as Van Furstin, John Herbert as Lindor, Caroline Rankley as Rosa, Mrs. Richard Barnett as Jella; Apr. 1857, with Mr. Vivian as Prince Ferdinand, R. H. Lingham as Donamar, T. Lyon as The Jew, James Worrell as Magliano, Charles Fenton as Stefano, Marianne Jackson as Rosa, Mary A. Victor as Jella.

JEW'S DAUGHTER, THE// D 2a// Edward Stirling// **Strand**, Jan. 1857.

JEWELLER OF ST. JAMES'S, THE// C 3a// Adap. by W. E. Suter fr F of H. de St. Georges & A. de Leuven// **Opera Comique**, Feb. 1862.

JEWESS, THE// D 4a// Adap. by Louis Ludovici fr G of Salomon Mosenthal, Deborah// **Shaftesbury**, June 1899, with Lester Lonergan as Father Joseph, Maclyn Arbuckle as Nathan, W. P. Carleton as Father Ignatius, George Barnum as Ludwig, McKee Rankin as Father Lorenz, Nance O'Neil as Leah, Julie Ring as Lena, Rose Snyder as Dame Groshen, E. A. Eberle as Mother Lisa, Miss Belmont as Rachel.

JEWESS, THE; OR, THE COUNCIL OF CONSTANCE// D// J. R. Planché// **Sad. Wells**, Aug. 1842, with C. J. Smith as Emperor Sigismund, Mr. Dry as Cardinal Brogny, Mr. Aldridge as Provost, Henry Marston as Eleazar, C. J. Bird as Leopold, Mr. Williams as Bishop, Caroline Rankeley as Rachel, Mrs. Henry Marston as Princess Eudosia; Nov. 1851, with Edward Knight as Emperor Sigismund, Frederic Robinson as Prince Leopold, George Bennett as de Brozny, Mr. Williamson as Bishop of Constance, Henry Marston as Elcazar, Eliza Travers as Princess Eudocia, Miss Goddard as Rachel/ **Victoria**, Mar. 1859, with Mr. Morrison as Emperor Sigismund, W. H. Pitt as Prince Leopold, S. Sawford as de Brogni, I. Cohen as St. Marc, F. H. Henry as Albert, J. H. Rickards as Mendizabel, Edwin Yarnold as Forester, James Howard as Bazil, Mr. Hitchinson as Karl, Miss Barroughcliffe [sic] as Empress Barba, Miss Honey as Princess Eudocia, Angelina Bathurst as Rachel, Miss Laporte as Abigail/ Scenery by Mildenhall & J. Wright/ Machines by Wood & Foster/ **Grecian**, July 1863, with W. Shirley, George Gillett, Henry Grant, Alfred Rayner, Marie Brewer, Ellen Hale.

JEWESS AND THE CHRISTIAN, THE; OR, THE LOVE THAT KILLS// D 4a// E. Manuel// **Britannia**, Apr. 1877.

JILT, THE// C 5a// Dion Boucicault// **Elephant & Castle**, July 1885/ **POW**, July 1886, with Dion Boucicault, John Billington, Myra Holme, Mary Barker, Roma Le Thière.

JILTED; AN OLD STORY RETOLD// C 2a// Alfred Maltby// **Criterion**, July 1879, with J. Russell, George Giddens, Caroline Harvey, Mary Rorke.

JIM ALONG JOSEY// F// n.a.// **Sad. Wells**, Feb. 1841, with Mr. Aldridge as Fitzsnooks, Mr. Elvin as Mortimer, Mr. Conquest as Josey, Mr. Richardson as Puffpaste, Charles Fenton as Pump, Mr. Stilt as Glutton, Miss Cooke as Mrs. Fitzsnooks, Mrs. Morgan as Julia, Mrs. Richard Barnett as Dolly, Miss Rose as Mrs. Glutton.

JIM CROW// C// n.a.// **Sad. Wells**, Mar. 1837, with J. Dunn as Jim Crow, Mr. Gay as Boots, Mr. Rogers as Sambo, Thomas Lee as Mealymouth, Mr. Scarbrow as Patchem, Mrs. Harris as Miss Rosa, Miss Lebatt as Dinah, Miss Hamilton as Mrs. Broom, Miss Wilson as Mrs. Patchem, Miss Jones as Mrs. Mealymouth.

JIM CROW IN HIS NEW PLACE// D// T. P. Taylor// **Haymarket**, Mar. 1839, with T. D. Rice as Jim Crow, William Strickland as Sir Solomon, T. F. Mathews as Grub, James Worrell as Seymour, Mrs. Gallot as Lady in White, Mrs. Frank Matthews as Deborah, Mrs. Partridge as Sally, Miss Gallot as Arabella.

JIM THE PENMAN// D 4a// Charles Young// **Haymarket**, Mar. 1886, with Arthur Dacre as Ralston, Yorke Stephens as Percival, M. Marius as Baron Hauteville, Charles Brookfield as Capt. Redwood, Edmund Maurice as Lord Drelincourt, Frank Rodney as George, Forbes Dawson as Chapstone, G. Farquhar as Netherby, P. Ben Greet as Pettywise, Helen Forsyth as Agnes, Henrietta Lindley as Lady Dunscombe, Mrs. E. H. Brooke as Mrs. Chapstone, Lady Monckton as Mrs. Ralston.

JIMMY WATT// D 3a// Dion Boucicault// **Elephant & Castle**, Aug. 1890.

JINGLE// FC 6a// Dram. by James Albery fr Charles Dickens, The Pickwick Papers// **Lyceum**, July 1878, with Henry Irving as Alfred Jingle, F. Lyons as Pickwick, W. Branscombe as Winkle, Mr. Andrews as Tupman, Mr. Hamilton as Snodgrass, Mr. Collett as Wardle, Arthur Wing Pinero as Perker, R. C. Lyons as Sam Weller, Georgina Pauncefort as Rachel Wardle, Miss Hammond as Arabella Nupkins, Isa Johnson as Emily/ Scenery by Hawes Craven/ Music by Robert Stoepel.

JINKS; OR, THE MAN WHO CAN'T HELP

IT// F// n.a.// **Grecian**, Jan. 1845, with Frederick Robson as Jinks, Mr. Campbell as Sly, Miss Atkins as Dolly, Annette Mears as Miss Flounce, Miss Merion as Mrs. Sly.

JO// D 3a// Dram. by J. P. Burnett fr novel of Charles Dickens, Bleak House// **Globe**, Mar. 1876, with Edward Price as Sir Leicester Dedlock, Charles Flockton as Tulkinghorn, J. B. Rae as Snagsby, C. Wilmot as Chadband, Charles Steyne as Guppy, J. P. Burnett as Bucket, Jennie Lee as Jo, Louise Hibbert as Lady Dedlock, Nelly Harris as Esther, Dolores Drummond as Hortense/ Scenery by W. Bruce Smith/ **Olympic**, Apr. 1881, with Gray Dolby as Sir Leicester Dedlock, J. A. Howell as Tulkinghorn, Percy Compton as Snagsby, Dalton Somers as Guppy, Henry Crisp as Chadband, J. P. Burnett as Bucket, Jennie Lee as Jo, Florence Bennett as Lady Dedlock, Dolores Drummond as Hortense, Florence Smithers as Guster, Miss C. Steele as Mrs. Snagsby, Mrs. C. Humphreys as Mrs. Rouncewell/ **Drury Lane**, May. 1896.

JOAN OF ARC// D 4a// Tom Taylor// **Queen's**, Apr. 1871.

JOAN OF ARC// D 5a// E. Villers// **East London**, Aug. 1871.

JOAN OF ARC// D// G. W. Innes// **Sad. Wells**, Sept. 1890.

JOAN OF ARC; OR, THE MAID OF ORLEANS// D 3a// Edward Fitzball// **Cov. Garden**, Nov. 1837, with Mr. Serle as Charles VII, John Pritchard as Dunois, Mr. Roberts as La Hire, Mr. Tilbury as Arnaud, Henry Howe as Montfort, George Bennett as Thibaut, Charles Diddear as Raimond, Edwin Yarnold as Colbert, C. J. Smith as Graville, Drinkwater Meadows as Wizard, W. H. Payne as Fiend Knight, Mrs. W. Clifford as Queen Isabel, Miss Huddart as Joan, Mrs. East as Madelon, Miss Garrick as Louise, James Anderson as Sir Lionel, Mr. Waldron as Talbot, John Ayliffe as Gargrave/ **Sad. Wells**, Apr. 1838, with Mr. Ranson as Prince Charles, Mr. Campbell as Beauvais, S. Smith as Scales, Mr. Gay as Richemont, Mr. Nunn as Chalons, James Worrell as Valiante, Miss Watkins as Joan, Miss Chartley as Lucelle.

JOAN OF ARC; OR, THE MAID, THE AMAZON, AND THE MARTYR// D 3a// Charles Clarke// **Victoria**, Aug. 1871.

JOCRISSE, THE JUGGLER// D 3a// Adap. fr F of A. P. D'Ennery & Jules Bresil// **Adelphi**, Apr. 1861.

JOE STERLING; OR, A RAGGED FORTUNE// D 3a// C. H. Hazlewood// **Victoria**, Nov. 1870.

JOE, THE ORPHAN// D// n.a.// **Marylebone**, Nov. 1846, with T. Lee.

JOHN-A-DREAMS// Play 4a// C. Haddon Chambers// **Haymarket**, Nov. 1894, with Herbert Beerbohm Tree as Wynn, Charles Cartwright as Sir Hubert, Charles Allan as Lord Barbridge, Nutcombe Gould as Rev. Wynn, Herbert Ross as De Coburn, Edmund Maurice as Wanklyn, Percival Stevens as George, Mrs. Patrick Campbell as Kate, Roma Le Thiere as Lady Barbridge, Janette Steer as Mrs. Wamklyn/ Scenery by Walter Johnstone & Walter Hann.

JOHN BULL// C // Adap. by Dion Boucicault fr orig, of George Colman the younger// **Gaiety**, July 1872.

JOHN BULL; OR, AN ENGLISHMAN'S FIRE-SIDE// C 5a// George Colman the younger// **Haymarket**, Sept. 1837, with William Dowton as Thornberry, Tyrone Power as Bulgruddery, E. W. Elton as Peregrine, Robert Strickland as Rochdale, Charles Selby as Frank, Frederick Vining as Shuffleton, J. B. Buckstone as Dan, T. F. Mathews as Burr, Mrs. Nisbett as Lady Caroline, Miss Allison as Mary, Mrs. Julia Glover as Mrs. Bulgruddery; May 1848, with William Creswick as Peregrine, Mr. Tilbury as Sir Simon, Henry Vandenhoff as Frank Rochedale, Alfred Wigan as Shuffleton, William Farren as Thornberry, Charles Hudson as Brulgruddery, T. F. Mathews as Dan, Mr. Rogers as Burr, Mrs. Julia Glover as Mrs. Brulgruddery, Mrs. Nisbett as Lady Caroline, Miss Fortescue as Mary; Nov. 1854, with W. H. Chippendale as Thornberry, Henry Howe as Peregrine, Mr. Rogers as Sir Simon, William Farren as Shuffleton, Edwin Villiers as Frank, Charles Hudson as Brulgruddery, Henry Compton as Dan, Ellen Chaplin as Lady Caroline, Miss Martindale as Mary, Mrs. Poynter as Mrs. Brulgruddery/ **Cov. Garden**, Dec. 1839, with Frank Matthews as Sir Simon, C. J. Mathews as Shuffleton, James Vining as Rochdale, Mr. Cooper as Peregrine, George Bartley as Thornberry, John Brougham as Brulgruddery, Drinkwater Meadows as Dan, Mr. Granby as Burr, Louisa Nisbett as Lady Caroline, Mrs. Charles Jones as Mrs. Brulgruddery, Mrs. Walter Lacy (Miss Taylor) as Mary/ **Sad. Wells**, Feb. 1841, with Henry Marston as Peregrine, Mr. Williams as Sir Simon, Mr. Elvin as Frank, Walter Lacy as Shuffleton, Alfred Rayner as Thornberry, Mr. Aldridge as Burr, Robert Honner as Dan, Thomas Lee as Brulgruddery, Miss Richardson as Lady Caroline, Miss Cocke as Mrs. Brulgruddery, Mrs. Robert Honner as Mary/ **Grecian**, Oct. 1844, with Edwin Dixon as Peregrine, Harry Chester as Shuffleton, Mr. Campbell as Thornberry, Frederick Robson as Dan, Mr. Kerridge as Simon, Mrs. Chester as Lady Caroline, Mary A. Crisp as Mary, Miss Merion as Mrs. Bulgruddery/ **Olympic**, Sept. 1846, with Mr. Hyde as Peregine, Mr. Purdy as Thornbury, "A Gentleman" as Rochdale, Mr. Fitzgerald as Dan, Mr. Jones as Burr, Mr. Hamersley as Shuffleton, J. S. Ward as Bulgruddery, "A Young Lady" as Lady Caroline, Miss Cobham as Mary, Mrs. Roberts as Mrs. Bulgruddery; May 1848, with George Bennett as Thornberry, H. Lee as Bulgruddery, Henry Mellon as Peregrine, Charles Perkins as Sir Simon, Lysander Thompson as Dan, Henry Holl as Shuffleton, Miss May as Mary, Kate Howard as Lady Caroline, Mrs. Parker as Mrs. Bulgruddery/ **Drury Lane**, Feb. 1851, with J. W. Ray as Sir Simon, Henry Butler as Rochdale, Walter Lacy as Shuffleton, Samuel Emery as Thornberry, Mr. Barrett as

Brulgruddery, Mr. Cooper as Peregrine, John Chester as Dan, Mr. Bisson as Burr, Mrs. Walter Lacy as Lady Caroline, Fanny Vining as Mary, Mrs. Bisson as Mrs. Brulgruddery.

JOHN DOBBS// F 1a// J. Maddison Morton// **Strand**, Apr. 1849/ **Haymarket**, June 1851, with Mr. Rogers as Fallowfield, John Parselle as Maj. Frankman, J. B. Buckstone as Paternoster, Leigh Murray as Dobbs, Mrs. L. S. Buckingham as Mrs. Chesterton, Amelia Vining as Lucy/ **Olympic**, May 1852, with Charles Bender as Fallowfield, John Kinloch as Maj. Frankman, Henry Compton as Paternoster, William Farren Jr. as John Dobbs, Miss Fielding as Mrs. Chesterton, Isabel Adams as Lucy; June 1862, with George Cooke as Fallowfield, Harwood Cooper as Frankman, Horace Wigan as Paternoster, Henry Neville as John Dobbs, Mrs. St. Henry as Mrs. Chesterton, Miss F. Haydon as Lucy/ **Sad. Wells**, Sept. 1852, with Henry Mellon as Fallowfield, Mr. Wallis as Maj. Frankman, Frederic Robinson as Dobbs, Lewis Ball as Paternoster, Miss T. Bassano as Mrs. Chesterton, Miss Mandelbert as Lucy/ **Grecian**, Mar. 1857, with Eaton O'Donnell as Fallowfield, C. Kelsey as Frankman, Richard Phillips as John Dobbs, John Manning as Paternoster, Jane Coveney as Miss Chesterton, Ellen Hale as Lucy.

JOHN DURNFORD, M.P.// Play 4a// Stuart Ogilvie// **Court**, Sept. 1901.

JOHN FELTON THE MAN OF THE PEOPLE; OR, THE MAID OF ERIN AND THE GRIFFIN OF THE THAMES// D 3a// Edward Stirling// **Victoria**, Apr. 1850, with Mr. Henderson as Buckingham, Mr. Hitchinson as Duke de Soubise, Mr. Richards as Sir Thomas, David Osbaldiston as Felton, James Howard as Lamb, J. Neville as Allnutt, Henry Dudley as Ferryman, J. T. Johnson as Griffin, Mr. Humphreys as L'Ennois, Miss Vincent as Kathleen, Miss Allford as Mme. de Hautefort, Mrs. Cooke as Dame Allnutt, Miss Barrowcliffe as Mog/ Scenery by Mildenhall/ Machines by Wood & Foster/ Music by Mr. Barrowcliffe.

JOHN FROCK; OR, THE PREJUDICE OF THE AGE// D 2a// John Courtney// **Grecian**, Aug. 1854, with Basil Potter as Maj. von Tulpen, Henry Grant as Count Maugeheim, Charles Horn as Burkhart, Richard Phillips as John Frock, Jane Coveney as Josephine, Harriet Coveney as Leonore.

JOHN GABRIEL BORKMAN// Play 4a// Transl. by William Archer fr Norw. of Henrik Ibsen// **Strand**, May 1897, with W. H. Vernon as Borkman, John Martin Harvey as Erhart Borkman, James Welch as Foldal, Genevieve Ward as Mrs. Borkman, Elizabeth Robins as Ella, Mrs. H. B. Tree as Mrs. Wilton, Dora Barton as Frida/ Scenery by Walter Bayes.

JOHN JASPER'S WIFE// C 4a// Frank Harvey// **Standard**, May 1876.

JOHN JONES// F 1a// J. B. Buckstone// **Haymarket**, June 1837, with William Farren as Goodluck, John Webster as Jones, Robert Strickland as Milton, Mrs. Humby as Eliza, Miss Gallot as Jenny; Apr. 1862, with Henry Compton as Goodluck, William Cullenford as Melton, Edwin Villiers as Jones, Mr. Weathersby as Cox, Eliza Weekes as Eliza, Mrs. Coe as Henny/ **Adelphi**, July 1853, with George Honey as Goodluck, William Cullenford as Melton, Mr. Parselle as John Jones, Emma Harding as Eliza/ **Sad. Wells**, Nov. 1857, with J. W. Ray as Goodluck, Mr. Williams as Melton, William Belford as Jones, James Lickfold as Cox, Mr. Walters as Trapper, Jenny Marston as Eliza, Caroline Parkes as Jenny.

JOHN OF PARIS// D// Isaac Pocock// **Victoria**, Sept. 1837, with James Vining as John of Paris, Frank Matthews as Chamberlain, Mr. Leffler as Theodore, Miss Lee as Olivia, Mr. Conquest as Pedrigo, Mr. Hitchinson as Gregory, Paul Bedford as Philip, Miss Betts as Princess of Navarre, Mrs. Frank Matthews as Rosa/ **Sad. Wells**, Dec. 1844, with Henry Marston as John of Paris, A. Younge as Chamberlain, Miss Lebatt as Olivia, R. Norman as Potts, Mr. Sharp as Gregory, Frank Graham as Philip, Mr. Sievier as Theodore, Miss Huddart as Queen of Navarre, Georgiana Lebatt as Rosa.

JOHN OF PROCIDA// Play 5a// Sheridan Knowles// **Cov. Garden**, Sept. 1840, with James Anderson.

JOHN OVERY; OR THE MISER OF SOUTHWARK FERRY// D 3a// Douglas Jerrold// **Sad. Wells**, Mar. 1840, with Mr. Williams as Overy, Mr. Dry as Shotbolt, Henry Hall as Bosk, Mr. Moreton as Baron Fitzgeffrey, Mr. Elvin as Mayfly, J. W. Collier as Parroquet, Miss Pincott as Tristan, Miss Hicks as Leonard, Miss Richardson as Mary/ **Grecian**, Mar 1847, with Mr. Campbell as John Overy, Charles Horn as Shotbolt, Frederick Robson as Bosk, Mr. Manley as Baron Fitzgeffery, Edwin Dixon as Mayfly, Eaton O'Donnell as Parroquet, Annette Mears as Tristan, Mary A. Crisp as Mary Overy.

JOHN SAVILE OF HAYSTEAD// D 5a// James White// **Sad. Wells**, Nov. 1847, with Henry Marston as Villiers, J. T. Johnson as Epslie, William Hoskins as Trivett, Henry Scharf as Sir Stephen, Mr. Stilt as Granville, Samuel Phelps as Savile, George Bennett as Felton, A. Younge as Clayton, Frank Graham as Soubise, Laura Addison as Lilian, Mrs. Henry Marston as Bridget/ Scenery by F. Fenton & Mr. Finlay.

JOHN SMITH// F 1a// William Hancock// **Strand**, Jan. 1862.

JOHN THURGOOD, FARMER// D 1a// Henry Byatt// **Globe**, June 1893, with Wilton Heriot as Armstrong, Cecil Thornbury as Thurgood, Henry Besley as Henry, Mabel Lane as Annie.

JOINT HOUSEHOLD, A// C 1a// Mrs. Hugh Bell// **Grand**, May 1892.

JOKER, THE// FC 3a// M. H. Tennyson// **Avenue**, Nov. 1894, with Fred Thorne as Miller, Henry Ashford as George,, Alfred Maltby as Crowe, Lewis Fitzhamon as Felix, Cosmo

Stuart as Brewster, Emily Thorne as Mrs. Crowe, Ethel Christine as Penelope.

JOLLIBOY'S WOES// F 1a// Charles Fawcett// **Olympic**, Dec. 1878, with Harry Proctor as Jolliboy, Herbert Beerbohm Tree as Gunter, C. A. Allbrook as Piggins, Miss Folkard as Deborah, Miss Beaumont as Susannah, Miss G. Marshall as Mary, Sophie Fane as Popsey, Massie Auber as Mrs. Gunter.

JOLLY JOE// D// C. H. Hazlewood Jr.// **Alexandra**, Nov. 1868.

JONATHAN BRADFORD; OR, THE MURDER AT THE ROADSIDE INN// D// Edward Fitzball// **Sad. Wells**, June 1837, with N. T. Hicks as Bradford, Mr. Campbell as Nelson, Mr. Rogers as Rackbottle, Mr. Conquest as Scrummidge, Thomas Lee as Dan, Mr. King as Haynes, Mrs. W. West as Ann, Lavinia Melville as Sally/ **Victoria**, Aug. 1854, with N. T. Hicks as Jonathan, E. F. Saville as Macraisy, Charles Rice as Scrummidge, T. E. Mills as Nelson, Mrs. Henry Vining as Anne, Miss Laporte as Sally/ **Grecian**, June 1861, with William James as Jonathan, Alfred Rayner as Dan, Mr. Jackson as Nelson, Walter Holland as Hayes, John Manning as Caleb Scrummidge, Henry Power as Jack, Mr. Costello as Dozey, Jane Coveney as Ann, Mrs. C. Fenton (Caroline Parkes) as Sally.

JONATHAN; OR, THE MAN WITH TWO MASTERS// F 1a// James Barber// **Astley's**, Mar. 1851, with Mr. Johnson as Ledgerly, Arthur Stirling as Alfred Morland, Thomas Barry as Jonathan, Mrs. Moreton Brookes as Caroline, Mrs. Beacham as Lucy.

JONATHAN WILD// Adap. by Henry Young fr novel of Harrison Ainsworth, Jack Sheppard// **Elephant & Castle**, Nov. 1886.

JONATHAN WILD; OR, THE STORM ON THE THAMES// D 4a// Mrs. H. Young// **East London**, July 1868.

JONES THE AVENGER// F 1a// Francis Talfourd// **Olympic**, Nov. 1856, with Frederick Robson as Jones, George Cooke as Tomlinson, Mr. Danvers as Doolan, James Rogers as Pipes, Miss Marston as Angelina.

JONES'S NOTES, THE// FC 3a// Joseph Tabrar// **Gaiety**, July 1886.

JOSIAH'S DREAM; OR, THE WOMAN OF THE FUTURE// FC 3a// Charles Rogers// **Strand**, May 1896, with Sidney Harcourt as Josiah, Graham Wentworth as Gushington, George Raiemond as Hardy, Richard Blunt as William, J. A. Bentham as Templeton, Ada Branson as Caroline, Lettice Fairfax as Georgina, Mary Allestree as Johanna, Florence Forster as Frederica.

JOSEPH CHAVIGNY// D// Watts Phillips// **Adelphi**, May 1856.

JOSEPH'S SWEETHEART// C 5a// Dram. by Robert Buchanan fr novel of Fielding// **Vaudeville**, Mar. 1888.

JOSEPHINE; OR, THE FORTUNE OF WAR// D 2a// Adap. by J. B. Buckstone fr Donizetti, La Fille du Regiment// **Haymarket**, Mar. 1844, with William Clark as Duke de Grandtete, James Bland as Sgt. Scalad, Mr. Tilbury as Pumpernickle, J. B. Buckstone as Guillot, Mr. Caulfield as Bernard, Mrs. Stanley as Duchess de Grandtete, Mrs. W. Clifford as Marchioness de Berkenfeldt, Mrs. Fitzwilliam as Josephine.

JOURNEY'S END, THE// Play 1a// Horace Newte// **Globe**, Jan. 1895, with H. Reeves Smith as Clements, Sydney Paxton as Blair, Cecil Thornbury as Briggs, Mabel Lane as Ethel, Emmie Merrick as Eleanor.

JOURNEYS END IN LOVERS MEETING// Play 1a// Mrs. P. Craigie ("John Hobbes") & George Moore// **Daly's**, June 1894, with Johnston Forbes Robertson as Sir Philip, William Terriss as Capt. Manamour, Ellen Terry as Lady Soupise.

JOY IS DANGEROUS// C 2a// James Mortimer// **Drury Lane**, Feb. 1872.

JUANA// T 4a// W. G. Wills// **Court**, May 1881, with Helena Modjeska, Johnston Forbes Robertson, Wilson Barrett, G. M. Anson, Ada Ward/ **Opera Comique** (rev. vers. in 3a), Apr. 1890.

JUDAEL// D 5a// Mrs. Julius Pollock// **Olympic**, May. 1885.

JUDAH// Play 3a// Henry Arthur Jones// **Shaftesbury**, May 1890, with Charles Fulton as Earl of Asgarby, Sant Matthews as Jopp, Frederick Kerr as Juxon Prall, Royce Carleton as Dethic, E. W. Thomas as Papworthy, E. S. Willard as Llewellyn, Bessie Hatton as Lady Eve, Gertrude Warden as Sophie, Adelaide Bowring as Mrs. Prall, Olga Brandon as Vashti/ Scenery by Walter Hann.

JUDGE, THE// FC 3a// Arthur Law// **Terry's**, July 1890, with W. S. Penley as Sir John, William Herbert as Stryver, Frank Fenton as Pringle, Mark Kinghorne as Mowle, William Lestocq as Shuttleworth, George Belmore as Ricketts, Cissy Grahame as Daphne, Emily Thorne as Mrs. Shuttleworth, Elsie Chester as Mrs. Ricketts, Helen Leyton as Chloe.

JUDGE JEFFREYS// Henry Spicer// **Sad. Wells**, Apr. 1846, with Henry Marston as Pomfret, George Bennett as Morgrave, Samuel Phelps as Jeffreys, Mr. Warde as Feversham, Edward Knight as Col. Kirke, E. Morton as L'Estrange, Henry Scharf as Tom, Henry Mellon as De Lisle, Mrs. Mary Warner as Lady Grace, Miss Cooper as Alice/ Scenery by F. Fenton & Mr. Finlay.

JUDGE NOT// D 5a// Frank Harvey// **Pavilion**, Aug. 1888.

JUDGEMENT// D Pro & 4a// John T. Douglass// **Standard**, Sept. 1885.

JUDITH SHAKESPEARE// D 1a// Dram. by E. B. Aveling ("Alec Nelson") fr novel of William Black// **Royalty**, Feb. 1894, with Rothbury Evans as Orridge, Frank Lacy as Quiny, Ernest Patterson as Evans, Lionel Calhaem as Hart, Eva Williams as Judith.

JUDITH OF GENEVA// D 3a// Thomas Morton Jr.// **Adelphi**, Jan. 1844, with Mr. Lyon as Advocat St. Val, George Maynard as Captain Henri St. Val, O. Smith as La Vogue, Edward Wright as Nicholas, John Sanders as the Butler, Mrs. Yates as Countess Malvoisine, Ellen Chaplin as Amy.

JUDY// Play 3a// Dram. by Roy Horniman fr novel of Percival Pickering, A life Awry// **POW**, May. 1899, with Arthur Lyle as Sir Edward, Wilfred Forster as Capt. Lilcot, Richard Lambart as Thornton, A. E. George as Choate, H. V. Surrey as Beales, Spencer Brunton as Maud, Jessie Bateman as Aline, Isabel Grey as Mrs. Dalton, Dorothy Heathcote as Mabel, Nina Boucicault as Judy/ Scenery by W. T. Hemsley.

JUGGLER OF PARIS, THE// D// n.a.// **Pavilion**, Sept. 1866.

JULIA// Play 3a// Arthur Sturgess// **Royalty**, Apr. 1898, with Robb Harwood as Minniver, Frank Atherley as Merridew, George Arliss as Bulpitt, Evelyn Dobell as Baggers, Louie Freer as Tom and as Julia Minniver, Maria Davis as Mrs. Merridew, Miss Furtado-Clarke as Clara/ Scenery by E. G. Banks/ Electrics by T. J. Digby/ Prod. by Arthur Sturgess.

JULIE LE MOINE; OR, THE ASSASSINS OF NANTES// D// C. Z. Barnett// **Victoria**, July 1850, with Mr. Morrison as Antoine Bruneau, Henry Frazer as Rodolphe Bruneau, J. T. Johnson as Myrtle, Mr. Humphries as Clarice, Mr. Henderson as Grimaud, John Hudspeth as Gull, Mr. Hitchinson as Voluys, James Howard as Briquet, Mrs. George Lee as Julie, Mrs. Cooke as Mere Grimaud, Georgiana Lebatt as Madelaine.

JULIET BY PROXY, A// C 1a// Hamilton Aidé// **St. James's**, June 1899, with Mrs. W. H. Kendal as Miss Oldfield, Annie Schletter as Kate, Gilbert Hare as Jervis.

JULIUS CAESAR// T// William Shakespeare// **Cov. Garden**, Apr. 1837, with W. C. Macready as Brutus, Mr. Vandenhoff as Cassius, Sheridan Knowles as Marc Antony, George Bennett as Caesar, John Pritchard as Octavius, Mr. Tilbury as Casca, John Webster as Decius, Miss Lee as Calpurnia, Mrs. W. West as Portia; May 1838, with W. C. Macready, Samuel Phelps, James Anderson, Helen Faucit/ **Sad. Wells**, June 1837, with John Pritchard as Marc Antony, Mr. King as Caesar, John Dale as Brutus, George Bennett as Cassius, Mr. Tilbury as Casca, C. H. Pitt as Decius, C. J. Smith as Octavius, Miss Williams as Calpurnia, Mrs. W. West as Portia; May 1846, with Henry Mellon as Caesar, E. Morton as Octavius, Henry Marston as Marc Antony, C. James as Lepidus, Samuel Phelps as Brutus, George Bennett as Cassius, Mr. Lacy as Casca, Mrs. Henry Marston as Calpurnia, Mrs. Mary Warner as Portia/ Scenery by F. Fenton, Mr. Finlay, & Mr. Brunning/ **Drury Lane**, June 1843, with John Ryder as Caesar, Charles Hudson as Octavius, James Anderson as Antony, W. C. Macready as Brutus, Samuel Phelps as Cassius, E. W. Elton as Casca, Mrs. Alfred Wigan as Lucius, Miss Ellis as Calpurnia, Helen Faucit as Portia; Feb. 1850, with Charles Fisher as Caesar, George Everett as Octavius, James Anderson as Antony, Mr. Vandenhoff as Brutus, Mr. Cathcart as Cassius, Mr. Cooper as Casca, Charles Diddear as Trebonius, William Montague as Decius, William Davidge as Soothsayer, Mrs. Ternan as Calpurnia, Miss Phillips as Portia/ **Princess's**, Apr. 1848, with Charles Fisher as Caesar, F. B. Conway as Octavius, W. C. Macready as Brutus, John Ryder as Cassius, Mr. Cooper as Marc Antony, J. Neville as Casca, John Gilbert as Decius, James Vining as Trebonius, Mrs. H. Hughes as Calpurnia, Emmeline Montague as Portia/ **Haymarket**, Nov. 1850, with Mr. Stuart as Caesar, John Parselle as Octavius, Henry Howe as Marc Antony, W. C. Macready as Brutus, E. L. Davenport as Cassius, Mr. Cooper as Casca, Charles Selby as Trebonius, Miss Reynolds as Calpurnia, Mrs. Mary Warner as Portia/ **City of London**, Nov. 1862, with G. V. Brooke as Brutus, John Ryder as Cassius, J. F. Young as Marc Antony/ **Olympic**, Apr. 1892, with Edmund Tearle as Brutus, Frederick Scarth as Cassius, W. S. Hardy as Marc Antony, A. Gow Bentinck as Julius Caesar, Jones Finch as Casca, Cyril Grier as Octavius, S. F. Walker as Trebonius, John Saunders as Metellus, Miss Glynne as Calpurnia, Theresa Osborne as Portia/ **Her Majesty's**, Jan. 1898 (in 3a), with Herbert Beerbohm Tree.

JUMBO JUM// F 1a// n.a.// **Grecian**, June 1865, with Dan Leeson as Jumbo Jum, J. Jackson as Gobbleton, George Gillett as Melville, W. Shirley as Cheatum, Miss Churchill as Adelaide, Mrs. J. W. Simpson as Hannah.

JUNIUS; OR, THE HOUSEHOLD GODS// Play 5a// Edward Bulwer-Lytton// **Princess's**, Feb. 1885, with Wilson Barrett as Junius, Mary Eastlake as Lucretia, E. S. Willard as Sextus Tarquin, Neville Doone as Aruns Tarquin, H. Evans as Valerius, Charles Fulton as Papinius, H. Besley as Titus, C. Burleigh as Lucius, Walter Speakman as Casca, Charles Hudson as Vindex, John Dewhurst as Sophronion, Clifford Cooper as Lucretius, Bernard Gould as Collantinus/ Scenery by Walter Hann, Stafford Hall, W. E. Beverley & W. L. Telbin/ Prod. by Wilson Barrett.

JUST IN TIME; OR, MURDER ON THE SEDGLEY ROAD (also subt. The Old Toll House)// D 3a// J. A. Cave// **Grecian**, Apr. 1865, with David Jones as Broxbourne, W. Howard as Beech, George Gillett as Burgess, J. Jackson as Fielding, Mr. Goodin as Miller, Henry Power as Rackstraw, John Manning as Bartlemy, George Conquest as Bunnage, J. B. Steele as Blackbourne, Lizzie Mandelbert as Phoebe, Mary A. Victor as Patty, Walter Holland as Lawrence, Henry Grant as Lying.

JUST LIKE A WOMAN// C 3a// A. W. Dubourg//

Gaiety, Nov. 1879, with John Maclean, Mrs. Chippendale, Louise Willes.

JUST LIKE ROGER// F 1a// W. Webster// **Adelphi**, May 1872, with C. H. Stephenson as Glubb, Henry Ashley as Snap, Brittain Wright as Jumph, Harwood Cooper as Blackman, A. C. Lilly as Edgar, Miss Stoker as Buttons, Miss Phillips as Lucy.

JUST MY LUCK// D// Alfred Rayner// **Sad. Wells**, July 1857, with Watkins Young as The Guest, John Chester as Cobb, R. Green as Landlord, Mr. Grey as Rigby, Alfred Rayner as Scatchard, G. Shore as Wilfred, Mrs. E. F. Saville as Rebecca, Mary A. Victor as Nelly, Mrs. Manders as Hester, Miss Chapman as Mrs. Scatchard.

JUST MY LUCK// F 1a// Alfred Maltby// **Lyceum**, Mar. 1878, with Edmund Lyons as Muffington Crumpets, Arthur Wing Pínero as Capt. Dunn, Mr. Branscombe as Mike, Mrs. St. John as Mrs. Crumpets, Eva Morley as Matilda.

*

KARIN// Play 2a// Trans. by Mrs. Hugh Bell fr Swed. of Alfhild Agrell// **Vaudeville**, May 1892, with Fuller Mellish as Hjerne, John Beauchamp as Milden, Herbert Ross as Niels, Ben Greet as Doctor, Elizabeth Robins as Karin, Kate Bateman as Mrs. Hjerne.

KARL; OR, THE LOVE THAT WINS// Play 5a// Herbert Mooney// **Standard**, June 1884.

KATAWAMPUS// Play// Louis Calvert & Judge Parry// **POW**, Dec. 1901.

KATE KEARNEY; OR, THE SPIRIT OF KILLARNEY// D// William Collier// **Grecian**, Feb. 1864, with Thomas Mead as Fairfield, Henry Grant as Rookwood, J. B. Steele as Capt. Cormorant, E. Howard as Buttens, J. Jackson as Lord Drobery, John Manning as H.B., Marie Brewer as Lady Emily, Louisa Graham as Mrs. Kearney, Mrs. Charles Dillon as Kate, Mary A. Victor as Nelly, Laura Conquest as Lurline/ Scenery by C. Smithers/ Prod. by George Conquest.

KATE PAYTON'S LOVERS// D 1a// Charles Reade// **Queen's**, Dec. 1883.

KATHERINE AND PETRUCHIO// C 3a// Alt. by David Garrick fr Shakespeare's <u>The Taming of the Shrew</u>// **Cov. Garden**, Mar. 1837, with John Pritchard as Petruchio, Mr. Thompson as Baptista, John Webster as Hortensio, Benjamin Webster as Grumio, Helen Faucit as Katherine, Mrs. Sarah Garrick as Curtis, Miss Lee as Bianca/ **Sad. Wells**, June 1837, with John Pritchard as Petruchio, Mr. Griffiths as Baptiste, C. J. Smith as Hortensio, C. H. Pitt as Biondello, Mr. Conquest as Grumio, Mr. Rogers as Tailor, Mr. Ennis as Pedro, Mrs. W. West as Katherine, Mrs. Harris as Curtis, Mrs. Rogers as Bianca; July 1844, with Henry Marston as Petruchio, Mr. Williams as Baptiste, G. F. Forman as Grumio, Mr. Sharp as Biondello, Mr. Evain as Pedro, Mr. Binge as Hortensio, Mrs. Mary Warner as Katherine, Emma Harding as Bianca, Mrs. Henry Marston as Curtis/ **Haymarket**, Dec. 1840, with James Wallack as Petruchio, Robert Strickland as Baptista, Henry Howe as Hortensio, James Worrell as Biondello, David Rees as Grumio, Mrs. Stirling as Katherine, Miss Grove as Bianca, Mrs. Stanley as Curtis; June 1885, with Johnston Forbes Robertson as Petruchio, Edmund Maurice as Baptista, Charles Eaton as Hortensio, Henry Kemble as Grumio, Charles Brookfield as Biondello, Mrs. Bernard Beere as Katharine, Maud Williamson as Bianca, Julia Gwynne as Curtis/ **Victoria**, Nov. 1842, with Mr. James as Baptiste, David Osbaldiston as Petruchio, William Seaman as Hortensio, C. Williams as Music Master, James Howard as Biodello, John Gardner as Grumio, Annette Vincent as Katherine, Miss Saddler as Bianca, Mrs. Griffith as Curtis/ **Princess's**, July 1845, with William Wallack as Petruchio, Mr. Granby as Baptista, James Ranoe as Hortensio, Henry Compton as Grumio, W. H. Oxberry as Tailor, Mrs. Stirling as Katherine, Miss E. Honner as Bianca, Mrs. Fosbroke as Curtis; Mar. 1881, with Edwin Booth as Petruchio, John Beauchamp as Baptista, John Gardiner as Biondello, W. Chamberlain as Pedro, Stanislaus Calhaem as Grumio, Miss Masson as Katherine, Miss Lyons as Curtis; June, 1875, with Helen Barry, William Rignold/ **Grecian**, Oct. 1845, with Harry Chester as Petruchio, John Collett as Baptista, Mr. Melvin as Hortensio, Frederick Robson as Grumio, Edmund Garden as Biondello, Mary A. Crisp as Katharine, Miss Johnstone as Bianca; July 1866, with Mr. Richards as Petruchio, George Gillett as Biondello, J. Jackson as Baptista, John Manning as Grumio, Lizzie Mandelbert as Katherine, Harriet Western as Bianca/ **Olympic**, Mar. 1848, with Henry Holl as Petruchio, Mr. Archer as Baptista, H. J. Turner as Grumio, Mrs. Brougham as Katherine, Mrs. H. Lee as Curtis/ **Drury Lane**, Dec. 1855, with Barry Sullivan as Petruchio, Mr. Tilbury as Baptista, Henry Ashley as Hortensio, A. Younge as Grumio, Miss Anderton as Katherine, Miss De Vere as Bianca, Mrs. Selby as Curtis; Feb. 1881, with Edwin Booth as Petruchio, John Beauchamp as Baptista, Bella Pateman as Katherine, John Gardiner as Biondello, Robert Pateman as Grumio, Mrs. Lyons as Curtis, Mr. Kendal as Cook/ **Astley's**, Feb. 1857, with James Holloway as Petruchio, Mr. Campbell as Baptista, J. T. Anderson as Hortensio, J. W. Anson as Grumio, Henry Reeves as Biondello, Mrs. J. W. Anson as Katharine, Mrs. William Dowton as Curtis, Miss Dowton as Bianca/ Scenery by T. Thompson/ Machines by E. Pryce/ Music by G. Phillips/ Horses trained by Wm. Cooke/ **Queen's**, Dec. 1867, with Henry Irving/ **Adelphi**, Feb. 1880, with Henry Neville as Petruchio, M. Byrnes as Baptista, Harwood

Cooper as Hortensio, F. W. Irish as Grumio, Robert Pateman as the Tailor, Bella Pateman as Katherine, Maria Harris as Bianca, Harriet Coveney as Curtis/ **Her Majesty's**, Nov. 1897.

KATHARINE HOWARD; OR, THE TOMB, THE THRONE, AND THE SCAFFOLD// D// n.a.// **Sad. Wells**, May 1869, with W. Thomas as Henry VIII, Frederick Maynard as Athelwold, Wade Clinton as Cranmer, Mr. Wilson as Sussex, Mr. Baxter as Norfolk, Mr. Monks as Chamberlain, Mr. Lawson as Fleming, P. Clifford as Martin, Carrie Clifford as Princess Margaret, Rose Gerard as Katherine, Miss J. Charles as Dame Kennedy, Louise Murray as Winifred.

KATHLEEN MAVOURNEEN; OR, ST. PATRICK'S EVE// D 4a// William Travers// **Sad. Wells**, Aug. 1866, with Agnes Burdett as Kathleen, Julia Summers as Dorothy, Annette Vincent as Meg, J. A. Cave as O'Moore, G. F. Warde as Kavanagh, F. Watts as Capt. Clearfield, Watty Brunton as O'Whack, W. M. Schofield as Fr. O'Cassidy, T. B. Bennett as McCullen/ Music by Leonard Giorgi, Machines by Mr. Tyrell, Electric light effects by Mr. Tyrell Jr.

KATTI, THE FAMILY HELP// C 3a// Adap. by Charles Fawcett fr F of Henri Meilhac, Gotte// **Strand**, Feb. 1888.

KATTY O'SHIEL; OR, THE FOLLOWER OF THE FAMILY// D// n.a.// **Victoria**, Nov. 1841, with John Dale as O'Dwyer, James Howard as Lenser, John Gardner as Twist, Mr. Paul as Card, William Seaman as Jessamy, C. Williams as O'Shiel, Mr. James as Gray, Annette Vincent as Katty, Mrs. George Lee as Lady Langham, Miss Wilton as Evelyn, Mrs. Garthwaite as Granny Twist/ Prod. by Mr. Osbaldiston.

KEELEY WORRIED BY BUCKSTONE// F 1a// Mark Lemon & Benjamin Webster// **Haymarket**, June 1852.

KEEP YOUR EYE ON HER// F 1a// T. J. Williams// **Olympic**, Sept. 1876, with Robert Pateman as Slowcoach, F. Cameron as Tomkins, T. G. Warren as Foster, Miss Beaumont as Phoebe, Lilly Cowell as Mary.

KEEP YOUR TEMPER// F 1a// J. P. Wooler// **Strand**, July 1862.

KEEPING A PLACE// F 1a// T. H. Reynoldson// **Princess's**, Nov. 1846, with Mr. Granby as Maj. Spikespur, Henry Compton as Crocus, Mrs. Fosbroke as Dorothea, Miss Laporte as Tidy.

KENILWORTH; OR, THE GENTLE AMY ROBSART// D 3a// n.a.// **Royal Alfred**, Nov. 1870.

KENILWORTH; OR, THE GOLDEN DAYS OF ENGLAND'S ELIZABETH (also subt., Golden Days of Queen Bess)// D// Dram. fr novel of Sir Walter Scott// **Drury Lane**, Apr. 1837, with Mr. Cooper as Leicester, Charles Diddear as Sussex, Frederick Cooke as Shrewsbury, Charles Fenton as Lee, Mr. Howell as Bowyer, Mr. Heath as Secretary, Mr. Henry as Blount, Mr. Warde as Varney, A. Brindal as Tressillian, Mr. Hooper as Raleigh, Mr. Mathews as Foster, Paul Bedford as Lambourne, Drinkwater Meadows as Smith, Fanny Huddart as Queen Elizabeth, Agnes Taylor as Amy Robsart, Miss Somerville as Countess of Rutland, Mrs. Humby as Janet, Miss Pincott as Cicely/ **Sad. Wells**, Aug. 1837, with N. T. Hicks as Leicester, Mr. Scarbrow as Sussex, Mr. Ennis as Hunsden, Mr. George as Sir Thomas, Mr. Williams as Sir Henry, Mr. Cussens as Burleigh, Mr. Pateman as Raleigh, C. H. Pitt as Varney, C. J. Smith as Tressilian, Mr. King as Lambourne, Mr. Campbell as Foster, Mr. Griffith as Smith, Mr. Ede as Gosling, Miss Williams as Queen Elizabeth, Lavinia Melville as Amy Robsart, Mrs. Harris as Janet; Apr. 1840, with Henry Marston as Leicester, Mr. Dry as Varney, W. D. Broadfoot as Hunsdon, Mr. Stilt as Essex, George Burt as Burleigh, Mr. Moreton as Raleigh, Mr. Elvin as Tresilian, J. W. Collier as Lamborne, Mrs. Robert Honner as Amy Robsart, Miss Richardson as Queen Elizabeth, Miss Pincott as Janet/ **Astley's**, June 1858, with James Holloway as Leicester, G. Clair as Varney, Mr. Rousilli as Sussex, J. T. Anderson as Tresilian, C. Bradbury as Raleigh, J. W. Anson as Lambourne, Mark Howard as Foster, Mrs. William Dowton as Queen Elizabeth, Miss Dowton as Amy, Julia Weston as Janet/ Scenery by Saunders & Thorne/ Machines by Mr. McLeod/ Music by G. Phillips/ Horses trained by Wm. Cooke.

KENNYNGTON CROSSE; OR, THE OLD HOUSE ON THE COMMON// D 2a// T. E. Wilks// **Surrey**, June 1848.

KENNSINGTON GARDENS; OR, QUITE A LADIES' MAN// C 2a// Adap. by Robert Brough fr F// **Strand**, May 1851.

KENT COAST SMUGGLERS, THE; OR, THE MURDER ON THE SEA BEACH// D// n.a.// **Victoria**, Feb. 1848, with Charles Morelli as Wyndham, Mr. Henderson as Thornton, N. T. Hicks as Brockman, T. H. Higgie as Brandon, G. F. Forman as Booth, James Howard as Jack, John Dale as Old Gaveston, Walter Searle as Mathew, F. H. Henry as Luke, Annette Vincent as Anne, Miss Burroughcliffe as Harriet, Miss Young as Maud, Miss Edgar as Jessie.

KENTUCKIAN, THE// F// W. Bayle Bernard// **Cov. Garden**, Feb. 1845, with James H. Hackett as Col. Wildfire, Mr. Bass as Freeman, J. C. Bird as Percival, George Braid as Jenkins, Mr. Rogers as Cacsan, Mrs. Watson as Mrs. Luminary, Miss Love as Caroline, Miss Carter as Mrs. Freeman, Miss Fitzjames as Mary.

KENYON'S WIDOW// C 3a// Charles Brookfield// **Comedy**, May 1900.

KERRY; OR, NIGHT AND MORNING// Play// Adap. by Dion Boucicault fr F of Madame de Girardin, La Joie Fait Peur// **Terry's**, Jan. 1893, with Edward Terry as Kerry, W. T. Lovell as Desmond, Alfred Kendrick as Capt. Coldham, William Calvert as Mellish, Clara Cowper as Blanche, Annie Hill as Kate.

KESA; THE WIFE'S SACRIFICE// Play// Transl. fr Jap// **Coronet**, July 1900/ **Criterion**, June 1901.

KEY OF THE STREET, THE// n.a.// **Surrey**, Mar. 1866.

KEY TO KING SOLOMON'S RICHES, LIMITED// D 4a// Abbey St. Ruth// **Opera Comique**, Dec. 1896, with E. H. Vanderfelt as Baring, F. MacDonnell as Coppall, J. A. Arnold as Lazarus, Gilbert Yorke as Crawler, Ernest Bertram as Grice, Frederick Lane as van Zyl, Percy Murray as Col. Yates, Harry Paulton as Murphy, John Manley as McLimo, Bernard Liell as Downey, Lawrence Sterner as Rhodes, Norman Graham as Sillytoe, Agnes Paulton as Sam, Thea Lesbrooke as Farni, Abbey St. Ruth as Ruth, Mabel Hardinge as Cissy, Mrs. Mat Robson as Matilda, Marianne Caldwell as Jane/ Scenery by Leolyn Hart.

KIDDLE A WINK, ONE AND ALL// D 2a// Brownlow Hill// **Victoria**, Feb. 1864, with James Howard as Sir Anthony, George Rose as Evelyn, Brownlow Hill as Eugene, Basil Potter as Ivan, Frederick Villiers as Red, George Yarnold as Muddlepate, Maria Daly as Robin, J. B. Johnstone as Fuller, George Stretton as Stubbs, R. Marchant as Andrew, Adelaide Bowering as Alice, Miss E. Farren as Becky/ Scenery by Frederick Fenton.

KILL OR CURE// F// Charles Dance// **Sad. Wells**, Oct. 1846, with Henry Mellon as Mildman, A. Younge as Brown, Henry Scharf as John, Mr. Wilkins as Apothecary, Mrs. Henry Marston as Mrs. Brown, Miss Stephens as Betty.

KILLING TIME// C 1a// J. Maddison Morton// **Haymarket**, Nov. 1871, with Frederick Everill as The Damp Stranger, Mr. Clark as David, Miss Francis as Susan, Amy Sedgwick as Lady Marmaduke.

KIND HEART WITH A ROUGH COVERING, A// D// W. H. Pitt// **Pavilion**, July 1875.

KIND TO A FAULT// C 2a// William Brough// **Strand**, Nov. 1867.

KING AND I, THE// F 1a// J. Maddison Morton// **Haymarket**, June 1845, with Henry Holl as Sir William, James Bland as Burchell, J. B. Buckstone as Pyefinch, Mr. Tilbury as Drake, Miss Telbin as Mistress Maylove, Julia Bennett as Jessie.

KING AND NO KING// D// Alt. fr Beaumont & Fletcher// **Sad. Wells**, Jan. 1847, with Samuel Phelps as Arbaces, Henry Marston as Tigranes, Henry Mellon as Gebrias, William Hoskins as Bacurine, A. Younge as Mardonius, George Bennett as Beseus, Frank Graham as Lygones, Mrs. Henry Marston as Arane, Laura Addison as Panthea, Miss Cooper as Spaconia.

KING AND THE DESERTER, THE (also titled Frederick the Great and the Deserter)// D// n.a.// **Victoria**, July 1879, with Charles Sennett as Frederick the Great, Charles Beverley as Schnoutzbard, Walter Lacy as De Reuter, J. G. Johnson as Morocco, Mr. Jameson as Baratto, W. T. Elworthy as Rolmar, Andy Robertson as Van Groat, Mrs. Lewis Nanton as Martha, Blanche Payne as Rosalie.

KING AND THE DUKE, THE; OR, THE SIEGE OF ALENCON// D// n.a.// **Cov. Garden**, Feb. 1839, with George Bartley as Governor, James Anderson as Count, Mr. Vining as St. Maurice, John Pritt Harley as Chapeanbas [sic], Thomas Lee as O'Whack, Drinkwater Meadows as Drug, Mr. Tilbury as Deuxmots, Mrs. W. Clifford as Mme. Alice, Miss Rainforth as Gabrielle, Miss Taylor as Laura/ Music by T. Cooke.

KING AND THE FREEBOOTER, THE; OR, THE KEEP OF CASTLE HILL// D// T. E. Wilks// **Sad. Wells**, Apr. 1842, with John Webster as King of Scotland, Mr. Lambe as Lumley, Mr. Williams as Todd, E. Morton as Burnette, John Herbert as McScrew, Mr. Dry as Elliot, Mr. Aldridge as Dunleary, Miss Richardson as Lady Margaret, Mrs. Richard Barnett as Ellen.

KING AND THE MILLER, THE; OR, CRAMOND BRIG (see also, Crammond Brig)// D 1a// W. H. Murray// **Lyceum**, Jan. 1880, with Mr. Elwood as James V, Charles Calvert as James Birkie, S. Johnson as Howieston, Georgina Pauncefort as Tibbie Howieston, Myra Holme as Marion; Apr. 1890, with Frank Tyars as James V, John Martin Harvey as Birkie, Samuel Johnson as Howieson, Georgina Pauncefort as Tibbie, Miss Foster as Marion.

KING AND THE PIPER, THE// D 2a// n.a.// **Princess's**, June 1847, with Henry Hughes as James I, Mr. Walton as Earl of Bridgetown, Mr. Barker as Sir George, Mr. Wynn as Col. Conyers, Mr. Devalanti as Capt. Everhill, Emma Stanley as Sandie, Mr. Granby as Spilepeg, Georgiana Smithson as Lady Katherine, Miss Marshall as Rosa/ Scenery by William Beverly, Mr. Wilson, & Mr. Sala/ Music by Joseph Duggan.

KING AND THE VETERAN, THE; OR, PITY THE BLIND// D 4a// n.a.// **Victoria**, Dec. 1860, with J. H. Rickards as Hildermar, Mr. Henderson as Duke Stenheim, W. Schofield as Adelbert, W. H. Pitt as Von Sonmenberg, James Howard as Count von Rosenberg, George Yarnold as Peperling, Mrs. Charles Boyce as Aurelia, Mrs. E. F. Saville as Benita, Mrs. F. Lauri as Martha, Lydia Pearce as Belia.

KING ARTHUR// Play Pro & 4a// J. Comyns Carr// **Lyceum**, Jan. 1895, with Henry Irving as King Arthur, Johnston Forbes Robertson as Lancelot, Frank Cooper as Mordred, Frank Tyars as Kay, Fuller Mellish as Bedevere, Sidney Valentine as Merlin, Genevieve Ward as Morgan Le Fay, Lena Ashwell as Elaine, Annie Hughes as Clarissant, Ellen Terry as Guinevere/ Scenery des. by Edward Burne-Jones, exec. by Hawes Craven & J. Harker/ Music comp. by Arthur Sullivan.

KING GEORGE'S SHILLING// D 3a// Edward Stirling// **Grecian**, Apr. 1879.

KING HAL'S EARLY DAYS// D 2a// n.a.// **Drury Lane**, Mar. 1837, with Mr. Cooper as

Henry VIII, A. Brindal as Lord Howard, Miss Taylor as Algernon, Mr. Hooper as Hawarde, Frederick Cooke as Wrangham, John Duruset as Carew, Drinkwater Meadows as Silvermark, George Bartley as Lambkin, Mrs. Hooper as Agnes, Mrs. Humby as Blanche.

KING HAROLD; OR, THE BATTLE OF HASTINGS// D 3a// J. T. Haines// **Victoria**, Sept. 1839.

KING JOHN// T 5a// William Shakespeare// **Sad. Wells**, Mar. 1837, with George Bennett as King John, Master Smith as Prince Henry, Thomas Lee as Pembroke, Mr. Gay as Essex, Mr. King as Salisbury, N. T. Hicks as Hubert, Mr. Jones as Gurney, John Pritchard as Faulconbridge, Benjamin Webster as Philip of France, C. H. Pitt as Dauphin, Miss Lane as Prince Arthur, Mr. Tilbury as Pandulph, Miss Williams as Queen Elinor, Miss Lebatt as Blanche, Mrs. W. West as Constance, Mrs. Harris as Lady Faulconbridge; Apr. 1840, with E. W. Elton as King John, Miss Hicks as Prince Henry, Mr. Aldridge as Salisbury, Mr. Stilt as Essex, Henry Marston as Faulconbridge, E. Morton as Robert Faulconbridge, J. W. Collier as Chatillon, Mr. Archer as Hubert, Mr. Dry as King Philip, Mr. Elvin as Dauphin, Miss O. Hicks as Prince Arthur, Miss Cooke as Queen Eleanor, Miss Richardson as Constance, Mrs. J. F. Saville as Blanche; Sept. 1844, with Samuel Phelps as King John, Miss Marston as Prince Henry, Miss Backous as Arthur, Charles Fenton as Pembroke, Mr. Coreno as Norfolk, George Bennett as Hubert, Mr. Raymond as Essex, E. Morton as Salisbury, Mr. Redburne as Fitzwalter, Mr. Williams as Faulconbridge, Henry Marston as Philip Faulconbridge, Charles Morelli as Gurney, T. H. Lacy as Philip of France, John Webster as Dauphin, A. Younge as Pandulph, Mrs. Henry Marston as Queen Elinor, Mrs. Mary Warner as Lady Constance, Miss Huddart as Blanch, Mrs. Francis as Lady Faulconbridge/ **Cov. Garden**, Apr. 1837, with W. C. Macready as King John, Mr. Vandenhoff as Faulconbridge, Miss Lacy as Prince Henri, James Worrell as Pembroke, Mr. Ransford as Essex, Mr. Thompson as Salisbury, Mr. Beckett as Robert Faulconbridge, George Bennett as Hubert, John Pritchard as Philip of France, John Webster as Dauphin, Mr. Tilbury as Pandulph, Charles Bender as Chatillon, Mrs. W. West as Queen Elinor, Helen Faucit as Lady Constance, Miss Lee as Blanche, Mrs. Sarah Garrick as Lady Faulconbridge/ **Drury Lane**, Oct. 1837, with Mr. Butler as King John, Miss Lacey as Prince Henry, Miss Poole as Prince Arthur, John Duruset as Pembroke, Charles Fenton as Sussex, Mr. King as Salisbury, H. Cooke as Hubert, Mr. Cooper as Faulconbridge, Mr. Baker as Philip of France, A. Brindal as Dauphin, Frederick Cooke as Pandulph, Mme. Simon as Queen Elinor, Mrs. Lovell as Lady Constance, Miss Fitzwalter as Blanche, Miss Somerville as Lady Faulconbridge; Sept. 1866, with Samuel Phelps as King John, Florence Bennett as Prince Henry, William McIntyre as Pembroke, Mr. Weaver as Essex, Edmund Phelps as Salisbury, Charles Warner as Norfolk, Thomas Swinbourne as Hubert, E. Clifton as Faulconbridge, Barry Sullivan as Philip Faulconbridge, Thomas Mead as Philip of France, Frank Barsby as Dauphin, Mr. Barrett as Pandulph, Charles Harcourt as Chatillon, Mrs. Henry Vandenhoff as Elinor, Mrs. Hermann Vezin as Constance, Adelaide Golier as Blanche, Mrs. G. Hodson as Lady Faulconbridge/ Scenery by William Beverley/ **Haymarket**, Dec. 1850, with W. C. Macready as King John, Mr. Caulfield as Pembroke, James Bland as Essex, John Parselle as Salisbury, Mr. Cooper as Hubert, E. L. Davenport as Faulconbridge, Mr. Stuart as France, Henry Howe as Dauphin, Charles Selby as Austria, Mrs. Stanley as Queen Elinor, Mrs. Mary Warner as Lady Constance, Mrs. Young as Lady Faulconbridge/ **Princess's**, Feb. 1852, with Charles Kean as King John, Miss Robertson as Prince Henry, Kate Terry as Arthur, Mr. Wynn as Pembroke, Mr. Stacey as Essex, James Vining as Salisbury, George Everett as Norfolk, John Ryder as Hubert, Drinkwater Meadows as Robert Faulconbridge, Alfred Wigan as Philip Faulconbridge, Charles Fisher as Philip of France, John Cathcart as Giles, Charles Wheatleigh as Chatillon, Frank Graham as Pandulph, Miss Phillips as Queen Elinor, Mrs. Charles Kean as Constance, Miss Murray as Blanche, Mrs. W. Daly as Lady Faulconbridge; Aug. 1863, with Walter Montgomery as King John, Ada Beverley as Prince Henry, Emily Maurice as Arthur, John Collett as Pembroke, G. Robinson as Essex, Mr. Meagreson as Salisbury, Charles Vincent as Hubert, Mr. Moreland as Robert Faulconbridge, Frederic Robinson as Philip Faulconbridge, W. R. Robins as Philip of France, Mr. Fitzjames as as Panduif, Mrs. Hodson as Queen Elinor, Miss Atkinson as Constance, Miss Murray as Blanche/ Scenery by W. Gordon & Mr. Dayes/ **Grecian**, Nov. 1866, with Alfred Rayner as King John, Emma Victor as Prince Henry, Kate Gill as Arthur, Charles Mortimer as Hubert, W. Shirley as Robert Falconbridge, William James as Philip Falconbridge, Henry Grant as Philip of France, George Gillett as the Dauphin, J. Jackson as Pandulph, Henry Power as Chatillon, Mrs. Atkinson as Elinor, Lizzie Mandelbert as Constance, Alice Denvil as Blanche, Mrs. Dearlove as Lady Falconbridge/ **Her Majesty's**, a vers. by Herbert Beerbohm Tree, Sept. 1899.

KING LEAR// T// William Shakespeare// **Drury Lane**, Feb. 1837, with Edwin Forrest as Lear, Mr. Hooper as Burgundy, Mr. Baker as Cornwall, A. Brindal as Albany, Mr. Mathews as Glo'ster, George Bartley as Kent, Drinkwater Meadows as Oswald, Mr. Cooper as Edgar, Mr. Warde as Edmund, Miss Taylor as Cordelia, Mrs. W. Clifford as Regan, Miss Somerville as Goneril; Mar. 1869, with Charles Dillon as Lear, Mr. O'Neill as France, Mr. Weaver as Burgundy, W. C. Temple as Cornwall, F. Charles as Albany, Mr. Barrett as Kent, James Johnstone as Glo'ster, John Ryder as Edgar, Henry Sinclair as Edmund, Harriet Coveney as Fool, John Rouse as Oswald, Miss Addison as Goneril, Marie O'Berne as Regan, Caroline Heath as Cordelia/ **Cov. Garden**, Jan. 1838, with W. C. Macready as Lear, Henry Howe as King of France, Charles Bender as Burgundy, Charles Diddear as Albany, Mr. Serle as Cornwall, George Bartley as Kent, George Bennett as

Glo'ster, E. W. Elton as Edgar, James Anderson as Edmund, Mr. Vining as Oswald, Priscilla Horton as Fool, Mrs. W. Clifford as Goneril, Mrs. Mary Warner (Miss Huddart) as Regan, Helen Faucit as Cordelia/ **Sad. Wells**, Dec. 1840, with Mr. Cathcart as Lear, George Burt as Burgundy, J. B. Hill as Cornwall, Mr. Stilt as Albany, Mr. Williams as Kent, Mr. Dry as Glo'ster, Henry Marston as Edgar, Mr. Elvin as Edmund, J. W. Collier as Oswald, Miss Cooke as Goneril, Miss Richardson as Regan, Mrs. Robert Honner as Cordelia; Nov. 1845, with Samuel Phelps as Lear, Edward Knight as France, Mr. Warde as Burgundy, Frank Graham as Cornwall, E. Morton as Albany, A. Younge as Kent, Henry Mellon as Glo'ster, Henry Marston as Edgar, George Bennett as Edmund, Samuel Buckingham as Oswald, Henry Scharf as Fool, Mrs. Henry Marston as Goneril, Miss Huddart as Regan, Miss Cooper as Cordelia/ Scenery by F. Fenton & Mr. Finlay/ Machines by Mr. Cawdery; Feb. 1868, with Charles Dillon as Lear, Mr. Foxcroft as King of France, Mr. Howard as Burgundy, Mr. Hamilton as Cornwall, Mr. Murray as Albany, Harry Chester as Glo'ster, C. W. Barry as Kent, J. L. Warner as Edgar, E. Morton as Edmund, Walter Searle as Oswald, Alice Dodd as Fool, Mrs. Walton as Goneril, Miss Fitzgerald as Regan, Alice Marriott as Cordelia/ **Princess's**, Mar. 1845, with Edwin Forrest as Lear, Frank Graham as Edgar, Mr. Archer as Edmund, Mr. Walton as Gloucester, Mr. Granby as Kent, James Ranoe as Burgundy, F. C. Courtney as Albany, Mr. Fitzjames as Cornwall, Walter Lacy as Oswald, Mrs. Stirling as Cordelia, Mrs. Fosbroke as Regan, Mrs. Brougham as Goneril; Oct. 1845, with W. C. Macready as Lear, Augustus Harris as Burgundy, Leigh Murray as Cornwall, James Vining as Albany, John Ryder as Gloucester, Mr. Cooper as Kent, William Wallack as Edgar, Charles Fisher as Edmund, Robert Roxby as Oswald, Miss Marshall as Fool, Mrs. Brough as Goneril, Mrs. Fosbroke as Regan, Mrs. Stirling as Cordelia; Apr. 1858, with Charles Kean as Lear, Mr. Brazier as King of France, Mr. Rolleston as Burgundy, Mr. Raymond as Cornwall, John Cathcart as Albany, Mr. Cooper as Kent, Frank Graham as Gloster, John Ryder as Edgar, Walter Lacy as Edmund, David Fisher as Oswald, Miss Poole as Fool, Caroline Heath as Goneril, Miss Bufton as Regan, Kate Terry as Cordelia/ Scenery by Grieve & Telbin/ Music by J. L. Hatton/ Machines by G. Hodsdon; May 1861, with Samuel Phelps as Lear, Edmund Garden as France, Mr. Chapman as Burgundy, J. G. Shore as Cornwall, Robert Cathcart as Albany, John Ryder as Kent, Basil Potter as Edmund, Mr. Raymond as Gloster, Edmund Phelps as Edgar, Maria Harris as Fool, T. H. Higgie as Oswald, Miss Atkinson as Goneril, Miss Murray as Regan, Caroline Heath as Cordelia; Feb. 1881, with Edwin Booth as Lear, W. Chamberlain as Burgundy, P. C. Beverley as Cornwall, John Beauchamp as Albany, John Ryder as Kent, Alfred Rayner as Glo'ster, William Redmund as Edgar, Charles Herberte as Edmund, Stanlslaus Calhaem as Oswald, F. Charles as Fool, Dolores Drummond as Goneril, Violet Temple as Regan, Maud Milton as Cordelia/ Scenery by Charles Brooke/ Gas by Mr. Jones/ Lime-light by Messrs. Kerr/ Prod. by Harry Jackson/ **Haymarket**, Oct. 1849, with W. C. Macready as Lear, A. Brindal as Burgundy, George Braid as Cornwall, B. Wentworth as Albany, Mr. Rogers as Glo'ster, Mr. Stuart as Kent, James Wallack as Edgar, Henry Howe as Edmund, Priscilla Horton as Fool, Charles Selby as Oswald, Henry Vandenhoff as France, Mrs. Mary Warner as Goneril, Mrs. L. S. Buckingham as Regan, Miss Reynolds as Cordelia/ Scenery by Mr. Johnstone & George Morris/ Machines by F. Heselton/ **Surrey**, Dec. 1859, with William Creswick, Edith Heraud, Miss Thorne/ **Grecian**, Oct. 1867, with Alfred Rayner as Lear, William James as Edgar, George Gillett as Edmund, J. Jackson as Gloster, Charles Mortimer as Kent, W. Shirley as Cornwall, Samuel Perfitt as Albany, John Manning as Oswald, Mary A. Victor as Fool, Mrs. Atkinson as Goneril, Alice Denvil as Regan, Lizzie Mandelbert as Cordelia/ **Lyceum**, Nov. 1892, with Henry Irving as Lear, William Terriss as Edgar, Frank Cooper as Edmund, Alfred Bishop as Gloster, W. J. Holloway as Kent, Frank Tyars as Albany, Mr. Haviland as Fool, Gordon Craig as Oswald, Ada Dyas as Goneril, Maud Milton as Regan, Ellen Terry as Cordelia/ Scenery by J. Harker & Hawes Craven/ Music by Hamilton Clarke and J. Meredith Ball.

KING O'NEIL; OR, THE IRISH BRIGADE// C 2a// Mrs. C. G. Gore// **St. James's**, Aug. 1867, with Marquis Townshend as Louis XV, Thomas Bowles as Richelieu, W. L. Maitland as Arundel, R. Roberts as Count Dillon, Charles Edwards as Maj. de Burgh, W. Maitland as Capt. O'Neil, Mrs. Leigh Murray as Countess Dillon, Eleanor Bufton as Marchioness de Clermont, Louisa Eden as Duchess de Mally.

KINGMAKER, THE// D 5a// J. W. Boulding// **Adelphi**, Apr. 1882, with E. H. Brooke as Neville, Edward Price as Edward IV, W. H. Perrette as Montague, Walter Brooks as Hastings, William Howell as Clarence, W. S. Parkes as Louis XI, Gertrude Doré as Countess of Warwick, Ellen Meyrick as Lady Isabel, Sophie Eyre as Lady Anne, Mrs. Edward Price as Margaret of Anjou/ Prod. by E. H. Brooke.

KING MAKER, THE; OR, THE LAST OF HIS RACE// D 4a// Robert Dodson// **Victoria**, Oct. 1873.

KING O' SCOTS// D 3a// Dram. by Andrew Halliday fr novel of Sir Walter Scott, Fortunes of Nigel// **Drury Lane**, Dec. 1868, with Samuel Phelps as James I and Trapbois, W. C. Temple as Prince Charles, F. Charles as Buckingham, Henry Sinclair as Delgarno, E. Price as Nigel, Mr. Addison as Heriot, James Johnstone as Ramsay, John Rouse as Sir Mungo, G. Cumming as Richie, Joseph Irving as Vin, Edith Stuart as Lady Hermione, Caroline Heath as Margaret, Mrs. Frank Matthews as Dame Ursula, Fanny Addison as Martha, William McIntyre as Hildebrod/ Scenery by William Beverley/ Music by W. C. Levey/ Prod. by Edward Stirling/ **Sadler's Wells**, Oct. 1869/ **Astley's**, Mar. 1870/ **Princess's**, Feb. 1871, with Samuel Phelps as James I and Trapbois, Henry Westland as Prince Charles, Herbert Crellin as Buckingham, William Rignold as Lord Dalgarno, John Clayton as Lord Glenvarloch, James Johnstone as Heriot, C. F. Marshall as Ramsay, Henry Clifford as Moniplies, John Murray as Vin, Annie Merton as Lady Hermione, Rose Leclercq as Margaret, Mrs. R. Power as Dame Ursula, Fanny Addison as Martha, Mr. Barrett as Hildebrod, Howard Russell as Capt. Colepepper.

KING OF DIAMONDS, THE; OR, THE HISTORY OF A ROUGH GEM// D// Paul Meritt & George Conquest// **Surrey**, Apr. 1884.

KING OF FOOLS, A// D// Dram. by H. J. Dam, C. Cartwright, & Benjamin Landeck fr F of Alexandre Dumas// **Grand**, Sept. 1899.

KING OF THE COMMONS, THE// Play 5a// James White// **Princess's**, May 1846, with W. C. Macready as James V of Scotland, John Ryder as Sir Adam, Mr. Cooper as Buckie, Leigh Murray as Young, Henry Compton as Laird Small, W. H. Oxberry as Mungo, Mr. Wynn as Archbishop, Robert Roxby as Lord Kilmaurs, Charles Fisher as Lord Seton, Mrs. Stirling as Madeline, Mrs. Fosbroke as Widow Barton/ Scenery by William Beverly, Mr. Smith, & Mr. Grey.

KING OF THE MINT, THE; OR, OLD LONDON BRIDGE BY NIGHT// D// n.a.// **Victoria**, Feb. 1873.

KING OF THE MIST, THE; OR, THE MILLER OF THE HARTZ MOUNTAINS// D 2a// Edward Fitzball// **Drury Lane**, Apr. 1839, with Henry Wallack as Martin, Henry Compton as Block, A. Brindal as Frederick, Mr. Harris as Colonel, Charles Fenton as Conrade, Mrs. C. Jones as Dame Elsey, Miss Poole as Gertrude/ Scenery by Grieve, T. Grieve & W. Grieve/ Music by G. F. Stansbury.

KING O'NEIL// C// Mrs. C. G. Gore// **Cov. Garden**, Sept. 1839, with Tyrone Power, Samuel Phelps.

KING RENE'S DAUGHTER// D// Adap. by Edmund Phipps fr Dan. of Henrik Herz// **Haymarket**, Dec. 1849, with James Wallack as King René, Charles Kean as Count Tristan, Benjamin Webster as Sir Geoffrey, B. Wentworth as Sir Almeric, Henry Howe as Jahia, Mr. Rogers as Bertrand, Mrs. Charles Kean as Iolanthe, Priscilla Horton as Martha/ **Lyceum**, May 1880 (in vers. by Henry Irving).

KING RENE'S DAUGHTER// D// Adap. by Theodore Martin fr Dan. of Henrik Herz// **Haymarket**, July 1855/ **Drury Lane**, Dec. 1859, with Samuel Emery as King René, Mr. Verner as Count Tristan, Mr. Delafield as Sir Geoffrey, Mr. Farrell as Sir Almeric, Mr. Peel as Jahia, Mr. Mellon as Bertrand, Miss Page as Iolanthe, Mrs. Dowton as Martha.

KING'S BARBER, THE// D 2a// Benjamin Webster// **Haymarket**, Feb. 1841, with Frederick Vining as King Alphonso, James Worrell as D'Aguilar, Mr. Caulfield as Villalba, Henry Wallack as Cardinal D'Almanzo, James Wallack as Gil Perez, J. W. Gough as Moreeno, Mr. Waldron as Father Joseph, John Webster as Juan, Mrs. W. Clifford as Pinehilla, Mrs. Stirling as Paghita/ Scenery by George Morris.

KING'S BUTTERFLY, THE// D// Adap. fr F of Paul Meurice, Fanfan, la Tulippe// **Lyceum**, Oct. 1864, with Charles Fechter as Fanfan, Henry Widdicomb as Ramponneau, John Ryder as Baron d'Alvera, F. Charles as Gabriel, William McIntyre as Maurepas, Carlotta Leclercq as Pompadour, Miss M. Henrade as Alice.

KING'S DEATH TRAP, THE// D 2a// C. H. Hazlewood// **Britannia**, Nov. 1867.

KING'S FIRST LESSON, THE// D 1a// n.a.// **Sad. Wells**, Mar. 1848, with Miss Huddart as Charles XII of Sweden, Henry Mellon as Count Waldemar, A. Younge as Gen. Piper, Mr. Harrington as Baron Stralheim, Julia St. George as Christine/ Music by W. Montgomery.

KING'S FRIEND, THE// D 5a// n.a.// **Sad. Wells**, May 1845, with Samuel Phelps as Henry IV of France, Henry Marston as Marquis de Remy, George Bennett as de Fresne, Samuel Buckingham as Victor, E. Morton as La Plume, Miss Cooper as Katherine, Mrs. Mary Warner as Mme. Chateaupers.

KING'S GARDENER, THE; OR, NIPPED IN THE BUD// C 1a// Charles Selby// **Sad. Wells**, May 1839, with Mr. Elvin as de Bussy, Mr. Dry as Ferdinand, J. W. Collier as Flicflac, Miss Pincott as Mme. Galochard, Mrs. J. F. Saville as Mme. de la Valliere, W. J. Hammond as Galochard; Sept. 1844, with Mr. Sharpe as Beuserade, E. Morton as de Busey, G. F. Forman as Galochard, Charles Fenton as Flicflac, Miss Huddart as Louise, Miss Lebatt as Mme. Galochard, Georgiana Lebatt as Nannette, Fanny Morelli as Susette/ **Haymarket**, Aug. 1840, with Henry Howe as Benserade, Mr. Caulfield as de Bussy, David Rees as Galochard, Mr. Clark as Flicflac, Priscilla Horton as Mme. Galochard, Miss Grove as Nanette, Mrs. Mattley as Louise.

KING'S HIGHWAY, THE// Adap. by George Roberts & Frank Gerald fr novel of Harrison Ainsworth, Rookwood// **Novelty**, Feb. 1897, with Frank Gerald as Dick Turpin.

KING'S MUSKETEERS, THE// D 3a// Dram. fr novel of Alexandre Dumas// **Lyceum**, Oct. 1856, with Mr. Normanton as Louis XIII, Mr. Stuart as Richelieu, J. G. Shore as Buckingham, G. H. Burt as Rochfort, Mr. Poynter as De Treville, Mr. McLien as Athos, Mr. Barrett as Porthos, Mr. Clifton as Aramis, Charles Dillon as D'Artagnan, Stanislaus Calhaem as Pouchet, Mrs. Buckingham White as Anne of Austria, Mrs. Weston as Lady de Winter, Mrs. Alfred Mellon (Sarah Woolgar) as Constance/ **Sad. Wells**, May 1857, with James Worrell as Louis XIII, J. G. Shore as Buckingham, Mr. Stuart as Richelieu, John Herbert as Rochfort, Charles Fenton as De Treville, Mr. Lingham as Athos, Mr. Barrett as Porthos, Charles Seyton as Aramis, Charles Dillon as D'Artagnan, Miss Portman as Anne of Austria, Mary A. Victor as Constance, Mrs. Weston as Lady de Winter/ **Drury Lane**, Mar. 1869, with Wilson Barrett as Louis XIII, James Johnstone as Richelieu, William McIntyre as Buckingham, F. Charles as de Rochefort, W. C. Temple as De treville, Henry Sinclair as Athos, Mr. Barrett as Porthos, Alfred Nelson as Aramis, Charles Dillon as D'Artagnan, John Rouse as Boniface, Edith Stuart as Anne of Austria, Mrs. Henry Vandenhoff as Lady de Winter, Harriet Coveney as Constance, Miss Seymour as Manette.

KING'S RIVAL, THE// Tom Taylor & Charles Reade// **St. James's**, Oct. 1854, with George Vandenhoff as Charles II, Thomas Mead as Richmond, F. Ede as Shaftesbury, Mr. Sidney as Buckhurst, Mr. Douglas as Etherege, George Burt as Ogle, J. L. Toole as Samuel Pepys, Fergus Tree as John Pepys, Miss Grey as Queen Katherine, Eleanore Glynn as Miss Stewart, Mrs. Seymour as Nell Gwynne, Miss Douglas as Mrs. Price, Miss Robertson as Mrs. Wells/ Scenery by Adams, Herbert & Fenoulhet/ Machines by Mr. Cassidy/ Music by Mr. Redl.

KING'S SEAL, THE// D 2a// H. R. Addison// **Drury Lane**, Jan. 1855.

KING'S WAGER, THE; OR, THE CAMP, THE COTTAGE AND THE COURT (also subtitled, The Castle and the Cottage)// D 3a// T. E. Wilks// **Victoria**, Dec. 1837, with Edward Hooper as Charles II, Mr. Powell as Sedley, Mr. Loveday as Clayford, Mr. Macdonald as Capt. Tattershall, Mr. Green as Col. Vane, Benjamin Wrench as Watch-and-Learn, Mr. Salter as Corp. Praying-for-Peace, Mr. Harwood as Proudflesh, Miss Richardson as Rosabelle, Miss Wilson as Eunice, William Davidge as Clarendon, Mr. Williams as Ormond, John Parry as Buckingham, W. H. Oxberry as Tybbe, Miss Bartlett as Duchess of Devonshire, Miss Wilson as Countess of Castlemaine, Mrs. Frank Matthews as Flora/ Scenery by C. J. James/ Music by Leigh Smith/ Prod. by T. E. Wilks; Apr. 1842, with David Osbaldiston as Charles II, E. F. Saville as Buckingham, Mr. Griffiths as Butler, Mr. James as Clarendon, William Seaman as Sedley, Mr. Franklin as Waller, John Dale as Vane, C. Williams as Mirondelle, Mr. Paul as Prayington, W. H. Oxberry as Tybbe, Mrs. George Lee as Rosabelle, Mrs. Frank Matthews.

KING'S WAGER, THE; OR, THE COTTAGE AND THE COURT// D 2a// n.a.// **Grecian**, May 1847, with Edwin Dixon as Charles II, Mr. Manley as Buckingham, Mr. Campbell as Herbert Vane, Eaton O'Donnell as Prayington, Frederick Robson as Tybbe, John Collett as Mirondelle, Annette Mears as Lilac, Miss Leclercq as Crystal, Mary A. Crisp as Flora, Madame Leclercq as Rosabelle, Miss Johnstone as Duchess of Devonshire, Ellen Crisp as Lady Debarre, Miss Merion as Countess Dorabella.

KIRKAULD'S POINT; OR, THE LEGEND OF THE THAMES// D// n.a.// **Sad. Wells**, July 1839, with John Webster as King John, Mr. Williams as Hubert, Robert Honner as De Bois, Mr. Stilt as Gilbert, Mr. Conquest as Kirkauld, Miss Pincott as Amy, Miss Cooke as Maude.

KISS, THE; OR, THE FESTIVAL OF ST. ROSAIRE// C 1a// n.a.// **Victoria**, Mar. 1843, with William Seaman as Delorme, John Gardner as Margot, Mr. James as Bretois, James Howard as Blaize, Mr. Hitchinson as Ambroise, Miss Saddler as Marchionesse de Merivale, Mrs. George Lee as Julienne, Miss Martin as Georgette, Mrs. Griffiths as Mme. Mag.

KISS, THE// Play 1a// Trans. by John Gray fr F of Théodore de Banville, Le Baiser// **Royalty**, Mar. 1892, with Bernard Gould as Pierrot, Edith Chester as Urgele.

KISS IN THE DARK, A// F 1a// J. B. Buckstone// **Haymarket**, June 1840, with J. B. Buckstone as Pettibone, John Webster as Fathom, Miss Mattley as Mary, Miss Partridge as Unknown Female, Mrs. W. Clifford as Mrs. Pettibone/ **Sad. Wells**, Oct. 1858, with Charles Young as Pettibone, William Belford as Fathom, Eliza Travers as Mrs. Pettibone, Rose Williams as Mary/ **Olympic**, Apr. 1884, with E. Hendrie as Pettibone, Fuller Mellish as Falhorn, Mlle. Carrara as Mrs. Pettibone/ **Adelphi**, July 1887, with F. Dagnall as Pettibone, R. Courtneidge as Fathom, Daisy England as Mrs. Pettibone.

KISS OF DELILAH, THE// Play 3a// George Grant & James Lisle// **Drury Lane**, Nov. 1896, with Hermann Vezin as Robespierre Brooke Warren as d'Herbois, Sam Johnson as Legendre, Edward O'Neill as Coupe Tete, Philip Darwin as Capuy, Arthur Vezin as Pierre, T. B. Thamberg as Talma, Hilda Spong as Herminie, Edith Jordan as Estelle.

KISSING GOES BY FAVOUR// F 1a// Edward Stirling// **Surrey**, Apr. 1847/ **Astley's**, Apr. 1863, with H. J. Montague as Duke de Bassompiere, Frederick Lloyd as Grillon, Mr. Weaver as Louis, Rose Leclercq as Marchionesse de Launey, Edith Stewart [sic] as Peroine, Miss Hayman as Jenny.

KIT MARLOWE// Play 1a// W. L. Courtney// **Shaftesbury**, July 1890, with Arthur Bourchier as Marlowe, Erskine Lewis as Alleyne, Cyril Maude as Chettle, Charles Fulton as Archer, R. G. Legge as Nash, Annie Irish as Nan/ **St. James's**, Oct. 1892.

KITCHEN GIRL, THE// F// James East// **Surrey**, Sept. 1900.

KITCHEN LOVE// F// Robert Courtneidge// **Olympic**, Sept. 1888.

KITTY CLIVE, ACTRESS// C 1a// Frankfort Moore// **Royalty**, Oct. 1895, with Henry Vibart as Bates, Fred Permain as Landlord, Irene Vanbrugh as Kitty/ **Strand**, Apr. 1897.

KITTY GREY// C 3a// Adap. by J. S. Pigott fr F of P. Mars & Maurice Henniquin, les Fétards// **Vaudeville**, Apr. 1900/ **Apollo**, Sept. 1901.

KLEPTOMANIA// FC 3a// Mark Melford// **Strand**, June 1888/ **Novelty**, Feb. 1890, with Edwin Brett as Gen. Blair, Mark Melford as

Prof. Smalley, Raymond Capp as Whatley, Roy Byford as Gathermoss, Ruth Rutland as Lady Josephine, Mrs. Mark Melford as Violet, Catherine Clair as Rosina, Bella Cuthbert as Mrs. Gathermoss.

KLONDYKE NUGGET, THE// D 5a// S. F. Cody// **Elephant & Castle**, Aug. 1899.

KLONDYKE RUSH, THE// D 4a// Henry Fielding// **Britannia**, May. 1898.

KLU, KLUX, KLAW// D 3a// G. H. Macdermott & H. A. Major// **Britannia**, May 1873.

KNAPSACK, THE; OR, TAKEN FROM THE RANKS// D// n.a.// **Elephant & Castle**, Apr. 1884.

KNIGHT AGAINST ROOK// C 4a// Gustave Soares ("Owen Dove") & J. G. Lefebre// **Gaiety**, July 1886.

KNIGHT ERRANT// Play 1a// Rutland Barrington// **Lyric**, Nov. 1894.

KNIGHT OF ARVA, THE// C 2a// Dion Boucicault// **Haymarket**, Nov. 1848, with Mr. Tilbury as Don Diego, Henry Vandenhoff as Duke de Chabannes, Mr. Rogers as Count Offenboer, Charles Hudson as Knight of Arva, Miss Reynolds as Princess Marina, Mrs. W. Clifford as Baroness Buckramstern/ Scenery by P. Phillips & George Morris/ **Adelphi**, July 1849, with Mr. Lambert as Don Diego, Charles Boyce as Duke de Chabannes, William Cullenford as Count Offenboer, Charles Hudson as the Knight, C. J. Smith as Manuel, Sarah Woolgar as Princess Marina.

KNIGHTS OF ST. ALBANS, THE; OR, THE CRYSTAL CROSS AND GLITTERING FOUNTAINS// D// T. P. Taylor// **Sad. Wells**, Sept. 1837, with Mr. King as De Lisle, Mr. Jephson as Montfalcon, C. J. Smith as de Clare, Mr. Scarbrow as Sir Stephen, Mr. Russell as Sir Robert, Mr. Morrison as Sir Maurice, Mr. Hicks as Wandering Knight, Mr. Rogers as Master Mathias, Mr. Griffith as Crab, Thomas Lee as Kildare, C. H. Pitt as Hornsey, Mr. Campbell as Overbery, Miss Williams as Helen, Mrs. Rogers as Mabel/ Scenery by Mr. Mildenhall/ Machines by Mr. Copping/ Prod. by B. S. Fairbrother.

KNIGHTS OF THE ROUND TABLE, THE// D 5a// J. R. Planché// **Haymarket**, May 1854, with William Farren as Sir Ralph, W. H. Chippendale as Gen. Grantley, Henry Howe as D'Arcy, George Vandenhoff as Capt. Cozens, J. B. Buckstone as Tittler, Henry Compton as Smith, Thomas Coe as Count Livonwitz, William Cullenford as Baron Griefenklaus, George Braid as de la Finesse, Miss Reynolds as Perdita, Ellen Grey as Francoise, Mrs. Fitzwilliam as Peggy, Miss Grantham as Duchess de Castelamare/ Scenery by W. Callcott, George Morris & John O'Conner/ Machines by Mr. Robertson/ Music by Edward Fitzwilliam.

KNIGHT OF THE SEPULCHRE, THE; OR, THE WIZARD CHIEF// D// George Almar// **Sad. Wells**, Oct. 1841, with Henry Marston as Sir Arundel, Mr. Aldridge as Sir Alberick, Miss Hicks as Edwayne, Mr. Dry as Sir Dominic, E. Morton as Candy, Charles Fenton as La Luce, Mr. Williams as Pennywise, John Herbert as Oddbody, George Almar as Edric, J. W. Collier as Orson, Mrs. Morgan as Ladye Elodie, Mrs. Richard Barnett as Winifred, Miss Cooke as Barbara, Miss Richardson as Helen/ Scenery by F. Fenton/ Machines by Mr. Cawdery/ Prod. by R. Honner.

KNIGHTS OF ST. JOHN, THE; OR, THE FIRE BANNER// D// George Almar// **Victoria**, Feb. 1852, with Mr. Morrison as Kondamar, J. T. Johnson as Sir Calydor, T. E. Mills as Sir Avelon, Mr. Richards as Sir Piers, I. Cohen as St. Clair, G. F. Forman as Rhymer, John Bradshaw as Kehama, F. H. Henry as Mustapha, James Howard as Mumbo Jumbo, Miss Fielding as Clarisse, Miss LaPorte as Belphoebe/ Scenery by Mr. Hawthorn/ Prod. by T. H. Higgie.

KNIGHTS OF THE CROSS, THE; OR, THE DOG AND THE STANDARD// D// Adap. fr novel of Sir Walter Scott// **Victoria**, Jan. 1845, with H. Howard as Coeur de Lion, Mr. Blanchard as Sir Kenneth, Mr. Hitchinson as Philip of France, Mr. Henry as Leopold of Austria, Mr. Coney as Conrade of Lombardy, Walter Searle as Beau Seant, Mr. Edgar as Sir Thomas, Miss Jefferson as Berengaria, Miss Treble as Edna, Miss Edgar as Calista, Dog Hector as Dog of the Standard.

KNIGHTS OF THE ROAD, THE; OR, THE GIPSY'S PROPHECY// D 3a// William Travers// **Marylebone**, Apr. 1868.

KNIGHTS OF THE ROUND TABLE, THE// D 5a// J. R. Planché// **Haymarket**, May 1854.

KNOW YOUR OWN MIND// C// Arthur Murphy// **Cov. Garden**, Apr. 1840, with Mr. Granby as Sir John, Alfred Wigan as Sir Harry, James Anderson as Millamour, C. J. Mathews as Dashwould, Frank Matthews as Bygrove, James Vining as Capt. Bygrove, Mr. Cooper as Malvil, Mme. Vestris as Lady Bell, Miss Lee as Lady Jane, Mrs. Orger as Mrs. Bromley, Emmeline Montague as Miss Neville, Mrs. Tayleure as Mme. La Rouge/ **Haymarket**, Oct. 1843, with Henry Holl as Millamour, C. J. Mathews as Dashwood, Mr. Stuart as Malvill, William Strickland as Bygrove, Howe Howe as Capt. Bygrove, Mr. Tilbury as Sir John, A. Brindal as Lovewit, Mme. Vestris as Lady Bell, Miss Lee as Lady Jane, Mrs. Julia Glover as Mrs. Bromley, Mrs. Edwin Yarnold as Miss Neville, Mrs. Stanley as Mme. La Rouge.

KNOWLEDGE// C 3a// n.a.// **Gaiety**, May 1883.

KNOWN TO THE POLICE// D Pro & 3a// John Douglass// **Surrey**, Mar. 1899.

KNUCKLE DUSTER, THE// F// J. C.Wilson// **Strand**, 1863.

KOHAL CAVE; OR, THE EVENTS OF A YEAR// D 3a// W. L. Rede// **Sad. Wells**, July 1898, with John Webster as Lord Hartville, Dibdin Pitt as Gordon, Mr. Mellor as Lt. Gough, Mr. Cathcart as Merriton, Robert Honner as Dally, C. J. Smith as West, Charles Montague as Ted, Mr. Harwood as Capstan, Mr. Phillips as Bill, Mr. Williams as Jeffery, Miss Richardson as Emily, Mrs. Robert Honner as Susan, Mr. Dry as Col. Brown, Mr. Conquest as Pawks, Mr. Wilkins as Sambo, Mrs. Harwood as Winifred, Miss Cooke as Rebecca/ Scenery by Mr. Telbin/ Machines by J. Sloman.

*

L.S.D // C 3a // Bertie Vyse // **Royalty**, June 1872.

L.S.D.; OR, FACE TO FACE// C 4a// n.a.// **Pavilion**, July 1889.

LA CATARINA// D 3a// Adap. fr F of Eugène Scribe// **Victoria**, Sept. 1844, with James Howard as Count Mayor, William Seaman as Don Henriquez, C. J. Bird as Don Sebastian, John Billington as Usher, Mr. Hitchinson as Andreas, John Dale as Rebelledo, Mr. Aldridge as Mugnoso, Annette Vincent as Lady Catarina, Miss Hamilton as Lady Diana, Miss M. Terry as Camillo, Miss E. Hicks as Albert, Miss Garrick as Juan.

LABOUR OF LOVE, A// Play 1a// Horace Newte// **Comedy**, July 1897, with Wilfred Draycott as Capt. Gayne, Cosmo Stuart as Capt. Laird, H. Deane as Sgt. Phipps, Harry Ford as Pvt. Hinks, Fred Thorne as Pearson, Maud Abbot as Violet.

LABOUR QUESTION, THE// D 1a// J. Courtney// **Grecian**, July 1861, with William James as Wilson, Mr. Jackson as Lt. Raymond, Thomas Mead as Tom Idle, R. H. Lingham as Ornshy, Jane Coveney as Rose, Miss Johnstone as Mrs. Wilson, Miss Wieland as Mary.

LACEMAKER OF PARIS, THE; OR, THE BRAND OF SHAME// D 2a// n.a.// **Grecian**, July 1868, with William James as Vivian, Charles Mortimer as Bertrand, John Manning as Jaques, Thomas Mead as Ramagean, Henry Power as Giriz, Lizzie Mandelbert as Pauline, Alice Denvil as Elise, Mary A. Victor as Terese.

LACKEY'S CARNIVAL, THE// C 4a// Henry Arthur Jones// **Duke of York's**, Sept. 1900.

LAD FROM THE COUNTRY, A// F 1a// J. Maddison Morton// **Olympic**, June 1857, with Henry Rivers as Cockletop, Robert Soutar as Peckover, Mr. Atkins as Chickabiddy, Miss Hayward as Laura, Miss J. Taylor as Patty/ **Adelphi**, Sept. 1881, with Mr. Goodrich, W. Avondale, Harwood Cooper, Miss E. Heffer, Clara Jecks.

LADDER OF LOVE, THE// C 1a// T. H. Bayly// **Olympic**, Dec. 1837, with C. J. Mathews as Chev. Duval, James Bland as Seneschal, Robert Keeley as Francois, Miss Murray as La Marquise de Vermont, Mme. Vestris as Suzanne.

LADIES AT HOME// F// J. G. Millingen// **Sad. Wells**, Sept. 1852, with Mrs. Henry Marston as Lady Antidote, Mrs. Barrett as Lady Lucretia, Eliza Travers as Mrs. Denter, Lizzie Mandelbert as Laura, Miss Pevensey as Mrs. Lenient.

LADIES' BATTLE, THE// C// Adap. by T. W. Robertson fr F of Eugène Scribe & Gabriel Legouvé// **Court**, Mar. 1879, with John Hare, W. H. Kendal, Mrs. Kendal.

LADIES' BATTLE, THE; OR, UN DUEL EN AMOUR// C 3a// Adap. by Tom Taylor & Charles Reade fr F of Eugène Scribe & Ernest Legouvé, La Bataille des Dames// **Olympic**, May 1851, with Henry Farren as Baron Montrichard, William Farren Jr. as de Flavigneul, Leigh Murray as de Grignon, Mrs. Stirling as Countess D'Autreval, Louisa Howard as Louise/ **Haymarket**, Nov. 1851, with Henry Howe as Baron de Montrichard, John Parselle as de Flavigneul, Leigh Murray as de Grignon, Mrs. Stirling as Countess D'Autreval, Amelia Vining as Leonie/ Scenery by George Morris & John O'Conner/ Machines by F. Hesselton; June 1879, with John Hare as Baron de Montrichard, W. Herbert as de Flavigneul, W. H. Kendal as de Grignon, Mr. Chevalier as Antoine, Cicely Grahame as Leonie, Mrs. Kendal as Countess d'Autreval/ **Sad. Wells**, Mar. 1856, with Leigh Murray as de Grignon, E. F. Edgar as Baron de Montrichard, Mr. Cooke as de Flavigneul, Mr. Moore as Brigadier, Miss M. Oliver as Countess d'Autreval, Jenny Marston as Leonie/ **Drury Lane**, Jan. 1857, with A. Younge as Baron de Montichard, Mr. Templeton as de Flavigneul, Leigh Murray as de Grignon, Mr. Parker as Brigadier, Mrs. Leigh Murray as Countess d'Autreval, Miss M. Oliver as Leoni/ **Opera Comique**, 1872; June 1891.

LADIES BEWARE// C// Adap. fr F, Une Femme qui se jette par la Fennetre// **Princess's**, June 1847, with Mr. Granby as Col. Vavasour, James Vining as Sir Charles, Miss Cooper as Matilda, Miss Winstanley as Lady Beauchamp, Emma Stanley as Grace/ **Olympic**, Oct. 1858, with George Vining as Sir Charles, George Cooke as Col. Vavasour, Miss Wyndham as Matilda, Miss Stevens as Lady Beauchamp, Mrs. W. S. Emden as Grace.

LADIES' CHAMPION, THE// C// H. Harold Gwindon// **Haymarket**, June 1868, with W. H. Kendal as Mightyman, Walter Gordon as Smythe, Mr. Johnson as Snuffles, Ione Burke as Beatrice, Fanny Wright as Chignon.

LADIES' CLUB, THE// C 2a// Mark Lemon// **Eng. Opera House** (Lyceum), July 1840, with Miss Brougham as Mrs. Fitzsmith, Miss Cooper as Mrs. Bookly, Miss R. Romer as Mrs. Mortar, Mme. Simon as Mrs. Twankay, Miss Fitzjames as Mrs. Cloudly, Miss Smithson as Mrs. Willing,

Mr. Turnour as Twankay, Mr. Baker as Mr. Derby, Thomas Green as Sir Charles Lavender, Mr. Granby as Maj. Mortar, Mr. Kerridge as Capt. Fitzsmith, Mr. Freeborn as Mr. Duke/ **Olympic**, Mar. 1840/ **Sad. Wells**, Feb. 1848, with A. Younge as Maj. Mortar, Mr. Harrington as Derby, Henry Mellon as Twankey, Charles Fenton as Bookly, Henry Scharf as Capt. Fitzsmyth, J. T. Johnson as Sir Charles Lavender, William Hoskins as Flammer, Mr. Williams as Fricandeau, Miss Cooper as Mrs. Fitzsmyth, Miss Marsh as Mrs. Mortar, Mrs. W. Watson as Mrs. Twankey, Miss Newcombe as Mrs. Bookly, Julia St. George as Susan.

LADIES OF THE CONVENT, THE// C// W. E. Suter// **Grecian**, Oct. 1853, with Richard Phillips as Viscount Roger, Basil Potter as Duke d'Angon, Edwin Dixon as Count d'Harcourt, Charles Rice as Hercule, Henry Power as Courtois, Jane Coveney as Charlotte, Harriet Coveney as Louise.

LADY AND GENTLEMAN IN A PECULIARLY PERPLEXING PREDICAMENT, A// F 1a// Charles Selby// **Engl. Opera House** (Lyceum), Aug. 1841/ **Olympic**, June 1844, with Charles Selby as the Gentleman, Miss Hamilton as the Lady, Mrs. Selby as Mme. Jobarde/ **Sad. Wells**, Aug. 1846, with William Hoskins as The Gentleman, Mrs. Leigh Murray as The Lady, Mrs. Francis as Mme. Jaborde/ **St. James's**, Apr. 1860, with Charles Young as The Gentleman, Miss Wyndham as The Lady, Mrs. Manders as Mme. Jobard.

LADY AND THE DEVIL, THE; OR, THE WIDOW AND THE RAKE// C 2a// William Dimond// **Sad. Wells**, Feb. 1842, with John Webster as Wildlove, John Herbert as Jeremy, Mr. Williams as Rafael, Mr. Elvin as Claudian, Mrs. Richard Barnett as Zephyra, Miss Cooke as Negombe; Aug. 1866, with F. Watts as Col. Wildlove, Watty Brunton as Jeremy, G. Carter as Claudian, Miss Neville as Zephyrina, Julia Summers as Negombe/ **Drury Lane**, Mar. 1851, with James Anderson as Wildlove, Walter Lacy as Jeremy, J. W. Ray as Rafael, Henry Butler as Claudian, Louisa Nisbett as Zephyrina, Mrs. Griffiths as Negombo/ **St. James's**, Mar. 1868, with Mr. Holman as Wildlove, Mr. Stretton as Claudian, Mr. Evans as Rafael, Thomas Bridgeford as Jeremy, Eleanor Bufton as Zephyrina, Kate Kearney as Negombo.

LADY ANNE'S WELL; OR, THE WARNING SPIRIT// D// William Travers// **Britannia**, July 1868.

LADY AUDLEY'S SECRET// D 2a// Dram. by W. E. Suter fr novel of Mrs. Braddon// **Queen's**, Feb. 1863/ **St. James's**, Mar. 1863, with Mr. Simpson as Sir Michael, Arthur Stirling as Robert, Gaston Murray as Talboys, Frank Matthews as Luke, Louisa Herbert as Lady Audley, Adeline Cottrell as Alice, Ada Dyas as Phoebe/ Scenery by William Beverley/ Music by Mr. Wallerstein/ Machines by Mr. Cassidy/ Prod. by George Ellis; June 1867, with T. C. Burleigh as Sir Michael, Henry Irving as Robert, Gaston Murray as Talboys, Frank Matthews as Luke, Louisa Herbert as Lady Audley, Eleanor Bufton as Alice, Ada Cavendish as Phoebe/ **Grecian**, May 1863, with J. Jackson as Sir Michael, Alfred Rayner as Robert, William James as Talboys, Henry Grant as Luke, John Manning as Bibbles, Mrs. Charles Dillon as Lady Audley, Ellen Hale as Alicia, Mary A. Victor as Phoebe/ **Sad. Wells**, Mar. 1869, with F. J. Howard as Sir Michael, Mr. Fitzwilliam as Robert, Charles Egerton as George, Harry Seed as Luke, Miss Wheeler as Lady Audley, Lizzie Dudley as Alicia, Miss Carrington as Phoebe.

LADY AUDLEY'S SECRET// D 2a// Dram. by George Roberts fr novel of Mrs. Braddon// **Globe**, 1874, with George Grainger as Sir Michael, G. R. Ireland as Robert, H. R. Teesdale as Talboys, Lionel Brough as Luke, Louisa Moore as Lady Audley, Blanche Colridge as Alice, Kathleen Irwin as Phoebe.

LADY AUDLEY'S SECRET// D 2a// Dram. by Robert Walters fr novel of Mrs. Braddon// **Drury Lane**, Mar. 1880, with J. B. Durham as Sir Michael, Mr. Boleyn as Robert, James Arnold as Talboys, Mr. Gibson as Luke, Louise Moodie as Lady Audley, Nelly Harris as Alice, Dolores Drummond as Phoebe.

LADY BARTER// C 3a// Charles Coghlan// **Princess's**, Feb. 1891, with Lewis Waller as Lord Brent, Frederick Everill as Short, Arthur Stirling as Gen. Peters, Charles Coghlan as Col. Pearce, Hubert Bruce as Wright, Lillie Langtry as Lady Barter, Helen Forsyth as Mary, Ethel Hope as Justine/ Scenery by Harry Potts/ Machines by J. Cawdery/ Gas & Limelight by Jones & Kerr.

LADY BOUNTIFUL// Play 4a// Arthur Wing Pinero// **Garrick**, Mar. 1891, with Johnston Forbes Robertson, Charles Groves, Gilbert Hare, Carlotta Addison, Kate Rorke, Marie Linden, John Hare.

LADY BROWNE'S DIARY// C 3a// Adap. by Minnie Bell fr F of Octave Feuillet, La Crise// **Strand**, June 1892, with Herbert Waring as Sir Philip, W. T. Lovell as Darrell, Ben Greet as Archibald, Basil Deane as Jack, Lily Hanbury as Lady Browne, Minnie Bell as Gilby, Hilary Deane as Margaret.

LADY BURGLAR, THE// C 1a// E. J. Malyon & Charles James// **Avenue**, Oct. 1897, with Frederick Volpé as Slumleigh, Arthur Helmore as Fluffington, Julie Ring as Miss Winthrop.

LADY CLANCARTY; OR, WEDDED AND WOOED// D 4a// Tom Taylor// **Olympic**, Mar. 1874, with Charles Neville as William III, Mr. Vollaire as Portland, W. H. Fisher as Woodstock, W. H. Vernon as Spencer, Henry Neville as Earl Clancarty, L. F. Lewis as Barclay, Mr. Canninge as Friend, G. W. Anson as Goodman, Ada Cavendish as Lady Clancarty, Miss Fowler as Lady Betty, Annie Taylor as Susannah, Mrs. Stephens as Mother Hunt.

LADY CLARA VERE DE VERE// D// n.a.// **POW**, June 1888.

LADY CLARE// D 5a// Adap. by Robert Buchanan fr F of Georges Ohnet, Le Maitre de Forges// **Globe**, Apr. 1883, with Philip Beck as Lord Ambermere, Alfred Bucklaw as Middleton, Horace Wigan as Smale, E. Hamilton Bell as Count Legrange, Lawrence Grey as Maj. O'Conner, Carlotta Leclercq as Countess Broadmeads, Harriet Jay as Miss Brookfield, Lydia Cowell as Mary, Mrs. Digby Willoughby as Melissa, Ada Cavendish as Lady Clare.

LADY DEADLOCK'S SECRET// Play 4a// Adap. by J. Palgrave Simpson fr novel of Charles Dickens, Bleak House// **Opera Comique**, Mar. 1884.

LADY DEANE// Play 4a// Alfred Wilmot// **St. Geo. Hall**, May 1887.

LADY FLIRT// C 3a// Adap. by Paul Gavault & G. Berr fr F, Mme. Flirt// **Haymarket**, 1901.

LADY FLORA// C 4a// Charles Coghlan// **Court**, Mar. 1875, with John Hare, W. H. Kendal, Mrs. Kendal, John Clayton, Charles Kelly.

LADY FORTUNE// Play 1a// Charles Thomas// **Globe**, Sept. 1887, with Graham Wentworth as Lord Ambleby, Norman Bent as Jessup, Frederick Glover as Guy Mallory, Milicent Mildmay as Mrs. Cunliffe, Cissy Grahame as Kate/ **Comedy**, Feb. 1892.

LADY FROM THE SEA, THE// D 5a// Trans. by Eleanor Marx-Aveling fr Norw. of Henrik Ibsen// **Terry's**, May 1891, with Oscar Ayde as Dr. Wangle, Leonard Outram as Arnholm, Herbert Sparling as Lyngstrand, Ernest Patterson as Ballested, Charles Dalton as Stranger, Rose Mellor as Ellida, Violet Armbruster as Bolette, Edith Kenward as Hilde.

LADY GLADYS// C// Robert Buchanan// **Opera Comique**, May 1894.

LADY GUIDE, THE// Play 3a// n.a.// **Terry's**, Apr. 1891.

LADY HUNTWORTH'S EXPERIMENT// C 3a// R. C. Carton// **Criterion**, Apr. 1900.

LADY IN DIFFICULTIES, A// C 2a// J. R. Planché// **Lyceum**, Oct. 1849, with C. J. Mathews as Count Natzmar, John Parselle as Herman, Frederick Cooke as Wetzlar, Frank Matthews as Puffengruntz, Robert Honner as Caspar, Miss H. Gilbert as Mme. Denhoff, Kathleen Fitzwilliam as Maria, Miss Clair as Betley/ Scenery by W. Beverly.

LADY JANE GREY// D// C. H. Hazlewood// **Britannia**, May 1874.

LADY JANE GREY// D 1a// William Poel// **St. Geo. Hall**, June 1885.

LADY KILLER, THE// FC 3a// Adap. by Charles Fawcett fr F of Alexandre Bisson, 115 Rue de Pigalle// **Strand**, Oct. 1893, with Cairns James as Chuckle, Charles Fawcett as Brown, Herbert Ross as Dr. Perfect, Harry Paulton as Robjohn, Willie Edouin as John Chuckle, Lillian Crauford as Sophie, Jenny Dawson as Carrie, Annie Goward as Mrs. Plumper, Mrs. G. B. Lewis as Mrs. Robjohn, Georgie Esmond as Ina, Mina Le Bert as Florence, Amy Gordon as Daisy, Venie Bennett as Sarah, Stella Berridge as May.

LADY LILIAN; OR, FLOWERS OF JOY AND FLOWERS OF SORROW// D 4a// Edward Towers// **Pavilion**, Mar. 1880.

LADY LOVINGTON; OR, A SOIREE DRAMATIQUE// C 1a// George Villars// **St. Geo. Hall**, June 1894.

LADY MARY WORTLEY MONTAGU// D// n.a.// **Lyceum**, 1839.

LADY OF BELLEISLE; OR, A NIGHT IN THE BASTILLE// D 3a// Adap. by J. M. Gully fr F of Alexandre Dumas, Mademoiselle de Belleisle// **Drury Lane**, Dec. 1839.

LADY OF LYONS, THE; OR, LOVE AND PRIDE// D 5a// Edward Bulwer-Lytton// **Cov. Garden**, Feb. 1838, with E. W. Elton as Beauseant, Drinkwater Meadows as Glavis, George Bartley as Col. Damas, Robert Strickland as Deschappelles, Henry Howe as Gervais, John Pritchard as Dupont, Mr. Roberts as Desmoulins, W. C. Macready as Claude Melnotte, Mrs. W. Clifford as Mme. Deschappelles, Helen Faucit as Pauline, Mrs. Griffith as Widow Melnotte, Mrs. East as Janet, Miss Garrick as Marian/ **Haymarket**, Nov. 1839, with John Webster as Beauseant, Benjamin Webster as Glavis, Robert Strickland as Col. Damas, Charles Perkins as Deschappelles, Henry Howe as Gervais, Mr. Cauldfield as Desmoulins, W. C. Macready as Claude Melnotte, Mrs. W. Clifford as Mme. Deschappelles, Helen Faucit as Pauline, Mrs. Danson as Widow Melnotte; Oct. 1845, with Mr. Stuart as Beauseant, A. Brindal as Glavis, James Anderson as Claude Melnotte, Mr. Tilbury as Col. Damas, James Bland as Deschappelles, Mrs. W. Clifford as Mme. Deschappelles, Helen Faucit as Pauline, Mrs. Stanley as Widow Melnotte; Apr. 1851, with Henry Howe as Beauseant, Charles Selby as Glavis, Mr. Lambert as Col. Damas, James Bland as Deschappelles, J. William Wallack as Claude Melnotte, George Braid as Gervais, Mrs. Stanley as Mme. Deschappelles, Laura Addison as Pauline, Mrs. Young as Widow Melnotte; Dec. 1871, with W. H. Chippendale as Damas, Walter Gordon as Beauseant, J. B. Buckstone Jr. as Glavis, George Braid as Deschappelles, George Conway Wilson as Claude Melnotte, Mrs. Edward Fitzwilliam as Widow Melnotte, Mrs. Hermann Vezin as Pauline/ **Drury Lane**, Jan. 1843; Mar. 1853, with Mr. White as Deschappelles, Mr. Moorhouse as Beauseant, James Lickfold as Glavis, Charles Selby as Col. Damas, E. L. Davenport as Claude Melnotte, Henry Lee as Gaspar, Fanny Vining as Pauline, Mrs. Griffith as Mme. Deschappelles, Kate Saxon as Widow Melnotte; Sept. 1856, with Barry Sullivan as Claude Melnotte, Charles Verner as Beauseant, C. Vincent as Glavis, A. Younge as Col. Damas, Mr. Tilbury as Deschappelles, Emma Waller as Pauline, Mrs. Selby as Mme. Deschappelles, Mrs. Montague as Widow Melnotte/ **Sad. Wells**, Nov. 1844, with Henry Marston as Beauseant, John Webster as Glavis, George Bennett as Deschappelles, A. Younge as Col. Damas, Samuel Phelps as Claude Melnotte, E. Morton as Demoulins, Mrs. Henry Marston as Mme. Deschappelles, Mrs. Mary Warner as Pauline, Mrs. Francis as Widow Melnotte/ Scenery by F. Fenton, Mr. Morelli & Mr. Finlay; May 1856, with W. Morgan as Beauseant, Mr. Swanborough as Glavis, Mr. Barrett as Col. Damas, Charles Dillon as Claude Melnotte, Walter Williams as Deschappelles, Mr. Laporte as Desmoulins, Mr. Shepherd as Gervais, Mrs. B. Bartlett as Mme. Deschappelles, Mrs. Charles Dillon as Pauline, Miss Sidney as Widow Melnotte, Emma Barnett as Jeanette; Mar. 1861, with T. C. Harris as Beauseant, Lewis Ball as Glavis, Samuel Phelps as Col. Damas, Mr. Josephs as Deschappelles, Edmund Phelps as Claude Melnotte, Webster Vernon as Desmoulin, Mrs. Charles Young (Mrs. Hermann Vezin) as Pauline, Mrs. Henry Marston as Mme. Deschappelles, Mrs. George Hodson as Widow Melnotte, Caroline Heath as Janet, Fanny Morelli as Marian/ **Adelphi**, Apr. 1847, with Charlotte Cushman as Claude Melnotte, Mr. Harker as Col. Damas, Mr. Mortimer as Beauseant, Benjamin Webster as Deschappelles, Mrs. Banks as Mme. Deschappelles, Susan Cushman as Pauline; Feb. 1898, with Kyrle Bellew as Claude Melnotte, Luigi Lablache as Col. Damas, H. A. Saintsbury as Beauseant, Arthur Lewis as Glavis, A. E. Drinkwater as Deschappelles, Miss Stirling as Mme. Deschappelles, Miss Crofton as Widow Melnotte, Mrs. Brown Potter as Pauline/ **Olympic**, Mar. 1848, with Henry Lee as Beauseant, Henry Holl as Glavis, E. L. Davenport as Claude Melnotte, William Davidge as Damas, Charles Perkins as Deschappelles, Mrs. Brougham as Mme. Deschappelles, Anna Cora Mowatt as Pauline, Mrs. H. Lee as Widow Melnotte; Dec. 1850 with William Farren Jr. as Beauseant, John Kinloch as Glavis, Charles Diddear as Deschappelles, George Cooke as Col. Damas, G. V. Brooke as Claude Melnotte, Mrs. B. Bartlett as Mme. Deschappelles, Helen Faucit as Pauline, Mrs. Griffiths as Widow Melnotte; July 1851 with same cast, except J. William Wallack as Claude Melnotte, Mrs. Charles Boyce as Widow Melnotte; Nov. 1851 with same cast except Henry Farren as Claude Melnotte, Laura Keene as Pauline; July 1866, with Henry Neville as Claude Melnotte, W. H. Stephens as Col. Damas, George Vincent as Beauseant, Horace Wigan as Glavis, Harwood Cooper as Deschappelles, Robert Soutar as Gaspar, Kate Terry as Pauline, Mrs. Stephens as Mme. Deschappelles, Miss Austin as Widow Melnotte; 1882, with F. H. Macklin as Claude Melnotte, E. F. Edgar as Beauseant, F. Charles as Glavis, A. T. Hilton as Col. Damas, G. Canninge as Deschappelles, Elinor Aickin as Mme. Deschappelles, Sally Clarke as Widow Melnotte, Miss De Grey as Pauline/ **Grecian**, Dec. 1853, with Henry Grant as Deschappelles, Basil Potter as Beauseant, Charles Horn as Glavis, Eaton O'Donnell as Col. Damas, Richard Phillips as Claude Melnotte, Miss Johnstone as Mme. Deschappelles, Ellen Crisp as Widow Melnotte, Jane Coveney as Pauline; Dec. 1863 with J. B. Steele as Beauseant, J. Jackson as Colonel Damas, Henry Grant as Deschappelles, Walter Holland as Gaspard, John Manning as Glavis, William James as Claude Melnotte, Rebecca Power as Pauline, Mme. Simon as Mme. Deschappelles, Marie Brewer as Widow Melnotte/ **St. James's**, Dec. 1854, with Mr. Stuart as Beauseant, Mr. Sidney as Glavis, W. Cooper as Col. Damas, F. Ede as Deschappelles, George Vandenhoff as Claude Melnotte, Mr. Johnson as Dumont, Mr. Forrester as Maj. Desmoulins, Mrs. Stanley as Mme. Deschappelles, Mrs. Seymour as Pauline, Miss Grey as Widow Melnotte; Aug. 1860, with J. G. Shore as Beauseant, T. H. Higgie as Glavis, Frank Matthews as Damas, Edmund Garden as Deschappelles, George Melville as Melnotte, Caroline Heath as Pauline, Mrs. Weston as Widow Melnotte; 1881, with W. H. Kendal as Claude Melnotte, John Hare as Col. Damas, T. N. Wenman as Beauseant, Mr. Mackintosh as Glavis, Robert Cathcart as Deschappelles, Mrs. Gaston Murray as Mme. Deschappelles, Louise Moodie as Widow Melnotte, Mrs. W. H. Kendal as Pauline/ **Victoria**, Sept. 1871, with Henry Mayhew as Beauseant, James Fawn as Glavis, Watty Brunton as Deschappelles, E. Fitzdavis as Col. Damas, R. Dodson as Claude Melnotte, Emma Barnett as Pauline, Harriet Farren as Mme. Deschappelles/ **Globe**, June 1873, with Charles Kelly as Beausant, Charles Neville as Glavis, Samuel Emery as Col. Damas, H. J. Montague as Claude Melnotte, E. W. Garden as Deschappelles, Mrs. Chippendale as Mme. Deschappelles, Rose Massey as Pauline, Mrs. Gaston Murray (Miss Hughes) as Widow Melnotte/ **Princess's**, Aug. 1876, with Ellen Terry, Charles Coghlan/ **Lyceum**, Apr. 1879, with Henry Irving as Claude Melnotte, Walter Lacy as Col. Damas, Mr. Forrester as Beausant, Kyrle Bellew as Glavis, C. Cooper as Deschappelles, Mrs. Chippendale as Mme. Deschappelles, Georgina Pauncefort as Widow Melnotte, Ellen Terry as Pauline; Oct. 1883, with Mary Anderson, J. H. Barnes, Frank Archer, Mrs. Arthur Stirling; Apr. 1885, with William Terriss as Claude Melnotte, Arthur Stirling as Col. Damas, Herbert Standing as Beausant, Arthur Lewis as Glavis, W. H. Stephens as Deschappelles, Carlotta Leclercq as Mme. Deschappelles, Mrs. Charles Calvert as Widow Melnotte, Mary Anderson as Pauline/ **POW**, Mar. 1886, with Charles Coghlan, Lillie Langtry/.

LADY OF OSTEND, THE// F 3a// Adap. by F. C. Burnand fr G of Oscar Blumenthal & Gustav Kadelburg// **Terry's**, July 1899, with Weedon Grossmith as Whertles, Charles Groves as Carbury, Wilfred Draycott as Blake, Edmund Gurney as Krockitt, Ellis Jeffreys as Dorothy, Mary A. Victor as Matilda, Violet Darrell as Millie, Eve Erskine as Jane, Ethel Clinton as Lady of Ostend/ Scenery by W. T. Hemsley.

LADY OF QUALITY, A// D 5a// Adap. by Frances Burnett & Stephen Townesend fr Burnett's novel// **Comedy**, Mar. 1899, with Alfred Kendrick as Sir John, William Farren Jr. as Sir Geoffrey, Gerald Lawrence as Duke of Osmonde, F. Rawson Buckley as Lord Eldershaw, Frank Hill as Sir Christopher, Richard Boleyn as Sir Joseph, Reginald Waram as

Gregory, Tom Heslewood as Hardy, Jerrold Robertshaw as Lord Ware, Charles Lander as Lord Lovelace, Walter Pearce as Sir Harry, Franklyn Walford as Jenifer, Eleanor Calhoun as Clorinda, Marie Linden as Anne, May Palfrey as Lady Betty, Margaret Myrtoun as Mistress Wimpole/ Scenery by Joseph Harker, T. E. Ryan & W. T. Hemsley.

LADY OF ST. TROPEZ, THE; OR, THE LAST LINK OF LOVE// D 4a// Adap. fr F// **Sad. Wells**, May 1857, with Edmund Falconer as Maurice, James Worrell as Count D'Auberine, John Chester as Langlois, J. G. Shore as D'Arbel, Mr. Lingham as Caussade, Charles Fenton as Gerfaut, Mr. Warren as Jerome, Emily Howard as Hortense, Mary A. Victor as Mme. Langlois, Miss Evans as Charlotte, Miss Weston as Mme. Jerome, Mr. Day as Justine.

LADY OF THE CAMELLIAS, THE// D 5a// Adap. fr F of Alexandre Dumas, Dame aux Camelias// **Vaudeville**, Feb. 1852/ **Sad. Wells** (in 4a), July 1862, with Henry Forrester as Armand, Ersser Jones as Duval, James Johnstone as Rieux, C. Lloyds as St. Gaudens, W. Mowbray as Gustave, Henry Butler as de Varville, Marian Jones as Marguerite, Miss Clements as Nichette, Emily Dowton as Prudence, Bessie Heath as Nanine, Miss Aldridge as Olympia, Rosa Nathan as Esther.

LADY OF THE LAKE, THE// D// Dram. by T. J. Dibdin fr Sir Walter Scott// **Sad. Wells**, Apr. 1837, with C. H. Pitt as Fitzjames, Thomas Lee as Grame, F. Ede as Brian, Mr. Hicks as Dhu, Mr. King as Douglas, Mr. Ennis as Rane, C. Smith as Murdock, Miss Williams as Ellen, Mrs. Harris as Lady Margaret, Miss Melville as Blanche.

LADY OF THE LAKE, THE// D 4a// Dram. by Andrew Halliday fr poem of Sir Walter Scott// **Drury Lane**, Oct. 1872, with James Fernandez as Fitzjames, J. Dewhurst as Douglas, William Terriss as Graeme, Henry Sinclair as Dhu, Mr. Milton as Bane, E. Rosenthal as Brian, J. H. Barnes as Lewis/ Scenery by William Beverley/ Music by W. C. Levey/ Machines by J. Tucker/ Prod. by author & F. B. Chatterton.

LADY OF THE LAKE, THE; OR, THE KNIGHT OF SNOWDOUN// D 2a// Dram. fr Sir Walter Scott// **Victoria**, Oct. 1843, with C. Williams as Earl Douglas, Mr. James as Bane, John Dale as Sir Roderick, Mr. Nantz as Fitzjames, William Seaman as Graeme, C. Baker as Brian, Mr. Hitchinson as John of Brent, Charles Morelli as Murdoch, Mr. Henry as Malise, Mrs. Atkinson as Ellen, Miss Ridgway as Blanche, Miss Saddler as Lady Margaret, Miss King as Jessie.

LADY OR THE TIGER, THE// D 3a// Adap. by Sidney Rosenfeld fr story of R. Stockton// **Elephant & Castle**, May 1888.

LADY VOLUNTEERS, THE// C 1a// Sidney Phelps// **Vaudeville**, Apr. 1900.

LADY WINDERMERE'S FAN// C 4a// Oscar Wilde// **St. James's**, Feb. 1892, with George Alexander as Lord Windermere, Nutcombe Gould as Lord Darlington, H. H. Vincent as Lord Lorton, A. Vane Tempest as Dumby, Ben Webster as Graham, Alfred Holles as Hopper, Fanny Coleman as Lady Windermere, Miss Granville as Lady Plimdale, Miss A. De Winton as Mrs. Cowper, Laura Graves as Lady Agatha, Marion Terry as Mrs. Erlynne/ Scenery by H. P. Hall, Walter Hann, & W. Harford.

LADY'S IDOL, THE// FC 3a// Arthur Law// **Vaudeville**, Apr. 1895.

LAGGARD IN LOVE, A// F// Horace Lennard// **Trafalgar Sq.**, Apr. 1893, with Alfred Balfour as Battersby, Harry Grattan as Lord Marigold, Harcourt Beatty as Rose, Mabel Hardy as Minnie, Millie Vere as Sarah.

LAID UP IN PORT; OR, SHARKS ALONG SHORE// D 3a// T. H. Higgie// **Victoria**, Apr. 1846, with James Ranoe as Capt. Stockton, T. Fredericks as Villanos, E. F. Saville as Chance, James Howard as Snakely, Alfred Raymond as Atherley, Roberts Tindell as Old Squalls, T. H. Higgie as Truefit, Walter Searle as Bopp, E. G. Burton as Pickles, Annette Vincent as Felicity, Miss Jefferson as Mrs. Crummy, Eliza Terrey as Hortensia, Mrs. George Lee as Jessey/ Scenery by Mildenhall/ Machines by Wood & Foster/ Music by W. J. Hill.

LALLA ROOKH; OR, THE GHEBIRS OF THE DESERT// D// Thomas Moore// **Sad. Wells**, Aug. 1842, with Alfred Rayner as Aranzebe, John Herbert as Fadladeen, W. D. Broadfoot as Aliria, Mr. Harwood as Himlah, C. J. Smith as Ziraffghan, Mrs. Hillier as Lalla, Mrs. Richard Barnett as Deelah, Mrs. Stickney as Mirrah/ Scenery by T. Pitt & G. Smithyes Jr./ Machines by Mr. Cawdrey/ Prod. by W. D. Broadfoot.

LAME EXCUSE, A// F 1a// Frederick Hay// **POW**, Apr. 1869, with William Terris, William Blakely, Augusta Wilton.

LAME LOVER, THE// C 3a// Samuel Foote// **Royalty**, 1872.

LAMED FOR LIFE// C 2a// Westland Marston// **Royalty**, June 1871.

LANCASHIRE LASS, THE; OR, TEMPTED, TRIED, AND TRUE// D Pro & 4a// H. J. Byron// **Queen's**, July 1868/ **Grecian**, Mar. 1869, with Thomas Mead as Redburn, George Gillett as Kirby, William James as Clayton, J. Jackson as Jellick, John Manning as Spotty, Lizzie Mandelbert as Ruth, Alice Denvil as Kate, Henry Grant as Danville, George Conquest as Johnson, Charles Mortimer as Donovan, Mary A. Victor as Fanny/ Scenery by Messender & Soames/ **Princess's**, Feb. 1875, with F. B. Egan as Kirby, J. B. Howard as Redburn, William Terriss as Clayton, Frederick Dewar as Jellick, George Belmore as Spotty, Lydia Foote as Ruth, Mrs. Alfred Mellon as Kate, J. G. Shore as Darvillo, Samuel Emery as Johnson, C. J. Smith as Milder, J. B. Johnstone as Kitely, P. C. Beverley as Andrews, Alma Murray as Fanny/ Scenery by F. Lloyds, W. Perkins, W. Leitch & E. Wigan.

LANCASHIRE LIFE; OR, POOR JOE THE FACTORY LAD// D// Edward Towers// **Pavilion,** May 1875.

LANCASHIRE SAILOR, THE// D 1a// Brandon Thomas// **Terry's,** June 1891, with W. L. Branscombe as Ormerod, Brandon Thomas as Alfred, Compton Coutts as Ellerby, Edith Chester as Alice, Dolores Drummond as Martha.

LANCERS, THE// F 1a// John Howard Payne// **Sad. Wells,** July 1844, with Mr. Williams as Adm. Etiquette, Charles Morelli as Crusty, John Webster as Belton, Mr. Coreno as Peter, Mr. Sharp as Short, Charles Hudson as Lenox, Emma Harding as Louisa/ **Grecian,** Sept. 1844, with Mr. Campbell as Adm. Etiquette, Edwin Dixon as Belton, Henry Horncastle as Lenox, Mr. Baldwin as Crusty, Frederick Robson as Peter, Miss M. A. Crisp as as Louisa.

LANCERS, THE; OR, THE GENTLEMAN'S SON// D 3a// Adap. by Leicester Vernon fr F// **Princess's,** Nov. 1853, with John Ryder as Col. De Franc-Epée, David Fisher as De Courcy, Henry Mellon as Moustache, Drinkwater Meadows as Blanchet, George Everett as Eugene, John Collett as Carabine, Carlotta Leclercq as Estelle, Mrs. Winstanley as Mme. D'Aplomb, Mrs. Walter Lacy as Pomponne, Maria Daly as Jeannette/ Scenery by Walter Gordon.

LAND AHEAD// D// George M. Fenn// **Astley's,** Oct. 1878, with Frank Cates as Brian Moore, Nelson Wheatcroft as Fitzgerald, H. Monte as Morrow, J. S. Delaney as Rooney, Edward Chamberlaine as Father Phelim, H. Cranston as Lanty, Virginia Blackwood as Honor Delaney, Fanny Wright as Biddy.

LAND AND LOVE// C 3a// A. W. Dubourg// **Globe,** May 1884.

LAND OF DIAMONDS, A// D// Louis Coen// **Sadler's Wells,** June 1884.

LAND OF GOLD, THE// D 6a// George Lander// **Elephant & Castle,** Feb. 1888.

LAND OF HEART'S DESIRE, THE// Play 1a// W. B. Yeats// **Avenue,** Mar. 1894, with James Welch as Michael Bruin, A. E. Mason as James Bruin, George Foss as Father Hart, Charlotte Morland as Bridget, Winifred Fraser as Mary.

LAND OF THE LIVING// D 5a// Frank Harvey// **Grand,** July 1889/ **Surrey,** June 1891.

LAND RATS AND WATER RATS// D 3a// Watts Phillips// **Surrey,** Sept. 1868.

LANDLADY, THE// C// Dram. by Alec Nelson// **Shaftesbury,** Apr. 1889.

LANGUAGE OF FLOWERS, THE// C 1a// J. P. Wooler// **Olympic,** May 1852, with John Kinloch as Sir Philip, Henry Compton as Robert, E. Clifton as Tom, Alfred Sanger as Heavywet, Mrs. B. Bartlett as Mrs. Martin, Isabel Adams as Harriet, Miss Fielding as Mary/ **Grecian,** Oct. 1857, with Richard Phillips as Sir Philip, John Manning as Robert, Henry Power as Tom, Mr. Coleman as Heavywet, Miss Johnstone as Mrs. Martin, Miss Chapman as Harriet, Harriet Coveney as Mary.

LANTERN LIGHT// D Pro & 4a// G. D'Arcy & C. H. Ross// **Elephant & Castle,** Feb. 1873.

LARA// D// n.a.// **Her Majesty's,** Jan. 1865.

LARK IN THE TEMPLE, THE// n.a.// **Alexandra,** Nov. 1866.

LARKINS' LOVE LETTERS// F// T. J. Williams// **Sad. Wells,** Apr. 1870, with R. Horsley Woods as Lynx, Cyril Mullett as Bobbins, Walter Cox as Col. Boyleover, Blanche Vaughn as Isabella, Fred Irving as Sally.

LAST APPEAL, THE// D// n.a.// **Britannia,** July 1859.

LAST CHANCE, THE// D 5a// G. R. Sims// **Adelphi,** Apr. 1885, with Charles Warner as Frank Daryll, James Fernandez as Barton, George Warde as Richard Daryll, Charles Glenney as Lisle, E. W. Garden as Day, J. G. Shore as West, Sidney Howard as Rawlings, J. D. Beveridge as Karasoff, Louise Moodie as Marion, Mary Rorke as Mary, Nelly Lyons as Nelly, Harriet Coveney as Mrs. "No. 22"/ Scenery by Bruce Smith, Walter Hann, & William Telbin/ Music by Henry Sprake.

LAST CHAPTER, THE// D 4a// G. H. Broadhurst// **Strand,** Sept. 1899, with Ben Webster as Stanley, Thomas Wise as Salter, John Beauchamp as Fairchild, Nicol Pentland as Boyden, Philip Cunningham as Morrison, Arnold Lucy as Blake, Harold Eden as Percivall, May Whitty as Katherine, Emma Gwynne as Mrs. Stanley, Jessie Bateman as Flora, Edith Stuart as Mrs. Watkins, Jessie Ferrar as Estelle.

LAST DAYS OF POMPEII, THE// D 5a// John Oxenford// **Queen's,** Jan. 1872.

LAST EXPRESS, THE// D 3a// W. H. Abel// **East London,** June 1871.

LAST GUERRILLA, THE// D 2a// n.a.// **Eng. Opera House** (Lyceum), July 1839, with George Bennett as Alvez, James Bland as Lt. Damien, Mr. Burnett as Lt. D'Avoux, John Sanders as Martin, Mr. Cullenford as Losquez, Miss Tyrer as Clara, Miss Goward as Mary, Miss Mears as Gianetta/ Scenery by Mr. Phillips/ Music by George Stansbury.

LAST HOPE, THE// D 3a// Adap. by John Oxenford fr F of Ferdinand Dugué, Les Amours Maudits// **Lyceum,** Feb. 1859, with Samuel Emery, Mme. Celeste, Mr. Barrett, Gaston Murray/ **Sad. Wells,** May 1863, with J. W. Collier as Sir William, Mr. Britten as Alfred, Mr. Chapman as Capt. Tintamarre, Mr. Stalman as Raymond, Frederick Morton as Michall, James Johnstone as Pierre, Bessie Heath as Mme. d'Antoine, Emma Leslie as Pierette, Mme. Celeste as Marie.

LAST HOPE, THE// D 3a// W. H. Abel// **East**

London, Dec. 1873.

LAST LINK OF LOVE, THE// D 2a// C. H. Hazlewood// **Britannia**, Feb. 1867.

LAST MAN, THE// D// n.a.// **Olympic**, Nov. 1845, with James Browne as Dale, Mr. Binge as Wentworth, Mr. Turnour as Battergate, Mr. D'Arcy as Mallard, Robert Romas as Weaver, Mr. Stevens as Henry, Mr. Astbury as David, Miss Treble as Lucy, Mrs. Griffith as Alice, Miss Hamilton as Barbara.

LAST MOMENT, THE// D 3a// William Travers// **East London**, Oct. 1867.

LAST OF THE DANDIES, THE// Play 4a// Clyde Fitch// **Her Majesty's**, Oct. 1901.

LAST OF THE PIGTAILS, THE// F 1a// Charles Selby// **Adelphi**, Jan. 1858, with Charles Selby as Sir Noah, J. L. Toole as Swellington, C. J. Smith as Doddles, Henrietta Simms as Lady Starchington, Kate Kelly as Mrs. Swellington, Mrs. Chatterley as Tabitha, Lydia Foote as Jane/ **Strand**, Sept. 1858/ **Drury Lane**, July 1860, with John Parselle as Sir Noah, James Bland as Doddles, John Clarke as Swellington, Eleanor Bufton as Mrs. Swellington, Mrs. Selby as Tabitha, Miss M. Oliver as Lady Starchington, Emily Turtle as Jane/ **Princess's**, May 1863, with Mr. Fitzjames as Sir Noah, Joseph Robins as Swellington, Robert Morton as Doddles, Mrs. St. Henry as Lady Starchington, Lydia Maitland as Mrs. Swellington, Mrs. Charles Selby as Tabitha.

LAST STRAW, THE// D 1a// C. H. Dickinson// **St. Geo. Hall**, Mar. 1888.

LAST STROKE OF MIDNIGHT, THE// D 4a// James Guiver// **Grecian**, Mar. 1879.

LAST WITNESS, THE; OR, THE FATE OF ST. MARC THE MURDERER// D 3a// n.a.// **Victoria**, Apr. 1842, with Mr. Griffith as Jaroche, C. Williams as D'Alambert, E. F. Saville as St. Marc, William Seaman as Lucksall, John Dale as Demane, Mr. Howard as Perlatti, John Gardner as Gibeau, Mrs. George Lee as Mme. Duval, Mrs. E. F. Saville as Marie, Miss Coveney as Mannette, Mrs. Griffith as Joan, Miss Saddler as Lisette/ Scenery by Fenton & Morelli.

LAST WORD, THE// C 4a// Adap. by Augustin Daly fr G of Franz von Schönthan// **Lyceum**, Sept. 1891, with John Drew as Rutherell, James Lewis as Airey, George Clark as Secretary, Charles Wheatleigh as Prof. Rutherell, Clarles Leclercq as Mossop, Sidney Herbert as Bouraneel, Sidney Bowkett as Baron Stuyve, Ada Rehan as Vera, Isabel Irving as Faith, Kitty Cheatham as Winnifred/ **Daly's**, Oct. 1893.

LASTING LOVE// D 3a// Edgar Newbound// **Britannia**, July 1878.

LATE LAMENTED, THE// D// Tom Taylor // **Haymarket**, Nov. 1859, with C. J. Mathews.

LATE LAMENTED, THE// F 3a// Adap. by Fred Horner fr F of Alexandre Bisson, Feu Toupinel// **Court**, May 1891, with Arthur Cecil as Crosse, Herbert Standing as Maj. Marshall, E. Allan Aynesworth as Webb, Gilbert Farquhar as Fawcett, Charles Rock as Smith, Rosina Filippi as Mrs. Webb, Mrs. Edmund Phelps as Kate, Florence Harrington as Mary.

LATE MR. CASTELLO, THE// F 3a// Sidney Grundy// **Comedy**, Dec. 1895, with Leonard Boyne as Capt. Trefusis, Cyril Maude as Sir Pinto, J. G. Grahame as Uniacke, Rose Leclercq as Mrs. Bickerdyke, Winifred Emery as Mrs. Castello, Esmé Beringer as Avice/ Scenery by Walter Johnstone/ Music by Alfred Caldicott.

LATE RALPH JOHNSON, THE// C 3a// Adap. by Sutherland Edwards fr F of Adolphe Bélot, Le Testament de César Girodot// **Royalty**, Feb. 1872.

LAUGH WHEN YOU CAN// C 3a// Frederic Reynolds// **Cov. Garden**, Oct. 1838, with Mr. Vining as Gossamer, George Bartley as Bonus, Charles Diddear as Mortimer, Drinkwater Meadows as Sambo, Henry Howe as Delville, Mr. Tilbury as Costly, Miss Male as Charles, Charlotte Vandenhoff as Mrs. Mortimer, Miss Charles as Emily, Mrs. Humby as Dorothy, Mrs. W. Clifford as Miss Gloomly/ **Sad. Wells**, Dec. 1852, with Henry Marston as Gossamer, Mr. Barrett as Bonus, Henry Mellon as Mortimer, Lewis Ball as Sambo, William Belford as Delville, C. Mortimer as Costly, Kate Mandelbert as Charles, Miss T. Bassano as Mrs. Mortimer, Eliza Travers as Emily, Mrs. Dixon as Dorothy, Mrs. Henry Marston as Miss Gloomily.

LAUGHING HYENA, THE// F 1a// Benjamin Webster Jr.// **Haymarket**, Nov. 1849, with Benjamin Webster as Fumer, J. B. Buckstone as Hornblower, Miss Reynolds as Mrs. Fumer, Mrs. Fitzwilliam as Popsy/ **Olympic**, July 1879, with Edith Bruce as Mrs. Fumier, Maria Davis as Popsy, Arthur Williams as Fumier, Luigi Lablache as Hornblower; Feb. 1886, with Frank Oswald as Fumier, Fred Irving as Hornblower, Ada Herbert as Mrs. Fumier, Nelly Daly as Popsy.

LAURA; OR, LOVE'S ENCHANTMENT// C 3a// n.a.// **Novelty**, June 1888.

LAURENCE'S LOVE SUIT// C 2a// J. P. Wooler// **Strand**, Jan. 1865.

LAURETTE'S BRIDAL// D// n.a.// **Britannia**, Nov. 1866.

LAVATER; OR, NOT A BAD JUDGE see, Not a Bad Judge.

LAVATER THE PHYSIOGNOMIST, AND A GOOD JUDGE TOO (see also Not a Bad Judge)// C 2a// Adap. by J. R. Planché fr F// **Haymarket**, Mar. 1848, with Benjamin Webster as Lavater, Mr. Rogers as Baron Wallenstein, Henry Vandenhoff as Theodore, Henry Howe as Marquis Rivarola, Mr. Tilbury as Puffendoff, James Bland as Katzencraft, Mr. Clark as Tunstein, Miss Fortescue as Agnes, Mrs. L. S. Buckingham as Diana, Miss E. Messent as Rose.

LAW AND LIONS// F 1a// n.a.// **Sad. Wells**, July 1837, with Mr. Griffiths as Suavy, C. J. Smith as Pudor, J. Dunn as Smoothface, Mr. Vale as Mammoth, C. H. Pitt as James, Thomas Lee as Robert, Mrs. Harris as Mrs. Mammoth, Lavinia Melville as Jane.

LAW FOR LADIES// C 1a// Alfred Wigan// **St. James's**, Apr. 1861, with Henry Ashley as Howard, Samuel Emery as Twizzleton, Garston Belmore as Peter, Mr. Terry as Edwards, Kate Terry as Mrs. Howard.

LAW, NOT JUSTICE// D// A. C. Calmour// **Surrey**, July 1882.

LAW OF THE LIPS// F// J. P. Wooler// **Sad. Wells**, Aug. 1851, with Mr. Barrett as Rattan, William Hoskins as Mornington, Henry Mellon as Nicholas, F. Younge as Jack, Mrs. Henry Marston as Mrs. Marigold, Lucy Rafter as Lucy, Mrs. Graham as Susan.

LAW VERSUS LOVE// C 1a// George Linley// **Princess's**, Dec. 1862, with Robert Roxby as Clifford, J. G. Shore as Mountnorris, Miss M. Oliver as Mrs. Harlowe, Miss Murray as Mrs. Belmont, Miss Gilbert as Rosetta.

LAWYERS, THE// C 3a// George Henry Lewis ("Slingsby Lawrence")// **Lyceum**, May 1853/ **Sad. Wells**, Apr. 1855, with Frank Matthews as Settle, Robert Roxby as Brown, Frederic Robinson as Court, C. Swan as Sgt. Broadgrin, Mr. Williams as Sgt. Bullyrag, Mr. Templeton as Rangle, Mrs. Frank Matthews as Mrs. Naggins, Frances Hughes as Mrs. Brown, Miss Wadham as Hannah.

LAYING A GHOST// F// n.a.// **Haymarket**, Nov. 1843, with Robert Strickland as Old Tremor, William Clark as Gimp, Mr. Tilbury as Old Risklove, Henry Holl as Young Risklove, Henry Widdicomb as Sam, Julia Bennett as Miss Tremor, Miss Carre as Flounce.

LEADER OF MEN, A// C 3a// Charles Ward// **Comedy**, Feb. 1895, with Will Dennis as Lord Killarney, Fred Terry as Llewellyn, Joseph Carne as Baldwin, H. B. Irving as Farquhar, William Wyes as Stone, Sydney Brough as Carnforth, Stuart Champion as Poole, Roma le Thière as Lady Solway, Alma Murray as Mrs. Alsager-Ellis, May Harvey as Barbara, Marion Terry as Mrs. Dundas/ Scenery by Walter Hann & Walter Johnstone.

LEADING LADY, THE (see Miss Frances of Yale)

LEADING STRINGS// C 3a// Adap. fr F of Eugène Scribe, Toujours// **Olympic**, Oct. 1857, with George Vining as Leveson, Mr. Addison as Binning, Harwood Cooper as John, F. Coney as Mitford, Mrs. Stirling as Mrs. Leveson, Miss Wyndham as Flora, Miss Swanborough as Edith.

LEAH// D 5a// Adap. fr G of Salomon Mosenthal, Deborah// **Haymarket**, Oct. 1868, with W. H. Kendal as Rudolph, Mr. Rogers as Lorentz, George Braid as Father Herman, William Clark as Ludwig, J. B. Buckstone Jr. as Hans, Mr. Weathersby as Fritz, Virginia Francis as Madelina, Miss Coleman as Mme. Groschen, Mrs. Laws as Dame Gertrude, Fanny Wright as Rosel, Kate Bateman as Leah, Henry Howe as Nathan, P. White as Abraham, Mrs. Edward Fitzwilliam as Sarah/ Scenery by John O'Conner, Mr. Morris, Mr. Barraud, & Mr. Maltby/ Machines by Oliver Wales/ Gas by F. Hope.

LEAH; OR, THE JEWISH WANDERER// D 4a// Adap. by Fanny Garthwaite fr G of Salomon Mosenthal, Deborah// **Sad. Wells**, Aug. 1866, with Philip Hannan as Father Lorenz, Walter Roberts as Adalbert, Mr. Jaques as Nathan, F. Watts as Father Bartholo, George Skinner as Hans, Watty Brunton as Fritz, G. Carter as Wilhelm, Agnes Burdett as Leah, Mrs. Philip Hannan as Elia, Julia Summers as Lotta, Miss George as Sarah, Annette Vincent as Frau Schnapps.

LEAH THE FORSAKEN// D 5a// Adap. by Augustin Daly fr G of Saloman Mosenthal, Deborah// **Adelphi**, Oct. 1863, with John Billington as Rudolf, Mr. Stuart as Lorrenz, Richard Phillips as Father Hermann, Arthur Wood as Ludwig, W. H. Eburne as Hans, Henrietta Simms as Madelena, Kate Kelly as Mme. Greschen, Kate Bateman as Leah, Mrs. Billington as Sarah, Arthur Stirling as Nathan, C. J. Smith as Abram/ **Lyceum**, May 1872/ **Opera Comique**, Apr. 1897.

LEAP YEAR// C 3a// J. B. Buckstone// **Haymarket**, Jan. 1850, with Robert Keeley as Sir Solomon, Charles Selby as Capt. Mouser, J. B. Buckstone as Dimple, Charles Kean as Walker, Mrs. Charles Kean as Mrs. Flowerdew, Mrs. Fitzwilliam as Sally, Mrs. W. Clifford as Miss Desperate, Mrs. Keeley as Mrs. Crisp/ Scenery by Mr. Johnstone & George Morris/ Machines by F. Heselton; Sept. 1880, with H. B. Conway as Sir William, John S. Clarke as Dimple, Henry Kemble as Capt. Mouser, Mrs. John Wood as Miss O'Leary, Linda Dietz as Lady Flowerdew, Mrs. Canninge as Mrs. Crisp, Miss Warden as Susan.

LEAR OF PRIVATE LIFE, THE; OR, FATHER AND DAUGHTER// D// W. T. Moncrieff// **Sad. Wells**, Feb. 1837, with Mr. Campbell as Fitzharden, Mr. King as Goodall, Mr. Hicks as Alvanley, C. H. Pitt as Kettleton, Mr. Rogers as Bachelor, Mr. Ray as Lord Saunter, Mr. Gay as Capt. Mowbray, Mr. Scarbrow as Adder, Miss Williams as Agnes, Miss Lebatt as Emily, Miss Julian as Muriel.

LEAVE IT TO ME// F 1a// C. H. Hazlewood & Arthur Williams// **Surrey**, Dec. 1870/ **Adelphi**, July 1885, with E. R. Fitzdavis as Easy, T. Fulljames as Courtley, E. Dagnall as Sprouts, Harwood Cooper as Quince, Jenny Rogers as Amelia.

LEAVES OF SHAMROCK// D 5a// J. P. Sullivan// **Sad. Wells**, June 1891.

LED ASTRAY// D 6a// Adap. by Dion Boucicault fr F of Octave Feuillet, La Tentation// **Gaiety**,

July 1874, with Charles Thorne, Stuart Robson/ **Olympic**, Mar. 1879, with William Rignold as Count Chandoce, J. A. Rosier as Placide, F. H. Macklin as Lesparre, John Maclean as Maj. O'Hara, Harry Proctor as Gosline, Helen Barry as Countess Chandoce, Maria Daly as Dowager Countess Chandoce, Mrs. Leigh Murray as Baroness de Rivonniere, Ruby Lonsdale as Mathilde, May Bulmer as Suzanne.

LEFT IN A CAB// F 1a// Edward Stirling// **Surrey**, Aug. 1851.

LEGACY, THE// C 1a// Frank Lindo// **Royalty**, Feb. 1894, with Douglas Gordon as Martyn, Robert Castleton as Atteboy, A. H. Brooke as Sparley, Mary Clayton as Agnes, Marjorie Christmas as Clara, Mary Bessle as Eliza.

LEGACY LOVE// C// Ernest Cuthbert// **Vaudeville**, Dec. 1872.

LEGACY OF HONOUR, THE// D 2a// Edward Stirling// **Drury Lane**, Apr. 1853.

LEGAL IMPEDIMENT, A// F 1a// John Oxenford// **Olympic**, Oct. 1861, with Frederick Robson as Blush, George Cooke as Grove, Gaston Murray as Blake, Harwood Cocper as Brownleigh, Henry Rivers as Fairleigh, Miss Marston as Justina, Miss Evans as Augustina, Mrs. Cooper as Clementina/ **Lyceum**, Oct. 1869, with Mr. Francis as Grove, Narcisse Garson as Blake, W. Howard as Fairleigh, Mr. Parry as Brownleigh, Helen Tory as Justina, Miss Egerton as Augustina, Miss Graham as Clementina.

LEGEND OF BEVILLE CASTLE; OR, THE LASS THAT LOVES A SAILOR// D// n.a.// **Grecian**, July 1864, with William James as Lancewood, J. B. Steele as Sir Walter, John Manning as Pipps, J. Jackson as Evergreen, Henry Grant as Tareseed, Jane Dawson as Ruth, Marie Brewer as Polly.

LEGEND OF FLORENCE, A// Play 5a// Leigh Hunt// **Cov. Garden**, Feb. 1840, with Mr. Moore as Agolanti, James Anderson as Rondinelli, George Vandenhoff as Colonna, George Bartley as Da Riva, Mrs. Walter Lacy (Miss Taylor) as Giulio, Ellen Tree as Ginevra, Miss Charles as Olimpia, Mrs. Brougham as Diana/ Scenery by Grieve, T. Grieve & W. Grieve/ **Sad. Wells**, Aug. 1850, with Samuel Phelps as Agolanti, Mr. Waller as Rondinelli, A. Younge as Da Riva, William Hoskins as Colonna, Eliza Travers as Giulo, Isabela Glyn as Ginevra, Mrs. Archbold as Olimpia, Miss Marston as Diana, Miss Mandelbert as Fiordilisa/ Scenery by F. Fenton.

LEGEND OF NOTRE DAME, A// D// J. C. Smith// **Surrey**, Nov. 1872.

LEGEND OF THE HEADLESS MAN, THE// D// Adap. by Benjamin Webster fr G// **Cov. Garden**, 1840, with James Anderson, George Vandenhoff, George Bartley, Ellen Tree, Mrs. T. H. Lacy/ **Adelphi**, Nov. 1857, with Benjamin Webster as Carl, John Billington as Count de Valberg, Edward Wright as Nickel, Charles Selby as Dr. Neiden, Edmund Garden as Martin, C. J. Smith as The Grey Man, Mme. Celeste as Christine, Marie Wilton as Nini, Mary Keeley as Agatha/ Scenery by Pitt & Brew/ Music by Thirlwall/ Machines by Ireland and Powell.

LEGEND OF VANDALE, A// C// Albert Drinkwater// **Grand**, Sept. 1890.

LEGEND OF WEHRENDORF, A// D// Edgar Newbound// **Britannia**, Dec. 1878.

LEIDA// Play 3a// Trans. by A. Teixeira de Mattos fr Dutch// **Comedy**, June 1893, with Basset Roe as Wielrave, Mervyn Herapath as Wertem, Marthy Conyngham as Leida, Charlotte Morland as Geertje, Henrietta Cowen as Saar.

LEIL, MAID OF THE ALHAMBRA; OR, THE SEIGE OF GRANADA// D 3a// n.a.// **Sad. Wells**, Oct. 1838, with Mr. Elvin as King Ferdinand, Mr. Mellor as Gonzago, Mr. Phillips as Hernando, Charles Montague as Ponce De Leon, Dibdin Pitt as Del Torquemada, Mrs. J. F. Saville as Queen Isabella, Miss Richardson as Donna Inez, Mr. Dry as El Chico, Robert Honner as Gazan, Mr. Harwood as Abdelmic, J. W. Collier as Hamet, Mr. Conquest as Sabdellec, Mrs. Harwood as Zaide, Miss Cooke as Zobedie, Miss Pitt as Selima, Mr. Cathcart as Almamen, Mr. Williams as Ximien, Mrs. Robert Honner as Leila/ Scenery by Mr. Telbin/ Music by Mr. Herbert/ Machines by B. Sloman/ Prod. by R. Honner.

LELA'S LOVE LETTERS// C// John Soden & Alfred Ganthony// **St. Geo. Hall**, May 1888.

LELIO// D 3a// George D'Arcy// **Olympic**, Aug. 1885.

LEND ME FIVE SHILLINGS// F 1a// J. Maddison Morton// **Haymarket**, Feb. 1846, with J. B. Buckstone as Golightly, Mr. Tilbury as Capt. Phobbs, A. Brindal as Capt. Spruce, Priscilla Horton as Mrs. Major Phobbs, Miss Telbin as Mrs. Captain Phobbs/ **Princess's**, Aug. 1863, with Mr. Fitzjames as Capt. Phobbs, Mr. Munro as Capt. Spruce, Sefton Parry as Golightly.

LENDING A HAND// F 1a// Gilbert à Beckett// **Strand**, Jan. 1866.

LEOLINE; OR, LIFE'S TRIALS// D 3a// n.a.// **Adelphi**, Feb. 1846, with Henry Howe as Darville, O. Smith as Mongerand, Edward Wright as Kit, George Munyard as Justin, Mrs. Yates as Leoline, Sarah Woolgar as Catherine, William Cullenford as M. Rozat.

LEON OF THE IRON MASK// D// W. Bayle Bernard// **Marylebone**, Feb. 1855, with J. W. Wallack.

LEONA; OR, LOVE AND STRATAGEM// D 3a// Oswald Brand & E. W. Linging// **Gaiety**, Mar. 1886/ **Sadler's Wells**, June 1892.

LEONI D'AUTRICHE; OR, THE MONK OF ST. JUST AND THE HEBREW MAID// D 3a// n.a.// **Victoria**, Aug. 1850, with John Ryder as Charles and Anselmo, Henry Frazer as Philip

II, J. T. Johnson as Leoni, J. Neville as Don Quessada, Mr. Humphries as Don Fernando, Mr. Morrison as di Monthelon, Georgiana Lebatt as Peblo, James Howard as Dominique, John Hudspeth as Babblo, Amelia Mercer as Leah, Mrs. Cooke as Dorothea, Miss Barrowcliffe as Sancha.

LEONIE THE SUTLER GIRL; OR, A COUNTESS IN DIFFICULTIES// D 3a// Horton Rhys// **Sad. Wells**, Feb. 1863, with Henry Forrester as Viscount Albert, Mr. Shelley as Capt. Beauregard, Mr. Dalton as Count d'Echo, Morton Price as Theodore, Lewis Ball as Andrew, A. Montague as Caesar, Harry Josephs as Antoine, C. Lloyd as Pettibody, Miss Farren as Grand Tete, Catherine Lucette as Bertha, Miss Dowton as Jeanette, Mrs. William Dowton as Dame Marguerite.

LEONTINE; OR, SIXTEEN YEARS AGO// D// n.a.// **Victoria**, Apr. 1844, with Mr. Osbaldiston as Earl of Fitzarlington, C. J. Bird as Arthur, Charles Freer as Clewine, Mr. Coreno as Dupoint, Annette Vincent as Leontine, Mrs. George Lee as Manie/ Scenery by Mr. Morelli/ Machines by Emmens, Wood & Fostler/ Music by J. W. Hill.

LESBIA// C 1a// Richard Davey// **Lyceum**, Sept. 1888, with Beatrice Cameron as Lesbia, John Sullivan as Catullus, Mrs. Sol Smith as Sibilla, Miss Bennett as Affra, Miss White as Claudia/ Scenery by Liverani Tancredi/ Music by W. H. Eayres.

LESSON, A// C 1a// Adap. by F. C. Burnand fr F of Henri Meilhac & Ludovic Halévy// **Haymarket**, Nov. 1881, with Charles Brookfield as Sir Thomas, H. B. Conway as Wentworth, Blanche Henri as Lady Duncan, Miss Warden as Markham, Mrs. Bancroft as Kate.

LESSON FOR LADIES, A// C 3a// J. B. Buckstone// **Haymarket**, Sept. 1838, with Walter Lacy as St. Val, Benjamin Webster as Gibelotte, J. B. Buckstone as Mathieu, Mrs. Julia Glover as Countess de Clairville, Miss Taylor as Mlle. Delbieux, Mrs. Fitzwilliam as Barbara.

LESSON FOR LIFE, A// C 3a// Tom Taylor// **Haymarket**, Dec. 1866, with E. A. Sothern as Henry, W. H. Chippendale as Vivian, Henry Howe as Greystoke, George Braid as Colepepper, Mr. Rogers as Baswitz, W. H. Kendal as Dacre, Walter Gordon as Horsley, Mr. Johnson as Stetcher, Mr. Weatherby as Crouch, Henry Vincent as Reredoss, Henry Compton as Raggett, Mrs. Chippendale as Lady Elizabeth, Miss Conran as Mabel, Miss Hill as Lady Gertrude, Fanny Wright as Miss Warblington, Nelly Moore as Mary, Mrs. Laws as Nanny/ Scenery by John O'Conner & George Morris/ Machines by Oliver Wales.

LESSON IN ACTING, A// F// Austin Fryers// **Sadler's Wells**, June 1883.

LESSON IN LOVE, A// C 3a// Charles Cheltham// **St. James's**, Dec. 1864, with Frederic Robinson as Capt. Freeman, C. J. Mathews as Middlemark, Frank Matthews as Bablebrook, Mrs. C. J. Mathews as Mrs. Sutherland, Mrs. Frank Matthews as Anastasia, Miss Wentworth as Edith.

LESSON OF LIFE, THE; OR, THE WOODMAN'S DREAM// D// Dram. fr story of Douglas Jerrold// **Sad. Wells**, June 1839, with John Webster as Rupert, Mr. Cathcart as Swithin, Mrs. Robert Honner as Narcisse, R. Honner as Ezra, J. W. Collier as Lankiman, John Webster as Chev. de Belleville, Mr. Conquest as Scamps, Mr. Elvin as de Loire, Miss Richardson as Lady Belleville/ Scenery by Mr. Fenton & G. Smithyes Jr./ Music by Mr. Herbert/ Machines by B. Sloman/ Prod. by Robert Honner/ **Marylebone**, Dec. 1877.

LESSON TO LANDLORDS, A// C 5a// n.a.// **Strand**, July 1888.

LET NOT YOUR ANGRY PASSIONS RISE// D 1a// James Schonberg// **Royalty**, June 1881.

LETTERS ADDRESSED HERE// F 1a// H. Chance Newton// **Shaftesbury**, Feb. 1893, with Albert James as Swire, Frank Walsh as Gillikins, Sam Hill as Clewidge, Harry Dorien as Tracshaw, Minnie Thurgate as Alfongs, J. Besborough as Mrs. Clewidge, Florence Leighton as Mrs. Tracshaw, Florence Barnes as Daisy, Hettie Hertzfield as Esther.

L'HOMME NOIR; OR, THE EXECUTIONER OF PARIS// D 4a// Adap. fr F// **Sad. Wells**, Aug. 1839, with W. L. Rede as Dormiley, Mr. Cathcart as Michell, Mr. Dry as Francois, Robert Honner as Ferdinand, Mr. Elvin as Charles, Miss Cooke as Mme. Douchett, Mrs. Robert Honner as Louise, Mr. Conquest as Batter, J. W. Collier as Caille, Mrs. J. F. Saville as Jannette.

LIAR, THE// C 2a// Alt. by Charles Mathews fr orig. of Samuel Foote// **Olympic**, Mar. 1867, with Mr. Addison as Wilding, C. J. Mathews as Jack Wilding, H. J. Montague as Sir James, Horace Wigan as Papillon, Mrs. C. J. Mathews as Mrs. Grantham, Mrs. Stephens as Miss Godfrey/ **Adelphi**, June 1868, with Henry Ashley as Sir James, C. H. Stephenson as Wilding, C. J. Mathews as Jack Wilding, Louisa Mocre as Miss Grantham, Mrs. Stoker as Miss Godfrey/ **Royalty**, July 1896.

LIARS, THE// C 4a// Henry Arthur Jones// **Criterion**, Oct. 1897, with Charles Wyndham as Col. Deering, T. B. Thalberg as Falkner, Herbert Standing as Gilbert Nepean, Leslie Kenyon as George Nepean, A. Vane Tempest as Tatton, Alfred Bishop as Coke, Janette Steer as Mrs. Crespin, Cynthia Brooke as Beatrice, Irene Vanbrugh as Lady Rosamund, Sarah Brooke as Dolly, Mary Moore as Lady Jessica/ Scenery by Walter Hann.

LIBERTINE'S BET, THE// D// n.a.// **St. James's**, Jan. 1857.

LIBERTINE'S LESSON, THE// D// Edward Fitzball// **Victoria**, Oct. 1848, with James Howard as Barton, J. T. Johnson as Seldon, Mr. Henderson as Murray, G. F. Forman as

Snacks, Mr. Hitchinson as Stapleton, Annette Vincent as Laura, Mrs. George Lee as Ellen, Miss Johnstone as Fanny, Miss Burroughcliffe as Polly.

LIBERTINE'S SHIP, THE// D 2a// Edward Fitzball// **Victoria**, May 1854, with N. T. Hicks as Lord William, F. H. Henry as Reuben, Alfred Saville as Gregory, James Howard as Solomon, T. E. Mills as Bilge, Miss Sutton as Margaret's Ghost, Mrs. Manders as Virtue, Mrs. Henry Vining as Madeline, Miss Laporte as Phoebe, Miss Dansor as Catherine.

LIBERTY; OR, THE DHU COLLEEN OF BALLY-FOYLE// D// Henry Richardson// **Victoria**, Sept. 1876/ **Elephant & Castle**, June 1879.

LIBERTY HALL// C 4a// R. C. Carton// **St. James's**, Dec. 1892, with George Alexander as Owen, Edward Righton as Todman, Ben Webster as Harringay, Nutcombe Gould as Pedrick, H. H. Vincent as Briginshaw, Vernon Sansbury as Luscombe, Alfred Holles as Mickson, Ailsa Craig as Miss Hickson, Fanny Coleman as Crafer, Maude Millet as Amy, Marion Terry as Blanche/ Scenery by H. P. Hall/ Music by Walter Slaughter.

LIFE// C 5a// B. Palmer// **Olympic**, Nov. 1846, with J. Cowell as Folair, Walter Lacy as Mentor, George Bolton as Smallwit, Leigh Murray as Frank Orston, Mr. Archer as Mr. Orston, John Howard as Newcombe, Mr. Wilkenson as Concord, George Maynard as Selwood, H. Lee as Turner, Miss C. Jones as Lady Bait, Mrs. R. Gordon as Emily, Mrs. Lacy as Fanny, Mrs. Griffiths as Mrs. Hookham, Miss Charles as Seraphina, Miss Ayres as Angelina.

LIFE; ITS MORN AND SUNSET// D 3a// C. H. Hazlewood// **Britannia**, Oct. 1872.

LIFE AFTER MARRIAGE (see Matrimony).

LIFE AND DEATH// D 5a// Adap. by Frank Harvey fr F of Hector Crémieux & A. P. D'Ennery, Germaine// **Grand**, Aug. 1886.

LIFE AND DEATH OF JACK SHEPPARD, THE// D 3a// Adap. by Isaac Brown fr novel of Harrison Ainsworth// **Sad. Wells**, Apr. 1857, with Mrs. Keeley as Jack Sheppard, R. H. Lingham as Jonathan Wild, John Chester as Blueskin, J. G. Shore as Darrell, James Worrell as Sir Rowland, Charles Fenton as Wood, Mr. Warren as Mendez, W. Williams as Arnold, George Burt as Capt. Kneebone, Mrs. Hill as Mrs. Wood, Miss Weston as Winifred, Miss Day as Bess, Miss Grant as Poll, Miss Evans as Rachel.

LIFE AND DEATH OF JAMES DAWSON, THE; OR THE REBEL OF 1745// D 3a// n.a.// **Victoria**, Sept. 1841, with William Seaman as Edward, C. Williams as Col. Townley, E. F. Saville as Dawson, John Dale as Lambourne, Mr. Howard as Dr. Pros, John Gardner as Simple, Mr. Paul as Boddy, Mr. Wilton as Standford, Mrs. George Lee as Kate, Mrs. Howard as Sarah, Mrs. Garthwaite as Peg/ Scenery by Telbin, Hawthorn, Morelli & Lancester.

LIFE AND HONOUR// D 4a// Dram. by William Calvert fr novel of Charles Gibbon, For the King// **Elephant & Castle**, Dec. 1893.

LIFE AS IT IS; OR, THE CONVICT'S CHILD// D 2a// T. G. Blake// **Sad. Wells**, July 1839, with Mr. Phillips as Eugene Neville, Mr. Cathcart as Franklin, Mr. Dry as Nugent Neville, Charles Montgomery as Morgan, Mr. Stilt as Dalton, Robert Honner as Twitch, Mr. Williams as Somers, Miss Richardson as Lady Walmsley, Mrs. J. F. Saville as Patty, Miss Norman as Mary, Mrs. Robert Honner as Martha/ Scenery by F. Fenton & G. Smithyes Jr./ Music by Mr. Herbert/ Machines by B. Sloman.

LIFE CHASE, A// D 5a// John Oxenford & Horace Wigan// **Gaiety**, Oct. 1869.

LIFE DOWN SOUTH// D 4a// R. F. Cantwell// **Britannia**, June 1874.

LIFE FOR LIFE// D 4a// Westland Marston// **Lyceum**, Mar. 1869, with Adelaide Neilson, Hermann Vezin, Charles Coghlan.

LIFE IN AUSTRALIA// n.a.// **Olympic**, Feb. 1853.

LIFE IN THE COAL-PITS// D 4a// J. C. Levey// **Victoria**, Feb. 1867.

LIFE OF A BEGGAR, THE; OR, FAITH, FORGERY, AND FALSEHOOD// D 3a// William Travers// **Sad. Wells**, Aug. 1866, with G. P. Jaques as Fitzgerald, Philip Hannan as Marot, Walter Roberts as Clark, F. Watts as Feron, George Skinner as Diver, Watty Brunton as Scrubbs, Miss Neville as Mary, Miss George as Edith, Julia Summers as Betsy, William Travers as Capt. Muddle, Mrs. Philip Hannan as Polly.

LIFE OF A SWELL MOBSMAN, THE; OR, THE OUTCAST, THE DETECTIVE, AND THE CAREER OF CRIME// D 3a// n.a.// **Grecian**, Dec. 1863, with J. Jackson as Scraper, J. B. Steele as Ormond, W. H. Pitt as Richmond, W. H. Courtley as Lout, Henry Grant as Dudley, Jane Dawson as Mildred, Mary A. Victor as Martha.

LIFE OF AN ACTRESS, THE// D 5a// Dion Boucicault// **Adelphi**, Mar. 1862, with Dion Boucicault as Grimaldi, Mrs. Dion Boucicault as Violet, Mrs. Billington as Julia, J. L. Toole as Wopshot, C. J. Smith as Hopkins, Mrs. H. Lewis as Mme. Hopkins/ **Sad. Wells**, Sept. 1865, with W. Nicholls as Duke, J. F. Stewart as Lord Arthur, Henry Lynn as Maltravers, Alfred Parry as Dawdle, Edward Winter as Wopshot, David Segdwick as Grimaldi, T. A. Weaver as Hopkins, Mr. Wilton as Leech, Kate Paxton as Julia, Clara Brookes as Violet, Mrs. Newbery as Countess Beaumaris, Miss Clifton as Miss Stingwell, Miss Williams as Mrs. Hopkins/ **Haymarket**, June 1879, with G. W. Anson as Grimaldi, F. H. Macklin as Lord Shafton, Henry Howe as Maltravers, Henry Crouch as Dawdle, David Fisher Jr. as Wopshot, Mr. Weathersby as Hopkins, Emily Fowler as Violet, Blanche

Henri as Julia, Miss E. Harrison as Mme. Hopkins.

LIFE OF DARE-DEVIL DICK, THE; OR, THE LEGEND OF THE LEAFLESS TREE// D 3a// n.a.// **Grecian**, May 1861, with Henry Grant as Claverton and as Chief Justice, Mr. Smithson as Woodfield, Alfred Rayner as Redwood, Mr. Jackson as Parchment, George Conquest as Sam Slider, William James as Fielder, John Manning as Green, Thomas Mead as Dick Palmer and as Dick Turpin, Henry Power as Bayes, Mrs. Charles Dillon as Mary, Jane Coveney as Susan, Harriet Coveney as Patty and as Mrs. Green, Lucreza Hill as Isabel, George Gillett as King.

LIFE OF PLEASURE, A// D 5a// Henry Pettitt & Augustus Harris// **Drury Lane**, Sept. 1893, with Mrs. Bernard Beere as Norah, Lily Hanbury as Lady Mary, Laura Linden as Phyllis, Roma Le Thiere as Lady Nellborough, Henry Neville as O'Brien, Arthur Dacre as Capt. Chandos, Frank Fenton as Lord Avondale, William Elton as Scasi, Robert Soutar as Sir John/ Scenery by Caney, W. Perkins, Joseph Harker, E. Ryan & J. Hicks/ Music by J. M. Glover/ Machines by E. Taylor.

LIFE POLICY, A// Play 4a// Adap. by Helen Davis fr her novel, For So Little// **Terry's**, July 1894, with Charles Rock as Col. Leigh, Herbert Flemming as Maber, Philip Cunningham as Dr. Langley, Rudge Harding as Lowthian, F. Percival Stevens as Govette, Harold Mead as Dr. Drew, E. G. Woodhouse as Detective, Winifred Fraser as Elsie, Mrs. Herbert Waring as Beatrice, Bertha Staunton as Mrs. Lothian, Mrs. Edward Saker as Nurse, Rose Dudley as Matilda.

LIFE RAFT, THE; OR, THE TWO REEFERS// D 3a// W. T. Townsend// **Victoria**, Nov. 1846, with Alfred Raymond as Capt. Manwaring, F. Wilton as Marquis Sabramonte, C. J. Bird as Watson, Walter Searle as Pembroke, James Ranoe as Lt. Trysail, Mr. Franklin as Wilson, E. Edwards as Cable, J. Howard as Splitbristle, Julia Vaughan as Felix, F. H. Henry as Jack, Mrs. George Lee as Estelle, Lydia Pearce as Peggy, Miss Edgar as Lamba, Mrs. Cooke as Mrs. Fricandeau.

LIFE SIGNAL, THE// D 2a// C. H. Hazlewood// **Britannia**, Apr. 1867.

LIFE WE LIVE, THE// D 4a// Fenton Mackay & Louis Denbigh// **Princess's**, Apr. 1892, with Charles Warner as Dick Redmond, Henry Bedford as Jonas Redmond, Ian Robertson as Esmond, Walter Gay as Harry, Wilfred Shine as O'Dowd, Harry Eversfield as Noodle, W. L. Abingdon as Burchill, Trant Fischer as Sgt. Thorndyke, H. N. Dickson as Silas Redmond, Alfred Phillips as Giles/ Scenery by Halley, Grimani & Julian Hicks/ Machines by J. W. Cawdrey/ Prod. by Charles Warner.

LIFE'S A LOTTERY; OR, JOLLY DICK THE LAMPLIGHTER// C 3a// W. L. Rede// **Olympic**, Nov. 1842, with Mr. Brookes as Lord Fawnington, Charles Baker as Col. Barrington, Mr. Halford as Lt. Frankville, Mr. Green as Charles, Mr. Fitzjames as Seedy, George Wild as Jolly Dick, Lavinia Melville as Agnes, Miss Hamilton as Sue, Miss Arden as Lucette, Miss Granby as Kitty, Mrs. Granby as Margery, Miss Lebatt as Bessie/ Scenery by R. W. Beverly & Mr. Scott/ Music by Mr. Calcott/ Machines by Mr. Mackintosh/ **Sad. Wells**, Aug. 1843, with Mr. Brookes as Lord Fawnington, Mr. Morton as Col. Barrington, C. J. Bird as Lt. Frankville, Mr. Lingham as Charles, Mr. Fitzjames as Seedy, Mr. Bologna as Dobson, C. J. Smith as Boler, George Wild as Jolly Dick, Caroline Rankley as Agnes, Miss Hamilton as Sue, Miss Stephens as Lucette, Miss Melville as Kitty, Miss Cooke as Margery, Mrs. Richard Barnett as Bessie, Fanny Morelli as Jane/ Scenery by F. Fenton/ Music by W. Montgomery, Machines by Mr. Cawdery, Prod. by George Wild.

LIFE'S BATTLE: A STORY OF THE RIVER THAMES// D 5a// Henry Saville// **Victoria**, Aug. 1878.

LIFE'S BONDAGE, A// D 4a// Harry Byrton & Arthur Shirley// **Marylebone**, May 1891.

LIFE'S DEVOTION, A// D Pro & 3a// W. H. Abel// **East London**, Nov. 1870.

LIFE'S HANDICAP// D 4a// W. J. Patmore// **Pavilion**, Sept. 1900.

LIFE'S RACE, A// Miss Evelyn// **Royal Alfred** [Marylebone], Feb. 1872, with Charles Harcourt, Thomas Swinbourne, Hermann Vezin.

LIFE'S RANSOM, A// D 5a// Westland Marston// **Lyceum**, Feb. 1857, with Charles Dillon as Lord Revesdale, Mr. Barrett as Matthew Ringwood, Mr. McLien as Arthur Ringwood, J. G. Shore as Richard, Mrs. Dillon as Felicia, Mrs. B. Tannett as Alicia/ Scenery by B. Tannett & F. Fenton/ **Sad. Wells**, May 1857, with Charles Dillon as Lord Revesdale, Mr. Barrett as Matthew Ringwood, J. G. Shore as Arthur Ringwood, Mr. Stuart as Bancroft, Mrs. Charles Dillon as Felicia.

LIFE'S REVENGE, A// D 4a// Walter Howard// **Shaftesbury**, June 1897.

LIFE'S REVENGE; OR, TWO LOVES FOR ONE HEART// D 3a// W. E. Suter// **Grecian**, Oct. 1858.

LIFE'S TRIAL, A// D 3a// W. Bayle Bernard// **Haymarket**, Apr. 1857, with William Farren as Wyndham, Henry Howe as Hawksworth, Edwin Villiers as Lambourne, J. B. Buckstone as Spicer, Henry Compton as Capt. Tatters, Mr. Rogers as Hookham, Miss Reynolds as Miss Rochdale, Ellen Sabine as Emily, Mrs. Edward Fitzwilliam as Mrs. Spicer, Mrs. Poynter as Mme. Ruspini/ Scenery by William Callcott, George Morris & John O'Conner/ Machines by Oliver Wales.

LIFEBOAT, THE; OR, SATURDAY NIGHT AT SEA// D// J. P. Taylor// **Sad. Wells**, Feb. 1837, with Mr. Ray as Capt. Hamilton, Mr.

Gay as Ned Bolt, Mr. Hicks as Weathergale, Mr. Scarbrow as Mainmast, Mr. Jones as Staysail, John Ayliffe as Ashbourne, Mr. Campbell as Blacklock, Miss Williams as Mary, Miss Julian as Barbara.

LIGHT// D 4a// Arthur Flaxman// **Gaiety**, Nov. 1877.

LIGHT AHEAD// D 4a// Herbert Leonard// **Surrey**, Nov. 1891.

LIGHT AND SHADE// C 3a// F. W. Broughton// **Imperial**, Oct. 1879, with E. F. Edgar, Lionel Brough, Kyrle Bellew, Fanny Addison.

LIGHT AND SHADOW// D// A. R. Slous// **Princess's**, May 1864, with Dominick Murray.

LIGHT DRAGOONS, THE// F 2a// Charles Dance// **Sad. Wells**, Dec. 1840, with Mr. Elvin, J. B. Hill, Mr. Williams, George Burt, Mrs. Richard Barnett, Miss Cooke/ **Lyceum**, Oct. 1847, with C. J. Mathews as Lord Alfred Martingal, Robert Roxby as Lovelorn, Frank Matthews as Dr. Rhatany, Mrs. Charles Jones as Mrs. Crowfoot, Louisa Howard as Matilda.

LIGHT FANTASTIC, THE// F// H. J. Byron// **Folly**, Nov. 1880, with J. L. Toole, Emily Thorne.

LIGHT IN THE DARK; OR, LIFE UNDERGROUND// D 4a// W. Sidney// **Sad. Wells**, Mar. 1869, with E. Butler as Oldenheart, Mr. Hallows as Charles, Mr. Gill as Brandon, Arthur Williams as Lightly, Mr. Isling as Mundic, W. Drury as Sretton, Mr. Beverley as Carter, Mr. Richmond as Closelock, W. Sidney as Trueworth, Charles Sennett as Drossheart, Fred Hughes as Johnny, Owen Ramsay as Maddox, Agnes Burdett as Kate, Clara Dillon as Lizzie, Louisa Summers as Susan, Miss Morone as Jane, Louisa Summerfield as Molly/ Scenery by Leitch, Burgess & Drury/ Machines by Mr. Thorne/ Prod. by W. Sidney.

LIGHT O' DAY// C 4a// Brien McCullough// **Novelty**, Aug. 1890.

LIGHT OF OTHER DAYS, THE; OR, THE LAST LEAF OF THE TREE// D// T. P. Taylor// **Sad. Wells**, Oct. 1837, with Mr. Wilkins as Gloomfield, C. H. Pitt as Henry, Mr. Campbell as Brown, S. Palmer as Mayfield, Thomas Lee as Gooseberry, Mr. Griffith as Purcel, Mr. King as Tim, Miss Williams as Mary, Miss Vernon as Bessy, Mrs. Rogers as Cicely.

LIGHT OF PENGARTH, THE// Play 1a// Ina Cassilis// **Opera Comique**, Dec. 1891.

LIGHT THAT FAILED, THE// Play 1a// Adap. by Cortenay Thorpe fr Rudyard Kipling// **Royalty**, Apr. 1898.

LIGHTHOUSE, THE// D 2a// Wilkie Collins// **Olympic**, July 1857, with Frederick Robson as Gurnock, Walter Gordon as Martin, Mr. Addison as Dale, George Cooke as Furley, Miss Swanborough as The Shipwrecked Lady, Miss Wyndham as Phoebe/ Scenery by J. Gray & Hawes Craven/ Music by Francesco Berger/ Machines by Mr. Sutherland.

LIGHTNING'S FLASH, THE// D 4a// Arthur Shirley// **Surrey**, Dec. 1891.

LIGHTS O' LONDON, THE// D 5a// G. R. Sims// **Princess's**, Sept. 1881, with G. R. Peach as Armytage, Wilson Barrett as Harold, E. S. Willard as Clifford, John Beauchamp as Marks, Walter Speakman as Preene, Charles Coote as Jack, Neville Doone as de Vere, George Barrett as Jarvis, Eugenie Edwards as Shakespeare, Mrs. Stephens as Mrs. Jarvis, Mary Eastlake as Bess, Emmeline Ormsby as Hetty, Maude Clitherow as Tottie, Lizzie Adams as Sal/ Scenery by Stafford Hall, W. Spong & Walter Hann/ Music by Michael Connolly/ **Olympic**, Feb. 1891, with Wilson Barrett as Harold Armytage, Winifred Emery as Bess, W. A. Elliott as Squire Armytage, H. Cooper Cliffe as Clifford, Stafford Smith as Marks, Austin Melford as Preene, Edward Irwin as Trotters, Ambrose Maning as Jack, George Barrett as Jarvis, Lily Hanbury as Hetty, Mrs. Henry Leigh as Mrs. Jarvis/ Scenery by Walter Hann & Stafford Hall/ Music by Michael Connelly.

LIGHTS OF HOME, THE// D 5a// G. R. Sims & Robert Buchanan// **Adelphi**, July 1892, with Charles Dalton as Carrington, G. W. Cockburn as Garfield, Thomas Kingston as Tredgold, Eardley Turner as Chowne, Howard Russell as Capt. Petherick, Evelyn Millard as Sybil, Mrs. Patrick Campbell as Tress Purvis, Clara Jecks as Martha/ Music by Henry Sprake/ Machines by H. Loftin/ Prod. by E. B. Norman.

LIKE FATHER LIKE SON// D 5a// J. Easton & E. E. Norris// **Globe**, Aug. 1901/ **Elephant & Castle**, Dec. 1901.

LIKENESS OF THE NIGHT, THE// Play 4a// Mrs. W. K. Clifford// **St. James's**, Oct. 1901.

LILIAN GERVAIS// D 3a// Morris Barnett// **Olympic**, Jan. 1853, with George Cooke as Marquis de Renneville, Charles Bender as Gervais, William Farren Jr. as Adolphe, William Hoskins as Bomard, Henry Compton as Pompon, Harriet Gordon as Marchioness de Renneville, Miss Anderton as Lilian Gervais/ Scenery by W. Shalders.

LILIAN THE SHOW GIRL// D// George Soane// **Sad. Wells**, Apr. 1842, with P. Williams as Maynard, Mr. Aldridge as Felten, John Webster as Everard, John Herbert as Diggs, Mr. Lyon as Morris, Mrs. Robert Honner as Lilian, Miss Richardson as Maude, Mrs. Richard Barnett as Susan.

LILIES; OR, HEARTS AND ACTRESSES// FC 3a// Harry Paulton// **Gaiety**, Nov. 1884.

LILY DAWSON; OR, A POOR GIRL'S STORY (also Lilly)// D 3a// Edward Stirling// **Surrey**, Mar. 1847/ **Victoria**, July 1857, with Mr. Hitchinson as Gen. Markham, Mr. Morrison as Ryland, W. H. Pitt as Philip, S. Sawford as Littlehams, Henry Dudley as Pefler, J. Howard as Old Able, J. H. Rickards as Luke,

George Pearce as Ambrose, Julia Seaman as Charlotte, Mrs. Robert Honner as Lilly, Mrs. J. H. Rickards as Anna, Miss Laporte as Winny, Phoebe Towers as Mary.

LILY'S LOVE; OR, WEARY OF WAITING// D// W. H. Abel// **Pavilion**, Aug. 1872.

LIMERICK BOY, THE// F// James Pilgrim// **Sad. Wells**, Mar. 1862, with Harry Linton as Paddy Miles, W. Cole as Dr. Coates, Mr. Chapman as Henry, C. Saunders as Job, Miss Heath as Mrs. Fidget, Fanny Morelli as Jane.

LINDA GREY// D 5a// Charles Young// **Princess's**, Apr. 1891, with Bernard Gould as Broughton, Herbert Standing as Lord Parkhurst, E. B. Norman as Sir Dennis, Fred Everill as Jay, S. H. Lechmere as Ashby, May Whitty as Lady Broughton, Laura Linden as Priscilla, Ethel Hope as Jane/ Scenery by Harry Potts/ Music by W. Corri Jr./ Machines by J. Cawdery/ Gas and limelight by Jones & Kerr.

LINEN DRAPER, THE// FC 3a// J. R. Brown & F. F. Thornthwaite// **Comedy**, Apr. 1890, with Edward Righton as Bazin, W. Scott Buist as Capt. de Broke, Walter McEwen as Maitland, Frank Wood as Lush, Cicely Richards as Sarah, Vane Featherston as Elinor, Susie Vaughan as Mrs. Maitland.

LINK BY LINK// D 4a// Frederick Hay & Fred Fenton// **Surrey**, Oct. 1870.

LINKED BY LOVE// C 3a// Paul Meritt// **Grecian**, July 1872.

LION HUNTER, THE// C 3a// J. T. Grein & Martha Leonard// **Terry's**, Mar. 1901, with H. B. Irving.

LION LIMB// D// Cecil Pitt// **Britannia**, Sept. 1867.

LION OF ENGLAND AND THE EAGLE OF FRANCE, THE; OR, OUR GALLANT SOLDIERS AND SAILORS IN THE CRIMEA// D 3a// T. Townsend & T. Younge// **Victoria**, Oct. 1854, with Mr. Morrison as Commander in Chief, E. F. Saville as Capt. Montague, N. T. Hicks as Martin, W. H. Pitt as Wilson, Charles Rice as Cutlet, J. Hicks as Prince Napoleon, Mr. Bradley as Marshal St. Arnaud, J. Howard as Ragout, Alfred Saville as Regan, Mr. Mandeville as the Sultan, Phoebe Johnson as Zer, Mrs. Henry Vining as Emmeline, Miss Laporte as Sukey, Mrs. Manders as Zabetta, Miss Edgar as Juliette.

LION QUEEN// D// n.a.// **Victoria**, Sept. 1852.

LION SLAYER, THE; OR, OUT FOR A PROWL// F 1a// T. J. Williams// **Haymarket**, Nov. 1860, with Henry Compton as Cumming, Mr. Rogers as Wiggleton, George Braid as Bantum, Mrs. Poynter as Mrs. Wiggleton, Florence Haydon as Sophia.

LIONESS OF THE NORTH, THE; OR, THE PRISONER OF SCHLUSSELBOURG// D 2a// Adap. by Charles Selby fr F// **Adelphi**, Dec. 1845, with Benjamin Webster as Alexis, Mr. Lambert as Major Puffendorf, Charles Selby as Count Schuvaloff, George Braid as Alexander Narciskoff, Mme. Celeste as Elizabeth, Ellen Chaplin as Feodora.

LION'S DEN, THE// D 3a// n.a.// **Victoria**, July 1871.

LION'S HEART, A// D Pro & 4a// Arthur Shirley & Benjamin Landeck// **Princess's**, Oct. 1895, with Charles Glenney as Rizardo, William Day as Dobre, Leslie Thompson as Puggs, Charles Baldwin as Ringmaster, E. Rochelle as Col. de Villefort, George Harker as Lorimore, Maitland Marler as Bealby, Frank Harding as Dobson, George Yates as Mason, Beaumont Collins as Louise, Josephine Woodin as Gilbert, Fanny Selby as Bessie, Harriet Clifton as Sister Gertrude.

LION'S LOVE, THE; OR, STILL IN THE TOILS// D 3a// George Conquest// **Grecian**, Aug. 1866, with Henry Grant as Duke de Novaille, George Gillett as Octave, William James as de Keral, Alfred Rayner as Phoenix, Chantil, and Crevecoeur, George Conquest as Roche, Boltreux and Deuxsous, John Manning as Leger, Jane Coveney as Marie and as Diane, Lizzie Mandelbert as Blanche, Mrs. Atkinson as Countess de Norvaille/ Scenery by Messender & Soames/ Music by W. Edroff/ Gas by Mr. Dimes/ Prod. by George Conquest.

LITTLE ANNOYANCES; OR, THE MISERIES OF HUMAN LIFE// F// n.a.// **Victoria**, June 1846, with J. Howard as Prettyman, T. Fredericks as Forrester, Mr. Wilton as Fubbins, Mr. Randall as Nebuchadnezzar, Mr. Hitchinson as Fantail, Miss Treble as Mrs. Dolby, Eliza Terrey as Betty, Miss Edgar as Donna Twiddlemeese.

LITTLE BACK PARLOUR, THE// F 1a// Edward Stirling// **Eng. Opera House** (Lyceum), Aug. 1839.

LITTLE CHANGE, A// C 1a// Sidney Grundy// **Haymarket**, July 1872.

LITTLE CRICKET// D 3a// James Mortimer// **Duke's**, June 1878.

LITTLE CULPRIT, THE// Play 1a// Russell Vaun & Alban Atwood// **St. Geo. Hall**, May 1898.

LITTLE DAISY// C 1a// T. J. Williams// **Haymarket**, Nov. 1863, with Henry Howe as Langdale, Thomas Coe as Curtspeech, Mr. Rogers as Robin, Mr. Clark as Dawdlegrass, George Braid as Sir Mathew, Mrs. Griffith as Janet, Maria Harris as Daisy/ **Her Majesty's**, Dec. 1865.

LITTLE DEVIL, THE// D// Benjamin Webster// **Haymarket**, Nov. 1846, with Lester Wallack.

LITTLE DOROTHY// D// n.a.// **City of London**, June 1863.

LITTLE EMILY'S TRIALS// D// E. H. Brooke// **Sad. Wells**, Mar. 1871.

LITTLE EM'LY// D 4a// Dram. by Andrew Halliday fr novel of Charles Dickens, David Copperfield// **Olympic**, Mar. 1873, with Samuel Emery as Peggotty, William Rignold as Ham, H. B. Conway as David Copperfield, Charles Peveril as Steerforth, Mr. Canninge as Traddles, Mr. Graeme as Wickfield, Arthur Wood as Uriah Heep, Joseph Eldred as Micawber, Marie Dalton as Little Em'ly, Miss C. Brabant as Agnes, Miss Griffiths as Barkis, Kate Rivers as Martha, Fanny Addison as Rosa, Jane Baber as Mrs. Micawber/ Scenery by Johnson, Ellerman, & Morris/ **Adelphi**, Nov. 1875, with Samuel Emery as Peggoty, William McIntyre as Ham, H. Vaughn as David Copperfield, Philip Day as Steerforth, W. Everard as Traddles, Harwood Cooper as Wickfield, John Clarke as Uriah Heep, James Fernandez as Micawber, Lydia Foote as Little Em'ly, Miss E. Phillips as Agnes, Miss Hudspeth as Martha, Edith Stuart as Rosa, Harriet Coveney as Betsy/ Scenery by F. Lloyds/ **Olympic**, Mar. 1880, with John Maclean as Pegotty, J. D. Beveridge as Ham, C. Fawcett as David Copperfield, Mr. Crauford as Steerforth, Mr. Alwin as Traddles, Mr. Murray as Wickfield, E. W. Royce as Uriah Heep, Edward Terry as Micawber, Gwynne Williams as Little Em'ly, Bella Howard as Agnes, Edith Bruce as Martha, Mrs. Ball as Mrs. Micawber, Mrs. Leigh as Betsy, Louisa Willes as Rosa.

LITTLE EM'LY// D 4a// Dram. by Andrew Halliday fr Charles Dickens's David Copperfield// **Olympic**, Oct. 1869/ **Adelphi**, 1875.

LITTLE EYOLF// D 3a// Trans. by William Archer fr Norw. of Henrik Ibsen// **Avenue**, Nov. 1896, with Courtenay Thorpe as Allmers, Master Stewart Dawson as Eyolf, C. M. Lowne as Borgheim, Janet Achurch as Rita, Elizabeth Robins as Asta, Mrs. Patrick Campbell as Ratwife.

LITTLE FLIRTATION, A// C 1a// T. J. Williams// **Princess's**, Dec. 1865, with John Maclean as Coaxer, Henry Forrester as Capt. Courtington, Robert Cathcart as Sim, Emma Barnett as Letty, Rachel Sanger as May.

LITTLE GIPSY, THE// F 1a// Mark Lemon// **Olympic**, Apr. 1841, with Mr. Brookes as Poz, Mr. Mulford as Duff, Charles Baker as Quilton, George Wild as Lovel, Miss Fortesque as Julia.

LITTLE JOCKEY, THE; OR, THE BOY IN YELLOW WINS THE DAY// F 1a// William Dimond// **Sad. Wells**, Apr. 1837, with John Ayliffe as Baron de Briancourt, C. H. Pitt as de Linval, Mr. Hicks as Florimond, Thomas Lee as Antoine, Mr. Scarbrow as Le Fleur, Miss Beresford as Arinette, Miss Lebatt as Clotilda, Miss Melville as Dora/ **Olympic**, Nov. 1846, with Mr. Hammersley as Florimond, H. Lee as De Linval, Robert Romer as Baron de Briancourt, Mr. Turnour as Antoine, Mr. Hollingsworth as La Fleur, Mr. Butler as Dennis, Miss Charles as Arinette, Lavinia Melville as Clotilda, Miss Ayres as Bona.

LITTLE LAUNDRESS, THE// C 2a// R. B. Peake// **Eng. Opera House** (Lyceum), Aug. 1837, with A. Brindal as Count de Lapierriere, Mr. Turnour as Prince de Soubise, Henry Compton as Tranquille, R. McIan as Philidor, Mr. Sanders as Raphael, Miss Rainforth as Madelon, Miss Pincott as Mlle. Guimard.

LITTLE LORD FOUNTLEROY// D 3a// Dram. by Mrs. E. H. Burnett fr her novel// **Princess's**, Dec. 1889, with Henry Edwards as Earl of Doricourt, Olive Berkely as Cedric, W. H. Leake as Havisham, George Leopold as Hobbs, S. Nelson as Dick, E. Gladstone as Higgins, Ethel Winthrop as Mrs. Errol, Louise Berkley as Minna, Miss D. Mainwaring as Mary/ Scenery by John Brunton.

LITTLE LORD FAUNTLEROY// D 3a// Adap. by E. V. Seebohm fr Mrs. Burnett's story// **POW**, Feb. 1888/ **Terry's**, May 1888/ **Wyndham's**, Dec. 1901.

LITTLE MADCAP, A// C 1a// C. S. Cheltnam// **Sad. Wells**, Mar. 1846, with Henry Scharf as Leonard, E. Morton as Maurice, Charles Fenton as Homeline, Miss Cooper as Georgette, Miss Huddart as Louise.

LITTLE MINISTER, THE// Play 4a// Dram. by J. M. Barrie fr his own novel// **Haymarket**, Nov. 1897, with W. G. Elliot as Earl of Rintoul, Cyril Maude as Dishart, C. M. Hallard as Capt. Halliwell, Brandon Thomas as Whamond, Mark Kinghorne as Hobart, F. H. Tyler as Tosh, E. Holman Clark as Mealmaker, Sidney Valentine as Dow, Miss Sidney Fairbrother as Micah, Nina Cadiz as Felice, Mary Mackenzie as Jean, Winifred Emery as Lady Babbie/ Scenery by Walter Hann & Joseph Harker.

LITTLE MISS CUTE// C 4a// Adap. by E. B. Norman fr orig. by C. T. Vincent// **Royalty**, Sept. 1894, with Gerald Spencer as Forrester, Frank Fenton as Sir Arthur, Eardley Turner as Adm. Leslie, Edward Broughton as Mountfort, Ivan Watson as Count Marani, A. H. Brooke as Filippo, Alexes Leighton as Lady Radcliffe, Violet Armbruster as Helen, Ethel Hope as Mrs. Leslie, Hope Booth as Miss Cute, Italia Conti as Edith.

LITTLE MISS MUFFET// C 3a// Adap. by James Albery fr F of Alfred Hennequin, La Femme à Papa// **Criterion**, Sept. 1882, with Herbert Beerbohm Tree, Lytton Sothern, Kate Rorke, Nelly Bromley.

LITTLE MOTHER// C 2a// J. Maddison Morton// **Royalty**, Apr. 1870/ **Gaiety**, Dec. 1880, with J. J. Wallus, Lottie Venne, Ethel Hughes.

LITTLE NELL; OR, THE OLD CURIOSITY SHOP// D// Adap. fr novel of Charles Dickens// **Sad. Wells**, Jan. 1841, with J. B. Hill as Trent, J. W. Collier as Swiveller, Mr. Williams as Single Gentleman, Henry Marston as Grandfather, Robert Honner as Quilp, Mrs. Robert Honner as Little Nell, Miss Cooke as Mrs. Jarley, Mrs. Morgan as Mrs. Jiniwin, Miss Hicks as Mrs. Quilp, Miss Louise as Sally,

Mrs. Richard Barnett as Polly.

LITTLE NELLY// D 4a// Murray Wood// **Surrey**, Nov. 1872.

LITTLE NOBODY// C 1a// Mary Righton// **Vaudeville**, July 1890.

LITTLE NUN, THE// F 1a// H. T. Craven// **Grecian**, Aug. 1847, with Richard Phillips as Capt. Latimer, Eaton O'Donnell as Sir Walter, Mr. Griffiths as Staunch, Miss Johnstone as Lady Abbess, Annette Mears as Adela, Miss Merion as Griselda, Mary A. Crisp as Patience.

LITTLE ONE, THE// D 1a// Arthur Ayers// **Vaudeville**, Jan. 1885.

LITTLE OUTCAST, A; A CHILD'S STORY// D 4a// C. A. Clarke & H. R. Silva// **Grand**, July 1901.

LITTLE PILGRIM, THE// D 2a// Dram. by W. G. Wills fr novel of Ouida, Two Little Wooden Shoes// **Criterion**, July 1886, with W. E. Gregory, Fred Emery, Miss F. Paget, Violet Vanbrugh.

LITTLE RAGAMUFFIN, THE; OR, THE WORLD'S WAIF// D 3a// n.a.// **Pavilion**, June 1868.

LITTLE RAY OF SUNSHINE, A// C 3a// Mark Ambient & Wilton Heriot// **Royalty**, Dec. 1898, with W. S. Penley as Lord Markham, Neville Doone as Carlton, Julius Royston as Dick Markham, E. H. Brooke as Ashton, Fred Epitaux as Dobbs, H. Reeves Smith as Sir Philip, Beatrice Selwyn as Lady Dorothy, Flossie Wilkinson as Evelyn, Jessie Bateman as Connie, Florence Leclercq as Madge.

LITTLE REBEL, THE// F 1a// Adap. by J. Stirling Coyne fr F// **Olympic**, Apr. 1861, with Horace Wigan as Poppincourt, Gaston Murray as Ormeston, Mrs. Stephen as Mrs. Wingrove, Louise Keeley as Laura, Mrs. W. S. Emden as Kitty.

LITTLE SAVAGE, THE// F 1a// J. Maddison Morton// **Strand**, Nov. 1858.

LITTLE SENTINEL, THE// C 1a// T. J. Williams// **St. James's**, May 1863/ **Haymarket**, Jan. 1883, with Frederick Everill as Coaxer, Mr. Medley as Courtington, Mr. Elliot as Sim, Florence Wade as Letty, Julia Gwynne as May/ **Adelphi**, Aug. 1890, with J. Northcote as Coaxer, James East as Courtington, W. Northcote as Sim, Miss Essex Dane as Letty, Clara Jecks as May.

LITTLE SQUIRE, THE// C 3a// Adap. by William Greet & Horace Sedger fr novel of Mrs. de la Pasture// **Lyric**, Apr. 1894.

LITTLE SUNBEAM// C// Mrs. Henry Wylde// **Lyric**, June 1892.

LITTLE SUPPER, A// F// Harold Ellis// **Globe**, Dec. 1900.

LITTLE TODDLEKINS// C 1a// Charles Mathews // **Lyceum**, Dec. 1852/ **Drury Lane**, Dec. 1855, with C. J. Mathews as Brownsmith, Mr. Tilbury as Babicombe, Henry Ashley as Capt. Littlepop, Mrs. Frank Matthews as Amanthis, Miss M. Oliver as Annie, Emma Wadham as Susan/ **Sad. Wells**, Apr. 1855, with Robert Roxby as Brownsmith, Frank Matthews as Babicombe, Gaston Murray as Capt. Littletop, Mrs. Frank Matthews as Amanthis, Miss M. Oliver as Anne, Emma Wadham as Susan/ **St. James's**, June 1864, with C. J. Mathews as Brownsmith, Frank Matthews as Babicombe, H. J. Montague as Capt. Littlepop, Mrs. Frank Matthews as Amanthia, Miss Wentworth as Anne.

LITTLE TREASURE, THE// C 2a// Augustus Harris// **Haymarket**, Oct. 1855, with Henry Howe as Sir Charles, J. B. Buckstone as Capt. Maydenblush, Edwin Villiers as Flattermore, George Braid as Allenbourne, Miss Swanborough as Lady Florence, Blanche Fane as Gertrude, Mrs. Poynter as Mrs. Meddleton/ Scenery by George Morris & John O'Conner/ Machines by Oliver Wales.

LITTLE VISCOUNT, THE// C 2a// Adap. by Hermann Vezin fr F of J. F. Bayard, Le Vicomte de Letorrières// **Gaiety**, Aug. 1884.

LITTLE VIXENS, THE// C 1a// George Neville// **Olympic**, Feb. 1878, with Robert Pateman as Capt. Farsea, T. G. Warren as John, G. Peyton as Adolphus, Clara May as Phillippa, Alma Stanley as Kate, Miss Beaumont as Julia.

LITTLE WIDOW, THE// FC 3a// Fred Jarman// **Royalty**, 1894, with Charles Sugden as Potter, Welton Dale as Dr. Potter, Frank Lacy as Capt. Rattlebrain, A. E. Mason as Bousieur, Ernest Patterson as Morton, Sydney Phelps as Mrs. Potter, Emilie Grattan as Emily, Jane Gray as Sophonisba, Minnie Palmer as Mrs. Rattlebrain.

LITTLE WILLIE THE WANDERER; OR, THE LIFE OF A POLICEMAN// D 2a// n.a.// **Sad. Wells**, June 1868, with Jenny Willmore as Willie, C. D. Pitt as Skinner, C. Arnold as Col. Vernon, Felix Rogers as Bobby, J. Davis as Slippers, C. Fisher as George, W. Willmore as Vernon, Eliza Gordon as Martha, Jenny Gordon as Nancy, Mrs. J. G. Beckett as Mrs. Caufield.

LITTLEST GIRL, THE// Play 1a// Dram. by Robert Hilliard fr story of R. H. Davis// **Court**, July 1896.

LIVING AT EASE// C 3a// George Rose ("Arthur Sketchley")// **Strand**, Oct. 1870.

LIVING OR DEAD// Play 5a// Dram. by Wilfred Stephens fr story of Hugh Conway// **Sad. Wells**, Oct. 1886.

LIVING TOO FAST; OR, A TWELVE-MONTH'S HONEYMOON// C 1a// A. C. Troughton// **Princess's**, Oct. 1854, with Walter Lacy as Prudent, George Everett as Capt. Plausible, John Chester as Cotton, Miss Murray as Mrs. Prudent, Miss J. Lovell as Mary.

LIZ; OR, THAT LASS O' LOWRIE'S// D Pro & 3a// Dram. by Arthur Matthison & Joseph Hatton fr Mrs. Burnett's novel// **Opera Comique**, Sept. 1877.

LIZZIE LEIGH; OR, THE MURDER NEAR THE OLD MILL// D 3a// W. R. Waldron// **City of London**, Aug. 1866.

LIZZIE LYLE; OR, THE FLOWER GIRL'S TEMPTATION (also subt. The Flower Makers of Finsbury)// D 3a// C. H. Hazlewood// **Grecian**, Oct. 1869/ **Marylebone**, Feb. 1874.

LOADSTONE, THE// D 4a// T. E. Pemberton & W. H. Vernon// **Lyceum**, Apr. 1888, with W. H. Vernon as Warburton, Fuller Mellish as Polwarth, Edward Sass as Dr. Pemberth, Leonard Outram as Rathbone, Dorothy Dene as Kate, Genevieve Ward as Lady Polwarth.

LOAN OF A LOVER, A// F 1a// J. R. Planché// **Eng. Opera House** (Lyceum), June 1837, with Mr. Cooper as Capt. Amersfort, William Vining as Swyzel, Mr. Wyman as Delve, C. J. Mathews as Spyk, Mme. Vestris as Gertrude/ **Haymarket**, Sept. 1837, with C. J. Mathews as Spyk, Charles Selby as Capt. Amersfort, T. F. Mathews as Delve, Robert Strickland as Swyzel, Mme. Vestris as Gertrude, Miss Wrighten as Ernestine; Nov. 1874, with G. Temple as Capt. Amerfort, Frederick Everill as Spyk, George Braid as Swyzel, Edward Osborne as Delve, Miss Walton as Gertrude, Linda Dietz as Ernestine/ **Olympic**, Sept. 1837, with James Vining as Amersfort, W. Vining as Swyzel, Mr. Wyman as Delve, Mr. Keeley as Spyk, Mme. Vestris as Gertrude; Sept. 1846, with "A Gentleman" as Amersfort, Mr. Hurlstone as Spyk, Mr. Jones as Swyzel, Mr. Johnson as Delve, Mrs. Nivett as Gertrude, Miss Leslie as Ernestine; Aug. 1852, with John Kinloch as Amersfort, William Farren Jr. as Spyk, George Cooke as Swyzel, Mr. Clifton as Delve, Harriet Gordon as Gertrude, Isabel Adams as Ernestine; Dec. 1862, with Walter Gordon as Amersfort, George Cooke as Swyzel, Harwood Cooper as Delve, Horace Wigan as Spyk, Miss Hughes as Gertrude, Mrs. St. Henry as Ernestine/ **Sad. Wells**, Sept. 1838, with John Webster as Amersfort, Robert Keeley as Spyke, Mr. Williams as Swyzel, J. W. Collier as Delve, Mrs. Keeley as Gertrude, Miss Murray as Ernestine/ **Cov. Garden**, Oct. 1839, with James Vining as Capt. Amersfort, Robert Keeley as Spyk, Mr. Granby as Swyzel, W. H. Payne as Delve, Miss Lee as Ernestine, Mme. Vestris as Gertrude/ **Princess's**, June 1846, with James Vining as Maj. Amersfort, C. J. Mathews as Spyk, Mr. Granby as Swyzel, Augustus Harris as Delve, Mme. Vestris as Gertrude, Mrs. H. Hughes as Ernestine; Feb. 1851, with James Vining as Capt. Amersfort, Robert Keeley as Spyk, Mr. Addison as Swyzel, Mr. Stacey as Delve, Mrs. Keeley as Gertrude, Miss Murray as Ernestine.

LOAN OF A WIFE, THE// F 1a// Adap. by Alfred Wigan fr F// **Lyceum**, July 1846, with Frank Matthews as Lobjoit, Alfred Wigan as Onesiphorus Lobjoit, John Kinloch as De Laine, Jane Turner as Alphonso, Mrs. Woollidge as Mrs. Fitzmontemar, Miss Howard as Bridget, Drinkwater Meadows as Mrs. Bandanna/ **St. James's**, Dec. 1860, with Samuel Emery as Lobjoit, Henry Ashley as Onesiphorous Lobjoit, Mr. Dawson as Delaine, Master Vokes as Alphonso, Mrs. Buckingham White as Mrs. Fitzmontemar, Nelly Mocre as Bridget, Charles Young as Mrs. Bandanna.

LOCHINVAR; OR, THE BRIDAL OF NETHERBY// D 2a// Dram. by W. T. Moncrieff fr Sir Walter Scott// **Sad. Wells**, Feb. 1841, with Mr. Dry as James VI, Mr. Aldridge as Lord Netherby, Mr. Stilt as Sir Heron, Mr. Elvin as Musgrave, Henry Marston as Lochinvar, Mr. Williams as Macbawnie, Mr. Priorson as Lord Chamberlain, J. W. Collier as Cromie, Miss Richardson as Lady Helen, Mrs. Richard Barnett as Mysie.

LOCK AND KEY// F// Prince Hoare// **Drury Lane**, Nov. 1839, with Mr. Addison as Brummagem, John Lee as Capt. Vain, Mr. Frazer as Cheerly, W. J. Hammond as Ralph, Miss Betts as Laura, Mrs. Waylett as Fanny, Miss Pettifer as Selina, Mrs. Melville as Dolly.

LOCKED IN (see also, Loan of a Lover)// F 1a// J. P. Wocler// **St. James's**, June 1863, with Charles Harcourt as Capt. Amersfort, Adeline Cottrell as Spyk, Charles Fenton as Swyzel, C. Western as Delve, Alice Dodd as Gertrude, Miss L. E. Wentworth as Ernestine/ **POW**, Sept. 1870.

LOCOMOTION// F// W. Bayle Bernard// **Haymarket**, Aug. 1842, with William Farren as Floss, Mr. Vining as Leicester, A. Brindal as Vernon, Mr. Clark as Dot, Miss Charles as Mrs. Leicester/ **Sad. Wells**, Oct. 1853, with William Hoskins as Floss, T. C. Harris as Vernon, William Belford as Leicester, Mr. Meagreson as Dot, Miss Portman as Mrs. Leicester.

LOCRINE// T 5a// A. C. Swinburne// **St. Geo. Hall**, Mar. 1899.

LODGERS, THE// F 3a// Adap. by Brandon Thomas & Maurice de Verney fr F.// **Globe**, Jan. 1887, with Charles Glenney as O'Blathagan, Wilfred Draycott as Sparker, W. S. Penley as Hundlebee, W. J. Hill as Muggridge, Blanche Horlock as Kitty, Miss Vane Featherston as as Amelia, Fanny Brough as Mrs. Muggridge/ Scenery by Bruce Smith/ Prod. by F. Glover.

LODGERS AND DODGERS// F 1a// Frederick Hay// **Strand**, May 1871.

LODGINGS FOR SINGLE GENTLEMEN// C// John Poole// **Haymarket**, Nov. 1855, with Edwin Villiers as Col. Stanmore, William Farren as Capt. Postlewaite, William Clark as Trusty, Ellen Chaplin as Mrs. Prattle, Miss Schott as Mrs. Stanmore, Amelia Vining as Mrs. Greville.

LODOISKA// D 2a// n.a.// **Cov. Garden**, Mar. 1839, with Mr. Waldron as Lupanski, Mr. Manvers as Floreski, James Anderson as Lovinski, John Pritt Harley as Farbel, Henry Howe as Adolphus, Miss Rainforth as Lodoiska, Samuel Phelps as Kera Khan.

as Floreski, James Anderson as Lovinski, John Pritt Harley as Farbel, Henry Howe as Adolphus, Miss Rainforth as Lodoiska, Samuel Phelps as Kera Khan.

LOLA MONTEZ; OR, A COUNTESS FOR AN HOUR// C// J. Sterling Coyne// **Haymarket**, Apr. 1848, with Mr. Tilbury as Prince Gruenasgras, Mr. Rogers as Baron von Stoutz, A. Brindal as Count Nottamagg, William Clark as Count Otzenay, Robert Keeley as Hedwiger, Mrs. Stanley as Baroness von Stoutz, Miss E. Messent as Mme. Sternfast, Mrs. L. S. Buckingham as Lola Montez, Mrs. Keeley as Netchen.

LOLAH; OR, THE WRECK LIGHT// D 2a// n.a.// **Haymarket**, Mar. 1844, with William Strickland as Com. Tempest, Henry Holl as Sir George, Henry Howe as Lord Erskine, A. Brindal as Grey, J. B. Buckstone as Custard, Mme. Celeste as Lolah.

LONDON ARAB, A// D 5a// Miles Wallerton & Francis Gilbert// **Surrey**, Apr. 1899.

LONDON ARAB, THE// D Pro & 4a// n.a.// **Victoria**, Apr. 1866, with W. D. Gresham as Walden, Henry Forrester as Hudson, James Fenton as Taptub, Emilie De Vigne as Mary, J. Howard as Villiers, J. C. Levey as Hardy, F. Thomas as Tatterboy, Maria Daly as Crazy Joe, George Yarnold as Jovial, John Bradshaw as Crabtree, R. Marchant as Daddy, Miss A. Mavis as Florence, Fanny Morgan as Sally/ **Grecian**, June 1878.

LONDON ASSURANCE// C 5a// Dion Boucicault// **Cov. Garden**, Mar. 1841, with William Farren as Sir Harcourt, George Bartley as Harkaway, James Anderson as Courtley, Robert Keeley as Spanker, C. J. Mathews as Dazzle, John Pritt Harley as Meddle, A. Brindal as Cool, W. H. Payne as Isaacs, Mme. Vestris as Grace, Louisa Nisbett as Lady Gay, Mrs. Humby as Pert/ Scenery by Grieve, T. Grieve & W. Grieve/ **Haymarket**, Sept. 1842, with William Farren as Sir Harcourt, Robert Strickland as Harkaway, Henry Holl as Charles, Mr. Vining as Dazzle, Benjamin Webster as Meddle, A. Brindal as Cool, Mrs. Nisbett as Lady Gay Spanker, Miss Charles as Grace, Miss Carre as Pert; Jan. 1852, with Mr. Lambert as Sir Harcourt, Mr. Rogers as Harkaway, Henry Howe as Charles, Mr. Buckstone as Spanker, Leigh Murray as Dazzle, Henry Bedford as Meddle, William Clark as Cool, George Braid as Isaacs, Mrs. Stirling as Lady Gay, Miss Reynolds as Grace, Mrs. Caulfield as Pert; Dec. 1860, with W. H. Chippendale as Sir Harcourt, Henry Howe as Charles, Henry Compton as Meddle, Mr. Rogers as Harkaway, J. B. Buckstone as Spanker, William Clark as Cool, William Farren as Dazzle, Amy Sedgwick as Lady Gay, Florence Haydon as Grace, Mrs. Edward Fitzwilliam as Pert/ **Sad. Wells**, Feb. 1854, with J. W. Ray as Sir Harcourt, Mr. Barrett as Harkaway, Henry Marston as Courtly, William Hoskins as Dazzle, Charles Fenton as Spanker, Lewis Ball as Meddle, William Belford as Cool, Miss Cooper as Lady Gay Spanker, Kate Hickson as Grace, Eliza Travers as Pert/ **Drury Lane**, Oct. 1856/ **Olympic**, Sept. 1858, with W. Cooper as Sir Harcourt Courtly, Walter Gordon as Charles, H. N. Chart as Spanker, George Vining as Dazzle, E. Marshall as Meddle, Mr. Sanger as Cool, J. H. Leffler as Isaacs, Miss Castleton as Lady Gay Spanker, Florence Haydon as Grace, Miss Hudson as Pert/ **Princess's**, Mar. 1860, with Frank Matthews as Sir Harcourt, Mr. Garden as Harkaway, William Farren as Dazzle, George Melville as Courtley, Robert Keeley as Spanker, Henry Widdicomb as Meddle, Henry Saker as Cool, J. W. Collier as Isaacs, Carlotta Leclercq as Lady Gay Spanker, Louise Keeley as Grace/ **Grecian**, June 1866, with J. Jackson as Sir Harcourt, William James as Charles, John Manning as Spanker, Henry Grant as Harkaway, Charles Mortimer as Meddle, Samuel Perfitt as Cool, Lizzie Mandlebert as Lady Gay, Mary A. Victor as Grace, Emma Victor as Pert/ **St. James's**, 1876, with W. H. Stephens as Sir Harcourt, Charles Warner as Charles, R. Markby as Dazzle, Clifford Cooper as Harkaway, Fred Mervin as Spanker, George Honey as Meddle, Mr. Benbrook as Cool, Mrs. John Wood as Lady Gay, Lydia Foote as Grace, Miss Telbin as Pert/ **Criterion**,. Nov. 1890.

LONDON BANKER, THE; OR, THE PROFLIGATE// D 2a// A. V. Campbell// **Grecian**, July 1845, with Mr. Campbell as Clayton, Henry Horncastle as Raymond Clayton, Harry Chester as Reckless, Edwin Dixon as Spade, Mr. Melvin as Scarlet, Frederick Robson as Tip, Annette Mears as Sally Rattle, Miss M. A. Crisp as Monimia.

LONDON BRIDGE 150 YEARS AGO; OR, THE OLD MINT// D 5a// Adap. by James Macnab fr F, Les Chevaliers du Brouillard// **Queen's**, Feb. 1873.

LONDON BY GASLIGHT// D 5a// Adap. by Miss Hazlewood fr Augustin Daly's Under the Gaslight// **Sad. Wells**, Sept. 1868, with J. H. Fitzpatrick as Trafford, Mr. Newbound as Snorkey, J. H. Loome as Bike, Mr. Sargent as Demilt, Mr. Harbourn as Windle, Mr. Weston as Bermudas, Miss Hazlewood as Laura, Miss Hill as Pearl, Miss Blackwood as Peach-Blossom, Mrs. G. Howe as Old Judas, Miss Marlborough as Mrs. Vandam.

LONDON CARRIER, THE// D 2a// n.a.// **Astley's**, Apr. 1849, with Mr. Johnson as Adm. Vanguard, Paul Bedford as Charles, Mr. Crowther as Jack, Mr. Adrian as Barney, S. Smith as David, Rosa Henry as Margaret, Helen Lane as Patience.

LONDON DAY BY DAY// D 4a// G. R. Sims & Henry Pettitt// **Adelphi**, Oct. 1889, with George Alexander as Frank Granville, J. L. Shine as Galloway, J. D. Beveridge as O'Brien, L. Rignold as Ascalon, W. L. Abingdon as Marks, James East as Lord Kempton, Alma Murray as Violet, Mary Rorke as Maud, Clara Jecks as Dolly, Charlotte Elliott as Mrs. Blossom, Madge Mildren as Rosie/ Scenery by Bruce Smith & W. Perkins/ Music by Henry Sprake/ Prod. by William Sidney.

LONDON FOG// F 1a// Mark Lemon// **Adelphi**, Apr. 1851, with Paul Bedford as Copal, Mr. Wright as Simple, Mrs. Laws as Mrs. Boarder, Emma Harding as Mrs. Brisk.

LONDON LADY, THE// C// n.a.// **Sad. Wells**, Nov. 1848, with William Hoskins as Jones, Henry Mellon as Maj. Wrangleton, Mr. Gladstone as Fitzarlington, Mr. Williams as Scrimmage, Miss Huddart as Emily, Mrs. Henry Marston as Mrs. Tubbs, Miss H. Berkley as Charlotte, Miss Garthwaite as Betty.

LONDON LIFE// D 4a// T. G. Clark// **Grecian**, Sept. 1881.

LONDON MYSTERY, A// D 4a// William Bourne// **Pavilion**, July 1895.

LONDON PRIDE// C// J. L. Kenney// **St. James's**, Nov. 1859, with Charles Young, Leigh Murray, Mrs. Frank Matthews.

LONDON'S CURSE// Play Pro & 3a// E. Hogan-Armadale// **Surrey**, July 1901.

LONE CHATEAU, THE; OR, THE SERGEANT'S WIFE// D 2a// John Banim// **Sad. Wells**, June 1857, with James Johnstone as Bertrand, George Cooke as Sgt. Bertrand, G. Pennett as Denuis, Mr. Edwin as Jaques, John Mordaunt as Francois, E. B. Gaston as Baptiste, G. B. Bigwood as Peter, Mrs. Robert Honner as Manette, Mary A. Victor as Estelle/ **Grecian**, Oct. 1865, with J. Jackson as Old Cartouche, William James as Frederick, W. Holland as Sgt. Louis, Mr. Goodin as Sgt. George, John Manning as Robin, Henry Grant as Dennis, J. B. Steele as Gaspard, Alice Denville as Lisette, Miss M. A. Victor as Margot.

LONELY LIVES// D 5a// Trans. by Mary Morrison fr G of Gerhart Hauptmann, Einsame Menschen// **Strand**, Apr. 1901.

LONELY MAN OF THE OCEAN, THE; OR, THE NIGHT BEFORE THE BRIDAL// D 3a// Thomas Blake// **Victoria**, Sept. 1848, with John Bradshaw as Bowyer, J. Howard as Hillington, J. T. Johnson as Lt. Bashford, E. Edwards as Jolly, G. F. Forman as Bloom, Mr. Hawkins as Bell, F. H. Henry as Marly, Mrs. George Lee as Eve, Miss Richardson as Helena, Miss Burroughcliffe as Becky, Miss Young as Peg/ **Olympic**, Dec. 1851, with William Norton as Bower, Mr. Sanger as Hillington, William Farren as Lt. Bashford, Charles Bender as Jack Jolly, W. Shalders as Bloom, Mr. Harris as Bell, Miss Fielding as Eve, Isabel Adams as Becky, Miss Wyndham as Peg/ **Grecian**, Aug. 1864, with George Gillett as Bowyer, W. Shirley as Hillington, William James as Bashford, Henry Grant as Jack Jolly, John Manning as Bloom, Mrs. Charles Dillon as Eve, Mary A. Victor as Becky, Jane Dawson as Helena.

LONELYE [sic] **SPOT, THE; OR, THE LEGEND OF THE ISLINGTON BRICK FIELD**// D// T. P. Taylor// **Sad. Wells**, Aug. 1837, with Mr. Griffiths as Morton, Mr. King as Plowden, C. H. Pitt as Peveril, Thomas Lee as Clay, Mr. Campbell as Hemlock, C. J. Smith as Mike, Miss Williams as Mario, Mrs. Harris as Harriet.

LONG AGO// D 1a// Arthur à Beckett// **Royalty**, Apr. 1882, with Kyrle Bellew, Hilda Hilton.

LONG DUEL, A// C 4a// Mrs. W. K. Clifford// **Garrick**, Aug. 1901.

LONG ODDS// C 3a// Conway Edwardes// **Opera Comique**, Feb. 1887.

LONG STRIKE, THE// D 4a// Found. by Dion Boucicault partly on Mary Barton and partly on Lizzie Leigh// **Lyceum**, Nov. 1866, with J. H. Fitzpatrick as Radley, Mr. Vivian as Aspinall, Samuel Emery as Learoyd, J. C. Cowper as Starkie, Edgar Newbound as Spurrier, Henry Widdicomb as Moneypenny, Miss Henrade as Jane, Miss Heally as Maggie, Miss Woodstone as Susan/ **Grecian**, Apr. 1867, with Henry Grant, Charles Mortimer, Mr. Dearlove, Mr. Dacey, Henry Power, W. Shirley, William James, Alfred Rayner, George Gillett, J. Jackson, Lizzie Mandelbert, Miss E. Victor, Mrs. Dearlove/ **Adelphi**, Nov. 1869, with Arthur Stirling as Radley, C. J. Smith as Aspinall, Harwood Cooper as Armitage, C. Locksley as Brooke, Benjamin Webster as Noah, William Rignold as Jem, George Belmore as Moneypenny, A. W. Powell as Slack, C. H. Stephenson as Crankshaw, Miss Furtado as Jane, Emily Turtle as Betsy/ Scenery by F. Lloyds & Maugham.

LOOK BEFORE YOU LEAP; OR, WOOINGS AND WEDDINGS// C 5a// George Lovell// **Haymarket**, Oct. 1846, with William Farren as Oddington, Charles Hudson as Rashleigh, Henry Holl as De Vere, Henry Howe as Brandon, Mr. Rogers as Hardman, Benjamin Webster as Spriggs, J. B. Buckstone as Filley, Mrs. Julia Glover as Miss Brown, Miss Fortescue as Claribel, Priscilla Horton as Mary, Mrs. Edwin Yarnold as Elinor, Julia Bennett as Fanny, Miss Carre as Mrs. Noggs/ Scenery by George Morris.

LOOSE TILES// FC 3a// J. P. Hurst// **Vaudeville**, Jan. 1885.

LORD AND LADY ALGY// C 3a// R. C. Carton// **Comedy**, Apr. 1898, with Charles Hawtrey as Lord Chetland, Henry Kemble as Duke of Droneborough, Arthur Williams as Tudway, Eric Lewis as Marquis of Quarmby, Lyston Lyle as Jethro, Frederick Volpé as Swepson, E. H. Kelly as Capt. Standidge, A. E. Matthews as Annesley, Henry Ford as Jemmett, Hugh Goring as Denton, Alec Weatherley as Jeal, Miss Compton as Lady Chetland, Marion Sterling as Lady Pamela, Mabel Hackney as Ottoline, Ethel Gain as Emily, Mrs. Charles Calvert as Mrs. Voskins, Fannie Ward as Mrs. Tudway/ Scenery by E. G. Banks.

LORD ANERLEY// Play 4a// Henry Hamilton & Mark Quinton// **St. James's**, Nov. 1891, with Nutcombe Gould as Earl of Edgehill, Arthur Bourchier as Lord Anerley, Ben Webster as Beaufort, George Alexander as Lee, Herbert Waring as Lester, F. W. Gardiner as Travers,

Alfred Holles as Evans, Laura Graves as Esme, Gertrude Kingston as Mme. de Sivon, Marion Terry as Evelyn/ Scenery by H. P. Hall/ Music by Walter Slaughter.

LORD DARNLEY; OR, THE KEEPER OF CASTLE HILL// D 2a// Thomas Wilks// **Surrey**, Sept. 1837.

LORD DOLLY// FC 3a// Charles Anderson// **Matinée**, Nov. 1898.

LORD DUNDREARY MARRIED AND DONE FOR// C// H. J. Byron & E. A. Sothern// **Haymarket**, Dec. 1864, with E. A. Sothern as Dundreary, J. B. Buckstone as Asa Trenchard, George Braid as Sir Edward, Thomas Coe as Buddicombe, William Clark as Binney, P. White as Murcott, Mr. Weathersby as Capt. Vernon, Walter Gordon as De Boots, James Worrell as Buggins, Caroline Hill as Lady Dundreary, Miss Snowdon as Lady Trenchard/ Scenery by John O'Conner & George Morris.

LORD HARRY, THE// D 5a// Henry Arthur Jones & Wilson Barrett// **Princess's**, Feb. 1886, with Wilson Barrett, Mary Eastlake, E. S. Willard, Lottie Venne.

LORD IN WAITING// C 1a// A. Bartholeyns// **Avenue**, July 1893, with Frank Worthing as Willoughby, J. B. Gordon as Sligo, Emilie Grattan as Fanny.

LORD MACNINNY// F// n.a.// **Vaudeville**, Dec. 1887.

LORD MARPLE'S DAUGHTER// C 3a// Adap. by Frank Harvey fr F// **Grand**, Nov. 1886.

LORD MAYOR, THE// C 3a// W. E. Bradley & Harry and Edward Paulton// **Strand**, Nov. 1895, with Harry Paulton as Sir Martin, W. Scott Buist as Marlow, Harold Child as Gratwick, James Welch as Bristol, Laurence Irving as Prof. Grimweed, Clinton Baddeley as Robbins, E. A. Coventry as Harris, Newman Maurice as Morgan, Stanley Betjemann as Jackson, Gladys Evelyn as Sabina, Agnes Paulton as Clarissa, Amy Elstob as Lady Muriel, Alice de Winton as Cora/ Scenery by E. G. Banks.

LORD MAYOR'S DAY, THE// FC 3a// n.a.// **Folly**, June 1879.

LORD MAYOR'S FOOL, THE// F 1a// n.a.// **Victoria**, Apr. 1847, with J. Howard as Sir Stephen, Alfred Raymond as Edward, J. B. Johnstone as Walbrook, Mr. Hitchinson as Osgood, F. H. Henry as Sir Richard, Mr. Fitzjames as Drawwell, John Gardner as Witless, Miss Edgar as Lady Mary, Mrs. George Lee as Margaret, Mrs. N. T. Hicks as Mabel, Mrs. Cooke as Lady Winifred.

LORD OF LOBINSKI, THE; OR, THE ZINGARI HORDE OF THE FOREST OF SCHEMNITZ// D 3a// n.a.// **Victoria**, Nov. 1850, with Mr. Richards as Grand Duke Maximilian, Henry Frazer as Hertzman, J. T. Johnson as Waldermar, J. Neville as Ivanhoff, Mr. Henderson as de Salvi, Mr. Humphreys as Echartoff, T. H. Higgie as Zingaro, Miss Alford as Alexis, Amelia Mercer as Miriam, Mrs. George Lee as Stella, Mrs. Cooke as Flametta,, Miss Barrowcliffe as Ullah, Miss Mildenhall as Fleeta.

LORD OF THE MANOR, THE// C// Charles Dibdin [?]// **St. James's**, Jan. 1837, with Robert Strickland as Sir John, Mr. Forester as Young Contrast, Mr. Bennett as Trumore, Mr. Leffler as Rashly, Mr. Hollingsworth as Rental, John Gardner as La Nippe, Miss Rainforth as Annette, Miss Smith as Sophia, Julia Smith as Peggy, John Pritt Harley as Moll Flaggon/ **Cov. Garden**, Oct. 1837, with George Bartley as Sir John, Mr. Vining as Young Contrast, Mr. Leffler as Rashley, Mr. Wilson as Truemore, Drinkwater Meadows as La Nippe, Mr. Tilbury as Rental, Mr. Roberts as Sgt. Sash, Edwin Yarnold as Corp. Drill, Miss Sherreff as Sophia, Priscilla Horton as Annette, Eliza Vincent as Peggy, W. J. Hammond as Moll/ .

LORD OF THE MANOR, THE// Play 3a// Dram. by Herman Merivale fr G novel, Wilhelm Meister// **Imperial**, Jan. 1880, with William Farren, Kyrle Bellew, Mr. Bannister, Lydia Cowell.

LORDS AND COMMONS// C 4a// Arthur Wing Pinero// **Haymarket**, Nov. 1883, with Johnston Forbes Robertson as Earl of Caryl, Charles Brookfield as Lord Lewiscourt, Mr. Elliot as Sir George, Squire Bancroft as Jervoise, Alfred Bishop as Smee, Mr. Girardot as Chadd, Albert Sims as Tredger, Percy Vernon as Pressenger, Stewart Dawson as Radbone, Mrs. Stirling as Countess of Caryl, Miss Calhoun as Lady Nell, Mrs. Bernard Beere as Mrs. Devenish, Mrs. Bancroft as Miss Maplebeck/ Scenery by Mr. Telbin & Walter Johnstone.

LORDS OF ELLINGHAM, THE// D 5a// Henry Spicer// **Olympic**, May 1848, with G. V. Brooke as Lawrency, E. L. Davenport as Latymer, Henry Holl as Vivian, Edward Stirling as Kensell, Mr. Lawrence as Watson, John Kinloch as Sir Griffin, Henry Mellon as Sir Edward, H. Lee as Bagot, Lizzie Mandelbert as Giovanni, Anna Cora Mowatt as Edith, E. Marie Duret as Marion, Kate Howard as Ethelind/ Scenery by Laidlaw, Cooper, Turner, & R. Laidlaw/ Music by W. Guernsey.

LORNA DOONE// Play 5a// Dram. by Mildred Dowling fr novel of R. D. Blackmore// **Royalty**, June 1901.

LORNA DOONE// D// Dram. by Mary Ford & Leonard Rayne fr novel of R. D. Blackmore// **Princess's**, Dec. 1901.

LOSS OF THE ROYAL GEORGE; OR, THE FATAL LAND BREEZE// D 2a// C. Z. Barnett// **Sad. Wells**, Sept. 1840, with Mr. Elvin as Capt. Effingstone, J. B. Hill as Lt. Trevor, Mr. Aldridge as Topsail, Mr. Stilt as Larboard, Robert Honner as Binnacle, J. W. Collier as Distich, Henry Marston as de Barossa, Mr. Dry as Gomez, Miss Melville as Patience, Miss Louise as Sister Agatha, Mrs. Robert Honner as Inez, Mr. Williams as Adm. Kempenfelt, Mr. Houghburt as as Capt.

Wagthorne, F. Fenton as Lt. Saunders/ Scenery by F. Fenton/ Music by Isaac Collins/ Machines by B. Sloman/ Prod. by R. Honner.

LOST// D// Lambert Thiboust// **Standard**, Oct. 1871.

LOST! A SOVEREIGN; OR, NEVER TRAVEL DURING A REVOLUTION// F// H. R. Addison// **Olympic**, Apr. 1848, with H. Lee as Lenoire, Mr. Conquest as Louis King, Mr. Lawrence as Charles, Miss Bromley as Louisa, Miss Young as Lizzy, Mrs. H. Lee as Mme. Dubois.

LOST AT SEA; A LONDON STORY// D 4a// Dion Boucicaut & H. J. Byron// **Adelphi**, Oct. 1869, with Arthur Stirling as Walter, J. D. Beveridge as Lord Alfred, George Belmore as Jessop, Mr. Atkins as Rawlings, C. H. Stephenson as Franklin, Eliza Johnstone as Smyley, C. J. Smith as Gabriel, Rose Leclercq as Katey, Mrs. Leigh Murray as Mrs. Jessop/ Scenery by Hawes Craven & Maugham/ Machines by Edward Charker/ Gas by G. Bastard/ Music by Edwin Ellis.

LOST CAUSE, THE// D 5a// Malcolm Boyd// **Olympic**, July 1884.

LOST CHILD, THE// F 1a// W. E. Suter// **Lyceum**, Oct. 1863, with E. Garden as Capt. Jones, Henry Widdicomb as William Jones, J. G. Shore as Chaffinch, F. Charles as Steadilad, Pauline Leclercq as Matilda Merton, Mrs. Lee as Mrs. Jones.

LOST DIAMONDS, THE// D 2a// Edward Stirling// **Olympic**, Feb. 1849, with Mr. Stuart as Darbert, Henry Compton as Vernieul, John Kinloch as Saville, William Norton as Freymn, Charles Bender as Loustall, Mrs. Stirling as Mme. Darbert, Mrs. Brougham as Mme. Vernieul, Mrs. H. J. Turner as Louise.

LOST EDEN, A// D 1a// Miss Hammond Hills// **Novelty**, June 1897, with Bernard Copping as King, Newman Maurice as Benjamin, Isa Bellington as Flora, V. St. Lawrence as Margaret.

LOST EM'LY// D 5a// Murray Wood// **Surrey**, Mar. 1873.

LOST FORTUNE, THE; OR, THE STORY OF A POCKETBOOK// D// Adolphe Faucquez// **Grecian**, July 1865, with J. B. Steele as Rolandson, John Manning as Butts, David Jones as Gordon, Walter Holland as Charles, William James as Sir William, Lizzie Mandlebert as Annie, Mary A. Victor as Carry, Marie Brewer as Amelia.

LOST HOME; OR, ALICE THE ORPHAN OF THE OLD FARM HOUSE// D 3a// Thomas Greenwood// **Sad. Wells**, Sept. 1840, with Mr. Elvin as Enfield, J. B. Hill as Falconer, J. W. Collier as Snagegrass, Mr. Williams as Glebeland, Henry Hall as Ralph, Mrs. Robert Honner as Alice/ Scenery by F. Fenton/ Machines by B. Sloman/ Music by Isaac Collins/ Prod. by R. Honner.

LOST HUSBAND, THE// D 4a// Adap. fr F// **Strand**, Apr. 1853.

LOST IN LONDON// D 3a// Watts Phillips// **Adelphi**, Apr. 1867, with Henry Ashley as Featherstone, Mr. Branscome as Sir Richard, Henry Neville as Armroyd, Paul Bedford as Longbones, J. L. Toole as Blinker, W. H. Eburne as Thomas, C. J. Smith as Tops, Miss Neilson as Nelly, Mrs. Billington as Tiddy, Miss A. Seaman as Florence/ Scenery by Messrs. Danson/ Music by Edwin Ellis/ Machines by Mr. Charker/ Gas by Mr. Bastard.

LOST IN NEW YORK// CD 5a// Leonard Grover// **Olympic**, Aug. 1896, with George Harker as Wilson, William Lee as Chester, A. B. Cross as George, Charles Edwards as Tramp, C. Stuart Johnson as Ally, Robert Escott as Dr. Arnold, Maggie Hunt as Mrs. Wilson, Lily Sinclair as Jenny, Lesley Bell as Caroline.

LOST INHERITANCE, THE; OR, THE IDIOT, THE ROUE, AND THE MISER// D 2a// n.a.// **Grecian**, Aug. 1864, with William James as de Saveuse, J. B. Steele as Malescot, J. Jackson as Bruno, Thomas Mead as Remy, John Manning as Martin, Henry Grant as Martial, Jane Dawson as Gabrielle, Mrs. Charles Dillon as Perine.

LOST LETTER, THE// F 1a// n.a.// **Princess's**, Apr. 1843, with J. S. Balls as Ardent, W. H. Oxberry as Le Beau, Augustus Harris as Scamper, Mr. Chicheley as Draft, Mrs. Anderson as Rosa, Miss Noel as Virginia; June 1860, with Henry Widdicomb as Lebeau, T. H. Higgie as Ardent, John Collett as Draft, Rose Leclercq as Virginia, Emma Wadham as Rose/ **Cov. Garden**, Dec. 1871.

LOST LOVE// D 4a// Mortimer Murdoch// **Pavilion**, Mar. 1879.

LOST ONE, THE; OR, THE LADY OF THE CAMELIAS// Adap. by Joseph Frippont fr F// **Sad. Wells**, Feb. 1865, with George Melville as Arthur, Alice Marriott as Violet, Lizzie Willmore as Fanchette, Lizzie Harrison as Amina, Ethel Somers as Mannette, Mrs. Stevenson as Marie.

LOST PARADISE, THE// Play 3a// Adap. by Henry De Mille fr G of Ludwig Fulda, Das Verloren Paradies// **Adelphi**, Dec. 1892, with Charles Warner as Maitland, Charles Dalton as Schwartz, George Cockburn as Benzel, W. L. Abingdon as Standish, W. A. Elliott as Andrew, T. B. Thalberg as Appleton, Sant Matthews as Fletcher, Howard Russell as Hyatt, Evelyn Millard as Polly, Clara Jecks as Cinders, Grace Warner as Nell, Ethel Hope as Mrs. Knowlton, Dorothy Dorr as Margaret.

LOST SHEEP, A// FC 3a// Walter Park & Arthur Shirley// **Opera Comique**, July 1892, with Arthur Wood as Duckweed, Orlando Barnett as Athanasius, Julian Cross as Capt. Rowser, G. E. Bellamy as Don Domingo, Sidney Burt as Maj. Bangs, Eardley Turner as Macgrab, Florence Tyrrell as Ada, Mrs. Beaumont Nelson as Mrs. Blacklock, Aimee Lowther as Donna Lola, Mary Mordaunt as Donna Xarfia, Henrietta

Cross as Mrs. Dedshott, Stella Brooke as Mme. Dazzle, Julia Warden as Eliza.

LOST SHIP, THE; OR, THE MAN O' WAR'S MAN AND THE PRIVATEER (alt. subt., The Sailor Buccaneers)// D 3a// W. T. Townsend// **Victoria**, Oct. 1854, with Mr. Morrison as Linden, W. H. Pitt as Martin, N. T. Hicks as Trennant, F. H. Henry as Vivian, C. H. Stephenson as Dousterswyvell, James Howard as Trim, Alfred Saville as Nibble, Mrs. Henry Vining as Ned, Miss Laporte as Sally/ **Sad. Wells**, Aug. 1863, with John Ennis as Linden, Edward Stanley as Martin, Henry Frazer as Trennant, Henry Reeves as Dunsterswyvell, G. Wilkinson as Nibble, Henry Bayley as Trim, Edward Palmer as Vivian, Marion Morton as Rose, Jessy Grey as Sally.

LOST TO THE WORLD// D Pro & 4a// Mrs. Talbot Hunter// **Marylebone**, July 1892.

LOST WIFE, THE; OR, A HUSBAND'S CONFESSION// D 3a// C. H. Hazlewood// **Britannia**, Aug. 1871.

LOST WITNESS, THE// D 4a// Henry Pettitt & Paul Meritt// **Grecian**, May 1880.

LOT No. 49// F 1a// Adap. by W. J. Fisher fr G of G. von Moser// **Gaiety**, Jan. 1888.

LOTA; OR, A MOTHER'S LOVE// D Pro & 4a// Fred Jarman// **Sadler's Wells**, Aug. 1892.

LOTTERY TICKET, THE; OR, THE LAWYER'S CLERK// C 1a// Samuel Beazley// **Drury Lane**, Jan. 1838, with W. Bennett as Capias, J. B. Buckstone as Wormwood, A. Brindal as Charles, Mrs. Charles Jones as Mrs. Corset, Mrs. Brindal as Susan; Mar. 1850, with William Davidge as Capias, W. H. Angel as Wormwood, George Everett as Charles, Mrs. Griffiths as Mrs. Corset, Clara Tellett as Susan/ **Victoria**, Mar. 1838, with William Bennett as Capias, J. B. Buckstone as Wormwood, A. Brindal as Charles, Mrs. Frank Matthews as Mrs. Corset, Mrs. Brindal as Susan/ **Sad. Wells**, Sept. 1838, with Dibdin Pitt as Capias, John Webster as Charles, Mr. Conquest as Wormwood, Miss Pincott as Susan, Miss Cooke as Mrs. Corset; June 1851, with Frank Graham as Capias, J. Williams as Charles, J. Simmonds as Wormwood, Mrs. J. Chester as Mrs. Corset, Mary A. Crisp as Susan/ **Engl. Opera House** (Lyceum), Apr. 1843, with Mr. Griffith as Capias, Samuel Emery as Wormwood, Mr. Young as Charles, Mrs. Griffith as Mrs. Corset, Mrs. Harris as Susan/ **Grecian**, Feb. 1844, with Edmund Garden as Capias, Frederick Robson as Wormwood, Edwin Dixon as Charles, Miss Merion as Mrs. Corset, Mary A. Crisp as Susan/ **Olympic**, Mar. 1863, with Horace Wigan as Capias, Walter Gordon as Charles, Frederick Robson as Wormwood, Mrs. Stephens as Mrs. Corset, Mrs. W. S. Emden as Susan/ **Princess's**, May 1871, with William Blakeley as Capias, John Renton as Wormwood, Mr. Herbert as Charles, Mrs. Leigh Murray as Mrs. Corset, Miss Hudspeth as Susan/ **Lyceum**, Feb. 1877, with Mr. Huntley as Capas, Mr. Archer as Wormwood, Mr. Carton as Charles, Mrs. Huntley as Mrs. Corset, Miss Clare as Susan.

LOTTIE// C 3a// n.a.// **Novelty**, Nov. 1884.

LOUIS XI// D 5a// Adap. by W. R. Markwell fr F of Casimir Delavigne// **Princess's**, Jan. 1855, with Charles Kean as Louis XI, Carlotta Leclercq as Dauphin, J. F. Cathcart as Nemours, Mr. Terry as D'Alby, Frank Graham as de Comines, John Ryder as Coitier, Henry Mellon as l'Hermite, James Vining as de Paule, Caroline Heath as Marie, Mrs. Winstanley as Marthe; June 1866, with Charles Kean as Louis XI, Miss Chapman as Dauphin, J. F. Cathcart as de Nemours, W. R. Robins as de Comines, George Spencer as de Dreux, Basil Potter as Coitier, George Everett as l'Hermite, J. C. Shore as de Paule, Katherine Rogers as Marie, Mrs. Charles Kean as Marthe/ **Drury Lane**, Feb. 1861, with Charles Kean as Louis XI, J. F. Cathcart as Duke de Nemours, Mr. Alton as Cardinal D'Alby, Frank Barsby as de Comines, Mr. Robinson as Count de Dreux, William Belford as Coitier, Henry Mellon as l'Hermite, Mr. Lambert as le Dain, George Everett as de Paule, Mrs. Charles Kean as Marthe, Miss N. Chapman as Marie.

LOUIS XI// D 5a// Adap. by Dion Boucicault fr F of Casimir Delavigne// **Lyceum**, Mar. 1878, with Henry Irving as Louis XI, Frank Tyars as Duke de Nemours, Mr. Collett as Cardinal D'Alby, F. Clements as de Commines, James Fernandez as Cotier, W. Bentley as l'Ermite, J. Archer as le Dain, Thomas Mead as de Paule, Walter Holland as de Lude, Edmund Lyons as Marcel, Virginia Francis as Marie, Mrs. Chippendale as Martha, Mrs. St. John as Jeanne/ Scenery by Hawes Craven/ Music by Robert Stoepel; May 1879, with Henry Irving, Arthur Wing Pinero, Alma Murray, Mrs. Chippendale; July 1901.

LOUISE; OR, THE WHITE SCARF// D 2a// H. Hall [?]// **Victoria**, Feb. 1838, with Edward Hooper as Felix, W. H. Oxberry as Andrew, Mr. Wilkins as Bernard, Mr. Loveday as Larplotte, Mr. Salter as Cainot, Mrs. Frank Matthews as Marie, Miss Lee as Susanne, Mrs. Loveday as Mme. Therese, Mrs. Hooper as Louise.

LOUISE DE LIGNOROLLES// D 3a// J. Bosworth// **Grecian**, Feb. 1854, with Eaton O'Donnell as Prince de Mire, Basil Potter as Henri de Lignorolles, Richard Phillips as de Givry, Henry Grant as Lagrange, H. R. Power as Charles, Jane Coveney as Louise de Lignorolles, Agnes De Warde as Countess de Givry, Miss Johnstone as Josephine.

LOUISE DE LIGNEROLLES; OR, A LESSON FOR HUSBANDS// D 3a// Miss Pardoe// **Adelphi**, Nov. 1838, with Frederick Yates, John Webster, Frank Matthews, O. Smith, Edmund Saville, William Cullenford, John Sanders, Mrs. Yates, Mrs. Young, Mrs. Honey.

LOUISON; OR, THE RECOMPENSE// D// W. Bayle Bernard// **Haymarket**, May 1843, with Henry Holl as Marquis de Reiulhiers, Benjamin Webster as Michel, Mr. Gallot as

Phillipe, Mr. Ennis as Antoine, Mme. Celeste as Louison, Miss Carre as Suzette, Miss C. Conner as Marie, Miss Kendall as Fanchon/ **Sad. Wells,** July 1843, with C. J. Bird as Marquis de Reiulhiers, John Webster as Michel, Mr. Lingham as Phillipe, Mr. Lambe as Antoine, Mme. Celeste as Louison, Miss Melville as Fauchon.

LOVE// Play 5a// J. Sheridan Knowles// **Cov. Garden,** Nov. 1839, with Mr. Cooper as Duke of Carinthia, Charles Selby as Prince of Milan, Charles Diddear as Count Ulrick, James Vining as Sir Rupert, Alfred Wigan as Sir Otto, Mr. Fitzjames as Sir Conrad, James Anderson as Huon, C. J. Smith as Herald, W. H. Payne as Stephen, Mrs. Brougham as The Empress, Ellen Tree as Countess of Eppenstein, Mme. Vestris as Katherine, Miss Lee as Christina, Mrs. Emden as Bertha/ Scenery by Mr. Grieve, T. Grieve, & W. Grieve/ **Sad. Wells,** July 1845, with George Bennett as Duke of Carenthia, E. Morton as Prince Frederick, Henry Mellon as Count Ulrick, Samuel Buckingham as Sir Rupert, Mr. Raymond as Sir Otto, Frank Graham as Sir Conrad, Henry Marston as Huon, Mrs. Henry Marston as The Empress, Mrs. Mary Warner as Countess of Eppenstein, Miss Cooper as Katherine, Miss Huddart as Christine, Georgiana Lebatt as Bertha/ Scenery by F. Fenton & Mr. Finlay; Sept. 1864, with W. Artaud as Duke of Carinthia, E. Foote as Prince Frederick, W. H. Drayton as Count Ulrick, George Melville as Huon, Charles Horsman as Sir Rupert, J. Mordaunt as Sir Otto, Mr. Bennett as Conrad, Mrs. Charles Horsman as The Empress, Alice Marriott as Countess of Eppenstein, Ellen Beaufort as Catherine, Lizzie Harrison as Christina/ Scenery by T. Robertson/ Machines by H. Ellis/ Music by T. Berry/ **Drury Lane,** Sept. 1856/ **Princess's,** Oct. 1862, with Henry Marston as Duke of Carinthia, Robert Cathcart as Prince Frederick, Charles Seyton as Count Ulric, J. G. Shore as Sir Rupert, Mr. Dugarde as Sir Otto, Mr. Brooke as Sir Conrad, Hermann Vezin as Huon.

LOVE A LA MODE// Charles Macklin// **Haymarket,** Aug. 1841, with Robert Maywood as Macsarcasm, J. W. Gough as Goodchild, Henry Wallack as O'Brallaghan, Frederick Vining as Groom, W. H. Oxberry as Mordecai, Miss Charles as Charlotte.

LOVE AND ART; OR, THE ARTIST'S GHOST// C 1a// Alfred Wilmot// **Novelty,** Mar. 1891, with J. G. Wilton as Sir Pompos, H. B. Clair as Durnstead, Madge Denzil as Mrs. Lestrange, Georgie Harris as Ethel, Dorothy Vernon as Smartly.

LOVE AND AVARICE// D 2a// Adap. by J. V. Bridgeman fr F// **Olympic,** June 1853, with Henry Farren as Heardall, Henry Marston as Herbert, George Cooke as Vellum, W. Shalders as Scribble, Miss Anderton as Jessie, Mrs. B. Bartlett as Margaret.

LOVE AND BE SILENT// Play 1a// Mrs. Charles Sim// **Garrick,** May 1901.

LOVE AND CHARITY// C 1a// n.a.// **Sad. Wells,** June 1854, with F. Charles as Edward, Agnes Elsworthy as Julia, Miss Parkes as Susan, Mrs. Barrett as Miss Withers.

LOVE AND CHARITY// D 1a// Mark Lemon// **Olympic,** Mar. 1840, with Mr. Halford as Amor, Mr. Ross as John, Mrs. Stirling as Julia, Phoebe, and Louis Bertrand, Mrs. Sarah Garrick as Miss Withers, Miss Stephens as Susan/ **St. James's,** Dec. 1854, with George Burt as Amor, Mr. Sidney as John, Miss Elsworthy as Julia, Phoebe, and as Louis, Mrs. Stanley as Miss Withers, Miss Robertson as Susan.

LOVE AND CRIME; OR, THE FATAL PASSION// D 3a// W. Kingdom// **Grecian,** May 1858/ **Victoria,** Feb. 1859, with John Bradshaw as De Valmont, J. H. Rickards as Mario, Frederick Byefield as Eugene, Mr. Henderson as Bernardo, George Pearce as Pierce, W. H. Pitt as de Roncourt, George Yarnold as Jerome, S. Sawford as Marcellus, John Howard as Croce, Mary Fielding as Beatrice, Angelina Bathurst as Lucretia, Mlle. Theodore as Andria, Miss Edgar as Lucetta.

LOVE AND FORTUNE// C// J. R. Planché// **Princess's,** Oct. 1859, with Louise Keeley as Love, Carlotta Leclercq as Fortune, Frank Matthews as Cassandre, Miss Clifford as Valere, Grace Darley as Leandre, Henry Saker as Arlequin and as Poltron, Robert Cathcart as Mezzetin, Rose Leclercq as Nicolas, J. G. Shore as Crispin, Helen Howard as Argentine, Emma Wadham as Diamantine, Kate Laidlaw as Nicolette/ Scenery by William Beverley.

LOVE AND HALFPENCE// C// Adap. by William Poel fr F of L. F. Clairville & Lambert Thilboust, L'Histoire d'un Sou// **St. Geo. Hall,** Jan. 1888.

LOVE AND HATE// D 2a// Horace Wigan// **Olympic,** June 1869/ **Britannia,** Apr. 1875.

LOVE AND HONOUR; OR, MONSIEUR ALPHONSE// C 3a// Trans. by Campbell Clarke fr F of Alexandre Dumas fils// **Globe,** Aug. 1875, with J. Carter-Edwards as de Montaiglin, Frank Harvey as Alphonse, H. Bennett as Reimy, C. A. Cowdery as Dieudonne, Mlle. Marie Beatrice as Raymonde, Charlotte Saunders as Mme. Guichard/ Music by M. Audibert.

LOVE AND HONOUR; OR, SOLDIERS AT HOME - HEROES ABROAD// D 3a// Adap. by J. E. Carpenter fr F of Alexandre Dumas fils, Monsieur Alphonse// **Surrey,** Nov. 1855/ **Globe,** Aug. 1875, with Mlle. Marie Beatrice, Frank Harvey, Mr. Carter-Edwards.

LOVE AND HUNGER// F 1a// J. Maddison Morton// **Adelphi,** Sept. 1859.

LOVE AND LIVERY// F 1a// n.a.// **Olympic,** Feb. 1849, with John Kinloch as Lord Sparkle, William Norton as Howard, Henry Compton as Patent, Mr. Lawrence as Thomas, Florence Gray as Violet, Mrs. H. J. Turner as Louisa.

LOVE AND LOYALTY// D 5a// William Robson//

Drury Lane, Mar. 1855, with R. H. Lingham as Lord Verney, James Ranoe as Wilderpate, Thomas Mead as Vermont, William Wallack as Marston, Frederick Belton as Fenton, Mr. Lickfold as Gamwell, Mrs. William Wallack as Juliet, Miss E. Arden as Margaret/ **Sad. Wells**, Oct. 1864, with W. H. Drayton as Lord Verney, William Artaud as Vermont, W. S. Foote as Wilderpate, George Melville as Marston, Charles Horsman as Fenton, T. B. Bennett as Gamwell, W. H. Courtley as Tremwell, William Ellerton as Anthony, John Mordaunt as Bovin, Walter Lacy as Medlicote, Alice Marriott as Juliet, Ellen Beaufort as Margaret, Maggie Campbell as Maud.

LOVE AND MONEY// D Pro & 5a// Charles Reade & Henry Pettitt// **Adelphi**, Nov. 1882, with John Ryder as Col. Clifford, J. A. Arnold as Bartley, W. R. Sutherland as Walter Clifford, A. C. Lilly as Monkton, J. W. Pigott as Fitzroy, Harry Proctor as Burnley, Harwood Cooper as Seaton, Sophie Eyre as Julia, Miss B. Farquhar as Lucy, Miss De Lacy as Rosa, Amy Roselle as Mary Bartley.

LOVE AND MURDER; OR, THE IRISHMAN IN SPAIN// F// John Brougham// **Princess's**, Oct. 1861, with John Brougham as Magra, Robert Cathcart as Don Manuel, Mr. Paulo as Don Garcia, Alfred Raymond as Don Andrea, John Collett as Don Leon, Rose Leclercq as Ninnette, Rebecca Powell as Anita, Marie Henderson as Isabella.

LOVE AND MURDER; OR, THE SCHOOL FOR SYMPATHY// C 3a// J. B. Buckstone// **Haymarket**, Aug. 1837, with J. B. Buckstone as Frigid, Robert Strickland as Col. Autumn, William Farren as Jubb, Edmund Saville as Stanly, Mrs. Nisbett as Mrs. Frigid, Miss Taylor as Emily, Mrs. Julia Glover as Mrs. Jumble, Mrs. Tayleure as Mrs. Green, Mrs. W. Clifford as Lady Teardrop, Mrs. Humby as Lappet.

LOVE AND POLITICS// C// H. T. Johnson// **Opera Comique**, Feb. 1888.

LOVE AND PRIDE// D// George Rodwell// **Adelphi**, Feb. 1843.

LOVE AND VENGEANCE; OR, THE CORSAIR AND HIS CREW// D// H. P. Grattan// **Sad. Wells**, Feb. 1843, with C. J. Bird as Hassan, Mr. Aldridge as Haroun, Henry Howe as Alcouz, Mr. Dry as Zeraldi, John Herbert as Sazan, Mr. Jones as Badour, Charles Fenton as Selim, Caroline Rankley as Hinda, Mrs. Richard Barnett as Zoda, Mrs. Andrews as Irene.

LOVE AND WAR// F 1a// R. Jephson// **Olympic**, Nov. 1842, with Mr. Fitzjames as Clapper, Mr. Halford as Wilton, Mr. Ross as Sage, Mrs. Granby as Virginia, Miss Lebatt as Philis, Miss Hamilton as Mary.

LOVE CHASE, THE// C 5a// Sheridan Knowles// **Haymarket**, Oct. 1837, with Robert Strickland as Fondlove, E. W. Elton as Master Waller, Benjamin Webster as Wildrake, Mr. Hemming as Trueworth, James Worrell as Neville, Mr. Hutchings as Humphrey, T. F. Mathews as Chargewell, Mrs. Julia Glover as Widow Green, Mrs. Nisbett as Constance, Charlotte Vandenhoff as Lydia, Mrs. Tayleure as Alice; Apr. 1847, with Louisa Nisbett; Jan. 1859, with Amy Sedgwick; July 1867, with W. H. Chippendale as Fondlove, W. H. Kendal as Master Waller, Henry Howe as Wildrake, Mr. Rogers as Trueworth, George Braid as Neville, Henry Vincent as Humphries, P. White as Chargewell, Mrs. Chippendale as Widow Green, Amy Sedgwick as Constance, Ione Burke as Lydia/ **Adelphi**, Mar. 1847, with Mr. Melbourne as Fondlove, Mr. Holmes as Master Waller, Mr. Mortimer as Trueworth, Mr. Hield as Wildrake, Mr. Harker as Neville, Charlotte Cushman as Constance, Susan Cushman as Lydia, Mrs. Banks as Widow Green/ **Princess's**, Dec. 1847, with Mr. Tilbury as Fondlove, Henry Howe as Master Waller, John Webster as Wildrake, William Creswick as Trueworth, Mrs. Julia Glover as Widow Green, Mrs. Seymour as Lydia, Louisa Nisbett as Constance, Mrs. Stanley as Alice/ **Sad. Wells**, Sept. 1849, with A. Younge as Fondlove, G. K. Dickinson as Master Waller, William Hoskins as Wildrake, Henry Marston as Trueworth, Frank Graham as Neville, William Belford as Humphreys, Charles Fenton as Lash, Edward Knight as Chargewell, Mrs. Henry Marston as Widow Green, Miss Fitzpatrick as Constance, Miss T. Bassano as Lydia, Mrs. G. Smith as Alice, Fanny Morelli as Phoebe, Mrs. Graham as Amelia/ Scenery by F. Fenton; Nov. 1855, with Mr. Barrett as Fondlove, Mr. Lunt as Trueworth, Henry Marston as Wildrake, Charles Seyton as Neville, T. C. Harris as Master Waller, Mr. Meagreson as Humphries, Mr. Lacy as Chargewell, Mrs. Henry Marston as Widow Green, Miss Fitzpatrick as Constance, Miss Rawlings as Alice, Margaret Eburne as Lydia, Miss Rose as Amelia; Apr. 1863, with James Johnstone as Fondlove, George Maynard as Master Waller, Hermann Vezin as Wildrake, Mr. Britten as Trueworth, Mr. Stalman as Lash, Mr. Norris as Chargewell, Mrs. Charles Young (Mrs. Hermann Vezin) as Constance, Miss Rawlings as Widow Green, Miss M. Fielding as Lydia, Bessie Heath as Alice, Miss Russelle as Phoebe, Miss Lucas as Amelia/ **Strand**, Jan. 1850, with Mrs. Julia Glover, Mrs. Stirling, William Farren/ **Drury Lane**, Jan. 1850, with Basil Baker as Sir William, William Montague as Master Waller, Charles Fisher as Wildrake, George Everett as Trueworth, Mr. Tyrrell as Neville, Mr. Frazer as Humphreys, Mrs. Winstanley as Widow Green, Louisa Nisbett as Constance, Fanny Huddart as Lydia/ **St. James's**, Jan. 1855, with W. Cooper as Fondlove, Mr. Herbert as Master Waller, Barry Sullivan as Wildrake, Mr. Stuart as Trueworth, Henry Rivers as Master Neville, Mr. Johnson as Master Humphreys, Mrs. Stanley as Widow Green, Mrs. Seymour as Constance, Miss Clifford as Lydia, Miss Grey as Alice; Oct. 1862, with Mr. Fitzjames as Fondlove, J. G. Shore as Master Waller, George Vining as Wildrake, Robert Cathcart as Trueworth, Mr. Brooke as Neville, Mr. Dugarde as Humphreys, Mrs. Henry Marston as Widow Green, Amy Sedgwick as Constance, Constance Aylmer as Lydia, Helen Honey as Amelia/ **Olympic**, Feb. 1879, with William Farren as Fondlove, Hermann

Vezin as Wildrake, W. Herbert as Master Waller, J. C. Buckstone as Trueworth, Mrs. Bernard Beere as Constance, Blanche Henri as Lydia, Mrs. Chippendale as Widow Green/ **Shaftesbury,** June 1891.

LOVE EXTEMPORE// F// James Kenney// **Haymarket,** Nov. 1841, with J. W. Gough as Sir Edmund, Frederick Vining as Sir Harry, David Rees as Titus, William Clark as Pax, Mrs. Stirling as Mrs. Courtney, Mrs. Stanley as Mrs. Oldstock, Priscilla Horton as Prudence, Miss Charles as Julia.

LOVE FOR LOVE// C 5a// "Adap. for representation" fr Congreve// **Drury Lane,** Nov. 1842, with Mr. Lambert as Legend, James Anderson as Valentine, Robert Keeley as Ben, Samuel Phelps as Scandal, Charles Hudson as Tattle, Henry Compton as Foresight, Charles Selby as Jeremy, W. Bennett as Trapland, Helen Faucit as Angelica, Mrs. Stirling as Mrs. Foresight, Mrs. Nisbett as Mrs. Frail/ **Haymarket,** June 1848, with Mr. Tilbury as Legend, Henry Howe as Scandal, Henry Farren as Valentine, Alfred Wigan as Tattle, Robert Keeley as Ben, William Farren as Foresight, Henry Vandenhoff as Jeremy, Miss Fortescue as Angelica, Mrs. Seymour as Mrs. Foresight, Mrs. Nisbett as Mrs. Frail, Mrs. Keeley as Miss Prue.

LOVE, LAW AND PHYSIC// F// James Kenney// **Sad. Wells,** Mar. 1855, with J. W. Ray as Dr. Camphor, William Belford as Capt. Danvers, E. Morton as Flexible, Mr. Barrett as Andrew, Mr. Maegreson as Brown, Edward Wright as Log, Eliza Travers as Mrs. Hilary, Miss Stuart as Laura.

LOVE IN A MAZE// C 5a// Dion Boucicault// **Princess's,** Mar. 1851, with Alfred Wigan as Lord Miniver, Mr. Addison as Sir Abel, Charles Kean as Col. Buckethorne, Robert Keeley as Nettletop, John Pritt Harley as Mopus, Drinkwater Meadows as Harrup, Mrs. Winstanley as Lady Aurora, Mrs. Charles Kean as Mrs. Buckethorne, Mrs. Keeley as Faith/ Scenery by Walter Gordon & F. Lloyds.

LOVE IN A SACK// F 1a// n.a.// **Haymarket,** Apr. 1844, with Robert Strickland as Quince, J. B. Buckstone as Pea, Mr. Tilbury as Tot, Mrs. Humby as Mrs. Quince, Miss Carre as Cleopatra, Mrs. Stanley as Jane.

LOVE IN A VILLAGE// C// Isaac Bickerstaff// **St. James's,** Jan. 1837, with Mr. Hollingsworth as Sir William, Mr. Bennett as Young Meadows, Robert Strickland as Woodcock, John Braham as Hawthorne, Edmund Saville as Eustace, John Pritt Harley as Hodge, Miss Rainforth as Rosetta, Miss Smith as Lucinda, Mrs. Penson as Deborah, Julia Smith as Madge/ **Princess's,** June 1845, with Mr. Granby as Eustice Woodcock, Robert Honner as Old Meadows, Mr. Allen as Young Meadows, Mr. Leffler as Hawthorn, C. E. Horn as Eustace, W. H. Oxberry as Hodge, Miss Grant as Rosetta, Miss E. Honner as Lucinda, Emma Stanley as Madge, Mrs. Fosbroke as Deborah.

LOVE IN HUMBLE LIFE// F 1a// John Howard Payne// **Olympic,** Mar. 1848, with Lysander Thompson as Ronslaus, Mr. Conquest as Carlitz, Mr. Pidgeon as Brandt, Miss Hill as Christine; Dec. 1873, with W. H. Vernon as Ronslaus, G. W. Anson as Carlitz, Marion Terry as Christine/ **Haymarket,** Aug. 1876, with Henry Howe as Ronslaus, Mr. Odell as Carlitz, Mr. Weathersby as Brandt, Maria Harris as Christine/ **Princess's,** 1878, with Howard Russell as Ronslaus, T. P. Haynes as Carlitz, Dolores Drummond as Christine.

LOVE IN IDLENESS// C 3a// L. N. Parker & Edward Goodman// **Terry's,** Oct. 1896, with Edward Terry as Pendlebury, W. E. Ashcroft as Frank, Gilbert Farquhar as Platt, Sydney Brough as Fenton, Herman de Lange as Gondinot, Hilda Rivers as Maggie, Beatrice Ferrar as Louise, Bella Pateman as Abigail, Kate Mills as Mrs. Trott, Jessie Danvers as Martha/ Scenery by Leolyn Hart/ Prod. by Edward Terry.

LOVE IN LIVERY// F 1a// J. P. Wooler// **Princess's,** May 1845, with Walter Lacy as Lord Sparkle, Augustus Harris as Howard, Henry Compton as Patent, T. Hill as Thomas, Mr. Franks as James, Emma Stanley as Countess Violet, Miss E. Honner as Louise, Miss Somers as Mary.

LOVE IN TANDEM// C 3a// Adap. by Augustin Daly fr F of Bocage & Decourcy, La Vie à Deux// **Daly's,** July 1893, with James Lewis as Skinastone, George Clarke as Littlejohn, Arthur Bourchier as Dymond, Herbert Gresham as Packer, William Greet as Barry, Thomas Bridgland as van Grooge, John Craig as Young Bristow, Herbert Bosworth as Pitthammer, Rankin Duval as Fiddley, Ada Rehan as Aprilla, Mrs. G. H. Gilbert as Countess Alticheff, Isabel Irving as Tetty, Violet Vanbrugh as Mme. Lauretta, Lucie Cleste as Mme. Rosareina, Florence Conron as Nadege, Olive Barry as Mrs. van Grooge.

LOVE IN THE EAST; OR, THE VOWS OF AUGUSTUS PORTARLINGTON AND CELESTINA BEVERLEY (see Tommy and Sally)

LOVE IS BLIND// C 2a// G. A. à Beckett// **St. James's,** Jan. 1837, with Edmund Saville as Sir Charles, Morris Barnett as Thistle, Mr. Hollingsworth as Claw, Julia Smith as Susan, Miss Allison as Mary, Miss Smith as Kitty, Mrs. Penson as Mrs. Dumps.

LOVE KNOT, THE// C 3a// J. Stirling Coyne// **Drury Lane,** Mar. 1858, with Robert Roxby as Lord George, Mr. Tilbury as Sir Croesus, John Kinloch as Wormley, Leigh Murray as Bernard, Mrs. Leigh Murray as Lady Lavender, Mrs. Frank Matthews as Lady Harbottle, Miss M. Oliver as Marian, Miss Innes as Ninette, Miss M. Barnes as Barbara.

LOVE LAUGHS AT LOCKSMITHS// F 2a// George Colman the younger// **Grecian,** Oct. 1847, with Richard Phillips as Capt. Beldare, John Webster as Risk, Mr. Baldwin as Vigil, Eaton O'Donnell as Totterton, Frederick Robson as Solomon Lob, Annette Mears as Lydia.

LOVE LETTER, A// D 1a// Mrs. E. Lonergan// **Strand**, May 1894, with Graham Wentworth as Capt. Damborough, Vincent Flexmore as John, Mary Stuart as Lady Torchester, Clara Greet as Hetty, Ethel Selwyn as Nurse.

LOVE LOCK, THE// D pro & 3a// H. F. Chorley// **Olympic**, Feb. 1854, with Samuel Emery as Mammon, Frederick Robson as Hardtmann, Alfred Wigan as Weinhart, J. H. White as Jacob, Priscilla Horton as Rose.

LOVE MAKES THE MAN// C// Colly Cibber// **Sad. Wells**, Sept. 1853, with Mr. Lunt as Governor, William Belford as Don Duart, Mr. Barrett as Don Antonio, J. W. Ray as Don Lewis, Henry Marston as Carlos, William Hoskins as Clodio, Miss Cooper as Angelina, Eliza Travers as Louisa, Mrs. Ternan as Elvira, Miss F. Younge as Honoria, Miss Lambe as Isabella.

LOVE ON CRUTCHES// C 3a// Adap. by Augustin Daly fr G of Heinrich Stobitzer// **Comedy**, July 1896, with Charles Richman as Austen, Sidney Herbert as Roverley, James Lewis as Quattles, Herbert Gresham as Bitteredge, William Haseltine as Podd, Robert Shephard as Bells, Ada Rehan as Annie, Mrs. G. H. Gilbert as Eudoxia, Sybil Carlisle as Mrs. Gwynn.

LOVE OR LIFE// D 3a// Dram. by Tom Taylor & Paul Merritt fr tale of Crabbe// **Olympic**, June 1878, with Johnston Forbes Robertson as Lockwood, Henry Neville as Richard Oakley, John Billington as John Oakley, G. W. Anson as Foxcote, Robert Pateman as Molesworth, Charles Flockton as Midhurst, George Yarnold as Rattenbury, J. G. Bauer as Harris, Mrs. Dion Boucicault as Hester, Kate Phillips as Bessien/ Scenery by Walter Hann.

LOVE STORY, THE// Play 4a// Pierre Leclercq// **Strand**, May 1888.

LOVE TEST, THE// C 1a// Walter Leslie // **Gaiety**, June 1873.

LOVE, THE MAGICIAN// Play 3a// Josephine Rae & Thomas Sidney// **Shaftesbury**, July 1892, with Frank Gillmore as Garth, Philip Cunningham as Crawford, Albert Bernard as Potts, Lawrance d'Orsay as Ferroll, H. T. Edgar as Brisetout, Fred Knight as Chetwoode, Irene Hayward as Hester, Esme Waldon as Lilith, Fanny Robertson as Mrs. Davisson, Marjorie Christmas as Lena, Florence Friend as Mary.

LOVE VERSUS LAW// D// n.a.// **Princess's**, Dec. 1862.

LOVE WINS// C 3a// Savile Clarke & H. F. du Terreaux// **Surrey**, May 1877.

LOVE WINS THE DAY// D 3a// Edward Towers// **Pavilion**, July 1879.

LOVE WISELY; OR, THE SETTING OF THE SUN// Charles Hannan// **Avenue**, Apr. 1898, with Victor Widdicombe as Rev. Moorfield, Edward Ferris as Lane, Alice Beet as Janet, Zeffie Tilbury as Lucy.

LOVER BY PROXY, A// F 1a// Dion Boucicault// **Haymarket**, Apr. 1842, with Benjamin Webster as Lawless, Mr. Tilbury as Bromley, Henry Howe as Blushington, Henry Widdicomb as Nibbs, Mrs. W. Clifford as Penelope, Miss Charles as Kate, Miss C. Conner as Harriet/ **Olympic**, Mar. 1849, with Henry Farren as Lawless, H. J. Turner as Bromley, C. Hale as Squibb, Mr. Norton as Blushington, Harwood Cooper as Nibbs, Mrs. Young as Penelope, Miss De Burgh as Kate, Miss Adams as Harriet/ **Sad. Wells**, Mar. 1862, with William Belford as Lawless, Mr. Smith as Bromley, Thomas Mowbray as Blushington, Lewis Ball as Squib, C. Dixon as Nibbs, Miss Rawlings as Penelope, Ada Dyas as Kate, Miss Mason as Harriet.

LOVERS IN ALL CORNERS// F 1a// n.a.// **Grecian**, Aug. 1861, with George Gillett as Moreland, Mr. Jackson as Quake, John Manning as Simon, R. H. Lingham as Capt. Bolding, Mr. Bell as Smart, Laura Conquest as Sophia, Helen Hale as Lucretia, Lucreza Hill as Rose.

LOVERS OF ALL SORTS; OR, THE ROMP, THE PRUDE, AND THE CHAMBERMAID// C// n.a.// **Sad. Wells**, Nov. 1837, with S. Palmer as Bolding, C. H. Pitt as Charles, Mr. Pateman as Smart, Mr. Gay as Quake, Mr. Rogers as Simon, Lavinia Melville as Sophia, Miss Williams as Lucretia, Miss Vernon as Rose.

LOVERS' QUARRELS; OR, LIKE MASTER LIKE MAN// F// Alt. fr Sir John Vanbrugh, The Mistake// **Sad. Wells**, Nov. 1841, with John Herbert as Don Carlos, Miss Richardson as Donnora, Mrs. Richard Barnett as Jacintha/ **St. James's**, Feb. 1868, with Mr. Holman as Don Carlos, Mr. Maskell as Sancho, Thomas Bridgeford as Lopez, Eleanore Bufton as Donna Leonora, Miss N. Nisbett as Jacintha.

LOVE'S ALARMS// C 1a// Charles Rae// **Royalty**, Jan. 1878.

LOVE'S ANGUISH// D 4a// Adap. by Oscar Schow fr F// **Adelphi**, May 1882.

LOVE'S ANNOYANCES// F 1a// n.a.// **Astley's**, Nov. 1850, with N. T. Hicks as Don Carlos, Thomas Barry as Sancho, Mr. Crowther as Lopez, Mrs. Moreton Brookes as Leonora, Mrs. Beacham as Jacintha.

LOVE'S COMPACK [sic]**; OR, THE DEATH PLEDGE**// D 3a// n.a.// **Victoria** May 1848, with John Bradshaw as Barton, E. Edwards as Lester, J. T. Johnson as Cameron, G. F. Forman as Puff, Mr. Hitchinson as Startem, Annette Vincent as Henriette, Mrs. Cooke as Susannah, Walter Searle as Dr. Machionelli, J. Howard as Benedetto, Mr. Hawkins as Roselio, Mrs. George Lee as Giannella, Julia Seaman as Clara.

LOVE'S CROSSES// C 1a// J. T. Day// **Olympic**, Aug. 1881, with David Gaunt, Henry Bennett, Ida Courtenay.

LOVE'S DISGUISES; OR, THE MOB CAP// D 2a// Howard Paul// **Drury Lane**, Apr. 1853/ **Sad. Wells**, Mar. 1867, with J. W. Lawrence as Tweezer, J. Collier as Capt. Trivet, John Rouse as Wigler, Alice Marriott as Miss Marchmont, Grace Edgar as Clipper.

LOVE'S DOCTOR// D 2a// Andrew Halliday// **Royalty**, Jan. 1870.

LOVE'S FRAILTIES; OR, PASSION AND REPENTENCE// D 2a// John Stafford// **Victoria**, Mar. 1838, with John Parry as Belgrade, W. H. Oxberry as John, William Davidge as Greenwell, Mr. Rayner as Lubin, Mr. Harwood as Michael, Miss E. Lee as Susan, Mrs. Frank Matthews as Jessy, Miss Wilson as Betty/ **Haymarket**, June 1838, with James Worrell as Squire Belgrade, Mr. Hutchings as John, Mr. Rayner as Lubin, J. W. Gough as Old Greenwell, T. F. Mathews as Bumblebee, Mrs. Fitzwilliam as Susan, Miss Gallot as Jessy, Mrs. Gallot as Dame Morton, Miss Beresford as Betty/ **Sad. Wells**, Aug. 1840, with Mr. Elvin as Belgrade, Mr. Aldridge as Old Greenwell, Mr. Rayner as Lubin, Mr. Richardson as Bumblebee, Mrs. Robert Honner as Susan, Mrs. J. F. Saville as Jessy, Miss Cooke as Dame Morton, Mrs. Richard Barnett as Betty.

LOVE'S LABOUR'S LOST// C// William Shakespeare// **Cov. Garden**, Sept. 1839, with Mr. Cooper as Ferdinand, James Anderson as Biron, Mr. Fitzjames as Longaville, James Vining as Dumain, Frank Matthews as Boyet, W. H. Payne as Mercade, John Pritt Harley as Don Adriano, Drinkwater Meadows as Sir Nathaniel, George Bartley as Holofernes, Mr. Granby as Dull, Robert Keeley as Costard, Miss Lee as Moth, Louisa Nisbett as Princess of France, Mme. Vestris as Rosaline, Miss E. Phillips as Maria, Miss Charles as Katherine, Mrs. Humby as Jaquenetta, Miss Rainforth as Ver/ **Sadler's Wells**, Sept. 1857, with Frederic Robinson as King Ferdinand, Henry Marston as Biron, William Belford as Longaville, Mr. Haywell as Dumain, J. W. Ray as Boyet, James Lickfold as Mercada, Samuel Phelps as Don Adriano, Charles Fenton as Sir Nathaniel, Lewis Ball as Gostard, Mrs. Charles Young as Princess of France, Miss Fitzpatrick as Rosaline, Caroline Parkes as Maria, Miss Rawlings as Katherine, Eliza Travers as Jaquenetta/ Scenery by Charles James/ Machines by Mr. Cawdery.

LOVE'S LABYRINTH// F 1a// W. S. Emden// **St. James's**, June 1865, with Frederic Robinson as Col. Ormond, Gaston Murray as Melton, H. J. Montague as Capt. Vernon, Eleanor Bufton as Miss Belford.

LOVE'S MARTYR// D 4a// Leicester Buckingham// **Olympic**, Apr. 1866, with Henry Neville as Evelyn, Robert Soutar as Mordant, George Vincent as Ryland, H. J. Montague as Sir Charles, Horace Wigan as Trevelyan, W. H. Stephens as Winwood, Kate Terry as Edith, Mrs. St. Henry as Lady Flora, Miss Elton as Marion, Miss H. Everard as Cordelia, Mrs. Stephens as Mrs. Spriggins/ Scenery by Hawes Craven/ Music by J. H. Tully/ Prod. by Horace Wigan/ **Criterion**, July 1886, with H. B. Conway, Fred Emery, Dorothy Dene, Miss F. Paget.

LOVE'S MARTYRDOM// D// John Saunders// **Haymarket**, June 1855.

LOVE'S MARTYRDOM// T 1a// Alfred Calmour// **Criterion**, July 1886.

LOVE'S MESSENGER// Play 1a// A. C. Calmour// **Novelty**, July 1884, with F. H. Macklin, Kate Rorke.

LOVE'S ORDEAL; OR, THE OLD AND NEW REGIME// D 5a// Edmund Falconer// **Drury Lane**, May 1865, with Walter Lacy as Duc de Chartreux, Henry Sinclair as Vicomte Lauzan, J. Neville as Comte d'Ostanges, Edmund Falconer as Robespierre, Edmund Phelps as de Morny, Alfred Rayner as Laverennes, Mr. Fitzjames as Sangfroid, George Belmore as Joconde, Mrs. Henry Vandenhoff as Comtesse d'Ostanges, Mrs. Hermann Vezin (Mrs. Charles Young) as Hortense, Rose Leclercq as Emelie, Miss C. Weston as Jeannette.

LOVE'S SACRIFICE; OR, THE RIVAL MERCHANTS// D 5a// G. W. Lovell// **Cov. Garden**, Sept. 1842, with George Vandenhoff as Aylmer, Mr. Cooper as Lafont, Charles Pitt as de Lorme, Walter Lacy as St. Lo, Alfred Wigan as Morluc, W. H. Payne as Du Viray, Charles Diddear as Friar Dominic, Drinkwater Meadows as Rusé, Miss Vandenhoff as Margaret, Mrs. Walter Lacy as Herminie, Mrs. Orger as Manou, Mrs. Humby as Jenny/ Scenery by Grieve, T. Grieve & W. Grieve/ **Sad. Wells**, Aug. 1846, with William Creswick as Aylmer, George Bennett as Lafont, William Hoskins as de Lorme, Henry Marston as St. Lo, Henry Mellon as Friar Dominic, Miss Cooper as Margaret, Mrs. Brougham as Herminie, Mrs. Henry Marston as Manou, Miss St. George as Jenny/ Scenery by F. Fenton & Mr. Finlay/ **Marylebone**, Mar. 1848, with Mrs. Mary Warner, Fanny Vining/ **Olympic**, June 1881, with Thomas Swinbourne as Elmore, E. F. Edgar as Lafont, Robert Mantell as Eugene de Lorme, J. H. Barnes as St. Lo, John Ryder as Friar Dominick, Stanislaus Calhaem as Ruse, E. T. Webber as Morluc, H. Hamilton as Du Viray, Miss Wallis as Margaret, Josephine St. Ange as Herminie, Miss Hudspeth as Jeannie, Mrs. R. Power as Manou.

LOVE'S SECRET// C 1a// J. R. Brown// **Haymarket**, Feb. 1886, with F. Gerard as Davenant, Arthur Darwin as Luttrell, Forbes Dawson as Matineau, Miss Norreys as Violet, Mrs. E. H. Brooke as Miss Morant.

LOVE'S TELEGRAPH// C 3a// Adap. fr F, Le Gant et l'Eventail// **Princess's**, Oct. 1846, with James Vining as Prince of Heinalt, C. J. Mathews as de Solberg, Henry Compton as Baron Pumpernickle, Mme. Vestris as Princess Blanche, Mrs. H. Highes as Alice, Emma Stanley as Marguerite; Oct. 1859, with Mrs. Charles Young, Kate Saville, Harcourt Bland.

LOVE'S VICTORY// D 3a// Thompson Townsend// **Grecian**, Mar. 1854, with Basil

Potter as Count de Preval, T. Roberts as Henri, Eaton O'Donnell as Jacques, Richard Phillips as Morin, Charles Rice as Narcissus, Jane Coveney as Blanche, Harriet Coveney as Mme. Susette, Miss Johnstone as Baroness de Courcy, Ellen Crisp as Mme. Dumas.

LOVE'S YOUNG DREAM// Play 1a// Eva Bright// **Strand**, Apr. 1891, with Acton Bond as Sir Geoffrey, Frederick Jacques as George, Amy McNeil as Edith, Florence Bright as Iris, Mrs. E. H. Brooke as Anne.

LOVER'S AMAZEMENT, THE// Leigh Hunt// **Lyceum**, Jan. 1858, with Charles Dillon, Mrs. Dillon, Sarah Woolgar, J. G. Shore.

LOVERS AT PLAY// n.a.// **Strand**, May 1856.

LOVING CUP, THE// C 2a// Andrew Halliday// **Royalty**, Nov. 1868.

LOVING HEARTS// C 3a// G. F. Neville// **Strand**, May 1870.

LOVING LEGACY, A// FC 3a// F. W. Sidney// **Strand**, Mar. 1895, with William Day as Kingsley, Oswald Yorke as Pomeroy, Alfred Maltby as Bird, Mark Kinghorne as Terence, J. A. Rosier as El Tebkir, Lizzie Henderson as Mrs. O'Rourke, May Whitty as Kitty, Nancy Noel as May/ Scenery by W. T. Hemsley.

LOVING WOMAN, THE// Play 3a// Mark Lemon// **Haymarket**, Dec. 1849, with Henry Howe as Wielfort, Charles Kean as Rosen, James Wallack as Hermann, Henry Vandenhoff as Max, Mr. Rogers as Groshen, Mrs. Charles Kean as Ottillia, Mrs. Caulfield as Martha/ Scenery by Mr. Johnstone & George Morris/ Machines by F. Heselton.

LOW WATER// C 3a// Arthur Wing Pinero// **Globe**, Jan. 1884, with Charles Cartwright as Lord George Ormolu, J. F. Young as Linklater, E. Hamilton Bell as Josey, J. L. Shine as Smallpage, Charles Smily as de Montfallet, Frank Evans as Charlesworthy, Harry Leigh as Medwin, E. W. Gardiner as Skilliter, Miss Compton as Anne, Miss Abington (Mrs. J. H. Barnes) as Rosamond, Maria Daly as Miss Butterworth.

LOWTHER ARCADE// F 1a// C. W. Brooks// **Lyceum**, Mar. 1845, with Charles Bender as Mornington, Mr. Bellingham as Capt. Mornington, Mr. Turner as Barnacle, Drinkwater Meadows as Premium, Robert Keeley as Bonus, Miss Dawson as Emma.

LOYAL// Play 1a// H. T. Johnson// **Vaudeville**, Sept. 1894, with Frederick Volpé as Col. Clulow, Thomas Kingston as Charles II, Arthur Helmore as Portsoken, T. A. Palmer as Sgt. Joel, Esmé Beringer as Lilian, Alice Beet as Cicely.

LOYAL LOVE// Play 4a// Ross Neil// **Gaiety**, Aug. 1887.

LOYAL LOVERS// C 4a// Adap. by C. Carick & A. F. Guibal fr F, Le Voyage de M. Perrichon// **Vaudeville**, Dec. 1885.

LOYAL TRAITOR, A// Play 1a// Beatrix De Burgh// **St. James's**, May 1900, with Helen Ferrers as Deborah, Winifred Emery as Esther, Sydney Valentine as Oliver Cromwell.

LOYALTY// CD 3a// H. P. Lyste// **Criterion**, Mar. 1876.

LUCILLE, A TALE OF THE HEART (also subt. The Story of a Heart)// D 3a// W. Bayle Bernard// **Victoria**, Oct. 1837, with Mr. Green as St. Cyr, Mr. Loveday as Vernet, John Parry as Dubois, L. Smith as Le Kain, W. H. Oxberry as Schuyp, Mrs. Hooper as Lucille, Mrs. Frank Matthews as Julie, William Davidge as Von Metz, Mr. Salter as Michael, Mr. Harwood as Clutz/ **Marylebone**, July 1848, with Robert & Mrs. Keeley/ **Olympic**, Oct. 1848, with Samuel Emery as St. Cyr and De Vavasour, Mr. Norton as Le Kain, H. J. Turner as Vernet, Frederick Vining as Dubious, Henry Compton as Schuyp, Mrs. Stirling as Lucille, Julia St. George as Julie, Charles Bender as Michael, Harwood Cooper as Clootz; May 1852, with Henry Farren as St. Cyr and De Vavasour, Charles Diddear as Vernet, John Kinloch as Le Kain, Mr. Clifton as Dubois, Mr. Edgar as Schuypt, Louisa Howard as Lucille, Miss Fielding as Julie and Mrs. Schuyp, C. Cooke as Von Metz, Alfred Sanger as Capt. de Lorme/ **Sad. Wells**, May 1854, with C. Poynter as Verney, F. Charles as Dubois, George Yarnold as Schuyp, Edwin Villiers as St. Cyr, Samuel Perfitt as Le Kain, Mr. Barrett as Von Ritz, Mr. Collier as Michel, Emily Norton as Lucille, Miss Lavine as Julie.

LUCK// C// Claude Templar// **Imperial**, Nov. 1870.

LUCK, OR A STORY OF PASTORAL LIFE// D// John Levey// **Britannia**, July 1869.

LUCK OF LIFE, THE// D 5a// J. K. Murray// **Standard**, Aug. 1898.

LUCKY DOG, A// C 1a// n.a.// **Sad. Wells**, May 1837, with John Ayliffe as Count Benini, Mr. King as Count Caliari, Thomas Lee as O'Rafferty, Mr. Scarbrow as Lupo, Mr. George as Malvolo, Mrs. Harris as Countess Viteria, Lavinia Melville as Ganette.

LUCKY DOG, A// F 3a// Walter Sapte Jr.// **Strand**, July 1892/ **Terry's**, Oct. 1892, with G. W. Anson as Woodcock, John Tresahar as Winyard, Lawrance d'Orsay as Jones, Charles Fawcett as Lucas, F. Hamilton Knight as Wiggs, Frederick Thorne as Barrable, Helen Forsyth as Marion, Mrs. George Canninge as Letitia, Eveline Faulkner as Jane, Rose Norreys as Atalanta.

LUCKY ESCAPE, A// C 1a// C. S. Cheltenham// **Strand**, Sept. 1861.

LUCKY FRIDAY, A// F 1a// Alfred Wigan// **Princess's**, May 1852, with Alfred Wigan as Raimbaut, Mr. Addison as Sharpe, Drinkwater Meadows as Joe, Hermann Vezin as Stapleton, John Chester as Hardnam, Mrs. John Chester as Bessie/ **Adelphi**, Feb. 1853, with Alfred Wigan as Raimbaut, John Parselle, C. J. Smith,

William Cullenford, James Rogers, Fanny Maskell/ **Olympic,** Mar. 1855, with Alfred Wigan as Raimbaut, E. Clifton as Joe Sharpe, Samuel Emery as Sharpe, Mr. Leslie as Stapleton, Miss Maskell as Bessie.

LUCKY HIT, A// C 1a// Edward Stirling// **Drury Lane,** Feb. 1858, with Miss M. Oliver as Duc D'Anjou, Mr. Tilbury as Villeblanche, John Kinloch as de Castagnac, Robert Roxby as la Tour, Mrs. Leigh Murray as Baroness de Villeblanche.

LUCKY HIT, A// C 1a// Howard Paul// **Sad. Wells,** June 1854, with Mr. Barrett as Baron de Ragone, E. L. Davenport as Chevalier Vilbrise, Fanny Vining as Marchioness de l'Espalier/ **Princess's,** May 1866, with Henry Mellon as Baron Bergonce, J. G. Shore as Vilbrac, Mr. Tressider as Nykon, Katherine Rogers as Marchioness de L'Espalier.

LUCKY HORSE SHOE, THE; OR, THE LONE CHAMBER OF THE SILENT HIGHWAY (also subt. Woman's Trials)// D 3a// Thomas Parry// **Drury Lane,** Nov. 1839/ **Victoria,** Mar 1842, with Mr. Griffiths as Col. Marchmont, John Dale as Graylingford, William Seaman as Frankton, E. F. Saville as Ruff, Mr. Howard as Gianini, C. Williams as Probyn, John Gardner as Hammer, Annette Vincent as Ellen, Miss Coveney as Kitty, Mrs. Seaman as Martha/ Scenery by Fenton & Morelli/ Music by W. J. Hill/ Prod. by E. F. Saville/ **Grecian,** July 1861, with Henry Grant as Graylingford, Mr. Jackson as Col. Marchmont, R. H. Lingham as Frankton, Henry Power as Barwell, J. B. Howe as Robert Ruff, John Manning as Hammer, Walter Holland as Trolign, Mr. Smithson as Glanino, Jane Coveney as Ellen, Lucreza Hill as Kitty, Miss Wieland as Betsy.

LUCKY SHILLING, THE// D 5a// n.a.// **Standard,** Feb. 1888.

LUCKY STAR, THE// D 4a// George Comer// **Elephant & Castle,** May 1889/ **Novelty,** Feb. 1896, with W. Robertson Foulis as Widdrington, Arthur Percy as Sir Richard, Herbert Princep as Esdaile, Reginald Vernon as Col. Ashmore, Sidney Proffit as Corp. Sharpe, Cecil Morand as Doyle, Emma Rainbow as Constance, Wanda Zaleska as Phoebe, Mabel Moore as Sally.

LUCKY STONE, THE// D// n.a.// **Britannia,** July 1877.

LUCREZIA BORGIA// D// Adap. by Frederick Belton fr F of Victor Hugo// **Standard,** Mar. 1859, with Mrs. W. C. Forbes/ **Sad. Wells,** Feb. 1866 (1n 3a), with E. H. Brooke as Don Alphonso, David Jones as Gennaro, James Johnstone as Gubetta, G. W. Warde as Orsini, Mr. Murray as Liveratto, Samuel Perfitt as Don Apostolo, Mr. Byrne as Vitellozo, Mr. Edwin as Petrucca, Alice Marriott as Lucretia, Miss Leigh as Princess Negroni/ **Sad. Wells,** Nov. 1871.

LUCREZIA BORGIA// D 4a// Adap. by William Young fr F of Victor Hugo// **Lyceum,** Aug. 1879, with J. H. Barnes as Alfonso, W. Herbert as Gennaro, Johnston Forbes Robertson as Orsini, J. Bradley as Liverotto, A. Andrews as Petrucci, Alfred Tapping as Vitelozzo, Ian Frank as Gazella, William McIntyre as Gubetta, J. Harwood as Rustighello, Genevieve Ward as Lucrezia Borgia, Miss Roland Phillips as Countess Negroni/ Scenery by Hawes Craven/ Music by Hamilton Clarke.

LUCY BRANDON// D 5a// Dram. by Robert Buchanan fr novel of Edward Bulwer-Lytton, Paul Clifford// **Imperial,** Apr. 1882, with James Elmore, Mrs. Chippendale, David Fisher, William Rignold, Harriet Jay.

LUCY GRAHAM// D 3a// n.a.// **Grecian,** Jan. 1855, with Basil Potter as Graham, Henry Grant as Smith, Mr. Marlow as Shanks, Richard Phillips as Faulkner, F. Charles as Trevor, Henry Power as Bawling Jack, Eaton O'Donnell as Phillipson, John Manning as Honeysuckle, Jane Coveney as Lucy, Harriet Coveney as Tattle.

LUCY HATTON// D// n.a.// **Marylebone,** Nov. 1863.

LUCY WOODBINE; OR, MURDER AT THE FOUR CROSS ROADS// D// n.a.// **Victoria,** Dec, 1860, with W. H. Pitt as Graham, Frederick Byefield as Sir John, Mr. Hitchinson as Barnes, George Pearce as Groves, N. Harrison as Hope, Mr. Henderson as Mowbray, W. Harmer as Burnley, Watty Brunton as Bristles, W. Schofield as Martin, John Bradshaw as Bill, Mrs. E. F. Saville as Lucy, Miss Glanville as Dame Woodbine, Mrs. F. Lauri as Betty, Lydia Pearce as Dolly.

LUGARTO THE MULATTO// D 4a// Charles O'Bryan// **Surrey,** May 1850.

LUKE THE LABOURER; OR, THE LOST SON// D 2a// J. B. Buckstone// **Haymarket,** Nov. 1837, with Benjamin Webster as Luke, Mr. Hutchings as Chase, J. W. Gough as Wakefield, T. P. Cooke as Philip, Mr. Worrell as Charles, Robert Strickland as Michael, J. B. Buckstone as Bobby Trot, Mrs. Tayleure as Dame, Miss Beresford as Clara, Mrs. Humby as Jenny/ **Sad. Wells,** Mar. 1839, with Mr. Cathcart as Luke, Dibdin Pitt as Wakefield, W. D. Broadfoot as Mike, Robert Honner as Phillip, Mr. Dry as Maydew, Mr. Elvin as Squire Chase, Mr. Conquest as Trot, Miss Cooke as Dame Wakefield, Mrs. J. F. Saville as Clara, Miss Pincott as Jenny; Dec. 1853, with William Belford as Squire Chase, Mr. Josephs as Wakefield, Wybert Rousby as Maydew, Mr. Lyon as Luke, T. P. Cooke as Phillip, Lewis Ball as Trot, William Searle as Mike, Miss Young as Dame Wakefield, Miss Wyatt as Clara, Eliza Travers as Jenny; July 1863, with T. W. Neale as Luke, Edmund Phelps as Philip, Kate Stonor as Clara, Minnie Davis as Jenny, E. R. Archer as Squire Chase, J. Johnson as Wakefield, J. Barnes as Dick, G. Clementson as Mayden, T. B. Bennett as Michael, Miss Rogers as Dame Wakefield.

LURED TO RUIN; OR, A HERO OF HEROES//

D 5a// J. W. Whitbread// **Britannia**, July 1892.

LYING IN ORDINARY// F 1a// J. B. Peake// **Engl. Opera House** (Lyceum), July 1838, with Mr. Baker as Adm. Fluke, Mr. Halford as Woodburn, A. Brindal as Achilles Aufait, W. Bennett as Peter Yarn, Mr. Wieland as Patrick, Mr. Turnour as Dominico, Mme. Simon as Miss Fluke, Miss Barnett as Hannah.

LYONS MAIL, THE// D 3a// Adap. by Charles Reade fr F of Emile Moreau, Paul Siraudin, & A. C. Delacour, Le Courier de Lyon// **Princess's**, June 1854/ **Lyceum**, May 1877, with Henry Irving as Joseph Lesurques and as Dubosc, Thomas Mead as Jerome, E. H. Brooke as Didier, Lydia Howard as Joliquet, Frank Tyars as Dorval, Virginia Francis as Julie, Isabel Bateman as Jeanette/ Scenery by Hawes Craven/ Music by Robert Stoepel.

LYRICAL LOVER, A// C 1a// H. S. Clarke// **Imperial**, Mar. 1881.

*

M.P// C 4a// T. W. Robertson// **POW**, Apr. 1870, with Squire Bancroft, Mrs. Bancroft, Carlotta Addison/ **Toole's**, July 1883, with A. Beaumont, E. D. Ward, Cora Stuart, Alice Thurston.

M.P. FOR PUDDLEPOOL; OR, THE BOROUGH ELECTION// F// Knight Summers// **Sad. Wells**, Nov. 1868, with Mr. Horton as Lord Hustings, W. H. Abel as Snapper, L. Smythe as Sir Frothy, J. H. Loome as Quintescence, Richard Edgar as Fleece, Miss Logan as Miss Hustings.

M.P. FOR THE ROTTEN BOROUGH// F 1a// Mark Lemon// **Eng. Opera House** (Lyceum), July 1838, with Henry Compton as Jerry, W. Bennett as Schemer, A. Brindal as Niceman, Mr. Turnour as Dabbs, Mr. Halford as Stubbs, Miss Poole as Peggy, Mrs. Allcroft as Miss Schemer/ **Sad. Wells**, Apr. 1850, with Mr. Williams as Schemer, Charles Fenton as Niceman, William Hoskins as Jerry, William Belford as Stubbs, Mr. Harris as Noteall, Mr. Wilkins as Dabbs, Miss Johnson as Miss Schemer, Miss A. Brown as Peggy, Fanny Morelli as Betty.

M.P.'S WIFE, AN// Play 4a// Dram. fr novel of Tenell, A Woman of Heart// **Opera Comique**, Feb. 1895, with William Herbert as Armytage, Frederic de Lara as Sir Richard, Rothbury Evans as Everard, Percy Bell as Sparrow, J. H. Batson as Jephson, Edward Rochelle as Venables, Charles Glenny as Fenwick, Alexis Leighton as Lady Calcott, Alice Dukes as Lucy, Ina Goldsmith as Rose, Dorothy Lawson as Elise.

MABEL// D 3a// Frederick Hay// **Olympic**, Oct. 1880, with David Fisher as Philip Fleetwood, Arthur Dacre as Leonard Fleetwood, W. H. Vernon as Gainsford, G. W. Anson as Redmund, Fred Moreland as Dawdell, Carlotta Leclercq as Mrs. Fleetwood, Carlotta Addison as Mabel, Bella Power as Susan, Fanny Thorne as Jane/ Scenery by W. Hann.

MABEL LAKE// D 3a// C. H. Hazlewood// **Britannia**, Feb. 1873.

MABEL'S CURSE// D 2a// Mrs. S. C. Hall// **St. James's**, Mar. 1837, with Mr. Hollingsworth as Burney, Mr. Bennett as Cleveland, John Pritt Harley as Flint, Mr. Halford as Brown, Miss C. Crisp as Caroline, Priscilla Horton as Annie, Miss Allison as Mad Mabel/ Music by Mrs. G. A. à Beckett.

MABEL'S LIFE; OR, A BITTER BARGAIN// D 4a// H. J. Byron// **Adelphi**, Nov. 1872.

MACBETH// T// William Shakespeare// **Cov. Garden**, Jan. 1837, with Mr. Thompson as Duncan, Mr. Roberts as Malcolm, W. C. Macready as Macbeth, John Pritchard as Macduff, George Bennett as Banquo, Mr. Harris as Lennox, John Webster as Ross, Mrs. W. West as Lady Macbeth, Mr. Ransford as Hecate/ Music of Matthew Locke; Jan. 1845, with Mr. Archer as Duncan, Mr. Bellingham as Malcolm, Henry Betty as Macbeth, James Vining as Macduff, Mr. Hield as Banquo, George Braid as Rosse, Mr. Lee as Lennox, Mr. Furtado as Hecate, Miss Vandenhoff as Lady Macbeth, Mrs. J. Cooke as Gentlewoman/ **Drury Lane**, Feb. 1837, with Charles Diddear as Duncan, A. Brindal as Malcolm, Mr. Baker as Lenox, Edwin Forrest as Macbeth, Mr. Cooper as Banquo, Mr. Warde as Macduff, Mr. Mathews as Rosse, Mr. Seguin as Hecate, Miss Huddart as Lady Macbeth; June 1843, with Mr. Waldron as Duncan, Frank Graham as Malcolm, W. C. Macready as Macbeth, James Anderson as Banquo, Samuel Phelps as Macduff, Edward Elton as Rosse, Mr. Roberts as Lenox, Mrs. Mary Warner as Lady Macbeth; Feb. 1844, with Charles Kean as Macbeth; Oct. 1847, with Charlotte Cushman as Lady Macbeth, W. C. Macready as Macbeth; Jan. 1852, with Mr. Swift as Duncan, Mr. Stirling as Malcolm, James Anderson as Macbeth, Mr. Cooper as Banquo, Frederick Belton as Macduff, Mr. Bellingham as Lenox, E. Morton as Rosse, Priscilla Horton as Hecate, Isabella Glyn as Lady Macbeth; Mar. 1855, with William Wallack as Macbeth, Frederick Belton as Macduff, R. H. Lingham as Banquo, James Worrell as Malcolm, Mr. Hall as Lennox, Mr. Jones as Rosse, Henri Drayton as Hecate, Mrs. William Wallack as Lady Macbeth; Dec. 1864, with Samuel Phelps as Macbeth, Helen Faucit as Lady Macbeth; Dec. 1876, with Barry Sullivan as Macbeth; July 1882, with William Rignold as Macbeth, J. H. Barnes as Macduff, H. R. Teesdale as Banquo, Arthur Dacre as Malcolm, Arthur Matthison as Duncan, A. C. Lilly as Rosse, W. D. Gresham as Physician, Harry Jackson as 1st Witch, Adelaide Ristori as Lady Macbeth/ **Sad. Wells**, May 1837, with Mr. King as Duncan, C. H. Pitt as Malcolm, C. J. Smith as Lenox, F. Ede as Rosse, Mr. Cobham Jr. as Macbeth, Mr. Campbell as Banquo, Mr. Hicks as Macduff, Miss Williams as Lady Macbeth, Mr. Bishop as Hecate, Mr. Rogers as 1st Witch, John Ayliffe as 2nd Witch, Thomas Lee as 3rd Witch; May 1844, with Mr. Williams as Duncan, Mr. Hield as Malcolm, Samuel Phelps as Macbeth, H. Lacy as Banquo, Henry Marston as Macduff, Mr. Raymond as Lennox, Mr. Aldridge as Rosse, Mrs. Mary Warner as Lady Macbeth, Clement White as Hecate/ Scenery by F. Fenton & Mr. Morelli; Feb. 1868, with Harry Chester as Duncan, Charles Dillon as Macbeth, J. L. Warner as Banquo, C. W. Barry as Macduff, Mr. Murray as Malcolm, E. Morton as Rosse, Mr. Hamilton as Lennox, Walter Searle as Hecate, R. Norman as 1st Witch, Alice Marriott as Lady Macbeth/ **Haymarket**, July 1840, with J. W. Gough as Duncan, John Webster as Malcolm, Charles Kean as Macbeth, Mr. Waldron as Banquo, Samuel Phelps as Macduff, Walter Lacy as Rosse, James Worrell as Lennox, Mrs. Mary Warner as Lady Macbeth, S. Jones as Hecate, Robert Strickland as 1st Witch, Benjamin Webster as 2nd Witch, O. Smith as 3rd Witch; Mar. 1851, with Mr. Rogers as Duncan, John Parselle as Malcolm, J. William Wallack as Macbeth, Henry Howe as Banquo, James Wallack as Macduff, Mr. Woolgar as Rosse, George Braid as Lennox, Laura Addison as Lady Macbeth, Priscilla Horton as Hecate, Mr. Stuart as 1st Witch/ Music by T. German Reed/ **Victoria**, Oct. 1842, with Mr. James as Duncan, Mr. Hamilton as Macduff, John Dale as Banquo, Frank Graham as Macbeth, C. J. Bird as Rosse, Mr. Ayres as Lenox, Mr. Millington as Physician, Mr. Hitchinson as Seyton, Mrs. W. West as Lady Macbeth, Mrs. Sarah Garrick as Gentlewoman, Eliza Vincent as 1st Witch; Aug. 1850, with John Bradshaw as Duncan, John Ryder as Macbeth, Henry Frazer as Banquo, J. T. Johnson as Macduff, T. H. Higgie as Rosse, Mr. Brunton as Lenox, Mr. Humphries as Seyton, Amelia Mercer as Lady Macbeth, J. Neville as Hecate, G. F. Forman as 1st Witch/ **Princess's**, Feb. 1845, with Edwin Forrest as Macbeth, Mr. Graham as Macduff, Mr. Granby as Duncan, F. C. Courtney as Malcolm, Henry Wallack as Banquo, James Ranoe as Lennox, Mr. Fitzjames as Rosse, Henry Compton as 1st Witch, W. H. Oxberry as 3rd Witch, Charlotte Cushman as Lady Macbeth, Miss E. Honner as Gentlewoman, Mr. Leffler as Hecate/ Music of Locke; add'l music by C. E. Horn; Nov. 1847, with W. C. Macready as Macbeth, Mr. Cooper as Macduff, John Gilbert as Duncan, F. B. Conway as Malcolm, James Vining as Rosse, Charles Fisher as Banquo, Mr. Bodda as Hecate, John Ryder as 1st Witch, Charlotte Cushman as Lady Macbeth, Miss Rourke as Gentlewoman; Feb. 1853, with F. Cooke as Duncan, Mr. Cathcart as Malcolm, Charles Kean as Macbeth, Frank Graham as Banquo, John Ryder as Macduff, George Everett as Lenox, James Vining as Rosse, Kate Terry as Fleance, Mr. Terry as Siward, Hermann Vezin as Wounded Officer, Mrs. Charles Kean as Lady Macbeth, Mrs. W. Daly as Gentlewoman, Henry Drayton as Hecate/ Scenery by Mr. Dayes, F. Lloyds, Walter Gordon, & Mr. Cuthbert/ Music by J. L. Hatton; Aug. 1860, with Mr. Garden as Duncan, J. G. Shore as Malcolm, James Anderson as Macbeth, James Fernandez as Banquo, Basil Potter as Macduff, Robert Cathcart as Lenox, Miss Elsworthy as Lady Macbeth, Rose Leclercq as Gentlewoman, Mr. Weiss as Hecate, Frank Matthews, T. H. Higgie & Henry Saker as Witches/ **Olympic**, Jan. 1848, with George Almar as Duncan, John Kinloch as Malcolm, Mr. Stuart as Macbeth, Mr. Archer as Banquo, Henry Holl as Macduff, E. Morton as Lennox, H. Lee as Rosse, Eleanore Glyn as Lady Macbeth, Mme. Delavanti as Hecate; Aug. 1851, with George Cooke as Duncan, R. Robinson as Malcolm, J. William Wallack as Macbeth, Mr. Norton as Banquo, Charles Diddear as Macduff, Mr. Mason as Lennox, John Kinloch as Rosse, William Farren Jr. as Hecate, Helen Faucit as Lady Macbeth/ **Grecian**, Nov. 1853, with Eaton O'Donnell as Duncan, Charles Horn as Malcolm, Basil Potter as Macbeth, Edwin Dixon as Banquo, Richard Phillips as Macduff, Charles Rice as First Witch, Jane Coveney as Lady Macbeth; Apr. 1861, with Henry Grant as Duncan, R. H. Lingham as Malcolm, George Gillett as Rosse, Thomas Mead as Macbeth, G. Kingston as Macduff, J. M. Cobden as Banquo, John Manning as First Witch, Jane Coveney as Lady Macbeth/ **Astley's**, Dec. 1856, with Mr. Campbell as Duncan, W. Cooke Jr. as Malcolm, James Holloway as Macbeth, Henry Reeves as Banquo, Mark Howard as Macduff, A. Palmer as Lenox, J. T. Anderson as Seyton, Mrs. Jackson as Lady Macbeth, Mrs. W. Dowton as Hecate/ Scenery by T. Thompson & Thorne/ Machines by E. Pryce/ Music by G. Phillips/ Horses trained by Wm. Cooke; Mar. 1870, with Henry Dudley as Duncan, Henry Fletcher as Malcolm, Samuel Phelps as Macbeth, Charles Harcourt as Banquo, Hermann Vezin as Macduff, W. Holland as Lennox, J. G. Rosiere as Ross, Mrs. Herman Vezin as Lady Macbeth, George Yarnold as First Witch/ Scenery by F. Fenton/ Machines by Mr. Lanham, Gas by Mr. Pepper/ **Surrey**, Mar. 1859, with William Creswick, Agnes Elsworthy/ **Standard**, May 1859, with Samuel Phelps as Macbeth, Isabel Glyn as Lady Macbeth/ **Lyceum**, Sept. 1875, with Henry Irving as Macbeth, Mr. Huntley as Duncan, Mr. Brooke as Malcolm, Mr. Forrester as Banquo, Thomas Swinbourne as Macduff, Kate Bateman as Lady Macbeth, Georgina Pauncefort as Hecate; Dec. 1888, with Henry Irving, George Alexander, Ellen Terry; Sept. 1898, with William Lugg as Duncan, John Martin Harvey as Malcolm, Johnston Forbes Robertson as Macbeth, Bernard Gould as Banquo, Robert Taber as Macduff, Ian Robertson as First Witch, Mrs. Patrick Campbell as Lady Macbeth/ Scenery by Hawes Craven, W. T. Helmsley, T. E. Ryan & Walter Hann/ Music by Carl Armbruster.

MACCARTHY MORE; OR, POSSESSION NINE POINTS OF THE LAW// C 2a// Samuel Lover// **Lyceum**, Apr. 1861.

MACHAGGIS, THE/ F 3a// Jerome K. Jerome & Eden Philpotts// **Globe**, Feb. 1897.

MACKINTOSH AND CO.// F// James Kenney// **Cov. Garden**, Jan. 1838, with Tyrone Power as Mackintosh, George Bartley as Henley,

Mr. Roberts as Leonard, Mrs. Humby as Mrs. Henley, Ellen Clifford as Sophy.

MAD// C// Edward Rose// **Olympic**, June 1880.

MAD AS A HATTER// F 1a// Francis Marshall/ **New Royalty**, Dec. 1863.

MAD MARRIAGE, A// D 4a// Adap. by Frank Harvey fr F// **Grand**, Aug. 1885.

MAD PAINTER, THE// F// n.a.// **Alhambra**, Oct. 1879.

MADAME BERLIOT'S BALL; OR, THE CHALET IN THE VALLEY// C 2a// F. C. Burnand// **New Royalty**, Dec. 1863.

MADAME BUTTERFLY// D 1a// Dram. by David Belasco fr story by John Long// **Duke of York's**, Apr. 1900.

MADAME DE RAIMONT// D 1a// Richard Butler & H. Chance Newton ("Richard Henry")// **Gaiety**, May 1883.

MADAME LAFARGE// D// n.a.// Adelphi, Nov. 1840.

MADAME SANS-GENE// C Pro & 3a// Adap. by J. Comyns Carr fr F of Victorien Sardou & Emile Moreau// **Lyceum**, Apr. 1897, with Henry Irving as Napoleon, Frank Cooper as Lefebvre, W. Macintosh as Fouché, Ben Webster as Comte de Neipperg, F. H. Macklin as Duc de Rovigo, Norman Forbes as Despréaux, Frank Tyars as Roustan, William Farren Jr. as Leroy, Fuller Mellish as Canouville, Gertrude Kingston as Caroline, Julia Arthur as Elisa, Mary Rorke as Mme. de Rovigo, Maud Milton as La Rousotte, Edith Craig as Toinon, Ellen Terry as Catherine/ Scenery by Hawes Craven & J. Harker; June 1901.

MADCAP// C 1a// E. B. Aveling ("Alec Nelson")// **Comedy**, Oct. 1890, with G. Kennedy as Read, P. S. Champion as Barton, Eleanor May as Ada, Helene Lambert as Mrs. Barton, Rhoda Larkin as Daphne.

MADCAP MADGE// C Pro & 4a// L. E. B. Stephens// **Imperial**, Oct. 1898.

MADCAP MIDGE// C 3a// Charles Fawcett// **Opera Comique**, Dec. 1889.

MADCAP PRINCE, A// C 3a// Robert Buchanan// **Haymarket**, Aug. 1874.

MADCAP VIOLET// C 4a// Dram. by Ella Stockton fr novel of Black// **Sadler's Wells**, Mar. 1882.

MADELAINE MOREL// D 5a// Daniel Bandmann// **Queen's**, Apr. 1878.

MADELEINE// D 3a// James Mortimer// **Vaudeville**, Feb. 1873.

MADELEINE, LA// Play 3a// H. W. Dam// **Shaftesbury**, Dec. 1901.

MADEMOISELLE DE BELLE ISLE// D 5a// Adap. by Frances Anne Kemble fr F of Alexandre Dumas// **Haymarket**, Oct. 1864, with Henry Howe as Richelieu, Walter Gordon as Duke de Aumont, Mr. Weathersby as D'Auvry, William Farren as D'Aubigny, Thomas Coe as Chamillac, George Braid as De Rosanne, Louisa Angel as Marchioness de Valcour, Mlle. Marie Beatrice as Gabriella, Miss Lovell as Marietta/ Scenery by John O'Conner & George Morris/ Machines by Oliver Wales.

MADEMOISELLE DE LIRA// Play 1a// Mrs. G. Thompson & Kate Sinclair// **Comedy**, Jan. 1890, with Royston Keith as Wild, A. Newroy as Reed, Mrs. G. Thompson as Eva Mayne, Kate Sinclair as Eva Ward, Mrs. E. H. Brooke as Mrs. Macdonald.

MADGE WILDFIRE// D 4a// Edward Stirling// **Standard**, Oct. 1868.

MAELSTROM, THE// D 4a// Mark Melford// **Shaftesbury**, Apr. 1892, with Mark Melford as Tierce, John Beauchamp as Sarcliff, H. Reeves Smith as Hartleigh, C. W. Garthorne as Aylward, G. L. Leith as Summerton, R. J. Pakenham as Ferguson, Giffard Stacey as Fabert, Decima Moore as Nora, Helen Leyton as Parker, Adeline Lester as Mrs. Grain, Claire Pauncefort as Esther, Maggie Bowman as Rhoda, Olga Brandon as Gertrude/ Scenery by Bruce Smith.

MAGDA// Play 4a// Trans. by L. N. Parker fr G of Hermann Sudermann, Heimat// **Daly's**, June 1895/ **Lyceum**, June 1896, with James Fernandez as Leopold Schwartze, Mrs. Patrick Campbell as Magda, Sarah Brooke as Marie, Mrs. E. H. Brooke as Augusta, Alice Mansfield as Franziska, Frank Gillmore as Lt. Wendlowski, Johnston Forbes Robertson as Hefferdingk, Murray Hathorne as Prof. Beckmann.

MAGGIE LORME// D 3a// n.a.// **Olympic**, Feb. 1873.

MAGGIE'S SITUATION// C 1a// J. Maddison Morton// **Court**, Jan. 1875.

MAGIC BOX, THE// F 1a// n.a.// **Astley's**, Feb. 1852, with Mr. Craddock as Aboun Hassan, Mr. Tannett as Binbi, Mr. Regan as Salem, Mr. Rivolti as Sadi, Mr. Johnson as Mother Winky, Miss Fenton as Amina, Mrs. Beacham as Zobide.

MAGIC HARP, THE; OR, THE GRAVE OF THE OLD RUINED ABBEY// D// R. St. Clair Jones// **Victoria**, July 1848, with John Bradshaw as Count Altenberg, Mr. Henderson as Ludolph, J. T. Johnson as Lt. Albert, E. Edwards as Herman, T. H. Higgie as Claude, J. Howard as Conrade, Walter Searle as Mathew, F. H. Henry as Francis, Mrs. Cooke as Countess Altenberg, Mrs. George Lee as Leonora, Miss Young as Agnes, Miss Burroughcliffe as Jeannette.

MAGIC TOYS// F 1a// John Oxenford// **Adelphi**, Mar. 1874, with Kate Vaughan as Valentine, Miss Hudspeth as Urgundula, Harwood Cooper as Merlin, J. Morris as Mother Goose.

MAGICIAN, THE// D 2a// Shirley Brooks// **Olympic**, Sept. 1848, with Mr. Norton as Charles of Anjou, A. Younge as Bruneau, Leigh Murray as Count d'Anglade, Mr. Neale as de Marigny, Henry Butler as de Serac, Alfred Sanger as Branzon, Charles Bender as Cardinal Ansaldo, Mr. Lawrence as Bure, H. J. Turner as Pincon, Miss Murray as Countess de Marigny, Miss St. George as Mignonelli, Mrs. Leigh Murray as Emilia.

MAGISTRATE, THE// F 3a// Arthur Wing Pinero// **Court**, Mar. 1885, with Arthur Cecil, John Clayton, Mrs. John Wood, Marion Terry.

MAGPIE AND THE MAID, THE// D 2a// Isaac Pocock// **Sad. Wells**, May 1854, with C. Poynter as Gervaise, F. Charles as Henry, George Yarnold as Martin, Mr. Barrett as as Kalerno, Edwin Villiers as Benjamin, James Worrell as Everard, Harriett Gordon as Annette, Mrs. Barrett as Mme. Gervaise.

MAGPIE AND THIMBLE, THE// F 1a// Thomas Smelt// **St. James's**, Feb. 1878, with W. H. Stephens as Ruggles, Robert Brennand as Doveton, Miss Chetwynd as Mrs. Doveton, Kate Rivers as Susan.

MAGPIE OR THE MAID, THE// D 3a// Isaac Pocock// **Sad. Wells**, July 1838, with Mr. Williams as Gerald, Robert Honner as Henry, Mr. Dry as Everard, Mr. Conquest as Martin, Dibdin Pitt as Malcour, Mr. Villiers as Benjamin, Mr. Harwood as Bertrand, Mr. Mellor as George, Mrs. Robert Honner as Annette, Mrs. Weston as Dame Gerald.

MAID AND THE MAGPIE, THE// D 3a// S. J. Arnold// **Victoria**, May 1838, with Mr. Loveday as Gerald, Charles Montague as Henry, Mr. King as Evrard, Mr. Vale as Martin, William Davidge as Malcour, John Parry as Benjamin, Mrs. Loveday as Dame Gerald, Mrs. John Parry as Annette/ Scenery by J. C. James/ **Sad. Wells**, June 1840, with Mr. Williams as Gerald, Mr. Elvin as Henry, Mr. Dry as Everard, Mr. Aldridge as Malcolm, Henry Hall as Martin, James Villiers as Benjamin, Charles Fenton as Bertrand, Mrs. Robert Honner as Annette, Miss Cooke as Dame Gerald.

MAID OF ARTOIS, THE// D// Alfred Bunn// **Drury Lane**, Dec. 1846, with D. W. King, Mrs. Bishop.

MAID OF BISCAY, THE// C 3a// n.a.// **Olympic**, Oct. 1841, with Mr. Brookes as Don Domingo, Mr. Thompson as Don Gomez, Mr. Green as Capt. Hernando, Mrs. Waylett as Leonora, Don Cesario, and Diavolino, Georgiana Le Batt [sic] as Donna Isabella/ Scenery by Mr. Wilson.

MAID OF CANADA, THE; OR, THE HAG OF THE RAPIDS// D// n.a.// **Sad. Wells**, Feb. 1838, with Mr. Forester as Capt. Fitzosburne, Mr. Ranson as the American, Mr. Nunn as Gates, Mr. Campbell as Gleg, S. Smith as Hackett, Mr. Rogers as Slick, Mr. Worrell as Jefferson, Mr. James as Pul-ta-Wella, Miss Chartley as Quita, Eliza Vincent as Imoinde, Mrs. Weston as Simaime, Miss Beresford as Mrs. Slick, Miss Watkins as Maude the Hag/ Scenery by Mr. Battie/ Music by W. Montgomery.

MAID OF CROISSEY, THE; OR, THE RETURN FROM RUSSIA (also subt., Theresa's Vow)// D 2a// Mrs. G. Gore// **Haymarket**, June 1837, with Frederick Vining as Francis, Mr. Ross as Walter, Benjamin Webster as Sgt. Austerlitz, Miss Taylor as Theresa, Mrs. Humby as Manette; Feb. 1850, with Henry Howe as Francis, Benjamin Webster as Sgt. Austerlitz, J. B. Buckstone as Walter, Mme. Celeste as Theresa, Mrs. Fitzwilliam as Manette/ **Adelphi**, July 1854, with John Parselle as Francis, Benjamin Webster as Sgt. Austerlitz, Robert Keeley as Walter, Mme. Celeste as Theresa, Mrs. Keeley as Manette; 1880, with E. H. Brooke as Francis, James Fernandez as Sgt. Austerlitz, Robert Pateman as Walter, Bella Pateman as Therese, Clara Jecks as Manette.

MAID OF GENOA, THE; OR, THE BANDIT MERCHANT// D 2a// John Farrell// **Sad. Wells**, Nov. 1838, with Mr. Elvin as Count Corveno, Mr. Dry as Antonio, Mr. Harwood as Jaspero, C. Montague as Desperetto, Dibdin Pitt as Justine, Mr. Conquest as Moso, T. Blanchard as Strapado, Miss Pincott as the Dumb Girl/ **Victoria**, June 1854, with Mr. Henderson as Count Corvenio, Alfred Saville as Justin, T. E. Mills as Antonio, N. T. Hicks as Strapado, J. Howard as Moco, F. H. Henry as Jaspero, Edwin Blanchard as Desperetta, Mrs. Henry Vining as Julietta, Miss Dansor as Bipeda.

MAID OF HONOUR// D// n.a.// **Adelphi**, Nov. 1841, with Frederick Yates, George Spencer, Mr. Forde, Mr. Freeborn, C. Morgan, John Sanders, Mrs. Yates, Mrs. Fosbroke, Ellen Chaplin.

MAID OF MARIENDORPT, THE// D 5a// J. Sheridan Knowles// **Haymarket**, Oct. 1838, with Robert Strickland as Gen. Kliener, Walter Lacy as Baron Idenstein, Sheridan Knowles as Muhldenau, J. B. Buckstone as Hans, Benjamin Webster as Joseph, Miss Elphinstone as Meeta, Miss Cooper as Adelpha, Mrs. Julia Glover as Esther, Mrs. Danson as Mme. Roselheim/ Scenery by George Morris.

MAID OF PLINLIMMON, THE (see Gwynneth the Maid of Plinlimmon)

MAID OF SWITZERLAND, THE// D// Mrs. C. B. Wilson// **Victoria**, Sept. 1837, with John Parry as Col. St. Leon, W. H. Oxberry as Rutley, William Davidge as Franz, L. Smith as Henrique, Mrs. Griffith as Mme. Werner, Mrs. Hooper as Generviere.

MAID WITH THE MILKING PAIL, THE// C// J. B. Buckstone// **Haymarket**, June 1849, with Mr. Tilbury as Lord Philander, Henry Howe as Algernon, J. B. Buckstone as Diccon, Mrs. Fitzwilliam as Milly.

MAIDEN AUNT, THE// C 5a// R. B. Knowles// **Haymarket**, Nov. 1845, with William Farren as Sir Simon, Mr. Tilbury as Wilmot, Charles Hudson as Sage, A. Brindal as Montague, Mrs. Julia Glover as Sarah, Mrs. Seymour as Catherine, Mrs. Stanley as Mrs. Matchwell, Mrs. L. S. Buckingham as Lady Spleen/ Scenery by George Morris.

MAIDS OF HONOUR// C // C. L. Kenney// **Mirror**, Apr. 1875.

MAIN CHANCE, THE// C 2a// H. B. Farnie// **Royalty**, Apr. 1874.

MAIN HOPE, THE// D Pro & 3a// George Comer// **Britannia**, Aug. 1886.

MAJOR AND MINOR// CD 2a// Walter Ellis// **Olympic**, Aug. 1881, with William McIntyre, Marie de Grey, Meggie Sharpe.

MAJOR MARIE ANNE// C 2a// Edgar Newbound// **Britannia**, May 1880.

MAJOR RAYMOND// Play 4a// Philip Havard// **Terry's**, June 1896, with W. L. Abingdon as Maj. Raymond, Frederick Volpé as Dyson, Julian Cross as Sir John, George Hippisley as Kennedy, Oswald Yorke as Fleming, C. M. Lowne as Viscount Ashbrooke, Sydney Burt as Rubenstein, Eva Moore as Molly, Madge Raye as Lady Dorothea, Nora Carewe as Mrs. Graham, Lena Cross as Rachel, Beatrice Baily as Maud.

MAKE THE BEST OF IT// C// John Oxenford// **Haymarket**, Mar. 1851, with J. B. Buckstone as Burr, Henry Howe as Driver, William Clark as Morgan, Priscilla Horton as Mrs. Driver, Mrs. Fitzwilliam as Constantia.

MAKE YOUR WILLS!// F 1a// E. Mayhew & G. Smith// **Haymarket**, July 1837, with Robert Strickland as Ireton, Charles Selby as Plotter, Mr. Worrell as Charles, T. F. Mathews as Process, J. B. Buckstone as Brag, Miss Wrighten as Clara, Mrs. W. Clifford as Foreright.

MAKE YOURSELF AT HOME// F// Alfred Maltby// **Mirror**, Apr. 1875.

MALCONTENT, THE// TC// John Marston// **Olympic**, Aug. 1850.

MAMA// FC 3a// Adap. by Sidney Grundy fr F of Alexandre Bisson & A. Mars, Les Surprises du Divorce// **Royalty**, Apr. 1888/ **Court**, Sept. 1888, with John Hare, Mrs. John Wood, Annie Hughes, Arthur Cecil/ **Criterion**, Mar. 1901.

MAMA'S OPINIONS// C 1a// n.a.// **St. Geo. Hall**, Jan. 1893.

MAMMON// C 3a// Sidney Grundy// **Strand**, Apr. 1877.

MAMMON AND GAMMON// C// n.a.// **Princess's**, Mar. 1848, with J. Neville as Featherdown, James Vining as Copperbrown, S. Cowell as Smudge, Mrs. Selby as Miss Featherdown, Mrs. H. Hughes as Julia, Miss Villars as Betty.

MAN ABOUT TOWN, THE// F// W. Bayle Bernard// **Victoria**, Sept. 1837, with Benjamin Wrench as Skirts, W. H. Oxberry as Topps, James Bland as St. Ledger, John Parry as Lord Aubrey, L. Smith as Mowbray, William Davidge as Dr. Mandible, Miss Waring as Lady Aubrey, Miss Fitzwalter as Fanny/ **Haymarket**, Apr. 1838, with Benjamin Wrench as Skirts, Mr. Hutchings as Lord Aubrey, Mr. Worrell as St. Ledger, Mr. Clark as Mawbray [sic], J. W. Gough as Dr. Mandible, T. F. Mathews as Tapps, Miss Gallot as Lady Aubrey, Miss Beresford as Fanny/ **Sad. Wells**, June 1844, with Mr. Binge as Lord Aubrey, Mr. Sharp as St. Leger, Charles Hudson as Skirts, Edward Knight as Mowbray, Charles Morelli as Dr. Mandible, Mr. Coreno as Tops, Emma Harding as Lady Aubrey, Georgiana Lebatt as Fanny.

MAN AND HIS MAKERS// Play 4a// Wilson Barrett & L. N. Parker// **Lyceum**, Oct. 1899, with Wilson Barrett as John Radleigh, J. H. Barnes as Sir Henry Faber, Ambrose Manning as Ripton, Horace Hodges as Faze, George Barrett Jr. as Goodson, Caleb Porter as Inspector Ferguson, Maud Jeffries as Jane Humphries, Lena Ashwell as Sylvia Faber, Daisy Belmore as Millicent, Alida Courtelyou as Diana, Stella Campbell as Sylvia.

MAN AND THE MARQUIS, THE; OR, THE THREE SPECTRES// F// Thomas Dibdin// **Grecian**, Jan. 1845, with John Collett as the Baron, Edwin Dixon as the Count, Mr. Melvin as the Marquis, Edmund Garden as Richard, Frederick Robson as Nicholas, Miss Atkins as Constantia, Miss M. A. Crisp as Lisette.

MAN AND THE SPIRIT, THE// D 1a// C. H. Hazlewood// **Britannia**, Feb. 1881.

MAN AND THE TIGER, THE (see also, P.P.)// F 1a// Thomas Parry// **Victoria**, Mar. 1842, with Tom Parry as Splashton, John Gardner as Buckskin, Mr. James as Startle, William Seaman as Somerhill, C. Williams as Lt. Fusil, Mrs. George Lee as Susan, Miss Collett as Crape, Mrs. Seaman as Duster.

MAN AND THE WOMAN// D 3a// Robert Buchanan// **Criterion**, Dec. 1889.

MAN AND WIFE// D 4a// Wilkie Collins// **POW**, Feb. 1873/ **Haymarket**, Mar. 1887, with Henry Kemble as Sir Patrick, E. S. Willard as Delamayne, William Herbert as Brinkworth, A. M. Denison as Speedwell, P. Ben Greet as Moy, Charles Collette as Bishipriggs, Ulick Winter as Duncan, Henrietta Lindley as Lady Lundie, Miss Russell Huddart as Blanche, Mrs. E. H. Brooke as Mistress Inchbare, Mrs. James Brown-Potter as Anne/ Scenery by Walter Johnstone.

MAN AND WIFE; OR, MORE SECRETS THAN ONE// C// S. J. Arnold// **Haymarket**, Apr. 1842, with Henry Howe as Lord Austincourt, Henry Wallack as Sir Rowland, Henry Holl as Charles, Robert Strickland as Sir Willoughby, Mr. Stuart as Growse, Benjamin Webster as Ponder, Malone Raymond as O'Dedimus, Mrs. W. Clifford as Lady Worrett, Mrs. Malone

Raymond as Helen, Mrs. Edwin Yarnold as Fanny, Mrs. Frank Matthews as Tiffany/ **Sad. Wells,** Dec. 1849, with G. K. Dickinson as Lord Austincourt, Frank Graham as Sir Rowland, A. Younge as Sir Willoughby, Henry Marston as Charles, George Bennett as Grouse, Henry Mellon as O'Dedimus, Henry Nye as Ponder, Mrs. G. Smith as Lady Worret, Miss Aldridge as Julia, Miss Fitzpatrick as Helen.

MAN AND WOMAN// C 4a// T. M. Watson ("H. C. de Mille") & David Belasco// **Opera Comique,** Mar. 1893, with Henry Neville as Rodman, Herbert Standing as Col. Kipp, Arthur Elwood as Cohen, Charles Fulton as Stedman, W. T. Lovell as Seabury, Sam Sothern as Delafield, Sant Matthews as Pendleton, Arthur Dacre as Prescott, Edgar Monson as Cannon, Gerald Godfrey as Webb, E. H. Kelly as Bergman, Arthur Wilmot as Wayne, Oscar Asche as Roberts, Eva Moore as Margery, Lena Ashwell as Dora, Amy Roselle as Agnes, Nancy Noel as Mrs. Delafield, Annie Constance as Lucy/ Scenery by Walter Johnstone & W. T. Hemsley.

MAN FROM BLANKLEY'S, THE// C 3a// Thomas Guthrie ("F. Anstey")// **POW,** Apr. 1901.

MAN IN A THOUSAND, THE// D 4a// Clarence Burnette// **Surrey,** Mar. 1892.

MAN IN BLACK, A// D 4a// Dram. by H. E. Williams fr novel of Stanley Weyman// **Vaudeville,** Sept. 1897.

MAN IN POSSESSION, THE// C 3a// James Albery// **Gaiety,** Dec. 1876.

MAN IN RAGS, THE// Play 1a// N. Monck// **St. Geo. Hall,** July 1901.

MAN IN THE CLOAK, THE; OR, THE ASSASSIN// D 2a// Frederick Marchant// **Victoria,** Feb. 1870.

MAN IN THE IRON MASK, THE// D// Dram. fr F of Alexandre Dumas// **Marylebone,** Feb. 1855.

MAN IN THE IRON MASK, THE// D 5a// Dram. by M. Goldberg fr F of Alexandre Dumas// **Adelphi,** Mar. 1899, with Norman Forbes as Louis XIV and as Marchiali, Charles Sugden as Mazarin, W. H. Vernon as D'Herblay, W. L. Abingdon as St. Mars, G. W. Anson as Gaspar, Genevieve Ward as Queen Anne, Dolores Drummond as Jean, Hilda Hanbury as Mlle. de Montalais, Kate Rorke as Louise de la Vallière/ Scenery by T. Ryan & W. Harford/ Music by John Crook.

MAN IN THE STREET, THE// Play 1a// L. N. Parker// **Strand,** May 1894, with James Welch as Gover, George Foss as Adare, Winifed Fraser as Minnie.

MAN IN THE ULSTER, THE// F// E. Manuel// **Britannia,** Nov. 1874.

MAN IS NOT PERFECT, NOR WOMAN NEITHER// C 1a// Adap. by Benjamin Webster Jr.// **Adelphi,** Oct. 1867, with George Belmore as Harry, C. H. Stephenson as Mike, J. G. Taylor as John Bunn, Mrs. Alfred Mellon (Sarah Woolgar) as Jane, Emily Pitt as Alice.

MAN O' AIRLIE, THE// D 4a// W. G. Wills// **Princess's,** July 1867/ **Globe,** May 1870/ **Grand,** Mar. 1890.

MAN OF ALL WORK, THE// F 1a// n.a.// **Victoria,** July 1854, with Henry Frazer as Sir Charles, Charles Rice as Sharpe, Miss Dansor as Lady Courtall, Miss Laporte as Grace.

MAN OF BUSINESS, A// Play 4a// Trans. by W. Olaf & W. Chapman fr Swed. of Björnsterne Björnson// **St. Geo. Hall,** Mar. 1887.

MAN OF DESTINY, THE// C 1a// George Bernard Shaw// **Comedy,** Mar. 1901.

MAN OF FORTY, THE// Play 4a// Walter Frith// **St. James's,** Mar. 1900, with George Alexander as Fanshawe, H. B. Irving as Roger Dunster and as Lewis Dunster, C. Aubrey Smith as Portman, Dennis Eadie as Capt. Garner, Alfred Bonnin as Barker, R. E. Goddard as Martin, Julie Opp as Mrs. Egerton, Carlotta Addison as Mrs. Jessop, Esmé Beringer as Claire, Miss Granville as Mrs. Portman, Fay Davis as Elsie.

MAN OF HIS WORD, A// Play 3a// Boyle Lawrence// **Imperial,** Aug. 1901, with H. B. Irving.

MAN OF LAW, THE// C 4a// Benjamin Webster// **Haymarket,** Dec. 1851, with Mr. Lambert as Marquis de la Seigliere, Leigh Murray as Count de Beaulieu, Benjamin Webster as Destournelles, Henry Howe as Bernard, Mrs. Stirling as Baroness de Vaubert, Amelia Vining as Helene/ Scenery by George Morris & John O'Conner/ Machines by F. Heselton.

MAN OF MANY FRIENDS, THE// C 3a// J. Stirling Coyne// **Haymarket,** Sept. 1855, with J. B. Buckstone as Popples, Henry Compton as Skrymsher, William Farren as Veneer, Mr. Howe as Capt. Hawkshaw, Mr. Rogers as Sir Jacob, Mr. Clark as Flapper, Miss Reynolds as Mrs. Popples, Ada Swanborough as Mrs. Beamish, Mrs. Poynter as Mrs. Martingale, Amelia Vining as Miss Nettley, Mrs. Griffiths as Miss Daw/ Scenery by George Morris & Mr. O'Conner, Machines by Oliver Wales.

MAN OF MYSTERY, A// D 4a// Roy Redgrave & A. Bell// **Grand,** Aug. 1901.

MAN OF QUALITY, THE// C// Adap. by John Holingshead fr John Vanbrugh's The Relapse// **Gaiety,** May 1870.

MAN OF THE RED HOUSE, THE// D 4a// n.a.// **Grecian,** May 1862, with William James as Linday, Thomas Mead as Lorin, George Gillett as the Chevalier, Alfred Rayner as Dizmer, Henry Grant as Simon, Mr. Shirley as Gen. Santerre, F. Smithson as Durand, John Manning as Waggles, Jane Dawson as Amalie, Miss Johnstone as Mme. Tison, Amelie Conquest as Heloise.

MAN OF THE RED MANSION, THE// Play 2a// C. Rice// **Grecian**, May 1854, with Richard Phillips as Alphonse, Basil Potter as Officer, Charles Horn as Giraffe, Eaton O'Donnell as Robespierre, Jane Coveney as Marie Antoinette.

MAN OF THE WORLD, THE// C 5a// Charles Macklin// **Haymarket**, Sept. 1840, with Robert Maywood as Sir Pertinax McSycophant, Samuel Phelps as Egerton, Robert Strickland as Lord Lumbercourt, John Webster as Sidney, Mr. Waldron as Melville, J. W. Gough as Plausible, T. F. Mathews as Eitherside, Mrs. Stanley as Lady McSycophant, Mrs. Edwin Yarnold as Constantia, Mrs. Stirling as Lady Rodolpha, Mrs. Frank Matthews as Betty/ **Olympic**, May 1845, with Mr. Bass as Macsycophant, Mr. Hollingsworth as Lumbercourt, Walter Grisdale as Egerton, Mr. Grafton as Sidney, George Grey as Melville, Mr. Turnour as Plausible, Mrs. W. Watson as Lady Rodolpha, Mrs. Griffiths as Lady Macsycophant, Miss Newcombe as Constantia, Miss M. A. Egan as Betty/ **Sad. Wells**, Nov. 1851, with Frederic Robinson as Egerton, Mr. Barrett as Lumbercourt, Samuel Phelps as McSycophant, Frank Graham as Sidney, Mr. Williams as Plausible, Henry Mellon as Melville, Miss Fitzpatrick as Lady Rodolpha, Mrs. Henry Marston as Lady McSycophant, Lucy Rafter as Constantia/ **Princess's**, Apr. 1860, with Frank Matthews as Lumbercourt, Samuel Phelps as Sir Pertinax Macsycophant, J. G. Shore as Egerton, Frank Graham as Sidney, Mr. Cathcart as Melville, Edmund Garden as Plausible, Miss Atkinson as Lady Rodolpha, Mrs. Weston as Lady Macsychophant, Rose Leclercq as Constantia, Emma Wadham as Betty; Jan. 1871, with Samuel Phelps as Sir Pertinax Macsycophant, Mr. Barrett as Lumbercourt, John Clayton as Egerton, Herbert Crellin as Sidney, John Vollaire as Melville, Henry Westland as Plausible, C. F. Marshall as Eitherside, Rose Leclercq as Lady Rodolpha, Mrs. Addie as Lady Macsycophant, Annie Merton as Constantia, Millie De Vere as Betty/ **Drury Lane**, May 1865, with Samuel Phelps as Sir Pertinax, Mr. Barrett as Lumbercourt, G. F. Neville as Egerton, John Neville as Plausible, Mr. Fitzjames as Sgt. Eitherside, Mr. Warde as Sidney, G. Weston as John, Mrs. Henry Vandenhoff as Lady Macsycophant, Miss Atkinson as Lady Rodolpha, Rose Leclercq as Constantia, Miss Hudspeth as Betty/ **Astley's**, Mar. 1870, with Henry Mellon as Lumbercourt, Samuel Phelps as Sir Pertinax, Charles Harcourt as Egerton, J. G. Rosier as Sidney, Margaret Eburne as Lady Rodolpha, Mrs. Charles Horseman as Betty, Mrs. Manders as Lady Macsyphocant/ **Adelphi**, Nov. 1879, with J. R. Gibson as Sir Pertinax, E. H. Brooke as Egerton, W. Holman as Sidney, Frank Barsby as Lumbercourt, Louise Moodie as Lady Rodolpha, Minnie Davis as Lady Macsycophant, Miss M. Thornton as Constantia.

MAN OF TWO LIVES, THE// Play 3a// Adap. by W. Bayle Bernard fr F of Victor Hugo, Les Miserables// **Drury Lane**, Mar. 1869.

MAN OR MONEY?// n.a.// **Surrey**, Mar. 1860.

MAN PROPOSES// C 1a// Sidney Grundy & G. R. Sims// **Duke's**, Mar. 1878/ **Globe**, Sept. 1883, with E. W. Gardiner as Capt. Huntington, Miss Valentine Noad as Dinah, Lottie Venne as Bell Huntington.

MAN THAT HESITATES, THE// D// Adap. by G. W. Godfrey fr Mrs. Hughes Bell, L'Indécis// **Royalty**, Nov. 1887.

MAN TO MAN// D 4a// William Bourne// **Surrey**, July 1887.

MAN WHO FOLLOWS THE LADIES, THE// F 1a// Howard Paul// **Strand**, July 1856.

MAN WITH A PAST, A// D// n.a.// **Strand**, Sept. 1895.

MAN WITH MANY FRIENDS, THE (see Man of Many Friends)

MAN WITH THE CARPET BAG, THE// F 1a// Gilbert à Becket// **Sad. Wells**, July 1845, with Frank Graham as Pluckwell, Edward Knight as Stokes, Charles Fenton as Coachman, Samuel Buckingham as Wrangle, Mr. Corrie as Grimes, Henry Scharf as Boots, Miss Huddart as Harriet/ **Olympic**, Feb. 1847, with R. Summerford as Pluckwell, J. Butler as Wrangle, Mr. Turnour as Grab, Mr. Robinson as John, Henry Butler as Stokes, T. Paine as Boots, Thomas Hughes as Grimes, Miss Penson as Harriet.

MAN WITH THREE WIVES, THE// F 3a// Adap. by Charles Rae fr F of Grenet Dancourt, Trois Femmes pour un Mari// **Criterion**, Mar. 1886, with George Giddens, Lytton Sothern, William Blakeley, Alfred Maltby, Fanny Coleman, Emily Vining, Annie Hughes, Helena Dacre, Rose Saker.

MAN WITHOUT A HEAD, A// F 1a// J. P. Wooler// **Princess's**, Oct. 1845, with Henry Compton as Top, Robert Roxby as Featherstone, Miss E. Honner as Kate, Mrs. Dugham as Mrs. Top/ **Sad. Wells**, Aug. 1949, with William Hoskins as Top, William Belford as Featherstone, Mr. Wilkins as William, Mrs. G. Smith as Mrs. Top, Mrs. Graham as Lucy, Miss T. Bassano as Kate.

MAN'S ENEMY; OR, THE DOWNWARD PATH// D 4a// C. H. Longden & Eric Hudson // **West London**, Apr. 1898.

MAN'S LOVE, A// Play 3a// Adap. by J. T. Grein & C. W. Jarvis fr Dutch of J. C. De Vos// **POW**, June 1889/ **Opera Comique**, Mar. 1895.

MAN'S SHADOW, A// D 4a// Adap. by Robert Buchanan fr F of Jules Mary & Georges Grisier, Roger la Honte// **Elephant & Castle**, Nov. 1888 (under French title)/ **Haymarket**, Sept. 1889, with Herbert Beerbohm Tree as Laroque, James Fernandez as Luversan, Charles Allan as Gerbier, Charles Collette as Picolot, E. M. Robson as Tristot, Mr. Hargreaves as Ricordot, Henry Kemble as President, Miss Robbins as Henriette, Minnie Terry as Suzanne, Miss Norreys as Victoire, Julia Neilson as Julie/ Scenery by Walter Johnstone & Walter

Hann/ **Her Majesty's**, Nov. 1897.

MAN'S TALISMAN - GOLD// D// Edgar Newbound// **Britannia**, Dec. 1877.

MANAGER, THE// FC 3a// Dram. by F. C. Burnand fr F of Henri Meilhac & Ludovic Halévy, Le Mari de la Débutante// **Court**, Feb. 1882, with John Clayton, G. W. Anson, D. G. Boucicault, Linda Dietz, Lottie Venne.

MANAGER IN DISTRESS; OR, THE PLAYHOUSE IN AN UPROAR// F 1a// George Colman the elder// **Sad. Wells**, Aug. 1840, with Mr. Dry as Manager, Mr. Birt [George Burt?] as Easy, Mr. Priorson as Bussleton, Mr. Richardson as Prompter, Mr. Elvin as Sir Jeffrey, J. W. Collier as O'Rog, Mr. Manders as Substitute.

MANAGER IN LOVE, THE// F// n.a.// **Haymarket**, Feb. 1873, with Mr. Rogers as Col. Sherman, Edward Arnott as George Washington, Walter Gordon as Capt. Russell, Mr. Clark as Thorneley, Mrs. Edward Fitzwilliam as Mrs. Sherman, Annie Merton as Augusta, Blanche Henri as Louisa, Miss Francis as Sarah.

MANAGER'S PERPLEXITIES, A (also titled A Manager In Perplexities)// F 1a// n.a.// **Sad. Wells**, Apr. 1862, with Catherine Lucette in 3 char. parts, Bessie Heath as Sally, Charles Crook in 3 char. parts.

MANDARIN, THE// D 5a// Alicia Ramsey & Rudolph De Cordova// **Grand**, Apr. 1901.

MANFRED// T 3a// Lord Byron// **Olympic**, June 1844, with Mr. Laws as the Hunter, J. Simpson as the Abbot, Mr. Scott as Manuel, Mr. France as Herman, Mr. Robertson as Arimanes, Mr. Wilson as Oreus, Miss France as Vesper, Mr. Green as Omorasdes, Mr. Sherrington as Astaroth, Mrs. Sarah Garrick as Nemesis, Miss Hamilton as Astarte, Caroline Rankley as the Witch/ **Drury Lane**, Oct. 1863, with Samuel Phelps as Manfred, John Ryder as Abbot, Alfred Rayner as Hunter, Mr. Neville as Manuel, G. Weston as Herman, Mr. Warde as Arimanes, Emma Heywood as Ariel, Miss Poole as Undine, Cicely Nott as Miserima, Mrs. Edmund Falconer as Nemises, Emma Atkinson as Clotho, Miss C. Weston as Lachesis, Rose Leclercq as Astarte, Miss Heath as Witch/ Scenery by W. Telbin, H. Telbin & Mr. Danson/ Machines by Mr. Tucker/ Music by Henry Bishop/ Prod. by Samuel Phelps/ **Grecian**, Sept. 1867, with Alfred Rayner as Manfred, Henry Grant as Abbot, Charles Mortimer as the Hunter, J. Jackson as Manwel, Samuel Perfitt as Arimanes, Mary A. Victor as Ariel, Alice Denvil as Hesper, Miss De Lacie as Undine, W. Shirley as Astaroth, Lizzie Mandelbert as Witch, Mrs. Atkinson as Clotho, Rosa Martineau as Astarte/ **Princess's**, Aug. 1873, with Mr. Dillon as Manfred, Mr. Palmer as Abbot, Mr. Brunton as Manuel, William Rignold as Hunter, Alfred Honey as Hermann, Mr. Egan as Arimanes, Alice Phillips as Ariel, Miss Russell as Hesper, Miss Villiers as Undine, Mr. Fenton as Astaroth, Jane Coveney as Nemesis/ Scenery by W. Telbin, W. L. Telbin, & F. Fenton.

MANHOOD// D 5a// J. James Hewson// **Marylebone**, July 1889/ **Sad. Wells**, Jan. 1891.

MANIAC LOVER, THE; OR, THE FAIR MAID OF LICHFIELD// D// n.a.// **Grecian**, Oct. 1866, with Charles Mortimer as Darville, George Gillett as Melville, John Manning as Adze, Henry Grant as Giraud, Frederick Marchant as Michael Erle, W. Shirley as Gillyflower, Harriet Western as Mary, Mrs. Atkinson as Dame Stapleton, Mary A. Victor as Julia.

MANKIND; OR, BEGGAR YOUR NEIGHBOR// D 7a// Paul Merritt & George Conquest// **Surrey**, Oct. 1881, with George Conquest, John Hewitt, Alice Ingram, Katie Barry/ **Globe**, Feb. 1882, with George Conquest as Groodge, C. Cruikshanks as Peter Sharpley, J. A. Rosier as Edmund Sharpley, Henry Hamilton as Pinpool, Kyrle Bellew as Warren, E. Shepherd as Melton, John Wilton as Bright, Frank Huntley as Monkeytrick, W. G. Carlile as Possett, Maria Litton as Alice, Katie Barry as Jessie, Harriet Claremont as Arabella, Lizzie Claremont as Kesiah.

MANOEUVERING// F// n.a.// **Sad. Wells**, Aug. 1846, with A. Younge as Whimsey, William Hoskins as Col. Random, E. Morton as Lt. Talbot, Henry Scharf as Spruce, Mrs. Leigh Murray as Clarisse.

MANOEUVERING// C// Adap. by J. R. Planché & Charles Dance fr F// **Haymarket**, June 1872, with Mr. Rogers as Count de Mayor, Walter Gordon as De Cernay, Frederick Everill as Finesse, Miss Francis as Costanza, Mrs. Edward Fitzwilliam as Janetta.

MANOEUVRES OF JANE, THE// Play 4a// Henry Arthur Jones// **Haymarket**, Nov. 1898, with Cyril Maude as Lord Bapchild, Frederick Harrison as Punshon, C. M. Hallard as Langton, W. G. Elliot as Nangle, Holman Clark as Bostok, F. H. Tyler as Pawsey, Sydney Valentine as Sir Robert, Gertrude Kingston as Constantia, Rose Leclercq as Mrs. Beechinor, Beatrice Ferrar as Pamela, Mrs. E. H. Brooke as Lady Bapchild, Fanny Holland as Mrs. Bostock, Winifred Emery as Jane/ Scenery by Walter Hann & Joseph Harker.

MANXMAN, THE// Play 5a// Dram. by Wilson Barrett fr novel of Hall Caine// **Shaftesbury**, Nov. 1895/ **Lyric**, Nov. 1896/ **Lyceum**, Nov. 1899.

MARBLE ARCH, THE// C 1a// Adap. by Edward Rose & Agnes Garraway fr G of G. von Moser, Versucherin// **POW**, Feb. 1882.

MARBLE HEART, THE; OR, THE SCULPTOR'S DREAM// D 5a// Adap. by Charles Selby fr F of Théodore Barrière & Lambert Thiboust, Les Filles de Marbre// **Adelphi**, May 1854, with Paul Bedford as Georgias and Chatenmargaux, John Parselle as Alcibiades and Octave, Leigh Murray as Phidias and Duchatlet, Benjamin Webster as Diogenes and Noel, Sarah Woolgar as Thea and Adrien, Mme. Celeste as Aspasia and Mme. des Aubiers, Emma Harding as Phryne, Mr. Hastings as Lord Merton,

Machines by Mr. Bartlett/ **Sad. Wells,** Mar. 1856, with Leigh Murray as Phidias and Duchatlet, Mr. Barrett as Gorgias and Chateaumargaux, Mr. Swanborough as Alcibiades and Venniere, E. F. Edgar as Diogenes and Volage, Miss M. Oliver as Thea and Marie, Jenny Marston as Marco, Emma Barnett as Phryne and Mariette; Oct. 1871, with Lewis Ball as Georgias and Chateaumargeaux, Mr. Dennistoun as Alcibades and de Courcey, F. Belton as Phidias and Duchatlet, J. Collier as Diogenes and Volage, Furness Rolfe as Alcimidon and Marquis le Grange, Emma Austin as Thea and Marie, Adelaide Lennox as Clementine, Miss Hervey as Aspasia and Mariette, Mrs. G. Hodgson as Mme. Duchatlet/ Prod. by F. Belton.

MARBLE MAIDEN, THE// D 3a// Adap. by W. E. Sutor fr F of Théodore Barrière & Lambert Thiboust// **Grecian,** Nov. 1866, with William James as Phideas and Raphael, Alfred Rayner as Diogenes and Desgenar, Henry Grant as Gorgias and Des Fresnes, George Gillett as Alcibiades and Julian, Henry Power as Strabon and Menleon, Lizzie Mandelbert as Aspasia and Marco, Alice Denvil as Thea and Mario, Mrs. Atkinson as Mme. Didier, Emma Victor as Lais and Josepha, Mrs. Dearlove as Phryne and Juliette/ Scenery by Messender and Soames/ Machines by Mr. Soutar/ Gas by Mr. Dimes/ Music by W. Edroff/ Prod. by George Conquest.

MARCH HARE HUNT, A// C 1a// Frankfort Moore// **Lyceum,** Aug. 1877, with Clifford Cooper as Grumball, Herbert Jenner as Capt. Wildrake, W. Branscombe as Thomas, Kate Pattison as Mrs. Grumball, Eva Morley as Julia.

MARCO SPADA// D 3a// Adap. by J. Palgrave Simpson fr F of Eugène Scribe// **Princess's,** Mar. 1853, with James Vining as Prince Orsini, George Everett as Prince Federico, Walter Lacy as Count Pepinelli, John Ryder as Baron di Torrida, Frank Graham as Fra Borromeo, John Collett as Giacomo, Mr. Terry as Gregorio, Carlotta Leclercq as Marchesa San Pietri, Caroline Heath as Andrea/ Scenery by F. Lloyds, Mr. Dayes, & Walter Gordon/ Music by R. Stöpel/ **Globe,** Oct. 1870, with E. J. Shepherd as Prince Orsini, Shafto Robertson as Prince Federico, Walter Lacy as Count Pepinelli, W. L. Branscombe as Giacomo, Ada Cavendish as Marchesa San Pietro, Clara Weston as Andrea/ Scenery by Frederick Fenton/ Music by Mr. Van Hamm/ Machines by Mr. Cawdery.

MARCORETTI// D// J. M. Kingdom// **Grecian,** Mar. 1854, with Richard Phillips as Baron de Toleda, Henry Grant as Fr. Anselmo, T. Roberts as Jerome, Eaton O'Donnell as Prince Orsini, Charles Rice as Count Pippipoppy, Basil Potter as Count Albert, Harriet Coveney as Marchionesse Sampietri, Jane Coveney as Angela.

MARDEN GRANGE// D// n.a.// **Queen's,** Dec. 1869.

MARE'S NEST, A// FC 3a// Adap. by Henry Hamilton fr G of Julius Rosen// **Vaudeville,** Nov. 1887.

MARGARET BYNG// Play 4a// F. C. Philips & Percy Fendall// **Criterion,** Dec. 1891, with Charles Brookfield as Bazano, John Beauchamp as Col. Heathcote, Ben Webster as Dornton, H. Dana as J. Dornton, Charles Milton as Francois, William Wyes as Braddick, Ernest Cosham as Sharker, A. W. Ayson as Gutteridge, William Herbert as Byng, Estelle Burney as Margaret, Helen Lambert as Mary, Maud Durand as Francine, Lizzie Webster as Mrs. Dornton.

MARGARET CATCHPOLE; OR, THE FEMALE HORSE-STEALER// D 3a// Edward Stirling// **Grecian,** Oct. 1861, with Mr. Jackson as Catchpole, Henry Power as Pip, R. H. Lingham as Barry, F. Smithson as Johnson, William James as Will Laud, Alfred Rayner as Luff, John Manning as Pegs, Miss Johnstone as Dame Catchpole, Miss Wieland as Mary, Jane Dawson as Margaret Catchpole, Mary A. Victor as Sally/ **Victoria,** Mar. 1864, with J. Howard as Catchpole, Brownlow Hill as Pip, Basil Potter as Laud, Frederick Villiers as Luff, George Yarnold as Pegs, George Rose as Barry, J. B. Johnstone as Chittenden, R. Marchant as Wilson, Maria Daly as Margaret, Mrs. W. Daly as Dame Catchpole, Miss E. Farren as Sally, Miss Marchant as Mary, Rose Roberts as Mrs. Palmer.

MARGARET CATCHPOLE, THE HEROINE OF SUFFOLK; OR, THE VICISSITUDES OF REAL LIFE// D 3a// Adap. by Edward Stirling// **Surrey,** Mar. 1845.

MARGARET MAYFIELD; OR THE MURDER OF THE LONE FARM HOUSE// D// C. Z. Barnett// **Sad. Wells,** Oct. 1841, with Mr. Aldridge as Longden, Henry Marston as Mayfield, Mr. Elvin as Watkins, John Herbert as Smallface, Mr. Dry as Garbett, E. Morton as Mackintosh, J. W. Collier as O'Trot, Miss Richardson as Margaret, Mrs. Richard Barnett as Jessy/ Scenery by F. Fenton, Machines by Mr. Cawdery, Music by Isaac Collins/ Prod. by R. Honner.

MARGATE// FC 3a// Barton White// **Terry's,** Feb. 1895, with Leslie Kenyon as Gen. Piercy, Richard Purdon as Beck, Harcourt Beatty as Vereker, E. H. Kelly as Willie, Robert Nainby as Dodd, Ells Dagnall as Stephens, Harry Norton as Inspector, Olga Noyle as Helen, Dolores Drummond as Mrs. Beck, Amelia Gruhn as Kitty, Ina Goldsmith as Pauline, Katie Neville as Mrs. Stephens, Mrs. B. M. de Solla as mme. Tulipon, Jessie Danvers as Eliza.

MARGATE SANDS// F 1a// William Hancock// **Strand,** Jan. 1864.

MARGERY DAW// F 1a// J. Maddison Morton// **Adelphi,** Jan. 1863, with John Billington, L. J. Sefton, C. H. Stephenson, Kate Kelly, Sarah Woolgar (Mrs. Alfred Mellon).

MARGERY'S LOVERS// C 3a// Brander Matthews// **Court,** Feb. 1884, with Edmund Maurice, John Clayton, Arthur Cecil, Mrs. Beerbohm Tree, Mrs. John Wood.

MARGOT// D Pro & 3a// E. Manuel// **Britannia**, Mar. 1875.

MARGUERITE'S COLOURS; OR, PASSING THE FRONTIER (alt. subt. All on the Frontier)// D 2a// Adap. by Thomas Archer fr F// **Lyceum**, July 1847/ **Grecian**, Aug. 1847, with Mr. Baldwin as Duke de Croissy, Eaton O'Donnell as Count Lannoy, J. H. Collins as Col. D'Aubreuil, Richard Phillips as Capt. Sanspeur, Mary A. Crisp as Marguerite, Annette Mears as Helen, Miss Merion as Mme. Thibaut.

MARIA PADILLA; OR, THE HUSBAND, THE KING, AND THE COURT FAVORITE// D 3a// C. Z. Barnett// **Sad. Wells**, May 1841, with Mr. Dry as King Pedro, Mr. Elvin as Don Frederique, Mr. Stilt as Don Tellos, George Ellis as Don Henrique, Mrs. Richard Barnett as Angelo, Henry Marston as Lucio, Robert Honner as Palmi, Mr. Aldridge as Nabal, Miss Richardson as Blanche, Mrs. Robert Honnor as Donna Maria/ Scenery by J. Wilson Jr./ Music by Isaac Collins/ Machines by B. Sloman.

MARIANA// Play 4a// Adap. by J. M. Graham fr Span. of José Echagaray// **Court**, Feb. 1897, with H. B. Irving as di Montoya, Hermann Vezin as Don Felipe, Edward O'Neill as Don Pablo, James Welch as Don Castulo, John Martin Harvey as Arturo, George Bancroft as Ramon, Beverley Sitgreaves as Dona Clara, Mary Keegan as Dona Luisa, Mabel Mackney as Claudia, Elizabeth Robins as Mariana/ Prod. by Elizabeth Robins.

MARIANNE THE CHILD OF CHARITY; OR, THE HEART OF A LAWYER// D// G. D. Pitt// **Victoria**, Jan. 1845, with David Osbaldiston as Capt. Sefton, T. Higgie as Sir Nicodemus, H. Howard as Mansfield, Ersser Jones as Grubwig, J. T. Johnson as Gayfand, John Herbert as Scroggs, Walter Searle as Nightshade, Annette Vincent as Marianne, Miss Jefferson as Bridget, Eliza Terrey as Charlotte.

MARIANNE THE VIVANDIERE; OR, THE MYSTERY OF TWENTY YEARS// D Pro & 3a// L. Phillips// **Standard**, Feb. 1851.

MARIE; OR, THE MANOR HOUSE OF MOUNT LOUVIER// D 2a// Adap. fr F of M. Rosier// **Sad. Wells**, Apr. 1839, with Mr. Cathcart as Count de Tirlemont, Robert Honner as de Limburg, J. W. Collier as Bruno, Mr. Phillips as Martigny, Mr. Conquest as Melchi, Miss Richardson as Countess Tirlemont, Miss Cooke as Abbess, Mrs. J. F. Saville as Martha, Mrs. Robert Honner as Marie/ Scenery by Mr. Fenwick & G. Smithyes Jr., Music by Mr. Herbert/ Prod. by R. Honner.

MARIE; OR, A REPUBLICAN MARRIAGE// C 5a// by "M. H."// **Olympic**, Aug. 1880, with Charles Harcourt as Gaston, Frederick Leslie as Henri, T. Lingham as Comte de Clisson, H. E. Teesdale as Joseph, Emma Chambers as Noel, A. Greville as Jacques, Lizzie Coote as Marie de Courcelles, Miss L. Stanhope as Blanche, Kate Neville as Mme. Jeanette, Louise Dalby as Mme. Maugé.

MARIE; OR, LIFE'S PROMOTION// D 2a// n.a.// **Grecian**, Oct. 1855, with Mr. Melvin as St. Valry, Henry Grant as Launay, Richard Phillips as Arthur St. Valry, Basil Potter as Arnald, John Manning as Mathurin, Eaton O'Donnell as Pierre, F. Charles as Jerome, Jane Coveney as Marie, Harriet Coveney as Therese, Ellen Crisp as Isabelle.

MARIE; OR, THE PEARL OF CHAMONNY// D 5a// n.a.// **Drury Lane**, Feb. 1855.

MARIE; OR, THE PEARL OF SAVOY// D// n.a.// **Adelphi**, Oct. 1843.

MARIE ANTOINETTE// D 4a// J. Palgrave Simpson// **Princess's**, Oct. 1868.

MARIE DE COURCELLES; OR, A REPUBLICAN MARRIAGE// D 5a// Mrs. Holford// **Olympic**, Nov. 1878.

MARIE DUCANGE// D 3a// W. Bayle Bernard// **Haymarket**, May 1841, with Robert Strickland as Bulkly, Samuel Phelps as Lascelles, Benjamin Webster as Rawdon, Henry Howe as Markland, Benjamin Wrench as Prong, George Bennett as Maj. Audley, John Webster as Duparc, Henry Wallack as Bitaube, Mlle. [sic] Celeste as Marie, Priscilla Horton as Susan, Mrs. Frank Matthews as Mrs. Pipes/ Scenery by Charles Marshall, Mr. Pitt & George Morris/ **Adelphi**, July 1845, with Charles Hudson as Edward Lascelles, O. Smith as Rawdon, Edward Wright as Prong, Charles Selby as Bitaube, William Cullenford as Audley, Mme. Celeste as Marie Ducange, Mrs. Frank Matthews as Mrs. Pipes, Ellen Chaplin as Susan/ Scenery by Pitt & Johnstone.

MARIE JEANNE; OR, THE CHILD OF THE FOUNDLING HOSPITAL// D 4a// n.a.// **Grecian**, May 1856, with Richard Phillips as Bertrand, Jane Coveney as Marie, Ellen Crisp as Marguerite, F. Charles as Roquebert, Miss E. Fowler as Pierre, John Manning as Fijeque; July 1863, with Thomas Mead, Alfred Rayner, John Manning, George Gillett, Mr. Howard, Mrs. Charles Dillon, Marie Brewer, Ellen Hale, Mary A. Victor.

MARINA// Play 4a// Dram. by John Coleman fr story by Archibald Gunter, Mr. Barnes of New York// **Gaiety**, Aug. 1888.

MARINER'S COMPASS, THE// D Pro & 3a// Henry Leslie// **Astley's**, Mar. 1865, with Basil Potter as Engleheart, Edward Atkins as Trafalgar Joe, W. S. Gresham as Scoaley, James Fernandez as Dayrell, Henry Frazer as Purvis, Mr. Friend as Brown, Minnie Clifford as Mrs. Proovis, Nelly Smith as Little Annie, Josephine Fiddes as Betty/ Scenery by Charles & William Brew/ Music by J. H. Tully/ Machines by Mr. Nash/ **Grecian**, July 1865, with David Jones as Engleheart, J. Jackson as Trafalgar Joe, Henry Grant as Scorley, William James as Dayrell, John Manning as Christopher, George Conquest as Brown, Mary A. Victor as Keziah, Marie Brewer as Mrs. Proovis, Lizzie Mandlebert as Hetty, Mrs. J. W. Simpson as Mrs. Engleheart/ Scenery by Mr. Messender/ Music by J. H. Tully/ Mise en scene by George Conquest.

MARINER'S DREAM, THE; OR, THE JEW OF PLYMOUTH// D 3a// C. Z. Barnett// **Sad. Wells,** Aug. 1840, with Mr. Dry as Waldorf, Mr. Aldridge as Grayling, Mr. Stilt as Dagan, Charles Fenton as Will, Mr. Houghburt as Capt. Manty, Henry Marston as Seaforth, J. B. Hill as Meriton, Mr. Priorson as Shroud, Mr. Elvin as Clairville, J. W. Collier as Perilous, Mrs. Robert Honner as Ellen, Mrs. Richard Barnett as Fanny/ Scenery by F. Fenton/ Music by Isaac Collins/ Machines by B. Sloman/ Prod. by R. Honner.

MARINERS OF ENGLAND, THE// D 4a// Robert Buchanan & Harriet Jay ("Charles Marlowe")// **Olympic,** Mar. 1897, with W. L. Abingdon as Nelson, Frederick Stanley as Adm. Talbot, W. H. Brougham as Adm. Collingwood, Geoffrey Weedall as Adm. White, Adam Alexander as Capt. Hardy, Herbert Sleath as Capt. Lebaudy, Ernest Mainwaring as Lt. Portland, Gilbery Wemys as Lestrange, Cyril Catley as Beaumont, E. M. Robson as Tom Trip, Julius Royston as Old Trip, Tom Taylor as Marston, Charles Fenton as Bucket, George Hareton as Appleyard, Charles Glenny as Dell, Keith Wakeman as Mabel, Florence Tanner as Nelly, Edith Bruce as Polly.

MARINO FALIERO, THE DOGE OF VENICE// T// Lord Byron// **Drury Lane,** May 1842, with W. C. Macready as Faliero, Charles Hudson as Bertuccio, James Anderson as Lioni, George Bennett as Benintende, Mr. Carle as Steno, Samuel Phelps as Israel, Helen Faucit as Angiolina, Miss Turpin as Marianna.

MARION// D 3a// Dram. by Walter Ellis & P. Greenwood fr Charles Dickens's Battle of Life// **Royalty,** Dec. 1898, with J. G. Taylor as Dr. Jeddler, Herbert Terry as Heathfield, Cooke Beresford as Warden, E. B. Payne as Snitchey, Blanche Eversleigh as Mrs. Craggs, Ruby Hallier as Clemency, Sidney Crowe as Marion.

MARION DE L'ORME [or DE LORME]// D 3a// Trans. fr F of Emile de la Roche// **Lyceum,** 1859, with Henry Vandenhoff, Edmund Falconer, Samuel Emery, Mme. Celeste.

MARION DE L'ORME// D 5a// Adap. by Richard Davey fr F of Victor Hugo// **Princess's,** June 1887.

MARION HAZLETON; OR, THE CHILD OF THE WRONGED// D// John Courtney// **Victoria,** June 1848, with Mr. Henderson as Leigh, David Osbaldiston as Lt. Hazleton, E. Edwards as Lester, J. T. Johnson as Edward Lester, F. H. Henry as Watts, G. F. Forman as Titler, Walter Searle as Wheeler, J. Howard as Crum, Annette Vincent as Marion, Miss Burroughcliffe as Agatha.

MARISHKA// D 5a// Wanda Zaleska// **Sad. Wells,** May 1891.

MARKED MAN, A// D 4a// J. J. Hewson// **Pavilion,** Sept. 1901.

MARKHAM AND GREENWOOD; OR, THE TWO BROTHERS' CAREER// D 3a// Dram. fr Reynolds' The Mysteries of London// **Victoria,** Apr. 1850, with J. T. Johnson as Richard, Mr. Henderson as Eugene (alias Greenwood), J. Neville as Prince Alberto, Mr. Humphreys as Chichester, John Bradshaw as Tidkins, Mr. Leake as Pocock, Watty Brunton as Filippo, J. Howard as Wicks, Henry Dudley as Cuffin, Miss Mildenhall as Henry, Mrs. Humphreys as Isabella, Mrs. George Lee as Ellen, Miss Barrowcliffe as Margaret, Mrs. Cooke as The Mummy, Mrs. Andrews as Mrs. Twiggs.

MARMION; OR, THE BATTLE OF FLODDEN FIELD// D// Found. on poem of Sir Walter Scott// **Sad. Wells,** May 1837, with Mr. Bishop as Surrey, Mr. King as Sir Hugh, Mr. Hicks as Marmion, Mr. Campbell as De Wilton, C. J. Smith as Sir Bertrand, C. H. Pitt as Eustace, Mr. Ennis as Corsley, Mr. Griffiths as Brag, Mr. Pateman as Warder, Mr. Scarbrow as Douglas, Miss Williams as Clare, Mrs. Harris as Constance, Lavinia Melville as Janet.

MARQUESA, THE// D 4a// John Uniacke// **Opera Comique,** July 1889.

MARRIAGE// C 5a// Robert Bell// **Haymarket,** Jan. 1842, with James Wallack as Sir Harry, Benjamin Wrench as Pause, Robert Strickland as Doubtful, Mr. Stuart as Baldwin, Henry Wallack as Wortley, Henry Howe as Wyndham, Benjamin Webster as Drouk, James Worrell as Sharp, F. Webster as Shadow, Mrs. Charles Pettingal as Adelaide, Miss C. Conner as Fanny, Miss Maywood as Mrs. Doubtful, Mrs. Edwin Yarnold as Clara, Mrs. W. Clifford as Lady Pierrepoint/ Scenery by George Morris.

MARRIAGE// Play 3a// Brandon Thomas & Henry Keeling// **Court,** June 1892, with W. G. Elliott as Sir Charles, C. P. Little as Chumbleigh, Brandon Thomas as Sir John, Gertrude Kingston as Mrs. Chumbleigh, Ellaline Terriss as Lady Belton/ Scenery by William Callcott.

MARRIAGE A LOTTERY// C 2a// Charles Dance// **Strand,** May 1858.

MARRIAGE AT ANY PRICE// F 1a// J. P. Wooler// **Strand,** July 1862/ **Sad. Wells,** July 1863, with Frank Murray as Brown, H. J. Montague (alt. with W. Taylor) as Gushington, H. Williams as Peppercorn, Mr. Hathrill as Tubbs, F. G. Gordon as Alick, Lizzie Harrison (alt. with Zoe Montague) as Kate, Rose Garland as Matilda, Maria Norton as Alice.

MARRIAGE BELLS// D 1a// Herbert Gough// **Vaudeville,** Nov. 1881/ **Opera Comique,** July 1892, with Henry Dana as Col. Belville, C. Cemally as Waldron, Cissie Wade as Jessie, Florence Wade as Mrs. Faulkner.

MARRIAGE BY FORCE// D// Adap. fr F// **Grecian,** Oct. 1855, with Henry Grant as Czar Paul, F. Charles as Grand Duke Alexandria, Eaton O'Donnell as Count Ozeroff, Mr. Hamilton as Count Altoff, John Manning as Alexis, Richard Phillips as Daniloff, Jane Coveney as Fedora,

Harriet Coveney as Catherine.

MARRIAGE CERTIFICATE, THE// D 3a// C. H. Hazlewood// **Britannia**, June 1867.

MARRIAGE, 1892// Play 3a & epil.// Clyde Fitch// **Royalty**, Oct. 1892.

MARRIAGE LINES// D 3a// J. D. Besemeres// **Court**, Mar. 1873.

MARRIAGE, NOT DIVORCE; OR, THE LOVE THAT BLOOMS FOREVER// D 3a// John Levey// **Britannia**, May 1870.

MARRIAGE OF CAMACHO, THE// n.a.// **Victoria**, 1868.

MARRIAGE OF CONVENIENCE, A// Play 4a// Adap. by Sidney Grundy fr F of Alexandre Dumas, Un Mariage sous Louis XV// **Haymarket**, June 1897, with William Terriss as de Candale, Cyril Maude as de Valclos, Sidney Valentine as The General, Holman Clark as Jasmin, Adrienne Dairolles as Marton, Winifred Emery as Comtesse de Candale.

MARRIAGE OF PRIDE, A; OR, THE COBBLER AND THE MARQUIS// C 2a// W. E. Suter// **Grecian**, Sept. 1854, with Richard Phillips as Marquis de Beauvilliers, Charles Horn as Viscount de Frettillon, F. Charles as Leonard, William Suter as Gobemouche, Jane Coveney as Mme. de Bellville, Harriet Coveney as Florestine.

MARRIAGE OF REASON, THE// D 2a// n.a.// **Haymarket**, Mar. 1844, with Mr. Stuart as Gen. Bremont, Henry Holl as Edward, Benjamin Webster as Bertrand, J. B. Buckstone as Pinchon, Mme. Celeste as Susette, Mrs. Humby as Mme. Pinchon.

MARRIED// C 3a// James Albery// **Royalty**, Nov. 1873.

MARRIED AND SINGLE// C 2a// J. Poole// **Sad. Wells**, Oct. 1852, with Mr. Barrett as Danvers, Frederic Robinson as Morton, Mr. Belford as Harwood, Mr. Wilkins as du Rore, Mr. Williams as Squeezem, Lewis Ball as Sharp, Miss T. Bassano as Mrs. Harwood, Miss Mandelbert as Eliza.

MARRIED ANOTHER// C 1a// Gerald Dixon// **Opera Comique**, Sept. 1877.

MARRIED BACHELOR, THE; OR, THE MAN OF ALL WORK// C 1a// P. P. O'Callaghan// **Haymarket**, Oct. 1837, with Mr. Hemming as Courtall, J. B. Buckstone as Sharp, Mr. Ray as Truss, Miss Beresford as Lady Courtall, Mrs. Fitzwilliam as Grace/ **Sad. Wells**, June 1842, with Mr. Lyon as Courtall, John Herbert as Sharpe, Mr. Richardson as Truss, Charles Fenton as John, Mrs. Morgan as Lady Courtall, Mrs. Richard Barnett as Grace/ **Victoria**, Aug. 1850, with T. H. Higgie as Courtall, G. F. Forman as Sharp, Georgiana Lebatt as Lady Courtall, Miss Barrowcliffe as Grace/ **Olympic**, May 1885, with Mr. Whitaker as Courtall, A. B. Tapping as Sharpe, Blanche Garnier as Lady Courtall, Miss E. Forbes as Grace.

MARRIED BY PROXY// F 3a// A. W. Yeuill// **Toole's**, Oct. 1894, with Clifford Bown as Maj. Chardin, Edward Compton as Albert Chardin, Robert Greville as Capt. Lumley, Harrison Hunter as Lt. Archer, Auriol Fitzroy as Lt. Pettigrew, Reginald Dartrey as Humphrey, Bessie Thompson as Mrs. Hudson, Sidney Crowe as Cecilia, Madeleine Meredith as Olive, Elsa Wylde as Hemma, Jessie Cross as Mrs. Bummer.

MARRIED DAUGHTERS AND YOUNG HUSBANDS// C 2a// John Daly// **Lyceum**, Nov. 1853, with Frank Matthews as Gadbury, Robert Roxby as Spooner, William Suter as Fagg, Henry Butler as Vacil, Mrs. Frank Matthews as Mrs. Carey, Julia St. George as Mrs. Fagg, Miss Martindale as Mary, Lydia Foote as Mrs. Dander/ **Grecian**, Aug. 1857, with Miss Johnstone as Mrs. Carey, John Manning as Fagg, Richard Phillips as Spooner, Eaton O'Donnell as Wee, W. H. Eburne as Vacil, Mr. Barrett as Gadbury, Jane Coveney as Mrs. Fagg, Harriet Coveney as Mrs. Spooner, Ellen Hale as Anna/ **Olympic**, Oct. 1861 (as Married Daughters), with Horace Wigan as Fagg, Gaston Murray as Spooner, Walter Gordon as Vacil, Harwood Cooper as Wee, George Cooke as Gadbury, Mrs. Leigh Murray as Mrs. Carey, Mrs. W. S. Emden as Mrs. Fagg, Miss Marston as Mrs. Spooner, Miss Cottrell as Anna, Mrs. Stephens as Mrs. Danvers.

MARRIED FOR MONEY// C 3a// Alt. by C. J. Mathews fr The Wealthy Widow// **Drury Lane**, Oct. 1855, with C. J. Mathews as Mopus, Robert Roxby as Royland, A. Younge as Sir Robert, Mr. Templeton as John, Mrs. Frank Matthews as Mrs. Mopus, Miss M. Oliver as Matilda, Miss Mason as Simpkins/ **Haymarket**, Aug. 1857, with W. H. Chippendale as Mellowboy, C. J. Mathews as Mopus, Henry Howe as Royland, Mrs. Poynter as Mrs. Mopus, Miss M. Oliver as Matilda, Mrs. Edward Fitzwilliam as Simpkins.

MARRIED FOR MONEY// D 4a// Edward Towers// **Pavilion**, Mar. 1873.

MARRIED IN HASTE// C 4a// H. J. Byron// **Haymarket**, Oct. 1875, with Henry Howe as Grainger, Hermann Vezin as Pendragon, H. J. Byron as Greene, Charles Warner as Augustus, Mr. Rogers as Mumchance, George Braid as Buffler, Edward Osborne as Rackstraw, Henry Rivers as Padstow, Carlotta Addison as Ethel, Emily Thorne as Mrs. Grainger/ **Folly**, Jan. 1880, with H. J. Byron.

MARRIED LIFE// C 3a// J. B. Buckstone// **Haymarket**, July 1837, with William Farren as Coddle, Frederick Vining as Lynx, J. B. Buckstone as Dove, John Webster as Younghusband, Robert Strickland as Dismal, Mrs. Julia Glover as Mrs. Coddle, Mrs. Nisbett as Mrs. Lynx, Mrs. W. Clifford as Mrs. Dove, Mrs. Humby as Mrs. Younghusband, Mrs. Tayleure as Mrs. Dismal; June 1870, with W. H. Chippendale as Coddle, Henry Howe as Lynx, W. H. Kendal as Younghusband, Mr. Rogers as Dismal, J. B. Buckstone as Dove,

Mrs. Chippendale as Mrs. Coddle, Caroline Hill as Mrs. Lynx, Mrs. Edward Fitzwilliam as Mrs. Younghusband, Mrs. Laws as Mrs. Dismal, Mrs. Frank Matthews as Mrs. Dove/ **Adelphi,** June 1849, with Mr. Lambert as Coddle, Edward Wright as Dove, Charles Boyce as Lynx, Charles Munyard as Younghusband, O. Smith as Dismal, Mrs. Julia Glover as Mrs. Coddle, Sarah Woolgar as Mrs. Lynx, Ellen Chaplin as Mrs. Younghusband/ **Sad. Wells,** May 1847, with J. B. Buckstone as Dove, John Saunders as Coddle, R. H. Lingham as Lynx, J. G. Shore as Younghusband, Charles Fenton as Dismal, Emily Howard as Mrs. Dove, Mrs. Weston as Mrs. Coddle, Miss Portman as Mrs. Lynx, Miss Weston as Mrs. Younghusband, Miss Evans as Mrs. Dismal/ **Lyceum,** May 1859, with Samuel Emery as Coddle, William Belford as Lynx, F. Charles as Younghusband, Mr. Barrett as Dismal, Charles Young as Henry Dove, Mrs. Newbury as Mrs. Coddle, Mrs. Manders as Mrs. Dove/ **Surrey,** Nov. 1869/ **Vaudeville,** Apr. 1880, with David James, C. W. Garthorne, Marie Illington, Kate Bishop, Cicely Richards, Sophie Larkin.

MARRIED LOVERS; OR, A WIFE'S LESSON// C// Tyrone Power// **Haymarket,** Oct. 1839, with Walter Lacy as Philippe d'Orleans, Benjamin Webster as Marquis de Meneville, Robert Strickland as Sir John, Tyrone Power as Col. O'Dillon, Miss Travers as Duchess d'Orleans, Mrs. Walter Lacy (Miss Taylor) as Mme. de Meneville, Priscilla Horton as Lady Ascot, Mrs. Frank Matthews as Annette.

MARRIED, NOT MATED// D 4a// Frank Harvey// **Olympic,** Apr. 1879.

MARRIED RAKE, THE// F// Charles Selby// **Cov. Garden,** June 1840, with Thomas Green as Flighty, Mrs. Brougham as Mrs. Trictrac, Miss Fitajames as Mrs. Flighty, Miss E. Honner as Susan/ **Adelphi,** Feb. 1841, with J. F. Saville, John Sanders, Mrs. Honey, Miss Lee, Mrs. Nailer/ **Victoria,** July 1846, with William Seaman as Flighty, Miss Fielding as Mrs. Trictrac, Mrs. J. Furzman as Mrs. Flighty, Mrs. Seaman as Susan/ **Sad. Wells,** Sept. 1846, with William Hoskins as Flighty, Mr. Franks as John, Mrs. Brougham as Mrs. Trictrac, Miss St. George as Susan, Mrs. Leigh Murray as Mrs. Flighty.

MARRIED UNMARRIED// F 2a// Morris Barnett// **Princess's,** Mar. 1854; May 1861, with John Ryder as Col. de Malfi, J. G. Shore as de Vilmain, Robert Cathcart as Goguenard, Caroline Heath as Adele, Miss Murray as Toinette.

MARSAC OF GASCONY// C 3a// Eduard Vroom// **Drury Lane,** Apr. 1900, with E. Dagnall as Richelieu, Julian Cross as Beaufort, Edward Vroom as de Marsac, William Devereux as de Lagarde, Charles Fulton as de Vertellac, J. A. Rosier as de Fontrailles, Fuller Mellish as Duroc, Edward O'Neill as Cardaize, Eva Moore as Louise, Lily Martin as Clarisse, Isa Dewar as Nichette/ Scenery by Bruce Smith, W. Johnstone, C. Caney & A Dixon/ Music by J. M. Glover/ Machines by E. A. Taylor/ Prod. by Arthur Collins.

MARTHA// C 3a// Wilford Field// **St. Geo. Hall,** Nov. 1894.

MARTIN CHUZZLEWIT// D 3a// Dram. by C. Webb fr novel of Charles Dickens// **Grecian,** Sept. 1844, with Edmund Garden as Martin Chuzzlewit, Mr. Delavanti as Tapley, John Collett as Old Chuzzlewit, Mr. Kerridge as Sweedlepipe, Edwin Dixon as Jonas, Henry Horncastle as Tigg, Frederick Robson as Young Bailey, Mr. Campbell as Pecksniff, Miss M. A. Crisp as Mary Graham, Ellen Crisp as Charity, Miss Merion as Betsy, Mrs. Dixon as Mrs. Lupin/ Scenery by Mr. Muir/ Music by Mr. Isaacson.

MARTIN CHUZZLEWIT// Play// Dram. by Edward Stirling fr novel of Charles Dickens// **Lyceum,** 1844, with Sarah Woolgar.

MARTIN CHUZZLEWIT// D 4a// Dram. by Horace Wigan fr novel of Charles Dickens// **Olympic,** Mar. 1868, with Mr. Stuart as Martin Chuzzlewit, C. J. Smith as Old Chuzzlewit, H. Vaughan as Young Martin, Horace Wigan as Jonas Chuzzlewit, Mr. Addison as Pecksniff, Robert Soutar as Tapley, J. G. Taylor as Pinch, George Vincent as Tigg, Harwood Cooper as Chuffy, Robert Romer as Poll Sweedlepipes, Ellen Farren as Bailey, John Clarke as Mrs. Gamp, Louisa Moore as Mary, Miss D'Este as Charity, Amy Burnette as Ruth, Mrs. Lennox Grey as Mercy, Mrs. Caulfield as Mrs. Todgers, C. J. Smith as Betsy Prig.

MARTINUZZI; OR, THE PATRIOT// D// George Stephens// **Lyceum,** May 1841, with Miss Fitzwalter as Sigismund, Samuel Phelps as Cardinal Martinuzzi, E. W. Elton as Castaldo, Mr. Morley as Turasc, Mrs. Mary Warner as Isabella, Miss Maywood as Czerina, Miss Collett as Bertha/ Scenery by Mr. Telbin/ Music by David Lee/ **Eng. Opera House** (Lyceum), Aug. 1841, with Miss Fitzwalter, Samuel Phelps, E. W. Elton, Mr. Morley, Charles Selby, Mrs. Mary Warner, Miss Maywood.

MARTYR, THE// F// Templeton Lucas// **Court,** (as Browne the Martyr), Jan. 1872.

MARY// C// H. J. Wynter// **Avenue,** Feb. 1897, with Frank Dyall as Rev. Selwyn, Leslie Norman as Sir Jasper, Clifford Soames as Sinclair, Marianne Caldwell as Mrs. Ferguson, Edyth Olive as Mary.

MARY BARTON; OR, THE WEAVERS' DISTRESS// D 3a// W. T. Townsend// **Grecian,** Nov. 1861, with Henry Grant as Carson, R. H. Lingham as Henry Carson, William James as Barton, F. Smithson as Wilson, Henry Power as Dodd, Thomas Mead as Jem, Mrs. Charles Dillon as Mary Barton, Mary A. Victor as Sally, Lucreza Hill as Peggy.

MARY CLIFFIORD, THE FOUNDLING APPRENTICE GIRL// D 3a// n.a.// **Victoria,** July 1850, with Mr. Neville as James Brownrigg, Mr. Henderson as John Brownrigg, J. Howard as Deacon, J. T. Johnson as Clipson, John Hudspeth as Dunbar, John Bradshaw as Clifford, G. F. Forman as Benham, Mrs. George Lee as Mrs. Brownrigg, Georgiana Lebatt as Kitty,

Amelia Mercer as Mary, Mrs. Cooke as Sarah, Miss Mildenhall as Ellen.

MARY EDMONSTONE// D// C. H. Hazlewood// **Britannia**, Dec. 1862.

MARY GRAHAM// D// n.a.// **Grecian**, Dec. 1862.

MARY JONES// C// n.a.// **Queen's**, Mar. 1868.

MARY LE MORE// D 3a// J. P. Hart// **Sad. Wells**, Aug. 1838, with John Webster as Heartman, Mr. Dry as Ineville, Mr. Harwood as Agrippa, Robert Honner as Connor, Dibdin Pitt as Old More, Mr. Conquest as Cleaver, Miss Cooke as Margaret, Mrs. Robert Honner as Mary le More.

MARY MELVYN; OR, THE MARRIAGE OF INTEREST// D 2a// Edward Fitzball// **Adelphi**, Mar. 1843, with Mr. Lyon as Mr. Melvyn, George Maynard as Capt. Marston, L. Smith as Sir Charles Grantley, H. T. Craven as Harry, Mr. Wilkenson as Maj. Lapwing, Mrs. Yates as Mary, Mrs. Frank Matthews.

MARY PENNINGTON, SPINSTER// C 4a// W. R. Walkes// **St. James's**, Apr. 1896, with Cyril Maude as Hale, Frank Fenton as Armstrong, Sidney Brough as Blomfield, Kate Rorke as Mary, Olga Brandon as Lady Maitland, Mary Jerrold as Prudence.

MARY, QUEEN OF SCOTS// D// Dra. fr novel of Sir Walter Scott, The Abbot// **Grecian**, June 1863, with Charles Vernon as Lord Douglas, J. Jackson as Drysdale, George Gillett as Graeme, Walter Holland as Lindsay, W. Shirley as Ruthven, John Manning as McFarlane, Jane Coveney as Queen Mary, Kate Seymour as Catherine, Miss Johnstone as Lady Douglas, Marie Brewer as Mattie.

MARY, QUEEN OF SCOTS// D 5a// W. G. Wills// **Lyceum**, Jan. 1870/ **Princess's**, Feb. 1874, with Mr. & Mrs. Rousby, Mr. Harcourt.

MARY, QUEEN OF SCOTS; OR, LOCH-LEVEN CASTLE// D// dram. fr novel of Sir Walter Scott, The Abbot// **Sad. Wells**, May 1839, with W. D. Broadfoot as Lord Lindsay, Mr. Phillips as Ruthven, Mr. Priorson as Sir Robert, Robert Honner as Douglas, Mr. Elvin as Roland, Mr. Williams as Sandy, Mr. Dry as Drysdale, Mrs. Robert Honner as Mary Stuart, Miss Richardson as Lady Douglas, Miss Nicholls as Catherine, Miss Green as Lady Fleming, Mrs. J. F. Saville as Mattie, Miss Norman as Moggie.

MARY STUART// T// James Haynes// **Drury Lane**, Jan. 1840, with Samuel Phelps as Darnley, George Bennett as Morton, W. C. Macready as Ruthven, Mr. Waldron as Lindsay, Mr. King as Chalmers, Edwin Yarnold as Bothwell, Mr. Heath as Huntley, Henry Marston as Maitland, E. W. Elton as Rizzo, J. W. Ray as Throgmorton, Mrs. Mary Warner as Mary Stuart, Mrs. W. West as Countess of Argyle, Emmeline Montague as Lady Catherine, Miss Cooper as Celine, Miss Pettifer as Marguerite/ Scenery by Mr. Marshall/ Music by Alexander Lee.

MARY STUART// D// Amer. adap. of F vers. of Schiller// **Haymarket**, May 1876, with Fanny Janauschek.

MARY STUART// D 5a// Adap. by Lewis Wingfield fr G of Friedrich von Schiller// **Court**, Oct. 1880, with John Clayton, J. D. Beveridge, Helena Modjeska, Louise Moodie

MARY STUART; OR, THE CASTLE OF LOCH-LEVEN// D// n.a.// **Drury Lane**, Mar. 1850, with Thomas Barry as Lord Lindsey, Charles Diddear as Ruthven, George Everett as Sir Robert, Charles Fisher as Douglas, William Montague as Graeme, Mr. Manderson as MacFarlane, Mr. Cathcart as Drysdale, Laura Addison as Mary Stuart, Miss Phillips as Lady Margaret, Miss Morant as Catherine, Miss Wyndham as Lady Fleming, Miss Grey as Mattie.

MARY WARNER// D 4a// Tom Taylor// **Haymarket**, June 1869, with Henry Howe as Warner, W. H. Kendal as Levitt, Mr. Clark as Dutton, P. White as Downes, Henry Compton as Tollit, Mr. Rogers as Tunks, George Braid as Scriven, Kate Bateman as Mary Warner, Caroline Hill as Milly, Mrs. Laws as Mrs. Floyd, Miss Coleman as Mrs. Frenwick/ Scenery by John O'Conner, Mr. Morris, Mr. Maltby, & Mr. Soutten/ Machines by Oliver Wales/ Gas by F. Hope/ **Olympic**, May 1870, with W. H. Vernon as George Warner, George Belmore as Levitt, David Fisher as Dutton, Walter Roberts as Downes, George Elliott as Tollit, William Blakely as Tunks, H. Vaughan as Scriven, Kate Bateman as Mary Warner, Miss V. Francis as Milly, Mrs. Poynter as Mrs. Floyd, Willa Brown as Little Mary, Jessie Earle as Mrs. Frenwick/ Scenery by John Johnson/ Music by John Winterbottom, Gas by Mr. Pepall/ Prod. by Mrs. W. H. Liston/ **Lyceum**, Sept. 1877, with Kate Bateman as Mary Warner, John Billington as George Warner, James Fernandez as Bob Levitt, S. Johnson as Tollitt, Edmund Lyons as Tunks, Arthur Wing Pinero as Scriven, Mrs. St. John as Mrs. Floyd, Virginia Francis as Milly Rigg.

MARY WHITE; OR, THE MURDER AT THE 'OLD TABBARD'// D 3a// n.a.// **Victoria**, Feb. 1842, with Mr. Cullen as Dove, John Dale as Baynard, C. Williams as Lenmore, William Seaman as Allworth, E. F. Saville as Sam the Padder, Mr. Paul as Hal, Mr. Hitchinson as Tom, John Gardner as Giddywig, Mr. James as Boddy, Mr. Howard as Stubbs, Annette Vincent as Mary White, Mrs. Garthwaite as Dame Dove, Mrs. George Lee as Bet, Miss Sadler as Annie, Miss King as Margaret.

MARY'S DEVOTION// D 1a// Charles Frere// **Surrey**, Apr. 1898.

MARY'S DREAM; OR, FAR, FAR AT SEA// D 3a// Thompson Townsend// **Pavilion**, July 1837.

MARY'S HOLIDAY// F// W. F. Vandervell// **Surrey**, June 1879.

MARY'S SECRET// CD// Arthur Matthison// **Criterion**, May 1876.

MASANIELLO: OR, THE DUMB GIRL OF PORTUGAL (also subt. The Dumb Girl of Portici)// D// Dram. vers. of Auber's opera// **Sad. Wells**, Mar. 1844, with C. J. Bird as Alfonso, Mr. Williams as Duke of Matolini, Mr. Wilson as Magistrate, Mr. Grammani as Lorenzo, Mr. Lamb as Gonzalo, Henry Marston as Masaniello, Charles Fenton as Borella, Mr. Coreno as Guiseppe, C. J. Smith as Pietro, Caroline Rankley as Elvira, Mme. Leoni as the Dumb Girl, Miss Cooke as Buelia/ Prod. by C. J. Smith/ **Victoria**, July 1857, with W. H. Pitt as Alfonzo, Mr. Henderson as Lorenzo, Mr. Hitchinson as Magistrate, Mr. Morrison as Duke, J. H. Rickards as Masaniello, Charles Rice as Aniello, Miss Bailey as Fenella, Julia Seaman as Elvira, Mrs. J. H. Rickards as Briella.

MASANIELLO; OR, THE FISH'O'MAN OF NAPLES// F 1a// Robert Brough// **Olympic**, July 1857.

MASK OF GUILT, THE// D 4a// Sutton Vane & Arthur Shirley// **Surrey**, June 1894.

MASKED// D 4a// n.a.// **Britannia**, Apr. 1870.

MASKED BALL, THE// F 3a// Adap. by Clyde Fitch fr F of Alexandre Bisson & Albert Carré// **Criterion**, Jan. 1900.

MASKED BALL, THE// F 1a// n.a.// **Sad. Wells**, Aug. 1850, with William Hoskins as Mouser, Charles Wheatleigh as Towser, Charles Fenton as Muff, F. Younge as Brisk, Eliza Travers as Mrs. Mouser, Miss Marston as Emily, Mrs. Hanson as Mary.

MASKS AND FACES; OR, BEFORE AND BEHIND THE CURTAIN// C 2a// Charles Reade & Tom Taylor// **Haymarket**, Nov. 1852, with Leigh Murray as Sir Charles, John Parselle as Vane, Mr. Lambert as Colly Cibber, James Bland as Quin, Benjamin Webster as Triplet, Mr. Stuart as Snarl, Mr. Caulfield as Soaper, Mr. Rogers as Burdock, Rosa Bennett as Mrs. Vane, Mrs. Stirling as Peg Woffington, Fanny Maskell as Kitty Clive, Mrs. Leigh Murray as Mrs. Triplet/ Scenery by George Morris & John O'Conner; Feb. 1881, with H. B. Conway as Sir Charles, Arthur Dacre as Vane, Mr. Teesdale as Quin, Arthur Cecil—alt with Squire Bancroft as Colly Cibber, Squire Bancroft—alt. with Arthur Cecil as Triplet, Henry Kemble as Snarl, Charles Brookfield as Soaper, Steward Dawson as Burdock, Mrs. Bancroft as Peg Woffington, Marion Terry as Mabel, Miss Wade as Kitty, Mrs. Canninge as Mrs. Triplet, Mabel Grattan as Roxalana/ Scenery by Walter Hann & Mr. Harford; Feb. 1885, with Johnston Forbes Robertson, Maurice Barrymore, Squire Bancroft, Mrs. Bancroft, Mabel Grattan; Oct. 1889, with Herbert Beerbohm Tree as Triplet, Johnston Forbes Robertson as Sir Charles, Edmund Maurice as Vane, Charles Brookfield as Colly Cibber, Charles Allan as Quin, Henry Kemble as Snarl, Frederick Harrison as Soaper, Stewart Dawson as Burdock, Mrs. Beerbohm Tree as Mistress Vane, Mrs. Bernard Beere as Peg Woffington, Miss Aubrey as Kitty Clive, Miss Ayrtoun as Mrs. Triplet, Dorothy Harwood as Roxalana/ **Adelphi**, Apr. 1853, with Leigh Murray as Sir Charles, John Parselle as Ernest, George Honey as Colly Cibber, Paul Bedford as Quin, Benjamin Webster as Triplet, O. Smith as Snarl, C. J. Smith as Soaper, Mme. Celeste as Peg Woffington, Sarah Woolgar as Mrs. Vane, Fanny Maskell as Kitty Clive, Mrs. Leigh Murray as Mrs. Triplet; Feb. 1859, with Mrs. Alfred Mellon (Sarah Woolgar), Henrietta Sims/ **Olympic**, Aug. 1859, with Mrs. C. J. Mathews, Benjamin Webster; Apr. 1869, with Henry Neville as Sir Charles, Henry Ashley as Vane, C. J. Smith as Colly Cibber, C. H. Stephenson as Quin, Benjamin Webster as Triplet, Harwood Cooper as Snarl, H. Vaughan as Soaper, Robert Romer as Burdock, Mrs. Alfred Mellon as Peg Woffington, Miss Furtado as Mrs. Vane, Mrs. St. Henry as Kitty Clive, Miss Schavey as Mrs. Triplet/ Scenery by Hawes Craven/ Machines by T. Staines/ Music by Edwin Ellis/ **POW**, Oct. 1875, with Mrs. Bancroft, Charles Coghlan, Ellen Terry, Squire Bancroft.

MASQUERADE BALL, THE; OR, TICKETS ON TICK// C// R. W. Pelham// **Sad. Wells**, June 1854, with R. W. Pelham as Sambo, James Worrell as Dash, C. Poynter as Richard III, Edwin Dixon as Macbeth, Mr. Galli as Ghost of Hamlet's Father, Samuel Perfitt as Othello, Miss Lavine as Ophelia, Miss Rawlings as Lady Macbeth, Miss E. Sherriter as Agnes.

MASQUERADERS, THE// Play 4a// Henry Arthur Jones// **St. James's**, Apr. 1894, with George Alexander as David Remon, Herbert Waring as Sir Brice, Mr. Elliot as Lushington, H. V. Esmond as Eddie Remon, Ian Robertson as Crandover, A. Vane Tempest as Blanchflower, Graeme Goring as Sir Winchmore, Ben Webster as Copeland, Arthur Roylston as Fancourt, Mrs. Patrick Campbell as Dulcie, Miss Granville as Helen, Irene Vanbrugh as Charley, Beryl Faber as Lady Clarice, Mrs. Edward Saker as Lady Crandover/ Scenery by H. P. Hall/ Music by Walter Slaughter.

MASTER, THE// C 3a// G. S. Ogilvie// **Globe**, Apr. 1898, with John Hare as Thomas Faber, Frank Gillmore as Dick Faber, Herbert Ross as Charles Faber, Gilbert Hare as Thurkettle, Charles Cherry as Dugdale, Frederick Kerr as Maj. Hawkwood, Kate Terry (Mrs. Arthur Lewis) as Mrs. Faber, Mabel Terry Lewis as Mary Faber/ Scenery by W. Harford.

MASTER AND MAN// D 4a// Henry Pettitt & G. R. Sims// **Pavilion**, Sept. 1889/ **Princess's**, Dec. 1889.

MASTER BUILDER, THE// D 3a// Trans. by William Archer & E. Goese fr Norw. of Henrik Ibsen// **Trafalgar Sq.**, Feb. 1893/ **Vaudeville**, Mar. 1893, with Herbert Waring as Solness, John Beauchamp as Dr. Herdal, Philip Cunningham as Ragnar, H. Athol Forde as Knut, Louise Moodie as Mrs. Solness, Marie Linden as Kala, Elizabeth Robins as Hilda/ Prod. by Herbert Waring & Elizabeth Robins.

MASTER CLARKE// Play 5a// T. J. Serle// **Haymarket**, Sept. 1840, with W. C. Macready as Cromwell, Samuel Phelps as Gen. Disbrowe, Walter Lacy as Col. Ingolsby, James Worrell as Falconberg, George Bennett as Capt. Darnel, Mr. Caulfield as Capt. Berry, J. W. Gough as Thurloe, Robert Strickland as Sir Jacob, Benjamin Webster as Deagle, John Webster as Charles II, Mr. Waldron as Lord Hyde, Henry Howe as Sir Richard, W. H. Oxberry as Smoothly, Helen Faucit as Lady Dorothy, Mrs. W. Clifford as Lady Chubb, Miss Grove as Patience.

MASTER HUMPREY'S CLOCK// D 2a// F. F. Cooper// **Victoria**, June 1840, with Charles Bender as Toddyhigh, Mr. Harding as Humphrey, John Dale as Hartley, Mr. Hicks as Gray, Mr. Burton as Tradelove, Mr. Manders as Curious, Mr. Macdonald as Hubert, Mrs. Howard as Elinor, Adelaide Cooke as Alice/ **Sad. Wells**, June 1840, with Mr. Williams as Humphrey, Henry Marston as Gray, Mr. Dry as Hargrave, Mr. Aldridge as Tradelove, J. W. Collier as Curious, J. B. Hill as Dyke, Mr. Houghburt as Hubert, Mrs. J. F. Saville as Elinor, Miss Richardson as Alice.

MASTER JONES'S BIRTHDAY// F 1a// J. Maddison Morton// **Princess's**, Aug. 1868, with Dominick Murray as Fitztopper, Mr. Maclean as Maj. Muzzle, Emma Barnett as Mrs. Jones, Polly Marshall as Martha.

MASTER OF RAVENSWOOD, THE (see also Ravenswood)// D// J. Palgrave Simpson// n.t., Dec. 1865, with Charles Fechter, Carlotta Leclercq, Miss Elsworthy, Hermann Vezin, Samuel Emery.

MASTER PASSION, THE// C 2a// Mrs. Alfred Phillips// **Olympic**, Sept. 1852, with George Cooke as Buscoyne, E. F. Edgar as Randolph, William Farren as Jacob, William Hoskins as Caleb, W. Shalders as Tobias, Mr. Clifton as Thomas, Mrs. B. Bartlett as Mrs. Buscoyne, Miss Vernon as Julia, Mrs. Walter Lacy as Mildred, Mrs. Alfred Phillips as Polly.

MASTER PASSION, THE; OR, THE OUTLAW OF THE ADRIATIC// D 3a// Adap. by Edmund Falconer fr F of Victor Séjour// **Princess's**, Nov. 1859, with John Collett as Doge, John Ryder as Orseolo, George Melville as Faliero, Robert Cathcart as Beppo, J. W. Collier as Vitatelli, Carlotta Leclercq as Olympia, Mrs. Charles Young as Morosina, Frank Graham as Spolatro, Edmund Garden as Ottofax, Rose Leclercq as Zingara/ Scenery by Grieve & Telbin/ Machines by Mr. Hodsdon/ Music by W. H. Montgomery/ Prod. by Augustus Harris.

MASTER'S LODGE NIGHT// F// G. S. Hodgson// **Surrey**, Feb. 1872.

MASTER'S RIVAL; OR, A DAY AT BOULOGNE// F 1a// R. B. Peake// **Eng. Opera House** (Lyceum), Aug. 1837, with Henry Compton as Paul Shack, A. Brindal as Peter Shack, Mr. Turnour as Sir Colly, W. Bennett as Aldgate, Mr. Baker as Capt. Middleton, Mr. Sanders as Robin, Priscilla Horton as Tibby, Mrs. Emden as Mrs. Aldgate/ **Victoria**, May 1838, with William Davidge as Aldgate, Mr. Loveday as Sir Colley, Mr. Forester as Peter Shack, Mr. Harwood as Capt. Middleton, Mr. Johnstone as Ralph, Mr. Vale as Paul Shack, Mrs. Loveday as Mrs. Aldgate, Miss Williamson as Amelia, Mrs. Vale as Tibby/ **Sad. Wells**, June 1839, with W. D. Broadfoot as Aldgate, Mr. Elvin as Capt. Middleton, John Webster as Peter Shack, Mr. Conquest as Paul Shack, Mr. Williams as Sir Colley, Mr. Phillips as Barnes, J. W. Collier as Robin, Miss Cooke as Mrs. Aldgate, Miss Pincott as Tibby, Mrs. J. F. Saville as Amelia/ **Olympic**, Mar. 1851, with George Cooke as Sir Colley, Charles Bender as Aldgate, John Kinloch as Capt. Middleton, Leigh Murray as Peter Shack, Henry Compton as Paul Shack, Mrs. B. Bartlett as Mrs. Aldgate, Miss Adams as Amelia, Mrs. Alfred Phillips as Tibby.

MASTERPIECE, THE// C 1a// Mrs. Hugh Bell// **Royalty**, Apr. 1893, with Herbert Flemming as Bromley, Gertrude Kingston as Mrs. Bromley, Hetty Lawrence as Sarah.

MATCH FOR A KING, A// C 2a// Adap. by C. J. Mathews fr Don Caesar de Bazan// **Haymarket**, Nov. 1844, with Mr. Stuart as King Charles, C. J. Mathews as Don Sebastian, Henry Holl as Don Fernando, Robert Strickland as Marquese de Tornados, Miss Lee as Pedrillo, J. W. Gough as Governor, Julia Bennett as Marquita, Mrs. Stanley as Marquesa de Tornados.

MATCH HER WHO CAN// C// n.a.// **Haymarket**, Oct. 1842, with Robert Strickland as Chasewell, Mr. Tilbury as Old Loveall, Henry Howe as Capt. Belmore, Henry Holl as Jack, Mrs. Honey in 5 char. parts, Miss Charles as Mary, Miss C. Conner as Olivia, Mrs. W. Clifford as Miss Wou'dwed, Mrs. Malone Raymond as Prue.

MATCH IN THE DARK, A// F 1a// Charles Dance// **Cov. Garden**, June 1840, with Thomas Green as Capt. Courtney, Mr. Granby as Clements, Mr. Collier as Vellum, John Brougham as O'Flynn, Mrs. Brougham as Ellen, Mrs. Orger as Prudence/ **Haymarket**, Nov. 1842, with Mr. Tilbury as Clements, Henry Holl as Capt. Courtnay, Malone Raymond as O'Flynn, Henry Widdicomb as Vellum, Mrs. W. Clifford as Prudence, Mrs. Honey as Ellen/ **Grecian**, July 1844, with Mr. Campbell as Clements, Frederick Robson as Vellum, Henry Horncastle as Capt. Courtney, Edmund Garden as Terence, Miss M. A. Crisp as Ellen, Miss Johnstone as Prudence/ **Sad. Wells**, Mar. 1846, with Henry Marston as Capt. Courtney, Henry Scharf as Vellum, Henry Mellon as O'Flynn, Mr. Williams as Clement, Mrs. Henry Marston as Mrs. McIntyre, Miss Cooper as Clara.

MATCH-MAKER, A// C 4a// Clothilde Graves & Gertrude Kingston// **Shaftesbury**, May 1896, with Lewis Waller as Rolles, C. P. Little as Marquess of Westbourne, E. W. Gardiner as Soper, Kenneth Black as Bishop of Dorminster, Lesly Thompson as Earl of Cranboisie, Alfred Maltby as Bligh, Florence West as Wilhelmina, Beatrice Ferrar as Georgiana, Spencer Brunton as Flora, Daisy Brough as Ethel, Nina Boucicault as Betty, Fanny Coleman as Lady Holdawle, Mrs. Arthur Ayres as Mrs. Waite, Lena Ashwell as Margaretta, Gertrude Kingston as Mrs. Lane.

MATCH MAKING// C 1a// n.a.// **Haymarket**,

Aug. 1956, with W. H. Chippendale as Matchem, William Farren as Col. Rakely, Leighton Walter as Capt. Belmont, Mr. Clark as Shuffle, Miss Talbot as Lady Emily.

MATCHES// C 3a// Charles Glenney & A. E. Bagot// **Comedy**, Jan. 1899, with Edmund Maurice as Maj. Glossop, Charles Troode as Schriver, W. E. Sauter as Duncan, F. G. Thurstans as Hall, Harry Nicolls as Hogan, Sophie Larkin as Lady Bicester, Sybil Carlisle as Eleanor, Henrietta Cowen as Miss Oswald, Mrs. Henry Leigh as Mrs. Hogan, Annie Hughes as Kitty/ Prod. by Edmund Maurice.

MATED// C 3a// Mrs. Vaughn// **Criterion**, June 1879.

MATEO FALCONI AND HIS SON// D// n.a.// **Sad. Wells**, June 1861, with Mr. Mattocks as Falconi, J. B. Johnstone as Sampiero, Mr. Stretton as Alezzio, Mr. Brinsley as Nicolo, Miss Ferguson as Guiseppa, Clara Denvil as Fortunato.

MATERNAL INSTINCT, THE// Play 3a// Thomas Bedding// **Duke of York's**, June 1898, with Charles Cherry as Jedward, Fred Grove as Vosper, H. A. Saintsbury as Sir Charles, Hubert Willis as Dr. Roach, Sydney Paxton as Gen. Emerett, Eardley Turner as Rev. Knowles, Herbart Jarman as Prof. Ouvry, Arthur Rowlands as Cruge, Maude Clifford as Miss Pulteney, Genevra Campbell as Ladt Aftonby, Mary Allentree as Mrs. Walsham, Octavia Kenmore as Cynthia.

MATHEWS & CO.// C 1a// C. J. Mathews// **Princess's**, Mar. 1846, with C. J. Mathews as Mathews, Henry Compton as Gagger, Mr. Walton as Gulling, W. H. Oxberry as Cumming, Miss E. Honner as Dolly.

MATRIMONIAL// C 3a// n.a.// **Novelty**, June 1891.

MATRIMONIAL - A GENTLEMAN, ETC// F 1a// J. V. Bridgeman// **Olympic**, Feb. 1852.

MATRIMONIAL AGENCY, THE// Play 1a// Emily Beauchamp// **Strand**, Dec. 1897.

MATRIMONIAL NOOSE, THE// FC 3a// M. H. Spier// **Princess's**, May. 1885.

MATRIMONIAL PROSPECTUSES// C 1a// J. Palgrave Simpson// **Strand**, Mar. 1852.

MATRIMONY// F 1a// James Kenney// **Cov. Garden**, May 1838, with Mr. Vining as Delaval, Mr. Tilbury as Baron de Limburg, Mr. Macarthy as O'Clogherty, Helen Faucit as Clara/ **Sad. Wells**, May 1840, with Henry Marston as Capt. Delaval, Henry Hall as O'Clogerty, Mr. Williams as Baron de Limberg, Mrs. Richard Barnett as Ninette, Mrs. Robert Honner as Clara.

MATTEO FALCONE; OR, THE BRIGAND AND HIS SON// D 1a// Adap. by W. H. Oxberry fr F// **Victoria**, Mar. 1838, with Mr. Wilkins as Matteo, Mr. Harwood as Sampiero, William Davidge as Corp. Gamba, Mr. King as Brozzi, Mrs. Harwood as Nina, Miss Le Vite as Fortunato/ **Sad. Wells**, Oct. 1841, with E. Morton as Capt. Alessio, J. W. Collier as Corp. Nicolo, Mr. Dry as Falcone, C. J. Smith as Sampiere, Charles Fenton as Brozzo, Mrs. Robert Honner as Fortunato, Miss Cooke as Guiseppa, Mrs. J. W. Collier as Marie.

MAUDE HARVEY; OR, THE WOLF AND THE LAMB// D 2a// n.a.// **Grecian**, Nov. 1867, with J. Jackson as Hugh Lindsay, William James as Charles Lindsay, Charles Mortimer as Robert Lindsay, Samuel Perfitt as Wharton, Alfred Rayner as Beagle, John Manning as Friz, Lizzie Mandelbert as Maude Harvey, Alice Denvil as Anale, Mary A. Victor as Mrs. Apollo.

MAUD'S PERIL// C 4a// Found. by Watts Phillips on story of Charles De Bernard// **Adelphi**, Oct. 1867, with John Billington as Sir Ralph, Henry Ashley as Gerald, George Belmore as Toby, C. J. Smith as Burrell, W. H. Eburne as Doctor, Miss Herbert as Lady Challoner, Amy Sheridan as Miss Sefton, Mrs. Billington as Susan/ Machines by Mr. Charker/ Gas by G. Bastard/ Prod. by Benj. Webster.

MAY; OR, DOLLY'S DELUSION// D 3a// Robert Reece// **Strand**, Apr. 1874.

MAY AND DECEMBER// C 3a// Adap. by Sidney Grundy fr F of Henri Meilhac & Ludovic Halévy, La Petite Marquise// **POW**, 1865/ **Criterion**, Apr. 1887/ **Comedy**, Nov. 1890, with Charles Hawtrey as Capt. L'Estrange, Charles Brookfield as Sir Archibald, J. F. Graham as Jones, Rose Norreys as Lady Ffolliott, Lydia Cowell as Jane, Ethel Mathews as Dolly, Lottie Venne as Judy.

MAY MARTIN THE MAID OF THE GREEN MOUNTAINS; OR, THE MONEY DIGGERS OF VERMONT PRAIRIE// D 3a// n.a.// **Victoria**, Nov. 1842, with C. Williams as Sheriff Johnson, Mr. Cullen as Martin, E. F. Saville as Gow, William Seaman as Ashley, Mr. Howard as Harwood, Mr. James as Mundle, John Dale as Colvin, Annette Vincent as May, Mrs. George Lee as Mrs. Martin, Mrs. Griffith as Widow Butler.

MAY MORNING; OR, THE MYSTERY OF 1715 AND THE MURDER// D 3a// n.a.// **Victoria**, Feb. 1850, with Henry Dudley as Sir George, Mr. Henderson as Capt. Elmore, J. T. Johnson as Stanmore, J. Neville as Ritter, John Dale as Heartland, John Bradshaw as Mendicant, John Hudspeth as Soak, J. Howard as Jobbins, Mr. Humphreys as Slink, F. H. Henry as Potts, Annette Vincent as May, Miss Mildenhall as Estella, Mrs. George Lee as Manuella, Miss Barrowcliffe as Dorothy.

MAYFAIR// Play 5a// Adap. by Arthur Wing Pinero fr F of Victorien Sardou, Maison Neuve// **St. James's**, Oct. 1885, with C. Cartwright as Lord Sulgrave, Charles Brookfield as Capt. Jekyll, John Hare as Barrable, W. H. Kendal as Roydant, John Maclean as Perricarp, E. Hendrie as Jowett, A. Elwood as Rufford, H. Reeves Smith as Moorcroft, W. T. Lovell as Ogilvy, Mrs. W. H. Kendal as Agnes, Miss

Webster as Edna, Fanny Enson as Hilda, Mrs. Gaston Murray as Priscilla, Linda Dietz as Louison/ Scenery by W. Harford.

MAYFAIR AND RAGFAIR// D 2a// Joseph Mackay// **Globe**, Aug. 1878.

MAYFLOWER, THE// C 4a// Dram. by F. F. Moore fr Longfellow// **Opera Comique**, Jan. 1892, with J. S. Blythe as Miles Standish, Sydney Paxton as Brewster, Lewis Ball as Jones, Clarence Blakiston as Couant, Edward Compton as John Alden, Elinor Aickin as Elizabeth, Evelyn McNay as Prudence/ Scenery by Joseph Harker.

MAYOR OF GARRATT, THE// F 2a// Samuel Foote// **St. James's**, Feb. 1837, with Mr. Hollingsworth as Sir Jacob, Robert Strickland as Maj. Sturgeon, Mr. Gardner as Sneak, Mr. Daly as Bruin, Mr. Sidney as Heeltap, Mr. Hart as Scuffle, Mme. Sala as Mrs. Sneak, Miss Stuart as Mrs. Bruin/ **Drury Lane**, June 1839, with Mr. Hughes as Sir Jacob, Mr. Dowton as Maj. Sturgeon, Mr. Russell as Sneak, Mr. Manders as Bruin, Mme. Simon as Mrs. Sneak, Miss Somerville as Mrs. Bruin/ **Haymarket**, July 1841 (in 1a), with Mr. Russell as Sneak, Robert Strickland as Maj. Sturgeon, T. F. Mathews as Sir Jacob, Mr. Gallot as Bruin, Mrs. W. Clifford as Mrs. Sneak, Miss Mattley as Mrs. Bruin/ **Sad. Wells**, Apr. 1843, with T. Peters as Sneak, Mr. Commodore as Maj. Sturgeon, Mr. Aldridge as Bruin/ **Olympic**, Sept. 1846, with Mr. George as Jalap, J. S. Ward as Maj. Sturgeon, Mr. Alexander as Sneak, Mr. Bright as Bruin, Mr. Frazier as Heeltap, Mrs. Roberts as Mrs. Sneak, Mrs. Smith as Mrs. Bruin/ **Astley's** (in 1a), May 1852, with S. Smith as Maj. Sturgeon, Mr. Johnson as Sir Jacob, Thomas Barry as Sneak, Mr. Craddock as Bruin, Miss Fenton as Mrs. Bruin, Lydia Pearce as Mrs. Sneak.

MAZEPPA; OR, THE WILD HORSE OF TARTARY// D 3a// Lord Byron// **Grecian**, Aug. 1862, with Henry Grant as Castellan, George Gillett as Count Palatine, J. Jackson as Rudsoloff, John Manning as Drolinsko, Mrs. Charles Dillon as Olinska, Miss Johnstone as Agatha, Mary A. Victor as Zemila, Alfred Rayner as Abder Kahn, Walter Edwin as Mazeppa, Walter Holland as Thamar, Laura Conquest as Opeiza/ **Sad. Wells**, Sept. 1865, with George Pearce as Castellan, John Gardiner as Count Premislaus, Mr. Wallis as Rudzoloff, J. Russell as Drolinska, Nellie Jones as Olinska, Miss Jones as Zemila, Mrs. Wallis as Agatha, Charles Moorhouse as Abder Khan, Julia Masters as Mazeppa, John Mordaunt as Thamar, Amy Stanley as Onezia; May 1868, with Harry Rignold as Castellan, Walton Chamberlain as Premislaus, Mr. Wilson as Rudzoloff, Mat Robson as Brolinsko, Lottie Brennan as Olinsko, Marie Willis as Agatha, Mrs. Henry Powell as Zemila, George Maynard as Abder Khan, Ada Isaacs Menken as Mazeppa, Mr. Hammonde as Thamar, Rita Percy as Oneiza.

MAZEPPA AND THE WILD HORSE; OR, THE CHILD OF THE DESERT// D// n.a.// **Sad. Wells**, July 1842, with Mr. Harwood as Castallan, John Herbert as Drolinski, Mr. Lamb as Count Premislaus, Mr. Richardson as Rudzoloff, Miss Richardson as Olinska, Mrs. Richard Barnett as Zemila, Mr. Dry as Abderkhan, W. D. Broadfoot as Mazeppa/ **Astley's**, July 1850, with G. Nelson as the Castellan, Arthur Stirling as Premislaus, Mr. Johnson as Rudzoloff, Thomas Barry as Drolinsko, Miss E. Neil as Olinska, Lydia Pearce as Zemila, W. West as Abder Khan, N. T. Hicks as Mazeppa, S. Smith as Thamar, Mrs. Moreton Brookes as Oneiza/ Scenery by Mr. Dalby/ Machines by Richard Smith/ Music by Mr. Phillips.

MAZOURKA// C 1a// n.a.// **Sad. Wells**, July 1839, with Mr. Elvin as Capt. Belmont, John Webster as Dr. Ardent, J. W. Collier as Robin, Mr. Conquest as Dobleton, Mrs. Honey in 3 char. parts.

MEADOW SWEET// C 1a// C. M. Prevost ("Terra Cotta")// **Vaudeville**, Mar. 1890, with J. S. Blythe as Barnes, Cyril Maude as John, Frank Gillmore as Topliffe, Fred Thorne as Jokel, Lily Hanbury as Julia, Ella Banister as Margery.

MEASURE FOR MEASURE// C// William Shakespear// **Sad. Wells**, Nov. 1846, with Samuel Phelps as Vincentio, George Bennet as Angelo, Henry Mellon as Escalus, Henry Marston as Claudio, Mr. Hoskins as Lucio, Charles Fenton as Abberson, Henry Scharf as Pompey, Laura Addison as Isabella, Miss Huddart as Mariana, Mrs. Henry Marston as Mrs. Overdone/ Scenery by Mr. Finlay/ **Haymarket**, Apr. 1876, with Henry Howe as Vincentio, Charles Harcourt as Angelo, George Braid as Escalus, Charles Warner as Claudio, H. B. Conway as Lucio, Mr. Weathersby as Frederick, F. Webster as Leopold, J. B. Buckstone as Pompey, Henry Rivers as Froth, Adelaide Neilson as Isabella, Edith Challis as Mariana, Mrs. Edward Osborne as Francesca, Mrs. Edward Fitzwilliam as Mrs. Overdone.

MEDDLE AND MUDDLE// F 1a// Henry Bellingham & William Best// **Terry's**, Oct. 1887.

MEDEA// T// Adap. by J. A. Heraud fr F of Gabriel Legouvé// **Sad. Wells**, 1857; Apr. 1863, with H. Dalton as Creon, Henry Forrester as Jason, Charles Vandenhoff as Orpheus, Miss Atkinson as Medea, Catherine Lucette as Creusa, Bessie Heath as Ianthe/ **Standard**, June 1859, with Edith Heraud.

MEDEA// T 3a// Trans. by Matilda Heron fr F of Gabriel Legouvé// **Drury Lane**, Nov. 1861, with Henry Mellon as Creon, R. Younge as Jason, L. J. Sefton as Orpheus, Avonia Jones as Medea, Henrietta Sims as Creusa, Mrs. Dowton as Ianthe.

MEDEA// T 5a// Trans. fr F of Ernest Legouvé// **Olympic**, Mar. 1883, with W. H. Vernon as Jason, A. C. Hatton as Creon, J. A. Rosier as Orpheus, Lucy Buckstone as Creusa, Genevieve Ward as Medea.

MEDEA// T 4a// Adap. fr G. of Franz Grillparzer, <u>Das Goldene Fliess</u>// **Haymarket**,

May 1876, with Fanny Janauschek as Medea.

MEDEA; OR, A LIBEL ON THE LADY OF COLCHIS// F 1a// "Freely adapted fr Mr. Thomas Williams's translation of Signor Joseph Montanelli's reproduction of M. Ernest Legouvé's imitation of Euripides"// **Adelphi**, Aug. 1856, with James Bland as Creon, Mary Keeley as Orpheus, Miss Wyndham as Jason, Paul Bedford as Glauce, Edward Wright as Medea.

MEDEA IN CORINTH// F 1a// "freely trans." fr Euripides// **Lyceum**, Oct. 1852, with Frank Matthews as Creon, Julia St. George as Jason, Mme. Vestris as Medea, Lydia Foote as Pouche, C. J. Mathews as Chorus.

MEDEA IN CORINTH// T 3a// Adap. fr F of Gabriel Legouvé// **Sad. Wells**, Aug. 1857, with Edith Heraud as Medea, Kate May as Creusa, Mrs. E. F. Saville as Ismene, R. Green as Nicippi, Alfred Rayner as Jason, Mr. Lyon as Aegeus, Charles Seyton as Creon.

MEDEA IN CORINTH// T 3a// Adap. by W. G. Wills fr F of Gabriel Legouvé// **Lyceum**, July 1872, with John Ryder as Creon, Thomas Swinbourne as Jason, Charles Warner as Orpheus, W. L. Branscombe as Xanthus, Isabel Bateman as Medea, Virginia Francis as Glaucea.

MEDICAL MAN, A// W. S. Gilbert// **St. Geo. Hall**, Oct. 1872.

MEDICAL STUDENT, THE// C 3a// Beard Francis & H. J. Laeland// **Strand**, July 1893, with Fred Everill as Burton, James Welch as Tim, Lawrance d'Orsay as Sir Giles, John Tresahar as Dick, Mrs. Henry Leigh as Mrs. Burton, Mary Kingsley as Alice, Annie Hill as Sophie, Fanny Marriott as Sarah, Henrietta Cross as Anne.

MEDICINE MAN, THE// C 5a// H. D. Traill & Robert Hichens// **Lyceum**, May 1898, with Henry Irving as Dr. Tregenna, Nutcombe Gould as Lord Belhurst, Frank Cooper as Col. Anson, Norman Forbes as Canon Slade-Smith, Ben Webster as Warrington, Rose Leclercq as Mrs. Culling, Maud Milton as Lady Agatha, Ellen Terry as Sylvia, Ian Macintosh as Burge, Fuller Mellish as Cheeseman, Dolores Drummond as Mrs. Burge/ Scenery by Hawes Craven, W. Harford & William Telbin/ Music comp. by Valérie White.

MEDUSA// C 1a// Dram. by Frederick Hay fr a story// **St. James's**, Jan. 1882, with T. N. Wenman as Col. Delfield, Mr. Draycott as George, Mr. Mackintosh as Vanstone, Mrs. Gaston Murray as Miss Medusa, Kate Bishop as Carry.

MEET ME BY MOONLIGHT; OR, THE IRISH ASTROLOGER// F// Thomas Parry// **Sad. Wells**, Mar. 1837, with Mr. King as Pedigree, Mr. Ennis as Planet, C. H. Pitt as Harcourt, Thomas Lee as O'Grady, Lavinia Melville as Emmeline, Miss Lebatt as Peggy, Mrs. Harris as Mrs. Plum/ **Olympic**, May 1839, with Thomas Green as Capt. Hampton, Charles Selby as Burfield, Mr. Granby as Lexicon, Robert Keeley as Timothy Trotter, Mrs. Macnamara as Miss Craw, Mrs. Franks as Jenny, Miss Murray as Sophia.

MEG MURNOCH; OR, THE FATAL GLEN// D// William Barrymore// **Astley's**, Apr. 1850, with G. Nelson as Walter, N. T. Hicks as Fitz Arran, Mr. Johnson as Lord Dunbar, Arthur Stirling as Murdyn, Master Rochester as Lord Malcolm, Ely Loveday as Lady Bertha, Mrs. Moreton Brookes as Meg.

MEG'S DIVERSION// C 2a// H. T. Craven// **Royalty**, Oct. 1866/ **Sad. Wells**, Apr. 1870, with C. Mortimer as Sir Ashley, W. Nicholls as Crow, C. A. White as Jasper Pidgeon, J. C. Hawksley as Roland Pidgeon, C. Jepson as Eytem, Miss Victor as Mrs. Netwell, Lizzie Dudley as Amelia, Miss S. Mills as Margaret.

MEHALAH; OR, THE POWER OF WILL// D 5a// Adap. by William Poel & W. H. G. Palmer fr novel of Baring-Gould// **Gaiety**, June 1886.

MEM. 7// C// Walter Lisle// **Royalty**, Oct. 1879.

MEMBER FOR SLOCUM// C 3a// Adap. by G. R. Sims fr F, Le Supplice d'un Homme// **Royalty**, May 1881, with Arthur Williams, Elise Ward, Harriet Coveney, Kate Lawler/ **Olympic**, Jan. 1882, with F. W. Irish as Epps, H. J. Lethcourt as Smith, D. Somers as Gunning, Miss J. Vernon as Fanny, Miss L. Fane as Madeline, Harriet Coveney as Mrs. Jeffs, Miss L. Telbin as Arathusa/ **Globe**, Mar. 1884, with J. L. Shine as Epps, H. J. Lethcourt as Smith, Florence Trevelyan as Madeline, Carlotta Leclercq as Mrs. Jeffs, Fanny Brough as Arethusa.

MEMOIRS OF AN UMBRELLA; OR, THE SILENT OBSERVER// C 3a// Dram. by Charles Dance fr novel of G. H. Rodwell// **Adelphi**, 1846, with Mr. Lambert as Mr. Stutters, Henry Howe as Quickly, O. Smith as Mr. Rant, Charles Selby as Spiff, George Braid as Lord Toodle, Paul Bedford as Swifts, Edward Wright as Mr. Chickweed, William Cullenford as Clear, Sarah Woolgar as Mrs. Colonel Seymore, Mrs. Edwin Yarnold as Alice, Ellen Chaplin as Ellen, Mrs. Frank Matthews as Lotty/ Scenery by Pitt & Johnstone/ Music by Alfred Mellon.

MEMOIRS OF THE D— C—; OR, THE MYSTIC BELL OF RONQUEROLLES// D 3a// James Barber// **Surrey**, Aug. 1842.

MEMOIRS OF THE D—L// D// J. Barber// **Grecian**, Mar. 1854, with Charles Horn as Marquis Lormias, Basil Potter as Chev. Rapinierre, Richard Phillips as Robert, T. Roberts as Count Corny, Eaton O'Donnell as Gauthier, Charles Rice as Valentine, Ellen Crisp as Baroness Rouquerolles, Agnes De Warde as Countess Gerny, Jane Coveney as Marie, Miss Johnstone as Mme. Giraud.

MEMORIES// C 3a// T. A. Palmer// **Court**, Oct. 1878.

MEN AND MONEY// D Pro & 3a// C. A.

Clarke// **Pavilion**, July 1890.

MEN AND WOMEN// D 6a// Mrs. R. Fairbairn// **Surrey**, July 1882.

MEN OF METAL// D 4a// C. A Clarke & H. R. Silva// **Pavilion**, July 1891.

MERCHANT OF VENICE, THE// C// William Shakespeare// **Cov. Garden**, Apr. 1837, with Mr. Thompson as Duke, John Pritchard as Bassanio, John Webster as Gratiano, Mr. Collins as Lorenzo, Charles Bender as Salanio, Mr. Worrell as Salarino, George Bennett as Antonio, Mr. Hyde as Shylock, Mr. Tilbury as Gobbo, Benjamin Webster as Launcelot, Helen Faucit as Portia, Eliza Vincent as Jessica, Miss Lee as Nerissa/ **Sad. Wells**, June 1837, with Mr. King as Duke, Mr. Campbell as Antonio, Mr. S. King as Lorenzo, John Dale as Bassanio, John Pritchard as Gratiano, George Bennett as Shylock, Mr. Tilbury as Old Gobbo, Mr. Conquest as Launcelot, Mrs. W. West as Portia, Miss Williams as Nerissa, Miss Land as Jessica; June 1844, with Samuel Phelps as Shylock, Henry Marston as Bassanio, T. H. Lacy as Antonio, Mr. Binge as Lorenzo, Charles Hudson as Gratiano, Mr. Coreno as Launcelot, Mr. Williams as Old Gobbo, Edward Knight as Duke, Mrs. Mary Warner as Portia, Miss Cooper as Nerissa, Georgiana Lebatt as Jessica/ **Haymarket**, Aug. 1837, with Samuel Phelps as Shylock, J. W. Gough as Duke, Mr. Saville as Bassanio, Frederick Vining as Gratiano, Mr. Collins as Lorenzo, Charles Selby as Salanio, J. T. Haines as Antonio, Benjamin Webster as Launcelot, T. F. Mathews as Old Gobbo, Miss Huddart as Portia, Miss E. Phillips as Nerissa, Eliza Vincent as Jessica; Sept. 1839, with Mr. Perkins as Duke, Samuel Phelps as Antonio, Walter Lacy as Bassanio, Mr. Hemming as Solanio, Henry Howe as Salarino, Benjamin Webster as Gratiano, W. C. Macready as Shylock, J. B. Buckstone as Launcelot, Robert Strickland as Old Gobbo, Helen Faucit as Portia, Miss Travers as Nerissa, Priscilla Horton as Jessica/ Scenery by Phillips & Morris; Dec. 1841 (J. P. Kemble's vers.), with George Bennett as Duke, Henry Wallack as Antonio, John Webster as Bassanio, Henry Howe as Salarino, James Worrell as Solanio, James Vining as Gratiano, James Wallack as Shylock, David Rees as Launcelot, Robert Strickland as Gobbo, Helen Faucit as Portia, Miss Charles as Nerissa, Priscilla Horton as Jessica; Jan. 1849, with A. Brindal as Duke, Mr. Rogers as Antonio, Alfred Wigan as Bassanio, Henry Vandenhoff as Salanio, George Braid as Salarino, Benjamin Webster as Gratiano, Charles Kean as Shylock, Robert Keeley as Launcelot, Mr. Tilbury as Gobbo, Mrs. Charles Kean as Portia, Mrs. Keeley as Nerissa, Priscilla Horton as Jessica; Sept. 1861, with William Cullenford as Duke, Mr. Rogers as Antonio, Henry Howe as Bassanio, James Worrell as Salanio, George Braid as Salarino, William Farren as Gratiano, Edwin Villiers as Lorenzo, Edwin Booth as Shylock, J. B. Buckstone as Launcelot, W. H. Chippendale as Old Gobbo, Mrs. Charles Young as Portia, Miss M. Oliver as Nerissa, Henrietta Lindley as Jessica/ **Victoria**, Oct. 1837, with William Davidge as Duke, Mr. Green as Bassanio, John Parry as Antonio, Mr. Roland as Solario, Mr. Denvil as Shylock, W. H. Oxberry as Gobbo, Mr. Loveday as Old Gobbo, Mrs. Hooper as Portia, Miss Lee as Jessica, Mrs. Frank Matthews as Nerissa; July 1842, with David Osbaldiston as Shylock, E. F. Saville as Gratiano, William Seaman as Bassanio, John Gardner as Launcelot, John Dale as Antonio, Miss Martin as Nerissa/ **Drury Lane**, Oct. 1837, with Mr. Baker as Duke, Mr. Cooper as Bassanio, H. Cooke as Antonio, A. Brindal as Solanio, Frederick Cooke as Salarino, J. S. Balls as Gratiano, Mr. Templeton as Lorenzo, Mr. Ternan as Shylock, Henry Compton as Launcelot, Mr. Hughes as Gobbo, Mrs. Lovell as Portia, Miss Fitzwalter as Nerissa, Miss H. Cawse as Jessica; Dec. 1841, with George Bennett as Duke, Samuel Phelps as Antonio, James Anderson as Bassanio, E. W. Elton as Lorenzo, Charles Hudson as Gratiano, Henry Marston as Salarino, Charles Selby as Salanio, W. C. Macready as Shylock, Henry Compton as Launcelot, W. Bennett as Old Gobbo, Mrs. Mary Warner as Portia, Mrs. Keeley as Nerissa, Miss E. Phillips as Jessica/ Scenery by C. Marshall & Mr. Tomkins; Dec. 1849, with Charles Diddear as Duke, Mr. Cooper as Antonio, Charles Fisher as Bassanio, Mr. Frazer as Salanio, George Everett as Salarino, Frederick Vining as Gratiano, William Montague as Lorenzo, James Anderson as Shylock, W. H. Angel as Launcelot, William Davidge as Gobbo, Laura Addison as Portia, Clara Tellett as Nerissa, Fanny Huddart as Jessica; May 1883, with Henry Irving as Shylock, William Terriss as Bassanio, James Fernandez as Antonio, Henry Howe as Duke, Frank Tyars as Gratiano, Louisa Payne as Nerissa, Ellen Terry as Portia/ **Grecian**, Nov. 1844, with John Collette as Duke, Edmund Garden as Antonio, Edwin Dixon as Bassanio, John Chester as Gratiano, Mr. Campbell as Shylock, Coplestone Hodges as Lorenzo, Mr. Baldwin as Gobbo, Frederick Robson as Launcelot Gobbo, Miss M. A. Crisp as Portia, Annette Mears as Nerissa, Miss Johnstone as Jessica; Feb. 1856, with Richard Phillips as Gratiano, T. Roberts as Duke, Mr. Melvin as Tubal, Mr. Hustleby as Bassanio, Basil Potter as Shylock, Henry Grant as Antonio, F. Charles as Lorenzo, Eaton O'Donnell as Old Gobbo, John Manning as Launcelot Gobbo, Jane Coveney as Portia, Harriet Coveney as Nerrisa, Ellen Hale as Jessica/ **Princess's**, June 1845, with James Ranoe as Duke, Mr. Archer as Antonio, Leigh Murray as Bassanio, Mr. Wallack as Shylock, Walter Lacy as Gratiano, F. C. Courtney as Solanio, Mr. Granby as Old Gobbo, Henry Compton as Launcelot Gobbo, Charlotte Cushman as Portia, Miss Grant as Jessica, Emma Stanley as Nerissa; Jan. 1851, with Charles Fisher as Duke, John Ryder as Antonio, Mr. King as Bassanio, Mr. Cathcart as Salanio, George Everett as Salarino, Alfred Wigan as Gratiano, Charles Kean as Shylock, John Pritt Harley as Launcelot Gobbo, Mr. Addison as Old Gobbo, Mrs. Charles Kean as Portia, Miss Robertson as Nerissa, Mary Keeley as Jessica; July 1860, with Edmund Garden as Duke, Frank Graham as Antonio, Frederic Robinson as Bassanio, J. G. Shore as Gratiano, Robert Cathcart as Lorenzo, Samuel Phelps as Shylock, Drinkwater Meadows as Old Gobbo,

Henry Widdicomb as Launcelot Gobbo, Miss Atkinson as Portia, Carlotta Leclercq as Nerissa, Rose Leclercq as Jessica; June 1866, with Henry Mellon as Duke, Thomas Mead as Antonio, J. F. Cathcart as Bassanio, Charles Kean as Shylock, Dominick Murray as Gobbo, John Vollaire as Old Gobbo, Mrs. Charles Kean as Portia, Miss Chapman as Nerissa, Miss Stonor as Jessica; Mar. 1881, with Edwin Booth as Shylock, John Ryder as Antonio, William Redmund as Bassanio, F. Charles as Gratiano, P. C. Beverley as Lorenzo, Alfred Rayner as Duke, Stanislaus Calhaem as Launcelot, Mr. Darton as Old Gobbo, Maud Milton as Nerissa, Violet Temple as Jessica, Miss Masson as Portia/ **Olympic**, Mar. 1847, with J. R. Scott as Shylock, George Maynard as Bassanio, Mr. Butler as Antonio, Mr. Binge as Lorenzo, Mr. Fortesque as Solanio, Mr. Johnston as Old Gobbo, Robert Romer as Gobbo, Mr. Darcie as Duke, Mrs. R. Gordon as Portia, Mrs. Boyce as Nerissa, Miss Penson as Jessica; Mar. 1848, with George Almar as Duke, Mr. Archer as Antonio, Henry Holl as Bassanio, J. Binge as Lorenzo, John Kinloch as Gratiano, G. V. Brooke as Shylock, Mr. Conquest as Gobbo, H. J. Turner as Old Gobbo, Miss May as Portia, Miss J. Gould as Nerissa, Susan Kenneth as Jessica; Jan. 1852, with George Cooke as Duke, Charles Diddear as Antonio, William Farren Jr. as Antonio, William Hoskins as Gratiano, R. Norton as Lorenzo, Charles Bender as Tubal, Henry Farren as Shylock, Henry Compton as Gobbo, Alfred Sanger as Old Gobbo, Mrs. Mead as Portia, Mrs. Lingham as Nerissa, Miss Adams as Jessica; Sept. 1866, with T. B. Bennett as Duke, Walter Joyce as Bassanio, Charles Horsman as Gratiano, Robert Soutar as Gobbo, Henry Rivers as Old Gobbo, H. Dalton as Antonio, Morgan Smith as Shylock, Miss Delaville as Portia, Ellen Farren as Nerissa, Miss E. Wilson as Jessica; May 1897/ **POW**, Apr. 1875, with Charles Coghlan, Ellen Terry, Frank Archer, Squire Bancroft, Carlotta Addison/ **Lyceum**, Nov. 1879, with Henry Irving as Shylock, A. Beaumont as Duke of Venice, Frank Tyars as Prince of Morocco, Mr. Forrester as Antonio, J. H. Barnes as Bassanio, Arthur Wing Pinero as Salarino, F. Cooper as Gratiano, Norman Forbes as Lorenzo, Charles Calvert as Clerk, Florence Terry as Nerrisa, Alma Murray as Jessica, Ellen Terry as Portia/ Scenery by Hawes Craven, W. Cuthbert, W. Hann, & William Telbin/ Music by Hamilton Clarke/ Machines by Mr. Mather; June 1893, with Henry Irving as Shylock, William Terriss as Bassanio, Mr. Howe as Duke, Mr. Haviland as Antonio, Frank Tyars as Morocco, Gordon Craig as Lorenzo, S. Johnson as Launcelot, Mr. Reynolds as Old Gobbo, Kate Phillips as Nerissa, Miss Coleridge as Jessica, Ellen Terry as Portia/ Scenery by Hawes Craven & William Telbin/ Music by J. Meredith Ball/ **Adelphi**, Nov. 1879, with J. R. Gibson as Shylock, Howard Russell as Antonio, E. H. Brooke as Bassanio, R. S. Boleyn as Gratiano, H. Reeves Smith as Lorenzo, J. G. Taylor as Gobbo, W. Holman as Old Gobbo, Frank Barsby as Duke, Louise Moodie as Portia, May Burney as Nerissa, Fanny Brough as Jessica/ **Comedy**, Jan. 1901.

MERCHANT'S DAUGHTER, THE; OR, WEALTH AND PRIDE// D 2a// C. Z. Barnett// **Sad. Wells**, Sept. 1839, with Mr. Aldridge as Lord Squanderfield, Robert Honner as Viscount Squanderfield, Mr. Dry as Silver Tongue, Mr. Phillips as Brief, Mr. Cathcart as Freeland, J. W. Collier as Paragraph, Mr. Elvin as Morland, Mr. Conquest as Snowball, Mr. Williams as Thrifty, Mrs. Robert Honner as Arabella, Miss Cooke as Susan, Mrs. J. F. Saville as Fanny.

MERCHANT'S CLERK, THE: A LOVE STORY// D 3a// G. D. Pitt// **Victoria**, Oct. 1847, with John Dale as Hillary, T. H. Higgie as de Grey, N. T. Hicks as Elliot, Charles Morelli as Sir James, Mr. Henderson as Jeffries, Walter Searle as Dimwig, G. F. Forman as Shackpole, J. Howard as Just, Alfred Raymond as Sandon, Annette Vincent as Mary, Mrs. George Lee as Mrs. Gubley, Mrs. Cooke as Mrs. Crout.

MERCHANT'S WEDDING, THE; OR, LONDON FROLICS IN 1638// Play 5a// J. R. Planché// **Sad. Wells**, Sept. 1852, with Mr. Barrett as Warehouse, Mr. Williams as Seathrift, Henry Marston as Plotwell, Frederic Robinson as Lt. Valentine, Lewis Ball as Timothy, William Belford as Bright, Charles Fenton as Salewit, Henry Mellon as Capt. Quarterfield, Miss Cooper as Aurelia, Miss T. Bassano as Penelope, Eliza Travers as Dorcas, Mrs. Dixon as Mrs. Seathrift.

MERE CHILD, A// C 1a// J. W. Marston// **Haymarket**, Dec. 1866, with Henry Howe as Grantley, Walter Gordon as Merion, P. White as Col. Whitby, Mr. Johnson as Brown, Mrs. Laws as Mrs. Radnor, Mrs. Chippendale as Mrs. Dampier, Miss Coleman as Mrs. Whitby, Rebecca Powell as Rose, Mrs. Edward Fitzwilliam as Gwyn.

MERELY PLAYERS// D 1a// Edward Rose// **POW**, July 1882, with Herbert Beerbohm Tree, Norman Forbes, Edward Rose, Myra Holme.

MERRIFIELD'S GHOST// C 1a// H. M. Paull// **Vaudeville**, Nov. 1895, with Frederick Volpé as Merrifield, Sydney Warden as John Gordon, Wilfred Draycott as Will Gordon, Kate Serjeantson as Sylvia.

MERRY CHRISTMAS, A// C 1a// Adap. by Clement Scott fr F, Je Dine Chez Ma Mère// **Strand**, Feb. 1897, with Alex Bradley as Duke of Maresfield, C. Garth as Sir Ralph, Charles Weir as Little, Agnes Paulton as Marion, Florence Gerard as Rose.

MERRY MARGATE// F 3a// Sidney Grundy// **Comedy**, Mar. 1889.

MERRY MEETING, A// F 1a// W. Lestocq// **Opera Comique**, Feb. 1887.

MERRY TERRY; OR, A REEFER'S WRONGS// D 3a// n.a.// **Victoria**, Oct. 1841, with William Seaman as Lt. Campley, C. Williams as Lt. Kennedy, John Dale as Rattline, Mr. Wilton as Starling, Mr. Cullen as Mizen, E. F. Saville as Merry Terry, John Gardner as Mac Shane, Charles Morelli as Ronnady, Mrs. George Lee as Ellen, Miss Sadler as Lydia, Mrs. Howard as Judy, Mrs. Garthwaite as Meg, Mrs. Seaman as Neil/ Scenery by Hawthorn, Morelli & Lancaster/ Machines by Wood & Foster/ Prod. by E. F. Saville.

MERRY WIDOW, THE// C 2a// Adap. by Leicester Buckingham fr F, Jeanne qui Pleure et Jeanne qui rit// **St. James's**, Jan. 1863, with Arthur Stirling as Aylwyn, Frank Matthews as Dockett, S. Johnson as Capias, Mrs. Frank Matthews as Mrs. Mildmay, Louisa Herbert as Mrs. Charles Mildmay, Patti Josephs as Florence, Adeline Cottrell as Mrs. Delamere, Ada Dyas as Lucy.

MERRY WIVES OF WINDSOR, THE// C// William Shakespeare// **Drury Lane**, Oct. 1837, with Mr. Dowton as Falstaff, Mr. Templeton as Fenton, Mr. Cooper as Ford, A. Brindal as Page, Henry Compton as Slender, Mr. Hughes as Shallow, W. Bennett as Evans, John Duruset as Caius, R. McIan as Pistol, Paul Bedford as Host, Miss Romer as Mrs. Ford, Miss H. Cawse as Mrs. Page, Miss Poole as Anne, Mrs. C. Jones as Dame Quickly/ **Cov. Garden**, Apr. 1840, with George Bartley as Falstaff, Frank Matthews as Shallow, C. J. Mathews as Slender, Mr. Cooper as Ford, Charles Diddear as Page, W. Harrison as Fenton, James Bland as Caius, Drinkwater Meadows as Sir Hugh, Mr. Granby as Host, R. McIan as Pistol, W. H. Payne as Nym, John Ayliffe as Bardolph, Rebecca Isaacs as Robin, Louisa Nisbett as Mrs. Ford, Mme. Vestris as Mrs. Page, Miss Rainforth as Anne, Mrs. C. Jones as Mrs. Quickly/ **Haymarket**, Jan. 1844, with Robert Strickland as Falstaff, Mr. Tilbury as Shallow, James Bland as Caius, C. J. Mathews as Slender, Henry Howe as Page, Mr. Stuart as Ford, Mr. Caulfield as Fenton, Benjamin Webster as Sir Hugh, T. F. Mathews as Nym, Mr. Gallot as Bardolph, A. Brindal as Pistol, Mme. Vestris as Mrs. Page, Mrs. Nisbett as Mrs. Ford, Mrs. Julia Glover as Mrs. Quickly, Miss Mattley as Anne; May 1851, with James H. Hackett as Falstaff, E. L. Davenport as Ford, Henry Howe as Page, J. B. Buckstone as Slender, Mr. Lambert as Shallow, A. Brindal as Fenton, Henry Bedford as Sir Hugh, James Bland as Caius, Mr. Rogers as Host, Charles Selby as Pistol, George Braid as Nym, Mr. Caulfield as Bardolph, Miss Reynolds as Mrs. Ford, Mrs. Fitzwilliam as Mrs. Page, Mrs. Stanley as Mrs. Quickly, Amelia Vining as Anne; Nov. 1888, with Herbert Beerbohm Tree as Falstaff, Fuller Mellish as Fenton, P. Percival Clarke as Shallow, Charles Brookfield as Slender, F. H. Macklin as Ford, Fred. Harrison as Page, Henry Kemble as Caius, Edward Righton as Sir Hugh, Charles Allan as Pistol, Robb Harwood as Nym, H. Crisp as Bardolph, Henrietta Lindley as Mrs. Ford, Rose Leclercq as Mrs. Page, Mrs. Tree as Anne, Mrs. Edmund Phelps as Mistress Quickly/ Scenery by Walter Johnstone; Feb. 1890, with Herbert Beerbohm Tree as Falstaff, James Fernandez as Ford, Charles Brookfield as Slender, Henry Kemble as Caius, Charles Collette as Host, E. M. Robson as Sir Hugh, Charles Allan as Pistol, Mr. Perceval-Clarke as Shallow, Mr. Gurney as Page, Mr. Hargreaves as Bardolph, Miss Lingard as Mrs. Ford, Rose Leclercq as Mrs. Page, Mrs. Beerbohm Tree as Anne, Henrietta Lindley as Mrs. Quickly/ Music by Arthur Sullivan; Dec. 1894, with Herbert Beerbohm Tree as Falstaff, C. M. Hallard as Fenton, Holman Clark as Shallow, Herbert Ross as Slender, Henry Neville as Ford, Edmund Maurice as Page, Henry Kemble as Caius, E. M. Robson as Sir Hugh, Charles Allan as Host, F. Percival Stevens as Pistol, Gayer Mackay as Nym, Mr. Willes as Bardolph, Maud Milton as Mrs. Ford, Lily Hanbury as Mrs. Page, Violet Armbruster as Anne, Mrs. E. H. Brooke as Mrs. Quickly/ **Grecian**, Mar. 1844, with Mr. Frazer as Fenton, Mr. Campbell as Falstaff, Edwin Dixon as Ford, Mr. Delavanti as Page, Edmund Garden as Slender, Frederick Robson as Shallow, John Collett as Sir Hugh Evans, Mr. Goldsmith as Bardolph, G. Norman as Nym, Henry Bedford as Pistol, Annette Mears as Mrs. Ford, Miss M. A. Crisp as Mrs. Page, Marian Taylor Anne Page, Miss Merion as Mrs. Quickly/ **Princess's**, July 1846, with Mr. Granby as Falstaff, Mr. Wallack as Ford, John Ryder as Page, C. J. Mathews as Sir Hugh, Mr. Walton as Shallow, Henry Compton as Slender, S. Smith as Host, Mme. Vestris as Mrs. Page, Mrs. Stirling as Mrs. Ford, Georgiana Smithson as Anne Page, Mrs. Fosbroke as Mrs. Quickly; Nov. 1851, with George Bartley as Falstaff, John Cathcart as Fenton, Drinkwater Meadows as Shallow, John Pritt Harley as Slender, Charles Kean as Ford, James Vining as Page, Robert Keeley as Sir Hugh, Alfred Wigan as Dr. Caius, John Ryder as Pistol, Mr. Wynn as Bardolph, Kate Terry as Robin, Mrs. Charles Kean as Mrs. Ford, Mrs. Keeley as Mrs. Page, Mary Keeley as Anne, Mrs. Winstanley as Mrs. Quickly/ Scenery by Walter Gordon & F. Lloyds; June 1860, with Samuel Phelps as Falstaff, George Melville as Ford, J. G. Shore as Page, Frank Matthews as Shallow, Drinkwater Meadows as Sir Hugh, Edmund Garden as Dr. Caius, Henry Widdicomb as Slender, Mr. Paolo as Bardolph, Henry Saker as Pistol, Carlotta Leclercq as Mrs. Ford, Mrs. Winstanley as Mrs. Page, Rose Leclercq as Anne Page, Mrs. Weston as Mrs. Quickly/ **Sad. Wells**, Apr. 1848, with Samuel Phelps as Falstaff, William Hoskins as Slender, A. Younge as Shallow, J. T. Johnson as Fenton, Henry Marston as Ford, Mr. Harrington as Page, Henry Scharf as Sir Hugh, Mr. Williams as Caius, Edward Knight as Bardolph, Henry Mellon as Host, Charles Fenton as Pistol, Miss Cooper as Mrs. Ford, Mrs. Henry Marston as Mrs. Page, Miss Marsh as Anne, Mrs. W. Watson as Mrs. Quickly/ Scenery by A. Finlay/ **Lyceum**, Nov. 1848, with Mr. Granby as Falstaff, Frank Matthews as Shallow, C. J. Matthews as Slender, Mr. Cooper as Ford, Mr. Bellingham as Page, Drinkwater Meadows as Hugh Evans, Charles Selby as Caius, Robert Honner as Bardolph, Frederick Cooke as Pistol, Mme. Vestris as Mistress Ford, Mrs. Yates as Mistress Page, Kathleen Fitzwilliam as Anne, Mrs. Macnamara as Mistress Quickly/ **Adelphi**, May 1853, with Benjamin Webster as Falstaff, Robert Keeley as Sir Hugh, Leigh Murray as Ford, John Parselle as Page, George Honey as Shallow, Sarah Woolgar as Slender, Alfred Wigan as Caius, Paul Bedford as Host, Fanny Maskell as Fenton, Robert Romer as Bardolph, William Cullenford as Pistol, Henry Bedford as Nym, Mme. Celeste as Mrs. Ford, Mrs.

Keeley as Mrs. Page, Mary Keeley as Anne, Mrs. Laws as Mrs. Quickly/ Scenery by Pitt & Turner; Feb. 1881, with Mr. Gresham as Shallow, F. W. Irish as Slender, Hermann Vezin as Ford, Mr. Palmer as Page, David Fisher as Host, Henry Murray as Falstaff, W. McIntyre as Pistol, Mr. Fenton as Nym, Mr. Russell as Bardolph, J. W. Anson as Sir Hugh, Horace Wigan as Caius, Mrs. Arthur Stirling as Mrs. Ford, Miss Williams as Mrs. Page, Mrs. Leigh as Dame Quickly/ **Gaiety**, Dec. 1874, with Samuel Phelps, Arthur Cecil, Hermann Vezin, Johnston Forbes Robertson, Mrs. John Wood, Rose Leclercq/ **Comedy**, Dec. 1900.

MESMERIC MYSTERY, A// F// W. R. Osman// **Victoria**, Aug. 1867.

MESMERISM// F 1a// Carrol Clyde// **Opera Comique**, May. 1890, with Eric Thorne as Shy, Maitland Marler as Sharp, Florance Lonsdale as Mrs. Grey.

MESMERISM; OR, AN IRISHMAN'S SYMPATHY// F// n.a.// **Sad. Wells**, Sept. 1841, with Mr. Williams as Old Phantom, Mr. Elvin as Plotwell, Mr. Aldridge as Dr. Nogo, J. Sloan as Murphy, Mrs. Richard Barnett as Mary, Mrs. Morgan as Charlotte.

MESMERIST, THE// D// George Conquest & Henry Robinson// **Grecian**, Oct. 1879.

MESSAGE FROM MARS, A// Play 3a// Richard Ganthony// **Avenue**, Nov. 1899, with Charles Hawtrey as Parker, Arthur Williams as Tramp, George Titherage as Messenger, C. M. Lowne as Dicey, H. Stephenson as Dr. Chapman, E. W. Tarver as Ferguson, Gayer MacKay as Sir E. Vivian, George Grossmith as Wright, Bella Pateman as Miss Parker, Hilda Hanbury as Mrs. Clarence, Jessie Bateman as Minnie/ Scenery by Walter Hann.

MESSAGE FROM THE SEA, A// D 3a// Dram. fr story of Charles Dickens// **Surrey**, Feb. 1873/ **Astley's**, Oct. 1878, with N. Wheatcroft as Hugh Raybrock, G. Murray Wood as Silas, Harry Cornwall as Tom, H. Monte as Lawrence, Frank Cates as Alfred, Edward Chamberlaine as Tregarthen, Fanny Wright as Mrs. Raybrock, Hilda Dunbar as Kitty, Emilie Blackwood as Margaret, Virginia Blackwood as Mog.

METAMORA, THE LAST OF THE WAMPANOAGS// T 5a// J. A. Stone// **Princess's**, Apr. 1845, with Mr. Archer as Lord Fitz-Arnold, Mr. Granby as Sir Arthur, Henry Wallack as Mordaunt, Mr. Walton as Errington, Mr. Hield as Walter, James Ranoe as Capt. Church, Mr. Fitzjames as Wolf, Emma Stanley as Oceana, Edwin Forrest as Metamora, F. C. Courtney as Kaneshine, Augustus Harris as Otah, Mr. Turnour as Anahwandah, Mrs. Stirling as Nahmeokee.

METHINKS I SEE MY FATHER// C 2a// C. J. Mathews// **Lyceum**, Nov. 1849, with Mr. Granby, Frank Matthews, C. J. Mathews, Mr. Bellingham, Mr. Charles, Mrs. Humby, Mrs. Macnamara, Mrs. Julia Glover.

MICHAEL AND CHRISTINE; OR, LOVE IN HUMBLE LIFE// D// n.a.// **Sad. Wells**, Jan. 1843, with Henry Marston as Ronclass, John Herbert as Carlitz, Caroline Rankley as Christine.

MICHAEL AND HIS LOST ANGEL// Play 5a// Henry Arthur Jones// **Lyceum**, Jan. 1896, with Johnston Forbes Robertson as Rev. Feversham, M. Hathorn as Sir Lyolf, Ian Robertson as Lashmar, W. Macintosh as Gibbard, Joseph Carne as Rev. Docwray, Marion Terry as Audrie, Sarah Brooke as Rose, Henrietta Watson as Mrs. Cantelo/ Scenery by Hawes Craven/ Music comp. by Edward German.

MICHAEL CENO; OR, THE MORNING STAR AND THE ROVER OF THE OCEAN// D 3a// n.a.// **Victoria**, June 1854, with Alfred Saville as Earl of Barnsbury, Henry Frazer as Lord Launcelot, Watty Brunton as Villars, J. T. Johnson as Ferrardo, Miles, and as Michael Ceno, N. T. Hicks as Gale, T. E. Mills as Capt. Bellaire, Charles Rice as Rashly, Mrs. Henry Vining as Lady Harriet, Miss Sutton as Lady Julia, Miss Dansor as Maud, Miss Laporte as Letty/ Prod. by J. T. Johnson.

MICHAEL ERLE, THE MANIAC LOVER; OR, THE FAYRE LASS OF LICHFIELD// D 2a// T. E. Wilks// **Surrey**, Dec. 1839/ **Victoria** June 1850, with Mr. Henderson as D'Arville, J. T. Johnson as Erle, Henry Frazer as Melville, J. Neville as Gilliflower, Mr. Morrison as Giraud, John Hudspeth as Adze, Mrs. Cooke as Dame Stapleton, Amelia Mercer as Mary, Miss Barrowcliffe as Julia.

MICHAEL STROGOFF// D Pro & 5a// Adap. by H. J. Byron fr F of A. P. Dennery & Jules Verne// **Adelphi**, Mar. 1881, with Charles Warner as Michael Strogoff, James Fernandez as Ogareff, J. A. Rosier as Governor, T. A. Palmer as Kiezoff, H. J. Byron as John Blunt, F. W. Irish as Jollivet, Howard Russell as Feofar, A. H. Warren as Grand Duke, Mrs. Hermann Vezin as Olga Strogoff, Mrs. Bernard Beere as Sangarre/ Music by Mr. Stoepel/ Machines by Edward Charker/ Prod. by Charles Warner.

MICHAELMAS DAY: A ROMANCE OF THE THAMES// F// n.a.// **Princess's**, Mar. 1848, with James Vining as Larkspur, Henry Compton as Broad, J. Neville as Donnywetter, Mr. Wynn as Drinkwater, S. Cowell as Pipey, Mrs. Selby as Susan/ Scenery by Mr. Gray.

MICHEL PERRIN// D 2a// A. Younge// **Sad. Wells**, Sept. 1850, with A. Young as Perrin, Charles Wheatleigh as Adolphe, Henry Mellon as Fouche, Mr. Williams as Bilette, Frank Graham as de Fancou, Miss Marston as Hulie.

MIDDLE TEMPLE, THE// F// R. B. Peake// **Sad. Wells**, May 1841, with John Herbert, Mr. Williams, Mr. Elvin, Mr. Richardson, Miss Garrick, Mrs. Richard Barnett.

MIDDLEMAN, THE// Play 4a// Henry Arthur Jones// **Shaftesbury**, Aug. 1889, with E. S. Willard as Blenkarn, Sant Matthews as Sir Seaton, C. Harbury as Chandler, E. W. Gardiner as Pegg, Charles Fulton as Capt. Chandler, H. Cane as Todd, E. W. Thomas as Danks, Bessie Hatton as Nancy, Annie Hill as Maud, Adelaide Bowering as Mrs. Chandler, Josephine St. Ange as Lady Umfraville, Mrs. E. S. Willard as Mary.

MIDDY ASHORE, THE// F 1a// W. Bayle Bernard// **Haymarket**, Aug. 1837, with Mr. Fitzwilliam as Halcyon, O. Smith as Cringle, Mr. Saville as Lt. Morton, T. F. Mathews as Limberback, Mrs. W. Clifford as Lady Starchington, Miss E. Phillips as Emily, Mrs. Humby as Anne; July 1861, with Mrs. Edward Fitzwilliam as Halcyon, George Braid as Lt. Morton, Mr. Rogers as Cringle, William Cullenford as Limberback, James Worrell as Tonnish, Mrs. Poynter as Lady Starchington, Miss Henrade as Emily, Eliza Weekes as Anne/ **Adelphi**, Nov. 1857, with Marie Wilton as Harry, F. Hall as Lt. Morton, Paul Bedford as Tom, Robert Romer as Limberback, Mrs. Chatterley as Lady Starchington, Miss Hayman as Emily; same cast at **Sad. Wells**, June 1858/ **Grecian**, Sept. 1861, with Mary A. Victor as Harry Halcyon, George Gillett as Lt. Morton, Henry Grant as Cringle, Mr. Smithson as Limberback, R. H. Lingham as Tennish, Miss Johnstone as Lady Starchington, Ellen Hale as Emily, Lucreza Hill as Anne/ **Astley's**, Mar. 1867, with Caroline Parkes as Harry Halcyon, W. T. Richardson as Lt. Morton, W. H. Stephens as Cringle, Mr. Arthur as Limberback, Mrs. Caulfield as Lady Starchington, Miss Marion as Emily, Ellen Thirlwall as Anne/ **Adelphi**, Aug. 1881, with Clara Jecks as Harry Halcyon, E. J. Henley as Morton, Harry Proctor as Cringle, Harwood Cooper as Limberback, E. Travers as Tonnish, Sophie Miles as Lady Starchington, Maud Howard as Emily.

MIDGE// C 3a// R. J. Martin & J. P. Burnett// **Royalty**, Jan. 1880, with J. P. Burnett, Jennie Lee.

MIDNIGHT; OR, THE BELLS OF NOTRE DAME// D 4a// Arthur Shirley & Benjamin Landeck// **Surrey**, Dec. 1892/ **Novelty**, Sept. 1896 (retitled King of Crime), with Samuel Livesay as Ronjarne, Gustavus Livesey as Gandelu, Albert Ward as Simon, Clarence Temple as Marcarot, Sam Roberts as Malony, Oswald Douglas as Folgat, Edwin Mayhew as Perpignan, S. S. Wilford as Taberet, Fred Lawrence as Toto, Madge Devereux as Henriette, Frances Alleyne as Mathilde, Violet Vivian as Mere Crochard, Rose Maitland as Clarisse, Susie Gordon as Mme. Maurivert, Rosie Leigh as Mimi.

MIDNIGHT; OR, THE WOOD CARVER OF BRUGES// D// J. W. Furrell & E. C. Stafford// **Princess's**, May 1888.

MIDNIGHT HOUR, THE// F// Mrs. Inchbald// **Cov. Garden**, June 1838, with James Anderson as The Marquis, Drinkwater Meadows as Sebastian, George Bartley as The General, John Pritt Harley as Nicholas, John Ayliffe as Ambrose, Mr. Tilbury as Mathias, Miss E. Clifford as Julia, Mrs. Sarah Garrick as Cecily, Mrs. Humby as Flora/ **Sad. Wells**, Feb. 1868, with J. L. Warner as The Marquis, Walter Searle as Sebastian, Harry Chester as General, J. W. Lawrence as Nicholas, Mr. Hamilton as Ambrose, Miss Leigh as Julia, Mrs. Walton as Cicily, Grace Edgar as Flora.

MIDNIGHT PARIS// D 4a// Adap. by Arthur Shirley fr F of M. La Rose & A. Levy, La Legion Etrangère// **Pavilion**, May 1900.

MIDNIGHT, THE THIRTEENTH CHIME; OR, OLD ST. PAUL'S// D 3a// C. Z. Barnett// **Surrey**, Feb. 1845.

MIDNIGHT TRUST, A// D 5a// W. R. Waldron & Lionel Ellis// **Britannia**, May 1899.

MIDNIGHT WATCH, THE// D 1a// J. Maddison Morton// **Marylebone**, Oct. 1848, with Fanny Vining, H. T. Craven, James Johnstone.

MIDSUMMER DAY// C 1a// Walter Frith// **St. James's**, Mar. 1892.

MIDSUMMER NIGHT'S DREAM, A// C// William Shakespeare// **Cov. Garden**, Nov. 1840, with Mr. Cooper as Theseus, Charles Diddear as Egeus, James Vining as Lysander, A. Brindal as Demetrius, Mr. Hemming as Philostrate, George Bartley as Quince, George Pritt Harley as Bottom, Robert Keeley as Flute, Drinkwater Meadows as Snout, Frank Matthews as Snug, W. H. Payne as Starveling, Mrs. Brougham as Hippolyta, Louisa Nisbett as Hermia, Miss Cooper as Helena, Mme. Vestris as Oberon, Mrs. Walter Lacy (Miss Taylor) as Titania, Miss Marshall as Puck/ Scenery by Grieve, T. Grieve & W. Grieve/ Machines by Mr. Sloman/ Music by T. Cooke/ **Princess's**, May 1847, with Henry Hughes as Theseus, John Ryder as Egeus, James Vining as Lysander, Charles Fisher as Demetrius, Mr. Wynn as Philostrate, Mr. Granby as Quince, Henry Compton as Bottom, S. Cowell as Flute, S. Smith as Snout, Mr. Walton as Snug, Robert Honner as Starveling, Miss Winstanley as Hippolyta, Mrs. Stirling as Hermia, Mrs. Henry Hughes as Helena, Sara Flower as Oberon, Anne Romer as Titania, Miss Marshall as Puck/ Music by T. Cooke; Oct. 1856, with John Ryder as Theseus, Frank Graham as Egeus, John Cathcart as Lysander, Mr. Brazier as Demetrius, Mr. Butler as Philostrate, Frank Matthews as Quince, Frederick Cooke as Snug, John Pritt Harley as Bottom, Henry Saker as Flute, Drinkwater Meadows as Snout, Miss Murray as Hippolyta, Maria Ternan as Hermia, Eleanor Bufton as Helena, Fanny Ternan as Oberon, Carlotta Leclercq as Titania, Ellen Terry as Puck, Kate Terry as Fairy, Rose Leclercq as Another Fairy/ Scenery under dir. of Mr. Grieve/ Music by J. L. Hatton, Machines by G. Hodsdon/ **Sad. Wells**, Oct. 1853, with Henry Marston as Theseus, Mr. Lunt as Egeus, Wybert Rousby as Lysander, William Belford as Demetrius, C. Mortimer as Philostrate, J. W. Ray as Quince, Mr. Barrett as Snug, Samuel Phelps as Bottom, Lewis Ball as Snout, Miss Portman as Hippolyta, Eliza Travers as Hermia, Miss Cooper as Helena, Katherine Hickson as Oberon, Miss Wyatt as Titania/ Scenery by F. Fenton/ Music by W. Montgomery/ Machines by Mr. Cawdery;

July 1880, with R. C. Lyons, Edmund Lyons, Rosa Kenny, Ella Dietz, Kate Barry/ **Lyceum**, Jan. 1888, with James Fernandez as Theseus, Mrs. F. H. Macklin as Hippolyta, F. H. Macklin as Philostrate, William Herbert as Lysander, Wilfred Draycott as Demetrius, Gabrielle Goldney as Hermia, Mary Ayerton as Helena, Henry Kemble as Quince, Edward Terry as Bottom, Edward Righton as Flute, Charles Collette as Snout, Lionel Brough as Snug, W. J. Hill as Starveling; Feb. 1900, with G. Fitzgerald as Theseus, E. A. Warburton as Egeus, F. R. Benson as Lysander, E. Lyall Swete as Quince, G. R. Weir as Bottom, Oscar Ashe as Snug, Miss L. Brayton as Helena, Ada Ferrar as Hermia, Miss E. Kirby as Hippolyta, Frank Rodney as Oberon, Mrs. F. R. Benson as Titania, Kitty Loftus as Puck, Isadora Duncan as Fairy/ **Globe**, Jan. 1890, with Sydney Price as Theseus, Alfred Brydone as Egeus, F. R. Benson as Lysander, Herbert Ross as Demetrius, G. M. Howard as Philostrate, H. A. Forde as Quince, G. R. Weir as Bottom, Marion Grey as Hippolyta, Ada Ferrar as Hermia, Kate Rorke as Helena, Otho Stuart as Oberon, Mrs. F. R. Benson as Titania, Grace Geraldine as Puck/ Scenery by Mr. Hemsley/ Prod. by Hugh Moss/ **Daly's**, July 1895.

MIGHT AND RIGHT// D// n.a.// Dec. 1852, with Samuel Phelps as Obolenski, George Bennett as Belski, Henry Mellon as Viavode, William Belford as Boscaria, Mrs. Ternan as Helena, Miss Cooper as Olga, Mrs. Dixon as Beatrice/ Scenery by F. Fenton/ Music by W. Montgomery.

MIGHT OF RIGHT, THE; OR, THE SOUL OF HONOR// D 3a// John Brougham// **Astley's**, Jan. 1864, with Henry Loraine as Paul Deveril and Ralph Deveril, Mr. Frazer as Raikes, A. C. Lilley as Downes, Frank Matthews as Claypole, Walter Chamberlaine as St. Leger, Stanislaus Calhaem as Peter Puffin, Miss Desborough as Clara, Miss Clifford as Alice/ Scenery by J. Gates & C. James.

MIGHTY DOLLAR, THE// C 4a// B. E. Woolf// **Gaiety**, Aug. 1880, with W. J. Florence, F. W. Wyndham, Mrs. W. J. Florence, Kate Vaughn.

MIGHTY ERROR, A// D 2a// Dram. by Leonard Outram fr poem by Robert Browning// **Avenue**, July 1891, with Leonard Outram as Amadis, Frank Worthing as Miguel, Sydney Herberte as Xante, Frances Ivor as Joan, Mary Ansell as Inez.

MIKE; OR, THE MILLER'S TRIALS// D// M. Pletts// **Albion**, May 1876.

MILADY// D 3a// Oswald Brand// **Avenue**, May 1885.

MILESTONES OF LIFE, THE// D 5a// Frank Harvey// **Pavilion**, Aug. 1901.

MILITARY MANOEUVRE, A// F// J. J. Dilley & Lewis Clifton// **Vaudeville**, Dec. 1879, with C. W. Garthorne, W. Hargreaves, Miss E. Palmer, Cicely Richards.

MILITARY MOVEMENTS// F// n.a.// **Sad. Wells**, Nov. 1838, with J. Lee as Col. Bakely, Mr. Elvin as Capt. Belmont, Mr. Williams as Match'em, Robert Honner as Shuffle, Miss Pincott as Lady Emily.

MILITARY PROMOTION; OR, THE YOUNG COLONEL// D// Adap. fr F// **Haymarket**, July 1843, with Mme. Celeste as Jules, Robert Strickland as Laplomb, Henry Howe as Henri de Cartouche, James Worrell as Octave de Cartouche, Mr. Ireland as Lafleur, Julia Bennett as Ernestine.

MILKY WHITE// C 2a// H. T. Craven// **Strand**, Sept. 1864/ **St. James's**, June 1871, with Miss H. Everard as Mrs. Sadrip, Fanny Brough as Annie, Lionel Brough as Duggs, F. Mervyn as Good, H. T. Craven as Milky White/ **Royalty**, 1872.

MILL OF BEREZINA, THE; OR, THE DESERTER OF THE BLACK FOREST// D 2a// G. D. Pitt// **Victoria**, May 1843, with Mr. Hitchinson as Count Carloff, William Seaman as Welsdorf, E. F. Saville as Count Romanoff, John Gardner as Bran, John Dale as Mercandoff, Miss Ridgeway as Catherine, Miss Saddler as Claudine, Miss Martin as Ulrica.

MILL OF WYNDYKE, THE// D// n.a.// **Haymarket**, Dec. 1843, with J. W. Gough as Maj. van Beet, Mr. Carle as Lt. Deitrick, Henry Howe as Lt. Victor, T. F. Mathews as Groot, Mr. Leonard as Sgt. O'Dillon, Miss Lee as Estelle, Miss Mattley as Gertrude.

MILLER AND HIS MEN, THE// D 2a// Isaac Pocock// **Sad. Wells**, June 1837, with Mr. Campbell as Grindhoff, Mr. Hicks as Lothair, C. H. Pitt as Count Friberg, Mr. Rogers as Karl, Mr. Griffiths as Kelmar, C. J. Smith as Riber, Mr. Jefferini as Golotz, T. G. Flowers as Zingra, Mr. Bishop as Schampt, Miss Williams as Ravina, Lavinia Melville as Claudine, Mrs. Harris as Laurette/ Music by H. R. Bishop; May 1854, with Mr. Barrett as Grindhoff, F. Charles as Count Frederick, George Yarnold as Karl, J. H. Delafield as Lothair, Mr. Poynter as Kalmar, Harriett Gordon as Claudine, Miss Woolf as Lauretta, Mrs. Barrett as Ravina/ **Cov. Garden**, Oct. 1837, with George Bennett as Grindoff, James Anderson as Lothaire, Mr. Roberts as Friberg, Drinkwater Meadows as Karl, Mr. Tilbury as Kelmar, W. H. Payne as Riber, C. J. Smith as Golotz, Eliza Vincent as Claudine, Mrs. W. Clifford as Ravina, Mrs. East as Lauretta/ **Olympic**, May 1848, with George Bennett as Grindoff, E. Morton as Count Frederick, Mr. Attwood as Karl, John Kinloch as Lothair, Mr. Butler as Kelmar, Miss Jones as Kruitz, Miss May as Claudine, Miss F. Hamilton as Lauretta, Mrs. Parker as Ravina/ scenery by Laidlaw & Cooper/ **Grecian**, Apr. 1855, with Basil Potter as Grindoff, F. Charles as Count Frederick, John Manning as Karl, Eaton O'Donnell as Kelmar, Richard Phillips as Lothair, Percy Corri as Riber, Jane Coveney as Ravina, Maria Simpson as Claudine, Ellen Crisp as Laurette/ **Haymarket**, Apr. 1861, with Henry Howe as Grindoff, William Farren as Lothair, Edwin Villiers as Count Friberg, Henry Compton as Karl, Mr. Rogers as Kelmar, James Worrell as Golotz, Charles Leclercq as Riber, Florence Haydon as Claudine, Miss Coleman as Laurette, Mrs. Poynter as Ravina, Louise Leclercq as Zara/ Scenery by Frederick Fenton/ Machines by Oliver Wales/ **Drury Lane,** Sept. 1867, with John Ryder as Grindoff, Edmund Phelps as Lothair, Charles Harcourt as Count Friberg, Mr. Barrett as Kelmar, Edith Stuart as Claudine, Miss Stafford as Ravena, Miss Grattan as Christine/ Scenery by J. Johnson.

MILLER OF DERWENT WATER, THE// D 3a// Edward Fitzball// **Olympic,** May 1853, with G. Cooke as Sir Marcus, Mr. Charles as Charles Lister, Frederick Robson as Dr. Prussic, Henry Farren as Ambroise, W. Shalders as Grist, Ellen Turner as Patty, Miss Anderton as Mercy.

MILLER'S DAUGHTER, THE// n.a.// **Haymarket,** May 1865.

MILLER'S MAID, THE// D// J. S. Faucit// **Sad. Wells,** Dec. 1837, with Mr. Campbell as the Miller, Mr. Rogers as Old Granger, Samuel Buckingham as Giles, C. H. Pitt as George, William Smith as Marvellous, Mr. Pateman as Ralph, Miss R. Honner as Phoebe/ **Victoria,** Mar. 1838, with Mr. Rayner as Giles, William Davidge as Miller, John Parry as George, W. H. Oxberry as Marvellous, Mr. Loveday as Granger, Mrs. Loveday as Dame, Mrs. Hooper as Phoebe/ **Grecian,** Mar. 1844, with John Collett as the Miller, Edmund Garden as Giles, Edwin Dixon as George, Frederick Robson as Matty, Mr. Baldwin as Old Grainger, Miss Merion as Dame, Miss M. A. Crisp as Phoebe.

MILLER'S WIFE, THE; OR, THE FALLS OF CLACKMULLIN// D 2a// Edward Fitzball// **Victoria,** Jan. 1843, with William Seaman as Ronald, C. Williams as Barvooden, John Dale as Cornock, John Gardner as McCraw, Mr. James as Nichol, Mr. Hitchinson as Roderick, Charles Morelli as Noah, Mrs. George Lee as Lady Julia, Miss Vincent as Ecky.

MILLINER'S HOLIDAY, THE// F 1a// J. Maddison Morton// **Haymarket,** June 1844, with Henry Holl as Lt. Bowling, J. B. Buckstone as Sparkes, Robert Strickland as Pennywig, Julia Bennett as Fanny, Mrs. Humby as Miss Potts, Miss Carre as Miss Dotts, Mrs. Caulfield as Miss Totts, Mrs. L. S. Buckingham as Miss Watts, Miss Conner as Miss Lotts, Mrs. Worrell as Miss Scotts/ **Adelphi,** June 1859, with John Billington as Lt. Bowling, J. L. Toole as Sparkes, Charles Selby as Pennywig, Mary Keeley as Fanny, Mrs. Alfred Mellon (Sarah Woolgar) as Miss Potts, Kate Kelly as Miss Dotts/ **Sad. Wells,** Sept. 1859, with William Belford as Lt. Bowling, Lewis Ball as Sparkes, Mr. Williams as Pennywig, Miss Phillips as Fanny, Caroline Parkes as Miss Dotts, Miss Howard as Miss Potts, Miss Morton as Miss Totts, Fanny Morelli as Miss Watts, Miss Taylor as Kitty.

MILLINER TO THE KING, THE// C 1a// Adap. by C. J. Mathews fr F of J. F. Bayard & P. F. Dumanoir, La Vicomtesse Lolotte// **Haymarket,** Mar. 1859, with C. J. Mathews.

MILLION OF MONEY, A// D 5a// Augustus Harris & Henry Pettitt// **Drury Lane,** Sept. 1890, with Charles Warner as Dunstable, Herbert Standing as Maj. Belgrave, Harry Nicholls as Cricklewood, Charles Glenney as St. Clair, Fred Shepherd as Bounder, Allen Beaumont as Rev. Maythorne, Mark Quinton as Hastings, Jessie Millward as Mary, Fanny Brough as Hetty, Alice Lingard as Stella, Helena Dacre as Elsie, Lilian Audrie as Lady Sandson, Alfred Phillips as Whetstone, Stanislaus Calhaem as Boulter, May Palfrey as Mme. Ribob/ **Grand,** Feb. 1891.

MILLIONAIRE, THE// D 4a// Edward Towers// **Pavilion,** May 1874.

MILLIONAIRE, THE// C 4a// Adap. by G. W. Godfrey fr novel of Edmund Yates, Kissing the Rod// **Court,** Sept. 1883, with Arthur Cecil, John Clayton, Marion Terry, Mrs. Beerbohm Tree, Mrs. John Wood.

MIMI// D 3a// Adap. by Dion Boucicault fr F of Henri Merger, Scènes de la Vie de Bohème// **Court,** Oct. 1881, with John Clayton, Henry Neville, Kyrle Bellew, Mrs. Bernard Beere, Carlotta Leclercq, Carlotta Addison, Marion Terry.

MIND YOUR OWN BUSINESS// C 3a// Mark Lemon// **Haymarket,** Apr. 1852, with J. B. Buckstone as Oddiman, Benjamin Webster as Verdon, Leigh Murray as Orgrave, Mr. Stuart as Morrison, Henry Howe as Mowbray, Robert Keeley as Smythe, John Parselle as Capt. Fowler, Mr. Rogers as Weazle, Mrs. Stirling as Fanny, Miss Reynolds as Marian, Mrs. L. S. Buckingham as Mrs. Smythe, Amelia Vining as Jane/ Scenery by George Morris & John O'Conner/ Machines by F. Heselton.

MINE GIRL OF KEBAL, THE; OR, THE RANSOM OF THE ROSE DIAMOND// D// G. D. Pitt// **Victoria,** Mar. 1846, with, T. Fredericks as Count Hansdorf, John Dale as Col. Sigismund, James Ranoe as Prince Maximilian, E. F. Saville as Durant, E. F. Edgar as Dubartz, Walter Searle as Vendosa, John Herbert as Blaire, Annette Vincent as Adela, Miss Jefferson as Bedina.

MINE OF WEALTH, A// D 3a// Edward Towers// **City of London,** July 1867.

MINERALI// D// H. P. Grattan// **Victoria,** Oct. 1837, with Mr. Denvil as Martelli, Mr. Green as Francisco, John Parry as Antonio, Mr. Macdonald as Marco, Mr. Roland as Bartolo, Mr. Harwood as Ricardo, William Davidge as Nicolo, Mr. Salter as Pietro, Miss Richardson as Leila, Mrs. Frank Matthews as Annette.

MINGLED THREADS// Play 1a// H. Farrington// **St. Geo. Hall,** Feb. 1901.

MINISTER OF FINANCE, THE// D// n.a.// **Sad. Wells,** Apr. 1849, with Frank Graham as Duke of Ferrara, Mr. Harrington as Marquis di Castelli, Henry Mellon as Count Marinni, A. Younge as Bambino, Miss Huddart as Paulina,

Miss Stephens as Susanna.

MINISTER OF SPAIN, THE// n.a.// **Standard,** Feb. 1863.

MINISTER'S CALL, THE// Play 1a// Dram. by Arthur Symons fr story of Frank Harris// **Royalty,** Mar. 1892, with Frank Worthing as Letgood, Rudge Harding as Knowell, W. Bonney as Deacon Hooper, Gertrude Kingston as Mrs. Knowell.

MINNIE; OR, LEONARD'S LOVE// D 3a// H. J. Byron// **Globe,** Mar. 1869.

MINNIE GREY// D 4a// George Roberts & Henry Young// **Elephant & Castle,** June 1886.

MINT OF MONEY, A// FC 3a// Arthur Law// **Toole's,** Jan. 1884.

MIRACLE, THE// D 4a// W. Howell-Poole// **Surrey,** Mar. 1883.

MIRAGE// Play 4a// Dram. by Edwin Cleary fr novel of F. C. Philips, As in a Looking Glass// **Princess's,** Feb. 1888.

MIRIAM, QUEEN OF JERUSALEM// D 4a// Dr. Sifert// **Standard,** July 1896.

MIRIAM'S CRIME// D 3a// H. T. Craven// **Strand,** Oct. 1863/ **Grecian,** Oct. 1868, with J. Jackson as Muffin, William James as Reynolds, George Conquest as Biles, Charles Mortimer as Scumley, Henry Power as Daniel, Lizzie Mandelbert as Miriam West, Mrs. Atkinson as Mrs Raby.

MIRZA// D 4a// W. Bryant// **Opera Comique,** Nov. 1893, with Ivan Watson as Montal, Philip Cunningham as Ritz, Charles Rutland as Voinoff, Maria Saker as Countess Dobronovska, Henrietta Cowen as Mme. de Montal, Carlotta Zerbini as Mme. Lesperon, Rose Dupré as Lezitre, Nadage Doree as Mirza.

MISCARRIAGE OF JUSTICE// D 4a// George Roy// **Sadler's Wells,** May 1882.

MISCHIEF// C 3a// Cunningham Bridgman// **Gaiety,** June 1886.

MISCHIEF MAKER, THE// FC 3a// Edith Henderson// **Globe,** June 1891, with W. Scott Buist as Loggerhead, Frederic Jacques as Middleton, Reginald Stockton as Denby, A. E. Drinkwater as Tapperton, Frank Damer as John, Mary Ansell as Mrs. Loggerhead, Phyllis Ayrian as Lucy, Sallie Booth as Anastasia, Madge Herrick as Alice, Eva Murray as Mary.

MISCHIEF MAKING// F 1a// J. B. Buckstone// **Haymarket,** Sept. 1837, with Mr. Saville as Desgrais, T. F. Mathews as Guiot, J. B. Buckstone as Nicholas, Mrs. Fitzwilliam as Mannette, Mrs. Tayleure as Jaquette, Miss E. Phillips as Therese/ **Sad. Wells,** Aug. 1845, with R. H. Lingham as Desgrais, Mr. Williams as Guise, Henry Scharf as Dovetail, Miss Huddart as Therese, Miss Lebatt as Mme. Manette, Miss Stephens as Jaquette, Georgiana Lebatt as Louise/ **Victoria,** July 1846, with Harry Lewis as Dovetail, Mr. Green as Guiot, James Lawson as Degrals, Eliza Terrey as Mme. Mannette, Miss M. Terrey as Therese, Mrs. Andrews as Louise, Miss Gregory as Jannette/ **Astley's,** Nov. 1852, with R. Dolman as Degrais, S. Smith as Guiot, Mr. Johnson as Dovetail, Lydia Pearce as Mme. Manetto, Miss Fenton as Therese/ **Olympic,** Oct. 1861, with Gaston Murray as Desgrais, Henry Rivers as Guiot, Horace Wigan as Dovetail, Miss Cottrell as Therese, Mrs. Stephens as Jacquette, Miss Evans as Louise, Miss Hughes as Mme. Manette/ **Princess's,** Sept. 1877.

MISER, A// D 1a// Julian Cross// **Globe,** June 1890, with Julian Cross as Brandon, Frederick Knight as Harold, H. Eden as Philip, Walter Russell as Wilding, T. Enfield as Butler, Ruby West as Amy.

MISER, THE// D 3a// Adap. by Henry Fielding fr F of Moliere// **Sad. Wells,** Mar. 1854, with Samuel Phelps as Lovegold, Wybert Rousby as Frederick, William Belford as Ramilie, C. Mortimer as Furnish, Charles Fenton as Sparkle, Miss F. Younge as Mrs. Wisely, Katherine Hickson as Mariana, Eliza Travers as Leggit.

MISER MERCHANT, THE; OR, GOLD AND ITS CURSE// D// n.a.// **Victoria,** Sept. 1850, with Henry Frazer as Luke Wynter, Mr. Neville as Morris Wynter, Mr. Henderson as Gaveston, J. T. Johnson as Careless, G. F. Forman as Sprouts, John Bradshaw as Hempseed, John Hudspeth as O'Donovan, J. Howard as Portlaven, Mrs. George Lee as Ruth, Amelia Mercer as Aleen, Miss Barrowcliffe as Patty.

MISER OF SHOREDITCH, THE// D 2a// T. P. Prest// **Standard,** Nov. 1854.

MISER OF WESTMINSTER, THE; OR, THE SOLDIER, THE LAWYER, AND THE CLERGYMAN// D// n.a.// **Victoria,** July 1857, with Mr. Henderson as Sir Richard, George Pearce as Edward, W. H. Pitt as Trevanion, J. H. Rickards as Gray, Capt. Flash, and William Gray, Mr. Morrison as Graham, Charles Rice as Dicky, S. Sawford as Quin, Henry Dudley as Miles, Julia Seaman as Bet, Mrs. J. H. Rickards as Therese, Miss Laporte as Polly, Mrs. A. Saville as Mrs. Bustle.

MISER'S DAUGHTER, THE// D 3a// Dram. by Edward Stirling fr novel of Harrison Ainsworth// **Adelphi,** Oct. 1842, with Mr. Freeborn as Beau Villiers, Mr. Henry as Sir Singleton, George Maynard as Beechcroft, John Sanders as Mr. Jukes, O. Smith as Post, Mr. Wilkinson as Pokerich, Mrs. H. Beverly as Lady Brabazon, Mrs. H. P. Grattan as Thomasine, Miss Faucit as Hilda// Prod. by Edward Stirling.

MISER'S DREAM, THE; OR, THE SEVENTH VICTIM AND THE DENOUNCER'S DOOM// D 2a// n.a.// **Grecian,** Dec. 1866, with Frederick Marchant as Claude, John Manning as Simon, William James as de Briancourt, Samuel Perfitt as Gustavus, Lizzie Mandelbert as Victorine.

MISER'S TREASURE, THE// C 2a// Adap. by James Mortimer fr F, La Fille de l'Avare, found. on Balzac's Eugenie Grandet// **Olympic**, Apr. 1878, with G. W. Anson as Clenchard, Miss Gerard as Nelly, George Yarnold as Pickett, Robert Pateman as Benjamin, Johnston Forbes Robertson as Goodwin, Clara May as Nancy.

MISER'S WELL, THE// D 2a// Dram. by R. B. Peake fr story of Washington Irving// **Lyceum**, Feb. 1844, with Mrs. Keeley as Dolph Heyliger, Mr. Turner as Knipperhausen, Mr. Yarnold as de Groodt, Robert Keeley as Claus, Mr. Griffith as Van Spiegel, Samuel Emery as Anthony, Jane Mordaunt as Marie, Mrs. Usher as Dame Heyliger, Mrs. Griffith as Frau Ilsy/ Scenery by Mr. Marshall.

MISER'S WILL, THE// D 4a// Tom Craven// **Surrey**, Nov. 1889.

MISERIES OF HUMAN LIFE, THE// F// Benjamin Webster// **Haymarket**, Nov. 1845, with Benjamin Webster as Croaker, Mr. Tilbury as Mildmay, Mr. Harcourt as Nabs, Mrs. Humby as Margaret, Mrs. L. S. Buckingham as Mrs. Courtney.

MISLED// F// A. A. Wilmot// **St. Geo. Hall**, May 1887.

MISOGYNIST, THE// Play 1a// G. W. Godfrey// **St. James's**, Nov. 1895, with George Alexander as Corquodale, Allan Aynesworth as Denison, H. H. Vincent as Royd, Ellis Jeffreys as Kitty.

MISS CINDERELLA// C 1a// W. R. Walkes// **Avenue**, Mar. 1890, with Nutcombe Gound as Wriothesley, Ben Webster as Lord Raemore, Mrs. Leston as Mrs. Wriothesley, Lillie Young as Hester, Laura Graves as Margery.

MISS CINDERELLA// C// Gertrude Warden// **Strand**, May 1900.

MISS FRANCES OF YALE// F 3a// Michael Morton// **Globe**, Sept. 1897, with Weedon Grossmith as Frank Staynor, H. Reeves Smith as Fred Anderson, Arthur Playfair as Byron McStuff, C. P. Little as FitzAllen, Mark Kinghorne as Soaper, Miss Spencer Brunton as Vesta, May Palfrey as Edna, Ethel Hope as Miss Mann, Beatrice Ferrar as Cosette/ Scenery by H. W. Owen/ Music by Carl Keifert/ Prod. by E. B. Norman.

MISS GALATEA OF OREGON// Play Pro & 3a// E. A. Cleveland// **Avenue**, Nov. 1894.

MISS GWILT// D 5a// Dram. by Wilkie Collins fr his novel, Armadale// **Globe**, Apr. 1876, with R. C. Lyons as Allan Armadale, Leonard Boyne as Midwinter, Arthur Cecil as Downward, Charles Collette as Maj. Milroy, E. D. Lyons as Capt. Manuel, Arthur Wing Pinero as Darch, H. Sainsbury as Francis, Ada Cavendish as Miss Gwilt, Augusta Wilton as Miss Milroy, Miss M. Anderson as Louisa/ Scenery by Julian Hicks & W. Bruce Smith/ Music by H. J. Loveday.

MISS HOBBS// C 4a// Jerome K. Jerome// **Duke of York's**, Dec. 1899, with Herbert Waring as Wolf Kingsearl, E. Allan Aynesworth as Percival Kingsearl, Cosmo Stuart as Jessop, J. W. Macdonald as Capt. Sands, George Curtiss as Charles, Evelyn Millard as Miss Hobbs, Agnes Miller as Mrs. Kingsearl, Susie Vaughan as Susan, Ida Yeoland as Millicent, Genevra Campbell as Jane/ Scenery by Cecil Hicks & Henry Brooke.

MISS HOYDEN'S HUSBAND// C 1a// Arr. by Augustin Daly fr Sheridan's Trip to Scarborough// **Shaftesbury**, July 1900, with Charles Leclercq as Lord Foppington, George Clarke as Young Fashion, Charles Wheatleigh as Clumsy, Eugere Ormond as Col. Townley, Frederick Bond as Lory, Hobart Bosworth as Nicodemus, Ada Rehan as Miss Hoyden, May Sylvie as Nurse, Adelaide Prince as Mistress Coupler.

MISS IMPUDENCE// C 1a// Edward Morton// **Terry's**, June 1892, with George Foss as Baxter, Annie Hughes as Miss Goslin, Lillian Lee as Knight.

MISS IN HER TEENS; OR, THE MEDLY OF LOVERS// F 2a// David Garrick// **Sad. Wells**, Apr. 1866, with Mr. Neilson as Sir Simon, Charles Warner as Capt. Loveit, George Belmore as Fribble, Frank Barsby as Capt. Flash, H. Courtley as Puff, Fanny Gwynne as Biddy, Mrs. Bishop as Aunt, Miss Hudspeth as Tag.

MISS MULTON// D 5a// **Duke's**, Nov. 1878.

MISS RUTLAND// Play 3a// Richard Pryce// **Gaiety**, Apr. 1894, with William Herbert as Marston, W. T. Lovell as Massareen, Miles Brown as Le Marchant, Guy Coulson as Warburton, John Byron as Morrisson, James Welch as Jackson, Frances Ivor as Helen, Henrietta Lindley as Lady Wroxeter, Helen Forsyth as Mildred, Mrs. B. M. de Solla as Miss Jordan, Evelyn Faulkner as Ethel, Olga Garland as Florry, Mabel Hardy as Wilson, Mrs. E. H. Brooke as Margaret, Ettie Williams as Eleanor.

MISS TOMBOY// C 3a// Adap. by Robert Buchanan fr Vanbrugh's The Relapse// **Vaudeville**, Mar. 1890, with Thomas Thorne as Foppington, Cyril Maude as Lory, Frank Gillmore as Fashion, J. S. Blythe as Matcham, Fred Thorne as Clumsy, Winifred Emery as Fanny, Sylvia Hodson as Mrs. Sentry, Lily Hanbury as Nancy, Mary Collette as Dolly.

MISSING; OR, SAVED FROM THE SCAFFOLD// D 4a// Edgar Newbound// **Britannia**, June 1881.

MISSING LINK, THE// F// Arthur Shirley// **Surrey**, Mar. 1894.

MISSIS IS OUT// F// n.a.// **Princess's**, Dec. 1901.

MISSIVE FROM THE CLOUDS, A// F// n.a.// **Princess's**, Oct. 1871, with Charles Seyton as Diffident, F. Charles as Heartsease, Bernard Cullen as Muggs, Edith Stuart as Violet, Miss Lennox Grey as Cissy, Miss Hudspeth as Mrs.

Rubynose.

MISTAKEN IDENTITY// F// Alfred Murray// **Gaiety**, Feb. 1886.

MISTAKEN STORY, A// F 1a// T. E. Wilks// **Princess's**, May 1844, with W. H. Oxberry as Picaninny, Mr. Fitzjames as Smith, Paul Bedford as Williams, Emma Stanley as Mrs. Pickaninny, Miss Noel as Amelia, Miss Brooks as Betty/ **Grecian**, Oct. 1847, with Frederick Robson as Picaninny, Mr. Manley as Smith, John Webster as Williams, Annette Mears as Seraphina, Miss Johnstone as Amelia, Miss Leclercq as Betsy/ **Victoria**, June 1850, with J. Howard as Piccaninny, Mr. Henderson as Smith, G. F. Forman as Williams, Georgiana Lebatt as Seraphina/ **Olympic**, Sept. 1853, with Frederick Robson as Piccannini, F. Charles as Smith, W. Shalders as Williams, Mrs. B. Bartlett as Seraphina, Miss Adams as Amelia, Ellen Turner as Betsy.

MR. AND MRS. DAVENTRY// Play 4a// Frank Harris// **Royalty**, Oct. 1900.

MR. AND MRS. PRINGLE// F 1a// J. T. De Trueba// **Sad. Wells**, Jan. 1840, with Mr. Williams as Pringle, J. W. Collier as Timothy, Mr. Elvin as Brush, W. D. Broadfoot as Charles Robinson, Mr. Aldridge as Henry Robinson, Miss Cooke as Mrs. Pringle, Mrs. Morgan as Clarissa, Mrs. J. F. Saville as Miss Pringle, Miss Pincott as Kitty/ **Grecian**, Feb. 1845, with Frederick Robson as Pringle, Harry Chester as Brush, Mr. Melvin as Timothy, Miss Merion as Mrs. Pringle, Miss Norman as Polly, Mrs. Dixon as Kitty/ **Astley's**, Sept. 1851, with Mr. Johnson as Peter Pringle, Mr. Crowther as Brush, Mr. Rivolta as Timothy, Arthur Stirling as Robinson, Mrs. Moreton Brookes as Mrs. Pringle, Miss Fenton as Clarissa, Mrs. Beacham as Mrs. Bustle.

MR. AND MRS. WHITE// F 1a// n.a.// **Astley's**, Mar. 1856, with Mr. Campbell as Maj. Pepper, W. Milborne as Brown, J. W. Anson as Peter White, Mrs. Jackson as Widow White, Mrs. W. Dowton as Mrs. White, Mrs. J. W. Anson as Kitty Clover/ **Grecian** Nov. 1856, with Eaton O'Donnell as Maj. Pepper, Richard Phillips as Brown, John Manning as Peter White, Miss Johnstone as Mrs. White, Jane Coveney as Widow White, Harriet Coveney as Kitty/ **Olympic**, July 1866, with John Maclean as Maj. Pepper, Robert Soutar as Brown, David James as Peter White, Maria Simpson as Widow White, Ellen Farren as Mrs. White, Mrs. Henry Farren as Kitty/ **Victoria**, Sept. 1871, with Watty Brunton as Major Pepper, Henry Mayhew as Brown, J. A. Cave as Peter White, Florence Farren as Widow White, Harriet Farren as Kitty, Bella Goodall as Mrs. White/ **Globe**, Mar. 1876, with Ellen Farren as Mrs. White, Eliza Johnstone as Kitty Clover, Rachel Sanger as Widow White, J. H. Avondale as Maj. Pepper, Henry Crouch as Brown, J. A. Cave as Peter White/ Music by Edward Solomans/ **Princess's**, Sept. 1876, with H. Jackson as White, J. W. Ford as Maj. Pepper, C. Furtado as Brown, Fannie Leslie as Mrs. White, Lilian Adair as Kitty, Mabel Hayes as Widow White.

MR. BARNES OF NEW YORK// C Pro & 3a// Dram. by Rutland Barrington fr novel of A. C. Gunter// **Olympic**, May 1888, with E. S. Willard as Count Danella, Julian Cross as Thomasso, Yorke Stephens as Barnes, H. Reeves Smith as Anstruther, Harry Halley as Phillips, James G. East as Arthur, F. Hamilton Knight as Capt. de Belloc, Matthew Brodie as Paoli, George Claremont as Mateo, Gertrude Kingston as Enid, Mrs. Billington as Lady Chartris, Helen Leyton as Maud, Maude Graves as Isola, Sophie Eyre as Marita/ Music by Charles Hargitt/ Prod. by Rutland Barrington & Yorke Stephens.

MR. CYNIC// C 1a// W. J. Locke & Garnham Roper// **Trafalgar Sq.**, May. 1893, with Basset Roe as Gargrave, Herbert Ross as Hamblyn, Winifred Fraser as Mrs. Forsyth, Eleanor Haddon as Eva.

MR. FERGUSON, YOU DON'T LODGE HERE// C// n.a.// **Sad. Wells**, Oct. 1837, with Mr. Rogers as Ferguson, Thomas Lee as Crupper, C. H. Pitt as Frankley, Mr. Griffith as Grummer, Mr. Pateman as Sharp, Mr. Ennis as Simon, Mr. Morrison as Lively, Mrs. Rogers as Mrs. Gregory, Lavinia Melville as Jane, Miss Vernon as Wilhelmina, Miss Pitt as Carolina, Miss Young as Araminta, Mrs. Andrews as Jemima, Miss Melville as Eleanore.

MR. GREENFINCH// F 2a// T. H. Bayly// **Haymarket**, Nov. 1838, with Robert Strickland as Greenfinch, Benjamin Webster as Wallop, J. B. Buckstone as Wigsby, Mr. Hemming as Forrester, Mrs. Julia Glover as Mrs. Wigsby, Miss Williams as Mrs. Wallop, Miss Gallot as Caroline, Mrs. Frank Matthews as Betty, Mrs. Fitzwilliam as Mrs. Mizzleminx.

MR. JOFFIN'S LATCHKEY// F 1a// Nugent Robinson// **Haymarket**, June 1873, with J. B. Buckstone as Joffins, Mr. Rogers as Bubb, Mrs. Chippendale as Mrs. Bubb, Mrs. Edward Fitzwilliam as Elizabeth.

MR. MARTIN// Play 3a// Charles Hawtrey// **Comedy**, Oct. 1896, with Henry Kemble as Sir Charles, W. T. Lovell as Sinclair, Charles Hawtrey as Heathcote, Charles Brookfield as Martin, Frederick Volpé as Bamfylde, Alfred Matthews as Pakenham, William Hawtrey as Kilfoyle, Jessie Bateman as Mona, Marjorie Griffiths as Mrs. Bamfylde, Nina Boucicault as Tiny, Rose Leclercq as Sophia, Lottie Venne as Maudie.

MR. PETER PIPER; OR, FOUND OUT AT HOME// C 3a// n.a.// **Haymarket**, May 1846, with William Farren as Piper, Mr. Tilbury as Sir Chevey, Charles Hudson as Maj. Owen, J. B. Buckstone as Facias, Mrs. Julia Glover as Mrs. Piper, Mrs. Seymour as Lady Janet, Mrs. W. Clifford as Galatea, Mrs. Humby as Busk/ Scenery by George Morris.

MR. RICHARDS// Play 3a// Arthur Bourchier & James Blair// **Shaftesbury**, Mar. 1892, with H. Reeves Smith as Chambers, Arthur Bourchier as Richards, E. W. Gardiner as Viscount Wordsham, Ian Robertson as Earl of Cromer,

Ells Dagnall as Bentley, Edward Righton as Leggatt, Lady Monckton as Mrs. Chambers, Rose Norreys as Lady Alice, Mrs. E. H. Brooke as Mrs. Leggatt, Helen Leyton as Felicia, Sophie Larkin as Isabella/ Scenery by Bruce Smith.

MR. RIGHTON'S ADVENTURES WITH A RUSSIAN PRINCESS// F// G. H. Lewis ("Slingsby Lawrence")// **Olympic**, Mar. 1874, with G. W. Anson as Prince Louis, Mr. Culver as Count Bangski, L. F. Lewis as Gen. Boshaky, Mr. Vincent as Capt. Larsky, Annie Taylor as Princess Cascowisky, Emma Chambers as Miss Smith/ Scenery by Julian Hicks.

MR. SCROGGINS; OR, CHANGE OF NAME// F 1a// William Hancock & Arthur Moore// **Sad. Wells**, Sept. 1867.

MR. SMITH// FC 1a// Stanley Dark// **Alexandra**, Apr. 1900.

MR. SYMPKYN// F 3a// A. J. Flaxman & William Younge// **Globe**, May 1897, with Sydney Paxton as Selwyn, Cecil Thornbury as Humbolt, George Shelton as Sympkyn, Mabel Lane as Mrs. Selwyn, Madge Johnstone as Mrs. Strickley.

MR. V. MRS// C 1a// Arthur Bourchier & F. B. Coutts// **St. James's**, June 1899, with Arthur Bourchier as Robert, Violet Vanbrugh as Mrs. Featherleigh

MISTLETOE BOUGH, THE; OR, YOUNG LOVEL'S BRIDE// D// Frederick Marchant// **Grecian**, Dec. 1865, with J. Jackson as Baron de Clifford, William James as Lovell, Charles Mortimer as Sir Reginald, Walter Holland as Kobo, John Manning as Crotchet, Marie Brewer as Lady Agnes, Mrs. Edwards as Dame Winnifred, Miss M. A. Victor as Maud.

MRS. ANNESLEY// Play 3a// J. F. Cooke// **Criterion**, July 1891.

MRS. BROWN// C// Miss J. H. Wilton// **Britannia**, May. 1874.

MRS. CAUDLE'S CURTAIN LECTURES// F 1a// H. Horncastle// **Grecian**, July 1845, with Frederick Robson as Job Caudle, Edwin Dixon as Prettyman, Mr. Baldwin as Spottletoe, Mr. Delavanti as Grubb, Mr. Kerridge as Alphonse, Henry Horncastle as Mrs. Caudle, Annette Mears as Miss Prettyman, Mrs. W. Watson as Mrs. Galdart/ Music by Mr. Isaacson.

MRS. CAUDLE'S CURTAIN LECTURES// D 1a// Douglas Jerrold// **Haymarket**, Aug. 1845, with J. B. Buckstone as Caudle, A. Brindal as Prettyman, Mr. Harcourt as Wittles, Mr. Caulfield as Leanly, Mr. Carle as Joskins, Mrs. W. Clifford as Mrs. Caudle.

MRS. DANE'S DEFENCE// D 4a// Henry Arthur Jones// **Wyndham's**, Oct. 1900, with Charles Wyndham, Alfred Bishop, Lena Ashwell, Alfred Kendrick, Marie Illington.

MRS. DEXTER// FC 3a// J. H. Darnley// **Strand**, Feb. 1894.

MRS. GREEN'S SNUG LITTLE BUSINESS// F 1a// C. S. Cheltnam// **Strand**, Jan. 1865.

MRS. HARRIS// F 1a// Edward Stirling// **Lyceum**, Oct. 1846, with Mr. Turner as Mugbolt, Alfred Wigan as Masker, Frank Matthews as Slickly, Drinkwater Meadows as Shivers, Miss Arden as Fanny, Robert Keeley as Mrs. Harris.

MRS. HILARY REGRETS// C 1a// S. Theyre Smith// **Criterion**, June 1892.

MRS. JOHNSON// F// I. R. O'Neil// **Drury Lane**, July 1852, with Frederick Vining as Lushington, Mr. Percival as Fast, William Suter as Tomkins, Henry Butler as Broadcloth, Mrs. Lewis as Lucy, Clara Tellett as Polly, Mrs. Harris as Mrs. Johnson.

MRS. JORDAN; OR, ON THE ROAD TO INGLEFIELD// Play 1a// Constance Smedley// **Royalty**, Feb. 1900.

MRS. LESSINGHAM// Play 4a// Constance Fletcher ("George Fleming")// **Garrick**, Apr. 1894, with John Hare.

MRS. M.P.// F// Adap. by Hermann Vezin fr G of Julius Rosen// **Opera Comique**, Dec. 1891.

MISTRESS OF THE MILL, THE// C 1a// Trans. by W. T. Moncrieff fr F, La Munière de Marly// **Sad. Wells**, Oct. 1849, with Henry Mellon as Pretengil, Henry Nye as Poppy, Mr. Franks as Clem, Mrs. G. Smith as Marchioness, Julia St. George as Flora/ **Lyceum**, 1867, with Henry Mellon as Pretengil, Stanislaus Calhaem as Poppy, Mr. Regan as Clem, Miss Ritter as Marchiness, Miss Montgomery as Flora/ **Holborn**, May 1869.

MISTRESS OF THE SEAS, THE// D 4a// John Douglass// **West London**, Feb. 1899.

MRS. OTHELLO// F 3a// Adap. by Fred Leslie & Arthur Shirley fr F of Maxime Boucheron & M. Morel// **Toole's**, Nov. 1893.

MRS. PONDERBURY'S PAST// FC 3a// Adap. by F. C. Burnand fr F of Ernest Blum & Raoul Touché, Madame Mongodin// **Avenue**, Nov. 1895/ **Court**, Feb. 1896.

MRS. WEAKLY'S DIFFICULTY// C// William Poel// **Vaudeville**, July 1887.

MRS. WHITE// C 1a// R. J. Raymond// **St. James's**, Oct. 1837, with Mr. Brookes as Maj. Pepper, Mr. Sidney as Brown, Mr. Wright as White, Mme. Sala as Mrs. White, Miss Smith as Widow White, Annette Mears as Kitty/ **Sad. Wells**, Apr. 1840, with Mr. Williams as Maj. Pepper, Mr. Elvin as Brown, Mr. Conquest as White, Mrs. J. F. Saville as Widow White, Miss Cooke as Kitty, Miss Pincott as Mrs. White; June 1854, with Mr. Barret as Maj. Pepper, F. Charles as Brown, A. Judd as White, Miss Lavine as Mrs. White, Miss Mandelbert as Widow White, Caroline Parkes as Kitty/ **Haymarket**, Oct. 1850, with Mr. Rogers as

Maj. Pepper, John Parselle as Brown, Henry Bedford as White, Mrs. L. S. Buckingham as Widow White, Mrs. Caulfield as Kitty, Priscilla Horton as Mrs. White.

MRS. WIGGINS// F// J. T. Allingham// **Haymarket**, Sept. 1842, with Robert Strickland as Old Wiggins, James Worrell as Young Wiggins, T. F. Mathews as Potsup, Henry Widdicomb as Trim, Miss Stanley as Mrs. Wiggins, Miss C. Conner as Mrs. Tom Wiggins, Mrs. Stanley as Mrs. Chloe Wiggins/ **Grecian**, Feb. 1844, with Edmund Garden as Old Wiggins, Frederick Robson as Trim, H. Bedford as Potsup, Edwin Dixon as Young Wiggins, Mrs. Dixon as Mrs. Wiggins, Ellen Crisp as Mrs. Tom Wiggins, Miss Merion as Mrs. Chloe Wiggins.

MIZPAH// D 4a// Wood Lawrence, H. W. Hatchman, & J. B. Mulholland// **Britannia**, May 1891.

MOB CAP, THE; OR, LOVE'S DISGUISES// D 2a// Howard Paul// **Drury Lane**, Apr. 1853.

MOCK MARRIAGE, THE; OR, THE BLACKSMITH ASSASSIN// D 3a// n.a.// **Victoria**, June 1850, with Mr. Henderson as Squire Harley, Mr. Hitchinson as Rev. Mason, Henry Frazer as Kurdiston, John Bradshaw as Red Ralph, J. Neville as Dr. Midge, J. T. Johnson as Anderson, G. F. Forman as Pledge, J. Howard as Mutchkkin, Georgiana Lebatt as Julia, Mrs. Andrews as Mrs. Anderson, Mrs. George Lee as Clara, Mrs. Cooke as Miss Bustleton, Miss Barrowcliffe as Sally.

MODEL HUSBAND, A// F 1a// J. P. Wooler// **Sad. Wells**, Sept. 1853, with Mr. Barrett as Shanky, J. W. Ray as Simon Shanky, Charles Fenton as Fitz Blazington, Master Righton as Joe, Eliza Travers as Mrs. Shanky, Mrs. Henry Marston as Mrs. Mannington.

MODEL HUSBAND, THE// C// Miss Braddon// **Surrey**, Oct. 1868.

MODEL OF A WIFE, A// F 1a// Adap. by Alfred Wigan fr F// **Lyceum**, Apr. 1845, with Alfred Wigan as Bonnefoi, Frank Matthews as Stump, Drinkwater Meadows as Tom, Mrs. Woollidge as Sarah, Miss Fairbrother as Clara/ **Princess's**, Oct. 1850, with Mr. Addison as Stump, Drinkwater Meadows as Tom, Alfred Wigan as Bonnefoi, Miss Somers as Mrs. Stump, Miss Murray as Clara/ **Olympic**, Oct. 1854, with J. H. White as Stump, Samuel Emery as Tom, Alfred Wigan as Bonnefoi, Mrs. Chatterley as Mrs. Stump, Miss Marston as Clara/ **St. James's**, Apr. 1876, with F. Strickland as Stump, G. Shelton as Tom, G. W. Anson as Bonnefoi, Miss E. Toms as Mrs. Stump, Miss A. Forrest as Clara.

MODEL UNCLE, A// F// G. L. M. Strauss// **Drury Lane**, Nov. 1868, with Mr. Barrett as Smith, Alfred Nelson as Barnton, F. Charles as Saltley, John Rouse as Strop, Kate Harfleur as Grace, Miss Hudspeth as Mary Jane.

MODERN CRAZE, THE// C// Mrs. Henry De La Pasture// **St. Geo. Hall**, Nov. 1899.

MODERN EVE, A// Play 3a// M. C. Salaman// **Haymarket**, July 1894, with Charles Allan as Sir Gerald, Fred Terry as Hereford, Herbert Beerbohm Tree as Wargrave, Mrs. H. B. Tree as Vivian, Lottie Venne as Mrs. Meryon, Mrs. Dion Boucicault as Mrs. Malleson.

MODERN HERCULES, A// F// Trans. by Oliver Brand fr G, Monsieur Herkules// **Grand**, Oct. 1886.

MODERN HYPATIA, A; OR, A DRAMA OF TODAY// Play// Mabel Collins// **Terry's**, June 1895, with Edmund Gurney as Lord Davenant, Acton Bond as Alexis, Frank Adair as Martyn, Rudge Harding as Francis, Charles Sugden as Tylden, Edith Crauford as Rose, Agnes Hill as Mrs. Tylden, Mrs. Theodore Wright as Marcia.

MODERN JUDAS, A// D 4a// Nellie Guion// **Vaudeville**, Feb. 1892, with Frank Worthing as Capt. St. John, Alfred Harding as Judas, Julian Cross as Slegman, W. S. Parkes as Dare, A. Wellesley as Gen. Grant, Douglas Gordon as Karl, W. A. Chandler as Grimes, Amy McNeil as Madge, Violet Russell as Esther, Mrs. W. Aubrey as Grandma, May Conrade as Edna, Henrietta Cross as Chloe.

MODERN MARRIAGE, A// Play 4a// Neville Doone// **Comedy**, May 1890, with Lewis Waller as Edwards, Sydney Basing as Capt. Gossett, Royce Carleton as Trevor, John Beauchamp as Sir Richard, Julian Cross as Middleton, Alma Murray as Lilian, Robertha Erskine as Lady Blessington, Ellaline Terriss as Eva.

MODERN ORPHEUS, THE; OR, MUSIC THE FOOD OF LOVE// F// Benjamin Webster// **Cov. Garden**, Apr. 1837, with William Farren as Dumont, Mr. Tilbury as Picote, John Webster as Philippe, Mrs. Julia Glover as Mme. Picote, Miss Lee as Cecile, Miss Nicholson as Jaquette/ **Haymarket**, June 1837, with William Farren as Dumont, Robert Strickland as Picote, John Webster as Philippe, Mrs. Julia Glover as Mme. Picote, Miss Allison as Cecile, Miss Gallot as Jaquette.

MODERN WIVES// FC 3a// Adap. by Ernest Warren fr F of Albin Valabrègne// **Royalty**, Jan. 1887.

MOHICANS OF PARIS, THE// D Pro & 2a// n.a.// **Britannia**, July 1873.

MOLIERE// Play 1a// Walter Frith// **St. James's**, July 1891, with George Alexander as Moliere, Ben Webster as Marquis, Alfred Holles as Baron, Herbert Waring as Dacquin, Laura Graves as Catherine, Marion Terry as Armande.

MOLLY OF THE DUKE'S// D// G. R. Sims & Arthur Shirley// **Court**, Mar. 1901.

MOMENT OF TERROR, THE// D 3a// George Conquest// **Grecian**, June 1862, with Alfred Rayner as Clayton, Thomas Mead as Kenny, William James as Ryan, John Manning as Wagtail, Henry Power as Tight, George Gillett as Montrose, Mrs. Charles Dillon as Adelaide,

Mary A. Victor as Mary, Miss Johnstone as Mrs. Burnett.

MOMENTOUS QUESTION, THE// D 2a// Edward Fitzball// **Lyceum**, June 1844/ **Sad. Wells**, June 1845, with Henry Mellon as Greenfield, Henry Marston as Shelley, Henry Scharf as Jack, Miss Cooper as Rachel, Mrs. Henry Mellon as Fanny/ **Olympic**, Dec. 1851, with William Farren Jr. as Greenfield, Henry Farren as Shelley, Charles Bender as Chalk, Alfred Sanger as Moletrap, W. Shalders as Union Jack, Louisa Howard as Rachael, Ellen Turner as Fanny/ **Grecian**, June 1855, with Basil Potter as Shelby, Mr. Hamilton as Moletrap, Richard Phillips as Greenfield, John Manning as Jack, Henry Power as Chalk, Jane Coveney as Ryland, Harriet Coveney as Fanny.

MONASTARY OF ST. JUST, THE// Play 3a// Adap. by John Oxenford fr F of Casimir Delavigne// **Princess's**, June 1864, with George Vining as Philip II, John Nelson as Juan, J. W. Ray as Don Quexada, Henry Mellon as Don Gomez, Henry Marston as Anselmo, W. R. Robins as Prior, Stella Colas as Peblo and as Donna Florinda, Charles Seyton as Raphael, Mrs. Henry Marston as Dorothea,

MONEY// C 5a// Edward Bulwer-Lytton// **Haymarket**, Dec. 1840, with Frederick Vining as Glossmore, Robert Strickland as Vesey, Walter Lacy as Blount, David Rees as Stout, W. C. Macready as Evelyn, Benjamin Webster as Graves, Benjamin Wrench as Smooth, Mrs. Julia Glover as Lady Franklin, Priscilla Horton as Georgina, Helen Faucit as Clara; Mar. 1852, with John Parselle as Glossmore, Mr. Lambert as Sir John, Leigh Murray as Blount, J. B. Buckstone as Stout, Barry Sullivan as Evelyn, Benjamin Webster as Graves, Henry Howe as Smooth, James Bland as Sharpe, Mrs. Fitzwilliam as Lady Franklyn, Mrs. L. S. Buckingham as Georgina, Mrs. Stirling as Clara; Aug. 1865, with Walter Gordon as Glossmore, W. H. Chippendale as Vesey, William Farren as Blount, J. B. Buckstone as Stout, Henry Howe as Evelyn, Henry Compton as Graves, George Braid as Smooth, Thomas Coe as Sharpe, Miss Snowdon as Lady Franklyn, Louisa Angel as Clara, Caroline Hill as Georgina; Jan. 1880, with Johnston Forbes Robertson as Glossmore, Mr. Odell as Vesey, Squire Bancroft as Blount, Mr. Archer as Smooth, Arthur Cecil as Graves, H. B. Conway as Evelyn, Henry Kemble as Stout, Charles Brookfield as Sharp, Mrs. Bancroft as Lady Franklin, Linda Dietz as Georgina, Marion Terry as Clara/ **Sad. Wells**, Mar. 1846, with E. Morton as Glossmore, Henry Scharf as Blount, A. Younge as Vesey, George Bennett as Stout, Henry Mellon as Graves, Henry Marston as Smooth, Samuel Phelps as Evelyn, Mr. Williams as Sharp, Mrs. Henry Marston as Lady Franklin, Miss Cooper as Georgina, Mrs. Mary Warner as Clara/ Scenery by F. Fenton & Mr. Finlay; July 1863, with Walter Joyce as Evelyn, Scott Ramsay as Stout, H. J. Montague as Blount, H. Williams as Graves, Frank Graham as Sharp, G. Wyld As Glossmore, W. Taylor as Smooth, H. Seymore as Vesey, Zoe Montague as Clara, Mrs. Newbury as Lady Franlin, Miss Norton as Georgina/ **Olympic**, May 1851, with William Farren Jr. as Glossmore, George Cooke as Vesey, Henry Farren as Blount, Henry Compton as Stout, W. Shalders as Graves, H. Lee as Smooth, Leigh Murray as Evelyn, Charles Diddear as Sharp, Charles Bender as Old Member, Mrs. Leigh Murray as Lady Franklin, Louisa Howard as Georgina, Mrs. Stirling as Clara; May 1866, with W. M. Terrott as Glossmore, W. H. Stephens as Vesey, Robert Soutar as Blount, Edward Atkins as Stout, Horace Wigan as Graves, Henry Neville as Alfred, H. J. Montague as Smooth, Henry Rivers as Sharp, Mrs. St. Henry as Lady Franklin, Lydia Foote as Georgina, Kate Terry as Clara/ **Grecian**, Jan. 1854, with T. Roberts as Lord Glossmore, Charles Horn as Blount, Eaton O'Donnell as Vesey, Charles Rice as Graves, Basil Potter as Smooth, Richard Phillips as Evelyn, Henry Power as Sharp, Jane Coveney as Clara, Miss Johnstone as Lady Franklin, Harriet Coveney as Georgina; **Olympic**, Mar. 1878, with Henry Neville as Evelyn, Charles Flockton as Vesey, J. G. Bauer as Glossmore, Johnston Forbes Robertson as Blount, Robert Pateman as Stout, G. W. Anson as Graves, J. R. Crawford as Smooth, Mr. Warren as Sharp, G. Hammond as Old Member, Bella Pateman as Clara, Mrs. John Wood as Lady Franklin, Alma Stanley as Georgina/ **Lyceum**, Feb. 1858, with J. Robertson as Glossmore, Mr. Barrett as Vesey, J. G. Shore as Blount, J. L. Toole as Stout, Mr. Stuart as Graves, C. F. Fortescue as Evelyn, C. Webb as Smooth, Mr. Poynter as Sharp, Mr. Holston as Old Member, Eliza Webb as Georgina, Maria Ternan as Clara, Mrs. Weston as Lady Franklin/ **Princess's**, Feb. 1860, with George Melville as Evelyn, Mr. Garden as Glossmore, J. G. Shore as Blount, Frank Matthews as Vesey, Henry Widdicomb as Stout, Harcourt Bland as Smooth, Frank Graham as Sharp, John Ryder as Graves, Carlotta Leclercq as Lady Franklin, Miss Clifford as Georgina, Mrs. Charles Young as Clara; Dec. 1862, with J. P. Herbert as Glossmore, H. Seymour as Vesey, Ernest Granville as Blount, Joseph Eldred as Smooth, Walter Joyce as Evelyn, Scott Ramsey as Stout, H. Williams as Graves, Constance Aylmer as Clara, Mrs. Buckingham White as Lady Franklin, Fanny Haldane as Georgina/ **POW**, May. 1872/ **Vaudeville**, May 1882, with Henry Neville, William Farren, Frank Archer, J. R. Crauford, Ada Cavendish, Alma Murray, Mrs. John Wood/ **Garrick**, May 1894, with Arthur Cecil, Johnston Forbes Robertson, Arthur Bourchier, Henry Kemble, Gilbert Hare, Kate Rorke, John Hare/ **Comedy**, Jan. 1900.

MONEY AND MISERY; OR, THE PHANTOM IN THE SNOW// D 3a// J. H. Wilkins// **Victoria**, July 1879, with Charles Sennett as Lord Clement, Lloyd Townrow as Morley, Walter Lacy as Wayland, Charles Beverley as Bianchi, Harry Bolton as Jem, Andy Robertson as Groggins, J. G. Johnson as Falcon, Lizzie Ballantyne as Lady Grace, Blanche Payne as Lady Rosamond, Mrs. Lewis Nanton as Rachael, Jessie Garratt as Polly.

MONEY BAGS// FC 3a// Adap. by. T. Edgar Pemberton & Mr. Shannon// **Novelty**, Nov. 1885.

MONEY MAD// D 5a// Steele Mackay// **Surrey**, Apr. 1893.

MONEY SPINNER, THE// C 2a// Arthur Wing Pinero// **St. James's**, Jan. 1881, with W. H. Kendal as Lord Kengussie, John Hare as Baron Croodle, John Clayton as Boycott, Mr. Mackintosh as Faubert, Mrs. W. H. Kendal as Millicent, Kate Phillips as Dorinda, Mrs. Gaston Murray as Margot/ Scenery by Gordon & Harford.

MONK OF CLERKE'S WELL, THE; OR, ISLINGTON IN OLDEN TIMES (see Clerke's Well)

MONK-KING, THE; OR, THE FATE OF THE HEBREW MAID// D 3a// n.a.// **Sad. Wells**, Jan. 1838, with Mr. Rumball as Charles V, Mr. Campbell as Philip II, Mr. Forester as Don Ferdinand, Mr. James as Don Quessada, Mr. Rogers as Peblo, S. Smith as Don Sylvestro, Mrs. Weston as Dorothea, Eliza Vincent as Donna Florinda/ Scenery by Mr. Battie.

MONK'S ROOM, THE// D Pro & 3a// John Lart// **POW**, (in Pro & 4a) Dec. 1887/ **Olympic**, Apr. 1888/ **Globe**, Nov. 1888, with E. S. Willard as Sir Darrell, Hermann Vezin as Lazanski, Forbes Dawson as Hargrave, Ivan Watson as Count Zoroff, Edward Rose as Potter, Edwin Shepherd as Brandon, Alma Murray as Elanor, Helen Leyton as Sophie, Mrs. E. H. Brooke as Mrs. Kulp/ Scenery by Bruce Smith/ Prod. by W. Sutney.

MONOMANIA; OR, THE DELUSION// D 2a// n.a.// **Haymarket**, Aug. 1838, with E. W. Elton as Sir Bernard, James Worrell as Lord Belmond, Mr. Hutchings as Dashton, Robert Strickland as Dr. Anodyne, J. W. Gough as David, J. B. Buckstone as Bobby, Miss Cooper as Lady Emily, Miss Gallot as Marian.

MONSEIGNEUR; OR, PARIS IN 1720// D 2a// n.a.// **Princess's**, Jan. 1845, with James Wallack as Monseigneur, Mr. Granby as Labarre, Augustus Harris as Methiew, W. H. Oxberry as Germaine, Mr. Walton as Bernard, James Ranoe as Gringot, Emma Stanley as Rosaline, Miss Marshall as Annette, Miss Somers as Lisette/ Scenery by William Beverley, Mr. Nichols, & Mr. Aglio/ Music by W. L. Phillips.

MONSEIGNEUR; OR, THE ROBBERS OF PARIS// D 4a// Adap. by T. H. Reynoldson fr F// **Grecian**, Jan. 1845, with Harry Chester as Monseigneur, C. Hodges as Gaspard, Mr. Campbell as Lamartellier, Mr. Baldwin as Ladoucine, Frederick Robson as Martial, Annette Mears as Fideline, Miss M. A. Crisp as Antoinette/ Scenery by Mr. Muir/ Music by Mr. Isaacson.

MONSIEUR DE PARIS// Play 1a// Alicia Ramsey & Rudolph de Cordova// **Royalty**, Apr. 1896, with Mark Kinghorne as Delpit, Henry Vibart as Le Febvre, Mrs. Henry Leigh as Mére Lisette, Violet Vanbrugh as Jacinta.

MONSIEUR JACQUES// D 1a// Adap. by Morris Barnet fr F of Cogniard, Le Pauvre Jacques// **St. James's**, Apr. 1837, with Morris Barnett as Jacques, Mr. Sidney as Sequence, Mr. Hollingsworth as Antonio, Mr. Halford as Vivid, Priscilla Horton as Nina/ **Sad. Wells**, Apr. 1841, with Morris Barnett as Jacques, Mr. Williams as Sequence, F. B. Conway as Vivid, Charles Fenton as Anton/ **Olympic**, July 1848, with H. J. Turner as Sequence, Mr. Lawrence as Antonio, Alfred Wigan as Jacques, Henry Butler as Vivid, Miss St. George as Nina.

MONSIEUR LE DUC// D 1a// Val Prinsep// **St. James's**, Oct. 1879, with John Hare as Richelieu, William Terriss as Comte de la Roque, John Cathcart as Le Chevalier, Mr. Draycott as Le Baron, Cicely Grahame as Marguerite/ Scenery by Gordon & Harford.

MONSIEUR MALLET; OR, THE POST OFFICE MISTAKE// F 3a// W. T. Moncrieff// **Drury Lane**, Dec. 1839/ **Cov. Garden**, Feb. 1845, with James H. Hackett as Mallet, J. C. Bird as Franklin, Mr. Griffiths as Baxter, Mr. Rogers as Postmaster, Miss Fitzjames as Marie, Mrs. Griffiths as Mrs. Baxter/ **Haymarket**, May 1845 (in 1a), with James H. Hackett as Mallet, Henry Howe as Franklin, William Clark as Howe, Mr. Tilbury as Baxter, Mr. Carle as Taffrail, Miss Telbin as Marie, Mrs. Stanley as Mrs. Baxter.

MONSIEUR MOULON; OR, THE SHADOW OF DEATH// Play 4a// Charles Hannon// **Shaftesbury**, Oct. 1890, with Luigi Lablache as Moulon, Sydney Basing as Rochefort, C. M. Hallard as Henri Raymond, Frank Fenton as Victor Raymond, M. Herapath as Vicomte Ongré, Charles Sugden as Carot, Arthur Wood as Grandfather Lupin, E. M. Robson as Jean, Adrienne Dairolles as Jeannette, Georgina Kuhe as Justine, Mary Barton as Adèle, Amy Bowen as Cherie, Alma Murray as Marie.

MONSIEUR TONSON// C// W. T. Moncrieff// **Sad. Wells**, Oct. 1837, with Mr. Campbell as Morblieu, Mr. Bathurst as King, E. Morton as Ardourly, Thomas Lee as Useful, Mr. Ennis as Thompson, Mr. Scarbrow as Nap, Miss Murray as Adolphine, Miss Vernon as Mme. Bellegarde.

MONT BLANC// C 3a// Adap. by H. & Athol Mayhew partly fr F of E. Labiche & E. Martin, Le Voyage de M. Perrichon// **Haymarket**, May 1874, with W. H. Chippendale as Dr. Majoribanks, W. H. Kendal as Harold, J. B. Buckstone Jr. as Silverspoon, George Braid as Earl of Osborne, Henry Howe as Centilivre, J. B. Buckstone as Chirpey, Mr. Rogers as Capt. Broadside, T. S. Jerrold as Fortinbras, Frederick Everill as Windbeutel, Edward Osborne as Lavigne, Mrs. Chippendale as Mrs. Chirpey, Amy Roselle as Florence, Helen Massey as Miss Jetsam/ Scenery by John O'Conner & George Morris/ Machines by Oliver Wales/ Gas by F. Hope/ Prod. by Mr. Coe.

MONT ST. MICHEL; OR, THE FAIRY OF THE SANDS// D 2a// W. Bayle Bernard// **Princess's**, Oct. 1852, with Frank Graham as Count de Rochemont, George Everett as St. Prie, John Ryder as Fortbras, John Pritt Harley as Le Sage, John Chester as Tronchet, Carlotta

Leclercq as Claire, Miss Marshall as Ninon, Miss Daly as Suzanne, Miss Vivash as Jeanette/ Scenery by Walter Gordon & F. Lloyds/ Music by Mr. Stöpel.

MONTCALM// D 5a// Charles Young// **Queen's**, Sept. 1872.

MONTE CHRISTO// D// Dram. by George Conquest fr novel of Alexandre Dumas// **Grecian**, Nov. 1864, with David Jones as Edmund Dantes, William James as Fernand, Henry Grant as Dangless, George Conquest as Caderousse, J. Jackson as Abbe Faria, George Gillett as Albert, Lizzie Mandlebert as Mercedes.

MONTE CRISTO// D 10a// Adap. fr F of Alexandre Dumas & A. Magret// **Drury Lane**, [first part, in 5a] June 1848.

MONTE CRISTO// D 5a// Dram. fr F of Alexandre Dumas// **Adelphi**, Oct. 1868, with Henry Ashley as Villefort, C. H. Stephenson as Morel, Richard Phillips as Danglars, Benjamin Webster as Van Gripp (and 3 other parts), Arthur Stirling as Fernand, Charles Fechter as Edmund Dantes (and 2 other parts), C. J. Smith as Old Dantes, Mrs. Alfred Mellon as de Morcerf, George Belmore as Caderousse, Carlotta Leclercq as Mercedes, Mrs. Leigh Murray as Carconte, Maria Harris as Mlle. Danglars/ Scenery by Hawes Craven/ Machines by Mr. Charker/ Gas by G. Bastard/ Music by Edwin Ellis/ Prod. by Charles Fechter/ **Avenue**, Feb. 1891.

MONTH AFTER DATE, A// C 1a// Silvanus Dauncey// **Globe**, Mar. 1891, with A. E. Drinkwater as Cumber, Frank Vancrossen as Clive, Charles Goold as Whimple, Mary Ansell as Rosy.

MONTRALTO; OR, THE MOUNTAIN PASS// D// Dram. fr Tales of the O'Hara Family// **Sad. Wells**, Jan. 1837, with Mr. King as Di Viglio, John Ayliffe as di Biraglio, Mr. Hicks as Montralto, C. H. Pitt as Storberg, Mr. Ray as Martsan, Mr. Campbell as Cavallo, Miss Lebatt as Garcia, Miss Julian as Flavilla, Miss Williams as Maretta.

MOONLIGHT BLOSSOM, THE// Play 3a// Adap. fr Jap. by Chester Fernald// **POW**, Sept. 1899, with Johnston Forbes Robertson as Arumo, James Welch as Bummawashi, Frank Mills as Sakata, Arthur Brumley Davenport as Yamakichi, Sydney Warden as Morikame, Mrs. Patrick Campbell as Inamura, Eleanor Calhoun as Dodan, Rosina Filippi as Mitsu, Beatrice Milani as Ibo, Rose Margaret as Biwa/ Scenery by William Telbin.

MOONLIGHT JACK; OR, THE KING OF THE ROAD// D// William Travers// **Sad. Wells**, Aug. 1866, with G. P. Jaques as Lord Clifford, F. Watts as Edmond, Philip Hannan as Rasper, William Travers as Jack, W. Carter as Carbyam, Watty Brunton as Potts, George Skinner as Gabriel, Mrs. Philip Hannan as Madge, Miss Neville as Bess, Julia Summers as Chrystabel.

MOONSHINE// C 5a// E. Stuart-Wartley// **Haymarket**, Aug. 1843, with Henry Holl as Ravendale, C. J. Mathews as Fitzosborne, Benjamin Webster as Rochegarde, William Farren as Batenbille, Henry Howe as Deloraine, Mr. Tilbury as Turnour, William Clark as Flash, James Worrell as Giovanni, Mrs. Julia Glover as Countess of Clanarlington, Mrs. Stanley as Lady Mordaunt, Mme. Vestris as Lady Maria, Miss Lee as Lady Juliana, Julia Bennett as Lady Geraldine, Mrs. W. Clifford as Mrs. Turnour, Mrs. Edwin Yarnold as Miss Montgomery/ Scenery by George Morris.

MOONSTONE, THE// D 4a// Dram. by Wilkie Collins fr his novel// **Olympic**, Sept. 1877, with Henry Neville as Blake, Charles Harcourt as Ablewhite, Thomas Swinbourne as Sgt. Cuff, J. W. Hill as Betteredge, Robert Pateman as Candy, Bella Pateman as Rachel, Mrs. Seymour as Miss Clack, Miss Gerard as Penelope/ Scenery by W. Hann.

MORDEN GRANGE// D 4a// F. C. Burnand// **Queen's**, Dec. 1869.

MORE BLUNDERS THAN ONE// F 1a// G. H. Rodwell// **Adelphi**, Mar. 1838, with William Cullenford, Mr. Saville, Mr. Sanders, Tyrone Power Sr., Agnes Taylor, Miss Shaw, Mrs. Nailer/ **Cov. Garden**, June 1840, with Mr. Brookes as Melborne, S. Smith as Trap, Mr. Pelham as Young Melborne, John Brougham as Hoolaghan, Miss Baker as Louisa, Mrs. Emden as Letty, Miss E. Honner as Susan/ **Grecian**, Nov. 1844, with John Collett as Old Melbourne, Harry Chester as Young Melbourne, Edmund Garden as Trap, Mr. Hodson as Hoolagan, Miss Johnstone as Louisa, Miss M. A. Crisp as Susan/ **Sad. Wells**, Mar. 1870, with Mr. Howard as Old Melbourne, Edgar Newbound as Young Melbourne, Mr. Byrne as Trap, Richard Edgar as Hoolagan, Florence Gerald as Louisa, Grace Edgar as Susan, Miss Fitzgerald as Jenny.

MORE PRECIOUS THAN GOLD// C 2a// C. S. Cheltnam// **Strand**, July 1861.

MORMON, THE// FC 3a// W. D. Calthorpe// **Vaudeville**, Mar. 1887/ **Comedy**, Mar. 1887.

MORMONS, THE; OR, ST. ABE AND HIS SEVEN WIVES (first titled Exiles of Erin)// C 4a// Adap. partly fr Amer. play// **Olympic**, May 1881, with William Redmund as Henry Desmond, Harry St. Maur as Fitzgerald, J. A. Arnold as Corcoran, Mr. Macartney as Rory, Mr. Daniels as Andy, Mr. Dolman as Brigham Young, William McIntyre as Swayne, Tully Thornton as Black Jack, Percy Compton as Clewson, Stanislaus Calhaem as Chingachook, Harriet Jay as Hester, Mrs. Digby Willoughby as Norah, Lizzie Williams as Biddy, Anges Clifton as Tabitha/ Scenery by Bruce Smith & J. Johnson.

MORNA, THE HAG OF THE CLIFF; OR, THE CHIEF OF ULVA'S ISLE// D// Found. on ballad, Lord Ullin's Daughter// **Sad. Wells**, June 1837, with Mr. Hicks as Roderick, Mr. Campbell as Lord Ullin, C. H. Pitt as Baron Monteith, C. J. Smith as Dougal, Mr. Griffiths as Gordon, Mr. Conquest as Sandie, Stuart King as Ronald,

Lavinia Melville as Lady Margaret, Mrs. Harris as Maggie, Miss Williams as Morna.

MORNING CALL, A// C 1a// Charles Dance// **Drury Lane**, Mar. 1851/ **Sad. Wells**, Dec. 1853, with E. L. Davenport as Sir Edward, Fanny Vining as Mrs. Chillington/ **Olympic**, Sept. 1859, with George Vining as Sir Edward, Mrs. Stirling as Mrs. Chillingtone; Apr. 1884, with James Nelson as Sir Edward, Mlle. Carrara as Mrs. Chillingtone/ **St. James's**, Aug. 1867, with Arthur P. Clinton as Sir Edward, Eleanor Bufton as Mrs. Chillington.

MORTGAGE DEEDS, THE// D// C. H. Hazlewood// **Britannia**, Feb. 1875.

MOSES AND SON// C 3a// J. Gordon// **Royalty**, June 1892, with Edward Righton as Solomon Moses, Harry Eversfield as Montagu, Gerald Maxwell as Bunting, Fred Shepherd as Col. Gore, Lennox Pawle as Howard, Annie Irish as Belle, Maria Davis as Mrs. Moses, Emma Ritta as Ruby, Florence Birchell as Rachel/ Scenery by R. C. Durant.

MOST UNWARRANTABLE INTRUSION, A// C 1a// J. Maddison Morton// **Adelphi**, June 1849.

MOTH AND THE CANDLE, THE// Play 3a// Violet Greville & Mark Ambient// **Wyndham's**, Dec. 1901.

MOTHER, THE// D 2a// Douglas Jerrold// **Haymarket**, May 1838, with Edmund Glover as Capt. Davenant, Robert Strickland as Compass, Charles Perkins as Foxglove, J. B. Buckstone as Larceny, Benjamin Webster as Barnaby, Mlle. [sic] Celeste as Eulalie, Miss Cooper as Fringella.

MOTHER, THE// D 5a// Adap. by Frank Harvey fr F// **Olympic**, Apr. 1879, with Frank Harvey as Armand, J. H. Barnes as Beizard, James Carter-Edwards as Father Gabriel, T. B. Appleby as Granier, H. Andrews as Pierre, H. Bennett as Nichaolas, Annie Baldwin as Hortense, Helena Ernstone as Marguerite, Lizzie Baldwin as Mariette/ Music by M. Buziau.

MOTHER AND CHILD ARE DOING WELL// F 1a// J. Maddison Morton// **Haymarket**, Aug. 1848, with Mr. Lambert as Snugsby, Paul Bedford as Lt. O'Scupper, James Worrell as Maxwell, Mr. Lindon as Mungo, Edward Wright as Fluffy, Mrs. Laws as Penelope, Emma Harding as Emily/ **Adelphi**, Jan. 1852, with William Cullenford as Snugsby, Paul Bedford as Lt. Scupper, Edward Wright as Felix, Emma Harding as Emily, Mrs. Laws as Penelope.

MOTHER BROWNRIGG; OR, MARY CLIFFORD, THE FOUNDLING APPRENTICE GIRL// D// n.a.// **Grecian**, June 1863, with J. Jackson as Brownrigg, W. Shirley as Elveston, George Gillett as William, Walter Holland as John, Alfred Rayner as Noah, John Manning as Wiggins, Henry Power as Hucklebridge, Miss Johnston as Mrs. Brownrigg, Mrs. Charles Dillon as Mary, Edith Randall as Emma, Mary A. Victor as Doll.

MOTHER OF THREE, A// F 3a// Clothilde Graves// **Comedy**, May 1896, with Felix Morris as Murgatroyd, Cyril Maude as Sir Wellington, Stuart Champion as Port, Clarence Blakiston as Capt. Tuckle, Cosmo Stuart as Thrupp, Rose Leclercq as Lady Port, Annie Goward as Sooza, Esmé Beringer as Cassiopeia, Lily Johnson as Vesta, Audrey Ford as Aquila, Fanny Brough as Mrs. Murgatroyd.

MOTHER'S DREAM, A// D 2a// Douglas Jerrold// **Adelphi**, Mar. 1850, with Charles Boyce as Capt. Davenant, Paul Bedford as Compass, O. Smith as Foxglove, Edward Wright as Larceny, Henry Hughes as Ratesby, Mme. Celeste as Eulalie, Ellen Chaplin as Pringella.

MOTHER'S DYING CHILD, THE// D 3a// C. H. Hazlewood// **Britannia**, Oct. 1864.

MOTHER'S SIN, A// D 6a// Walter Reynolds// **Elephant & Castle**, July 1885/ **Grand**, July 1886.

MOTHER-IN-LAW// C 3a// G. R. Sims// **Opera Comique**, Dec. 1881.

MOTHERS AND DAUGHTERS// C 5a// Robert Bell// **Cov. Garden**, Jan. 1843, with George Vandenhoff as Lord Merlin, George Bartley as Sir Gregory, Mr. Cooper as Sandford, John Pritt Harley as Capt. Montague, Alfred Wigan as Loop, J. Ridgway as Tom, Drinkwater Meadows as Blount, Mr. Granby as Cushion, Mrs. Orger as Lady Manifold, Mrs. Walter Lacy as Emily, Miss Vandenhoff as Mabel, Mrs. Humby as Rose/ Scenery by Grieve, T. Grieve & W. Grieve.

MOTHS// D 4a// Dram. by Henry Hamilton fr novel of Ouida// **Globe**, Mar. 1882, with Herbert Standing, Kyrle Bellew, Carlotta Addison/ **Olympic**, Apr. 1882, with C. Cartwright as Prince Zouroff, Henry Hamilton as Duke of Mull, J. A. Rosier as Lord Jura, Kyrle Bellew as Raphael, Miss Claremont as Princess Nadine, Maud Brennan as Duchess de Sonnaz, Carlotta Addison as Lady Dolly, Miss Litton as Vere, Louise Willis as Fuschia/ **Sad. Wells**, Sept. 1882, with E. N. Hallows as Raphael, George Stretton as Prince de Zouroff, J. E. Kellerd as Lord Jura, F. Owen as Duke of Mull, Lissie Lily as Fuschia, Alice Denvil as Lady Dolly, Helen Grahame as Duchess de Sonnaz, Miss M. Blandford as Princess Nadina, Marie Forde as Vera/ Scenery by W. T. Hemsley.

MOTHS// D 4a// Mervyn Dallas// **Strand**, June 1884.

MOTTO ON THE DUKE'S CREST, THE: "I AM HERE"// D 3a// George Conquest// **Grecian**, July 1863, with George Gillett as Regent of France, Walter Holland as Duc de Nevers, Alfred Rayner as Duc de Gonzaque, Thomas Mead as Henri de Lagardere, J. Jackson as Cocardasse, Henry Grant as Feyrolles, John Manning as Passepoil, W. Shirley as Nathaniel, Henry Power as Aesop, Jane Dawson as Blanche de Caylna, Mrs. Charles Dillon as Blanche de Nevers, Mary A. Victor as Flora.

MOUNT ST. BERNARD; OR, THE GOLDSMITH OF GRENOBLE// D 4a// n.a.// **Adelphi**, Oct. 1839.

MOUNTAIN HEIRESS, A// Gilbert à Beckett// **St. Geo. Hall**, Mar. 1883.

MOUNTAIN JUDGE, THE// D 3a// n.a.// **Victoria**, Nov. 1853, with T. E. Mills as Emanuel, Mr. Moreland as Henri, N. T. Hicks as Amboise, Mr. Green as Bishop, Mr. Richards as D'Albigny, J. Howard as Birchonback, Mrs. Henry Vining as Agatha, Miss Dansor as Angeline, Mrs. Manders as Bridgetta, Miss Sutton as Annetti, Miss Edgar as Lisetta.

MOUNTAINEERS, THE; OR, LOVE AND MADNESS// D 3a// George Colman the younger// **Grecian**, Oct. 1845, with Edwin Dixon as Count Virolet, Mr. Baldwin as Sadi, Frederick Robson as Tocho, Harry Chester as Octavian, F. Ede as Muley, Edmund Garden as Kilmallock, John Collett as Pietro, Miss M. A. Crisp as Floranthe, Annette Mears as Agnes, Miss Johnstone as Zorayda/ **Sad. Wells**, May 1850, with Samuel Phelps as Octavian, G. K. Dickinson as Count Virolet, Henry Mellon as Kilmallock, Frank Graham as Roque, A. Younge as Tocho, George Bennett as Muley, Miss Edwardes as Floranthe, Miss T. Bassano as Zorayda, Miss A. Brown as Agnes.

MOUNTEBANK, THE (a vers. of Belphegor)// D// Adap. fr F of A. P. Dennery & M. Fourier, La Paillasse// **Lyceum**, Apr. 1865, with Charles Fechter as Belphegor, Henry Widdicomb as Farfayou, John Ryder as Lavarennes, Samuel Emery as Duke of Montbazon, Charles Horsman as Viscount de Blangy, Carlotta Leclercq as Violette, Mrs. Charles Horsman as Catherine, Mlle. Marie Beatrice as Madeleine.

MOUSE, THE// F 1a// n.a.// **Victoria**, July 1850, with J. Neville as Badger, Mr. Morrison as Grab, G. F. Forman as Queerchance, J. Howard as Calculate, John Hudspeth as Mooneye, T. H. Higgie as Swiftfoot, Georgiana Lebatt as Grace, Mrs. Cooke as Mrs. Calculate, Miss Barrowcliffe as May.

MOUSETRAP, THE// C 3a// J. White// **Haymarket**, May 1853, with Mr. Tilbury as Lord Winterdell, W. H. Chippendale as Sir Clerimont, Mr. Rogers as Gen. Borolift, J. B. Buckstone as Marling, William Farren as George, Mr. Edwards as William, Mrs. Poynter as Lady Serena, Miss A. Woulds as Sophronia, Louisa Howard as Helen, Mrs. Fitzwilliam as Judith, Mrs. Stanley as Camomile.

MOUSTACHE MOVEMENT, THE// F 1a// Robert Brough// **Adelphi**, Mar. 1854, with O. Smith as Simon, John Parselle as Capt. Kidd, Robert Keeley as Soskins, Mrs. Keeley as Louisa, Mary Keeley as Eliza.

MOVE ON; OR, THE CROSSING SWEEPER// D 3a// Dram. by James Mortimer fr Charles Dickens, Bleak House// **Grand**, Sept. 1883.

MOVING TALE, A// F 1a// Mark Lemon// **Adelphi**, June 1854, with Robert Keeley as Grandison, Robert Romer as Chelsea, Mrs. Keeley as Mrs. Grandison, Mary Keeley as Keziah.

MOYNA A-ROON; OR, THE RAPPAREE'S BRIDE// D// J. C. Levey// **Elephant & Castle**, Nov. 1875.

MOYRA THE DOOMED; OR, THE FORGED WILL AND THE MALEDICTION OF THE DEAD// D 3a// n.a.// **Victoria**, May 1854, with Alfred Saville as Dunovan, Phoebe Johnson as Gilbert, Mr. Henderson as Mark O'Bryant, N. T. Hicks as William O'Bryant, Mr. Green as Father Gerald, John Hudspeth as Filgarlic, T. E. Mills as Fitzbaun, Mrs. Henry Vining as Moyra, Miss Laporte as Dora, Mrs. Manders as Shelah.

MUCH ADO ABOUT NOTHING// C// William Shakespeare// **Drury Lane**, Nov. 1839, with George Bennett as Don Pedro, Mr. Archer as Leonato, Mr. Waldron as Don John, John Lee as Claudio, Henry Marston as Benedick, W. Bennett as Antonio, Mr. Roberts as Balthazar, Mr. Baker as Borachio, William Dowton as Dogberry, Henry Compton as Verges, W. H. Oxberry as Sexton, Jane Mordaunt as Hero, Miss Barnett as Ursula, Mrs. Stirling as Beatrice; Mar. 1843, with Charles Hudson as Don Pedro, Mr. Lynne as Don John, James Anderson as Claudio, W. C. Macready as Benedict, Samuel Phelps as Leonato, W. Bennett as Antonio, George Bennett as Borachio, Charles Selby as Conrade, Henry Compton as Dogberry, Robert Keeley as Verges, Miss Fortescue as Hero, Louisa Nisbett as Beatrice, Miss Fairbrother as Margaret, Miss Ellis as Ursula; Oct. 1856, with C. Verner as Don Pedro, R. H. Lingham as Don John, C. Vincent as Claudio, Barry Sullivan as Benedict, Mr. Tilbury as Antonio, Mr. Carter as Leonato, James Worrell as Borachio, A. Younge as Dogberry, George Honey as Verges, Emma Waller as Beatrice, Miss M. Oliver as Hero, Emma Wadham as Ursula, Miss Florence as Margaret/ **Cov. Garden**, Apr. 1840, with Mr. Cooper as Don Pedro, James Bland as Don John, George Vandenhoff as Claudio, Charles Diddear as Leonato, George Bartley as Antonio, Charles Kemble as Benedick, William Farren as Dogberry, Robert Keeley as Verges, Emmeline Montague as Hero, Louisa Nisbett as Beatrice, Mme. Simon as Ursula, Miss Garrick as Margaret/ **Haymarket**, Jan. 1843, with Henry Vandenhoff as Pedro, A. Brindal as Don John, Henry Howe as Claudio, Benjamin Webster as Benedick, Mr. Tilbury as Antonio, Mr. Rogers as Leonato, William Farren as Dogberry, Robert Keeley as Verges, Mrs. Nisbett as Beatrice, Mrs. Seymour as Hero, Mrs. Caulfield as Ursula; Nov. 1853, with William Farren as Pedro, George Braid as Don John, Henry Howe as Claudio, George Vandenhoff as Benedick, Mr. Rogers as Leonato, Mr. Tilbury as Antonio, Henry Corri as Borachio, Edwin Villiers as Conrade, Henry Compton as Dogberry, William Clark as Verges, Louisa Howard as Hero,, Miss Reynolds as Beatrice, Miss E. Romer as Margaret, Miss Hollingsworth as Ursula/ **Drury Lane**, Feb. 1843, with W. C. Macready, Louisa Nisbett, Henry Compton, Robert Keeley, Samuel Phelps; Feb. 1858, with Amy Sedgwick, Henry Compton/ **Princess's**,

Apr. 1845, with Henry Wallack as Don Pedro, Mr. Hield as Claudio, Mr. Fitzjames as Don John, James Wallack as Benedick, Mr. Archer as Leonato, Mr. Granby as Antonio, Charles Horn Jr. as Borachio, Augustus Harris as Conrad, Henry Compton as Dogberry, W. H. Oxberry as Verges, Charlotte Cushman as Beatrice, Mrs. Brougham as Hero, Miss E. Honner as Ursula; Nov. 1852, with Charles Kean as Benedick, James Vining as Don Pedro, Mr. Terry as Don John, John Cathcart as Claudio, John Ryder as Leonato, Mr. Addison as Antonio, George Everett as Borachio, Frederick Cooke as Conrad, John Chester as Seacoal, George Bartley as Dogberry, Drinkwater Meadows as Verges, Mrs. Charles Kean as Beatrice, Caroline Heath as Hero, Miss Daly as Ursula, Miss J. Lovell as Margaret/ Scenery by Walter Gordon & F. Lloyds; Sept. 1863, with Charles Vincent as Don Pedro, Mr. Brooke as Don John, E. F. Edgar as Claudio, Walter Montgomery as Benedick, W. R. Robins as Leonato, John Collett as Antonio, Mr. Raymond as Borachio, Mr. Fitzjames as Dogberry, Robert Cathcart as Verges, Miss Atkinson as Beatrice, Agnes Ansell as Hero, Miss Frazer as Ursula, Lizzie Harrison as Margaret/ **Marylebone**, Sept. 1849, with Anna Cora Mowatt/ **Sad. Wells**, Nov. 1852, with William Belford as Don Pedro, Mr. Wallis as Don John, Frederic Robinson as Claudio, Henry Mellon as Antonio, Henry Marston as Benedick, George Bennett as Leonato, C. Mortimer as Balthazar, Miss Cooper as Beatrice, Miss T. Bassano as Hero, Mrs. Dixon as Margaret, Miss Mandelbert as Ursula; Mar. 1868, with Mr. Murray as Don Pedro, R. Norman as Don John, J. L. Warner as Claudio, C. W. Barry as Leonato, Charles Dillon as Benedick, J. W. Lawrence as Antonio, Walter Searle as Dogberry, Harry Chester as Verges, Miss Leigh as Hero, Alice Marriott as Beatrice/ **Grecian**, Sept. 1856, with Henry Grant as Don Pedro, Mr. Coleman as Don John, F. Charles as Claudio, Richard Phillips as Benedict, Mr. Hustleby as Leonato, Eaton O'Donnell as Dogberry, John Manning as Verges, Jane Coveney as Beatrice, Ellen Hale as Hero/ **St. James's**, Apr. 1866, with F. Charles as Don Pedro, Walter Joyce as Don John, John Clayton as Claudio, Walter Lacy as Benedick, Mr. Rolfe as Leonato, Edward Dyas as Antonio, Frank Matthews as Dogberry, Frederick Robson as Verges, Gaston Murray as the Friar, Louisa Herbert as Beatrice, Eleanor Bufton as Hero/ Scenery by T. Grieve/ Machines by Mr. Mathews/ Music by Frank Musgrave; Feb. 1898, with Fred Terry as Don Pedro, H. B. Irving as Don John, Robert Loraine as Claudio, George Alexander as Benedick, W. H. Vernon as Leonato, J. D. Beveridge as Antonio, Arthur Royston as Borachio, J. Nutcombe Gould as Friar Francis, H. H. Vincent as Dogberry, H. V. Esmond as Verges, Fay Davis as Hero, Julia Neilson as Beatrice, Winifred Dolan as Margaret, Hilda Rivers as Ursula/ Scenery by Walter Hann, T. E. Ryan, H. P. Hall & William Telbin/ Music by Edward German/ Machines by Mr. Cullen/ Electrics by Mr. Barbour/ **Adelphi**, Aug. 1867, with Henry Ashley as Don Pedro, Richard Phillips as Don John, Henry Neville as Benedick, Mr. Stuart as Leonardo, C. H. Stephenson as Antonio, Emily Pitt as Balthazar, W. H. Eburne as Borachio, John Clarke as Dogberry, C. J. Smith as Verges, Miss Hughes as Hero, Kate Terry as Beatrice, Miss A. Seaman as Ursula/ **Lyceum**, Nov. 1882, with Henry Irving as Benedick, William Terriss as Don Pedro, Charles Glenney as Don John, Johnston Forbes Robertson as Claudio, James Fernandez as Leonato, Henry Howe as Antonio, Frank Tyars as Borachio, S. Johnson as Dogberry, Stanislaus Calhaem as Verges, Jessie Millward as Hero, Louisa Payne as Ursula, Ellen Terry as Beatrice/ Scenery by Hawes Craven, William Cuthbert & William Telbin/ Music by Meredith Ball/ Machines by Mr. Knight.

MUCH TOO CLEVER; OR, A FRIEND INDEED// C 1a// Adap. fr F by Joseph Hatton & John Oxenford// **Gaiety**, Feb. 1874.

MUDBOROUGH ELECTION// F 1a// William Brough and Andrew Halliday// **POW**, July 1865.

MUDDLES// FC 3a// Mr. Jessup & William Gill// **Imperial**, Mar. 1885.

MUFF OF THE REGIMENT, THE (see Good Bye, by Johnson)

MUGWUMP, THE// C 1a// n.a.// **Court**, Oct. 1898, with Cyril Vernon as Marston, Aubrey Fitzgerald as Barrymore, Ferdinand Gottschalk as Ferguson, Grace Dudley as Emily, Janet Evelyn as Kate.

MULDOON'S PICNIC; OR, IRISH LIFE IN AMERICA// F// Harry Pleon// **Marylebone**, Nov. 1886.

MULETEER OF TOLEDO, THE; OR, KING, QUEEN, AND KNAVE// C 2a// Adap. by J. Maddison Morton fr F// **Princess's**, Apr. 1855, with James Vining as Don Pedro, George Everett as Don Scipio, John Pritt Harley as Count do Pompolo, Walter Lacy as Manuel, Ffrederick Cooke as Pablo, Mr. Raymond as Jose, Carlotta Leclercq as Elvira, Miss Murray as Carmen, Mrs. Winstanley as Countess de Pompolo/ Scenery by Walter Gordon & F. Lloyds/ **Grecian**, May 1856, with F. Charles as Manuel, Mr. Hustleby as Don Pedro, Henry Grant as Don Sallust, John Manning as Don Caesar, Amelie Conquest as Elvira, Harriet Coveney as Donna Carmen, Miss Johnstone as Donna Beatrice.

MUMMY, THE// F 1a// W. Bayle Bernard// **Olympic**, June 1854, with J. H. White as Mandragon, Mr. Leslie as Capt. Canter, Henry Rivers as Old Tramp, Frederick Robson as Toby Tramp, Alfred Wigan as Dithershin, Harwood Cooper as Pole, Miss Marston as Fanny, Ellen Turner as Susan.

MUMMY, THE// FC 3a// G. D. Day & Arthur Reed// **Comedy**, July 1896, with Lionel Brough as Rameses, William Cheesman as Garsop, Robb Harwood as Smythe, Stuart Champion as Tibbs, Clarence Blakiston as Marston, Alice Mansfield as Alvena, Lily Johnson as Eva, Jessie Bateman as Mabel, Annie Goward as Cleopatra, Charlotte Walker as Hattie.

MUMMY AND THE HUMMING BIRD, THE//

Play 4a// Isaac Henderson// **Wyndham's**, Oct. 1901.

MUMPS THE MASHER// F// Tom Craven & R. Nelson// **Pavilion**, Aug. 1884.

MURDERER'S DREAM, THE; OR, THE DARK POOL OF THE AVENUE// D// n.a.// **Sad. Wells**, July 1837, with Mr. King as Norton, Mr. Hicks as Ross, C. H. Pitt as Stanley, Mr. Rogers as Pathos, C. J. Smith as Haversack, Thomas Lee as Sawney, Lavinia Melville as Fanny, Mrs. Harris as Peggy, Miss Williams as Janet, Miss Pitt as Jessy/ Scenery by Mr. Mildenhall.

MURPHY THE DRUMMER// C 2a// n.a.// **Sad. Wells**, Aug. 1843, with Thomas Lee as Paddy Murphy, R. H. Lingham as Rusti, Mr. Williams as Foxi Fum, Mr. Coreno as Ski Hi, Mr. Lamb as Phaster, Miss Lee as Ko Ket, Miss Stephens as Sing Smahl.

MURPHEY'S WEATHER ALMANAC; OR, ANNO. DOMINI 1838// F// n.a.// **Sad. Wells**, Feb. 1838, with Mr. James as Weatherguage, Mr. Rogers as Murphy, Mr. Scarbrow as Gregory, Miss Beresford as Charlotte, Miss Chartley as Cicely.

MUSE AND THE MERCHANT, THE// D// n.a.// **Olympic**, Mar. 1840, with Mr. Brookes as Pigalt, Mr. Baker as Bureau, Mr. Hull [Henry Holl?] as Dian, George Wild as Slickton Swop, Mr. Halford as Folarte, Miss Fitzwalter as Rose, Mrs. Anderson as Lisette/ Scenery by Mr. Wilson.

MUSETTE// D// Fred Marsden// **Opera Comique**, Dec. 1883.

MUSIC HATH CHARMS// F 1a// David Fisher// **Princess's**, June 1856, with David Fisher as Pertinax, Mr. Raymond as Capt. Bremont, John Pritt Harley as de Beauval, Mr. Brazier as Rabinel, Carlotta Leclercq as Mathilde, Maria Ternan as Lucille, Miss Clifford as Victoire/ **Olympic**, May 1870, with David Fisher as Pertinax, Alfred Sanger as Capt. Bremont, Mr. St. Maur as Babinel, Henry Vaughan as de Beauval, Mattie Reinhardt as Mme. de la Roche, Jessie Earle as Lucille, Nellie Joy as Victoire.

MUSICAL BOX, THE// F// F. C. Burnand// **Gaiety**, Oct. 1877.

MUSKETEERS, THE// Play 10a// Adap. by Sidney Grundy fr F of Alexandre Dumas// **Her Majesty's**, Nov. 1898, with Herbert Beerbohm Tree as D'Artagnan, Franklyn McLeay as Richelieu, Louis Calvert as Porthos, Herbert Ross as Louis XIII, Frank Mills as Athos, Gerald du Maurier as Aramis, Charles Allan as Bonacieux, Alfred Brydone as Stranger, F. P. Stevens as De Treville, Lewis Waller as Buckingham, Mrs. H. B. Tree as Anne of Austria, Mabel Love as Constance, Mona Harrison as Claudette, Alice Kingsley as Zoe, Mrs. Brown Potter as Milady/ Scenery by Walter Johnstone, William Telbin, Joseph Harker & Walter Hann/ Music by Raymond Roze.

MUTINY AT THE NORE, THE// D// Douglas Jerrold// **Sad. Wells**, Dec. 1838, with W. D. Broadfoot as Adm. Colpoys, Mr. Harwood as Capt. Griffith, Mr. Mellor as Capt. Loch, Mr. Dry as Capt. Arlington, J. W. Collier as Adams, Mr. Cathcart as Parker, Dibdin Pitt as Bubble, Mr. Conquest as Chicken, Miss Sims as William, Miss Pincott as Molly, Miss Cooke as Dame Goose, Mrs. Robert Honner as Mary.

MUTUAL MISTAKE, A// F 1a// W. H. Denny// **Court**, Mar. 1891, with Charles Rock as John, John Clulow as Smith, Susie Vaughan as Letitia.

MY ARTFUL VALET// FC 3a// Adap. by James Mortimer fr F of M. Chivot & Alfred Duru, Le Truc d'Arthur// **Globe**, Nov. 1891, retitled as Gloriana// **Terry's**, Aug. 1896; Dec. 1901.

MY ASTRAL BODY// F 3a// W. C. Hudson & Nicholas Colthurst// **Court**, Apr. 1896, with Yorke Stephens as Cariston, C. M. Lowne as Thayer, Ernest Hendrie as J.P., J. F. Cornish as Phu, Fanny Coleman as Mildred, Miss Fairbrother as Meredith, Helen Petrie as Kate.

MY AUNT'S ADVICE// Adap. by E. A. Sothern fr F of Pierron & La Ferriere, Livre III, Chap. 1// **Haymarket**, Dec. 1861, with Henry Howe as Arundel, E. A. Sothern as Capt. Leslie, Miss M. Oliver as Mrs. Arundel, Miss Coleman as Jane/ **St. James's**, May 1867, with Henry Irving as Arundel, Louisa Herbert as Mrs. Arundel, Miss Guiness as Mary/ **Drury Lane**, Mar. 1890, with E. S. Willard as Capt. Leslie, Herbert Waring as Arundel, Mrs. E. S. Willard as Lucy.

MY AUNT'S HUSBAND// D 1a// Charles Selby// **Strand**, Sept. 1858.

MY AWFUL DAD// C 2a// Adap. by C. J. Matthews fr F of Alexandre Dumas, Un Père Prodigue// **Gaiety**, Sept. 1875, with C. J. Mathews.

MY BACHELOR PAST// C 3a// Adap. by James Mortimer fr F of Eugène Labiche & A. C. Delacour, Celimare le Bien-Aimé// **Wyndham's**, Aug. 1901.

MY BEAUX; OR, THE FIRST OF APRIL// F// T. A. Stack// **Marylebone**, Apr. 1868.

MY BENEFACTOR// F 1a// Edward Rose// **Strand**, Nov. 1883.

MY BONNY BOY (also Bonnie)// FC 3a// T. G. Warren// **Criterion**, Dec. 1886, with William Blakeley, J. H. Darnley, Miss. F. Paget, Annie Hughes.

MY BOY// C 3a// Adap. by G. A. Lubinoff fr G of Adolphe L'Arronge, Mein Leopold// **Vaudeville**, Jan. 1888.

MY BRAVE LITTLE WIFE// CD 1a// A. M. Seaton// **Toole's**, July 1882.

MY BROTHER'S SISTER// Play 3a// Leonard Grover// **Gaiety**, Feb. 1890, with John Maclean as Bernadet, Wallace Erskine as Livingstone, Herbert Sparling as Grosserby, C. W. Allison as Parker, Minnie Palmer in 4 char. parts, Helen Palgrave as Mrs. Livingstone, Gladys Homfrey as Geraldine, Cecilia Beaucliffe as Mary.

MY COOK AND HOUSEKEEPER// F// n.a.// **Drury Lane**, Mar. 1854.

MY COUSIN// C 1a// J. J. Hewson// **Olympic**, Mar. 1887.

MY DARLING// C 3a// E. R. Callender// **Gaiety**, Feb. 1883.

MY DAUGHTER// Play 1a// Adap. by Marie Bancroft fr G// **Garrick**, Jan. 1892, with W. Scott Buist as Capt. Blake, Charles Rock as Rochie, Einifred Fraser as Rosie, Louise Moodie as Mrs. Blake, Minna Blakiston as Lucy.

MY DAUGHTER THE DUCHESS// C 4a// A. Meadow// **Vaudeville**, Oct. 1884.

MY DAUGHTER-IN-LAW// C 3a// Adap. fr F of F. Carré & P. Bilhaud, Ma Bru// **Criterion**, Sept. 1899, with Seymour Hicks as Reginald Mainwaring, Herbert Standing as Mainwaring Sr., C. P. Little as Bulstrode, Alfred Bishop as Brown, J. L. MacKay as Sweeting, A. Vane Tempest as Osesimus Bulstrode, Fanny Brough as Mrs. Mainwaring Sr., Cynthia Brooks as Countess Lodoiska, Ellaline Terriss as Mrs. Mainwaring Jr./ Scenery by Walter Hann.

MY DRESS BOOTS// F 1a// T. J. Williams// **Royalty**, Sept. 1854.

MY ENEMY// C 2a// Adap. by Robert Reece fr F// **Olympic**, Jan. 1880, with Edward Righton as Omen, J. D. Beveridge as Luxmore, John Maclean as Langford, Gwynne Williams as Sybil, Miss Howard as Sarah.

MY FATHER DID SO BEFORE ME// C 1a// n.a.// **Lyceum** Oct. 1848, with Charles Selby as Lord Flippington, John Reeve as Trot, Mrs. Yates as Countess de Clairville, Kathleen Fitzwilliam as Laura.

MY FELLOW CLERK (see also, Clerk of Islington)// F 1a// John Oxenford// **Victoria**, Sept. 1837, with William Davidge as Hooker, W. H. Oxberry as Victim, Benjamin Wrench as Tactic, John Parry as Fag, Mr. Hitchinson as Knitbrow, Mrs. Griffith as Mrs. Dobson, Miss Wilson as Fanny, Mrs. Frank Matthews as Juliet, Miss Bartlett as Betty/ **Sad. Wells**, July 1854, with Mr. Williams as Hooker, Robert Roxby as Tactic, Mr. Templeton as Victim, Mr. Swan as Fag, Mr. Henry as Knitbrow, Mrs. Foote as Mrs. Dobson, Emma Wadham as Miss Dobson, Miss M. Oliver as Juliet/ **Grecian**, Apr. 1857, with Eaton O'Donnell as Hoskey, Mr. Smithson as Bailiff, Mr. Melvin as Knitbrow, Richard Phillips as Tactic, John Manning as Victim, Henry Power as Fag, Miss Johnstone as Mrs. Dobson, Ellen Hale as Fanny, Ellen Crisp as Juliet/ **Adelphi**, Jan. 1873, with B. Egan as Hooker, A. C. Lilly as Victim, Harwood Cooper as Fag, J. G. Shore as Tactic, Mr. Smithson as Bailiff, Mrs. Addie as Mrs. Dobson, Maud Howard as Fanny, Miss Hudspeth as Juliet, Ada Dyas as Betty.

MY FIRST BRIEF// F// n.a.// **Sad. Wells**, Nov. 1861, with Lewis Ball as Jones, Edmund Phelps as Skimford, Mr. Williams as Buckles, Mr. Chapman as William, Miss Heath as Mrs. Buckles, Ada Dyas as Jemima, Mrs. Barrett as Aunt Mary, Mrs. Lingard as Mrs. Jones.

MY FRIEND// C// Joseph Tabrar// **Vaudeville**, Nov. 1885.

MY FRIEND FROM LEATHERHEAD// F 1a// Edmund Yates & N. H. Harrington// **Lyceum**, Feb. 1857.

MY FRIEND IN THE STRAPS// F// n.a.// **Haymarket**, Oct. 1850, with Mr. Lambert as Nupkins, James Bland as Maj. Capiscum, John Parselle as Frederick, Charles Hudson as O'Blarney, Mr. Rogers as Grumpy, Mrs. L. S. Buckingham as Caroline, Mrs. Stanley as Mrs. Capiscum.

MY FRIEND JARLET// C 1a// Arnold Goldsworthy & E. B. Norman// **Terry's**, Nov. 1890, with Julian Cross as Jarlet, Henry Dana as Latour, Arthur Wellesley as Prussian, Elinore Leyshon as Marie.

MY FRIEND THE CAPTAIN// F// J. Stirling Coyne// **Haymarket**, July 1841, with Benjamin Wrench as Brown, David Rees as Snoxell, Robert Strickland as Tidmarsh, Henry Howe as Selborne, William Clark as Trigg, Mrs. Stanley as Mrs. Tidmarsh, Miss Charles as Sophia, Miss Grove as Clara, Mrs. Frank Matthews as Patty/ **Sad. Wells**, Oct. 1847, with William Hoskins as Brown, Henry Scharf as Snexel, Mr. Williams as Tidmarsh, Frank Graham as Selborn, G. Maskell as Tom Trigg, Mrs. W. Watson as Mrs. Tidmarsh, Miss Marsh as Sophia, Miss Newcombe as Clara, Julia St. George as Patty, Fanny Morelli as Sally.

MY FRIEND THE MAJOR// F 1a// Charles Selby// **St. James's**, Oct. 1854, with W. Cooper as Broadacre, George Burt as Chizzleton, J. L. Toole as Weazel, F. Ede as Sir Pilbury, Mr. Jones as Playfair, Mr. Herbert as Jenks, Miss Douglas as Miss Todhunter, Miss Waterhouse as Miss Tiverton, Miss Wheeler as Lady Bloomfield, Miss Harford as Mrs. Playfair.

MY FRIEND THE PRINCE// Play 3a// Adap. by J. H. McCarthy fr Amer. F, My Friend from India// **Garrick**, Feb. 1897, with Percy Lyndal as Prince Maurice, Paul Arthur as Godolphin, Fred Kaye as Jannaway, Aubrey Boucicault as Pink, Herbert Ross as Hertzlein, Ells Dagnall as Shottery, James Welch as Pinning, Miriam Clements as Princess Brunhilde, Sybil Carlisle as Poppy, Blanche Massey as Pansy, Juliette Nesville as Gilberte/ Scenery by Joseph Harker/ Prod. by Dion Boucicault.

MY GRANDMOTHER// F 1a// n.a.// **St. James's**, Apr. 1837, with Mr. Hollingsworth as Sir Matthew, Mr. Halford as Vapour, Mr. Sidney as Souffrance, Mr. Moore as Tom, John Pritt

Harley as Gossip, Miss Rainforth as Florella, Miss C. Crisp as Charlotte.

MY HEART'S IDOL; OR, A DESPERATE REMEDY// C 2a// J. R. Planché// **Lyceum**, Oct. 1850, with George Vining as Count Leopold, C. J. Mathews as Baron Borrowitz, Mr. Bellingham as Col. Reichard, Mr. Harcourt as Maj. Waldeck, Mme. Vestris as Mme. Reinstein, Miss Kenworthy as Louise, Isabel Dickenson as Baroness Borrowitz.

MY HEART'S IN THE HIGHLANDS// F 1a// William Brough & Andrew Halliday// **Drury Lane**, May 1864, with George Belmore as Muggins, G. Weston as MacWalker, Mr. Neville as O'Groat, Mr. Warde as Gray/ **Princess's**, Apr. 1872, with Mr. Barrett as O'Groat, William Terriss as Gray, Stanislaus Calhaem as Nuggins, Charles Seyton as Walker, J. Morriss as Gillie, Mrs. Addie as Tibble, Miss O'Hara as Caledonia.

MY HUSBAND'S GHOST// F// J. Maddison Morton// **Haymarket**, June 1837, with Benjamin Webster as Corp. Musket, Mr. Ross as Gilkes, Mr. Gallot as Sgt. Bumpus, Eliza Vincent as Mrs. Musket, Mrs. Humby as Fanny, Mrs. W. Clifford as Mrs. Jabber; Nov. 1861, with George Braid as Sgt. Bumpus, Edwin Villiers as Corp. Musket, William Clark as Gilks, Eliza Weekes as Mrs. Musket, Mrs. Griffith as Mrs. Jabber, Henrietta Lindley as Fanny.

MY HUSBAND'S SECRET// F 1a// W. D. Whitty// **Vaudeville**, Apr. 1874, with Nelly Walters, Mr. Lilly.

MY INNOCENT BOY// FC 3a// G. R. Sims & Leo Merrick// **Royalty**, May 1898, with Charles Rock as Smith, Herman de Lange as de Moulin, Sidney Drew as Valentine, Frank Atherley as Jellicoe, Harry Farmer as Tremlett, Doris Templeton as Dulcie, Mrs. Furtado-Clark as Hypatia, Helen Rous as Miss Magnus, Dora Barton as Dora, Constance Mori as Mabel, Kate Bishop as Mrs. Jutsam.

MY JACK// C 1a// Emily Coffin// **Princess's**, Oct. 1887.

MY JACK// D 5a// Benjamin Landeck// **Surrey**, Sept. 1889.

MY KNUCKLEDUSTER// n.a.// **Strand**, Feb. 1863.

MY LADY HELP// C 1a// Arthur Macklin// **Shaftesbury**, May 1890, with John Beauchamp as Pennygrass, H. V. Esmond as Desborough, Florence West as Lady Desborough.

MY LADY'S ORCHARD// Play 1a// Mrs. Oscar Beringer & G. P. Hawtrey// **Avenue**, Oct. 1897, with Charles Brookfield as John of Courtenay, Frederick Volpé as Dennis, Sydney Warden as Pierre, Vera Beringer as Azalais, Katherine Stewart as Lisette, Esmé Beringer as Bertrand/ Scenery by Walter Johnstone.

MY LIFE// D 4a// Miss Archer// **Gaiety**, Dec. 1882.

MY LITTLE ADOPTED// C// T. H. Bayly// **Haymarket**, Dec. 1838, with J. B. Buckstone as Dibbs, Mr. Hemming as Maj. Seymore, Walter Lacy as Summers, Miss Taylor as Laurette, Mrs. Fitzwilliam as Rose, Mrs. Frank Matthews as Becky.

MY LITTLE GIRL// C 1a// Dram. by Dion Boucicault fr novel of W. Besant & James Rice// **Court**, Feb. 1882, with John Clayton as Venn, Carlotta Addison as Aunt Janet/ **Drury Lane**, Mar. 1882, with John Clayton as Venn, Henry Kemble as Jones, D. G. Boucicault as Durnford, Carlotta Addison as Aunt Janet, Miss Measor as Gladys.

MY LORD ADAM// C 3a// Mrs. De Lacy// **Royalty**, Jan. 1901.

MY LORD AND MY LADY; OR, IT MIGHT HAVE BEEN WORSE// C 5a// J. R. Planché// **Haymarket**, July 1861, with C. J. Mathews as Lord Fitzpatrick, Henry Howe as Sir Harry, Mr. Andrews as Louis, J. B. Buckstone as Groundsell, Mrs. C. J. Mathews (Lizzie Davenport) as Lady Fitzpatrick, Henrietta Lindley as Mrs. Groundsell, Mrs. Edward Fitzwilliam as Slip, Eliza Weekes as Betty, Mrs. Wilkins as Mrs. Round.

MY LORD IN LIVERY// F 1a// S. Theyre Smith// **Princess's**, Sept. 1886, with Wilfred Draycott as Lord Thirlmere, Stewart Dawson as Spiggott, Vane Featherston as Sybil, Grace Arnold as Laura, Emily Calhaem as Rose.

MY MAN TOM AND SISTER KATE// C 1a// Mark Lemon// **Olympic**, Feb. 1840, with Mr. Baker as Unit, Mr. Halford as Morton, George Wild as Tom Chaff, Mrs. Anderson as Mrs. Morton, Mrs. Norton as Miss Pemberton, Miss Conner as Emily/ **Sad. Wells**, June 1841, with Mr. Elvin as Unit, George Ellis as Morton, John Herbert as Chaff, Mrs. Richard Barnett as Kate, Mrs. Morgan as Miss Pemberton, Miss Garrick as Emily, Miss Cooke as Mrs. Scrubber/ **Drury Lane**, Spr. 1853.

MY MILLINER'S BILL// C 1a// G. W. Godfrey// **Drury Lane**, June 1884, with Arthur Cecil as Merridew, Mrs. John Wood as Mrs. Merridew.

MY MISSIS// D// Catherine Lewis & Donald Robertson// **Opera Comique**, Oct. 1886.

MY MOTHER// F 3a// Amy Steinberg// **Toole's**, Apr. 1890, with Yorke Stephens as Featherfield, James Nelson as Meredith, B. P. Seare as Sir Dallas, A. Ellis as Sparkle, Henry Bedford as Turner, Harry Monkhouse as McCarthy, Vane Featherston as Amy, Jean Vanderbilt as Florence, Eva Eden as Mary Jane, Elsie Chester as Mrs. Compass, Amy Steinberg as Felicité.

MY MOTHER'S MAID// F// C.J. Mathews// **Haymarket**, Nov. 1858, with C. J. Mathews as Prettyboy, Mr. Rogers as Softpip, William Cullenford as Quilltwiddle, Mrs. Poynter as Mrs. Prettyboy, Ellen Ternan as Flora, Mrs. C. J. Mathews as Pamela.

MY NEIGHBOR'S WIFE// F 1a// Alfred Bunn// **Drury Lane**, Mar. 1837, with Mr. Cooper as Somerton, Drinkwater Meadows as Brown, George Bartley as Smith, Miss Taylor as Mrs. Somerton, Miss Pincott as Mrs. Brown, Miss Lee as Mrs. Smith/ **Eng. Opera House** (Lyceum), June 1837, with Mr. Cooper as Somerton, Drinkwater Meadows as Brown, George Bartley as Smith, Miss Murray as Mrs. Somerton, Miss Lee as Mrs. Smith/ **Cov. Garden**, Feb. 1840, with Mr. Cooper as Somerton, Drinkwater Meadows as Brown, George Bartley as Smith, Mrs. Walter Lacy (Miss Taylor) as Mrs. Somerton, Miss Lee as Mrs. Brown, Mrs. Brougham as Mrs. Smith/ **Astley's**, Feb. 1863, with Henry Vandenhoff as Somerton, Mr. Worboys as Brown, B. Ryan as Smith, Rose Leclercq as Mrs. Somerton, Julia Craven as Mrs. Brown, Edith Stuart as Mrs. Smith.

MY NEIGHBOR'S WIFE// F// n.a.// **Sad. Wells**, Sept. 1839, with Mr. Elvin as Aubery, J. W. Collier as Brittle, Mr. Conquest as Simmons, Miss Pincott as Mrs. Aubery, Mrs. J. F. Saville as Mrs. Simmons, Miss Cooke as Mrs. Brittle.

MY OLD LUCK// C 1a// n.a.// **Sad. Wells**, Nov. 1858, with J. W. Ray as Goodbody, Charles Seyton as Valentine, Mr. Williams as Thrifty, Mr. Meagreson as Grasp, Charles Fenton as Timothy, Caroline Parkes as Mabel.

MY OWN GHOST// F 1a// n.a.// **Adelphi**, Dec. 1875, with Stanislaus Calhaem as Pearlbutton, Mr. Smithson as Thimble, Frederick Moreland as Clipper, Ernest Travers as Die, Cicely Nott as Mrs. Cribber.

MY PARTNER// D 4a// Bartley Campbell// **Olympic**, Apr. 1884, with George Rignold as Joe, Philip Beck as Ned, Harry Courtaine as Maj. Britt, W. H. Stephens as Brandon, Howard Russell as Venables, J. G. Wilton as Lee, Ernest Hendrie as Bowler, Alma Murray as Mary, Laura Linden as Grace, Mrs. Ernest Clifton as Posie.

MY POLL AND MY PARTNER JOE// D 3a// J. T. Haines// **Cov. Garden**, Feb. 1837, with Mr. Thompson as Capt. Oakheart, George Bennett as Brandon, T. P. Cooke as Hallyard, Henry Wallack as Tiller, Benjamin Webster as Watchful, John Webster as Zinga, James Worrell as Lt. Manly, Charles Bender as Bowse, Eliza Vincent as Mary, Mrs. Sarah Garrick as Dame Hallyard, Miss Lee as Abigail, Miss Lane as Zamba/ **Haymarket**, Nov. 1837, with J. W. Gough as Capt. Oakheart, Mr. Hutchings as Lt. Manly, Mr. Ray as Bowse, Mr. Gallot as Brandon, James Worrell as Zinga, T. P. Cooke as Hallyard, J. T. Haines as Tiller, J. B. Buckstone as Waxend, T. F. Mathews as Snatchem, Mrs. Waylett as Mary, Mrs. Humby as Abagail, Miss Wrighten as Zamba, Mrs. Gallot as Dame Hallyard/ **Sad. Wells**, Apr. 1841, with Mr. Elvin as Capt. Oakheart, Mr. Archer as Lt. Manly, Mr. Hamilton as Zingra, George Maynard as Brandon, Mr. Stilt as Bowse, T. P. Cooke as Hallyard, Robert Honner as Tiller, W. Smith as Waxend, Mr. Lewis as Old Sam, Mr. Turnour as Snatch'em, Mrs. Richard Barnett as Abigail, Mrs. Robert Honner as Mary/ **Victoria**, Feb. 1850, with Mr. Humphreys as Capt. Oakheart, Mr. Hitchinson as Lt. Manly, John Dale as Brandon, John Bradshaw as Bowse, Henry Dudley as Zingra, J. T. Johnson as Hallyard, Mr. Henderson as Toiler, John Hudspeth as Waxend, J. Neville as Old Sam, Annette Vincent as Mary, Miss Barrowcliffe as Abigale, Miss Mildenhall as Zamba, Mrs. Cooke as Dame Hallyard/ **Grecian**, Oct. 1856, with C. Kelsey as Capt. Oakheart, Mr. Coleman as Bowse, Richard Phillips as Hallyard, Henry Grant as Brandon, Henry Power as Snatch'em, Eaton O'Donnell as Old Sam, Mr. Hustleby as Tiller, John Manning as Waxend, Jane Coveney as Mary Maybud, Harriet Coveney as Abigale.

MY PRECIOUS BETSY// F 1a// J. Maddison Morton// **Adelphi**, Feb. 1850, with Edward Wright as Bobtail, Paul Bedford as Wagtail, James Worrell as Langford, Emma Harding as Mrs. Bobtail, Mrs. Frank Matthews as Mrs. Wagtail, Mrs. Laws as Nancy/ **Sad. Wells**, May 1854, with Mr. Barrett as Wagtail, Edward Wright as Bobtail, F. Charles as Langford, Caroline Parkes as Mrs. Bobtail, Harriett Gordon as Mrs. Wagtail. Mrs. Barrett as Mary; Aug. 1869, with Henry Atkins as Bobtail, C. J. Smith as Wagtail, E. C. Locksley as Langford, Emily Turtle as Mrs. Bobtail, Mrs. H. Lewis as Mrs. Wagtail, Miss D'Aubeny as Nancy.

MY PRESERVER// C 1a// H. T. Craven// **Strand**, Mar. 1863.

MY QUEEN// Play Pro & 3a// W. H. Poole// Gaiety, Mar. 1884.

MY QUEENIE// C 4a// H. W. Williamson// **Vaudeville**, Apr. 1889.

MY SISTER FROM INDIA// F 1a// Charles Selby// **Strand**, Jan. 1852.

MY SISTER'S SECRET// C// n.a.// **Princess's**, Jan. 1848, with James Vining as Lovechace, Henry Compton as Torpid, Thomas Hill as Whitethorn, Emmeline Montague as Margaret, Miss Villars as Alice.

MY SOLDIER BOY// FC 3a// Alfred Maltby & Frank Lindo// **Criterion**, Jan. 1899.

MY SON DIANA// F 1a// Augustus G. Harris// **Haymarket**, June 1857, with W. H. Chippendale as Culpepper, J. B. Buckstone as Smith, William Clark as John, Miss M. Oliver as Diana, Ellen Sabine as Louisa.

MY SON'S A DAUGHTER// C 2a// J. Parselle// **Strand**, Sept. 1862.

MY SPOUSE AND I// C 1a// C. I. Dibdin// **Victoria**, May 1838, with Mr. Harwood as Squire Wilton, Mr. Forester as Frisk, John Parry as Dick, Mr. Loveday as Paddock, William Davidge as Scorem, Mrs. Loveday as Dame Paddock, Mrs. Maddocks as Harriet, Mrs. Corry as Janet.

MY THREE CLERKS (a sequel to My Fellow Clerk)// F 1a// John Oxenford// **Victoria**, Feb. 1838, with William Davidge as Hooker,

Benjamin Wrench as Tactic, W. H. Oxberry as Victim, John Parry as Fag, Mr. Wilkins as O'Flasham, Miss E. Lee as Mrs. Victim, Mrs. Frank Matthews as Julia.

MY TURN NEXT// F 1a// T. J. Williams// **Lyceum**, Sept. 1872, with George Belmore as Twitters, F. W. Irish as Bolus, Robert Markby as Trap, John Collett as Wheatear, Miss E. Mayne as Lydia, Rose James as Cicely, Mrs. F. B. Egan as Peggy/ **Adelphi**, Dec. 1881, with Mr. Goodrich & Harry Proctor alt. as Paraxicum and Twitters, W. Howell as Tom Trap, Harwood Cooper as Wheatear, Miss Heffer as Lydia, Clara Jecks as Peggy, Miss Cruikshank as Cicely.

MY UNCLE// FC 3a// Amy Steinberg// **Terry's**, July 1889.

MY UNCLE'S CARD; OR, THE BARRISTER BEWILDERED// F 1a// H. P. Grattan// **Olympic**, Oct. 1841, with Mr. Brookes as Quiet, George Wild as Squil, Mr. Thompson as Testy, Mrs. Granby as Mrs. Quiet, Miss Fitzjames as Emily, Miss Le Batt [sic] as Sharp/ **Astley's**, Aug. 1855, with J. W. Anson as Quiet, W. Milborne as Hairbrain, George Wild as Sam Squills, Mrs. Dowton as Mrs. Quiet, Fanny Williams as Sharp.

MY UNCLE'S CARD; OR, THE FIRST OF APRIL// F// H. P. Grattan// **Surrey**, Jan. 1873.

MY UNCLE'S PET// C 2a// Thomas Archer// **Sad. Wells**, Apr. 1846, with Mr. Williams as Gen. Hermilly, Henry Scharf as Zurich, Frank Graham as D'Orville, Miss Cooper as Jules, Charles Fenton as Andre, Miss Huddart as Isadore, Mrs. Francis as Mme. Bertrand/ **Grecian**, June 1847, with Eaton O'Donnell as Gen. d'Hermilly, Frederick Robson as Zurich, Annette Mears as Jules, John Collett as Dorville, Miss M. A. Crisp as Isadora, Miss Merion as Mme. Bertrand.

MY UNCLE'S SUIT// F 1a// Martin Becher// **Drury Lane**, 1871, with William Terris, Miss D'Arcy.

MY UNCLE'S WILL// F 1a// S. Theyre Smith// **Haymarket**, 1873, with W. H. Kendal, Madge Robertson (Mrs. Kendal).

MY VALET AND I// F 1a// T. E. Wilks// **Olympic**, Nov. 1842, with Mr. Brookes as Mountain, Mr. Turnour as Claret, Mr. Fitzjames as Ardent, George Wild as Whisper, Miss Hamilton as Corelia, Georgiana Lebatt as Finesse/ **Sad. Wells**, July 1844, with Mr. Williams as Mountain, Charles Morelli as Claret, John Webster as Ardent, G. F. Forman as Whisper, Emma Harding as Corelia, Georgiana Lebatt as Finesse/ **Grecian**, May 1847, with Eaton O'Donnell as Mountain, John Collett as Claret, Richard Phillips as Ardent, Frederick Robson as Whisper, Miss M. A. Crisp as Corelia, Annette Mears as Finesse.

MY WIFE! WHAT WIFE?// F// E. S. Barrett// **Drury Lane**, May 1837, with George Bartley as Capt. Temptest R.N., Mr. Cooper as Capt. Tempest, Dragoons, Paul Bedford as Blunt, Drinkwater Meadows as Pym, Mr. Baker as Staunch, Mrs. C. Jones as Lady Longpurse, Miss Lee as Louisa/ **Sad. Wells**, Oct. 1844, with A. Young as Capt. Tempest, John Webster as Hector, G. F. Forman as Pym, Mr. Coreno as Staunch, Mr. Williams as Blunt, Mr. Sharpe as Allsauce, Charles Fenton as Thomas, Mrs. Henry Marston as Lady Longpurse, Miss Huddart as Louisa.

MY WIFE'S BABY// F// Fred Hughes// **Royalty**, Sept. 1872.

MY WIFE'S BONNET// F 1a// J. Maddison Morton// **Olympic**, Nov. 1864, with J. G. Taylor as Topknot, D. Evans as Cutwater, Robert Soutar as Jones, Miss Melvin as Mrs. Topknot, Miss Harland as Mrs. Cutwater, Miss Sheridan as Mrs. Appleby.

MY WIFE'S COME// F 1a// J. Maddison Morton// **Drury Lane**, Oct. 1843, with John Pritt Harley as Prettyjohn, Drinkwater Meadows as Plummy, Charles Selby as Simmons, Mrs. Stirling as Mrs. Prettyjohn, Miss Somerville as Dorothy, Mrs. Alfred Wigan as Clementina.

MY WIFE'S DAUGHTER// C 2a// J. Stirling Coyne// **Olympic**, Oct. 1850, with Henry Farren as Ormonde, William Farren as Ivyleafe, William Farren Jr. as Apsley, Henry Compton as Gilliflower, Mrs. Stirling as Mrs. Ormonde, Louisa Howard as Clara, Mrs. Leigh Murray as Mrs. Ivyleaf, Ellen Turner as Rose/ Scenery by W. Shalders/ **Sad. Wells**, Nov. 1852, with Frederic Robinson as Ormonde, William Belford as Apsley, Mr. Barret as Ivyleaf, Lewis Ball as Gillyflower, Kate Mandelbert as Tittums, Mrs. Ternan as Mrs. Ormonde, Miss T. Bassano as Mrs. Ivyleaf, Miss Mandelbert as Clara, Eliza Travers as Rose.

MY WIFE'S DENTIST// F 1a// T. E. Wilks// **Haymarket**, May 1839, with Mr. Cooper as Sir John, Robert Strickland as Gen. Squadron, Benjamin Wrench as Hazard, T. F. Mathews as David, Miss Mordaunt as Cicely, Miss Grove as Lady Letitia, Mrs. Frank Matthews as Rhoda; Apr. 1857, with W. H. Chippendale as Ivyleafe, Henry Howe as Ormond, Edwin Villiers as Apsley, Henry Compton as Gillyflower, Miss Talbot as Mrs. Ormond, Miss M. Oliver as Clara, Mrs. Edward Fitzwilliam as Mrs. Ivyleafe, Bella Copeland as Rose/ **Sad. Wells**, June 1844, with Mr. Binge as Beauville, Mr. Williams as Gen. Squadron, Charles Hudson as Hazard, Mr. Sharp as David, Emma Harding as Lady Letitia, Miss Thornbury as Cicely, Miss Lebatt as Rhoda; June 1857, with George Cooke as Sir John, J. Gates as Gen. Squadron, Frederick Morton as Hazard, G. B. Bigwood as David, Miss Stuart as Lady Letitia, Emma Barnett as Cicely, Mary A. Victor as Rhoda/ **Lyceum**, Aug. 1879, with J. H. Barnes as Sir John, W. Herbert as Dick Hazard, William McIntyre as Gen. Squadron, Miss Layton as Cicely, Miss Lang as Lady Letitia.

MY WIFE'S FIRST HUSBAND// F 1a// W. E. Suter// **Grecian**, June 1855, with F. Charles as Muttonhead, Percy Corri as Frisky, Miss Johnstone as Matilda, Harriet Coveney as

Molly.

MY WIFE'S JOURNAL// F 1a// Adap. by W. Robertson fr F of A. P. Dennery & L. F. Clairville, Les Memoires de deux Jeunes Mariées// **Olympic**, 1854.

MY WIFE'S MAID// F 1a// T. J. Williams// **Adelphi**, Aug. 1864.

MY WIFE'S MOTHER// C// C. J. Mathews// **Haymarket**, June 1837, with William Farren as Foozle, Frederick Vining as Budd, John Webster as Waverly, James Worrell as Thomas, Mrs. Julia Glover as Mrs. Quickfidget, Miss E. Phillips as Mrs. Fitzosborne, Mrs. Nisbett as Mrs. Budd/ **Cov. Garden**, Apr. 1842, with William Farren as Uncle Foozle, Walter Lacy as Budd, A. Brindal as Waverly, John Ayliffe as Thomas, Mrs. Julia Glover as Mrs. Quickfidget, Mrs. Walter Lacy as Mrs. Budd, Miss Cooper as Mrs. Fitzosborne.

MY WIFE'S OUT// F 1a// G. H. Rodwell// **Cov. Garden**, Oct. 1843, with Robert Keeley as Scumble, Alfred Wigan as Dobbs, Jane Mordaunt as Mrs. Scumble, Mrs. Keeley as Betty/ **Lyceum**, Apr. 1844, with Robert Keeley as Scumble, Alfred Wigan as Dobbs, Ellen Chaplin as Mrs. Scumble, Mrs. Keeley as Betty/ **Princess's**, Apr. 1860, with Henry Widdicomb as Scumble, Frederick Villiers as Dobbs, Emma Wadham as Mrs. Scumble, Louise Keeley as Betty/ **Globe**, Dec. 1871, with E. W. Garden as Scumble, J. H. Barnes as Adolphus Dobbs, Nelly Harris as Mrs. Scumble, Maria Harris as Betty.

MY WIFE'S RELATIONS// C 1a// William Gowing ("Walter Gordon")// **Olympic**, Dec. 1862, with Walter Gordon as Lambe, Harwood Cooper as Tyrrel, Henry Rivers as Uncle Dobson, Horace Wigan as Hector, Miss Hughes as Mrs. Lambe, Mrs. St. Henry as Mrs. Frankland, Florence Haydon as Emma, Mrs. Leigh Murray as Aunt Patience, Mrs. Stephens as Aunt Charity.

MY WIFE'S SECOND FLOOR// F 1a// J. Maddison Morton// **Princess's**, May 1845, with Mr. Granby as Capt. Topheavy, Walter Lacy as Toddle, Henry Compton as Close, Augustus Harris as Tim, Mrs. Brougham as Mrs. Topheavy, Miss E. Honner as Fanny, Mrs. Fosbroke as Mrs. Downy/ **Olympic**, Mar. 1851, with George Cooke as Topheavy, Henry Farren as Toddle, Henry Compton as Jacob Close, Mrs. Leigh Murray as Mrs. Topheavy, Louisa Howard as Fanny, Mrs. B. Bartlett as Mrs. Downey/ **Princess's**, June 1853.

MY YOUNG WIFE AND MY OLD UMBRELLA// C// Benjamin Webster// **Haymarket**, June 1837, with William Farren as Grizzle, Robert Strickland as Prog, John Webster as Allen, Benjamin Webster as Tompkins, Miss E. Phillips as Dianah.

MYSTERIES OF AUDLEY COURT// n.a.// **Astley's**, Aug. 1866.

MYSTERIES OF LONDON, THE// D 4a// Lewis Gilbert// **Surrey**, Aug. 1901.

MYSTERIES OF LONDON, THE; OR, THE BROTHERS' CAREER// D 3a// n.a.// **Victoria**, Oct. 1846, with T. H. Higgie as Prince Alberto, Mr. Hitchinson as Chichester, James Ranoe as Harborough, F. C. Courtney as Greenwood, C. J. Bird as Markham, Mr. Archer as Stephens, Walter Searle as Tidkins, E. G. Burton as Pocock, Mrs. George Lee as Isabella, Mrs. Henry Vining as Ellen, Miss Fielding as Eliza, Mrs. Cooke as Margaret.

MYSTERIES OF PARIS, THE// D 3a// Charles[?] Dillon// **Marylebone**, Sept. 1844/ **Grecian**, Sept. 1861, with Henry Grant as Ferrand, R. H. Lingham as Maitre d'Ecole, Henry Power as Tortillard, William James as Rodolphe, John Manning as Murphy, Alfred Rayner as Chourineur, George Gillett as Sir Thomas, Mr. Johnstone as Francois, Miss Johnstone as Mme. Seraphin, Mrs. Charles Dillon as Fleur, Jane Coveney as Sarah, Lucreza Hill as Rigolette/ **Victoria**, Mar. 1873, with Henry Dudley as Ferraud, F. Shepherd as Chourineur, Walter Lacy as Maitre d'Ecole, George Roberts as Tortilard, H. C. Sidney as Rodolphe, John Hudspeth as Murphy, Mr. Hamilton as Francois, Mr. Glenville as Bras Rouge, Miss P. Cross as Seraphin, Miss Lee as Mme. Georget, Marie Henderson as Fleur, Mrs. C. H. Stephenson as Countess Sarah, Marie Bramah as Rigolette.

MYSTERIES OF THE CHAMBER, THE// C// n.a.// **Sad. Wells**, Sept. 1837, with C. H. Pitt as Dupré, C. J. Smith as Valere, Mr. Pateman as Simon, Mr. Rogers as Thomas, Lavinia Melville as Mme. Dupré, Mrs. Rogers as Angelica.

MYSTERIOUS FAMILY, THE// F 2a// G. H. Rodwell// **Haymarket**, Oct. 1837, with Robert Strickland as Twaddledale, J. B. Buckstone as Daffodil, James Worrell as Frederick, Mr. Hutchings as Charles, T. F. Mathews as Bob Short, Benjamin Webster as Gregory, Mrs. Waylett as Caroline, Miss Beresford as Laura, Mrs. Tayleure as Arabellinda, Mrs. Humby as Fidget.

MYSTERIOUS HOME OF CHELSEA, THE// D 3a// J. A. Cave & George Roberts// **Marylebone**, Sept. 1876.

MYSTERIOUS LADY, THE; OR, WORTH MAKES THE MAN// C 2a// J. R. Planché// **Lyceum**, Oct. 1852, with Frank Matthews as Amaranth Fitz-Ape, C. J. Mathews as Hector Fitz-Ape, Frederick Belton as Valentine, Basil Baker as Blackstone, Henry Horncastle as Matthew, Henry Butler as Peter, Miss M. Oliver as Dorothea.

MYSTERIOUS MR. BUGLE, THE// F 3a// Madeleine Ryley// **Strand**, May 1900.

MYSTERIOUS STRANGER, THE// D 2a// Adap. by Charles Selby fr F of Clarville & Damarin, Satan; ou le Diable à Paris// **Adelphi**, Nov. 1844, with Charles Hudson as Beausoliel, Charles Selby as Vanille, Mme. Celeste as the Stranger, O. Smith as Chechoré, John Sanders as Loupy, Emma Harding as Mlle.

de Nantelle, Ellen Chaplin as Madeline, Mrs. Frank Matthews as Mme. de Luceval/ **Haymarket**, Aug. 1848, with Henry Hughes as Count Beausoleil, Charles Boyce as Count Vanille, James Worrell as Capt. Gasconade, Mme. Celeste as Stranger, Mr. Cullenford as Duplumet, Edward Wright as Créquet, Emma Harding as Mlle. de Nantelle, Ellen Chaplin as Madeline.

MYSTERY, THE// D// n.a.// **Surrey**, Sept. 1863.

MYSTERY; OR, GREED FOR GOLD// D 4a// Walter Stephens// **Olympic**, Apr. 1873.

MYSTERY OF A GLADSTONE BAG, THE// F// F. H. Francks// **Pavilion**, June 1889.

MYSTERY OF A HANSOM CAB, THE// D 4a// Dram. by Fergus Hume & Arthur Law fr novel by Hume// **Princess's**, Feb. 1888, with J. H. Barnes as Fitzgerald, James Fernandez as Frettlby, W. L. Abingdon as Moreland, Harry Parker as Kilsip, Frank Wright as Gorbey, Basset Roe as Whyte, Forbes Dawson as Rolleston, A. R. Hodgson as Calton, Henry De Solla as Dr. Chinston, Eva Sothern as Madge, Grace Hawthorne as Sal, Mrs. Frank Huntley as Mother Guttersnipe, Miss Cooper-Parr as Rosanna, Dolores Drummond as Mrs. Sampson, Cicely Richards as Mrs. Rolleston/ Scenery by R. C. Durant/ Machines by R. E. Warton/ Prod. by Arthur Law & Frank Wright.

MYSTERY OF EDWIN DROOD, THE// D 4a// Walter Stephens// **Surrey**, Nov. 1871.

MYSTERY OF EDWIN DROOD, THE// D 4a// G. H. Macdermott// **Britannia**, July 1872.

MYSTERY OF THE SEVEN SISTERS// D 4a// F. A. Scudamore// **Surrey**, Oct. 1890.

MYSTICAL MISS, THE// C// n.a.// **Shaftesbury**, Jan. 1900.

*

NABOB FOR AN HOUR, A// F// John Poole// **Haymarket**, Feb. 1841, with John Webster as Frampton, David Rees as Dumpy, Robert Strickland as Hobbs, Miss Charles as Emma, Mrs. Frank Matthews as Nanny.

NADESHTA THE SLAVE GIRL; OR, THE CRUELTIES OF RUSSIAN TYRANNY// D// G. D. Pitt// **Victoria**, May 1850, with Mr. Henderson as Prince Ivan, J. T. Johnson as Count Montresson, David Osbaldiston as Lascelles, Mr. Hitchinson as Count Berkendorf, Mr. Richards as Count Lockendorf, Watty Brunton as Count Gaspodier, R. H. Kitchen as Count Darakoff, John Bradshaw as Petrovitch, Henry Frazer as Dieddritche, J. Neville as Vasili, Mr. Hitchinson as Mortimer, John Hudspeth as Bridle, J. Howard as Hans, Annette Vincent as Nadeshta, Mrs. George Lee as Blanche, Miss Barrowcliffe as Katinka, Miss Mildenhall as Trutchen/ Scenery by Mr. Mildenhall/ Machines by Wood & Foster/ Music by Mr. Barrowcliffe/ Prod. by Mr. Osbaldiston.

NADIA// Play 4a// Dram. by Violet Greville fr novel of H. Greville, Les Epreuves de Raissa// **Lyric**, May 1892, with Arthur Bourchier as Count Rezof, Frank Gillmore as Count Gretzky, E. J. Malyon as Svensky, Charles Thursby as Sabatrine, Frank Wood as Fadei, George Mudie as Gen. Kleine, Julian Cross as Porof, Helen Forsyth as Princess Adine, Henrietta Lindley as Countess Gretsky, Adelaide Newton as Mme. Porof, Olga Brandon as Nadia.

NADINE// Play 4a// Frank Rogers// **Vaudeville**, Mar. 1885.

NADJEZDA// Play Pro & 3a// Maurice Barrymore// **Haymarket**, Jan. 1886, with Emily Rigl as Nadjezda and Nadine, Lydia Foote as Praxeda, Robert Pateman as Janoush, Mr. Mackintosh as Khorvitch, Herbert Beerbohm Tree as Prince Zabouroff, Edmund Maurice as Lord Alsager, Maurice Barrymore as Devereux, Forbes Dawson as O'Hara, Georgina Drew as Eureka.

NAIDA; OR, THE GODDESS OF ELDORADO// D 3a// n.a.// **Princess's**, Feb. 1848, with Charles Fisher as Capt. Fleurville, Mr. Wynn as Lafolle, J. Neville as Trincoli, Mr. Cooper as Marondel, Augustus Harris as Selino, Henry Compton as Salaam, Mrs. Fosbroke as Marchioness de Montauron, Miss Villars as Hortense, Emma Stanley as Zilia/ Scenery by Brunning & Grey/ Music by Mr. Loder.

NAMESAKES// F 1a// Horace Lennard// **Toole's**, Feb. 1883.

NAN DARRELL; OR, THE GIPSY, THE MANIAC, AND THE FELON// D 3a// n.a.// **Victoria**, Oct. 1857, with Mr. Henderson as Morven, Frederick Byefield as Sir Herbert, J. H. Rickards as Darrell, John Dale as Bell, S. Sawford as Old John, F. H. Henry as Millar, Mr. Morrison as Payne, J. Howard as Plushbrass, James Francis as Binks, Mrs. J. H. Rickards as Elinor, Mrs. E. F. Saville as Katherine, Miss Richardson as Nan, Miss Halford as Mrs. Millar.

NANA SAHIB// D// n.a.// **Victoria**, Nov. 1863.

NANCE// D Pro & 3a// J. T. Douglass// **Pavilion**, Nov. 1893.

NANCE OLDFIELD// C 1a// Charles Reade// **Olympic**, Apr. 1883, with W. H. Vernon as Oldworthy, Philip Beck as Alexander, Janet Achurch as Sarah, Genevieve Ward as Nance Oldfield/ **Lyceum**, Mar. 1888, with W. H. Vernon as Nathan Oldworthy, Fuller Mellish as Alexander Oldworthy, Genevieve Ward as Nance Oldfield.

NANCY AND COMPANY// C 4a// Adap. by

Augustin Daly fr G of Julius Rosen// **Strand**, July 1886, with James Lewis, John Drew, Otis Skinner, William Gilbert, Mrs. G. H. Gilbert, May Irwin, Ada Rehan/ **Lyceum**, June 1890, with James Lewis as Griffing, John Drew as O'Kiefe, Eugene Ormond as Capt. Renseller, Frederick Bond as Stockslow, Burr Macintosh as Brasher, Mrs. G. H. Gilbert as Huldah, Edith Crane as Oriana, Isabel Irving as Daisy, Ada Rehan as Nancy/ **Daly's**, July 1895.

NANCY OLDFIELD see Nance Oldfield.

NANCY SIKES// D 5a// Cyril Searle// **Olympic**, July 1878.

NANNIE// C 2a// T. G. Warren// **Opera Comique**, Nov. 1895, with Edward Sass as Burge, Oscar Ayde as Wynne, J. G. Taylor as Geen, Emily Cudmore as Nannie Geen, Emma Gwynne as Jessie, Stella Leigh as Rose/ Scenery by E. G. Banks.

NAOMI, THE GIPSY GIRL// D 3a// C. H. Hazlewood// **Britannia**, Aug. 1872.

NAPOLEON; OR, THE STORY OF A FLAG// D 5a// C. H. Hazlewood// **Britannia**, Apr. 1873.

NARCISSE// D 3a// Trans. fr G. of A. E. Brachvogel// **Lyceum**, Feb. 1868, with Daniel Bandmann as Narcisee Rameau, George Jordan as Duc de Choiseul, William Farren as Comte du Barri, James Fernandez as Comte de St. Lambert, Basil Potter as Baron D'Holbach, Mr. Dalton as Diderot, Louisa Herbert as Pompadour, Teresa Furtado as Marquise d'Epinay, Milly Palmer as Doris, Miss Roselle as Colette/ Scenery by James Gates & Darran/ Music by W. H. Montgomery/ Machines by Mr. Lanham.

NARCISSE, THE VAGRANT// T 5a// Trans. by J. Schönberg fr G of A. E. Brachvogel// **Vaudeville**, July 1883 (in 4a).

NATIONAL QUESTION, A// F// Robert Reece// **Globe**, Mar. 1878.

NATURAL MAGIC// F 1a// Charles Selby// **St. James's**, Oct. 1837, with Mrs. Stirling as Countess Heloise and as Heloise de Mirancourt, Mr. Hollingsworth as Champignon, Mr. Forester as Ferdinand.

NATURE AND ART// F 1a// n.a.// **Sad. Wells**, Feb. 1844, with J. Dunn as Gabbleton, Miss Vincent in 5 char. parts.

NATURE AND PHILOSOPHY// C 1a// n.a.// **Lyceum**, Apr. 1876, with Mr. Archer, Mr. Huntley, Mr. Carter, Lucy Buckstone, Mrs. Huntley.

NATURE'S ABOVE ART// C// Edmund Falconer// **Drury Lane**, Sept. 1863.

NAULAHKA, THE// Play// Dram. fr novel of Kipling & Balostier// **Opera Comique**, Oct. 1891.

NAVAL ENGAGEMENTS// C 2a// Charles Dance// **Olympic**, May 1838, with William Farren as Adm. Kingston, C. J. Mathews as Lt. Kingston, Mr. Wyman as Short, John Brougham as Dennis, Mrs. Orger as Mrs. Pontifex, Mme. Vestris as Miss Mortimer; Jan. 1859 (in 1a), with Mr. Addison as Adm. Kingston, George Vining as Lt. Kingston, Harwood Cooper as Short, Horace Wigan as Dennis, Mrs. Stirling as Mrs. Pontifex, Miss Hughes as Miss Mortimer/ **Haymarket**, June 1838, with Robert Strickland as Adm. Kingston, C. J. Mathews as Lt. Kingston, T. F. Mathews as Short, John Brougham as Dennis, Mrs. Orger as Mrs. Pontifex, Mme. Vestris as Miss Mortimer/ **Drury Lane**, June 1838, with William Farren as Adm. Kingstone, C. J. Mathews as Lt. Kingstone, Mr. Wyman as Short, John Brougham as Dennis, Mrs. Orger as Mrs. Pontifex, Mme. Vestris as Mrs. Mortimer/ **Cov. Garden**, Oct. 1839, with William Farren as Adm. Kingston, C. J. Mathews as Lt. Kingston, Mr. Granby as Short, John Brougham as Dennis, Mrs. Orger as Mrs. Pontifex, Mme. Vestris as Miss Mortimer/ **POW**, Sept. 1865, with Squire Bancroft, John Hare/ **Globe**, May 1869, with David Fisher as Adm. Kingston, W. H. Vernon as Capt. Kingston, H. Andrews as Short, J. Tindale as Dennis, Lydia Foote as Miss Mortimer, Mrs. Stephens as Mrs. Pontifax/ **Olympic**, May 1876, with John Vollaire as Adm. Kingston, Randal Roberts as Lt. Kingston, Mr. Winstanley as Short, W. J. Hill as Dennis, Mrs. Stephens as Mrs. Pontifex, Fanny Josephs as Mary.

NEARLY LOST// D// William Travers// **City of London**, Aug. 1867.

NEARLY SEVERED// Play 1a// J. P. Hurst// **Vaudeville**, Sept. 1885.

NECK OR NOTHING// D 3a// George Conquest & Henry Pettitt// **Grecian**, Aug. 1876.

NED DAUNTLESS OF DAGENHAM DELL; OR, THE LOST ONE FOUND// D// n.a.// **Victoria**, Dec. 1853, with Mr. Green as Watkins, T. E. Mills as Saunders,, N. T. Hicks as Dauntless, John Bradshaw as Jem, J. Howard as Stalk, John Hudspeth as Everslow, Alfred Saville as Hazelburn, Georgiana Lebatt as Sally, Mrs. Henry Vining as Emily, Miss Sutton as Carry, Miss Edgar as Milly, Miss Laporte as Nelly.

NED KNOWLES// C// T. G. Warren// **Opera Comique**, Feb. 1887.

NED'S CHUM// C 3a// D. C. Murray// **Globe**, Aug. 1891.

NEEDFUL, THE// C 5a// H. T. Craven// **St. James's**, Jan. 1868, with D. Evans as Meek, G. Maskell as Lax, H. T. Craven as Store, G. W. Blake as Yellowchase, William Belford as Capt. Daly, Thomas Bridgeford as Scriplie, Sophie Larkin as Mrs. Meek, Eleanor Bufton as Amelia, Louisa Herbert as Kate, Miss M. Ellsworthy as Tabitha, Miss Marion as Esther/ Scenery by Frederick Fenton.

NE'ER DO-WEEL// C 3a// W. S. Gilbert// **Olympic**, Feb. 1878, with Charles Flockton as Seton, Johnston Forbes Robertson as Gerard, Henry Neville as Rollestone, G. W. Anson as O'Hara, Robert Pateman as Quilt, J. G. Bauer as Jakes, George Yarnold as David, Marion Terry as Maud, Mrs. St. Henry as Mrs. Parminter, Miss Gerard as Jessie/ Scenery by W. Hann/ Prod. by W. S. Gilbert. (Re-written, and title changed to The Vagabond Mar. 1878, with same cast.)

NEIGHBORS// C 2a// John Oxenford// **Strand**, Nov. 1866.

NELL; OR, THE OLD CURIOSITY SHOP// D 4a// Dram. by Andrew Halliday fr Charles Dickens// **Olympic**, Nov. 1870.

NELL GWYNNE// C// Douglas Jerrold// **Haymarket**, July 1838, with John Pritchard as Charles II, Mr. Hutchings as Rochester, J. W. Gough as Hart, James Worrell as Maj. Mohun, Thomas Green as Betterton, T. F. Mathews as Joe Haines, Frank Matthews as Crowsfoot, Miss Taylor as Nell Gwynne, Robert Keeley as Orange Moll, Mrs. Gallot as Mrs. Snowdrop, Miss Patridge as Queen; Feb. 1850, with Benjamin Webster as Charles II, Henry Howe as Berkley, Henry Vandenhoff as Hart, James Bland as Maj. Mohun, Mr. Stuart as Betterton, Charles Selby as Joe Haynes, Mr. Tilbury as Crowsfoot, Mr. Rogers as Stockfish, Miss Reynolds as Nell, Robert Keeley as Orange Moll, Mrs. Stanley as Mrs. Snowdrop.

NELL GWYNNE// C 4a// W. G. Wills// **Royalty**, May. 1878, with Miss Fowler, Edmund Leathes.

NELL SNOOKS// D 4a// C. Russell & J. Lawson// **West London**, Apr. 1899.

NELLIE'S TRIALS// D// n.a.// **Strand**, Jan. 1866.

NELSON'S ENCHANTRESS// Play 4a// Richard Horne// **Avenue**, Feb. 1897, with Charles Goodheart as Ferdinand, Nutcombe Gould as Sir William, Sidney Brough as Sir John, Johnston Forbes Robertson as Nelson, Arthur Elwood as Greville, Ben Greet as Romney, C. M. Lowne as Capt. Blackwood, Frank Dyall as Capt. Hardy, Clifford Soames as Lt. Lapenotiere, E. H. Brooke as Lt. Nisbet, Clara Denman as Queen of Naples, Mrs. E. H. Brooke as Mrs. Cadogan, Marianne Caldwell as Bridget, Mrs. Patrick Campbell as Emma/ Scenery by E. G. Banks, William Perkins, Joseph Harker & William Harford/Prod. by Johnston Forbes Robertson.

NERVES// FC 3a// Adap. by J. Comyns Carr fr F of Ernest Blum & R. Toché, Les Femmes Nerveuses// **Comedy**, June 1890, with Henry Kemble as Brittle, Edward Righton as Caramel, Charles Hawtrey as Capt. Armitage, William Wyes as Commissionaire, Maude Millett as Violet, Sophie Larkin as Mrs. Brittle, Lydia Cowell as Emma, Ethel Matthews as Iphigenie, Lottie Venne as Mme. Elaine.

NERVOUS MAN AND THE MAN OF NERVE, THE// F 2a// W. Bayle Bernard// **Haymarket**, Aug. 1837, with William Farren as Aspen, Tyrone Power as McShane, Charles Selby as Lord Lounge, Mr. Harris as Vivian, J. W. Gough as Dr. Oxyden, Mr. Gallot as Brown, Mr. Saville as Burnish, James Worrell as Merton, T. F. Mathews as Topknot, Mrs. W. Clifford as Lady Leach, Miss E. Phillips as Emily, Miss Wrighten as Betty, Mrs. Tayleure as Mrs. Clacket; Nov. 1854, with W. H. Chippendale as Aspen, Charles Hudson as Shane, William Farren as Lounge, William Cullenford as Vivian, George Braid as Brown, Edwin Villiers as Burnish, Mrs. Poynter as Lady Leach, Miss Schott as Emily, Ellen Chaplin as Mrs. Clackit/ **Cov. Garden**, Mar. 1838, with Robert Strickland as Aspen, Tyrone Power as MacShane, Mr. Roberts as Lord Lounge, Henry Howe as Burnish, Paul Bedford as Vivian, John Pritchard as Merton, John Ayliffe as Oxygen, C. J. Smith as Brown, Mr. Holmes as Topknot, Mrs. W. Clifford as Lady Leach, Miss E. Phillips as Emily, Mrs. Humby as Mrs. Clackit, Mrs. East as Betty, Miss Garrick as Mary/ **Sad. Wells**, Sept. 1844, with A. Younge as Aspen, Mr. Collins as McShane, John Webster as Lord Lounge, Mr. Morton as Capt. Burnish, Charles Morelli as Vivian, Charles Fenton as Merton, Mrs. Henry Marston as Lady Leech, Miss Huddart as Emily, Georgiana Lebatt as Mrs. Clackit, Miss Thurnbury as Mary; Mar. 1861, with Malone Raymond as McShane, Mr. Barrett as Aspen, Mr. Meagreson as Vivian, Charles Seyton as Capt. Burnish, Webster Vernon as Lounge, Caroline Parkes as Lady Leach, Fanny Josephs as Emily, Kate Saxon as Mrs. Clacket, Miss Heath as Betty/ **Princess's**, July 1845, with Mr. Granby as Aspen, Mr. Collins as McShane, Robert Honner as Vivian, Augustus Harris as Capt. Burnish, James Ranoe as Merton, Mrs. Fosbroke as Lady Leech, Miss E. Honner as Emily, Miss Somers as Mrs. Clacket/ **Grecian**, Dec. 1845, with Mr. Campbell as Aspen, John Collett as Vivian, Edwin Dixon as Burnish, Harry Chester as Lounge, G. Hodson as McShane, Frederick Robson as Biggs, Mrs. W. Watson as Lady Leech, Miss M. A. Crisp as Mrs. Clacket.

NETTLE, THE// C 1a// Ernest Warren// **Court**, Oct. 1886, with Miss Cudmore, F. Kerr.

NEUTRAL GROUND// C// F. Brodie// **Princess's**, Aug. 1875.

NEVER AGAIN// FC 3a// Adap. fr F of Maurice Desvallières & Ann Mars, Le Truc de Séraphin// **Vaudeville**, Oct. 1898, with George Giddens as Ribot, E. Allan Aynesworth as Vignon, Hubert Willis as Planchette, Ferdinand Gottschalk as Katzenjammer, Robb Harwood as Lavrille, Cairnes James as Séraphin, Maggie Holloway as Mme. Ribot, Mary Clayton as Marceline, Agnes Miller as Octavie, Helen Rous as Mme. Lavrille, Dorothy Drake as Maud, Marion Wakeford as Désirée/ Scenery by William Harford.

NEVER DESPAIR// D 4a// Walter James// **Grecian**, Dec. 1871.

NEVER DESPAIR// D Pro & 4a// George Comer// **Novelty**, Nov. 1890, with Brien

McCullough as Spriggins, Edwin Fergusson as Harry Brierly, Charles Lerigo as Dan Brierly, Alfred Tate as Dyson, H. B. Clair as Adair, King Bolton as Phipps, Nellie Nelson as Lottie, Julia Listelle as Ned, Mrs. Edward Hallows as Mary.

NEVER DESPAIR, FOR OUT OF EVIL COMETH GOOD// D 4a// C. H. Stephenson// **Victoria**, Aug. 1869.

NEVER RECKON YOUR CHICKENS BEFORE THEY'RE HATCHED// C 1a// W. E. Suter// **Grecian**, June 1861, with Alfred Rayner as Wilful, Webster Vernon as Clitheree, Robert Bell as Bernard, Henry Grant as Maj. Bolder, John Manning as Pettifog, Miss E. Miller as Mrs. Osborne, Mrs. Charles Dillon as Emily.

NEVER RECKON YOUR CHICKENS BEFORE THEY ARE HATCHED// F 1a// Wybert Reeve// **Olympic**, Dec. 1871.

NEVER TOO LATE TO MEND// (see It's Never Too Late to Mend).

NEW BABY, THE// F 3a// Adap. by Arthur Bourchier fr G of H. J. Fischer & J. Jarno, Der Rabenvater// **Royalty**, Jan. 1896, with Arthur Bourchier as Col. Walker, William Blakeley as Commodore van Gutt, W. G. Elliott as Gomez, Charles Troode as Harry, Alice Mansfield as Drusilla, Mrs. B. M. de Solla as Patience, Irene Vanbrugh as Faith, Katherine Stewart as Kate, Lilian Millward as Pascoe.

NEW BABYLON// D Pro. & 4a// Paul Meritt & G. F. Rowe// **Duke's**, Feb. 1879, with Caroline Hill, Charles Wilmot.

NEW BOY, THE// FC 3a// Arthur Law// **Terry's**, Feb. 1894, with Weedon Grossmith as Rennick, John Beauchamp as Dr. Candy, J. D. Beveridge as Roach, Sydney Warren as de Brissac, Kenneth Douglas as Major, Gladys Homfrey as Mrs. Rennick, May Palfrey as Nancy, Esmé Beringer as Susan/ Scenery by T. W. Hall/ Prod. by Fred Terry.

NEW CINDERELLA, THE// C 2a// J. P. Simpson// **Royalty**, Jan. 1879.

NEW DON QUIXOTE, THE// Play 4a// Robert Buchanan & Harriet Jay ("Charles Marlowe")// **Royalty**, Feb. 1896.

NEW EAST LYNNE, THE// D Pro & 4a// Dram. by Edmund Gurney fr novel of Mrs. Henry Wood// **Standard**, July 1898.

NEW FOOTMAN, THE// C 1a// Charles Selby// **Grecian**, Feb. 1856, with Eaton O'Donnell, John Manning, F. Charles, Henry Power, Harriet Coveney, Miss Johnstone.

NEW LAMPS FOR OLD// C 3a// Jerome K. Jerome// **Terry's**, Feb. 1890, with W. S. Penley as Buster, Bernard Gould as Honeydew, William Lestocq as Jorkins, Frederick Kerr as Postlewaite, Cissy Grahame as Elvira, Gertrude Kingston as Octavia.

NEW LEAF, A// D 1a// J. H. Darnley// **Royalty**, Nov. 1897, with Charles Bell as Lord Annerly, Harry Parker as Parker, Grace Vicat as Lady Annerly.

NEW LIFE, THE// Play 1a// W. G. Mackay// **Avenue**, July 1894, with William MacKay as Wylde, Herbert Flemming as Capper, Mary Allestree as Vera.

NEW LIGHTS; OR, THE IRISH PEGAGOGUE// F 1a// n.a.// **Astley's**, Oct. 1850, with Mr. Johnson as Tillwell, Arthur Stirling as Charles, Mr. Crowther as Flail, Thomas Barry as Terry, Miss E. Neil as Rose, Mrs. Beacham as Mary.

NEW MAGDALEN, THE// D Pro & 3a// Wilkie Collins// **Olympic**, May 1873, with Ada Cavendish as Mercy Merrick, Miss Ernstone as Grace, C. H. Peveril as Holmcroft, David Evans as Wetzel, Mrs. St. Henry as Lady Janet, Mr. Archer as Gray/ **Globe**, July 1876, with Ada Cavendish as Mercy Merrick, Kate Rivers as Grace Roseberry, R. C. Lyons as Horace Holmcroft, E. D. Lyons as Wetzel, Roma Le Thière as Lady Janet, Leonard Boyne as Julian Gray/ **Novelty**, Jan. 1884, with Frank Archer, Ada Cavendish, Roma Le Thière.

NEW MAZEPPA, THE// D Pro & 3a// Frederick Cooke & W. R. Waldron// **Sadler's Wells**, Sept. 1890.

NEW MEN AND OLD ACRES; OR, A MANAGING MAMMA// C 3a// Tom Taylor & A. W. Dubourg// **Haymarket**, Nov. 1869, with W. H. Chippendale as Vavasour, Henry Howe as Brown, J. B. Buckstone as Bunter, Mr. Rogers as Blazenbalg, J. B. Buckstone Jr. as Bertie, Mrs. Chippendale as Lady Matilda, Madge Robertson as Lillian, Mrs. Edward Fitzwilliam as Mrs. Bunter, Caroline Hill as Fanny/ Scenery by John O'Conner/ Machines as Oliver Wales/ Gas by F. Hope/ **Court**, Dec. 1876, with John Hare, Ellen Terry.

NEW NOTIONS// F// W. Bayle Bernard// **Haymarket**, July 1838, with Mr. Hill as Maj. Wheeler, Robert Strickland as Ledger, Mr. Hemming as Markham, Mr. Hutchings as Bates, Mrs. W. Clifford as Mrs. Ledger, Miss Cooper as Ellen, Miss Gallot as Susan, Miss Patridge as Mrs. Smith, Miss Holmes as Miss Hawkins.

NEW SERVANT, THE// F 1a// J. R. Planché// **Olympic**, Sept. 1837, with Robert Keeley as Mastico, James Bland as Sebastian, Mrs. Keeley as Xarifa/ Scenery by W. Marchall.

NEW SUB, THE// Play 1a// Seymore Hicks// **Court**, Apr. 1892, with Brandon Thomas as Maj. Ensor, W. G. Elliott as Capt. Champion, C. P. Little as Capt. Blount, Compton Coutts as Lt. Crookenden, Ernest Bertram as Lt. Dartlington, Wilfred Draycott as Maj. Carruthers, Gertrude Kingston as Mrs. Dartlington.

NEW TRIAL, A// D 4a// Adap. by Charles Coughlan fr Ital. of Paolo Giacometti, La Morte Civile// **POW**, Dec. 1880, with Charles Coghlan, James Fernandez, Amy Roselle,

Mrs. Leigh Murray.

NEW WAY TO PAY OLD DEBTS, A// C 5a// Philip Massinger// **Sad. Wells,** Apr. 1837, with Mr. King as Lovell, Mr. Hicks as Wellborn, C. H. Pitt as Allworth, J. B. Booth as Sir Giles Overreach, John Ayliffe as Marrall, Mr. Rodgers as Greedy, Miss Seymour as Lady Allworth, Miss Melville as Margaret, Mrs. Harris as Froth, Miss Young as Tabitha, Miss Pitt as Abigale; Sept. 1844, with George Bennett as Lovel, Samuel Phelps as Sir Giles Overreach, Henry Marston as Welborn, T. H. Higgie as Allworth, Mr. Coreno as Furnace, A. Younge as Marrall, G. F. Forman as Greedy, Mrs. Mary Warner as Lady Allworth, Miss Cooper as Margaret, Mrs. Henry Marston as Froth, Georgiana Lebatt as Tabitha, Fanny Morelli as Abigail/ **Haymarket,** Sept. 1837, with E. W. Elton as Sir Giles Overreach, Frederick Vining as Wellborn, Benjamin Webster as Marrall, Mr. Saville as Lovel, Charles Selby as Allworth, Robert Strickland as Greedy, Mrs. W. Clifford as Lady Allworth, Mrs. Tayleure as Froth, Miss Allison as Margaret; June 1839, with Charles Perkins as Lovell, Charles Kean as Sir Giles Overreach, Mr. Cooper as Wellborn, Mr. Hemming as Allworth, J. W. Gough as Willdo, Robert Strickland as Greedy, William Farren as Marrall, Miss Pelham as Lady Allworth, Miss Travers as Margaret, Mrs. Gallot as Abigail, Mrs. Frank Matthews as Froth, Miss Partridge as Tabitha; Oct. 1861, with Henry Howe as Lord Lovell, Edwin Booth as Sir Giles Overreach, William Farren as Wellborn, Henry Compton as Marrall, Edwin Villiers as Allworth, W. H. Chippendale as Greedy, William Cullenford as Tapwell, Mrs. Wilkins as Lady Allworth, Mrs. Griffith as Froth, Miss M. Oliver as Margaret/ **Drury Lane,** Mar. 1838, with H. Cooke as Lord Lovell, Charles Kean as Sir Giles Overreach, Mr. Cooper as Wellborn, A. Brindal as Allworth, Charles Fenton as Welldo, William Dowton as Greedy, Henry Compton as Marrall, Mr. Hughes as Tapwell, Mrs. Ternan as Lady Allworth, Miss Poole as Margaret, Mme. Simon as Froth, Miss Somerville as Tabitha, Mrs. Brindal as Abigail/ **Cov. Garden,** Oct. 1842, with Charles Diddear as Lord Lovel, George Vandenhoff as Sir Giles Overreach, Mr. Cooper as Wellborn, James Vining as Allworth, Frank Matthews as Greedy, Drinkwater Meadows as Marrall, Mrs. Salzberg (Miss Phillips) as Lady Allworth, Miss Cooper as Margaret, Mrs. Emden as Abigail/ **Victoria,** 1844/ **Princess's,** Nov. 1846, with John Ryder as Lovel, John R. Scott as Sir Giles Overreach, James Vining as Wellborn, Mr. Granby as Justice Greedy, Henry Compton as Marrall, Robert Roxby as Allworth, Charles Fisher as Tapwell, Miss Harrington as Lady Allworth, Mrs. Stirling as Margaret, Mrs. Fosbroke as Froth/ **Olympic,** Jan. 1847, with John R. Scott, Mrs. Stirling; Jan 1848, with Mr. Archer as Lovell, G. V. Brooke as Sir Giles Overreach, Henry Holl as Wellborn, William Davidge as Marral, Mr. Conquest as Greedy, Mr. Morton as Allworth, Mr. Somerford as Tapwell, Mrs. Brougham as Lady Allworth, Miss Hill as Margaret/ **Marylebone,** Jan. 1848, with Frank Graham/ **Grecian,** Nov. 1854, with Basil Potter as Sir Giles Overreach, Henry Grant as Lord Lovell, F. Charles as Allworth, Eaton O'Donnell as Justice Greedy, Henry Power as Tapwell, William Suter as Marrall, Jane Coveney as Margaret, Ellen Crisp as Martha, Miss Johnstone as Froth; Nov. 1862, with Henry Grant as Lovel, Thomas Mead as Sir Giles Overreach, William James as Wellborn, George Burton as Allworth, John Manning as Greedy, J. Jackson as Marrall, Mrs. Charles Dillon as Margaret, Jane Dawson as Lady Allworth, Marie Brewer as Abigale/ **City of London,** Oct. 1862, with G. V. Brooke/ **St. James's,** Apr. 1877, with Robert Markby as Lovell, Hermann Vezin as Sir Giles Overreach, John Clayton as Wellborn, Charles Cooper as Allworth, Clifford Cooper as Greedy, Charles Flockton as Marrall, Roma Le Thière as Lady Allworth, Kate Pattison as Margaret, Maria Daly as Froth/ Music by George Richardson.

NEW WING, THE// FC 3a// H. A. Kennedy// **Strand,** May 1890, with Charles Collette as Slab, Frank Gillmore as Strangeways, H. Athol Forde as Gen. Singleside, Eardley Turner as Jobbings, Herbert Ross as Bobbie, Gertrude Lovell as Hester, Mrs. Henry Leigh as Priscilla.

NEW WOMAN, THE// C 4a// Sidney Grundy// **Comedy,** Sept. 1894, with Fred Terry as Cazenove, Cyril Maude as Col. Cazenov, J. G. Graham as Capt. Sylvester, William Wyes as Armstrong, Stuart Champion as Pettigrew, Rose Leclercq as Lady Wargrave, Alma Murray as Mrs. Sylvester, Laura Graves as Enid, Gertrude Warden as Victoria, Irene Rickards as Dr. Bevan, Winifred Emery as Margery/ Scenery by Walter Johnstone & Walter Hann.

NEW WORLD, THE// D 4a// Fred Darcy// **West London,** May 1898.

NEW YORK DIVORCE// F 3a// Adap. by Walter Clarke fr F// **Strand,** Aug. 1895.

NEWINGTON BUTTS// F 2a// J. Maddison Morton// **St. James's,** Sept. 1866, with F. Charles as Butts, J. D. Stoyle as Jogtrot, T. C. Burleigh as Capt. Clincher, Carlotta Addison as Mrs. Thrillington, Ellen McDonnell as Martha.

NEWS FROM CHINA// C 1a// J. Maddison Morton// **Haymarket,** Sept. 1843, with Robert Strickland as Splicem, J. B. Buckstone as Soft, James Worrell as Canvass, C. J. Mathews as Finchley, Mr. Tilbury as Growl, Miss C. Conner as Maria, Mrs. Humby as Patty.

NEWSPAPER NUPTIALS// C// Ellie Norwood// **Strand,** Aug. 1901.

NEXT DOOR// F 1a// Alfred Wigan// **St. James's,** Dec. 1860, with Charles Young as Skylark, Mr. Dawson as Alfred Walker, Mr. Terry as Walker, Kate Terry as Emily, Clara St. Casse as Jemima.

NEXT OF KIN// C 2a// Edmund Falconer// **Lyceum,** Apr. 1860, with Mr. Tilbury as Montjoy, Henry Butler as Facile, Samuel Emery as Grubton, Stanislaus Calhaem as Chump, Kate Saxon as Clara Mountjoy, Eliza Travers as

Mrs. Chump/ **Drury Lane**, Dec. 1862.

NICANDRA// F 3a// Russell Vaun// **Avenue**, Apr. 1901.

NICE FIRM, A// C 1a// Tom Taylor// **Lyceum**, Nov. 1853, with C. J. Mathews, Frank Matthews.

NICE GIRL, A// C// n.a.// **Gaiety**, Feb. 1873.

NICE QUIET DAY, A// F 1a// H. J. Hipkins// **Royalty**, Dec. 1861.

NICE YOUNG LADIES, THE// F 1a// Edward Stirling// **Lyceum**, Oct. 1878, with Edward Terry, D. Evans, Mr. Everard, Miss A. Goodall, Millie Sidney, Caroline Parkes.

NICHOLAS FLAM, ATTORNEY AT LAW// F 1a// J. B. Buckstone// **Haymarket**, June 1837, with William Farren as Flam, J. W. Gough as Pedigree, Charles Selby as Fitzsmith, Mr. Ross as Shrimp, Robert Strickland as Dr. Birch, Miss E. Phillips as Harriet, Mrs. Tayleure as Mrs. Nibble, Mrs. W. Clifford as Mary/ **Sad. Wells**, Mar. 1845, with Samuel Phelps as Flam, Mr. Sharp as Shrimp, A. Younge as Dr. Birch, Mr. Rae as Lord Pedigree, Mr. Morton as Fitzsmith, Mrs. Henry Marston as Mary, Mrs. Francis as Mrs. Nibble, Miss Huddart as Harriet/ **Princess's**, July 1860, with Samuel Phelps as Flam, Henry Widdicomb as Shrimp, Edmund Garden as Lord Pedigree, Robert Cathcart as Fitzsmith, Drinkwater Meadows as Dr. Birch, Rose Leclercq as Harriet, Mrs. Wallis as Mrs. Nibble, Mrs. Weston as Mary.

NICHOLAS NICKLEBY// C 2a// Dram. by Edward Stirling fr novel of Charles Dickens// **Astley's**, May 1863, with Henry Mellon as Ralph Nickleby, H. J. Montague as Nicholas Nickleby, Edward Stirling as Noggs, Henry Vandenhoff as Mantalini, Edith Stuart as Smike, Frederick Dewar as Squeers, Rose Leclercq as Mme. Mantalini, Julia Craven as Miss Squeers, Mrs. Chatterly as Mrs. Squeers.

NICHOLAS NICKLEBY// D 3a// Dram. by Andrew Halliday fr novel of Charles Dickens// **Adelphi**, Nov. 1838; Apr. 1875, with William Terriss as Nicholas, James Fernandez as Ralph, John Clarke as Squeers, George Belmore as Noggs, Samuel Emery as Browdie, J. G. Shore as Broaker, C. J. Smith as Snawley, Lydia Foote as Smike, Mrs. Addie as Mrs. Nickleby, Edith Stuart as Kate, Miss Hudspeth as Tilda, Harriet Coveney as Miss Squeers, Mrs. Alfred Mellon as Mrs. Squeers; Oct. 1879, with E. H. Brooke, James Fernandez, Hermann Vezin, Henry Neville, Robert Pateman, Lydia Foote, Mrs. Alfred Mellon.

NICHOLSON'S NIECE// FC 3a// Mrs. Hugh Bell// **Terry's**, May 1892, with George Giddens as Burton, Frank Atherley as Rev. Grigg, Arthur Dacre as Lee, Ernest Hendrie as Jenks, Adria Hill as Mrs. Tamworth, Henrietta Cowen as Mrs. Burton, Irene Rickards as Lucy, Ethel Hope as Mrs. Gradden, Maggie Grant as Milly.

NICK OF THE WOODS// D// n.a.// **Standard**, Oct. 1859, with Joseph Proctor.

NICOLETTE// Play 1a// Edward Ferris & Arthur Stuart// **Criterion**, Jan. 1899, with Edward Ferris as Villiars, Wilfred Forster as Lamont, Margaret Halstan as Helene, Elsie Cross as Mme. Margot.

NIGGER WHAT SWEEPS THE CROSSINGS, THE// F 1a// n.a.// **Victoria**, Dec. 1838, with E. R. Harper as Jim Crow, Mr. Melville as Capt. Hector, John Parry as Pads, W. Vining as Skinflint, Master J. B. Parry as Ellen, Miss Darion as Mrs. Smith.

NIGHT; OR, PERILS OF THE ALPS// D// n.a.// **Pavilion**, Jan. 1863.

NIGHT AND DAY; OR, THE HAUNTS OF THE HUNTED DOWN// D// n.a.// **Pavilion**, Oct. 1868.

NIGHT AND MORN// D// Edmund Falconer// **Drury Lane**, Jan. 1864, with Alfred Rayner as Duke of Ferrara, Samuel Phelps as di Vivaldi, John Ryder as Santoni, George Spencer as Mercuriali, G. Weston as Tomaso, Mr. Meagerson as Jacopo, Mr. Fitzjames as Ugolino, Mr. Warde as Felice, Miss Atkinson as Duchess, Miss Heath as Princess Olympia, Rose Leclercq as Lady Olivia.

NIGHT AND MORN; OR, THE REBEL CHIEF// D// n.a.// **Grecian**, June 1866, with Henry Grant as Gen. Danville, George Gillett as Lt. Somers, J. Jackson as Corp. Dickey, William James as Capt. Blakely, John Manning as Tape, George Conquest as Squall, Alfred Rayner as O'Brien, Charles Mortimer as O'Donnell, Lizzie Mandlebert as Norah, Harriet Western as Kathleen.

NIGHT AND MORNING// D 2a// n.a.// **Grecian**, Oct. 1861, with William James as Morton, Henry Grant as Beaufort, George Gillett as Lilburne, John Manning as Plaskwill, R. H. Lingham as Arthur, Alfred Rayner as Gawtry, George Conquest as Bill Smith, Lucreza Hill as Mrs. Plaskwill, Jane Dawson as Mrs. Morton, Mrs. Charles Dillon as Fanny.

NIGHT AND MORNING// D 1a// Adap. by Dion Boucicault fr F, La Joie fait Peur// **Gaiety**, Nov. 1871.

NIGHT AT NOTTING HILL, A// F 1a// N. H. Harrington & Edmund Yates// **Adelphi**, Jan. 1857, with Edward Wright as Syllabub, Paul Bedford as Leathers, Frank Hall as O'Mutton, Mrs. Chatterley as Mrs. Chutney, Mary Keeley as Lizzy.

NIGHT AT THE BAL MASQUE// n.a.// **Surrey**, Mar. 1866.

NIGHT GUARD, THE; OR, THE SECRET OF THE FIVE MASKS// D// Cecil Pitt// **Britannia**, Sept. 1868.

NIGHT HAG, THE; OR, THE EVE OF HALLOW MASS// D// William Barrymore// **Sad. Wells**, June 1840, with Mr. Elvin as Fergus Campbell, J. B. Hill as Donald Campbell, Mr. Richardson as McGoran, Mr. Williams as Cameron, Henry

Hall as Logan, Mr. Dry as McDufith, Mr. Aldridge as Gildy Grey, Miss Cooke as Lady Margaret, Miss Richardson as Jennie.

NIGHT IN THE BASTILLE, A// Play 3a// Thomas Archer// **Drury Lane**, Dec. 1839, with Mr. Vining as Richelieu, E. W. Elton as de Croissy, Mr. Addison as Gramont, Mr. Roberts as d'Auterre, George Cooke as Mezieres, Charles Fenton as Antoine, Mrs. W. West as Countess de Prie, Mrs. Stirling as Gabrielle, Miss Pettifer as Juliette.

NIGHT IN TOWN, A// FC 3a// H. A. Sherburn// **Strand**, Apr. 1891/ **Royalty**, June 1894.

NIGHT OF THE PARTY, THE// FC 3a// Weedon Grossmith// **Avenue**, May 1901.

NIGHT OFF, A; OR, A PAGE FROM BALZAC// C 4a// Adap. by Augustin Daly fr G of Franz von Schönthan, Der Raub der Sabinerinnen// **Strand**, May 1886, with Otis Skinner, John Drew, William Gilbert, Charles Leclercq, Mrs. G. H. Gilbert, May Irwin, Ada Rehan/ **Lyceum**, Sept. 1891, with James Lewis as Babbitt, Herbert Gresham as Damask, John Drew as Mulberry, Charles Wheatleigh as Lord Mulberry, Charles Leclercq as Snap, Mrs. G. H. Gilbert as Mrs. Babbitt, Adelaide Prince as Angelica, Isabel Irving as Susan, Ada Rehan as Nisbe/ Prod. by Augustin Daly.

NIGHT OUT, A// FC 3a// Adap. by Charles Klein fr F of Georges Feydeau & Maurice Desvallières, Hôtel du Libre Echange// **Vaudeville**, Apr. 1896.

NIGHT PORTER OF TOWER HILL, THE; OR, THE DARK HEARTS// D// Alfred Rayner// **Grecian**, Nov. 1861, with Thomas Mead as Lafarge, William James as Merville, Henry Grant as Conard, Walter Holland as Tacit, John Manning as Sudge, R. H. Lingham as Ruse, Henry Power as Jocelyn, Laura Conquest as Dwaff, Jane Dawson as The Linda, Ellen Hale as Althea, Lucreza Hill as Silverbell, Mary A. Victor as Penelope.

NIGHT SESSION, A// F 1a// Adap. fr F of Georges Feydeau// **Globe**, Nov. 1897, with Percy Lyndal as Gentillac, J. R. Crawford as Fauconnet, Helen Fordyce as Clarisse, May Protheroe as Artemise, Mary Vernon as Emelie.

NIGHT WATCH, THE; OR, A SMUGGLER'S FATE// D// n.a.// **Sad. Wells**, Feb. 1837, with Mr. King as Allworth, C. H. Pitt as Harfield, Mr. Ray as Lt. Seabrook, Mr. Scarbrow as Thorncliffe, John Ayliffe as Old Brockman, Mr. Hicks as Will Brockman, Mr. Rogers as Mudlark, T. Lee as Sly, Miss Williams as Rose, Mrs. Harris as Mrs. Harfield, Miss Julian as Nelly.

NIGHTINGALE, THE// D 5a// T. W. Robertson// **Adelphi**, Jan. 1870, with Arthur Stirling as Harold, Benjamin Webster as Ismael, Mrs. Alfred Mellon as Chepstow, J. D. Beveridge as William, Harwood Cooper as Maj. Pomeroy, Miss Furtado as Mary, Eliza Johnstone as Keziah/ Scenery by Hawes Craven.

NIGHTINGALE, THE// D 5a// Mark Melford// **Standard**, Aug. 1884.

NIGHT'S ADVENTURE, A// D// T. W. Robertson// **Olympic**, 1851.

NIGHT'S FROLIC, A// FC 3a// Adap. by Augustus Thomas & Helen Barry fr G of G. von Moser// **Strand**, June 1891, with Willie Edouin as Comodore Stanton, Percy Marshall as Sedley, Charles Fawcett as Capt. Chandon, Sydney Barraclough as Claude, William Lugg as Sawyer, Florence West as Mrs. Sedley, Georgie Esmond as Nellie, Venie Bennett as Sarah, Alice Atherton as Lady Betty.

NIGHT'S SURPRISE, A// West Cromer & German Reed// **St. Geo. Hall**, 1865[?].

NILSSON OR NOTHING// F// n.a.// **St. James's**, 1876, with George Honey as Gag, Clifford Cooper as Leatherlungs, Fred Mervin as Bury, George Darrell as Scheroot, Mrs. John Wood as Jenny Leatherlungs.

NIMBLE SHILLING, THE// D// J. Levey// **Elephant & Castle**, June 1877.

NINA; OR, THE STORY OF A HEART// Play 5a// Dram. by Mrs. Kennion fr portions of Emile Zola's Nana & Alexandre Dumas fils's La Dame aux Camélias// **Strand**, July 1887.

NINA SFORZA// T 5a// R. Z. Troughton// **Haymarket**, Nov. 1841, with James Wallack as Doria, W. C. Macready as Spinola, George Bennett as Grimoalda, Henry Wallack as Sforza, Henry Howe as Bizzaro, Mr. Caulfield as Villetri, John Webster as D'Estala, J. W. Gough as del Borgo, Helen Faucit as Nina, Mrs. W. Clifford as Brigitta, Miss Charles as Gioconday/ Scenery by Charles Marshall & George Morris.

NINE DAYS' QUEEN, THE// D 4a// Robert Buchanan// **Gaiety**, Dec. 1880, with Louise Willes, Arthur Dacre, Herbert Beerbohm Tree, David Fisher, Mrs. Leigh Murray.

NINE DAYS' WONDER, A// C 3a// Hamilton Aïdé// **Court**, June 1875, with W. H. Kendal, Mrs. Kendal, John Hare, John Cathcart.

NINE POINTS OF THE LAW// C 1a// Dram. by Tom Taylor fr story of Savage// **Olympic**, Apr. 1859, with Mr. Addison as Ironside, Horace Wigan as Cunninggame, George Vining as Rolling- stone, Walter Gordon as Britton, Mrs. Stirling as Mrs. Smylie, Miss Cottrell as Kate, Miss Seymour as Sarah Jane/ **Haymarket**, Aug. 1874, with T. N. Wenman as Ironsides, H. Bennett as Britton, James Carter-Edwards as Rollingstone, H. Andrews as Cunninghame, Annie La Fontaine as Mrs. Smylie, Ida Courtenay as Katie, Nelly Lingham as Sarah/ **Sad. Wells**, Sept. 1880, with J. Durham as Ironsides, Walter Brooks as Rollingstone, G. Canninge as Cunninghame, Mr. Wheatcroft as Britton, Mrs. Charles Calvert as Mrs. Smylie, Ada Clare as Kate.

NINETY-NINE// Play 5a// Dion Boucicault//

Standard, Oct. 1891.

NINON// D 4a// W. G. Wills// **Adelphi**, Feb. 1880, with Henry Neville as St. Cyr, F. H. Brooke as Marat, James Fernandez as Baget, J. G. Taylor as Simon, F. W. Irish as Beaugras, Jenny Rogers as the Dauphin, Maria Harris as Josephine, Miss Wallis as Ninon, Harriet Coveney as Nanette/ Scenery by Julian Hicks/ Music by W. C. Levey.

NIOBE, ALL SMILES// C 3a// Harry & Edward Paulton// **Strand**, Apr. 1892, with Harry Paulton as Dunn, Forbes Dawson as Griffin, George Hawtrey as Tompkins, Herbert Ross as Innings, Alec MacKenzie as Sillocks, Beatrice Lamb as Niobe, Ina Goldsmith as Caroline, Carlotta Zerbini as Helen, Georgie Esmond as Hattie, Eleanor May as Beatrice.

NITA'S FIRST// FC 3a// T. G. Warren// **Novelty**, Mar. 1884.

NITOCRIS// Play 5a// Edward Fitzball// **Drury Lane**, Oct. 1855, with E. F. Edgar as Mesphra, Mr. Stuart as Amenophis, Barry Sullivan as Tihrak, Miss Anderton as Koephed, George Wild as Cuzar, James Worrell as Kenos, Miss Cleveland as Kaphna/ Scenery by Cuthbert, Nicholls, Cooper, Gordon & Aglio/ Machines by Mr. Tucker/ Music by Henri Laurent/ Prod. by Robert Roxby.

NIXIE// Play 3a// Mrs. Hodgson Burnett & Stephen Townsend// **Terry's**, Apr. 1890, with Lewis Waller as Belasys, Julian Cross as Hutchens, Walter Russell as Dr. Armstead, William Herbert as Lawrence, Helen Forsyth as Kitty, Ruth Rutland as Mrs. Belasys, Caroline Ewell as Miss Pinch, Charlotte Morland as Miss Macgregor, Lucy Webling as Nixie/ Trans. to **Globe** May 1890.

NO! (also as No! No! No!)// F// n.a.// **Cov. Garden**, Jan. 1837, with John Pritchard as Sir George, Mr. Tilbury as Com. Hurricane, Mr. Collins as Frederick, Mr. Ross as Smart, Charles Bender as Thomas, John Collett as John, Mrs. W. West as Lady Doubtful, Mrs. Sarah Garrick as Deborah, Eliza Vincent as Maria/ **Haymarket**, July 1837, with Charles Selby as Sir George, Robert Strickland as Commodore, John Webster as Frederick, T. F. Mathews as Andrew, James Worrell as Smart, Eliza Vincent as Maria, Miss Wrighten as Lady Doubtful, Mrs. Tayleure as Deborah/ **Grecian**, Oct. 1844, with Edwin Dixon as Sir George, Mr. Melvin as Frederick, W. Saker as Com. Hurricane, Edmund Garden as Smart, Frederick Robson as Andrew, Paul Herring as William, Mrs. Chester as Lady Doubtful, Miss M. A. Crisp as Maria/ **Princess's**, Mar. 1848, with Mr. Bodda as Sir George, J. Neville as Com. Hurricane, Mr. Barker as Frederick, Mr. Palmer as Doublelock, Mr. Mucklow as William, S. Cowell as Smart, Miss Villars as Lady Doubtful, Emma Stanley as Maria, Mrs. Selby as Mrs. Doublelock/ **Astley's**, Mar. 1852, with Mr. Hustleby as Sir George, Mr. Johnson as Com. Hurricane, Mr. Craddock as Smart, Mr. Tannett as Doublelock, Miss Maclean as Lady Doubtful, Miss Fenton as Maria, Mrs. Beacham as Mrs. Doublelock/ **Sad. Wells**, June 1854, with Edwin Dixon as Sir George, F. Charles as Frederick, Mr. Barrett as Com. Hurricane, J. W. Collier as Smart, Mrs. Barrett as Lady Doubtful, Miss Lavine as Marie, Miss Rawlings as Deborah/ **Olympic**, May 1866, with Robert Soutar as Sir George, W. H. Stephens as Com. Thunder [sic], H. Vincent as Frederick, Miss Sheridan as Lady Doubtful, Mrs. Stephens as Deborah.

NO ACTRESS// H. H. Bartlett// **Surrey**, June 1898.

NO CARDS// F// John Oxenford// **Adelphi**, Nov. 1872.

NO CREDIT// C 1a// Emily Coffin// **Strand**, Apr. 1892, with George Hawtrey as Grant, Herbert Ross as Gordon, Alec MacKenzie as Sir George, Georgie Esmond as Kitty, Venie Bennett as Barbara.

NO MAN'S LAND// D 5a// J. T. Douglass// **Grand**, Apr. 1893.

NO MERCY// D 5a// Mark Melford// **Elephant & Castle**, May. 1885.

NO SONG NO SUPPER// F 2a// Prince Hoare// **Cov. Garden**, Mar. 1838, with Mr. Manvers as Col. Detonator, Drinkwater Meadows as Sir Jacob, James Anderson as Mowbray, Mr. Vining as Nonpareil, Edwin Yarnold as Solomon, Priscilla Horton as Emily/ **Grecian**, Apr. 1844, with Mr. Frazer as Frederick, Mr. Baldwin as Crop, Mr. Campbell as Robin, Frederick Robson as Endless, Edmund Garden as Thomas, Annette Mears as Margaretta, Miss Johnstone as Louisa, Miss M. A. Crisp as Dorothy, Miss Merion as Nelly/ **Olympic**, Nov. 1852, with William Farren Jr. as Crop, Henry Compton as Endless, William Hoskins as Robin, E. F. Edgar as Frederick, Harriet Gordon as Margaretta, Lucy Rafter as Dorothy, Mrs. B. Bartlett as Nelly, Miss Pitt as Louisa.

NO THOROUGHFARE// D Pro & 5a// Charles Dickens & Wilkie Collins// **Adelphi**, Dec. 1867, with John Billington as Wilding, George Belmore as Mr. Bintrey, Benjamin Webster as Ladle, Henry Neville as Vendale, Charles Fechter as Jules Obenreizer, Carlotta Leclercq as Marquerite, Mrs. H. Lewis as Madame Dor/ Scenery by T. Grieve & Son/ Machines by Mr. Charker/ Gas by G. Bastard/ Music by E. Ellis/ Prod. by Charles Fechter/ **Standard**, June 1868/ **Olympic**, Nov. 1873, with T. G. Warren as Wilding and as Jean Marie, Charles Flockton as Bintrey, W. J. Hill as Ladle, Henry Neville as Vendale, Arthur Stirling as Jules Obenreizer, Miss Carlisle as Marguerite, Fanny Morelli as Madame Dor, Mr. Arnauld as Jean Paul, Dibdin Culver as Father Francis/ Scenery by Mr. Hann/ Machines by Mr. Collins/ Gas by Mr. Hinckley/ Music by Edwin Ellis/ Prod. by Mrs. Seymour & Henry Neville.

NOAH'S ARK// C 3a// Henry Paulton// **Royalty**, Oct. 1886, with Charles Ashford, Harry Paulton, Julia Seaman, Marion Morris, Dorothy Dene.

NOBLE ART, THE// F 3a// Eille Norwood//

Terry's, May 1892, with Arthur Williams as Andrew Fullalove, H. Reeves Smith as Charles Fullalove, Sydney Brough as Brady, Julian Cross as Prof. Tranz, Sydney Valentine as Sledge, May Whitty as Gertie, Katie Leechman as Winifred, Lille Belmore as Tilly.

NOBLE ATONEMENT, A// D 4a// Ina Cassilis// **Opera Comique**, Jan. 1892, with Charles Lander as Locksley, H. Athol Forde as Melville, E. W. Thomas as Smith, Howard Sturge as West, D. G. English as Dolly, Bernard Copping as Fendale, Frederic Jacques as Snedger, Annie Cathew as Marguerite, Florence Fordyce as Emily, Leila Rivers as Dabbs, Adelaide Grace as Norris, Lesley Bell as Rosamond.

NOBLE BROTHER, A// C 4a// W. J. Summers// **Opera Comique**, Feb. 1890, with George Herbert as Col. Leigh, E. Rochelle as Travers, Charles Weir as Ellsworth, Henry Vaughan as Howard, W. J. Summers as Jerry, Ellen Boucher as Nana, Clara Rose as Rosie.

NOBLE FALSEHOOD, A// Play 1a// Edwin Drew// **St. Geo. Hall**, June 1894.

NOBLE HEART, THE// T 5a// George H. Lewis// **Olympic**, Feb. 1850, with G. V. Brooke as Don Gomez, E. L. Davenport as Don Leon, H. Lee as Don Guzman, Frederick Belton as Don Antonio, John Kinloch as Don Garcia, John Ryder as Herman, J. Johnstone as Reinaldos, J. Howard as Lizzardo, Anna Cora Mowatt as Juanna/ Scenery by Dayes & Gordon/ Machines by B. Sloman.

NOBLE LORD, THE// FC 3a// Robert [?] Marshall// **Criterion**, Oct. 1900.

NOBLE LOVE// D 4a// C. A. Clarke & J. J. Hewson// **Elephant & Castle**, July 1891.

NOBLE VAGABOND, THE// D 4a// Henry Arthur Jones// **Princess's**, Dec. 1886, with Charles Warner as Lester, John Beauchamp as Sir Godfrey, Julian Cross as Joseph Scorier, C. Cartwright as Ralph Scorier, George Barrett as Vimpany, Alfred Phillips as Baldock, Dorothy Dene as Maud, Bella Titheredge as Mary, Annie Hughes as Dinah/ Scenery by Walter Hann/ Music by Isadore de Solla.

NOBODY IN LONDON// F 1a// E. L. Blanchard// **Drury Lane**, Sept. 1873, with Frederick Moreland as Cranky, Brittain Wright as Skid, Fred Evans as Fresco, T. Lovell as Clump, Harriet Coveney as Arabella,, Miss Hudspeth as Sally, Amy Rosalind as Dolly.

NOBODY'S CHILD// D 3a// Watts Phillips// **Surrey**, Sept. 1867/ **Princess's**, 1868.

NOBODY'S FORTUNE// D 3a// H. P. Grattan// **Surrey**, Feb. 1872.

NOEMIE THE VILLAGE ORPHAN// D 2a// n.a.// **Grecian**, June 1857, with Basil Potter as Count d'Avrigny, Richard Phillips as d'Avrigny, W. H. Eburne as Viscount de Normas, Mr. Smithson as Francois, Ellen Hale as Marie, Harriet Coveney as Annette, Jane Coveney as Noemie, Miss Johnstone as Mme. Marguerite.

NONE BUT THE BRAVE DESERVE THE FAIR// C 2a// Benjamin Webster// **Haymarket**, June 1850, with Henry Howe as King, Benjamin Webster as Don Flores, J. B. Buckstone as Don Pachico, Charles Selby as Don Rococo, Mr. Rogers as Don Gomez, Mrs. L. S. Buckingham as Queen, Miss Reynolds as Isabella, Miss Woulds as Inez/ Scenery by George Morris/ Machines by F. Heselton.

NORA// Play// Adap. fr G vers. of Henrik Ibsen's A Doll's House// **St. Geo. Hall**, Oct. 1900.

NORAH// C 1a// Re Henry// **Grand**, Oct. 1897.

NORAH O'DONNELL; OR, THE SYBIL OF THE CAMP// D 2a// H. P. Grattan// **Sad. Wells**, Jan. 1840, with Mr. Aldridge as Gen. Darville, W. D. Broadfoot as Lt. Somers, Mr. Elvin as Capt. Blakely, J. W. Collier as Corp. Dickey, Henry Hall as Tape, Robert Honner as Squall, Mr. Cathcart as O'Brien, Mr. Dry as O'Donnell, Mrs. Robert Honner as Norah, Miss Pincott as Kathleen.

NORAH O'NEAL// D// William Travers// **East London**, Dec. 1876.

NORTH POLE, THE// D// n.a.// **Victoria**, 1868.

NORTHERN STAR, THE; OR, RUSSIAN TYRANNY// D 4a// Dram by J. Maddison Morton fr Meyerbeer's opera, L'Etoile du Nord// **Sad. Wells**, Mar. 1855, with Marcus Elmore as Emperor of Russia, Mr. Herbert as Prince Menschikoff, Charles Vincent as de la Rosiere, Mr. Sidney as Browne, Miss St. Clair as Carlowitz, Mr. Johnson as Yermoloff, Miss Elsworthy as Empress Ekaterina, Suey Elsworthy as Princess Alexina.

NORWEGIAN WRECKERS, THE// D// Edward Fitzball// **Victoria**, Dec. 1853, with T. E. Mills as Angerstoff, F. H. Henry as Frederick, John Bradshaw as Junk, J. Howard as Weignstadt, R. H. Kitchen as Ormoloff, Mr. Morrison as Maurice, Mrs. Henry Vining as Mariette, Georgiana Lebatt as Christine.

NOT A BAD JUDGE (also titled, Laviter; or, Not a Bad Judge)// C 2a// Adap. by J. R. Planché fr F// **Lyceum**, Mar. 1848, with Robert Roxby as Marquis de Treval, Charles Diddear as Count de Steinberg, C. J. Mathews as Lavater, John Parselle as Christian, John Pritt Harley as Betman, Drinkwater Meadows as Zug, Mr. Bellingham as Rutly, Louisa Howard as Louise, Miss Lee as Mme. Betman; / **Drury Lane**, Mar. 1856, with Robert Roxby as Marquis de Treval, Charles Vincent as Count de Steinberg, C. J. Mathews as Lavale, Henry Ashley as Christian, Miss M. Oliver as Louise, Miss Adams as Mme. Betman/ **Princess's**, Aug. 1863, with Mr. Fitzjames as Count de Steinberg, Charles Vincent as Marquis de Treval, Walter Montgomery as Lavater, Mr. Brooke as Christian, Mr. Moreland as Betman, Mr. Doyne as Zug,

Miss Murray as Louise, Lizzie Harrison as Mme. Betman/ **Olympic**, Mar. 1867, with Mr. Stuart as Count de Steinberg, John Clayton as Marquis de Treval, C. J. Mathews as Lavater, H. J. Montague as Christian, Dominick Murray as Betman, Jerrold Reeves as Zug, Harwood Cooper as Nutley, Milly Palmer as Louise, Nelly Harris as Mme. Betman/ **Royalty**, July 1894.

NOT A WORD// FC 3a// Adap. by G. De Meirelles Soares ("Owen Dove") fr F of M. Civot & Alfred Duru, Le Carnaval d'un Merle Blanc// **Avenue**, Apr. 1884.

NOT ALONE// D 5a// George Lander & Mrs. Weldon// **Grand**, Oct. 1885.

NOT ALL THAT JEALOUS// F 1a// T. W. Robertson// **Court**, May 1871.

NOT FOUND// D 3a// Edward Towers// **East London**, Feb. 1870.

NOT GUILTY// D 4a// Watts Phillips// **Queen's**, Feb. 1869.

NOT IF I KNOW IT// F 1a// J. Maddison Morton & A. W. Young// **Haymarket**, June 1871, with E. A. Sothern as Thrillington, Frederick Everill as Dr. Chirper, Mr. Rogers as Gubbins, Caroline Hill as Mrs. Thrillington, Mrs. Chippendale as Mrs. Pecker, Miss Francis as Mary, Amy Roselle as Clementina.

NOT IN VAIN// D// Paul Meritt// **Grecian**, Oct. 1871.

NOT REGISTERED// D 2a// Arthur Matthison// **Royalty**, Apr. 1882.

NOT SO BAD AS WE SEEM; OR, MANY SIDES TO A CHARACTER// Play// Edward Bulwer-Lytton// **Haymarket**, Feb. 1853, with Mr. Stuart as Duke of Middlesex, George Braid as Earl of Loftus, Leigh Murray as Lord Wilmot, Robert Keeley as Softhead, Barry Sullivan as Hardman, Benjamin Webster as Sir Geoffrey, J. B. Buckstone as Easy, Mr. Rogers as Tonson, Rosa Bennett as Lucy, Amelia Vining as Barbara.

NOT SUCH A FOOL AS HE LOOKS// C 3a// H. J. Byron// **Globe**, Oct. 1869/ **Adelphi**, Feb. 1870/ **Olympic**, Aug. 1871, with John Carter as Murgatroyd, C. H. Peveril as Grantley, H. J. Byron as Sir Simon Simple, George Belmore as Mould, Maria Harris as Felicia, Miss Hughes as Mrs. Merton.

NOT TO BE DONE// F 1a// H. T. Craven// **Olympic**, Nov. 1850, with Charles Bender as Sturnbrowe, Henry Farren as Downeywag, Leigh Murray as Quick, John Kinloch as Fipsey, Mrs. B. Bartlett as Mrs. Sturnbrowe, Miss Adams as Elizabeth, Isabel Adams as Miss Stuccop, Mrs. Alfred Phillips as Sally.

NOTE FORGER, THE; OR, A FATHER'S CRIME// D 2a// Edward Fitzball// **Sad. Wells**, Aug. 1839, with Mr. Cathcart as Brastoun, Mr. Dry as Cresfield, John Webster as Glebeland, Mr. Conquest as Ducket, Mrs. Robert Honner as Diana, Miss Richardson as Mrs. Glebeland, Miss Pincott as Phillis.

NOTE OF HAND, THE// Play 1a// Herbert Keith// **Vaudeville**, Jan. 1891, with Fred Grove as Merton, Fred Thorne as Solomon, Annie Hill as Mabel, Coralie Owen as Mrs. Peckover.

NOTHING TO NURSE// F 1a// C. M. Walcot// **St. James's**, Apr. 1876, with G. W. Anson as Muddle, G. Shelton as Brads, F. Strickland as Ashton, Amy Forrest as Mrs. Foxingen, Miss M. Brown as Bessie, Miss E. Toms as Fanny.

NOTHING VENTURE, NOTHING WIN// C 2a// J. Stirling Coyne// **Strand**, Apr. 1858.

NOTICE TO QUIT; OR, IN THE CLUTCH OF THE LAW// D 3a// George Conquest & Henry Pettitt// **Grecian**, Apr. 1878.

NOTORIOUS MRS. EBBSMITH, THE// D 4a// Arthur Wing Pinero// **Garrick**, Mar. 1895, with John Hare as Duke of St. Olpherts, Ian Robertson as Sir Sandford, Johnston Forbes Robertson as Cleeve, C. Aubrey Smith as Rev. Winterfield, Joseph Carne as Sir John, Fred Thorne as Dr. Kirke, Gerald du Maurier as Fortune, Mrs. Patrick Campbell as Agnes, Ellis Jeffreys as Gertrude, Eleanor Calhoun as Sybil/ Scenery by William Harford.

NOTRE DAME; OR, THE GIPSY GIRL OF PARIS// D 3a// Dram. by Andrew Halliday fr novel of Victor Hugo// **Adelphi**, Apr. 1871, with T. C. King as Quasimodo, James Fernandez as Claude Frollo, A. C. Lilley as de Chateaupers, F. Stainforth as Jehan Frollo, Brittain Wright as Gringoire, M. D. Byrnes as Tristan, Harwood Cooper as Olivier, C. H. Stephenson as Clopin, Miss Furtado as Esmeralda, Mrs. Addie as Mme. Gondelaurier, Miss Hibbert as Fleur de Lys, Mrs. Alfred Mellon as Gudale/ Scenery by F. Lloyds & Maugham/ Machines by Edward Charker/ Gas by G. Bastard/ Music by Edwin Ellis.

NOUGHTOLOGY; OR, NOTHING// C 4a// Frederick Stanford// **St. Geo. Hall**, Nov. 1889.

NOVEL EXPEDIENT, A// C 1a// Benjamin Webster// **Haymarket**, June 1852, with Leigh Murray as Damon, Henry Howe as Moore, Mrs. Stirling as Maria/ **Adelphi**, Apr. 1853, with Leigh Murray as Damon, John Parselle as Moore, Sarah Woolgar as Maria/ **Sad. Wells**, Nov. 1855, with Leigh Murray as Damon, William Belford as Moore, Margaret Eburne as Maria/ **Drury Lane**, Feb. 1858.

NOVEL READER, THE// C 3a// Adap. by Joseph Mackay & Sidney Grundy fr F of Henri Meilhac & Ludovic Halévy, La Petite Marquise// **Globe**, Aug. 1882, with Clifford Cooper, Arthur Wood, Lydia Cowell, Maria Davis, Alice Corri, Kate Mortimer.

NOVICE, THE// D 3a// William Dimond// **Cov. Garden**, Oct. 1837, with Mr. Warde as Elector, George Bartley as Baron Solomons, Mr. Vining as Count Carolstadt, John Pritchard as Rosenheim, Mr. Roberts as Dornberg, Mr. Harris as Arnheim, Charles Bender as Hoffman, Drinkwater Meadows as Margrave of Anspach, W. H. Payne as Stiffenbach, James Anderson as Verstein, Mrs. Sarah Garrick as Lady Griffenclaw, Mrs. East as Lady Dragondorf, Miss Garrick as Minna, Mrs. W. Clifford as Mme. Polnitz, Helen Faucit as Clotilda.

NOW OR NEVER!// F 1a// George Dance// **Drury Lane**, Jan. 1839, with Henry Compton as Puffenheim, Mr. Hughes as Wiggendorf, J. S. Balls as Waldrick, A. Brindal as Von Alterberg, Miss Fitzwalter as Laurine, Miss Poole as Rose.

NOW-A-DAYS: A TALE OF THE TURF// D 4a// Wilson Barrett// **Princess's**, Feb. 1889, with Wilson Barrett as Saxton, Lewis Waller as Tom, Julian Cross as Harper, George Barrett as Dowling, Horace Hodges as Fressingwold, H. Cooper Cliffe as Sir Harry, Austin Melford as Bleater, Miss Webster as Amy, Miss Norreys as Kitty, Harrietta Polini as Peggy, Grace Hawthorne as Jenny/ Scenery by Walter Hann, Stafford Hall & R. C. Durant/ Music by Michael Connolly.

No. 49// C 1a// Frederick Lawrence// **St. James's**, Mar. 1860, with Mr. Barrett as Whimsical, Charles Young as Nofees, George Spencer as Selby, F. Craxford as Smith, James Francis as Charles, Henry Reeves as Bootmaker, Eliza Arden as Emily, Alice Evans as Susan, Mrs. Manders as Dame Jones.

NUMBER ONE 'ROUND THE CORNER// F 1a// William Brough// **Lyceum**, Mar. 1854/ **Sad. Wells**, Apr. 1855, with Robert Roxby as Nobbler, Mr. Swan as Flipper, Mr. Templeton as Jem, Mr. Williams as Old Man/ **Drury Lane**, Nov. 1855, with C. J. Mathews as Flipper, Robert Roxby as Nobbler, Mr. Templeton as Jem/ **Princess's**, Mar. 1867, with J. G. Shore as Flipper, Henry Forrester as Nobbler/ **Adelphi**, June 1879, with Edward Compton as Flipper, E. J. George as Nobbler, Harwood Cooper as Lodger; Dec. 1898, with Arthur Bawtree as Flipper, W. St. John as Nobbler.

NUMBER SIX DUKE STREET// F// Martin Becher// **Drury Lane**, Sept. 1871, with James Francis as Judd, William Terriss as Jarvis, Ersser Jones as Noakes, Mrs. Power as Mrs. Clapper, Maud Howard as Lottie.

No. 12// C// James Francis// **Novelty**, July 1886.

NUMBER 20; OR, THE BASTILLE OF CALVADOS// D 4a// James Albery & Joseph Hatton// **Princess's**, 1878, with Charles Warner as Lestouche, J. H. Barnes as Neron, W. Travers as Duke de Némours, W. Hargreaves as de Longueville, William Redmund as Father Laval, T. P. Haynes as Francois, F. Strickland as Pierre, Harry Jackson as Chadron, Miss Fowler as Blanche, Rose Berends as Mimi, Marie Daly as Anna, Miss Abington as Jeannette/ Scenery by Julian Hicks/ Machines by Mr. Warton/ Lime-light by Mr. Kerr/ Music by J. L. Hatton/ Prod. by Harry Jackson.

NO. 23, JOHN STREET, ADELPHI// F// n.a.// **Sad. Wells**, July 1843, with Mr. Thompson as Sir Charles, Mr. Lingham as Capt. Smith, Mr. Lamb as Spencer, John Webster as Tompkins, Mr. Williams as Phelim, Mr. Coreno as Skulk, Miss Lane as Lady Crazy, Miss Stephens as Eliza, Miss Melville as Mary.

NUMBER TWO// FC 3a// H. C. Hiller// **Vaudeville**, Mar. 1890, with Fred Shepherd as O'Larrigan, Charles Medwin as Jump, Norman Norman as Darcy, Richard Brennand as Brompton, Adolphus Ellis as Cramp, Mary Stuart as Lady Magrath, Mrs. Henry Leigh as Emily Jemima, Gertrude Lovell as Emily, Rose Dearing as Mabel, Vinnie Bennett as Daisy.

NURSE// F 2a// Clotilde Graves// **Globe**, Mar. 1900, with Sidney Brough as Fastnet, Mark Kinghorne as Sims, Alfred Maltby as Hopper, Fred Eastman as Maj. Walker-Wilson, Lawrance D'Orsay as Lord Colchicum, William Cheesman as Bittles, Ethel Clinton as Mrs. Walker-Wilson, Carlotta Zerbini as Caroline, Lottie Venne as Dorothy Ffinch.

NURSEY CHICKWEED// F 1a// T. J. Williams// **Princess's**, Nov. 1859, with Henry Widdicomb as Chickweed, Henry Saker as Barnes, Mr. Meadows as Mountsorrel, Mrs. Weston as Clementina, Louise Keeley as Nelly.

*

OAKLEAVES AND EMERALDS; OR, THE TITLED GRISETTE// D 2a// n.a.// **Grecian**, Feb. 1856, with Mr. Hustleby as Count Liancourt, F. Charles as Chev. Beauregard, Richard Phillips as Achille, John Manning as Nicolet, Jane Coveney as Madeline, Harriet Coveney as Marguerite, Ellen Hale as Blanche.

OATH, THE// D Pro & 4a// J. A. Meade// **Strand**, June 1887.

OBED SNOW'S PHILANTHROPY// Play 3a// George Newton// **POW**, July 1887.

OBI; OR, THREE FINGERED JACK (see also, Three Fingered Jack)// D// n.a.// **Victoria** Mar. 1845, with Mr. Griffiths as Sandford, Mr. James as Capt. Orford, Mr. Deering as Quashee, Mr. Grove as Cunningham, Mr. Torning as Three Fingered Jack, W. H. Douglass as Jonkanoo, Mme. Torning as Rosa, Mrs. Gibbs as Ulalee, Mrs. Bushelle as Fatatoo, Charles Fenton as Obi Woman, Mme. Louise as Yanina.

OBJECT OF INTEREST, AN// F 1a// J. H. Stocqueler// **Lyceum**, July 1845/ **Olympic**, Sept. 1848, with Samuel Emery as Primrose,

Charles Bender as Maj. Culverin, Mr. Norton as Simmerton, S. Cowell as O'Dwyer, Clara Wynne as Mrs. Vernon, Mrs. H. J. Turner as Mrs. Culverin, Mrs. C. A. Tellet as Fanny; Jan. 1859, with J. Howard as Maj. Culverin, George Cooke as Primrose, F. Charles as Simmerton, Horace Wigan as O'Dwyer, Miss Cottrell as Mrs. Vernon, Mrs. Leigh Murray as Mrs. Culverin, Mrs. W. S. Emden as Fanny; May 1872, with Mr. Bennett as Simmerton, Mr. Wood as Primrose, Mr. Andrews as Barney, Miss Chapman as Mrs. Vernon, Mrs. Parker as Mrs. Culverin, Eva Hamilton as Fanny; Feb. 1878, with T. G. Warren as Simmerton, G. Harmond as Maj. Culverin, George Yarnold as Primrose, Robert Pateman as O'Dwyer, Alma Stanley as Mrs. Vernon, Ida Beaumont as Mrs. Culverin, Miss Gerard as Fanny.

OBLIGING A FRIEND// F 1a// Adap. by George Conquest// **Grecian**, Nov. 1867, with John Manning as Sheepshanks, Henry Grant as Smith, George Gillett as Keating, Mary A. Victor as Matilda, Miss De Lacie as Rose.

OBSERVATION AND FLIRTATION// C 1a// Horace Wigan// **Strand**, July 1860.

OBSTINATE FAMILY, THE// F 1a// Adap. fr G// **Sad. Wells**, Feb. 1853, with Frederic Robinson as Harford, Mr. Barrett as Harwood, Lewis Ball as James, Mrs. Henry Marston as Mrs. Harwood, Miss T. Bassano as Mrs. Harford, Eliza Travers as Lucy.

OCEAN GRAVE, THE// D// n.a.// **Sad. Wells**, May 1839, with W. D. Broadfoot as Will Starboard, John Webster as Tom Starboard, Mr. Dry as Col. Campbell, Mr. Williams as Bane, J. W. Collier as Barlow, Mr. Phillips as Lt. Dart, Mrs. J. F. Saville as Helen, Miss Cooke as Dame Starboard, Miss Nicholls as Miss Primrose.

OCEAN OF LIFE, THE; OR, EVERY INCH A SAILOR// D 3a// J. T. Haines// **Sad. Wells**, July 1843, with Mr. Coreno as Sir Timothy, R. H. Lingham as Morville, C. J. Bird as Capt. Blundell, Mr. Starmer as Westfield, Mr. Lambe as Allensby, C. J. Smith as Herefield, Henry Marston as Mat, John Herbert as Tommy, Caroline Rankley as Isabella, Mrs. Richard Barnett as Jemima, Miss Cooke as Mrs. Morville, Mrs. Andrews as Miss Skinrat, Miss Stephens as Fanny/ Scenery by F. Fenton/ Machines by Mr. Cawdery/ Music by W. Montgomery/ **Victoria**, May 1854, with Alfred Saville as Sir Timothy, Mr. Henderson as Capt. Blundell, Mr. Morrison as Morville, Mr. Green as Westfield, Mr. Hitchinson as Allensby, T. E. Mills as Horsfiels, N. T. Hicks as Meriton, John Hudspeth as Jumble, J. Howard as Skinrat, Mrs. Henry Vining as Miss Morville, Miss Dansor as Mrs. Morville, Miss Sutton as Mrs. Skinrat, Miss Laporte as Jemima, Mrs. Manders as Mrs. Fubbs.

OCTOROON, THE; OR, LIFE IN LOUISIANA// D 4a// Dion Boucicault// **Adelphi**, Nov. 1861, with Delmon Grace as Salem Scudder, John Billington as Peyton, Robert Romer as Sunnyside, Samuel Emery as Jacob, Paul Bedford as Capt. Ratts, C. H. Stephenson as Col. Poindexter, C. J. Smith as Lafourche, Mrs. Billington as Thibodeaux, Clara Denvil as Picayune, George Jamison as Pete, Mrs. Henry Marston as Dora, Mrs. Dion Boucicault as Zoe, Mrs. H. Lewis as Dido/ **Grecian**, June 1864, with Thomas Mead as Salem Scudder, Henry Grant as Peyton, J. B. Steele as McCloskey, J. Jackson as Sunnyside, William James as Wahnotee, D. W. Leeson as Pete, Louisa Graham as Mrs. Peyton, Marie Brewer as Dora, Mrs. Charles Dillon as Zoe/ Scenery by Mr. Messender/ **Princess's**, Feb. 1868, with Dion Boucicault as Wahnotee, G. F. Neville as Peyton, Mr. Maclean as Sunnyside, George Vining as McClosky, J. S. Clarke as Salem Scudder, J. G. Shore as Capt. Ratts, Henry Forrester as Poindexter, Emma Barnett as Thibodeux, Rachel Sanger as Little Paul, Dan Leeson as Pete, Miss K. Stafford as Mrs. Peyton, Mrs. Dion Boucicault as Zoe, Miss Hubert as Mrs. Claiborne, Miss Russell as Grace/ Scenery by F. Lloyds/ **Astley's**, June 1870, with Mr. Manley as Salem Scudder, T. B. Bennett as Jacob, Walter Holland as Wahnotree, Henry Pitt as Payton, Mr. Young as Sunnyside, Clingan Jones as Pete, Mary Sanders as Zoe, Lotty Reynolds as Dora.

ODD LOT, AN// F 1a// William Gowing ("Walter Gordon")// **Royalty**, Mar. 1864.

ODD, TO SAY THE LEAST OF IT// FC 3a// Edward Rose// **Novelty**, Nov. 1886.

ODETTE// C 4a// Adap. fr F of Victorien Sardou// **Haymarket**, July 1882, with Squire Bancroft as Lord Henry, Stewart Dawson as Lord Arthur, Frank Cooper as Lord Shandon, Mr. Smedley as Prince Troubitzkoy, Arthur Cecil as Stratford, H. B. Conway as Eden, Owen Dove as Wilkes, Arthur Wing Pinero as Hanway, Helena Modjeska as Lady Trevene, Florence Wade as Lady Walker, Cicely Grahame as Eva, Miss Measor as Margaret, Maria Daly as Princess de Goertz, Mrs. Mitford as Countess Karola, Ruth Francis as Mrs. Hanway/ Scenery by Mr. Johnstone, Walter Hann & William Telbin.

ODETTE// C 4a// Adap. by Clement Scott fr F of Victorien Sardou// **Princess's**, Sept. 1894, with Charles Warner as Lord Henry, Bernard Gould as Stratford, Herbert Flemming as Eden, Paul Berton as Narcisse, Sheridan Lascelles as Lord Shandon, Eardley Howard as Lord Arthur, Rothbury Evans as Prince Nobitskoy, Ettie Williams as Eva, Marie Cecil as Margaret, Miss Brinsley Sheridan as Lady Walker, Mrs. W. L. Abingdon as Countess Varola, Mrs. B. M. De Solla as Mrs. Hanway, Anna Rupert as Odette.

O'DOWD, THE// D 4a// Dion Boucicault// **Adelphi**, Oct. 1880, with Dion Boucicault as O'Dowd, Henry Neville as Mike, Edward Compton as Talboys, Harry Proctor as Col. Muldoon, J. G. Taylor as Leake, Robert Pateman as Chalker, Bella Pateman as Lady Rose, Lydia Foote as Kitty, Roma Le Thière as Bridget.

O'FLAHERTYS, THE; OR, THE DIFFICULTY OF IDENTIFYING AN IRISHMAN// C// Edmund Falconer// **Drury Lane**, Nov. 1864, with Edmund Falconer as O'Flaherty, Mr. Barrett as Constant, George Belmore as Gammon, Mr. Fitzjames as Theophilus, Miss E. Falconer as Mary, Miss Seymour as Peggy, Miss Hudspeth as Betty, Mrs. Henry Vandenhoff as Angelica.

OF AGE TOMORROW// F 1a// Thomas Dibdin// **Sad. Wells**, July 1841, with J. S. Balls as Baron Willinghurst, Mr. Williams as Baron Piffleberg, Mr. Aldridge as Molkus, Miss Cooke as Lady Brumback, Mrs. Richard Barnett as Marie, Mrs. Morgan as Sophia/ **Haymarket**, Jan. 1843, with Mr. Tilbury as Baron Biffleberg, Mr. Bishop as Molkus, John Webster as Baron Willinghurst, Mrs. Stanley as Lady Brumback, Miss Kelly as Maria; Aug. 1861, with William Farren as Baron Willinhurst, W. H. Chippendale as Baron Piffleberg, Henry Compton as Molkus, Mr. Weatherby as Friz, Mrs. Poynter as Lady Brumback, Miss Henrade as Sophia, Miss M. Oliver as Maria.

OFF DUTY// C 1a// T. E. Pemberton// **Toole's**, Sept. 1884/ **Lyceum**, July 1890, with Lionel Brough as Ben Bloss, Percy Everard as Negus, Alfred Matthews as Sam Medley, Percy Brough as Scrope, Kate Hodson as Mrs. Tinklar, Mary Brough as Millie.

OFF THE LINE// C 1a// Clement Scott// **Gaiety**, Apr. 1871/ **Lyceum**, June 1888, with J. L. Toole as Harry Coke, G. Shelton as Jem Brass, Watty Brunton as Puffy, Eliza Johnstone as Lizzie Coke, Blanche Wolseley as Mary Coke.

OFFER OF MARRIAGE, AN// C. Leslie Fomm// **Wyndham's**, June 1900 (orig. prod. at the **Globe**, Apr. 1899, as Ambition).

OH! MY HEAD// F// Francis Allen// **Alhambra**, Apr. 1871.

OH, SUSANNAH!// FC 3a// Mark Ambient, Alban Atwood, & Russell Vaun// **Royalty**, Oct. 1897, with Charles Glenney as Sheppard, Alfred Maltby as Plant, L. Power as Lt. Merry, Harry Farmer as Vane, Mary Milton as Flora, Alice Mansfield as Susannah, Bella Graves as Ruby, Grace Vicat as Pearl, Kate Kearney as Mrs. O'Hara, Clara Jecks as Tupper, Louie Freear as Aurora.

OH! THESE WIDOWS// F 3a// Adap. by James Mortimer fr F of Marc Michel & Eugène Labiche// **Terry's**, May 1889.

OIL AND VINEGAR// C 2a// H. J. Byron// **Gaiety**, Nov. 1874.

OLD ADMIRER, AN// Play 1a// C. H. Brookfield// **Avenue**, Sept. 1899, with Wilfred Draycott as Maj. Lacy, Arthur Holmes-Gore as Lawford, Miss Dolan as Cynthia.

OLD AND YOUNG// F// John Poole// **Haymarket**, Oct. 1837, with Robert Strickland as Wilton, James Worrell as Mowbray, Mr. Ross as Peter, Mr. Ray as William, Miss Davenport in 4 char. parts, Miss Wrighten as Peggy.

OLD AND YOUNG STAGER, THE// C// W. L. Rede// **Haymarket**, Oct. 1861, with W. H. Chippendale as Sir Pompadour, William Farren as Clement, William Cullenford as Stocks, Henry Compton as Tapple, C. J. Mathews as Timothy, Mr. Weathersby as James, Mrs. Griffith as Lady Puffendale, Henrietta Lindley as Laura, Miss Lovell as Miss Stocks, Eliza Weekes as Lucy.

OLD BISHOPSGATE// D// n.a.// **City of London**, Aug. 1851.

OLD BLUE LION IN GRAY'S INN LANE, THE; OR, DEATH ON THE TAVERN STAIRS// D 2a// T. E. Wilks// **Sad. Wells**, Jan. 1843, with Mr. Williams as Sir Acton, C. J. Bird as Sir Paul, Mr. Lambe as Neville, Henry Marston as Grey, Mr. Aldridge as Hoon, Mr. Dry as Noreton, John Herbert as Pilgrim, Charles Fenton as Arden, Caroline Rankley as Fan, Mrs. Henry Marston as Dame Margaret, Mrs. Richard Barnett as Ursula/ Scenery by F. Fenton/ Prod. by Henry Marston.

OLD BOGEY OF THE SEA, THE// n.a.// **Britannia**, Dec. 1891.

OLD BOOTY, THE BAKER OF BISHOPSGATE; OR THE FIEND OF THE VOLCANO// D// T. Mildenhall// **Grecian**, July 1861, with Mr. Jackson as Old Booty, Walter Holland as Capt. Barnaby, George Gillett as Lt. Belrose, R. H. Lingham as St. Clair, John Manning as Crumpet, Alfred Rayner as Dodge, Jane Coveney as Alice, Helen Hale as Adela, Miss Johnstone as Mrs. Barnaby, Miss Love as Mariana, Lucreza Hill as Jenny.

OLD CHATEAU, THE; OR, A NIGHT OF PERIL// D 3a// J. Stirling Coyne// **Haymarket**, July 1854, with Henry Howe as Marquis de Leyrac, Mr. Rogers as Domville, William Farren as Armand, J. B. Buckstone as Sammson, Henry Marston as Lalouette, William Clark as Pierre, Miss Reynolds as Julie, Mrs. Fitzwilliam as Jeannette, Mrs. Poynter as Gertrude/ Scenery by George Morris & John O'Conner, Machines by Mr. Wales, Music by Edward Fitzwilliam/ **Grecian**, July 1857, with Richard Phillips as Gen. de Leyrac, W. H. Eburne as Armand, Henry Grant as Domville, Basil Potter as Laluette, John Manning as Sammson, Jane Coveney as Julie, Harriet Coveney as Jeannette, Miss Johnstone as Gertrude.

OLD CHUMS// C 3a// H. J. Byron// **Opera Comique**, Dec. 1876.

OLD CHURCH WALLS, THE// D// n.a.// **Marylebone**, Nov. 1852.

OLD COMMODORE, THE// C// Adap. fr Dibdin's The Birthday// **Haymarket**, Nov. 1837, with Robert Strickland as Com. Bertram, J. W. Gough as Bertram, T. P. Cooke as Jack Junk, Mr. Hemming as Harry, T. F. Mathews as Capias, Miss Beresford as Emma, Mrs. Tayleure as Mrs. Moral.

OLD CRONIES// C 1a// S. Theyre Smith// **St. James's**, Mar. 1880, with T. N. Wenman as Capt. Pigeon, Mr. Mackintosh as Dr. Jacks.

OLD CURIOSITY SHOP, THE// D 2a// Dram. by Edward Stirling fr novel of Charles Dickens// **Adelphi**, Nov. 1840.

OLD CURIOSITY SHOP, THE// D// Dram. fr novel of Charles Dickens// **Drury Lane**, Oct. 1853.

OLD CURIOSITY SHOP, THE// D// Dram. by Charles Dickens Jr., from his father's novel// **Opera Comique**, Jan. 1884.

OLD FLAME, AN// C// Adap. by W. T. Blackmore fr F, Le Passé de Nichette// **Gaiety**, Sept. 1882.

OLD FLAMES// F 3a// Adap. by Alfred Maltby fr F of Alexandre Bisson, No. 115, Rue Pigalle// **Opera Comique**, Feb. 1884.

OLD FOLKS, THE// C// Howard Paul// **Strand**, Sept. 1867.

OLD FORGE, THE// D 3a// Charles Osborne// **Gaiety**, June 1872.

OLD FOX INN, THE// D 3a// C. H. Hazlewood// **Britannia**, Aug. 1875.

OLD FRIENDS// C 1a// Violet Greville// **St. James's**, June 1890, with Laurence Cautley as Fitzroy, Gilbert Farquhar as Capt. Mowbray, Annie Irish as Alice, Marie Illington as Dolly.

OLD GARDEN, AN// C 1a// Hill Davies// **Terry's**, Nov. 1895, with W. J. Robertson as Brice, John Buckstone as Melville, Mona Oram as Mildred, Doris Templeton as Rose/ Prod. by Edward Terry.

OLD GENTLEMAN, THE// C 1a// Benjamin Webster// **Olympic**, Apr. 1837, with Frank Matthews as Oldham, James Vining as Nat, Charles Selby as Benedick, Miss Murray as Angelina, Mrs. Orger as Bell.

OLD GOOSEBERRY// F 1a// T. J. Williams// **Olympic**, Oct. 1869.

OLD GRIMEY; OR, LIFE IN THE BLACK COUNTRY// D Pro & 3a// J. M. Murlock// **Grecian**, Sept. 1872.

OLD GUARD, THE// D 1a// Dion Boucicault// **Princess's**, Oct. 1843, with Mr. Walton as Lord Beauville, Mr. Fitzjames as Lefebvre, Robert Honner as Rawson, Morris Barnett as Naverane, Miss Noel as Lady Beauville, Eugenie Prosper as Melanie/ **Haymarket**, July 1869, with Sol Smith as Haversack, Gaston Murray as Lord Beauville, Mr. Trafford as Henry, H. Naylor as Rawson, Mag Lewellyn as Melanie.

OLD HEADS AND YOUNG HEARTS// C 5a// Dion Boucicault// **Haymarket**, Nov. 1844, with Mr. Tilbury as Earl of Pompion, William Strickland as Col. Rocket, Henry Holl as Lord Roebuck, C. J. Mathews as Littleton Coke, Benjamin Webster as Tom Coke, J. B. Buckstone as Bob, William Farren as Jesse Rural, T. F. Mathews as Stripe, Mrs. W. Clifford as Countess of Pompion, Mme. Vestris as Lady Alice, Julia Bennett as Miss Rocket/ Scenery by George Morris.

OLD HOME, THE// C 3a// Robert Buchanan// **Vaudeville**, June 1899.

OLD HONESTY// C 2a// J. Maddison Morton// **Haymarket**, Apr. 1848, with Benjamin Webster as Michael Bradshaw, Henry Vandenhoff as Joseph Bradshaw, Henry Howe as Sir Perkins, Mr. Tilbury as Hook, Robert Keeley as Perch, Mrs. Julia Glover as Dame Bradshaw, Miss Reynolds as Mary/ Scenery by P. Phillips & George Morris.

OLD HOUSE AT HOME, THE (also titled, Our Old House at Home)// D 3a// J. Sterling Coyne// **Sad. Wells**, July 1840, with Mr. Elvin as Middleton, Henry Marston as Greenland, Henry Hall as Wright, J. W. Collier as Maybush, J. B. Hill as Rutley, Mr. Richardson as Jenkins, Mr. Dry as Davy, Mrs. Robert Honner as Fanny, Mrs. J. F. Saville as Sophy, Mrs. Richard Barnett as Becky, Miss Richardson as Mabel/ Scenery by F. Fenton/ Machines by B. Sloman/ Music by Isaac Collins/ Prod. by R. Honner; Mar. 1862 (in 2a), with Ernest Granville as Middleton, Mr. Meagreson as Greenland, Alfred Raynor as Wright, C. Walters as Maybush, Mr. Chapman as Rutley, Charles Seaton [Seyton?] as Jenkins, Jane Coveney as Fanny, Miss C. Phillips as Sophia, Miss Morelli as Betty/ **Grecian**, Nov. 1853, with Charles Horn as Middleton, Basil Potter as Greenland, Richard Phillips as Michael Wright, Charles Rice as Maybush, R. Power as Jemmy Jenkins, Edwin Dixon as Dark Davy, Jane Coveney as Fanny, Miss Morgan as as Sophia, Harriet Coveney as Becky, Ellen Crisp as Mabel; Sept. 1861, with John Manning, Alfred Rayner, Mr. Jackson, Henry Power, Walter Holland. George Gillett, Jane Coveney, Ellen Hale, Miss Johnstone, Mary A. Victor.

OLD JEW, AN// C 5a// Sidney Grundy// **Garrick**, Jan. 1894, with John Hare as Sterne, Gilbert Hare as Venables, W. L. Abingdon as Burnside, Eugene Mayeur as Craik, Charles Rock as Walsingham, G. W. Anson as Slater, William Day as Brewster, W. Scott Buist as Wandle, Gilbert Farquhar as Finucane, Herman de Lange as Polak, Gerald du Maurier as Fritz, Mrs. Theodore Wright as Mrs. Venables, Italia Conti as Eliza, Kate Rorke as Ruth/ Scenery by William Harford.

OLD JOE AND YOUNG JOE; OR, A MEMBER FOR THE BOROUGH// C 2a// John Courtney// **Surrey**, Oct. 1853/ **Grecian**, Jan. 1855, with Eaton O'Donnell as Beresford, F. Charles as Alfred, Richard Phillips as Young Joe, Basil Potter, Mr. Hamilton as Richard, Maria Simpson as Charlotte, Jane Coveney as Marion, Henry Grant as Dobbs, John Manning as Old Joe, Basil Potter as Martin.

OLD LADY, THE// C 3a// C. Haddon Chambers// **Criterion**, Nov. 1892, with Herbert Standing as Count de Chartres, Fred Kerr as Arathoon, Sydney Valentine as Barker, David James as McDoggerty, Herman de Lange as Croupier, Rosina Filippi as Mlle. le Grande, Ellis Jeffreys as Margery, Mrs. John Wood as Miss Lund/ Scenery by H. Potts.

OLD LONDON// D Pro & 3a// Dram. by Arthur Shirley & W. M. Tilson fr novel of Harrison Ainsworth// **Marylebone**, Aug. 1892.

OLD LONDON BRIDGE IN THE DAYS OF JACK SHEPPARD AND JONATHAN WILD// Dram. fr novel of Harrison Ainsworth// **Standard**, Mar. 1894.

OLD LOVE, THE// C 3a// J. S. Pigott// **Globe**, May 1900, with J. S. Pigott as Lord Melton, Mark Kinghorne as Sir Timothy, Sidney Brough as Rivers, F. H. Macklin as Brainsby, Frank Cooper as John Angerstein, Oswald Yorke as Cecil Angerstein, Cynthia Brooke as Mrs. Brainsby, Dora Barton as Minnie, Ethel Clinton as Mrs. Fleming.

OLD LOVE AND NEW FORTUNE// H. F. Chorley// **Surrey**, Feb. 1850.

OLD LOVE AND THE NEW, THE// C// Robert Sullivan// **Drury Lane**, Jan. 1851, with Mr. Cooper as Sir Algernon, Samuel Emery as Maj. Stock, James Anderson as Capt. Courtoun, Mr. Barrett as Haythorn, Stephen Artaud as Stubbs, Mrs. Ternan as Miss Trimmer, Louisa Nisbett as Camilla, Mrs. Walter Lacy as Cherry Bounce.

OLD LOVE AND THE NEW, THE// C 5a// Adap. by James Albery fr orig. of Bronson Howard// **Court**, Dec. 1879, with Charles Coghlan, Edmund Lethes, Arthur Dacre, David Fisher, Amy Roselle, Winifred Emery/ **Princess's**, July 1881, with Wilson Barrett as Stratton, Edmund Leathes as Comte de Carojac, Arthur Dacre as Kenyon, David Fisher as Westbrook, G. W. Anson as Phipps, Allen Thomas as Babbage, Neville Doone as Montvillais, C. Cathcart as Dr. Beaumarchais, Mary Eastlake as Lilian, Emmeline Ormsby as Florence, Miss M. A. Giffard as Aunt Fanny, Maud Clitherow as Natalie, Alice Cooke as Lisette/ Scenery by Walter Hann & Stafford Hall.

OLD MAIDS// C 5a// J. Sheridan Knowles// **Cov. Garden**, Oct. 1841, with C. J. Mathews as Sir Philip, Frank Matthews as Blount, John Pritt Harley as John, George Vandenhoff as Thomas, Walter Lacy as Robert, W. H. Payne as Stephen, Alfred Wigan as Jacob, John Ayliffe as Bernard, Robert Honner as Harris, Mme. Vestris as Lady Blanche, Louisa Nisbett as Lady Anne, Mrs. W. West as Mistress Blount, Mrs. Humby as Charlotte, Miss Lee as Jane/ Scenery by Grieve, T. Grieve & W. Grieve.

OLD MAID'S WOOING, AN// C 1a// Arnold Goldsworthy & E. B. Norman// **St. Geo. Hall**, Jan. 1888/ **Lyric**, July 1890, with E. B. Norman as Rev. Braithwaite, Ernest Hendrie as Higgins, Henry Bayntun as Gammon, Ethel Hope as Hester, Beatrice Ferrar as Naomi.

OLD MAIDS// C 5a// J. Sheridan Knowles// **Cov. Garden**, 1841.

OLD MAN, AN// D 2a// Robert Reece// **Duke's**, Mar. 1876.

OLD MAN'S BLESSING, AN// D// n.a.// **Gal. of Illust.**, June 1868.

OLD MAN'S BRIDE, THE; OR, THE MURDER AT NORWOOD VILLA// D 3a// Charles Webb// **Victoria**, Apr. 1844, with John Dale as Phillipson, William Seaman as Faulkner, Charles Freer as Grantly, Mr. James as Marlow, C. J. Bird as Trevor, Mr. Nantz as Smith, Smooth, and Tony, John Gardner as Laurel, Mr. Paul as Jack, Annette Vincent as Lucy, Miss Arden as Tattle/ Scenery by Mr. Morelli, Machines by Emmens, Wood & Foster/ **Grecian**, Nov. 1867, with Alfred Rayner as Graham, Charles Mortimer as Smith, William James as Faulkner, Samuel Perfitt as Trevor, John Manning as Honeysuckle, J. Jackson as Phillipson, Lizzie Mandelbert as Lucy, Mary A. Victor as Tattle.

OLD MAN'S DARLING, AN// C 1a// Henry Pettitt// **Grecian**, Nov. 1879.

OLD MASTER, AN// C 1a// Henry Arthur Jones// **Princess's**, Nov. 1880, with C. Garthorne, Harriet Coveney.

OLD MILL STREAM, THE// D// C. H. Hazlewood// **Britannia**, June 1875.

OLD MINT OF SOUTHWARK, THE// D// J. B. Johnstone// **Grecian**, Sept. 1863, with J. Jackson as Col. Walton, Walter Holland as Walton, Henry Grant as Kitely, Henry Power as Count Nobody, John Manning as Brand, J. Elphinstone as Steady, Mary A. Victor as Frank, Ellen Hale as Mabel, Miss Johnstone as Babet, Marie Brewer as Bella.

OLD MORTALITY; OR, THE HEIR OF MILNWOOD// D 3a// Dram. by W. E. Suter fr novel of Sir Walter Scott// **Sad. Wells**, Sept. 1869, with Mr. Stuart as Grahame, Edgar Newbound as Lord Evondale, Mr. Howard as Fairfax, T. W. Ford as Sgt. Bothwell, Mr. Goodwin as Corp. Halliday, Edmund Phelps as Morton, George Weston as Headrigg, Mr. Lacey as Grindsaw, J. G. Rosiere as Balfour, Mrs. E. F. Edgar as Lady Margaret, Margaret Eburne as Edith, Florence Gerald as Lady Emily, Julia Summers as Jeanie, Richard Edgar as Manse/ Scenery by William Gowrie, Machines by Mr. Hoare & Mr. Oats/ Music by T. Berry/ Prod. by Robert Edgar.

OLD OAK CHEST, THE// D// J. M. Scott// **Sad. Wells**, Sept. 1842, with C. J. Smith as Count Lanfranco, Mr. Lambe as Almanza, C. J. Bird as Rosalva, Mr. Williams as Nicholas di Lasso, Mr. Aldridge as Paulo di Lasso, John Herbert as Tinoco di Lasso, Mr. Dry as Rodolph, Charles Fenton as Shabrice, Miss Richardson as Adriana, Mrs. Richard Barnett as Roda.

OLD OFFENDER, AN// C 2a// Adap. by J. R. Planché fr F, Le Captaine Voleur// **Adelphi**, July 1859, with J. L. Toole, Mrs. Billington.

OLD, OLD STORY, THE; OR, THE FALL OF A SHATTERED FLOWER// D// Frederick Marchant// **Britannia**, Oct. 1868.

OLD PARR// D 2a// Mark Lemon// **Haymarket**, Oct. 1843, with William Farren as Parr, Robert Strickland as Kite, Mr. Stuart as Cheetham, J. B. Buckstone as Griffiths, James Worrell as Fairside, Julia Bennett as Mildred, Henry Howe as Earl of Arundel, Miss Conner as Mistress Loveall.

OLD PHIL HARDY// C 2a// George Conquest// **Grecian**, Aug. 1863, with J. Jackson as Capt. Rough, William James as Reckless, Henry Grant as Grip, George Conquest as Old Phil, Walter Holland as Harry, Mrs. Charles Dillon as Amy, Miss Johnstone as Mrs. Hardy.

OLD PHIL'S BIRTHDAY// C 2a// J. P. Wooler// **Strand**, Jan. 1862.

OLD RAG SHOP, THE// D Pro & 3a// Frederick Marchant// **Victoria**, Oct. 1869.

OLD SAILORS// C 3a// H. J. Byron// **Strand**, Oct. 1874.

OLD SCHOOL, THE// C 2a// n.a.// **Haymarket**, Feb. 1846, with Henry Holl as Duke de Choiseul, William Farren as Louis, A. Brindal as Capt. Saville, Mrs. W. Clifford as Countess of Bloomsbury, Mrs. Edwin Yarnold as Estelle.

OLD ST. PAULS; OR, THE THIRTEENTH CHIME// D 3a// n.a.// **Grecian**, July 1863, with W. Shirley as Sir Mark, Walter Holland as Albert, Henry Grant as Capt. Lisle, Charles Warner as Walter, Alfred Rayner as Cyprian, John Manning as Peter, Emma Robberds as Sybil, Miss Clarrisse as Maude.

OLD SALT, THE// D// John Besemeres ("John Daly")// **Strand**, Jan. 1868.

OLD SCAPEGOAT, AN// C 2a// "Austin Fryers"// **Imperial**, Nov. 1884.

OLD SCORE, AN// C 3a// W. S. Gilbert// **Gaiety**, July 1869.

OLD SCROOGE; OR, THE MISER'S DREAM// D 3a// Dram. fr Charles Dickens// **Sad. Wells**, Feb. 1844, with Henry Marston as Scrooge, C. J. Bird as Pleasant, Mr. Coreno as Cratchit, C. J. Smith as Christmas Present, Mr. Dry as Christmas Future, Mr. Williams as Marley, Caroline Rankley as Ellen, Mr. Richardson as Fezzewig, Miss Cooke as Mrs. Fezzewig, Mrs. Richard Barnett as Mrs. Cratchit, Miss Backhouse as Martha, Miss Stephens as Mrs. Pleasant, Mr. Lamb as Topper, Mr. Williamson as Old Joe, Mrs. Wilton as Mrs. Dibbler, Mrs. Andrews as Mrs. Mangle, Charles Fenton as Berry/ Scenery by F. Fenton/ Music by W. Montgomery/ Prod. by Henry Marston.

OLD SINNERS// D 4a// Adap. by James Mortimer fr F of Victorien Sardou, Les Vieux Garçons// **Gaiety**, June 1886.

OLD SOLDIER, THE// D 1a// Mark Lemon// **Haymarket**, June 1845, with A. Brindal as Sir Lionel, Mr. Tilbury as Cramp, William Farren as Lethersole, James Bland as Buff, Henry Howe as Bowyer, Mr. Harcourt as Quillet, Mrs. Stanley as Patience, Miss Telbin as Helen.

OLD SOLDIERS// C 3a// H. J. Byron// **Strand**, Jan. 1873.

OLD SONG, AN// D 1a// Freeman Wills & A. F. King// **Criterion**, Dec. 1896, with John Martin Harvey as de Lisle, Lionel Belmore as Ravachol, May Whitty as Sara, N. de Silva as Angele.

OLD SPADE GUINEA, THE; OR, KATE OF DOVER// D 2a// n.a.// **Victoria**, Jan. 1858, with John Dale as Conwell, Frederick Byefield as Seabold, Mr. Henderson as Morton, W. H. Pitt as Flint, F. H. Henry as Capt. Oakley, Mr. Hitchinson as Lt. Wilson, J. H. Rickards as Albatross, Jane Dawson as Kate, Miss Laporte as Polly.

OLD STEADY// D 4a// J. Mortimer Murdoch// **Pavilion**, Sept. 1881.

OLD STORY, THE// C 2a// H. J. Byron// **Strand**, Apr. 1861.

OLD TOLL HOUSE, THE// D// n.a.// **Marylebone**, Sept. 1861.

OLD TRUSTY// C 1a// Adap. by William Gowing ("Walter Gordon") fr F, Un Vieux de la Vieile Roche// **Olympic**, Jan. 1861, with Walter Gordon as Herbert Daventry, Gaston Murray as Lionel Daventry, Horace Wigan as Dingle, Mr. Addison as Briar, Miss Marston as Mrs. Daventry, Miss Evans as Patty, Mrs. W. S. Emden as Hutchinson.

OLDEST INHABITANT, THE// F 1a// n.a.// **Olympic**, Sept. 1850, with William Farren, Henry Compton, Charles Diddear, Mr. Norton, Miss Adams, Mrs. B. Bartlett, Ellen Turner.

OLISKA; OR, THE MILL OF GLARIS// D// n.a.// **Sad. Wells**, Nov. 1841, with Mr. Elvin as Count Vedalmar, Mr. Williams as Ulrick, John Herbert as Malcoff, J. W. Collier as Risler, Mr. Aldridge as Yermach, Miss Richardson as Oliska.

OLIVER CROMWELL'S SOFA// F// n.a.// **Queen's**, Dec. 1877.

OLIVER TWIST// D// Dram. fr Novel of Charles Dickens// **Adelphi**, Mar. 1839.

OLIVER TWIST// D 3a// Dram. by John Oxenford fr novel of Charles Dickens// **Queen's**, Apr. 1868.

OLIVER TWIST// D// Dram. fr novel of Charles Dickens// **Grecian**, May 1868, with Mary A. Victor as Oliver Twist, W. Shirley as Brownlow, Mr. Goodin as Sowerberry, Henry Grant as Bumble, Henry Power as Claypole, Samuel Perfitt as Monks, Charles Mortimer as Sykes, Thomas Mead as Fagin, John Manning as Dodger, Mr. Donne as Bates, Lizzie Mandelbert as Nancy, Mrs. Dearlove as Rose.

OLIVER TWIST// D// Dram. by J. B. Buckstone fr novel of Charles Dickens// **Surrey**, May 1868.

OLIVER TWIST// D// Dram. by John Mordaunt fr novel of Charles Dickens// **Alexandra**, Apr. 1869.

OLIVER TWIST// D 5a// Dram. by George Collingham fr novel of Charles Dickens// **Olympic**, Dec. 1891.

OLIVER TWIST; OR, THE PARISH BOY'S PROGRESS// D 3a// Dram. fr novel of Charles Dickens// **Pavilion**, May 1838/ **Sad. Wells**, Dec. 1838, with Mrs. Robert Honner as Oliver, Mr. Conquest as Bumble, Mrs. J. F. Saville as Mrs. Mann, Mr. Harwood as Sowerberry, Master Gardener as Claypole, Miss Pitt as Mrs. Sowerberry, Mrs. Harwood as Charlotte, J. W. Collier as Dawkins, Robert Honner as Fagin, Mr. Williams as Brownlow, Charles Montague as Crackit, Miss Pincott as Rose, Mr. Elvin as Monks/ **Victoria**, Sept. 1842, with Annette Vincent as Oliver Twist, E. F. Saville as Sykes, Miss Martin as Nance/ **Grecian**, Sept. 1855, with Harriet Coveney as Oliver Twist, Richard Phillips as Brownlow, T. Roberts as Grimwig, Mr. Melvin as Sowerberry, B. O. Conquest as Bumble, Basil Potter as Sikes, Mr. Hynes as Toby, F. Charles as Monks, George Conquest as the Artful Dodger, Jane Coveney as Nancy, Miss Chapman as Rose, Miss Johnstone as Mrs. Corney/ **Sad. Wells**, June 1857, with John Mordaunt as Brownlow, Mrs. Robert Honner as Oliver Twist, James Johnstone as Sikes, E. B. Gaston as Fagin, G. Pennett as Grimwig and Fang, Mr. Edwin as Sowerberry, John Gates as Bumble, John Hudspeth as Artful Dodger, G. B. Bigwood as Claypole, Miss Stewart as Nancy, Emma Barnett as Rose, Mrs. J. Gates as Mrs. Bumble, Miss Actman as Charlotte.

OLIVIA// Play 4a// Dram. by W. G. Wills fr novel of Oliver Goldsmith, The Vicar of Wakefield// **Court**, Mar. 1878, with Hermann Vezin, Frank Archer, William Terriss, Ellen Terry, Kate Aubrey/ **Lyceum**, May 1885, with Henry Irving as Dr. Primrose, Norman Forbes as Moses, William Terriss as Squire Thornhill, Frank Tyars as Leigh, Henry Howe as Flamborough, Miss L. Payne as Mrs. Primrose, Winifred Emery as Sophia, Ellen Terry as Olivia/ Scenery by Hawes Craven, William Cuthbert & S. Hall/ Music by Meredith Ball/ Machines by Mr. Knight; Apr. 1891; Jan. 1897; June 1900.

OMADHAUN, THE; OR, MY POOR DOG TRAY// D 3a// H. P. Grattan// **Sad. Wells**, Aug. 1841, with Mr. Aldridge as Godfrey, Mr. Elvin as Connelly, J. W. Collier as Sullivan, E. L. Blanchard as Patrick, Mr. Cony as Andy, Miss Richardson as Shelah, Mrs. Richard Barnett as Bridget, Miss Cooke as Cauth, Mrs. Morgan as Minny, Dog Hector as Dog Tray/ **Queen's**, Nov. 1877.

OMENS AND ODD COINCIDENCES// C 3a// Thomas Parry// **Haymarket**, June 1848, with William Farren as Token, Alfred Wigan as Gayhurst, Mr. Tilbury as Grubb, Robert Keeley as Foil, Henry Vandenhoff as Harlencourt, Mr. Rogers as Trace, A. Brindal as Mordax, Mrs. Nisbett as Mrs. Fitzmarshall, Mrs. Julia Glover as Miss Prune, Mrs. Humby as Mrs. Provender, Emma Harding as Emmeline, Mrs. Keeley as Susan/ Scenery by P. Phillips & George Morris.

OMNIBUS, THE; OR, A CONVENIENT DISTANCE// F 1a// Isaac Pocock// **Haymarket**, Aug. 1837, with T. F. Mathews as Ledger, Robert Strickland as Dobbs, J. B. Buckstone as Tom, Tyrone Power as Rooney, Miss E. Phillips as Julia, Mrs. Tayleure as Mrs. Dobbs, Miss Partridge as Miss Damper, Mrs. Gallot as Jemima/ **Cov. Garden**, Feb. 1838, with Robert Strickland as Ledger, George Bartley as Dobbs, Drinkwater Meadows as Tom Dobbs, Tyrone Power as Rooney, Miss E. Phillips as Julia, Mrs. Griffith as Mrs. Dobbs, Miss Seymour as Miss Damper, Mrs. Brown as Jemima/ **Sad. Wells**, May 1839, with T. F. Matthews as Ledger, Mr. Cullenford as Old Dobbs, Thomas Lee as Rooney, W. H. Oxberry as Tom Dobbs, Mrs. J. F. Saville as Julia, Miss Cooke as Mrs. Dobbs, Miss Norman as Miss Damper, Mrs. Phillips as Jemima/ **Grecian**, Nov. 1844, with Mr. Hodson as Pat Rooney, John Collett as Ledger, Frederick Robson as Tommy Dobbs, Mr. Campbell as Mr. Dobbs, Miss Merion as Mrs. Dobbs, Miss Johnstone as Julia; Mar 1856, with Henry Power as Old Ledger, Henry Grant as Dobbs, Thomas Lee as Rooney, John Manning as Tommy Dobbs, Ellen Hale as Julia, Miss Johnstone as Mrs. Dobbs./ **Olympic**, Aug. 1880, with Mr. Domican as Lodger, Mr. Medwin as Dobbs, Mr. Wilton as Tom Dobbs, Mr. Reynolds as Rooney, Miss R. Dudley as Julia, Miss Brindly as Mrs. Dobbs.

ON ACTIVE SERVICE// D// Herbert Leonard// **Surrey**, Oct. 1899.

ON AN ISLAND// C 1a// J. W. Jones// **Vaudeville**, Feb. 1882.

ON AND OFF// F 1a// T. J. Williams// **Strand**, June 1861.

ON AND OFF// C 3a// Adap. by Catherine Riley fr F of Alexandre Bisson, Le Contrôleur des Wagons-Lits// **Vaudeville**, Dec. 1898, with George Giddens as George Godfray, Paul Arthur as Alfred Godfray, William Wyes as Randolphe, Harry Cane as Martel, George Arliss as Brumaire, J. L. MacKay as du Patty, Elliott Page as Madelaine, Elsie Chester as Mme. Brumaire, Lucie Milner as Rosa, Robertha Erskine as Mme. Martel, Marie Yorke as Lizette, Evelyn Harrison as Julie/ Scenery by William Harford.

ON BAIL// F 3a// Adap. by W. S. Gilbert fr F, Le Reveillon// **Criterion**, Feb. 1877.

ON 'CHANGE// F 3a// Adap. by Eweretta Lawrence fr G of G. von Moser, Ultimo// **Strand**, July 1885, with William Farren, Yorke Stephens, David Fisher, Robertha Erskine, Harriet Coveney, Lottie Venne, Mary Burton/ **Toole's**, Aug. 1885/ **Strand**, Feb. 1896.

ON DUTY// D 2a// n.a.// **Lyceum**, Apr. 1845, with Frank Matthews as Baron Saldorf, Frederick Vining as Count Lowenstein, Robert Keeley as Fritz, Edwin Yarnold as Schwartz, Mrs. Woollidge as Mme. Deutelle, Miss Villars as Henrietta.

ON GUARD// C 3a// W. S. Gilbert// **Court**, Oct. 1871.

ON LEAVE// F 3a// Adap. fr F of M. Sylvane & Jean Gascoigne, Le Sursis// **Avenue**, Apr. 1897.

ON PROBATION// C 4a// Brander Matthews & G. H. Jessop// **Elephant & Castle**, Sept. 1889.

ON STRIKE// Play// Arthur à Beckett// **Court**, Oct. 1873.

ON THE CARDS// C 3a// Adap. fr F, L'Escamoteur// **Gaiety**, Dec. 1868.

ON THE JURY// D 4a// Watts Phillips// **Princess's**, Dec. 1871, with Samuel Phelps as Sanderson, Benjamin Webster as Tibbetts, J. G. Shore as Robert Sanderson, Henry Forrester as Curlett, Henry Ashley as Prof. Schmidt, Theresa Furtado as Edith, Miss F. Lynd as Rosa, Julia Daly as Miss Nippingale, Miss Hudspeth as Tilda, Jenny Lovell as Miss Winch.

ON THE SLY// F 1a// J. Maddison Morton// **Haymarket**, Oct. 1864, with J. B. Buckstone as Dibbits, Mr. Rogers as Maj. Growler, Walter Gordon as Wagstaff, Miss Snowdon as Mrs. Dibbits, Mrs. Edward Fitzwilliam as Martha.

ON THE TILES// F 1a// Edward Stirling// **Surrey**, Apr. 1846.

ON THE TRACK// D 4a// Edward Towers// **East London**, Nov. 1877.

ON TOAST// C 1a// Fred Horner// **Avenue**, July 1888/ **Toole's**, Oct. 1889.

ON TOUR// C// Adap. by James Mortimer fr F// **Strand**, Mar. 1886.

ONCE AGAIN// C// Ernest Cuthbert// **Vaudeville**, Jan. 1879.

ONCE AGAIN// C 1a// F. W. Broughton & George Browne// **Toole's**, Aug. 1885.

ONCE UPON A TIME// Play 4a// Adap. by L. N. Parker & H. B. Tree fr G of Ludwig Fulda, Der Talisman// **Haymarket**, Mar. 1894, with Herbert Beerbohm Tree as The King, Luigi Lablache as Berengar, Nutcombe Gould as Diomede, Gilbert Farquhar as Niccola, Charles Allan as Stefano, Holman Clark as Panfilio, Fred Terry as Omar, Lionel Brough as Habakuk, Julia Neilson as Magdalena, Mrs. Beerbohm Tree as Rita/ Scenery by Walter Hann, Music by C. Armbruster.

ONE BLACK SPOT// D 2a// C. H. Hazlewood// **Britannia**, Apr. 1870.

ONE CRIME, THE; OR, THE ADVOCATE OF ROUEN AND THE PRESIDENT'S DAUGHTER// D 3a// Adap. fr F by Thompson Townsend// **Sad. Wells**, Jan. 1839, with Mr. Cathcart as Loubet, Mr. Conquest as Nolis, Mr. Harwood as Fontenelle, Mr. Elvin as Capt. de Bionville, Mrs. Robert Honner as Marchioness de Pontarlier, Miss Pincott as Louise, Dibdin Pitt as President/ Scenery by Fenwick & Smithyes/ Machines by B. Sloman.

ONE FALSE STEP// D 1a// W. J. Mackay// **Sad. Wells**, Feb. 1893.

ONE FALSE STEP; OR, THE PERILS OF A BEAUTY// D 4a// Walter Travers// **Pavilion**, July 1874.

ONE FOR HIS NOB; OR, 39 HONEYSUCKLE VILLAS, N.W.// C// E. Manuel// **Britannia**, Feb.1874.

ONE GOOD TURN DESERVES ANOTHER// C 2a// J. Maddison Morton// **Princess's**, Nov. 1862, with George Vining as Topper, W. H. Stephens as Sir Timothy, Charles Seyton as Capt. Fritterly, Amy Sedgwick as Phoebe, Marian Jones as Lady Clementina, Mrs. Henry Marston as Mrs. Woodpecker.

ONE HOUR; OR, A CARNIVAL BALL// C// T. H. Bayly// **Haymarket**, June 1838, with C. J. Mathews as Swiftly, John Brougham as O'Leary, Mrs. Gallot as Mrs. Bevil, Miss Gallot as Mrs. Smith, Mme. Vestris as Miss Dalton/ **Drury Lane**, June 1839, with C. J. Mathews as Swiftly, John Brougham as O'Leary, Mrs. Macnamara as Mrs. Bevil, Miss Lee as Mrs. Smith, Mme. Vestris as Miss Dalton/ **Cov. Garden**, Oct. 1839, with C. J. Mathews as Swiftly, John Brougham as O'Leary, Mrs. Macnamara as Mrs. Bevil, Miss Lee as Miss Smith, Mme. Vestris as Miss Dalton/ **Princess's**, Mar. 1846, with C. J. Mathews as Swiftly, Mr. Collins as O'Leary, Mrs. Fosbroke as Mrs. Bevil, Miss Grey as Fanny, Mme. Vestris as Miss Dalton.

ONE HUNDRED AND TWO; OR, THE VETERAN AND HIS PROGENY// D 1a// H. M. Milner// **Drury Lane**, June 1838, with William Davidge as Gabois, W. Bennett as Jerome, R. McIan as Pierre, Henry Compton as Francois, Mrs. Anderson as Isabel, Mrs. Brindal as Mme. Lerond, Miss Hatton as Louise.

£100 NOTE, THE// F// R. B. Peake// **Haymarket**, Sept. 1837, with Frederick Vining as Montmorency, J. W. Gough as Paperfund, T. F. Mathews as James, Tyrone Power as O'Shocknessy, Robert Strickland as Morgan, Benjamin Webster as Black, Mrs. Waylett as Mrs. Arlington, Mrs. Tayleure as Lady Pedigree/ **Cov. Garden**, Feb. 1843, with James Vining as Montmorency, Drinkwater Meadows as Morgan, Frank Matthews as Janus, Alfred Wigan as O'Shaugnessy, John Pritt Harley as Black, Mr. Granby as Paperfund, W. H. Payne as Bilker, Mrs. Tayleure as Lady Pedigree, Mrs. H. P. Grattan as Harriet, Miss Lee as Honoria/ **Sad. Wells**, Nov. 1838, with J. Lee as Montmorency, J. W. Collier as O'Shocknessy,

Mr. Williams as Morgan, Dibdin Pitt as Janus, Mr. Conquest as Blank, Miss E. Honner as Miss Arlington, Mrs. J. F. Saville as Mrs. Darlington, Miss Cooke as Lady Pedigree; Feb. 1850, with William Hoskins as Montmorency, Mr. Williams as Janus, A. Younge as Morgan, Henry Nye as Black, Henry Mellon as O'Shaughnessey, William Belford as Paperfund, Charles Fenton as Bilker, Mrs. G. Smith as Lady Pedigree, Miss Fitzpatrick as Harriet, Miss Johnstone as Mrs. Arlington/ **Grecian** Oct. 1857, with Richard Phillips as Montmorency, Henry Power as Morgan, Mr. Coleman as Paperfund, Henry Grant as Janus, George Conquest as Billy Black, Eaton O'Donnell as Grady, Miss Johnstone as Harriet; Sept 1862 with William James as Montmorency, George Conquest as Billy Black, Henry Power as Morgan, Walter Holland as Janus, Mary A. Victor as Harriet, Ellen Hale as Mrs. Arlington, Miss Johnstone as Lady Pedigree.

117 ARUNDEL STREET, STRAND// F 1a// H. R. Addison// **Lyceum**, Mar. 1860, with Walter Lacy as Charles Ludlow, John Rouse as Belton, Kate Saville as Mrs. Ludlow, Mrs. Keeley as Betsy, Mrs. H. Campbell as Mrs. Smith.

£100 A-SIDE// F// J. R. Brown// **Sad. Wells**, as Blower Jones, Feb. 1881/ **Pavilion**, Dec. 1890.

ONE HUNDRED YEARS AGO// D// n.a.// **Olympic**, July 1875.

ONE LAW FOR MAN// F pro & 2a// Adap. by Charles Brookfield fr F of Paul Hervieu, La Loi de l'Homme// **Criterion**, Dec. 1899, with Norman McKinnel as Sylvester, Hermann Vezin as Gen. Blaney, C. M. Lowne as Cottrell, Duncan McRae as Hugh Blaney, Lawrance d'Orsay as Torrington, A. C. Grand as Doughty, Lottie Venne as Fannie, Keith Wakeman as Lady Blaney, Muriel Varna as Eva.

ONE O'CLOCK; OR, THE KNIGHT AND THE WOOD DEMON// D 3a// n.a.// **Victoria**, June 1843, with Miss Wilton as Leolyn, E. F. Saville as Hardyknute, Mr. James as Guelpho, John Gardner as Willikind, William Seaman as Oswy, C. Williams as Auriol, John Dale as Sangrida, Miss Ridgeway as Clotilde, Miss Saddler as Pauline, Mrs. George Lee as Una.

ONE OF OUR GIRLS// C 4a// Bronson Howard// **Elephant & Castle**, Nov. 1885.

ONE OF THE BEST// D 4a// Seymore Hicks & George Edwardes// **Adelphi**, Dec. 1895, with William Terriss as Dudley Keppel, W. L. Abingdon as Ellsworth, Charles Fulton as Gen. Coventry, J. D. Beveridge as Sir Archibald, Julian Cross as Dr. Penrose, L. Delorme as de Gruchy, Miss Millward as Esther, Edith Ostlere as Mary, Miss Vane Featherston as Kitty/ Scenery by Joseph Harker, Bruce Smith, & W. Harford/ Music by John Crook/ Prod. by Fred Latham/ **Princess's**, June 1899.

ONE SUMMER'S DAY// C 3a// H. V. Esmond// **Comedy**, Sept. 1897, with Charles Hawtrey as Maj. Rudyard, Henry Kemble as Bendyshe, Cosmo Stuart as Marsden, Ernest Hendrie as Hoddesden, Kenneth Douglas as Tom, Lyston Lyle as Seth, Eva Moore as Maysie, Lettice Fairfax as Irene, Constance Collier as Chiara, Mrs. Charles Calvert as Mrs. Bendyshe/ Scenery by Walter Hann.

ONE SUMMER'S NIGHT// C 1a// F. W. Broughton// **Comedy**, Nov. 1889.

ONE TOO MANY// F 1a// Desmond Ryan// **Princess's**, Apr. 1872.

ONE TOO MANY FOR HIM// F 1a// T. J. Williams// **Olympic**, Feb. 1868, with C. J. Mathews as de Walker, Henry Ashley as Brompton, Mrs. Caulfield as Euphemia/ **Surrey**, Feb. 1868.

ONE TOUCH OF NATURE// C 1a// Benjamin Webster// **Adelphi**, Aug. 1859; Mar. 1871, with Benjamin Webster as Pen Holder, John Billington as Fletcher, Henry Ashley as Belgrave, Harwood Cooper as Jones, Miss Furtado as Constance Belmour/ **St. James's**, Mar. 1864, with Benjamin Webster as Penn Holder, Henry Ashley as Fletcher, H. J. Montague as Belgrave, Henrietta Simms as Constance/ **Olympic**, May 1869, with Benjamin Webster as William Penn Holder, H. Vaughan as Fletcher, W. H. Eburne as Belgrave, Miss Furtado as Constance.

ONE TREE HILL// D 2a// H. T. Craven// **Strand**, Apr. 1865/ **Royalty**, Apr. 1865.

ONE TREE SQUARE// D// Dram. fr tale publ. in "New Bells"// **Grecian**, Apr. 1865, with J. B. Steele as Sewerly, Mr. Allison as Lindsay, David Jones as Shearman, Henry Power as Bob, Marie Brewer as Eugenie, Louise Graham as Mrs. Warjuice, William James as Barrington, J. Jackson as Jarvis, Lizzie Mandlebert as Emeline.

ONLY A CLOD// C 1a// J. Palgrave Simpson// **Lyceum**, May 1851, with C. J. Mathews as Thorncote, Mr. Bellingham as Sir Cyril, Robert Roxby as Babbleton, William Suter as Owlet, Miss M. Oliver as Grace/ **Sad. Wells**, Apr. 1855, with Frederic Robinson as Thorncote, Gaston Murray as Beaumorris, Robert Roxby as Babbleton, Mr. Templeton as Owlet, Miss M. Oliver as Mrs. Thorncote/ **St. James's**, Oct. 1867, with Henry Irving as Thorncote, Walter Joyce as Sir Cyril, G. W. Blake as Babbleton, J. H. Allen as Owlet, Eleanore Bufton as Grace.

ONLY A DREAM// Play 1a.// Jocylyn Brandon// **Criterion**, Dec. 1888.

ONLY A HALFPENNY// F 1a// John Oxenford// **Haymarket**, June 1855, with J. B. Buckstone as Jones, W. H. Chippendale as Plantagenet, Ada Swanborough as Henrietta, Ellen Chaplin as Bridget/ **Sad. Wells**, Apr. 1856, with Mr. Barrett as Plantagenet, J. B. Buckstone as Jones, Miss M. Oliver as Henrietta, Miss Cuthbert as Bridgett/ **St. James's** Nov. 1870, with Miss Adair as Henrietta, Sallie Turner as Bridget, A. W. Young as Jones, G. P. Grainger as Plantagenet.

ONLY A HEAD; OR, THE HEMPEN CRAVAT// D 4a// Edgar Newbound// **Britannia**, Nov. 1880.

ONLY A PLAYER// C// Daniel Bandmann// **Princess's**, Mar. 1873.

ONLY A SHILLING// D 3a// W. H. Abel// **Pavilion**, Apr. 1872.

ONLY FOR LIFE; OR, A CONVICT'S CAREER// D// C. H. Hazlewood// **Britannia**, Aug. 1877.

ONLY MY COUSIN// C// Edgar Newbound// **Britannia**, Apr. 1880.

ONLY THREE YEARS AGO// Play 1a// C. H. Dickinson// **Duke of York's**, Nov. 1898, with W. R. Staveley as Meredith, F. J. Nettlefold as Wilson, J. Cooke-Beresford as Lord Archdall, Graeme Goring as Emmett, Winifred Fraser as Kate.

ONLY WAY, THE: A TALE OF TWO CITIES// D Pro & 4a// Dram. by Freeman Wills fr novel of Charles Dickens// **Lyceum**, Feb. 1899, with John Martin Harvey as Sydney Carton, Holbrook Blinn as Defarge, J. G. Taylor as Lorry, Sam Johnson as Stryver, Frederick Everill as Dr. Manette, Herbert Sleath as Darnay, Frank Tyars as President, Frank Vernon as Prosecutor, Ben Webster as Comte de Fauchet, Grace Warner as Lucy, Alice Marriott as The Vengeance/ Scenery by Joseph Harkins, Walter Hann & Hawes Craven/ Music by Hamilton Clarke/ **Apollo**, May 1901.

OONAGH// D 5a// Edmund Falconer// **Her Majesty's**, Nov. 1866.

OPAL RING, THE// C 2a// Adap. by G. W. Godfrey fr F of Octave Feuillet, Péril en la Demeure// **Court**, Jan. 1885, with John Clayton, Arthur Cecil, H. B. Conway, Marion Terry, Lydia Foote.

OPEN GATE, THE// D 1a// C. Haddon Chambers// **Comedy**, Mar. 1887.

OPEN HOUSE; OR, THE TWIN SISTERS// F// J. B. Buckstone// **Haymarket**, June 1837, with Frederick Vining as Villers, Charles Selby as Foster, Benjamin Webster as Tod, Mr. Ross as Jacob, Robert Strickland as Matcher, T. F. Mathews as White, Mrs. Julia Glover as Mrs. Matcher, Mrs. Humby as Jane, Eliza Vincent as Fanny, Mrs. Tayleure as Mrs. Pocock.

OPEN HOUSE// F 3a// H. J. Byron// **Vaudeville**, Apr. 1885, with William Farren Jr., Cissy Crahame, Kate Phillips.

OPEN TO CONVICTION// F 1a// Robert Brough// **Adelphi**, Jan. 1870, with George Belmore as Pheeble, C. H. Stephenson as Popthorne, C. J. Smith as Jogmerton, J. D. Beveridge as Brown, Miss Lennox Grey as Arabella, Mrs. Leigh Murray as Mrs. Bright.

OPERA CLOAK, THE// C 1a// L. D. Powles & Augustus Harris// **Drury Lane**, Aug. 1883, with Harry Jackson as Malt, Henry George as O'Brien, William Morgan as Fitz-Jones, Fanny Enson as Mrs. Malt, Mary A. Victor as Mrs. Abinger-Smith, John Ridley as Abinger-Smith, Harry Nicholls as Kettle, Alice Denvil as Mrs. O'Brien, Lillie Young as Lucy, Addie Gray as Mary/ **Royalty**, Jan. 1890, with J. Wilson as Malt, John Clulow as Smith, Guy Fane as Jones, G. B. Prior as Kettle, Augustus Wheatman as O'Bruin, Hettie Bennett as Mrs. Malt, Amy Liddon as Mrs. Smith, Miss G. Price as Mrs. O'Bruin, Kate Price as Lucy.

OPPOSITE NEIGHBORS// F 1a// Howard Paul// **Strand**, July 1854.

ORANGE BLOSSOMS// C 1a// J. P. Wooler// **Strand**, Feb. 1862.

ORANGE GIRL, THE// D Pro & 3a// Henry Leslie & Nicholas Rowe// **Surrey**, Oct. 1864/ **Grecian**, May 1865, with David Jones as Fryer, Henry Grant as ----, W. Shirley as Langley, Lizzie Mandelbert as Jane, Mary A. Victor as Sally, Marie Brewer as Ellie, John Manning as Gyngell, Henry Power as Partridge, William James as Underwood, J. Jackson as Frost, Laura Conquest as Jenny/ **East London**, May 1870.

ORDEAL BY TOUCH// C 5a// Richard Lee// **Queen's**, May 1872.

ORDER OF THE NIGHT, THE; OR, TWENTY YEARS OF A SOLDIER'S LIFE// D// Thomas Mead// **Elephant & Castle**, Sept. 1873.

ORGAN OF ORDER, THE// F 1a// n.a.// **Haymarket**, June 1839, with William Farren as Primshaw, Robert Strickland as Prankley, Mrs. Danson as Mrs. Prankley, Mrs. Fitzwilliam as Mme. Rosignol, Mrs. Gallot as Mrs. Fitchet, Miss Mattley as Mrs. Brown.

ORGANIC AFFECTION, AN// F 1a// Mrs. Alfred Phillips// **Olympic**, Jan. 1852, with Henry Compton as Bun, George Cooke as Doctor, Mr. Norton as Longwind, John Kinloch as Fleecemraw, Mrs. Alfred Phillips as Mlle. Jolliejambe, Mrs. Julia Glover as Penelope.

ORIANA// C 3a// James Albery// **Globe**, Feb. 1873.

ORIENT EXPRESS, THE// C 3a// Adap. by F. C. Burnand fr G of Oscar Blumenthal & Gustav Kadelburg, Die Orient Reise// **Daly's**, Oct. 1893, with James Lewis as Jellaby, George Clarke as Dioskobobulus, W. G. Elliott as Featherston, E. Allan Aynesworth as Trevor, William Owen as Sir Jasper, Herbert Gresham as Glibb, Ada Rehan as Hettie, Mrs. G. H. Gilbert as Mrs. Jellaby, Isabel Irving as Nina, Catherine Lewis as Katrina, Adelaide Sterling as Frances/ Scenery by Walter Johnstone/ Electrics by F. Hinton/ Prod. by Augustin Daly.

ORIGINAL, THE// F 1a// J. Maddison Morton// **Cov. Garden**, Nov. 1837, with George Bartley as Col. Detonator, Drinkwater Meadows as

Sir Jacob, James Anderson as Mowbray, Mr. Vining as Nonpareil, Edwin Yarnold as Solomon, Priscilla Horton as Emily/ **Sad. Wells**, Mar. 1842, with Mr. Williams as Col. Detonator, P. Williams as Sir Jacob, Mr. Moreton as Mowbray, John Webster as Nonpareil, Mrs. Richard Barnett as Emily.

ORLANDO THE OUTCAST; OR, THE KNIGHT OF THE SILVER CROSS// D// n.a.// **Grecian**, Sept. 1863, with Thomas Mead as Orlando, Alfred Rayner as Manfred, Walter Holland as Lodovic, W. Shirley as de Castro, George Gillett as de Modena, William James as Theodore, F. Smithson as Gaston, John Manning as Perez, Clara Middleton as Princess Rosabella, Mary A. Victor as Lucetta, Marie Brewer as Cynthia, Miss Johnstone as Hyppolita/ Scenery by C. Smithers/ Machines by Mr. Smithers Sr./ Music by W. Edroff.

ORPHAN HEIRESS, THE// D 4a// Arthur Jefferson// **Surrey**, Sept. 1899.

ORPHAN OF GLENCOE, THE// D// J. Parselle// **Sad. Wells**, Dec. 1863, with W. D. Gresham as Drummond, George Fisher as McDougal, Miss Mandelbert as Effie.

ORPHAN'S LEGACY, THE; OR, A MOTHER'S DYING WORDS// D 4a// Adolphe Fancquez// **Grecian**, June 1867, with Henry Grant as Bourdonnais, John Gardiner as Charles, Alfred Rayner as Martin, Charles Mortimer as Carton, John Manning as Chaffinch, Mary A. Victor as Cecile, Miss De Lacie as Lizzy, Mrs. Atkinson as Dame Rivere.

ORPHANS, THE; OR, THE BRIDGE OF NOTRE DAME// D 4a// Adap. by Arthur Shirley & C. H. Longdon fr F// **Pavilion**, July 1898.

ORSON// C// H. P. Grattan// **Adelphi**, Aug. 1876.

OSCAR AND MALVINA// D// n.a.// **Victoria**, Oct. 1846, with F. C. Courtney as Cathullin, Walter Searle as Morren, C. J. Bird as Conlath, F. H. Henry as Brian, Mr. Fitzjames as Dronadhu, Mrs. Henry Vining as Morna, F. Wilton as King Fingal, Alfred Raymond as Oscar, Mr. Archer as Toscar, James Ranoe as Ruro, J. Howard as Starno, Miss Fielding as Matrina, Lydia Pearce as Cathlin.

OSTLER AND THE ROBBER, THE; OR, THE MURDER AT THE LONE INN// see Innkeeper of Abbeville.

OSTLER'S VISION, THE// D// Alfred Rayner// **Grecian**, Sept. 1861, with Henry Grant as The Guest, Walter Holland as Frothwell, Alfred Rayner as Isaac, William James as Wilfred, John Manning as Cobbs, R. H. Lingham as Rigby, Jane Coveney as Rebecca, Ellen Hale as Hester, Miss Chapman as Nelly, Miss Johnstone as Mrs. Scratchard.

OSWALD THE BRIGAND// D 3a// n.a.// **Sad. Wells**, Aug. 1857, with Mr. Gladstone as Walmer, R. Green as Goldstadt, Mr. Wakely as Largent, Mr. Testo as Poverall, George Clair as Oswald, Mr. Lyon as La Loup, Charles Seyton as Herman, John Chester as Bumps, Mrs. E. F. Saville as The Countess, Kate May as Caroline, Miss Chapman as Minette.

OTHELLO, THE MOOR OF VENICE// T// William Shakespeare// **Drury Lane**, Feb. 1837, with Mr. Baker as Duke, Mr. Mathews as Brabantio, Edwin Forrest as Othello, Mr. Warde as Iago, Mr. Cooper as Cassio, Mr. Hooper as Roderigo, A. Brindal as Montano, Miss Taylor as Desdemona, Miss Huddart as Emilia; May 1838, with Mr. Baker as Duke, H. Cooke as Brabantio, Charles Fenton as Gratiano, Charles Kean as Othello, Mr. Ternan as Iago, Mr. Cooper as Cassio, A. Brindal as Roderigo, Mr. King as Montano, F. Cooke as Lodovico, Miss Allison as Desdemona, Mrs. Ternan as Emilia/ Scenery by Grieve, T. Grieve & W. Grieve; Sept. 1853, with Mr. Evans as Duke, George Bennett as Brabantio, G. V. Brooke as Othello, E. L. Davenport as Iago, Mr. Leslie as Roderigo, Mr. Moorhouse as Ludovico, Frederick Belton as Cassio, Mr. Hustleby as Antonio, Mr. Harcourt as Gratiano, Miss Anderton as Desdemona, Mrs. Leslie as Emilia; Oct. 1861, with G. V. Brooke as Othello, Edwin Dixon as Duke, Henry Mellon as Brabantio, Mr. Hope as Gratiano, Frank Barsby as Ludovico, H. Farrell as Montano, R. Younge as Iago, J. Rogers as Cassio, Robert Roxby as Roderigo, T. Matthews as Antonio, Henrietta Sims as Desdemona, Mrs. W. Sidney as Emilia; Mar. 1869, with James Johnstone as Duke, Mr. Barrett as Brabantio, Samuel Phelps as Othello, Charles Dillon as Iago, James Lickfold as Gratiano, Alfred Nelson as Roderigo, Henry Sinclair as Cassio, W. C. Temple as Lodovico, Caroline Heath as Desdemona, Fanny Huddart as Emelia [sic]/ Scenery by William Beverley; May 1881, with John McCullough as Othello, Hermann Vezin as Iago, John Ryder as Brabantio, J. H. Barnes as Cassio, Augustus Harris as Roderigo, A. L. Baron as Duke, Bella Pateman as Desdemona, Mrs. Arthur Stirling as Emelia [sic]/ **Sad. Wells**, May 1837, with Mr. King as Duke, John Ayliffe as Brabantio, Mr. Bishop as Gratiano, Mr. Scarbrow as Ludovico, Mr. Cobham Jr. as Othello, C. H. Pitt as Cassio, J. B. Booth as Iago, Miss Melville as Desdemona, Miss Williams as Emilia; Mar. 1840, with Mr. Archer as Othello, Henry Marston as Iago, Mr. Dry as Brabantio, Robert Honner as Roderigo, Mr. Elvin as Cassio, W. D. Broadfoot as Duke, Mrs. Robert Honner as Desdemona, Miss Richardson as Emilia; June 1844, with Edward Knight as Duke, H. Lacy as Brabantio, Charles Morelli as Gratiano, Mr. Raymond as Ludovico, Samuel Phelps as Othello, Charles Hudson as Cassio, Henry Marston as Iago, John Webster as Roderigo, Miss Cooper as Desdemona, Mrs. Mary Warner as Emilia/ Scenery by F. Fenton & Mr. Morelli; Sept. 1880, with G. Canninge as Duke, Mr. Durham as Brabantio, Mr. Graeme as Gratiano, Mr. Wheatcroft as Ludovico, Charles Aarner as Othello, E. H. Brooke as Cassio, Hermann Vezin as Iago, Walter Brooks as Roderigo, Isabel Bateman as Desdemona, Mrs. Charles Calvert as Emilia/ **Haymarket**, June 1837, with W. C. Macready as Othello, E. W. Elton as Iago, Frederick Vining as Cassio, J. W. Gough as Duke, Mr. Haines as Brabantio, Benjamin

Webster as Roderigo, Mr. Saville as Lodovico, James Worrell as Gratiano, John Webster as Montano, Miss Allison as Desdemona, Miss Huddart as Emilia; Sept. 1837, with Samuel Phelps as Othello; July 1839, with Charles Kean as Othello, Mr. Cooper as Iago, Charles Perkins as Brabantio, Mr. Hemming as Montano, Walter Lacy as Cassio, A. Brindal as Roderigo, J. W. Gough as Duke, Mrs. Walter Lacy (Miss Taylor) as Desdemona, Mrs. Julia Glover as Emilia; Jan. 1842, with J. W. Gough as Duke, Henry Wallack as Brabantio, James Worrell as Gratiano, James Wallack as Othello, Mr. Vining as Cassio, John Webster as Rodorigo [sic], Mr. Stuart as Iago, Helen Faucit as Desdemona, Mrs. W. Clifford as Emilia; Feb. 1849, with A. Brindal as Duke, Mr. Rogers as Brabantio, J. W. Gough as Gratiano, Henry Vandenhoff as Ludovico, James Wallack as Othello, Charles Kean as Iago, William Creswick as Cassio, Alfred Wigan as Roderigo, Laura Addison as Desdemona, Mrs. Charles Kean as Emilia; Mar. 1851, with Mr. Rogers as Duke, Mr. Stuart as Brabantio, James Bland as Gratiano, Mr. Caulfield as Ludovico, J. William Wallack as Othello, Henry Howe as Cassio, James Wallack as Iago, Charles Selby as Roderigo, Miss Reynolds as Desdemona, Laura Addison as Emilia; Aug. 1865, with J. Neville as Duke, Ira Aldridge as Othello, Walter Montgomery as Iago, John Vollaire as Brabantio, Lewis Wingfield as Roderigo, James Fernandez as Cassio, Alfred Raymond as Ludovico, John Collett as Gratiano, Madge Robertson as Desdemona, Miss Atkinson as Emilia; May 1892, with Edmund Tearle as Othello, Charles Pond as Iago, James Cooke as Duke, Arthur Lennard as Gratiano, Alfred Paumier as Montano, Frederick Scarth as Cassio, R. Parlby as Antonio, Naomi Hope as Emilia, Kate Clinton as Desdemona/ **Cov. Garden,** Oct. 1837, with W. C. Macready, Samuel Phelps, James Anderson, Helen Faucit, Miss Huddart; Nov. 1838, with W. C. Macready, John Vandenhoff, James Anderson, Mrs. Mary Warner, Helen Faucit, Henry Howe, John Cooper, Walter Lacy, Samuel Phelps; May 1842, with James Anderson; Feb. 1845, with Henry Betty as Othello, Mr. Rae as Duke, George Vandenhoff as Iago, Mr. Archer as Cassio, James Vining as Roderigo, George Braid as Montano, Mr. Lee as Ludovico, Mr. Rogers as Brabantio, Miss Vandenhoff as Desdemona, Mrs. W. Watson as Emilia/ **Princess's,** Feb. 1845, with Edwin Forrest as Othello, Frank Graham as Iago, Henry Wallack as Cassio, Walter Lacy as Roderigo, James Ranoe as Duke, Mr. Granby as Brabantio, Mr. Fitzjames as Montano, Augustus Harris as Ludovico, Robert Honner as Gratiano, Charlotte Cushman as Emilia, Mrs. Stirling as Desdemona; May 1860, with Edmund Garden as Duke, Frank Graham as Brabantio, John Collett as Gratiano, Samuel Phelps as Othello, Harcourt Bland as Cassio, John Ryder as Iago, J. G. Shore as Roderigo, Caroline Heath as Desdemona, Miss Atkinson as Emilia; Mar. 1862, with Edmund Garden as Doge, Basil Potter as Brabantio, John Ryder as Othello, Charles Fechter as Iago, George Jordan as Cassio, J. G. Shore as Roderigo, Carlotta Leclercq as Desdemona, Rose Leclercq as Bianca, Miss Elsworthy as Emilia; June 1863, with J. G. Warde as Duke, Mr. Fitzjames as Brabantio, Mr. Brooke as Gratiano, Walter Montgomery as Othello, Henry Marston as Iago, Charles Verner as Cassio, Robert Roxby as Roderigo, Miss E. Terrey as Desdemona, Miss Atkinson as Emilia; Sept. 1873, with Mr. Dolman as Duke, H. Russell as Gratiano, Ernest Travers as Ludovico, Samuel Phelps alt. with William Creswick as Othello/ Iago, H. Crellin as Cassio, Mr. Northcote as Antonio, Rose Leclercq as Desdemona, Fanny Huddart as Emilia; Jan. 1881, with Edwin Booth as Othello/ Iago, alternating with Henry Forrester, John Beauchamp as Duke, John Ryder as Brabantio, Mr. Chamberlain as Gratiano, P. C. Beverley as Ludovico, William Redmund as Cassio, F. Charles as Roderigo, C. W. Garthorne as Montano, Maud Milton as Desdemona, Mrs. Hermann Vezin as Emelia/ Scenery by Charles Brooke/ Machines by Mr. Warton, Lime-light by Messrs. Kerr/ Prod. by Harry Jackson/ **Olympic,** Mar. 1847, with J. R. Scott as Othello, George Bolton as Iago, George Maynard as Cassio, Mr. Binge as Roderigo, Mr. Johnstone as Brabantio, Mr. Fortesque as Duke, Mrs. R. Gordon as Desdemona, Mrs. Boyce as Emilia; Jan. 1848, with George Almar as Duke, Mr. Archer as Brabantio, H. Lee as Ludovico, Mr. Darcie as Gratiano, G. V. Brooke as Othello, Mr. Stuart as Iago, Henry Holl as Cassio, Miss Stuart as Desdemona, Mrs. Brougham as Emilia; Feb. 1852, with George Cooke as Duke, Charles Diddear as Brabantio, Mr. Norton as Lodovico, Henry Farren as Othello, William Farren Jr. as Cassio, William Hoskins as Iago, W. Shalders as Roderigo, Charles Bender as Gratiano, Louisa Howard as Desdemona, Mrs. Barrett as Emilia; Aug. 1866, with Morgan Smith as Othello, J. Walters as Duke, John Maclean as Brabantio, Henry Rivers as Gratiano, T. B. Bennett as Lodovico, W. J. Collens as Montano, James Craig as Cassio, Charles Horsman as Iago, Robert Soutar as Roderigo, Emma Barnett as Desdemona, Miss Atkinson as Emelia/ **Grecian,** Apr. 1855, with Eaton O'Donnell as Brabantio, Henry Grant as Duke of Venice, Master G. Branch as Othello, Basil Potter as Iago, F. Charles as Montano, John Manning as Roderigo, Master Righton as Cassio, Jane Coveney as Desdemona, Miss Johnstone as Emilia; Aug. 1862, with J. Jackson, Henry Grant, G. C. Kingston, Thomas Mead, William James, John Manning, Mrs. Charles Dillon, Jane Dawson; June 1866, with J. Jackson as Duke of Venice, Henry Grant as Brabantio, Alfred Rayner as Othello, Charles Mortimer as Iago, William James as Cassio, John Manning as Roderigo, Lizzie Mandlebert as Desdemona, Harriet Western as Emilia/ **Lyceum,** Feb. 1857, with Mr. Holston as Duke, Mr. Barrett as Brabantio, Mr. Clifton as Ludovico, Mr. Poynter as Gratiano, Charles Dillon as Othello, Mr. McLien as Cassio, Mr. Stuart as Iago, J. G. Shore as Roderigo, Mrs. Dillon as Desdemona, Mrs. Weston as Emilia; July 1858, with Ira Aldridge; Mar. 1859, with James Bennett, Edmund Falconer; Feb. 1876, with Henry Irving as Othello, John Collett as Duke, Thomas Mead as Brabantio, Mr. Carton as Roderigo, Mr. Brooke as Cassio, H. Forrester as Iago, Isabel Bateman as Desdemona, Kate Bateman as Emilia; May 1881 with Edwin Booth as

Othello, Henry Irving as Iago, William Terriss as Cassio, Thomas Mead as Brabantio, Arthur Wing Pinero as Roderigo, Mr. Beaumont as Duke, Georgina Pauncefort as Emilia, Helen Terry as Desdemona/ **Surrey**, Dec. 1859, with William Creswick, Edith Heraud, Basil Potter/ **Astley's**, Feb. 1870, with J. Russell as Duke, E. St. Albyn as Antonio, Samuel Phelps as Othello, Charles Harcourt as Cassio, Hermann Vezin as Iago, Mrs. Hermann Vezin as Desdemona, Fanny Huddart as Emilia/ **Drury Lane**, Apr. 1875, with Tomasso Salvini/ **Lyric**, May 1897, with Wilson Barrett.

OTHER FELLOW, THE// F 3a// Adap. by Fred Horner fr F of Georges Feydeau & Maurice Desvallières, Champignol Malgré lui// **Court**, Sept. 1893/ **Strand**, Nov. 1893.

OTTO, A GERMAN// C 3a// J. F. Marsden// **Sadler's Wells**, July 1880, with George Knight, Robert Mantell, Maude Reenie.

OUGHT WE TO VISIT HER?// C 3a// Mrs. Edwards & W. S. Gilbert// **Royalty**, Jan. 1874.

OUR ACCOMPLISHED DOMESTIC// F// E. Dale// **Strand**, Aug. 1878.

OUR AMERICAN COUSIN// C 4a// Tom Taylor// **Haymarket**, Nov. 1861, with E. A. Sothern as Lord Dundreary, J. B. Buckstone as Asa Trenchard, George Braid as Sir Edward, Edwin Villiers as Lt. Vernon, Mr. Weathersby as Capt. De Boots, Mr. Rogers as Coyle, W. H. Chippendale as Murcott, Mrs. Charles Young as Florence, Miss M. Oliver as Mary, Mrs. Griffith as Mrs. Mountchessington, Henrietta Lindley as Augusta, Miss Henrade as Georgina/ Scenery by George Morris & John O'Conner/ Machines by Oliver Wales/ **Drury Lane**, July 1872, with E. A. Sothern as Dundreary, Edmund Coles as Asa Trenchard, G. Grainger as Sir Edward, Lytton Sothern as Lt. Vernon, Gaston Murray as Capt. De Boots, Thomas Coe as Biddicombe, J. F. Cathcart as Murcott, W. Blakeley as Coyle, A. W. Young as Binney, Miss Kemp as Florence, Fanny Gynne as Mary, Mrs. St. Henry as Mrs. Mountchessington, Amy Roselle as Georgina/ **Novelty**, Feb. 1890, with George Turner as Dundreary, Graham Wentworth as Asa Trenchard, Norman Clark as Sir Edward, D. D. Betterton as Murcott, Aida Valde as Georgina, Clare Greet as Florence, Essex Dane as Mary.

OUR ANGELS// D 3a// G. H. R. Dabbs & Edward Righton// **Vaudeville**, Mar. 1891.

OUR AUTUMN MANOEUVERS// F// C. L. Kenney// **Adelphi**, Oct. 1871.

OUR BITTEREST FOE: AN INCIDENT OF 1870// D 1a// G. C. Herbert// **Globe**, Apr. 1874/ **Astley's**, Sept. 1881, with F. Fowler as Gen. von Rosenberg, E. Hughnott as de la Fere, Marie Forde as Blanche/ **Princess's**, June 1890, with Edward Sass as Gen. Rosenberg, H. Diver as de la Fere, Helen Kinnaird as Blanche/ **Globe**, Sept. 1897, with H. Athol Forde as Von Rosenberg, Herbert Sleath as de la Fére, Miss A. L'Aumonier as Blanche.

OUR BOYS// C 3a// H. J. Byron// **Vaudeville**, Jan. 1875, with Arthur James, William Farren, Charles Warner, Kate Bishop, Amy Roselle, Cecily Richards/ **Criterion**, Feb. 1890, with David James as Perkyn, Leonard Boyne as Charles, Arthur Elwood as Sir Geoffrey, E. W. Gardiner as Champneys, Olga Brandon as Mary, E. Brunton as Clarissa, F. Frances as Violet, Emily Vining as Belinda/ **Terry's**, July 1898/ **Vaudeville**, Sept. 1892.

OUR CLERKS; OR, No. 3, FIG TREE COURT TEMPLE// F 1a// Tom Taylor// **Princess's**, Mar. 1852, with George Everett as Meacock, Alfred Wigan as Hazard, Robert Keeley as Puddicomb, Mrs. Keeley as Sharpus, Mr. Addison as Bulpit, Miss Robertson as Emily, Miss Vivash as Mary, Miss Daly as Jane, Mrs. W. Daly as Mrs. Chowser/ **Adelphi**, Aug. 1862, with John Sefton as Job Meacock, David Fisher as Hazard, J. L. Toole as Puddicomb, Louise Keeley as Edward, Paul Bedford as Bulpit, Robert Romer as Docket, C. J. Smith as Jerimiah, Kate Bland as Emily, Lydia Foote as Jane/ **Globe**, Apr. 1878, with Henry Westland as Richard Hazard, J. L. Toole as Puddicomb, Fannie Leslie as Sharpur, Charles Collette as Mouldicot, Miss Vivian as Emily Harden, Isabel Clifton as Mrs. Chauser.

OUR CLUB// C 3a// F. C. Burnand// **Strand**, May 1878.

OUR DAUGHTERS// C 3a// T. G. Warren & W. Edouin// **Strand**, Apr. 1891.

OUR DEAR OLD HOME// D// William Archer// **City of London**, June 1868.

OUR DOCTORS// F 3a// R. H. Roberts & Joseph Mackay// **Terry's**, Mar. 1891.

OUR DOMESTICS// F 2a// Adap. by Frederick Hay// **Strand**, June 1867.

OUR ELDORADO// D 4a// F. A. Scudamore// **Pavilion**, Aug. 1894.

OUR EMMIE// Play 1a// Marwood Clark// **Opera Comique**, Aug. 1892.

OUR FARM// C// Edward Rose// **Queen's**, June 1872.

OUR FEMALE AMERICAN COUSIN// C 2a// Charles Gaylor// **Adelphi**, May 1860, with Mr. Stuart as Sir William, W. H. Eburne as Fitzherbert, John Billington as Gerald, Charles Selby as Peter Neff, J. G. Warde as Capt. Granville, Mrs. Chatterley as Lady Appleby, Kate Kelly as Clara Appleby, Mrs. Billington as Lady Blanche, Julia Daly as Pamela.

OUR FLAT// F 3a// Mrs. Musgrave// **POW**, June 1889/ **Opera Comique**, June 1889/ **Strand**, July 1894.

OUR FRENCH LADY'S MAID// F 1a// J. Maddison Morton// **Adelphi**, May 1858, with Benjamin Webster as Sparkins, Charles Selby as Folley, C. J. Smith as Pevot, Mrs. Chatterley as Mrs. Puddifoot, Mme. Celeste as Mlle.

Zephyone/ **Sad. Wells,** June 1858, with Benjamin Webster as Sparkins, Charles Selby as Folley, C. J. Smith as Pevot, Mrs. Chatterley as Mrs. Puddifoot, Miss Hayman as Fanny, Miss Aldridge as Mary, Mme. Celeste as Zephyone.

OUR FRIENDS; OR, NOS INTIMES// C 4a// Adap. by George March fr F of Victorien Sardou// **Olympic,** May 1872, with Henry Sinclair as Dr. Tholosan, T. N. Wenman as Marécat, Horace Wigan as Caussade, Frank Harvey as Maurice, John S. Wood as Vigneux, Mlle. Marie Beatrice as Cécile, Patty Chapman as Mme. Vigneux, Agnes Barnett as Benjamine.

OUR GAL// F 1a// G. D. Johnson// **Adelphi,** July 1856, with John Parselle as Edward, J. G. Shore as Henry, Mrs. Barney Williams as Caroline, Mrs. Stoker as Mrs. Winterblossom/ **Sad. Wells,** July 1858, with Walter Vernon as Mason, Mr. Butler as Seymour, James Bland as Winterblossom, Edward Wright as Sam, Mrs. Barney Williams as Our Gal, Mrs. Barnett as Mrs. Winterblossom/ **Drury Lane,** Feb. 1859, with Henry Butler as Seymour, Mr. Templeton as Mason, Mr. Tilbury as Winterblossom, Mrs. Barney Williams as Caroline, Mrs. Barrett as Miss Winterblossom.

OUR GIRLS// C// H. J. Byron// **Vaudeville,** Apr. 1879.

OUR GUARDIAN ANGEL// D 4a// Clarence Burnett // **Novelty,** Jan. 1896, with Clarence Burnett as Capt. Massey, Edward Bicker as Darrell, L. R. Montgomery as Peggs, Horace Barma as Sambo, Wallace Eastlake as Gambier, Gilbert Sandys as Crawl, Ellen Cranston as Zadia, Nita Snow as Eliza, Kittie Lofting as Cora, Clara Reid as Sarah.

OUR HOUSE; OR, LODGINGS IN LONDON// F// n.a.// **Sad. Wells,** Jan. 1842, with Mr. Williams as Briarton, Mr. Aldridge as Capt. Clayton, John Webster as Banner, J. W. Collier as O'Done, John Herbert as Slack, Miss Cooke as Widow Wolfus, Mrs. Morgan as Mrs. Clayton, Mrs. Richard Barnett as Sally.

OUR JOAN// D 3a// Mr. & Mrs. Herman Merivale// **Grand,** Oct. 1887.

OUR JOHN// Play 1a// Percy Murray// **Garrick,** June 1899, with Frank Emery as Briley, Leonard Buttress as Wilson, Mrs. Gordon Gray as Mrs. Briley.

OUR LADY OF THE WILLOW; OR, THE WIFE WITH TWO HEADS// D// G. D. Pitt// **Victoria,** Mar. 1854, with Mr. Henderson as Count Fabian, Mr. Hitchinson as Don Diago, J. T. Johnson as Felix, J. Howard as Sancho, Watty Brunton as Don Fusile, Mr. Morrison as Jacomo, Annette Vincent as Olivia and as Sabrina, Miss Dansor as Queen Isabella.

OUR LASS// D Pro & 4a// W. S. Salford// **POW,** Apr.1886/ **Sadler's Wells,** July 1888.

OUR LOT IN LIFE; OR, BRIGHTER DAYS IN STORE// D// C. H. Hazlewood// **Britannia,** 1862.

OUR MARY ANNE// F 1a// J. B. Buckstone// **Drury Lane,** Jan. 1838, with Mr. Cooper as Col. Albert, J. B. Buckstone as Tunks, Henry Compton as Solomon, Mr. Mears as Thomas, Mrs. Ternan as Ernestine, Miss Poole as Mary Anne, Mrs. Brindal as Aunt Winifred/ **Haymarket,** Nov. 1839, with John Webster as Col. Albert, J. B. Buckstone as Tunks, T. F. Mathews as Solomon, Priscilla Horton as Ernestine, Miss Gallot as Mary Anne, Mrs. Danson as Aunt Winifred/ **Sad. Wells,** Apr. 1841, with Mr. Dry as Col. Albert, Mr. Poole as Tunks, A. Richarson as Solomon, Miss Vivian as Ernestine, Mrs. Maddocks as Mary Anne.

OUR NATIONAL DEFENCES; OR, THE COCKSHOT YEOMANRY// F// n.a.// **Adelphi,** Mar. 1852, with Samuel Emery as Maj. Snapdragon, Ellen Chaplin as Adrien, Edward Wright as Marrofat, Paul Bedford as Geeup, Sarah Woolgar as Sarah, Emma Harding as Emily.

OUR NATIVE HOME// D 5a// Charles Whitlock & John Sargent// **Surrey,** Sept. 1892.

OUR NELLY// D 2a// H. T. Craven// **Surrey,** 1853/ **Astley's,** Apr. 1861, with Mr. Johnson, T. J. Anderson, H. Lewis, F. Charles, Henry Widdicomb, Mrs. Dowton, Rebecca Isaacs, Kate Rivers, Julia Craven.

OUR NEW GOVERNESS// C 2a// C. W. Brooks// **Lyceum,** May 1845, with Mr. Stanton as Trelawney, Frank Matthews as Biggs, Alfred Wigan as Fitz-Duval, Robert Keeley as Scroop, Mrs. Woollidge as Mrs. Biggs, Mrs. Alfred Wigan as Miss St. Ursula, Mrs. Keeley as Lizzy.

OUR NEW LADIES' MAID// C 1a// H. C. Coape// **Haymarket,** July 1852, with Leigh Murray as Baron d'Arbel, J. B. Buckstone as Babillard, Henry Bedford as Michonnet, Mrs. L. S. Buckingham as Countess de Rougemont, Mrs. Temple as Blanche.

OUR NURSE DOROTHY// F// n.a.// **Drury Lane,** Jan. 1855.

OUR OLD HOUSE AT HOME (see Old House at Home)

OUR PLAY// C// R. G. Graham// **Vaudeville,** Mar. 1893.

OUR POLLY// D 3a// Edward Towers// **Pavilion,** Apr. 1881.

OUR QUIET CHATEAU// Robert Reece// **Gal. of Illust.,** Dec. 1867.

OUR REGIMENT// FC 3a// Adap. by Henry Hamilton fr G of G. von Moser, Kriegim Frieden// **Vaudeville,** Feb. 1883/ **Globe,** Jan. 1884, with Edward Henley as Dobbinson, J. F. Young as Ellaby, H. J. Lethcourt as Capt. Featherston, Gerald Moore as Warrener, E. W. Gardiner as Rev. Talbot, Carlotta Leclercq as Mrs. Dobbinson, Florence Trevelyan as Olive, Fanny Brough as Enid Thurston, Miss Abington (Mrs. J. H. Barnes) as Maud Ellaby/

Toole's, Jan. 1891.

OUR RELATIVES// C 1a// Walter Ellis// **Olympic**, Dec. 1880, with H. Pery, Muriel Campbell.

OUR SILVER WEDDING// D 5a// J. T. Douglass ("James Willing")// **Standard**, Mar. 1885.

OUR SQUARE// F 3a// Edward Rose// **Gaiety**, Apr. 1884.

OUR STRATEGISTS// F 4a// Dr. Sayre// **Opera Comique**, May. 1886, with Henry Bell, John Burke, Katie Gilbert, Lottie Harcourt.

OUR VILLAGE; OR, LOST AND FOUND (also subt. The Lost Ship)// D 3a// Leman Rede// **Olympic**, Apr. 1843, with C. Baker as Earl of Marlington, Mr. Rogers as Sneaky, George Wild as Tulloch, Mr. Bologna as Giles, Mr. Brookes as Hobson, Walter Searle as Bowyer, Lavinia Melville as Fanny, Miss Lebatt as Polly, Miss Granby as Jenny, Mrs. W. West as Florence/ Scenery by W. R. Beverly & Mr. Scott/ Music by Mr. Calcott/ Machines by Mr. Mackintosh.

OUR WIFE; OR, THE ROSE OF AMIENS// C 2a// J. Maddison Morton// **Princess's**, Nov. 1856, with John Ryder as Marquis de Ligny, David Fisher as Count de Brissac, John Pritt Harley as Pomaret, Mr. Raymond as Dumont, Carlotta Leclercq as Rosine, Miss Murray as Mariette/ **Olympic**, July 1867, with H. J. Montague as Marquis de Ligny, John Clayton as Count de Brissac, Dominick Murray as Pomaret, Harwood Cooper as Dumont, Louisa Moore as Rosine, Ellen Farren as Manette/ **Haymarket**, July 1867, with H. J. Montague as Marquis de Ligny, John Clayton as Count de Brissac, Dominick Murray as Pomaret, Jasper Redgrave as Dumont, Mr. Cowdery as Officer, Nelly Mocre as Rosine, Carlotta Addison as Mariette.

OUR WIFE// F 1a// Thomas Archer// **Grecian**, Sept. 1847, with Eaton O'Donnell as Muff, Frederick Robson as Short.

OURANG OUTANG; OR, THE INDIAN MAID AND THE SHIPWRECKED MARINER// D 2a// n.a.// **Olympic**, Mar. 1843, with Mr. Fitzjames as Capt. Sinclair, Mr. Green as Harcourt, Mr. Ross as Peter, Miss Arden as Madame Sinclair, Walter Searle as Tschikoh, Mr. Bologna as Ghaffo, Mr. Bartland as Bazeff, Lavinia Melville as Orah.

OURS// C 3a// T. W. Robertson// **POW**, Sept. 1866/ **Haymarket**, Jan. 1882, with Arthur Cecil as Prince Perovski, Arthur Wing Pinero as Sir Alexander, H. B. Conway as MacAlister, Squire Bancroft as Chalcot, Mr. Smedley as Capt. Samprey, Charles Brookfield as Sgt. Jones, Roma Le Thière as Lady Shendryn, Lillie Langtry as Blanche, Mrs. Bancroft as Mary Netley/ Scenery by Hawes Craven, Mr. Harford, Mr. Johnstone & Walter Hann; Apr. 1885, with Henry Kemble, Maurice Barrymore, Squire Bancroft, Mary A. Victor, Mrs. Bancroft/ **Globe**, Feb. 1899, with John Hare as Prince Perovsky, Gilbert Hare as Shendryn, Charles Cherry as Samprey, Frank Gillmore as MacAlister, Frederick Kerr as Chalcot, Fanny Coleman as Lady Shendryn, Mabel Terry Lewis as Blanche, May Harvey as Mary Netley/ Scenery by W. Harford.

OURSELVES// C 3a// F. C. Burnand// **Vaudeville**, Jan. 1880.

OUT AT ELBOWS// F 1a// Aylmer Dove// **Toole's**, Mar. 1882.

OUT OF LUCK; OR, HIS GRACE THE DUKE// F 1a// E. Stirling// **Sad. Wells**, Apr. 1839, with Mr. Williams as Sir Guffin, Mr. Elvin as Flippant, John Webster as Slip, Robert Honner as Slack, Mrs. J. F. Saville as Emily, Miss Pincott as Pigeon.

OUT OF PLACE// F// Mark Lemon// **Haymarket**, Mar. 1844, with J. W. Gough as Walnut, James Worrell as Capt. Merrivale, William Clark as John, Henry Widdicomb as Pommel, Henry Howe as Dovenap, Miss Carre as Mrs. Merrivale, Miss C. Conner as Lucy, Mrs. Fitzwilliam as Sophy Sollikins.

OUT OF THE BEATEN TRACK// C 4a// Adap. by Meyrick Milton fr G of E. Wichert// **Strand**, July 1889.

OUT OF THE FRYING PAN INTO THE FIRE// F// Brittain Wright// **City of London**, July 1867.

OUT OF THE HUNT// F 3a// Adap. by Robert Reece & T. Thorpe fr F of Théodore Barrière & Tristan[?] Bernard// **Royalty**, Oct. 1881, with G. W. Anson, Richard Mansfield, Lytton Grey, E. Sothern, Lynda Cowell, Lottie Venne.

OUT OF SIGHT OUT OF MIND// F 1a// Adap. by C. J. Mathews fr F, Les Absences de Monsieur// **Haymarket**, Aug. 1859, with C. J. Mathews/ **St. James's**, May 1864, with C. J. Mathews as Gatherwool, Frank Matthews as Spongeman, H. J. Montague as Prettyman, Miss Wentworth as Mrs. Gatherwool, Miss Willars as Meggy.

OUT ON THE LOOSE// F 1a// Morris & Benjamin Barnett// **Strand**, Mar. 1850.

OUTCAST LONDON// D 4a// Henry Young & George Roberts, rev. by Albert West// **Elephant & Castle**, Oct. 1886/ **West London**, Feb. 1898.

OUTCAST MOTHER, THE; OR, THE WILD WOMAN OF THE VILLAGE// D 3a// n.a.// **Sad. Wells**, Dec. 1840, with Mr. Williams as Ramble, Mr. Dry as Lister, Henry Marston as Richard, Mr. Elvin as Kennilson, J. W. Collier as Barleycorn, Miss Richardson as Wardock, Mrs. Richard Barnett as Maude, Mrs. Morgan as Alice.

OUTCAST POOR; OR, THE BYEWAYS OF LONDON// D 4a// Julian Cross// **Surrey**, Aug. 1884.

OUTCAST OF THE STREETS// D// n.a.// **City of London**, Feb. 1886.

OUTWITTED// C 3a// Mrs. Vaughn// **St. Geo. Hall**, July 1871.

OVER THE GARDEN WALL// F 1a// Sidney Grundy// **Folly**, July 1881, with J. L. Tocle, Emily Thorne.

OVER THE WAY// F// Paul Meritt// **Strand**, Feb. 1878.

OVER THE WAY// C 1a// Adap. by T. W. Robertson fr F of Henri Murger, Bonhomme Jadis// **Court**, Jan. 1893, with W. G. Elliott as Chirrup, Wilfred Draycott as Hardy, Ellaline Terriss as Jessie.

OVERLAND MAIL, THE (see Overland Route)

OVERLAND ROUTE, THE// C 3a// Tom Taylor// **Haymarket**, Feb. 1860, with W. H. Chippendale as Colepepper, Henry Compton as Sir Solomon, Mr. Rogers as Maj. McTurk, C. J. Mathews as Dexter, J. B. Buckstone as Levibond, Edwin Villiers as Capt. Claveriag, George Braid as Capt. Smart, Mrs. Wilkins as Mrs. Levibond, Mrs. C. J. Mathews, Maria Ternan as Miss Colepepper/ Scenery by John O'Conner & George Morris/ Machines by Oliver Wales; Oct. 1882, with Alfred Bishop, Squire Bancroft, Mrs. Bancroft, Mrs. John Wood, Maria Daly.

OWEL SISTERS, THE; OR, THE HAUNTED ABBEY RUINS// D// Edward Fitzball// **Adelphi**, Sept. 1842.

*

P.P.; OR, THE MAN AND THE TIGER// F// Thomas Parry// **Sad. Wells**, Feb. 1841, with J. S. Balls as Splasher, J. W. Collier as Buckskin, Mr. Aldridge as Old Startle, Mr. Elvin as Somerhill, George Ellis as Lt. Fusil, Mrs. Richard Barnett as Crape, Mrs. Morgan as Susan.

PACHA OF EGYPT, THE; OR, THE SIGNET RING// D// n.a.// **Sad. Wells**, Oct. 1840, with Henry Marston as Ali, Mr. Elvin as Selim, Mr. Dry as Zenocles, J. W. Collier as Hassan, Mr. Stilt as Ismail, J. B. Hill as Talathon, Mr. Aldridge as Mouctar, Mrs. Richard Barnett as Helena.

PADDY CAREY; OR, THE BOY OF CLOGHEEN// F// Tyrone Power// **Haymarket**, Aug. 1837, with Tyrone Power as Paddy, James Worrell as Fitzroy, T. F. Mathews as Tims, Mr. Harris as Sgt. Snap, Mrs. Tayleure as Mrs. Leary, Miss E. Phillips as Catherine, Miss E. Honner as Mary.

PAINLESS DENTISTRY// F// Martin Becher// **Adelphi**, June 1875.

PAINTER OF GHENT, THE// D 1a// Douglas Jerrold// **Sad. Wells** n.d., with Mr. Cathcart as Roderick, Mr. Williams as Ichabod, Mr. Harwood as Anson, Mr. Dry as Father Francis, Mrs. Robert Honner as Euphemia.

PAIR OF BOOTS, A// F// n.a.// **Olympic**, Oct. 1873.

PAIR OF KNICKERBOCKERS, A// C 1a// Eden Phillpotts// **St. Geo. Hall**, Dec. 1899.

PAIR OF SPECTACLES, A// C 3a// Adap. by Sidney Grundy fr F of Eugène Labiche & A. C. Delacour, Les Petites Oiseaux// **Garrick**, Feb. 1890, with John Hare as Goldfinch, Charles Groves as Uncle Gregory, Rowley Cathcart as Joyce, Sidney Brough as Dick, Charles Dodsworth as Lorimer, F. Hamilton Knight as Bartholomew, Blanche Horlock as Lucy, Kate Rorke as Mrs. Goldfinch/ Scenery by William Harford.

PALACE OF TRUTH, THE// C 3a// W. S. Gilbert// **Haymarket**, Nov. 1870, with J. B. Buckstone as King Phanor, W. H. Kendal as Prince Philamir, Frederick Everill as Chrysal, Mr. Clark as Zoram, Mr. Rogers as Aristoeus, George Braid as Gélanor, Mrs. Chippendale as Queen Altemire, Madge Robertson (Mrs. Kendal) as Princess Zeolide, Caroline Hill as Mirza, Fanny Wright as Palmis, Fanny Gwynne as Azéma/ Scenery by John O'Conner & George Morris/ **Prince's**, Jan. 1884, with G. W. Anson, Kyrle Bellew, Herbert Beerbohm Tree, John Maclean, Florence Marryat, Miss Lingard, Sophie Eyre.

PALE JANET// D 4a// C. H. Hazlewood// **Pavilion**, Aug. 1867.

PALMISTRY// C 1a// R. R. Lumley// **POW**, Apr. 1888.

PAMELA'S PRODIGY// C 3a// Clyde Fitch// **Court**, Oct. 1891, with George Giddens as Serious, Donald Robertson as Bogle, Charles Rock as Sir Timothy, Seymour Hicks as Jennings, John Clulow as James, Percy Brough as Hamilton, Edward Righton as Todd, Mrs. Edmund Phelps as Lady Iggins, Emily Miller as Lucinda, Mary Jocelyn as Clarissa, Marianne Caldwell as Marie, Mrs. John Wood as Mrs. Podkins, Daisy Stratton as Seraphina.

PAN; OR, THE LOVES OF ECHO AND NARCISSUS// H. J. Byron// **Adelphi**, Apr. 1865.

PANEL PICTURE, THE// Play 4a// W. O. Tristram// **Opera Comique**, Mar. 1889.

PAOLO; OR, THE CORREGIDOR'S DAUGHTER// D 3a// n.a.// **Sad. Wells**, June 1857, with John Mordaunt as Don Raymond, George Cooke as Don Sylvio, Mr. Lyon as Paolo, E. B. Gaston as Sangrillo, G. B. Bigwood as

Perez, G. Pennett as Jerome, Mrs. Robert Honner as Helena, Mary A. Victor as Juanna.

PAPA'S HONEYMOON// C 3a// Adap. by Silvain Mayer & W. B. Tarpey fr G// **Criterion**, June 1890, with George Giddens as Hale, William Blakeley as Bush, Sydney Valentine as Martin, S. Hewson as Emden, J. T. Graham as Sniffle, Mary A. Victor as Amelia, Angela Cudmore as Ida, Helen Forsyth as Annette, Ellaline Terriss as Agnes, Mabel Hardinge as Lucy, Emily Vining as Caroline.

PAPER CHASE, THE// F 3a// Charles Thomas// **St. Geo. Hall**, May 1888/ **Strand**, June 1888/ **Toole's**, July 1888/ **Royalty**, Aug. 1888.

PAPER WINGS// C// Watts Phillips// **Adelphi**, Feb. 1860, with Alfred Wigan as Sir Arthur, David Fisher as Jonothan Garroway, Paul Bedford as Sir Peter, Robert Romer as Fungus, Mr. Stuart as Transfer, W. H. Eburne as Coupon, John Billington as Owen Percival, J. L. Toole as Kite, Charles Selby as Flimsey, C. J. Smith as Hammer, Mrs. Alfred Wigan as Mrs. Chicane, Henrietta Sims as Blanche, Mrs. Chatterley as Mme. Kalydore, Kate Kelly as Tawdry/ **Olympic**, Feb. 1869.

PAQUITA// D 5a// Bartley Campbell// **Elephant & Castle**, Aug. 1884.

PARALLEL ATTACKS// C// Fred James// **Strand**, July 1893, with Laurence Cautley as Capt. Adair, C. Aubrey Smith as Capt. Annersley, J. R. Crauford as Lt. Brunderson, Beryl Faber as Violet, Mina le Bert as Madge.

PARIS AND PLEASURE; OR, HOME AND HAPPINESS// D 4a// Adap. by Charles Selby fr F of de Beauvoir and Thibault, Les Enfers de Paris// **Lyceum**, Nov. 1859, with Frederick Villiers as George Kerven, Walter Lacy as Desgenais, James Johnstone as Champi, Mr. Forrester as de Veauroti, Henry Butler as Chaumiere, James Vining as Jacobus, Mme. Celeste in 7 char. parts, Miss Hudspeth as Madeline, Julia St. George as Tronquette, Kate Saville as Carmen/ Scenery by W. Callcott & May/ Music by Nargeot and Palati, adap. by G. Loder.

PARISIAN ROMANCE, A// D 5a// Trans. fr F of Octave Feuillet, Un Roman Parisien// **Lyceum**, Oct. 1888, with John Sullivan as Henri de Targy, D. H. Harkins as Dr. Chesnel, Richard Mansfield as Baron Chevrial, Joseph Frankau as Signor Juliani, John Buckstone as Tirandel, W. H. Crompton as Labauniere, J. B. Booth as Suraise, Mrs. Sol Smith as Mme. de Targy, Beatrice Cameron as Marcelle, Emma Sheridan as Baroness Chevrial, Maude White as Rosa, Ada Marsh as Mme. de Luce, Adelaide Emerson as Estelle.

PARLOURS// F 3a// Adap. by Robert Reece fr F// **Royalty**, July 1880, with Charles Sugden, Edward Righton, Kate Lawler.

PAROLE OF HONOR, THE// D 2a// T. J. Serle// **Cov. Garden**, Nov. 1837, with Mr. Waldron as Lord Glenmere, George Bartley as Sir Lionel, Mr. Tilbury as Maj. Stock, Charles Diddear as Capt. Andrews, James Anderson as Capt. Raby, George Bennett as Hartley, Drinkwater Meadows as Corp. Slink, John Pritchard as Gen. Harrison, Helen Faucit as Jane, Miss Taylor as Ruth.

PARSON, THE// F 3a// S. Adair Fitzgerald// **Globe**, Oct. 1891, with J. G. Wilton as Scuggles, Charles Barrett as Hedgehog, William Glenney as Simpleton, Norman Clark as Sharpe, Mabel Pate as Matilda, Lydia Lisle as Jane, Winifred Elliott as Miss Bootleby, Cissy Farrell as Maria.

PARSON JIM// D 1a// Dram. fr Amer. story// **Terry's**, May 1889.

PARSON WYNN'S TRUST// Play 1a// Paul Heriot// **Comedy**, Apr. 1898, with Acton Bond as Rev. Wynn, Edward Ferris as Heythrop, Laura Graves as Grace.

PARSON'S PLAY, THE// C 1a// J. Scott Battams// **Grand**, July 1889.

PARTED AND REUNITED// D 3a// C. H. Hazlewood// **Britannia**, June 1872.

PARTED ON THE BRIDAL HOUR// D 4a// L. J. Libbey// **Sad. Wells**, Feb. 1888.

PARTING OF THE WAYS, THE// C 1a// Frederick Bowyer & E. Edwardes-Sprange// **Terry's**, Feb. 1890, with Oscar Ayde as Rev. Ellis, Yorke Stephens as Conybeare, Miss M. A. Giffard as Margaret, Helen Leyton as Edith, Rose Dearing as Nance.

PARTNERS// C 5a// Adap. by Robert Buchanan partly fr F novel of Alphonse Daudet// **Haymarket**, Jan. 1888, with Herbert Beerbohm Tree as Borgfeldt, Laurence Cautley as Derwentwater, Henry Kemble as Parr, Charles Brookfield as Bellair, Stewart Dawson as Somerville, Stratton Rodney as Boker, Charles Allan as Dickinson, Marion Terry as Claire, Janet Achurch as Alice, Minnie Terry as Gretchen, Emilie Grattan as Mary, Roma Le Thiere as Lady Silverdale, Gertrude Kington as Mrs. Harkaway/ Scenery by Walter Johnstone/ Music by Hamilton Clarke/ Machines by Oliver Wales.

PARTNERS FOR LIFE// C 3a// H. J. Byron// **Globe**, May 1871, with H. J. Montague as Gilroy, David Fisher as Mervyn, Henry Compton as Muggles, Charles Neville as Ernest, F. W. Garden as Sir Archibald, Charles Flockton as Maj. Billiter, Maria Harris as Emily, Carlotta Addison as Fanny/ **Olympic** Apr. 1880, with E. W. Royce as Mervyn, J. D. Beveridge as Gilroy, Edward Terry as Muggles, Mr. Crauford as Sir Archibald, John Maclean as Maj. Billiter, C. Fawcett as Ernest, Fanny Josephs as Emily, Louise Willes as Fanny, Mrs. Leigh as Miss Priscilla.

PARVENU, THE// C 3a// G. W. Godfrey// **Court**, Apr. 1882/ **Globe**, Feb. 1891, with Harry Paulton as Ledger, Charles Sugden as Tracey, William Herbert as Glynne, Ian Robertson as Sir Fulke, Fanny Coleman as Lady Pettigrew,

Laura Linden as Mary, Lucy Buckstone as Gwendolyn.

PAS DE FASCINATION, THE; OR, CATCHING A GOVERNOR// F 1a// J. Sterling Coyne// **Sad. Wells**, May 1855, with Mrs. Keeley as Katherine, James Rogers as Browsky, Mr. Barrett as Muffenuff, George Fisher as Kyboshki, Mr. Moreland as Slickwitz, C. Kelsey as Maj. Kutznoff, Miss Robertson as Tittlebatz, Robert Soutar as Grippenhoff, F. Tree as Stiffenbach, Miss Cleveland as Cephyrine, Kate Kelly as Mme. Volkerchalks, Mrs. Leman Rede as Mme. Kyboshki/ **Haymarket**, May 1848, with Mr. Tilbury as Count Muffenuff, Mr. Rogers as Kyboshki, A. Brindal as Slickwitz, J. W. Gough as Maj. Kutzoff, William Clark as Galopsky, Miss Woulds as Tittlebatz, Robert Keeley as Browsky, Emma Harding as Zephirine, Miss E. Messent as Mme. Volkerchawks, Mrs. Stanley as Mme. Kyboshki, Mrs. Keeley as Katherine/ **Drury Lane**, Oct. 1856, with Mr. Tilbury as Count Muffineff, Mr. Carter as Kyboski, R. H. Lingham as Slickwitz, C. Walton as Maj. Kutzoff, Mr. Templeton as Golopski, Miss Ennis as Tittlebatz, George Honey as Browski, James Worrell as Grippenhoff, Mr. Walton as Stiffenbach, Miss E. Warden as Zephirine, Miss Barnes as Mme. Volkerchawks, Mrs. Selby as Mme. Kyboski, Mrs. Keeley as Katherine/ **Grecian**, Sept. 1861, with Mr. Jackson as Count Muffenuff, Henry Grant as Kybashki, Mr. Smithson as Slickwitz, Walter Holland as Maj. Kutzoff, Henry Power as Galopski, John Manning as Browski, Lucreza Hill as Zephrine, Miss Oxlee as Mme. Velkerchawks, Amelie Conquest as Katherine.

PASCAL BRUNO// D 2a// Adap. fr Theodore Hook's trans. fr F of Alexandre Dumas// **St. James's**, Jan. 1838, with Mrs. Stirling as Pascal Bruno, Mr. Brookes as Prince Butera, Mr. Sidney as Prince Carini, Edward Wright as Capt. Altaville, John Webster as Paolo, Mr. Hollingsworth as Carlo, Miss C. Booth as Ali, Miss Allison as Gemma, Miss Stuart as Teresa/ Music by G. F. Stansbury/ Scenery by Mr. Nicholls.

PASQUIN// C// Henry Fielding// **Olympic**, Aug. 1850.

PASSING CLOUD, THE// D 2a// W. Bayle Bernard// **Drury Lane**, Apr. 1850, with Mr. Vandenhoff as Hartzmann, Mr. Cooper as Col. Rheinberg, William Montague as Gellert, Charles Diddear as Kruger, John Parry as Sturmthal, Frederick Vining as Flims, James Anderson as Schaddow, Miss Vandenhoff as Linda, Annie Lonsdale as Katrin.

PASSING THROUGH THE FIRE// D 4a// T. Mead// **Elephant & Castle**, Sept. 1883.

PASSION// D 4a// Walter Stephens// **Vaudeville**, Feb. 1873.

PASSION AND PRINCIPLE// D 5a// Leopold Wagner// **Sad. Wells**, June 1883.

PASSION FLOWER, THE// Play 1a// Charles Thursby & A. Applin// **Wyndham's**, June 1900.

PASSION FLOWER, THE; OR, WOMAN AND THE LAW// D 3a// Adap. fr Span. of Leopoldo Cano, La Passionara// **Olympic**, Mar. 1885.

PASSION OF LIFE// D 5a// Hubert Fuller// **West London**, Mar. 1901.

PASSION'S PERIL; OR, THE BROKEN MARRIAGE// D// Adolphe Faucquez// **Britannia**, May 1874.

PASSION'S SLAVE// D 4a// J. A. Stevens// **Standard**, Aug. 1887.

PASSIONS OF THE HEART; OR, NATURE AGAINST THE WORLD// D// n.a.// **Albion**, June 1876.

PASSPORT, THE// C 3a// Dram. by B. C. Stephenson & W. Yardley partly fr novel of Savage// **Globe**, Oct. 1894/ **Terry's**, Apr. 1895, with Yorke Stephens as Sinclair, Alfred Maltby as Christopher Coleman, Roland Atwood as Bob Coleman, Cecil Ramsey as Grey, Compton Coutts as Harris, Richard Blunt as Pattison, J. L. MacKay as Schmirkoff, George Giddens as Greenwood, Fanny Coleman as Mrs. Coleman, Kate Tully as Mildred, Grace Lane as Violet, Cicely Richards as Markham, Gertrude Kingston as Mrs. Darry.

PAST AND PRESENT// D 3a// John Poole// **Olympic**, Jan. 1852, with Charles Diddear as Marquis de St. Victor, Henry Farren as Count de Florville, Louisa Howard as Julian and as Ferdinand, William Farren as Larose, Mrs. B. Bartlett as Marchioness de St. Victor, Miss Adams as Celestine, Miss Rawlings as Baroness de Nermont, Isabel Adams as Countess d'Elmar, W. Shalders as Placid, George Cooke as Pierre, Ellen Turner as Rosalie, Mrs. Alfred Phillips as Marie.

PAST MIDNIGHT// F 1a// George Conquest// **Grecian**, Mar. 1855, with Richard Phillips as Flapper, John Manning as Snapper.

PAST TEN O'CLOSK AND A RAINY NIGHT// F// T. J. Dibdin// **Sad. Wells**, Sept. 1851, with Henry Mellon as Sir Peter, Charles Wheatleigh as Harry, Mr. Williams as Old Snaps, Charles Fenton as Young Snaps, Mr. Wilkins as Wildfire, F. Younge as Rantam, J. W. Ray as Squibb, Fanny Huddart as Nancy, Lucy Rafter as Lucy, Mrs. Henry Marston as Mrs. Silence.

PAT, THE IRISH LANCER// D 3a// n.a.// **Sad. Wells**, Mar. 1888.

PAT'S VAGARIES// F 1a// n.a.// **Sad. Wells**, Oct. 1839, with Mr. Elvin as Melbourne, Mr. Williams as Old Melbourne, Charles Montgomery as Trap, Henry Hall as Hoolagin, Mrs. J. F. Saville as Louisa, Miss Pincott as Susan, Miss Cocke as Letty.

PATCHED-UP AFFAIR, A// Play 1a// Florence Warden// **St. James's**, Mar. 1900, with George Alexander as Col. Dixon, H. B. Warner as Eames, Carlotta Addison as Mrs. Merridew, Fay Davis as Mrs. Dixon.

PATIENCE; OR, THE PURPOSE OF A LIFE// D// C. H. Hazelwood// **Sad. Wells**, Nov. 1866, with J. H. Slater as Robert Ross, Walter Holland as Edwin Ross, J. L. Warner as Wolverton, R. Norman as Cheetham, John Rouse as Ainslie, J. Collier as Hart, Alice Marriott as Patience, Louise Pereira as Totty, Miss Leigh as Charlotte, Mrs. J. F. Saville as Mrs. Selby/ Scenery by Mr. Gowrie.

PATRICIAN'S DAUGHTER, THE// D 5a// Westland Marston// **Drury Lane**, Dec. 1842, with Samuel Phelps as Earl of Lynterne, Charles Selby as Lord Chatterly, Morris Barnett as Sir Archer, Charles Hudson as Capt. Pierpoint, W. C. Macready as Mordaunt, E. W. Elton as Heartwell, George Bennett as Lister, W. H. Bland as Deancourt, John Ryder as Physician, Mrs. Mary Warner as Lady Lydia, Helen Faucit as Lady Mabel, Miss Ellis as Lady Chatterly, Mrs. Selby as Lady Taunton/ **Sad. Wells**, Aug. 1846, with George Bennett as Lord Lynterne, William Hoskins as Capt. Pierpoint, Henry Mellon as Heartwell, Samuel Phelps as Mordaunt, Mr. Morton as Lister, Mr. Stilt as Deancourt, Charles Fenton as Colville, Laura Addison as Lady Mabel, Mrs. Brougham as Lady Lydia, Miss Stephens as Lady Chatterly, Mrs. Francis as Lady Taunton/ **Haymarket**, Oct. 1848, with William Creswick as Mordaunt, Mr. Rogers as Earl of Lyntern, Henry Vandenhoff as Capt. Pierpoint, Henry Holl as Hartwell, A. Brindal as Lister, George Braid as Deancourt, Mr. Caulfield as Colville, James Bland as Physician, Laura Addison as Lady Mabel, Mrs. W. Clifford as Lady Lydia/ Scenery by P. Phillips & George Morris/ **Grecian**, Sept. 1864, with J. B. Steele as Earl of Lysterne, George Gillett as Capt. Pierpoint, Walter Holland as Lister, Henry Grant as Heartwell, Thomas Mead as Mordaunt, Jane Dawson as Lady Lydia, Fanny Bennett as Lady Mabel, Louisa Graham as Lady Chatterly, Marie Brewer as Lady Taunton.

PATRIOTIC SPY, THE// D// n.a.// **Standard**, Mar. 1866.

PATRON SAINT, A// C 1a// Dram. by Charles Thomas fr F of Edmond About, Le Chapeau de St. Catherine// **St. James's**, Oct. 1888, with Georgina Hermon as Lilian, Eleanore Leyshon as Mrs. Helmsley, Millicent Mildmay as Lady Petersfield, Clarence Blakiston as Melton, Nutcombe Gould as Lord Petersfield.

PATRONAGE// D 1a// n.a.// **Olympic**, Nov. 1848, with F. Vining as Lord Snipe, Leigh Murray as Clavering, Samuel Emery as Rockley, Mr. Norton as Frisby, Mrs. Stirling as Edith.

PATTER VERSUS CLATTER// F 1a// Charles Mathews// **Olympic**, May 1838, with C. J. Mathews as Capt. Patter, Mr. Wyman as Parker, Mr. Kerridge as Perker, Miss Beresford as Patty, Miss Jackson as Polly/ **Haymarket**, June 1838, with C. J. Mathews as Patter, T. F. Mathews as Parker, Mr. Green as Pytter, Mr. Bishop as Pouter, Mr. Kerridge as Perker, Miss Holmes as Patty, Miss Partridge as Polly/ **Cov. Garden**, July 1838, with C. J. Mathews as Patter, T. F. Mathews as Parker, Mr. Green as Pytter, Mr. Bishop as Pouter, Mr. Kerridge as Perker, Miss Holmes as Patty, Miss Partridge as Polly; Sept. 1841, with C. J. Mathews as Patter, Mr. Granby as Parker, Mr. Kerridge as Perker, Miss Charlton as Patty, Miss Jackson as Polly/ **Princess's**, Mar. 1846, with C. J. Mathews as Patter, Mr. Granby as Parker, Augustus Harris as Perker, Miss Hodson as Patty, Miss Taylor as Polly/ **Lyceum**, Jan. 1850, with C. J. Mathews as Capt. Patter, Mr. Granby as Parker, Mr. De Courcy as Peitter, George Burt as Ponter, Mr. Kerridge as Perker, Miss Clair as Patty, Miss A. Cushnie as Polly/ **Drury Lane**, Dec. 1855, with C. J. Mathews as Patter, Mr. Tilbury as Parker, Mr. Laporte as Peitter, Mr. Tanner as Pouter, Mr. Templeton as Perker, Miss Box as Patty, Miss Barnes as Polly/ **Olympic**, Mar. 1867, with C. J. Mathews as Capt. Patter, Harwood Cooper as Parker, Mr. Hawkins as Pelter, Mr. Franks as Pouter, Mr. Cowdery as Perker, Miss Lewis as Patty, Miss Schavey as Polly.

PAUL AND VIRGINIA// D 5a// Dram. by Richard Davey fr F novel of Bernardin de St. Pierre// **Novelty**, Nov. 1886.

PAUL CLIFFORD; OR, THE DAYS OF 1770// D 3a// Dram. fr novel of Edward Bulwer-Lytton// **Cov. Garden**, May 1837, with Mr. Collins as Clifford, John Webster as Lord Mauleverer, Mr. Ransford as Jack, Mr. Ross as Dunnaker, Mr. Harris as Ned, James Worrell as Tomlinson, Mr. Huckle as George, Mr. Tilbury as Slopperton, John Collett as Valentine, Eliza Vincent as Terpsichore, Mrs. Sarah Garrick as Mrs. Slopperton, Miss Lee as Lucy/ **Sad. Wells**, Mar. 1838, with Mr. James as Lord Mauleverer, Mr. Ranson as Sir William, Eliza Vincent as Paul, Mr. Gay as Jack, S. Smith as Ned, Mr. Scarbrow as George, H. George as Tomlinson, Mr. Rogers as Dunmaker, Mrs. Weston as Margery, Miss Young as Sally/ **Victoria**, Sept. 1854, with Alfred Saville as Lord Maulevrer, Mr. Morrison as Brandon, Mr. Gay as Muskwell, Mr. Henderson as Burnflat, J. Howard as Slopperton, T. E. Mills as Sir William, N. T. Hicks as Clifford, E. F. Saville as Tomlinson, JohnBradshaw as Pepper, Charles Rice as Dunmaker, Mrs. Henry Vining as Lucy Brandon, Miss Dansor as Lack Backbite, Miss Sutton as Miss Sneerwell/ Prod. by J. T. Johnson.

PAUL CLIFFORD; OR, THE HIGHWAYMAN OF LIFE// D 4a// H. M. Pitt// **Victoria**, July 1870.

PAUL DUCANGE; OR, THE OUTCASTS OF APPELZEL// D 2a// n.a.// **Victoria**, May 1848, with Mr. Henderson as Marquis Daumont, John Bradshaw as Clement, E. Edwards as Ducange, J. Howard as Grosnez, G. F. Forman as Julien, F. H. Henry as Maurice, Mrs. George Lee as Marie, Miss Burroughcliffe as Therese, Mrs. Cooke as Dame Marguerite.

PAUL JONES// C 3a// Adap. by Henry Farnie fr F of M. Chivet & Alfred Duru// **POW**, Jan. 1889.

PAUL KAUVAR// D 4a// Steele Mackaye// **Drury Lane**, May 1890, with Laurence Cautley as Kauvar, Henry Neville as Maxime, Arthur

Stirling as Gen. Delaroche, Charles Hudson as Marquise de Vaux, Victor Stevens as Potin, Ernest Hendrie as Carrac, Jessie Millward as Diane, Edith Bruce as Nanette, Mrs. Clifton as Scarlotte.

PAUL LAFARGE; OR, SELF-MADE// D 2a// Adap. by Dion Boucicault fr F// **Princess's,** Mar. 1870, with Rose Leclercq as Countess Marie, George Belmore as Remy, William Rignold as Lafarge, John Vollaire as Malhard, Alfred Tapping as Chapion.

PAUL LAZARO// D// n.a.// **Drury Lane,** Jan. 1854.

PAUL PRY// C 3a// J. Poole// **Haymarket,** Sept. 1837, with Robert Strickland as Col. Hardy, Charles Selby as Frank, J. T. Haines as Witherton, Mr. Saville as Somers, J. W. Gough as Stanley, J. B. Buckstone as Pry, Frederick Vining as Harry, Mr. Gallot as Grasp, Mrs. Julia Glover as Mrs. Subtle, Miss E. Phillips as Eliza, Miss Wrighten as Marian, Mrs. Humby as Phoebe; Sept. 1848, with Charles Boyce as Harry Stanley, William Cullenford as Witherton, Mr. Lambert as Col. Hardy, James Worrell as Somers, Mr. Thomas as Mr. Stanley, Mr. Stoker as Frank, Edward Wright as Paul Pry, C. J. Smith as Simon, O. Smith as Grasp, Miss M. Taylor as Eliza, Emma Harding as Marian, Mrs. Yates as Mrs. Subtle, Sarah Woolgar as Phoebe/ Scenery by Pitt & Johnstone/ Machines by Mr. Cooper/ **Adelphi,** Mar. 1852, with George Braid as Harry Stanley, William Cullenford as Witherton, Samuel Emery as Col. Hardy, James Worrell as Somers, C. J. Smith as Mr. Stanley, Edward Wright as Paul Pry, Mr. Wayne as Doubledot, Laura Honey as Eliza, Emma Harding as Marian, Sarah Woolgar as Phoebe/ **Globe,** May 1874, with J. L. Toole as Paul Pry, Samuel Emery as Col. Hardy, Mr. Teesdale as Frank Hardy, George Temple as Stanley, Arthur Cecil as Witherton, J. H. Allen as Grasp, Eliza Johnstone as Phoebe, Maria Harris as Eliza.

PAUL PRY// F 1a// C. J. Mathews// Haymarket, Sept. 1859, with C. J. Mathews, Mrs. Mathews (Lizzie Davenport).

PAUL PRY// C// n.a.// **Sad. Wells,** Nov. 1837, with C. H. Pitt as Sir Spangle, Mr. Gay as Oldbutton, Mr. Pateman as Pommade, F. Ede as Hazleton, Mr. Campbell as Paul Pry, Mr. Rogers as Billy, Mr. Ennis as Tankard, Miss Vernon as Laura, Lavinia Melville as Crimp.

PAUL PRY MARRIED AND SETTLED// F 1a// Charles Mathews// **Haymarket,** Oct. 1861, with C. J. Mathews as Pry, Mr. Rogers as Knibbs, Edwin Villiers as Pegtop, Mr. Clark as Toby, Henrietta Lindley as Emily.

PAUL THE BRAZIER; OR, THE REIGN OF TERROR// D// R. J. Raymond// **Sad. Wells,** Dec. 1840, with Mr. Dry as Duval, Mr. Elvin as Valcour, Mr. Williams as Leroe, J. S. Balls as Legay, J. W. Collier as Frontin, J. B. Hill as Francois, Mrs. Robert Honner as Louise, Miss Richardson as Mme. Duval.

PAUL THE PILOT; OR, THE WRECK OF THE RAVEN IN 1692// D 4a// T. L. Greenwood// **Sad. Wells,** Sept. 1839, with W. D. Broadfoot as Lord Carlingford, Mr. Williams as Capt. Longueville, Mr. Cathcart as Wilson, Miss Hicks as Edward, Mr. Dry as Johnson, J. W. Collier as Jones, Mr. Elvin as Lt. Howard, Robert Honner as Toughyarn, Miss Cooke as Dame Wilson, Mrs. Robert Honner as Mary, Mr. Aldridge as Capt. Transon, Mr. Conquest as Swallow/ Scenery by F. Fenton & G. Smithyes Jr./ Machines by B. Sloman/ Music by Mr. Herbert/ Prod. by R. Honner/ **Victoria,** Oct. 1849, with T. H. Higgie as Capt. Froissart, J. Neville as Lord Curlingford, Mr. Humphreys as Capt. Transon, Mr. Henderson as Lt. Howard, J. T. Johnson as Paul, Henry Frazer as Johnson, Mr. Morrison as Jones, John Bradshaw as Toughyarn, J. Howard as Swallow, Mrs. Cooke as Dame Wilson, Amelia Mercer as Mary.

PAUL THE POACHER// D// n.a.// **Sad. Wells,** Nov. 1843, with Robert Romer as Broadfield, Mr. Williams as Stapleton, C. J. Bird as George, Mr. Lamb as Barnsley, Henry Marston as Copsley, W. H. Williams as Birch, Charles Fenton as Tibbs, Caroline Rankley as Margaret, Miss Stephens as Lucy, Miss Cooke as Mrs. Scor'em.

PAUL THE REPROBATE; OR, THE LAW IN 1656// D 2a// n.a.// **Sad. Wells,** Oct. 1837, with S. Palmer as Dangerfield, Mr. Campbell as Bill, Mr. Rogers as Pringle, F. Ede as Inderling, Mr. King as Brown, Mr. Griffith as Dr. Gallipot, Mr. Scarbrow as Jemmy, Mr. Ennis as Ratlin, Miss Williams as Mrs. Howard, Lavinia Melville as Lucy, Miss Vernon as Dame Dangerfield, Mrs. Rogers as Mrs. Pringle.

PAUL ZEGERS; OR, THE DREAM OF RETRIBUTION// D 3a// F. C. Burnand// **Alfred,** Nov. 1871.

PAUL'S RETURN// C 3a// Watts Phillips// **Princess's,** Feb. 1864, with George Vining as Richard Goldsworthy, Charles Seyton as Geoffrey Goldsworthy, Henry Mellon as Flyntaken, John Nelson as Paul Goldsworthy, Henry Forrester as Herbert, David Fisher as Honeydew, Robert Cathcart as Beeswing, Mrs. Henry Marston as Zenobia, Caroline Carson as Mrs. G. Goldsworthy, Kate Saville as Beatrice, Rebecca Powell as Blanche/ Scenery by F. Lloyds, Walter Hann, Mr. Gray.

PAULA LAGARRO; OR, THE LADRONE'S DAUGHTER// D 3a// Mark Lemon// **Drury Lane,** Jan. 1852.

PAULINE// D 3a// Adap. by John Oxenford fr F// **Princess's,** Mar. 1851, with Charles Kean as Count de Beaupre, James Vining as de Norval, John Cathcart as de Socqueville, Mr. Wynn as Brissac, Mr. Daly as Mont Louis, John Ryder as Max, Frederick Cooke as Henri, George Everett as Ali, Miss Phillips as Mme. de Norval, Miss Robertson as Gabrielle, Mrs. Charles Kean as Pauline, Carlotta Leclercq as Harriet; Mar. 1860, with George Melville as Count de Beuzeval, J. G. Shore as de Nerval, Robert Cathcart as de Beauchamp, Mr. Daly as de Montlouis, Frank Graham as Max, J. W. Collier as Henri, Edmund Garden as Inghi, Mrs. Weston as Mme. de Nerval, Mrs. Charles Young as Pauline, Rose Leclercq as Harriett, Miss Laidlaw as Gabrielle, Mrs. J. W. Collier as Hostess.

PAULINE; OR, THE CONSCRIPT'S BRIDE// D// Adap. fr F// **Sad. Wells**, Mar. 1843, with Henry Howe as Francois, John Herbert as Jocrise, Charles Fenton as Theodore, Henry Marston as Moustache, Caroline Rankley as Pauline, Mrs. Richard Barnett as Fanchette.

PAUPER OF LAMBETH, THE// D// n.a.// **Victoria**, Apr. 1851.

PAVED WITH GOLD// D 3a// J. B. Johnstone// **City of London**, May 1868.

PAY ME! OR IF YOU DON'T—// F// n.a.// **Princess's**, July 1848, with W. H. Oxberry as Penguin, John Gilbert as Dingle, Charles Fisher as Taunton, Mr. Wynn as Joseph, Mr. Paulo as William, Mrs. Selby as Mrs. Penguin, Miss Temple as Harriet.

PAY TO THE BEARER A KISS// F// Walter Gordon// **Haymarket**, July 1868.

PAYABLE ON DEMAND// C 2a// Tom Taylor// **Olympic**, July 1859, with Frederick Robson as Goldsched, Walter Gordon as Marquis de St. Cast, Mr. Franks as Leonidas, Horace Wigan as Bricabrac, Harwood Cooper as Brutus, George Cooke as Menasseh, Miss Wyndham as Lina, Frederick Vining as Lyons, F. B. Conway as Lacquerstein.

PEACE AND QUIET// F 1a// T. J. Williams// **Strand**, June 1861.

PEACEFUL WAR// Adap. by Sophie Scotti & Leopold Wagner fr G of G. von Moser & Franz Schönthan, Krieg im Frieden// **POW**, May 1887.

PEACOCK'S HOLIDAY// F 2a// Henry Merivale// **Court**, Apr. 1874.

PEASANT DUKE, THE// D// n.a.// **Victoria**, Mar. 1838, with Edward Hooper, W. H. Oxberry, Mr. Hicks, Mr. Salter, Mr. Loveday, William Davidge, Mrs. Hooper, Mrs. Frank Matthews, Mrs. Loveday, Miss Lee.

PECKSNIFF// C 3a// Henry Paulton// **Folly**, Oct. 1876.

PECULIAR POSITION, A// F 1a// J. R. Planché// **Olympic**, May 1837, with John Liston as Champignon, Charles Selby as Lascart, James Bland as Carlo, W. H. Oxberry as Pepito, Miss Murray as Countess de Novara, Miss M. A. Crisp as Mme. Champignon, Miss Fitzwalter as Barbara/ **Sad. Wells**, Mar. 1842, with John Webster as Maj. Lascari, Mr. Peters as Champignon, Mr. Aldridge as Carlo, J. W. Collier as Pepito, Miss Richardson as Countess de Novara, Miss Cooke as Mme. De Champignon, Mrs. Richard Barnett as Barbara/ **Eng. Opera House** (Lyceum), June 1837, with John Liston as Champignon, James Bland as Carlo, W. H. Oxberry as Pepito, Charles Selby as Major Lascari, Miss Murray as Countess de Novara, Miss Crisp as Mme. Champignon, Miss Fitzwaller as Barbara.

PEDIGREE// C 3a// C. C. Bowring & F. H. Court// **Toole's**, Mar. 1900, with Yorke Stephens as Calthorpe, Compton Coutts as Spavin, Luigi Lablache as Capt. Pollard, E. B. Robson as Robert, Lawrence d'Orsay as Martingale, Edward Righton as Sir Jabez, Vane Featherston as Kitty, Robertha Erskine as Mrs. Fitzpatrick, Helen Leyton as Jane/ Prod. by W. H. Vernon.

PEDLAR BOY, THE; OR, THE OLD MILL RUIN// D// Richard Harrington// **Standard**, Jan. 1862/ **Sad. Wells**, Jan. 1866, with R. Norman as Flemming, John Rouse as Croak, James Johnstone as Wadheim, Mr. Murray as Bethold, Mr. Byrne as Rudolph, Alice Marriott as Carl, Samuel Perfitt as Galliard, Miss Leigh as Louise, Mrs. E. F. Edgar as Eleanore.

PEDRILLS; OR, A SEARCH FOR TWO FATHERS// D 2a// Adap. by J. B. Johnstone fr F// **Marylebone**, May 1857.

PEEP O'DAY; OR, SAVOURNEEN DEELISH// D 4a// Edmund Falconer// **Lyceum**, Nov. 1861, with Hermann Vezin as Harry Kavanagh, Henry Neville as Mr. Grace, George Spencer as Stephen Purcell, Walter Lacy as Capt. Howard, Edmund Falconer as Barney O'Toole, Mr. Addison as Rev. O'Clery, C. Arthur as Maj. O'Grady, Charles Selby as Black Mullins, J. B. Johnstone as Darby, Mrs. D. P. Bowers as Kathleen, Mrs. Stephenson as Mrs. Kavanagh, Miss M. Morton as Widow Mahone, Clara Weston as Mary Grace/ Scenery by Grieve & Telbin/ Music by John Barnard/ **Drury Lane**, Feb. 1870, with J. B. Howard as Kavanagh, Lewis Nanton as Purcell, Mr. Barrett as O'Cleary, J. Neville as Grace, F. Charles as Capt. Howard, C. Moore as Lt. Graham, William McIntyre as Mullins, J. Reynolds as O'Toole, Edith Stuart as Kathleen, Amy Roselle as Mary, Mrs. Barrett as Widow Kavanagh, Miss Hastings as Widow Mahone, Rosina Vokes as Shelah/ **Princess's**, Oct. 1870, with William Rignold as Kavanagh, E. F. Edgar as Purcell, John Vollaire as O'Cleary, C. F. Marshall as Grace, H. Crellin as Capt. Howard, Henry Westland as Lt. Graham, Alfred Rayner as Black Mullins, Shiel Barry as O'Toole, Rose Leclercq as Kathleen, Mrs. R. Power as Widow Kavanagh, Miss Lennox Grey as Mary, Mrs. Addie as Molshee, Miss Hubert as Widow Malone/ **Adelphi**, Jan. 1876, with James Fernandez as Harry Kavanagh, J. G. Shore as Stephen, Frederick Moreland as Mr. Grace, Edmund Falconer as Barney O'Toole, Samuel Emery as Rev. O'Cleary, W. Everard as Lt. Graham, William Terriss as Capt. Howard, William McIntyre as Black Mullins, Ernest Travers as Phelim, Lydia Foote as Kathleen, Cicely Nott as Widow Kavanagh, Miss Hudspeth as Mary Grace.

PEEPING TOM OF COVENTRY// F 1a// John O'Keefe// **Haymarket**, Dec. 1837, with Benjamin Webster as Tom, Robert Strickland as Mayor, James Worrell as Earl Mercia, Mr. Hemming as Harold, Mr. Hutchings as Count Louis, T. F. Mathews as Crazy, Miss Wrighten as Lady Godiva, Miss Beresford as Emma, Mrs. Tayleure as Mayoress, Mrs. Humby as Maud/ **Drury** Lane, Dec. 1837, with Henry Compton as Tom, William Dowton as Mayor, A. Brindal as Harold, Mr. Baker as Earl Mercia, Frederick Cooke as Count Lewis, William Bennett as Crazy, Miss Somerville as Lady Godiva, Miss Poole as Maud.

PEEPSHOW MAN, THE// D 2a// T. J. Williams// **Surrey**, Feb. 1868.

PEER AND THE PEASANT, THE// D// W. T. Moncrieff// **Victoria**, Aug. 1857, with George Pearce as Prince Leopold, Mr. Morrison as Baron Leibheim, Mr. Henderson as Count Hartenstein, W. H. Pitt as Maurice, S. Sawford as Petrovitch, Henry Dudley as Lynx, Rosalie Young as Fritz, Julia Seaman as Marie, Miss Vaul as Lotta.

PEER AND THE PEASANT, THE// D// Anna Cora Mowatt// **Sad. Wells**, Jan. 1864, with E. H. Brook as Louis XV, W. D. Gresham as Richelieu, Samuel Perfitt as Duke D'Antim, David Jones as Armand, T. B. Bennett as Le Sage, Miss Mandelbert as Victor, Alice Marriott as Blanche, Mrs. H. Wallis as Dame Babette, Miss Grainger as Jaqueline.

PEER AND THE TAR, THE; OR, PRIDE AND ITS FALL// D// n.a.// **Grecian**, June 1866, with William James as Vernon, Samuel Perfitt as Sir Charles, John Manning as Neptune, Harry Rignold as Reuben Bell, Charles Mortimer as Col. St. Clair, Henry Grant as Blake, Lizzie Mandlebert as Lillian, Mrs. Atkinson as Dame Bozzle, Mary A. Victor as Mary.

PEER OR PAUPER// D Pro & 4a// A. M. Green// **Olympic**, Sept. 1885.

PEG WOFFINGTON// Play 3a// Adap. fr novel of Charles Reade// POW, Feb. 1901.

PEG WOFFINGTON; OR, THE STATE SECRET// C 2a// n.a.// **Adelphi**, June 1845, with Charles Selby as Marquis de Mousseux, Paul Bedford as Baron Stuph, Charles Hudson as George Tarleton, Edward Wright as Jacob Merestick, John Sanders as Frizz, Emma Harding as Lady Anne, Sarah Woolgar as Peg Woffington/ Scenery by Pitt & Johnstone.

PEGGY// D 3a// Joseph Mackay// **Royalty**, Feb. 1881, with Kate Lawler, Harriet Coveney, Amy Crawford.

PEGGY GREEN// C 1a// Charles Selby// **Lyceum**, Dec. 1847, with Mr. Granby as Tippins, C. J. Mathews as Edward Roverly, John Pritt Harley as Nicholas, Mr. Kerridge as Hedge, Mrs. Macnamara as Mrs. Clover, Kathleen Fitzwilliam as Peggy, Louisa Howard as Kate, Miss Laidlaw as Caroline.

PELLEAS AND MELISANDE// T 5a// Trans. by J. W. Mackail fr F of Maurice Maeterlinck// **POW**, June 1898/ **Lyceum**, Oct. 1898, with James Hearn as Arkel, Miss Cecil Cromwell as Queen Genevieve, Johnston Forbes Robertson as Golaud, John Martin Harvey as Pelleas, Mrs. Patrick Campbell as Melisande/ Music comp. by Gabriel Fauré/ **Royalty**, June 1900.

PENAL LAW// D 3a// R. Hodson// **Britannia**, Mar. 1879.

PENALTY, THE// Play 3a// Julian Cross// **Terry's**, Dec. 1890, with Julian Cross as Antonelli, Henry Bedford as Bentry, Robert Soutar as Sir Lionel, Graham Wentworth as Drillinghurst, Henry Dana as Loombe, Arthur Wood as Barnard, George Belmore as Sam, Marie Linden as Alice, Kate Bealby as Lawretta, Elinore Leyshon as Iris, Rose Dearing as Lizzie, Ruth Rutland as Cora.

PEOPLE'S HERO, A// D 4a// Dram. by W. H. Poole fr novel of Ouida, Triçotrin// **Vaudeville**, June 1890, with B. P. Searle as Duke de Vigne, E. Hoggan-Armadale as Charteris, Arthur Raynor as Viscount Lascelles, W. Howell-Poole as Lioncoeur, Wallace Moir as Rio, William Felton as Rienzi, Charles Hargrave as Daudet, A. E. Maskell as Garton, James Adams as Alphonse, Alice Raynor as Héloise, Gertrude Lesage as Duchess de Vigne, Laura Hanson as Lola, Etta Claire as Florette, Emily Turtle as Mere Verite.

PEOPLE'S IDOL, THE// D 4a// Wilson Barrett & Victor Widnell// **Olympic**, Dec. 1890, with Wilson Barrett as Lawrence St. Aubrey, H. Cooper Cliffe as Arthur St. Aubrey, T. W. Percyval as Maj. Duncan, Edward Irwin as Dolroyd, W. Lionel Belmore as Dr. Wheeler, Austin Melford as Stevens, Ambrose Manning as Hackett, W. A. Elliott as The Buster, Horace Hodges as Sneedon, George Barrett as Gabriel, Lillie Belmore as Myra, Maud Jefferies as Lydia, Alice Cooke as Mrs. St. Aubrey, Louie Wilmot as Blanche, Lily Hanbury as Rose, Alice Belmore as Mrs. Melway, Winifred Emery as Grace/ Scenery by Walter Hann, Stafford Hall & Bruce Smith/ Music by Michael Connelley.

PEPPER'S DIARY// C 1a// Arthur Morris// **Royalty**, Oct. 1890, with Ernest Hendrie as St. John, H. V. Esmond as Maj. Bunderput, F. Smithson as Pepper, Jenny McNulty as Mrs. Pringle, Mary Jocelyn as Letty.

PERCY// D 3a// Leonard Towne// **Globe**, Apr. 1877.

PEREGRINATIONS OF PICKWICK, THE// C// Adap. fr novel of Charles Dickens// **Adelphi**, 1837.

PERFECT CONFIDENCE// F// n.a.// **Olympic**, July 1854, with Frederick Robson as Easy, Samuel Emery as Johnson, Frederic Robinson as Atherley, Miss Marston as Mrs. Easy, Miss Ormonde as Julia, Ellen Turner as Susan.

PERFECTION; OR, THE LADY OF MUNSTER// F 1a// T. H. Bayly// **Drury Lane**, June 1838, with William Bennett as Sir Lawrence, J. S. Balls as Paragon, Mrs. Honey as Kate, Mrs. Brindal as Susan/ **Haymarket**, Nov. 1842, with Robert Strickland as Paragon, Henry Holl as Charles, Henry Widdicomb as Sam, Mrs. Honey as Kate, Miss Conner as Susan; Apr. 1867, with P. White as Sir Lawrence, Mr. Kendal as Paragon, William Clark as Sam, Ione Burke as Kate, Mrs. Edward Fitzwilliam as Susan/ **Princess's**, Apr. 1843, with F. Williams as Sir Lawrence, J. S. Balls as Paragon, W. H. Oxberry as Sam, Mrs. H. P. Grattan as Rory, Miss Noel as Susan; June 1853, with Mr. Addison as Sir Lawrence, Walter Lacy as Paragon, Henry Saker as Sam, Carlotta Leclercq as Kate, Miss Vivash as Susan; May 1863, with Mr. Fitzjames as Sir Lawrence, Robert Roxby as Paragon, George Belmore as Sam, Miss M. Oliver as Kate, Miss Murray as Susan/ **Sad. Wells**, Dec. 1844, with A. Younge as Sir Lawrence, John Webster as Paragon, Mr. Coreno as Sam, Mr. Franks as John, Jane Mordaunt as Kate, Miss Lebatt as Susan; Oct. 1850, with A. Younge as Sir Lawrence, William Hoskins as Paragon, F. Young as Sam, Mr. Dolman as John, Lucy Rafter as Kate, Mrs. Harris as Susan/ **Olympic**, May 1845, with Mr. Turnour as Sir Lawrence, Mr. Roarke as Paragon, W. Gomersal as Sam, Amelia Mercer as Kate, Miss M. A. Egan as Susan/ **Lyceum**, Nov. 1867, with J. Neville as Sir Lawrence, Mr. Dalton as Charles Paragon, J. Francis as Sam, Miss Edgar as Susan, Maud Shelley as Kate.

PERICLES, PRINCE OF TYRE// T// William Shakespeare// **Sad. Wells**, Oct. 1854, with T. C. Harris as Antiochus, William Belford as Thaliard, Samuel Phelps as Pericles, Mr. Barrett as Halicanus, Mr. Thompson as Escanes, Henry Marston as Cleon, Miss Atkinson as Dyonyza, Mr. Lunt as Simonides, Miss Cooper as Thaisa, Mrs. Henry Marston as Lychorida, J. W. Ray as Cerimon, Charles Mortimer as Philemon, Edith Heraud as Marina, Frederic Robinson as Lysimachus, Teresa Bassano as Diana/ Scenery by F. Fenton/ Music by W. Montgomery/ Prod. by Samuel Phelps.

PERIL// Play 4a// Adap. by B. C. Stephenson & Clement Scott ("Saville Rowe") fr F of Victorien Sardou, Nos Intimes// **POW**, 1876/ **Haymarket**, Feb. 1884, with Johnston Forbes Robertson as Sir George, Alfred Bishop as Sir Woodbine, H. B. Conway as Capt. Bradford, Squire Bancroft as Thornton, Charles Brookfield as Beck, H. Eversfield as Percy Grafton, Percy Vernon as Meadows, Stewart Dawson as Kemp, Mrs. Bernard Beere as Lady Ormond, Julia Gwynne as Lucy, Mrs. Canninge as Mrs. Beck, Augusta Wilton as Sophie/ Scenery by Mr. Telbin & Walter Johnstone; Apr. 1892, with Augusta Wilton as Sophie/ Scenery by Mr. Telbin & Walter Johnstone; Apr. 1892, with F. H. Macklin as Sir George, Herbert Beerbohm Tree as Sir Woodbine, Fred Terry as Capt. Bradford, Charles Allan as Thornton, Henry Kemble as Beck, A. Wigley as Percy, Julia Neilson as Lady Ormond, Lizzie Webster as Lucy, Rose Leclercq as Mrs. Beck/ **Prince's**, Apr. 1885, with Joseph Carne, Herbert Beerbohm Tree, Henry Grattan, Charles Coghlan, Lillie Langtry, Annie Rose, Helena Dacre/ **Garrick**, Feb. 1901.

PERILOUS PASS, THE// D// n.a.// **Britannia**, 1862.

PEROUROU, THE BELLOWS MENDER AND THE BEAUTY OF LYONS// D 3a// W. T. Moncreiff// **Sad. Wells**, Feb. 1842, with Mr. Williams as Daubigny, John Webster as Perourou, Mr. Elvin as Theodor, Mr. Aldridge, John Herbert, P. Williams, Mr. Richardson, Mrs. Robert Honnor as Julia, Mrs. Richard Barnett as Barbelliere/ Scenery by F. Fenton/ Music by Isaac Collins/ Prod. by R. Honner/ **Grecian**, Sept. 1847, with Eaton O'Donnell as D'Aubigny, John Webster as Perourou, John Collett as Pere Massillon, Edwin Dixon as Le Brun, Mr. Manley as Dunois, Frederick Robson as Jaques, Annette Mears as Julia, Miss Leclercq as Bachelette.

PERUVIAN, THE// Play 1a// Adap. by Anna de Naucaze// **Opera Comique**, Nov. 1891.

PET LAMB, THE// C 1a// Charles Selby// **Strand**, Sept. 1860.

PET OF THE PUBLIC, A// F 1a// Edward Stirling// **Strand**, 1853/ **Sad. Wells**, June 1855, with F. Coney as Dorville, Mr. Kelsy as Discount, Robert Soutar as Stubbs, Rebecca Isaacs as Emily, Fanny Beaumont as Louise.

PETER AND PAUL// C 2a// Benjamin Webster// **Haymarket**, July 1842, with William Farren as Peter, Robert Strickland as Paul, Mr. Tilbury as Lord Dandelion, Mr. Vining as Schemer, Henry Howe as Willoughby, James Worrell as Bennet, Mrs. Julia Glover as Mrs. Britton, Mrs. Edwin Yarnold as Emma.

PETER BELL THE WAGGONER; OR, THE MURDERERS OF MASSIAC// D 3a// J. B. Buckstone// **Victoria**, Sept. 1850, with J. Howard as Arnold, Mr. Humphreys as Dubois, J. T. Johnson as Durand, John Bradshaw as Baptiste, John Hudspeth as Martin, J. Neville as Peter Bell, Mr. Hitchinson as Robert, Miss Vaul as Adolphe, Georgiana Lebatt as Amelia, Amelia Mercer as Catherine.

PETER THE GREAT// D 5a// Laurence Irving// **Lyceum**, Jan. 1898, with Henry Irving as Peter the Great, Robert Taber as Alexis, H. Cooper-Cliffe as Menshikoff, W. Mackintosh as Tolstoi, William Farren Jr. as Adm. Apraxin, W. L. Belmore as Dolgorovki, Fuller Mellish as Mansouroff, Ben Webster as Kikine, Frank Tyars as Ignatieff, F. H. Macklin as Daun, Norman Forbes as Col. Bauer, S. Johnson as Maj. Steinmetz, Ethel Barrymore as Euphrosine, Suzanne Sheldon as Masha, Ellen Terry as Catherine.

PETER THE GREAT; OR, THE STORMING OF MARIENBOURG// D 2a// **Astley's**, Aug. 1852, with John Ryder as Peter the Great, F. Hustleby as Prince Alexis, S. Smith as Ivan, C. Leclercq Jr. as Count Olga, Mr. Craddock as Baron Menzekoff, Mr. Lawrence as Count Adelsdoff, Thomas Barry as Paul, Mr. Johnson as Joseph, Miss Fenton as Catharine, Mrs. Moreton Brookes as Princess Eudocia, Lydia Pearce as Giffa/ Scenery by Thorne & Mildenhall/ Machines by Richard Smith/ Music by Mr. Phillips/ Prod. by C. Leclercq.

PETER WILKINS; OR, THE FLYING INDIANS// D 2a// C. I. Dibdin// **Sad. Wells**, Sept. 1838, with Mrs. Robert Honner as Wilkins, Mr. Conquest as Crowquill, J. W. Collier as O'Scud, Mr. Dry as Adams, Mr. Harwood as Colombat, Mrs. Harwood as Hallycarnia, Miss E. Honner as Yourankee, Charles Montague as Wild Man/ Scenery by Mr. Telbin/ Music by Mr. Watson/ Prod. by R. Honner.

PETS// C// Brandon Ellis// **St. Geo. Hall**, May 1889.

PETS OF THE PARTERRE, THE; OR, LOVE IN A GARDEN// C 1a// J. Stirling Coyne// **Lyceum**, Nov. 1860, with Henry Neville as Leon Dorville, John Rouse as Pomponne, J. Morris as Pierre, Maria Ternan as Albertine, Lydia Thompson as Fanchette, Miss Neville as Cecile, Miss Hudspeth as Louise/ Scenery by William Callcott/ Music by George Loder.

PETTYCOAT GOVERNMENT// F// Charles Dance// **Sad. Wells**, Aug. 1846, with A. Younge as Hectic, Henry Scharf as Stump, Mr. Williams as Clover, Henry Mellon as Bridoon, Mrs. Henry Marston as Mrs. Carney, Miss Stephens as Annabella.

PETTICOAT GOVERNMENT// F// Charles Dance// **Cov. Garden**, Apr. 1837, with William Farren as Hectic, Mr. Ransford as Clover, Mr. Tilbury as Stump, Mr. Thompson as Bridoon, Mrs. Julia Glover as Mrs. Carney, Miss Lee as Annabella.

PETTICOAT PERFIDY// C 1a// Charles Young// **Court**, May 1885/ **St. James's**, Nov. 1887, with Grace Arnold as Mrs. Mountrevor, Maud Cathcard as Mrs. Jones, Alexes Leighton as Juliette.

PHANTOM BREAKFAST, THE// F 1a// Charles Selby// **Adelphi**, Jan. 1846.

PHANTOM CAPTAIN, THE// D// George Conquest// **Grecian**, Sept. 1864, with David Jones as Cabanil, George Conquest as Flonflon, John Manning as Josse, Henry Grant as Grosserine, J. B. Steele as Manoel, J. Jackson as Lazarillo, Lizzie Mandlebert as Lilias, Marie Brewer as Georgina, Louise Graham as Barbara.

PHANTOM VOICE, THE; OR, THE DOOMED ONE OF THE HULK// D// n.a.// **Sad. Wells**, Mar. 1838, with Mr. Ranson as Macmoran, Mr. Campbell as Ironheart, S. Smith as Bloodhound, James Worrell as Kempstane, Mr. Gay as Lammie, Mr. Nunn as Gilbert, H. George as Davey, Mr. Rogers as Splinter, Mrs. Weston as Bridget, Miss Watkins as Barbara.

PHANTOMS// D 5a// George Conquest & Arthur Shirley// **Surrey**, Oct. 1894.

PHARISEE, THE// Play 3a// Malcolm Watson & Mrs. Lancaster Wallis// **Shaftesbury**, Nov. 1890, with Lewis Waller as Lord Helmore, Herbert Waring as Landon, Mr. Marius as Capt. Darrell, John Beauchamp as Pettifer, H. V. Esmond as Maxwell, Sydney Basing as Brooke, Mrs. Lancaster Wallis as Kate, Sophie Larkin as Miss Maxwell, Marion Lea as Maud, Minnie Terry as Katie/ Scenery by Walter Hann.

PHEDRE// T// Trans. by A. W. Momerie fr F of Jean Racine// **Princess's**, Apr. 1888.

PHENOMENON IN A SMOCK FROCK, A// C 1a// William Brough// **Lyceum**, Dec. 1852, with Frank Matthews as Sowerberry, C. J. Mathews as Buttercup, Henry Horncastle as Barker, Fanny Baker as Mrs. Barker, Miss C. Mitchell as Cecily/ **Sad Wells**, Nov. 1855, with J. W. Ray as Sowerberry, Lewis Ball as Buttercup, William Belford as Barker, Mr. Righton as James, Miss Macarthy as Mrs. Barker, Eliza Travers as Betsey/ **Olympic**, July 1862, with Horace Wigan as Sowerberry, William Worboys as Buttercup, Gaston Murray as Barker, Harwood Cooper as James, Florence Haydon as Mrs. Barker, Mrs. W. S. Emden as Betsey/ **St. James's**, 1875, with Clifford Cooper as Sowerberry, W. J. Hill as Buttercup, E. S. Vincent as Barker, E. A. Russell as James, Miss Murielle as Mrs. Barker, Millie Cook as Betsey/ **Globe**, Sept 1884, with W. F. Hawtrey as Sowerberry, Frederick Glover as Buttercup, H. W. Lambert as Barker, Miss Vane Featherston as Mrs. Barker, Miss M. Siddons as Betsey.

PHIL'S FOLLY// Ca.// Fred Hawley ("Frederick Haywell")// **Royalty**, Apr. 1877.

PHILANTHROPHY// F// Alice Chandos ("A. V. Livondals")// **Princess's**, Sept. 1888.

PHILIP// D 4a// Hamilton Aïdé// **Lyceum**, Feb. 1874, with Henry Irving as Count Philip de Miraflore, John Clayton as Count Juan de Miraflore, H. B. Conway as Count de Flamarens, F. Charles as de Beauport, Mr. Brennand as Aignau, Mr. Beaumont as de Brimont, John Carter as Thibult, Mr. Harwood as Kitchakoff, W. L. Branscombe as de Charente, Virginia Francis as Mme. de Privoisin, Georgina Pauncefort as Countess de Miraflore, Isabel Bateman as Marie/ Scenery by Hawes Craven & H. Cuthbert/ Music by Robert Stoepel/ Prod. by H. L. Bateman.

PHILIP OF FRANCE AND MARIE DE MERANIE// T 5a// Westland Marston// **Olympic**, Nov. 1850, with G. V. Brooke as Philip Augustus, Charles Diddear as Guerin, Henry Farren as De Fontaine, Mr. Norton as De Tournet, John Kinloch as De la Roche, W. Shalders as Archbiship of Reims, George Cooke as Bishop of Paris, William Farren Jr. as Lucien de Larrante, Charles Bender as Briorn, Miss Adams as Ingerburge, Helen Faucit as Meranie, Mrs. Leigh Murray/ Scenery by W. Shalders & Mr. Mildenhall.

PHILIP STRONG; OR, IN HIS STEPS// D 4a// G. F. Neilson// **Garrick**, Nov. 1899.

PHILIP VAN ARTEVELDE// Play// Henry Taylor// **Princess's**, Nov. 1847, with W. C. Macready as Van Artevelde, John Ryder as Van den Bosch, Mr. Cooper as Sir Guy, Mr. Palmer as Ackerman, Miss Somer as Henry,

Charles Fisher as Van Ryk, John Gilbert as Van Muck, Mr. Wynn as Steensel, F. C. Courtney as Sir Simon, Walter Lacy as Sir Guisebert, James Vining as Earl of Flanders, F. B. Conway as Sir Walter, J. Neville as Matthew, Emmeline Montague as Adriana, Susan Cushman as Clara/ Scenery by Brunning & Grey/ Machines by Mr. Breckell.

PHILLIS MAYBURN// D// C. H. Hazlewood// **Britannia**, July 1873.

PHILOMEL// D 3a// H. T. Craven// **Globe**, Feb. 1870.

PHOBUS'S FIX// F// n.a.// **Drury Lane**, Feb. 1870.

PHILOSOPHERS, THE; OR, LAUGH WHEN YOU CAN// F 1a// n.a.// **Sad. Wells**, Dec. 1840, with J. S. Balls as Gossamer, Mr. Williams as Bonus, Henry Marston as Mortimer, Mr. Elvin as Delville, J. W. Collier as Sambo, J. B. Hill as Costly, Miss Richardson as Mrs. Mortimer, Mrs. Richard Barnett as Dorothy, Miss Cooke as Miss Gloomly, Mrs. Robert Honner as Emily.

PHILOSPHERS OF BERLIN, THE// C 2a// W. Bayle Bernard// **Haymarket**, May 1841, with Benjamin Webster as Frederick II of Prussia, James Wallack as Voltaire, Henry Wallack as Maupertuis, T. F. Mathews as La Beaumelle, Samuel Phelps as Ludolph, Robert Strickland as Hertschild, David Rees as Ephraim, Mrs. Stirling as Amelia, Priscilla Horton as Rachel.

PHOBUS' FIX// F 1a// n.a.// **Drury Lane**, Oct. 1870, with W. F. Vokes as Charles, F. Vokes as Jeremiah, Jessie Vokes as Maud, Victoria Vokes as Beatrice, Rosina Vokes as Amy.

PHOEBE HESSEL; OR, THE STRUGGLES OF SEVENTY YEARS// D 3a// J. B. Johnstone// **Victoria**, July 1850, with Mr. Humphreys as Musgrave, T. H. Higgie as Watkins, John Bradshaw as Umberstone, Henry Frazer as Charles, Mr. Henderson as Davidson, J. T. Johnson as Golding, G. F. Forman as Strangeways, J. Howard as Oldworth, Miss Mildenhall as Bella, Amelia Mercer as Phoebe, Mrs. George Lee as Lydia, Miss Barrowcliffe as Bessy, Georgiana Lebatt as Matty, Mrs. Cooke as Mrs. Carroway/ Scenery by Mr. Mildenhall/ Prod. by T. H. Higgie.

PHOTOGRAPHIC FRIGHT, A// F 1a// J. E. Soden// **Princess's**, Sept. 1881, with George Barrett as Kettleby, Neville Doone as Beecher, Charles Cathcart as Sprouts, Emily Waters as Mary, Miss N. Vincent as Clara.

PHYLLIS// Play 4a// Frances Hodgson Burnett// **Globe**, July 1889.

PHYSICIAN, THE// Play 4a// Henry Arthur Jones// **Criterion**, Mar. 1897, with Charles Wyndham as Dr. Carey, Alfred Bishop as Rev. Hinde, T. B. Thalberg as Amphiel, Leslie Kenyon as Dr. Brooker, J. G. Taylor as Gurdon, Kenneth Douglas as Hebbings, A. E. George as Dibley, Marion Terry as Lady Valerie, Emily Vining as Mrs. Bowden, Carlotta Addison as Mrs. Dibley, Mary Moore as Edana/ Scenery by Walter Hann.

PHYSICIAN AND APOTHECARY, THE; OR, A TRIAL OF SKILL// F// n.a.// **Sad. Wells**, May 1837, with John Ayliffe as Dolus, Mr. Ennis as Mulberry, C. H. Pitt as Dunall, Mr. Rogers as Harry, Thomas Lee as O'Larragon, Miss Lebatt as Charlotte, Miss Julian as Lucy.

PHYSICIAN'S WIFE, THE// D 3a// Charles Webb// **Grecian**, Oct. 1858; Sept. 1865, with David Jones as Lauriston, John Manning as Lovely, J. B. Steele as Audley, Henry Power as Lynx, J. Jackson as Heartboy, Lizzie Mandlebert as Mrs. Lauriston, Mary A. Victor as Mrs. Heartboy.

PICKING UP THE PIECES// C 1a// Julian Sturgis// **Court**, Nov. 1882, with Arthur Cecil, Carlotta Addison.

PICKPOCKET, THE// F 3a// Adap. by G. P. Hawtrey fr G of G. von Moser, Mit Vernügen// **Globe**, Apr. 1886, with W. J. Hill as Grumbledon, Charles Allen as Frederick Hope, Wilfred Draycott as Hewitt, T. Squire as Johnson, A. G. Andrews as Dr. Shaw, W. S. Penley as Andrew, Miss Vane Featherston as Freda, Cissy Grahame as Mrs. Hope, Mrs. Stephens as Maria Trumper/ Scenery by Bruce Smith/ Prod. by F. Glover.

PICKWICK// C 4a// Dram. by James Albery fr novel of Charles Dickens// **Lyceum**, Oct. 1871, with Mr. Addison as Samuel Pickwick, Henry Irving as Alfred Jingle, George Belmore as Sam Weller, Mr. Odell as Trotter, Frank Hall as Old Weller, F. W. Irish as Perker, Gaston Murray as Nupkins, Minnie Sidney as Arabella, Marion Hill as Emily, Caroline Ewell as Miss Witherfield, Kate Manor as Rachel, Maud Morice as Miss Smithers, Annie Lafontaine as Mary, Maude Middleton as Ellen/ Prod. by H. L. Bateman.

PICTURE DEALER, THE// F 3a// Arnold Goldsworthy & Henry Reichardt// **Strand**, July 1892.

PIERRE BERTRAND// D// Frederic Lawrance// **Haymarket**, Dec. 1837, with Mr. Ranger as Pierre, Robert Strickland as Col. Lacy, Mr. Hutchings as Albert, Mr. Ray as Hardheart, Mrs. Julia Glover as Mme. Clement, Mrs. Waylett as Agnes.

PIERRE THE FOUNDLING// D// Adap. by Dion Boucicault fr F of Mme. Dudevant// **Adelphi**, Dec. 1854, with Benjamin Webster, Mme. Celeste, Sarah Woolgar, Robert Keeley, Mrs. Keeley.

PIETRA// D 3a// Adap. by John Oxenford fr G of Salomon Mosenthal// **Haymarket**, Dec. 1868, with W. H. Chippendale as di Campetri, Henry Howe as Gaspardo, Walter Gordon as Lionisio, W. H. Kendal as Manfred, Kate Bateman as Pietra, Mrs. Edward Fitzwilliam as Marca/ Scenery by John O'Conner, George Morris, Mr. Barraud, & Mr. Maltby/ Machines by Oliver Wales/ Gas by F. Hope.

PIGEONS AND HAWKS// F 2a// n.a.// **Grecian**, Feb. 1856, with Eaton O'Donnell as Gander, Mr. Hustleby as Fitzfalcon, Richard Phillips as Larkey, John Manning as Poppy, Henry Power as Flush, Jane Coveney as Miss Fitzfalcon, Harriet Coveney as Ellen.

PIKE O'CALLAGHAN; OR, THE IRISH PATRIOT// D 3a// Wybert Reeve// **Surrey**, Feb. 1870.

PILGRIM'S PROGRESS, THE// Play 4a// Found. on tale of Paul Bunyan// **Olympic**, June 1896, with W. L. Abingdon as Apollyon, Frank Celli as Gloriosus, Arnold Lucy as Fairspeech, Quinton Pearson as Holdworld, Gilbert Buckton as Thankless, W. F. Sauter as Vainhope, Jack Cole as Dives, Gilbert Porteous as Pamper, Edwin Shepherd as Graspall, Courtenay Thorpe as Raphael, George Cockburn as Faithful, Lesly Thomson as Death, John Webb as Despair, H. J. Cole as Simple, Dudley Clinton as Mammon, Esmé Beringer as Speranza, Roma Brenon as Isolde, Frances Innes as Iris, Laura Johnson as Malignily, Juliette d'Ervieux as Sabra, Maud St. John as Crafty, Nettie Hooper as Dame Gossip, Vera Beringer as Florimond/ Scenery by Bruce Smith, William Harker, E. G. Banks, Richard Durant & William Perkins/ Electrics by T. J. Digby/ Music by W. Meyer Lutz & Henry Leslie.

PILKERTON'S PEERAGE// C 4a// Anthony Hope// **Garrick**, Mar. 1901.

PILLARS OF SOCIETY, THE// Play 4a// Trans. by William Archer fr Norw. of Henrik Ibsen// **Opera Comique**, June 1889.

PILOT, THE: A TALE OF THE SEA// D 3a// Dram. by Edward Fitzball fr novel of Cooper// **Cov. Garden**, Feb. 1837, with George Bennett as The Pilot, John Pritchard as Capt. Barnstable, Benjamin Webster as Capt. Boroughcliffe, Mr. Thomas as Capt. Manson, Mr. Thompson as Col. Howard, T. P. Cooke as Long Tom Coffin, John Webster as Lt. Griffith, Eliza Vincent as Kate, Miss Land as Cicilia/ **Haymarket**, Oct. 1837 (in 2a), with T. P. Cooke as Long Tom Coffin, Mr. Haines as The Pilot, Mr. Hemming as Barnstable, J. B. Buckstone as Boroughcliff, J. W. Gough as Col. Howard, Mrs. Waylett as Kate, Miss E. Honner as Cecilia/ **Victoria**, Dec. 1838, with T. P. Cocke as Long Tom Coffin, Mr. Hicks as the The Pilot, Mr. Forester as Lt. Barnstaple, Mr. King as Col. Howard, W. J. Hammond as Capt. Boroughcliffe, Lavinia Melville as Kate, J. B. Hill as Cicilia, Charles Montague as Young Merry; June 1843, with Mr. Glindon as Capt. Howard, William Seaman as Barnstable, John Gardner as Boroughcliffe, Mr. Paull as Sgt. Drill, E. F. Saville as Long Tom Coffin, C. Williams as Griffith, John Dale as The Pilot, Charles Morelli as Capt. Saynor, Miss Ridgeway as Katherine, Mrs. George Lee as Cecilia, Mrs. Franklin as Nelly/ **Princess's**, May 1853, with T. P. Cooke as Long Tom Coffin, John Ryder as The Pilot, Frank Graham as Col. Howard, Walter Lacy as Lt. Barnstable, George Everett as Lt. Griffith, Edward Wright as Capt. Boroughcliffe, Henry Saker as Sgt. Drill, Miss Vivash as Merry, Mrs. Walter Lacy as Kate, Miss Desborough as Cecilia/ **Adelphi**, Sept. 1857, with T. P. Cooke as Long Tom Coffin, John Billington as Barnstable, James Bland as Col. Howard, Frank Hall as Lt. Griffith, Edmund Garden as Sgt. Drill, Edward Wright as Capt. Burroughcliffe, Charles Selby as The Pilot, Mary Keeley as Kate, Miss Arden as Cecilia.

PILOT'S GRAVE, THE; OR, REVENGE AND RETRIBUTION// D 2a// n.a.// **Grecian**, Dec. 1862, with Alfred Rayner as Black Ned, J. Jackson as as Jonas, Henry Grant as Stephen, William James as Moran, Thomas Mead as as Malliard, John Manning as Higginbottom, Jane Dawson as Ellen, Miss Johnstone as Widow Moran, Mary A. Victor as Nancy.

PILOT'S SON, THE; OR, THE FATHER'S RANSOM AND THE FALSE KEY// D 3a// Adap. by J. Ebsworth fr F// **Sad. Wells**, Nov. 1840, with Mr. Dry as Montesquieu, Henry Marston as Dubriel, Mr. Elvin as Edward, Mr. Williams as Brice, Mr. Aldridge as Robert, J. W. Collier as Phillip, Mrs. Robert Honner as Pauline, Mrs. Richard Barnett as Emelie, Miss Richardson as Mme. Robert/ Scenery by F. Fenton & G. Smithyes Jr./ Music by Isaac Collins/ Machines by B. Sloman/ Prod. by R. Honner.

PINDEE SINGH// D// C. H. Hazlewood// **Royal Alfred** (Marylebone), Oct. 1868, with Neil Warner, George Melville, Amy Sedgwick.

PINK DOMINOS, THE// F// Adap. by James Albery fr F of Maurice Hennequin & A. C. Delacour, Les Dominos Roses// **Criterion**, Mar. 1877, with Charles Wyndham, Mary Eastlake, Fanny Josephs.

PINK OF POLITENESS, THE// C// Charles Selby// **Olympic**, Feb. 1840, with R. Jones as Duc de Coyllin, Mr. Halford as Duc d'Humieres, Mr. Baker as Duc de Lauzun, Mr. Beckett as De Beaufort, C. J. Pitt as Plumette, Mr. Turnour as Casserole, Mrs Anderson as Mme. Kirgoet.

PIPKIN'S RUSTIC RETREAT// F 1a// T. J. Williams// **Adelphi**, Jan. 1866.

PIQUILLO ALLIAGA; OR, THE ADVENTURER// D 3a// C. Webb// **Grecian**, Sept. 1861, with William James as Philip of Spain, Mr. Jackson as Duke de Lermes, Mr. Costello as Delascar, Thomas Mead as Piquillo, Henry Grant as Baptista, Henry Power as Diaz, George Conquest as Spinello, Ellen Hale as Queen Marguerite, Mrs. Charles Dillon as Carmen, Miss Johnstone as Countess Altamina, Lucreza Hill as Pepita.

PIRATE OF SCIO, THE; OR, A GREEK'S REVENGE// D// n.a.// **Victoria**, May 1850, with Mr. Neville as Harcourt, Mr. Humphreys as Capt. Morton, J. T. Johnson as Mavricordoti, Mr. Henderson as Alexis, Mr. Hitchinson as Constantine, J. Howard as Mumps, John Hudspeth as Mag, Mrs. George Lee as Emily,

Miss Barrowcliffe as Phillis, Mrs. Cooke as Dame Briarly.

PIRATE'S LOVE, THE// D// n.a.// **Grecian**, Sept. 1860.

PITY THE SORROWS OF A POOR OLD MAN// D// n.a.// **Strand**, 1862.

PIZARRO; OR, THE DEATH OF ROLLA// T 5a// Adap. by Richard Brinsley Sheridan fr G of August von Kotzebue, The Spaniard in Peru// **Drury Lane**, Feb. 1837, with Charles Diddear as Ataliba, Edwin Forrest as Rolla, George Bartley as Orozembo, Mr. Shuter as Hualpa, Mr. Mears as Orano, Miss Marshall as Topac, Mr. Honner as Husca, Agnes Taylor as Cora, S. Jones as High Priest, Mr. Warde as Pizarro, Mr. Cooper as Alonzo, Mr. Mathews as Las Casas, A. Brindal as Valverde, Mr. Howell as Gomez, Frederick Cooke as Almagro, Miss Huddart as Elvira/ **Sad. Wells**, Mar. 1837, with Mr. King as Pizarro, C. H. Pitt as Alonzo, C. J. Smith as Valverde, Mr. Ennis as Almagro, Mr. Ray as Davilla, Mr. Jones as Gomez, Miss Hicks as Elvira, Mr. Gay as Ataliba, Mr. Campbell as Orozembo, Mr. Hicks as Rolla, Mr. Scarbrow as Orano, Mr. Young as Almatro, Miss Julian as Cora; Oct. 1845, with George Bennett as Pizarro, Mr. Warde as Valverde, Frank Graham as Las Casas, Henry Marston as Alonzo, Edward Knight as Almagro, Charles Fenton as Gonzalo, R. H. Lingham as Davilla, Mr. Franks as Gomez, Mrs. Mary Warner as Elvira, Henry Mellon as Ataliba, Samuel Phelps as Rolla, A. Younge as Orozembo, Mr. Bologna as Hualpa, Miss Cooper as Cora/ Scenery by Mr. Finlay & F. Fenton/ **Victoria**, Mar. 1838, with Mr. Wilkins as Pizzaro, John Parry as Alonzo, Mr. Harwood as Valverde, Mr. Macdonald as Almagro, Mr. Phillips as Gomez, Miss Richardson as Elvira, Mr. Hicks as Rolla, Mr. King as Ataliba, Mr. Loveday as Orozembe, Mrs. Hooper as Cora/ **Haymarket**, Dec. 1841, with J. W. Gough as Ataliba, Robert Strickland as Orozembo, James Wallack as Rolla, Mrs. Stirling as Cora, Mr. Vining as Alonzo, J. Worrell as Davilla, Benjamin Webster as Las Cases, Henry Wallack as Pizarro, John Webster as Valverde, Henry Howe as Almagro, Mrs. W. Clifford as Elvira/ **Marylebone**, Feb. 1846, with J. R. Scott; Feb. 1848, with E. L. Davenport, Anna Cora Mowatt, Fanny Vining/ **Princess's**, May 1846, with John Ryder as Pizarro, Mr. Wynn as Valverde, Augustus Harris as Almagro, Leigh Murray as Alonzo, Mr. Granby as Las Casas, Mr. Honner as Gomez, Mrs. Ternan as Elvira, Charles Fisher as Ataliba, James Wallack as Rolla, F. C. Courtney as Orano, S. Smith as Hualpa, Mr. Cooper as Orozembo, Mrs. Stirling as Cora, Mr. Leffler as High Priest; Sept. 1856, with Mr. Raymond as Ataliba, Charles Kean as Rolla, Mr. Cooper as Orozembo, Kate Terry as Boy, Caroline Heath as Core, John Ryder as Pizzaro, John Cathcart as Alonzo, Mr. Terry as Almagro, George Everett as Valverde, Mrs. Charles Kean as Elvira/ **Olympic**, Jan. 1847, with George Maynard as Pizarro, Mr. Binge as Alonzo, Mr. Johnstone as Ataliba, J. Cowell as Orozembo, J. R. Scott as Rolla, Mr. Darcie as High Priest, Mr. Palmer as Valverde, Mrs. R. Gordon as Elvira, Mrs. Boyce as Cora/ **Grecian**, Apr. 1856, with Professor Anderson as Rolla, Richard Phillips as Ataliba, F. Charles as Valverde, Eaton O'Donnell as Orozembo, Mr. Hustleby as Pizarro, Percy Corri as High Priest, Jane Coveney as Elvira, Mrs. Charles Montgomery as Cora; Dec. 1866, with Henry Grant as Ataliba, J. Jackson as Orozemba, Alfred Rayner as Rolla, Charles Mortimer as Pizzaro, William James as Alonzo, W. Shirley as Valverde, Henry Power as Gomez, Mr. Goodin as Almaga, Lizzie Mandelbert as Cora, Alice Denvil as Elvira/ **City of London**, Jan. 1866.

PLACE HUNTER, THE// F 1a// n.a.// **Haymarket**, May 1840, with John Webster as Colbert, Benjamin Wrench as Renard, Robert Strickland as Uncle Noset, O. Smith as Friend, Miss Charles as Mme. Renard, Miss Travers as Mme. Colbert, Priscilla Horton as Babille.

PLAGUE OF PLYMOUTH, THE// C 1a// n.a.// **Olympic**, Mar. 1844, with Robert Roxby as Penny, Mr. Turnour as Snooks, Mr. Darcie as Lt. Coxhead, Henry Bedford as Thomas, Mrs. Griffith as Mrs. Snooks, Miss Fielding as Emma.

PLAGUE OF THE FAMILY, THE// C 3a// Adap. by W. E. Suter fr F// **Grecian**, Feb. 1854, with Basil Potter as Tourbillion, Henry Grant as Haversac, Richard Phillips as de Croissac, Charles Horn as Eustace, Mr. Hamilton as Leblanc, Charles Rice as Tintamarre, Jane Coveney as Genevieve, Harriet Coveney as Perpignone, Agnes De Warde as Susette, Miss Johnstone as Mme. Latouche.

PLANTER, THE// F 3a// Adap. by W. Yardley fr F of M. Ordinneau, La Plantation Thomassin// **POW**, Oct. 1891.

PLATONIC ATTACHMENTS// F 1a// W. Bayle Bernard// **Princess's**, Sept. 1850, with Robert Keeley as Thistledown, Alfred Wigan as Rawlings, Frederick Cooke as Diggs, Mrs. Keeley as Mrs. Thistledown, Miss Murray as Ellen, Miss Somers as Mary, Miss Cuchnie as Susan.

PLAY// C 4a// T. W. Robertson// **POW**, Feb. 1868, with Squire Bancroft, Mrs. Bancroft, John Hare/ **Court**, May 1884, with John Clayton, Mr. Mackintosh, H. B. Conway, Arthur Cecil, Edmund Maurice, Amy Roselle, Mary A. Victor.

PLAY ACTRESS, THE// Play// Adap. by R. D. Scott fr novel of S. R. Crockett// **Grand**, Jan. 1890.

PLAY IN A LITTLE, A// Play 1a// Ian Robertson// **Shaftesbury**, June 1892.

PLAYING AT LOO-LOO// F// G. H. Macdermott// **Grecian**, May 1871.

PLAYING FIRST FIDDLE// C// n.a.// **Adelphi**, Apr. 1850.

PLAYING THE GAME// F 3a// William Young & A. J. Flaxman// **Strand**, June 1896.

PLAYING WITH FIRE// C 5a// John Brougham// **Princess's**, Sept. 1861, with George Jordan as Waverly, John Brougham as Dr. Savage, John Ryder as Uncle Timothy, Henry Widdicomb as Pinchbeck, Rose Leclercq as Mrs. Waverly, Carlotta Leclercq as Mrs. Savage, Mrs. Weston as Widow Crabstick, Ellen Honey as Perkins/ Scenery by H. Cuthbert/ **Lyceum**, Apr. 1864, with John Brougham, Samuel Emery, J. G. Shore, Carlotta Leclercq.

PLEASANT COURTSHIP, A// F 1a// n.a.// **Grecian**, May 1845, with Mr. Baldwin as Winbrass, Harry Chester as Wildrove, Frederick Robson as Dipagain, Mr. Kerridge as Joe, Annette Mears as Tugwell, Frank, and Peacock, Miss M. A. Crisp as Sally.

PLEASANT NEIGHBOR, A// F 1a// Mrs. J. R. Planché// **Sad. Wells**, July 1837, with J. Dunn as Christopher, Mr. George as Thomas, C. H. Pitt as Sir George, Mrs. Orger as Nancy Strap, Miss Williams as Lady Elizabeth; Oct. 1848, with Mr. Gladstone as Sir George, Charles Fenton as Thomas, A. Younge as Strap, Miss Huddart as Lady Elizabeth, Mrs. Henry Marston as Nancy Strap/ **Globe**, May 1871, with Frederick Hughes, Harriet Coveney, Miss Jordan.

PLEASURE// C 6a// Paul Meritt & Augustus Harris// **Drury Lane**, Sept. 1887, with Edward Gardiner as Lovel, Harry Nicholls as Doddipods, Percy Lyndal as Prince Valvasia, Basil West as Blessington, Walter Unridge as Tommy, Frank Harrison as Willie, Napier Barry as Sir Samuel, Lionel Rignold as Alderman Doddipods, George Melville as Carey, Alma Murray as Jessie, Fanny Brough as Geraldine, Lily Miska as Rose, Jenny Dawson as Phillis/ Scenery by Henry Emden & Mr. Frampton/ Machines by James Skinner/ Music by Walter Slaughter.

PLEBIAN, THE// C 4a// n.a.// **Vaudeville**, Jan. 1886.

PLEBEIANS// C 3a// Joseph Derrick// **Vaudeville**, Jan. 1886, with Thomas Thorne, William Lestocq, Charles Groves, Kate Phillips, Maude Millet, Kate Rorke.

PLIGHTED TROTH// D 2a// George Darley// **Drury Lane**, Apr. 1842, with W. C. Macready as Sir Gabriel, James Anderson as Willoughby, Charles Hudson as Joybel, Samuel Phelps as Wormall, E. W. Elton as Folio, Mr. Lynne as Siftwell, Charles Selby as Probit, George Bennett as Maurice, Helen Faucit as Maddalene, Mrs. Stirling as Lady Barbara, Miss Floyd as Winifred.

PLOT AND COUNTERPLOT// C// Charles Kemble// **Sad. Wells**, Nov. 1841, with Mr. Williams as Hernandez, Mr. Elvin as Don Leon, George Ellis as Don Fernando, Mr. Aldridge as Don Gaspard, Mr. Richardson as Isadore, J. W. Collier as Fabio, John Herbert as Pedrillo, Mrs. Morgan as Donna Lorenza, Mrs. Richard Barnett as Joanna, Miss Cooke as Beatrice/ **Victoria**, Mar. 1848, with Charles Morelli as Don Gaspard, T. H. Higgie as Don Leon, Mr. Henderson as Don Fernando, J. Howard as Hernandez, Walter Searle as Fable, G. F. Forman as Pedrillo, F. H. Henry as Isidore, Mrs. N. T. Hicks as Donna Lorenza, Miss Burroughcliffe as Juana, Mrs. Cooke as Beatrice.

PLOT AND PASSION// D 3a// Tom Taylor & John Lang// **Olympic**, Oct. 1853, with Mr. White as Berthier, Samuel Emery as Duke of Otranto, Frederick Robson as Desmaretz, Mr. Leslie as Marquis de Chevennes, Alfred Wigan as de Neuville, Harwood Cooper as Grisboulle, Mrs. Stirling as Mme. de Fontanges, Ellen Turner as Cecile; Nov. 1875, with John Vollaire as Duke of Otranto, G. W. Anson as Desmarets, Alfred Nelson as Marquis de Chevennes, Mr. Westall as Berthier, Charles Harcourt as De Neuville, Mr. Crichton as Grisboulle, Carlotta Leclercq as Marie, Annie Taylor as Cecile/ **Sad. Wells**, Mar. 1863, with James Johnstone as Duke of Otranto, Henry Forrester as Desmarets, Alfred Montague as Marquis de Chevennes, Mr. Stalman as Berthier, Morton Price as De Neuville, Julia Seaman as Mme. de Fontanges, Miss Farren as Cecile; Nov. 1868, with Miss Hazlewood as Mme. de Fontagnes, L. Smythe as Duke of Otranto, J. H. Loome as Desmarets, Mr. Newbound as Marquis de Cevennes, W. H. Abel as Berthier, J. H. Fitzpatrick as de Neuville, Miss Herbert as Cecile/ **Haymarket**, Nov. 1881, with Squire Bancroft as Fouché, Arthur Cecil as Desmarets, Arthur Wing Pinero as Marquis de Cevennes, Mr. Teesdale as Berthier, H. B. Conway as de Neuville, Stewart Dawson as Grisboulle, Ada Cavendish as Marie, Augusta Wilton as Cecile/ Scenery by Walter Hann, Mr. Johnstone & Mr. Harford/ Music by Mr. Bucalossi.

PLOT OF HIS STORY, THE// Play 1a// Dram. by Mrs. Oscar Berringer fr story of Morley Roberts// **St. James's**, May 1899, with H. B. Irving as Windover, Arthur Elwood as Lomax, George Hawtrey as Batson, Esmé Beringer as Margaret/ **Garrick**, Dec. 1899.

PLOTS FOR PETTICOATS// F 1a// J. P. Wooler// **Sad. Wells**, Sept. 1849, with Mr. Williams as Sir Andrew, William Hoskins as Finish, Mr. Clinton as Atherton, Teresa Bassano as Rose, Julia St. George as Caroline/ **Olympic**, Dec. 1851, with George Cooke as Sir Andrew, John Kinloch as Atherton, William Hoskins as Finish, Miss Adams as Rose, Isabel Adams as Caroline.

PLOWDENS, THE// C 4a// Edward Rose & O. Benyon// **POW**, Mar. 1892.

PLUCK: A STORY OF £50,000// D 7a// Henry Pettitt & Augustus Harris// **Drury Lane**, Aug. 1882, with J. H. Barnes as Clinton, Arthur Dacre as Maitland, Harry Jackson as Marks, H. Parker as Templeton, Harry Nicholls as Keene, A. Cook as Martin, James Elmore as Locke, Augustus Harris as Springfield, Caroline Hill as Florence, Agnes Thomas as Mary, Mary A. Victor as Polly, Gretchen Lyons as Nellie, Lydia Foote as Ellen/ Scenery by Henry Emden & Thomas Hall/ Music by Oscar Barrett/ Prod. by Augustus Harris.

PLUNGE IN THE DARK, A// D 4a// George Roberts// **Sad. Wells**, Mar. 1888.

PLUNGER, THE// D 5a// D. H. Higgins// **Elephant & Castle**, Oct. 1893.

POACHER BILL; OR, THE GIPSY OUTCAST// D// Alfred Coates// **Britannia**, Apr. 1872.

POET, THE// C 1a// F. W. Broughton// **Vaudeville**, Jan. 1889.

POET'S SLAVE, THE// D// n.a.// **Olympic**, Feb. 1850.

POETIC PROPOSAL, A// F 1a// Martin Becher// **Globe**, May 1871, with Charles Flockton as John Fletcher, J. H. Barnes as Charles Harper, Charles Neville as Timothy Knight, Maria Harris as Lucy Fletcher.

POINT OF HONOUR, THE// C 3a// Adap. by Charles Kemble fr F of L. S. Mercier, Le Deserteur// **Drury Lane**, Jan. 1842, with James Anderson, Samuel Phelps/ **Sad. Wells**, Mar. 1842, with Mr. Dry as St. Franc, R. Norton as Durimel, J. W. Collier as Steinberg, John Webster as Valcour, Miss Richardson as Mrs. Melfort, Mrs. Robert Honner as Bertha/ **Marylebone**, Oct. 1849, with E. L. Davenport, Fanny Vining.

POINTSMAN, THE// D Pro & 3a// R. C. Carton & Cecil Raleigh// **Olympic**, Aug. 1887, with E. S. Willard as Dugdale, J. G. Grahame as Lidstone, Bernard Gould as Fordyce, F. G. Darbishire as Franklin, J. P. Burnett as Bastick, F. Motley Wood as Collins, Frank Wright as George, E. E. Blatchley as Dr. Raeburn, Phillip Cunningham as Johnson, Alfred Rayner as Hathernut, Maud Milton as Lizzie, Agnes Hewitt as Esther, Helen Ferrers as Geraldine.

POISON FLOWER, THE// Play 3a// Adap. by John Todhunter fr story of Nathaniel Hawthorne// **Vaudeville**, June 1891.

POLICE SPY, THE; OR, THE BRAND OF SHAME// D// Thompson Townsend// **Sad. Wells**, Aug. 1866, with F. Watts as Vivian, Philip Hannan as Bertrand, Watty Brunton as Jacques, J. Baker as Giltz, William Travers as Hamagan, G. Carter as Moret, Miss Neville as Pauline, Mrs. Philip Hannan as Elise, Julia Summers as Theresa.

POLICEMAN, THE// F 3a// Walter Helmore & Eden Philpotts// **Terry's**, Nov. 1888.

POLICY OF THE OSTRICH, THE// Play 1a// Cosmo Hamilton// **Terry's**, Jan. 1900.

POLISH JEW, THE// D// J. R. Ware// **Grecian**, Mar. 1872.

POLKA, THE// C// Russell Vaun// **Grand**, June 1895.

POLL AND PARTNER JOE// C 4a// F. C. Burnand// **Astley's**, May 1865, with Basil Potter as Hallyard, Edward Atkins as Waxend, W. S. Gresham as Teller, Walter Holland as Bowse, Henry Frazer as Brandon, Mrs. Poynter as Dame Hallyard, Miss Nesbitt as Abigale, Josephine Fiddes as Mary Maybud.

POLLY'S BIRTHDAY// C// Charles Fawcett// **Gaiety**, Mar. 1884.

POLLY'S VENTURE// C 1a// T. Malcolm Watson// **Gaiety**, Aug. 1888/ **Adelphi**, Oct. 1899, with Howard Russell as Sir Jabez, Ronald Bayne as Frank Merton, S. Wilfred as Reuben, Charlotte Elliott as Polly, Edith Vyse as Cris.

POMONA// D Pro & 3a// Edward Towers// **East London**, Jan. 1877.

POMPADOUR, THE// Play 4a// Adap. by W. G. Wills & Sidney Grundy partly fr G of Brachvogel & fr F of Diderot// **Haymarket**, Mar. 1888, with H. Ashley as Louis XV, Royce Carleton as Duc de Choiseul, E. Harrison as Maupeau, F. Russell as Comte du Barri, George Honey as Marquis de Silhouet, F. Jarrard as Terray, Fred Terry as Lambert, Charles Brookfield as Voltaire, Charles Allan as Grimm, Herbert Beerbohm Tree as Rameau, Rose Leclercq as Queen Marie, Janet Achurch as Mathilde, Roma Le Thière as Marquise D'Epinay, Mrs. Herbert Beerbohm Tree as Marquise de Pompadour/ Scenery by Walter Johnstone & Mr. Telbin/ Music by Hamilton Clarke/ Machines by Oliver Wales.

PONTER'S WEDDING// F 1a// J. Maddison Morton// **St. James's**, June 1865.

POOR COUSIN WALTER// D 1a// J. Palgrave Simpson// **Strand**, Apr. 1850, with Mrs. Stirling, William Farren Jr., Leigh Murray.

POOR DOG TRAY// D// n.a.// **Victoria**, June 1854, with Alfred Saville as Godfrey, Mr. Morrison as Rogan, N. T. Hicks as Patrick, J. Howard as Sullivan, Mr. Green as Colgan, Edwin Blanchard as Andy, Mrs. Henry Vining as Shelah, Miss Laporte as Cauth, Miss Greville as Mina, Mrs. Manders as Bridget, Dog Hector as Dog Tray.

POOR GENTLEMAN, THE// C// George Colman the younger// **Drury Lane**, June 1838, with William Dowton as Sir Robert, A. Brindal as Sir Charles, H. Cooke as Lt. Worthington, J. S. Balls as Frederick, Henry Compton as Ollapod, Mr. Baker as Corp. Foss, R. McIan as Harrowby, William Bennett as Dobbins, Miss Fitzwalter as Emily, Mrs. Charles Jones as Lucretia McTab, Mme. Simon as Dame Harrowby, Mrs. Allcroft as Mary/ **Cov. Garden**, June 1840, with William Dowton as Sir Robert, George Bartley as Dobbins, William Farren as Corp. Foss, John Pritt Harley as Ollapod, Benjamin Webster as Harrowby, Drinkwater Meadows as Stephen, Thomas Green as Sir Charles, Mr. Cooper as Lt. Worthington, Frederick Vining as Frederick, Ellen Tree as Emily, Mrs. Julia Glover as Lucretia McTab, Mrs. Tayleure as Dame Harrowby, Mrs. Humby as Mary/ **Sad. Wells**, Oct. 1841, with Mr. Dry as Lt. Worthington, Mr. Aldridge as Corp. Foss, Mr. Moreton as Sir Charles, Mr. Williams as Sir Robert, Henry Marston as Frederick, J. W. Collier as Dobbins, John Herbert as Ollapod, Robert Honner as Harrowby, Mrs.

Robert Honner as Emily, Miss Cooke as Lucretia McTab, Mrs. Phillips as Dame Harrowby, Mrs. Richard Barnett as Mary/ **Haymarket**, Oct. 1846, with William Farren as Sir Robert, Charles Hudson as Frederick, A. Brindal as Sir Charles, Mr. Tilbury as Corp. Foss, Mr. Stuart as Lt. Worthington, Benjamin Webster as Ollapod, J. B. Buckstone as Harrowby, Mr. Rogers as Dobbins, Mrs. Julia Glover as Lucretia McTab, Miss Fortescue as Emily, Mrs. Stanley as Dame Harrowby, Miss Carre as Mary; July 1864, with Henry Howe as Lt. Worthington, George Braid as Corp. Foss, Walter Gordon as Sir Charles, W. H. Chippendale as Sir Robert, Mr. Rogers as Dobbins, John Dale as Harrowby, Henry Compton as Dr. Ollapod, William Farren as Bramble, Nelly Moore as Emily, Miss Snowden as Lucretia McTab, Miss Coleman as Dame Harrowby, Mrs. J. Rogers as Mary/ **Princess's**, July 1847, with John Gilbert as Sir Robert, John Webster as Sir Charles, Henry Hughes as Lt. Worthington, Henry Compton as Ollapod, James Vining as Frederick, John Ryder as Corp. Foss, Mr. Honner as Harrowby, S. Cowell as Stephen, Charles Fisher as Humphrey, Miss Cooper as Emily, Miss Winstanley as Lucretia MacTab, Mrs. Fosbroke as Dame Harrowby, Miss Rourke as Mary/ **Olympic**, Jan. 1848, with William Davidge as Sir Robert, Henry Holl as Frederick, Mr. Conquest as Ollipod, Mr. Buxton as Harrowby, Henry Lee as Cropland, John Kinloch as Sir Charles, Mr. Archer as Lt. Worthington, Miss C. Lacy as Emily, Mrs. Brougham as Lucretia McTab, Mrs. H. Lee as Dame Harrowby, Miss Honey as Mary/ **Grecian**, Nov. 1854, with Basil Potter as Lt. Worthington, T. Roberts as Capt. Foss, F. Charles as Sir Charles, Richard Phillips as Frederick, Henry Grant as Bramble, Eaton O'Donnell as Ollapod, Jane Coveney as Emily, Miss Johnstone as Lucretia MacTab, Harriet Coveney as Mary/ **Imperial**, Oct. 1879, with William Farren, Lionel Brough, E. F. Edgar, Kyrle Bellew, Mrs. Stirling.

POOR GENTLEMAN, THE// C 2a// Adap. by Alfred Wigan fr F of F. P. F. Dumanoir & M. Lafargue, Le Gentilhomme Pauvre// **St. James's**, 1861.

POOR GIRL'S TEMPTATIONS, A.; OR, A VOICE FROM THE STREETS// D// William Travers// **City of London**, 1857/ **Victoria**, May 1858, with James Elphinstone as Bolton, S. Sawford as Groaner, Mr. Henderson as Lord Edward, Mr. Hitchinson as Warmheart, George Yarnold as Nobbilini, Henry Dudley as Jack, W. H. Pitt as Warren, George Pearce as Sgt. Wallop, John Dale as Stony, Miss Burroughcliffe as Bridget, Julia Seaman as Jessie, Jane Dawson as Elinor, Phoebe Towers as Mme. Nobbilini, Mrs. Alfred Saville as Mrs. Groaner/ **Grecian**, Sept. 1861, with Mr. Jackson as Luke, Henry Grant as Lord Weatherton, F. Smithson as Timothy, John Manning as Snivel, Walter Holland as Warren, R. H. Lingham as Nobbilini, Alfred Rayner as Eelskin Jack, Sophia Mordecai as Elinor, Jane Coveney as Jessie, Miss Johnstone as Bridget, Fanny Branch as Mme. Nobbilini/ **Sad. Wells**, Aug. 1866, with Walter Roberts as Jack, Philip Hannan as Bolton, Mr. Jaques as Lord Wetherton, Watty Brunton as Groaner, F. Watts as Warren, William Travers as Nobbilini, George Skinner as Mite, Miss Neville as Eleanore, Annette Vincent as Bridget, Mrs. Philip Hannan as Jessie, Julia Summers as Slop.

POOR HUMANITY// D Pro & 4a// Nugent Robinson// **Surrey**, Apr. 1868/ **Grecian**, July 1868, with Charles Mortimer as Gifford, Mr. Donne as Mudgeson, W. Shirley as Dr. Rivera, Alice Denvil as Augusta, Lizzie Mandelbert as Nolla, Mrs. Atkinson as Mrs. Carr, Mrs. Dearlove as Mrs. Mudgeson, Thomas Mead as Hewitt, J. Jackson as Mother Wisby, Mary A. Victor as Sally, George Gillett as Horace Essenden, William James as Paul Essenden, Thomas Mead as Carr.

POOR JACK; OR, THE WIFE OF A SAILOR// D 3a// Dram. by J. B. Buckstone fr The Bride of Obeydah// **Adelphi**, Feb. 1840; June 1845, with William Cullenford as Mark Williams, T. P. Cooke as Jack Somerton, Paul Bedford as Sam Griffin, John Sanders as Flipper, O. Smith as Mrs. Mendoza, Charles Munyard as Mrs. Orinoco, Mrs. Edwin Yarnold as Eleanore/ Music by G. H. Rodwell.

POOR JOE THE MARINE OF WOOLWICH, AND SWEET POLL OF HORSELYDOWN// D// G. D. Pitt// **Victoria**, July 1855, with Mr. Hitchinson as Parker, Frederick Byefield as Capt. Oakem, Watty Brunton as Lt. Wilson, Harry Carles as Sgt. Jenkins, W. H. Pitt as Ardent, J. Howard as Roselip, G. W. Sims as Johnson, R. H. Lingham as Hawser, Henry Dudley as Bowse, Jane Dawson as Mary, Mrs. Manders as Mrs. Bowse, Miss Laporte as Pretty Jane.

POOR MR. POTTON// F 3a// Clarence Hamlyn & H. M. Paull// **Vaudeville**, Oct. 1895.

POOR NEEDLEWOMAN OF LONDON, THE// D// n.a.// **Marylebone**, June 1858.

POOR NOBLEMAN, THE// C 2a// Charles Selby// **St. James's**, Nov. 1861, with Alfred Wigan as Marquis de Belleterre, Frank Matthews as Robineau, F. Charles as Oscar, Mr. Dewar as Brilart, George Belmore as Blaisot, Mrs. Alfred Wigan as Mme. Bonbon, Miss Herbert as Hortense, Miss Tunbridge as Justine/ **Queen's**, May 1868.

POOR OF LAMBETH, THE// D// n.a.// **Astley's**, May 1879, with G. Bradfield as Capt. Fairweather, R. H. Lingham as Bloodgood, Augustus Glover as Badger, J. Hayes as Livingstone, Nelson Wheatcroft as Paul Fairweather, Walter Goodman as Puffy, Marie Marlitt as Mrs. Fairweather, Madge Johnstone as Mrs. Puffy, Miss A. Desmond as Alida, Miss Louie Maunders as Lucy/ Scenery by G. Lingham/ Machines by R. Gilbert/ Music by T. Berry/ Gas by Mr. Pepper/ Prod. by Augustus Glover.

POOR OF LONDON, THE (also titled, Lives of the Poor of London)// D 3a// W. E. Suter// **Grecian**, May 1864, with William James as Edmonds, J. B. Steele as Massingham, George Conquest as Grabworm, Thomas Mead as Walton,

J. Jackson as Mouldy, John Manning as Cropp, Marie Brewer as Emma, Mrs. Charles Dillon as Caroline, Laura Conquest as Lizzy, Louisa Graham as Miss Kafibbs, Mary A. Victor as Patsey.

POOR OF THE LONDON STREETS, THE// D 5a// n.a.// **Grecian**, Apr. 1866, with Henry Grant as Capt. Birkheim, Alfred Rayner as Badger, George Gillett as Lester, William James as Blenheim, J. Jackson as Paste, Charles Mortimer as Sharkley, John Manning as Bob, Mrs. Atkinson as Mrs. Blenheim, Mrs. Dearlove as Mrs. Paste, Lizzie Mandlebert as Isabelle, Harriet Western as Agatha/ Scenery by Messender & Soames/ Machines by Mr. Sowtar/ Gas by Mr. Dimes/ Music by W. Edroff/ Prod. by George Conquest.

POOR OLD PERKINS// F 3a// Percival Sykes// **Strand**, Nov. 1896.

POOR PARISHEEN, THE; OR, THE FUGITIVES OF DERRINANE// D 3a// J. B. Howe// **Britannia**, Sept. 1869.

POOR PILLICODDY// F 1a// J. Maddison Morton// **Lyceum**, July 1848, with J. B. Buckstone, Henry Hall, Louisa Howard, Miss Lee, Miss Marshall/ **Sad. Wells**, Nov. 1855, with Lewis Ball as Pillicoddy, Mr. Barrett as Capt. O'Scuttle, Emily Ormonde as Mrs. Pillicoddy, Caroline Parkes as Mrs. O'Scuttle, Eliza Travers as Sarah/ **Olympic**, Aug. 1861, with George Cooke as Capt. Scuttle, Frederick Robson as Pillicoddy, Miss Marston as Mrs. Pillicoddy, Miss Cottrell as Mrs. Scuttle, Mrs. W. S. Emden as Sarah/ **Princess's**, Sept. 1867, with Dominick Murray as Pillicoddy, W. D. Gresham as Capt. O'Scuttle, Emma Barnett as Mrs. Pillicoddy, Mrs. Addie as Mrs. O'Scuttle, Polly Marshall as Sarah/ **Adelphi**, Apr. 1876, with Stanislaus Calhaem as Mr. Pillicoddy, Frederick Moreland as Capt. O'Scuttle, Cicely Nott as Mrs. O'Scuttle, Miss Hudspeth as Sarah.

POOR SOLDIER, THE// F// John O'Keefe// **Cov. Garden**, Oct. 1841, with W. Harrison as Patrick, Mr. Hemming as Capt. Fitzroy, George Horncastle as Dermot, John Pritt Harley as Darby, John Brougham as Father Luke, Alfred Wigan as Bagatelle, Miss Rainforth as Norah, Mrs. Walter Lacy as Kathleen/ **Haymarket**, Feb. 1871, with Walter Gordon as Capt. Fitzroy, Fanny Wright as Patrick, E. Osborne as Dermot, Frederick Everill as Darby, William Clark as Father Luke, Fanny Gwynne as Norah, Miss Landre as Kathlane/ Scenery by John O'Conner.

POOR STROLLERS, THE// D 3a// Watts Phillips// **Adelphi**, Jan. 1858, with Edmund Garden as Michael, Charles Selby as Lawson, Benjamin Webster as Leroux, Paul Bedford as Samson, Mme. Celeste as Marie, Edward Wright as Ritts, John Billington as Walter/ Scenery by Pitt & Brew/ Machines by Powell/ Music by J. W. Thirlwall/ **Sad. Wells**, May 1866, with Mr. Holland as Cassidy, William McIntyre as Lawson, Thomas Swinbourne as Leroux, Mr. Barrett as Samson, Ada Dyas as Marie, Miss Ella as Katrine, George Belmore as Ritts, Charles Warner as Walter, Mrs. Bishop as Judy.

POOR SUSAN; OR, THE FATE OF A VILLAGE MAID// D 4a// G. D. Pitt// **Victoria**, June 1842, with John Dale as Chesterton, C. Williams as Capt. Manson, William Seaman as Mapleton, John Gardner as Tony, Annette Vincent as Susan, Miss Saddler as Lady Manson, Jane Coveney as Cicely, Mrs. Griffith as Joan, Mrs. Seaman as Bridget/ Scenery by Fenton & Morelli/ Machines by Mr. Emmens/ Music by W. J. Hill/ Prod. by Mr. Osbaldiston.

POPPING THE QUESTION// F 1a// J. B. Buckstone// **Haymarket**, June 1837, with William Farren as Primrose, Charles Selby as Thornton, Miss E. Phillips as Ellen, Mrs. Tayleure as Miss Winterblossom, Mrs. Julia Glover as Miss Biffin, Mrs. Humby as Bobbin; Nov. 1853, with Mr. Tilbury as Primrose, George Braid as Thornton, Mrs. Stanley as Miss Biffin, Mrs. Poynter as Miss Winterblossom, Amelia Vining as Ellen, Mrs. Caulfield as Bobbin; Feb. 1870, with W. H. Chippendale as Primrose, Walter Gordon as Thornton, Miss Francis as Ellen, Mrs. Chippendale as Miss Biffin, Mrs. Laws as Miss Winterblossom, Mrs. Edward Fitzwilliam as Bobbin/ **Cov. Garden**, Oct. 1841, with William Farren as Primrose, A. Brindal as Thornton, Mrs. Julia Glover as Miss Biffin, Miss Lee as Ellen, Mrs. Tayleure as Miss Winterblossom, Mrs. Orger as Bobbin/ **Grecian**, Jan. 1845, with Frederick Robson as Primrose, Edwin Dixon as Henry, Miss E. Mears as Ellen, Miss Merion as Miss Biffin, Miss Johnstone as Miss Winterblossom, Annette Mears as Bobbin/ **Sad. Wells**, Apr. 1846, with A. Younge as Primrose, Mr. Morton as Thornton, Mrs. Henry Marston as Miss Biffin, Georgiana Lebatt as Miss Murray, Miss Stephens as Miss Winterblossom, Miss Lebatt as Bobbin/ **Drury Lane**, Mar. 1847/ **Strand**, 1851/ **Olympic**, Apr. 1861, with George Cooke as Primrose, Gaston Murray as Thornton, Miss Evans as Ellen, Mrs. Leigh Murray as Miss Biffin, Mrs. Stephens as Miss Winterblossom, Mrs. W. S. Emden as Bobbin.

POPPLETON'S PREDICAMENTS// F 1a// C. M. Rae// **Olympic**, 1870, with William Blakely as Poppleton, Henry Vaughan as Hardup, George Elliott as Thomas, Miss Ashton as Mrs. Trapeen, Miss Eversfield as Fanny, Miss Alma as Mrs. Walker, Alice Fanshaw as Jemima/ **Royalty**, July 1870.

PORK CHOPS// F// E. L. Blanchard// **Olympic**, Feb. 1843, with George Wild as Snooks, Walter Searle as Dabbs, Mr. Rogers as Pilfer, Miss Hamilton as Miss Chubb/ Scenery by W. R. Beverly/ Music by Mr. Calcott.

PORTER'S KNOT, THE// C 2a// Adap. by John Oxenford fr F, Les Crochets du Père Martin// **Olympic**, Dec. 1858, with George Cooke as Capt. Oakham, Frederick Robson as Samson Burr, Walter Gordon as Augustus Burr, Horace Wigan as Smirk, George Vining as Scatter, Harwood Cooper as Bob, J. H. White as Binnacle, Mrs. Leigh Murray as Mrs. Burr, Miss Hughes as Alice.

PORTRAIT, THE; OR, THE BIRTHDAY// George Colman the elder// **Sad. Wells**, Nov. 1838, with Mr. Dry as Bertram, Mr. Elvin as Henry, Mr. Williams as Capt. Bertram, Robert Honner as Junk, Dibdin Pitt as Capias, Miss E. Honner as Emma, Miss Richardson as Mrs. Moral.

PORTRAIT, THE// C// Walter Sapt Jr.// **Olympic**, May 1888.

PORTRAIT OF CERVANTES, THE// F// n.a.// **Cov. Garden**, Dec. 1838, with George Bartley as Murillo, Henry Howe as Don Guzman, Mr. Roberts as Merida, Mr. Tilbury as Fr. Benito, Drinkwater Meadows as Scipio, John Pritt Harley as Sancho, Miss E. Phillips as Isabella, Mrs. Humby as Lucetta/ **Haymarket**, Dec. 1839, with Robert Strickland as Murillo, Henry Howe as Don Guzman, J. Worrell as Don Carlos, J. B. Buckstone as Sancho, T. F. Mathews as Scipio, Miss Grove as Isabella, Mrs. Frank Matthews as Lucetta; July 1852, with Mr. Lambert as Murillo, Henry Bedford as Sancho, John Parselle as Don Guzman, George Braid as Don Carlos, William Clark as Scipio, Mr. Rogers as Father Benito, Amelia Vining as Isabella, Mrs. Caulfield as Lucetta.

POST BOY, THE// D 2a// H. T. Craven// **Strand**, Oct. 1860/ **Princess's**, Dec. 1862, with W. H. Stephens as Sir John, J. G. Shore as Bingley, James Rogers as Spurritt, Mr. Cockrill as Fubbs, Mr. Brooke as Fesac, Miss M. Oliver as Maria, Marian Jones as Miss Wharton, Miss Murray as Lacet.

POST OF HONOUR, THE// D 1a// T. Mildenhall// **Lyceum**, May 1844, with Mr. Turner as Burgomaster, John Kinloch as Raymond, J. Collier as Skipps, Edwin Yarnold as Captain, Robert Keeley as Yerks, Miss Grove as Adela, Sarah Woolgar as Trudchen/ **Olympic**, Feb. 1845, with Mr. Pardy as Burgomaster, C. Howard as Vandaleur, Mr. Mestayer as Skipps, Mr. Henry as Capt. Cranecaer, Mr. Dunn as Montelieu, Mr. Robinson as Yorks, Mrs. G. Jones as Trudchen, Mrs. Mestayes as Adela.

POSTMAN, THE// C// T. E. Pemberton// **Strand**, July 1892.

POSTSCRIPT, THE// C 1a// F. H. Knight// **POW**, Feb. 1888/ **Vaudeville**, Aug. 1889.

POUL A-DHOIL; OR, THE FAIRY MAN// D 3a// C. H. Hazlewood// **Britannia**, Oct. 1865.

POUTER'S WEDDING// F// J. Maddison Morton// **St. James's**, June 1865, with Frank Matthews as Marrowfat, H. J. Montague as Capt. Latimer, Frederick Robson as Pouter, James Johnstone as Pickings, Mr. Smithson as Joseph, Mrs. Frank Matthews as Mrs. Marrowfat, Miss Mason as Alice, Miss Weber as Kitty.

POWDER AND BALL// F// n.a.// **Adelphi**, 1845.

POWER AND PRINCIPLE// D 3a// Adap. by Morris Barnett fr G of Friedrich Schiller, Kabale und Liebe// **Strand**, June 1850.

POWER OF ENGLAND, THE// D// Adap. by C. E. Dering fr novel of Ouida// **Imperial**, June 1885.

POWER OF HATE, THE; OR, HONESTY IS THE BEST POLICY// D 3a// W. R. Osman// **Surrey**, Feb. 1870.

POWER OF LOVE, THE// D 4a// Adap. by Henrietta Lindley fr novel of Michael Connelly// **POW**, Mar. 1888.

POWERFUL PARTY, A// F// n.a.// **Olympic**, Aug. 1862, with George Cooke as Bagwell, Alfred Wallace as Ladylove, William Worboys as Headstrong, Florence Haydon as Mrs. Bagwell, Mrs. W. S. Emden as Hannah.

PRACTICAL JOKER, A// C// C. L. Hume// **Comedy**, June 1895.

PRACTICAL MAN, A// F 1a// W. Bayle Bernard// **Lyceum**, Oct. 1849, with C. J. Mathews as Cloudsley, Mr. Granby as Rockstone, Frederick Cooke as Horton, Mr. Kerridge as Biggs, Mrs. Macnamara as Mrs. Mildmay/ **Grecian**, July 1862, with Charles Lambert as Cloudsley, Henry Power as Horton, George Gillett as Rockstone, Miss Johnstone as Mrs. Mildmay.

PRACTICAL MAN, A// D// n.a.// **Drury Lane**, Mar. 1856.

PRAYER IN THE STORM, THE; OR, THE THIRST FOR GOLD (see Thirst of Gold)

PREDICTION, THE// D// n.a.// **Princess's**, Dec. 1844, with Walter Lacy as de Mauleon, Augustus Harris as Verinville, Mr. Fitzjames as de Estigny, W. H. Oxberry as de Hauterive, Mr. Granby as Diquedon, James Ranoe as Colasse, Mr. Turnour as La Fleur, Mrs. Brougham as Mme. Laura, Emma Stanley as The Uninvited, Mrs. Fosbroke as Mme. de Clarincourt, Miss Charlton as Mme. de Lenneville, Mrs. Lacy as Mme. de Savigny.

PRESENTED AT COURT// C 2a// J. Stirling Coyne// **Haymarket**, Feb. 1851, with Mr. Stuart as Charles II, Henry Howe as Capt. Montague, E. L. Davenport as Rochester, George Braid as Sedley, Mr. Woolgar as Etheridge, Charles Selby as Marquis de Flamareus, Mr. Lambert as Pepys, John Parselle as Killgrew, J. B. Buckstone as Wedderburne, Miss Reynolds as Anne, Mrs. L. S. Buckingham as Lady Castlemaine, Miss Young as Lady Shrewsbury, Amelia Vining as Mrs. Middleton, Mrs. Stanley as Lady Trumpington.

PRESS GANG, THE// D 3a// Douglas Jerrold// **Victoria**, May 1850, with Mr. Neville as The Stranger, J. Howard as Adm. Oakwood, Mr. Henderson as Graham, Mr. Humphreys as Capt. Crosbie, J. T. Johnson as Lansdown, John Bradshaw as Tough, John Hudspeth as Twist, Mr. Morrison as Snare, Mrs. George Lee as

Rachel, Miss Barrowcliffe as Mary, Miss Mildenhall as Kate.

PRESUMPTION; OR, THE FATE OF FRANKENSTEIN// D 3a// R. B. Peake// **Victoria**, Mar. 1840, with O. Smith as X, Mr. Hicks as Frankenstein, Mr. Frampton as Clerval, Mr. Manders as Fritz, Mr. King as De Lacy, Mr. Reynolds as Felix, Mr. Johnstone as Tanskin, Mr. Howard as Hammerpan, Mrs. Howard as Elizabeth, Miss Stoker as Agatha, Mrs. France as Mme. Ninon/ **Lyceum**, June 1847, with Leigh Murray as Frankenstein, Charles Bender as De Lacey, Mr. Bellingham as Felix, John Kinloch as Clerval, W. H. Oxberry as Fritz, Samuel Emery as XXX, Miss May as Elizabeth, Miss Bromley as Agatha, Mary Keeley as Saffe.

PRESUMPTIVE EVIDENCE; OR, MURDER WILL OUT// D 2a// J. B. Buckstone// **Victoria**, Nov. 1837, with William Davidge as Hammond, John Parry as Dorgan, Mr. Green as Kinchela, Mr. Salter as Madigan, Mr. Harwood as Fed, Mrs. Hooper as Penny, Miss Bartlett as Shelah, Mrs. Griffith as Judith, Mrs. Loveday as Cathleen/ **Sad. Wells**, May 1842, with Mr. Aldridge as Hammond, Robert Honner as Dorgan, John Herbert as Madigan, John Brougham as Kinshela, Mrs. Robert Honner as Pennie, Mrs. Richard Barnett as Nelly, Mrs. Morgan as Shelah, Mrs. Henry Marston as Judith, Miss Richardson as Cauthleen/ **Grecian**, Oct. 1861, with Henry Grant as Hammoud, Walter Holland as Madigan, Thomas Mead as Dorgan, Alfred Rayner as Kinchela, Jane Dawson as Pennie, Miss Taylor as Nelly, Lucreza Hill as Judith, Miss Johnstone as Cathleen.

PRESUMPTIVE EVIDENCE// D 2a// Dion Boucicault// **Princess's**, May 1869, with John Parselle as Sir Bertie, G. F. Neville as Reginald, Louisa Moore as Sybil, Mme. Celeste as Josephine, J. G. Shore as Dodd, Emma Barnett as Mercy, William Rignold as Coveney, Dominick Murray as Saker, Mr. Moreland as Brassey.

PRETENDER, THE// Play 3a// George Duncan// **Princess's**, May 1876.

PRETTY GIRLS OF STILBERG, THE// C 1a// Adap. by Benjamin Webster fr F// **Haymarket**, Apr. 1842, with Benjamin Webster as Ernest, Henry Holl as Alfred, Mr. Vining as Jules, Henry Howe as Gustavus, J. Worrell as Theodore, Henry Widdicomb as Popplewig, William Strickland as Bobb, Mlle. [sic] Celeste as Margot, Miss Mattley as Betty, Mis Charles as Crettle/ Scenery by George Morris/ Music by T. German Reed/ **Adelphi**, Aug. 1845, with Benjamin Webster as Napoleon, Edward Wright as Bob, Charles Munyard as Popplewig, Mme. Celeste as Margot, Sarah Woolgar as Christina.

PRETTY HORSEBREAKER, THE; OR, SEE 'EM AT A GLANCE// F 1a// Andrew Halliday & William Brough// **Adelphi**, Aug. 1862, with Paul Bedford as Maj. Lollipop, J. L. Toole as Spout, Mrs. Henry Marston as Lady Stilton, Kate Kelly as Cherubina, Mrs. Alfred Mellon (Sarah Woolgar) as Belia/ **Globe**, June 1878, with J. L. Toole as Spaut, Fanny Josephs as Bella, Charles Collette as Maj. Lollipop, Isabel Clifton as Lady Creamly.

PRETTY PIECE OF BUSINESS, A// C 1a// Thomas Morton// **Haymarket**, Nov. 1853, with Henry Howe as Capt. Merryweather, J. B. Buckstone as Shee, Miss Reynolds as Mrs. Grantley, Mrs. L. S. Buckingham as Mrs. Shee, Mrs. Fitzwilliam as Dobson/ **Lyceum**, July 1876, with Evan Gordon as Capt. Merryweather, H. Moxon as Dr. Shee, Amy Lionel as Mrs. Grantley, Frances Ryan as Charlotte, Mrs. E. Fitzwilliam as Dobson/ **Vaudeville**, Mar. 1890, with Frank Atherley as Capt, Merryweather, George Giddens as Shee, Fanny Moore as Mrs. Grantley, Eleanore Leyshon as Charlotte, Emily Vining as Dobson/ **Criterion**, Oct. 1899.

PRETTY POLL// C 1a// Robert Reece// **St. James's**, Jan. 1876, with Mr. Crawford as Sir Robert, George Robinson as Tom Jones, Miss Spiller as William, Caroline Hill as Mrs. Beauchamp, Constance Brabant as Paget.

PREVIOUS ENGAGEMENT, A// Play 1a// Blanche Chandler// **Avenue**, Nov. 1900.

PRICE OF EXISTENCE, THE// D// C. H. Hazlewood// **Britannia**, Dec. 1872.

PRICE OF PEACE, THE// D 4a// Cecil Raleigh// **Drury Lane**, Sept. 1900, with Henry Neville as Earl of Derwent, Charles Allan as Addiscott, Charles Lowne as Sir Henry, Alfred Bucklaw as Sir George, H. Cooper Cliffe as Benton, Frank Atherley as Vincent, Lettice Fairfax as Lady Kathleen, Mrs. Raleigh as Baroness Blanco, Vane Featherston as Lady St. Azuline, Birdie Sutherland as Lady Stagge, Mary Brough as Mrs. Tulk/ Scenery by Henry Emden, W. Perkins, Mr. McLeery, Bruce Smith, Julian Hicks & R. Caney/ Machines by E. Taylor/ Music by J. M. Glover/ Prod. by Arthur Collins.

PRIDE// C 3a// James Albery// **Vaudeville**, Apr. 1874.

PRIDE OF THE MARKET, THE// C 3a// J. R. Planché// **Lyceum**, Oct. 1847, with Leigh Murray as de Volange, Mr. Granby as Troptard, John Parselle as Bellerive, J. B. Buckstone as Farine, Miss H. Gilbert as Mlle. Volange, Mme. Vestris as Marton.

PRIDE; OR, THE USURER'S DAUGHTER// D 4a// Edward Towers// **Pavilion**, May 1872.

PRIEST HUNTER, THE// D 4a// Hubert O'Grady// **Grand**, Apr. 1893.

PRIEST OR PAINTER// C 3a// Adap. by William Poel fr novel of W. D. Howell// **Olympic**, July 1884.

PRIEST'S DAUGHTER, THE// D// T. J. Serle// **Sad. Wells**, Jan. 1845, with Henry Marston as Count Robert, Mr. Raymond as De Stateville, Edward Knight as De Crussel, Samuel Phelps as Ambroise, John Webster as Luitgrand, Mr. Morton as D'Angeville, Mr. Williams as Huguis, Mrs. Henry Marston as Sybilla, Mrs. Mary Warner as Madeline.

PRIMA DONNA, THE// C 2a// Dion Boucicault// **Princess's**, Sept. 1852, with John Cathcart as Count von Mansfeldt, Mr. Addison as Dr. Holbein, Walter Lacy as Rouble, Caroline Heath as Stella, Miss Robertson as Margaret/ Scenery by Mr. Dayes.

PRIMROSE FARM// D// H. A. Major// **Grecian**, July 1871.

PRIMROSE PATH, THE// Play 4a// W. W. Lindon// **Vaudeville**, May 1892.

PRINCE AND THE CHIMNEY SWEEP, THE// F// n.a.// **Grecian**, Oct. 1845, with Harry Chester as Prince D'Oresca, Mr. Melvin as Don Cesar, Mr. Kerridge as Lopez, Edwin Dixon as Guzman, Frederick Robson as Barago, Miss M. A. Crisp as Donna Sancha.

PRINCE AND THE PAUPER, THE// Play 4a// Dram. by Mrs. Oscar Berringer fr novel of Mark Twain// **Gaiety**, Apr. 1890, with W. H. Vernon as Henry VIII, J. H. Barnes as Hendon, J. G. Taylor as Canty, Edmund Gurney as Hertford, Ernest Hendrie as St. John, John Beauchamp as Father Andrews, Master Alfred Field-Fisher as Prince Edward, Annie Irish as Mrs. Canty, Ethel Mathews as Lady Jane Grey/ Prod. by W. H. Vernon.

PRINCE AND THE PAUPER, THE// Play 4a// Adap. by Joseph Hatton fr novel of Mark Twain// **Vaudeville**, Oct. 1891.

PRINCE FOR AN HOUR, A// F 1a// J. Maddison Morton// **Princess's**, Mar. 1856, with Miss Desborough as Prince Lorenzo, Carlotta Leclercq as Beppo, George Everett as Col. Pazzi, Frederick Cooke as Geronimo, Ellen Ternan as Carlotta.

PRINCE KARL// C 4a// A. C. Gunter// **Lyceum**, Oct. 1888, with Richard Mansfield as Prince Karl, W. H. Crompton as Spotts, J. Burrows as Davis, John Parry as Briggs, Joseph Frankau as Dragoon, Carlotta Leclercq as Daphne, Emma Sheridan as Alicia, Beatrice Cameron as Florence.

PRINCESS AND THE BUTTERFLY; OR, THE FANTASTICS// C 5a// Arthur Wing Pinero// **St. James's**, Mar. 1897, with George Alexander as Sir George, H. B. Irving as Oriel, H. V. Esmond as St. Roche, C. Aubrey Smith as Col. Eave, Ivo Dawson as Denstroude, R. Dalton as Velleret, George Bancroft as Mylls, Gerald Gurney as Levan, A. Vane Tempest as Ord, Arthur Royston as Demailly, H. H. Vincent as Gen. Chichele, S. Hamilton as Count Reviczky, Robert Soutar as Kara Pasha, Julia Neilson as Princess Pannonia, Dorothy Hammond as Annis, Rose Leclercq as Lady Ringstead, Pattie Bell as Lady Chichele, Mrs. Cecil Raleigh as Mrs. Sabiston, Miss Granville as Mrs. St. Roche, Julie Opp as Mrs. Ware/ Scenery by Walter Hann, H. P. Hall & William Telbin.

PRINCESS CARO'S PLOT// C 3a// Hilda Hilton// **Novelty**, Jan. 1887.

PRINCESS GEORGE// D 3a// Adap. by Charles Coghlan fr F of Alexandre Dumas fils// **Prince's**, Jan. 1885, with Charles Coghlan, Lillie Langtry, Amy Roselle, Kate Pattison.

PRINCESS OF ORANGE, A// Play 1a// Fred James// **Lyceum**, Dec. 1896.

PRINCESS TARAKANOFF, THE; OR, THE NORTHERN NIGHT// Play 5a// Clotilde Graves// **POW**, July 1897.

PRINTER'S DEVIL, THE// F 1a// J. R. Planché// **Olympic**, Oct. 1838, with Thomas Green as Count de Maurepas, Charles Selby as Duke de Bringhen, Mr. Granby as Griffet, Robert Keeley as Pierre, Mrs. Macnamara as Mme. Girard, Miss Lee as Cecile/ Scenery by W. Telbin/ **Cov. Garden**, Oct. 1839, with Thomas Green as Count de Maurepas, Charles Selby as Duke de Bringhen, Mr. Granby as Griffet, Robert Keeley as Pica, Mrs. Macnamara as Mme. Girard, Miss Lee as Cecile/ **Haymarket**, Aug. 1841, with John Webster as Count de Maurepas, Henry Wallack as Duke de Bringhen, Robert Keeley as Pica, Mrs. Woulds as Mme. Girard, Miss Grove as Cecile/ **Lyceum**, June 1847, with Mr. Bellingham as Count Maurepas, John Kinloch as Duke de Bringhen, Mr. Turner as Griffen, Robert Keeley as Pica, Mrs. Woollidge as Mme. Girard, Miss Arden as Cecile/ **Sad. Wells**, Apr. 1848, with J. T. Johnson as Count de Maurepas, Henry Mellon as Duke de Bringhen, Mr. Williams as Griffet, John Scharf as Pica, Mrs. W. Watson as Mme. Girard, Miss Marsh as Cecile.

PRISONER OF ROCHELLE, THE// D// G. D. Pitt// **Victoria**, June 1841, with David Osbaldiston as Florival, Mr. James as Count Larole, John Gardner as Guichard, William Seaman as Capt. Le Blanque, Mr. Hitchinson as Lt. Delavigne, Annette Vincent as Beatrice, Miss J. Howard as Amile.

PRISONER OF TOULON, THE; OR, THE PEASANTS' REVENGE// D 3a// A. B. Richards// **Drury Lane**, Mar. 1868, with William McIntyre as Didier, Henry Sinclair as Rouvray, J. Irving as Cochet, Mr. Barrett as Marquis de Villetaneuve, Charles Harcourt as Count Henri, Charles Webb as Col. Montani, W. C. Temple as Capt. de Lestagnes, Edith Stuart as Genevieve, Kate Harfleur as Leontine, Mrs. Henry Vandenhoff as Mme. Rouvray, Mrs. Charles Harcourt as Josephine/ Music by W. C. Levey/ Prod. by Edward Stirling.

PRISONER OF WAR, THE// C 2a// Douglas Jerrold// **Drury Lane**, Feb. 1842, with Samuel Phelps as Capt. Channel, James Anderson as Lt. Firebrace, Charles Hudson as Heyday, George Bennett as Beaver, Robert Keeley as Pall-Mall, Henry Mellon as Forest, Charles Selby as Cheille, Morris Barnett as Boaz, Mrs. Charles Jones as Mme. La Rose, Mrs. Selby as Mme. Violette, Miss Turpin as Babette, Mrs. Keeley as Polly, Miss Fortesque as Clarina/ **Sad. Wells**, Oct. 1844, with A. Young as Capt. Channel, John Webster as Firebrace, E. Morton as Heyday, G. F. Forman as Pallmall, Edward Knight as Chenille, Mr. Raymonde as Beaver,

Mr. Sharp as Boaz, Miss Cooper as Clarina, Miss Lebatt as Polly, Mrs. Henry Marston as Mme. La Rose, Mrs. Francis as Mme. Violet, Georgiana Lebatt as Babella/ **Princess's**, Feb. 1851, with John Ryder as Capt. Channel, Charles Kean as Firebrace, Robert Keeley as Pallmall, Frederick Belton as Heyday, Mr. King as Beaver, Drinkwater Meadows as Boaz, Mr. Wynn as Chenille, Mrs. Charles Kean as Clarina, Mrs. Keeley as Polly, Mrs. Alfred Wigan as Mme. La Rose, Mrs. W. Daly as Mme. Violette, Mary Keeley as Babette/ **Haymarket**, Feb. 1850, with Benjamin Webster as Capt. Channel, Charles Kean as Lt. Firebrace, Henry Vandenhoff as Heyday, Mr. Stuart as Beaver, Mr. Rogers as Boaz, Robert Keeley as Pall-Mall, Charles Selby as Chenille, Mrs. Charles Kean as Clarina, Mrs. W. Clifford as Mme. la Rose, Mrs. Stanley as Mme. la Violette, Mrs. L. S. Buckingham as Babette/ **Grecian**, Apr. 1856, with W. H. Tilbury as Capt. Channell, Richard Phillips as Firebrace, F. Charles as Heyday, Mr. Hustleby as Beaver, John Manning as Pallmall, Jane Coveney as Clarisa, Harriet Coveney as Polly, Miss Johnstone as Mme. la Rose, Ellen Hale as Babette.

PRISONER OF ZENDA, THE// D Pro & 4a// Dram. by Edward Rose fr novel of Anthony Hope// **St. James's**, Jan. 1896, with George Alexander as Prince Rudolf, Herbert Waring as Duke Woligang and as Rudolf Rassendyll, Charles Glenney as Earl of Rassendyll, Vincent Sternroyd as Glyn, Mabel Hackney as Countess Amelia, W. H. Vernon as Col. Sapt, Arthur Royston as Fritz, Laurence Cautley as Hentzau, Allan Aynesworth as Bertram, George Hawtrey as Teppich, George Bancroft as Lord Topham, Frank Dyall as Josef, Evelyn Millard as Princess Flavia, Lily Hanbury as Antoinette, Olga Brandon as Frau Teppich/ Scenery by H. P. Hall, William Telbin & Walter Hann/ Music by Walter Slaughter.

PRIVATE DETECTIVE, A// F 1a// S. Leigh & M. Pemberton// **St. Geo. Hall**, Apr. 1886.

PRIVATE INQUIRY,A// F 3a// Adap. by F. C. Burnand fr F of A. Valabrègue, La Securité des Familles// **Adelphi**, Mar. 1862, with David Fisher as Charles Madison, J. L. Toole as Worricow, John Billington as Carder, Kate Bland as Emily, Kate Kelly as Laura.

PRIVATE SECRETARY, THE// F 4a// Adap. by C. H. Hawtrey fr G of G. von Moser, Der Bibliothekar// **Prince's**, Mar. 1884, with W. J. Hill, Herbert Beerbohm Tree, G. W. Anson, Lucy Buckstone, Mrs. Leigh Murray/ **Globe**, (in 3a), 1884, with A. Beaumont as Mr. Marsland, Reeves Smith as Harry Marsland, W. J. Hill as Cattermole, C. H. Hawtrey as Douglas Cattermole, W. S. Penley as Rev. Spalding, Julian Cross as Gibson, Miss Vane Featherston as Edith Marsland, Maude Millett as Eva, Mrs. Leigh Murray as Mrs. Stead/ **Comedy**, July 1892/ **Avenue**, Sept. 1895/ **Grand**, July 1900.

PRIVATEER, THE; OR, THE LADY OF ST. TROPEZ// D 4a// C. Long// **Grecian**, Feb. 1845, with Harry Chester as Frank Stemwell, John Collett as Count St. Armand, Edmund Garden as Seymore, Mr. Baldwin as Loverule, Edwin Dixon as Dr. Gerald, Frederick Robson as Hinton, Miss M. A. Crisp as Mlle. Blanche, Annette Mears as Kate Loverule, Miss Merion as Jeanne/ Scenery by Mr. Muir.

PRIVATEER'S VENTURE, THE// D Pro & 2a// H. Hayman// **Victoria**, June 1876.

PRODIGAL DAUGHTER, THE// D 4a// Henry Pettitt & Augustus Harris// **Drury Lane**, Sept. 1892, with Henry Neville as Sir John, James Fernandez as Deepwater, Leonard Boyne as Capt. Vernon, Julius Knight as Belford, Harry Nicholls as Lord Banbury, J. L. Shine as Roper, Arthur Williams as Blinker, Charles Dodsworth as Jim, Jessie Millward as Rose, Blanche Horlock as Violet, Fanny Brough as Dorcas, Mrs. B. De Solla as Concierge/ Scenery by Caney, W. Perkins & Harker/ Machines by J. Taylor/ Music by John Crook.

PRODIGAL FATHER, THE// F 3a// Glen Macdonough// **Strand**, Feb. 1897.

PRODIGAL PARSON, THE; OR, FOR EVER AND EVER// D 4a// F. L. Connyngham & C. A. Clarke// **Standard**, June 1899.

PROFESSIONAL BEAUTY, A// C 3a// Vincent Ambrose// **Imperial**, June 1880.

PROFESSOR'S LOVE STORY, THE// C 3a// J. M. Barrie// **Comedy**, June 1894/ **Garrick**, Aug. 1894.

PROFESSOR'S WOOING, THE// C 4a// William Gillette// **Royalty**, Feb. 1887.

PROFLIGATE, THE// D 3a// Leman Rede// **Olympic**, Feb. 1844, with Mr. Scott as Lord Villiers, Charles Fenton as Sir Tittleby, John Webster as Viscount Ormonde, Mr. Brookes as Dr. Merton, Mr. Turnour as Bill Badger, George Wild as Harry, Lavinia Melville as Emmeline, Miss Hamilton as Lady Massingham, Miss Lebatt as Kate, Mrs. Sarah Garrick as Mrs. Dearlet, Miss Yates as Susan/ Scenery by W. R. Beverly & Mr. Scott/ Music by Mr. Calcott/ Machines by Mr. Mackintosh.

PROFLIGATE, THE// Play 4a// Arthur Wing Pinero// **Garrick**, Apr. 1889, with Kate Rorke, Olga Nethersole, Lewis Waller, John Hare, Sidney Brough, Johnston Forbes Robertson.

PROGRESS// C 3a// Adap. by T. W. Robertson fr F of Victorien Sardou, Les Gamaches// **Globe**, Sept. 1869/ **St. James's**, May 1874, with Arthur Knight as Lord Mompesson, R. S. Boleyn as Arthur, George Barrett as Dr. Brown, Francis Fairlie as Bunnythorne, Leonard Boyke as Fenne, Gilmer Greville as Danby, Rose Coghlan as Eva, Mrs. Buckingham White as Miss Myrnie/ Prod. by Francis Fairlie & George Barrett.

PROMISE, A// Play 1a// S. B. Lawrence// **Globe**, Oct. 1889.

PROMISE OF MAY, THE// D 3a// Alfred Tennyson// **Globe**, Nov. 1882, with Charles

Kelly as Dobson, Hermann Vezin as Edgar, H. Cameron as Steer, E. T. March as Wilson, Mrs. Bernard Beere as Dora Steer, Emmeline Ormsby as Eva, Alexes Leighton as Sally, Maggie Hunt as Milly/ Scenery by W. Hann, Spong, & Perkins/ Music by Hamilton Clarke.

PROMISED IN PIQUE// Play 3a// n.a.// **Globe**, Apr. 1885.

PROMISED LAND, THE; OR, THE SEARCH FOR THE SOUTHERN STAR// D// Henry Pettitt// **Grecian**, Sept. 1875.

PROMISSORY NOTE, THE; OR, A RACE TO HAMPSTEAD// F// Samuel Beazley// **Sad. Wells**, Aug. 1845, with Mr. Morton as Scamper and as Markham, Charles Fenton as Nicks, Mrs. Henry Marston as Mrs. Markham, Miss Huddart as Caroline, Miss Lebatt as Cicely.

PROMPTER'S BOX, THE: A STORY OF THE FOOTLIGHTS AND THE FIRESIDE (see also Crushed Tragedian)// D 4a// H. J. Byron// **Adelphi**, Mar. 1870, with C. H. Stephenson as Sir Michael, J. D. Beveridge as Ernest, Benjamin Webster as Bristowe, H. J. Byron as Fitzaltamount, Harwood Cooper as Mandaville, J. G. Taylor as Ned, Mr. Ashley as Gadsby, Richard Phillips as Capt. Racket, W. H. Eburne as Phipps, Miss Furtado as Florence, Mrs. Alfred Mellon as Miss Montcashel/ Scenery by Hawes Craven & Maugham/ Machines by Edward Charker.

PROOF; OR, A CELEBRATED CASE// D Pro & 3a// Adap. by F. C. Burnand fr F of A. P. Dennery & Eugène Cormon, Une Cause Célèbre// **Adelphi**, Dec. 1872, with Hermann Vezin as Pierre, Edward George as Chamboran, Arthur Stirling as Lazare, James Johnstone as Seneschal, Louise Moodie as Madeleine, Jane Coveney as Martha, Kate Barry as Adrienne, Charles Harcourt as Aubeterre, Luigi Lablache as Victor, Mrs. Billington as Duchesse d'Aubterre, Bella Pateman as Adrienne, Mrs. Arthur Stirling as Mme. Deprets, Mrs. Bandmann as Valentine, Clara Jecks as Julie.

PROOF POSITIVE// C 3a// F. C. Burnand// **Opera Comique**, Oct. 1875.

PROPHET OF THE MOOR, THE// D 3a// George Almar// **Victoria**, Aug. 1853, with N. T. Hicks as White, T. E. Mills as Gayton, John Bradshaw as Peynet, Mr. Raymond as Col. Leelyn, F. H. Henry as Hardenbrass, Mr. Richards as Talbot, J. Howard as Stokes, Mr. Hitchinson as Brown, John Hudspeth as Johnny, Mrs. Henry Vining as Crazy Ruth, Georgiana Lebatt as Catherine, Miss Sutton as Honor, Mrs. Manders as Dame Horner.

PROPOSALS// F 3a// J. F. Gilmore// **Vaudeville**, Dec. 1887.

PROVED TRUE// D 5a// J. Mortimer Murdoch// **Sadler's Wells**, May 1883.

PROVISIONAL GOVERNMENT, THE// C 1a// J. H. Stocqueler// **Olympic**, July 1848, with Frederick Vining as Grand Duke Frederick, Mr. Norton as Prince Sigismund, H. J. Turner as Baron Clackmann, Charles Bender as Baron Pepinstern, A. Younge as Flip-Flap, C. Cowell as Floreston, Mr. Lawrence as Cuefail, Harwood Cooper as Gagton, Mrs. H. J. Turner as Baroness Wilhemina, Miss Richards as Princess Matilda, Miss Marsh as Azoline.

PROVOKED HUSBAND, THE; OR, A JOURNEY TO LONDON// C 5a// John Vanbrugh// **Haymarket**, Aug. 1837, with W. C. Macready as Lord Townly, William Farren as Sir Francis, J. B. Buckstone as Richard, Benjamin Webster as Moody, J. T. Haines as Manly, Charles Selby as Count Basset, Mrs. Nisbett as Lady Townly, Mrs. Julia Glover as Lady Wronghead, Eliza Vincent as Lady Grace; Jan. 1842, with Mr. Stuart as Lord Townly, Henry Howe as Manly, William Strickland as Sir Francis, David Rees as Richard, Benjamin Webster as Moody, J. Worrell as Count Basset, J. W. Gough as Poundage, Lucy Bennett as Lady Townly, Mrs. W. Clifford as Lady Wronghead, Miss Charles as Lady Grace, Mrs. Stanley as Mrs. Motherly, Mrs. Frank Matthews as Trusty/ **Cov. Garden**, Oct. 1837, with W. C. Macready as Townly, George Bartley as Wronghead, Drinkwater Meadows as Richard, W. J. Hammond as Moody, Mr. Warde as Manly, John Pritchard as Basset, Helen Faucit as Lady Townly, Mrs. W. Clifford as Lady Wronghead, Miss Huddart as Lady Grace, Miss Taylor as Jenny/ **Drury Lane**, May 1842, with W. C. Macready as Townly, Samuel Phelps as Manly, Henry Compton as Sir Francis, Robert Keeley as Richard, William Bennett as Moody, Charles Selby as Basset, Mr. Hughes as Poundage, Helen Faucit as Lady Townly, Mrs. Charles Jones as Lady Wronghead, Mrs. Stirling as Lady Grace, Mrs. Sarah Garrick as Mrs. Motherly, Miss Turpin as Trusty, Miss Phillips as Myrtilla, Mrs. Keeley as Jenny/ **Sad. Wells**, Aug. 1844, with Samuel Phelps as Lord Townley, A. Younge as Sir Francis, G. F. Forman as Richard, Henry Marston as Moody, John Webster as Manly, Mr. Morton as Count Basset, Mrs. Mary Warner as Lady Townley, Miss Cooper as Lady Grace, Mrs. Henry Marston as Lady Wronghead, Georgiana Lebatt as Myrtilla, Miss Lebatt as Jenny, Miss Stephens as Mrs. Trusty, Mrs. Francis as Mrs. Motherly; Sept. 1858, with Samuel Phelps, Mrs. Charles Young, Henry Marston/ **St. James's**, Dec. 1854, with George Vandenhoff as Lord Townly, Henry Rivers as Manly, W. Cooper as Wronghead, J. L. Toole as Richard, Mr. Robertson as Moody, George Burt as Basset, Mr. Ennis as Poundage, Mrs. Seymour as Lady Townly, Mrs. Stanley as Lady Wronghead, Miss Bulmer as Lady Grace, Miss Marshall as Jenny.

PROVOST OF BRUGES, THE// T// George Lovell// **Sad. Wells**, June 1847, with Henry Mellon as Earl Charles, Samuel Phelps as Bertulphe, George Bennett as Thanemar, Henry Marston as Bouchard, Mr. Morton as Gautier, William Hoskins as St. Prieux, Mr. Towers as Albert, Charles Fenton as Hackel, Edward Knight as Hebert, Frank Graham as Charente, A. Younge as Philippe, Mr. Williams as Antoine, John Scharf as Denis, Laura Addison as Constance, Mrs. Henry Marston as Ursula.

PRUDE'S PROGRESS, THE// C 3a// Jerome K. Jerome & Eden Phillpotts// **Comedy**, May 1895/ **Terry's**, July 1895.

PRUDES AND PROS// F 2a// Adelene Voteere// **St. Geo. Hall**, June 1891.

PUDDENHEAD WILSON// Dram. by Frank Mayo fr novel of Mark Twain// **Elephant & Castle**, Apr. 1895.

PUMP, THE// C// W. L. Clowes// **Toole's**, Mar. 1886.

PUNCH// C 3a// H. J. Byron// **Vaudeville**, May 1881, with David James, William Lestocq, William Farren, John Maclean, Kate Bishop, Sophie Larkin, Cicely Richards.

PUNCH AND JUDY// C 1a// Rachel Penn & M. E. Jones// **Savoy**, June 1893.

PUNCHINELLO// Play 1a// G. H. Dabbs// **Avenue**, June 1890.

PUNCTURED// C 1a// T. G. Warren// **Strand**, Aug. 1900.

PURE AS DRIVEN SNOW; OR, TEMPTED IN VAIN// D 3a// C. H. Hazlewood// **Britannia**, Nov. 1869.

PURE GOLD// Play 4a// Westland Marston// **Sad. Wells**, Nov. 1863, with Edmund Phelps as Sir Gerard, T. B. Bennett as Brackenbury, David Jones as Gilbery, Samuel Perfitt as Langley, Henry Marston as Rochford, W. D. Gresham as Lancia, E. H. Brooke as Rinaldo, George Vining as Schmidt, T. Robinson as Neuner, A. Baildon as Morley, Alfred Denial as Jackson, Miss Mandelbert as Evelyn, Mrs. Buckingham White as Miss Fortescue.

PURITAN, THE// Play 4a// D. C. and Henry Murray & J. L. Shine// **Trafalgar**, July 1894.

PURSER, THE/ F 3a// J. T. Day// **Strand**, Sept. 1897.

PUSS; OR, METEMPSYCHOSIS// F 1a// Adap. fr F// **Princess's**, Nov. 1859, with J. G. Shore as Carl, Edmund Garden as Schamp, Mrs. Weston as Bonne, Louise Keeley as Adelaide/ **Olympic**, Oct. 1860, with Gaston Murray as Carl, Harwood Cooper as Schamp, Mrs. Stephens as Bonne, Miss Seymour as Liza, Louise Keeley as Adelaide.

PUT ASUNDER// D 4a// Freeman Wills// **Gaiety**, May 1883.

PUT TO THE TEST// D 1a// Adap. by Westland Marston fr F// **Olympic**, Mar. 1873, with William Rignold as Count Pietra, George Canninge as Prior, W. Conway as Flavio, Ada Cavendish as Countess de Tolomei, Kate Rivers as Mila.

PUT YOURSELF IN HIS PLACE// D 4a// Charles Reade// **Adelphi**, 1870, with John Chute as Raby, Henry Ashley as Coventry, Mr. Neville as Cheetham, Henry Neville as Little, G. F. Sinclair as Grotait, Richmond Kyrle as Cole, Mrs. Leigh Murray as Mrs. Little, Margaret Young as Grace, Robertha Erskine as Jael/ Scenery by Hawes Craven/ Music by Edwin Ellis/ Machines by Edward Charker/ Stage Dir. Henry Neville.

PUZZLED AND PLEASED// F 1a// Henry Spry// **Grecian**, Nov. 1855, with Eaton O'Donnell as Argus-Eye, F. Charles as Capt. Lovel, John Manning as Thin, Richard Phillips as Tight, Mrs. Charles Montgomery as Rosa, Harriet Coveney as Mary.

PYGMALION AND GALATEA// C 3a// W. S. Gilbert// **Haymarket**, Dec. 1871, with W. H. Kendal as Pygmalion, Henry Howe as Leucippe, J. B. Buckstone as Chrysos, Madge Robertson as Galatea, Caroline Hill as Cynisca, Miss Merton as Myrine, Mrs. Chippendale as Daphene/ **Lyceum**, Dec. 1883, with J. H. Barnes as Pygmalion, F. H. Macklin as Leucippe, Henry Kemble as Crysos, E. T. March as Agesimos, Arthur Lewis as Mimos, Amy Roselle as Cynisca, Mrs. Arthur Stirling as Daphne, Mary Anderson as Galatea/ Scenery by Hawes Craven and W. G. Cuthbert/ Music by Andrew Levey/ Prod. by W. S. Gilbert/ **Comedy**, June 1900.

PYRAMUS AND THISBE// F// C. H. Stephenson// **Sad. Wells**, Sept. 1866, with John Rouse as Slabs, W. Cameron as Robinson, Louisa Periera as Sally.

*

Q.E.D.; OR, ALL A MISTAKE// F 1a// Frank Marshall// **Court**, Jan. 1871.

Q.Q.// C 4a// H. T. Johnson// **Terry's**, Mar. 1898.

QUACKS, THE// FC 3a// Adap. by Louis Honig fr G of G. von Moser// **Royalty**, Sept. 1887.

QUADROON SLAVE, THE// D 2a// Benjamin Webster// **Haymarket**, Oct. 1841, with John Webster as St. George, Frederick Vining as Pelham, Benjamin Webster as Heartley, William Clark as Von Vipper, Mrs. Stanley as Mrs. Heartley, Mlle. [sic] Celeste as Julie.

QUAKER, THE// C 1a// Charles Dibden// **St. James's**, Jan. 1837, with Mr. Leffler as Steady, Mr. Bennett as Lubin, Mr. Hollingsworth as Easy, John Pritt Harley as Solomon, Miss Rainforth as Gillian, Miss Smith as Floretta, Mrs. Penson as Cecily/ **Cov. Garden**, May 1838, with Mr. Leffler as Steady, Mr. Wilson as Lubin, Drinkwater Meadows as Solomon, John Ayliffe as Easy, Mrs. Sarah Garrick as Cicely, Mrs. Humby as Floretta, Priscilla Horton as Gillian.

QUARTER OF MILLION OF MONEY, A// D 3a// Edward Towers// **East London**, Feb. 1868.

QUARTER TO NINE, A// F 1a// R. B. Peake// **Eng. Opera House** (Lyceum), Aug. 1837, with A. Brindal as Capt. Nearshot, Mr. Baker as Killrush, William Bennett as Mustyroll, R. McIan as Rook, Mr. Turnour as Tom, Henry Compton as Frolick, Mrs. Frank Matthews as Mrs. Major Petule, Mrs. East as Mrs. Jervis.

QUASIMODO; OR, THE GIPSEY GIRL OF NOTRE DAME// D// Edward Fitzball// **Cov. Garden**, Feb. 1837, with George Bennett as Frollo, Mr. Thompson as Provost, Mr. Collins as Chateaupers, John Webster as Ernest, Henry Wallack as Quasimodo, Benjamin Webster as Gringoire, Eliza Vincent as Esmeralda, Miss Pelham as Mme. Gondelaurier, Miss Lacy as Fleur de Lys, Mrs. W. West as Gudule, Mrs. Sarah Garrick as Julie.

QUEEN AND CARDINAL// D 5a// W. S. Raleigh// **Haymarket**, Oct. 1881, with Mrs. Scott-Siddons, Blanche Henri, Kate Pattison, Henry Kemble, Mr. Swinbourne.

QUEEN AND THE YEOMAN, THE// D// n.a.// **City of London**, Jan. 1852.

QUEEN ELIZABETH; OR, AT THE QUEEN'S COMMAND// Play 4a// Frances Leightner// **Vaudeville**, Sept. 1901.

QUEEN MAB// C 3a// G. W. Godfrey// **Haymarket**, Mar. 1874, with W. H. Chippendale as Sir Grevile, W. H. Kendal as Gerald, J. B. Buckstone as Curnick, Henry Howe as Brent, Frederick Everill as Prince Brulendorf, J. B. Buckstone Jr. as Earl of Quorn, Mrs. Chippendale as Mrs. Carew, Helen Massey as Clara, Madge Robertson (Mrs. Kendal) as Mab/ Scenery by John O'Conner & George Morris/ Machines by Oliver Wales.

QUEEN MARY// D 5a// Alfred Tennyson// **Lyceum**, Apr. 1876, with Henry Irving as Philip of Spain, Thomas Swinbourne as Gardiner, Mr. Brooke as Renard, Walter Bentley as Noailles, Mr. Carton as Courtenay, Thomas Mead as Howard, Mr. Huntley as Sir Thomas, Virginia Francis as Princess Elizabeth, Kate Bateman as Queen Mary, Georgina Pauncefort as Lady Clarence, Isabel Bateman as Alice/ Scenery by Hawes Craven & H. Cuthbert/ Music by Robert Stoepel.

QUEEN MARY; OR, THE TOWER OF LONDON// D 3a// n.a.// **Adelphi**, 1840.

QUEEN MARY'S BOWER// C 3a// Adap. by J. R. Planché fr F, Les Mouquetaires de la Reine// **Haymarket**, Oct. 1846, with Benjamin Webster as Killicrankie, Charles Hudson as Capt. O'Donoghue, George Braid as Capt. Norris, Henry Howe as Lt. Ormond, A. Brindal as Lt. Wentworth, Mrs. Seymour as Lady Arabella, Miss Fortescue as Lucy/ Scenery by George Morris.

QUEEN OF AN HOUR// D 5a// J. T. Douglass & Frank Stainforth// **Standard**, Oct. 1877.

QUEEN OF ARRAGON, THE// C 1a// Howard Paul// **Sad. Wells**, June 1854, with C. Poynter as Don Mendos, E. L. Davenport as de Alaide, Mr. Barrett as Hernando, Fanny Vining as Queen.

QUEEN OF BOHEMIA, THE; OR, LONDON IN 1664// D 3a// E. L. Blanchard// **Olympic**, Oct. 1845, with Thomas Archer as Maynard, James Browne as Malefant, Mr. Waldron as Zaubergoldt, George Wild as John, Mr. Smithson as Richard, Mr. Binge as Atherley, Mr. Turnour as Beedroll, Robert Romer as Harte, Lavinia Melville as Queen Elizabeth of Bohemia, Kate Howard as Lucille/ Scenery by Laidlaw & Hodson/ Machines by Mr. Mackintosh/ Music by Mr. Griesbach.

QUEEN OF CONNAUGHT, THE// C 4a// Dram. by Harriet Jay & Robert Buchanan fr novel of same name// **Olympic**, Jan. 1877, with John Vollaire as O'Mara, J. A. Arnold as Dooneen, Mr. Byatt as Blake, Mr. Raemond as Mackey, Mr. Bauer as Father Flynn, Charles Flockton as Dunbeg, Henry Neville as Darlington, W. J. Hill as O'Kelly, Dibdin Culver as Hagan, T. G. Warren as Croghan, Trevor Glyndon as Monaghan, Ada Cavendish as Kathleen, Camille Dubois as Norah, Miss Carlisle as Nannie, Miss Beaumont as Bridget/ Scenery by W. Hann/ Music by M. Buziau/ Prod. by Henry Neville, Mrs. Seymour, & the authors.

QUEEN OF DIAMONDS, THE; OR, THE SHADOWS OF LIFE// D 5a// Arthur Shirley// **Standard**, Nov. 1894.

QUEEN OF FASHION, THE// D Pro & 4a// T. Cannam & J. T. Preston// **Sad. Wells**, Mar. 1888/ **Vaudeville**, June 1888.

QUEEN OF MANOA, THE// Play 4a// C. Haddon Chambers & W. O. Tristram// **Haymarket**, Sept. 1892, with Lewis Waller as Sevarro, Cyril Maude as Baron Finot, Herbert Flemming as Lord Chudleigh, Edmund Maurice as Malvern, Charles Collette as Maj. Garrett, Rudge Harding as Hill, W. Cheesman as Wildrake, J. H. Batson as McNair, Lillie Langtry as Lady Violet, Marie Linden as Dorothy, Henrietta Lindley as Lady Helmore, Emily Cross as Mrs. Clover, Rose Nesbitt as Lady Dashley/ Scenery by Walter Johnstone/ Electrics by E. Wingfield Bowles.

QUEEN OF SPADES, THE// D 2a// Adap. by Dion Boucicault fr F, La Dame de Pique// **Drury Lane**, Apr. 1851, with Walter Lacy as Prince Moskau, H. T. Craven as Klamberg, James Anderson as Ivan, Mr. Barrett as Kopeck, Julia Bleaden as Ludwig, Louisa Nisbett as Katinka, Mrs. Walter Lacy as Olga, Mrs. Bisson as Princess Beresina/ Scenery by Jones & Cuthbert/ Machines by J. Sloman/ Music by Henri Laurent.

QUEEN OF THE BEGGARS, THE// D 2a// T. J. Serle// **Haymarket**, Sept. 1837, with Mr. Saville as de Burgh, J. W. Gough as Sir

John, E. W. Elton as Ormsby, Mr. Harris as Corby, J. Worrell as Hugh, J. T. Haines as Hogson, Mr. Ross as Dull, Robert Strickland as Archbishop, Benjamin Webster as Jack, J. B. Buckstone as Nibble, T. F. Mathews as Snoose, Miss Huddart as Margaret/ Scenery by Morris & Fenton.

QUEEN OF THE MARKET, THE// Pro & 3a// Adap. fr F, La Dame de la Halle// **Adelphi**, Apr. 1852, with J. Worrell as Count de Salnalies, Samuel Emery as Leonard, O. Smith as Lorrain, George Honey as Robishon, C. J. Smith as Jean, William Cullenford as Chauvel, Ellen Chaplin as Albert, Paul Bedford as Blaise, Mrs. Keeley as Louise, Emma Harding as Duchess de Cerny/ Scenery by Pitt & Turner.

QUEEN OF THE ROSES, THE// Arthur Calmour// **Court**, Jan. 1900.

QUEEN STORK// F// F. Waller// **POW**, Sept. 1870.

QUEEN'S BENCH, THE// F 2a// W. L. Rede// **Strand**, Nov. 1848/ **Sad. Wells**, Feb. 1849, with A. Younge as Hughes, William Hoskins as Edward, Frank Graham as Tristy, William Belford as Brereton, Charles Fenton as Skylark, Miss Murray as Kate, Miss Garthwaite as Betty, Miss Stephens as Mary.

QUEEN'S CHAMPION, THE// D 2a// Mrs. C. G. Gore// **Haymarket**, Aug. 1837, with Frederick Vining as Malvoisy, Charles Selby as Duc de Lauzun, Robert Strickland as Marquis de Vassan, Benjamin Webster as Dr. Bourdillac, Miss Taylor as Marie Antoinette, Miss E. Phillips as Princess de Guemence, Mrs. Humby as Louise.

QUEEN'S COLOURS, THE// D 4a// George Conquest & Henry Pettitt// **Grecian**, May 1879.

QUEEN'S COMMAND, THE// D 4a// n.a.// **Lyceum**, July 1838.

QUEEN'S COUNSEL// F 3a// Adap. by James Mortimer fr F of Victorien Sardou, Les Pommes du Voisin// **Comedy**, May 1890.

QUEEN'S DOUBLE, THE// Play 4a// n.a.// **Garrick**, Apr. 1901.

QUEEN'S EVIDENCE// D 4a// George Conquest & Henry Pettitt// **Grecian**, June 1876/ **Princess's**, 1878, with J. G. Shore as Sydney, Leonard Boyne as Wynford, Charles Warner as Medland and Stanfield, William Rignold as Thorntorn, Harry Jackson as Isaacs and Levant, T. W. Thorne as Joe, Marie Litton as Kate, Fannie Leslie as Ada and Miss Sydney, Maud Milton as Laura, Kate Barry as Arthur/ Scenery by Julian Hicks/ Machines by Mr. Warton/ Lime-light by Mr. Kerr/ Music by W. C. Levey/ Prod. by Harry Jackson.

QUEEN'S FAVOURITE, THE// C 4a// Adap. by Sidney Grundy fr F of Eugene Scribe, Le Verre d'Eau// **Olympic**, June 1883, with W. H. Vernon as St. John, T. C. Blindloss as Masham, Hamilton Knight as Marquis de Torcy, Gertrude Kellogg as Queen, Lucy Buckstone as Abegail, Janet Achurch as Lady Albemarle, Genevieve Ward as Duchess of Marlborough.

QUEEN'S HORSE, THE; OR, THE BREWER OF PRESTON// F 1a// Adap. fr F// **Olympic**, Dec. 1838, with Robert Keeley as Tubbs, John Brougham as Corp. Murphy, Charles Selby as Capt. Forecastle, Miss Lee as Mary/ Scenery by William Telbin & Mr. Cuthbert/ Music by J. H. Tully/ **Cov. Garden**, Oct. 1839, with Robert Keeley as Tubbs, Charles Selby as Capt. Forecastle, Robert Honner as Adjutant, John Brougham as Corp. Murphy, Miss Lee as Mary/ **Eng. Opera House** (Lyceum), June 1843, with Mr. Thornton as Capt. Forecastle, Charles Fenton as Adjutant, Mr. Burton as Corp. Murphy, J. Courtney as Sam, Samuel Emery as Tom Tubbs, Miss Taylor as Mary.

QUEEN'S JEWELS, THE; OR, THE PURITAN'S BRIDE// D 3a// Robert Dodson// **East London**, Nov. 1876.

QUEEN'S MESSENGER, A// Play 1a// J. H. Manners// **Haymarket**, June 1899, with C. Aubrey Smith as Officer, Miss Granville as Lady/ **Avenue**, Oct. 1899.

QUEEN'S PRIZE, THE// C// R. Fenton Mackay// **Strand**, Nov. 1894.

QUEEN'S PROCTOR, THE; OR, DECREE NISI// C 3a// Adap. by Herman Merivale fr F of Victorien Sardou & E. de Najac, Divorçons// **Royalty**, Feb. 1896/ **Strand**, Apr. 1897.

QUEEN'S ROOM, THE// Play 1a// F. F. Moore// **Opera Comique**, Oct. 1891.

QUEEN'S SECRET, THE; OR, THE IRON MASK// D 3a// Benjamin Webster// **Adelphi**, Sept. 1851, with Mme. Celeste as Roland, Benjamin Webster as de Rosarges, Paul Bedford as Neauwitz, C. J. Smith as St. Mars, Sarah Woolgar as Countess de Chevreuse, Kathleen Fitzwilliam as Aline.

QUEEN'S SHILLING, THE// C 3a// Adap. by G. W. Godfrey fr F of J. F. Bayard & M. Bieville, Le Fils de Famille// **Court**, Apr. 1879, with John Hare, W. H. Kendal, Mrs. Kendal/ **St. James's**, Oct. 1879, with John Hare as Col. Daunt, William Terriss as Gambier, W. H. Kendal as Frank Maitland, Mr. Mackintosh as Sam, T. N. Wenman as Sgt. Sabretache, Robert Cathcart as Doolan, Mrs. Kendal as Kate Greville, Mrs. Gaston Murray as Mrs. Ironsides, Kate Phillips as Jenny/ Scenery by Gordon & Harford.

QUEEN'S TRAGEDY, THE// Play 2a// M. A. Curtois// **St. Geo. Hall**, Oct. 1899.

QUEEN'S VENGEANCE, A// D 4a// Brandon Ellis// **Britannia**, July 1898.

QUEER STREET// D 2a// Richard Butler & H. Chance Newton ("Richard Henry")// **Gaiety**, Mar. 1892.

QUEEN SUBJECT, THE// F// J. Stirling Coyne//

Adelphi, 1837.

QUESTION OF MEMORY, A// D 4a// Katherine Bradley & Emma Cooper ("Michael Field")// **Opera Comique**, Oct. 1893.

QUICKSANDS// C 4a// Adap. by Charlotte Morland fr novel of Lovett Cameron, The Devout Lover// **Comedy**, Feb. 1890, with Walter Russell as Dane, Edwin Gilbert as Halliday, Laurence Cautley as Geoffrey, Gilbert Yorke as Trichet, Charlotte Morland as Angel, Florence Bright as Dulcie, Mrs. B. M. de Solla as Martine.

QUICKSANDS; OR, THE PILLARS OF SOCIETY// Adap. by William Archer fr Norw. of Henrik Ibsen// **Gaiety**, Dec. 1880.

QUICKSANDS AND WHIRLPOOLS// D 4a// Robert Soutar// **Victoria**, Mar. 1868.

QUICKSANDS OF LIFE, THE; OR, THE LABYRINTH OF DEATH// D 4a// T. Mead// **Grecian**, Oct. 1865, with David Jones as Denis Treghorn, J. Jackson as Bertram Treghorn, J. B. Steele as Penruth, William James as St. Leven, John Manning as Abel, Henry Grant as Zamerman, Lizzie Mandlebert as Marion.

QUID PRO QUO; OR, THE DAY OF DUPES// C// Mrs. Gore// **Haymarket**, June 1844, with Mr. Stuart as Earl of Hunsdon, Mrs. Nisbett as Lord Bellamont, William Strickland as Grigson, Henry Holl as Henry, J. B. Buckstone as Capt. Sippet, William Farren as Sir George, Henry Howe as Rivers, Mr. Tilbury as Cogit, Henry Widdicomb as Spraggs, Mrs. W. Clifford as Countess of Hunsdon, Mrs. Julia Bennett as Lady Mary, Julia Glover as Mrs. Grigson, Mrs. Edwin Yarnold as Ellen, Mrs. Humby as Bridget/ Scenery by George Morris.

QUIET DAY, A// F 1a// John Oxenford// **Olympic**, Oct. 1837, with Robert Keeley as Somerday, John Brougham as O'Reilly, Mr. Stoker as Marsden, Miss Murray as Mrs. O'Reilly, Miss Lee as Emma, Mrs. Keeley as Mrs. Somerday/ **Cov. Garden**, Oct. 1839, with Robert Keeley as Somerday, John Brougham as O'Reilly, Robert Honner as Marsden, Mrs. Orger as Mrs. Somerday, Mrs. Brougham as Mrs. O'Reilly, Miss Lee as Emma.

QUIET DAY A// F 1a// H. T. Hipkins & Gaston Murray// **Haymarket**, July 1869, with C. Swan as Col. Brimstone, W. H. Vernon as Poodle, Mr. Trafford as St. Bernard, R. Ross as Mongrel, Polly Marshall as Mrs. Brimstone, Miss Coleman as Emily, Bella Fawsette as Susan.

QUIET FAMILY, A// F// W. E. Suter// **Surrey**, 1857/ **Olympic**, Nov. 1866, with Harwood Cooper as Benjamin Bibbs, Dominick Murray as Barnaby Bibbs, J. Reeves as Parker, Henry Rivers as Grumpy, Mrs. Stephens as Mrs. Benj. Bibbs, Miss Sheridan as Mrs. Barn. Bibbs, Miss E. Wilson as Selina, Miss Schavey as Snarley/ **Globe**, Sept. 1876, with E. Shepherd as Benjamin Bibbs, Harry Cox as Barnaby Bibbs, A. Evans as Peter Parker, F. Lyons as Grumpy, Rose Roberts as Mrs. Benj. Bibbs, Miss F. Gray as Mrs. Barn. Bibbs, Annie Campbell as Selina Summers.

QUIET IN HARNESS// C 2a// Leonard Rae// **Standard**, Oct. 1876.

QUIET LODGINGS// F// n.a.// **Princess's**, Dec. 1865, with Gaston Murray as Cranky, Robert Cathcart as Dozy.

QUIET PIPE, A// C 1a// Miss Cowen & S. M. Samuel// **Folly**, Mar. 1880, with F. H. Macklin, Miss B. Henri.

QUIET RUBBER, A// C 1a// Adap. by Charles Coghlan fr F, La Partie de Piquet// **Globe**, June 1878, with John Hare as Lord Kilcare, C. Kelly as Sullivan, Mr. Herbert as Charles, Miss Plowden as Mary Sullivan/ **Court**, Jan. 1879, with John Hare, Miss M. Cathcart/ **St. James's**, Apr. 1885, with John Hare as Lord Kilcare, F. Rodney as Charles, John Maclean as Sullivan, Miss Webster as Mary/ **Haymarket**, May 1888, with John Hare as Kilcare, W. Herbert as Charles, T. N. Wenman as Sullivan, Maud Cathcart as Mary.

QUITE BY ACCIDENT// F// Frank Walters// **POW**, Sept. 1869.

QUITE CORRECT// C// n.a.// **Haymarket**, Sept. 1840, with John Webster as Sir Harry, Henry Howe as Milford, David Rees as Grojan, J. Worrell as Butler, William Clark as John, Mrs. Julia Glover as Lady Almeria, Mrs. Stanley as Mrs. Rosemore, Mrs. Edwin Yarnold as Maria, Mrs. W. Clifford as Miss Leech.

QUITS; OR, WAR VERSUS LAW// C 1a// George Dance// **Cov. Garden**, Oct. 1843, with Mr. Hamilton as O'Corny, Mr. Hemming as Wilson, Mr. Attwood as Pounce, Mrs. Selby as Miss Moreland, Jane Mordaunt as Amy, Miss Turpin as Janet.

QUIXOTE, JUNIOR// F 1a// Leicester Buckingham// **Strand**, July 1859, with John Clarke, Maria Simpson.

QUO VADIS?// D 6a// Dram. by S. Strange fr novel of Henryk Sienkiewicz// **Adelphi**, May 1900.

QUONG III// FC 3a// Fenton Mackay// **Terry's**, June 1895/ **Avenue**, July 1895.

*

RABBI'S SON, THE; OR, THE LAST LINK IN THE CHAIN// D 4a// E. Manuel// **Britannia**, Apr. 1879.

RACE AT HAMPSTEAD, A// F 1a// n.a.//

Sad. Wells, June 1840, with Mr. Elvin as Scamper, J. B. Hill as Markham, J. W. Collier as Nick, Miss Richardson as Mrs. Markham, Mrs. J. F. Saville as Caroline, Mrs. Richard Barnett as Cicely.

RACE FOR A DINNER, A// F// J. T. Rodwell// **Sad. Wells**, Dec. 1843, with Mr. Williams as Grumpy, Robert Romer as Homely, Henry Marston as Sponge, Mr. Lamb as Fawnwell, M. Hill as Squire Flint, C. J. Bird as Discount, Mr. Coreno as Diggory, Miss Stephens as Mrs. Discount, Miss Cooke as Mrs. Grumpy, Mrs. Richard Barnett as Dolly, Mrs. Andrews as Deborah.

RACE FOR A DINNER, A// F// n.a.// **Sad. Wells**, July 1844, with Mr. Williams as Doric, Mr. Sharpe as Measureton, Mr. Binger as Dalton, Charles Hudson as Sponge, Edward Knight as Lovel, Charles Morelli as Feedwell, Miss Thornbury as Harriet, Miss Morelli as Jane.

RACE FOR A RARITY, A// F// n.a.// **Adelphi**, Oct. 1838, with John Webster, Mr. Wilkinson, Frederick Yates, John Sanders, Mr. Landsdowne, Mrs. Young.

RACE FOR A WIDOW, A// F 1a// T. J. Williams// **Strand**, Apr. 1860.

RACE FOR A WIFE, A// C 1a// Frederick Cooper// **Adelphi**, Aug. 1876, with Frederick Moreland as Sir Peckham, W. Everard as Richard Green, Ernest Travers as Roland Green, Henry Vaughn as Robert, Cicely Nott as Lady Wry, Miss E. Phillips as Isabella.

RACE TO HAMPSTEAD, A// F// n.a.// **Sad. Wells**, Dec. 1840, with Mr. Elvin as Scamper, J. B. Hill as Markham, J. W. Collier as Nick, Miss Richardson as Mrs. Markham, Mrs. Morgan as Caroline, Mrs. Richard Barnett as Cicely.

RACHEL// D Pro & 3a// Adap. by Sidney Grundy fr F of E. P. Grange & Lambert Thiboust, La Voleuse d'Enfants// **Olympic**, Apr. 1883, with W. H. Vernon as Sir Philip, Hermann Vezin as Capt. Craven, W. E. Blatchley as Sgt. Matthews, F. Staunton as Adams, Mrs. Leigh Murray as Margaret, Genevieve Ward as Rachel and as Mrs. Athelstan, T. C. Blindloss as Lee, Lucy Buckstone as Gladys.

RACHEL THE REAPER// D 2a// Charles Reade// **Queen's**, Mar. 1874.

RACHEL'S MESSENGER// C 1a// T. Malcolm Watson// **Princess's**, Feb. 1891, with E. B. Norman as Gleddin, S. H. Lechmere as Hedley, Oscar Adye as Holden, Ethel Hope as Ruth, Hetty Dene as May, Amy McNeil as Rachel.

RACHEL'S PENANCE; OR, A DAUGHTER OF ISRAEL// D 4a// E. Manuel// **Britannia**, Apr. 1878.

RACKET COURT; OR, LODGINGS FOR A SINGLE MAN// F 1a// Adap. by Thomas Greenwood fr F// **Sad. Wells**, June 1841, with John Herbert as Dozyman, J. S. Balls as Crankyman.

RADICAL CURE, A// F 1a// Dion Boucicault// **Haymarket**, Nov. 1850, with J. B. Buckstone as Bumptious, George Braid as Doctor, Mrs. Fitzwilliam as Rose.

RAFAEL THE LIBERTINE// D// George Almar// **Olympic**, May 1841, with J. S. Balls as Don Rafael, Mr. Halford as Don Alphonso, Mr. Freeborn as Juan, Mr. Harry as Roderique, Samuel Buckingham as Pedro, Miss Fortesque as Maria, Miss Hamilton as Inezelia, Miss Bartlett as Joanna.

RAFFAELLE THE REPROBATE; OR, THE SECRET MISSION AND THE SIGNET RING// D 2a// T. E. Wilks// **Victoria**, Sept. 1841/ **Sad. Wells**, Oct. 1842, with Henry Marston as Raffaelle, C. J. Bird as di Monti, Charles Fenton as Montmorency, P. Williams as Gablin, John Herbert as Jumble, Mr. Dry as Lorienne, Caroline Rankley as Pauline, Mrs. Henry Marston as Mme. Bonbon/ **Grecian**, Feb. 1852, with Basil Potter as Count Achille, Mr. Douglas as Montmorency, Richard Phillips as Raffaelle, Charles Horn as Titus, J. W. Collier as Jumble, Eaton O'Donnell as Gablin, Miss M. A. Crisp as Pauline, Miss Johnstone as Mme. Bonbon.

RAFFLE FOR LIFE, THE; OR, A MAIDEN'S HAZARD// D 2a// n.a.// **Victoria**, July 1870, with J. H. Fitzpatrick as St. Dumont, E. Fitzdavis as Marquis of Croixville, James Fawn as Marquis de le Fresbete, G. Skinner as Simpion, J. Baker as Borwin, J. H. Doyne as Marquis de la Rosiere, G. Carter as Malfois, Mrs. J. F. Young as Genevieve, Julia Summers as Baretta, Florence Farren as Madeline.

RAG FAIR// D 5a// Horace Wigan// **Victoria**, May 1872.

RAG PICKERS OF PARIS AND THE DRESS MAKERS OF ST. ANTOINE, THE// D 3a// Edward Stirling// **Olympic**, Mar. 1849, with Edward Stirling as Jean, Mr. Norton as Garousse, Mr. Mazzoni as Didier, John Kinloch as Berville, Mr. Lawrence as Comte St. Antoine, Mrs. Henry Vining as Marie Didier, Miss De Burgh as Marie Hoffman, Mrs. England Young as Mme. Potard.

RAGGED ROBIN// Play 4a// Adap. fr F of Jean Richepin, Le Chemine// **Her Majesty's**, June 1898.

RAGS AND BONES// D// Frank Scudamore// **Surrey**, July 1883.

RAID IN THE TRANSVAAL, THE; OR, THE KING OF DIAMONDS// D// a rev. of King of Diamonds by Paul Merritt & George Conquest// **Surrey**, Apr. 1884.

RAILROAD OF LOVE, THE// C// Adap. by Augustin Daly fr G of Franz Schönthan & G. Kadelberg, Goldfische// **Gaiety**, May 1888/ **Daly's**, June 1895.

RAILROAD STATION, THE// F 1a// T. E. Wilks// **Olympic**, Oct. 1840/ **Sad. Wells**, Sept. 1844, with A. Younge as Jones, Mr. Williams as William Smith, Mr. Morton as Charles Smith, Henry Marston as Robins, Mr. Sharpe as Grabbins, Charles Fenton as Sleeper, Mr. Franks as Trap, Edward Knight as Shutup, Mrs. Henry Marston as Mrs. W. Smith, Miss Huddart as Mrs. C. Smith/ **Grecian,** Nov. 1846, with Frederick Robson as Sampson Jones, John Collett as William Smith, Mr. Manley as Charles Smith, Edwin Dixon as Robins, Miss Merion as Mrs. W. Smith, Miss Johnstone as Mrs. C. Smith.

RAILROAD TRIP, A; OR, LONDON, BIRMINGHAM & BRISTOL// F 2a// Thomas Morton Jr. & J. Maddison Morton// **Haymarket,** Oct. 1843, with Mr. Tilbury as Toby Bristle, J. B. Buckstone as Blondel Bristle, Henry Howe as Charles, Henry Holl as Gag, William Strickland as Buffer, Miss C. Conner as Lydia, Mrs. W. Clifford as Penelope, Miss Lee as Laura.

RAILWAY BELLE, THE// F 1a// Mark Lemon// **Adelphi,** Nov. 1854.

RAILWAY BUBBLES// F// J. Stirling Coyne// **Haymarket,** Nov. 1845, with Charles Hudson as Hudson, Mr. Tilbury as Gen. Bungalow, A. Brindal as Braggs, Mr. Caulfield as Lord Fitz-Flam, Mr. Carle as Sir Seamperly, T. F. Mathews as Bam, Miss Telbin as Ellen, Miss Carre as Kitty.

RAILWAY KING, THE// F 1a// Edward Stirling// **Olympic,** Oct. 1845, with Mr. Brookes as Sir Jacob, Mr. Turnour as Shirk, George Wild as Sam Stag, Mr. Richardson as Inspector, Kate Howard as Sally, Miss Beauchamp as Clara.

RAILWAY STATION, THE// F 1a// n.a.// **Sad. Wells,** Dec. 1854, with Lewis Ball as Jones, Mr. Barrett as William Smith, Charles Mortimer as Charles Smith, William Hoskins as Robins, Mrs. Henry Marston as Mrs. W. Smith, Teresa Bassano as Mrs. C. Smith.

RAISED FROM THE ASHES// D// Frank Fuller// **Elephant & Castle,** May 1879.

RAISING THE WIND// F 1a// James Kenney// **Victoria,** Sept. 1837, with Edward Hooper as Jeremy Diddler, W. H. Oxberry as Sam, John Parry as Fainwould, William Davidge as Plainway, L. Smith as Richard, Miss Fitzwalter as Peggy, Mrs. Griffith as Lucretia/ **Cov. Garden,** Dec. 1838, with Mr. Vining as Jeremy Diddler, Mr. Tilbury as Plainway, Drinkwater Meadows as Fainwood, John Pritt Harley as Sam, W. H. Payne as Walter, Mr. Bannister as Richard, John Collett as John, Mrs. W. Clifford as Miss Durable, Miss Charles as Peggy/ **Drury Lane,** Feb. 1840, with Mr. Vining as Jeremy Diddler, William Bennett as Old Plainway, W. H. Oxberry as Fainwould, W. J. Hammond as Sam, Miss Daly as Peggy, Mrs. Selby as Miss Durable/ **Sad. Wells,** Mar. 1850, with Mr. Williams as Plainway, Henry Nye as Fainwou'd, Samuel Phelps as Jeremy Diddler, William Hoskins as Sam, Teresa Bassano as Peggy, Mrs. Brougham as Miss Durable/ **Princess's,** Dec. 1862, with W. H. Stephens as Plainway, George Belmore as Fainwould, Robert Roxby as Jeremy Diddler, Charles Seyton as Sam, Mr. Cockrill as Richard, Marian Jones as Peggy, Mrs. Henry Marston as Miss Durable/ **Olympic,** Aug. 1866, with Henry Rivers as Plainway, Robert Soutar as Fainwould, George Vincent as Jeremy Diddler, Annie Florence as Peggy, Mrs. Poynter as Laura/ **Grecian,** Sept. 1866, with J. Jackson as Plainway, Henry Power as Fainwould, John Manning as Sam, Frederick Marchant as Jeremy Diddler, Mrs. Atkinson as Laura, Harriet Western as Peggy; Feb. 1875, with Mr. Raemond as Plainway, T. G. Warren as Fainwould, Johnston Forbes Robertson as Jeremy Diddler, Robert Pateman as Sam, Miss Beaumont as Peggy, Amy Crawford as Laurelia/ **Lyceum,** June 1874, with Henry Irving as Jeremy Diddler, John Clayton as Fainwould, Gaston Murray as Plainway, F. W. Irish as Sam, W. L. Branscombe as John, Miss Ewell as Miss Durable, Virginia Francis as Peggy.

RAKE'S PROGRESS, THE// D 3a// W. L. Rede// **Sad. Wells,** Aug. 1837, with C. H. Pitt as Rakewell, Mr. Mercer as Markham, Mr. Ray as Florid, Thomas Lee as Slap, Mr. Pateman as Frank, Mr. Rogers as Nokes, Miss Beresford as Fanny, Mrs. Harris as Betty, Miss Williams as Lady Blazon, Mrs. Griffiths as Mrs. Dabbleditch, Miss H. Pitt as Martha.

RAKE'S WILL, THE// Play 1a// H. P. Grattan// **Princess's,** Feb. 1881, with C. W. Somers as Jeremy Diddler, Henry Leigh as Plainway, Fred Terry as Richard, J. C. Buckstone as Fainwould, Miss B. Huntley as Miss Durable, Miss Measor as Peggy/ **Terry's,** July 1889.

RALPH GASTON// D// n.a.// **Surrey,** Sept. 1860.

RANDALL'S THUMB// C 3a// W. S. Gilbert// **Court,** Jan. 1871.

RANELAGH// C 2a// J. Palgrave Simpson & Cecil Wray// **Haymarket,** Feb. 1854, with George Vandenhoff as Sir Robert, William Farren as Lord Pryington, J. B. Buckstone as Dr. Coddlelove, Mr. Tilbury as Col. Crawfish, Mr. Rogers as Bramble, Edwin Villiers as Sir Lorimer, William Clark as Fluster, George Braid as Flegmorton, Miss Reynolds as Lady Rovely, Mrs. Fitzwilliam as Mrs. Coddlelove/ Scenery by George Morris & Mr. O'Conner.

RANK AND FAME// D 5a// Leonard Rae & Frank Stainforth// **Standard,** Mar. 1875.

RANK AND RICHES// D 4a// Wilkie Collins// **Adelphi,** June 1883, with Charles Sugden as Duke of Heathcote, J. W. Pigott as Earl of Laverock, Miss Lingard as Lady Calista, Mrs. Billington as Lady Sherlock, G. W. Anson as Dominic, George Alexander as Cassilis, Myra Holme as Alice, Harry Proctor as Jessup/ Scenery by Prodger & Smith/ Prod. by Wilkie Collins and G. W. Anson.

RANSOM, THE// D 2a// Mrs. J. R. Planché// **Haymarket,** June 1837, with Charles Selby as President, Mr. Harris as Capt. Bordier, J. T. Haines as Durvalle, Mr. Saville as Edward,

Mr. Gallot as le Blanc, T. F. Mathews as Phillipe, Miss E. Phillips as Estelle, Mrs. W. Clifford as Gertrude, Miss Allison as Pauline/ Nov. 1848, with Henry Howe as President, Mr. Rogers as Durvalle, Henry Holl as Edward, Henry Vandenhoff as Capt. Bordier, James Bland as Le Blanc, Mrs. L. S. Buckingham as Estelle, Mrs. W. Clifford as Gertrude, Mrs. Charles Kean as Pauline.

RAPID THAW, A// C 2a// Adap. by T. W. Robertson// **St. James's**, Mar. 1867, with Henry Irving.

RAPPAREE; OR, THE TREATY OF LIMERICK// D 3a// Dion Boucicault// **Princess's**, Sept. 1870, with Hermann Vezin as O'Malley, William Rignold as Duquesne, John Clayton as Gen. Ginckel, Alfred Rayner as Col. O'Hara, E. F. Edgar as McMurragh, Shiel Barry as Doctor, John Reynolds as Roe, Katherine Rogers as Grace, Margaret Cooper as Patrice.

RAPPINGS AND TABLE-MOVINGS// F 1a// Howard Paul// **Haymarket**, June 1853, with J. B. Buckstone as Toots, Mr. Rogers as Mummy, George Braid as Podger, Mr. Vincent as Tyson, William Clark as Rummy, Mrs. Fitzwilliam as Misery, Mrs. Poynter as Mrs. Marabout, Mrs. Coe as Mrs. Gummy, Amelia Vining as Pauline, Miss E. Bromley as Blanche.

RATS OF RATS CASTLE, THE// D// J. B. Johnstone [?]// **Grecian**, Nov. 1863, with William James as Louis, Thomas Mead as Robin, John Manning as Bobby, J. B. Steele as Sir Ralph, Henry Grant as Redruth, Walter Holland as Rosethorn, Jane Dawson as Maud, Harriet Coveney as Jenny, Ellen Crisp as Dame Goodbody.

RAVEN'S NEST, THE; OR, THE BRIDE OF THE GRAVE// D 2a// T. E. Wilks// **Victoria**, Oct. 1846, with J. C. Bird as Marsden, Mr. Archer as Shirley, Walter Searle as Shawe, F. H. Henry as David, G. F. Forman as Finewebb, J. Howard as Sam, E. G. Burton as Regular, Mrs. Henry Vining.

RAVENS OF ORLEANS, THE// D// W. T. Moncrieff// **Sad. Wells**, Aug. 1843, with Mr. Williams as Dorville, C. J. Bird as Frederick, Mr. Morion as Provost, C. J. Smith as Dunoir, R. H. Lingham as Clairfranc, Mr. Bologna as Dumont, Henry Marston as Bruno Dunoir, Mr. Coreno as Antoine, Caroline Rankley as Louisa, Miss Cooke as Isabella, Miss Stephens as Margot.

RAVENSWOOD// Play 4a// Dram. by Herman Merivale fr novel of Sir Walter Scott, The Bride of Lammermoor// **Lyceum**, Sept. 1890, with Henry Irving as Edgar, William Terriss as Hayston, Alfred Bishop as Sir William, F. H. Macklin as Marquis of Athole, Henry Howe as Bide-the-Bent, Gordon Craig as Henry Ashton, Frank Tyars as Moncrieff, Roma Le Thière as Lady Ashton, Georgina Pauncefort as Annie Winnie, Ellen Terry as Lucy Ashton/ Scenery by Hawes Craven & J. Harker/ Music by A. C. Mackenzie.

RAYMOND AND AGNES; OR, THE BLEEDING NUN OF LINDENBURG// D 2a// Dram. by Edward Fitzball fr M. T. Lewis's The Monk// **Sad. Wells**, May 1837, with C. H. Pitt as Don Raymond, Mr. Griffiths as Don Felix, Mr. Rogers as Theodore, Mr. Campbell as Baptiste, Mr. Hicks as Robert, C. J. Smith as Jacques, Miss Williams as Marguerite, Lavinia Melville as Agnes, Mrs. Worrell as Bleeding Nun, Mrs. Harris as Ursula, Mrs. Rogers as Abbess/ **Victoria**, May 1859, with W. H. Pitt as Don Raymond, Mr. Henderson as Don Felix, J. Howard as Theodore, John Bradshaw as Baptiste, Miss Donaldson as Agnes, Miss Barrowcliffe as Ursula, Mrs. E. F. Saville as Marguerite, Miss James as Annette/ **Haymarket**, Jan. 1874, with Mr. James as Don Felix, Mr. Teesdale as Don Raymond, Frederick Everill as Theodore, George Braid as Baptista, Mr. Rogers as Robert, Walter Gordon as Jaques, Mr. Weathersby as Claude, Benjamin Webster as Marco, Helen Massey as Agnes, Mrs. Chippendale as Ursula, Mrs. Edward Fitzwilliam as Marguerite, Blanche Henri as Spectre/ Scenery by John O'Conner & George Morris/ Music by Mr. Hermann.

READING FOR THE BAR// F// Sidney Grundy// **Strand**, Oct. 1876.

READY AND WILLING// F 1a// F. Grove// **Astley's**, Aug. 1881, with George Stretton as Ready, E. Hughnott as Alphonso, Jennie Vernon as Galushiana, Nelly Grahame as Aurelia Willing.

READY-MONEY MORTIBOY// D 4a// Dram. by Walter Besaant & James Rice fr novel of same// **Court**, Mar. 1874, with George Rignold, Clifford Cooper, Miss Henderson, Miss Litton, Edger Bruce.

REAL AND IDEAL// C 1a// Adap. by Horace Wigan fr F// **Olympic**, Sept. 1862, with George Cooke as Bonus, Horace Wigan as Hargrave, Henry Neville as Herbert, Harwood Cooper as John, Mrs. St. Henry as Mrs. Hargrave, Miss Hughes as Lucy Brandon/ **Princess's**, Jan. 1874, with Edwin Yarnold as Bonus, P. C. Beverley as Hargrave, J. R. Crauford as Herbert, Constance Brabant as Lucy Brandon, Mrs. St. Henry as Sophy/ **Globe**, Apr. 1873, with E. W. Garden as Bonus, Charles Flockton as Hargrave, Charles Neville as Herbert, Sophie Larkin as Mrs. Hargrave, Mrs. Gaston Murray (Miss Hughes) as Lucy Brandon/ **St. James's**, Feb. 1876, with Mr. Leigh as Bonus, Horace Wigan as Hargrave, Mr. Crauford as Herbert, George Yarnold as John, Constance Brabant as Lucy Brandon, Mrs. St. Henry as Sophy.

REAL LIFE// D 4a// Robert Dodson// **Surrey**, Aug. 1882.

REAL LITTLE LORD FAUNTLEROY, THE// Play 3a// Adap. by Mrs. Frances Hodgson Burnett fr her own novel// **Terry's**, May 1888.

REALISM// C 1a// Madeleine Ryley// **Garrick**, Oct. 1900.

REALITIES OF LIFE, THE; OR, THE THIEF!

THE ARTIST! THE DOCTOR! AND THE BANKER!// D 4a// George Conquest// **Grecian,** Apr. 1862, with Thomas Mead as Morel, Mr. Jackson as Dupont, Henry Power as Remy, Walter Holland as Rousseau, Henry Grant as the Stranger, Mrs. Charles Dillon as Adele, Jane Dawson as Louise, George Conquest as Darcy, Amilie Conquest as Susanne.

REALMS OF JOY, THE// F// F. L. Tomline// **Royalty,** Oct. 1873.

REAPERS, THE; OR, FORGET AND FORGIVE// D 2a// Edward Stirling// **Strand,** Aug. 1856.

REAPING THE HARVEST// D Pro & 3a// Alfred Stafford// **Elephant & Castle,** Dec. 1887.

REAPING THE WHIRLWIND// C// Horace Lennard// **Novelty,** Apr. 1884.

REAR ADMIRAL, THE// F 1a// W. S. Emden// **Princess's,** Feb. 1845, with Mr. Granby as Admiral, Mr. Fitzjames as Sir Everard, Henry Compton as Andrew, Augustus Harris as Speedwell, Mr. Matlow as Hawser, Emma Stanley as Harriet/ **St. James's,** May 1866, with Edward Dyas as Admiral, Frederick Robson as Andrew, Alfred Sanger as Longford, Thomas Bridgeford as Speedwell, Ellen McDonnell as Harriet.

REBECCA// D 4a// Dram. by Andrew Halliday fr Sir Walter Scott, Ivanhoe// **Drury Lane,** Sept. 1871, with E. Rosenthal as King Richard, S. Dyneley as Prince John, Mr. Dolman as Rotherwood, J. B. Howard as Ivanhoe, Mr. Bruton as Athelstane, Mr. Dewhurst as Brian de Bois, B. Egan as de Boeuf, Mr. Milton as Beaumanoir, William Terriss as Robin Hood, Samuel Phelps as Isaac, Ersser Jones as Friar Tuck, Adelaide Neilson as Rebecca, Miss M. Reinhardt as Lady Rowena, Miss F. Addison as Ulrica, Miss K. Ryan as Elgitha/ Scenery by William Beverley/ Music by W. C. Levey/ Machines by J. Tucker/ Prod. by Edward Stirling.

REBEL SWEDE, THE; OR, THE MONARCH AND THE MINE// D// n.a.// **Sad. Wells,** June 1840, with Henry Marston as King Gustavus, Mr. Aldridge as Rubenski, Mr. Dry as Carlowitz, J. B. Hill as Ufo, Mr. Houghburt as Brannomar, Mr. Elvin as Calmar, Mr. Williams as Gabriel, Henry Hall as Mardoff, Miss Richardson as Princess Gunilda, Mrs. J. F. Saville as Frederica, Miss Cooke as Abbess, Miss Louise as Paulina, Mrs. Richard Barnett as Alexa, Mrs. Morgan as Ulrica/ Scenery by F. Fenton/ Machines by B. Sloman/ Music by Isaac Collins.

REBEL'S WIFE, THE// D 3a// Fred Jarman// **Britannia,** June 1899.

RECKONING, THE// Play 4a// "Sylvanus Dauncey"// **Globe,** Dec. 1891/ **Grand,** May 1895.

RECLAIMED// C 4a// Adap. by James Mortimer fr F of Victorien Sardou, Les Vieux Garçons// **Haymarket,** Sept. 1881, with Hermann Vezin as Col. Abercrombie, Arthur Dacre as Capt. Llewellyn, Alfred Bishop as Sir John, Harry St. Maur as Lord Frothingham, Morton Selten as Delafield, George Weathersby as Redfern, Lottie Venne as Mrs. Delafield, Miss J. Clifford as Mrs. Redfern, Rose Doré as Mrs. Markwicke, Rosalie Taylor as Jenny, Lydia Cowell as Grace.

RECOMMENDED TO MERCY// D Pro & 4a// Dram. by J. Wilson Jones fr novel of Mrs. Braddon// **Pavilion,** July 1883.

RECONCILIATION, THE// C 1a// G. F. Neville// **Olympic,** Feb. 1876, with John Vollaire as Moreland, Lytton Sothern as Arnold, Miss Hazleton as Jessy, Miss Taylor as Bobkins.

RECRUITING OFFICER, THE// C 5a// George Farquhar// **Lyceum** (in 3a.), Mar. 1845, with Frederick Vining as Capt. Plume, Mr. Bellingham as Capt. Brazen, Frank Matthews as Balance, Alfred Wigan as Sgt. Kite, Robert Keeley as Pearmain, Samuel Emery as Bullock, Drinkwater Meadows as Appletree, Miss Villars as Sylvia, Mrs. Keeley as Rose.

RECTOR, THE: A STORY OF FOUR FRIENDS// Play 4a// Arthur Wing Pinero// **Court,** Mar. 1883, with John Clayton, Henry Kemble, Arthur Cecil, Marion Terry, Kate Rorke.

RED CAP, THE; OR, THE PRISONER OF VINCENNES// D 2a// Adap. by Thomas Archer fr F, Le Chaperon Rouge// **Olympic,** Nov. 1846, with Leigh Murray as Duke de Beaufort, John Howard as Duke de Bassompiere, Mr. Fortesque as Count de Lannay, Mr. Butler as Mazarin, Thomas Archer as Count de Chavigny, H. Lee as Croisey, Robert Romer as Sgt. Laramee, George Maynard as Grimaud, Mr. Turnour as Marteau, Mr. Darcie as Noirmont, Miss Penson as Catherine de Medicis, Miss Charles as Countess de Montbazon.

RED COAT, THE// C 4a// Barry Williams// **West London,** June 1900.

RED DWARF, THE; OR, MYSTERY AND VENGEANCE// D// n.a.// **Elephant & Castle,** Apr. 1873.

RED FARM, THE; OR, THE WELL OF ST. MARIE// D 2a// Adap. by W. T. Moncrieff fr F of A. P. Dennery & M. Lemoine// **Sad. Wells,** Aug. 1842, with Mr. Lyon as Leclerc, Mr. Dry as Eustache, C. J. Bird as Dervillier, John Herbert as La Queue, Mr. Richardson as Jean, Mrs. Henry Marston as Mme. Leblanc, Miss Richardson as Dame Marçon, Mrs. Richard Barnett as Jeannette.

RED HANDS// D Pro & 3a// Gilbert à Beckett// **St. James's,** Jan. 1869.

RED HUNTSMAN, THE; OR, THE PHANTOM OF THE BLACK VALLEY// D 3a// John Bradshaw// **Victoria,** May 1858, with John Dale as Rushleim, S. Sawford as Wolfrich, Henry Dudley as Bronson, Mr. Morrison as Albert, George Yarnold as Stichbacque, J. Howard as Grunthoof, W. H. Pitt as Adolph, Mr. Henderson as Gruff, James Elphinstone as Red Huntsman, Jane Dawson as Bertha, Julia Seaman as Agatha, Miss Laporte as

Trudgekin/ Scenery by James Gates.

RED JOSEPHINE// D// Mrs. S. Lane// **Britannia**, Nov. 1880.

RED LAMP, THE/ D 4a// W. O. Tristram// **Comedy**, Apr. 1887/ **Haymarket**, Sept. 1887, with Herbert Beerbohm Tree as Demetrius, C. H. Brookfield as Gen. Morakoff, Charles Sugden as Villiers, Laurence Cautley as Prince Alexis, Robert Pateman as Zazzulic, Charles Allan as Kertch, Sant Matthews as Count Bohrenheim, Cecil Thornbury as Turgan, J. Nutcombe Gould as Rheinveck, Janet Achurch as Princess Claudia, Marion Terry as Olga, Rosina Filippi as Félise, Mrs. Conyers D'Arcy as Mme. Dannenberg/ Scenery by Walter Johnstone/ Machines by Oliver Wales/ **Her Majesty's**, June 1897.

RED LAMP, THE; OR, THE DARK DENS OF THE CITY// D 2a// Eliza Clayton// **Grecian**, June 1863, with Alfred Rayner as Schiller, J. Jackson as Boorme, Walter Holland as Schuggi, Henry Grant as Faust, Henry Power as Nervski, F. Smithson as Spitzer, John Manning as Prongh, Eliza Clayton as Constance, Harriet Coveney as Barbarissa, Maria Brewer as Nancy/ Music by B. Isaac.

RED MAN'S RIFLE, THE// D// C. H. Hazlewood// **Britannia**, Dec. 1874.

RED POTTAGE// D// F. Kinsey Peile & D. M. Cholmondeley// **St. James's**, Oct. 1900.

RED RAG, A// C// Adap. by J. H. McCarthy fr F of G. Ohnet// **Toole's**, Feb. 1888.

RED REPUBLICANS, THE; OR, THE FLAG OF LIBERTY// D// J. B. Johnstone// **Sad. Wells**, Aug. 1866, with Philip Hannan as Robert, G. P. Jaques as Boutard, J. Baker as St. Cyr, Walter Roberts as Henri, Watty Brunton as Cuchard, Miss Neville as Madeline.

RED RIDING HOOD; OR, WALTER OF WALSDORF THE WOLF// D 2a// Charles Dibdin// **Victoria**, Jan. 1840, with Walter Searle as Vaschen, Mr. Hitchinson as Vasbeth, Mr. Reynolds as Varlhen, Mr. Harding as Snakesnarl, Mrs. Hicks as Crimsonetta, H. Hicks as Walter, Charles Bender as Ulric, Mr. Johnson as Gurther, Mr. Foster as Albert, Mr. Manders as Slibbs, Mrs. France as Dame Bernardine, Mrs. H. Beverley as Gwynette, Mrs. Harris as Leza/ Scenery by Dearlove & Son/ Machines by Mr. Moulds/ Prod. by C. Bender.

RED RIVEN THE BANDIT// D// n.a.// **Victoria**, Feb. 1850, with John Dale as Count Vandermer, J. T. Johnson as Riven, John Bradshaw as Rister, Mr. Leake as Yermeck, J. Howard as Ulrick, John Hudspeth as Dalcoff, Mrs. George Lee as Olinska.

RED ROB, THE COINER// D// n.a.// **Marylebone**, June 1863.

RED RONALD THE REIVER; OR, THE DOOM OF THE LEONARDS// D// n.a.// **Victoria**, Nov. 1848, with J. T. Johnson as Red Ronald, J. Howard as Old Adam, Mr. Henderson as Albert, Mr. Hitchinson as Donald, John Dale as Steenie, Mr. Macdonald as Alison, G. F. Forman as Guy, John Bradshaw as Brand, F. H. Henry as Wylie, Mrs. George Lee as Laurette, Miss Mildenhall as Jessie, Miss Devere as Annot, Miss Sharpe as Moggy.

RED ROVER, THE; OR, THE MUTINY OF THE CAROLINE// D 2a// Edward Fitzball// **Sad. Wells**, Sept. 1837, with Mr. King as Bignal, C. H. Pitt as Lt. Wilder, Mr. Campbell as Fid, C. J. Smith as Africa, Mr. Hicks as Red Rover, Thomas Lee as Homespun, Mr. Griffith as Bunt, Mr. Pateman as Corp. Ramrod, Miss Williams as Mme. de Lacey/ **Victoria**, Mar. 1842, with John Dale as Red Rover, William Seaman as Lt. Wilder, Mr. Paul as Guinea, E. F. Saville as Fid, Mr. Scarbrow as Corp. Stiff, C. Williams as Cutreef, John Gardner as Homespun, Mrs. George Lee as Madame de Lacey, Miss Saddler as Gertrude.

RED ROVER, THE; OR, THE TIGER OF THE SEAS// D// n.a.// **Grecian**, July 1865, with David Jones, William James, Henry Power, John Manning, Mrs. J. W. Simpson, Miss E. Churchill.

RED SQUADRON// D 4a// T. Harkins & J. Macmahon// **Pavilion**, Feb. 1895.

RED TAPE// C 2a// H. J. Byron// **Adelphi**, Sept. 1874, with J. S. Clarke as Redmond Tape, James Fernandez as Rawdon, Augustus Glover as Sheldrake, Frederick Moreland as Richard Rawdon, A. C. Lilly as Harry, Edith Stuart as Ethel, Miss Hudspeth as Nutmeg, Fanny Morelli as Mrs. Tape/ **Olympic**, Feb. 1880, with John S. Clarke as Redmond Tape, John Ryder as Jasper Rawdon, Charles Harcourt as Sheldrake, John Maclean as Richard Rawdon, F. H. Macklin as Harold Rawdon, Blanche Henri as Ethel, Gwynne Williams as Kate, Mrs. Leigh as Mrs. Tape, Miss Smith as Miss Tape, Edith Bruce as Nutmeg.

RED VIAL, THE// D 3a// Wilkie Collins// **Olympic**, Oct. 1858, with Mr. Addison as Rodenberg, Frederick Vining as Keller, Walter Gordon as Karl, Frederick Robson as Hans Grimm, J. H. White as Dr. Hetzel, George Cooke as Schwartz, Harwood Cooper as Duntzer, Mrs. Stirling as Widow Bergmann, Miss Marston as Ninna.

REEFER'S WRONGS, THE; OR, THE WRECK OF THE AURORA// D 3a// n.a.// **Victoria**, Apr. 1847, with C. J. Bird as Lt. Campley, Alfred Raymond as Kennedy, John Dale as Rattlin, N. T. Hicks as Merrivale, Walter Searle as Dhudierick, John Gardner as McShane, J. B. Johnstone as Father O'Done, J. Howard as Block, F. H. Henry as Mizen, Mrs. George Lee as Ellen, Mrs. N. T. Hicks as Lady Lydia, Miss Young as Judy, Mrs. Cooke as Nelly.

REFEREE, THE// C 3a [rev. vers. of The Undergraduates]// W. O. Tristram// **Opera Comique**, Oct. 1886/ **Vaudeville**, Dec. 1886.

REFUGEES, THE// C 1a// J. M. Campbell//

Adelphi, Jan. 1888, with Harry Halley as Linklater, Dalton Somers as Poddleson, Howard Russell as Pompouseau, Eleanor Bufton as Mme. Nanichette, Agnes Miller as Marie.

REGIMENT, THE// C 3a// S. Osborn// **Elephant & Castle,** May 1888.

REGIMENT OF TARTARS, A; OR, THE PRETTY GIRLS OF STILBERG// F// n.a.// **Sad. Wells,** Mar. 1842, with John Herbert as Maj. Victor, Mr. Dry as Lagloire, Mr. Morton as Laurencon, Mr. Lambe as St Léon, Charles Fenton as De Berry, Mr. Aldridge as Morbleu, Mr. Richardson as Buzman, Mrs. Richard Barnett as Cecile, Miss Melville as Marie, Miss Anderson as Louise, Miss Morgan as Annette, Miss Pitt as Lisette, Miss Couch as Theresa.

REGULAR FIX, A// F 1a// J. Maddison Morton// **Olympic,** Oct. 1860; Dec. 1883, with C. W. Somerset as Hugh de Brass, E. Hendrie as Surplus, W. St. Clair as Charles, L. Norman as Quick, Miss Ashford as Mrs. Surplus, Miss M. Gordon as Emily, Miss Ballard as Mrs. Carter, Miss A. Forrest as Matilda/ **Haymarket,** Dec. 1862, with E. A. Sothern as Hugh De Bras, Mr. Rogers as Surplus, George Braid as Charles, Mr. Weathersby as Quick, Mrs. Griffith as Mrs. Surplus, Henrietta Lindley as Emily, Mrs. Coe as Mrs. Carter, Miss Lovell as Matilda/ **Lyceum,** 1874, with John Clayton as Hugh de Brass, John Carter as Surplus, F. Charles as Charles Surplus, Mr. Brennand as Quick, Miss Ewell as Mrs. Surplus, Miss Hampden as Emily/ **Globe,** June 1878, with E. A. Sothern as Hugh de Bras, George Holland as Surplus, H. B. Conway as Charles, John Clarke as Smiler, Isabel Clifton as Mrs. Carter, Edith Challis as Matilda Jane.

REGULAR TURK, A// F// Robert Soutar// **Gaiety,** Feb. 1877.

REIGN OF BLOOD, THE// D 4a// Edgar Newbound// **Britannia,** May 1880.

REIGN OF TERROR// D 3a// Mark Melford// **Avenue,** Apr. 1885.

REIGNING FAVOURITE, THE// D 3a// John Oxenford// **Strand,** Oct. 1849.

RELAPSE, THE// C 5a// John Vanbrugh// **Olympic,** Oct. 1846, with Walter Lacy as Foppington, Mr. Clifford as Friendly, Mr. Wilkenson as Clumsy, George Bolton as Young Fashion, Leigh Murray as Loveless, Thomas Archer as Worthy, Robert Romer as Syringe, John Howard as Foretop, Mrs. R. Gordon as Amanda, Miss Charles as Berinthia, Mrs. Lacy as Hoyden, Mrs. Charles Jones as Nurse.

RELEASED// D 1a// C. H. Dickenson// **Comedy,** Apr. 1890, with Luigi Lablache as Capt. Vallete, Bassett Roe as Leroux, Julian Cross as Corp. Georges, Ada Neilson as Mme. Lasalle.

RELIEF OF LUCKNOW, THE// D// Dion Boucicault// **Drury Lane,** Oct. 1862, with Thomas Swinbourne as Randal, Charles Vandenhoff as Geordie, Henry Mellon as O'Grady, Dion Boucicault as Cassidy, Edward Atkins as Sweeney, Mme. Celeste as Mrs. Campbell, Mrs. Dion Boucicault as Jessie, Julia Craven as Alice, Miss Kinglake as Mary, John Ryder as Rajah, H. Farrell as Mour-ed-deen, Mr. Edwin as Achmet/ Scenery by W. Beverley/ Prod. by Dion Boucicault.

RELY ON MY DISCRETION// F// T. A. Palmer// **Royalty,** Jan. 1870/ **Globe,** Jan. 1870, with W. H. Vernon as Robert Bashville, R. Rolfe as Maj. Bloggins, W. L. Branscombe as Roots, Henry Rignold as Walker, Emily Burns as Mrs. Squance, Isabella Armour as Miss Cantingham, Miss R. Roberts as Mrs. Roots, Clara Weston as Sarah Sims.

REMARKABLE CURE, A// F// Paul Heriot// **Vaudeville,** Mar. 1883.

REMEMBRANCE// Play 1a// Adap. by Maurice Robinson fr novel of Miss Harraden// **Terry's,** June 1895.

REMININI; OR, THE BRIGAND'S BRIDE// D// n.a.// **Sad. Wells,** June 1837, with Mr. Hicks as Reminini, C. H. Pitt as Count Loridano, Mr. Tilbury as Miseltoe, Mr. George as Pietro, C. J. Smith as Gasparino, Miss Land as Lady Isabel, Mrs. W. West as Antonia, Lavinia Melville as Clotilde.

REMORSE; OR, THE PERILS OF A NIGHT// D 4a// G. I. Whiting// **Victoria,** Nov. 1873.

RENAISSANCE// C 3a// Adap. by Augustin Daly fr G of Franz von Schönthan & F. Coppell-Ellfield// **Daly's,** July 1897/ **Comedy,** Nov. 1900.

RENDEZVOUS, THE; OR, A HOUSE TURNED UPSIDE DOWN// F 1a// R. Ayton// **Sad. Wells,** Dec. 1838, with J. Lee as Capt. Bolding, Mr. Elvin as Charles, J. W. Collier as Smart, Mr. Williams as Quake, Mr. Conquest as Simon, Miss Pincot as Sophia, Miss Richardson as Lucretia, Mrs. J. F. Saville as Rose/ **Olympic,** Feb. 1848, with Mr. Somerford as Quake, Mr. Conquest as Simon, Mr. Morton as Capt. Bolding, Mr. Harcourt as Charles, John Kinloch as Smart, Miss H. Walcott as Sophia, Miss Lovatt as Lucretia/ **Victoria,** May 1850, with Mr. Neville as Quake, Mr. Humphreys as Capt. Holding, Mr. Henderson as Morland, J. Howard as Smart, John Hudspeth as Simon, Mrs. George Lee as Lucretia, Georgiana Lebatt as Sophia, Miss Barrowcliffe as Mose/ **Grecian,** Jan. 1855, with Eaton O'Donnell, F. Charles as Charles, Henry Power as Smart, Richard Phillips as Capt. Bolding, John Manning, Jane Coveney as Lucretia, Harriet Coveney as Sophia/ **Princess's,** Sept. 1861, with Drinkwater Meadows as Quake, T. H. Higgie as Bolding, Alfred Raymond as Charles, Frederick Moreland as Simon, Robert Cathcart as Smart, Rebecca Powell as Sophia, Marie Henderson as Lucretia, Miss Lavenu as Rose.

RENT DAY, THE// C 3a// Douglas Jerrold// **Sad. Wells,** Oct. 1838, with Mr. Dry as Grantly, Mr. Williams as Old Crumbs, J. Lee as Heywood, Mr. Cathcart as Martin Heywood, R. Horner as Jack, Mr. Conquest as Bullfrog, Charles Montague as Hyssop, Dibdin Pitt as Beanstalk, Mrs. Robert Honnor as Rachel, Mrs. J. F. Saville as Polly; July 1863, with T. W. Neal (alt. with Edmund Phelps) as Heywood, Edmund Phelps (alt. with G. Clarence) as Toby, Kate Stonor as Rachel, Minnie Davis as Polly, T. B. Bennett as Crumbs, Mr. Williams as Bullfrog, Charles Mowbray as Jack, F. Warboys as Squire Grantley/ **Victoria**, June 1840, with Mr. Frampton as Grantley, Mr. Burton as Crumbs, Mr. Rogers as Bullfrog, Mr. Willing as Martin Heywood, Charles Bender as Toby, Mr. Harding as Silver Jack, Mr. Morton as Hyssop, F. B. Conway as Beanstalk, Adelaide Cooke as Rachel, Mrs. Harris as Polly/ **Haymarket**, Feb. 1841, with Henry Howe as Grantley, Robert Strickland as Old Crumbs, James Wallack as Martin Heywood, John Webster as Toby Heywood, Henry Wallack as Silver Jack, David Rees as Bullfrog, Mrs. Stirling as Rachel, Priscilla Horton as Polly; Mar. 1849, with James Wallack as Heywood, Henry Howe as Toby, Benjamin Webster as Bullfrog, Alfred Wigan as Silver Jack, James Bland as Hyssop, Mr. Rogers as Old Crumbs, Henry Vandenhoff as Grantley, Mrs. Keeley as Rachel, Mrs. Humby as Polly/ **Princess's**, Dec. 1844, with James Wallack as Heywood, Augustus Harris as Grantley, Mr. Granby as Crumbs, Mr. Fitzjames as Toby, Henry Compton as Bullfrog, Walter Lacy as Jack, James Ranoe as Hyssop, Robert Honner as Beanstalk, Mrs. Stirling as Rachel, Mrs. Brougham as Polly; Mar. 1861, with Robert Cathcart as Grantley, Basil Potter as Heywood, J. G. Shore as Toby, Henry Widdicomb as Bullfrog, John Collett as Beanstalk, Caroline Heath as Rachel, Miss Murray as Polly/ **Olympic**, July 1852, with Mr. Edgar as Grantly, George Cooke as Old Crumbs, William Hoskins as Martin Heywood, William Farren Jr. as Toby Heywood, Henry Compton as Bullfrog, W. Shalders as Jack, Charles Bender as Hyssop, John Kinloch as Stephen, Mrs. Walter Lacy as Rachael, Ellen Turner as Polly/ **Grecian**, Oct 1856 (in 2a), with William Shuter as Grantly, C. Kelsey as Toby Heywood, Richard Phillips as Martin Heywood, Eaton O'Donnell as Silver Jack, Henry Grant as Hyssop, Mr. Hustleby as Old Crumbs, Henry Power as Beanstalk, John Manning as Bullfrog, Jane Coveney as Rachel, Harriet Coveney as Polly/ **Adelphi**, July 1857, with Frank Hall as Grantley, Charles Selby as Crumbs, Benjamin Webster as Martin Heywood, John Billington as Toby, Henry Wallack as Silver Jack, Paul Bedford as Hyssop, Edward Wright as Bullfrog, Mme. Celeste as Rachel, Mrs. Keeley as Polly.

REPARATION// Play 5a// Adap. fr G of Salomon Mosenthal// **Gaiety**, May 1882.

REPENTANCE, A// D 1a// J. O. Hobbes// **St. James's**, Feb. 1899.

REPRIEVE, THE; OR, LIFE FOR LIFE// D 3a// W. Travers// **Grecian**, July 1861, with J. Jackson as Isaac, Thomas Mead as Henry, William James as Maurice, Alfred Rayner as Nightsblade, John Manning as Volkes, Henry Power as Button, Mr. Holland as Pleadwell, Mr. Coleman as Sheriff, Mr. Costello as Waxend, Jane Coveney as Ellen, Miss Chapman as Patty, Miss Johnstone as Dame Armstrong.

REPUBLICAN MARRIAGE, A// Mrs. Holford// **Olympic**, Nov. 1878.

RESCUE ON THE RAFT, THE; OR, SUNLIGHT THROUGH THE MIST// D pro & 3a// George Conquest// **Grecian**, June 1867, with Alfred Rayner as Gilbert, J. Jackson as Capt. Kerval, John Manning as Ponolpot, Charles Mortimer as de Poville, Henry Grant as de Besaval, Henry Power as Hanetin, Samuel Perfitt as Roquet, Lizzie Mandelbert as Helen, Mary A. Victor as Jacquinette, Miss De Lacie as Diana.

RESCUED// D 4a// Dion Boucicault// **Adelphi**, Sept. 1879, with E. H. Brooke as Earl of Mt. Audley, Hermann Vezin as Count Ruskov, Henry Neville as Weatherby, J. G. Taylor as Tarbox, Robert Pateman as Manifold, James Fernandez as O'Reilly, Clara Jecks as Dan, Bella Pateman as Lady Sybil, Lydia Foote as Midge, Maria Harris as Jenny/ Scenery by Julian Hicks/ Music by W. C. Levey/ Prod. by Charles Harris.

RESCUED HONOUR, A// C 3a// A. Fay// **Avenue**, June 1896.

RESEMBLANCE// D Pro & 4a// Mme. C. Scotte// **Vaudeville**, Dec. 1885.

REST// Play 1a// H. V. Esmond// **Avenue**, June 1892.

RESTLESS NIGHT, A// F// Frederick Hay// **Holborn**, Mar. 1873.

RETAINED FOR THE DEFENCE// F 1a// Adap. by John Oxenford fr F of Eugène Labiche & M. Lefrana, L'Avocat d'un Grec// **Olympic**, May 1859, with George Cooke as de Windsor, George Vining as Whitewash, Harwood Cooper as Ferguson, Horace Wigan as Thwaites, Frederick Robson as Pawkins, Miss Cottrell as Agatha.

RETALIATION: A MYSTERY OF TWENTY YEARS// D 3a// n.a.// **Grecian**, Oct. 1855, with R. Phillips as Marquis de Sivry, Mr. Melvin as de Rochemore, T. Roberts as Duc de Daniville, Eaton O'Donnell as Huguenin, Basil Potter as Stocq, Henry Grant as Abbe de Fleury, F. Charles as Fergus, Henry Power as Bertrand, John Manning as Seul, Jane Coveney as Artimes, Harriet Coveney as Camille, Mrs. Charles Montgomery as Louise.

RETALIATION// C 1a// Adap. by Rudolph Dircks fr G// **Grand**, July 1891.

RETIRED FROM BUSINESS// C// Douglas Jerrold// **Haymarket**, May. 1851, with Mr. Lambert as Pennyweight, Mr. Rogers as Puffins, Charles Selby as Jubilee, J. B. Buckstone as Creepmouse, James Wallack as Lt. Tackle, Benjamin Webster as Capt. Gunn, Mrs. Fitzwilliam as Paul, Henry Howe as Woodburn, Miss Reynolds as Amy, Mrs. Stanley as Mrs. Pennyweight, Annie Romer as Kitty, Mrs. Laws as Narcissa, Mrs. Caulfield as Mrs. Puffins,

Amelia Vining as Susan.

RETIRING// D 3a// H. W. Williamson// **Globe**, May 1878.

RETRIBUTION// Play 5a// Dram. by George Bennett fr novel of Sir Walter Scott// **Sad. Wells**, Feb. 1850, with A. Younge as Sir Robert, George Bennett as Sir Baldwin, Samuel Phelps as Blackbourn, G. K. Dickinson as Edwin, Henry Marston as Philip, William Belford as Capt. Rowley, Frank Graham as Humphrey, Isabela Glyn as Alice, Miss Johnstone as Amy.

RETRIBUTION// D 4a// Dram. by Tom Taylor fr F novel of C. de Bernard// **Olympic**, May 1856, with George Vining as de Beaupre, Alfred Wigan as Count Prinli, Samuel Emery as Morisset, Gaston Murray as de Mornac, Mr. Leslie as Garnier, Miss Marston as Mme. de Pomenars, Miss Herbert as Mme. de Beaupre.

RETURN OF THE TICKET OF LEAVE, THE// D 2a// n.a.// **Sad. Wells**, Oct. 1863, with E. H. Brooke as Hardy, David Jones as Travers, Henry Haynes as George, W. D. Gresham as Beswick, T. B. Bennett as Joe, George Fisher as Todd, Alfred Denial as Rummins, Mrs. Edmund Phelps (Miss Hudspeth) as Hayward, Mr. Routledge as Lewes, Mrs. Wallis as Mrs. Haywood, Miss Mandelbert as Ellen.

RETURN TICKET, A// F 1a// George Spencer & J. W. Jones// **St. James's**, Aug. 1862.

RETURNED BILL, THE; OR, AMERICAN NOTES AND ENGLISH CHANGE// F// W. T. Moncrieff// **Sad. Wells**, Sept. 1843, with Mr. Williams as Bullcalf, W. H. Williams as Star, C. J. Bird as Badger, Mr. Coreno as Ochre, Mr. Bologna as Nozzle, Mr. Lamb as Shearman, Miss Hamilton as Bella, Mrs. Richard Barnett as Kitty.

RETURNED KILLED// F 2a// J. R. Planché// **Sad. Wells**, Dec. 1847, with Mr. Harrington as Frederick the Great, A. Younge as Baron Von Lindorf, J. T. Johnson as Ernest Lindorf, Edward Knight as Capt. Brumenfeld, Henry Scharf as Rauvogel, Charles Fenton as Sgt. Milligan, G. Maskell as Fritz, Mrs. W. Watson as Mme. Lisburg, Mrs. Charles Boyce as Victorine.

REVELATIONS OF THE WORLD WE LIVE IN (alt. title Revelations of London)// D 3a// C. H. Stevenson// **Grecian**, July, 1868, with W. Shirley as Tom Cropps, J. Jackson as Father McKeon, Samuel Perfitt as Rutts, Thomas Mead as Savage, Henry Grant as Hardman, George Gillett as Willie, Charles Mortimer as Foxcraft, John Manning as Snapail, Miss De Lacie as Barbara, Alice Denvil as Nancy, Lizzie Mandelbert as Maude and as Mable, Mary A. Victor as Nelly, Mrs. Dearlove as Susan.

REVERSES// D 2a// H. B. Farnie// **Strand**, July 1867.

REVIEW, THE; OR, THE WAGS OF WINDSOR// F 1a// George Colman the younger// **Sad. Wells**, Nov. 1837, with David Rees as Mactwolter, C. H. Pitt as Capt. Beaugard, Mr. Gay as Bull, Mr. Campbell as Caleb Quotem, Mr. Rogers as Lump, Mr. Ennis as Dubbs, Miss Williams as Grace, Lavinia Melville as Lucy; Nov. 1852, with Mr. Belford as Capt. Beaugard, Mr. Williams as Bull, Lewis Ball as Lump, Henry Mellon as McTwolter, Mr. Barrett as Caleb Quotem, Mr. Franks as Dubbs, Mr. Wallis as Whitethorn, Teresa Bassano as Grace, Eliza Travers as Lucy, Miss Mandelbert as Phoebe/ **Grecian**, June 1846, with Edwin Dixon as Capt. Beaugard, Richard Saker as Deputy Bull, Eaton O'Donnell as Mactwolter, Frederick Robson as Calem Quotem, Miss M. A. Crisp as Grace, Miss Johnstone as Lucy/ **Olympic**, Oct. 1846, with John Howard as Beaugard, Mr. Turnour as Bull, John Ward as McTwolter, Robert Romer as Lump, Mr. Fortesque as William, J. Cowell as Caleb Quotem, Miss Ayres as Lucy, Lavinia Melville as Grace.

REVOLTED DAUGHTER, THE// C 3a// Israel Zangwill// **Comedy**, Mar. 1901.

RIBSTON'S RIDE// F 3a// W. A. Chandler// **Novelty**, May 1897.

RICH AND POOR; OR, THE UP-HILL GAME OF LIFE// D 3a// W. E. Suter// **Grecian**, May 1854, with Mr. Melvin as Crawford, Charles Horn as Augustus, Richard Phillips as Arnold, Basil Potter as Bullfinch, Henry Power as Richard, T. Roberts as Welford, William Suter as Peter Plummy, Miss Chapman as Emily, Miss Johnstone as Mrs. Wetherall, Harriet Coveney as Sally, Jane Coveney as Fanny.

RICH IN LOVE BUT POOR IN POCKET// C 1a// George Conquest// **Grecian**, Oct. 1857, with John Manning as Briggs, Henry Grant as Bradbury, Mr. De Solla as Evans, William Shuter as Thornburne, Harriet Coveney as Mrs. Bradbury, Miss Chapman as Hermance; June 1863, with John Manning, Henry Grant, George Gillett, Mary A. Victor, Ellen Hale.

RICHARD COEUR DE LION// D 4a// Dram. by Andrew Halliday fr Sir Walter Scott, The Talisman// **Drury Lane**, Sept. 1874, with James Anderson as Richard, William Creswick as Saladin, William Terriss as Sir Kenneth, S. Parkes as De Vaux, Mr. Matthison as Blondel, H. Naylor as Marrabout, Henry Kemble as Philip of France, R. Dolman as Austria, Henry Sinclair as Conrad, Henry Vaughan as Beauseant, Bessie King as Queen Berengaria, Miss Wallis as Edith, Miss Marshall as Calista, Jane Macauley as Florise/ Scenery by William Beverley/ Music by Karl Meyder/ Machines by James Tucker/ Prod. by Andrew Halliday & F. B. Chatterton.

RICHARD SAVAGE// Play 4a// J. M. Barrie & H. B. Watson// **Criterion**, Apr. 1891.

RICHARD II// T// William Shakespeare// **Adelphi**, Apr. 1844, with Mr. Cathcart as Richard, W. Johnstone as Henry VI, J. Grey as Richmond, Mr. Starke as Buckingham, Mr. Freeman as Norfolk, Mrs. J. Grey as the Queen, Mrs. De Bourgh as Lady Anne, Mrs. Lovegrove as Duchess of York/ **Haymarket**, Dec. 1850, with W. C. Macready as Richard II, Mr. Stuart as John of Gaunt, Mr. Cooper as York, E. L. Davenport as Bolingbroke, Mr. Harrington as Norfolk, Henry Howe as Northumberland, John Parselle as Aumerle, Mr. Rogers as Carlisle, James Bland as Scroop, Charles Selby as Bagot, Miss Reynolds as Queen, Mrs. Mary Warner as Duchess of York, Mrs. Stanley as Duchess of Glo'ster/ **Princess's**, Mar. 1857, with Charles Kean as Richard II, Mr. Cooper as York, Walter Lacy as Lancaster, John Ryder as Bolingbroke, Mr. Brazier as Aumerle, John Cathcart as Norfolk, Mr. Raymond as Surry, George Everett as Salisbury, John Collett as Berkley, Henry Mellon as Northumberland, Eleanor Bufton as Henry Percy, Mrs. Charles Kean as Queen, Mrs. Ternan as Duchess of Gloucester, Miss Desborough as Duckess of York, Kate Terry as Boy/ Scenery under dir. of Mr. Grieve/ Music by J. L. Hatton/ Machines by G. Hodsdon/ **Lyceum**, Mar. 1899, with F. R. Benson as Richard II, E. A. Warburton as John of Gaunt, Alfred Brydone as Edmund of Langley, Frank Rodney as Bolingbroke, Oscar Ashe as Thomas Mowbray, E. Harcourt Williams as Henry Percy, H. H. Ainley as Scroop, Lily Brayton as Queen, Frances Wetherall as Duchess of Gloster/ **Comedy**, May 1901.

RICHARD III// T// William Shakespeare// **Cov. Garden**, Jan. 1837, with George Bennett as King Henry, John Pritchard as Buckingham, Mr. Vandenhoff as Richard III, Miss Lane as Prince of Wales, Henry Wallack as Richmond, John Webster as Tressel, Mr. Ransford as Norfolk, Mr. Thompson as Stanley, Charles Bender as Catesby, Mr. Harris as Ratcliffe, John Collett as Oxford, J. Smith as Tyrrell, Eliza Vincent as Lady Anne, Mrs. W. West as Queen, Mrs. Sarah Garrick as Duchess of York/ **Drury Lane**, Feb. 1837, with Mr. Mathews as Henry VI, Miss Poole as Prince of Wales, Edwin Forrest as Glo'ster, Mr. Cooper as Buckingham, Mr. Warde as Richmond, Frederick Cooke as Norfolk, Mr. Howell as Oxford, Charles Diddear as Stanley, Mr. Baker as Ratcliffe, Mr. Henry as Catesby, Miss Huddart as Queen, Miss Taylor as Lady Anne, Mrs. W. Clifford as Duchess of York; Feb. 1838, with Mr. Baker as Henry VI, Miss Poole as Prince of Wales, Charles Kean as Glo'ster, Mr. Cooper as Buckingham, John Duruset as Norfolk, Mr. Howell as Oxford, F. Sutton as Hastings, Mr. Harris as Stanley, Mr. King as Richmond, Mr. Mears as Blunt, Frederick Cooke as Ratcliffe, A. Brindal as Catesby, Mrs. Lovell as Queen, Mme. Simon as Duchess of York, Mrs. Ternan as Lady Anne/ Scenery by Grieve, T. Grieve & W. Grieve; Jan. 1844, with Charles Diddear as Henry VI, Miss Newcombe as Prince of Wales, Charles Kean as Gos'ster, Mr. Cooper as Buckingham, George Horncastle as Norfolk, Mr. Mott as Surrey, Mr. Beckett as Rivers, Charles Selby as Stanley, Charles Hudson as Richmond, Mr. Howell as Oxford, W. H. Payne as Catesby, Henry Horncastle as Ratcliffe, Mrs. Mary Warner as Queen Elizabeth, Mrs. Selby as Duchess of York, Mrs. Stirling as Lady Anne/ Scenery by Grieve, T. Grieve & W. Grieve/ Prod. by W. West; Sept. 1876, with J. F. Cathcart as Henry VI, Miss Grattan as Prince of Wales, Barry Sullivan as Glo'ster, Henry Sinclair as Richmond, Charles Vandenhoff as Buckingham, Howard Russell as Stanley, Frank Tyars as Norfolk, H. M. Clifford as Oxford, Mr. Douglas as Blount, Henry Evans as Ratcliffe, G. R. Ireland as Catesby, Mrs. Hermann Vezin as Queen Elizabeth, Fanny Huddart as Duchess of York, Edith Stuart as Lady Anne/ Scenery by William Beverley/ **Sad. Wells**, Apr. 1837, with Mr. King as Henry VI, C. H. Pitt as Buckingham, Mr. Cobham as Glo'ster, Miss Pitt as Prince of Wales, Mr. Scarbrough as Norfolk, Mr. Hicks as Richmond, F. Ede as Stanley, Thomas Lee as Catesby, C. J. Smith as Ratcliff, H. George as Blunt, Miss Williams as Queen, Miss Beresford as Lady Anne, Mrs. Harris as Duchess of York; Mar. 1844, with R. Young as Henry VI, Miss Stephens as Prince of Wales, Henry Marston as Glo'ster, C. J. Bird as Buckingham, Mr. Mepham as Richmond, C. Lamb as Norfolk, Mr. Franks as Oxford, Mr. Williams as Stanley, C. J. Smith as Catesby, Charles Fenton as Ratcliffe, Mr. Grammani as Blunt, Caroline Rankley as Queen Elizabeth, Mrs. Richard Barnett as Lady Anne, Miss Cooke as Duchess of York; Mar. 1845, with Mr. Ward as Edward IV [sic], Miss Backous as Prince of Wales, Henry Marston as Clarence, Samuel Phelps as Glo'ster, Mr. Seale as York, George Bennett as Buckingham, Mr. Raymond as Norfolk, Mr. Franks as Surrey, Mr. Williams as Rivers, John Webster as Richmond, James Villiers as Ely, Mr. Sharpe as Ratcliffe, Mr. Morton as Catesby, A. Younge as Stanley, Mrs. Henry Marston as Elizabeth, Mrs. Mary Warner as Queen Margaret, Jane Mordaunt as Lady Anne, Mrs. Francis as Duchess of York/ Scenery by F. Fenton/ **Haymarket**, June 1837, with W. C. Macready as Glo'ster, Robert Strickland as Henry VI, Miss Gallot as Prince of Wales, Mr. Saville as Buckingham, Mr. Harris as Norfolk, J. T. Haines as Richmond, Mr. Hart as Oxford, J. W. Gough as Stanley, Charles Selby as Catesby, J. Worrell as Ratcliffe, Miss Huddart as Queen Elizabeth, Eliza Vincent as Lady Anne, Mrs. W. Clifford as Duchess of York; Oct. 1837, with much of same cast, except Samuel Phelps as Glo'ster, Julia Glover as Queen Elizabeth, and Charlotte Vandenhoff as Lady Anne; June 1839, with Charles Kean as Glo'ster, Charles Perkins as Henry VI, Miss Gallot as Prince of Wales, Mr. Cooper as Buckingham, Walter Lacy as Richmond, Mr. Green as Norfolk, William Clark as Oxford, J. W. Gough as Stanley, Mr. Caulfield as Catesby, J. Worrell as Ratcliffe, Miss Pelham as Queen Elizabeth, Miss Taylor as Lady Anne, Mrs. Danson as Duchess of York; Apr. 1851, with Mr. Stuart as King Henry, J. William Wallack as Glo'ster, Henry Howe as Buckingham, E. L. Davenport as Richmond, James Bland as Norfolk, Mr. Clark as Oxford, Mr. Caulfield as Catesby, Mr. Braid as Ratcliffe, Laura Addison as Queen Elizabeth, Miss Reynolds as Lady Anne, Mrs. Stanley as Duchess of York; Oct. 1861, with Mr. Rogers as Henry VI, S. Henrade as Prince of Wales, Edwin Booth as Glo'ster, Henry Howe as Richmond, R. Dolman as Buckingham, Mr. Andrews as Norfolk, Mr. Weathersby as Oxford, William Cullenford as Stanley, J. Worrell as Ratcliffe, George

Braid as Catesby, Mrs. Charles Young as Queen Elizabeth, Miss M. Oliver as Lady Anne, Mrs. Griffith as Duchess of York/ **Victoria**, Feb. 1838 (in vers. "founded on Shakespeare"), with Mr. Wilkins as Henry VI, Miss Levete as Prince of Wales, Miss Brian as Duke of York, Mr. Latto as Glo'ster, John Parry as Buckingham, Leigh Smith as Norfolk, William Davidge as Stanley, Eaton Bernard as Trassell, Mrs. Hooper as Lady Anne, Mrs. Loveday as Duchess of York/ **Adelphi**, Apr. 1844, with Mr. Cathcart, W. Johnston, J. Grey, Miss Lovegrove, Mr. Starke, Mr. Freeman, Mrs. J. Grey, Mrs. De Bourgh, Mrs. Lovegrove/ **Olympic**, Jan. 1847, with Mr. Johnstone as King Henry, Mr. Binge as Buckingham, Mr. Fortesque as Stanley, J. R. Scott as Glo'ster, George Maynard as Richmond, Mr. Butler as Catesby, Mr. Palmer as Norfolk, Mrs. R. Gordon as Queen Elizabeth, Mrs. Boyce as Lady Anne, Mrs. Griffiths as Duchess of York; Feb. 1848, with Mr. Archer as King Henry, G. V. Brooke as Glo'ster, Henry Lee as Buckingham, Mr. Harcourt as Norfolk, Henry Holl as Richmond, George Almar as Stanley, Mrs. Brougham as Queen Elizabeth, Mrs. H. Lee as Duchess of York, Miss May as Lady Anne; Apr. 1892/ **Princess's**, Nov. 1846, with John Ryder as Henry VI, Miss Somers as Prince of Wales, John R. Scott as Glo'ster, James Vining as Buckingham, Augustus Harris as Norfolk, Henry Hughes as Richmond, Mr. Granby as Lord Stanley, Robery Roxby as Tressel, Charles Fisher as Catesby, Mr. Wynne as Ratcliffe, Mrs. H. Hughes as Queen, Mrs. Fosbroke as Duchess of York, Mrs. Stirling as Lady Anne; Aug. 1863, with Charles Vincent as King Henry, Lizzie Harrison as Prince of Wales, Walter Montgomery as Glo'ster, E. F. Edgar as Buckingham, W. E. Robins as Norfolk, John Collett as Oxford, Mr. Fitzjames as Stanley, Mr. Raymond as Catesby, Frederic Robinson as Richmond, Miss Atkinson as Queen, Clara Nash as Lady Anne, Mrs. Hodson as Duchess of York/ **City of London**, Feb. 1847, with J. R. Scott/ **Astley's**, Aug. 1856, with James Holloway as Richard, Henry Reeves as Richmond, Mark Howard as Buckingham, J. Craddock as Norfolk, A. Bridges as Surrey, E. Cooke as Pembroke, A. Palmer as Oxford, A. Bradbury as Hastings, W. Gomersal as Ratcliffe, J. W. Anson as Catesby, Mrs. Jackson as Queen Elizabeth, Mrs. J. W. Anson as Lady Anne, Mrs. William Dowton as Duchess of York/ Scenery by T. Thompson & Thorne/ Machines by E. Pryce/ Music by G. Phillips/ Horses trained by Wm. Cooke/ **St. James's**, Aug. 1860, with Alfred Rayner as Henry VI, Miss Griffith as Prince of Wales, Miss Vokes as Duke of York, Barry Sullivan as Glo'ster, E. Green as Buckingham, Henry Butler as Norfolk, Mr. Lever as Oxford, Mr. Sinclair as Richmond, J. B. Johnstone as Blunt, Mr. Chapman as Ratcliffe, Mr. Rourke as Catesby, Katharine Hickson as Queen Elizabeth, Mrs. Sherrard as Duchess of York, Miss Percy as Lady Anne/ **Drury Lane**, Feb. 1868; Sept. 1876, [in Colly Cibber's vers.], with Barry Sullivan, Mrs. Hermann Vezin, Mr. Cathcart/ **Lyceum**, Jan. 1877, with Allen Beaumont as Edward IV, Walter Bentley as Clarence, Henry Irving as Richard, E. H. Brooke as Richmond, Thomas Swinbourne as Buckingham, Mr. Harwood as Norfolk, Mr. Carton as Rivers, R. C. Lyons as Hastings, Arthur Wing Pinero as Stanley, Arthur Dillon as Lord Grey, Kate Bateman as Queen Margaret, Georgina Pauncefort as Queen Elizabeth, Isabel Bateman as Lady Anne/ Music by Robert Stoepel; Dec. 1896/ **Globe**, Mar. 1889, with Allen Beaumont as Henry VI, Richard Mansfield as Glo'ster, James Fernandez as Buckingham, W. R. Staveley as Norfolk, Luigi Lablache as Richmond, D. H. Harkins as Lord Stanley, Reginald Stockton as Ratcliffe, Leonard Calvert as Blount, Norman Forbes as Catesby, W. H. Crompton as Hastings, Mary Rorke as Queen Elizabeth, Carlotta Leclercq as Duchess of York/ Scenery by Bruce Smith, William Telbin, & E. G. Banks/ Music by Edward German.

RICHARD'S PLAY// C 1a// Mary Rowsell & J. J. Dilley// **Terry's**, Feb. 1891.

RICHELIEU; OR, THE CONSPIRACY// D 5a// Edward Bulwer-Lytton// **Cov. Garden**, Mar. 1839, with E. W. Elton as Louis XIII, Charles Diddear as Gaston, W. C. Macready as Richelieu, Mr. Warde as Baradas, James Anderson as de Mauprat, Mr. Roberts as de Clermont, Mr. Vining as de Beringhen, Samuel Phelps as Father Joseph, George Bennett as Huguet, Henry Howe as Francois, Helen Faucit as Julie, Miss Charles as Marion de Lorme/ Music by T. Cooke/ **Haymarket**, Apr. 1840, with Benjamin Webster as Louis XIII, J. W. Gough as Orleans, W. C. Macready as Richelieu, Mr. Warde as Baradas, John Webster as de Mauprat, J. Worrell as de Clermont, Walter Lacy as de Behringen, Samuel Phelps as Father Joseph, Henry Howe as Francois, Mrs. Edwin Yarnold as Julie, Miss Charles as Marion de Lorme/ Scenery by Charles Marshall; Nov. 1850, with Mr. Stuart as Louis XIII, Mr. Woolgar as Gaston, W. C. Macready as Richelieu, Henry Howe as Baradas, E. L. Davenport as de Mauprat, John Parselle as de Clermont, Charles Selby as de Beringhen, James Bland as Huguet, Priscilla Horton as Francois, Miss Reynolds as Julie,, Mrs. L. S. Buckingham as Marian de Lorme; Nov. 1861, with R. Dolman as Louis XIII, Edwin Villiers as Orleans, Edwin Booth as Richelieu, Henry Howe as Baradas, William Farren as De Mauprat, J. Worrell as De Clermont, Mr. Andrews as Beringhen, George Braid as Huguet, Eliza Weekes as Francois, Mrs. Charles Young as Julie, Miss Henrade as Marian de Lorme/ **Sad. Wells**, June 1845, with Henry Mellon as Louis XIII, Mr. Raymond as Orleans, George Bennett as Barradas, Samuel Phelps as Richelieu, Henry Marston as de Mauprat, Samuel Buckingham as de Beringhen, A. Younge as Joseph, Edward Knight as Huguet, Mr. Morton as Francois, Mrs. Mary Warner as Julie, Mrs. Henry Marston as Marion de Lorme/ Scenery by Mr. Finlay & F. Fenton; Feb. 1868, with Charles Dillon as Richelieu, J. L. Warner as de Mauprat, C. W. Barry as Baradas, R. Norman as Joseph, Walter Searle as de Beringhen, Mr. Howard as Orleans, Alice Marriott as Julie, Miss Fitzgerald as Marion de Lorme/ **Princess's**, Feb. 1846, with Charles Fisher as Louis XIII, Mr. Walton as Orleans, Mr. Cooper as Baradas, W. C. Macready as Richelieu, Leigh Murray as de Mauprat, James

Vining as de Beringhen, Mr. Granby as Joseph, John Ryder as Huguet, Mr. Wynn as Francois, Mrs. Stirling as Julie, Mrs. Brougham as Marion de Lorme/ Scenery by William Beverley & Mr. Nicholls; June 1860, with Harcourt Bland as Louis XIII, T. H. Higgie as Orleans, J. G. Shore as Beringhen, Samuel Phelps as Richelieu, Frank Graham as Joseph, Edmund Garden as Huguet, George Melville as de Mauprat, Emma Wadham as Francois, Frederic Robinson as Baradas, Caroline Heath as Julie, Rose Leclercq as Marion de Lorme/ **Drury Lane,** Oct. 1852; Mar. 1869, with W. Hampton as Louix XIII, John Ryder as Baradas, T. C. King as Richelieu, Henry Sinclair as de Mauprat, Alfred Nelson as de Beringhen, Mr. Barrett as Joseph, Mr. Cumming as Huguet, F. Charles as Francois, Bessie King as Julie, Marie O'Berne as Marion de Lorme/ **Grecian,** Dec. 1853, with Charles Horn as Louis XIII, T. Roberts as Gaston, Henry Grant as Baradas, Basil Potter as Richelieu, Richard Phillips as de Mauprat, Eaton O'Donnell as Joseph, Edwin Dixon as Huguet, Harriet Coveney as Francois, Jane Coveney as Julie, Agnes De Warde as Marian de Lorme; Oct. 1866 with Samuel Perfitt as Louis XIII, Mr. Goodin as Gaston, Charles Mortimer as Baradas, Alfred Rayner as Richelieu, William James as de Mauprat, George Gillett as de Beringhen, J. Jackson as Joseph, Henry Grant as Huguet, Mary A. Victor as Francois, Lizzie Mandelbert as Julie, Mrs. Dearlove as Marion de Lorme/ **Astley's,** Mar. 1870, with Walter Holland as Louis XIII, Harry Pritchard as Orleans, Charles Horsman as Baradas, Samuel Phelps as Richelieu, Charles Harcourt as de Mauprat, Henry Fletcher as de Beringhen, J. G. Rosiere as Joseph, Henry Dudley as Huguet, Mrs. Hermann Vezin as Julie, Mrs. Charles Horsman as Marion de Lorme/ **Lyceum,** May 1879, with Henry Irving, Kyrle Bellew, Georgina Pauncefort, Alma Murray; Nov. 1880, with Edwin Booth as Richelieu, Edmund Leathes as Louis XIII, P. C. Beverley as Orleans, William Redmund as Baradas, Charles Cartwright as de Mauprat, F. Charles as de Beringhen, John Ryder as Joseph, John Beauchamp as Huguet, W. Younge as Francois, Miss Gerard as Julie, Violet Temple as Marian de Lorme/ Scenery by Charles Brooke, Walter Hann, W. Greaves & Bruce Smith/ Machines by Mr. Warton/ Gas by Mr. Jones/ Lime-light by Messrs. Kerr/ Prod. by Harry Jackson; Apr. 1884, with Lawrence Barrett as Richelieu, Mark Quinton as Louis XIII, Mervyn Dallas as Orleans, Louis James as de Mauprat, James Fernandez as Baradas, Philip Ben Greet as De Beringhen, F. W. Irish as Joseph, Mr. Hamilton-Bell as Francois, Marie Wainwright as Julie de Mortimer, Mrs. Digby Willoughby as Marion de Lorme; Sept. 1873, with Henry Irving as Richelieu, John Clayton as Louis XIII, Allen Beaumont as Orleans, Henry Forrester as Baradus, J. B. Howard as De Mauprat, F. Charles as De Beringhen, John Carter as Joseph, E. F. Edgar as Huguet, H. B. Conway as Francois, Roma Le Thière as Marion de Lorme, Isabel Bateman as Julie/ Scenery by Hawes Craven & Cuthbert/ Costumes by Alfred Thompson/ Music by Robert Stoepel/ Prod. by H. L. Bateman/ **Adelphi,** July 1879, with J. G. Shore as Louix XIII, G. H. Weston as Orleans, E. F. Edgar as Baradas, Hermann Vezin as Richelieu, E. H. Brooke as De Mauprat, H. B. Conway as Francois, Mrs. Bernard Beere as Julie, Miss Compton as Marion de Lorme; June 1882, with Edwin Booth as Richelieu, J. G. Shore as Louis XIII, Samuel Fisher as Orleans, E. H. Brooke as Baradas, Eben. Plympton as de Mauprat, Robert Pateman as Joseph, Bella Pateman as Julie, Ellen Meyrick as Marion de Lorme/ Scenery by Charles Brooke.

RICHELIEU IN LOVE// C 3a// E. Robinson// **Haymarket,** Oct. 1852, with Henry Howe as Louis XIII, John Parselle as Prince Charles, Leigh Murray as Buckingham, Benjamin Webster as Richelieu, James Bland as Lord Herbert, Mr. Rogers as Joseph, Mrs. L. S. Buckingham as Mignon, Mrs. Stirling as Anne of Austria, Amelia Vining as Princess Henriette, Mrs. Selby as Countess le Dragon/ Scenery by George Morris & Mr. Conner.

RICHES; OR, THE WIFE AND BROTHER// D 3a// Adap. fr Massinger's The City Madam// **Cov. Garden,** Nov. 1837, with Charles Diddear as Sir John, George Bartley as Sir Maurice, James Anderson as Lacey, Mr. Vining as Heartwell, W. C. Macready as Luke, Mr. Roberts as Invoice, John Pritchard as Ledger, Drinkwater Meadows as Holdfast, W. H. Payne as Venture, Miss Taylor as Lady Traffic, Priscilla Horton as Maria, Miss E. Phillips as Eliza, Mrs. Sarah Garrick as Furbish/ **Haymarket,** Sept. 1841, with Henry Wallack as Sir John, William Strickland as Sir Maurice, John Webster as Lacey, Frederick Vining as Heartwell, W. C. Macready as Luke, J. Worrell as Invoice, Mr. Caulfield as Ledger, J. W. Gough as Risk, T. F. Mathews as Holdfast, Mrs. Stirling as Lady Traffic, Priscilla Horton as Maria, Miss Charles as Eliza, Mrs. Frank Matthews as Furbish.

RIENZI// T 5a// Mary Mitford// **Sad. Wells,** Dec. 1839, with Mr. Cathcart as Rienzi, Mr. Williams as Stephen Colonna, Mr. Elvin as Angelo Colonna, Mr. Dry as Ursini, Charles Montgomery as Savilli, Mr. Aldridge as Caparello, W. D. Broadfoot as Frangipani, J. W. Collier as Paulo, Miss Richardson as Lady Colonna, Mrs. Robert Honner as Claudia, Mrs. Morgan as Bertha.

RIFLE AND HOW TO USE IT, THE// F 1a// J. V. Bridgeman// **Haymarket,** Oct. 1859, with J. B. Buckstone as Floff, Mr. Rogers as Jubkins, Henry Compton as Muttins, J. Worrell as Pad, Mrs. Buckingham White as Mrs. Floff, Mrs. Wilkins as Mrs. Jubkins, Mrs. Edward Fitzwilliam as Mary/ **Sad. Wells,** Mar. 1860, with J. B. Buckstone as Floff, William Belford as Mutton, Mr. Williams as Tubkins, Mrs. Wilkins as Mrs. Tubkins, Grace Darley as Mrs. Floff, Emily Scott as Mary.

RIFLE BRIGADE, THE// F 1a// Charles Selby// **Haymarket,** Mar. 1852, with Leigh Murray as Doddleton, Henry Howe as Capt. Nugent, J. B. Buckstone as Simple, Amelia Vining as Mrs. Doddleton, Mrs. Fitzwilliam as Mrs. Masterman, Mrs. Caulfield as Perker/ **Adelphi,** Oct. 1860, with David Fisher as Doddleton,

Charles Selby as Capt. Nugent, William Smith as Peter, Mrs. Billington as Mrs. Doddleton, Kate Kelly as Perker, Mrs. Alfred Mellon (Sarah Woolgar) as Mrs. Major Masterman.

RIFT WITHIN THE LUTE, THE// Play 1a// C. H. Dickenson & Arthur Griffiths// **Duke of York's**, Nov. 1898/ **Avenue**, Jan. 1899/ **Terry's**, July 1899.

RIGHT// Play 3a// J. M. Killick// **St. Geo. Hall**, Feb. 1881.

RIGHT AGAINST MIGHT// C 3a// M. White// **Novelty**, July 1891.

RIGHT OR WRONG// C 1a// J. J. Bidford// **Criterion**, May 1887.

RIGHT OR WRONG// D 4a// F. Jerman// **Britannia**, July 1898.

RIGHTFUL HEIR, THE// D 5a// Alt. by Edward Bulwer-Lytton fr his own play The Sea Captain// **Lyceum**, Oct. 1868, with G. F. Neville as Lord Beaufort, Hermann Vezin as Sir Grey, Frank Lawlor as Wreckliffe, George Peel as Sir Godfrey, Daniel Bandmann as Vyvyan, Lin Rayne as Faulknor, T. Anderson as Harding, Basil Potter as Alton, Mrs. Hermann Vezin (Mrs. Charles Young) as Lady Montreville, Milly Palmer as Eveline/ Scenery by Charles & William Brew/ Music by John Barnard/ Machines by Mr. Lanham/ Prod. by E. T. Smith & T. H. Friend.

RIGHTS AND WRONGS OF WOMAN// F 1a// J. Maddison Morton// **Haymarket**, May 1856, with J. B. Buckstone as Sir Brian, Henry Howe as Col. Marchmont, Miss Talbot as Mrs. Marchmont, Bella Copeland as Stacey.

RIGHTS OF WOMAN, THE// C 1a// Emma Schiff// **Globe**, Jan. 1870, with H. Vernon as Charles Clifford, Ada Cavendish as Celia Steadfast, Emily Fowler as Kate Bertrand, Isabella Armour as Louisa, Nelly Nesbitt as Polly.

RING MISTRESS, THE// F 3a// Richard Ganthony// **Lyric**, Dec. 1900.

RING OF DEATH, THE; OR, THE BURIED BRIDE// D// n.a.// **Sad. Wells**, Jan. 1837, with Mr. Burton as Burgomaster, Mr. Campbell as Ephraim, Mr. Hicks as Laban, C. H. Pitt as Theodore, Mr. Rogers as Bolt, Miss Williams as Adelhaide, Miss Julian as Nina, Miss Hamilton as Bitha.

RING OF IRON, A// D 5a// Frank Harvey// **Grand**, Aug. 1885/ **Olympic**, Nov. 1886, with Lawrence Cautley as Sir John, George Temple as Meredith, Frank Wood as Thorpe, Hubert Byron as Timothy, P. C. Beverly as Mike, Alfred Davis as Dr. Grant, Olga Brandon as Nancy, Lydia Cowell as Selina, Lizzie Fletcher as Geraldine, Alice Chandos as Florence, Fanny Heath as Bland, Grace Hawthorne as Mary.

RINGDOVES, THE// C 1a// C. J. Mathews// **Olympic**, Dec. 1837, with Frank Matthews as Sir Harry, C. J. Mathews as Harry, John Brougham as Moony, Mr. Kerridge as Hobnail, Miss Lee as Cecilia, Mrs. Orger as Miss Longlackit/ **Cov. Garden**, Oct. 1839, with Frank Matthews as Sir Harry, C. J. Mathews as Harry, John Brougham as Mooney, Mr. Kerridge as Hobnail, Mrs. Orger as Mrs. Longclackit, Miss Lee as Cecilia/ **Lyceum**, Dec. 1847, with Frank Matthews as Sir Harry, C. J. Mathews as Harry, Henry Hall as Moony, Mr. Kerridge as Hobnail, Mrs. Charles Jones as Mrs. Longelackit, Miss Lee as Cecilia/ **Drury Lane**, July 1852/ **Sad. Wells**, July 1854, with Frank Matthews as Sir Harry, Mr. Williams as Rooney, Mr. Gladstone as Ringdove, Mr. Templeton as Hobnail, Mrs. Frank Matthews as Mrs. Longlackitt, Miss M. Oliver as Cecilia.

RINGING THE CHANGES// C 1a// [Horton Rhys?]// **Sad. Wells**, June 1862, with Catherine Lucette in 2 char. parts, Bessie Heath as Dame Moritz, Horton Price in 2 char. parts.

RIP VAN WINKLE; OR, THE SLEEP OF TWENTY YEARS// D 3a// Dram. by Dion Boucicault fr story of Washington Irving// **Adelphi**, Sept. 1865, with Joseph Jefferson as Rip, Richard Phillips as Derrick, Paul Bedford as Nick Vedder, Felix Rogers as Cockles, Mrs. Billington as Gretchen/ Scenery by Mr. Gates/ Music by Mr. Riviere/ Machines by Mr. Charker/ **Sad. Wells**, Apr. 1867, with Basil Potter as Haarlam, Mr. Andrews as Von Brummel, E. Shepherd as Vedder, Mr. Bellair as Krootz, Mr. Edwin as Hartz, Charles Rice as Rip, Fanny Gwynne as Carline, Annette Solomon as Annie, Louise Laidlaw as Gertude, Henry Crouch as Frederick, Nelly Burton as Annie (as adult), Miss Gilbert as Susan/ Scenery by John Johnson/ Machines by Mr. Caudery [sic], Music by Frank Musgrave/ Prod. by W. H. Swanborough/ **Princess's**, Nov. 1875, with Joseph Jefferson as Rip, E. F. Edgar as Derrick, E. Shepherd as Vedder, F. W. Irish as Cockles, J. B. Johnstone as Rory, T. W. Thorne as Stein, Mrs. Alfred Mellon as Gretchen, Miss Grattan as Meenie, Osmond Tearle as Hendrick, Miss A. Hamilton as Meenie (adult), Miss J. Lee as Katchen/ **Her Majesty's**, May 1900.

RIP VAN WINKLE: A LEGEND OF THE KAATSKILL MOUNTAINS// D 2a// Dram. fr novel of Washington Irving// **Cov. Garden**, Feb. 1845, with James H. Hackett as Rip, Mr. Griffiths as Von Tassel, Mr. Hollingsworth as Vedder, Mr. Bass as Von Brunt, Mr. Henry as Van Clump, Mr. Hann as Hudson, Mr. Butler as Jewett, Mrs. Griffiths as Dame Van Winkle, Miss L. Lyons as Alice, George Braid as Herman, J. C. Bird as Gustaff, Mr. Lee as Judge, Mr. Taylor as Young Rip, Miss Fitzjames as Gertrude.

RIPPLINGS// C// Charles Balcour// **Sadler's Wells**, Mar. 1883.

RISE OF DICK HALWARD, THE// Play 3a// Jerome K. Jerome// **Garrick**, Oct. 1895.

RIVAL ARTISTES, THE// F// M. Kinghorne// **Surrey**, May 1873.

RIVAL BROTHERS, THE; OR, A MEXICAN'S REVENGE// D// n.a.// **Sad. Wells**, Oct. 1837, with Mr. King as Don Gomez, Mr. Pateman as Sebastian, Thomas Lee as Diego, Mr. Scarbrow as Leandro, Mr. Campbell as Bowline, Mr. Ennis as Perez, Mr. Russell as Fernando, Miss Young as Donna Lorenza, Miss Vernon as Leonora, Mrs. Worrell as Morane, S. Palmer as Xalva, Mr. Wilkins as Tiasella, Miss Pitt as Morano, Mr. Griffith as Sarad, Miss Williams as Oreana.

RIVAL CANDIDATES// C 4a// G. R. Douglas// **Folly**, Mar. 1880, with F. H. Macklin, Mrs. Leigh Murray, Miss B. Henri.

RIVAL FOUNTAIN// D// n.a.// **Britannia**, Oct. 1859.

RIVAL ROMEOS// F 1a// H. B. Farnie// **St. James's**, Apr. 1871, with Marian Inch as Gloriana, Sallie Turner as Mrs. Snooks, Harry Cox as Snooks, Gaston Murray as Smudge, George Grainger as Peppercorn.

RIVAL SERGEANTS, THE// F// Charles Dance// **Sad. Wells**, Apr. 1847, with John Scharf as Sgt. Charles, Henry Mellon as Sgt. O'Lynn, Julia Wallack as Margaretta, Fanny Morelli as Louisa, Miss Graham as Janette.

RIVAL VALETS, THE// F 1a// Joseph Ebsworth// **Grecian**, Oct. 1847, with Eaton O'Donnell as Ms. Perkins, Richard Phillips as Capt. Welford, John Webster as Frank, Frederick Robson as Anthony, Ada Harcourt as Sophia, Miss Merion as Dorothy.

RIVALS, THE// C 5a// Richard Brinsley Sheridan// **Haymarket**, June 1837, with William Farren as Sir Anthony, Frederick Vining as Capt. Absolute, Mr. Daly as Sir Lucius, E. W. Elton as Faulkland, Benjamin Webster as Acres, Charles Selby as Fag, Mrs. Julia Glover as Mrs. Malaprop, Miss Huddart as Julia, Mrs. Nisbett as Lydia, Miss Wrighten as Lucy; Nov. 1839, with Robert Strickland as Sir Anthony, Samuel Phelps as Faulkland, Walter Lacy as Capt. Absolute, Tyrone Power as Sir Lucius, Benjamin Webster as Acres, Mrs. Julia Glover as Mrs. Malaprop, Mrs. Walter Lacy (Miss Taylor) as Lydia, Mrs. Mary Warner as Julia, Priscilla Horton as Lucy; Aug. 1841, with Robert Strickland as Sir Anthony, George Bennett as Faulkland, Henry Wallack as Sir Lucius, James Wallack as Capt. Absolute, Mr. Placide as Acres, David Rees as David, J. Worrell as Fag, Mrs. Julia Glover as Mrs. Malaprop, Mrs. Stirling as Lydia, Helen Faucit as Julia, Mrs. Frank Matthews as Lucy/ Jan. 1848, with William Farren as Sir Anthony, Henry Farren as Capt. Absolute, William Creswick as Faulkland, Benjamin Webster as Acres, Alfred Wigan as Sir Lucius, A. Brindal as Fag, Robert Keeley as David, Mrs. Julia Glover as Mrs. Malaprop, Mrs. Nisbett as Lydia, Miss Fortescue as Julia, Mrs. Humby as Lucy; Mar. 1853, with W. H. Chippendale as Sir Anthony, William Farren as Capt. Absolute, Henry Howe as Faulkland, Henry Compton as Acres, H. Corri as Sir Lucius, Mr. Clark as Fag, Mrs. Poynter as Mrs. Malaprop, Mrs. L. S. Buckingham as Julia, Miss Reynolds as Lydia, Ellen Chaplin as Lucy; Feb. 1861, with W. H. Chippendale as Sir Anthony, William Farren as Capt. Absolute, Henry Howe as Faulkland, J. B. Buckstone as Acres, John Brougham as Sir Lucius, Fanny Stirling as Lydia, Mrs. Poynter as Mrs. Malaprop, Florence Haydon as Julia, Mrs. Edward Fitzwilliam as Lucy; Oct. 1878, with Henry Howe as Sir Anthony, Charles Kelly as Faulkland, William Terriss as Capt. Absolute, Robert Pateman as Sir Lucius, David Fisher Jr. as David, Henry Crouch as Fag, John S. Clarke as Acres, Emily Thorne as Mrs. Malaprop, Bella Pateman as Lydia, Carlotta Addison as Julia, Kate Phillips as Lucy; Apr. 1879, with similar cast except Mrs. Bernard Beere as Lydia, Blanche Henri as Julia; May 1884, with Arthur Wing Pinero as Sir Anthony, Alfred Bishop as Sir Lucius, Johnston Forbes Robertson as Capt. Absolute, Squire Bancroft as Faulkland, Lionel Brough as Acres, Charles Brookfield as David, Mr. Elliot as Fag, Mrs. Stirling as Mrs. Malaprop, Mrs. Bernard Beere as Julia, Miss Calhoun as Lydia, Julia Gwynne as Lucy/ Scenery by Mr. Telbin, Walter Johnstone & Walter Hann; Mar. 1900, with Sydney Valentine as Sir Anthony, Paul Arthur as Capt. Absolute, Frederick Harrison as Faulkland, Cyril Maude as Acres, J. D. Beveridge as Sir Lucius, Holman Clark as Fag, Mrs. Charles Calvert as Mrs. Malaprop, Winifred Emery as Lydia, Lily Hanbury as Julia, Beatrice Ferrar as Lucy/ Scenery by Joseph Harker & Walter Hann/ **Cov. Garden**, Nov. 1839, with William Farren as Sir Anthony, James Anderson as Capt. Absolute, John Brougham as Sir Lucius, Mr. Cooper as Faulkland, John Pritt Harley as Acres, Thomas Green as Fag, Drinkwater Meadows as David, Mrs. Charles Jones as Mrs. Malaprop, Mme. Vestris as Lydia, Louisa Nisbett as Julia, Mrs. Humby as Lucy; Sept. 1841, with William Farren as Sir Anthony, Walter Lacy as Capt. Absolute, Mr. Cooper as Faulkland, John Pritt Harley as Acres, John Brougham as Sir Lucius, A. Brindal as Fag, Mrs. Julia Glover as Mrs. Malaprop, Louisa Nisbett as Julia, Mme. Vestris as Lydia, Mrs. Humby as Lucy/ **Sad. Wells**, July 1844, with Samuel Phelps as Sir Anthony, John Webster as Capt. Absolute, Charles Hudson as Sir Lucius, Henry Marston as Faukland, G. F. Forman as Acres, Mr. Coreno as Fag, Mrs. Henry Marston as Mrs. Malaprop, Miss Cooper as Lydia, Mrs. Mary Warner as Julia, Georgiana Lebatt as Lucy; May 1866, with Mr. Barrett as Sir Anthony, Charles Warner as Capt. Absolute, William McIntyre as Faulkland, Mr. Holland as Fag, Garston Belmore as Acres, Frank Barsby as Sir Lucius, Mrs. Poynter as Mrs. Malaprop, Ada Harland as Julia, Fanny Gwynne as Lydia, Lizzie Wilmore as Lucy/ **Grecian**, May 1845, with F. Ede as Sir Anthony, Harry Chester as Capt. Absolute, Edwin Dixon as Faulkland, Edmund Garden as Sir Lucius, Frederick Robson as Acres, Annette Mears as Lydia Languish, Miss M. A. Crisp as Julia, Miss Merion as Mrs. Malaprop; Oct. 1856, with H. Somerville as Sir Anthony, Eaton O'Donnell as Sir Lucius, Mr. Hustleby as Faukland, Richard Phillips as Capt. Absolute, John Manning as Acres, Miss Johnstone as Mrs. Malaprop, Harriet Coveney as Lydia, Jane Coveney as Julia;

July 1866, with Henry Marston as Sir Anthony, William James as Capt. Absolute, George Gillette as Faulkland, John Manning as Acres, Charles Mortimer as Sir Lucius, Mrs. Henry Marston as Mrs. Malaprop, Harriet Western as Julia, Mary A. Victor as Lucy, Lizzie Mandelbert as Lydia/ **Olympic**, Oct. 1846, with J. Cowell as Sir Anthony, Mr. Hammersley as Sir Lucius, Leigh Murray as Captain Absolute, Henry West Betty as Faulkland, Walter Lacy as Acres, Mr. Wilkenson as David, Mrs. Charles Jones as Mrs. Malaprop, Mrs. Lacy as Lydia, Miss Ayres as Lucy; Nov. 1850, with William Farren as Sir Anthony, Mr. Norton as Sir Lucius, Henry Farren as Capt. Absolute, Leigh Murray as Faulkland, Henry Compton as Acres, William Farren Jr. as Fag, Mrs. Stirling as Lydia Languish, Mrs. Leigh Murray as Julia, Mrs. B. Bartlett as Mrs. Malaprop, Mrs. Alfred Phillips as Lucy/ **Drury Lane**, Feb. 1850, with Basil Baker as Sir Anthony, William Montague as Sir Lucius, Frederick Vining as Capt. Absolute, Mr. Cooper as Faulkland, Stephen Artaud as Acres, John Parry as Fag, Mrs. Winstanley as Mrs. Malaprop, Laura Addison as Julia, Louisa Nisbett as Lydia, Clara Tellett as Lucy/ **Princess's**, Oct. 1853, with Mr. Addison as Sir Anthony, Walter Lacy as Capt. Absolute, John Cathcart as Faulkland, Henry Mellon as Sir Lucius, John Pritt Harley as Acres, Mrs. Winstanley as Mrs. Malaprop, Carlotta Leclercq as Lydia, Caroline Heath as Julia, Mrs. Walter Lacy as Lucy; Mar. 1860, with Frank Matthews as Sir Anthony, Leigh Murray as Capt. Absolute, George Melville as Faulkland, Henry Widdicomb as Acres, Harcourt Bland as Sir Lucius, J. W. Collier as Fag, Mrs. Frank Matthews as Mrs. Malaprop, Carlotta Leclercq as Lydia, Miss Clifford as Julia, Louise Keeley as Lucy/ **Sad. Wells**, 1866/ **St. James's**, May 1866, with Frank Matthews as Sir Anthony, F. Charles as Captain Absolute, Gaston Murray as Faulkland, Walter Lacy as Acres, Fourness Rolfe as Sir Lucius, John Clayton as Fag, Frederick Robson as David, Edward Dyas as Thomas, Mrs. Frank Matthews as Mrs. Malaprop, Louisa Herbert as Lydia, Eleanor Bufton as Julia, Ellen McDonnell as Lucy/ Scenery by T. Grieve/ Machines by Mr. Mathews/ Music by Frank Musgrave/ **Globe**, Sept. 1877, with John Ryder as Sir Anthony, Charles Warner as Capt. Absolute, F. H. Macklin as Falkland, Edward Righton as Acres, John Maclean as Sir Lucius, Emma Ritta as Lydia, Miss Compton as Julia, Isabel Clifton as Lucy, Mrs. Stirling as Mrs. Malaprop/ **St. James's**, Feb. 1878, with William Farren Jr. as Sir Anthony, Charles Warner as Capt. Absolute, Henry Forrester as Faukland, Edward Righton as Acres, J. D. Beveridge as Sir Lucius, Mrs. Chippendale as Mrs. Malaprop, Helen Barry as Lydia Languish, Mrs. Bernard Beere as Julia, Miss Chetwynd as Lucy; Mar. 1881, with W. H. Chippendale as Sir Anthony, C. W. Somerset as Capt. Absolute, H. Templeton as Sir Lucius, Philip Beck as Faulkland, Mr. Fosbrooke as Acres, J. C. Buckstone as Fag, Marie De Grey as Lydia, Miss Measor as Julia, Miss B. Huntley as Lucy, Mrs. Chippendale as Mrs. Malaprop/ **Vaudeville**, Dec. 1882, with William Farren, Henry Neville, Frank Archer, John Maclean, Winifred Emery, Alma Murray, Kate Phillips, Mrs. Stirling/ **Strand**, Sept. 1885, with Edward Compton, Lewis Ball, Sidney Valentine, Dora Vivian, Elinor Aickin/ **Court**, Nov. 1895.

RIVERSIDE STORY, A// Play 2a// Marie Wilton Bancroft// **Haymarket**, May 1890.

ROAD OF LIFE, THE; OR, THE CABMAN'S CAREER// D 3a// E. L. Blanchard// **Olympic**, Nov. 1843, with Mr. Salter as Welford, Mr. Green as Arlingford, James Ranoe as Gutler, Mr. Brookes as Pivot, John Webster as Humbug, Mr. Turnour as Bilk, Walter Searle as Scowl, George Wild as Turnstile, Lavinia Melville as Caroline, Miss Hamilton as Emily, Miss Lebatt as Dolly/ Scenery by W. R. Beverly, Mr. Wilson & Mr. Scott/ Machines by Mr. Mackintosh/ Music by Mr. Calcott.

ROAD TO FAME, THE// C 3a// Adap. by A. White & P. Grunfeld fr G of von Kneisel, Der Kuchnek// **Vaudeville**, May 1885.

ROAD TO RUIN, THE// C 5a// Thomas Holcroft// **Drury Lane**, Oct. 1837, with William Dowton as Old Dornton, Mr. Cooper as Harry, J. S. Balls as Goldfinch, William Bennett as Sulky, Henry Compton as Silky, A. Brindal as Milford, Mr. Baker as Smith, Mr. Hughes as Jacob, Mrs. Charles Jones as Widow Warren, Miss Charles as Sophia, Mrs. Brindal as Jenny, Mme. Simon as Mrs. Ledger; Oct. 1842, with Samuel Phelps as Dornton, James Anderson as Harry, Frank Graham as Milford, Mr. Lambert as Sulky, C. J. Mathews as Goldfinch, Henry Compton as Silky, Mrs. Charles Jones as Widow Warren, Mrs. Stirling as Sophia, Mrs. Sarah Garrick as Mrs. Ledger, Mrs. Selby as Jenny; Dec. 1849, with Basil Baker as Dornton, James Anderson as Harry, William Davidge as Sulky, Samuel Emery as Silky, Frederick Vining as Goldfinch, Charles Fisher as Milford, Mr. Darcie as Smith, Mrs. Winstanley as Widow Warren, Miss Baker as Sophia, Annie Lonsdale as Jenny, Mrs. Foster as Mrs. Ledger/ **Haymarket**, Sept. 1840, with Samuel Phelps as Old Dornton, J. Waldron as Sulky, James Wallack as Harry Dornton, William Strickland as Silky, Benjamin Wrench as Goldfinch, Henry Howe as Milford, J. Worrell as Smith, Mrs. Julia Glover as Widow Warren, Mrs. Gallot as Mrs. Ledger, Mrs. Frank Matthews as Jenny, Mrs. Stirling as Sophia/ **Sad. Wells**, Apr. 1841, with Mr. Williams as Old Dornton, Henry Marston as Dornton, Mr. Turnour as Silky, Mr. Salter as Sukly, John Webster as Goldfinch, George Ellis as Milford, Mr. Aldridge as Smith, Mr. Archer as Hosier, Miss Cooke as Widow Warren, Mrs. Morgan as Mrs. Ledger, Mrs. Robert Honner as Sophia; Aug. 1844, with Samuel Phelps as Dornton, Henry Marston as Harry Dornton, A. Younge as Silky, Mr. Williams as Sulky, John Webster as Goldfinch, Mr. Morton as Milford, Mrs. Henry Marston as Widow Warren, Miss Cooper as Sophia, Miss Lebatt as Jenny, Mrs. Francis as Mrs. Ledger/ **Drury Lane**, Dec. 1849/ **Adelphi**, July 1851, with Benjamin Webster as Goldfinch, William Cullenford as Sulky, Samuel Emery as Silky, C. J. Smith as Smith, Leigh Murray as Harry Dornton, Mr. Woolgar as Mr. Dornton, Sarah Woolgar as Sophia, Mrs. Laws as Widow Warren, Ellen Chaplin as Jenny/ **Olympic**,

Nov. 1851, with William Farren as Dornton, William Farren Jr. as Harry Dornton, Henry Farren as Goldfinch, Henry Compton as Silky, Charles Diddear as Sulky, Mr. Norton as Milford, Mrs. Alfred Phillips as Widow Warren, Louisa Howard as Sophia, Isabel Adams as Jenny, Mrs. B. Bartlett as Mrs. Ledger/ **Haymarket**, Sept. 1859, with C. J. Mathews, Mrs. Mathews (Lizzie Davenport)/ **St. James's**, Feb. 1867, with Henry Irving/ **Vaudeville**, 1873/ **Vaudeville**, Dec. 1879, with Henry Howe, C. W. Garthorne, Sophie Larkin, Marie Illington, Cicely Richards/ **Sadler's Wells**, Nov. 1880, with Charles Warner, Isabel Bateman, Edmund Lyons/ **Opera Comique**, Dec. 1891.

ROAD TO TRANSPORTATION, THE// D 3a// Dram. by John Courtney fr tale of E. F. Roberts// **Victoria**, Oct. 1848, with J. Howard as Carpenter, J. T. Johnson as Wildeye, Mr. Hitchinson as Whitworth, Mr. Henderson as Timmins, John Bradshaw as Mudge, G. F. Forman as Starter, E. Edwards as Slammers, Mr. Hawkins as Lump, F. H. Henry as Slicker, Annette Vincent as Frances, Miss Richardson as Mrs. Wildeye, Mrs. Cooke as Mrs. Carpenter, Miss Burroughcliffe as Biddy/ Prod. by Mr. Osbaldiston & T. H. Higgie.

ROADSIDE INN// D// n.a.// **Lyceum**, Jan. 1865.

ROB ROY// D 3a// Dram. fr novel of Sir Walter Scott// **Cov. Garden**, Jan. 1837, with Mr. Thompson as Sir Frederick, Mr. Tilbury as Owen, George Bennett as Rashleigh Osbaldistone, Mr. Collins as Francis Osbaldistone, Mr. Vandenhoff as Rob Roy, John Webster as Capt. Thornton, Mr. Ransford as Maj. Galbraith, William Farren as Jarvie, Miss Turpin as Diana, Mrs. W. West as Helen, Miss Nicholson as Martha/ **Sad. Wells**, June 1837, with Mr. King as Sir Frederick, Mr. Hicks as Rashleigh, Mr. Manvers as Francis, John Pritchard as Rob Roy, C. H. Pitt as Capt. Thornton, Mr. Griffiths as Owen, Mr. Tilbury as Jarvie, C. J. Smith as Dougal, Mrs. W. West as Helen, Mrs. Harris as Jean, Mrs. Rogers as Martha, Miss Land as Diana, Lavinia Melville as Mattie; Oct. 1879, with Walter Bentley as Rob Roy, Richard Drummond as Francis Osbaldistone, N. Wheatcroft as Rashleigh Osbaldistone, E. Smart as Sir Frederick, F. W. Wyndham as Capt. Thornton, A. Redwood as Maj. Galbraith, Edmund Lyons as Jarvie, Mr. Fosbrooke as Owen, Kate Bateman as Helen, Maud Irvine as Diana, Miss K. Mildenhall as Mattie, Miss B. Montague as Martha/ Scenery by Gordon, Harford, J. Brunton, T. W. Hall, & John O'Conner/ Music by W. C. Levey/ **Cov. Garden**, Nov. 1837, with Samuel Phelps/ **Grecian**, (in 3a), Nov. 1853, with Basil Potter as Rashleigh, Charles Horn as Francis, Richard Phillips as Rob Roy, Eaton O'Donnell as Bailie Nicol, Percy Corri as Maj. Galbraith, T. Roberts as Capt. Thornton, Charles Rice as Dougal, Harriet Coveney as Diana, Jane Coveney as Helen, Ellen Crisp as Mattie/ **Astley's**, Feb. 1857, with Mr. Campbell as Sir Frederick, Mark Howard as Osbaldistone, W. H. Eburne as Francis, Clarance Lindon as Owen, Henry Reeves as Capt. Thornton, Mr. Vokes as Maj. Galbraith, James Holloway as Rob Roy, J. W. Anson as Jarvie, H. Hemmings as Dougal, Miss Dowton as Robert, Julia Weston as Diana, Mrs. J. W. Anson as Mattie, Mrs. William Dowton as Helen/ Scenery by T. Thompson & Thorne/ Machines by E. Pryce/ Music by G. Phillips/ Horses trained by Wm. Cooke.

ROB ROY// D// Dram fr novel of Sir Walter Scott// **Victoria**, Sept. 1871, with Thomas Swinbourne as Rob Roy, George Harvey as Osbaldiston, John Maclean as Jarvie, J. A. Cave as Maj. Galbraith, William McIntyre as Dougal, Henry Mayhew as Capt. Thornton, E. Fitzdavis as Rashleigh, A. Stile as Sir Frederick, James Fawn as Owen, Mrs. Henry Leigh as Helen, Lizzie Branch as Diana.

ROB ROY// D// Dram. by Isaac Pocock fr novel of Sir Walter Scott// **Sad. Wells**, Oct. 1879, with Walter Bentley, Edward Cotte, Mrs. Charles Calvert.

ROB ROY; OR, AULD LANG SYNE// D// n.a.// **Sad. Wells**, June 1854, with F. Charles as Capt. Thornton, James Worrell as Osbalistone, Mr. Barrett as Jarvie, W. Williams as Maj. Galbraith, E. L. Davenport as Rob Roy, Miss Lavine as Diana, Miss Rawlings as Mattie, Mrs. Barrett as Helen.

ROB ROY MACGREGOR; OR, THE DAYS OF AULD LANG SYNE// D 3a// Dram. fr novel of Sir Walter Scott// **Drury Lane**, Jan. 1850, with Charles Diddear as Sir Frederick, William Montague as Rashleigh Osbaldistone, Mr. Rafter as Francis Osbaldistone, William Davidge as Owen, Mr. Frazer as Capt. Thornton, James Anderson as Rob Roy, Samuel Emery as Jarvie, Mr. Manderson as Dougal, Mr. Clifford as McStuart, Mr. Priorson as Willie, Robert Romer as Fairservice, Lucy Rafter as Diana, Mrs. Ternan as Helen, Miss Morant as Mattie, Annie Lonsdale as Martha, Mrs. Griffiths as Jean/ **Grecian**, Apr. 1856, with Professor Anderson as Rob Roy, William Shuter as Vernon, Mr. Hustleby as Rashleigh Osbaldiston, F. Charles as Francis, Eaton O'Donnell as Owen, Percy Corri as Maj. Galbraith.

ROBBERS, THE// D 5a// Adap. by James Anderson fr G of Friedrich Schiller// **Drury Lane**, Apr. 1851.

ROBBER'S BRIDE, THE (see Robber's Wife)

ROBBER'S WIFE, THE (also titled Robber's Bride)// D 2a// Isaac Pocock// **Sad. Wells**, Nov. 1838, with Mr. Williams as Briarly, Dibdin Pitt as Penfuddle, J. W. Collier as O'Gig, J. Lee as Redland, Mr. Conquest as Macfile, Mr. Dry as Rody, Mr. Harwood as Drosset, Mrs. Robert Honner as Rose; Sept. 1845, with A. Younge as Briarly, Mr. Williams as Punfuddle, George Bennett as Redland, Henry Mellon as O'Gig, Miss Cooper as Rose/ **Olympic**, Dec 1846, with Mr. Johnstone as Briarley, Robert Romer as Penfuddle, J. Cowell as O'Gig, Charles Maynard as Redland, Mr. Wilkenson as Macfile, Mr. Darcie as Rody, Mrs. R. Gordon as Rose/ **Victoria**, Jan. 1850, with John Dale as Briarly, J. T. Johnson as Redland, J. Howard as

Penfuddle, Mr. Leake as Rody, J. Neville as O'Gig, John Hudspeth as MacFile, F. H. Henry as Drosset, Mr. Humphreys as Clipem, Mrs. George Lee as Rose.

ROBBERY UNDER ARMS// D 5a// Adap. by Alfred Dampier & Garnet Walch fr Austral. orig. of B. Boldrewood// **Princess's**, Oct. 1894.

ROBERT EMMET, THE PATRIOT OF IRELAND// D// n.a.// **Adelphi**, June 1867, with C. King as Robert Emmet, J. W. Lawler as O'Gaff, G. James as Leary, Eliza Rudd as Maria.

ROBERT LE GRANGE; OR, ONE NIGHT OF THE FRENCH REVOLUTION// D 1a// Charles Webb// **Sad. Wells**, Sept. 1843, with C. J. Bird as de Courcy, Mr. Lyon as Le Grange/ **Grecian**, Aug. 1861, with Mrs. Charles Dillon as Mariette, R. H. Lingham as Chevalier, William James as Robert.

ROBERT MACAIRE; OR, THE AUBERGE DES ADRETS// D 2a// Adap fr F, L'Auberge des Adrêts// **Sad. Wells**, Oct. 1838, with Dibdin Pitt as Germeuil, Mr. Dry as Dumont, Mr. Elvin as Charles, J. Lee as Robert Macaire, Mr. Conquest as Jacques Strop, Mr. Harwood as Sgt. Loupy, Mr. Phillips as Louis, Mr. Priorson as Francois, Miss Richardson as Marie, Mrs. J. F. Saville as Clementine/ **Victoria**, Nov. 1841, with Mr. James as Dumont, Mr. Wilton as Germouil, William Seaman as Charles, Mr. Chapino as Louis, C. Williams as Sgt. Loupy, E. F. Saville as Robert Macaire, John Gardner as Jaques Strop, C. Pitt as Francois, Mr. Hitchinson as Ducape, Miss Sadler as Clementine, Mrs. George Lee as Marie, Miss Edgar as Selina, Mrs. Seaman as Rosina/ **Cov. Garden**, Oct. 1843, with Mr. Lambert as Germeuil, Frank Matthews as Dumont, Henry Wallack as Robert Macaire, Robert Keeley as Jacques Strop, Mr. Craven as Charles, Mr. Priorson as Francois, Edwin Yarnold as Sgt. Loupy, Mr. Ross as Pierre, Mrs. Selby as Marie, Miss Grove as Clementine/ **Olympic**, Aug. 1855, with J. H. White as Germeuil, Frederick Vining as Dumont, Samuel Emery as Macaire, Frederick Robson as Jacques Strop, Mr. Leslie as Charles, Harwood Cooper as Sgt. Loupy, Mrs. Fitzallan as Marie, Miss Bromley as Clementine/ **Grecian**, Jan. 1856, with Eaton O'Donnell as Germeiul, Henry Grant as Dumont, Richard Phillips as Robert Macaire, John Manning as Jacques Strop, F. Charles, Jane Coveney as Marie, Ellen Hale as Clementina/ **Gaiety**, Feb. 1877, with J. L. Toole, Henry Widdicomb/ **Lyceum**, May 1888, with Henry Irving as Robert Macaire, Weedon Grossmith as Jacques Strop, Henry Howe as Dumont, Mr. Harbury as Germeuil, Frank Tyars as Sgt. Loupy, Mrs. Macklin as Marie, Miss F. Harwood as Clementine/ Scenery by Hawes Craven/ Music by J. Meredith Ball.

ROBERT MACAIRE; OR, THE TWO MURDERERS// D 2a// n.a.// **Sad. Wells**, Aug. 1858, with Mr. Taylor as Germeuil, Mr. Williams as Dumont, J. Turner as Macaire, John Price as Jacques Strop, Walter Cambell as Charles, Mr. Hollingberry as Louis, Mr. Fredericks as Francois, Mrs. Henderson as Marie, Miss Wright as Clementine.

ROBERT RABAGAS// C 3a// Stephen Fiske// **St. James's**, Feb. 1873.

ROBESPIERRE; OR, TWO DAYS OF THE REVOLUTION// D 2a// W. Bayle Bernard// **Adelphi**, Oct. 1840, with Frederick Yates, J. F. Saville, Mr. Freeborn, William Cullenford, Mr. Lyon, George Maynard, Mr. Wilkinson, J. F. Smith, John Sanders, Paul Bedford, Mrs. Yates, Mrs. Fosbroke.

ROBESPIERRE// D 5a// Trans. by L. B. Irving fr F of Victorien Sardou// **Lyceum**, Apr. 1899.

ROBIN GOODFELLOW// Play 3a// R. C. Carlton// **Garrick**, Jan. 1893.

ROBIN HOOD; OR,. THE HUNTRESS OF ARLINGFORD// D// n.a.// **Sad. Wells**, Mar. 1838, with Mr. Ranson as Richard II, F. Ede as Prince John, Mr. James as Baron Fitzwalter, J. Worrell as Sir Ralph, Mr. Forester as Robin Hood, Mr. Rogers as Abbott, Mr. Campbell as Friar Tuck, Mr. Gay as Sir William, S. Smith as Scarlet, Mr. Moore as Little John, Mr. Nunn as Allen o' Dale, Mr. Williams as Sheriff, Eliza Vincent as Maid Marian, Miss Beresford as Alice, Miss Chartley as Matilde.

ROBINSON CRUSOE; OR, THE BOLD BUCCANEERS// D// n.a.// **Sad. Wells**, Apr. 1843, with C. J. Smith as Crusoe, T. Matthews as Friday, Mr. Dry as Iglou, C. J. Bird as Diego, Mr. Williams as Windlass, J. W. Collier as Bluff, Mr. Aldridge as Swivel, John Herbert as Nipcheese, Miss Melville as Inez.

ROBUR RAGABAS; OR, 1792// D// n.a.// **Elephant & Castle**, Mar. 1873.

ROBUST INVALID, THE// C 3a// Adap. by Charles Reade fr F of Moliere, Malade Imaginaire// **Adelphi**, June 1870, with Mr. Vining as Argan, G. F. Sinclair as Beroalde, George Pearce as Diafoirus, W. Worboys as Thomas, Richmond Kyrle as Purgon, Harwood Cooper as Fleurant, Henry Ashley as Cleantes, Constance Georgi as Mme. Beline, Phillis Glover as Angelique, Florence Terry as Louison/ Asst. Act. Mgr. George Coleman.

ROCAMBOLE; OR, THE KNAVES OF HEARTS AND THE COMPANIONS OF CRIME// D Pro & 3a// W. E. Suter// **Grecian**, Mar. 1866, with Dacre Baldie as Andrea, Mr. Goodin as Venture, John Manning as Guignon, J. Jackson as Chamery, William James as Fippart, Walter Holland as Armand, W. Shirley as Sallendrera, Marie Brewer as Carmen, Mrs. Dearlove as Fanchette, Lizzie Mandlebert as Baccarat, Mrs. Atkinson as Mme. Fippart, Mary A. Victor as Cerise/ prod. under title of Baccarat, **Sad. Wells**, Mar. 1865.

ROCHESTER; OR, KING CHARLES THE SECOND'S MERRY DAYS// C 3a// W. J. Moncrieff// **Sad. Wells**, May 1839, with Mr. Dry as Charles II, Mr. Elvin as Buckingham, John Webster as Rochester, Mr. Aldridge as

Dunstable, W. D. Broadfoot as Starvemouse, Mr. Conquest as Balaam, Miss Píncott as Countess Lovelaugh, Mrs. J. F. Saville as Silvia, Mrs. Phillips as Lady Gay, Miss Cooke as Aunt Rebecca, Miss Norman as Bell/ **Olympic**, Apr. 1842, with Mr. Baker as Charles II, Mr. Fitzjames as Rochester, Mr. Halford as Buckingham, Mr. Green as Dunstable, Mr. Turnour as Starvemouse, Mr. Ross as Balaam, Walter Searle as Squeak, Miss Hamilton as Countess of Lovelaugh, Miss Arden as Lady Gay, Miss Fitzjames as Silvia, Mrs. Granby as Aunt Rebecca/ **Victoria**, Oct. 1843, with Mr. Grove as Charles II, Mr. Lazar as Rochester, Mr. Griffiths as Buckingham, Mr. Thomson as Dunstable, Charles Fenton as Starvemouse, Mr. Peat as Thin, Mr. Coppin as Muddle, Mr. Simes as Squeak, Mr. Deering as Balaam, Mrs. Coppin as Countess of Lovelaugh, Mme. Louise as Lady Gay, Mme. Torning as Bell/ **Grecian**, Nov. 1856, with Henry Grant as Charles II, Richard Phillips as Rochester, C. Kelsey as Dunstable, Mr. Hustleby as Buckingham, John Manning as Balaam, George Conquest, Eaton O'Donnell as Muddle, Jane Coveney as Lovelaugh, Ellen Hale as Gay, Miss Chapman as Silvia, Miss Johnstone as Aunt Rebecca.

ROCK OF ARPENNAZ, THE// D// n.a.// **Sad. Wells**, Aug. 1842, with Mr. Lyon as Count Romaldi, C. J. Smith as Francisco, Mr. Dry as Benamo, W. D. Broadfoot as as Stephano, Mr. Williams as Montano, John Herbert as Michelli, Miss Richardson as Selina, Mrs. Richard Barnett as Fiametta.

ROCK OF ST. HELENA, THE; OR, NAPOLEON IN EXILE// D// W. Gomersal// **Sad. Wells**, Mar. 1839, with W. Gomersal as Napoleon, Mr. Dry as Sir Hudson, Mr. Harwood as Bertrand, Mr. Elvin as Montholon, Dibdin Pitt as Balcombe, Charles Montgomery as Casas, J. W. Collier as Capriani, Mr. Phillips as Lt. Montgomery, Miss Cooke as Mme. Bertrand, Mrs. Harwood as Mme. Montholon, Mrs. J. F. Saville as Rose.

ROCK OF SKULLS, THE; OR, THE HIDDEN TREASURE// D// n.a.// **Sad. Wells**, Jan. 1837, with Mr. Campbell as Paoley, C. H. Pitt as Walfram, Mr. Hicks as Hacarth, Mr. Burton as Lictover, Mr. Rogers as Peterpo, Miss Williams as Helena, Miss Julian as Semina, Miss Wilson as Lerena.

ROCKET, THE// C 3a// Arthur Wing Pinero// **Gaiety**, Dec. 1883, with Edward Terry, Maria Jones, Dolores Drummond.

ROGER O'HARE// n.a.// **Victoria**, Aug. 1865.

ROGUE'S COMEDY, THE// Play 3a// Henry Arthur Jones// **Garrick**, Apr. 1896.

ROGUES AND VAGABONDS// D 4a// E. H. Mitchelson & F. Brenton// **Surrey**, July 1899.

ROLAND FOR AN OLIVER, A// F 2a// J. Maddison Morton// **Drury Lane**, May 1837, with George Bartley as Sir Mark, A. Brindal as Selborne, Mr. Hooper as Highflyer, Drinkwater Meadows as Fixture, Miss Taylor as Maria, Mrs. Humby as Mrs. Fixture, Miss Lee as Mrs. Selborne/ **Cov. Garden**, Sept. 1837, with George Bartley as Sir Mark, Mr. Vining as Highflyer, Mr. Roberts as Selborne, Drinkwater Meadows as Fixture, Miss Taylor as Maria, Priscilla Horton as Mrs. Selborne, Mrs. Sarah Garrick as Mrs. Fixture/ **Sad. Wells**, Mar. 1838, with Mr. James as Sir Mark, J. Worrell as Selborne, Mr. Forester as Highflyer, Henry Hall as Fixture, S. Smith as Gamekeeper, Eliza Vincent as Maria, Miss Watkins as Mrs. Selborne, Miss Beresford as Mrs. Fixture; Oct. 1849, with A. Younge as Sir Mark, Henry Marston as Highflyer, Frank Graham as Selborne, Henry Nye as Fixture, Miss Fitzpatrick as Maria, Teresa Bassano as Mrs. Selborne, Mrs. G. Smith as Mrs. Fixture; Apr. 1856, with E. F. Edgar as Highflyer, Mr. Swanborough as Selborne, Mr. Barrett as Sir Mark, Charles Swan as Fixture, Harriet Gordon as Maria, Jenny Marston as Mrs. Selborne, Miss Cuthbert as Mrs. Fixture/ **Victoria**, Apr. 1838, with Edward Hooper as Highflyer, Mr. Loveday as Sir Mark, John Parry as Selborn, Alfred Rayner as Fixture, Miss Lee as Mrs. Selborn, Mrs. Frank Matthews as Mrs. Fixture, Miss Melville as Maria/ **Olympic**, Nov. 1845, with Walter Lacy as Highflyer, Mr. Brookes as Sir Mark, Mr. Binge as Selbourne, Robert Romer as Fixture, Mrs. Lacy as Maria, Miss Treble as Mrs. Selbourne, Mrs. Griffiths as Mrs. Fixture/ **Haymarket**, July 1851, with Mr. Lambert as Sir Mark, Walter Lacy as Highflyer, John Parselle as Selbourne, Mr. Rogers as Fixture, Mrs. Walter Lacy as Maria, Mrs. L. S. Buckingham as Mrs. Selbourne, Mrs. Caulfield as Mrs. Fixture/ **Princess's**, Sept. 1852, with Mr. Addison as Sir Mark, George Everett as Selborne, Walter Lacy as Highflyer, Drinkwater Meadows as Fixture, Mr. Terry as Gamekeeper, Carlotta Leclercq as Marie, Jenny Marston as Mrs. Selborne, Miss Vivash as Mrs. Fixture; Nov. 1862, with Mr. Fitzjames as Sir Mark, Robert Cathcart as Selborne, Robert Roxby as Highflyer, W. H. Stephens as Fixture, Miss M. Oliver as Maria, Marian Jones as Mrs. Selborne, Miss Gilbert as Mrs. Fixture.

ROLL OF THE DRUM, THE// D 3a// T. E. Wilks// **Sad. Wells**, Nov. 1843 (in 2a), with C. J. Bird as Viscount d'Obernay, Mr. Lamb as Capt. Aubri, Robert Romer as Brutus, Henry Marston as Oscar, Mr. Coreno as Valentine, W. H. Williams as Peaflower, Caroline Rankley as Emilie, Miss Cooke as Martha, Mrs. Richard Barnett as Rosalie; July 1862 (in 3a), with Henry Forrester as Viscount D'Obernay, A. Baildon as Capt. Aubri, C. Lloyds as Brutus, Charles Crook as Peaflower, Morton Price as Oscar, Lewis Ball as Valentine, Emily Dowton as Rosalie, Mrs. Ersser Jones as Martha, Catherine Lucette as Emilie.

ROLLING STONE SOMETIMES GATHERS MOSS, A// D 4a// Frederick Marchant// **Victoria**, Oct. 1870.

ROLLO THE MINSTREL; OR, THE DEVIL'S IN IT// D 3a// T. E. Wilks// **Sad. Wells**, June 1843, with Mrs. Fitzwilliam as Rollo, C. J. Bird as Grand Duke, R. H. Lingham as Baron Gompertz, John Webster as Honstein, John Herbert as Bunne, Mr. Lambe as Magdall,

Mr. Franks as Count Melstein, Caroline Rankley as The Duchess, Mrs. Richard Barnett as Felicia/ Scenery by F. Fenton, Machines by Mr. Cawdery, Music by Mr. Montgomery/ Prod. by Henry Marston.

ROMA; OR, THE DEPUTY// D 4a// Adap. by A. Lubimoff fr F of Victorien Sardou, Daniel Rochat// **Adelphi**, Nov. 1885.

ROMANCE AND REALITY// C 2a// John Brougham// **Princess's**, June 1847, with John Webster as Capt. Montague, James Vining as Dunbar, Mrs. Stirling as Florence, Emma Stanley as Emily, Mrs. Henry Hughes as Isabella, Miss E. Honner as Lappet/ **Haymarket**, Oct. 1860 (characters renamed), with Mr. Rogers as Oliver Manly, W. H. Chippendale as Jasper Manly, Henry Howe as Meredith, William Farren as Kydd, John Brougham as Swift, Mr. Clark as Badger, Florence Haydon as Rosabel, Mrs. Wilkins as Barbara, Mrs Edward Fitzwilliam as Blossom.

ROMANCE AND REALITY// F// n.a.// **Grecian**, Sept. 1861, with Thomas Mead as Travers, John Manning as Barnaby, Henry Grant as Sir Tympany, Mr. Jackson as Brown, Henry Power as Timothy, Jane Coveney as Amelia, Miss Johnstone as Miss Oldbustle, Lucreza Hill as Mary/ **Sad. Wells**, Apr. 1865, with Thomas Mead as Travers, T. B. Bennett as Brown, John Mordaunt as Sir Tympany, William Ellerton as Barnaby, T. Sidney as Timothy, Mr. Dearlove as James, Ellen Beaufort as Amelia, Mrs. Stevenson as Miss Oldbustle, Lizzie Willmore as Mary.

ROMANCE OF THE RHINE, A// D// n.a.// **Princess's**, Oct. 1847, with James Vining as Dumarteau, Mr. Palmer as Schafscopf, J. Neville as Rossekraut, Henry Compton as Fritz, Emma Stanley as Constance, Miss Villars as Lucille.

ROMANCE OF THE SHOPWALKER, THE// C 3a// Robert Buchanan & Harriet Jay// **Vaudeville**, Feb. 1896.

ROMANTIC ATTACHMENT, A// C// P. A. Wood// **Haymarket**, Feb. 1866, with Ada Cavendish as Emmeline, Miss Coleman as Mrs. Chatsworth, Mrs. Edward Fitzwilliam as Selina, William Farren as Morton, Henry Compton as Dewlap, Mr. Johnson as John.

ROMANTIC IDEA, A// C// J. R. Planché// **Lyceum**, Mar. 1849, with C. J. Mathews as Hans Skelter, Henry Hall as Rogueingrain, Charles Selby as Franz, Robert Roxby as Karl, Kathleen Fitzwilliam as Mme. Rogueingrain, Louisa Howard as Therese/ Scenery by W. Beverly & Mr. Grey/ **Olympic**, Mar. 1867, with C. J. Mathews as Skelter, Mr. Addison as Rogueingrain, Dominick Murray as Franz, George Vincent as Karl, Mrs. C. J. Mathews as Mme. Rogueingrain, Ellen Farren as Therese/ Scenery by Hawes Craven/ Music by Edward Fitzwilliam.

ROMANTIC WIDOW, THE// C 2a// n.a.// **Haymarket**, Oct. 1837, with Mr. Ranger as Marquis St. Croix, Benjamin Webster as Lord Cool, Mr. Hemming as Hartman, Robert Strickland as Allright, J. W. Gough as Count Ecartini, T. F. Mathews as York, Mrs. Nisbett as Ernestine, Miss Beresford as Lady Caroline, Miss Gallot as Olivia, Mrs. Humby as Ninette, Mrs. Gallot as Mrs. Cosy.

ROMANY RYE, THE// D 5a// G. R. Sims// **Princess's**, July 1882, with Wilson Barrett as Hearne, Mary Eastlake as Gertie, E. S. Willard as Royston, Robert Markby as Marsden, Walter Speakman as Heckett, George Barrett as Knivett, John Beauchamp as Goliath, Brian Darley as Nathan, Charles Coote as Duck, G. R. Peach as Capt. David, Neville Doone as Morgan, Miss Masson as Kiomi, Emmeline Ormsby as Lura, Mrs. E. S. Willard as Miss Adrian, Mrs. Huntley as Mother Shipton/ Scenery by William Beverley, Walter Hann, Bruce Smith & Stafford Hall/ Music by James Weaver.

ROMEO AND JULIET// D// "founded on Shakespeare's tragedy"// **Victoria**, Jan. 1838, with Mr. Cobham Jr. as Romeo, Edward Hooper as Mercutio, John Parry as Benvolio, Mr. King as Tybalt, Mr. Harwood as Paris, William Davidge as Capulet, Mr. Wilkins as Friar Lawrence, Mrs. Hooper as Juliet, Miss Richardson as Lady Capulet, Mrs. Loveday as Nurse.

ROMEO AND JULIET// T// William Shakespeare// **Cov. Garden**, Feb. 1837, with Charles Bender as Escalus, Mr. Tilbury as Montague, Mr. Thompson as Capulet, George Bennett as Romeo, Mr. Roberts as Paris, Henry Wallack as Mercutio, John Webster as Tybalt, Helen Faucit as Juliet, Mrs. W. West as Lady Capulet, Mrs. Julia Glover as Nurse; Mar. 1840, with Alfred Wigan as Escalus, Mr. Fitzjames as Paris, Charles Diddear as Capulet, Mr. Granby as Montague, James Anderson as Romeo, George Vandenhoff as Mercutio, James Vining as Benvolio, Mr. Cooper as Friar Lawrence, Charles Selby as Tybalt, Jane Mordaunt as Juliet, Miss Penley as Lady Capulet, Mme. Simon as Lady Montague, Mrs. Charles Jones as Nurse/ Scenery by Grieve, T. Grieve & W. Grieve; Mar. 1840, with same cast except Charles Kemble as Mercutio/ **Sad. Wells**, Mar. 1837, with Charles Bender as Prince Escalus [sic], Mr. Gay as Montague, John Ayliffe as Capulet, George Bennett as Romeo, C. H. Pitt as Paris, J. Worrell as Tybalt, Mr. Harris as as Benvolio, John Pritchard as Mercutio, Mrs. W. West as Juliet, Mrs. Sarah Garrick as Lady Capulet, Mrs. Julia Glover as Nurse; Mar. 1843, with Caroline Rankley as Romeo, Mr. Dry as Tybalt, C. J. Bird as Benvolio, Mr. Lambe as Paris, Mr. Cowle as Mercutio, Mr. Aldridge as Capulet, Henry Howe as Friar Lawrence, Mrs. Cowle as Juliet, Mrs. Henry Marston as Nurse, Mrs. Wilson as Lady Capulet; Sept. 1846, with Edward Knight as Escalus, Mr. Morton as Paris, Mr. Williams as Montague, Henry Mellon as Capulet, William Creswick as Romeo, Samuel Phelps as Mercutio, William Hoskins as Benvolio, Frank Graham as Tybalt, George Bennett as Friar Lawrence, Mrs. Francis as Lady Montague, Mrs. Brougham as Lady Capulet, Laura Addison as Juliet, Mrs. Henry Marston as Nurse/ Scenery by Mr. Finlay &

F. Fenton; Mar. 1861, with Mr. Chapman as Escalus, Charles Seyton as Paris, James Lickfold as Montague, Mr. Meagreson as Capulet, Hermann Vezin as Romeo, Samuel Phelps as Mercutio, Webster Vernon as Benvolio, T. C. Harris as Tybalt, Mrs. Charles Young (Mrs. Hermann Vezin) as Juliet, Mrs. G. Hodson as Lady Capulet, Miss Heath as Lady Montague, Mrs. Henry Marston as Nurse; Sept. 1866, with W. Lacey as Escalus, Mr. Murray as Paris, Mr. Hamilton as Montague, E. Shepherd as Capulet, J. H. Slater as Romeo, J. L. Warner as Mercutio, J. Collier as Benvolio, Walter Holland as Tybalt, Alice Marriott as Juliet, Miss Fitzgerald as Lady Capulet, Mrs. J. F. Saville as Nurse/ **Haymarket**, Mar. 1840, with James Anderson; July 1841, with Mr. Caulfield as Escalus, John Webster as Paris, J. W. Gough as Montague, George Bennett as Capulet, Charles Kean as Romeo, James Wallack as Mercutio, J. Worrell as Benvolio, Henry Howe as Tybalt, Henry Wallack as Friar Laurence, Mrs. Stanley as Lady Capulet, Ellen Tree as Juliet, Mrs. W. Clifford as Nurse/ Scenery by Charles Marshall, Mr. Pitt & George Morris/ Music by T. German Reed; Dec. 1845, with Mr. Caulfield as Escalus, Mr. Carle as Paris, J. W. Gough as Montague, James Bland as Capulet, Charlotte Cushman as Romeo, Henry Holl as Mercutio, A. Brindal as Benvolio, Henry Howe as Tybalt, Mr. Stuart as Friar Lawrence, Susan Cushman as Juliet, Mrs. Stanley as Lady Capulet, Mrs. Powell as Lady Montague, Mrs. Julia Glover as Nurse; Oct. 1848, with same cast except William Creswick as Romeo, Laura Addison as Juliet; Feb. 1855, with Thomas Coe as Escalus, Edwin Villiers as Paris, William Cullenford as Montague, Mr. Tilbury as Capulet, Charlotte Cushman as Romeo, Henry Howe as Mercutio, William Farren as Tybalt, Ada Swanborough as Juliet, Mrs. Poynter as Lady Capulet, Miss Grantham as Lady Montague, Mrs. Griffith as Nurse; Sept. 1867, with Thomas Coe as Escalus, Henry Vincent as Paris, P. White as Montague, W. H. Chippendale as Capulet, W. H. Kendal as Romeo, Henry Howe as Mercutio, George Braid as Benvolio, Walter Gordon as Tybalt, Mrs. Laws as Lady Capulet, Miss Coleman as Lady Montague, Mrs. Mary Scott-Siddons as Juliet, Mrs. Chippendale as Nurse/ Scenery by John O'Conner & George Morris/ Machines by Oliver Wales/ Gas by J. Hope; Jan. 1876, with C. Allbrook as Escalus, Harold Kyrle as Paris, Edward Osborne as Montague, George Braid as Capulet, H. B. Conway as Romeo, Charles Harcourt as Mercutio, A. Matthison as Benvolio, Walter Gordon as Tybalt, Miss E. Harrison as Lady Montague, Mrs. Edward Osborne as Lady Capulet, Adelaide Neilson as Juliet, Emily Thorne as Nurse/ Scenery by John O'Conner & George Morris/ **Victoria**, Oct. 1841, with Charles Dillon, Miss E. Montague/ **Adelphi**, Mar. 1847, with Charlotte Cushman as Romeo, Mr. Charles as Paris, Mr. McGregor as Montague, Miss Aitkin as Lady Montague, Mr. Harker as Capulet, Mrs. Lewis as Lady Capulet, Mr. Hield as Mercutio, Mr. Ball as Benvolio, Mr. Mortimer as Tybalt, Mr. Holmes as Frair Lawrence, Susan Cushman as Juliet./ **Princess's**, Oct. 1847, with Mr. Howard as Escalus [sic], Mr. Palmer as Montague, J. Neville as Capulet, Charlotte Cushman as Romeo, Augustus Harris as Paris, Charles Fisher as Benvolio, James Vining as Mercutio, F. B. Conway as Tybalt, John Ryder as Friar Lawrence, Susan Cushman as Juliet, Mrs. Fosbroke as Lady Capulet, Miss Rourke as Lady Montague, Mrs. Selby as Nurse; May 1866, with Mr. Robins as Escalus, Mr. Brooke as Paris, James Lickfold as Montague, Henry Mellon as Capulet, John Nelson as Romeo, James Vining as Mercutio, Charles Seyton as Tybalt, Henry Forrester as Friar Laurence, David Fisher as Peter, Miss Stafford as Lady Capulet, Stella Colas as Juliet; June 1863, with Walter Montgomery as Romeo, George Vining as Mercutio, Henry Marston as Friar Laurence, Gaston Murray as Benvolio, J. G. Warde as Paris, Mrs. Fitzjames as Capulet, Mr. Terry as Montague, Charles Seyton as Tybalt, Henrietta Sims as Lady Capulet, Mrs. Henry Marston as Nurse, Stella Colas as Juliet/ **Olympic**, July 1851, with Charles Bender as Escalus, George Cooke as Capulet, Mr. Mason as Montague, J. William Wallack as Romeo, William Farren Jr. as Paris, Mr. Orton as Tybalt, Henry Farren as Mercutio, Charles Diddear as Friar Lawrence, Mrs. Charles Boyce as Lady Capulet, Miss Rawlings as Lady Montague, Helen Faucit as Juliet, Mrs. B. Bartlett as Nurse; June 1881, with Henry Hamilton as Paris, Charles Arnold as Capulet, Robert Mantell as Romeo, E. F. Edgar as Mercutio, E. T. Webber as Benvolio, James Wheeler as Tybalt, John Ryder as Friar Laurence, Stanislaus Calhaem as Peter, Cicely Nott as Lady Capulet, Miss Wallis as Juliet, Mrs. R. Power as Nurse/ **Sad. Wells**, Mar. 1859, with Mrs. Charles Young, Frederic Robinson, Henry Marston, Samuel Phelps; Sept. 1859, with Frederic Robinson, Samuel Phelps, Caroline Heath, Mrs. Marston/ **Grecian**, Aug. 1861, with Robert Bell as Paris, J. Jackson as Capulet, William James as Romeo, Thomas Mead as Mercutio, Walter Holland as Benvolio, Henry Grant as Tybalt, Alfred Rayner as Friar Laurence, Emma Robberds as Juliet, Ellen Hale as Lady Capulet, Miss Johnstone as Nurse/ **Astley's**, Oct. 1866, with Mr. Denial as Capulet, George Webster as Paris, Walter Joyce as Mercutio, W. Ryder as Benvolio, Henry Vandenhoff as Romeo, John Ryder as Friar Lawrence, Sophie Young as Juliet, Mrs. Russell as Lady Capulet, Mrs. Barrett as Nurse/ **Lyceum**, Nov. 1867, with Miss Vestvalli as Romeo, Mr. Stuart as Paris, J. Neville as Capulet, Walter Lacy as Mercutio, W. Ryder as Benvolio, Mr. Dalton as Tybalt, John Ryder as Friar Lawrence, Mrs. Hodson as Lady Capulet, Milly Palmer as Juliet, Mrs. Marston as Nurse; Mar. 1882, with Henry Irving as Romeo, William Terriss as Mercutio, George Alexander as Paris, Henry Howe as Capulet, James Fernandez as Friar Laurence, Ellen Terry as Juliet, Mrs. Stirling as Nurse, Helen Matthews as Lady Montague, Louisa Payne as Lady Capulet/ Scenery by Hawes Craven, W. Cuthbert, Walter Hann &William Telbin/ Music by Julius Benedict/ Machines by Mr. Knight; Nov. 1884, with Mary Anderson as Juliet, William Terriss as Romeo, James Anderson, Edmund Maurice, Ben Greet, Mrs. Charles Calvert, Mrs. Stirling; Sept. 1895, with Arthur Grenville as Paris, Alfred Brydone as Montague, George Warde as Capulet, Johnston

Forbes Robertson as Romeo, Charles Coghlan as Mercutio, Frank Gillmore as Benvolio, Will Dennis as Tybalt, Mrs. Edward Saker as Lady Capulet, Mrs. Patrick Campbell as Juliet, Dolores Drummond as Nurse/ Scenery by William Harford, Hawes Craven & T. E. Ryan/ Music comp. by Edward German/ **Drury Lane**, Dec. 1870, with Mr. Stainforth as Escalus, Mr. Lilley as Paris, Thomas Mead as Montague, J. Neville as Capulet, J. B. Howard as Romeo, T. C. King as Mercutio, Frederick Moreland as Tybalt, Alfred Rayner as Friar Lawrence, Miss Kemp as Lady Capulet, Miss Timbrell as Lady Montague, Adelaide Neilson as Juliet, Mrs. Power as Nurse; Dec. 1874, with Mr. Fenton as Paris, James Johnstone as Capulet, James Anderson as Mercutio, William Terriss as Romeo, Henry Kemble as Benvolio, Stanislaus Calhaem as Peter, John Ryder as Friar Lawrence, R. Dolman as Tybalt, Miss Wallis as Juliet, Cicely Nott as Lady Capulet, Mrs. Manders as Nurse/ **Court**, Mar. 1881, with Johnston Forbes Robertson, Helena Modjeska, Wilson Barrett, John Ryder, Roma Le Thière.

RONALD THE REIVER; OR, THE BRIDAL OF THE BORDER// **Sad. Wells**, July 1839, with Mr. Dry as Stranger, Mr. Williams as Old Adam, John Webster as Albert, Mr. Conquest as Guy, Mr. Elvin as Glenbrae, Mr. Cathcart as Steenie, Mr. Aldridge as Brand, Charles Montgomery as Wylie, Miss Richardson as Laurette, Miss Pincott as Jessie, Mrs. J. F. Saville as Amy.

ROOF SCRAMBLERS, THE// F 1a// G. A. á Becket// **Victoria**, Feb. 1838, with John Parry as Rodolpho, Mr. Salter as Sexton, Leigh Smith as Bobbo, W. H. Oxberry as Molly, Mrs. Loveday as Lizzy, Miss Wilson as Theresa.

ROOM 70// F// Percy Fitzgerald// **Haymarket**, Jan. 1886.

RORY O'MORE// D 3a// Dram. by Samuel Lover fr his own novel// **Adelphi**, Oct. 1837; Jan. 1838, with Mr. Saville, Frederick Yates, O. Smith, John Sanders, Tyrone Power, Agnes Taylor/ **Sad. Wells**, June 1857, with Mr. Lyon as Rory O'More, George Cooke as De Lacy, G. Pennett as Col. Thunder, James Johnstone as De Welskin, G. B. Bigwood as Scrubs, E. B. Gaston as Shan Dhu, Miss Stewart as Kathleen, Emma Barnett as Mary, Mrs. J. Gates as Widow O'More, Miss M. A. Murry as Betty.

ROSALIE; OR, THE CHAIN OF CRIME// D 3a// n.a.// **Astley's**, Apr. 1864, with E. F. Edgar as Horace Belton, R. Norman as Mr. Belton, H. Frazer as Vernon, F. Wallace as Clifton, J. A. Shaw as Dredger, W. S. Gresham as Dimsdale Hawk, Miss Furtado as Rosalie, Fanny Clifford as Mrs. Beauchamp, Miss Bodenham as Fanny, Mrs. J. W. Simpson as Mrs. Jenks/ Scenery by J. Gates.

ROSE CLINTON, VICTIM OF CIRCUMSTANTIAL EVIDENCE// D 3a// John Courtney// **Victoria**, May 1848, with John Bradshaw as Wheatfield, J. T. Johnson as Walton, Walter Searle as Hawk, Mr. Henderson as Shye, J. Howard as Stone, G. F. Forman as Poodle, Mr. Hitchinson as Whinston, Annette Vincent as Rose, Mrs. George Lee as Marian, Miss Burroughcliffe as Polly, Mrs. Cooke as Mrs. Walton, Miss Young as Betty/ Scenery by Mildenhall & Macdonald/ Music by W. J. Hill/ Machines by Wood & Foster/ Prod. by T. H. Higgie.

ROSE LINDED; OR, THE OLD CHAPEL RUINS// D// C. Z. Barnett// **Sad. Wells**, Feb. 1842, with Mr. Norton as Marsden, Mr. Elvin as Capt. Caleb, Mr. Dry as Linden, John Webster as Merivale, Robert Honner as Col. Morrison, J. W. Collier as Pilfer, Mr. Aldridge as Kilvert, Charles Fenton as Stiles, John Herbert as Serious, Mrs. Robert Honner as Rose, Miss Hicks as Alice, Mrs. Morgan as Dame Stiles/ Scenery by F. Fenton/ Prod. by R. Honner.

ROSE MICHEL// D 5a// Campbell Clarke// **Gaiety**, Mar. 1875.

ROSE OF ARRAGON, THE// D 5a// J. Sheridan Knowles// **Haymarket**, June 1842, with Henry Howe as King, Henry Holl as Alonzo, Mr. Wilsone as Andreas, J. Worrell as Carlos, J. W. Gough as Pedro, Mr. Stuart as Ruphino, Charles Kean as Alasco, Samuel Phelps as Almagro, Mr. Vining as Valasquez, Mrs. Charles Kean (Ellen Tree) as Olivia, Miss Partridge as Theresa/ Scenery by Mr. Danson & George Morris.

ROSE OF CORBEIL, THE; OR, THE FOREST OF SENART// D 2a// Edward Stirling// **City of London**, Nov. 1838.

ROSE OF DEVON, THE; OR, THE SPANISH ARMADA// D 4a// Adap. by John Jourdain fr novel of Charles Kingsley, Westward Ho!// **Elephant & Castle**, Feb. 1889.

ROSE OF ETTRICK VALE, THE; OR, THE BRIDAL OF THE BORDERS// D// T. J. Lynch// **Sad. Wells**, July 1839; May, 1856, with Basil Potter as Ronald, Mr. Barrett as Old Adam, Mr. Laporte as Glenbrae, James Rogers as Guy, Professor Anderson as Steenie, W. Morgan as Brand, Miss E. Morton as Laurette.

ROSEMARY// Play 4a// L. N. Parker & S. Murray Carson// **Criterion**, May 1896.

ROSENCRANTZ AND GUILDENSTERN// T 3a// W. S. Gilbert// **Vaudeville**, June 1891/ **Court**, Apr. 1892.

ROSMERSHOLM// D 4a// Trans. by Charles Archer fr Norw. of Henrik Ibsen// **Vaudeville**, Feb. 1891.

ROUGE ET NOIR// D 5a// Adap. fr F, La Vie d'un Joueur// **Lyceum**, Dec. 1866, with Charles Fechter as Maurice D'Arbel, Samuel Emery as de Layrac, J. C. Cowper as Gautier, J. H. Fitzpatrick as Remy, Frederick Moreland as Everard, Mr. Reynolds as Martin, Carlotta Leclercq as Pauline, Mrs. Leigh Murray as Mme. D'Arbel, Miss Henrade as Sarah, Miss Gratton as Frau Schopp/ Scenery by T. Grieve/ Music by W. H. Montgomery/ Machines by E. Godin.

ROUGH AND READY// D 3a// Paul Meritt// **Adelphi**, Jan. 1874/ **Globe**, July 1875, with A. D. Anderson as John Norman, Cecil Beryl as Harry Valentine, John Billington as Mark Musgrave, J. Jackson as Hickory, Mrs. Billington as Mrs. Valentine, Miss E. Meyrick as Alice, Camille Dubois as Amelia.

ROUGH DIAMOND, A// C 1a// J. B. Buckstone// **Lyceum**, Nov. 1847/ **Haymarket**, Apr. 1849, with Mr. Rogers as Plato, Henry Howe as Evergreen, J. B. Buckstone as Joe, Henry Vandenhoff as Capt. Blenheim, Emma Harding as Lady Plato, Mrs. Fitzwilliam as Margery/ **Sad. Wells**, July 1853, with Mr. White as Lord Plato, F. Morton as Sir William, Mr. Edgar as Capt. Blenheim, J. B. Buckstone as Cousin Joe, Miss Adams as Lady Plato, Mrs. Fitzwilliam as Margery/ **Princess's**, Aug. 1863, with Robert Cathcart as Sir William, Mr. Fitzjames as Lord Plato, Mr. Brooke as Capt. Blenheim, Sefton Parry as Cousin Joe, Emily Frazer as Lady Plato, Lizzie Harrison as Margaret/ **Olympic**, Mar. 1866, with J. T. King as Capt. Blenheim, W. J. Collins as Sir William, Mr. Fitzjames as Lord Plato, Mr. Granville as Joe, Rose Melborne as Lady Plato, Lizzie Harrison as Margery/ **Adelphi**, Aug. 1868, with C. H. Stephenson as Plato, Henry Ashley as Sir William, W. H. Eburne as Capt. Blenheim, George Belmore as Joe, Miss Lennox Grey as Lady Plato, Mrs. Billington as Margery/ **Olympic** Nov. 1877, with Mr. Bauer as Lord Plato, Charles Harcourt as Sir William, Johnston Forbes Robertson as Capt. Blenheim, W. J. Hill as Joe, Miss Beaumont as Lady Plato, Miss Gerard as Margery.

ROUND OF WRONG, THE// D// W. Bayle Bernard// **Haymarket**, Dec. 1846.

ROUND THE CLOCK// F 3a// J. F. McArdle// **Surrey**, June 1879.

ROUND THE RING// Play// Paul Meritt// **Surrey**, Nov. 1891.

ROUND THE WORLD IN 80 DAYS// D 14sc// Adap. fr F of A. P. Dennery & Jules Verne// **Princess's**, June 1875, with Henry Sinclair as Milford, Brittain Wright as Ready, Mr. Morgan as Partgon, Mr. Claremont as Flanagan, P. C. Beverley as Sullivan, William McIntyre as Spreadeagle, Augustus Glover as Fix, Miss Carlisle as Aouda, Miss Macdonald as Nemea, Jenny Lovell as Margaret, Alma Murray as Slave, Cicely Nott as Makaira/ Scenery by Robecchi, Cornil & Poisson.

ROUNDHEAD, THE// D 3a// B. F. Bussey & W. T. Blackmore// **Terry's**, Feb. 1891.

ROUSED LION, THE// C 2a// Adap. by Benjamin Webster fr F of Bayard & Jaime, Le Réveil du Lion// **Haymarket**, Dec. 1847, with Benjamin Webster as de Fonblanche, Henry Howe as Ernest, Alfred Wigan as Mauleon, Henry Vandenhoff as d'Herbelin, Mr. Rogers as de Luxeuil, Mrs. Keeley as Suzanne, Miss Reynolds as Leonie, Mrs. Seymour as Mme. de St. Luc, Mrs. Stanley as Baroness Cabrion/ **Princess's**, Dec. 1847, with John Webster as de Fonblanche, Henry Howe as Ernest, Alfred Wigan as Mauleon, Henry Vandenhoff as d'Herbelin, Mr. Rogers as de Luxeuil, Mrs. Keeley as Suzanne, Miss Reynolds as Leonie, Mrs. Seymour as Mme. de St. Luc, Mrs. Stanley as Baroness Cabrion/ **Adelphi**, May 1853, with Benjamin Webster as Stanislas, John Parselle as Ernest, Alfred Wigan as Hector, Robert Romer as Antinous, Mrs. Keeley as Mlle. Suzanne, Fanny Maskell as Léonie, Mrs. Leigh Murray as Mme. de St. Luc.

ROVER'S BRIDE, THE; OR, THE BITTERN'S SWAMP// D 2a// George Almar// **Sad. Wells**, Mar. 1844, with Henry Marston as Glennon, C. J. Bird as Bellerton, C. J. Smith as Von Voorn, Mr. Coreno as Magog, Caroline Rankley as Alice, Miss Cooke Bellerton, Miss Stephens as Mary, Charles Fenton as Barbelot, Mrs. Richard Barnett as Bella, Miss Melville as Betty.

ROVING COMMISSION, A// C// John Besemeres **Royalty**, Apr. 1869.

ROW IN THE BUILDINGS, A// F 1a// Thomas Greenwood// **Sad. Wells**, May 1844, with Mr. Williams as Chubb, Mr. Hield as Paragraph, John Webster as Nibbs, Emma Harding as Norma, Mrs. Henry Marston as Mrs. Chubb, Miss Lebatt as Mary.

ROW IN THE HOUSE, A// F 1a// T. W. Robertson// **Toole's**, Aug. 1883.

ROYAL BERKSHIRE REGIMENT, THE// D 1a// H. T. van Laun & Félix Remo// **Comedy**, June 1886.

ROYAL BETROTHAL, A// Play 1a// Edward Ferris & B. P. Matthews// **St. James's**, Dec. 1900.

ROYAL DIVORCE, A// D 5a// W. G. Wills & G. G. Collingham// **Olympic**, Sept. 1891, with Murray Carson as Napoleon, T. W. Percyval as Tallyrand, G. W. Cockburn as Marquis de Beaumont, Eardley Turner as Gen. Augereau, J. A. Welch as Grimand, Frederick Victor as Murat, J. G. East as Ney, Lesley Bell as Marie Louise, Miss G. Esmond as Stephanie, Louie Wilmot as Blanche, Ethel Patrick as Empress Josephine/ Prod. by Henry Herman/ **Princess's**, July 1892.

ROYAL FAMILY, A// C 3a Robert Marshall// **Court**, Oct. 1899.

ROYAL MAIL, THE// D Pro & 3a// J. T. Douglas// **Standard**, Aug. 1887.

ROYAL MARRIAGE, A// F//John Douglass Jr// **Standard**, Apr. 1868.

ROYAL NECKLACE, A// Play 4a// Paul & E. C. Berton// **Imperial**, Apr. 1901.

ROYAL OAK, THE// D 2a// William Dimond// **Cov. Garden**, Nov. 1838, with Mr. Vandenhoff as Charles II, Mr. Warde as Col. Wyndham, James Anderson as William, George Bennett as Cavendish, Charles Diddear as Fairfax,

Drinkwater Meadows as Capt. Reuben, George Bartley as Maythorn, Mrs. Mary Warner as Lady Matilda, Charlotte Vandenhoff as Elinor, Mrs. W. Clifford as Dame Maythorn, Miss Rainforth as Claribel.

ROYAL OAK, THE// D 5a// Henry Hamilton & Augustus Harris// **Drury Lane**, Sept. 1889.

ROYAL PARDON, A; OR, THE HOUSE ON THE CLIFF// D 4a// George Conquest & Henry Pettitt// **Grecian**, Oct. 1878.

ROYAL RIVAL, A// Play 3a// Adap. by Gerald du Maurier fr F of P. F. Dumanoir & A. P. Dennery, Don César de Bazan// **Coronet**, May 1901/ **Duke of York's**, Aug. 1901.

ROYALIST AND THE REPUBLICAN, THE// D 1a// n.a.// **Grecian**, Jan. 1857, with Richard Phillips as Glornaud, C. Kelsey as Julius, Jane Coveney as Marie.

RUBBER OF LIFE, THE; OR, ST. JAMES'S AND ST. GILES'S// D// Edward Stirling// **Sad. Wells**, Feb. 1844, with Mr. Williams as Boughton, C. J. Bird as Faulkland, Mr. Watson as Lord Westend, Mr. Raymond as Shelbourn, Charles Fenton as Hazeldine, Mr. Harvey as Capt. Snooks, Mr. Jones as Pigeon, Mr. Hutchings as Coryton, Henry Hall as Footman, Mrs. Andrews as Mrs. Boughton, Miss Stephens as Clara, Caroline Rankley as Julia, Miss Cooke as Mrs. Maggs, Mrs. Richard Barnett as Nancy, Mrs. Henry Marston as Mary, Miss Melville as Betty.

RUBBER OF LIFE, THE; OR, THE BEST OF THREE GAMES// C Pro & 4a// A. G. & F. R. Bagot// **Strand**, Nov. 1885.

RUBY// D 5a// Edwin France// **Sad. Wells**, Jan. 1885.

RUBY RING, THE; OR, THE MURDER AT SADLER'S WELLS// D 3a// T. E. Wilks// **Sad. Wells**, June 1840, with Mr. Dry as Lord Arendale, Mr. Aldridge as Forcer, Mr. Richardson as Junket, J. W. Collier as Motley, Mr. Elvin as Waite, Henry Marston as French, J. B. Hill as Willoughby, Robert Honner as Featherley, Mr. Williams as Levy, Mrs. J. F. Saville as Adeline, Mrs. Robert Honner as Barbara, Mrs. J. W. Collier as Espagnolia/ Scenery by F. Fenton/ Machines by B. Sloman/ Prod. by R. Honner.

RUDOLPHO THE HUNGARIAN; OR, THE THRONE, THE TOMB, AND THE COTTAGE// D 4a// Thomas Mead// **Victoria**, Apr. 1871.

RUGANTINO; OR, THE BRAVO OF VENICE// D 2a// M. G. Lewis// **Sad. Wells**, July 1840, with Mr. Dry as Doria, Mr. Aldridge as Lomello, Mr. Houghburt as Manfroni, Mr. Wilson as Patriarch, Henry Marston as Rugantino, Mrs. J. F. Saville as Rosabella, Miss Cooke as Camilla, Miss Louise as Laura, Miss Rose as Bellina/ Music by Dr. Busby/ **Victoria**, Apr. 1850, with J. Neville as Duke Andreas, Mr. Leake as Lomellino, Mr. Brunton as Manfrone, J. T. Johnson as Rugantino, Francisco, Friar, Flodoardo, and as Prince of Milan, John Bradshaw as Concartino, Jane Trafford as Rosabella, Mrs. Cooke as Camilia, Miss Leigh as Laura, Miss Edgar as Bettina.

RUINED HOUSE OF MILLBANK, THE; OR, THE MURDER OF THE LONELY CREEK// D// n.a.// **Victoria**, Jan. 1846, with Mr. Fredericks as Montague, Walter Searle as Witherly, Mr. Wilton as Cripps, John Dale as Thornley, T. H. Higgie as Butler, F. H. Henry as Spencer, Mr. Edgar as Mutton, John Herbert as Nubbles, Miss Edgar as Alice, Miss Richardson as Mary, Mrs. George Lee as Thomasine, Miss Jefferson as Mrs. Cripps, Eliza Terrey as Barbara/ Scenery by Mildenhall & McDonald/ Machines by Wood & Foster/ Music by W. J. Hill.

RUINED LIFE, A// D Pro & 4a// Arthur Goodrich & J. R. Crauford// **Grand**, Sept. 1884.

RULE A WIFE AND HAVE A WIFE// C// Alt. fr Beaumont & Fletcher// **Cov. Garden**, Oct. 1839, with Charles Diddear as Duke of Medina, Charles Selby as Juan, C. J. Mathews as Perez, George Bartley as Cacafogo, Mr. Fitzjames as Alonzo, James Bland as Sancho, George Vandenhoff as Leon, W. H. Payne as Lorenzo, John Collett as Diego, Mr. Honner as Vasco, Mrs. Brougham as Margarita, Annie Taylor as Victoria, Louisa Nisbett as Estifania, Miss E. Phillips as Isabel, Frank Matthews as Old Woman, Drinkwater Meadows as Daughter/ **Sad. Wells**, Oct. 1848, with Henry Mellon as Duke, Samuel Phelps as Leon, Mr. Gladstone as Joan, Frank Graham as Alonzo, Mr. Harrington as Sancho, William Hoskins as Perez, Edward Knight as Cacafogo, Miss Huddart as Margaritta, Miss Stephens as Clara, Miss Williams as Altea, Miss Cooper as Estifania, Miss Warde as Victoria, Fanny Morelli as Isabella, Henry Scharf as Old Woman, Mr. Williams as Daughter/ Scenery by F. Fenton & A. Finlay; Mar. 1860, with Mr. Haywell as Duke, William Belford as Perez, Frederic Robinson as Leon, Mr. Meagreson as Cacafogo, Mr. Chapman as Lorenzo, Eliza Travers as Estafania, Miss Hart as Victoria, Caroline Hill as Isabel, Mrs. J. B. Hill as Alica, Miss Phillips as Margaritta, Caroline Parkes as Clara, Lewis Ball as Old Woman, J. W. Ray as Daughter/ **Grecian**, Mar. 1855, with Henry Grant as Duke of Medina, F. Charles as Don Juan, Mr. Marlow as Don Sanchia, Richard Phillips as Don Michael, T. Roberts as Don Alonzo, Basil Potter as Leon, Maria Simpson as Margarita, Ellen Crisp as Altea, Jane Coveney as Astifania, Eaton O'Donnell as Old Woman, John Manning as Daughter.

RULE BRITANNIA// F 1a// M. Becher// **Drury Lane**, Feb. 1871, with Frederick Moreland as Hobby, F. Charles as Rashleigh, Charles Steyne as de Chemin, Miss Kemp as Maria.

RULE OF THREE, THE// C 1a// Francis Talfourd// **Strand**, Dec. 1858.

RULE OF THREE, THE// Play 4a// Pierre Leclercq// **Shaftesbury**, June 1891.

RULING PASSION, THE// D Pro & 5a// J. T. Douglass ("James Willing")// **Standard**, Nov. 1882.

RUMOUR// Play 3a// J. S. Winter// **Vaudeville**, Apr. 1889.

RUN OF LUCK, A// D 4a// Henry Pettitt & Augustus Harris// **Drury Lane**, Aug. 1886, with J. G. Grahame as Harry Copsley, J. Beauchamp as John Copsley, William Rignold as Selby, E. W. Gardiner as George, Charles Cartwright as Capt. Trevor, Harry Nicholls as Sandown, Victor Stephens as Ladybird, Basil West as Lord Earlswood, Arthur Yates as Duke, Louis Calvert as Parsons, Alma Murray as Daisy, Miss Compton as Mabel, Mary A. Victor as Aunt Mary, Edith Bruce as Phoebe, Sophie Eyre as Lucy.

RUN TO EARTH; OR, A GOLDEN FORTUNE// D 4a// George Roberts// **Elephant & Castle**, Apr. 1887.

RUN WILD// C 3a// Emily Coffin// **Strand**, June 1888.

RUNAWAY HUSBANDS, THE// C 3a// Adap. fr F// **Haymarket**, May 1849, with Henry Howe as Duke of Anjou, James Wallack as Viscount St. Herem, Henry Vandenhoff as Duke d'Harcourt, J. B. Buckstone as Dubouloy, George Braid as Comtois, Miss Reynoldson as Charlotte, Mrs. Fitzwilliam as Louise, Mrs. Stanley as Therese.

RUNAWAYS, THE// Ca.// Eliza Aria// **Criterion**, May 1898.

RUPERT OF HENTZAU// Play 4a// Anthony Hope// **St. James's**, Feb. 1900, with George Alexander as King Rudolf and as Rudolf Rassendyll, W. H. Vernon as Col. Sapt, H. V. Esmond as von Tarlenheim, Sidney Brough as von Bernenstein, H. B. Irving as Rupert of Hentzau, Basset Roe as Rischenheim, George Hawtrey as von Diekerk, Fay Davis as Queen Flavia, Esmé Beringer as Helga, Henrietta Leverett as Mother Holf, Julia Opp as Rosa/ Music by Walter Slaughter.

RURAL FELICITY// C// J. B. Buckstone// **Haymarket**, July 1837, with Mr. Collins as Layton, Frederick Vining as Unit, J. B. Buckstone as Sly, Robert Strickland as Twaddle, T. F. Mathews as Spike, Mr. Bishop as Dr. Squills, Mrs. Julia Glover as Mrs. Colpepper, Mrs. W. Clifford as Mrs. Whiley, Mrs. Tayleure as Miss Spike, Mrs. Humby as Jemima, Miss E. Honner as Cecilia, Eliza Vincent as Harriet.

RUSSIA; OR, THE EXILES OF SIBERIA// D Pro & 3a// H. B. Farnie & Robert Reece// **Queen's**, Oct. 1877.

RUSSIAN BRIDE, THE// D// C. H. Hazlewood// **Britannia**, Mar 1874.

RUSTIC'S CRIME, THE; OR, THE PEASANT AND THE PEER// D 3a// "Founded on" Thomas Morton's School of Reform// **Sad. Wells**, Aug. 1840, with Mr. Dry as Lord Avondale, Mr. Williams as Gen. Tarragon, Mr. Elvin as Frederick, Mr. Rayner as Tyke, Henry Marston as Ferment, Mr. Aldridge as Old Tyke, Mrs. J. F. Saville as Julia, Miss Richardson as Mrs. St. Clair, Mrs. Richard Barnett as Mrs. Ferment, Miss Cooke as Mrs. Nicely.

RUTH// D 3a// Adap. by Reginald Moore fr G of Salomon Mosenthal, Deborah// **Princess's**, July 1868, with Basil Potter as Factor, John Maclean as Bernhard, J. G. Shore as Ernest, Robert Cathcart as Peter, Brandon Ellis as Nathan, W. D. Gresham as Abraham, Frank Crellin as David, Trissy Marston as Gertrude, Emma Barnett as Gretchen, Kate Saville as Ruth, Miss Kemp as Esther.

RUTH; OR, A POOR GIRL'S LIFE IN LONDON// D// C. H. Ross & P. Richards// **Surrey**, Feb. 1871.

RUTH; OR, THE LASS THAT LOVES A SAILOR// D 3a// J. T. Haines// **Victoria**, Jan. 1843, with C. Williams as Lord Glenmuir, Mr. Wilton as De Retz, E. F. Saville as Jasper, John Dale as Amboine, William Seaman as Dereveigne, John Gardner as Whitethorn, Annette Vincent as Ruth, Miss Saddler as Lady Ernestine, Mrs. Griffith as Dame Whitethorn, Mrs. Seaman as Polly/ Scenery by Mildenhall & Morelli/ Machines by Emmens, Moon, Wood & Foster/ Music by J. B. Hill.

RUTH OAKLEY// D 3a// Thomas Williams & Augustus Harris (the elder)// **Marylebone**, Jan. 1857.

RUTH TUDOR// D// n.a.// **Adelphi**, 1837.

RUTH UNDERWOOD// Play 1a// L. E. Mitchell// **Strand**, May 1892.

RUTH'S ROMANCE// C 1a// F. W. Broughton// **Olympic**, Jan. 1885, with Miss Tilbury as Ruth, W. Howell-Poole as Jack, H. Parry as Capt. Wilton.

RUTHVEN// D 4a// Augustus Harris (the elder)// **Grecian**, Apr. 1862, with Thomas Mead as Ruthven, George Gillett as Marquis de Lurac, Henry Grant as Count de Vivrey, Walter Holland as D'Aubigny, William James as Count de Tiffanges, John Manning as Lazare, Henry Power as Botaro, Mr. Jackson as Roso, Jane Dawson as The Unknown, Amilie Conquest as Helene, Mary A. Victor as Juanna, Ellen Hale as Antonia.

RUY BLAS// D 3a// Adap. by Edmund Falconer fr F of Victor Hugo// **Princess's**, Oct. 1860, with Walter Lacy as Don Salluste, Augustus Harris as Don Caesar, Drinkwater Meadows as Marquis of Santa Cruz, Edmund Garden as Codavenga, Robert Cathcart as Marquis of Priego, John Collett as Don Antonio, Charles Fechter as Ruy Blas, Caroline Heath as Princess of Neuberg, Rose Leclercq as Casilda, Mrs. Weston as Duchess of Albuquerque/ Scenert by Mr. Gates/ Machines by Mr. Burgess/ Music by W. H. Montgomery/ **Grecian**, Jan. 1861, with Alfred Rayner as Sallustro, Thomas Mead as Ruy Blas, Mr. Smithson as del Basto, Walter

Holland as Covandenga, William James as Don Caesar de Bazan, Jane Coveney as Queen, Lucreza Hill as Casilda, Miss Johnstone as Duchess/ **Adelphi**, Mar. 1872, with James Fernandez as Don Sallust, Mr. Barrett as Santa Cruz, A. C. Lilly as Don Caesar, M. D. Byrnes as Don Manuel, F. Stainforth as Count de Camporeal, Robert Romer as de Priego, C. H. Stephenson as Codavenga, Charles Fechter as Ruy Blas, Rose Leclercq as Princess de Neubourg, Mrs. R. Power as Duchess of Albaquerque, Maud Howard as Casilda.

RUY BLAS// D// Adap. fr F. by C. Webb// **Sad. Wells**, Feb. 1866, with R. Norman as Don Sallustie, J. W. Warde as Don Caesar, Samuel Perfitt as Marquis del Bastio, Mr. Sidney as Don Pedro, Mr. Murray as Don Manuel, David Jones as Ruy Blas, Miss M. A. Bellair as Princess Maria, Miss Leigh as Casilda, Mrs. E. F. Edgar as Duchess of Alberquerque.

RYE-HOUSE PLOT, THE; OR, THE MALTSTER'S DAUGHTER// D// J. T. Haines// **Sad. Wells**, Junt 1838, with Mr. Cathcart as Charles II, Mr. Jones as Halifax, Mr. Wilton as Ormond, Mr. Faulkland as Sir Hugh, Mr. Harwood as Jenkins, Mr. Mellor as Monmouth, W. D. Broadfoot as Essex, Mr. Ray as Russell, Mr. Townley as Howard, Dibdin Pitt as Hampden, Mr. Hitchinson as Sydney, Robert Honner as Lee, Mr. Williams as Rumbald, Mr. Conquest as Stagg, C. J. Smith as Keiling, Mrs. Robert Honner as Ruth, Miss Pincott as Joan/ Scenery by T. Pitt, Machines by Mr. Sloman/ Prod. by R. Honner.

*

SABLE MARINER, THE; OR, MAMOUND THE EVIL ONE// D// n.a.// **Sad. Wells**, Apr. 1837, with C. H. Pitt as Walter Forrester, Mr. King as Oswald Forrester, Mr. Rogers as Swallow, John Ayliffe as Derwent, Mr. Campbell as Allan, F. Ede as Capt. Preston, C. J. Smith as Black Will, Miss Beresford as Adeline, Miss Lebatt as Lucy, Mrs. Harris as Mabel, Mrs. Rogers as Jenny/ Scenery by Mr. Mildenhall/ Music by Mr. Nicholson/ Machines by Mr. Copping.

SACRAMENT OF JUDAS, THE// Play 3a// Adap. by L. N. Parker fr F of Louis Tiercelin// **POW**, Oct. 1899, rev. vers. at **Comedy**, May 1901.

SACRED TRUST, THE; OR, THE OATH MADE ON THE FIELD OF BATTLE// D 3a// Adolph Faucquez// **Victoria**, Feb. 1861, with Frederick Byefield as De Lisle, Henry Frazer as Gen. Jourdon, J. Johnson Towers as Corp. Francois, George Pearce as Roquet, John Bradshaw as Robert, Mrs. E. F. Saville as Juliette, Lydia Pearce as Rose, Fanny Boyce as Adele, W. H. Pitt as Edouard Francois, W. Harmer as Fircaundeau, George Yarnold as Jeanotte, Mrs. Charles Boyce as Isabelle.

SACRED VOW, THE; OR, THE ORPHAN OF THE BATTLE FIELD// D 3a// n.a.// **Sad. Wells**, July 1866, with T. B. Bennett as Gen. Roquebert, George Skinner as Capt. Travenny, J. F. Young as Corp. Simon, S. Carter as Pigoche, J. Baker as Picard, Philip Hannan as Frochard, F. Watts as Lucien, W. M. Schofield as Germond, Watty Brunton as Potichon, Annette Vincent as Catherine, Etty Brandon as Geneviere, Julia Summers as Mariette.

SACRIFICED// D 1a// Mabel Lloyd// **Vaudeville**, July 1891.

SAILOR AND HIS LASS, A// D 5a// Robert Buchanan & Augustus Harris// **Drury Lane**, Oct. 1883, with Augustus Harris, William Morgan, James Fernandez, A. C. Lilly, Charles Sennett, Arthur Chudleigh, Mr. Villiers, Harriet Jay, Sophie Eyre, Mary A. Victor, Clara Jecks, Cissy St. George, Mrs. Barrett/ Scenery by Grieve & Emden/ Music by Oscar Barrett.

SAILOR AND THE PEDLAR, THE; OR, THE ANCHOR OF HOPE// D// Edward Stirling// **Victoria**, June 1857, with Mr. Morrison as Dunmore, Mr. Henderson as Capt. Walton, Mr. Hitchinson as Mumps, S. Sawford as Hargrave, Henry Dudley as Topreef, Frederick Byefield as Moonshine, Charles Rice as Crabstick, Rosalie Young as Joe, Phoebe Towers as Emily, Julia Seaman as Susan, Mrs. J. H. Rickards as Dame Wheatly.

SAILOR OF FRANCE, THE; OR, THE REPUBLICANS OF BREST// D 2a// J. B. Johnstone// **Surrey**, Nov. 1854.

SAILOR'S KNOT, A// D 4a// Henry Pettitt// **Drury Lane**, Sept. 1891, with Charles Warner as Jack, Charles Glenney as Harry, Harry Nicholls as Strawbones, Julian Cross as Pennycad, Edmund Gurney as Delaunay, W. Lugg as Capt. Vernon, Thomas Terriss as Seafield, Frank Macvickars as Col. Scarlett, Ethel Bland as Josephine, Jessie Millward as Marie, Fanny Brough as Margery/ Scenery by Caney, W. Perkins & J. Harker/ Music by John Crook/ Machines by J. Taylor.

ST. ANN'S WELL; OR, A CENTURY GONE// D 2a// F. C. Nantz// **Sad. Wells**, Jan. 1840, with Mr. Aldridge as Col. Jackson, J. W. Collier as O'Devilskin, Mr. Dry as Hutchinson, Henry Hall as Gobble, Mr. Elvin as Goodfellow, Mr. Cathcart as Booth, Miss Cooke as Dame Malison, Mrs. Robert Honner as Mary.

ST. BARTHOLOMEW; OR, A QUEEN'S LOVE// D// Mrs. S. Lane// **Britannia**, May 1877.

ST. CLAIR OF THE ISLE; OR, THE OUTLAW OF BARRA// D 3a// Elizabeth Polack// **Victoria**, Apr. 1838, with Mr. Wilkins as Lord John, Mr. Maddocks as St. Clair, Mr. Johnstone as Hamilton, Mr. Rayner as De Bourgh, Charles

Montague as Rosa, Mrs. Loveday as Randolph, Mr. Harwood as Sir James, John Parry as Donald, Mrs. Maddocks as Ambrosine, Mrs. Corry as Bridget.

ST. CUPID; OR, DOROTHY'S FORTUNE// C 3a// Douglass Jerrold// **Princess's**, Jan. 1853, with James Vining as Zero, Walter Lacy as Sir Valentine, John Pritt Harley as Dr. Budd, George Everett as Bellefleur, John Ryder as Checker, Frederick Cooke as Hawke, John Chester as Trundle, Mrs. Charles Kean as Dorothy, Edward Wright as Queen Bee, Mrs. Walter Lacy as Juno.

ST. JOHN'S PRIORY; OR, ISLINGTON IN THE OLDEN TIME// D// n.a.// **Sad. Wells**, Feb. 1839, with Mr. Williams as Sir Robert, Mr. Cathcart as de la Marck, Mr. Dry as Philip, Mr. Conquest as Sit Wynkin, Mr. Harwood as Prior, Robert Honner as Hugo, Mrs. Robert Honner as Patience, Miss Pincott as Cicely/ Scenery by Fenwick & Smithyes/ Machines by B. Sloman/ Music by Mr. Herbert.

ST. MARC; OR, A HUSBAND'S SACRIFICE// D// n.a.// **Drury Lane**, June 1853.

ST. MARY'S EVE; A STORY OF THE SOLWAY// D 2a// W. Bayle Bernard// **Adelphi**, Dec. 1837; Jan. 1838, with Mr. Lyon, Harry Beverly, O. Smith, Mr. Wilkinson, William Cullenford, Mlle. [sic] Celeste/ **Haymarket**, Apr. 1838, with Edmund Glover as Maj. Wentworth, Mr. Hemming as Vaughan, Mr. Hutchings as Lt. Manly, J. B. Buckstone as Bags, Robert Strickland as Chalk, Mr. Gallot as Sharpe, Mme. Sala as Dame Mayfield, Miss Beresford as Mary, Mrs. Gallot as Dame Ferns, Mlle. [sic] Celeste as Madeline/ Scenery by George Morris/ Music by Mr. Eliason; Mar. 1853, with Henry Howe as Maj. Wentworth, George Braid as Vaughan, Mr. Caulfield as Lt. Manley, Henry Bedford as Biggs, Mr. Lambert as Chalk, O. Smith as Sharpe, Mr. Rogers as Grayling, Mrs. Laws as Dame Mayfield, Mrs. Caulfield as Mary, Miss Woulds as Dame Ferns, Mme. Celeste as Madeline/ **Lyceum**, Dec. 1859, with Mr. Morton as Maj. Wentworth, Frederick Villiers as Robert Vaughn, Henry Forrester as Lt. Manley, James Johnstone as Sharp, Mme. Celeste as Madeline, Miss Stuart as Mary/ **Astley's**, Feb. 1861, with Frederick Morton as Maj. Wentworth, Frederick Villiers as Robert Vaughn, J. Francis as Bags, James Johnstone as Sharpe, T. E. Lyon as Chalk, Mme. Celeste as Madeline, Emily Scott as Mary, Mrs. Thorne as Dame Mayfield/ **Sad. Wells**, May 1863, with Frederick Morton as Maj. Wentworth, Mr. Britten as Vaughan, Mr. Pugh as Lt. Manly, W. Worboys as Bags, James Johnstone as Sharpe, J. W. Collier as Chalk, Mme. Celeste as Madeline, Kate Lemmon as Mary, Bessie Heath as Dame Mayfield.

SAINT OR SINNER// D Pro & 4a// Dram. by Alfred Dampier fr F of Victor Hugo, Les Miserables// **Surrey**, Mar. 1881.

ST. PATRICK'S EVE; OR, THE ORDER OF THE DAY// D 3a// Tyrone Power// **Haymarket**, Sept. 1837, with Benjamin Webster as Frederick II, Mr. Harris as Count Gotha, Tyrone Power as Maj. O'Dogherty, Charles Selby as Capt. Schonfeldt, J. Worrell as Capt. Brandt, J. T. Haines as Baron Trenck, Miss E. Phillips as Catherine, Mrs. W. Clifford as Mme. Schonfeldt, Miss Wrighten as Mechi, Mrs. Tayleure as Mrs. Blitz.

ST. RONAN'S WELL// D 4a// Dram. by Richard Davey & W. H. Pollock fr novel of Sir Walter Scott// **Trafalgar**, June 1893.

ST. VALENTINE'S DAY; OR, THE FATAL CHOICE// D 3a// William Travers// **East London**, July 1869.

SAINTS AND SINNERS// Play 5a// Henry Arthur Jones// **Vaudeville**, Sept. 1884, with Thomas Thorne, Henry Neville, H. B. Conway, E. M. Robson, William Lestocq, Kate Phillips, Miss M. Giffard.

SAIREY GAMP// F 1a// n.a.// **Adelphi**, Mar. 1873, with J. Clarke, C. J. Smith.

SALLY IN OUR ALLEY// Play 3a// Fred Lister & Paul Heriot// **Sad. Wells**, Aug. 1888.

SALT TEARS// C 1a// T. W. Speight// **Royalty**, July 1873/ **Haymarket**, Oct. 1880, with Henry Howe as Briny, Stewart Dawson as Shingle, Edith Bruce as Ruth, Winifred Emery as Lady Janet/ **Strand**, Mar. 1895.

SALVATORI// D// n.a.// **Olympic**, Mar. 1853.

SALVINIANA// F// G. L. Gordon// **Opera Comique**, June 1877.

SAM WELLER; OR, THE PICKWICKIANS// D// Dram. by William Moncrieff fr sketch by Charles Dickens// **Strand**, July 1837.

SAM'S ARRIVAL// F 1a// John Oxenford// **Strand**, Sept. 1862.

SAMPLE VERSUS PATTERN// F 1a// Walter Sapte Jr.// **POW**, June 1887.

SAMPSON'S WEDDING// F 1a// G. F. Rowe// **Lyceum**, Apr. 1870, with Charles Wilmot as Sampson Green, Miss J. Lee as Cleaver, G. F. Neville as Horatio Figgins, H. Morton as Maj. McIntosh, W. C. Williams as Chuckles, Miss Lisle as Patty Smallweed, Miss Love as Sophonisba, Laura Morgan as Mrs. McIntosh, Susan Rignold as Dinah.

SAMUEL IN SEARCH OF HIMSELF// F 1a// J. Stirling Coyne// **Princess's**, Apr. 1858, with David Fisher as Shirkington, John Pritt Harley as Pounce, Henry Saker as Dearlove, Mrs. Winstanley as Mrs. Peckham, Miss Murray as Mrs. Dearlove, Maria Daly as Lucy/ **Sad. Wells**, Sept. 1859, with William Belford as Shirkington, Lewis Ball as Dearlove, J. W. Ray as Sir Paul, Caroline Hill as Tippy, Mrs. Henry Marston as Mrs. Peckham, Caroline Parkes as Mrs. Dearlove, Miss German as Lucy.

SAMUEL OF POSEN// C 4a// G. H. Jessop// **Gaiety**, July 1895.

SANCTUARY, THE; OR, ENGLAND IN 1415// D 2a// J. E. Carpenter// **Surrey**, Oct. 1855.

SANDFORD AND MERTON// Play 1a// F. C. Burnand// **Comedy**, Dec. 1893.

SARAH BLANGI// D 5a// Adap. by Morris Barnett fr F, Sarah le Créole// **Olympic**, Oct. 1852, with William Farren as Col. Dumont, Henry Compton as Vanoris, William Hoskins as de Cerney, William Farren Jr. as Duplessis, W. Shalders as Dr. Robert, George Cooke as Jerome, Fanny Wallack as Sarah Blangi, Harriet Gordon as Alice/ Scenery by W. Shalders.

SARAH, THE FAIR MAIDEN OF THE RHINE// T// R. J. Blyth// **St. Geo. Hall**, July 1879.

SARAH'S YOUNG MAN// F 1a// W. E. Suter// **Surrey**, Apr. 1856/ **Grecian**, June 1866, with J. Jackson as Moggridge, George Gillett as Fielding, George Conquest as Sloeleaf, Mrs. Atkinson as Mrs. Moggridge, Harriet Western as Araminta, Mary A. Victor as Sarah/ **POW**, Apr. 1867/ **Adelphi**, Dec. 1872, with Frederick Moreland as Moggeridge, Edward George as Slowleaf, Mr. Waring as Fielding, Jane Coveney as Mrs. Moggeridge, Miss K. Bentley as Araminta, Clara Jecks as Sarah/ **Globe**, Sept. 1876, with Henry Leigh as Moggridge, A. Evans as Fielding, James Fawn as Sam Sloeleaf, Miss F. Gray as Mrs. Moggridge, Alice Mowbray as Araminta, Miss C. Wallace as Sarah Tibbs.

SARDANAPALUS, KING OF ASSYRIA// T 5a// Lord Byron// **Princess's**, ("considerably abridged"), June 1853, with Charles Kean as Sardanapalus, George Everett as Arbaces, Frank Graham as Beleses, John Ryder as Salemenes, Mr. Rolleston as Altada, John Cathcart as Pania, John Collett as Balea, Caroline Heath as Zarina, Mrs. Charles Kean as Myrrha/ Scenery under direction of Mr. Grieve/ Machines by G. Hodsdon/ Music by J. L. Hatton.

SATAN; OR, THE STRANGE INTRUDER// D// Adap. fr F// **Grecian**, June 1867, with Charles Mortimer as D'Estigny, Samuel Perfitt as de Varinville, George Gillett as de Bravadeau, William James as Count de Mauleon, Lizzie Mandelbert as the Strange Intruder, Unknown Princess, Boy, Mysterious Stranger and Roy Vay, Alice Denvil as Mme. de Mantelles, Miss De Lacie as Mme. de Cerecourt, Mrs. Dearlove as Mme. de Denneville.

SATAN IN PARIS; OR, THE MYSTERIOUS STRANGER// D 2a// Adap. by Charles Selby fr F// **Adelphi**, 1844, with Mme. Celeste, Charles Selby.

SATISFACTION; OR, THE DUELISTS// Thomas Blake// **Grecian**, Oct. 1845, with Edwin Dixon as Somers, Harry Chester as Bellamy, Frederick Robson as Tom Tap, Annette Mears as Kate, Sally, and as Capt. Marmaduke Musk, Miss Johnstone as Patty.

SAUCY LASS, THE; OR, THE LOG OF A BRITISH TAR// D 3a// J. T. Haines// **Victoria**, Aug. 1843, with John Dale as Ellerton, Mr. Wilton as Capt. Armstrong, Mr. James as Magnus, William Seaman as Grey, E. F. Saville as Heaveline, C. Williams as Kedge, Mr. Paul as Corp. Jolly, Annette Vincent as Gillian, Mrs. Atkinson as Eunice, Miss Ridgeway as Jennet.

SAUCY SALLY// C 3a// Adap. by F. C. Burnand fr F of Maurice Hennequin, La Flamboyante// **Comedy**, Mar. 1897.

SAVAGE AND THE MAIDEN, THE; OR, CRUMMELS AND HIS DAUGHTER// F// Dram. by J. H. Horncastle fr Charles Dickens, Nicholas Nickleby// **Grecian**, June 1844, with Henry Horncastle as Vincent Crummles, Edwin Dixon as Nicholas Nickleby, Annette Mears as Smike, Frederick Robson as Mr. Lenville, Edmund Garden as Mr. Folair, Miss Merion as Mrs. Crummles, Mary A. Crisp as Miss Snivellici/ Music by G. Loder.

SAVAGE AS A BEAR// F 1a// Adap. by Horace Wigan fr F// **Olympic**, Sept. 1860, with Frederic Robinson as Griffin, Horace Wigan as Jujube, Miss Marston as Mrs Griffin, Mrs. W. S. Emden as Bustle.

SAVANNAH, THE// D 5a// "arranged" by C. J. Mathews// **Drury Lane**, Mar. 1861, with Mr. McLein as Sebastian, John Ryder as Oliveirez, Robert Roxby as Col. Pennypecker, George Honey as Pestletop, C. J. Mathews as Wander, George Spencer as Loiter, Mr. Cormack as Walker, Henry Mellon as Pascalez, Edwin Dixon as Fabio, Mrs. C. J. Mathews as Rita, Mrs. Dowton as Leonora, Miss Thirlwall as Zara, Miss Egan as Meg.

SAVED// D 3a// H. S. Granville// **St. Geo. Hall**, Dec. 1868/ **Astley's**, June 1869, with H. S. Granville as Ben Bisset, Hudson Liston as Tom Bisset, A. H. Roberts as Sharpe, Clara Tellett as Mrs. Bisset, Nellie Clifton as Emily.

SAVED; OR, A WIFE'S PERIL// D// Adap. by Arthur Shirley fr F, La Maison du Mari// **Holborn**, Dec. 1885.

SAVED BY A WORD// D// Edgar Newbound// **Britannia**, Feb. 1877.

SAVED FROM THE SEA// D 4a// Arthur Shirley & Benjamin Landeck// **Pavilion**, Mar. 1895/ **Princess's**, Aug. 1895.

SAVED FROM THE STREETS; OR, WAIFS AND STRAYS// D 4a// George Conquest & R. H. Eaton// **Surrey**, Oct. 1886.

SAVOURNEEN DEELISH; OR, THE GIRL OF MY HEART AND THE SOLDIER'S BRIDE// D// T. G. Blake// **Sad. Wells**, June 1839, with Mr. Williams as Byrne, Mr. Cathcart as Fitzsimmons, Robert Honner as Van Hilden, Charles Montgomery as Oliver, John Webster as Barton, J. W. Collier as O'Loughlin, Mr. Conquest as Proudfoot, Mrs. Robert Honner as Ellen, Miss Richardson as Meg, Miss Norman as Mary, Miss Pincott as Norah/ Scenery by Mr. Fenwick & G. Smithyes Jr./ Music by Mr.

Herbert. Machines by B. Sloman.

SAYINGS AND DOINGS; OR, THE RULE OF CONTRARY// F 1a// J. Maddison Morton// **Cov. Garden**, Apr. 1839, with Drinkwater Meadows as Titmouse, Mr. Vining as Nightingale, John Pritt Harley as Merrypegs, Thomas Lee as Bourke, Mrs. W. Clifford as Mrs. Wilful, Miss Charles as Lucy, Mrs. East as Phoebe.

SCALES OF JUSTICE, THE// D 4a// W. R. Waldron// **Standard**, Dec. 1894.

SCAMPS OF LONDON, THE; OR, THE CROSS-ROADS OF LIFE// D// Arr. by Frederick Marchant fr W. J. Moncreiff's adap. fr F// **Sad. Wells**, Nov. 1848/ Orig. vers. at **Grecian**, Nov. 1868, with Charles Mortimer as Devereux, W. Shirley as Dorrington, William James as Danvers, J. Jackson as Shabner, John Manning as Yorkney, George Gillett as Herbert, Thomas Mead as Tom Fogg, Henry Power as Brindle, Henry Grant as Onion, Lizzie Mandelbert as Louisa, Mary A. Victor as Charlotte, Mrs. Dearlove as Miss Dorrington.

SCANDAL// C 2a// Adap. by Arthur Matthison fr F, Les Scandales d'Hier// **Royalty**, June 1878.

SCAPEGOAT, THE// D 4a// Dram. by J. W. Jones fr novel of Gertrude Warden// **Globe**, July 1891.

SCAPEGOAT, THE// F 1a// J. Poole// **Sad. Wells**, Sept. 1839, with W. D. Broadfoot as Old Eustace, Mr. Elvin as Charles, J. W. Collier as Robin, Mr. Williams as Polyglot, Mrs. J. F. Saville as Harriet, Miss Pincott as Molly; Oct. 1848, with Mr. Williams as Eustace, Mr. Gladstone as Charles, A. Younge as Polyglot, Charles Fenton as Robin, Miss Huddart as Harriet, Mrs. C. A. Tellet as Molly/ **St. James's**, Nov. 1854, with F. Ede as Eustace, Mr. Moreland as Charles, Mr. Sidney as Robin, W. Cooper as Polyglot, Miss Clifford as Harriet, Miss Robertson as Molly/ **Olympic**, July 1860, with Frederick Vining as Eustace, Walter Gordon as Charles, Harwood Cooper as Robin, Mr. Addison as Polyglot, Miss Cottrell as Harriet, Mrs. W. S. Emden as Molly/ **Haymarket**, July 1861, with William Cullenford as Old Eustace, Edwin Villiers as Charles, W. H. Chippendale as Polyglot, Mr. Clark as Robin, Henrietta Lindley as Harriet, Mrs. Fitzwilliam as Molly/ **Globe**, Feb 1877, with T. Balfour as Eustace, Paul Gray as Charles, W. H. Stephens as Polyglot, Francis Harcourt as Robin, Nellie Harris as Harriet, Rosine Power as Molly.

SCAPEGRACE, THE// C// Samuel Beazley// **Sad. Wells**, June 1845, with Henry Marston as Col. Aubrey, Miss Cooper as Darlington, Henry Scharfe as Bustle, Mr. Williams as Perequet, Miss Huddart as Mrs. Aubrey, Miss Lebatt as Tucker.

SCAR ON THE WRIST, THE// D Pro & 3a// J. Palgrave Simpson & Claude Templar// **St. James's**, Mar. 1878, with Mr. Titheradge as Sir Reginald, Henry Vaughan as Marsden, Edmund Leathes as Capt. Onslow, W. H. Stephens as Lord Snowbery, Henry Forrester as Claypole, Ada Cavendish as Alice, Emily Fowler as Ethel, Kate Rivers as Martha, Mrs. Leigh Murray as Mrs. Sweetapple/ Scenery by H. Potts.

SCARECROW, THE// C 3a// Charles Thomas// **Strand**, May 1889.

SCARLET DICK, AND THE ROAD AND ITS RIDERS// D 3a// J. B. Howe// **Britannia**, July 1867; Oct. 1878 under title of Scarlet Dick, The King's Highwayman.

SCARLET DYE, THE// D 3a// Julia Masters// **St. Geo. Hall**, May 1888.

SCARLET LETTER, THE; OR, LOST IN THE SNOW// D 3a// Alfred Rayner// **Grecian**, Oct. 1863, with Henry Grant as Sir Roland, J. B. Steele as Owen, William James as Arundel, J. Jackson as Jacob, Thomas Mead as Shingles, John Manning as Caleb, Mrs. Charles Dillon as Lilian, Jane Dawson as Phoebe, Mary A. Victor as Letty, Miss C. Crisp as Lady Agatha.

SCARLET LETTER, THE// D 5a// Dram. by Norman Forbes & Stephen Coleridge fr novel of Nathaniel Hawthorne// **Royalty**, May 1888.

SCARLET LETTER, THE// Play Pro & 4a// Dram. by E. B. Aveling fr novel of Nathaniel Hawthorne// **Olympic**, June 1888.

SCARLET MANTLE, THE// D 3a// T. E. Wilks// **Victoria**, Oct. 1854, with E. F. Savile as de Gayenne, Alfred Saville as Gen. Victor, Mr. Morrison as Capt. Waldman, N. T. Hicks as Von Ankerstroll, W. H. Pitt as Rubalt, Charles Rice as Wimbleton, J. Howard as MacMurrough, Miss Dansor as Countess Maria, Mrs. Henry Vining as Agnese, Mrs. Manders as Gertrude.

SCARLET MARK, THE; OR, THE WITCH, THE ROVER, AND THE MYSTERY// D 3a// C. H. Hazlewood// **Britannia**, Nov. 1868.

SCATTERED LEAVES// D// R. H. Lingham// **Grecian**, Sept. 1861, with Mr. Jackson as Jessie Dale, F. Smithson as Weasley, Walter Holland as Squire Hastings, Henry Grant as Leslie, William James as Hastings, R. H. Lingham as Laurence, Alfred Rayner as Leicester, John Manning as Rusty, Jane Dawson as Bess and as Bell, Mary A. Victor as Rachael, Miss Johnstone as Mrs. Dale, Lucreza Hill as Snubbs.

SCENE OF CONFUSION, A// F// Thomas Wilks// **Victoria**, Sept. 1839.

SCHAMYL// D// Adap. by J. Palgrave Simpson// **Princess's**, Nov. 1854.

SCHOLAR, THE// C// J. B. Buckstone// **Haymarket**, July 1837, with William Farren as Bookworm, Mr. Ross as Krackjaw, Robert Strickland as Wurtzburg, Benjamin Webster as Dr. Kepplecranck, Mr. Saville as Frederick, Mrs. W. Clifford as Mrs. Wurtzburg, Miss Taylor as Helen.

SCHOOL// C 4a// Adap. by T. W. Robertson fr G of Roderich Benedix, Aschenbrödel//

POW, Jan. 1869, with Squire Bancroft, Mrs. Bancroft, Carlotta Addison, H. J. Montague, John Hare/ **Haymarket,** May 1880, with H. B. Conway as Lord Beaufoy, Henry Kemble as Sutcliffe, Arthur Cecil as Farintosh, Squire Bancroft as Poyntz, Charles Brookfield as Krux, Mrs. Canninge as Mrs. Sutcliffe, Mrs. Bancroft as Naomi Tighe, Marion Terry as Bella/ Scenery by Hawes Craven, Mr. Harford & Walter Hann/ **Garrick,** Nov. 1880; Sept. 1891, with H. B. Irving, Gilbert Hare, Fanny Robertson, Kate Rorke, William Mackintosh/ **Globe,** Feb. 1899, with Frank Gillmore as Beaufoy, William Day as Sutcliffe, John Hare as Farintosh, Frederick Kerr as Poyntz, Gilbert Hare as Krux, Henry Abbott as Vaughan, Fanny Coleman as Mrs. Sutcliffe, Mabel Terry Lewis as Bella, May Harvey as Naomi Tighe.

SCHOOL FOR COQUETTES, THE// C 1a// Adap. by J. Palgrave Simpson fr F of La Marquise Senneterre// **Strand,** July 1859, with Ada Swanborough, W. H. Swanborough.

SCHOOL FOR GROWN CHILDREN, A// C 5a// Thomas Morton// **Haymarket,** Aug. 1845 (in 3a), with Henry Holl as Sir Arthur, William Farren as Old Revel, CharlesHudson as Young Revel, Benjamin Webster as Ryeland, A. Brindal as Dexter, J. B. Buckstone as Buttercup, T. F. Mathews as Randal, Mrs. Julia Glover as Dame Ryeland, Julia Bennett as Lady Stanmore, Miss Fortescue as Mrs. Revel, Miss Carre as Fanny, Mrs. Stanley as Miss Raven.

SCHOOL FOR INTRIGUE, THE// C 4a// "Imitated from Beaumarchais" by James Mortimer// **Olympic,** Dec. 1873, with Henry Neville as Almaviva, Edward Righton as Figaro, W. H. Fisher as Cherubino, John Vollaire as Dr. Bartholo, G. Canninge as Don Bazile, A. Estcourt as Don Gusman, J. G. Bauer as Antonio, Edith Gray as Countess Almaviva, Miss Fowler as Suzanne, Mrs. Stephens as Marceline, Elsie Pearce as Fanchette/ Scenery by Julian Hicks/ Music by J. Mallandaine.

SCHOOL FOR KINGS, THE// D 3a// C. A. Somerset// **Drury Lane,** Mar. 1853, with E. L. Davenport as Heldomar, Mr. White as Duke Sternheim, Mr. Moorhouse as Herman, Mr. Halford as Gotfried, Mr. Wilson as Adelbert, James Lickfold as Rosenheim, Charles Selby as Rittmeister, Henry Lee as Bruthart, Mr. Anderson as Marco, Mr. King as Hans, George Yarnold as Pufferling, Miss Malcolm as Lady Abbess, Fanny Vining as Aurelia, Mrs. Griffiths as Benita, Kate Saxon as Bella, Miss Honey as Anna, Miss Florence as Martha.

SCHOOL FOR MUFFS, THE// C// Robert Dodson// **Surrey,** Feb. 1876.

SCHOOL FOR SAINTS, A// C 3a// J. O. Hobbes// **Lyceum,** Mar. 1896.

SCHOOL FOR SCANDAL, THE// C 5a// Richard Brinsley Sheridan// **Haymarket,** June 1837, with William Farren as Sir Peter, John Webster as Backbite, Robert Strickland as Sir Oliver, E. W. Elton as Joseph Surface, Frederick Vining as Charles Surface, T. F. Mathews as Crabtree, J. Worrell as Careless, Benjamin Webster as Moses, E. F. Saville as Snake, Charles Selby as Trip, Mrs. Nisbett as Lady Teazle, Mrs. Julia Glover as Mrs. Candour, Mrs. W. Clifford as Lady Sneerwell, Miss E. Phillips as Maria; Oct. 1839, with Mme. Vestris , William Farren, George Bartley, Robert Keeley; Dec. 1846, with Mme. Celeste; Dec. 1849, with Samuel Phelps, James Wallack, Helen Faucit, Mrs. Julia Glover/ **Drury Lane,** June 1837, with William Farren as Sir Peter, William Dowton as Sir Oliver, C. J. Mathews as Charles Surface, Mr. Cooper as Joseph Surface, Drinkwater Meadows as Crabtree, James Vining as Backbite, Mr. Wilson as Sir Harry, Mr. Henry as Careless, Mr. Baker as Snake, Mr. Shuter as Moses, Mrs. Julia Glover as Mrs. Candour, Miss Murray as Maria, Mme. Vestris as Lady Teazle, Miss Somerville as Lady Sneerwell; Feb. 1850, with Basil Baker as Sir Peter, William Davidge as Sir Oliver, Frederick Vining as Backbite, W. H. Angel as Crabtree, Samuel Emery as Moses, Mr. Barry as Rowley, Mr. Cooper as Joseph Surface, James Anderson as Charles Surface, John Parry as Trip, Mr. Everett as Careless, Mr. Frazer as Snake, Louisa Nisbett as Lady Teazle, Miss Phillips as Lady Sneerwell, Mrs. Winstanley as Mrs. Candour; Apr. 1864, with Samuel Phelps as Sir Peter, Mr. Addison as Sir Oliver, C. J. Mathews as Charles Surface, William Creswick as Joseph Surface, J. B. Buckstone as Backbite, Henry Compton as Crabtree, J. L. Toole as Moses, Walter Montgomery as Careless, Horace Wigan as Trip, Benjamin Webster as Snake, Frank Matthews as Rowley, Mrs. Charles Mathews as Lady Teazle, Mrs. Billington as Lady Sneerwell, Mrs. Stirling as Mrs. Candour, Henrietta Sims as Maria/ **Cov. Garden,** June 1837, with William Farren as Sir Peter, William Dowton as Sir Oliver, Frederick Vining as Charles Surface, E. W. Elton as Joseph Surface, James Vining as Backbite, J. Worrell as Careless, Charles Bender as Snake, Robert Strickland as Crabtree, Benjamin Webster as Moses, John Webster as Trip, Mme. Vestris as Lady Teazle, Mrs. Julia Glover as Mrs. Candour, Miss Murray as Maria, Mrs. W. West as Lady Sneerwell; Oct. 1839, with William Farren as Sir Peter, George Bartley as Sir Oliver, John Pritt Harley as Backbite, Mr. Cooper as Joseph Surface, C. J. Mathews as Charles Surface, Drinkwater Meadows as Crabtree, Mr. Fitzjames as Careless, Charles Selby as Snake, Robert Keeley as Moses, Mme. Vestris as Lady Teazle, Mrs. Brougham as Lady Sneerwell, Mrs. Orger as Mrs. Candour; Apr. 1840, with same cast except Charles Kemble as Charles Surface/ **Sad. Wells,** July 1837, with Benjamin Webster as Sir Peter, Mr. Hicks as Joseph Surface, Mr. Griffiths as Sir Oliver, John Pritchard as Oliver Surface, C. H. Pitt as Backbite, Mr. Collins as Sir Harry, Mr. Ross as Moses, F. Ede as Snake, C. J. Smith as Careless, Mr. Rogers as Crabtree, Mrs. W. West as Lady Teazle, Lavinia Melville as Maria, Mrs. Harris as Lady Sneerwell, Miss Williams as Mrs. Candour; June 1844, with Samuel Phelps as Sir Peter, Mr. Williams as Sir Oliver, John Webster as Backbite, Henry Marston as Joseph Surface, Charles Hudson as Charles Surface, G. F. Forman as Crabtree, Mr. Binge as Careless, Mr. Sharp as Moses,

Edward Knight as Snake, Mrs. Mary Warner as Lady Teazle, Emma Harding as Lady Sneerwell, Mrs. Henry Marston as Mrs. Candour; Nov. 1865, with James Johnstone as Sir Peter, J. C. Cowper as Charles, R. Norman as Sir Oliver, E. F. Edgar as Joseph, E. H. Brooke as Backbite, John Rouse as Moses, Samuel Perfitt as Crabtree, Mr. Murray as Careless, H. Sidney as Trip, Alice Marriott as Lady Teazle, Miss Graham as Lady Sneerwell, Mrs. E. F. Edgar as Mrs. Candour; Dec. 1880, with Hermann Vezin as Sir Peter, Charles Warner as Charles Surface, E. H. Brooke as Joseph Surface, Edmund Lyons as Sir Oliver, Rowland Buckstone as Backbite, William Farren Jr. as Crabtree, Arthur Wood as Moses, G. Canninge as Snake, Mr. Wheatcroft as Careless, Virginia Bateman as Lady Teazle, Miss M. Bell as Lady Sneerwell, Mrs. W. Sidney as Mrs. Candour/ **Princess's**, June 1845, with Henry Compton as Sir Peter, Mr. Granby as Sir Oliver, James Wallack as Charles Surface, Mr. Lynne as Joseph Surface, Walter Lacy as Backbite, Mr. Walton as Crabtree, W. H. Oxberry as Moses, Charles Horn Jr. as Carless, Charlotte Cushman as Lady Teazle, Mrs. Fosbroke as Lady Sneerwell, Emma Stanley as Mrs. Candour, Mrs. Brougham as Maria; Jan. 1873, with Benjamin Webster as Sir Peter, James Fernandez as Joseph Surface, J. C. Cowper as Charles Surface, John Clarke as Moses, E. Shepherd as Sir Oliver, F. Barsey as Crabtree, F. Charles as Backbite, Charles Seyton as Trip, C. H. Fenton as Careless, Theresa Furtado as Lady Teazle, Edith Stuart as Maria, Mrs. Alfred Mellon as Mrs. Candour, Cicely Nott as Lady Sneerwell; Feb. 1881, with W. H. Chippendale as Sir Peter, Mr. Fosbrooke as Sir Oliver, J. C. Buckstone as Backbite, Henry Leigh as Crabtree, H. Templeton as Careless, C. W. Somerset as Joseph Surface, Philip Beck as Charles Surface, Mr. Bennett as Moses, Fred Terry as Trip, Mr. Williamson as Snake, Marie De Grey as Lady Teazle, Miss B. Huntley as Lady Sneerwell, Mrs. Chippendale as Mrs. Candour/ **Olympic**, Dec. 1850, with William Farren as Sir Peter, George Cooke as Sir Oliver, William Farren Jr. as Backbite, Leigh Murray as Joseph Surface, Henry Farren as Charles Surface, Henry Compton as Moses, Charles Bender as Snake, Mrs. Stirling as Lady Teazle, Mrs. Leigh Murray as Lady Sneerwell, Mrs. Alfred Phillips as Mrs. Candour, Miss Adams as Maria; July 1855, with Samuel Emery as Sir Peter, Frederick Vining as Sir Oliver, George Vining as Charles Surface, Alfred Wigan as Joseph Surface, Mr. Danvers as Backbite, Frederick Robson as Moses, Mr. Gladstone as Snake, J. H. White as Crabtree, Mr. Leslie as Careless, Mrs. Stirling as Lady Teazle, Miss Castleton as Lady Sneerwell, Mrs. Alfred Wigan as Mrs. Candour, Miss Marston as Maria; May 1861, with Mr. Addison as Sir Peter, Frederick Vining as Sir Oliver, Horace Wigan as Joseph Surface, Frederic Robinson as Charles Surface, George Cooke as Crabtree, Walter Gordon as Backbite, F. B. Conway as Moses, Harwood Cooper as Trip, Gaston Murray as Snake, Amy Sedgwick as Lady Teazle, Miss Cottrell as Maria, Miss Marston as Lady Sneerwell, Mrs. Leigh Murray as Mrs. Candour; Feb. 1879, with W. H. Stephens as Sir Peter, Frederick Everill as Sir Oliver, Henry Neville as Charles Surface, Hermann Vezin as Joseph Surface, Rowland Buckstone as Trip, Lionel Brough as as Moses, Mr. Chapman as Snake, W. Herbert as Careless, Harry Proctor as Crabtree, J. C. Buckstone as Backbite, Mrs. Bernard Beere as Lady Teazle, Blanche Henri as Maria; July 1881, with W. H. Chippendale as Sir Peter, Horace Wigan as Sir Oliver, J. C. Buckstone as Backbite, Arthur Wood as Crabtree, C. W. Somerset as Joseph Surface, Philip Beck as Charles Surface, Edward Righton as Moses, E. T. Webber as Carless, J. B. Rae as Snake, Marie De Grey as Lady Teazle, Helen Mathews as Lady Sneerwell, Miss Measor as Maria, Mrs. Chippendale as Mrs. Candour/ **Grecian**, Oct. 1854, with Eaton O'Donnell as Sir Peter, Richard Phillips as Charles Surface, Henry Grant as Sir Oliver, Henry Power as Trip, Basil Potter as Joseph Surface, F. Charles as Sir Benjamin Backbite, T. Roberts as Snake, William Suter as Moses, Jane Coveney as Lady Teazle, Miss Johnstone as Mrs. Candour, Agnes De Warde as Maria, Harriet Coveney as Lady Sneerwell/ **St. James's**, Dec. 1854, with Mr. Ranger as Sir Peter, W. Cooper as Sir Oliver, Mr. Stuart as Joseph Surface, George Vandenhoff as Charles Surface, Mr. Herbert as Backbite, Mr. Sanger as Crabtree, Mr. Sidney as Moses, Mr. Ennis as Snake, Henry Rivers as Careless, Mrs. Seymour as Lady Teazle, Miss Bulmer as Maria, Miss Grey as Lady Sneerwell, Mrs. Stanley as Mrs. Candour; Nov 1867, with Frank Matthews as Sir Peter, Edward Dyas as Sir Oliver, F. Charles as Backbite, Henry Irving as Joseph Surface, Walter Lacy as Charles Surface, T. C. Burleigh as Crabtree, Gaston Murray as Careless, J. D. Stoyle as Moses, Thomas Bridgeford as Snake, Louisa Herbert as Lady Teazle, Mrs. Frank Matthews as Mrs Candour, Eleanore Bufton as Lady Sneerwell, Ada Cavendish as Maria; Dec. 1877, with W. H. Stephens as Sir Peter, Edward Atkins as Sir Oliver, Lin Rayne as Backbite, Henry Forrester as Joseph Surface, W. Herbert as Charles Surface, Mr. Holman as Crabtree, W. J. Selby as Careless, Mr. Odell as Moses, Mr. Chapman as Snake, Ada Cavendish as Lady Teazle, Sallie Turner as Mrs. Candour, Mrs. Bernard Beere as Lady Sneerwell, Beatrice Strafford as Maria/ **Vaudeville**, July 1872; Jan. 1890, with Fred Thorne as Moses, T. B. Thalberg as Charles Surface, Cyril Maude as Joseph Surface, Frank Gillmore as Backbite, J. S. Blythe as Sir Oliver, Fred Grove as Crabtree, Oswald Yorke as Careless, John Maclean as Sir Peter, J. Horton as Snake, Winifred Emery as Lady Teazle, Mary Collette as Maria, Coralie Owen as Mrs. Candour, L. Bryer as Lady Sneerwell/ Scenery by Walter Hann/ **POW**, Apr. 1874, with Charles Coghlan, Squire Bancroft, Mrs. Bancroft, John Hare, Miss Josephs, Mrs. Murray/ **Adelphi**, May 1879, with Charles Flockton as Sir Peter, Horace Wigan as Sir Oliver, Edward Compton as Backbite, Hermann Vezin as Joseph Surface, Henry Neville as Charles Surface, Robert Pateman as Moses, Harwood Cooper as Snake, Adelaide Neilson as Lady Teazle, Mrs. Alfred Mellon as Candour, Bella Pateman as Sneerwell, Lydia Foote as Maria/ Scenery by Julian Hicks/ **Prince's**, Feb. 1885, with William Farren Jr., Herbert Beerbohm Tree, Charles Coghlan,

Lillie Langtry, Mrs. Arthur Stirling, Kate Pattison/ **Strand**, Oct. 1886, with Lewis Ball, Charles Dodsworth, Sidney Valentine, Edward Compton, Angela Fenton, Dora Vivian, Elinor Aickin/ **Globe**, Feb. 1889, with James Fernandez as Sir Peter, D. H. Harkins as Sir Oliver, Weedon Grossmith as Backbite, J. T. Sullivan as Joseph Surface, William Herbert as Charles Surface, W. H. Crompton as Crabtree, Lionel Brough as Moses, Kate Vaughan as Lady Teazle, Carlotta Leclercq as Mrs. Candour, May Whitty as Lady Sneerwell, Maude White as Maria/ **Criterion**, Apr. 1891 [in vers. by Charles Wyndham]/ **Daly's**, Nov. 1893/ **Lyceum**, July 1896, with William Farren Jr. as Sir Peter, Edward Righton as Sir Oliver Surface, Cyril Maude as Sir Benjamin Backbite, Johnston Forbes Robertson as Joseph Surface, Fred Terry as Charles Surface, Arthur Wood as Crabtree, Frank Gillmore as Careless, Fred Thorne as Moses, Sydney Warden as Snake, Mrs. Patrick Campbell as Lady Teazle, Rose Leclercq as Mrs. Candour, Henrietta Watson as Lady Sneerwell, Sarah Brooke as Maria/ **Terry's**, July 1898.

SCHOOL FOR SCHEMING, A// C// Dion Boucicault// **Haymarket**, Feb. 1847.

SCHOOL FOR THE KINGS, THE// D 3a// n.a.// **Drury Lane**, Mar. 1853.

SCHOOL FOR TIGERS; OR, THE SHILLING HOP// F// Mark Lemon// **Adelphi**, Nov. 1850, with Charles Boyce as Capt. Kiteflyer, J. Worrell as Maj. Stiff, Edward Wright as Mr. Panels, Ellen Chaplin as Alexander Panels, Miss Turner as David, C. J. Smith as Firkins, Sarah Woolgar as Tom Crop, Laura Honey as Traces, Fanny Young as Blinkers; Nov. 1867, with W. H. Eburne as Capt. Kiteflyer, Mr. Branscombe as Major Stiff, Garston Belmore as Panels, Nelly Harris as David, C. J. Smith as Firkins, Mrs. Alfred Mellon as Tom Croft, Emily Pitt as Mary Panels.

SCHOOL OF REFORM, THE// C// Thomas Morton// **Haymarket**, Mar. 1839, with Charles Perkins as Lord Avondale, Robert Strickland as Gen. Tarragon, Walter Lacy as Ferment, Mr. Cooper as Frederick, J. W. Gough as Old Tyke, Benjamin Webster as Robert Tyke, Mrs. W. Clifford as Mrs. St. Clair, Mrs. Fitzwilliam as Mrs. Ferment, Mrs. Gallot as Nicely, Mrs. Frank Matthews as Shelah, Miss Mordaunt as Julia/ **Eng. Opera House** (Lyceum), June 1843, with George Maynard as Lord Avondale, Mr. Thornton as Frederick, J. Neville as Gen. Tarragon, Samuel Emery as Tyke, Thomas Green as Ferment, Miss Taylor as Julia, Amelia Mercer as Mrs. Ferment/ **Olympic**, Feb. 1848, with Charles Perkins as Avondale, William Davidge as Tarragon, Henry Holl as Ferment, Mr. Morton as Frederick, Lysander Thompson as Tyke, H. Lee as Old Tyke, Mr. Buxton as Timothy, Mrs. Brougham as Mrs. Ferment, Miss C. Lacy as Julia, Mrs. H. Lee as Mrs. Nicely, Mrs. Leman Rede as Mrs. St. Clair/ **Sad. Wells**, Mar. 1849 (in 3a), with Henry Mellon as Lord Avondale, A. Younge as Gen. Tarragon, William Hoskins as Tyke, Mr. Harrington as Old Tyke, Henry Marston as Ferment, G. K. Dickinson as Frederick, Miss Huddart as Mrs. St. Clair, Miss Murray as Julia, Miss Cooper as Mrs. Ferment, Mrs. Henry Marston as Mrs. Nicely, Miss Stephens as Shelah/ **Grecian**, Aug. 1861, with R. H. Lingham as Lord Avondale, Mr. Jackson as Gen. Tarragon, William James as Ferment, Mr. Bell as Frederick, Alfred Rayner as Tyke, Henry Grant as Old Man, Helen Hale as Mrs. St. Clair, Lucreza Hill as Julia, Jane Coveney as Mrs. Ferment, Miss Johnstone as Mrs. Nicely/ **St. James's**, Nov. 1867, with Henry Irving.

SCHOOLBOY FROLICS// F 1a// n.a.// **Princess's**, Jan. 1847, with Mr. Granby as Sir Gabriel, James Vining as Capt. Masterton, Miss Marshall as Albert, Samuel Cowell as Wildgoose, Mrs. H. Hughes as Clara, Miss E. Honner as Matilda, Miss Somers as Mary.

SCHOOLFELLOWS// D 2a// Douglas Jerrold// **Grecian**, June 1856, with Eaton O'Donnell as Cedar, Richard Phillips as Jasper, F. Charles as Horace, Mr. Hustleby as Nicholas, John Manning as Tom Drops, Jane Coveney as Esther, Ellen Hale as Marion, Amelie Conquest as Phillis.

SCHOOLMASTER OF LYNN, THE// D 3a// n.a.// **Marylebone**, Aug. 1879.

SCHOOLMISTRESS, THE// F 3a// Arthur Wing Pinero// **Court**, Mar. 1886, with Arthur Cecil, John Clayton, Mrs. John Wood.

SCHRIFTEN, THE ONE-EYED PILOT// D// George Conquest & Henry Pettitt// **Grecian**, Apr. 1877.

SCORNFUL LADY, THE// C// Adap. by T. J. Serle fr Beaumont & Fletcher// **Marylebone**, Nov. 1847, with Mrs. Mary Warner, Frank Graham, George Vining, James Johnstone, Miss Huddart.

SCOTCH MIST, A// F 3a// Edwin Shepherd// **Vaudeville**, Nov. 1886.

SCOTTISH CHIEF, THE// D// n.a.// **Britannia**, Mar. 1866.

SCRAP OF PAPER, A// D 3a// Adap. by J. Palgrave Simpson fr F of Victorien Sardou, Les Pattes de Mouche// **St. James's**, Apr. 1861, with Alfred Wigan as Couramont, Samuel Emery as de la Glacier, Garston Belmore as Brisemouche, Henry Ashley as Anatole, Mr. Terry as Baptiste, Miss Herbert as Louise, Mrs. Alfred Wigan as Suzanne, Nelly Moore as Mathilde, Miss Rainforth as Zenobia, Mrs. Manders as Mme. Dupont/ Scenery by F. Lloyds & Walter Hann/ Music by Mr. Wallerstein/ **Court**, Mar. 1876, with W. H. Kendal, Mrs. Kendal, John Hare; Jan. 1897, with W. H. Kendal, Kate Pattison, Mrs. Kendal/ **St. James's**, Dec. 1883, with Herbert Waring as Sir John, W. H. Kendal as Col. Blake, John Hare as Dr. Penguin, D. G. Boucicault as Archie, Robert Cathcart as Thomas, Linda Dietz as Lady Ingram, Mrs. W. H. Kendal as Susan, Miss Webster as Lucy, Mrs. Gaston Murray as Mrs. Penguin, Ada Murray as Mrs. Perkins/ Scenery by W. Harford.

SCREW LOOSE, A// F 3a// Mark Melford// **Vaudeville**, Nov. 1893.

SCUTTLED SHIP, THE// D Pro & 5a// Dram. by Charles Reade fr novel of Charles Reade & Dion Boucicault// **Olympic**, Apr. 1877, with Mr. Bauer as Wardlaw, Johnston Forbes Robertson as Arthur, Mr. Raiemond as Penfold, Henry Neville as Rev. Robert Penfold, Mrs. Seymour as Nancy, W. Avondale as Gen. Rolleston, Robert Pateman as Wylie, Bella Pateman as Helen, Agnes Bennett as Sarah.

SEA, THE// D 2a// C. A. Somerset// **Olympic**, May 1842, with Mr. Halford as Capt. Mandeville, Mr. Walton as Capt. Sturdy, Charles Baker as Harry Helm, Walter Searle as O'Trott, Mr. Hartland as Kohrek, Mr. Ross as Dr. Poultice, Miss Mitchell as Mary, Mrs. Granby as Margery.

SEA AND LAND// D 3a// Mark Lemon// **Adelphi**, May 1852, with Henry Hughes as Sir Thomas, O. Smith as Crouch, J. Worrell as Maj. Brownlow, Edward Wright as Poppy, Paul Bedford as Potts, William Cullenford as Davy, C. J. Smith as Will, Samuel Emery as Ned Bradley, Ellen Chaplin as Miss Burton, Mrs. Keeley as Wild Meg, Kathleen Fitzwilliam as Mary Thorncliffe/ Scenery by Pitt & Turner/ Music by Alfred Mellon/ Machines by Mr. Cooper/ **Sad. Wells**, May 1855, with Mrs. Keeley as Wild Meg, E. F. Edgar as Crouch, Frederick Moreland as Maj. Brownlow, Mr. Barrett as Burton, James Rogers as Mr. Poppy, W. Shalders as Potts, George Fisher as David, Robert Soutar as Will, Henry Butler as Bradley, Miss Cleveland as Miss Burton, Kate Kelly as Mary, Mrs. Leman Rede as Mrs. Blake.

SEA CAPTAIN, THE; OR, THE BIRTHRIGHT// D 5a// Edward Bulwer-Lytton// **Haymarket**, Oct. 1839, with John Webster as Lord Ashdale, Robert Strickland as Sir Maurice, W. C. Macready as Norman, Henry Howe as Falkner, O. Smith as Gaussen, Samuel Phelps as Onslow, Mrs. Mary Warner as Lady Arundel, Helen Faucit as Violet, Mrs. W. Clifford as Prudence/ Scenery by Phillips & Morris.

SEA DEVIL, THE; OR, THE FREEBOOTER'S BOY// D// n.a.// **Sad. Wells**, Dec. 1839, with Mr. Cathcart as D'Orville, Mr. Williams as Duke de Lisle, Mr. Elvin as Capt. Fabio, Henry Hall as Sabotte, Mr. Dry as Jacques, J. W. Collier as Ralph, Mr. Aldridge as Peter, Charles Montgomery as Francois, Mrs. Robert Honner as Paul, Miss Richardson as Eugenia, Mrs. J. F. Saville as Pauline, Miss Pincott as Jacqueline, Miss Cooke as Marguerite, Mrs. Morgan as Annette.

SEA FLOWER, THE// Play 4a// Arthur Law// **Comedy**, Mar. 1898.

SEA GULLS// F// Arthur Maltby & Frank Stainforth// **Royalty**, Aug. 1869.

SEA IS ENGLAND'S GLORY, THE// D// Frederick Marchant// **Britannia**, Sept. 1875.

SEA KING'S VOW, THE; OR, A STRUGGLE FOR LIBERTY// D 3a// Edward Stirling// **Surrey**, Feb. 1846.

SEA OF ICE, THE; OR, THE ORPHAN OF THE FROZEN SEA (also subt., The Wild Flower of Mexico)// D// T. W. Robertson// **Grecian**, Apr. 1867 (in 4a), with William James as Capt. de Lascours, Alfred Rayner as Carlos, Samuel Perfitt as Medoc, John Manning as Barabas, Lizzie Mandelbert as Louise and Ogarita, Henry Grant as de Brienne, Mrs. Atkinson as Countess de Thoringe, Alice Denvil as Diane/ **Sad. Wells**, Apr. 1867 (in 5a), with J. L. Warner as Capt. de Lascours, J. H. Slater as Carlos, Mr. Hamilton as Pacombe, R. Norman as Medoc, Mr. Ewing as Castille, Walter Lacy as Boufflard, J. W. Lawrence as Souri, John Rouse as Barabas, Alice Marriott as Louise and Ogarita, Miss Levettez as Marie, Mrs. J. F. Saville as Countess.

SEALED TO SILENCE// D 4a// Dram. by F. M. Bussy & H. M. Holles fr novel of F. Freeland & S. Norton// **Strand**, Apr. 1896.

SEATS OF THE MIGHTY, THE// D Pro & 3a// Dram. by Gilbert Parker fr his own novel// **Her Majesty's**, Apr. 1897.

SECOND IN COMMAND// C 4a// Robert Marshall// **Haymarket**, Nov. 1900, with Allan Aynesworth as Anstruther, Cyril Maude as Bingham, Herbert Sleath as Mannering, G. M. Graham as Barker, H. G. Oughterson as Medenham, G. A. Trollope as Hartopp, A. Vane-Tempest as Carstairs, Sybil Carlisle as Muriel, Fanny Coleman as Lady Harburgh, Muriel Beaumont as Norah.

SECOND LOVE// C 3a// J. Palgrave Simpson// **Haymarket**, Aug. 1856, with J. B. Buckstone as Thornhill, Henry Howe as Capt. Dangerfield, Henry Compton as Hawbuck, Miss Reynolds as Ellinor, Miss M. Oliver as Mildred, Mrs. Edward Fitzwilliam as Lucy/ Scenery by William Callcott, George Morris & John O'Conner/ Machines by Oliver Wales.

SECOND MRS. TANQUERAY, THE// Play 4a// Arthur Wing Pinero// **St. James's**, May 1893, with George Alexander as Tanqueray, A. Vane Tempest as Orreyed, Ben Webster as Capt. Ardale, Cyril Maude as Drummle, Nutcombe Gould as Misquith, Murray Hathorn as Jayne, Edith Chester as Lady Orreyed, Amy Roselle as Mrs. Cortleyon, Mrs. Patrick Campbell as Paula, Maude Millet as Ellean/ Scenery by Walter Hann & H. P. Hall/ **Royalty**, Sept. 1901.

SECOND SIGHT; OR, THE TWO DROVERS// D// n.a.// **Sad. Wells**, Aug. 1840, with Alfred Rayner as Wakefield, Henry Hall as McCombeck, Mr. Dry as Morrison, Mr. Aldridge as Heskitt, J. B. Hill as Ireby, Mr. Richardson as Dumpkin, Miss Richardson as Elspet, Mrs. Richard Barnett as Martha, Miss Cocke as Mrs. Heskitt.

SECOND THOUGHTS// C 1a// J. C. Herbert// **Court**, Apr. 1874.

SECOND TO NONE// D// n.a.// **Standard**, Nov. 1864.

SECRET, A// Ca.// Adap. by Constance Beerbohm fr F// **St. Geo. Hall**, June 1888.

SECRET, THE (also subt. Hole in the Wall)// F 1a// n.a.// **Grecian**, July 1844, with Henry Horncastle as Dupuis, Edwin Dixon as Valeri, Frederick Robson as Thomas, Mr. Glennaire as Porter, Annette Mears as Cecile, Ellen Crisp as Angelica; June 1863, with William James as Dupuis, George Gillett as Valeri, Charles Rice as Thomas, F. Cranford as Porter, Mrs. Charles Dillon as Mrs. Dupuis, Ellen Hale as Angelica/ **Olympic**, Mar. 1844, with Robert Roxby as Dupuis, Henry Bedford as Moses, F. Burton as Valaire, Miss Fitzjames as Mrs. Dupuis, Miss Fielding as Angelica/ **Drury Lane**, Nov. 1864, with Charles Vandenhoff as Dupuis, Mr. Bennoe [sic] as Valere, S. Johnson as Thomas, Miss Emmeline Montague as Mme. Dupuis, Miss A. Bourke as Angelica/ **Princess's**, Feb. 1869, with C. H. Fenton as Dupuis, Alfred Tapping as Valare, William Holston as Thomas, Mr. Chapman as Porter, Emma Barnett as Cecile, Miss Kemp as Angelica/ **Sad. Wells**, Sept. 1882, with J. E. Kellerd as Dupuis, Mr. Gregory as Valere, Mr. Williams as Porter, Lizzie Lilly as Mrs. Dupuis, Helen Grahame as Angelina.

SECRET AGENT, THE// F 2a// Adap. fr G by J. Stirling Coyne// **Haymarket**, Mar. 1855, with Henry Howe as Duke Victor, J. B. Buckstone as Count Steinhausen, Henry Compton as Baron Standbach, William Farren as Count Oscar, Mrs. Poynter as Dowager Duchess, Caroline White as Ernestine, Ellen Chaplin as Nettchen/ Scenery by William Callcott, George Morris & John O'Conner.

SECRET AGREEMENT, A// C Pro & 4a// Edmund Gregory// **Novelty**, July 1886.

SECRET FOE, A// D 4a// J. A. Stevens// **Opera Comique**, Aug. 1887.

SECRET LOVE; OR, THE MAIDEN QUEEN// T// John Dryden// **Court**, Jan. 1886, with W. T. Lovell, Bernard Gould, Miss Webster, Rose Dearing.

SECRET OF A LIFE, A// D 4a// Arthur Williams & George Roberts// **Grand**, Nov. 1886.

SECRET OF THE KEEP, THE// C// Cecil Raleigh// **Garrick**, Sept. 1898.

SECRET SERVICE// D 2a// J. R. Planché// **Cov. Garden**, Mar. 1840, with Mr. Cooper as Fouché, Charles Diddear as Desaunais, William Farren as Perrin, Mr. Fitzjames as de Crussac, James Bland as Bernard, Miss Lee as Thérese/ **Olympic**, Sept. 1860 (as comedy), with Frederick Robson as Fouché, Horace Wigan as Desaunais, Mr. Addison as Perrin, Gaston Murray as de Crussac, W. Gordon as Bernard, Miss Hughes as Therese/ **St. James's**, May 1871, with Fanny Brough as Therese, William Farren Jr. as Perrin, Alfred Young as Fouché, Lionel Brough as Desaunais, Gaston Murray as de Crussac, Frederick Mervin as Bernard, Charles Otley as Alphonse.

SECRET SERVICE// D 4a// William Gillette// **Terry's**, May 1895/ **Adelphi**, May 1897, with Joseph Brennan as Gen. Randolph, Ida Waterman as Mrs. Varney, Blanche Walsh as Edith, Henry Woodruff as Wilfred, Odette Tyler as Caroline, William Gillette as Lewis Dumont, M. L. Alsop as Henry, Campbell Gollan as Arrelsford, Ethel Barrymore as Miss Kittridge, Francis Neilson as Lt. Maxwell/ Music by William Furst.

SECRETARY, THE// Play// Dram. by J. Sheridan Knowles fr novel of H. P. Grattan// **Drury Lane**, Apr. 1843, with John Ryder as Wiliam III, George Bennett as Gaveston, Samuel Phelps as Byerdale, Mr. Waldron as Sunbury, Charles Hudson as Sherbrooke, Frank Graham as Sir George, W. C. Macready as Col. Green, James Anderson as Brown, George Ellis as Harrison, Charles Selby as Armstrong, Helen Faucit as Lady Laura, Mrs. Alfred Wigan as Emmeline.

SECRETS OF THE POLICE// D 4a// Mark Melford// **Surrey**, Nov. 1886.

SECRETS OF WAR// F 1a// n.a.// **Astley's**, Sept. 1855, with C. Shaw as Hugh Neville, W. Milborne as Hal, J. W. Anson as Thimblewell, Mrs. William Dowton as Maud, Mrs. J. W. Anson as Letty.

SECRETS WORTH KNOWING// C// Thomas Morton// **Haymarket**, May 1844, with Henry Howe as Greville, Mr. Tilbury as Undermine, Mr. Stuart as Egerton, C. J. Mathews as Rostrum, William Strickland as April, J. B. Buckstone as Plethora, William Farren as Rue, Mrs. Edwin Yarnold as Mrs. Greville, Julia Bennett as Rose, Mrs. Julia Glover as Sally/ **Sad. Wells**, Sept. 1851, with Frederic Robinson as Greville, Henry Mellon as Egerton, WilliamHoskins as Rostrum, J. W. Ray as Undermine, Mr. Barrett as April, F. Younge as Plethora, Mr. Williams as Rue, Mrs. Barrett as Mrs. Greville, Lucy Rafter as Rose, Mrs. Henry Marston as Sally.

SEDGEMOOR// Play 4a// W. G. & F. C. Wills// **Sad. Wells**, Aug. 1881, with R. P. Steele, H. J. Barrett, Miss C. Robinson, Marie de Grey.

SEE SAW// C 3a// George Capel & J. R. Phillips// **Terry's**, Feb. 1889.

SEE SAW, MARGERY DAW// E. L. Blanchard// **Drury Lane**, Dec. 1856.

SEEING FROU-FROU// C 1a// Adap. fr F by Alfred Murray// **Globe**, June 1881, with Charles Ashford as Perkins, George Temple as Pribble, Miss Deacon as Talboys, Miss K. Graham as Littlego, J. Anderson as Bodger, H. Tempest as Vavasour, Miss Avondale as Mrs. Pribble, Nellie Maxwell as Mrs. Perkins, Miss F. Thornton as Kate Bodger.

SELF// D 4a// Adap. by John Oxenford & Horace Wigan fr F of Victorien Sardou, Les Diables Noirs// **Mirror**, Sept. 1875, with John Clayton, Rose Coghlan, Horace Wigan.

SELF; OR, MAN'S INHUMANITY// D 5a//

Brian McCullough// **Britannia**, July 1886.

SELF-ACCUSATION; OR, A BROTHER'S LOVE// D 2a// Mark Lemon// **Eng. Opera House** (Lyceum), Sept. 1838, with Mr. Halford as Justice Kindly, A. Brindal as Edward, Mr. Howell as Dawson, Mr. Baker as Brandon, HenryCompton as Joe Raby, Lavinia Melville as Mary Brandon, Miss Poole as Patty/ **Sad. Wells**, Nov. 1843, with Mr. Lamb as Justice Kindly, C. J. Bird as Howard, C. J. Smith as Dawson, Mr. Coreno as Raby, Henry Marston as Brandon, W. H. Williams as Darvill, Mr. Williams as Dyke, Caroline Rankley as Mary, Mrs. Richard Barnett as Patty.

SELF AND LADY// F 3a// Adap. fr F of Pierre Decourcelle// **Vaudeville**, Sept. 1900.

SELF MADE// D 3a// George Vining// **St. James's**, Jan. 1862, with W. H. Stephens as de Boulonne, Frederick Dewar as Baron de Tréval, F. Charles as Vicompte de Morlière, George Vining as St. Georges, Mr. Terry as Plato, Garston Belmore as Julien, Miss Herbert as Countess de Presle, Miss A. St. Clair as Fanchette, Miss Willard as Marie/ Scenery by F. Lloyds/ Music by Mr. Wallerstein.

SELFISHNESS// D// n.a.// **City of London**, Feb. 1856.

SEMPSTRESS, THE// D 2a// Mark Lemon// **Haymarket**, May 1844, with William Strickland as Goldring, Henry Howe as Gusset, J. B. Buckstone as Bobbin, Henry Holl as Debit, Mr. Stuart as Plainword, Priscilla Horton as Mercy and Mary, Julia Bennett as Lucy, Mrs. Stanley as Mrs. Goodheart.

SENATOR, THE// C 4a// D. D. Lloyd & Sidney Rosenfeld// **Elephant & Castle**, Oct. 1889.

SEND HER VICTORIOUS// D 4a// Alt. & rev. by Sutton Vane fr his D, For England// **Pavilion**, Nov. 1899.

SEND THIRTY STAMPS// F 1a// J. K. Angus// **Sad. Wells**, Apr. 1884, with C. H. Kenney as Vincent, F. Hamilton Knight as Timbs, Nellie Davis as Polly.

SENT TO THE TOWER// F 1a// J. Maddison Morton// **Princess's**, Oct. 1850, with John Pritt Harley as Puddyfoot, Robert Keeley as Banks.

SENTENCED TO DEATH// D 4a// George Conquest & Henry Pettitt// **Grecian**, Oct. 1875.

SENTIMENTALIST, THE// Play Pro & 4a// H. V. Esmond// **Duke of York's**, Oct. 1901.

SENTINEL, THE// C 1a// J. Maddison Morton// **Olympic**, Feb. 1837, with Charles Mathews, James Vining, Frank Matthews, Charles Selby, Mme. Vestris/ **Lyceum**, Oct. 1849, with Frank Matthews as King Frederick William, John Parselle as Prince Frederick, Mr. Granby as Vonderbushel, C. J. Mathews as Maximilian Schloppsen, Kathleen Fitzwilliam as Linda/ **Olympic**, Feb. 1861, with Horace Wigan as King Frederick, Walter Gordon as Prince Frederick, George Cooke as Vonderbushel, Frederic Robinson as Schloppsen, Louise Keeley as Linda.

SENTINEL OF THE ALMA, THE// C// Samuel Lover// **Haymarket**, Nov. 1854, with William Cullenford as Col. Steel, William Farren as Capt. Fitzgerald, Charles Hudson as Tim, Mr. Woodfield as Capt. le Vaillant, Henry Compton as Prince Mendaciokoff, Mr. Rogers as Gen. Bragadociokoff, Mr. Edwards as Maj. Scribbleowski, Mrs. Coe as Mme. Tremolowski, Miss E. Woulds as Mme. Scamperoffski, Ellen Chaplin as Katharine/ Scenery by George Morris & John O'Conner, Machines by Oliver Wales/ Music by Edward Fitzwilliam.

SEPARATE MAINTAINANCE, THE// F 1a// J. Stirling Coyne// **Haymarket**, Mar. 1849, with Robert Keeley as Pennipother, Mrs. Keeley as Mrs. Pennipother, Mrs. Humby as Jane, Miss E. Messent as Lord Brompton, Mrs. L. S. Buckingham as Sir Toppleton, Miss Duval as Lipscombe, Miss Woulds as Capt. Featheredge.

SEPARATION AND REPARATION// C// Thomas Morton// **Haymarket**, July 1837, with Frederick Vining as Baron Malamour, William Farren as Von Grotius, John Webster as Col. Esplanade, Benjamin Webster as Poppinoff, Mrs. Nisbett as Angelique, Mrs. Tayleure as Mme. Gilderland.

SEQUEL, THE// Play 1a// L. N. Parker// **Vaudeville**, July 1891.

SERF, THE; OR, LOVE LEVELS ALL// D 3a// Tom Taylor// **Olympic**, 1865, with E. F. Edgar as Prince Khovalenski, George Vincent as Count Karateff, Henry Neville as Khorvich, Horace Wigan as Khor, Charles Coghlan as Mistigris, John Maclean as Steinhardt, Harwood Cooper as Chasseur, Kate Terry as Countess de Mauléon, Mrs. Stephens as Princess Bariatinski, Miss Lindley as Acoulina.

SERGE PANINE// Play 5a// Adap. by J. H. Thorp fr F of Georges Ohnet// **Gaiety**, June 1883/ **Avenue**, June 1891.

SERGEANT'S WEDDING, THE// C 1a// T. E. Wilks// **Prince's**, Nov. 1840/ **Victoria**, May 1848, with Walter Searle as Frederick the Great, G. F. Forman as Gen. Omelette, T. H. Higgie as Sgt. Orloff, J. Howard as Poomple, Miss Burroughcliffe as Tietzia, Mrs. George Lee as Katrina, Mrs. Cooke as Frow Dumnicks/ **Olympic**, Jan. 1876, with Alfred Nelson as Frederick II of Prussia, John Vollaire as Gen. Omelette, Mr. Darley as Sgt. Orloff, Mr. St. Alban as Poomple, Mr. Westall as Sgt. Krautz, Mrs. Stephens as Frow Dumnicke, Miss Hazleton as Teltzia, Nellie Phillips as Katrina.

SERGEANT'S WIFE, THE// D 2a// S. J. Arnold// **Victoria**, Sept. 1837, with Frank Matthews as Old Cartouch, Charles Perkins as Dennis, Paul Bedford as Gaspard, James Bland as Sergeant, Mr. Conner as Sgt. Louis/ **Lyceum**, Mar. 1860, with T. Lyon as Old Cartouch, Frederick Villiers as Sgt. Cartouch, James

Vining as Dennis, James Johnstone as Gaspard, J. Rouse as Robin, Mr. Forrester as Sgt. Louis, Mme. Celeste as Lisette, Mrs. Keeley as Margot.

SERIOUS FAMILY, THE// C 3a// Adap. fr F, Le Mari à la Compagne// **Haymarket**, Oct. 1849, with Benjamin Webster as Torrens, James Wallack as Capt. Maguire, Henry Vandenhoff as Vincent, J. B. Buckstone as Sleek, Mrs. W. Clifford as Lady Creamley, Miss Reynolds as Mrs. Torrens, Mrs. L. S. Buckingham as Emma, Mrs. Fitzwilliam as Mrs. Delmaine, Mrs. Caulfield as Graham/ Scenery by Mr. Johnstone & George Morris/ Machines by F. Heselton; July 1863, with William Farren as Torrens, Henry Howe as Capt. Maguire, Walter Gordon as Vincent, Henry Compton as Sleek, Mrs. Wilkins as Lady Creamly, Louisa Angel as Mrs. Torrens, Mrs. Edward Fitzwilliam as Mrs. Delamaine, Blanche Percy as Emma/ **St. James's**, 1867, with Henry Irving.

SERPENT OF THE NILE, THE; OR, THE BATTLE OF ACTIUM// D 2a// Edward Stirling// **Adelphi**, Apr. 1840, with Mr. Lyon, Paul Bedford, J. F. Saville, Mr. Freeborn, George Maynard, E. H. Butler, Mr. Wilkinson, J. B. Buckstone, William Cullenford, Caroline Darling, Mrs. Fosbroke, Mrs. Keeley.

SERPENT ON THE HEARTH, THE// D// Thomas Mead// **Grecian**, Aug. 1861, with Thomas Mead as Count de Lugarto, R. H. Lingham as De Rochgune, Mr. Jackson as Gonrean, Walter Holland as de Kranmont, William James as de Lancy, Alfred Rayner as Secherin, John Manning as Fritz, Jane Coveney as Mathilde, Mrs. Charles Dillon as Ursula, Lucreza Hill as Mme. de Condeau.

SERPENT ON THE HEARTH, THE// D 3a// J. Palgrave Simpson// **Adelphi**, Aug. 1869, with Mr. Stuart as Sir Simeon, Mr. Dalton as Capt. Trevor, W. H. Eburne as Claude, C. H. Stephenson as Dr. Mildmay, Richard Phillips as Barak, Edward Atkins as Mark, Robert Romer as Slobberiboski, Mrs. Leigh Murray as Lady Sykes, Margaret Eburne as Marie, Mrs. Stoker as Barbara, Eliza Johnstone as Polly/ Scenery by Hawes Craven & Maugham/ Machines by Edward Charker/ Gas by G. Bastard/ Prod. by R. Phillips/ **Sad. Wells**, Aug. 1869, with the Adelphi cast.

SERPENT'S COIL, THE// D 5a// E. H. Mitchelson & C. H. Longden// **Surrey**, June 1896.

SERVANT OR SUITOR// F// n.a.// **Royalty**, May 1872.

SERVE HIM RIGHT!// C 2a// C. J. Mathews & Morris Barnett// **Lyceum**, Oct. 1850, with Frank Matthews as Shuttleworth, C. J. Mathews as Barry Bellamy, Robert Roxby as Greenfinch, William Suter as Hobbs, Mrs. Charles Horn as Mrs. Shuttleworth, Miss H. Oliver as Julia, Mrs. Frank Matthews as Mrs. Charity Smith.

SERVING THE QUEEN// D 5a// Herbert Leonard// **Surrey**, Oct. 1898.

SETH GREEN; OR, STRUCK OIL AT LAST// D// n.a.// **Elephant & Castle**, Oct. 1884.

SETTLED OUT OF COURT// C 4a// Estelle Burney// **Globe**, June 1897.

SETTLING DAY// Play 4a// F. A. Scudamore// **Surrey**, June 1895.

SETTLING DAY: A STORY OF THE TIME// Play 5a// Tom Taylor// **Olympic**, Mar. 1865, with Henry Neville as Markland, Horace Wigan as Maiklam, George Vincent as Frank, Charles Coghlan as Harrington, John Maclean as Molesworth, Robert Soutar as Rocket, Harwood Cooper as Laxton, D. Evans as Fermor, Kate Terry as Mrs. Markland, Lydia Foote as Miss Hargrave, Mrs. Leigh Murray as Mrs. Vernon, Miss Dacy [Daly?] as Miss Vernon/ Scenery by Hawes Craven/ Machines by Mr. Chapman, Prod. by Horace Wigan.

SEVEN MAIDS OF MUNICH, THE; OR, THE GHOST'S TOWER// C// G. H. Rodwell// **Princess's**, Jan. 1847, with Charles Fisher as Col. Bertrand, Augustus Harris as Capt. D'Armincourt, Mr. Delavanti as Capt. Bellejambe, Mr. Wynn as Lt. Adolphe, Henry Compton as Grosdos, Mr. Walton as Baron Bristlebach, S. Smith as Gaspard, Mrs. Fosbroke as Mme. Groutz, Miss Marshall as Uriel, Sara Flower as Ernestine, Miss Rourke as Eva, Miss E. Honner as Marian, Louisa Marshall as Carlotta, Miss Laporte as Mathilde.

SEVEN POOR TRAVELLERS, THE// Pro & 2a// Dram. by C. Duval fr story of Charles Dickens// **Grecian**, Mar. 1855, with Henry Grant as Philanthropist, Basil Potter as Outcast and as Davager, John Manning as the Pedlar, Eaton O'Donnell as Fox, Richard Phillips as Gatcliff, John Manning as Mug, F. Charles as Cool, Jane Coveney as Mrs. Gatcliff, Maria Simpson as Ellen, Harriet Coveney as Prudence.

SEVEN SINS; OR, PASSION'S PARADISE// D 4a// George Conquest & Paul Meritt// **Grecian**, Aug. 1874.

SEVEN YEARS' SECRET, THE// D 2a// C. H. Hazlewood// **Britannia**, Oct. 1870.

SEVEN YEARS AGO// D// H. P. Grattan// **Grecian**, Mar. 1879.

SEVENTY AND SEVENTEEN// C// Charles Dance// **Haymarket**, Jan. 1838, with Mrs. Honey as Rose, Mrs. Young as Phillis, T. Green as Capt. Vivid, Mr. Vale as Stephen/ **Sad. Wells**, July 1839, with John Webster as Capt. Vivid, Mr. Conquest as Stephen, Mrs. Honey in 3 char. parts, Miss Pincott as Phillis.

SEVERINE// Play// Adap. fr F of Alexandre Dumas fils, La Princesse Georges// **Gaiety**, May 1885.

SEWING MACHINE ON EASY TERMS, A// F// H. Hayman// **Elephant & Castle**, Sept. 1876.

SEXTON OF COLOGNE, THE; OR, THE

BURGOMASTER'S DAUGHTER// D 2a// Edward Fitzball// **Cov. Garden**, Apr. 1837, with George Bennett as Ibraim, John Pritchard as Laban, J. Worrell as Simeon, Benjamin Webster as Bolt, John Webster as Theodore, Mr. Thompson as Denderweldt, Eliza Vincent as Adelhaide.

SHADE, THE; OR, BLOOD FOR BLOOD// D// C. P. Thompson// **Olympic**, May 1842, with Mr. Hambleton as Rousseau, Mr. Thompson as Blondel, Mr. Watson as Spirit, Mr. Boyd as Theodore, Mr. Harold as Dessein, Mr. Rogers as La Fleur, Mrs. Harold as Eugenia, Mrs. Watson as Therese, Miss Watson as Louise.

SHADES OF NIGHT, THE// Play 1a// Robert Marshall// **Lyceum**, Mar. 1896.

SHADOW DANCE, THE// D 4a// Adap. by Benjamin Landeck fr F of Victor Hugo, Notre Dame de Paris// **Grand**, Oct. 1901/ **Princess's**, Nov. 1901.

SHADOW OF DEATH, THE// D// J. R. Walrond// **Victoria**, Sept. 1876.

SHADOW OF THE SWORD, THE// D 5a// Robert Buchanan// **Olympic**, Apr. 1882, with Brittain Booth as Pipriac, John Collier as Corp. Derval, H. Dalton as Gildas Derval, Henry George as Arfoll, Theodore Balfour as Grallon, Harry Dundas as Gwenfern, John Coleman as Rohan, Robertha Erskine as Widow Gwenfern, Clarissa Ash as Guinevere, Margaret Young as Marcelle/ Scenery by George Tweddell, M. Gompertz, Charles Brew & Charles Maltby/ Music by Ferdinand Kessler/ Prod. by John Coleman.

SHADOW OF WRONG, THE; OR, THREAT FOR THREAT// D 3a// George Conquest// **Grecian**, Feb. 1863, with J. Jackson as George Duverel, Thomas Mead as Jerome Duverel, Walter Holland as Charles, Alfred Rayner as Eugene, William James as Etienne, Miss Johnstone as Gertrude, Mrs. Charles Dillon as Marie.

SHADOW ON THE HEARTH, THE// D// C. H. Hazlewood// **Britannia**, June 1874.

SHADOW-TREE SHAFT// D 3a// T. W. Robertson// **Princess's**, Feb. 1867, with Charles Verner as Kenyon, George Vining as Sampson, Henry Forrester as Woodyat, Frederick Villiers as Richard, J. G. Shore as Capt. Mildmay, Henry Mellon as Thorniwork, Robert Cathcart as Moddershall, Miss Montague as Lady Kenyon, Katherine Rogers as Katie/ Scenery by F. Lloyds/ Music by King Hall, Machines by R. E. Warton/ Prod. by T. W. Robertson.

SHADOWS// D Pro & 4a// Charles Young// **Princess's**, May 1871, with Henry Dalton as Charles II and as Auberon, Charles Coghlan as Stephen Iredell and as Martin Iredell, John Nelson as Flemyng and as Col. Marwood, Mrs. Hermann Vezin as Lady Inez and as Beatrice, Alfred Neldon as Rochfort, Mr. Herbert as Farquhar, Alice Austin as Lady Etherege/ Mise en scene by John Cormack/ Music by J. M. Ball.

SHADOWS OF A GREAT CITY// D 5a// Joseph Jefferson & L. R. Shewell// **Princess's**, July 1887, with J. H. Barnes as Cooper, J. L. Shine as Farren, Harry Parker as Nathan, W. L. Abingdon as Benson, Forbes Dawson as Arkwright, Donald Robertson as Hammond, T. C. Dwyer as Downey, Lizzie Fletcher as Annie, Mary Rorke as Helen, Cicely Richards as Biddy, Alice Chandos as Mrs. Higgins/ Scenery by R. C. Durant.

SHADOWS OF CRIME// D// n.a.// **Surrey**, Feb. 1876.

SHADOWS OF LIFE; OR, THE HAND OF FATE// D 4a// Arthur Shirley// **Elephant & Castle**, Sept. 1887.

SHADOWS ON THE BLIND// F 3a// J. H. Darnley & Harry Bruce// **Terry's**, Apr. 1898.

SHADRAGH, THE HUNCHBACK// D// H. W. Williamson// **Elephant & Castle**, July 1880.

SHAKE HANDS// F 1a// Leicester Buckingham// **St. James's**, May 1864, with Henry Ashley as Sir Arthur, John Clarke as Fidget, J. Johnstone as Bullion, Fanny Josephs as Emma, Patti Josephs as Susan.

SHAKESPEARE// C 4a// E. E. Greville// **Globe**, June 1892, with T. B. Thalberg as Shakespeare, Henry Vernon as John Shakespeare, Matthew Brodie as Tom Green, G. Lyon-Leith as Ben Jonson, Douglas Gordon as Gabriel Spencer, Hugh Warren as Hemynge, Charles Medwin as Southampton, Arthur Helmore as Sir Thomas Lucy, Robert Soutar as Giles, Mrs. Dion Boucicault as Mary Shakespeare, Mary Keegan as Elizabeth, Beatrice Selwyn as Queen Elizabeth, Miss Norreys as Anne Hathaway.

SHALL WE FORGIVE HER?// D 5a// Frank Harvey// **Adelphi**, June 1894, with Fred Terry as Oliver West, F. H. Macklin as Elsworth, Charles Dalton as Garth, Julian Cross as McKerrow, Herbert Flemming as Stapleton, Julia Neilson as Grace, Mrs. Henry Leigh as Aunt Martha, Ada Neilson as Joanna, Mabel Hardinge as Nellie/ Scenery by Bruce Smith/ Music by Edward Jones/ Prod. by H. H. Vincent.

SHALL WE REMEMBER?// D 1a// W. Turnbull & R. C. Ellis// **St. Geo. Hall**, Oct. 1899.

SHAME// D 1a// Alice Chapin & E. H. Oliphant// **Vaudeville**, July 1892.

SHAMEFUL BEHAVIOUR// C 2a// A. C. Troughton// **Strand**, Nov. 1859, with Mr. Swanborough, H. J. Turner, Miss M. Oliver.

SHAMROCK AND THE ROSE, THE// D 4a// Walter Reynolds// **Grand**, Sept. 1892.

SHAMROCK OF IRELAND, THE// D 3a// J. B. Howe// **Britannia**, May 1867.

SHAMUS-NA-LENA; OR, THE SPEIDHOR// D 4a// Edward Towers// **Pavilion**, Oct. 1876.

SHAMUS O'BRIEN; OR, THE BOULD BOY OF GLENGALL// D 4a// Fred Maeder & C. Vernon// **West London**, Apr. 1897.

SHANK'S MARE// F// W. A. Vicars// **Duke's**, Feb. 1878.

SHARPS AND FLATS; OR, THE RACECOURSE OF LIFE// D 3a// Frederick Marchant// **Britannia**, Aug. 1870.

SHAUGHRAUN, THE// D 4a// Dion Boucicault// **Drury Lane**, Sept. 1875, with William Terriss as Capt. Molyneux, J. B. Howard as Ffolliott, David Fisher as Fr. Dolan, Henry Sinclair as Kinchela, Shiel Barry as Duff, Dion Boucicault as Conn, Ernest Travers as Sgt. Jones, Rose Leclercq as Claire, Marie Dalton as Arte, Mrs. Dion Boucicault (Agnes Robertson) as Moya, Miss Everard as Mrs. O'Kelly, Mrs. J. Carter as Bridget/ Scenery by William Beverley/ **Adelphi**, Dec. 1875, with William Terriss as Molineux, Philip Day as Ffolliott, James Fernandez as Father Dolan, Samuel Emery as Corry, Shiel Barry as Harvey, Dion Boucicault as Conn, Ernest Travers as Sgt. Jones, Fanny Josephs as Claire, Lydia Foote as Arte, Cicely Nott as Mrs. O'Kelly, Mrs. Dion Boucicault as Moya/ Scenery by F. Lloyd & W. Hann/ Music by Edwin Ellis; Apr. 1880, with Henry Neville, James Fernandez, Robert Pateman, Dion Boucicault, Bella Pateman, Lydia Foote, Mrs. Alfred Mellon.

SHE// D Pro & 5a// Dram. by Edward Rose fr novel of Rider Haggard// **Haymarket**, May 1888/ New vers. by W. Sidney & Clotilde Graves, **Novelty**, May 1888/ **Gaiety**, Sept. 1888.

SHE STOOPS TO CONQUER; OR, THE MISTAKES OF A NIGHT// C 3a// Oliver Goldsmith// **Drury Lane**, Oct. 1837, with William Bennett as Sir Charles, J. S. Balls as Marlowe, William Dowton as Hardcastle, A. Brindal as Hastings, Henry Compton as Lumpkin, Mr. Hughes as Diggory, Mrs. C. Jones as Mrs. Hardcastle, Miss Charles as Miss Hardcastle, Miss Fitzwalter as Miss Neville/ **Sad. Wells**, Mar. 1842, with Mr. Aldridge as Sir Charles, John Webster as Marlow, Mr. Williams as Hardcastle, Mr. Moreton as Hastings, John Herbert as Lumpkin, Mr. Richardson as Diggory, Miss Cooke as Mrs. Hardcastle, Mrs. Robert Honner as Miss Hardcastle, Mrs. Richard Barnett as Miss Neville; Mar. 1859, with Mr. Cullenford as Sir Charles, Charles Seyton as Hastings, William Farren [Jr.] as Young Marlow, Mr. Barrett as Hardcastle, J. B. Buckstone as Lumpkin, Charles Fenton as Diggory, Mrs. Charles Young as Kate, Annie Ness as Miss Neville, Mrs. Barrett as Mrs. Hardcastle/ **Haymarket**, Sept. 1842, with William Farren as Hardcastle, Mr. Tilbury as Sir Charles, A. Brindal as Hastings, Mr. Vining as Young Marlow, Benjamin Webster as Lumpkin, Mrs. Julia Glover as Mrs. Hardcastle, Miss C. Conner as Miss Neville, Mrs. Nisbett as Miss Hardcastle; Dec. 1860, with W. H. Chippendale as Hardcastle, William Cullenford as Sir Charles, J. B. Buckstone as Lumpkin, Henry Howe as Young Marlowe, Edwin Villiers as Hastings, Fanny Stirling as Miss Hardcastle, Mrs. Poynter as Mrs. Hardcastle, Mrs. Edward Fitzwilliam as Miss Neville, Miss Henrade as Dolly; Nov. 1871, with W. H. Chippendale as Hardcastle, Edward Osborne as Sir Charles, Walter Gordon as Hastings, W. H. Kendal as Young Marlow, J. B. Buckstone as Lumpkin, Mrs. Chippendale as Mrs. Hardcastle, Madge Robertson (Mrs. Kendal) as Miss Hardcastle, Mrs. Edward Fitzwilliam as Miss Neville; Jan. 1900, with F. H. Tyler as Sir Charles, Cyril Maude as Hardcastle, Paul Arthur as Young Marlow, Graham Brown as Hastings, George Giddens as Lumpkin, Mary A. Victor as Mrs. Hardcastle, Winifred Emery as Miss Hardcastle, Beatrice Ferrar as Miss Neville/ **Princess's**, Oct. 1847, with Mr. Wynn as Sir Charles, John Gilbert as Hardcastle, James Vining as Young Marlow, Henry Compton as Lumpkin, Charles Fisher as Hastings, R. Hughes as Stingo, Samuel Cowell as Diggory, Emmeline Montague as Miss Hardcastle, Miss Villars as Miss Neville, Mrs. Selby as Mrs. Hardcastle/ **Olympic**, Dec. 1848, with H. J. Turner as Sir Charles, Mr. Harvey as Hardcastle, Leigh Murray as Young Marlow, Henry Compton as Lumpkin, John Howard as Hastings, C. Hale as Diggory, Mrs. Stirling as Miss Hardcastle, Mrs. England Young as Mrs. Hardcastle, Miss Acosta as Miss Neville; Apr. 1852, with George Cooke as Sir Charles, William Farren as Hardcastle, Henry Compton as Tony Lumpkin, Henry Farren as Young Marlow, William Farren Jr. as Hastings, Mrs. B. Bartlett as Mrs. Hardcastle, Mrs. Walter Lacy as Miss Hardcastle, Miss Fielding as Miss Neville/ **St. James's**, Oct. 1869, with Sophie Larkin as Mrs. Hardcastle, Louisa Herbert as Miss Hardcastle, Miss Henrade as Miss Neville, G. P. Grainger as Marlow, Mark Smith as Mr. Hardcastle, Barton Hill as Young Marlow, J. G. Shore as Hastings, Lionel Brough as Lumpkin, Gaston Murray as Stingo, A. W. Young as Diggory/ Scenery by Grieve, Lloyds, & O'Conner/ **Imperial**, Feb. 1879, with John Ryder, William Farren, Lionel Brough, Mrs. Stirling, Miss Litton/ **Globe**, Dec. 1881, with John Ryder as Hardcastle, C. Medwin as Sir Charles, Arthur Dacre as Young Marlow, G. W. Anson as Tony Lumpkin, Henry Hamilton as Hastings, Mrs. Stirling as Mrs. Hardcastle, Miss Litton as Miss Hardcastle, Ellen Meyrick as Miss Neville, Maria Harris as Lucy/ **Vaudeville**, Apr. 1890/ in vers. by Charles Wyndham, **Criterion**, May 1890/ **Terry's**, June 1898.

SHE WOULD AND SHE WOULD NOT; OR, THE KIND IMPOSTER// C 5a// Adap. by Colly Cibber fr Span// **Cov. Garden**, Sept. 1841, with William Farren as Don Manuel, Mr. Cooper as Don Philip, Walter Lacy as Don Octavio, John Pritt Harley as Trappanti, A. Brindal as Don Lewis, Drinkwater Meadows as Soto, John Collett as Corrigidore, Mr. Hughes as Alguazile, Louisa Nisbett as Hypolyta, Mrs. Walter Lacy as Flora, Miss Cooper as Rosara, Mrs. Orger as Viletta/ **Haymarket**, Nov. 1843, with William Strickland as Don Manuel, Henry Holl as Don Philip, A. Brindal as Don Octavio, Henry Howe as Don Lewis, Benjamin Webster as Trappanti, J. Worrell as Alguazil, Louisa Nisbett as Hypolita, Mrs. Edwin Yarnold as Rosara, Mrs. Julia Glover as Viletta, Julia Bennett as Flora; July 1868, with W. H.

Chippendale as Don Manuel, Henry Howe as Don Philip, W. H. Kendal as Don Octavio, Walter Gordon as Don Luis, J. B. Buckstone as Trappanti, Mr. Clark as Soto, P. White as Diego, Mr. Weathersby as Corrigidore, Madge Robertson as Hypolita, Ione Burke as Flora, Miss Dalton as Rosara, Mrs. Edward Fitzwilliam as Viletta/ **Sad. Wells**, Sept. 1849, with A. Younge as Don Manuel, Henry Marston as Don Phillip, G. K. Dickinson as Don Octavio, William Belford as Don Louis, William Hoskins as Trappanti, Miss Fitzpatrick as Hypolita, Miss T. Bassano as Rosara, Julia St. George as Flora, Mrs. G. Smith as Villetta; Mar. 1857, with William Belford as Don Philip, Mr. Haywell as Don Octavio, J. W. Ray as Don Manuel, Charles Seyton as Don Louis, Charles Fenton as Soto, Henry Marston as Trappanti, Emma Fitzpatrick as Hypolita, Jenny Marston as Flora, Miss C. Parkes as Rosara.

SHE WOULD AND HE WOULD NOT// C 2a// J. Maddison Morton// **St. James's**, Sept. 1862, with George Vining as Count di Villani, F. Charles as Ascanio, Frank Matthews as Baron di Pompolino, Garston Belmore as Spadillo, Mr. Cockrill as Majordomo, Miss Herbert as Marchioness di Villafranca, Clara St. Casse as Zinetta/ Scenery by F. Lloyds/ Music by J. H. Tully.

SHEEP IN WOLF'S CLOTHING, A// C 1a// Adap. by Tom Taylor fr F of Mme. de Girardin, Une Femme qui déteste son Mari// **Olympic**, Feb. 1862, with Mr. Addison as Col. Kirke, Mr. Leslie as Col. Churchill, George Vining as Jasper, George Cooke as Chedzoy, J. H. White as Corp. Flintoff, Mrs. Stirling as Anne, Mrs. Melfort as Dame Carew, Miss Conway as Sibyl, Miss Maskell as Keziah; Nov. 1865 with John Maclean as Col. Kirke, H. J. Montague as Col. Churchill, Robert Soutar as Chedzoy, Henry Neville as Carew, Harwood Cooper as Corp. Flintoff, Henry Rivers as Zoyland, Kate Terry as Anne, Mrs. Beauclerc as Dame Carew, Florence Terry as Sibyl, Ada Harland as Keziah/ **St. James's**, June 1864, with James Johnstone as Capt. Kirke, H. J. Montague as Col. Churchill, Frederic Robinson as Carew, John Clarke as Chedzoy, Mr. Branscombe as Corp. Flintoff, Mr. Smithson as Zoyland, Mrs. Stirling as Anne, Mrs. Stoker as Dame Carew, Miss Conran as Sibyl; 1881, with T. N. Wenman as Col. Kirke, Mr. Draycott as Churchill, W. H. Kendal as Carew, Mr. Denny as Chedzoy, Mr. Brandon as Flintoff, Robert Cathcart as Zoyland, Mrs. W. H. Kendal as Anne, Miss Cowle as Dame Carew, Miss Fenton as Sybil, Kate Phillips as Keziah/ Scenery by Gordon & Harford/ **Princess's**, Jan. 1876, with David Fisher as Col. Kirke, P. C. Beverley as Col. Churchill, J. H. Barnes as Carew, F. W. Irish as Chedzoy, Mr. Dormar as Corp. Flintoff, Mr. Warne as Zoyland, Rose Coghlan as Anne, Mrs. St. Henry as Dame Carew, Miss Brunton as Sibyl, Miss C. Brabant as Keziah/ **Lyceum**, Dec. 1883, with F. H. Macklin as Col. Kirke, Joseph Anderson as Col. Churchill, J. H. Barnes as Jasper Carew, F. W. Irish as Chedzoy, Mrs. F. H. Macklin (Blanche Henri) as Anne Carew, Mrs. J. F. Young as Dame Carew/ Music by Andrew Levey.

SHEPPARD (see Tom Sheppard)

SHERIFF OF THE COUNTY, THE// C 3a// R. B. Peake// **Haymarket**, Mar. 1845, with William Farren as Hollylodge, William Strickland as Smirker, Henry Holl as Capt. Oswald, A. Brindal as Ens. Tardigrade, J. B. Buckstone as Pansy, Henry Howe as Firedrake, J. W. Gough as Maj. Blandman, Mrs. Julia Glover as Mrs. Hollylodge, Mrs. W. Clifford as Lady Winkleworth, Mrs. Humby as Miss Crawley, Julia Bennett as Ellen, Mrs. L. S. Buckingham as Grace, Miss Telbin as Marian, Mrs. Stanley as Mrs. Benson, Mrs. Edwin Yarnold as Mrs. Forrester/ Scenery by George Morris; Mar. 1853, with Mr. Tilbury as Hollylodge, Mr. Rogers as Smirker, William Farren as Capt. Oswald, H. Corri as Ens. Tardigrade, J. B. Buckstone as Pansy, Henry Compton as Nonpareil, A. Payne as Firedrake, George Braid as Blandman, Mrs. Stanley as Mrs. Hollylodge, Mrs. Poynter as Lady Winkleworth, Amelia Vining as Grace, Eleanor Bromley as Marian, Ellen Chaplin as Miss Crawley, Louisa Howard as Ellen, Mrs. Coe as Mrs. Forrester, Miss A. Woulds as Mrs. Benson.

SHERLOCK HOLMES// D 4a// Dram. by William Gillette & Arthur Conan Doyle, fr Doyle's novel The Strange Case of Miss Faulkner// **Lyceum**, Sept. 1901.

SHE'S MINE FOR A THOUSAND// C 2a// W. J. [?] Lucas// **Grecian**, Oct. 1847, with Eaton O'Donnell as Earl of Woodfield, Richard Phillips as Viscount Erneston, John Webster as Lord Finikin, Edwin Dixon as Capt. Charge, Frederick Robson as Rubycorn, Annette Mears as Lady Helen, Ada Harcourt as Mabel.

SHIELD OF DAVID, THE// D// n.a.// **West London**, Apr. 1899.

SHILLING DAY AT THE EXHIBITION// F 1a// Andrew Halliday & William Brough// **Adelphi**, June 1862.

SHILLY-SHALLY// C 3a// Charles Reade & Anthony Trollope// **Gaiety**, Apr. 1872.

SHIP AHOY// D 3a// George Roberts// **Surrey**, Oct. 1874.

SHIP BOY, THE; OR, THE WHITE SLAVE OF GUADALOUPE// D 2a// n.a.// **Victoria**, June 1854, with T. E. Mills as Dumasse, Mr. Henderson as Lenoir, J. Howard as Franville, Charles Rice as Balancez, Annette Vincent as Julien, Alfred Saville as Gardeau, F. H. Henry as Rouget, Miss Dansor as Jennie, Mrs. Manders as Mme. Gardeau.

SHOCKING EVENTS// F 1a// J. B. Buckstone// **Olympic**, Jan. 1838, with Robert Keeley as Puggs, Charles Selby as Capt. Spoff, William Farren as Griffinhoof, Miss Crisp as Dorothy, Miss Lee as Kitty; Aug. 1856, with Samuel Emery as Griffinhoof, Gaston Murray as Capt. Spoff, Mr. Danvers as Puggs, Miss Bromley as Dorothy, Fanny Ternan as Kitty/ **Haymarket**, Aug. 1843, with William Farren as Griffinhoof,

A. Brindal as Capt. Spoff, J. B. Buckstone as Puggs, Miss C. Conner as Dorothy, Miss Lee as Kitty/ **Adelphi**, May 1848, with Mr. Lambert as Griffinhoof, J. Worrell as Capt. Spoff, Charles Munyard as Puggs, Emma Harding as Dorothy, Ellen Chaplin as Kitty; Oct. 1880, with W. H. Stephens as Dr. Griffenhoof, Mr. Norman as Capt. Spoff, Clara Jecks as Kitty, Miss Mathews as Dorothy, Robert Pateman as Puggs/ **Sad. Wells**, Nov. 1855, with Mr. Barrett as Griffenhoof, William Belford as Capt. Spoff, Lewis Ball as Puggs, Caroline Parkes as Dorothy, Eliza Travers as Kitty.

SHOOTING THE MOON// F 1a// F. F. Cooper// **Strand**, Oct. 1850/ **Astley's**, Dec. 1858, with J. W. Anson as Col. Brownless, J. T. Anderson as Jack, H. Hemmings as Hartley, Mrs. William Dowton as Mrs. Ogre, Miss Dowton as Drusilda, Julia Weston as Betty.

SHORT AND SWEET// D 1a// A. C. Troughton// **Strand**, Oct. 1861/ **Court**, Mar. 1875.

SHORT EXPOSURE, A// F// J. Anstey// **Criterion**, June 1901.

SHOULD THIS MEET THE EYE// F 1a// Alfred Maltby// **Lyceum**, July 1872, with W. L. Branscombe as Lionel Long, F. W. Irish as Louder, John Collett as Skinflint, L. Fredericks as Teddy, Rose James as Maud, Miss Middleton as Polly; Aug. 1877, with Edmund Lyons as Louder, Arthur Wing Pinero as Lionel Long, W. L. Branscombe as Teddy, Kate Pattison as Maud, Eva Morley as Polly.

SHOWMAN'S DAUGHTER, THE// C 3a// Frances Hodgson Burnett// **Royalty**, Jan. 1892.

SHRIMPS FOR TWO// F 1a// n.a.// **Adelphi**, Dec. 1872, with Frederick Moreland as Muddlebank, Mr. Waring as Alexander, Harwood Cooper as Jenkins, Miss K. Bentley as Mrs. Muddlebank.

SHUTTLECOCK, THE// F 3a// H. J. Byron & J. A. Sterry// **Toole's**, May. 1885.

SHYLOCK; OR, THE MERCHANT OF VENICE PRESERVED// F 4sc// Francis Talfourd// **Olympic**, June 1853, with Charles Bender as Duke, Mr. Harris as Morocco, Mr. Laporte as Arragon, George Cooke as Antonio, John Kinloch as as Bassanio, W. Shalders as Gratiano, Frederick Robson as Shylock, Mr. Marchant as Tubal, F. Charles as Lorenzo, Isabel Adams as Portia, Harriet Gordon as Nerissa, Ellen Turner as Jessica.

SHYLOCK AND CO.// F 3a// Adap. by George Canning & Alfred Chevalier fr F of Henri Bataille & M. Fengère, L'Article 7// **Criterion**, June 1892.

SI SLOCUM; OR, THE AMERICAN TRAPPER AND HIS DOG// D 5a// Clifton Tayleure// **Olympic**, Dec. 1876, with Frank Frayne as Si Slocum, Mrs. Frank Frayne as Ruth, Master Frankie Frayne as Little Freddie, James M. Butler as Tobe, Robert Frayne as Blackburn, Camille Dubois as Patsy, Charles Flockton as Vasquez, Robert Pateman as Doran, John Vollaire as Townsend, Dibdin Culver as Bledsoe, T. G. Warren as U Bet, Miss Carlisle as Grace, Amy Crawford as Mrs. Bledsoe, Agnes Bennett as Pasquita.

SIAMESE TWINS// F// G. A. à Becket// **Sad. Wells**, July 1844, with Mr. Williams as Forceps, Mr. Binge as Capt. Vivid, G. F. Forman as Slow, Charles Hudson as O'Glib, Georgiana Lebatt as Sally, Fanny Morelli as Marian.

SIBERIA// D 5a// Bartley Campbell// **Princess's**, Dec. 1887, with J. H. Barnes as Neigoff, W. L. Abingdon as Jaracoff, James Meade as Sparta, Harry Parker as Trolsky, Forbes Dawson as Ivan, Edwin Cleary as Count Stanislaus, Basset Roe as Lt. Smailoff, A. R. Hodgson as Governor, Henry De Solla as Janoski, Philip Darwin as Poluski, T. C. Dwyer as Lt. Prudoff, Sackville West as Christovitch, Mary Rorke as Marie, Cicely Richards as Vera, Bertie Willis as Phedora, Alice Chandos as Drovna, Grace Hawthorne as Sara/ Scenery by R. C. Durant & E. G. Banks/ Machines by R. E. Warton/ Music by Thomas Fish & Fred Lyster/ Prod. by Grace Hawthorne & J. H. Barnes.

SID// C// Paul Meritt// **Grecian**, June 1871.

SIDONIA DI MOLINA; OR, RUSE DE GUERRE// D 3a// n.a.// **Adelphi**, Dec. 1844, with Charles Hudson as the Duke de Saavedra, Charles Selby as Baron de Madly, Edward Wright as Nunoz, J. Worrell as Ratalto, Paul Bedford as La Rose, Mr. Freeborn as the Alcade, Mme. Celeste as Sidonia di Molina, Sarah Woolgar as Maraquita, Miss M. Taylor as Fidelia/ Scenery by Messrs. Pitt & Johnstone/ Machinery by Mr. Cooper.

SIDONIE// D 3a// Fred Lyster & Paul Heriot// **Novelty**, Dec. 1887.

SIEGE OF TROY, THE// D// n.a.// **Lyceum**, Dec. 1858.

SIGHT AND SOUND// D// n.a.// **Britannia**, Nov. 1876.

SIGN OF THE CROSS, THE// D 4a// Wilson Barrett// **Lyric**, Jan. 1896, with Wilson Barrett, Maud Hoffman/ **Lyceum**, Oct. 1899, with Wilson Barrett as Marcus, J. H. Barnes as Nero, J. Carter-Edwards as Tigellinus, Edward Irwin as Licinius, Ambrose Manning as Glabrio, Basil Gill as Philodemus, Stafford Smith as Signinius, Horace Hodges as Servillius, Alida Cortelyou as Berenis, Daisy Belmore as Dacia, Alice Gambier as Poppea, Rose Pendennis as Ancaria, Maude Jeffries as Mercia.

SIGNAL, THE// D 3a// J. Stirling Coyne// **Olympic**, Apr. 1844.

SIGNAL LIGHTS// D 5a// W. J. Thompson// **Pavilion**, Sept. 1894.

SIGNAL ROCKET, THE; OR, SAILORS AND BUSH-RANGERS// D// G. D. Pitt// **Victoria**, May 1842, with C. Williams as Old Hartly,

John Dale as Scowling, William Seaman as Edmund Hartly, E. F. Saville as Haulyard, John Gardner as Fidge, Mr. Hitchinson as Capt. Wortley, Mr. James as Maj. Noble, Mrs. George Lee as Rose, Mrs. Griffith as Hannah, Mrs. King as Jabne.

SILAS BRUTON; OR, THE MURDER AT THE OLD CROOK FARM// D// H. Hayman// **Victoria**, Apr. 1877.

SILENCE// D 4a// C. H. Ross// **Holborn**, May 1871.

SILENCE OF A CHATTERBOX, THE// Play 1a// Dram. by Constance Prevost fr story of Miss Wilford// **Terry's**, Oct. 1899.

SILENT BATTLE, THE// Play 3a// Isaac Henderson (prev. titled Agatha)// **Criterion**, May 1892.

SILENT PROTECTOR, A// C 1a// T. J. Williams// **POW**, Mar. 1868.

SILENT SHORE, THE// D Pro & 4a// Dram. by J. Bloundelle-Burton fr his own novel// **Olympic**, May 1888.

SILENT SYSTEM, THE// F 1a// T. J. Williams// **Strand**, July 1862.

SILENT WITNESS, A// D 4a// John Coleman// **Olympic**, May 1889.

SILENT WOMAN, THE// F 1a// Adap. by T. H. Lacy// **Sad. Wells**, Aug. 1846, with Mr. Williams as Sandford, William Hoskins as Merton, Miss Cooper as Miss Sandford/ **Olympic**, Jan. 1883, with Mr. Cameron as Sandford, W. E. Blatchley as Merton, Kate Lee as Marianne.

SILKEN FETTERS// C 3a// Leicester Buckingham// **Haymarket**, Nov. 1863, with Henry Howe as Earl of Windermere, William Farren as Trevanion, C. J. Mathews as Codicil, W. H. Chippendale as Hazelton, Mrs. C. J. Mathews as Countess of Windermere, Maria Harris as Clara, Miss Coleman as Lucy.

SILVER BULLET, THE// D// William Seaman// **Britannia**, Aug. 1875.

SILVER CRESCENT, THE// D// n.a.// **Lyceum**, 1839.

SILVER FALLS, THE// D 4a// Henry Pettitt & G. R. Sims// **Adelphi**, Dec. 1888, with William Terriss as Eric Normanhurst, Charles Cartwright as Valles, J. L. Shine as Slingsby, J. D. Beveridge as Maguire, Royce Carleton as Redmayne, Wallace Erskine as José, Howard Russell as Robjohn, Miss Millward as Primrose, Olga Nethersole as Loia, Clara Jecks as Norah, Adrienne Dairolles as Marie/ Scenery by Bruce Smith & Walter Johnstone/ Music by Henry Sprake/ Machines by Benjamin Burns/ Prod. by William Sidney.

SILVER HONEYMOON, A// C// Richard Butler & H. Chance Newton ("Richard Henry")// **Trafalgar**, May 1894.

SILVER HORSESHOE, THE// D 4a// St. A. Miller// **Novelty**, Feb. 1896.

SILVER KEY, THE// D 4a// Dram. by Sidney Grundy fr F of Alexandre Dumas, Mlle. de Belle Isle// **Her Majesty's**, July 1897.

SILVER KING, THE// D 5a// Henry Arthur Jones & Henry Herman// **Princess's**, Nov. 1882, with Wilson Barrett as Denver, Mary Eastlake as Nellie, George Barrett as Jaikes, Neville Doone as Selwyn, Brian Darley as Ware, Walter Speakman as Baxter, E. S. Willard as Capt. Skinner, Charles Coote as Corkett, Clifford Cooper as Coombe, Frank Huntley as Cripps, John Beauchamp as Parkyn, Dora Vivian as Olive, Mrs. Huntley as Tabitha, Miss Woodworth as Susy, Mrs. Beckett as Mrs. Gammage/ Scenery by William Beverley, Stafford Hall, Bruce Smith & Walter Hahn/ Music by Michael Connolly/ Prod. by Wilson Barrett/ **Olympic**, Jan. 1891, with Wilson Barrett as Denver, Winifred Emery as Nellie, George Barrett as Jaikes, Edward Irwin as Selwyn, T. W. Percyval as Ware, Stafford Smith as Baxter, Cooper Cliffe as Capt. Skinner, Ambrose Manning as Corkett, Austin Melford as Coombe, W. A. Elliott as Cripps, Miss M. C. Jeffries as Olive, Alice Cooke as Tabitha, Lille Belmore as Susy/ **Lyceum**, Sept. 1899, with Wilson Barrett as Denver, Maud Jeffries as Nellie, Horace Hodges as Jakes, T. Wigney Percyval as Capt. Skinner, Edward Irwin as Ware, Caleb Porter as Baxter, Ambrose Manning as Coombe, Henry Rivers as Pottle, Alida Cortelyou as Olive, Daisy Belmore as Susy, May Relph as Tabitha.

SILVER LINING, THE// C 3a// Leicester Buckingham// **St. James's**, Jan. 1864, with Frederic Robinson as Merivale, C. J. Mathews as Fairleigh, Henry Ashley as Maj. Eversley, H. J. Montague as Chester, Mr. Smithson as Robert, Mrs. C. J. Mathews as Helen, Mrs. Stirling as Mrs. Dorrington, Mrs. Frank Matthews as Mrs. Maltravers, Adeline Cottrell as Dora/ Scenery by Wilson & Maugham.

SILVER SHELL, THE// Play 4a// H. J. Dam// **Avenue**, Apr. 1893.

SILVER SHIELD, THE// C 3a// Sidney Grundy// **Strand**, May 1885, with Arthur Dacre, Charles Groves, Amy Roselle, Mrs. Leigh Murray, Kate Rorke.

SILVER THIMBLE, THE; OR, LIGHT AND SHADE// D// Mark Lemon// **Sad. Wells**, Sept. 1841, with Mr. Williams as Lord Lottleton, Mr. Dry as Harvey, John Herbert as Dabble, Henry Hall as Nabbs, J. W. Collier as Gentle, Miss Cooke as Lady Lottleton, Mrs. Richard Barnett as Mary, Mrs. Robert Honner as Jane.

SILVER TOWER, THE// D// n.a.// **Standard**, Apr. 1857.

SIMON LEE; OR, THE MURDER AT THE 5 FIELDS COPSE// D 3a// G. D. Pitt// **City of London**, Apr. 1839/ **Victoria**, Nov. 1850, with Henry Frazer as Hatherleigh, Mr. Henderson as Meltington, J. T. Johnson as Simon Lee,

G. F. Forman as Jones, John Hudspeth as Dring, J. Howard as Old Martin, J. Neville as Todd, Annette Vincent as Grace, Mrs. George Lee as Annie, Miss Barrowcliffe as Mrs. Jones, Miss Mildenhall as Winifred, Miss Edgar as Mary.

SIMON THE TANNER// D// n.a.// **Victoria**, Apr. 1856.

SIMPSON AND COMPANY// C 2a// John Poole// **Sad. Wells**, Apr. 1841, with Mr. Williams as Simpson, Thomas Green as Bromley, Charles Fenton as Foster, Miss Richardson as Mrs. Simpson, Mrs. W. L. Rede as Mrs. Bromley, Miss Grant as Mrs. Fitzallan, Mrs. Brougham as Mme. La Trappe; Apr. 1856, with Mr. Barrett as Simpson, E. F. Edgar as Bromley, C. Kelsey as Foster, Charlotte Cushman as Mrs. Simpson, Harriet Gordon as Mrs. Bromley, Jenny Marston as Mrs. Fitzallan, Miss Cuthbert as Mme. La Trappe/ **Adelphi**, Apr. 1847, with Mr. Melbourne as Peter Simpson, Mr. Hield as Bromley, Susan Cushman as Mrs. Simpson, Miss Aitken as Mrs. Fitzallen, Mrs. Lewis as Mrs. Bromley/ **Drury Lane**, Mar. 1851/ **Haymarket**, Mar. 1861, with W. H. Chippendale as Simpson, Henry Howe as Bromley, Mr. Weathersby as Foster, Mrs. Wilkins as Mrs. Simpson, Mrs. Fitzwilliam as Mrs. Bromley, Henrietta Lindley as Mrs. Fitzallan, Fanny Wright as Mme. la Trappe/ **Olympic**, June 1865, with W. H. Stephens as Simpson, Robert Soutar as Bromley, Harwood Cooper as Foster, Kate Terry as Mrs. Simpson, Lydia Foote as Mrs. Bromley, Amy Sheridan as Mrs. Fitzallan, Mrs. Stephens as Mme. La Trappe/ **Lyceum**, Feb. 1874, with John Carter as Simpson, J. D. Beveridge as Bromley, Alfred Tapping as Foster, Georgina Pauncefort as Mrs. Simpson, Miss J. Henri as Mrs. Bromley, Miss St. Ange as Mrs. Fitzallan.

SIMPSON AND DELILAH// C 1a// H. Sutherland Edwards// **Avenue**, June 1882.

SIMSON'S LITTLE HOLIDAY// F// Harry Nichols// **Drury Lane**, Sept. 1884.

SIN AND THE SORROW, THE// D Pro & 3a// Henry Leslie// **Grecian**, Sept. 1866, with Alfred Rayner as Harland, William James as Pedro, Charles Mortimer as Marduke, J. Jackson as Patterson, Henry Power as Hobson, John Manning as Vinney, Lizzie Mandelbert as Anita, Jane Coveney as Olivia, Mary A. Victor as Veronico, Emma Victor as Miss Timmins, Mrs. Atkinson as Nina/ Scenery by Messender & Soames/ Machines by Mr. Soutar/ Gas by Mr. Dimes/ Music by W. Edroff/

SIN OF A LIFE, THE// D 3a// Nelson Lee// **Victoria**, Sept. 1867.

SIN OF A LIFE, A// D 4a// Dram. by Walter Reynolds fr novel of Ouida, Wanda// **Princess's**, Sept. 1901.

SIN OF ST. HULDA, THE// D 4a// G. S. Ogilvie// **Shaftesbury**, Apr. 1896.

SINBAD THE SAILOR; OR, THE ALLEY OF DIAMONDS// D// n.a.// **Cov. Garden**, Apr. 1838, with Mr. Macarthy as Hamet, George Bennett as Joniah, George Bartley as Kabob, James Anderson as Sinbad, Paul Bedford as Knocknoc, Edwin Yarnold as Guffarah, John Ayliffe as Gazna, Mr. Manvers as Ali, Miss E. Clifford as Leila.

SINGLE LIFE// C 3a// J. B. Buckstone// **Haymarket**, July 1839, with Benjamin Webster as Niggle, Robert Strickland as Damper, J. B. Buckstone as Pinkey, Walter Lacy as Boss, Mr. Hemming as Chester, Mrs. W. Clifford as Caroline, Mrs. Julia Glover as Maria, Mrs. Fitzwilliam as Kitty, Mrs. Danson as Sarah, Miss Travers as Jessy; July 1873, with W. H. Kendal as Niggle, W. H. Chippendale as Damper, J. B. Buckstone as Pinkey, Walter Gordon as Boss, Mr. Weathersby as Chester, Mrs. Edward Fitzwilliam as Miss Coy, Mrs. Chippendale as Maria, Madge Robertson as Kitty, Miss Harrison as Sarah, Helen Massey as Jessy.

SINK OR SWIM// C 2a// Thomas Morton// **Olympic**, Aug. 1852, with William Hoskins as Lord Yawnly, George Cooke as Sir Felix, Charles Bender as Debit, Henry Compton as Stunty, Mrs. B. Bartlett as Mrs. Sterling, Mrs. Walter Lacy as Ellen.

SINLESS SECRET, A// D 5a// Dram. by Frank Lindo fr novel of Rita// **Comedy**, Jan. 1890, with Oscar Ayde as Leroux, Royston Keith as Col. von Brandstein, Frank Lindo as Moprat, Ronald Power as Bohmer, Henry Arncliffe as Wiesman, Miss F. Mellon as Rose, Marion Denvil as Gretchen, Marion Lea as Ninette.

SINS OF A CITY, THE// D// George Conquest & Paul Meritt// **Surrey**, Sept. 1884.

SINS OF THE FATHERS, THE// D 1a// William Lestocq// **Globe**, Jan. 1886, with William Lestocq, Kate Tyndell.

SINS OF THE FATHERS; OR, THE UNNATURAL BROTHERS// D 6a// Mark Melford// **Pavilion**, May 1885.

SINS OF THE NIGHT// D 5a// Frank Harvey// **Grand**, May 1893.

SIR JOHN OLDCASTLE// C// Thomas Brereton// **Olympic**, Mar. 1848, with Henry Holl as Henry V, Mr. Stuart as Lord Cobham, Mr. Archer as Bishop of Rochester, William Davidge as Sir John, Mr. Harcourt as Suffolk, Mr. Warde as Huntington, John Kinloch as Harpool, Mr. Butler as Scroop, Mr. Lee as Acton, Mr. Darcie as Herbert, Lysander Thompson as Murley, Miss Laidlaw as Owen, Miss Hill as Davy, Miss Lovatt as Lady Powis, Miss Matthews as Lady Cobham.

SIR ROGER DE COVERLEY; OR, THE WIDOW AND HER WOOERS// D 4a// Tom Taylor// **Olympic**, Apr. 1851, with William Farren as Sir Roger, George Cooke as Sir Andrew, Henry Farren as Honeycombe, H. Lee as Grecian, William Farren Jr. as Capt. Sentry, Henry Compton as Wimble, W. Shalders as Touchy, Leigh Murray as Cooper, Ellen Turner as Josh, Mrs. Stirling as Lady Bellasis, Louisa Howard as Sylvia, Isabel Adams as Mrs. Cosey, Miss Adams as Susan, Mrs. B. Bartlett as Honor/ Scenery by W. Shalders/ Music by J. Barnard/ Machines by J. Matthews.

SIREN, THE// D 3a// J. Palgrave Simpson// **Lyceum**, Nov. 1869.

SISTER AND I// F// T. Mildenhall// **Lyceum**, June 1846, with Frank Matthews, Mr. Bellingham, Alfred Wigan, Samuel Emery, Drinkwater Meadows, Mrs. Alfred Wigan, Miss Forster, Ellen Daly.

SISTER GRACE// C// J. S. Buttams// **Avenue**, June 1884.

SISTER MARY// Play 4a// Wilson Barrett & Clement Scott// **Comedy**, Sept. 1886.

SISTER'S PENANCE, A// D 3a// Tom Taylor & A. W. Dubourg// **Adelphi**, Nov. 1866, with Hermann Vezin as Markham, John Billington as Ammedoolah, C. H. Stephenson as Col. Leslie, Henry Ashley as Handyside, J. A. Shaw as Stubbs, Robert Romer as Maj. McWort, W. H. Eburne as Ens. Dodds, Kate Terry as Alice Vernon, Miss Hughes as Marion Vernon, Emily Pitt as Pamela.

SISTER'S SACRIFICE, A// D// Adap. fr novel of Lamartine, Geneviève// **Lyceum**, 1857, with Mr. Barrett as Mons. Girard, Samuel Emery as Cyprian Girard, James Rogers as Pierre, Mr. Haynes as Jerome, E. L. Davenport as Soldier, Mme. Celeste as Genevieve, Julia St. George as Josette, Mrs. Keeley as Catherine, Mrs. Weston as Mme. Belan.

SISTER'S SACRIFICE, A// D 4a// St. A. Miller & M. Turner// **Surrey**, June 1901.

SISTER'S SIN, A// D 4a// Mrs. F. G. Kimberley// **Elephant & Castle**, Aug. 1901.

SISTERLY SERVICE// C 1a// J. P. Wooler// **Strand**, Feb. 1860.

SISTERS, THE// D 4a// C. H. Hazlewood// **Britannia**, June 1878.

SIX DEGREES OF CRIME, THE// D// C. Z. Barnett// **Marylebone**, Nov. 1846.

SIX MONTHS AGO// C 1a// Adap. fr F by H. C. Merivale ("Felix Dale")// **Olympic**, July 1867, with John Clayton as Bliss, H. J. Montague as Deedes, Milly Palmer as Angelina.

SIX YEARS AFTER; OR, THE TICKET-OF-LEAVE MAN'S WIFE (see also, Ticket of Leave Man's Wife)// D 3a// C. S. Cheltnam// **Olympic**, Aug. 1866, with Charles Horsman as Brierly, Edward Atkins as Dalton, George Vincent as Moss, James Craig as Hawkshaw, Lizzie Wilmore as Sam, Robert Soutar as Jones, John Maclean as Gibson, Harwood Cooper as Totty, Henry Rivers as Cooper, W. J. Collins as Biggles, Emma Barnett as May, Miss Austin as Mrs. Jones, Mrs. Poynter as Mrs. Willoughby, Miss Wilson as Seraphina/ Scenery by Hawes Craven/ Machines by Mr. Chapman/ Prod. by E. Hastings.

SIXES// C // Alfred Lindsay// **Vaudeville**, Aug. 1893.

SIXTEEN, NOT OUT// C 2a// James Blair// **POW**, Feb. 1892.

SIXTEEN-STRING JACK; OR, RANN THE RIEVER// C 3a// Dram. by Leman Rede fr story "The Royal Rake"// **Olympic**, Nov. 1841, with C. Baker as Colville, Mr. Green as Frederick, Mr. Thompson as Manby, Mr. Brookes as Theophilus, Leman Rede as John Rann, Walter Searle as Long Jerry, Mr. Turnour as Draggle, George Wild as Clayton, Miss Fitzjames as Constance, Miss Lebatt as Mary, Miss Bartlett as Nelly, Miss Granby as Sophia/ Scenery by Mr. Wilson Jr./ Music by Mr. Callcott.

SIXTEEN-STRING JACK; OR, THE KNAVES OF KNAVES' ACRE// D// n.a.// **Sad. Wells**, Nov. 1842, with C. J. Bird as Grantley, Mr. Williams as Millhurst, Mr. Dry as Mordaunt, Charles Fenton as Daunton, Henry Marston as Jack Rann, Mr. Lambe as Davis, Mr. Aldridge as Bowes, John Herbert as Pattypan, Caroline Rankley as Rosalie, Fanny Morelli as Phyllis, Miss Melville as Elizabeth.

SIXTEEN YEARS AGO// D// Joseph Wolff// **East London**, Mar. 1871.

SIXTH COMMANDMENT, THE// D 5a// Dram. by Robert Buchanan partly fr novel of Dostoievski, Crime and Punishment// **Shaftesbury**, Oct. 1890.

SIXTUS V (see Broken Vow)

SKELETON, THE// C 3a// Adap. by Yorke Stephens & A. Stannus fr G of G. von Moser// **Vaudeville**, May 1887.

SKELETON WITNESS, THE; OR, THE MURDER OF THE MOUNT// D// W. L. Rede// **Sad. Wells**, Feb. 1841, with Mr. Aldridge as Moore, Mr. Williams as Dormer, Henry Marston as Danvers, Mr. Elvin as Lt. Dorrington, Robert Honner as Watterley, J. W. Collier as Jerningharn, Mr. Villiers as Levy, Miss Richardson as Celia, Mrs. Richard Barnett as Joan, Mrs. Morgan as Maud, Miss Hicks as Esther.

SKETCHES IN INDIA// F 1a// n.a.// **Olympic**, with James Browne as Tom Tapes, Kate Howard as Sally Scraggs/ **Sad. Wells**, Mar. 1846, with A. Younge as Sir Mathew, Mr. Williams as Count Glorieux, R. H. Lingham as Capt. Dorrington, Henry Scharf as Tom Tape, Charles Fenton as Melton, Mrs. Francis as Lady Scraggs, Miss Stephens as Poplin, Miss Lebatt as Sally.

SKYROCKETS OF HER MAJESTY'S SERVICE, THE// F// Edward Stirling// **St. James's**, Feb. 1868, with Mr. Evans as Adm. Trunnion, Mr. Allen as Herbert, Mr. Blake as Binnacle, Thomas Bridgeford as Chaser, Arthur Brown as Jacko, Eleanor Bufton as Fanny, Miss N. Nisbett as Betsy.

SKYWARD GUIDE, THE// D 4a// Mrs. A.

Bradshaw & Mark Melford// **Royalty**, May 1895.

SLASHER AND CRASHER// F 1a// J. Maddison Morton// **Adelphi**, Nov. 1848/ **Olympic**, Dec. 1868, with George Vincent as Blowhard, Edward Atkins as Slasher, J. G. Taylor as Crasher, H. Vaughan as Lt. Brown, Mrs. Caulfield as Miss Blowhard, Miss Schavey as Rose.

SLATE PENCILINGS; OUT OF SPIRITS// F// Frederick Hay// **Globe**, Oct. 1876.

SLAVE, THE; OR, THE MOTHER AND HER CHILD (also subt., The Revolt of Surinam)// D// Thomas Morton// **Drury Lane**, May 1837, with Mr. Methews [sic] as Governor, A. Brindal as Col. Lindenberg, Mr. Cooper as Gambia, John Duruset as Capt. Clifton, Mr. Hooper as Sharpset, James Anderson as Capt. Malcolm, Mr. Bedford as Sam, Drinkwater Meadows as Fogrum, Miss Romer as Zelinda, Mrs. W. Clifford as Mrs. Lindenberg, Miss Poole as Stella, Mrs. Charles Jones as Miss Von Frump/ **Sad. Wells**, June 1837, with Mr. King as Col. Lindenberg, George Bennett as Gambia, Mr. Conquest as Fogrum, C. H. Pitt as Clifton, Mr. Tilbury as Governor, John Pritchard as Sharpset, Mr. Manvers as Capt. Malcolm, Miss Land as Zelinda, Mrs. Rogers as Stella, Miss Williams as Mrs. Lindenberg, Mrs. Harris as Mrs. Von Frump; Aug. 1857, with R. Green as Gvernor, F. Charles as Capt. Clifton, Mr. Gladstone as Malcolm, Charles Seyton as Col. Lindenburg, Edward Wright as Somerdyke, Watkins Young as Sharpset, John Chester as Fogrum, Alfred Rayner as Sam Sharpset, Miss Heath as Mrs. Lindenburg, Mary A. Victor as Zelinda, Mrs. J. B. Johnson as Miss Von Frump, Miss Murry as Stella/ **Cov. Garden**, Apr. 1839, with George Bartley as Governor, Mr. Manvers as Capt. Clifton, Mr. Frazer as Capt. Malcolm, George Bennett as Col. Lindenburg, Mr. Vining as Matthew Sharpset, John Pritt Harley as Fogrum, Drinkwater Meadows as Sam Sharpset, Mr. Vandenhoff as Gambia, Mrs. Griffiths as Mrs. Lindenburg, Mrs. W. Clifford as Miss Von Frump, Priscilla Horton as Stella, Miss Rainforth as Zelinda/ **Olympic**, Jan. 1847, with Mr. Turnour as Governor, Mr. Darcie as Clifton, Mr. Binge as Malcolm, Mr. Johnstone as Lindenburg, George Maynard as Gambia, Mr. Wilkenson as Fogrum, J. Cowell as Sharpset, Robert Romer as Sam, Miss Charles as Zelinda, Miss Penson as Stella, Mrs. Griffiths as Miss Von Frump, Mrs. Bland as Mrs. Lindenburg/ **Grecian**, July 1863, with J. Jackson as Governor, George Gillett as Clifton, Walter Holland as Malcolm, Henry Grant as Col. Linderburg, William James as Matthew, John Manning as Fogrum, Alfred Rayner as Sharpset, F. Smithson as Somedyke, Henry Power as Planter, Thomas Mead as Gambia, Jane Dawson as Mrs. Linderburg, Miss Johnstone as Miss Von Trump, Ellen Hale as Zelinda, Marie Brewer as Stella.

SLAVE BRIDE, THE; OR, THE QUADROON AND THE SECRET TREE CAVERN// D 2a// H. Young// **Victoria**, Oct. 1857, with Frederick Byefield as Antoine, Samuel Sawford as Gayarre, F. H. Henry as Larkins, Henry Dudley as Ruffin, J. H. Rickards as Rochfort, W. H. Pitt as Scipio, George Yarnold as Capt. Brazer, Mrs. E. F. Saville as Eugenie, Angelina Bathurst as Auroure, Miss Laporte as Fid, Julia Seaman as Melinda, Mrs. J. H. Rickards as Aunt Aggy, Phoebe Towers as Little Aggy, Rosalie Young as Phillis.

SLAVE HUNTER, THE// D// n.a.// **City of London**, Aug. 1866.

SLAVE LIFE; OR, UNCLE TOM'S CABIN// D// Tom Taylor// **Adelphi**, Nov. 1852, with William Cullenford as Shelby, Samuel Emery as Legree, Alfred Wigan as George, O. Smith as Uncle Tom, C. J. Smith as Loker, Mme. Celeste as Casey, Sarah Woolgar as Liza, Mrs. Keeley as Topsy, Emma Harding as Mrs. Shelby, Laura Honey as Rosa/ Scenery by Pitt & Turner/ Music by Alfred Mellon/ Machines by T. Ireland.

SLAVE SALE, THE; OR, NATURE, BONDAGE, AND LIBERTY// D// Edward Bulwer-Lytton// **Victoria**, Apr. 1838, with Mr. Wilkins as Sir Walter, Alfred Rayner as Capt. Manley, Mr. Archer as Ubino, Mr. Harwood as Quashquedo, William Davidge as Samioba, Mr. King as Wolf, Charles Montague as Ziba, Mrs. Maddocks as Adelade, Mrs. Loveday as Wadnoo, Miss Levite as Chiclum/ Scenery by C. James.

SLAVES OF THE RING// Play 3a// Sidney Grundy// **Garrick**, Dec. 1894.

SLEEP-WALKER, A// F// Walter Ellis// **Royalty**, Dec. 1898.

SLEEP WALKER, THE// F 1a// n.a.// **Strand**, July 1893.

SLEEPING DOGS// F 3a// Mark Melford// **Imperial**, May 1898.

SLEEPING DRAUGHT, THE// F 2a// Samson Penley// **Sad. Wells**, Jan. 1840, with Henry Hall, Mr. Williams, Mr. Elvin, Miss Pincott, Mrs. J. F. Saville; Dec. 1861, with Mr. Williams as Dr. Vincolo, Mr. Barrett as Bruno, W. Mowbray as Rinaldo, Lewis Ball as Popolino, Charles Seyton as Gabriotto, Ada Dyas as Francesca, Miss Hudspeth as Nonna/ **Grecian**, June 1846, with John Collett as Dr. Vincolo, Eaton O'Donnell as Bruno, Edwin Dixon as Rinaldo, Frederick Robson as Popolino, Miss Johnstone as Francesca, Miss M. A. Crisp as Nonna/ **Princess's**, May 1847, with Mr. Granby as Dr. Vincolo, Mr. Walton as Bruno, Charles Fisher as Rinaldo, Henry Compton as Popolino, Samuel Cowell as Gabriotte, S. Smith as Yaldo, Mrs. Henry Hughes as Francesca, Emma Stanley as Nonna/ **Olympic**, Mar. 1849, with H. J. Tutner as Dr. Vincolo, Charles Bender as Bruno, John Kinloch as Rinaldo, Henry Compton as Popolino, Miss Acosta as Francesca, Mrs. H. J. Tutner as Nonna/ **Drury Lane**, Apr. 1851/ **Princess's**, Nov. 1873 (in 1a), with Mr. Bruton as Vincolo, Mr. Palmer as Bruno, Mr. Fenton as Rinaldo, Stanislaus Calhaem as Popolino, Mr. A. Honey as Gabriotto, Mr. Clarke as Yaldo, Miss Kemp as Francisca, Miss Everard as Nonna.

SLEEPING PARTNER, THE// C 3a// Adap.

fr Martha Morton's dram fr G, His Wife's Father// **Criterion**, Aug. 1897.

SLICE OF LUCK, A// F 1a// J. Maddison Morton// **Adelphi**, June 1867, with John Clarke as Twitter, C. J. Smith as Dr. Barnacles, C. H. Stephenson as Capt. O'Slash, J. G. Taylor as Joseph, Miss A. Seaman as Mrs. O'Slash, Emily Pitt as Julia.

SLIGHT MISTAKES// F// Henry Herman// **Folly**, Jan. 1876.

SLIGHT MISTAKES// F 1a// J. Maddison Morton// **Cov. Garden**, Oct. 1843, with Robert Keeley as Paternoster, Mr. Hemming as Baxter, Frank Matthews as Fallowfield, Mr. Attwood as Martin, Mr. Howell as Pounce, Mr. King as Grab, Mrs. H. Beverly as Mrs. Marmalade, Jane Mordaunt as Fringe.

SLIGHTLY SUSPICIOUS// F// Josiah Byron// **Globe**, Oct. 1891.

SLOW AND SURE// D 3a// W. H. Abel// **Pavilion**, Aug. 1876.

SLOW MAN, THE// F 1a// Mark Lemon// **Adelphi**, Nov. 1854, with Robert Romer as Dr. Dix, Robert Keeley as Watts, G. Lee as Fillip, John Parselle as Rackett, Miss Wyndham as Lucinda, Miss Cuthbert as Betty, Mrs. Garden as Mrs. Rumble.

SLOWTOP'S ENGAGEMENTS// C// Adap. by C. S. Cheltnam fr F// **Olympic**, Jan. 1862, with Henry Neville as Greyleaf, Horace Wigan as Bang, Miss Marston as Mme. Wappshott, Mrs. W. S. Emden as Mary.

SLUMS OF LONDON, THE// D 4a// C. A. Aldin// **Britannia**, Apr. 1893.

SMITHS OF NORWOOD// n.a.// **St. James's**, Jan. 1863.

SMOKE// C 1a// Benjamin Webster Jr// **Adelphi**, Dec. 1870/ **Opera Comique**, Nov. 1890.

SMUGGLERS, THE; OR, THE INNKEEPER'S DAUGHTER// D// n.a.// **Victoria**, May 1838, with Mr. Maddocks as Harrop, John Parry as Richard, Mr. King as Ketzler, Mr. Loveday as Tricksey, Mr. Harwood as Langly, Mr. Scriven as Franklin, William Davidge as Monkton, H. Lewis as Wentworth, Mr. Johnstone as William, Mrs. John Parry as Mary.

SNAE FELL, THE// D 3a// Paul Meritt & Henry Spry// **Gaiety**, June 1873.

SNAKE IN THE GRASS, THE// D 3a// n.a.// **Grecian**, June 1856, with Henry Grant as Col. Dumont, Richard Phillips as Vandris, Mr. Hustleby as de Gerney, F. Charles as Jullien, William Shuter as Roland, Eaton O'Donnell as Jerome, Jane Coveney as Sarah, Amelie Conquest as Louise/ **City of London**, Nov. 1858.

SNAPPING TURTLES, THE; OR, MATRIMONIAL MASQUERADING// F 1a// J. B. Buckstone// **Haymarket**, Nov. 1842, with J. B. Buckstone in 3 char. parts, Mrs. Fitzwilliam in 3 char. parts/ **Olympic**, Apr. 1845, with J. B. Buckstone as Mr. Turtle, Mrs. Fitzwilliam as Mrs. Turtle.

SNATCHED FROM DEATH// D 1a// Stephanie Baring & Walter Beaumont// **Novelty**, Oct. 1896.

SNATCHED FROM THE GRAVE// D// George Conquest & Henry Pettitt// **Grecian**, Mar. 1876.

SNEAKING REGARD, A// F// Ada Moore// **Surrey**, Apr. 1870.

SNOW DRIFT, THE; OR, THE CROSS ON THE BOOT// D 2a// Alfred Coates// **Britannia**, Feb. 1869.

SNOWBALL, THE// F 3a// Sidney Grundy// **Strand**, Feb. 1879, with W. H. Vernon, Ada Swanborough/ **Globe**, Mar. 1887, with Charles Hawtrey as Felix Featherstone, Stewart Dawson as Uncle John, Wilfred Draycott as Harry Prendergast, Norman Bent as Saunders, Miss Vane Featherston as Mrs. Featherstone, Blanche Horlock as Ethel, Fanny Brough as Penelope/ Prod. by F. Glover.

SNOWSTORM, THE// Play 1a// Sidney Bowkett// **Gaiety**, Oct. 1892.

SO RUNS THE WORLD AWAY// Play 1a// G. Phillipson// **St. Geo. Hall**, Jan. 1889.

SOCIAL PEST, A// D 4a// Frederick Vanneck// **Novelty**, Jan. 1891.

SOCIALIST, A// Adap. by Henry Bellingham fr Swed// **Royalty**, Apr. 1887.

SOCIETY// C 3a// T. W. Robertson// **POW**, Nov. 1865; 1868, with Squire Bancroft, Mrs. Bancroft, Carlotta Addison/ **Haymarket**, July 1881, with Arthur Cecil as Lord Ptarmigant, Mr. Smedley as Lord Cloudwrays, H. B. Conway as Daryl, Squire Bancroft as Stylus, Henry Kemble as Chodd Sr., Charles Brookfield as Chodd Jr., Mr. Teesdale as O'Sullivan, Mrs. Canninge as Lady Ptarmigant, Miss Cavalier as Maud, Kate Grattan as Little Maud/ Scenery by W. Harford, Walter Hann & John O'Conner.

SOCIETY BUTTERFLY, A// C// Robert Buchanan & Henry Murray// **Opera Comique**, May 1894.

SOCIETY SAINT, A// Play 3a// J. R. Wallace// **St. Geo. Hall**, Jan. 1892.

SOCIETY'S VERDICT// Play 4a// n.a.// **Shaftesbury**, Mar. 1900.

SOFT SEX, THE// C 3a// C. J. Mathews// **Haymarket**, Aug. 1861, with J. B. Buckstone as Boilover Biggins, C. J. Mathews as Solon Biggins, Henry Compton as Mandwindle, George Braid as Count Martinofski, Edwin Villiers as Goodenough, Mrs. C. J. Mathews (Lizzie Davenport) as Ida, Mrs. Edward Fitzwilliam as Mrs. Mandwindle, Mrs. Wilkins as Columbia,

Mrs. Poynter as Priscilla, Henrietta Lindley as Harriet, Miss Henrade as Julia.

SOLD AGAIN// F 1a// Robert Soutar// **Gaiety**, Aug. 1876.

SOLD TO ADVANTAGE// F// J. P. Wooler// **Sad. Wells**, Nov. 1853, with William Belford as Tarleton, Mr. Lunt as Dr. Darwin, J. W. Ray as Christopher, Mr. Josephs as Docket, Charles Mortimer as Merton, Mr. Lloyd as Hartly, Miss Portman as Madeline, Miss Wyatt as Lucy.

SOLDIER OF 102, THE// C 1a// n.a.// **Olympic**, Mar. 1851, with William Farren as Phillipe, George Cooke as Jerome, W. Shalders as Pierre, John Kinloch as Antoine, Henry Compton as Francois, Mrs. B. Bartlett as Mme. Le Ronde, Louisa Howard as Isabeau.

SOLDIER, A SAILOR, A TINKER AND A TAILOR, A// C 1a// n.a.// **Sad. Wells**, May 1837, with John Ayliffe as Bombshell, Mr. Campbell as Barnacle, Thomas Lee as Charcoal, Mr. Rogers as Botch, Mrs. Harris as Dame Bombshell, Miss Melville as Barbara.

SOLDIER'S BRIDE, THE; OR, THE BATTLE OF AUSTERLITZ// D 3a// J. T. Haines// **Victoria**, July 1842, with Mr. James as Col. Le Froi, John Dale as Capt. Roué, John Gardner as Pontoon, Mr. Paul as Index, William Seaman as St. Louis, C. Williams as Meriet, E. F. Saville as Marcel, Annette Vincent as Constance, Miss Martin as Merial, Mrs. Griffiths as Dame Canteen, Miss Saddler as Antoinette, Mrs. Seaman as Lucille/ Scenery by Fenton & Morelli/ Machines by Emmens, Wood & Foster/ Prod. by E. F. Saville.

SOLDIER'S BRIDE, THE; OR, WOMAN'S FIDELITY// D// n.a.// **Grecian**, Feb. 1855, with Mr. Melvin as Gen. Mortimer, F. Charles as Francois, Eaton O'Donnell as Sgt. Jacques, John Manning as Corp. de Fot, Basil Potter, Richard Phillips as Andre, Jane Coveney, Harriet Coveney as Fanchette.

SOLDIER'S COURTSHIP, A// C 1a// John Poole// **Olympic**, July 1858, with George Vining as Col. Clayton, Miss Castleton as Lady Melford, Mrs. W. S. Emden as Fanny.

SOLDIER'S DAUGHTER, THE// C 3a// Andrew Cherry// **Haymarket**, July 1837, with William Farren as Gov. Heartall, J. W. Gough as Malfort, J. T. Haines as Malfort Jr., Frederick Vining as Frank, John Webster as Capt. Woodley, Robert Strickland as Ferret, Benjamin Webster as Quaint, Miss Huddart as Mrs. Malfort, Miss M. Gallot as Julia, Mrs. Gallot as Mrs. Townley, Miss Wrighten as Susan, Mrs. Tayleure as Mrs. Fidget, Mrs. Nisbett as Widow Cheerly; May 1848, with William Farren as Heartall, Henry Farren as Frank, Henry Howe as Malfort, Mr. Tilbury as Ferret, Robert Keeley as Quaint, Henry Vandenhoff as Capt. Woodley, Mrs. Nisbett as Widow Cheerly, Mrs. Seymour as Mrs. Malfort, Mrs. Stanley as Mrs. Fidget, Miss Robins as Julia/ **Sad. Wells**, Apr. 1845, with A. Younge as Gov. Heartall, Samuel Phelps as Frank Heartall, Mr. Rae as Malfort Sr., Henry Marston as Malfort Jr., Mr. Morton as Capt. Woodly, Mr. Williams as Ferret, G. F. Forman as Quaint, Mrs. Mary Warner as Widow Cheerly, Miss Huddart as Mrs. Malfort, Miss Backous as Julia, Mrs. Francis as Mrs. Townly, Georgiana Lebatt as Susan, Mrs. Henry Marston as Mrs. Fidget/ **Grecian**, Nov. 1854, with Richard Phillips as Frank Heartall, Eaton O'Donnell as Governor Heartall, Henry Grant as Ferret, Mr. Melvin as Malfort Sr., Henry Power as Simon, Basil Potter as Malfort Jr., William Suter as Timothy Quaint, Jane Coveney as Widow Cheerly, Miss Johnstone as Mrs. Fidget, Harriet Coveney as Susan, Ellen Crisp as Mrs. Townly/ **Haymarket**, Jan. 1859, with Mrs. W. C. Forbes.

SOLDIER'S FAITH, A// F 1a// n.a.// **Princess's**, May. 1881, with H. Evans as Fritz, Allen Thomas as Carlitz, Maud Milton as Christine.

SOLDIER'S PROGRESS, THE; OR, THE HORRORS OF WAR// D 4a// John Courtney// **Victoria**, Nov. 1849, with John Bradshaw as Hathaway, Mr. Leake as Mouthpiece, Mr. Henderson as Sgt. Trap, Mr. Humphreys as Capr. Snap, J. T. Johnson as Drummond, John Dale as Bloomley, John Hudspeth as Plump, F. H. Henry as Slinker, J. Howard as Slush, Miss Richardson as Mrs. Drummond, Annette Vincent as Mary, Miss Barrowcliffe as Polly, Mr. Neville as Nancy/ Scenery by Mr. Mildenhall/ Prod. by Mr. Osbaldiston & Mr. Neville.

SOLDIER'S RETURN, THE// D// T. E. Hook// **Grecian**, Nov. 1862, with J. Jackson as Hamilton, William James as Redland, Henry Power as Corp. Simpkins, Alfred Rayner as Springfield, John Manning as Dauber, Mrs. Charles Dillon as Kate, Mary A. Victor as Grace.

SOLDIER'S WIDOW, THE; OR, THE MILL IN RUINS// D 2a// Edward Fitzball// **Grecian**, Nov. 1842, with Mr. Turnour as Bertrand, Henry Hall as de Tourney, Mr. Fitzjames as Sanguard, Mr. Ross as Couteau, Mr. Seymour as Jacob, Miss Hamilton as Lisette, Lavinia Melville as Jaqueline/ Scenery by Mr. Scott.

SOLE SURVIVOR, THE; OR, A TALE OF THE GOODWIN SANDS// D 4a// George Conquest & Henry Pettitt// **Grecian**, Oct. 1876.

SOLICITOR, THE// F 3a// J. H. Darnley// **Toole's**, July 1890.

SOLITARY OF LAMBETH, THE; OR, THE MURDER IN ST. GEORGE'S FIELDS// D// n.a.// **Astley's**, July 1849, with Mr. Johnson as Sir Valentine, Mr. Bedford as Master Martin, Mr. Adrian as Barnaby Dry, Mr. Crowther as Master Percy, B. Norton as the Solitary, Rosa Henry as Maude, Ellen Lane as Bess Dry.

SOLITARY OF THE HEATH, THE; OR, THE IDIOT WITNESS// D// J. T. Haines// **Victoria**, Aug. 1854, with T. E. Mills as Armand, Mr. Henderson as Robert, Mr. Morrison as Ratcliffe, Alfred Saville as Tugscull, N. T. Hicks as Gilbert, Miss Laporte as Walter, Mrs. Manders as Dame Tugscull, Miss Dansor as Janet.

SOLOMON'S TWINS// F 3a// F. K. Peile// **Vaudeville**, May 1897.

SOLON SHINGLE// C 1a// Adap. by John Owens// **Adelphi**, July 1865, with John E. Owens as Solon Shingle, John Billington as Howard, Richard Phillips as Winslow, W. H. Eburne as Ellsley, C. H. Stephenson as Tripper, C. J. Smith as Judge, Mrs. H. Lewis as Mrs. Otis, Miss Godsall as Grace.

SOME DAY// Play 3a// Mrs. Newton Phillips & John Tresahar// **St. Geo. Hall**, May 1889.

SOMEBODY ELSE// C 1a// J. R. Planché// **Haymarket**, Dec. 1844, with C. J. Mathews as Horitz, Henry Howe as Waldburg, A. Brindal as Flitterman, Miss Lee as Louise, Mme. Vestris as Minnie/ **Olympic**, July 1860, with Gaston Murray as Waldburg, Frederick Robinson as Moritz, Harwood Cooper as Flitterman, Miss Cottrell as Louise, Louise Keeley as Minnie.

SOMETHING TO DO// F 1a// J. Maddison Morton// **Haymarket** (in rev. vers.) Apr. 1884.

SOMNAMBULIST, THE; OR, THE SPIRIT OF THE HILLSIDE// D 2a// W. T. Moncrieff// **Sad. Wells**, June 1837, with Mr. Hicks as de Rosambert, C. H. Pitt as Edmund, Mr. Rogers as de Trop, Mr. Griffiths as Notaire, John Dunn as Oliver, Mr. George as Ranger, Mrs. W. West as Ernestine, Mrs. Harris as Dame Marchand, Mrs. Andrews as Marceline, Lavinia Melville as Dame Gertrude/ **Victoria**, Aug. 1846, with William Seaman as de Resambert, J. W. Walton as Edmund, E. G. Burton as de Trop, F. Wilton as Notaire, Mr. Hitchinson as Ranger, J. Howard as Oliver, Mrs. Henry Vining as Ernestine, Mrs. Cooke as Dame Marchand, Lydia Pearce as Gertrude, Miss Backhous as Marceline, Miss Wilson as Justine.

SON OF NIGHT, THE// D 4a// n.a.// **Sadler's Wells**, Sept. 1872.

SON OF THE DESERT AND THE DEMON CHANGELING, THE// D// W. L. Rede// **Sad. Wells**, Feb. 1843, with Mr. Dry as Jacopo Sforza, C. J. Bird as Leonato Sforza, Signor Nano as Kardi-ab-dello, Henry Marston as Padre Tormichelle, C. Centon [Fenton?] as Baptiste, Mr. Freeman as Son of the Desert, John Herbert as Pamplino, Mr. Aldridge as Torpietre.

SON OF THE SEA, THE// D// n.a.// **Grecian**, Sept. 1866, with J. Jackson as Allsorts, Mr. Goodin as Basil, William James as Breezeley, Charles Mortimer as Tritton, John Manning as Roberts, Mrs. Atkinson as Mrs. Allsorts, Mary A. Victor as Sally, Lizzie Mandelbert as Morna.

SON OF THE SOIL, A// Play 3a// Adap. by Herman Merivale fr F of Pousard, Lion Amoreux// **Court**, Sept. 1872.

SONG OF THE RIVER, THE// Play Pro & 3a// Mlle. Coquelicot// **St. Geo. Hall**, Aug. 1900.

SONS AND SYSTEMS// C 2a// Charles Dance// **Olympic**, Oct. 1838, with William Farren as Lemon Sowerby, T. Green as George Sowerby, Charles Selby as Sweetman, W. H. Oxberry as Roots, John Brougham as McSweeney, Mrs. Orger as Mrs. Sweetman, Miss Murray as Blanche, Louisa Nisbett as Laura/ **Cov. Garden**, Oct. 1839, with William Farren as Lemon Sowerby, T. Green as George Sowerby, Charles Selby as Sweetman, Drinkwater Meadows as Roots, John Brougham as McSweeney, Mrs. Orger as Mrs. Sweetman, Mrs. Brougham as Blanche, Louisa Nisbett as Laura/ **Sad. Wells**, Nov. 1851, with J. W. Ray as Leman Sowerby, William Hoskins as George Sowerby, Charles Wheatleigh as Sweetman, F. Younge as Roots, Henry Mellon as O'Macsweeny, Mrs. Henry Marston as Mrs. Sweetman, Miss Fitzpatrick as Laura, Lucy Rafter as Blanche.

SONS OF COLUMBIA// n.a.// **Britannia**, Mar. 1862.

SONS OF ERIN// D 4a// W. J. Patmore// **Surrey**, Sept. 1893.

SONS OF FREEDOM// D// A. Faucquez// **City of London**, June 1868.

SONS OF MARS// C 2a// n.a.// **Adelphi**, Oct. 1849, with Mr. Lambert as Col. Dorville, Charles Boyce as Capt. Forigras, Mr. Hughes as Lt. Louis, Paul Bedford as Caesar, Mme. Celeste as Trim, Sarah Woolgar as Nedige, Mrs. Frank Matthews as Mme. Pompeux, Ellen Chaplin as Harriette.

SONS OF THE EMPIRE, THE// D 4a// W. J. Mackay// **Britannia**, Nov. 1899.

SONS OF THE FORGE; OR, THE BLACKSMITH AND THE BARON// D// C. H. Hazlewood// **Britannia**, Aug. 1870.

SONS OF THE SEA// D 4a// Matt Wilkinson// **West London**, May 1898.

SONS OF TOIL, THE; OR, ENGLISH HEARTS AND HOMES// D 3a// John Levey// **Marylebone**, Nov. 1873.

SOPHIA// C 4a// Found. by Robert Buchanan on incidents in Fielding's Tom Jones// **Vaudeville**, Apr. 1886, with Charles Glenney, Fred Thorne, Kate Rorke, Sophie Larkin, Lottie Venne, Rose Leclercq.

SOPHIA'S SUPPER// F 1a// H. R. Addison// **Surrey**, Apr. 1849.

SORROWS OF SATAN, THE// Play 4a// Dram. fr stories by G. A. Sala & Marie Corelli// **Court**, July 1901.

SOUR GRAPES// C 4a// H. J. Byron// **Olympic**, Nov. 1873.

SOUTHERN CROSS, THE// D Pro & 2a// George Peel// **Victoria**, Aug. 1873.

SOUTHERNER, JUST ARRIVED, A// F 1a// Horace Wigan// **Olympic**, Nov. 1862, with George Cooke as Franchise, Henry Neville as Foister, Horace Wigan as Julep, Harwood Cooper as Doeskin, Florence Haydon as Mary, Mrs. W. S. Emden as Spry.

SOVEREIGN REMEDY, A// F 1a// S. Woodroofe// **Princess's**, July 1847, with John Ryder as Capt. Pendragon, Mr. Granby as Bottleby, C. J. Mathews as Quackit, John Webster as Alfred, Mrs. Fosbroke as Mrs. Bottleby, Miss Marshall as Mary.

SOWING AND REAPING// C 2a// C. Vernon// **Criterion**, July 1890.

SOWING THE WIND// C 4a// Sidney Grundy// **Comedy**, Sept. 1893.

SPAE WIFE// D 4a// Dram. by Dion Boucicault fr novel of Sir Walter Scott, Guy Mannering// **Elephant & Castle**, Mar. 1886.

SPAN OF LIFE, THE// D 4a// Sutton Vane// **Princess's**, May 1896.

SPANISH CURATE, THE// C// Alt. fr Beaumont & Fletcher// **Cov. Garden**, Oct. 1840, with Mr. Cooper as Don Henrique, James Anderson as Don Juan, C. J. Mathews as Leandro, William Farren as Lopez, George Bartley as Bartolus, Robert Keeley as Diego, Mrs. Brougham as Violante, Mme. Vestris as Amaranta, Mrs. W. West as Jacintha, Miss Lane as Egla/ Scenery by Grieve, T. Grieve & W. Grieve.

SPANISH GIRL, THE// n.a.// **City of London**, Apr. 1857.

SPANISH GIPSIES, THE// C// William Rowley & Thomas Middleton// **Matinee**, Apr. 1898.

SPANISH MARRIAGES, THE// C 2a// n.a.// **Princess's**, June 1848, with James Vining as Don Hernandez, John Gilbert as Count San Lucca, F. B. Conway as Don Gaspar, T. Hill as Chief, Mrs. Stirling as Elizabeth, Miss Cooper as Donna Beatrice, Emma Stanley as Griselda.

SPANKING LEGACY, A// F 1a// T. G. Blake// **Grecian**, May 1845, with Frederick Robson as Manglo, F. Ede as Ursino, Edwin Dixon as Rinaldini, Harry Chester as Leoni, Miss M. A. Crisp as Columba.

SPARE ROOM, THE// Play 1a// Leopold Montague// Royalty, June 1894.

SPARE THE ROD AND SPOIL THE CHILD// n.a.// **Marylebone**, Mar. 1859.

SPEAKING LIKENESS, A// C 1a// n.a.// **Princess's**, Mar. 1846, with Mr. Granby as Baron de Rancy, James Vining as Alfred, Henry Compton as Coco, Mme. Vestris as Manette.

SPECIAL PERFORMANCES// F 1a// Wilmot Harrison// **Holborn**, Apr. 1868.

SPECTRE BRIDEGROOM, THE; OR, A GHOST IN SPITE OF HIMSELF// F 2a// W. T. Moncreiff// **Sad. Wells**, Oct. 1837, with Mr. Griffith as Aldwinkle, F. Ede as Capt. Vauntington, Mr. Wilkins as Nicodemus, Mr. Rogers as Dickery, T. Lee as Paul, Miss Vernon as Georgina, Lavinia Melville as Lavinia/ **Victoria**, Oct. 1842, with John Dale as Nicodemus, Mr. James as Aldwinkle, William Seaman as Capt. Vauntington, John Herbert as Dickory, C. J. Bird as Paul/ **Grecian**, July 1847, with Richard Phillips as Nicodemus, Edwin Dixon as Capt. Vauntington, Frederick Robson as Dickory, W. Saker as Aldwinkle, Eaton O'Donnell as Paul, Annette Mears as Georgiana, Miss M. A. Crisp as Lavinia/ **Princess's**, Oct. 1847, with Mr. Cooper as Nicodemus, J. Neville as Aldwinkle, Mr. Howard as Capt. Vauntington, Henry Compton as Dickory, Miss Villars as Georgiana, Emma Stanley as Lavinia/ **Haymarket**, Nov. 1867, with Walter Gordon as Nicodemus, Mr. Rogers as Aldwinkle, Mr. Weathersby as Capt. Vauntington, J. T. Raymond as Dickory, William Clark as Paul, Fanny Wright as Georgiana, Miss Dalton as Lavinia.

SPECTRE SKIFF, THE; OR, THE PHANTOM OF THE SEA// D 3a// n.a.// **Victoria**, Oct. 1846, with Mr. Archer as Allerton, C. J. Bird as Rullock, Walter Searle as Jansein, G. F. Forman as Plainbody, Alfred Raymond as Gordon, Miss Backhous as Gerald, Annette Vincent as Abel Allerton, Mrs. Cooke as Dame Plainbody, Lydia Pearce as Tabitha/ Prod. by T. H. Higgie.

SPECULATION// C 3a// William Sapte Jr// **POW**, Jan. 1886.

SPEED THE PLOUGH// C 5a// Thomas Morton// **Haymarket**, Nov. 1838, with Robert Strickland as Sir Abel, Walter Lacy as Bob, Charles Perkins as Sir Philip, Benjamin Webster as Ashfield, J. W. Gough as Morrington, T. F. Mathews as Evergreen, Miss Taylor as Miss Blandford, Mrs. Danson as Lady Handy, Miss Williams as Susan, Mrs. Julia Glover as Dame Ashfield; Mar. 1845, with William Farren as Abel Handy, Henry Holl as Bob Handy, Mr. Stuart as Sir Philip, Benjamin Webster as Ashfield, T. F. Mathews as Evergreen, Mrs. Julia Bennett as Miss Blandford, Mrs. W. Clifford as Lady Handy, Mrs. Edwin Yarnold as Susan, Julia Glover as Dame Ashfield/ **Sad. Wells**, Mar. 1839, with Mr. Williams as Sir Abel, Mr. Cathcart as Sir Philip, Mr. Dry as Mornington, E. F. Saville as Bob Handy, Alfred Rayner as Ashfield, Robert Honner as Henry, Dibdin Pitt as Evergreen, Mrs. J. F. Saville as Miss Blandford, Miss Cooke as Dame Ashfield, Miss Richardson as Lady Handy, Miss Pincott as Susan; Dec. 1848 (in 3a), with A. Younge as Sir Abel, Henry Mellon as Sir Philip, Henry Marston as Bob Handy, Frank Graham as Henry, William Hoskins as Ashfield, Edward Knight as Gerald, Mr. Williams as Evergreen, Mr. Harrington as Mornington, Miss Cooper as Miss Blandford, Miss Huddart as Lady Handy, Mrs. Henry Marston as Dame Ashfield, Miss Garthwaite as Susan; Mar. 1857, with J. W. Ray as Sir Abel, Alfred Rayner as Sir Phillip, Henry Marston as Handy, Lewis Ball as Ashfield, T. C. Harris as Morrington, Mr. Lacy as Evergreen, Jenny Marston as Miss Blandford, Miss Rawlings as Lady Handy, Eliza Travers as Susan, Mrs. Henry Marston as Dame Ashfield/

Grecian, Oct. 1847, with Edwin Dixon as Sir Philip, Mr. Manley as Morrington, Eaton O'Donnell as Sir Abel Handy, John Webster as Bob Handy, Richard Phillips as Henry, Mr. Baldwin as Farmer Ashfield, Miss Johnstone as Miss Blandford, Annette Mears as Lady Handy, Miss Merion as Dame Ashfield, Ada Harcourt as Susan/ **Olympic**, (in 3 acts), May 1848, with William Davidge as Abel Handy, Henry Holl as Bob Handy, Charles Perkins as Sir Philip, Lysander Thompson as Farmer Ashfield, Mr. Morton as Henry, Mr. Butler as Evergreen, Mrs. Parker as Dame Ashfield, Miss F. Hamilton as Miss Blandford, Mrs. Beverley as Lady Handy, Miss May as Susan.

SPEED THE PLOUGH// C// Rev. by Arthur Matthison, Edward Righton, & H. J. Byron fr orig. of Thomas Morton// **Globe**, Oct. 1877, with William Farren as Sir Abel Handy, John Ryder as Sir Phillip Blanford, Charles Warner as Bob Handy, Edward Righton as Farmer Ashfield, A. H. Warren as Morrington, John Billington as Gerald, John Clarke as Evergreen, F. H. Macklin as Henry, Charles Collette as Peter, Marie Litton as Susan, Emma Ritta as Miss Blanford, Isabel Clifton as Lady Handy.

SPENDTHRIFT, THE; OR, THE SCRIVENER'S DAUGHTER// C 5a// James Albery// **Olympic**, May 1875, with G. W. Anson as Sir Howard, John Vollaire as Dr. Cramp, W. H. Stephens as Capt. Decker, Charles Harcourt as Tingle, Henry Neville as Burleigh, Johnston Forbes Robertson as Borders, Mrs. Charles Viner as Mrs. Tingle, Mrs. Stephens as Mrs. Daws, Annie Taylor as Peggy, Nellie Phillips as Mary, Miss Fowler as Deborah/ Scenery by Julian Hicks, Music by J. Mallandaine, Prod. by Henry Neville & James Albery.

SPHINX, THE// D 4a// Adap. by Campbell Clarke fr F of Octave Feuillet// **Haymarket**, Aug. 1874, with T. N. Wenman as Adm. de Chelles, Frank Harvey as de Savigny, J. Dewhurst as Lord Astley.

SPIDERS AND FLIES; OR, CAUGHT IN THE WEB// D 4a// Elliott Galer// **Grecian**, Oct. 1868, with Henry Grant as Fairlight, William James as Walter, Charles Mortimer as Hardman, George Gillett as Hartley, Thomas Mead as Sharp, John Manning as Jacob, Lizzie Mandelbert as Grace, Mary A. Victor as Nelly, Mrs. Dearlove as Mrs. Brown.

SPIDER'S WEB, THE// D 4a// Henry Pettitt// **Olympic**, Dec. 1883, with G. W. Anson as Wragby, J. F. Younge asa Greenfield, H. H. Vincent as Manby, Philip Beck as Staunton, C. W. Somerset as Leverett, E. Hendrie as Baldock, Minnie Rayner as Tom Titley, Alma Murray as Mabel, Laura Linden as Susan.

SPIDERS AND FLIES; OR, CAUGHT IN THE WEB// D 4a// Elliot Galer// **Grecian**, Oct. 1868.

SPIRIT CHILD'S PRAYER, THE// n.a.// **City of London**, Feb. 1865.

SPIRIT OF GOLD, THE// D 3a// n.a.// **Princess's**, June 1848, with F. B. Conway as Albert, Mr. Norton as Julio, Charles Fisher as Montani, John Gilbert as Van Guildergutten, James Vining as Ulric, W. H. Oxberry as Knockertop, Mlle. Leclercq as Spirit, Mrs. Stirling as Aline, Miss Temple as Virginia, Emma Stanley as Lina/ Scenery by Mr. Nichols/ Machines by Mr. Breckell/ Music by Mr. Loder.

SPIRIT-TRAPPER, THE; OR, THE RAPPAREE'S MYSTERY: A TALE OF ALL-HALLOWS// D 2a// n.a.// **Victoria**, Aug. 1853, with Mr. Morrison as Brady, Mr. Raymond as Morris, F. H. Henry as Duncan, John Hudspeth as Tinker, T. E. Mills as Roundhead, John Bradshaw as White, N. T. Hicks as The Spirit, Mrs. Henry Vining as Hester, Miss Clinton as Rose, Georgiana Lebatt as Norah, Miss Laporte as Aileen, Mrs. Manders as Mrs. Brady.

SPITALFIELDS WEAVER, THE// C 1a// T. H. Bayley// **St. James's**, Feb. 1838, with John Webster as Brown, Edward Wright as Simmons, Mr. Sidney as Darville, Mr. Hart as Dawson, Miss Allison as Adelle/ **Sad. Wells**, Mar. 1839, with John Webster as Brown, Mr. Conquest as Simmons, Alfred Wigan as Darville, Mr. Phillips as Dawson, Miss Pincott as Adele; Oct. 1850, with Charles Wheatleigh as Brown, F. Younge as Simmons, Charles Fenton as Darville, Edward Knight as Dawson, Miss Marston as Adele; Sept. 1882, with G. Stretton as Brown, G. Irwin as Simmons, J. F. Kellerd as Darville, Mr. Edwins as Dawson, Nellie Grahame as Adele/ **Haymarket**, Oct. 1839, with John Webster as Brown, J. B. Buckstone as Simmons, Henry Howe as Darville, J. Worrell as Dawson, Priscilla Horton as Adelle; July 1852, with John Parselle as Brown, J. L. Toole as Simmons, George Braid as Darville, Amelia Vining as Adele/ **Princess's**, May 1844, with Mr. Fitzjames as Brown, Edward Wright as Simmons, T. H. Higgie as Darville, Robert Honner as Dawson, Miss Noel as Adelle; Oct. 1852, with Walter Lacy as Brown, Edward Wright as Simmons, George Everett as Darville, John Collett as Dawson, Miss Murray as Adelle/ **Olympic**, July 1866, with Henry Neville as Brown, Edward Atkins as Simmons, H. J. Montague as Darville, Henry Rivers as Dawson, Mrs. St. Henry as Adele/ **Globe**, May 1874, with H. J. Montague as Brown, J. L. Toole as Simmons, George Temple as Darville, Carlotta Addison as Adele.

SPITFIRE, THE// F 1a// J. Maddison Morton// **Engl. Opera House** (Lyceum), Sept. 1837, with S. Jones as Capt. Shortcut, A. Brindal as Lt. Seaworth, Henry Compton as Tobias, William Bennett as Bobstay, Mr. Turnour as Sam, Priscilla Horton as Margaret, Mme. Simon as Mrs. Fidget/ Scenery by Mr. Pitt/ **Cov. Garden**, Oct. 1837, with Mr. Roberts as Capt. Shortcut, James Anderson as Lt. Seaworth, Drinkwater Meadows as Bobstay, Edwin Yarnold as Sam, George Bartley as Tobias, Priscilla Horton as Margaret, Mrs. Sarah Garrick as Mrs. Fidget/ **Sad. Wells**, Mar. 1845, with Edward Knight as Capt. Shortcut, John Webster as Lt. Seaworth, Mr. Williams as Bobstay, Mr. Sharpe as Sam, A. Younge as Tobias, Miss Lebatt as Margaret, Mrs. Francis as Mrs. Fidget.

SPLENDID INVESTMENT, A// F 1a// W. Bayle Bernard// **OLympic**, Feb. 1857, with George Vining as Rockingham, George Cooke as Boddy, J. Rogers as Fulgent, Harwood Cooper as Joe, Miss Marston as Emily, Miss Stevens as Mrs. Winterton, Miss Castleton as Fanny.

SPOILED CHILD, THE// F 1a// Isaac Bickerstaff// **Haymarket**, Sept. 1837, with Robert Strickland as Old Pickle, Miss Davenport as Little Pickle, J. B. Buckstone as Tag, Mrs. Tayleure as Miss Pickle/ **Sad. Wells**, Feb., 1844, with Elizabeth Backous as Little Pickle, Mr. Williams as Old Pickle, Mr. Richardson as John, Mr. Franks as Thomas, Mr. Grammani as William, Miss Cooke as Miss Pickle, Miss G. Marston as Maria, Mrs. Andrews as Margery, Miss Stephens as Susan; Dec. 1866, with Master Percy Roselle as Little Pickle, Robert Soutar as Tagg, Mrs. Poynter as Miss Pickle, Ame Roselle as Maria/ **Grecian**, June 1846, with Carlotta Leclercq as Little Pickle, John Collett as Old Pickle, Frederick Robson as Tagg, Mrs. W. Watson as Miss Pickle, Miss Johnstone as Maria/ **Drury Lane**, Feb. 1850, with William Davidge as Old Pickle, W. H. Angel as Tag, John Parry as John, Maria Ternan as Little Pickle, Mrs. Winstanley as Miss Pickle, Miss Baker as Maria, Annie Lonsdale as Susan/ **Astley's**, July 1860, with Mr. Johnson as Old Pickle, Mr. Henry as James, Amelia Smith as Little Pickle, Mrs. Moreton Brookes as Miss Pickle, Walter Carle as Tag, Miss A. Seaman as Maria/ **Olympic**, Aug. 1866, with John Maclean as Old Pickle, Robert Soutar as Tagg, Mr. Cowdery as John, Master Percy Roselle as Little Pickle, Mrs. Poynter as Miss Pickle, Miss Lewis as Margery, Miss Schavey as Susan, Amy Roselle as Maria.

SPORTING LIFE// D 4a// Cecil Raleigh & Seymore Hicks// **Shaftesbury**, Jan. 1898.

SPORTSMAN, THE// F 3a// Adap. by W. Lestocq fr F of Georges Feydeau, Monsieur Chasse// **Comedy**, Oct. 1892.

SPOTTED LION, THE// F// William Sapte Jr// **Gaiety**, Oct. 1888.

SPRIG OF SHILLELAH, THE// F// J. Mildenhall// **Sad. Wells**, Apr. 1837, with John Ayliffe as Sternly, C. H. Pitt as Frank, Mr. Ennis as Dodgebrain, Thomas Lee as O'Lynn, Mr. Rogers as Slyboots, Miss Lebatt as Julia, Miss Melville as Betty, Miss Pitt as Cook.

SPRING AND AUTUMN// C// James Kenny// **Haymarket**, June 1837, with William Farren as Sir Simon, John Webster as Maj. Osmond, Mr. Ross as John, Frederick Vining as Rattle, Mrs. W. Clifford as Mrs. Rattle, Miss E. Phillips as Clara, Mrs. Julia Glover as Mrs. Dartmouth; Jan. 1842, with William Strickland as Sir Simon, Henry Howe as Maj. Osmond, T. F. Mathews as John, Mr. Vining as Rattle, Mrs. W. Clifford as Mrs. Rattle, Miss Maywood as Clara, Miss Charles as Mrs. Dartmouth.

SPRING AND FALL OF LIFE, THE// D 3a// F. S. Stanley// **Grecian**, May 1866, with William James as Treherne, John Manning as Tompkins, Alfred Rayner as Dubois, Charles Mortimer as Father Jean, Lizzie Mandlebert as Annette, Henry Grant as Slinker, Henry Power as Brown, Mrs. Atkinson as Lady Superior/ Scenery by Mr. Messender.

SPRING GARDENS// F// J. R. Planché// **Haymarket**, Oct. 1846, with Henry Holl as Courtington, Henry Howe as Sir Arthur, J. B. Buckstone as Scoreup, Mrs. L. S. Buckingham as Lady Clarissa, Julia Bennett as Mrs. Scoreup; Oct. 1875, with H. B. Conway as Lord Courtington, Walter Gordon as Sir Arthur, J. B. Buckstone as Scoreup, Mr. Weathersby as Lightfoot, Henry Rivers as Tim, Edith Challis as Lady Clarissa, Minnie Walton as Mrs. Scoreup/ **Sad. Wells**, Sept. 1854, with Frederic Robinson as Lord Courtington, William Belford as Sir Arthur, Lewis Ball as Scoreup, Charles Mortimer as Lightfoot, Teresa Bassano as Lady Clarissa, Eliza Travers as Mrs. Scoreup.

SPRING HEEL'D JACK; OR, THE MYSTERIES OF THE OLD RED GRANGE// D// Douglas Stewart (withdrawn, and new version subtitled The Felon's Wrongs by George Conquest introduced. Second version characters and cast following in brackets) // **Grecian**, June 1863, with George Conquest as Jack Dalton, William James as Brace, Alfred Rayner as Everard, Henry Grant as Hornby, Mr. Shirley as Leslie, John Manning as Frankleton, Marie Brewer as Clara, Mary A. Victor as Kitty [Alfred Rayner as Sir Joseph, William James as Hatton, George Conquest as Hardy, Henry Grant as Harker, J. Jackson as Mayfield, Henry Power as Nickey, Mrs. Charles Dillon as Adelie, Marie Brewer as Mary].

SPRING LEAVES// Ca.// Adap. by J. T. Grein & C. W. Jarvis fr Dutch// **Court**, Mar. 1891.

SPRING-HEELED JACK// D 4a// William Travers// **Marylebone**, June 1868.

SPUR OF THE MOMENT, THE// C 4a// H. J. Byron// **Globe**, May 1871, with H. J. Montague as Walker, Mr. Compton as Gulp, E. W. Garden as Lenitive, David Fisher as Jasper Jones, Louisa Manders as Mrs. Gridley, Nelly Harris as Charlotte.

SPY, THE// Play 1a// Cecil Raleigh// **Comedy**, Sept. 1888.

SPY, THE; A STORY OF THE AMERICAN REBELLION// D 5a// George Turner// **Novelty**, Nov. 1889.

SPY OF THE REPUBLIC, THE// pro & D 3a// Dram. by Edward Stirling// **Astley's**, May 1864, with W. S. Gresham as Danville, E. F. Edgar as Frudaine, Edward Stirling as Lomaque, Mrs. J. W. Simpson as Mme. Danville, J. A. Shaw as Sabot, W. Templeton as Satine, Henry Frazer as St. Mark, Josephine Fiddes as Rose, Miss L. Stuart as Jacquiline.

SQUARING THE CIRCLE// C 1a// Francis Drake// **Globe**, July 1876, with H. Sainsbury as Gregory, V. Robinson as Blount, Henry Deane as George, E. D. Lyons as Joseph Marshall, Augusta Wilton as Mrs. Marshall, Kate Rivers as Mrs. Fearon.

SQUIRE, THE// Play 3a// Arthur Wing Pinero// **St. James's**, Dec. 1881, with John Hare as Rev. Dormer, W. H. Kendal as Lt. Thorndyke, T. N. Wenman as Hythe, Mr. Mackintosh as Gunnion, T. W. Robertson as Haggerston, Mrs. W. H. Kendal as Kate, Ada Murray as Christina, Miss Brereton as Felicity/ Scenery by W. Harford/ Music by Frederic Clay.

SQUIRE OF DAMES, THE// Adap. by R. C. Carton fr F of Alexandre Dumas fils, L'Ami des Femmes// **Criterion**, Nov. 1895.

SQUIRE OF RINGWOOD CHASE, THE// n.a.// **Royalty**, May 1865.

STAFF OF DIAMONDS, THE// D 2a// C. H. Hazlewood// **Surrey**, Jan. 1861.

STAGE, THE// C 1a// West Digges// **Duke's**, May 1877.

STAGE COACH, A// C 1a// Frederic de Lara// **Globe**, May 1892.

STAGE LAND// C 3a// G. R. Douglas// **Vaudeville**, Jan. 1875.

STAGE STRUCK; OR, THE AFRICAN ROSCIUS// F 1a// William Dimond// **Olympic**, Apr. 1837, with James Vining as Stubborn, Charles Selby as Forrester, W. H. Oxberry as Jeronymo, Mrs. Macnamara as Mrs. Stubborn, Miss Fitzwalter as Juliet/ **Sad. Wells**, Dec. 1840, with Mr. Aldridge as Stubborn, Mr. Elvin as Forrester, Thomas Dillon as Jeronymo, Miss Cooke as Mrs. Stubborn, Mrs. Morgan as Juliet.

STAGE STRUCK// F 1a// n.a.// **Astley's**, May 1859, with J. W. Anson as Scraggs, J. T. Anderson as Dorrington, Mr. Herbert as Glorious, Mr. Worboys as Tape, Mrs. William Dowton as Lady Scraggs, Miss Bathurst as Sally, Miss Dowton as Poplia/ **Princess's**, Nov. 1862, with W. H. Stephens as Scraggs, Mr. Fitzjames as Count Glorieux, George Belmore as Tape, Marian Jones as Sally, Mrs. Sims as Lady Scraggs, Marie Henderson as Poplin/ **Sad. Wells**, Oct. 1869, with Mr. Blythe as Milton, Mr. Goodwin as Dorrington, J. Johnston as Sir Matthew, Richard Edgar as Tape, Edgar Newbound as Count Glorieux, Miss Summers as Sally, Mrs. Howard as Poplin, Mrs. E. F. Edgar as Lady Scraggs/ **Adelphi**, Apr. 1878, with Frederick Moreland as Scraggs, Fred Hughes as Count Glorieux, Edward George as Tape, Jane Coveney as Lady Scraggs, Miss Hudspeth as Sally/ **Astley's**, Oct. 1881, with E. Fowler as Scraggs, G. Stretton as Glorieux, G. Hardynge as Dorrington, G. Irwin as Tape, Alice Chandos as Sally, Mrs. Henry Blandford as Lady Scraggs, Nelly Grahame as Poplin.

STAND AND DELIVER; OR, THE PERILS OF THE ROAD// D 3a// W. J. Archer// **Elephant & Castle**, Nov. 1885.

STANDING TOAST, THE; OR, THE LASS THAT LOVES A SAILOR// D// T. P. Taylor// **Sad. Wells**, Jan. 1837, with Mr. Burton as Harding, John Ayliffe as Capt. Crosby, Mr. Campbell as Ratline, Thomas Lee as Toaster, Mr. King as Thornton, Mr. Ray as Bligh, H. George as Breakwater, Mr. Hicks as Hornet, Mr. Scarbrow as Masthead, C. H. Pitt as Gray, Miss Williams as Lucy, Miss Julian as Susan, Mrs. Harris as Mrs. Walker/ Scenery by R. Glindon.

STAR OF INDIA, THE// D 5a// G. R. Sims & Arthur Shirley// **Princess's**, Apr. 1896.

STAR OF THE NORTH, THE// D// Adap. by F. W. Pratt fr F of Meyerbeer// **Court**, Feb. 1889.

STATE SECRETS// F// T. E. Wilks// **Sad. Wells**, Apr. 1846, with Frank Graham as Neville, Mr. Morton as Hal, Henry Scharf as Thimblewell, Mr. Williams as Hedgehog, Charles Fenton as Robert, Mrs. Francis as Maude, Miss Huddart as Letty.

STATION HOUSE, THE// F 1a// Charles Dance// **Victoria**, June 1837, with Frank Matthews as Wheatly, Benjamin Wrench as Quill, Morris Barnett as Millefleurs, Mr. Kerridge as Tracker, Miss Fitzwalter as Fanny, Miss Crisp as Miss Buckram/ **Olympic**, Feb. 1849, with Leigh Murray as Quill, H. J. Turner as Wheatley, B. Barnett as Millefleurs, Harwood Cooper as Tracker, Mrs. Leigh Murray as Fanny, Miss Egan as Miss Buckram/ **Sad. Wells**, Dec. 1848, with Mr. Williams as Wheatley, William Hoskins as Quill, Henry Scharf as Millefleurs, Charles Fenton as Tracker, Mr. Wilkins as Tracer, Miss Garthwaite as Fanny, Miss Stephens as Miss Buckram.

STATUE GALLERY, THE (see Hercules, King of Clubs)

STAY AT HOME// C 2a// George Henry Lewis// **Olympic**, Feb. 1856, with George Vining as Lauriston, Samuel Emery as Dr. Metcalf, Frederick Vining as Letheridge, Henry Leslie as Chanoit, Gaston Murray as Fleming, Fanny Ternan as Mrs. Lauriston, Mrs. Stirling as Mrs. Metcalf, Miss Bromley as Mary.

STEEL HAND AND HIS NINE THIEVES// n.a.// **Britannia**, May 1857.

STEEPLECHASE, THE; OR, IN THE PIG SKIN// F 1a// J. Maddison Morton// **Adelphi**, Mar. 1865/ **Drury Lane**, Feb. 1881, with J. L. Toole as Tittums, Watty Brunton as Buzzard, John Billington as Dr. Clipper, Walter Brunton as Cummings, Madeline Santon as Mrs. Clipper, Effie Liston as Mrs. Tittums.

STELLA// C 3a// B. W. Lindon// **St. Geo. Hall**, Nov. 1889.

STEPHEN DIGGES// n.a.// **Adelphi**, Sept. 1874.

STEPSISTER, THE// C 1a// William Sapte Jr// **Comedy**, June 1887.

STEWARD, THE// C// Samuel Beazley// **Haymarket**, June 1837, with William Farren as Item, E. W. Elton as Mordent, Frederick Vining as Cheveril, John Webster as Lennox, Charles Selby as Clement, Benjamin Webster as Winter, Robert Strickland as Grime, Mrs. W. Clifford as Lady Anne, Mrs. Nisbett as Joanna, Mrs. Tayleure as Mrs. Penfold, Mrs. Julia Glover as Mrs. Sarsnet/ **Sad. Wells**, Dec. 1847, with A. Younge as Item, Henry Marston as Mordent, William Hoskins as Cheveril, J. T. Johnson as Lennox, Mr. Williams as Grimes, Henry Scharf as Winter, Frank Graham as Clements, Miss Cooper as Joanna, Mrs. Charles Boyce as Lady Anne, Mrs. Henry Marston as Mrs. Saranet, Mrs. W. Watson as Mrs. Pinfold, Miss Newcombe as Betty/ Scenery by Mr. Finlay.

STILL ALARM, THE// C 4a// Joseph Arthur & J. C. Wheeler// **Princess's**, Aug. 1888, with Harry Lacy as Manley, W. L. Abingdon as Bird, Harry Nicholls as Willie, Harry Parker as Wilbur, Basset Roe as Fordham, Frank Wright as Jones, Henry De Solla as Jenkins, T. C. Dwyer as Nozzle, Mary Rorke as Elinore, Fannie Leslie as Carrie, Cicely Richards as Mrs. Manley/ Scenery by R. C. Durant/ Prod. by Harry Lacy/ **Grand**, Dec. 1888.

STILL WATERS RUN DEEP// C 3a// Adap. by Tom Taylor fr F of de Bernard, Le Gendre// **Olympic**, May 1855, with Samuel Emery as Potter, George Vining as Hawksley, Alfred Wigan as John Mildmay, Mr. Danvers as Dunbilk, Mr. Gladstone as Longford, J. H. White as Markham, Harwood Cooper as Gimlet, Miss Maskell as Mrs. Mildmay, Mrs. Melfort as Mrs. Sternhold; Nov. 1856, with Horace Wigan, Samuel Emery, George Vining; June 1866, with Horace Wigan as Potter, George Vincent as Hawksley, Henry Neville as Mildmay, W. M. Terrott as Dunbilk, Mr. Cowdery as Langford, Harwood Cooper as Gimlet, Lydia Foote as Mrs. Mildmay, Mrs. St. Henry as Mrs. Sternhold/ **Sad. Wells**, Mar. 1859, with Mr. Williams as Potter, Henry Marston as Mildmay, William Belford as Capt. Hawksley, Charles Seyton as Dunbilk, Mrs. Charles Fenton as Mrs. Mildmay, Mrs. Henry Marston as Mrs. Sternhold/ **Adelphi**, Feb. 1860, with Charles Selby as Potter, John Billington as Capt. Hawksley, Alfred Wigan as John Mildmay, W. H. Eburne as Dunbilk, C. J. Smith as Gimlet, Mrs. Alfred Wigan as Mrs. Sternhold, Mrs. Billington as Mrs. Mildmay/ **St. James's**, June 1862, with W. H. Stephens as Potter, George Vining as Hawksley, Alfred Wigan as Mildmay, Garstin Belmore as Dunbilk, Mr. Mellvine as Langford, Mr. Terry as Gimlet, Isabel Adams as Mrs. Mildmay, Mrs. Alfred Wigan as Mrs. Sternhold; Mar. 1880, with John Hare as Potter, W. H. Kendal as Mildmay, William Terriss as Capt. Hawksley, T. N. Wenman as Dunbilk, Mr. Denny as Gimlet, Cicely Grahame as Mrs. Mildmay Mrs. Kendal as Mrs. Sternhold/ **Haymarket**, Apr. 1863, with W. H. Chippendale as Potter, William Farren as Capt. Hawksley, Alfred Wigan as Mildmay, George Braid as Dunbilk, J. Worrell as Langford, Mr. Weathersby as Markham, Thomas Coe as Gimblet, Louisa Angel as Mrs. Mildmay, Mrs. Alfred Wigan as Mrs. Sternhold/ **Globe**, Nov. 1873, with H. J. Montague as John Mildmay, George Temple as Capt. Hawksley, Samuel Emery as Potter, E. W. Garden as Dunbilk, Frank Selby as Langford, Carlotta Addison as Mrs. Mildmay, Maria Daly as Mrs. Sternhold/ Music by T. Gough/ **Criterion**, Oct. 1890.

STOCK EXCHANGE, THE; OR, THE GREEN BUSINESS// F 1a// Charles Dance// **Princess's**, June 1858, with Walter Lacy as Grasshopper, Drinkwater Meadows as Gresham, David Fisher as Paks, Caroline Heath as Mrs. Grasshopper, Miss Murray as Mrs. Free, Maria Daly as Catherine.

STOLEN; OR, THE STREET BALLAD SINGER// D Pro & 3a// n.a.// **Sad. Wells**, Nov. 1868, with J. H. Fitzpatrick as Harker, J. Robertson as Carrington, L. Smythe as Sir Oswald, J. H. Loome as Milsom, H. Perry as Eversleigh, Richard Edgar as Wayman, W. H. Abel as Capt. Gernam, Miss Hazlewood in 3 char. parts, Miss Logan as Pauline, Miss Hill as Lydia, Miss Herbert as Jane, Mrs. Howe as Mrs. Willet/ Scenery by T. Evans.

STOLEN; OR, £20 REWARD// F 1a// William Hancock// **Royalty**, Dec. 1863.

STOLEN AWAY// D 3a// Robert Dodson// **Britannia**, Mar. 1875.

STOLEN FROM HOME; OR, HUMAN HEARTS// D 3a// n.a.// **Sad. Wells**, Oct. 1891.

STOLEN JEWESS, THE; OR, THE TWO ISRAELITES// D 3a// C. H. Hazlewood// **Britannia**, Apr. 1872.

STOLEN KISSES; OR, THE LION AND THE MOUSE// D 3a// Paul Meritt// **Globe**, July 1877, with John Ryder as Walter Temple, H. H. Vincent as Viscount Trangmar, Edmund Leathes as Felix, A. Garner as Tom Spirit, B. D'Arley as Fred Gay, Emma Ritter as Cherry, Kate Manor as Mrs. Jawkins, Lydia Foote as Jenny.

STONE BROKE// C // R. S. Sievier// **Grand**, Mar. 1892.

STONE JUG, THE// D 4a// Dram. by J. B. Buckstone fr novel of Harris Ainsworth, Jack Sheppard// **Adelphi**, 1873, with Harwood Cooper as Marquis de Chatillion, J. G. Shore as Sir Neville, B. Egan as Benjamin, A. C. Lilly as Richard, Miss Hudspeth as Robert Chance, F. Roland as Buckhurst, James Fernandez as Savage, Augustus Glover as Jim, Robert Romer as Kennedy, C. J. Smith as Moses, Mrs. Addie as Mrs. Bevel, Miss Marston-Leigh as Mrs. Chance, Miss M. Howard as Millicent/ Scenery by F. Lloyds/ Prod. by Edw. Stirling.

STOP, THIEF!// F 3a// Mark Melford// **Strand**, Nov. 1889.

STORM BEATEN// D Pro & 5a// Robert Buchanan// **Adelphi**, Mar. 1883, with E. F. Edgar as Squire Orchardson, J. H. Barnes as Richard Orchardson, Mrs. Billington as Dame

Christianson, Charles Warner as Christian, Amy Roselle as Kate, J. G. Shore as Sefton, Eweretta Lawrence as Priscilla, Clara Jecks as Sally, Herbert Beerbohm Tree as Jabez, Harry Proctor as Johnnie, E. R. Fitzdavis as Capt. Higginbotham/ Scenery by W. R. Beverley/ Music by Henry Sprake/ Machines by Edward Charker/ Prod. by Charles Warner.

STORM DEED, THE; OR, BLACK GANG CHINE, THE// D 3a// William Seaman// **Elephant & Castle**, Apr. 1877.

STORM IN A TEACUP, A// F 1a// W. Bayle Bernard// **Princess's**, Mar. 1854, with Walter Lacy as Summerley, Mrs. Walter Lacy as Mrs. Summerley, John Chester as Respected Parent, Miss Vivash as Servant.

STORM OF LIFE, THE; OR, THE LAST CHANCE// D// n.a.// **Sad. Wells**, July 1866, with Walter Roberts as St. Drumont, W. M. Schofield as Marquis de Croixville, Watty Brunton as de la Tresbete, Philip Hannan as Marquis de la Rosiere, T. B. Bennett as Malvois, Miss Neville as Genevieve, Julia Summers as Marbetta, Annette Vincent as Mme. St. Dumont.

STORM SIGNAL, THE; OR, DRIFTING TO LEEWARD// D// n.a.// **Grecian**, Oct. 1866, with Samuel Perfitt as Graham, Mr. Dearlove as Lot Graham, George Conquest as Grit Arnott, William James as Jack Arnott, Charles Mortimer as Richards, Henry Grant as Heavysides, John Manning as Bullseye, Henry Power as Pilecoke, Mrs. Atkinson as Margaret, Lizzie Mandelbert as Bessie, Mary A. Victor as Honor, Emma Victor as Clara, Mrs. Dearlove as Mrs. Hartley/ Scenery by Messender and Soames/ Machines by Mr. Soutar/ Gas by Mr. Dimes/ Music by W. Edroff/ Prod. by George Conquest.

STORM-BEATEN// D Pro & 5a// Dram. by Robert Buchanan fr his own novel// **Adelphi**, Mar. 1883, with E. F. Edgar, J. H. Barnes, Charles Warner, Amy Roselle, Clara Jecks, Herbert Beerbohm Tree.

STORM COAST// D 4a// Frederick Vanneck// **Globe**, Dec. 1888.

STORY OF A NIGHT, THE; OR, THE CONVICT BROTHER// D// T. Mead// **Victoria**, July 1855, with Samuel Sawford as Harden, Frederick Byefield as Bennett, Henry Dudley as Bancroft, W. H. Pitt as Allen, W. H. Simms as Jerry, Mr. Morrison as Barney, J. Howard as Old Boney, Mrs. Henry Vining as Ellen Harden, Miss Dansor as Mrs. Barney, Miss Laporte as Ellen Barney, Mrs. Manders as Peggy/ **Grecian**, Feb. 1861, with Henry Grant as John Harden, George Gillett as Bennett, Mr. Smithson as Beal, Mr. Jackson as Old Boney, John Manning as Jerry Wattle, Thomas Mead as William Bancroft, Alfred Rayner as Allen, Henry Power as Barney, Miss Chapman as Mrs. Barney, Miss Johnstone as Peggy, Jane Coveney as Ellen, Harriet Coveney as Clesly.

STORY OF A POOR YOUNG MAN, THE// D 4a// Adap. by John Oxenford fr F of Octave Feuillet// **Princess's**, Sept. 1859, with Harcourt Bland, Kate Saville, Mrs. Charles Young, Frank Matthews.

STORY OF PROCIDA, A// D 1a// n.a.// **St. James's**, Nov. 1867.

STORY OF THE FORTY-FIVE, A// D// Watts Phillips// **Adelphi**, Nov. 1860.

STORY OF WATERLOO, A// Play 1a// Arthur Conan Doyle// **Lyceum**, May 1895, with Henry Irving as Corp. Brewster, Fuller Mellish as Sgt. McDonald, Ben Webster as Col. Midwinter, Annie Hughes as Nora.

STORY TELLING// C// Adap. by J. R. Planché fr F// **Haymarket**, Dec. 1846, with William Farren.

STOWAWAY, THE// D 5a// Tom Craven// **Sadler's Wells**, Feb. 1885.

STRAFFORD// T 5a// Robert Browning// **Cov. Garden**, May 1837, with John Dale as Charles I, Mr. Huckle as Holland, Mr. Tilbury as Saville, Mr. Thompson as Vane, W. C. Macready as Strafford, Mr. Vandenhoff as Pym, George Bennett as Hollis, John Webster as Vane the Younger, J. Worrell as Fiennes, Mr. Harris as Hampden, John Pritchard as Rudyard, Eliza Vincent as Queen Henrietta, Helen Faucit as Lucy.

STRAIGHT FROM THE HEART// D 4a// Sutton Vane & Arthur Shirley// **Pavilion**, Aug. 1896.

STRAIGHT TIP, THE// F 1a// n.a.// **Drury Lane**, Sept. 1873, with Frank Barsby as Capt. Fitzfiggins, Frederick Moreland as Wiseacre, Brittan Wright as Fetlock, A. M. Denison as Fairleigh, Clara Jecks as Short, Charlotte Saunders as Mrs. Bandoline, Maud Howard as Julia.

STRANGE ADVENTURES OF MISS BROWN, THE// F// Robert Buchanan & Charles Marlowe// **Vaudeville**, June 1895/ **Terry's**, Oct. 1895/ **Court**, Sept. 1901.

STRANGE BUT TRUE; OR, THE CONVICT'S WIFE// D 3a// Sidney Daryl// **Grecian**, July 1866, with Alfred Rayner as Henri, Charles Mortimer as Muelou, Henry Grant as Irange, John Manning as Jacquee, J. Jackson as Godin, Samuel Perfitt as Col. Launay, Lizzie Mandlebert as Christine, Mary A. Victor as Louise.

STRANGE GUEST, A// C 1a// Adap. by Frank Lange fr F// **Globe**, Apr. 1892, with Charles Grayson as Bloghead, Kate Mills as Lady Pommeridge, Cecily Banyard as Susan.

STRANGE HISTORY, A// D 8a// G. H. Lewis ("Slingsby Lawrence") & C. J. Mathews// **Lyceum**, Mar. 1853, with C. J. Mathews as Jerome Leverd, Frank Matthews as Legros, Robert Roxby as Nicolas, Mr. Cooper as Bellisle, James Bland as Dominique, Frederick Belton as de Mirecour, Basil Baker as Brigard, J. G. Rosiere as Amedée, Henry Butler as Beausire,

Mme. Vestris as Christine, Mrs. Frank Matthews as Mme. Legros, Julia St. George as Nicotte, Miss M. Oliver as Estelle/ Scenery by W. Beverly & Mr. Meadows/ Music by J. H. Tully/ Machines by H. Sloman.

STRANGER, THE; OR, MISANTHROPY AND REPENTENCE// D 5a// Adap. fr G of August von Kotzebue// **Sad. Wells**, Nov. 1838, with J. Lee as The Stranger, Mr. Elvin as Baron Steinfort, Robert Honner as Francis, Mr. Harwood as Count Wintersen, Mr. Conquest as Peter, Dibdin Pitt as Tobias, Mr. Williams as Solomon, Mrs. Robert Honner as Mrs. Haller, Mrs. J. F. Saville as Countess Wintersen, Miss Pincott as Charlotte; June 1844, with Samuel Phelps as The Stranger, Henry Marston as Baron Steinfort, Mr. Minor as Count Wintersen, Charles Hudson as Francis, G. F. Forman as Solomon, T. H. Lacy as Tobias, Mrs. Mary Warner as Mrs. Haller, Miss Cooper as Countess Wintersen, Miss Lebatt as Charlotte, Emma Harding as Annette, Miss Thornbury as Pauline; June 1854, with E. L. Davenport as The Stranger, Davis Baldie as Baron Steinfort, Mr. Barrett as Solomon, Samuel Perfitt as Count Wintersen, C. Poynter as Tobias, F. Charles as Francois, Fanny Vining as Mrs. Haller, Mrs. Barrett as Countess Wintersen, Miss Rawlings as Charlotte, Miss Lavine as Annette/ **Haymarket**, Oct. 1840, with W. C. Macready, Samuel Phelps, Helen Faucit; July 1848, with Charles Kean as The Stranger, William Creswick as Baron Steinfort, Henry Howe as Count Wintersen, William Farren as Solomon, Robert Keeley as Peter, Benjamin Webster as Francis, Mrs. Charles Kean as Mrs. Haller, Miss Fortescue as Countess Wintersen, Mrs. Keeley as Charlotte; Jan. 1854, with George Vandenhoff as The Stranger, Edwin Villiers as Count Wintersen, Henry Howe as Baron Steinfort, William Farren as Francis, Mr. Rogers as Tobias, W. H. Chippendale as Solomon, Henry Compton as Peter, Charlotte Cushman as Mrs. Haller, Mrs. L. S. Buckingham as Countess Wintersen, Ellen Chaplin as Charlotte; Aug. 1879 (in vers. rev. by Barry Sullivan), with Barry Sullivan as The Stranger, Charles Harcourt as Steinfort, Mr. Langley as Wintersen, John Ryder as Tobias, H. J. Turner as Solomon, David Fisher Jr. as Peter, Charles Cooper as Francis, Rose Eytinge as Mrs. Haller, Blanche Henri as Countess Wintersen, Emily Thorne as Charlotte, Lucy Millais as Annette/ **Victoria**, Nov. 1841, with William Seaman as Steinfort, C. Williams as Wintersein, David Osbaldiston as The Stranger, Mr. James as Solomon, John Dale as Tobias, John Gardner as Peter, Eliza Vincent as Mrs. Haller, Mrs. George Lee as Countess Wintersein, Mrs. Howard as Charlotte/ **Princess's**, Mar. 1845, with James Wallack as The Stranger, Mr. Fitzjames as Baron Steinfort, F. C. Courtney as Count Wintersen, Walter Lacy as Francis, W. H. Oxberry as Peter, Mr. Granby as Solomon, Mr. Walton as Tobias, Charlotte Cushman as Mrs. Haller, Mrs. Brougham as Countess Wintersen, Emma Stanley as Charlotte, Miss E. Honner as Claudine; May 1847, with William Creswick as Stranger, John Ryder as Steinfort, Charles Fisher as Count Wintersen, Mr. Walton as Tobias, John Webster as Francis, Mr. Granby as Solomon, Mrs Butler (Fanny Kemble) as Mrs. Haller, Miss Winstanley as Countess Wintersen, Emma Stanley as Charlotte, Miss Rourke as Annette, Miss E. Honner as Claudine; Oct. 1850, with Charles Kean as The Stranger, Charles Fisher as Steinfort, Frederick Cooke as Count Wintersen, James Vining as Francis, Mr. Addison as Solomon, John Pritt Harley as Peter, Drinkwater Meadows as Tobias, Mrs. Charles Kean as Mrs. Haller, Miss Phillips as Countess Wintersen, Mrs. Alfred Wigan as Charlotte/ **Olympic**, Apr. 1848, with George Bennett as The Stranger, Mr. Morton as Count Wintersen, H. Lee as Steinfort, William Davidge as Mr. Solomon, Charles Perkins as Tobias, John Kinloch as Francis, Miss Acosta as Mrs. Haller, Mrs. Beverley as Countess Wintersen, Miss F. Hamilton as Charlotte, Susan Kenneth as Annette; Jan. 1891 (in 3a), with Wilson Barrett as The Stranger, T. W. Percyval as Count Wintersen, W. A. Elliott as Baron Steinfort, Austin Melford as Solomon, George Barrett as Peter, Stafford Smith as Tobias, Cooper Cliffe as Francis, Lily Hanbury as Countess Wintersen, Winifred Emery as Mrs. Haller, Lillie Belmore as Charlotte, Maud Jefferies as Annette/ **Drury Lane**, Dec. 1849, with James Anderson as The Stranger, Mr. Frazer as Count Wintersen, Charles Fisher as Baron Steinfort, Wwilliam Davidge as Solomon, W. H. Angel as Peter, Charles Diddear as Tobias, William Montague as Francis, Laura Addison as Mrs. Haller, Miss Phillips as Countess Wintersen, Clara Tellett as Charlotte, Fanny Huddart as Annette, Aliza Nelson as Claudine/ **Grecian**, Jan. 1856 (in 3 acts), with T. Roberts as Count Wintersen, Henry Grant as Baron Steinfort, F. Charles as Francis, Richard Phillips as the Stranger, Eaton O'Donnell, John Manning as Peter, Jane Coveney as Mrs. Haller, Harriet Coveney as Charlotte, Ellen Crisp as Countess Wintersen; July 1862, with Thomas Mead as the Stranger, Henry Grant as Steinfort, Walter Holland as Wintersen, George Gillett as Francis, J. Jackson as Soloman, John Manning as Peter, Jane Dawson as Mrs. Haller, Miss Johnstone as Countess Wintersen, Mary A. Victor as Charlotte, Ellen Hale as Annette/ **Surrey**, Dec. 1859, with William Creswick, Edith Heraud; Feb. 1865.

STRANGERS YET// D// C. O. Allen// **Grecian**, May 1872.

STRANGLERS OF PARIS, THE// D 5a// Adap. by Arthur Shirley fr F of Adolphe Belot// **Surrey**, Oct. 1887.

STRATHLOGAN// D 3a// Charles Overton & Hugh Moss// **Princess's**, June 1892.

STRATHMORE; OR, LOVE AND DUTY// T 4a// Westland Marston// **Haymarket**, June 1849, with Henry Hughes as Sir Rupert, Henry Vandenhoff as Henry Lorn, Charles Kean as Strathmore, Mr. Rogers as Balfour, Mr. Stuart as Hamilton, Henry Holl as Craigburn, Henry Howe as Brycefield, J. B. Buckstone as Roland, James Bland as Keith, Mr. Caulfield as Robert, Mrs. Charles Kean as Katharine, Miss Reynolds as Isabella, Mrs. Fitzwilliam as Fanchette/ Scenery by P. Phillips & George Morris/

Machines by F. Heselton.

STRAYED AWAY// D 4a// William Travers// **East London**, Aug. 1870.

STRAYED AWAY FROM THE FOLD// D 4a// Mortimer Murdoch// **Pavilion**, June 1878.

STREETS, THE; OR, A TALE OF WICKED LONDON// D 4a// George Gordon// **Sad. Wells**, Dec. 1884.

STREETS OF LONDON, THE// D Pro & 3a// Adap. by Dion Boucicault fr F of E. L. Brisbarre & Eugène Nus, Les Pauvres de Paris// **Princess's**, Aug. 1864, with J. W. Ray as Crawley, Henry Mellon as Capt. Fairweather, George Vining as Badger, W. R. Robins as Edwards, John Nelson as Livingstone, David Fisher as Puffy, Dominick Murray as Dan, Henry Forrester as Paul Fairweather, Mr. Brooke as Count de Montebello, Fanny Gwynne as Lucy, Emma Barnett as Alida, Mrs. Henry Marston as Mrs. Puffy/ Scenery by F. Lloyds, F. Fenton & Walter Hann/ Music by Charles Hill/ Machines by Mr. Garnett/ **Adelphi**, May 1877, with William McIntyre as Crawley, H. Evans as Capt. Fairweather, Samuel Emery as Badger, W. S. Parkes as Edwards, J. G. Shore as Livingstone, Frederick Moreland as Puffy, Mrs. Alfred Mellon as Dan, Ernest Travers as Count de Montebello, Miss Hudspeth as Lucy Fairweather, Edith Stuart as Alida; May 1891/ **Princess's**, June 1900.

STREETS TO THE HULKS, THE; OR, THE OLD WORLD AND THE NEW// D 3a// George Conquest// **Grecian**, May 1869, with William James as Keeting, Charles Mortimer as Fulton, J. Jackson as Farmley, John Manning as Giblets, Thomas Mead as Cooper, Samuel Perfitt as Moorehouse, Lizzie Mandelbert as Ada, Mary A. Victor as Patty/ Scenery by Messender & Soames/ Machines by Mr. Soutar/ Prod. by George Conquest.

STRIKE, THE// D// Dion Boucicault// **Lyceum**, Sept. 1866/ **Novelty**, Aug. 1896.

STRIKE, THE; OR, HEADS, HANDS, AND HEARTS// D// Herbert Stanley// **Albion**, May 1875.

STRIKE AT ARLINGFORD, THE// Play 3a// George Moore// **Opera Comique**, Feb. 1893.

STRIKING SIMILARITY, A// F// Frederick Hay// **Surrey**, Oct. 1870.

STRIKING THE HOUR// D// W. H. Pitt// **City of London**, May 1867.

STRING OF PEARLS, THE// D// n.a.// **Grecian**, Dec. 1867, with Frederick Marchant as Sweeney Todd, George Gillett as Capt. Thornhill, William James as Willis, Henry Grant as Big Ben, J. Jackson as Oakley, Samuel Perfitt as Stranger, John Manning as Ragg, Lizzie Mandelbert as Johanna, Mary A. Victor as Arabella, Mrs. Atkinson as Mrs. Lovett.

STRUCK OIL; OR, THE PENNSYLVANIA DUTCHMAN// D 3a// n.a.// **Adelphi**, Apr. 1876, with J. C. Williamson as John Stofel, Samuel Emery as Deacon Skinner, H. Vaughn as Dr. Pearson, J. G. Shore as Sgt. Flynn, Frederick Moreland as Corp. Sharp, W. Everard as Capt. Warren, Ernest Travers as Peter Rowley, Maggie Moore as Lizzie, Mrs. Alfred Mellon as Mrs. Stofel.

STRUGGLE FOR GOLD, THE; OR, THE SEA OF ICE (see also, Sea of Ice)// D 5a// Edward Stirling// **Sad. Wells**, Apr. 1869, with E. Butler as de Lascours, Arthur Williams as Barabas, O. Ramsay as Medoc, Charles Sennett as Carlos, Agnes Burdett as Louise and Ogarita, W. H. Abel as Laval, E. N. Hallows as de Brienne, Miss Spencer as Mme. de Theringe, Annie Merton as Diana/ Scenery by Mr. Drury.

STRUGGLE FOR LIFE, THE// D 4a// Adap. by Robert Buchanan fr F of Alphonse Daudet, La Lutte pour la Vie// **Avenue**, Sept. 1890.

STRUGGLE FOR LIFE, A; OR, A BURGLAR'S FATE// D// E. Drayton// **Sad. Wells**, Sept. 1884.

STRUGGLING FOR WEALTH// C Pro & 3a// W. A. Gosnay// **Surrey**, Dec. 1880.

SUBSTITUTE, A// C // James Payn// **Court**, Sept. 1876.

SUBTERFUGE, A// C 1a// n.a.// **Olympic**, Aug. 1857, with G. Murray as Edward, George Vining as Oliver, Mrs. Stirling as Lucy.

SUCCESS// Play 1a// F. H. Knight// **Elephant & Castle**, Apr. 1892.

SUCH A GOOD MAN// C 3a// Walter Besant & James Rice// **Olympic**, Dec. 1879, with John Maclean as Sir Jacob, F. H. Macklin as Carteret, J. D. Beveridge as Gower, Edward Righton as Bodkin, Fanny Josephs as Rose, Mrs. Leigh as Mrs. Sampson.

SUCH IS LIFE// D// n.a.// **Elephant & Castle**, Feb. 1885.

SUCH IS LOVE// C 1a// A. M. Mond// **Avenue**, July 1894.

SUCH IS THE LAW// D 3a// Tom Taylor & Paul Meritt// **St. James's**, Apr. 1878, with Mr. Titheradge as Capt. Saxby, Leonard Boyne as Belfoy, Mr. Carton as Fossbrooke, W. H. Stephens as Halifax, Charles Kelly as Goatcher, Katie Brown as Little Georgy, Miss Compton as Lucy, Kate Rivers as Miss Osbaldiston, Ada Cavendish as Ruth/ Scenery by H. Potts.

SUCH STUFF AS DREAMS ARE MADE OF// D 4a// Adap. by Edward Fitzgerald fr Span. of Calderon, La Vida es Sueño// **St. Geo. Hall**, May 1899.

SUDDEN THOUGHTS// F 1a// T. E. Wilks// **City of London**, Oct. 1837/ **Victoria**, Mar. 1840, with Mr. Burton as Gen. Dornton, Charles Bender as Impulse, Mr. Hitchinson as Sims, Walter Searle as Nobbs, Mr. Vale as Jack

Cabbage, Mrs. France as Mrs. Impulse, Mrs. Howard as Sophia, Miss Stoker as Chrissa/ **Sad. Wells,** Oct. 1840, with Mr. Elvin as Impulse, J. W. Collier as Cabbage, Mr. Williams as Gen. Dornton, Mr. Richardson as Sims, Charles Fenton as Nabbs, Miss Cooke as Mrs. Impulse, Mrs. Richard Barnett as Sophia, Mrs. Morgan as Clarissa/ **Grecian,** May 1847, with Edwin Dixon as Impulse, Eaton O'Donnell as Gen. Dornton, Frederick Robson as Jack Cabbage, Miss Merion as Mrs. Impulse, Miss M. A. Crisp as Sophia, Miss Johnstone as Clarissa.

SUE// Play 3a// Dram. by T. E. Pemberton & Bret Hart fr story of Hart, The Judgement of Bolivas Plain// **Garrick,** June 1898.

SUGAR AND CREAM// C 1a// J. P. Hurst// **Globe,** Mar. 1884.

SUGGS IN DANGER// F// Thomas Atkinson Jr// **Sad. Wells,** Oct. 1882, with George Stretton as Jones, Mr. Lawson as Suggs, Mr. Edwards as Bloggs, Lizzie Lilly as Mrs. Jones, Mrs. G. Sennett as Mrs. Flappleton, Helen Grahame as Betsy.

SUIT OF TWEEDS, A// F 1a// Frederick Hay// **Strand,** Jan. 1867.

SUITOR AND SERVANT// D// Adap. fr F of Henri Meilhac & Ludovic Halévy// **Royalty,** 1872.

SUMACHAUM, THE// D 3a// Barry Conner// **Britannia,** Aug. 1878.

SUMMER CLOUD, A// C// n.a.// **Strand,** Sept. 1880.

SUMMER CLOUDS// Play 1a// Neville Doone// **Toole's,** Feb. 1891.

SUMMER'S DREAM, A// Play 1a// Rose Meller// **Avenue,** July 1891.

SUMMONED TO COURT// F// J. J. Dillay & Lewis Clifton// **Imperial,** Mar. 1880/ **Sad. Wells,** Mar. 1880.

SUNBURY SCANDAL, THE// F 3a// Fred Horner// **Terry's,** June 1896.

SUNDOWN TO DAWN// D// James Mortimer// **Britannia,** July 1876.

SUNLIGHT AND SHADOW// Play 3a// R. C. Carton// **Avenue,** Nov. 1890/ **St. James's,** Feb. 1891, with Nutcombe Gould as Dr. Latimer, Yorke Stephens as Denvil, George Alexander as Addis, Ben Webster as Datafield, Marion Terry as Helen, Maude Millet as Maud, Ada Neilson as Juliet.

SUNNY SIDE, THE// C 1a// Adap. by C. M. Rae fr F of About, Risette// **Strand,** May 1885.

SUNNY SOUTH, THE// D 5a// George Darrell// **Surrey,** Sept. 1898.

SUNNY-VALE FARM// D 4a// Adap. by J. V. Bridgeman fr G of Mosenthal// **Haymarket,** Dec. 1864, with William Farren as Valentine, Henry Howe as Matthias, George Braid as Fr. Ernst, William Clark as Fritz, Mlle. Marie Beatrice as Hilda, Miss Snowdon as Monica, Mrs. Edward Fitzwilliam as Dorothy, Maria Harris as Franzl/ Music by Miss V. Gabriel.

SUNSET// C 1a// Dram. by Jerome K. Jerome fr Alfred Tennyson, The Sisters// **Comedy,** Feb. 1888.

SUNSHINE// C 1a// F. W. Broughton// **Strand,** June 1884.

SUNSHINE AND SHADE// D 3a// W. L. Rede// **Olympic,** Nov. 1842, with C. Baker as Algernon, Mr. Green as Capt. Garton, Mr. Halford as Sir James, Mr. Robins as Lt. Gorget, Mr. Fitzjames as Graves, Mr. Bologna as Benjamin, George Wild as Dobbs, Lavinia Melville as Jane, Miss Fitzjames as Louisa, Miss Lebatt as Arabella.

SUNSHINE THROUGH THE CLOUDS// D 1a// Adap. by George Henry Lewis ("Slingsby Lawrence") fr F, La Joie fait Peur// **Lyceum,** July 1854, with J. G. Rosiere as Lt. Cleveland, Mr. Gladstone as Julian, Frank Matthews as Old Sandford, Mme. Vestris as Mrs. Cleveland, Miss M. Oliver as Emily, Miss Martindale as Harriet/ **Sad. Wells,** Apr. 1855, with Frederic Robinson as Lt. Cleveland, Gaston Murray as Julian, Frank Matthews as Sandford, Mrs. Frank Matthews as Mrs. Cleveland, Frances Hughes as Emily, Miss Martindale as Harriet.

SUPER, THE// Play 1a// A. M. Heathcote// **Criterion,** May 1894.

SURE TO WIN// Play 1a// W. H. Goldsmith// **Novelty,** Nov. 1896.

SURGEAON OF PARIS, THE; OR THE YOUNGER DAYS OF THE CARPENTER OF ROUEN// D// Jacob Jones// **Victoria,** June 1854, with Mr. Morrison as Charles IX, F. H. Henry as Count de Rets, Henry Frazer as Duke de Saubigne, N. T. Hicks as Surgeon, Charles Rice as Balladin, T. E. Mills as Michael, Watty Brunton as Antoine, Miss Laporte as Rosignol, Mrs. Henry Vining as Madelon, Miss Dansor as Queen Catherine, Mrs. Manders as Mme. Balladin.

SUSAN HOPLEY; OR, THE VICISSITUDES OF A SERVANT GIRL// D 3a// G. D. Pitt// **Victoria,** May 1841, with Mr. Wilton as Wentworth, John Dale as Gaveston, William Seaman as Remorden, Mr. Howard as Cripps, Mr. Hitchinson as Sir Thomas, E. F. Saville as Dean, Mr. Paul as Dicky Dean, Mr. Ross as Grigsby, C. Williams as Andrew, Miss G. Lee as Fanny, Annette Vincent as Susan, Miss Warde as Caroline, Miss Clifford as Mrs. Simpson/ Scenery by Telbin & Hawthorn/ Prod. by Mr. Osbaliston/ **Grecian,** Feb. 1857, with Mr. Melvin as Wentworth, Henry Grant as Gaveston, Mr. Hustleby as Remorden, Henry Power as Cripps, Richard Phillips as Dean, John Manning as Spraggs, Eaton O'Donnell as Jeremy Dobbs, Jane Coveney as Susan Hopley, Harriet Coveney as Sarah, Miss Johnstone as Mrs. Dobbs/ **Sad. Wells,** Dec. 1868, with Mr. Matthews as Sir Thomas, Mr. Horton as Cripps, Mr. Harris as Wentworth, Mr. Smythe as Gareston, W. H. Abel as Remarden, J. H. Loome as Simpson, Mr. Lacey as Hopley, H. Perry as Deane, T. H. Bridgeford as Dicky, Richard Edgar as Larkune, Mrs. Howe as Mrs. Dobbs, Miss Herbert as Caroline, Miss Hill as Fanny, Miss Logan as Susan, Miss Gibson as Gimp.

SUSAN SMITH// C 1a// Augustus Harris// **Princess's,** Oct. 1860, with Frank Matthews as Sir Exeter, J. G. Shore as Lavender, Frederick Moreland as Joe, Miss Murray as Arabella.

SUZANNE// D// W. J. Lucas// **Haymarket,** May 1838, with Charles Perkins as Col. Maddison, Benjamin Webster as Bounceby, J. B. Buckstone as Swallow, Mlle. [sic] Celeste as Suzanne, Mrs. Julia Glover as Mrs. Lignum, Miss Beresford as Sally/ Music by T. German Reed.

SUZANNE; OR, THE POWER OF LOVE// D// n.a.// **Lyceum,** Mar. 1860, with Frederick Villiers, Walter Lacy, John Rouse, Mme. Celeste, Miss H. Campbell, Miss M. A. Hatton.

SWALLOW'S NEST, THE// n.a.// **Marylebone,** May 1863.

SWASHBUCKLER, THE// C 4a// L. N. Parker// **Duke of York's,** Nov. 1900.

SWEENEY TODD, THE BARBER OF FLEET STREET; OR, THE STRING OF PEARLS// D 3a// Frederick Hazleton// **Bower Saloon,** 1862.

SWEET AND TWENTY// C 3a// Basil Hood// **Vaudeville,** Apr. 1901.

SWEET BELLS JANGLED// C 3a// Gilbert Hastings// **Olympic,** June 1879.

SWEET CUPID'S NET// C 3a// Julian Cross// **Strand,** Apr. 1892.

SWEET LAVENDER// C 3a// Arthur Wing Pinero// **Terry's,** Mar. 1888.

SWEET NANCY// C 3a// Adap. by Robert Buchanan fr story of Rhode Broughton// **Lyric,** July 1890/ **Royalty,** Oct. 1890/ **Court,** Feb. 1897/ **Avenue,** Jan. 1898.

SWEET NELL OF OLD DRURY// Play 4a// Paul Kester// **Haymarket,** Sept. 1900, with Fred Terry as Charles II, Louis Calvert as Lord Jeffreys, C. M. Hallard as Fairfax, Arthur Royston as Rochester, Sydney Brough as Lovelace, Lionel Brough as Percival, Constance Collier as Lasy Castlemaine, Lillian Jefferds as Duchess of Portsmouth, Lilian Braithwaite as Lady Olivia, Julia Neilson as Nell Gwyn/ Scenery by Joseph Harker & Walter Johnstone.

SWEET PRUE// D 1a// Claude Dickens// **Court,** Feb. 1901.

SWEET REVENGE; OR, ALL IN HONOUR// D 3a// Joseph Fox & J. F. McArdle// **Pavilion,** June 1878.

SWEET WILL// C 1a// Henry Arthur Jones// **Shaftesbury,** June 1890.

SWEETHEART, GOOD-BYE// C 1a// Mrs. R. Fairbairn ("May Holt")// **Strand,** Dec. 1884/ **Criterion,** Feb. 1890, with W. S. Buist as Rothsey, Guy Stanton as Penryhn, Henry Saker as Wort, E. Brunton as Mrs. Wort, Ellaline Terriss as Effie, Emily Vining as Martha.

SWEETHEARTS// D 2a// W. S. Gilbert// **POW,** Nov. 1874, with Charles Coghlan, Mrs. Bancroft; May 1879, with Squire Bancroft as Spreadbrow, Mrs. Bancroft as Jenny, Ida Hertz as Ruth/ **Haymarket,** June 1885, with Squire Bancroft as Spreadbrow, Mrs. Bancroft as Jenny, Maud Williamson as Ruth.

SWEETHEARTS AND WIVES// C 2a// James Kenney// **Sad. Wells,** Nov. 1838, with Mr. Williams as Adm. Franklin, J. Lee as Charles Franklin, Mr. Elvin as Sandford, Dibdin Pitt as Curtis, Mr. Conquest as Lackaday, Mrs. Robert Honner as Eugenia, Mrs. J. F. Saville as Susan, Miss Richardson as Mrs. Bell; July 1853, with W. H. Chippendale as Adm. Franklin, Henry Butler as Charles, Mr. Clinton as Sandford, Mr. White as Curtis, Henry Bedford as Lackaday, Fanny Wallack as Eugenia, Miss Dyer as Mrs. Bell, Miss Young as Susan, Julia Harland as Laura; Sept. 1866, with E. Shepherd as Adm. Franklin, J. H. Slater as Charles, J. Collier as Sandford, J. W. Lawrence as Curtis, John Rouse as Lackaday, Miss Mason as Laura, Miss Leigh as Eugenia, Grace Edgar as Susan, Mrs. J. F. Saville as Mrs. Bell/ **Haymarket,** Aug. 1840, with Robert Strickland as Adm. Franklyn, John Webster as Charles, David Rees as Lackaday, Mr. Caulfield as Sandford, T. F. Mathews as Curtis, Mrs. Edwin Yarnold as Eugenia, Priscilla Horton as Laura, Mrs. Frank Matthews as Mrs. Bell, Miss Mattley as Susan; Oct. 1850, with Mr. Lambert as Adm. Franklin, Henry Howe as Charles, Henry Bedford as Lackaday, Mr. Caulfield as Sandford, Mr. Rogers as Curtis, Mrs. Stanley as Mrs. Bell, Priscilla Horton as Laura, Miss Reynolds as Eugenia, Mrs. Caulfield as Susan; Oct. 1854, with W. H. Chippendale as Adm. Franklin, William Farren as Charles, Edwin Villiers as Sandford, Edward Wright as Lackaday, William Cullenford as Curtis, Mrs. L. S. Buckingham as Eugenia, Ellen Chaplin as Laura, Mrs. Poynter as Mrs. Bell, Miss E. Woulds as Susan/ **Adelphi,** Aug. 1845, with Mr. Lambert as Admiral Franklin, Charles Selby as Charles Franklin, Edward Wright as Billy Lackaday, William Cullenford as Curtis, Mrs. Frank Matthews as Mrs. Bell, Mrs. Yates as Eugenia, Sarah Woolgar as Laura/ **Princess's,** Oct. 1852, with Mr. Addison as Amd. Franklin, James Vining as Charles, John Cathcart as Sandford, Edward Wright as Lackaday, John Chester as Curtis, Miss Murray as Eugenia, Carlotta Leclercq as Laura, Mrs. W. Daly as Mrs. Bell, Miss Daly as Susan.

SWELLS FROM TOWN// F// n.a.// **Sad. Wells,**

Nov. 1866, with J. Collier as Capt. Rambleton, Walter Holland as Varnish, John Rouse as Tom, Louise Pereira as Ellen.

SWINDLER, THE; OR, THE CAPTIVE MAID// D// A. V. Campbell// **Britannia**, Aug. 1873.

SWISS COTTAGE, THE (also titled Why Don't She Marry?)// C 1a// T. H. Bayly// **Princess's**, Aug. 1845, with W. H. Oxberry as Tieck, Mr. Walton as Corp. Max, Miss Grant as Lisette, Miss Somers as Ninette, Miss Taylor as Louise, Miss Mott as Mariette/ **Drury Lane**, Jan. 1852, with Ellen Bateman as Tieck, Mr. Bateman as Max, Kate Bateman as Lisette, Jane Coveney as Louise, Harriet Coveney as Janet/ **Olympic**, Aug. 1852, with Henry Compton as Tieck, William Farren Jr. as Corp. Max, Harriet Gordon as Lisette.

SWORD OF DAMOCLES, THE// F// Adap. by Philip Darwin fr G// **St. Geo. Hall**, Jan. 1890.

SWORDSMAN'S DAUGHTER, THE// D 5a// Adap. by Brandon Thomas & Clement Scott fr F of Jules Mary & Georges Grisier, Le Maitre d'Armes// **Adelphi**, Aug. 1895, with William Terriss as Vibrac, Charles Fulton as Olgan, Harry Nicholls as de Chantoisel, J. R. Crauford as Dubarry, Julian Cross as Wilkins, Richard Purdon as Breton, G. R. Foss as Melvil, W. L. Abingdon as de Rochefiere, Jessie Millward as Madeleine, Miss Vane Featherston as Thérese, Alice Marriott as Mrs. Wilkins, Kate Kearney as Mme. Breton, Mrs. E. H. Brooke as Lisette/ Scenery by Joseph Harker & Bruce Smith/ Music by John Crook/ Prod. by Fred Latham.

SYBIL, THE HUNCHBACK// D Pro & 3a// F. Ford// **Marylebone**, June 1874.

SYBILLA; OR, STEP BY STEP// C 3a// J. Palgrave Simpson// **St. James's**, Oct. 1864, with Frederic Robinson as King Christian, Henry Ashley as Count Wolfenstiern, Frank Matthews as Joachim Barke, Walton Chamberlaine as Petrus Barke, C. J. Mathews as Flemming, H. J. Montague as Wilfred, W. H. Eburne as Jansen, Mrs. C. J. Mathews as Sybilla, Miss Percival as Suzanne.

SYLVENA, OF ATHLONE; OR, THE PASS OF RATHCONNELL// D// n.a.// **Sad. Wells**, May 1839, with Mr. Williams, C. J. Smith as Sir Richard, Robert Honner as Capt. Greville, W. D. Broadfoot as Sir James, Mr. Elvin as Capt. Hope, Mr. Phillips as Don Diego, Mr. Cathcart as Neil O'Gorm, John Webster as Michael O'Gorm, Mr. Dry as O'Brian, Mr. Conquest as Durfy, J. W. Collier as Dickens, Mrs. Robert Honner as Sylvena, Miss Pincott as Katty/ Scenery by Mr. Fenwick & G. Smithyes Jr./ Music by Mr. Herbert/ Machines by B. Sloman.

SYLVIA; OR, THE FOREST FLOWER// n.a.// **Royalty**, Feb. 1866.

SYNDICATE, THE// F 2a// Adeline Votieri// **St. Geo. Hall**, June 1897.

SYREN, THE// D// Adap. by J. Palgrave Simpson fr F of Octave Feuillet, Dalilah// **Lyceum**, 1869, with Kate Saville, Charles Coghlan.

SYREN OF PARIS, THE// D 2a// Adap. by W. E. Suter fr F// **Queen's**, Apr. 1861.

*

TABITHA'S COURTSHIP// C// n.a.// **Comedy**, Feb. 1890.

TABLES, THE// Play 1a// Marie Wilton Bancroft// **Criterion**, June 1901.

TAILOR MAKES THE MAN, THE// J. E. Soden// **Globe**, Mar. 1876, with Edward Price as Lambkin, Charles Wilmot as Pods, Charles Steyne as Orts, Miss F. Robertson as Virginia Dander, Nelly Harris as Emma, Dolores Drummond as Mary.

TAILOR OF TAMWORTH, THE; OR, STATE SECRETS (see also, State Secrets// D// T. E. Wilks// **Sad. Wells**, Mar. 1839, with Mr. Elvin as Neville, Dibdin Pitt as Hal, Mr. Williams as Hodgehog, W. Smith as Thimblewell, Miss Cooke as Maud, Miss Pincott as Lucy.

TAINT IN THE BLOOD, A; OR, THE POISONED PEARL// D 4a// n.a.// **Grecian**, Oct. 1856, with Mr. Hustleby as Brigand, Richard Phillips as Morland, Henry Grant as de Lafure, Mr. Melvin as de Launay, John Manning as Grizzle, Eaton O'Donnell as Gaspard, Jane Coveney, Harriet Coveney, Ellen Hale, Miss Johnstone.

TAKE CARE OF DOWB// F// J. Maddison Morton// **Haymarket**, Nov. 1857, with William Farren as Dowbiggin, Edwin Villiers as Ramsay, J. B. Buckstone as Wallop, Thomas Coe as John, Miss Lavine as Mrs. Dowbiggin, Ellen Ternan as Fanny, Mrs. Edward Fitzwilliam as Mrs. Wallop.

TAKE THAT GIRL AWAY!// C// C. J. Mathews// **Drury Lane**, Dec. 1855, with A. Younge as Poddle, C. J. Mathews as Rocket, Charles Swan as Scollop, Mr. Tilbury as Cuttle, Miss M. Oliver as Isabel, Miss Mason as Jenny, Emma Wadham as Dinah.

TAKEN BY FORCE// n.a.// **Novelty**, Mar. 1897.

TAKEN BY SURPRISE// F 1a// John Courtney// **Princess's**, June 1844, with Mr. Fitzjames as Metaphor, Walter Lacy as Single, W. H. Oxberry as Martin, T. Hill as Keeper, Miss Noel as Mrs. Preston, Emma Stanley as Laura, Miss E. Honner as Faith, Miss Brooks as Patty, Miss Somers as Mrs. Nibble.

TAKEN FROM LIFE// D 5a// Henry Pettitt// **Adelphi**, Dec. 1881, with Charles Warner as Walter Lee, J. D. Beveridge as Philip Radley, E. H. Brooke as Maguire, Fred Thorne as Titus, Edward Price as Denby, Harry Proctor as Gallon, Miss Gerard as Kate Denby, Florence Chalgrove as Bella, Edith Bruce as Mary/ Scenery by F. Lloyds/ Machines by Edward Charker/ Music by Karl Meyder/ Prod. by Charles Warner.

TAKEN FROM MEMORY// n.a.// **Britannia**, Nov. 1873.

TAKING BY STORM// D// G. H. Lewis// **Lyceum**, June 1852, with C. J. Mathews as Buff, William Suter as Piper, Isabel Dickenson as Betsy, Julia St. George as Fanny/ Scenery by W. Beverley/ Music by J. H. Tully/ Machines by H. Sloman/ **Haymarket**, July 1861, with C. J. Mathews as Buff, William Clark as Piper, Mrs. Edward Fitzwilliam as Betsy, Henrietta Lindley as Fanny, Miss Lovell as Martha.

TAKING IT EASY// F 1a// n.a.// **Drury Lane**, Apr. 1884, with Mr. Cheesman as Scatterbrain, Lewis Waller as Jack, Henry Westland as Sam, Miss K. Carlyon as Lucinda, Miss Wolseley as Lucy/ **Toole's**, Nov. 1882.

TAKING THE PLEDGE// F 1a// n.a.// **Princess's**, Oct. 1844, with W. H. Oxberry as Larkins, Walter Lacy as Pops, Robert Honner as Affidavit, T. Hill as Holden, Miss Noel as Rosabella, Emma Stanley as Emily.

TAKING THE WATERS// n.a.// **St. Geo. Hall**, Nov. 1886.

TAKING THE VEIL// D 3a// C. H. Hazlewood// **Britannia**, July 1870.

TALBOT'S TRUST// D 2a// T. A. Tharp// **Globe**, Sept. 1875, with Lin Rayne as Harold Garnet, Mr. Hallows as Julius Ambrose, Henry Deane as Needle, Ada Ward as Catherine Talbot, Miss Hathaway as Mrs. Biscoe, Miss Ges. Smythe as Minnie.

TALE OF A COAT, A// William Brough// **Haymarket**, Nov. 1858, with Edwin Villiers as Baron de Meremont, C. J. Mathews as Molinet, William Cullenford as Don Gomez, George Braid as Minister, Mrs. Poynter as Mme. de Meremont, Ellen Ternan as Adele, Miss Fitzinman as Inez, Mrs. Edward Fitzwilliam as Paquita.

TALE OF A COMET, THE// F// Lennox Horne// **Drury Lane**, Feb. 1873, with William Terriss as Payback, E. Jones as Softdown, Stanislaus Calhaem as Forcem, Mr. Douglas as Jobson, Charlotte Saunders as Miss Tabitha, Miss Alma as Florence, Miss D'Arcy as Jenny.

TALE OF A TELEPHONE, A// n.a.// **Drury Lane**, Jan. 1879.

TALE OF A TUB, A// D 2a// Mrs. C. Gore// **Haymarket**, July 1837, with Frederick Vining as Lauzun, Mr. Saville as Louis XV, J. West as St. Vallier, Charles Selby as Jolicoeur, J. Worrell as Rattan, T. F. Mathews as Bronze, Mrs. Humby as Jeannette, Mrs. Nisbett as Mme. du Barry, Mrs. W. Clifford as Countess de Grammount.

TALE OF A TUB// C 1a// Paul Merritt & H. Ginnet// **Duke's**, Mar. 1876/ **Olympic**, Dec. 1879, with Nelly Bromley as Phyllis, F. H. Macklin as Cyril, Edward Righton as Antonio.

TALE OF MYSTERY, THE// D// Thomas Holcroft// **Sad. Wells**, July 1843, with Mr. Williams as Bonamo, Mr. Lamb as Stephano, C. J. Bird as Montano, R. H. Lingham as Malvoglio, C. J. Smith as Francisco, Caroline Rankley as Selina, Mrs. Richard Barnett as Fiametta.

TALE OF THE THAMES// n.a.// **Surrey**, Oct. 1895.

TALE OF TWO CITIES, A// Pro & 2a// Dram. fr novel of Charles Dickens// **Lyceum**, Feb. 1860, with Walter Lacy as Marquis de St. Evremond, Mr. Forrester as Chevalier de St. Evremond, James Vining as Dr. Manette, Mme. Celeste as Colette and as Therese Defarge, Frederick Villiers as Sidney Carton, T. Lyon as Lorry, James Johnstone as Defarge, Henry Butler as Gaspard, Kate Saville as Lucie/ Scenery by William Callcott/ Machines by Mr. Bare/ Music by George Loder.

TALK OF THE TOWN, THE// F 3a// Ellie Norwood (a rev. vers. of The Noble Art)// **Strand**, Aug. 1901.

TAM O'SHANTER// F// H. R. Addison// **Haymarket**, Aug. 1837, with William Farren as O'Shanter, Robert Strickland as Johnnie, J. Worrell as Roderick, Benjamin Webster as David, Mrs. Fitzwilliam as Maggie, Miss E. Phillips as Jeannie, Miss Wrighten as Mrs, Mucklewee, Mrs. Tayleure as Dame Shanter.

TAME CAT, A// C// L. N. Parker// **Matinee**, June 1898.

TAME CATS// C 3a// Edmund Yates// **POW**, Dec. 1868.

TAMING A TIGER// F 1a// Adap. fr F// **Globe**, June 1880, with Charles Morton as Chutnee, J. S. Blythe as Beeswing, L. Williams as Jacob.

TAMING OF THE SHREW, THE// C// William Shakespeare// **Haymarket**, Jan. 1848, with Mr. Lambert as Sly, Mrs. Caulfield as Hostess, J. W. Gough as Baptista, Mr. Tilbury as Vincentio, Henry Vandenhoff as Lucentio, Henry Howe as Hortensio, James Bland as Gromio, Benjamin Webster as Petrucio, Robert Keeley as Grumio, Mrs. Nisbett as Katherine, Mrs. Seymour as Bianca; Oct. 1867, with Henry Howe as Petruchio, P. White as Baptista, Walter Gordon as Hortensio, George Braid as Biondello, Henry Compton as Grumio, Mrs. Mary Scott-Siddons as Katherine, Miss Matthews as Bianca, Mrs. Laws as Curtis/ **Sad. Wells**, Nov. 1856, with Alfred Rayner as Lord, Samuel Phelps as Sly, Mr. Williams as Baptista, T. C. Harris as Vincentio, William Belford as

Lucentio, Henry Marston as PetruchioJ. W. Ray as Gremio, Mr. Haywell as Hortensio, Frederic Robinson as Tranio, Miss Atkinson as Katharina, Jenny Marston as Bianca/ Scenery by F. Fenton & C. Fenton/ Machines by Mr. Cawdery/ **Olympic**, Apr. 1864, with Henry Neville as Petruchio, Harwood Cooper as Baptiste, Robert Soutar as Biondello, Horace Wigan as Tailor, Edward Atkins as Grumio, Miss Hughes as Katherine, Florence Haydon as Bianca/ **Grecian**, Dec. 1865, with Mr. Richards as Petruchio, George Gillett as Biondello, J. Jackson as Baptista, John Manning as Givorneo, Walter Holland as Hortenzio, Mr. Goodin as Pedro, Miss D'Aubeny as Katherine, Marie Brewer as Bianca/ **Globe**, Oct. 1870 [in vers. arr. by David Garrick & rev. by John Kemble, entitled Taming The Shrew], with Mr. Fairclough, E. J. Shepherd, Shafto Robertson, W. L. Branscombe, Rowley Cathcart, Bessie Alleyne, Isabelle Armour, Emily Burns; Jan. 1880, with F. R. Benson as Petruchio, George Black as Baptista, Henry Athol as Vincentio, G. R. Weir as Grumio, Mrs. F. R. Benson as Katherina, Marion Grey as Bianca, Alice Denvil as Curtis/ **Gaiety**, May 1888 in vers. by Augustin Daly/ **Lyceum**, July 1890, "rearranged" by Augustin Daly, with George Clarke as a Lord, Charles Wheatleigh as Christopher Sly, Charles Fisher as Baptista, John Moore as Vincentio, Eugene Ormond as Lucentio, John Drew as Petruchio, Charles Leclercq as Gremio, Sidney Herbert as Hortensio, James Lewis as Grumio, Edward Wilks as Biondello, Ada Rehan as Katherine, Edith Crane as Bianca, Mrs. G. H. Gilbert as Curtis/ **Daly's**, June 1893/ **Comedy**, Jan. 1901.

TAMING THE TRUANT// C 3a// Adap. by Horace Wigan fr F// **Olympic**, Mar. 1863, with Henry Neville as Flutter, Horace Wigan as Blush, Walter Gordon as Pertinax, Harwood Cooper as Fringe, Miss Hughes as Aurelia, Miss Latimer as Florence, Miss Conway as Mary.

TANGLED CHAIN, A// Adap. by Henrietta Lindley fr novel of Mrs. Panton// **POW**, Mar. 1888.

TANGLED SKEIN, A// D 3a// Oswald Allen & Dudley Fleck// **Grecian**, Aug. 1872.

TANGLED WEB, A// C 4a// Vere Chester// **Criterion**, July 1884.

TARANTULA, THE// D// Mary Scott// **Haymarket**, Sept. 1897.

TARES// Play 3a// Mrs. Oscar Beringer// **POW**, Jan. 1888/ **Opera Comique**, Jan. 1889.

TARTAR WITCH AND PEDLAR BOY, THE// D 2a// n.a.// **Sad. Wells**, Feb. 1839, with J. W. Collier as Azim, Mr. Conquest as Chinque le Too, Mr. Walton as Kien-Long, Mr. Phillips as Orasming, Mrs. Robert Honner as Zamfi, Mrs. Harwood as Zepherenza, Miss Pincott as Ebra, Charles Montgomery as Banaska, John Gardiner as Manghi, Miss Richardson as Maga/ Scenery by Fenwick & Smithyes/ Music by G. Stansbury/ Machines by B. Sloman/ Prod. by R. Honner.

TARTUFFE// C// Adap. by John Oxenford fr F of Moliere// **Haymarket**, Mar. 1851, with Mr. Lambert as Orgon, E. L. Davenport as Damis, Henry Howe as Valere, Mr. Rogers as Cleante, Benjamin Webster as Tartuffe, Charles Selby as Loyal, Mrs. Stanley as Mme. Pernelle, Miss Reynolds as Elmire, Laura Addison as Marianne, Mrs. Fitzwilliam as Dorine/ Scenery by George Morris/ Machines by F. Neselton/ **Adelphi**, July 1856, with Charles Selby as Orgon, John Parselle as Damis, J. G. Shore as Cléante, Benjamin Webster as Tartuffe, C. J. Smith as Loyal, Mrs. Leigh Murray as Mme. Pernelle, Mme. Celeste as Elmire, Mary Keeley as Mariane, Kate Kelly as Dorine/ **Sad. Wells**, July 1858, with Benjamin Webster as Tartuffe, Charles Selby as Orgon, John Billington as Damis, Frederick Moreland as Valere, Edmund Garden as Cleante, C. J. Smith as Loyal, Mme. Celeste as Elmire, Mrs. Chatterley as Mme. Pernelle, Mary Keeley as Mariane, Marie Wilton as Dorine, Mrs. Conran as Flipete.

TEA// F 3a// Maurice Noel// **Criterion**, May 1887.

TEACHER TAUGHT, THE// F 1a// Edward Stirling// **Sad. Wells**, Oct. 1850, with A. Younge as Aubrey, William Hoskins as Henry, Charles Fenton as Tom, Lucy Rafter as Charlotte, Mrs. Archbold as Mrs. Plausible.

TEARS// C// B. C. Stephenson ("Bolton Rowe")// **Opera Comique**, Feb. 1877.

TEARS, IDLE TEARS// D 1a// Adap. by Clement Scott fr F of Jules Sandeau & Pierre Decourselle, Marcel// **Globe**, Nov. 1872, with H. J. Montague as Wilfrid Cumberledge, Charles Flockton as Dr. Stone, Charles Neville as Davy Wright, Rose Massey as Mrs. Cumberledge, Mrs Gaston Murray (Miss Hughes) as Nurse.

TEDDY THE TILER// F 1a// G. H. Rodwell// **Sad. Wells**, Feb. 1837, with Mr. Ray as Henry, C. H. Pitt as Frederick, John Ayliffe as Lord Dunderford, Mr. Burton as Notary, Mr. Scarbrow as Tim, T. Lee as Teddy, Mrs. Harris as Lady Dunderford, Miss Lebatt as Oriel, Miss Julian as Flora; Sept. 1844, with Mr. Williams as Lord Dunderford, Mr. Morton as Henry, Mr. Collins as Teddy, Charles Fenton as Frederick, Mr. Sharpe as Bombardine, Mr. Coreno as Tim, Mr. Franks as Richard, Mrs. Henry Marston as Lady Dunderford, Miss Huddart as Oriel, Miss Thornbury as Julia, Georgiana Lebatt as Flora/ **Haymarket**, Aug. 1837, with Tyrone Power as Mullowny, J. W. Gough as Lord Dunderford, J. Worrell as Henry, Charles Selby as Frederick, T. F. Mathews as Bombardine, Mrs. Gallot as Lady Dunderford, Miss E. Phillips as Oriel, Miss Wrighten as Flora, Miss Gallot as Julia; Mar. 1845, with Mr. Collins as Mullowny, J. W. Gough as Dunderford, A. Brindal as Henry, Henry Howe as Frederick, Mrs. Stanley as Lady Dunderford, Mrs. L. S. Buckingham as Oriel, Miss Carre as Flora/ **Cov. Garden**, Feb. 1838, with Mr. Tilbury as Lord Dunderford, Mr. Roberts as Henry, Henry Howe as Frederick,

Edwin Yarnold as Scrivener, W. H. Payne as Bombardine, Tyrone Power as Mullowny, Mrs. Griffith as Lady Dunderford, Miss E. Phillips as Oriel, Mrs. Humby as Flora, Miss Garrick as Julia/ **Olympic**, Dec. 1841, with Mr. Walton as Frederick, Mr. Green as Henry, Mr. Brookes as Lord Dunderford, J. Burns as Tim, Mr. Fleming as George, Mr. Collins as Teddy, Mrs. Granby as Lady Dunderford, Miss Bartlett as Flora, Miss Fitzjames as Oriel/ **Princess's**, Aug. 1845, with Mr. Granby as Lord Dunderford, Augustus Harris as Henry, F. C. Courtney as Frederick, Robert Honner as Scrivener, Mr. Collins as Teddy, Mrs. Fosbroke as Lady Dunderford, Miss E. Honner as Oriel, Miss Somers as Flora, Miss Mott as Julia.

TEDDY'S WIVES// F 3a// Fergus Hume// **Strand**, Sept. 1896.

TEDDY THE TILER// F// n.a.// **Grecian**, Oct. 1844, with Mr. Campbell as Lord Dunderford, Harry Chester as Henry, Mr. Melvin as Frederick, Mr. Hodson as Teddy Malowney, Mr. Kerridge as Tim, Miss Merion as Lady Dunderford, Miss Johnstone as Oriel, Mrs. Chester as Flora.

TEKELI; OR, THE MILL OF KEBEN (also subt. The Siege of Montgatz)// D 1a// T. E. Hook// **Sad. Wells**, July 1842, with John Webster as Tekeli, Mr. Lingham as Count Caraffa, Henry Marston as Wolf, C. J. Smith as Maurice, John Herbert as Bras-de-fer, Mr. Bird as Edmund, Miss Lane as Christine/ **Astley's**, Sept. 1857, with James Holloway as Count Tekeli, Mr. Vokes as Conrad, Mark Howard as Wolf, H. Hemmings as Laidore, Julia Weston as Christine, J. T. Anderson as Edmund, J. W. Anson as Counr Caraffa, Henry Reeves as Maurice.

TELEGRAM, THE// Play// William Sapte Jr// **Globe**, Nov. 1888.

TELEPHONE, THE// F 1a// Arthur Clements// **Strand**, Apr. 1878.

TEMPEST, THE// D// William Shakespeare// **Cov. Garden**, Oct. 1838, with Mr. Warde as Alonzo, Charles Diddear as Sebastian, W. C. Macready as Prospero, Samuel Phelps as Antonio, James Anderson as Ferdinand, Mr. Waldron as Gonzalo, Charles Bender as Adrian, C. J. Smith as Francisco, George Bennett as Caliban, John Pritt Harley as Trinculo, George Bartley as Stephano, Helen Faucit as Miranda, Priscilla Horton as Ariel; Nov. 1842, with Mr. Cooper as Alonso, Charles Diddear as Sebastian, George Vandenhoff as Prospero, James Vining as Antonio, Charles Pitt as Ferdinand, Frank Matthews as Gonzalo, Alfred Wigan as Adrian, James Bland as Caliban, John Pritt Harley as Trinculo, Miss Vandenhoff as Miranda, Miss Rainforth as Ariel/ Scenery by Grieve, T. Grieve & W. Grieve/ Machines by Mr. Sloman/ **Sad. Wells**, Apr. 1847, with William Hoskins as Alonzo, Edward Knight as Sebastian, Samuel Phelps as Prospero, Henry Mellon as Antionio, Frank Graham as Gonzalo, Henry Marston as Ferdinand, George Bennett as Caliban, Henry Scharf as Trinculo, A. Younge as Stephano, Laura Addison as Miranda, Julia St. George as Ariel/ Scenery by F. Fenton & Mr. Finlay/ Machines by Mr. Cawdery/ **Princess's**, July 1857, with Mr. Cooper as Alonzo, Mr. Raymond as Sebastian, Charles Kean as Prospero, John Cathcart as Antonio, Miss Bufton as Ferdinand, Frank Graham as Gonzalo, John Ryder as Caliban, John Pritt Harley as Trunculo, Frank Matthews as Stephano, Carlotta Leclercq as Miranda, Kate Terry as Ariel/ Scenery under dir. of Mr. Grieve/ Music by J. L. Hatton, Machines by G. Hodsdon/ **Standard**, Mar. 1859, with Henry Marston/ **Lyceum**, Apr. 1899, with G. Fitzgerald as Alonzo, H. R. Hignett as Sebastian, Alfred Brydone as Prospero, E. A. Warburton as Antonio, Frank Rodney as Ferdinand, Arthur Whitby as Gonzalo, F. R. Benson as Caliban, Mrs. F. R. Benson as Miranda, Kitty Loftus as Ariel.

TEMPEST OF THE HEART// D 3a// William Travers// **East London**, Mar. 1868.

TEMPEST TOSSED// D 4a// Edward Darbey// **Marylebone**, Nov. 1886.

TEMPLAR, THE// D 5a// A. R. Slous// **Princess's**, Nov. 1850, with John Ryder as de la Roche, Frederick Belton as Bertrand, Charles Fisher as Beauvais, James Vining as St. Foix, Mr. Wynn as Clisson, George Everett as Fabian, John Cathcart as Eustace, Charles Kean as la Marche, Frederick Cooke as De Tancarville, Mrs. Charles Kean as Isoline.

TEMPLAR AND THE JEWESS, THE// D// J. P. Jackson// **Drury Lane**, May 1841.

TEMPTATION; OR, THE FATAL BRAND// D// n.a.// **Grecian**, Aug. 1866, with William James as Vivian, Charles Mortimer as Bertrand, John Manning as Jacques, Alfred Rayner as Ramagean, Lizzie Mandelbert as Pauline, Harriet Western as Elise, Mary A. Victor as Teresa.

TEMPTATION; OR, THE PROGRESS OF CRIME// D 2a// Dram. by J. P. Wilson fr tale of De Kock// **Sad. Wells**, June 1841, with Mr. Elvin as Edward Murville, Mr. Dry as James Murville, J. W. Collier as Sans Souci, Mr. Aldridge as Dupré, Henry Marston as Dufresne, Robert Honner as Lampine, Mrs. Robert Honner as Adeline, Miss Cooke as Mme. Germeuil, Mrs. Richard Barnett as Louise/ Scenery by F. Fenton & G. Smithyes/ Music by Isaac Collins/ Machines by B. Sloman/ Prod. by R. Honner.

TEMPTATION AND ATONEMENT// D 2a// George Conquest// **Grecian**, June 1861, with J. Jackson as Sir Clement, Mr. Costello as Wigswell, Henry Grant as Colston, Thomas Mead as Old Downing, John Manning as Carr, Henry Grant as Jukes, Jane Coveney as Esther; Apr. 1867, with Alfred Rayner, George Gillett, Mr. Goodin, John Manning, Samuel Perfitt, J. Jackson, Henry Grant, Lizzie Mandelbert.

TEMPTER, THE// Play 4a// Henry Arthur Jones// **Haymarket**, Sept. 1893, with Herbert Beerbohm Tree as The Tempter, Fred Terry as Prince Leon, Holman Clark as Earl of Rougemont, Fuller Mellish as Sir Gilbert, A.

H. Revelle as Sir Gaultier, F. A. Everill as Father Urban, G. W. Anson as Pound, Charles Allan as Host, Lilly Hanbury as Lady Isobel, Mrs. Beerbohm Tree as Lady Avis, Mrs. E. H. Brooke as Sarah, Irene Vanbrugh as Lettice/ Scenery by W. T. Hemsley & Walter Hann/ Music by Edward German/ Electrics by E. Wingfield Bowles.

TEMPTER, THE; OR, THE OLD MILL OF ST. DENIS// D// J. Greaves// **Sad. Wells**, June 1838, with Mr. Cathcart as Darville, Mr. Dry as Mongerand, C. J. Smith as Edward, Dibdin Pitt as Poncet, Mr. Conquest as Sam Snipe, J. W. Collier as Jacques, Mr. Montague as Malcour, Miss Richardson as Leonie, Mrs. J. F. Saville as Louise, Miss Cook as Mariette/ Scenery by Mr. Telbin.

TEMPTING BAIT, A// F// W. J. Austin// **Opera Comique**, Oct. 1875.

TEN THOUSAND A YEAR// D 4a// Dram. by R. B. Peake fr novel of S. Warren// **Adelphi**, Nov. 1841, with George Maynard, E. Morgan, Mr. Lyon, Mr. Wieland, John Sanders, Paul Bedford, William Cullenford, Mr. Freeborn, Mrs. H. P. Grattan, Mrs. Fosbroke, Mrs. Yates.

TEN THOUSAND TOPSAIL SHEET BLOCKS// C// J. Bosworth// **Grecian**, Dec. 1863, with J. Jackson as Acheson, W. Shirley as Vonestracht, Walter Holland as Dawes, Henry Grant as Dubois, John Manning as Dillydragge, William James as Blocks, George Gillett as Hernhausen, Jane Dawson as Caroline, Fanny Reynolds as Eugenia, Ellen Crisp as Widow Blocks, Marie Brewer as Alicia.

TENANT FOR LIFE// F 1a// n.a.// **Sad. Wells**, Nov. 1858, William Belford as Smith, Mr. Meagreson as Snap, Charles Seyton as Bibblecombe, Mr. Williams as Hayward, Grace Egerton as Mrs. Hayward Jr., Mrs. Henry Marston as Mrs. Hayward Sr., Mrs. J. B. Hill as Miss Skriggs, Eliza Travers as Mary.

TENDER CHORD, THE// Adap. by Alfred Maltby fr F// **Terry's** (L) June 1899.

TENDER PRECAUTIONS; OR, THE ROMANCE OF MARRIAGE// C 1a// T. J. Serle// **Princess's**, Nov. 1851, with Mr. Addison as Adm. Jollyboy, Robert Keeley as Gosling, Alfred Wigan as Sparkes, Mr. Wynn as Capt. Wildbore, George Everett as Chase, Frederick Cooke as Grab, Mrs. Keeley as Mrs. Gosling, Miss Murray as Lucy, Mrs. Alfred Wigan as Mrs. Souchong.

TENTERHOOKS// F 3a// Henry Paull// **Comedy**, May 1889.

TERAPH, THE// C 2a// Hedworth Williamson// **Court**, May 1900.

TERESA// Play 3a// G. P. Bancroft// **Garrick**, Sept. 1898.

TERMAGANT, THE// Play 4a// L. N. Parker & Murray Carson// **Her Majesty's**, Sept. 1898.

TERPSICHORE// Play 1a// Justin McCarthy// **Lyric**, July 1894.

TERRIBLE SECRET, A// F 1a// J. Stirling Coyne// **Drury Lane**, Oct. 1861, with Edward Atkins as Henpecker, Robert Roxby as Loosefish, Miss E. Arden as Mrs. Henpecker, Louise Keeley as Tilly.

TERRIBLE TINKER, A// F 1a// T. J. Williams// **Astley's**, Dec. 1869.

TERROR OF LONDON, THE// D// Walter James & Harold Whyte// **Grecian**, Oct. 1879.

TERROR OF PARIS, THE// D 4a// E. H. Mitchelson & Charles Longden// **Pavilion**, June 1895.

TESS// Play 4a// Dram. by H. A. Kennedy fr novel of Thomas Hardy, Tess of the D'Urbervilles// **Coronet**, Feb. 1900/ **Comedy**, Apr. 1900.

TESS OF THE D'URBERVILLES// D// Dram. by Lorimer Stoddart fr novel of Thomas Hardy// **St. James's**, Mar. 1897.

TEXAN, THE// Play 4a// Tyrone Power// **Princess's**, June 1894.

THAD; OR, LINKED BY LOVE// C 3a// Paul Meritt// **Grecian**, July 1872.

THAMES, THE; OR, ADRIFT ON THE TIDE// D 4a// Robert Dodson// **Surrey**, Sept. 1879.

THAT BEAUTIFUL BICEPS// F// H. S. Clarke// **Drury Lane**, Sept. 1876, with Brittain Wright as Boodles, Percy Bell as Smithini, F. W. Irish as Gubbins, Harriet Coveney as Belinda, Clara Jecks as Sally.

THAT BLESSED BABY// F 1a// F. Moore// **Adelphi**, Feb. 1856/ **Lyceum**, Aug. 1879, with Frank Tyars as Finnicke, Stanislaus Calhaem as John Thomas, S. Russell as Policeman, Miss Dolman as Mrs. Lever, Miss Roland Phillips as Mary Jane/ **Princess's**, Dec. 1880, with P. C. Beverley as Finnicke, Stanislaus Calhaem as Thomas, Dot Coombes as Flora, Violet Temple as Mrs. Lever, Maud Milton as Mary Jane.

THAT DOCTOR CUPID// C 3a// Adap. by Robert Buchanan partly fr Samuel Foote's The Devil Upon Two Sticks// **Vaudeville**, Jan. 1889.

THAT DREADFUL DOCTOR// C 1a// C. L. Young// **Haymarket**, Oct. 1888, with Angela Cudmore as Mrs. Beauchamp, Fred. Harrison as Beauchamp, Charles Allan as Dr. Mars.

THAT GIRL// C 3a// Dram. by Mrs. Oscar Beringer & Henry Hamilton fr story by Clementina Black// **Haymarket**, July 1890.

THAT HORRID BIGGINS// F// n.a.// **Royalty**, Jan. 1866.

THAT HOUSE IN HIGH STREET// n.a.// **Strand**, July 1856.

THAT ODIOUS CAPTAIN CUTTER// C 1a// J. Palgrave Simpson// **Olympic**, Feb. 1851, with George Cocke as Peregrine, John Kinloch as Valentine, Leigh Murray as Capt. Cutter, Mr. Tanner as James, Mrs. Stirling as Widow Harcourt, Mrs. B. Bartlett as Mistress Prudence, Miss E. Shalders as Mrs. Tippet.

THAT RASCAL JACK// F 1a// Thomas Greenwood// **Sad. Wells**, Feb. 1843, with C. J. Bird as Granby, John Herbert as John and as Jack, Mr. Williams as Waddleton, Miss Melville as Emily, Mrs. Richard Barnett as Lucy/ **Drury Lane**, June 1867, with J. Neville as Maddleton, Charles Warner as Granby, John Rouse as Jack, Paul Bedford as Walter, Bessie Alleyn as Amelia, Miss C. Thompson as Lucy.

THAT RING// F// V. C. Rolfe// **St. Geo. Hall**, May 1893.

THAT SISTER OF MINE// C // S. J. Adair-Fitzgerald// **St. Geo. Hall**, Dec. 1900.

THAT TELEGRAM (see Telegram)

THAT WRETCH OF A WOMAN// D 4a// Walter Melville// **Standard**, Nov. 1901.

THEMIS// F 3a// Adap. by H. P. Stevens fr F of Victorien Sardou// **Royalty**, Mar. 1880, with Charles Groves, Rose Cullen.

THEN FLOWERS GREW FAIRER// Play 1a// Sutton Vane// **Terry's**, Aug. 1894.

THEODORA// Play 6a// Adap. by Robert Buchanan fr F of Victorien Sardou// **Princess's**, May 1890/ **Olympic**, Aug. 1891.

THEODORA, ACTRESS AND EMPRESS// D 5a// Watts Phillips// **Surrey**, Apr. 1866.

THERE'S MANY A SLIP 'TWIXT CUP AND LIP// C 3a// Robert Hall// **St. Geo. Hall**, Jan. 1877.

THERESA VORSHNER; OR, THE TRAITOR OF THE TYROL PASS// D// G. D. Pitt// **Victoria**, Mar. 1848, with John Dale as Landberg, N. T. Hicks as Sebastian, Mr. Henderson as Affland, J. Howard as Vorshner, Charles Morelli as Waldeck, T. H. Higgie as Lutold, G. F. Forman as Titmouse, Walter Searle as Dr. Ap Grap, F. H. Henry as Sibert, Annette Vincent as Theresa, Miss Burroughcliffe as Jodette, Mrs. George Lee as Beatrice, Mrs. Cooke as Mrs. Ap Grub.

THERESE; OR, THE ORPHAN OF GENEVA// D 3a// John Howard Payne// **Sad. Wells**, June 1837, with Mr. Hicks as Fontaine, Mr. Rogers as Lavigne, Mr. King as Delpare, C. H. Pitt as Charles, Mr. Griffiths as Picard, Mrs. W. West as Therese, Miss Williams as the Countess, Miss Young as Annette, Mrs. Harris as Bridget; Mar. 1844, with Henry Marston as Carwin, R. Younge as Fontaine, Mr. Bird as Count de Morville, Mr. Williams as Picard, Mr. Coreno as Lavigne, Caroline Rankley as Therese, Mrs. Andrews as the Countess, Fanny Morelli as Mariette, Miss Cooke as Bridget, Miss Lee as Julia; Jan. 1863, with Henry Forrester as Carwin, E. F. Edgar as Fontaine, H. Dalton as Count Morville, C. Lloyd as Picard, Lewis Ball as Lavigne, A. Montague as Delparre, Sophie Miles as Therese, Mrs. William Dowton as the Countess, Bessie Heath as Bridget/ **Grecian**, May 1845, with Harry Chester as Carwin, F. Ede as Fontaine, Edwin Dixon as Count de Morville, Edmund Garden as Picard, Frederick Robson as Lavigne, Miss M. A. Crisp as Mariette, Miss Merion as Countess de Morville; Apr. 1865, with David Jones as Carwin, J. B. Steele as Foutain, George Gillett as Count de Morville, John Manning as Picard, Lizzie Mandlebert as Therese, Louise Graham as Countess de Morville, Mary A. Victor as Bridget.

THERESE RAQUIN// D 4a// Adap. by A. Teixeira de Mattos fr F of Emile Zola// **Royalty**, Oct. 1891.

THEY WERE MARRIED// C 4a// Adap. by J. R. Crauford & Frederick Hawley fr story by W. Besant// **Strand**, June 1892.

THIEF MAKER, THE// D Pro & 3a// Edward Towers// **East London**, Feb. 1878.

THIEVES! THIEVES!// F 1a// n.a.// **Olympic**, Mar. 1857, with George Vining as Lushington, Frederick Robson as Brown, Henry Leslie as Bludyer, Miss Swanborough as Mrs. Dashwood, Miss Bromley as Mary.

THIMBLE RIG, THE// F// J. B. Buckstone// **Haymarket**, Nov. 1844, with J. B. Buckstone as Ginger, Mr. Tilbury as Worrycow, William Strickland as Shindy, Mrs. W. Clifford as Mrs. Ginger.

THIRD CLASS AND FIRST CLASS// n.a.// **Britannia**, Aug. 1859.

THIRD TIME, THE// C// C. H. Dickinson// **St. Geo. Hall**, Feb. 1896.

THIRST FOR GOLD, A// D 5a// Adap. fr F of A. P. Dennery & Ferdinand Dugué// **Olympic**, June 1885, with Henry Nelson as Capt. de Lascours, Charles Ward as Carlos, Frank Dallas as Medoc, T. G. Bailey as Barabas, Ada Ward as Louise.

THIRST OF GOLD, THE; OR, THE LOST SHIP AND THE WILD FLOWER OF MEXICO (alt. title, The Prayer in the Storm; or, the Thirst for Gold)// D 5a// Adap. by Benjamin Webster fr F// **Adelphi**, Dec. 1853, with Benjamin Webster as Pedro and as Marquis D'Arvez, Charles Selby as Jules de Valois, Robert Keeley as Putney Bill, Paul Bedford as Porpus, C. J. Smith as Requin, John Sanders as Splice, Mme. Celeste as Blanche de Valois and as Unarita, John Parselle as Roland, Edmund Garden as Henri de Belcour, Mrs. Leigh Murray as Countess de Brissac, Fanny Maskell as Adèle; Mar. 1874, with James Fernandez as Pedro, Howard Russell as Jules de Valois, Brittain Wright as Putney Bill, Edmund Leathes as Roland, Augustus Glover as Porpus, Harwood Cooper as D'Aubery, Genevieve Ward as Blanche de Valois and as Unarita, Cicely Nott as

Countess de Brissac, Miss E. Phillips as Adel/ **Olympic**, Mar. 1889.

1313// C 2a// Frank Desprez// **Folly**, May 1879.

£30,000; OR, THE DREAD SECRET// D Pro & 2a// L. W. Harleigh// **Elephant & Castle**, Oct. 1875.

THIRTY, STRAND// F 1a// Mark Lemon// **Olympic**, Nov. 1841, with Mr. Fitzjames as Jingle, Mr. Halford as Felix, Mr. Turnour as Cutrie, Mr. Brookes as Snarling, Miss Hamilton as Mrs. Snarling, Georgiana Lebatt as Lucy.

THIRTY-THREE NEXT BIRTHDAY// F 1a// J. Maddison Morton// **Princess's**, Nov. 1858, with Mr. Cooper as Maj. Havoc, Frank Matthews as Cackleberry, George Everett as Beason, Miss Murray as Anastasia, Rose Leclercq as Cicely.

THIS HOUSE TO LET// D Pro & 3a// Edward Towers// **East London**, Sept. 1869.

THIS PLOT OF GROUND TO LET// F// n.a.// **Alexandra**, Jan. 1874.

THIS WOMAN AND THAT// Play 3a// Pierre Leclercq// **Globe**, Aug. 1890.

THIS WORLD OF OURS// D 4a// Seymore Hicks// **Pavilion**, Aug. 1892.

THOMPSON'S VISIT// F// J. T. Douglass// **Standard**, Sept. 1872.

THOROUGHBRED// C 3a// Ralph Lumley// **Toole's**, Feb. 1895.

THOSE HORRID GARROTERS// F 1a// n.a.// **Olympic**, Feb. 1873, with Arthur Wood as Whiffles, C. Parry as Beat, Jane Baber as Euphenia, Emma Chambers as Martha.

THOU SHALT NOT KILL// D 4a// F. A. Scudamore// **Shakespeare**, July 1899.

£1000 REWARD// Pro & 4a// George Roberts & Mr. Cordyce; vers. in 3a by Charles Rogers// **Pavilion**, July 1894/ **Novelty**, Feb. 1896.

THREAT FOR THREAT; OR, THE SHADOW OF WRONG// D 3a// George Conquest// **Grecian**, June 1869, with J. Jackson as George Duverel, Thomas Mead as Jerome Duverel, Samuel Perfitt as Charles, Charles Mortimer as de Beauvisin, William James as Etienne, Mrs. Atkinson as Gertrude, Lizzie Mandelbert as Marie.

THREE AND THE DEUCE// F 1a// Prince Hoare// **Haymarket**, Apr. 1839, with Robert Strickland as Touchet, J. B. Buckstone as Grizzle, W. R. Blake in 3 char. parts, J. W. Gough as MacFloggan, T. F. Mathews as Frank, Miss Grove as Emily, Miss Mattley as Taffine, Miss Gallot as Phoebe/ **Sad. Wells**, Dec. 1840, with J. S. Balls in 3 char. parts, Mr. Williams as Touchit, J. B. Hill as Renard, J. W. Collier as Woodbine, Robert Honner as Grizzle, Mr. Richardson as Floggin, Mrs. Morgan as Emily, Mrs. Richard Barnett as Taffline, Miss Cocke as Phoebe.

THREE AVENGERS, THE// D 2a// n.a.// **Victoria**, July 1848, with John Bradshaw as Duke de Valberg, Mr. Henderson as Count Henri, E. Edwards as Stranger Neider, J. T. Johnson as Carl, F. H. Henry as Frederick, G. F. Forman as Kreutzner, Mrs. George Lee as Agathe.

THREE BLACK SEALS, THE// D 4a// Adap. by Edward Stirling fr F// **Astley's**, Apr. 1864, with Mr. Elmore as Louis XIII, Henry Frazer as Harley, F. Wallace as Marshal d'Ancre, William Belton as St. Pierre, A. Denial as Duke d'Epernon, W. S. Gresham as Bernard, J. A. Shaw as Faubert, E. F. Edgar as Count d'Inglese, Mrs. J. W. Simpson as Mary de Medicis, Miss Burton as Anne of Austria, Teresa Furtado as Marguerite, Blanche Ellerman as Sylvie/ Scenery by W. Gates/ Music by J. H. Tully/ Machines by Mr. Sloman/ Prod. by Edward Stirling.

THREE BROTHERS OF BREVANNES, THE; OR, TRUTH MAY BE BLAMED BUT NEVER SHAMED// D 3a// J. Mead// **Sad. Wells**, Feb. 1863, with Alfred Montague as Marquis de Brevannes, Mr. Dalton as Count de Brevannes, Henry Forrester as Viscount de Brevannes, E. F. Edgar as de Marsy, James Johnstone as Pimopnelle, Lewis Ball as Babillard, Harry Josephs as Danton, Annie Lufton as Louise, Miss Heath as Cephese.

THREE CHRISTMAS NIGHTS; OR, THE MURDER NEAR THE OLD MILL// D 3a// Dram. fr novel, Lizzie Leigh// **Grecian**, July 1868, with Thomas Mead as Bantry, Charles Mortimer as Heywood, John Manning as Darwen, Henry Grant as Norris, W. Shirley as Ralington, Samuel Perfitt as Hindley, J. Jackson as Timothy, George Gillett as Middleton, Lizzie Mandelbert as Lizzie Leigh, Mary A. Victor as Bessy, Mrs. Atkinson as Ellen.

THREE CLERKS, THE// F 1a// W. H. Oxberry// **Princess's**, July 1845, with Walter Lacy as Fudge, W. H. Oxberry as Trudge, Mr. Granby as Drudge, Robert Honner as Grudge, F. C. Courtney as O'Slashem, Mrs. Brougham as Julia, Miss Somers as Mrs. Trudge.

THREE CUCKOOS, THE// F 1a// J. Maddison Morton// **Haymarket**, Mar. 1850, with J. B. Buckstone as Postlethwaite, Mr. Tilbury as Col. Cranky, Henry Howe as Capt. Dudley, Mrs. Fitzwilliam as Dolly, Mrs. L. S. Buckingham as Alice.

THREE DAYS IN TOWN// C 1a// n.a.// **Victoria**, May 1838, with Mr. Loveday as Sir Arthur, John Parry as George, Mr. Harwood as Macely, Mr. Forester as Sharp, Mr. Vale as Dan, Mrs. John Parry as Emily, Mrs. Loveday as Sally, Miss Corri as Nancy.

THREE FURIES, THE// C 1a// George Roberts// **St. James's**, Mar. 1865.

THREE GREAT WORTHIES// n.a.// **Standard**, Oct. 1866.

THREE HATS, THE// F 3a// Adap. by Gustave Soares ("Owen Dove") & Alfred Maltby fr F of Alfred Henniquin// **Royalty**, Dec. 1883.

THREE MILLIONS OF MONEY// C 4a// Fred Lyster & Joseph Mackay// **St. James's**, Oct. 1876, with Charles Warner as Daffy, George Clarke as Col. Denter, Clifford Cooper as Molar, Frederick Mervin as Smithers, George Darrell as Thomas, George Honey as John, Mrs. John Wood as Mrs. Desmond, Maria Daly as Lasy Ascot, Miss Oscar Byrne as Miss Featherstone.

THREE MUSKETEERS, THE// D// Dram. fr novel of Alexandre Dumas// **Grecian**//, May 1854, with T. Roberts, Charles Horn, Basil Potter, Richard Phillips, Henry Grant, Eaton O'Donnell, Jane Coveney, Miss Johnstone, Agnes De Warde.

THREE MUSKETEERS, THE// Play 3a// Dram. by Charles Dillon, Charles Rice, & Augustus Harris fr novel of Alexandre Dumas// **Lyceum**, Oct. 1856.

THREE MUSKETEERS, THE// Dram. fr novel of Alexandre Dumas// **City of London**, June 1857.

THREE MUSKETEERS, THE// D 4a// Dram. by W. Heron-Brown fr novel of Alexandre Dumas// **Imperial**, June 1898.

THREE MUSKETEERS, THE// D// Dram. by Henry Hamilton fr novel of Alexandre Dumas// **Globe**, Oct. 1898, with Walter Gay as Louis XIII, John Beauchamp as Richelieu, Vincent Sternroyd as Villiers, Arthur Wontner as de Rochefort, Hamilton Knight as de Treville, Basset Roe as Athos, Charles Goodheart as Porthos, Gerald Gurney as Aramis, H. V. Esmond as D'Artagnan, Kate Rorke as Anne of Austria, Mrs. Lewis Waller as Countess de Winter, Eva Moore as Gabrielle/ **Lyceum**, Nov. 1900, with Norman McKinnel as Louis XIII, William Mollison as Richelieu, Alexander Calvert as Villiers, W. Devereux as Rochefort, Hamilton Knight as Tréville, Basset Roe as Athos, Charles Godheart as Porthos, Gerald Gurney as Aramis, Lewis Waller as D'Artagnan, Frank Dyall as Felton, Evelyn McNay as Anne of Austria, Lily Hanbury as Countess de Winter, Eva Moore as Gabrielle.

THREE MUSKETEERS, THE; OR, THE QUEEN, THE CARDINAL, AND THE ADVENTURER// D 3a// Dram. by Charles Rice fr novel of Alexandre Dumas// **Grecian**, Nov. 1861, with George Gillett as Louis XIII, R. H. Lingham as Buckingham, Alfred Rayner as Richelieu, Walter Holland as de Rochfort, Mr. Costello as De Treville, Henry Grant as Athos, Mr. Jackson as Porthos, F. Smithson as Aramis, Henry Power as Boniface, Thomas Mead as D'Artagnan, Jane Dawson as Anne of Austria, Miss Johnstone as Lady de Winter, Mrs. Charles Dillon as Constance/ **Britannia**, Oct. 1898.

THREE PAIR OF LOVERS// F 1a// n.a.// **Astley's**, Oct. 1850, with Mr. Johnson as Quake, Mr. Danaville as Bolding, T. Barry as Simon, Arthur Stirling as Charles, Mr. Crowther as Smart, Mrs. Moreton Brookes as Lucretia, Miss E. Neil as Sophia, Mrs. Beacham as Rose.

THREE PERILS, THE; OR, WINE, WOMEN, AND GAMBLING// D 3a// Frederick Marchant// **Britannia**, Oct. 1870.

THREE PRINCES// n.a.// **Surrey**, Apr. 1850.

THREE SECRETS, THE// D 2a// Mark Lemon// **Lyceum**, May [?] 1840, with many of same cast following/ **Cov. Garden**, June 1840, with Mr. Baker as Darbert, Mr. Granby as Verneuil, Mr. Binge as Fremyn, Mr. Fitzjames as Laville, Mr. Turnour as Loustal, Mrs. Walter Lacy as Mme. Darbert, Miss Cooper as Mme. Verneuil, Miss Fitzjames as Lisette.

THREE SMUGGLERS OF KENT, THE; OR, THE MURDER ON THE SEA BEACH// D 3a// C. Z. Barnett// **Victoria**, June 1843, with Mr. James as Wyndham, William Seaman as Thornton, Mr. Glindon as Brandon, E. F. Saville as Brockman, J. W. Collier as Midnight, Charles Morelli as Old Gaveston, John Dale as Mathew, C. Williams as Luke, Mr. Henry as Robert, Annette Vincent as Ann, Miss Ridgeway as Harriet, Miss Saddler as Maud.

THREE SPECTRES, THE// F// n.a.// **Grecian**, Oct. 1857, with Eaton O'Donnell as The Baron, William Shuter as The Marquis, Mr. De Solla as The Count, Henry Power as Richard, George Conquest as Nicholas, Henry Grant as Serjeant, Ellen Hale as Constantia, Harriet Coveney as Lisette.

THREE THIEVES, THE; OR, THE BOHEMIAN AND THE MONKEY OF FRANKFORT// D 2a// J. B. Johnstone// **Victoria**, June 1851, with Mr. Morrison as Mremberg, Mr. Taylor as Zingare, J. Howard as Fruizmann, Mr. Coney as Karuneman, F. H. Henry as Mansen, Mr. Brunton as Estman, Miss Edgar as Isabel, Georgiana Lebatt as Rosa.

THREE WARNINGS, THE// D// Alfred Raynor// **Pavilion**, Mar. 1872.

THREE WAYFARERS, THE// Play 1a// Thomas Hardy// **Terry's**, June 1893.

THREE WEEKS AFTER MARRIAGE// C 1a// A. Murphy// **Victoria**, Mar. 1838, with William Dowton as Old Drugget, J. S. Balls as Rackett, Mrs. Ternan as Lady Rackett, Mrs. Loveday as Mrs. Drugget, Miss Wilson as Nancy, Miss Brothers as Divinity/ **Sad. Wells**, Apr. 1840, with Mr. Melville as Racket, Mr. Williams as Drugget, Mrs. W. West as Lady Racket, Miss Cooke as Mrs. Drugget, Miss Pettifer as Dimity; Nov. 1851, with Henry Marston as Rackett, Mr. Barrett as Drugget, Charles Wheatleigh as Lovelace, Frank Graham as Woodley, Miss Fitzpatrick as Lady Rackett, Mrs. Henry Marston as Mrs. Drugget, Lucy Rafter as Nancy.

THREE WOMEN, THE// n.a.// **Pavilion**, Nov. 1866.

THREE WORDS; OR, SILENT, NOT DUMB// D 2a// n.a.// **Grecian**, Oct. 1855, with Eaton O'Donnell as Rutter, Henry Grant as Hertzoff, Richard Phillips as Henrick, John Manning as Popp, Henry Power as Quibbleburg, Basil Potter as Baldwin, T. Roberts as Capt. Bertrand, Harriet Coveney as Suzette, Ellen Crisp as Mme. Popp.

THREEPENNY BITS// TF// Dram. by Isaac Zangwill fr his own story Old Maid's Club// **Garrick**, May 1895.

THRICE MARRIED// F 1a// Howard Paul// **Drury Lane**, Mar. 1854; **Princess's**, May 1861, with J. G. Shore as White, Drinkwater Meadows as Quaverly, Edmund Garden as Waddles, Mr. Hastings as Wilmot, Carlotta Leclercq in 4 character parts.

THOUGH A GLASS DARKLY// D 4a// E. M. Seymour// **Olympic**, Apr. 1896.

THROUGH FIRE AND WATER// C 3a// Walter Gordon// **Adelphi**, Aug. 1865, with J. L. Toole as Fireman, Henry Ashley as Biddles, John Billington as Coventry, Sarah Woolgar (Mrs. Alfred Mellon) as Bright.

THROUGH MY HEART FIRST// D 3a// J. M. Campbell// **Grand**, June 1884.

THROUGH THE FIRE// C 1a// William Lestocq & Yorke Stephens// **Strand**, Feb. 1888.

THROUGH THE FURNACE// D 4a// W. Howell-Poole// **Olympic**, July 1885.

THROUGH THE WORLD; OR, A BLIND CHILD'S PERIL// D Pro & 3a// Brandon Ellis// **Pavilion**, July 1901.

THROW OF THE DICE, A// Play 1a// H. A. Kennedy// **Strand**, May 1890.

THUMBSCREW, THE// D 5a// H. J. Byron// **Holborn**, Apr. 1874.

THUMPING LEGACY, A// F 1a// J. Maddison Morton// **Drury Lane**, Feb. 1843, with H. Bennett as Geronimo, Robert Keeley as Ominous, Charles Selby as Bambogetti, Charles Hudson as Leoni, George Bennett as Brigadier, Priscilla Horton as Rosetta/ **Sad. Wells**, Aug. 1844, with Mr. Williams as Geronimo, Mr. Morton as Bambagetti, Charles Fenton as Leoni, Edward Knight as Brigadier, G. F. Forman as Ominous, Miss Cooper as Rosetta; May 1868, with David Evans as Geronimo, John Royston as Ominous, J. C. Eldon as Leoni, Edgar Dallas as Bambogetti, Walter Tracey as Brigadier, Ada Courtenay as Rosetta/ **Olympic**, Nov. 1858, with George Cooke as Geronimo, J. Howard as Brigadier, Walter Gordon as Leoni, Horace Wigan as Bambozetti, Frederick Robson as Ominous, Miss Herbert as Rosetta.

THYRZA FLEMING// Play 4a// Dorothy Leighton// **Terry's**, Jan. 1895.

TICKET OF LEAVE, A// F 1a// Watts Phillips// **Adelphi**, Dec. 1862, with J. L. Toole as Aspen Quiver, C. H. Stephenson as Nuggets, Paul Bedford as Bottles, Miss Stoker as Joe, Mrs. Billington as Mrs. Quiver.

TICKET OF LEAVE, A// D// n.a.// **Grecian**, Sept. 1863, with Thomas Mead as Edmund Sorel, Henry Grant as Sluford, John Manning as Swigaly, Alfred Rayner as Huntley, William James as Loosely, Jane Dawson as Martha, Marie Brewer as Florinda, Mary A. Victor as Jerry.

TICKET-OF-LEAVE MAN, THE// D 4a// Adap. by Tom Taylor fr F of E. L. Brisbarre & Eugène Nus, Léonard// **Olympic**, June, 1857, with Henry Neville as Brierly, Edward Atkins as Dalton, Horace Wigan as Hawkshaw, George Vincent as Moss, Robert Soutar as Jones, Mr. Laclean as Gibson, Miss Raynham as Sam, Harwood Cooper as Maltby, Kate Saville as May, Miss Hughes as Emily, Mrs. Stephens as Mrs. Willoughby/ **Marylebone**, July 1866, with Henry Neville, H. J. Montague, Lydia Foote, Nellie Farren/ **Sad. Wells**, Sept. 1868, with George Melville as Brierly, Mr. Booth as Dalton, Mr. Hamilton as Hawkshaw, J. H. Loome as Moss, Mr. Newbound as Jones, Mr. Frazer as Gibson, Miss Choldmondley as May, Miss Stanley as Emily, Mrs. G. Howe as Mrs. Willoughby/ **Holborn**, 1873/ **Adelphi**, Aug. 1879, with Henry Neville as Robert Brierley, Robert Pateman as James Dalton, Hermann Vezin as Hawkshaw, F. W. Irish as Moss, F. Charles as Jones, E. J. George as Gibson, Clara Jecks as Sam Willoughby, Harwood Cooper as Maltby, Lydia Foote as May Edwards, Maria Harris as Emily St. Evremond, Harriet Coveney as Mrs. Willoughby/ **Astley's**, Nov. 1881, with E. N. Hallows, George Stretton, Mat Robson, Marie Forde.

TICKET OF LEAVE MAN'S WIFE; SIX YEARS AFTER (see also, Six Years After)// D// C. S. Cheltnam// **Sad. Wells**, Oct. 1866, with J. H. Slater as Brierly, Walter Holland as Dalton, E. Shepherd as Moss, J. L. Warner as Hawkshaw, Louise Periera as Willoughby, John Rouse as Jones, R. Norman as Gibson, J. W. Lawrence as Totty, Miss Leigh as May, Miss Nason as Mrs. Jones, Miss Mansfield as Anna/ Prod. by Alice Marriott.

TICKET OF LEAVE, THE ADVENTURES OF A// D// n.a.// **Grecian**, Sept. 1863, with Thomas Mead, Henry Grant, John Manning, Alfred Rayner, William James, Jane Dawson, Marie Brewer, Henry Power, Mary A. Victor.

TICKLE AND SCRUBBS// F// W. S. Penley & Frank Wyatt// **Trafalgar**, May. 1893.

TICKLISH TIMES// F 1a// J. Maddison Morton// **Olympic**, Mar. 1858, with Walter Gordon as Sir William, George Cooke as Bodkins, Frederick Robson as Griggs, Harwood Cooper as Jansen, Miss Marston as Mrs. Griggs, Miss Herbert as Winifred, Mrs. W. S. Emden (Miss Somers) as Dot/ **Drury Lane**, Feb. 1873, with William Terriss as Sir William, Ersser Jones as Bodkins,

Stanislaus Calhaem as Griggs, Miss Ryan as Mrs. Griggs, Miss Alma as Winifred, Miss D'Arcy as Dot.

TIDE AND TIME// D Pro & 3a// Henry Leslie// **Surrey**, Mar. 1867.

TIDE OF TIME, THE// C 3a// W. Bayle Bernard// **Haymarket**, Dec. 1858, with W. H. Chippendale as Pendarvis, Henry Compton as Sir Dorimer, J. B. Buckstone as Molehill, WilliamClark as Quillet, Mr. Rogers as Grainger, Henry Howe as Spalding, Miss Reynolds as Mildred, Ellen Ternan as Alice, Mrs. Poynter as Sabina/ Scenery by John O'Conner & George Morris.

TIGER OF MEXICO, THE; OR, A ROUGH ROAD TO A GOLDEN LAND// D 4a// J. B. Johnston// **Britannia**, Apr. 1881.

TIGHT CORNER, A// C 3a// Sidney Bowkett// **Terry's**, Oct. 1901.

TIGRESS, THE// D Pro & 4a// Adap. by Ramsey Morris fr novel, Crucify Her// **Comedy**, June 1889.

TILL DEATH DO US PART// D Pro & 4a// George Corner// **Surrey**, App. 1885.

TIME AND THE HOUR// D 3a// J. Palgrave Simpson & Felix Dale// **Queen's**, June 1868.

TIME AND TIDE; A TALE OF THE THAMES// D 3a// Henry Leslie// **Surrey**, Mar. 1867/ **Grecian**, Mar. 1868, with Henry Grant as Ingledew, John Manning as Mapleoft, Henry Power as Diggins, Charles Mortimer as Cannon, Thomas Mead as Barjohn, William James as Clement Morris, J. Jackson as Job Morris, Samuel Perfitt as Chalmers, Lizzie Mandelbert as Mildred, Mary A. Victor as Mrs. Mapleloft, Miss De Lacie as Letty.

TIME, HUNGER, AND THE LAW// Play 1a// Lawrence Irving// **Criterion**, May 1894.

TIME IS MONEY// C// Mrs. Hugh Bell & Arthur Cecil// **Comedy**, Apr. 1892.

TIME, THE AVENGER// D 4a// Tom Craven// **Surrey**, Oct. 1892.

TIME TRIES ALL// C 2a// Dram. by John Courtney// **Olympic**, Sept. 1848, with A. Younge as Leeson, Henry Butler as Clinton, Frederick Vining as Yawn, Leigh Murray as Bates, Samuel Cowell as Tact, Mr. Sanger as John, Mrs. Stirling as Laura, Mrs. C. A. Tellet as Fanny/ **Sad. Wells**, June 1851, with Frank Graham as Leeson, Charles Boyce as Bates, J. Williams as Clinton, John Chester as Tact, W. H. Oxberry as Yawn, Miss M. A. Crisp as Laura, Mrs. Charles Boyce as Fanny/ **Princess's**, Nov. 1862, with W. H. Stephens as Leeson, Hermann Vezin as Bates, J. G. Shore as Yawn, Mr. Brooke as Clinton, George Belmore as Tact, Constance Aylmer as Laura, Miss Murray as Fanny.

TIME WILL TELL// C 3a// Herbert Gardiner// **Trafalgar**, May 1893.

TIME WORKS WONDERS// C 5a// Douglas Jerrold// **Haymarket**, Apr. 1845, with Mr. Stuart as Sir Gilbert, Henry Holl as Norman, William Farren as Goldthumb, C. J. Mathews as Felix, Benjamin Webster as Prof. Truffles, Mr. Tilbury as Olive, J. B. Buckstone as Bantam, James Bland as Jugby, Mme. Vestris as Bessy, Miss Fortescue as Florentine, Mrs. Julia Glover as Miss Tucker, Mrs. W. Clifford as Mrs. Goldthumb, Mrs. Humby as Patty/ Scenery by George Morris/ Machines by W. Adams/ **Sad. Wells**, 1866/ **Globe**, Apr. 1873, with Charles Flockton as Sir Gilbert Norman, Charles Neville as Clarance Norman, H. J. Montague as Felix Goldthumb, Henry Compton as Prof. Truffles, E. W. Garden as Olive, J. H. Allen as Jugby, Rose Massey as Bessie Tulip, Sophie Larkin as Miss Tucker, Louisa Manders as Mrs. Goldthumb, Carlotta Addison as Florentine.

TIMES, THE// D 3a// John Besemeres ("John Daly"), **Sad. Wells**, Apr. 1854, with C. Poynter as Falconer, F. Charles as Sidney, William Suter as Bungle, Henry Farren as Eye, George Vining as Tangible, Mr. Barrett as Eden, Miss Mandelbert as Muffin, Charles Fenton as Moss, Miss Castleton as Francis, Miss A. Elsworthy as Emm, Miss Rawlings as Mrs. Focus, Mrs. Thomas as Martha.

TIME'S REVENGE// D// n.a.// **Britannia**, Oct. 1875.

TIME'S REVENGE// Play 1a// W. E. Sprange// **Toole's**, May 1890.

TIMES, THE// D 3a// John Daly// **OLympic**, July 1853, with George Cooke as Sir Arthur, W. Shalders as Sir William, Henry Marston as Falconer, Thomas Mead as Bye, William Farren as Tangible, Mr. [Henry?] Farren as Eden, Ellen Turner as Muffin, Miss Anderton as Frances, Harriet Gordon as Em, Mrs. R. Bartlett as Mrs. Focus, Isabel Adams as Martha.

TIMES, THE// C 4a// Arthur Wing Pinero// **Terry's**, Oct. 1891.

TIMKINS, THE TROUBADOUR// F 1a// n.a.// **Queen's**, Aug. 1868.

TIMON OF ATHENS// T// William Shakespeare// **Sad. Wells**, Sept. 1851, with Samuel Phelps as Timon, Frederic Robinson as Lucius, William Hoskins as Lucullus, Henry Mellon as Sempronius, Edward Knight as Ventidius, George Bennett as Apemantus, Frank Graham as Flavius, Henry Marston as Alcibiades, Charles Wheatleigh as Emalinius, Miss E. Bullen as Cupid, Mrs. Graham as Phrynia, Miss Jones as Timandra/ Scenery by F. Fenton.

TIMOTHY TO THE RESCUE// F 1a// H. J. Byron// **Strand**, May 1864.

TIMOUR THE TARTAR, THE// D// n.a.// **Sad. Wells**, July 1837, with C. H. Pitt as Timour, Mr. King as Bermeddin, Mr. Griffiths as Oglou, Mr. Jones as Abdallec, C. J. Smith as Kerim, Mrs. W. West as Zorilda, Mrs. Rogers as Selina.

TIN BOX, THE// F 3a// G. M. Fenn// **Globe**,

Apr. 1892, with Walter Everard as John Kedge, Austin Melford as Capt. Teale, E. Allan Aynesworth as Lt. Teale, Henry Vernon as Peach, Arthur Helmore as Buzzard, George Hughes as Brace, Annie Hughes as Bella Kedge, Eleanor Bufton as Mrs. Bolitho/ Scenery by Richard Durant.

TINSEL QUEEN, A// D Pro & 3a// W. E. Morton// **Sad. Wells**, Dec. 1883.

TIPPERARY LEGACY, THE// F// J. Sterling Coyne// **Adelphi**, Dec. 1847, with Edward Wright as Green, Charles Munyard as Bob Gills, Paul Bedford as Scrimmage, William Cullenford as Chubblock, Sarah Woolgar as Lissy Chubblock.

'TIS LOVE ALONE CAN FIX HIM// C// n.a.// **Sad. Wells**, Feb. 1841, with Mr. Williams as Old Fickle, J. W. Collier as Briefwit, George Ellis as Sneer, J. S. Balls as Tristram, Mrs. Richard Barnett as Variella, Miss Cooke as Ready.

'TIS SHE!; OR, THE MAID, THE WIFE, AND THE WIDOW// F 1a// T. E. Wilks// **St. James's**, Feb. 1838, with Mr. Brookes as Adm. Triton, John Webster as Col. Carleton, Edward Wright as Gabbleton, Mr. Sidney as Dorrington, John Gardner as Quickset, Mrs. Stirling as Sophia, Mrs. Gabbleton, and as Lady Eliza, Mrs. Penson as Mrs. Dabbleton.

TIT FOR TAT// C 2a// Francis Talfourd & Alfred Wigan// **Victoria**, Oct. 1843, with Mr. Griffiths as Col. Carleton, Mr. Grove as Adm. Triton, Mr. Coppin as Gabbleton, Mr. James as Dorrington, Charles Fenton as Quickset, Mrs. Coppin as Sophia, Mrs. Gabbleton and as Lady Eliza.

TIT FOR TAT// C 2a// n.a.// **Olympic**, Feb. 1855, with Samuel Emery as Frankland, Frederick Robson as Sowerby, Alfred Wigan as Thornby, E. Clifton as Bolter, Miss Maskell as Mrs. Frankland, Miss Bromley as Mrs. Sowerby, Ellen Turner as Rose/ **Sad. Wells**, Aug. 1855, with Samuel Emery as Frankland, Frederick Robson as Sowerly, Alfred Wigan as Thornby, E. Clifton as Belter, Miss Maskell as Mrs. Frankland, Miss Bromley as Mrs. Sowerby, Miss Marston as Rose.

TIT FOR TAT// F 1a// n.a.// **Sad. Wells**, Dec. 1862, with Henry Forrester as Markham, C. Lloyds as Borem, Charles Bender as John, Miss Clements as Harriet, Mrs. William Dowton as Mrs. Meddle, Bessie Heath as Polly.

TITLE DEEDS, THE// D 3a// R. B. Peake// **Adelphi**, June 1847, with Mr. Lambert as Polydore Fustic, William Cullenford as Mr. Morant, O. Smith as Humphrey Haywhisp, Edward Wright as Peter Hush, Paul Bedford as Turfy Goodwood, John Sanders as Hardware, Emma Harding as Matilda, Mrs. Yates as Mrs. Evergay, Ellen Chaplin as Rose, Sarah Woolgar as Sally Haywhisp/ Scenery by Pitt & Johnstone.

TO BE CONTINUED IN OUR NEXT// F// Walter James// **Marylebone**, June 1867.

TO MARRY OR NOT TO MARRY// C// Mrs. Inchbald// **Haymarket**, Aug. 1840, with W. C. Macready as Sir Oswin, Robert Strickland as Lord Danberry, Benjamin Wrench as Willowcar, Samuel Phelps as Lavensforth, Henry Howe as Amos, Miss Charles as Lady Susan, Mrs. Julia Glover as Sarah, Priscilla Horton as Hester.

TO OBLIGE BENSON// C 1a// Adap. by Tom Taylor fr F of M. Vaud, Un Service à Blanchard// **Olympic**, Mar. 1854, with Samuel Emery as Benson, Frederick Robson as Southdown, Henry Leslie as Meredith, Miss Marston as Mrs. Southdown, Ellen Turner as Mrs. Benson/ **Sad. Wells**, Aug. 1855, with Samuel Emery as Benson, Frederick Robson as Southdown, Henry Leslie as Meredith, Miss Marston as Mrs. Southdown, Miss Maskell as Mrs. Benson/ **St. James's**, Nov. 1870, with Miss H. Everard as Mrs. Southdown, Marion Inch as Mrs. Benson, Harry Cox as Mr. Southdown, G. P. Grainger as Benson, F. Mervin as Meredith/ **Drury Lane**, July 1872, with Edward Atkins as Southdown, Frank Barsby as Benson, F. Mervin as Meredith, Agnes Hargraves as Mrs. Benson, Miss Hughes as Mrs. Southdown/ **Olympic**, May 1873, with David Evans as Benson, Arthur Wood as Trotter, G. W. Garthorne as Meredith, Elise Melville as Mrs. Benson, Kate Rivers as Mrs. Trotter/ **Haymarket**, Aug. 1875, with John Chester as Benson, David Fisher Jr. as Trotter, J. C. Fuell as Meredith, Blanche Henri as Mrs. Trotter, Miss Hinton as Mrs. Benson/ **Lyceum**, Apr. 1884, with Philip Ben Greet as Benson, F. W. Irish as Trotter Southdown, Charles Hawthorne as John Meredith, Annie Rose as Mrs. Benson, Mrs. Digby Willoughby as Mrs. Southdown.

TO PARENTS AND GUARDIANS// C 1a// Tom Taylor// **Lyceum**, Sept. 1846, with Drinkwater Meadows as Mr. Swish, Alfred Wigan as Tourbillon, Mrs. Keeley as Robert Nettles, Robert Keeley as Waddilove, Ellen Turner as Skutler, Miss O. Hicks as Skraggs, Miss J. O. Young as Thompson, Mrs. Woollidge as Lady Nettles, Louisa Howard as Mary, Mrs. Alfred Wigan as Virginie/ **Princess's**, Dec. 1850, with Drinkwater Meadows as Swish, Alfred Wigan as Tourbillon, Mrs. Keeley as Nettles, Robert Keeley as Waddilove, Miss Robertson as Shuttler, Miss Daly as Scraggs, Miss Cushnie as Brown, Mr. Paulo as Doggett, Frederick Cooke as Nubbles, Mary Keeley as Mary, Mrs. Alfred Wigan as Virginie, Mrs. W. Daly as Lady Nettles/ **Adelphi**, Apr 1853, with Alfred Wigan as Tourbillon, William Cullenford as Swish, Mrs. Keeley as Nettles, Robert Keeley as Waddilove, Mr. Lindon as Dogget, Mrs. Laws as Lady Nettles, Mary Keeley as Mary Swish, Mrs. Alfred Wigan as Virginie/ **Sad. Wells**, Mar. 1859, with Mr. Williams as Swish, Leigh Murray as Tourbillon, Rose Williams as Herbert, C. Dickson as Waddilove, Miss Hill as Scutler, Mr. Chapman as Dogget, Miss Rawlings as Lady Nettles, Miss Mason as Mary, Annie Ness as Virginie/ **Astley's**, Dec. 1862, with Mr. Mellon as Swish, Mr. Ryan as Dogget, Dion Boucicault as

Tourbillon, Dan Leeson as Waddelove, Mr. Regan as Nubbles, Mrs. Dion Boucicault as Bob Nettles, Rose Leclercq as Virginie/ **Olympic**, July 1866, with Robert Soutar as Swish, Horace Wigan as Tourbillon, Ellen Farren as Robert Nettles, F. Head as Waddilove, Miss H. Farren as Scraggs, Miss F. Farren as Thompson, Harwood Cooper as Nubbles, Mrs. Farren as Lady Nettles, Alice Austin as Virginie.

TO PARIS AND BACK FOR FIVE POUNDS// F 1a// J. Maddison Morton// **Haymarket**, Feb. 1853, with J. B. Buckstone as Snozzle, Henry Howe as Markham, Mr. Lambert as Spriggins, Mr. Rogers as Lt. Spike, George Braid as Pounce, Amelia Vining as Fanny.

TO THE DEATH// D Pro & 3a// Adap. by Rutland Barrington fr novel of A. C. Gunther, Mr. Barnes of New York// **Olympic**, May 1888, under title of Mr. Barnes of New York.

TO THE RESCUE// C// Dora Greet// **POW**, June 1889/ **Court**, Dec. 1889.

TOBIT'S DOG// F// W. T. Moncrieff// **Sad. Wells**, Nov. 1846, with Henry Marston as Lord Rochester, Mr. Morton as Saville, Henry Scharf as Whittington, Mr. Branson as Jermyn, Miss Huddart as Lady Diana, Miss Cooper as Alice.

TODAY// C 3a// Adap. by C. H. Brookfield fr F of Victorien Sardou, Divorçons// **Comedy**, Dec. 1892.

TODAY// C 1a// Charles Vieson// **Avenue**, Aug. 1895.

TOFF JIM// Play 1a//Frederick Wright Jr// **Apollo**, May 1901.

TOILERS ON THE THAMES; OR, THE DARK SIDE OF LONDON LIFE// D 2a// W. E. Waldron// **Grecian**, Mar. 1869.

TOM AND JERRY; OR, LIFE IN LONDON (also subt., Sprees & Life in London)// C// W. T. Moncrieff// **Cov. Garden**, May 1837, with John Pritchard as Tom, Benjamin Webster as Jerry, William Farren as Logic, Mr. Ross as Green, John Webster as Trifle, Mr. Tilbury as Hawthorn, Mr. Sanders as Bob, Miss Lee as Kate, Miss Land as Sue, Miss Nicholson as Jane, Mrs. Sarah Garrick as Mrs. Tartar/ **Sad. Wells**, June 1837, with Mr. Hicks as Tom, Mr. Conquest as Jerry, Mr. Campbell as Logic, Mr. Rogers as Green, C. H. Pitt as Trifle, Mr. Griffiths as Hawthorn, T. G. Flowers as Dusty Bob, Mr. Ennis as Tattersall, Mr. Pateman as Gull'em, C. J. Smith as Primefit, Lavinia Melville as Kate, Miss Williams as Sue, Mrs. Worrell as Jane, Mrs. Harris as Mrs. Tartar, Mr. Scarbrow as African Sal/ **Victoria**, Feb. 1842, with E. F. Saville as Tom, John Gardner as Jerry, J. Howard as Logic, Mr. Paul as Jemmy, Mr. James as M'Lush, Mr. Scarbrow as Dusty Bob, Mr. Elliott as Tartan, C. Williams as Trifle, William Seaman as Primefit, Mr. Cullen as Hawthorn, Mr. Hitchinson as Tattersal, Mrs. George Lee as Kate, Miss Collett as Sue, Mrs. Seaman as Jane, Mrs. Garthwaite as Mrs. Tartar/ **Grecian**, July 1863, with William James as Tom, John Manning as Jerry, J. Jackson as Logie, Henry Power as Green, George Gillett as Trifle, Mrs. Charles Dillon as Kate, Mary A. Victor as Jane, Ellen Hale as Susan, Adelaide Russell as Miss Lightfoot.

TOM AND JERRY; OR, LIFE IN LONDON IN 1820// D 3a// Dram. by W. J. Moncrieff fr story of Pierce Egan// **Victoria**, Mar. 1870.

TOM BOWLING: THE DARLING OF OUR CREW// D// A. V. Campbell// **Sad. Wells**, Jan. 1837, with Mr. Burton as Tom Bowling, Mr. Ennis as John Bowling, John Ayliffe as Snapfee, Mr. Rogers as Takepart, Thomas Lee as Mainsheet, C. H. Pitt as Wellwish, Miss Williams as Lucy, Miss Julian as Polly.

TOM COBB// F 3a// W. S. Gilbert// **St. James's**, Apr. 1875, with Clifford Cooper as Col. O'Fipp, E. W. Royce as Tom Cobb, Edgar Bruce as Whiffle, Edith Challis as Matilda, Mr. De Vere as Effingham, Mrs. Chippendale as Mrs. Effingham, W. J. Hill as Bulstrode Effingham, Miss Litton as Caroline.

TOM CRINGLE; OR, THE LOG OF A BRITISH TAR// D// Edward Fitzball// **Victoria**, May 1848, with John Bradshaw as Staunton, Mr. Henderson as Alfred, J. T. Johnson as Black Walter, Walter Searle as Nat, E. Edwards as Tom Cringle, G. F. Forman as Jack, Mr. Hawkins as Surf, Mrs. George Lee as Elizabeth, Miss Burroughcliffe as Fanny.

TOM, DICK, AND HARRY// F 3a// Mrs. R. Pacheco// **Trafalgar**, Nov. 1893.

TOM NODDY'S SECRET// F 1a// T. H. Bayly// **Haymarket**, Sept. 1838, with Mr. Hemming as Capt. Ormond, Robert Strickland as Noddy, J. B. Buckstone as Inkpen, Miss Taylor as Gabrielle, Miss Cooper as Mary/ **Drury Lane**, June 1839, with Mr. Hemming as Capt. Ormond, Robert Strickland as Noddy, J. B. Buckstone as Inkpen, Miss Taylor as Gabrielle, Miss Gallot as Mary/ **Sad. Wells**, Apr. 1840, with Mr. Hemming as Capt. Ormond, Robert Strickland as Tom Noddy, Henry Hall as Inkpen, Mrs. Robert Honner as Gabrielle, Mrs. J. F. Saville as Mary/ **Grecian**, Mar. 1856, with F. Charles as Capt. Ormond, John Manning as Inkpen, Eaton O'Donnell as Tom Noddy, Mrs. Charles Montgomery as Gabrielle, Ellen Hale as Mary/ **Olympic**, Dec. 1859, with Walter Gordon as Capt. Ormond, Horace Wigan as Inkpen, Mr. Addison as Tom Noddy, Miss Cottrell as Mary, Miss Marston as Gabrielle.

TOM PINCH// C 3a// Dram. by J. J. Dilley & Lewis Clifton fr Charles Dickens, Martin Chuzzlewit// **Vaudeville**, Mar. 1881, with William Farren, John Maclean, Kate Bishop, Sophie Larkin.

TOM SHEPPARD; OR, THE BRIGHT PATH OF HONESTY AND THE DARK ROAD OF CRIME// D// n.a.// **Grecian**, June 1866, with J. Jackson as Goodwood, W. Shirley as Kneebone, Mary A. Victor as Jack, George Gillett as Darrell, Charles Mortimer as Jonathan Wild, John Manning as Blueskin, Henry Power as

Mendez, Samuel Perfitt as Sir Rowland, Mrs. Dearlove as Mrs. Goodwood, Miss Atkinson as Mrs. Sheppard.

TOM THRASHER// F 1a// Augustus Harris// **Adelphi**, July 1868.

TOM THUMB// C// Adap. fr. C of Fielding// **St. James's**, Feb. 1837, with Robert Strickland as King Arthur, John Pritt Harley as Grizzle, Morris Barnett as Allcash, Mr. Bennett as Lorenzo, John Parry as Giacomo, Mr. Hart as Matteo, G. Stansbury as Beppo, Miss Smith as Lady Allcash, Miss Rainforth as Zerlina.

TOM TRANSON; OR, UP THE MEDITERRANEAN// D 3a// Mr. Campbell// **Sad. Wells**, July 1837, with Mr. Griffiths as Tom Transom, Mr. Hicks as William Transon, C. J. Smith as Thomas, C. H. Pitt as Jack, Mr. Ennis as Answer, Mr. Campbell as Alias, Mr. King as di Vento, Mr. Rogers as Wassel, J. Dunn as Cacklequicki, F. Ede as Moreno, Mr. Scarbrow as Weatherwise, Mrs. Worrell as Cecini, Miss Williams as Neronna, Lavinia Melville as Phoebe, Mrs. Harris as Betsy, Mrs. Rogers as Sybilla/ Scenery by Mildenhall & Roberts/ Machines by Mr. Copping/ Music by Mr. Nicholson.

TOM TRUANT// D 4a// Douglas Stewart// **Marylebone**, Mar. 1874.

TOMB OF LUNEDA, THE; OR, THE FORCE OF TERROR// D// William Dimond// **Sad. Wells**, Apr. 1841, with Mr. Cobham as Estevan, John Dale as Col. Rigolio, Mr. Hollingsworth as Capt. Xavior, Charles Bender as The Baron, J. Richardson as Claudio, Mlle. Gooderham as Myrtillo, Mrs. Maddocks as Rosara, Miss Goodwin as Stella.

TOMKINS AND THE TROUBADOUR// F 1a// n.a.// **Queen's**, Aug. 1868.

TOMMY// C// Mrs. E. S. Willard// **Olympic**, Feb. 1891, with Horace Hodges as Peter, Ambrose Manning as Simpkins, Paul Belmore as Solomon, Alice Cooke as Rachel, Alice Gambier as Martha, Lillie Belmore as Tommy.

TOMMY AND HARRY// n.a.// **Britannia**, Dec. 1872.

TOMMY AND SALLY; OR, THE STAGE-STRUCK HEROES// F// n.a.// **Sad. Wells**, with S. Huffer as Sir Matthew, Mr. Stalman as Count Glorieux, T. T. Pugh as Capt. Dorrington, J. Felix Rogers as Top Tape, Jenny Willmore as Sally, Bessie Heath as Lady Scraggs, Miss Collier as Poplin.

TOMMY ATKINS// D 4a// Arthur Shirley & Benjamin Landeck// **Pavilion**, Sept. 1895/ **Duke of York's**, Sept. 1895, with Charles Cartwright, Constance Collier/ **Princess's**, July 1897.

TOMMY DODD// F 3a// Osmond Shillingford// **Globe**, Aug. 1898, with J. L. Shine as Louis Goodwin, Bertie Wright as Thomas Dodd, J. L. Mackay as Tresset, Watty Brunton Jr. as Abd-Er-Rahman, Eva Moore as Angelina, Milly Thorne as Amy, Cicely Richards as Jane/ Scenery by Harry Potts.

TON OF GOLD, A// n.a.// **Pavilion**, Oct. 1866.

TONGUE OF SLANDER// D 4a// T. G. Warren & J. T. Douglass// **Standard**, Oct. 1887.

TOO HAPPY BY HALF// C 1a// Julian Field// **St. James's**, May 1895, with H. V. Esmond as Verner, Arthur Royston as Fortesque, F. Benham as James, Evelyn Millard as Maud.

TOO LATE FOR DINNER// F// Richard Jones// **Victoria**, Nov. 1837, with Edward Hooper as Frank Poppleton, John Parry as Frederick Poppleton, Mr. Salter as Rafter, W. H. Oxberry as Twill, William Davidge as Farmet, Mr. Loveday as Pincroft, Mrs. Griffith as Mrs. Thompson, Mrs. Loveday as Letty, Miss Wilson as Emma, Miss Lee as Eliza/ **Sad. Wells**, July 1841, with J. S. Balls as Frank Poppleton, Mr. Elvin as Frederick Poppleton, John Herbert as Twill, J. W. Collier as Rafter, George Ellis as Fumet, Mr. Williams as Pincroft, Mrs. Richard Barnett as Emma, Miss Hicks as Miss Pincroft, Mrs. Morgan as Letty, Miss Cooke as Mrs. Thompson; Aug. 1851, with William Hoskins as Frank Poppleton, Charles Wheatleigh as Frederick Poppleton, F. Younge as Twill, J. W. Ray as Pincroft, Mr. Williams as Rafter, Mr. Wilkins as Fumet, Mr. Harris as Snip, Mrs. Henry Marston as Mrs. Thompson, Fanny Huddart as Emma, Lucy Rafter as Elizabeth.

TOO MANY COOKS SPOIL THE BROTH// F 1a// n.a.// **Princess's**, Jan. 1848, with Henry Compton as Granite, Mr. Granby as Badger, Mr. Woodfield as Chicory, W. H. Oxberry as George, Emma Stanley as Fanny, Mrs. Fosbroke as Anastasia, Miss E. Honner as Clara.

TOO MUCH FOR GOOD NATURE// F 1a// Edmund Falconer// **Drury Lane**, Nov. 1858.

TOO MUCH JOHNSON// C 3a// Adap. by William Gillette fr F of M. Ordonneau, La Plantation Thomassin// **Garrick**, Apr. 1898.

TOO MUCH OF A GOOD THING// C 1a// Augustus Harris// **Lyceum**, Dec. 1855/ **Drury Lane**, Jan. 1857, with Robert Roxby as Capt. Montgomery, A. Younge as Brandysnap, Mr. Templeton as Sam, Miss M. Oliver as Isabel, Mrs. Frank Matthews as Diana, Miss Barnes as Biddy/ **Adelphi**, Aug. 1869, with Mr. Dalton as Capt. Montgomery, C. H. Stephenson as Brandysnap, Harwood Cooper as Sam, Nelly Harris as Isabel, Maria Harris as Dianah, Emily Turtle as Betty/ **Princess's**, Nov. 1869, with Henry Ashley as Capt. Montgomery, Dan Leeson as Dr. Brandysnap, Alfred Tapping as Sam, Nelly Harris as Isabel, Maria Harris as Diana, Miss B. Schavey as Betty.

TOO TRUE// D 3a// H. T. Craven// **Duke's**, Jan. 1876, with Louisa Moore, H. T. Craven, Mr. Macklin.

TOODLES, THE// C 1a// R. J. Raymond// **Adelphi**, Sept. 1874, with J. S. Clarke as Timothy

Toodles, G. Temple, Howard Russell, Mrs. Addie, Mrs. Kemp/ **Haymarket**, Apr. 1879, with John S. Clarke as Toodles, Henry Howe as Acorn, Norman Forbes as Charles, Henry Crouch as Ghrymes, Mr. Weathersby as George, C. Allbrook as Fenton, Emily Thorne as Mrs. Toodles, Miss Abington as Mary/ Scenery by Thomas Hall.

TOPSAIL-SHEET BLOCKS; OR, THE GUNNER AND THE FOUNDLING// D 3a// Dram. by Thompson Townsend fr novel of Capt. Baker// **Sad. Wells**, Oct. 1838, with Dibdin Pitt as Breeze, Robert Honner as Blocks, Mr. Elvin as Topsail-Sheet, Mr. Conquest as Weatherspoon, Mr. Harwood as Hector, Mr. Mellor as Capt. Yorick, Mr. Priorson as Watts, Miss E. Honner as Grace, Mr. Cathcart as Wilson, C. Montague as Du Fay, Miss Richardson as Marie, W. D. Broadfoot as Earl of Wentworth, Mr. Dry as Acheson, Mrs. J. F. Saville as Alicia.

TOSCA, LA// D 5a// Adap. by F. C. Grove & Henry Hamilton fr F of Victorien Sardou// **Garrick**, Nov. 1889, with Mrs. Bernard Beere, Johnston Forbes Robertson, Lewis Waller, Rose Leclercq, Sidney Brough.

TOT// D 3a// Frederick Hazleton// **Grecian**, Apr. 1879.

TOTTLE'S// C 3a// H. J. Byron// **Gaiety**, Dec. 1875, with J. L. Toole, Miss Farren, Clifford Cooper, Mlle. Camille.

TOUCH AND TAKE; OR, THE LAW OF KISSES// C 2a// n.a.// **Haymarket**, Apr. 1839, with Tyrone Power as Sir Roderick, Robert Strickland as Blunderbussen, Benjamin Webster as Ludwig, J. Worrell as De Vere, T. F. Mathews as Sgt. Einvordt, Mrs. W. Clifford as Mme. Spartenheim, Miss Taylor as Linda, Mrs. Fitzwilliam as Nina/ Music by T. G. Reed.

TOUCH AND TAKE; OR, SATURDAY NIGHT AND SUNDAY MORNING// F// n.a.// **Drury Lane**, Jan. 1855.

TOURIST'S TICKET, A// F// T. J. Williams// **Globe**, Mar. 1872, with Charles Flockton as Starter Shunt, E. W. Garden as Fenchurch, J. H. Allen as Rasper, J. H. Barnes as Scruggins, Maria Harris as Lucinda, Nelly Harris as Mrs. Simperton, Mrs. Manders as Mrs. Cranky.

TOWER OF LONDON, THE; OR, THE DEATH OMEN AND THE FATE OF LADY JANE GREY// D 3a// T. J. Higgie & T. H. Lacy// **City of London**, Dec. 1840.

TOWER OF NESLE, THE; OR, THE DARK GONDOLA (also subt., Black Gondola)// D 5a// adap. by George Almar fr F of Galliardet// **Sad. Wells**, June 1837, with Mr. King as Louis X, F. Ede as de Marigny, C. H. Pitt as Count Savoisy, Mr. Huckel as De Pierrefonds, Mr. Pateman as Roual, Mr. Griffiths as Richard, Mr. Scarbrow as Simon, Mr. Williams as Jehan, George Bennett as de Bournonville, John Dale as D'Aulnay, J. Dunn as Philip, Mr. Campbell as Orsini, C. J. Smith as Landry, Ellen Townley as Marguerite, Miss Williams as Charlotte/ **Victoria**, Aug. 1844, with Mr. Hitchinson as Louis X, John Ryder as de Bournonville, J. T. Johnson as D'Aulnay, Henry Frazer as Philip, T. H. Higgie as Count Savoisy, Mr. Henderson as de Marigny, Mr. Morrison as Pierrefonds, Mr. Humphries as Raoul, J. Neville as Orsini, Mrs. George Lee as Marguerite, Miss Edgar as Janette, Miss Leigh as Matilde/ **Grecian**, Jan. 1862, with Thomas Mead as Buridan, Mr. Costello as Louis of France, Mr. Johnson as Savolay, R. H. Lingham as d'Aulnay, Walter Holland as de Marigay, William James as Gaultier d'Aulnay, Henry Power as Richarde, Jane Dawson as Queen Marguerite, Miss Oxley as Jeannette.

TOWN AND COUNTRY// C// Thomas Morton// **Cov. Garden**, Sept. 1838, with Mr. Vining as Plastic, Robert Strickland as Trot, George Bartley as Cosey, J. Waldron as Glenroy, Mr. Vandenhoff as Reuben, E. W. Elton as Capt. Glenroy, Edwin Yarnold as Armstrong, C. J. Smith as Dwindle, Mr. Tilbury as Ross, W. H. Payne as Williams, T. H. Mathews as Robin, John Pritt Harley as Hawbuck, Mrs. Mary Warner as Mrs. Glenroy, Charlotte Vandenhoff as Rosalie, Mrs. Humby as Mrs. Trot, Mrs. W. Clifford as Mrs. Moreen, Mrs. Sarah Garrick as Goody Hawbuck, Miss Wortley as Taffline/ **Haymarket**, Oct. 1840, with Walter Lacy as Plastic, David Rees as Trot, Robert Strickland as Cosey, J. Waldron as Glenroy, James Wallack as Reuben, John Webster as Capt. Glenroy, Miss Charles as Mrs. Glenroy, Mrs. Stirling as Rosalie, Mrs. Julia Glover as Mrs. Trot, Mrs. W. Clifford as Mrs. Moreen; Apr. 1849, with James Wallack as Rueben [sic] Glenroy, Alfred Wigan as Plastic, Henry Howe as Capt. Glenroy, Robert Keeley as Hawbuck, J. B. Buckstone as Trot, Benjamin Webster as Cosey, Mr. Rogers as Owen Glenroy, Mr. Caulfield as Armstrong, J. W. Gough as Ross, Mr. A. Brindal as Dwindle, Priscilla Horton as Mrs. Glenroy, Miss Reynolds as Rosalie, Mrs. Julia Glover as Mrs. Trot, Mrs. Stanley as Mrs. Moreen, Mrs. Caulfield as Taffine/ **Sad. Wells**, May 1847, with William Hoskins as Plastic, Mr. Williams as Trot, A. Younge as Cosey, George Bennett as Rev. Glenroy, Henry Marston as Capt. Glenroy, Samuel Phelps as Reuben Glenroy, Henry Mellon as Rosse, Miss Cooper as Mrs. Glenroy, Laura Addison as Rosalie, Mrs. Garthwaite as Mrs. Trot, Mrs. Henry Marston as Mrs. Moreen, Julia St. George as Taffline; Feb. 1867, with J. H. Slater as Reuben, J. L. Warner as Plastic, Mr. Hamilton as Owen, R. Norman as Cosey, J. W. Lawrence as Trot, J. Collier as Capt. Glenroy, John Rouse as Hawbuck, Miss Leigh as Rosalie, Mrs. J. F. Saville as Mrs. Glenroy, Miss Fitzgerald as Mrs. Moreen, Mrs. J. W. Lawrence as Mrs. Trot/ **Princess's**, Sept. 1851, with Alfred Wigan as Plastic, John Pritt Harley as Trot, Mr. Addison as Cosey, Drinkwater Meadows as Rev. Glenroy, William Belton as Capt. Glenroy, Charles Kean as Reuben Glenroy, Frederick Cooke as Ross, John Cathcart as Williams, Robert Keeley as Hawbuck, Miss Phillips as Mrs. Glenroy, Mrs. Charles Kean as Rosalie, Mrs. Winstanley as Mrs. Trot, Mrs. W. Daly as Mrs. Moreen, Miss Somers as Goody Hawbuck, Mary Keeley as Taffline.

TRADESMAN'S SON, THE// D 2a// n.a.// **Surrey**, Oct. 1862.

TRADESMEN'S BALL, THE// C 1a// G. A. á Beckett// **St. James's**, Jan. 1837, with John Parry as Villiers, John Pritt Harley as Bluster, Mr. Daly as O'Cornice, Julia Smith as Lady Revel, Mme. Sala as Mrs. Sturch, Miss Stuart as Eliza.

TRAFALGAR; OR, PORTSMOUTH IN 1805// D 1a// A. V. Campbell// **Grecian**, Oct. 1845, with Mr. Saker as Petulant, Frederick Robson as Jacob Bustle, Harry Chester as Bergamot, John Collett as Dismal Dark, Mr. Campbell as Meredith, Mrs. W. Watson as Mrs. Meredith, Miss M. A. Crisp as Emma, Miss Johnstone as Mary.

TRAFALGAR MEDAL, THE; OR, THE IRISH FORTUNE TELLER// D 2a// J. B. Buckstone [?]// **Victoria**, June 1857, with Alfred Saville as Hammond, J. Howard as Madigan, Henry Dudley as Duke, J. H. Rickards as Kinchola, Julia Seaman as Cathleen, Mrs. H. Wallis as Judith, Mrs. Henry Vining as Pennie, Rosalie Young as Nelly.

TRAGEDY, A// F 3a// C. S. Fawcett// **Royalty**, Apr. 1887.

TRAGEDY QUEEN, THE// F 1a// John Oxenford// **Lyceum**, Nov. 1847, with Frank Matthews as Edenezer Standfast, John Parselle as David Standfast, Mrs. Stirling as Mrs. Bracegirdle, Miss Marshall as Bridget; May 1859, with Mr. Barrett as Ebenezer Standfast, F. Charles as David Standfast, Mrs. Stirling as Mrs. Bracegirdle, Emma Neville as Bridget/ **Olympic**, Dec. 1857, with Mr. Addison as Ebenezer Standfast, Gaston Murray as David Standfast, Mrs. Stirling as Mrs. Bracegirdle, Mrs. W. S. Emden (Miss Somers) as Bridget/ **Drury Lane**, Oct. 1860, with Mr. Lambert as Ebenezer Standfast, George Spencer as David Standfast, Mrs. Stirling as Mrs. Bracegirdle, Miss Arden as Bridget/ **Adelphi**, Oct. 1863, with C. H. Stephenson as Ebenezer Standfast, John Billington as David Standfast, Mrs. Stirling as Mrs. Bracegirdle, Kate Kelly as Bridget.

TRAIL OF SIN, THE// D// Henry Leslie// **Victoria**, Sept. 1863.

TRAIL OF THE SERPENT, THE// D// George Lander// **Elephant & Castle**, Aug. 1879.

TRAINED TO CRIME// D 4a// Edward Towers// **Pavilion**, Sept. 1878.

TRAMPS, THE// D 1a// Wilfred Stephens & Brian McCullough// **West London**, Dec. 1896.

TRAMP'S ADVENTURE, THE; OR, TRUE TO THE LAST// D 2a// F. L. Phillips// **Surrey**, 1862.

TRANSGRESSOR, THE// C 4a// A. W. Gattie// **Court**, Jan. 1894.

TRANSPORTED FOR LIFE// D 4a// Mortimer Murdoch// **Elephant & Castle**, Oct. 1880.

TRAPPED AT LAST// C 3a// George Neville// **Royalty**, Mar. 1882.

TRAPPER, THE// D// George Roberts// **Sad. Wells**, Apr. 1888.

TRAPPING A TARTAR// C 1a// Edward Stirling// **Astley's**, June 1864, with Henry Frazer as Gen. Keichioff, Mr. Friend as Count Plotski, Frederick Belton as Ivan, Teresa Furtado as Zelia.

TREASURE, THE// F 3a// R. C. Carton & Cecil Raleigh// **Strand**, May 1888.

TREE OF KNOWLEDGE, THE// Play 5a// R. C. Carton// **St. James's**, Oct. 1897, with George Alexander as Stanyon, W. H. Vernon as Sir Mostyn, Fred Terry as Hollingworth, H. B. Irving as Roupell, H. V. Esmond as Maj. Blencoe, George Shelton as Sweadle, Carlotta Addison as Mrs. Stanyon, Fay Davis as Monica, Winifred Dolan as Deborah, Julia Neilson as Belle/ Scenery by H. P. Hall/ Machines by Mr. Cullen/ Electrics by Mr. Barbour.

TRELAWNEY OF THE "WELLS"// C 4a// Arthur Wing Pinero// **Court**, Jan. 1898, with Dion Boucicault Jr., Irene Vanbrugh, Hilda Spong, Isabel Bateman, Roma Le Thière.

TREVANION; OR, THE FALSE POSITION// D// n.a.// **Grecian**, May 1855, with Richard Phillips as Trevanion, Basil Potter as Langford, Henry Grant as Knightly, John Manning, Jane Coveney as Margaret, Miss Johnstone as Mrs. Langford, Maria Simpson as Mrs. Lorimer, Harriet Coveney as Hornet, Ellen Crisp as Williams.

TRIAL BY BATTLE, THE// D// William Barrymore// **Victoria**, Sept. 1871, with John Bradshaw as Baron Falconbridge, Watty Brunton as Albert, Henry Mayhew as Hubert, E. Fitzdavis as Ambrose, George Skinner as Rufus, George Carter as Henrie, A. Stilt as Barnard, Annie Bentley as Little Jem, James Fawn as Morrice, Miss Clements as Geralda.

TRIAL OF EFFIE DEANS, THE// D 3a// Dram. by Dion Boucicault fr Sir Walter Scott, The Heart of Midlothian// **Royal Westminster** (Astley's), Jan. 1863, with Mrs. Dion Boucicault as Jeannie Deans, Edith Stuart as Effie Deans, Dan Leeson as Dumbiedike, Henry Vandenhoff as Duke of Argyll, Miss Atkinson as Meg Murdochson, Rose Leclercq as Madge Wildfire, Mr. Worboys as Archibald, Thomas Swinbourne as Geordie, Charles Vandenhoff as Reuben, Montague Smythson as Cousel for the Crown, Dion Boucicault as Counsel for Defense/ Scenery by Mr. Roberts/ Prod. by Dion Boucicault.

TRIAL OF LOVE, THE// D 5a// G. W. Lovell// **Princess's**, June 1852, with George Everett as Prince Rupert, John Ryder as Col. Boswell, Frank Graham as Sir William, Charles Kean as Col. Tyrrel, Charles Wheatleigh as Maj. Offington, Drinkwater Meadows as Shirley, John Cathcart as Gilbert, Mrs. Charles Kean as Isabel, Miss Marshall as Margaretta.

TRIALS OF TOMKINS, THE// F 1a// T. J. Williams// **Adelphi**, Apr. 1863.

TRIALS OF GRACE HUNTLY, THE; OR, A WOMAN'S LIFE// D 3a// Dram. by C. Z. Barnett fr tale of Mrs. S. C. Hall// **Victoria**, Mar. 1844, with Charles Morelli as Western, Mr. James as Darley, William Seaman as Greenshaw, Mr. Freer as Huntly, John Gardner as Cramwell, John Dale as Butt, Mr. Franklin as Grab, Annette Vincent as Grace, Miss Arden as Rosa, Miss Howard as Dorothy, Miss Brookes as Patience.

TRICK OF ESMERALDAY, THE// W. E. Bailey & Edgar Ward// **West London**, Feb. 1897.

TRICKS OF THE TURF// D// n.a.// **Victoria**, May 1867.

TRILBY// D 4a// Dram. by Paul Potter fr novel of Gerald Du Maurier// **Haymarket**, June 1895, with Herbert Beerbohm Tree as Svengali, Edmund Maurice as Taffy, Lionel Brough as The Laird, H. V. Esmond as Little Billee, C. M. Hallard as Gecko, Herbert Ross as Zouzou, Gerald Du Maurier as Dodor, Berte Thomas as Oliver, Gayer Mackay as Lorimer, Dorothea Baird as Trilby, Frances Ivor as Mrs. Bagot, Adrienne Dairolles as Mme. Vinard, Cicely Turner as Angèle/ **Her Majesty's**, June 1897.

TRIP TO BRIGHTON, A// F// J. E. Soden// **Globe**, Nov. 1874.

TRIP TO GRETA, A// C 2a// W. B. D'Almeida// **Vaudeville**, June 1891.

TRIP TO HAMPTON, A// F// n.a.// **Princess's**, Nov. 1847, with Samuel Cowell as Dramagogue, J. Neville as Greenwig, Mr. Howard as Verjuice, Augustus Harris as Dapple, F. C. Courtney as Goldsby, Mrs. Selby as Miss Verjuice, Miss Villars as Clara, Miss Somers as Maria/ Scenery by Mr. Brunning.

TRIP TO KISSINGEN, A// F// Tom Taylor// **Lyceum**, 1844.

TRIP TO RICHMOND, A// F 1a// n.a.// **Victoria**, July 1857, with J. Howard as Maj. Pepper, W. H. Pitt as Brown, Charles Rice as White, Julia Seaman as Widow White, Miss Laporte as Mrs. White, Mrs. J. H. Rickards as Kitty/ **Grecian**, Sept. 1861, with Mr. Jackson as Maj. Pepper, R. H. Lingham as Brown, Henry Power as White, Matilda Mordecai as Mrs. White, Jane Coveney as Widow White, Mary A. Victor as Kitty.

TRIPLE ALLIANCE, THE// D 3a// Adap. by John Oxenford fr F// **Princess's**, Nov. 1862, with George Vining as Don Estevan, J. G. Shore as Don Miguel, Constance Aylmer as Donna Maria, Mrs. Buckingham White as Duchess of Marialva, Miss M. Oliver as Beatrix.

TRIPLE ALLIANCE, THE// F 3a// n.a.// **Strand**, Dec. 1897.

TRIUMPH OF ARMS, A// F// W. Foulton// **Olympic**, Dec. 1872.

TRIUMPH OF THE PHILISTINES, AND HOW MR. JORGAN PRESERVED THE MORALS OF MARKET PEWBURY UNDER VERY TRYING CIRCUMSTANCES// C 3a// Henry Arthur Jones// **St. James's**, May 1895, with George Alexander as Sir Valentine, H. V. Esmond as Hesselwood, Herbert Waring as Jorgan, E. M. Robson as Pote, Ernest Hendrie as Blagg, Arthur Royston as Modlin, James Welch as Skewitt, H. H. Vincent as Wapes, Lady Monckton as Lady Beauboys, Miss Elliott Page as Alma, Blanche Wilmot as Angela, Juliette Nesville as Sally/ Scenery by H. P. Hall.

TROILUS AND CRESSIDA// T// William Shakespeare.

TROTTY VECK// D 2a// Mrs. Charles Calvert// **Gaiety**, Dec. 1872.

TROUBLES// C 1a// B. W. Findon// **St. Geo. Hall**, Nov. 1888.

TROUBLESOME LODGER, A// F 1a// Henry Mayhew & H. Baylis// **St. James's**, Feb. 1839, with Mr. Brookes as Tetchy, Benjamin Wrench as Palaver, Mr. Hughes as Weasel, Mr. Canning as Howlett, F. Carlton as Inspector, Miss Williams as Cynthia, Mrs. Frank Mathews as Patty.

TROVATORE, IL// D// Adap. by W. E. Suter fr opera of Verdi// **Cov. Garden**, May 1855.

TRUE AS STEEL; OR, THE REGENT'S DAUGHTER// D 2a// C. H. Hazlewood// **Britannia**, Dec. 1869.

TRUE AT LAST// n.a.// **Marylebone**, Apr. 1866.

TRUE BLUE; OR, AFLOAT AND ASHORE// D 5a// L. S. Outram & Sidney Gordon// **Olympic**, Mar. 1896.

TRUE COLOURS// C 1a// J. P. Hurst// **Globe**, June 1888.

TRUE COLOURS// Play 4a// Charles Hartley// **Vaudeville**, June 1889.

TRUE HEARTS// C 3a// Frank Bell// **St. Geo. Hall**, May 1874.

TRUE STORY, A; TOLD IN TWO CITIES// D 5a// Eliot Galer// **Drury Lane**, June 1885, with Richard Mansfield as Lord Cholmondley, William Herbert as Capt. Melton, W. H. Day as Frederick, J. H. Clynds as Sternhold, C. H. Kenney as Rupert, Reuben Inch as Faithful, Harry Jackson as Smithers, Harry Nichols as Sam, Maude Fisher as Little Maude, Lizzie Claremont as Lady Vere, Fanny Brough as Edith, Emilt Duncan as Mabel, Amy McNeill as Polly/ Scenery by Henry Emden & Charles Frampton/ Music by E. J. Thomas.

TRUE TILL DEATH// D 4a// Adap. by Hugh Marston fr F// **Standard**, Oct. 1876.

TRUE TO THE CORE; A STORY OF THE ARMADA// D// A. R. Slous// **Surrey**, Sept. 1866/ **Princess's**, June 1867/ **Novelty**, Apr. 1897.

TRUE TO THE LAST// D 4a// J. W. Whitbread// **Elephant & Castle**, July 1888.

TRUE TO THE QUEEN// D 4a// Harold Whyte// **Grand**, July 1891.

TRUAND CHIEF, THE; OR, THE PROVOST OF PARIS// D 3a// W. H. Oxberry// **Victoria**, Oct. 1837, with John Parry as Emanuel, Mr. Denvil as Zarak, Mr. Green as d'Aubriot, Mr. Salter as Erie, L. Smith as De Samfia, Mr. Harwood as Aubray, Mrs. Hooper as Zabina, Mrs. Griffith as Rachel, William Davidge as Godfrey/ Scenery by C. J. James.

TRUMPET CALL, THE// D 4a// G. R. Sims & Robert Buchanan// **Adelphi**, Aug. 1891, with Leonard Boyne as Cuthbertson, J. D. Beveridge as Sgt.-Maj. Milligan, Lionel Rignold as Prof. Ginnifer, Charles Dalton as Featherston, Richard Douglass as Dutton, Howard Russell as Col. Englehardt, Arthur Leigh as Sir William, Elizabeth Robins as Constance, Mrs. Patrick Campbell as Bertha, Miss E. Heffer as Lucy, Clara Jecks as Lavinia/ Scenery by Bruce Smith & W. Hann/ Music by Henry Sprake/ Machines by H. Loftin/ Prod. by Frederick Glover.

TRUMPETER'S DAUGHTER, THE: OR, LOVE AND THE POLKA// C// J. Sterling Coyne// **Haymarket**, Dec. 1843, with Benjamin Webster as Phillipot, William Strickland as Muller, William Clark as Robin, J. W. Gough as Laplomb, Mme. Celeste as Madelon.

TRUST AND TRIAL// D 4a// A. C. Calmour// **Gaiety**, Oct. 1880.

TRUSTEE, THE// D 2a// n.a.// **Olympic**, Oct. 1854, with Frederick Vining as Baron de Maugirolles, Samuel Emery as Caussade, Alfred Wigan as Deslandes, Henry Leslie as Armand, Miss Maskell as Angeline, Miss Stephens as Marguerite.

TRUTH, THE// C. J. Mathews// **Olympic**, Oct. 1837, with James Vining, James Bland, Charles Selby, Mr. Stoker, Mrs. Keeley.

TRUTH; OR, A GLASS TOO MUCH// D// Charles Mathews// **Olympic**, Oct. 1837.

TRUTH// C 3a// Bronson Howard// **Criterion**, Feb. 1879, with Charles Wyndham, Mary Rorke; Sept. 1890.

TRUTH AGAINST THE WORLD// D// George Spencer// **East London**, Apr. 1870.

TRUTH AND FICTION// C// T. J. Williams & Augustus Harris// **Princess's**, May 1861, with Frank Matthews as Brown, Robert Cathcart as Arthur, Edmund Garden as Fitzcrushington, Henry Widdicomb as Feedem, John Collett as St. Clare, Carlotta Leclercq as Margaret, Mrs. Weston as Mrs. Walters, Rose Leclercq as Angelina, Maria Harrisnas Rose.

TRUTHFUL JAMES// C 3a// James Mortimer & Charles Klein// **Royalty**, Oct. 1894.

TRYING IT ON// F 1a// William Brough// **Lyceum**, May 1853, with C. J. Mathews as Potts, Basil Baker as Jobstock, Henry Butler as Tittlebat, Miss Robertson as Fanny, Miss C. Mitchell as Mrs. Jobstock/ **Drury Lane**, Dec. 1855, with C. J. Mathews as Potts, A. Younge as Jobstock, Henry Butler as Tittlebat, Mrs. Selby as Mrs. Jobstock, Miss M. Oliver as Fanny, Emma Wadham as Lucy/ **St. James's**, 1875, with Charles Wyndham as Walsingham Potts, Mr. De Vere as Jobstock, Charles Steyne as Tittlebat, Miss M. Davis as Mrs. Jobstock, Rose Egan as Fanny.

TUFELHAUSEN// D 2a// J. B. Johnstone// **Surrey**, Mar. 1856.

TUPPINS AND CO.// E. M. Watson & Edward Solomon// **St. Geo. Hall**, Mar. 1889.

TURF, THE// C 2a// Mark Lemon// **Cov. Garden**, Oct. 1842, with Frank Matthews as Warren, Walter Lacy as Capt. Flatooker, Alfred Wigan as Siney, George Bartley as Culpepper, Drinkwater Meadows as Gallop, Mr. Granby as Doo, John Pritt Harley as Tret, Mrs. Humby as Mrs. Culpepper, Miss Lee as Miss Warren, Mrs. Emden as Fanny/ Scenery by Grieve, T. Grieve & W. Grieve.

TURKISH BATH, A// F 1a// Montague Williams & F. C. Burnand// **Adelphi**, Apr. 1861/ **Sad. Wells**, June 1861, with Paul Bedford as Spriggs, J. L. Toole as Griggs, W. H. Eburne as Fitzmortimer, Miss Laidlaw as Amelia.

TURN HIM OUT// F 1a// T. J. Williams// **Strand**, Aug. 1863/ **Adelphi**, Nov. 1875, with Frederick Moreland as Moke, James Fawn as Nobbs, W. Everard as Roseleaf, Miss E. Phillips as Julia; Oct. 1883, with Harwood Cooper as Nobbs, Frederick Moreland as Moke, Ernest Travers as Roseleaf, Miss Heffer as Julia, Harriet Coveney as Susan/ **Princess's**, June 1881, with G. W. Anson as Nobbs, Edward Price as Moke, Brian Darley as Roseleaf, Dora Vivian as Julia, Eugenie Edwards as Susan.

TURN OF THE TIDE, THE// D 4a// Dram. by F. C. Burnand fr novel of Mrs. Edwards// **Grecian**, Mar. 1870, with Henry Grant as Assheton, Thomas Mead as Mortimer, William James as Earnecliffe, John Manning as Danby, Samuel Perfitt as Maj. Podmore, George Gillett as Neville, W. Shirley as Sir George, Henry Power as Blaisot, Lizzie Mandelbert as Marguerite, Alice Denvil as Lady Clara, Mrs. Atkinson as Lady Templemore, Mrs. Dearlove as Lady Lorrimore, Mary A. Victor as Mrs. Danby/ **Olympic**, Dec. 1877, with J. G. Bauer as Assheton, Henry Neville as Earnscliffe, Johnston Forbes Robertson as Greville, Frank Barsby as Sir George, Charles Harcourt as Dr. Mortimer, G. W. Anson as Danby, G. Harmond as Doldrum, T. G. Warren as Pere Blaisot, George Yarnold as William, Florence

Terry as Marguerite, Sophie Young as Lady Clara, Mrs. Leigh Murray as Lady Templemore, Alma Stanley as Lady Lorrimer, Mrs. John Wood as Mrs. Danby, Miss Gerard as Georgy, Mme. Herbert as Manon, Ida Beaumont as Susan/ Scenery by W. Hann & H. Potts/ Machines by Mr. Collins/ Lime Light and Gas by Mr. Sabin/ Music by Victor Buziau.

TURN OUT// F// James Kenney// **Sad. Wells**, Apr. 1840, with Mr. Williams as Restive, Mr. Elvin as Somerville, Mr. Aldridge as Dr. Truckle, J. W. Collier as Forage, Henry Hall as Gregory, Charles Fenton as Cook, Mrs. R. Barnett as Marian, Miss Cooke as Mrs. Ramsay/ **Princess's**, Mar. 1848, with J. Neville as Restive, Mr. Barker as Somerville, John Gilbert as Dr. Truckle, Samuel Cowell as Forage, Henry Compton as Gregory, Emma Stanley as Marian, Mrs. Fosbroke as Mrs. Ramsay, Miss Somers as Peggy.

TURNED HEAD, THE// F 1a// G. A. à Beckett// **Victoria**, Apr. 1838, with Mr. Loveday as Fitzirundle, M. Forester as Ferdinand, William Davidge as Mulrent, Mr. Vale as Dick, John Parry as Dampley, Mrs. Maddocks as Laura; Mar. 1844, with Mr. James as Fitzfiggins, William Seaman as Ferdinand, Charles Morelli as Mulgent, F. H. Henry as Spoutling, John Gardner as Dick, Mr. Paul as Dampley, Miss Arden as Laura/ **Globe**, Sept. 1873, with Edmund Garden, Frank Selby, J. H. Allen, E. W. Garden, Nelly Harris.

TURNED OUT TO STARVE; OR, THE HAND THAT GOVERNS ALL// D 2a// Thomas Webb// **Britannia**, Feb. 1870.

TURNED UP// F 3a// Mark Melford// **Vaudeville**, May 1886/ **Strand**, Feb. 1891.

TURNING THE TABLES// F 1a// J. Poole// **D.L**, Mar. 1837, with Mr. Cooper as Bumps, Drinkwater Meadows as Humphries, Mrs. Charles Jones as Patty/ **Sad. Wells**, Mar. 1843, with Henry Marston as Bumps, C. J. Bird as de Courcy, Mr. Lambe as Thornton, Mr. Aldridge as Knibbs, John Herbert as Humphries, Miss Melville as Miss Knibbs, Mrs. Henry Marston as Mrs. Humphries, Mrs. Richard Barnett as Patty; Feb. 1851, with Mr. Williams as Old Knibbs, A. Younge as Humphries, Charles Wheatleigh as De Courcy, Frank Graham as Thornton, Samuel Phelps as Bumps, Lucy Rafter as Sally, Mrs. Graham as Mrs. Humphries, Eliza Travers as Patty/ **Olympic**, Nov. 1850, with H. Buckland as Jeremiah Bumps, Charles Bender, Mr. Berton as Edgar, John Kinloch as Thurston, W. Shalders as Humphreys, Miss Adams as Miss Squibbs, Isabel Adams as Mrs. Humphreys, Ellen Turner as Patty/ **Princess's**, May 1853, with John Chester as Knibbs, James Vining as Bumps, John Pritt Harley as Humphries, George Everett as de Courcey, Hermann Vezin as Thornton, Miss Daly as Mrs. Humphries, Carlotta Leclercq as Miss Knibbs, Mrs. Walter Lacy as Patty/ **Grecian**, June 1857, with Henry Grant, W. H. Eburne, William Shuter, Ellen Hale, Miss Johnstone, Harriet Coveney/ **Haymarket**, Mar. 1861, with William Cullenford as Knibbs, Henry Compton as Bumps, William Farren as de Courcy, George Braid as Thornton, Henry Howe as Humphries, Marie Nolan as Miss Knibbs, Mrs. Griffiths as Mrs. Humphries, Ella Staunton as Patty; July 1876, with Henry Rivers as Knibbs, H. B. Conway as Bumps, Walter Gordon as De Conray, Mr. Weathersby as Thornton, Frederick Everill as Humphries, Mrs. Edward Osborne as Miss Knibbs, Miss E. Harrison as Mrs. Humphries, Maria Harris as Patty/ **Lyceum**, Mar. 1878, with J. Archer as Nibbs, Arthur Wing Pinero as de Courcy, Mr. Holland as Thornton, R. C. Lyons as Bumps, Edmund Lyons as Humphreys, Eva Morley as Miss Nibbs, Mrs. St. John as Mrs. Humphreys.

TURNPIKE GATE, THE; OR, THE OLD ADMIRAL// F 2a// T. Knight// **Sad. Wells** (in 1a), Aug. 1840, with Mr. Elvin as Sir Edward, Mr. Richardson as Smart, J. B. Hill as Blunt, Alfred Rayner as Crack, J. W. Collier as Maythorn, Mr. Aldridge as Standfast, Miss Roberts as Mary, Mrs. Richard Barnett as Pegy/ **Grecian**, July 1846, with Mr. Melvin as Sir Edward, Mr. Kerridge as Smart, Mr. Manley as Maythorn, Charles Horn as Blunt, Frederick Robson as Crack, Miss M. A. Crisp as Mary, Mrs. W. Watson as Landlady/ **Olympic**, Oct. 1846, with C. Cowell as Crack, Mr. Clifford as Sir Edward, Mr. Binge as Blunt, Charles Maynard as Standfast, Robert Romer as Maythorne, Mis Madden as Mary, Miss Hamblin as Peggy, Mrs. Johnstone as Landlady/ **Astley's**, Nov. 1860, with Walter Carle as Dashaway, G. B. Ellis as Blunt, J. Francis as Crack, C. Johnson as Standfast, Henry Reeves as Smart, Miss Thompson as Mary, Emily Scott as Peggy.

TURPIN'S RIDE TO YORK; OR, THE DEATH OF BONNY BLACK BESS// D// George Conquest// **Grecian**, July 1862, with Walter Edwin as Dick Turpin, George Gillett as Rookwood, Walter Holland as Tom King, Henry Grant as Luke, Mr. Jackson as Simon, John Manning as Timothy, R. Summersby as Sharpset, Mary A. Victor as Dolly Dudgeon, Ellen Hale as Sybil.

TUTOR'S ASSISTANT, THE// C 2a// Charles Selby// **Lyceum**, July 1848, with Charles Selby AS Grand Duke Stiffenback Squidlitz, C. J. Mathews as Prince Ludwig, Frederick Cooke as Slockenhausen, Robert Roxby as Capt. Fredrick, Mr. Granby as von Florisberg, Mrs. Charles Jones as Mlle. de Boulancourt, Louisa Howard as Theresa.

'TWAS I// C 1a// John Howard Payne// **Olympic**, Feb. 1876, with E. N. Hallows as Delorme, Albert Bernard as Marcel, Mr. Winstanley as Mayor, Mr. St. Alban as Clerk, Myra Hope as Marchioness de Merville, Miss Beaumont as Julienne, Maud Branscombe as Georgette, Mrs. Stephens as Madame Mag.

'TWAS IN TRAFALGAR'S BAY// D 5a// John Henderson// **Marylebone**, Nov. 1891.

TWEEDIE'S RIGHTS// C 2a// James Albery// **Vaudeville**, May 1871.

TWEEDLETON'S TAIL COAT// F// T. J.

Williams// **Lyceum**, Oct. 1866.

TWELFTH NIGHT; OR, WHAT YOU WILL// C// William Shakespeare// **Haymarket**, Sept. 1839, with Mr. Cooper as Orsino, Henry Howe as Sebastian, Charles Perkins as Antonio, J. Worrell as Valentine, William Clark as Curio, Robert Strickland as Sir Toby, J. B. Buckstone as Aguecheek, William Farren as Malvolio, Benjamin Webster as Clown, Mrs. Walter Lacy (Miss Taylor) as Olivia, Ellen Tree as Viola, Mrs. Fitzwilliam as Marian; Nov. 1848, with Henry Howe as Duke, A. Brindal as Valentine, Mr. Tilbury as Sir Toby, Robert Keeley as Sir Andrew, Henry Vandenhoff as Sebastian, Mr. Rogers as Antonio, Benjamin Webster as Malvolio, Alfred Wigan as Clown, Miss Reynolds as Olivia, Mrs. Charles Kean as Viola, Mrs. Humby as Maria; Aug. 1864, with Henry Howe as Orsino, Mr. Weatherby as Sebastian, George Braid as Antonio, Walter Gordon as Roberto, J. Worrell as Valentine, Mr. Rogers as Sir Toby, J. B. Buckstone as Aguecheek, W. H. Chippendale as Malvolio, William Farren as Fabian, Henry Compton as Clown, Nelly Moore as Olivia, Louisa Angel as Viola, Mrs. Edward Fitzwilliam as Maria; Feb. 1878, with Harold Kyrle as Orsino, Mr. Fielder as Valentine, F. Webster as Curio, Frederick Everill as Sir Toby, Charles Harcourt as Aguecheek, H. B. Conway as Sebastian, Henry Howe as Malvolio, David Fisher Jr. as Clown, Miss Ernstone as Olivia, Adelaide Neilson as Viola, Kate Phillips as Maria/ Scenery by John O'Conner/ **Cov. Garden**, May 1840, with Mr. Cooper as Orsino, Mr. Fitzjames as Valentine, Alfred Wigan as Curio, George Bartley as Sir Toby, Drinkwater Meadows as Aguecheek, James Vining as Sebastian, Charles Diddear as Antonio, William Farren as Malvolio, John Pritt Harley as Clown, Mrs. Walter Lacy (Miss Taylor) as Olivia, Ellen Tree as Viola, Mrs. Humby as Maria/ **Sad. Wells**, Jan. 1848, with Henry Marston as Duke Orsini, Frank Graham as Sebastian, Mr. Harrington as Antonio, George Bennet as Sir Toby, A. Younge as Aguecheek, Samuel Phelps as Malvolio, Henry Mellon as Fabian, Henry Scharf as Clown, Miss Cooper as Olivia, Laura Addison as Viola, Mrs. Henry Marston as Maria; Apr. 1884, with Pascoe Bioletti as Orsino, Arthur Wood as Sir Toby, F. Hamilton Knight as Aguecheek, C. H. Kenney as Sebastian, Charles Medwin as Antonio, Frank Hinde as Clown, Henry Vernon as Malvolio, Nina Walpole as Olivia, Mrs. Anderson as Maria, Rose De Vane as Viola/ **Marylebone**, Dec. 1849, with Anna Cora Mowatt, E. L. Davenport/ **Princess's**, Sept. 1850, with Frederick Belton as Orsino, John Cathcart as Sebastian, John Ryder aas Antonio, Frederick Cooke as Roberto, Mr. Addison as Sir Toby, Robert Keeley as Aguecheek, Drinkwater Meadows as Malvolio, James Vining as Fabian, John Pritt Harley as Clown, Miss Phillips as Olivia, Mrs. Charles Kean as Viola, Mrs. Keeley as Maria/ **Olympic**, July 1865, with Charles Coghlan as Orsino, Kate Terry as Viola and Sebastian, E. F. Edgar as Antonio, Harwood Cooper as Valentine, Robert Soutar as Sir Toby Belch, Horace Wigan as Aguecheek, George Vincent as Malvolio, Ellen Farren as Clown, Miss A. Bowering as Olivia, Lydia Foote as Maria/ **Lyceum**, July 1884, with Henry Irving as Malvolio, William Terriss as Duke Orsino, David Fisher as Sir Toby Belch, Francis Wyatt as Sir Andrew Aguecheek, Stanislaus Calhaem as Clown, Fred Terry as Sebastian, Henry Howe as Antonio, Rose Leclercq as Olivia, Louise Payne as Maria, Ellen Terry as Viola/ Scenery by Hawes Craven, William Hann, William Cuthbert, T. W. Hall, J. Selby Hall, J. Harker, & William Telbin/ Music by Meredith Ball/ Machines by Mr. Knight; Mar. 1900/ **Daly's**, Jan. 1894/ **Her Majesty's**, Feb. 1901.

TWELVE ANGELS// D 3a// Edward Towers// **East London**, Nov. 1869.

TWELVE LABOURS OF HERCULES, THE// C 2a// Robert Brough// **Strand**, Dec. 1851.

TWENTY-FOURTH OF MAY, THE// D 1a// n.a.// **Olympic**, Feb. 1844, with Mr. Scott as Gen. Bensengen, Mr. Thornton as Col. Romanoff, Mr. Green as Count Orloff, Mr. Cook as Capt. Versloffky, Mr. Sherrington as Benowsky, Mr. Turnour as Kroff, Mr. Salter as Nicholas, Miss Morton as Ulrica, Miss Hamilton as Katherina.

TWENTY MINUTES' CONVERSATION UNDER AN UMBRELLA// C 1a// A. W. Dubourg// **Haymarket**, July 1873, with W. H. Kendal as Will, Madge Robertson as Madge.

TWENTY MINUTES WITH A TIGER// F 1a// Adap. fr F// **Drury Lane**, Oct. 1855, with A. Younge as Chutnee, C. J. Mathews as Beeswing, Charles Swan as Jacob, Miss De Vere as Arabella, Emma Wadham as Dolly/ **Olympic**, Aug. 1874, with Charles Harcourt as Beeswing, John Vollaire as Chutnee, Mr. Canninge as Mutter, Miss Emmerson as Arabella, Annie Taylor as Dolly.

£20 A YEAR, ALL FOUND// F// H. J. Byron// **Folly**, Apr. 1876.

TWENTY THOUSAND POUNDS A YEAR// D// Edward Towers// **Pavilion**, Sept. 1871.

23, JOHN STREET, ADELPHI// F 1a// n.a.// **Grecian**, June 1844, with Frederick Robson as Tomkins, John Collett as Spencer, Edwin Dixon as Sir Charles, Mr. Shaw as Capt. Smith, Henry Bedford as James, G. Norman as Phalim, Edmund Garden as Snatch, Miss M. A. Crisp as Lady Crazy, Miss Johnstone as Eliza, Miss Merion as Mary/ **Sad. Wells**, Apr. 1845, with Mr. Rae as Sir Charles Crazy, John Webster as Tomkins, Mr. Morton as Capt. Smith, Mr. Raymond as Spencer, Mr. Evain as Snatch, Edward Knight as Fogle, Charles Fenton as Phelim, Miss Huddart as Lady Crazy, Fanny Morelli as Eliza, Georgiana Lebatt as Mary.

TWENTY YEARS IN A DEBTORS' PRISON// D// n.a.// **City of London**, Sept. 1858.

22A CURZON STREET// Play 3a// Brandon Thomas & John Edwards// **Garrick**, Mar. 1898.

TWENTY-FOURTH OF GEORGE II, THE// n.a.// **Royalty**, May 1866.

TWICE KILLED// F 1a// John Oxenford// **Olympic**, Nov. 1837, with Robert Keeley as Facile, John Brougham as Reckless, Mr. Stoker as Tom, W. Vining as Holdfast, Mr. Wyman as Fable, Miss Murray as Mrs. Facile, Miss Crisp as Julia, Mrs. Orger as Fanny Pepper/ **Cov. Garden**, July 1838, with Robert Keeley as Facile, John Brougham as Reckless, T. F. Mathews as Tom, J. W. Gough as Holdfast, Mr. Clarke [sic] as Fable, Mr. Kerridge as Robert, Mrs. Orger as Fanny, Miss Beresford as Mrs. Facile, Miss Gallott as Julia/ **Haymarket**, Feb. 1848, with Robert Keeley as Facile, Henry Howe as Reckless, George Braid as Tom, Mr. Rogers as Holdfast, Mr. Clark as Fable, Mrs. L. S. Buckingham as Mrs. Facile, Miss E. Messent as Julia, Mrs. Keeley as Fanny/ **Princess's**, Nov. 1850, with Robert Keeley as Facile, James Vining as Reckless, Frederick Cooke as Tom, Mr. Addison as Holdfast, Drinkwater Meadows as Fable, Miss Vivash as Mrs. Facile, Miss A. Cushnie as Julia, Mrs. Keeley as Fanny Pepper/ **Drury Lane**, Sept. 1856, with Robert Keeley as Facile, C. Vincent as Reckless, Mr. Walton as Tom, Mr. Tilbury as Holdfast, Mr. Templeton as Fable, Miss Cleveland as Mrs. Facile, Miss Bulmer as Julia, Mrs. Keeley as Fanny/ **Grecian**, Nov. 1857, with George Conquest as Facile, Richard Phillips as Reckless, Henry Power as Tom, Henry Grant as Holdfast, Eaton O'Donnell as Fable, Jane Coveney as Mrs. Facile, Ellen Hale as Julia, Harriet Coveney as Fanny/ **Lyceum**, Sept. 1871, with George Belmore as Facile, Herbert Crellin as Reckless, John Royston as Tom, John Collett as Holdfast, Georgiana Pauncefort as Mrs. Facile, Ellen Leigh as Julia, Mrs. F. B. Egan as Fanny.

TWICE MARRIED// C 3a// Clement O'Neill & H. Sylvester// **Gaiety**, Apr. 1887.

TWICE-TOLD TALE, A// C 1a// J. P. Wooler// **Olympic**, Sept. 1858, with Walter Gordon as Gauntlett, Lewis Ball as Breezely, Miss Wyndham as Mrs. Breezly, Miss Hughes as Miss Mannerly.

TWIG FOLLY// D 4a// Robert Dodson// **Pavilion**, Apr. 1878.

TWIN BROTHERS, THE; OR, THE WARNING VISION// D// W. Paul// **Marylebone**, Feb. 1874.

TWINS// F 3a// Joseph Derrick// **Olympic**, Aug. 1884, with Edward Righton as Titus Spinach and as Timothy Spinach, W. H. Wallace as Billings, Lawrence Cautley as Adolphus, Mr. Teesdale as O'Haversack, Charles Steyne as Arrack, J. W. Bradbury as Rampunkah, Carlotta Leclercq as Mrs. Granby, Anna Conover as Edith, Ethel Hope as Mrs. Billings, Gabrielle Goldney as Lydia, Kate Kearney as Matilda/ Scenery by Perkins & Spong.

TWINE THE PLAIDEN; OR, THE IMPROVISATORE// D 4a// G. R. Walker// **Globe**, May 1878.

'TWIXT AXE AND CROWN; OR, THE LADY ELIZABETH// D 5a// Tom Taylor// **Princess's**, 1873.

'TWIXT CUP AND LIP// C 3a// "C. A. De La Plume"// **Olympic**, June 1873, with David Evans as Lord Minton, A. Ellwood as Capt. Winter, C. W. Garthorne as Worcester, Mr. Baker as Maj. Fotheringay, Arthur Wood as Quibble, J. K. Murray as Pussifat, Miss E. Lander as Mrs. Shuttleton, Miss E. Chambers as Mary, Kitty Fisher as Kate.

'TWIXT CUP AND LIP// C 2a// William Sapte Jr.// **Strand**, Nov. 1893.

'TWIXT KITH AND KIN// D 4a// Adap. by J. J. Blood fr novel of Miss Braddon, Cut by the County// **Grand**, Oct. 1887.

'TWIXT NIGHT AND MORN// D 2a// E. M. Seymore// **Avenue**, May 1896.

TWO BLINDS, THE// F// A. Clements// **Drury Lane**, Feb. 1881, with E. Royce as Black, John Maclean as White.

TWO BONNYCASTLES, THE// F 1a// J. Maddison Morton// **Haymarket**, Nov. 1851, with Mr. Lambert as Smuggins, Henry Howe as Johnson, J. B. Buckstone as Bonnycastle, Mrs. L. S. Buckingham as Mrs. Bonnycastle, Amelia Vining as Helen, Mrs. Caulfield as Patty.

TWO BOYS, THE// D// Adap. by G. R. Sims & Arthur Shirley fr F, Les Deux Gosses// **Princess's**, May 1896.

TWO BROTHERS, THE// C// W. E. Suter// **Grecian**, Nov. 1861, with Alfred Rayner as Wilfred Wilful, William James as Clitheroe, R. H. Lingham as Bernard, Henry Grant as Maj. Bolder, John Manning as Pettifog, Mary A. Victor as Mrs. Clitheroe Osborne, Mrs. Charles Dillon as Emily.

TWO BUZZARDS, THE// F 1a// n.a.// **Drury Lane**, Nov. 1864, with Mr. Odell as Benjamin, Wyke Moore as Glimmer, S. Johnson as Small, Mrs. E. F. Saville as Lucretia, Mrs. F. Huntley as Sally.

TWO CAN PLAY AT THAT GAME// C 1a// Arthur Wing Pinero// **Lyceum**, Sept. 1877, with J. Archer as Capt. Bunyard, Arthur Wing Pinero as Clutterbuck, Edmund Lyons as Tummus, Miss Sedley as Kate Clutterbuck.

TWO CAN PLAY AT THAT GAME// C 1a// n.a.// **Olympic**, June 1881, with E. T. Webber as Howard, H. Hamilton as Charles, Josephine St. Ange as Lucy.

TWO FIGAROS, THE// C 2a// J. R. Planché// **Olympic**, Mar. 1837, with James Bland as Almaviva, C. J. Mathews as Col. Cherubino, Charles Selby as Toribio, W. H. Oxberry as Scribleros, John Liston as Figaro, Mrs. Knight as Countess Almaviva, Miss Crawford as Seraphina, Miss Murray as Susanna, Mme. Vestris as Susannetta/ Scenery by Mr. Hilliard/ Music by Mr. Tully/ **Cov. Garden**, Oct. 1839, with James Bland as Almaviva, Thomas Green as Figaro, C. J. Mathews as Col. Cherubino, Mr. Granby as Scribleros, Mr. Ireland as Antonio,

John Ayliffe as Basilio, Mrs. Macnamara as Countess Almaviva, Miss A. Taylor as Seraphina, Mrs. Humby as Susanna, Mrs. Emden as Barbarina, Mme. Vestris as Susanetta.

TWO FLATS AND A SHARP// F 1a// Alfred Matlby// **Globe**, Dec. 1873, with George Temple as Major Keye, Linda Deitz; Mar. 1874, with George Temple as Major Keye, Nelly Harris as Mrs. Keye, Maria Daly as Mrs. Minor.

TWO FOSCARI, THE// D// Lord Byron// **Cov. Garden**, Apr. 1838, with W. C. Macready as Francis Foscari, James Anderson as Jacopo Foscari, Mr. Warde as Loredano, E. W. Elton as Barbarigo, George Bennett as Chief, Charles Diddear as Memmo, J. Waldron as Macenigo, John Pritchard as Gradenigo, Henry Howe as Salvati, Edwin Yarnold as Bianchi, W. H. Payne as Benedetto, C. J. Smith as Giulio, Helen Faucit as Marina.

TWO GALLEY SLAVES, THE; OR, THE MILL OF ST. ALDERVON// D 2a// Transl. by John Howard Payne fr F// **Sad. Wells**, Aug. 1842, with Mr. Lyon as Henry, Mr. Lambe as Maj. De Lisle, Mr. Dry as Bonhomme, P. Williams as La Route, C. J. Smith as Unknown, Miss Richardson as Louise/ **Victoria** May 1848, with John Bradshaw as Maj. de Lisle, J. Howard as Bonhomme, J. T. Johnson as Henry, E. Edwards as The Unknown, Walter Searle as La Route, G. F. Forman as Basil, Julia Seaman as Felix, Mrs. George Lee as Louise, Miss Young as Annette, Miss Devere as Cephise.

TWO GENTLEMEN OF VERONA// C// William Shakespeare// **Drury Lane**, Jan. 1842, with Samuel Phelps as Duke, W. C. Macready as Valentine, James Anderson as Proteus, William Bennett as Antonio, George Bennett as Panthino, Henry Compton as Thurio, Henry Marston as Eglamour, Edwin Yarnold as Host, Henry Hall as Speed, Robert Keeley as Launce, Miss Fortesque as Julia, Miss Ellis as Silvia, Miss Turpin as Lucetta/ **Haymarket**, Dec. 1848, with Henry Howe as Duke, Charles Kean as Valentine, William Creswick as Proteus, Mr. Rogers as Antonio, Alfred Wigan as Thurio, Henry Vandenhoff as Eglamour, Benjamin Webster as Speed, Robert Keeley as Launce, Mrs. Charles Kean as Julia, Julia Bennett as Silvia, Mrs. Humby as Lucetta/ **Sad. Wells**, Feb. 1857, with Alfred Rayner as Duke, Henry Marston as Valentine, Frederic Robinson as Proteus, Mr. Haywell as Antonio, William Belford as Thurio, Charles Seyton as Eglamour, Lewis Ball as Launce, Margaret Eburne as Julia, Jenny Marston as Silvia, Eliza Travers as Lucetta/ Scenery by C. Fenton/ Machines by Mr. Cawdery.

TWO GREENS, THE// F// Leman Rede// **Olympic**, Feb. 1840, with Benjamin Wrench as James Green of the first floor, George Wild as James Green of the second floor, Mr. Ross as Samuel, Mrs. Julia Glover as Mrs. Green, Miss Treble as Fanny, Miss Norton as Miss Freelove.

TWO GREGORIES// F 1a// Charles Dibdin// **St. James's**, May 1877, with Mr. Burleigh as John Bull, Mr. Wyndham as Mr.Gregory, J. D. Stoyle as Gregory, Ada Cavendish as Mrs. Gregory, Kate Kearney as Fanchette/ **Globe**, Dec. 1876, with Richard Temple as John Bull, J. Edwards as Mr. Gregory, Charles Steyne as Gregory, Marian Carr as Mrs. Gregory, Rose Cullen as Fanchette.

TWO HEADS ARE BETTER THAN ONE// F 1a// F. L. Horne// **Lyceum**, Dec. 1854/ **Sad. Wells**, Apr. 1855, with Robert Roxby as Conquest, Edwin Villiers as Strange, Mr. Templeton as Maxwelton, Charles Swan as Sammy, Miss Hughes as Ellen/ **Drury Lane**, Dec. 1856, with Mr. Tilbury as Strange, Robert Roxby as Conquest, J. Worrell as Maxwelton, Mr. Templeton as Sammy, Emma Wadham as Ellen/ **Princess's**, Sept. 1873, with Mr. Shepherd as Strange, Frank Barsby as Conquest, Mr. Rories as Maxwelton, Charles Seyton as Sammy, Miss Bennett as Mrs. Strange.

TWO HEARTS// Play 1a// J. A. Fitzgerald// **Royalty**, Feb. 1894.

TWO HUNDRED A YEAR// C 1a// Arthur Wing Pinero// **Globe**, Oct. 1877, with F. H. Macklin as John Meadows, Mr. Bradbury as Fubby, Miss Compton as Mrs. Meadows, Miss J. Warden as Ellen Jane.

TWO HUNDRED YEARS AGO; OR, TWO LOVES AND TWO LIVES// D 3a// Robert Dodson// **Victoria**, Apr. 1872.

TWO HUSSARS, THE// D 4a// Harry Bruce & Walter Burnot// **Surrey**, June 1896.

TWO IN THE BUSH// F 1a// S. Murray Carson// **Olympic**, Aug. 1891/ **Globe**, Nov. 1891, with Henry De Solla as Cyrus Carr, James Welch as Maj. Frere, T. W. Percyval as Draycott, Georgie Esmond as Nettit.

TWO IN THE MORNING// F 1a// C. J. Mathews// **St. James's**, Mar. 1864, with C. J. Mathews as The Stranger, Frank Matthews as Newpenny.

TWO JACK SHEPPARDS, THE// C 1a// C. A. Somerset// **Olympic**, May 1841, with Mr. Halford as Mr. Sheppard, Mr. Mulford as Justice Quibble, Mr. Harry as Twitter, Mr. Thompson as Sturdy, Mr. Brookes as Muzzy, Mr. Turnour as Dozey, Thomas Lee as Paddy O'Swag, Mrs. Edmonds as Caroline, Miss Le Batt as Betty.

TWO JOHNNIES, THE// F 3a// Adap. by Fred Horner & Frank Wyatt fr F of M. Ordonneau & A. Valabrègue// **Comedy**, June 1889/ **Trafalgar**, Oct. 1893.

TWO LITTLE HEROES// n.a.// **Surrey**, May 1901.

TWO LITTLE VAGABONDS// D 5a// Adap. by G. R. Sims & Arthur Shirley fr F of Pierre Decourcelle, Les Deux Gosses// **Princess's**, Oct. 1896, with Ernest Leicester as Thornton, Lyston Lyle as Capt. Darville, Walter Howard as Scarth, Edmund Gurney as Mullins, Christopher Walker as Bunce, Edward Coleman as Cough Drop, Herbert Vyvyan as Leeson, Geraldine Cliffe as Marion, Mena Le Bert as Barbara, Eva Williams as Sister Randall, Sydney Fairbrother as Wally, Kate Tydall as Dick/ Scenery by Cecil Hicks, Henry Brooke, Ernest Howard, C. Noble, W. Muir & R. Flannagan/ Prod. by George Minshull.

TWO LOCKSMITHS OF LONDON, THE// D// G. D. Pitt// **Victoria**, Aug. 1846, with Mr. Archer as Hosper, J. Howard as Samuel Davis, G. W. Walton as George Davis, William Seaman as Burl, Alfred Raymond as Paul Davis, Walter Searle as Cly, E. G. Burton as Lively, F. Wilton as Old William, James Ranoe as West, Miss Fielding as Emily, Lydia Pearce as Rose.

TWO LODGERS TO ONE LODGING// F 1a// n.a.// **Grecian**, Oct. 1853, with Charles Rice as Allerton, Mr. Wilson as Wanchie, Harriet Coveney as Fanny, Miss Johnstone as Cribbage.

TWO LONDON LOCKSMITHS, THE; OR, THE BANKER, THE THIEF, AND THE WILL// D// G. D. Pitt// **Victoria**, Dec. 1841, with John Dale as Hosper, Mr. James as Samuel Davis, E. F. Saville as George Davis, William Seaman as Burl, C. Williams as Paul Davis, Mr. Paul as Cly, John Gardner as Lively, Mrs. George Lee as Emily, Mrs. Howard as Rose.

TWO LOVES AND A LIFE// D 4a// Charles Reade & Tom Taylor// **Adelphi**, Mar. 1854, with Charles Selby as Duke of Cumberland, Leigh Murray as Sir Gervase, Benjamin Webster as Father Radcliffe, John Parselle as Capt. Dormer, Robert Keeley as John Daw, O. Smith as Musgrave, C. J. Smith as Capt. Jansen, Mr. Braithwaite as Farmer Greystoke, Sarah Woolgar as Anne, Mme. Celeste as Ruth Ravensear/ Scenery by Pitt & Turner/ Music by Alfred Mellon/ **Sad. Wells**, Oct. 1868, with J. H. Fitzpatrick as Fr. Radcliffe, J. H. Loome as Musgrave, Mr. Newbound as Sir Gervase, Mr. Matthews as Gordon, Richard Edgar as Potts, Mr. McErnest as Capt. Dormer, Mr. Jackson as Farmer Greystoke, W. H. Abel as Capt. Jason, Miss Hazlewood as Ruth, Miss Logan as Ann/ Scenery by T. Evans.

TWO MEN// D 4a// William Bourne// **West London**, Dec. 1896.

TWO MEN AND A MAID// D 4a// F. H. Purchase & James Webster// **Comedy**, June 1893.

TWO MOTHERS, THE// D 5a// Mr. Mayer// **Duke's**, Mar. 1877.

TWO NIGHTS; OR, THE DUCHESS AND THE ASTROLOGER// D 2a// n.a.// **Grecian**, July 1855, with Richard Phillips as St. Megrin, Henry Grant as Duke of Guise, T. Roberts as d'Epernon, F. Charles as de Joyeuse, Basil Potter as Compte Ruggiere, Harriet Coveney as Arthur, Eaton O'Donnell as Durand, Jane Coveney as Suchess of Guise, Miss Johnstone as Mme. de Cosse.

TWO OLD BOYS// C 1a// Adap. by James Mortimer fr F of Henri Meilhac// **Court**, Dec. 1880, with G. W. Anson, Edward Price, Winnifred Emery/ **Princess's**, July 1881, with G. W. Anson as Merriweather, Allen Thomas as Chalmers, Neville Doone as Jocelyn, Miss G. Wright as Perkins, Dora Vivian as Kate.

TWO ORPHANS, THE// D 6a// Adap. by John Oxenford fr F of A. P. Dennery & D. E. Cormon, Les Deux Orphelines// **Olympic**, Sept. 1874, with Charles Harcourt as Count de Limiere, Frank Rowland as Marquis de Presles, Charles Sugden as de Vaudry, William Rignold as Jacques, Henry Neville as Pierre, John Vollaire as Doctor, G. W. Anson as Picard, Mrs. Charles Viner as Countess de Limiere, Miss Fowler as Louise, Miss Ernstone as Henriette, Mrs. Huntley as La Frochard, Mrs. Charles Harcourt as Genevieve, May Douglas as Marianne, Annie Taylor as Florette, Nellie Phillips as Julie/ Scenery by Julian Hicks/ Machines by J. Collins/ Limelight by Mr. Sabin/ Gas by Mr. Hinckley/ Music by J. Mallandaine/ Prod. by Henry Neville.

TWO PAGES OF FREDERICK THE GREAT, THE// C// John Poole// **Cov. Garden**, May 1837, with William Farren as Frederick, Eliza Vincent as Theodore, Miss Lee as Augustus, Mr. Tilbury as Phelps, John Collett as Carlo, Mrs. Julia Glover as Mme. Phelps, Mrs. W. West as Mme. Ritzburg, Miss Nicholson as Caroline, Mrs. Sarah Garrick as Lisbeth/ **Sad. Wells**, Feb. 1839, with Mr. Cathcart as Frederick the Great, Mr. Williams as Phelps, Mr. Phillips as Papilion, Miss Pincott as Theodore, Mrs. Robert Honner as Augustus, Miss Richardson as Mme. Ritzberg, Miss Cooke as Mrs. Phelps, Mrs. J. F. Saville as Caroline.

TWO PATHS IN LIFE, THE// D// E. R. Callender// **Victoria**, Apr. 1876.

TWO PETERS// F// Frederic Reynolds// **Sad. Wells**, Apr. 1847, with Henry Marston as Czar Peter, Henry Mellon as Baron Von Clump, Frank Graham as Count Varenshoff, Mr. Branson as Count de Morville, A. Younge as Van Dunder, Henry Scharf as Stanmitz, Julia Wallack as Bertha.

TWO PHOTOGRAPHS, THE// F 1a// Arthur Clements// **Strand**, Mar. 1884.

TWO POETS, THE// F 1a// John Courtnay// **Surrey**, Nov. 1850. (misreading of item below?)

TWO POLTS,THE// F 1a// John Courtney// **Princess's**, Oct. 1859, with Henry Widdicomb as Peter Polt, Edmund Garden as Col. Bumpus, Henry Irving as Jack, J. G. Shore as Thomas Polt, Helen Howard as Betsy, Emma Wadham as Amelia, Rose Leclercq as Caroline/ **Sad. Wells**, June 1861, with Mr. Shepherd as Col. Bumpus, G. Dawson as Jack Bumpus, William Belford as Thomas Polt, Hewnry Widdocomb as Peter Polt, Miss Hodson as Caroline, Miss Heath as Amelia, Bella Staunton as Betsy/ **Lyceum**, Jan. 1867, with Henry Widdicomb AS Peter Polt, J. H. Fitzpatrick as Tom Polt.

TWO PORTRAITS// D// n.a.// **Sad. Wells**, Nov. 1841, with Robert Honner as Jack Junk, Mr. Williams as Capt. Bertram, Mr. Elvin as Henry, Mr. Aldridge as Capais, Mr. Dry as

Bertram, Miss Richardson as Mrs. Moral, Mrs. Richard Barnett as Emma.

TWO PUDDIFOOTS// F 1a// Adap. by J. Maddison Morton// **Olympic**, Oct. 1867, with Mr. Addison as Puddifoot Sr., Horace Wigan as Puddifoot Jr., M. Robson as Buffles, Mrs. Caulfield as Mrs. Figsby, Miss Schavey as Caroline, Ellen Farren as Peggy.

TWO QUEENS// C 1a// J. B. Buckstone// **Haymarket**, Mar. 1853, with Henry Howe as Koller, Henry Compton as Lobb, Mr. Weathersby as Banner, Thomas Coe as James, Mrs. L. S. Buckingham as Queen Christine, Louisa Howard as Mary of Denmark.

TWO RECRUITS// C 3a// Frank Wyatt// **Toole's**, Nov. 1890.

TWO RAINBOWS, THE// C// n.a.// **Princess's**, Mar. 1847, with Mr. Granby as James Rainbow, Henry Compton as Peter Rainbow, Samuel Cowell as Frank, Mrs. Henry Hughes as Caroline, Miss E. Honner as Matilda.

TWO ROSES, THE// C 3a// James Albery// **Vaudeville**, June 1870; Sept. 1879, with Henry Howe, Thomas Thorne, Marie Illington, Kate Bishop/ **Lyceum**, Dec. 1879, with Henry Irving as Digby Grant, C. W. Garthorne as Caleb Deecie, Charles Warner as Jack Wyatt, Edward Righton as Furnival, J. W. Bradbury as Our Mr. Jenkins, Amy Roselle as Lottie, Kate Bishop as Ida, Sophie Larkin as Mrs. Jenkins, Cicely Richards as Mrs. Cupps; Dec. 1881, with Henry Irving, Henry Howe, William Terriss, George Alexander, Fanny Josephs, Winifred Emery, Georgina Pauncefort.

TWO SONS// D 4a// E. Manuel// **Britannia**, Sept. 1877.

TWO STARS; OR, THE FOOTLIGHTS AND THE FIRESIDE// n.a.// **Strand**, Oct. 1872.

TWO STUDENTS, THE// n.a.// **Surrey**, Feb. 1861.

TWO THORNES, THE// C 4a// James Albery// **St. James's**, Mar. 1871.

TWO TO ONE; OR, THE IRISH FOOTMAN// F 1a// Arthur Clements// **Sad. Wells**, Oct. 1872.

TWO WEDDING RINGS// D 4a// G. S. Bellamy & F. Romer// **Britannia**, Feb. 1882.

TWO WINTERS// n.a.// **Marylebone**, Mar. 1859.

TWO WOMEN// D 4a// Adap. by Edward Rose fr F of Victor Hugo, Marie Tudor// **Standard**, Apr. 1885.

TYRANNY OF TEARS, THE// C 4a// C. Haddon Chambers// **Criterion**, Apr. 1899, with Charles Wyndham, Alfred Bishop, Mary Moore, Maude Millet.

TYRANT OF ALGIERS, THE// D// n.a.// **Victoria**, Mar. 1838, with Mr. Hicks, John Parry, Mr. Wilkins, Mr. King, Mr. Harwood, Miss Richardson, Miss Desborough, Mrs. Loveday.

*

UNCLE DICK'S DARLING// D 3a// H. J. Byron// **Gaiety**, Dec. 1869.

UNCLE FOOZLE// F 1a// C. J. Mathews// **Haymarket**, May 1871, with W. H. Chippendale as Foozle, Henry Howe as Bud, Walter Gordon as Waverley, Mrs. Chippendale as Mrs. Quickfidget, Caroline Hill as Mrs. Bud, Fanny Wright as Miss Fitzosborne.

UNCLE JOHN// F// J. B. Buckstone// **Haymarket**, June 1837, with William Farren as Uncle John, Benjamin Webster as Hawk, Robert Strickland as Thomas, John Webster as Edward, Mrs. Julia Glover as Mrs. Hawk, Mrs. Humby as Eliza, Mrs. W. Clifford as Mrs. Comfort/ **Sad. Wells**, Nov. 1859, with J. W. Ray as Uncle John, Mr. Williams as Thomas, Charles Seyton as Easel, Mr. Chapman as Andrew, Lewis Ball as Hawk, Mrs. Henry Marston as Niece, Mrs. J. B. Hill as Mrs. Comfort, Caroline Parkes as Eliza.

UNCLE JOHN// C// G. R. Sims & Cecil Raleigh// **Vaudeville**, Apr. 1893.

UNCLE MARK// C 2a// A. Younge// **Sad. Wells**, Aug. 1850, with Henry Mellon as Fitzfog, Charles Wheatleigh as Mowbray, William Hoskins as Sharpman, Frank Graham as Frederick Chester, A. Younge as Mark Chester, Miss Marston as Emma, Mrs. Archbold as Sarah, Fanny Morelli as Betty.

UNCLE MIKE// Play 4a// Florence Warden// **Terry's**, Dec. 1892.

UNCLE RIP// F 2a// R. B. Peake// **Lyceum**, June 1842.

UNCLE SILAS// D 4a// Dram. by Seymore Hicks & Lawrence Irving fr novel of S. Le Fanu// **Shaftesbury**, Feb. 1893.

UNCLE THATCHER// Play 1a// Clive Brooke// **Court**, June 1896.

UNCLE TOM// D 4a// Adap. by Leonard Rae fr F vers. of novel of Mrs. Stowe// **Standard**, Sept. 1878.

UNCLE TOM// C// G. R. Sims & Cecil Raleigh// **Vaudeville**, Apr. 1893.

UNCLE TOM'S CABIN// D 3a// Dram. fr novel of Mrs. Stowe// **Victoria**, July 1854, with Mr. Morrison as Shelby, Mr. Henderson as Robert, Henry Frazer as Legree, F. H. Henry as Haley, Mr. Hitchinson as Wilson, T. E. Mills as Uncle

Tom, J. T. Johnson as George Harris, Charles Rice as Tickler, Miss Vaul as Little Harry, Miss Sutton as Mrs. Selby, Phoebe Johnson as Ruth, Mrs. Henry Vining as Lizzy/ **Adelphi**, Feb. 1875, with Frank Barsby as Shelby, William McIntyre as Simon Legree, Henry Sinclair as George, Howard Russell as Uncle Tom, Frederick Moreland as Sol, T. W. Thorne as Sambo, Harwood Cooper as Sam, Marie Henderson as Cassy, Edith Stuart as Eliza, Miss Hudspeth as Topsy/ Machines by E. Charker/ Music by Edwin Ellis.

UNCLE TOM'S CABIN// D 5a// Dram. fr novel of Mrs. Stowe// **Princess's**, 1878, with Charles Morton as Uncle Tom, Charles Warner as Harris, Harry Hawk as Marks, Harry Jackson as Fletcher, J. H. Rowe as Simon Legree, Mr. Brennand as St. Clair, William Rouse as Bird, Mr. Russell as Shelby, T. W. Thorne as Haley, Dolores Drummond as Eliza, Edith Wilson as Cassie, Marie Bates as Topsy, Carrie Coote as Eva, Fanny Denham as Emmeline, Agnes Hewitt as Marie, Mrs. William Rouse as Chloe/ Scenery by Julian Hicks/ Machines by Mr. Warton/ Gas by Mr. Kerr/ Music by Michael Connelly/ Prod. by Harry Jackson.

UNCLE TOM'S CABIN// D 3a// Dram. by Charles Hermann fr novel of Mrs. Stowe// **Princess's**, Oct. 1892.

UNCLE TOM'S CABIN// D 5a// Dram. by G. F. Rowe fr novel of Mrs. Stowe// **Princess's**, Aug. 1878.

UNCLE TOM'S CABIN// D 2a// Dram. by Edward Fitzball fr novel of Mrs. Stowe// **Olympic**, Nov. 1852, with Charles Bender as Shelby, C. Humphries as Bird, William Farren Jr. as Harris, George Cooke as Uncle Tom, William Hoskins as Haley, Mr. Edgar as Budd, Isabel Adams as Mrs. Shelby, Mucy Rafter as Mrs. Bird, Harriet Gordon as Eliza, Mrs. B. Bartlett as Chloe, Mr. Clifton as Topsy, Ellen Turner as Mrs. Budd/ Scenery by W. Shalders.

UNCLE TOM'S CABIN; OR, THE HORRORS OF SLAVERY// D 3a// Edward Fitzball// **Drury Lane**, Dec. 1852.

UNCLE TOM'S CABIN; OR, SLAVE LIFE IN SOUTH AMERICA// Dram. by Mark Lemon & Tom Taylor fr novel of Mrs. Stowe// **Sad. Wells**, May 1855, with George Fisher as Shelby, E. F. Edgar as Legree, T. C. Harris as Harris, Mr. Barrett as Uncle Tom, W. Shalders as Solomon, Robert Soutar as Loker, Mrs. Leman Rede as Mrs. Shelby, Miss Markham as Cassy, Kate Kelly as Eliza, Mrs. Keeley as Topsy.

UNCLE ZAC; OR, A WILD REVENGE// D 4a// G. R. Walker// **Standard**, June 1883.

UNCLE ZACHARY// C 2a// Adap. by John Oxenford fr F, L'Oncle Baptiste// **Olympic**, Mar. 1860, with Frederick Robson as Uncle Zachary, George Cooke as Clench, Frederick Vining as Highbury, Walter Gordon as Montgomery, Mrs. Leigh Murray as Tabitha, Miss Herbert as Amy.

UNCLE'S GHOST// F 3a// William Sapte Jr.// **POW**, June 1887/ **Opera Comique**, Jan. 1894.

UNCLE'S WILL// C 1a// S. Theyre Smith// **Haymarket**, Oct. 1870; May 1888, with W. H. Kendal as Cashmore, Mrs. Kendal as Florence, Charles Cathcart as Barker.

UNCLES AND AUNTS// F 3a// William Lestocq & Walter Everard// **Comedy**, Aug. 1888.

UNDER A VEIL// C// Randal Roberts// **Olympic**, May 1876, with Randal Roberts as Devereux, W. J. Hill as Prichard, Viola Dacre as Lucy, Miss C. Elise as Elizabeth.

UNDER ARREST// F// C. Z. Barnett// **Sad. Wells**, July 1845, with Henry Mellon as Col. Desmarais, Frank Graham as Brig, Francois, Samuel Buckingham as Ledoux, Mr. Corrie as Pristin, Miss Lebatt as Mariette, Miss Huddart as Clemence.

UNDER COVER// C// Adap. by Charles Bridgman fr F of Ernest Hervilly, La Céramique// **Gaiety**, Jan. 1886.

UNDER FALSE COLOURS// D 4a// Myles Wallerton & Frances Gilbert// **West London**, Mar. 1901.

UNDER FIRE// C 4a// Westland Marston// **Vaudeville**, Apr. 1885, with Thomas Thorne, Charles Sugden, Frank Archer, Amy Roselle, Cissy Grahame, Kate Phillips.

UNDER REMAND// D 4a// Reginald Stockton & Eric Hudson// **Surrey**, June 1896.

UNDER THE CZAR// D 4a// Fred Jarman// **Elephant & Castle**, Apr. 1896.

UNDER THE EARTH; OR, THE SONS OF TOIL// D// Dram. by W. H. Nation fr novel of Charles Dickens, Hard Times// **Astley's**, May. 1867, with James Elphinstone as Gradgrind, W. H. Stephens as Bounderby, T. W. Richardson as Harthouse, James Fernandez as Blackpool, Annie Richardson as Mrs. Sparset, Edith Stuart as Rachel, Miss Marion as Louise.

UNDER THE GASLIGHT; OR, LIFE AND LOVE IN THESE TIMES// D 4a// Augustin Daly// **Pavilion**, July 1868.

UNDER THE LAMPS; OR, THE GENTLEMEN OF THE NIGHT// D// Thomas Mead// **Grecian**, Oct. 1862, with Thomas Mead as Rio Santo, William James as Percival, Henry Grant as Dr. Moore, George Gillett as Sir Paul, J. Jackson as Capt. Patrick, Mr. Shirley as Falkener, Alfred Rayner as Garstang, Henry Power as Lantern, John Manning as Snail, Walter Holland as Mitchell, Marie Brewer as Lady Campbell, Ellen Hale as Mary, Mrs. Charles Dillon as Susan, Laura Conquest as Clara, Miss Johnstone as Mrs. Burnett, Mary A. Victor as Sally.

UNDER THE MASK OF TRUTH// D 4a// Sutton Vane & Arthur Shirley// **Surrey**, June 1894, under title of Mask of Guilt.

UNDER THE MISTLETOE// C Pro & 5 a// M. St. John & R. M. Jepson// **Imperial**, Dec. 1881.

UNDER THE OLD FLAG// C 4a// Adap. by Eliot Gregory fr F of Victorien Sardou// **Globe**, Apr. 1900.

UNDER THE RED ROBE// D 4a// Adap. by Edward Rose fr novel of Stanley Weyman// **Haymarket**, Nov. 1896, with Herbert Waring as de Berault, Sidney Valentine as Richelieu, Hamilton Revelle as de Cocheforet, J. L. Mackay as Marquis de Pombal, Albert Mayer as De Fargis, Cyril Maude as Capt. Larolle, Dawson Milward as Sir Thomas, E. Holman Clark as Clon, Granville Barker as Major-domo, Winifred Emery as Renée, Eva Moore as Mme. de Cocheforet, Fanny Coleman as Mme. Zaton/ Scenery by Walter Johnstone, J. Harker & Walter Hann/ Music by A. J. Caldicott.

UNDER THE ROSE// F 1a// George Roberts// **St. James's**, Mar. 1862, with Henry Ashley as Sheepshanks, Mr. Lever as Buttons, Kate Terry as Mrs. Magnet, Elizabeth Romer as Susan.

UNDER THE SCREW; OR, A YOUNG WIFE'S TROUBLES// D// Thomas Mead// **Elephant & Castle**, Oct. 1873.

UNDER THE SHADOW OF OLD ST. PAUL'S// D// Frederick Marchant// **East London**, Oct. 1872.

UNDER THE SNOW// D// n.a.// **Britannia**, Aug. 1877.

UNDER THE STARS; OR, THE STOLEN HEIRESS// D 4a// Walter Banks// **Marylebone**, Aug. 1880.

UNDER TWO FLAGS// D Pro & 4a// Dram. by George Daventry fr novel of Ouida// **Pavilion**, Aug. 1884.

UNDERCURRENT, THE// C 4a// R. C. Carton// **Criterion**, Sept. 1901.

UNDERGRADUATE, THE// D 4a// J. C. Freund// **Queen's**, June 1872.

UNDERGRADUATES, THE// F 3a// W. O. Tristram// **Opera Comique**, Oct. 1886.

UNDERGROUND JOURNEY, AN// C // Mrs. Hugh Bell & C. H. Brookfield// **Comedy**, Feb. 1893.

UNEQUAL MATCH, AN// C 3a// Tom Taylor// **Haymarket**, Nov. 1857, with William Farren as Arncliffe, W. H. Chippendale as Honeyweed, J. B. Buckstone as Botcherby, Henry Compton as Blenkinsop, Mr. Rogers as Grazebrook, George Braid as Capt. Chillingham, Amy Sedgwick as Hester, Mrs. Buckingham White as Mrs. Montresor, Miss Lavine as Lady Honeywood, Mrs. Edward Fitzwilliam as Bessy/ Scenery by George Morris & John O'Conner/ Machines by Oliver Wales.

UNFINISHED GENTLEMAN, THE// F// Charles Selby// **Sad. Wells**, May 1854, with Mr. Barrett as Lord Totterly, F. Charles as Flammer, Henry Ashley as Danvers/ **Grecian**, July 1857, with Eaton O'Donnell as Lord Totterly, Charles Harcourt as Flammer, Mr. Ramsay as Danvers, John Manning as Downy, Harry Hill as Miller, Miss Chapman as Louisa, Harriet Coveney as Mary Chintz.

UNFORTUNATE YOUTH, THE// F// Benjamin Webster// **Haymarket**, Oct. 1840, with Robert Strickland as Pierrepoint, Henry Howe as Charles, J. W. Gough as Pelham, David Rees as Cooper, W. H. Oxberry as Tom, Miss Travers as Rose, Mrs. Stanley as Deborah, Mrs. Frank Matthews as Mary.

UNION JACK, THE// D 4a// Henry Pettit & Sidney Grundy// **Adelphi**, July 1888, with William Terriss as Jack Medway, J. D. Beveridge as Sir Philip, Charles Cartwright as Capt. Morton, Laurence Cautley as Lt. Stanley, J. L. Shine as Peter Fly, Dalton Somers as Cuckles, Howard Russell as Stone, Harwood Cooper as Tompkins, Jessie Millward as Ethel, Helen Forsyth as Ivy, Olga Nethersole as Ruth Medway, Eleanor Bufton as Mrs. Stone, Dolores Drummond as Mrs. Pippin, Clara Jecks as Polly/ Scenery by Bruce Smith, W. Perkins, & William Telbin/ Music by Henry Sprake/ Machines by Benjamin Burns/ Prod. by William Sidney.

UNION JACK, THE; OR, THE CREW OF THE BRIGHT BLUE WATERS// D// n.a.// **Victoria**, Sept. 1850, with E. Edwards as Marli, Henry Frazer as Alvaradi, J. Howard as Twyford, H. Lewis as Maggs, John Douglass as Hatchway, Mr. Henderson as Holdworthy, Mr. Humphries as Black Frank, Eliza Terrey as Sukey, Mrs. George Lee as Mary, Miss M. Terrey as Miss Holdworthy.

UNITED HAPPY FAMILY, A// F 1a// n.a.// **Globe**, Jan. 1869, with H. Andrews as Benjamin Bibbs, E. Marshall as Barnaby Bibbs, Edgar Newbound as Peter Parker, J. Tindale as Grumpy, Mrs. Stephens as Mrs. Benjamin Bibbs, Laura Morgan as Mrs. Barnaby Bibbs, Clara Thorne as Snarley.

UNITED SERVICE, THE// F// n.a.// **Cov. Garden**, Dec. 1841, with William Farren as Capt. Whistleborough, George Bartley as Capt. Pacific, C. J. Mathews as Rivet, John Pritt Harley as Bam, Walter Lacy as Woodpecker, John Collett as John, Mrs. Julia Glover as Mrs. Coo, Mrs. Tayleure as Miss Polecon, Miss Lee as Fanny, Mrs. Orger as Mrs. Walker.

UNKNOWN, THE; OR, A RIVER MYSTERY// D 5a// J. A. Stevens// **Surrey**, July 1882.

UNLAWFUL PRESENT, THE// D 1a// C. H. Hazlewood// **Britannia**, June 1872.

UNLIMITED CASH// C 3a// Adap. by F. C. Burnand fr F, Trente Millions de Gladiateur// **Gaiety**, Oct. 1879, with E. W. Royce, Edward Terry, William Elton, Miss E. Farren.

UNLIMITED CONFIDENCE// D 1a// A. C. Troughton// **Strand**, Feb. 1864.

UNLUCKY FRIDAY// D 1a// Adap. by H. T. Craven fr F// **Sad. Wells**, Nov. 1858.

UNLUCKY MORTAL, AN// F 1a// n.a.// **Haymarket**, June 1863, with William Farren as Vincent, Mr. Tilbury as Corderoy, Mr. Weathersby as Bob, Maria Harris as Blanche, Mrs. Griffith as Mrs. Farmer.

UNMASKED, THE// D 4a// Clifford Merton// **Pavilion**, Nov. 1875.

UNPAID DEBT, AN// Play 4a// C. H. Dickenson// **St. Geo. Hall**, Dec. 1893.

UNPROTECTED FEMALE, AN// F 1a// J. Stirling Coyne// **Strand**, Feb. 1850, with John Wood, Mrs. John Wood, S. D. Johnson/ **Olympic**, Sept. 1851, with Charles Bender as Crisp, Mr. Norton as Temple, Mrs. Stirling as Polly/ **Sad. Wells**, May 1854, with Mr. Franks as Crisp, F. Charles as Temple, Miss Marshall as Polly.

UNSANCTIFIED GARMENT, AN// C 3a//. Mr. Gray & Mr. Martin// **St. Geo. Hall**, Dec. 1895.

UNSEEN HELMSMAN, THE// Play 1a// L. Alma Tadema// **Comedy**, June 1901.

UP A TREE// F 1a// T. J. Williams// **Adelphi**, Mar. 1873, with John Clarke, A. C. Lilly, F. Roland, Mr. Smithson, Miss Marston Leigh, Maud Howard.

UP AT THE HILLS// C 2a// Tom Taylor// **St. James's**, Oct. 1860, with Alfred Wigan as Maj. Standhurst, Charles Young as Capt. Slack, Henry Ashley as Lt. Greenway, Samuel Emery as Doctor, Edward [?] Terry as Nabichull, Mrs. Alfred Wigan as Mrs. McCann, Miss Herbert as Mrs. Eversleigh, Nelly Moore as Margaret, Kate Terry as Monee.

UP FOR THE CATTLE SHOW// F 1a// Harry Lemon// **Adelphi**, Dec. 1867, with C. J. Smith as Gabriel, W. H. Eburne as Paul, George Belmore as Peter Strollop, Emily Pitt as Phoebe, Miss Harris as Cecilia.

UP FOR THE JUBILEE// F// Joseph Bracewell// **Grand**, May 1887.

UP IN THE WORLD// F 1a// J. Worthington// **Surrey**, 1858/ **Sad. Wells**, Dec. 1862, with James Johnstone as Matthew Mudlark, Henry Widdicomb as Harry Mudlark, Alfred Montague as Livelydale, Mr. Dalton as Lester, Miss Dowton as Mrs. Mudlark, Miss Clements as Anne.

UP IN THE WORLD// C 3a// George Rose ("Arthur Sketchley")// **Strand**, Feb. 1871.

UP TO SNUFF; OR, A FRIEND AT A PINCH// F// n.a.// **Princess's**, Mar. 1848, with Henry Compton as Gadout, James Vining as Ramble, J. Neville as Gappletit, Emmeline Montague as Mrs. Gadout, Emma Stanley as Mrs. Ramble, Miss Taylor as Betty.

UP TRAIN, THE// C// Adap. by C. P. Colnagi fr F// **Haymarket**, May 1890.

UPPER CRUST, THE// C 3a// H. J. Byron// **Folly**, Apr. 1880, with John Billington, J. L. Toole, E. D. Ward, Lilian Cavalier, Emily Phillips/ **Toole's**, Apr. 1891.

UPPER HAND, THE// C 3a// Charles Winthorp & Walter Lisle// **Terry's**, May 1899.

UPS AND DOWNS OF LIFE, THE// D 4a// F. A. Scudamore// **Pavilion**, Aug. 1892.

UPSTAIRS AND DOWNSTAIRS; OR, THE GREAT PERCENTAGE QUESTION// F 1a// William Brough & Andrew Halliday// **Strand**, May 1865.

URGENT PRIVATE AFFAIRS// F 1a// J. Stirling Coyne// **Adelphi**, Jan. 1856, with Edward Wright as Dotts, Charles Selby as Maj. Polkinghorne, Paul Bedford as Joe, Robert Romer as Bagshaw, Miss Arden as Mrs. Dotts, Kate Kelly as Mrs. Polkinghorne, Mary Keeley as Sally.

USE OF POETS, THE// C// Alistair Tayler// **Comedy**, July 1901.

USED UP// C 2a// Adap. by C. J. Mathews fr F, L'Homme Blasé// **Haymarket**, Feb. 1844, with C. J. Mathews as Sir Charles Coldstream, Mr. Tilbury as Leech, A. Brindal as Saville, James Bland as Wurzel, Henry Howe as Ironbrace, J. W. Gough as Fennel, Julia Bennett as Mary, Mrs. Humby as Lady Clutterbuck/ **Princess's**, July 1847, with C. J. Mathews as Sir Charles Coldstream, Mr. Granby as Leech, Mr. Wynn as Saville, Mr. Walton as Wurzel, John Ryder as Ironbrace, Miss E. Honner as Lady Clutterbuck, Miss Marshall as Mary/ **Lyceum**, Jan. 1850, with C. J. Mathews as Sir Charles Coldstream, Mr. Granby as Adonis Leech, Mr. Bellingham as Tom Saville, Henry Hall as Ironbrace, Robert Honner as Fennel, Mrs. Humby as Lady Clutterbuck, Mrs. Julia Glover as Mary/ **Drury Lane**, Dec. 1855, with C. J. Mathews as Sir Charles Coldstream, Mr. Tilbury as Sir Adonis, C. Vincent as Saville, J. Worrell as Wurzel, Robert Roxby as Ironbrace, Mr. Hollingsworth as Fennel, Mrs. Frank Matthews as Lady Clutterbuck, Miss M. Oliver as Mary/ **St. James's**, June 1864, with C. J. Mathews as Sir Charles Coldstream, Walton Chamberlaine as Leech, H. J. Montague as Saville, James Johnstone as Wurzel, Henry Ashley as Ironbrace, Mr. Smithson as Fennell, Patti Josephs as Mary, Mrs. Frank Matthews as Lady Clutterbuck/ **Olympic**, Feb. 1868, with C. J. Mathews as Sir Charles Coldstream, Robert Soutar as Adonis Leech, H. Vaughan as Tom Saville, Harwood Cooper as Wurzel, George Vincent as Ironbrace, Ellen Farren as Mary, Mrs. St. Henry as Lady Clutterbuck.

USED UP// C 2a// Dion Boucicault// **Drury Lane**, Nov. 1855.

USURER'S DAUGHTER, THE// D// n.a.// **Grecian**, Oct. 1855, with F. Charles as Charles

II, Basil Potter as Goldthrift, Richard Phillips as Okebroke, Henry Grant as Smith, Henry Power as Barebones, John Manning as Gouge, Mrs. Charles Montgomery as Gilbert Gossamer, Jane Coveney as Marion, Harriet Coveney as May.

*

VAGABOND, THE// C 3a// W. S. Gilbert (see Ne'er Do Weel).

VAGABOND KING, THE// Play 4a// L. N. Parker// **Court**, Nov. 1897, with Murray Carson as Don Pedro XIV, Herbert Ross as Pandolfo, Gilbert Farquhar as Don Miguel, Lawrance d'Orsay as Marchese di Castelverano, Sydney Brough as Moffat, Fred Grove as Monsiegneur, Lewis Mannering as Benito, H. Athol Forde as Sammy, Kate Bateman as Donna Pia, Lena Ashwell as Stella, Ellis Jeffreys as Princess Zea, Ethel Verne as Lady Violet, Mrs. Henry Leigh as Mrs. Wallis/ Scenery by Joseph Hurst.

VAGRANT, THE// D 5a// Frederick De Lara// **Sad. Wells**, Oct. 1892.

VAIN SACRIFICE, A// C 3a// W. E. Grogan// **Strand**, Nov. 1893, with Norman V. Norman as Conway, C. L. Lane as Wylmer, H. N. Chart as Maclure, George Norman as Campbell, Hall Caine as Gwendoline, Violet Raye as Edith, Miss Olliffe as Madge, Adelaide Grace as Mrs. Wylmer.

VALENTINE, A// F 1a// William Brough & Andrew Halliday// **Adelphi**, Feb. 1863.

VALENTINE AND ORSON; OR, THE WILD MAN OF THE WOODS// D 2a// n.a.// **Sad. Wells**, Mar. 1837, with Mr. King as King Pepin, Mr. Ray as Henry, Mr. Gay as Haufrey, Mr. Hicks as Valentine, C. J. Smith as Orson, W. Smith as Hugo, Thomas Lee as Agramont, Miss Williams as Eglantine, Miss Lebatt as Belisanta, Miss Andrews as Florimonda, Miss Julian as Agatha/ **Drury Lane**, Mar. 1837, with Mr. Mathews as King Pepin, A. Brindal as Henry, Mr. Henry as Haufray, T. F. Matthews as Orson, Charles Diddear as Mandiman, Drinkwater Meadows as Hugo, Miss Taylor as Princess Eglantine, Miss Ballin as Florimonda, Miss Somerville as Dame Cicely, Miss Poole as Agatha, Mrs. W. Clifford as Empress, Frederick Cooke as Agramant, Mr. Perry as Iman/ Scenery by Grieve, T. Grieve & W. Grieve/ Music by Mr. Jouve, Machines by Mr. Nall/ **Victoria**, Nov. 1853, with Mr. Green as King Pepin, Mr. Morrison as Henry, Mr. Richards as Haufrey, Mr. Hitchinson as Blandman, J. T. Johnson as Valentine, R. H. Kitchen as Orson, J. Howard as Hugo, F. H. Henry as Agramont, Watty Brunton as Golden Oracle, Miss Dansor as Princess Eglantine, Mrs. Manders as Empress Belesanta, Miss Edgar as Pierimonda, Miss Laporte as Agatha.

VALET DE SHAM, THE// C 1a// Charles Selby// **St. James's**, Apr. 1838, with Mr. Brookes as Tweezer, John Webster as Trivit, Edward Wright as Wigler, Miss Allison as Miss Marchment, Mrs. Stirling as Clipper.

VALLEY OF ANDORRE, THE; OR, THE ORPHAN GIRL OF THE PYRENEES// D// n.a.// **Victoria**, Feb. 1850, with J. T. Johnson as Gautier, J. Neville as Sincere, Mr. Humpreys as d'Antour, John Bradshaw as Capt. Lejoyeux, Mr. Leake as L'Endormi, John Hudspeth as Nigaud, F. H. Henry as Coco, Mrs. George Lee as Theresa, Annette Vincent as Rose, Miss Barrowcliffe as Georgette, Miss Mildenhall as Agatha.

VAMPIRE, THE; OR, THE BRIDE OF THE ISLES// D// Adap. fr. story of Lord Byron// **Eng. Opera House** (Lyceum), Sept. 1837, with Charles Diddear as the Vampire and as Ruthven, Miss Rainforth as Lady Margaret, Miss Poole as Unda, Mrs. East as Ariel, Mr. Baker as Ronald, Mr. Frazer as Robert, Henry Compton as Swill, Mr. Turnour as Andrew, Mr. Sanders as Father Francis, Priscilla Horton as Effie/ Music by Mr. Moss/ Scenery by Mr. Pitt/ **Sad. Wells**, Nov. 1838, with Mrs. J. F. Saville as Unda, Mrs. Harwood as Uriel, Mrs. Robert Honner aas Lady Margaret, Mr. Cathcart as the Vampire and as Ruthven, Mr. Dry as Lord Ronald, Dibdin Pitt as Andrew, Mr. Conquest as Macswill, Miss Cooke as Bridget, Miss E. Honnor as Effie/ **Victoria**, Feb. 1841, with Mr. Hicks as the Vampire and as Ruthven, Miss Warde as Unda, Miss Hicks as Ariel, Emmeline Montague as Lady Margaret, John Dale as Ronald, Mr. Reynolds as Robert, Mr. Attwood as McSwill, Mr. Burton as Andrew, Mr. Hamilton as Father Francis, Mrs. Hicks as Effie, Miss B. Kemble as Bridget.

VAMPIRE, THE// D 3a// Dion Boucicault// **Princess's**, June 1852, with Dion Boucicault as Sir Alan, George Everett as Lord Arthur, Mr. Daly as Gwynne, Mr. Rolleston as Nevil, James Vining as Sir Guy, John Chester as Rhys, Frederick Cooke as Griffyths, Carlotta Leclercq as Lucy, Miss J. Lovell as Lady Ellen, Miss Daly as Maud, John Cathcart as Peveril, Hermann Vezin as Trevanion, Miss Phillips as Lady Peveril, Miss Robertson as Alice, Miss Marshall as Augusta, John Pritt Harley as Rees, Mrs. W. Daly as Mrs. Raby, Miss Desborough as Ada/ Scenery by Walter Gordon & F. Lloyds/ Music by R. Stopel.

VANDERDECKEN// D 4a// Dram. by W. G. Wills & Percy Fitzgerald fr Ger. tale, The Flying Dutchman// **Lyceum**, June 1878, with Henry Irving as Vanderdecken, James Fernandez, Walter Bentley, Edmund Lyons as Pastor Been, Arthur Wing Pinero as Jorgen, R. Lyons as Steffen, Georgina Pauncefort as Birgit, Mrs. St. John as Nancy, Isabel Bateman as Shekla/

Scenery by Hawes Craven/ Music by Robert Stoepel.

VANDYKE BROWN// F 1a// A. C. Troughton// **Strand**, Mar. 1859/ **Adelphi**, Dec. 1875, with John Clarke as Vandyke, J. G. Shore as Robins, H. Vaughn as Eastman, Miss E. Phillips as Mrs. Brown, Edith Stuart as Mrs. Bobbins, Miss Hudspeth as Rebecca/ **Lyceum**, Mar. 1888, with Charles Collette as Vandyke, Henry Sainsbury as Bobbins, Glen Winn as Fastman, Miss Staunton as Mrs. Brown, Helen Dacre as Mrs. Bobbins, Mary Ayerton as Rebecca/ **Globe**, May 1888, with Charles Collett as Vandyke, Gilbert Farquhar as Bobbins, A. J. Byde as Eastman, Miss Webster as Mrs. Bobbins, Maud Merrill as Mrs. Brown, Rose Evelyn as Rebecca.

VANITY// D// n.a.// **Grecian**, Dec. 1854, with Richard Phillips as Hastings, Henry Power as Slow, Basil Potter as Sir Henry, Eaton O'Donnell as Westland, William Suter as Floss, Jane Coveney as Miss Westland, Harriet Coveney as Peggy Sly, Miss Johnstone as Stinger, Ellen Crisp as Mrs. Leicester; Sept. 1861 with Mr. Jackson, Thomas Mead, William James, George Gillett, John Manning, Jane Coveney, Miss Johnstone, Lucrezia Hill.

VANITY CURED; OR, THE SCHOOL FOR OLD GENTLEMEN// C 2a// Mr. Ranger// **Sad. Wells**, May 1854, with Mr. Barrett as Col. Freewill, Mr. Ranger as Lord Witherly, F. Charles as de Montfort, Mr. James as Jem, Mrs. Barrett as Mrs. Maxman, Miss Mandelbert as Lucretia, Miss Rawlings as Mrs. Skepton/ **St. James's**, Oct. 1854, with Mr. Ranger as Lord Witherly, W. Cooper as Col. Frewill, George Burt as de Montfort, Miss Clifford as Lucretia, Mrs. Stanley as Mrs. Maxman, Miss Grey as Mrs. Kepton.

VANITY FAIR// C 3a// G. W. Godfrey// **Court**, Apr. 1895, with Arthur Cecil as Lord Nugent, Charles Sugden as Duke of Berkshire, William Wyes as Brabazon-Tegg, Charles Fawcett as Sir James, A. Vane Tempest as Bertie, Wilfred Draycott as Sir Richard, Howard Sturge as Villars, William Cheesman as Smiley, G. W. Anson as Feltoe, Helena Dacre as Lady Jacqueline, Nancy Noel as Violet, Frances Dillon as Mrs. Chetwynd, Lucy Bertram as Mrs. Walrond, Mrs. John Wood as Mrs. Brabazon-Tegg, Charlotte Granville as Viscountess of Castleblaney/ Scenery by T. W. Hall.

VARSITY BOAT RACE, THE// F// C. H. Stephenson & Frederick Robson// **Olympic**, Apr. 1870.

VEILED PORTRAIT, THE; OR, THE CHATEAU OF BEAUVAIS// F// n.a.// **Cov. Garden**, May 1838, with Mr. Warde as Duke de Lavalle, Mr. Vining as Count de St. Joie, John Pritt Harley as Babillard, Edwin Yarnold as Hercule, Mr. Tilbury as Pierre, Miss Taylor as Estelle, Mrs. W. Clifford as Mme. Marguerite.

VELASCO; OR, CASTILIAN HONOUR// T// Eps Sargent// **Marylebone**, Sept. 1848, with E. L. Davenport, James Johnstone, Fanny Vining.

VELVET AND RAGS// D Pro & 3a// Paul Meritt & George Conquest// **Grecian**, Apr. 1873.

VENDEAN GIRL, THE; OR, THE NOYADES// D// n.a.// **Sad. Wells**, Jan. 1868, with Alice Marriott as Carline, J. L. Warner as Capt. Lovetu, Walter Searle as Tardiff, Grace Edgar as Eugene.

VENDETTA// D// n.a.// **Victoria**, May 1863.

VENDETTA, THE; OR, LIFE'S CHANCES// D 5a// n.a.// **Britannia**, Aug. 1896.

VENDETTA; OR, THE NEW CORSICAN BROTHERS// D 5a// Dram. fr Alexandre Dumas// **Drury Lane**, Feb. 1854.

VENDETTA; OR, THE CORSICAN'S REVENGE// D 4a// Dram. by William Calvert fr novel of A. C. Gunter, Mr. Barnes of New York// **Sad. Wells**, Sept. 1888.

VENETIAN, THE; OR, THE COUNCIL OF TEN// D 3a// T. H. Reynoldson// **Sad. Wells**, Aug. 1843, with Mr. Lyon as Count Salfieri, C. J. Bird as Count di Bellamont, Henry Marston as di Romano, Mr. Williams as Maffeo, Mr. Lambe as Don Camillo, Caroline Rankley as Theodora, Miss Hamilton as Violetta, Miss Stephens as Michelmina.

VENGEANCE; OR, FAMILY FUDES AND A BUMPING LEGACY// C 1a// C. Z. Barnett// **Victoria**, Oct. 1843, with Mr. James as Joachim, John Gardner as Akim, William Seaman as Leoni, Mr. Paul as Gaspard, C. Williams as Moustache, Miss Ridgway as Lison.

VENGEANCE IS MINE// D 4a// Sutton Vane// **Pavilion**, Jan. 1892.

VENGEANCE IS THINE// D 5a// John Mill// **Britannia**, July 1895.

VENGEANCE OF MRS. VANSITTART, THE// C 3a// Arthur Hare & H. Eves// **Garrick**, July 1901.

VENICE PRESERVED; OR, A PLOT DISCOVERED// T 5a// Thomas Otway// **Sad. Wells**, May 1837, with Mr. King as Duke, Mr. Campbell as Priuli, C. H. Pitt as Bedamar, Mr. Cobham Jr. as Jaffiier, J. B. Booth as Pierre, John Ayliffe as Renault, Miss Williams as Belvidira; Aug. 1845, with Samuel Phelps as Jaffier, Henry Marston as Pierre, George Bennett as Renault, Henry Mellon as Priuli, Mrs. Mary Warner as Belvidera; Mar. 1857, with Mr. Lacy as Duke, J. W. Ray as Priuli, Henry Marston as Jaffier, Alfred Rayner as Pierre, T. C. Harris as Renault, Mr. Haywell as Bedamar, Charles Seyton as Spinosa, Miss Atkinson as Belvidera/ **Cov. Garden**, Dec. 1838, with Mr. Tilbury as Duke, Mr. Waldron as Priuli, Charles Diddear as Bedamar, E. W. Elton as Jaffier, Mr. Vandenhoff as Pierre, George Bennett as Renault, Henry Howe as

Spinosa, Helen Faucit as Belvidera/ **Drury Lane**, Feb. 1842, with E. W. Elton as Priuli, J. Waldron as Doge, George Bennett as Renault, James Anderson as Jaffier, Mr. Lynne as Bedamar, Henry Marston as Spinosa, Mr. Mellon as Elliot, Samuel Phelps as Pierre, Helen Faucit as Belvidera.

VENUS IN ARMS// F 1a// Mrs. C. B. Wilson// **Sad. Wells**, Dec. 1844, with Mr. Raymond as Sir Frederick, John Webster as Capt. Dashall, Edward Knight as Lt. Gorget, Mr. Sievier as Corp. Standard, Charles Fenton as O'Phalanx, G. F. Forman as Dan, Miss Lebatt as Arabella, Miss Huddart as Lady Melville.

VENUS VERSUS MARS// C// J. T. Douglass Jr.// **Standard**, Sept. 1870.

VENUS WITH A TIPPET ON// F 1a// C. A. Somerset// **Grecian**, Feb. 1855, with Eaton O'Donnell as Grattenbowl, F. Charles as Fortune, John Manning as Medard, Maria Simpson as Mme. Grattanbowl, Jane Coveney as Celeste; June 1863, with J. Jackson as Grattenbowl, John Manning as Medard, George Gillett as Fortune, Ellen Hale as Madame Grattenbowl, Mary A. Victor as Celeste.

VERA// D 4a// M. E. Smith// **Globe**, July, 1890 , with Edmund Gurney as Baron Alexis, Cecil Yorke as d'Arblay, Alfred Cross as Shapiroff, Roydon Erlynne as Gen. Vladimir, J. A. Bentham as Count Olgaff, Violey Thornycroft as Isadora, Therese Mayer as Mme. Petrolsky, Anna de Naucaze as Vera.

VERACITY// C 3a// Walter Parke// **Gaiety**, Apr. 1886.

VERBUM SAP// C// Alfred Maltby// **Criterion**, Mar. 1880, with Lytton Sothern, Mary Rorke.

VERDICT OF THE WORLD, THE// D 3a// George Lander// **Britannia**, Aug. 1872.

VERMONT WOOLDEALER, THE// F 1a// n.a.// **Olympic**, Apr. 1845, with Dan Marble as Deuteronomy, Mr. Mellon as Gormley, F. Burton as Capt. Oakley, Mr. Turnour as Waddle, Mr. Craven as Slap, Mr. Darcie as Bob, Miss Fielding as Amanda, Miss Martineau as Betty.

VERY SERIOUS AFFAIR, A// F 1a// Augustus Harris// **Lyceum**, Oct. 1857.

VERY SUSPICIOUS// C 1a// J. Palgrave Simpson// **Lyceum**, June 1852, with Mr. Milton as Col. Basely, Basil Baker as Buzzbite, Henry Butler as Sharp, Laura Keene as Lady Emily, Mrs. Frank Matthews as Lady Buzzbite, Miss Grove as Mary.

VERY SUSPICIOUS// C 1a// n.a.// **Grecian**, Oct. 1853, with Fanny Williams as Kate Montague, Tim Kelly, and as Winifred, George Wild as Ned Overall and as Mrs. Cummings

VESSEL OF LIFE, THE; OR, THE WITNESS OF THE WAVE// D// J. B. Johnstone// **Victoria**, Aug. 1848, with E. Edwards as Sir Launcelot, Mr. Henderson as Danton, T. H. Higgie as Blight, J. T. Johnson as Anster, Mr. Hawkins as Old Littlenut, G. F. Forman as Simon Littlenut, J. Howard as Tittlebat, F. H. Henry as Garnet, John Bradshaw as Jack, Mrs. George Lee as May, Mrs. Cooke as Dame Allerton, Miss Sharpe as Miss Spifflebustle, Miss Burroughcliffe as Cicely/ Prod. by T. H. Higgie.

VETERAN AND HIS FAMILY, THE// D 1a// n.a.// **Grecian**, Nov. 1863, with J. Jackson as Phillip, W. Shirley as Jerome, Henry Grant as Pierre, George Gillett as Antoine, John Manning as Francois, Ellen Crisp as Mme. Lerond, Marie Brewer as Isabel.

VETERAN AND HIS PROGENY, THE// D 1a// n.a.// **Haymarket**, Mar. 1839, with William Davidge as Garbois, J. W. Gough as Jerome, Charles Perkins as Pierre, Mr. Hemming as Antoine, Henry Compton as Francois, Mrs. Gallot as Mme. Lerond, Mrs. Frank Matthews as Isabel/ **Lyceum**, Nov. 1865, with Henry Widdicomb as Garbois, Mr. Clifford as Jerome, Mr. Raymond as Pierre, Mr. Fitzpatrick as Antoine, Miss Edmonds as Theodore, Mrs. G. Lee as Mme. Beroud, Miss E. Lavenu as Isabel.

VETERAN HUNTER, THE; OR, THE FRATRICIDE OF THE GALLENSTOCK// D 2a// n.a.// **Victoria**, Mar. 1838, with Mr. Loveday as Balser, Mr. Wilkins as Karl, John Parry as Franz, Mr. King as Krantz, Mrs. Loveday as Louise, Miss Wilson as Agatha, William Davidge as Paul Krantz, Mr. Harwood as Wilhelm, W. H. Oxberry as Frumptz, Leigh Smith as Stoss.

VETERAN OF 102, THE// F// n.a.// **Cov. Garden**, May 1837, with William Farren as Galliard, Mr. Thompson as Jerome, Mr. Tilbury as Pierre, Mr. Collins as Antoine, Benjamin Webster as Le Dru, Mrs. Sarah Garrick as Mme. La Ronde, Eliza Vincent as Isabeau.

VETERAN SERGEANT, THE; OR, THE GUNNER'S BOY AND THE FOUNDLING OF THE CAMP// D 2a// n.a.// **Sad. Wells**, Apr. 1839, with W. D. Broadfoot as Col. St. Ange, Mr. Williams as Regault, Mr. Elvin as Maurice, J. W. Collier as Moustach, Mr. Phillips as Barbenoir, Mr. Conquest as Giblou, Mrs. J. F. Saville as Paulina, Miss Pincott as Georgette.

VEVA// D Pro & 3a// Clement O'Neill// **Strand**, Apr. 1883.

VICAR OF WAKEFIELD, THE// D 3a// Dram. by J. Stirling Coyne fr novel of Oliver Goldsmith// **Strand**, Mar. 1850/ **Haymarket**, Apr. 1850, with Benjamin Webster as Dr. Primrose, Henry Vandenhoff as Thornhill, Mr. Stuart as Burchell, J. B. Buckstone as Moses, Henry Howe as Jenkinson, Charles Selby as Capt. Staggers, Mr. Rogers as Flamborough, William Clark as Pounce, James Bland as Shackles, Miss Reynolds as Olivia, Mrs. L. S. Buckingham as Sophia, Priscilla Horton as Lady Blarney, Mrs. Fitzwilliam as Carolina/ Scenery by Mr. Johnstone & George Morris/ Machines by F. Heselton/ **Olympic**,

May 1851, with William Farren as Dr. Primrose, William Farren Jr. as Moses, Ellen Turner as Dick, Miss Gilbert as Bill, Charles Diddear as Burchell, John Kinloch as Squire Thornhill, W. Shalders as Frank, Henry Farren as Jenkinson, Charles Bender as Flamborough, Mrs. Alfred Phillips as Mrs. Primrose, Mrs. Stirling as Olivia, Miss Adams as Sophia, Mrs. B. Bartlett as Lady Blarney, Mrs. Leigh Murray as Carolina, Isabel Adams as Dame Flamborough, Miss E. Shalders as Letty.

VICAR OF WAKEFIELD, THE// D 4a// Dram. by J. T. Douglass fr novel of Oliver Goldsmith// **Standard**, Oct. 1870.

VICAR'S DILEMMA, THE// C 3a// n.a.// **Terry's**, July 1898.

VICARAGE, THE; A FIRESIDE STORY// C 1a// Adap. by Clement Scott ("Saville Rowe") fr F of Octave Feiullet// **POW**, Mar. 1877, with Mrs. Bancroft as Mrs. Haygarth, Arthur Cecil as Haygarth, W. H. Kendal as Clarke/ **Haymarket**, Nov. 1880, with Arthur Cecil as Haygarth, Squire Bancroft as Clarke, Stewart Dawson as Mason, Mrs. Bancroft as Mrs. Haygarth.

VICTIM OF VICE, THE; OR, THE FELON SON (see also, Woman's Wrongs; or, the Felon Son)// D 3a// n.a.// **Victoria**, Sept. 1849, with Henry Frazer as de Vervey, J. Howard as de Passey, T. H. Higgie as Eugene, J. T. Johnson as de Brien, G. F. Forman as Jambonneau, John Bradshaw as Bronchette, Mr. Henderson as Trompeau, Mr. Kerridge as Murdot, Amelia Mercer as Pauline, Mrs. George Lee as Henriette, Mrs. Cooke as Mme. Rosier, Miss Barrowcliffe as Madelon, Mrs. Andrews as Mme. Graffe, Miss E. Morden as Mme. Rotin, Miss Mildenhall as Claudine.

VICTIMS// C 3a// Tom Taylor// **Haymarket**, July 1857, with Henry Howe as Merryweather, Mr. Rogers as Rowley, William Farren as Fitzherbert, J. B. Buckstone as Butterby, William Cullenford as Curdle, Miss Reynolds as Mrs. Merryweather, Mrs. Poynter as Miss Crane, Miss M. Oliver as Mrs. Fitzherbert, Miss Lavine as Satchell, Mrs. Griffiths as Mrs. Sharp/ **Court**, 1878, with John Hare, John Clarke, George Kelly, Ellen Terry, Mrs. Gaston Murray.

VICTOIRE// D// n.a.// **Adelphi**, Dec. 1837.

VICTOR AND HORTENSE; OR, FALSE PRIDE// D 2a// n.a.// **Haymarket**, Nov. 1843, with Benjamin Webster as Victor, Robert Strickland as Mallard, J. B. Buckstone as Pettipas, Mme. Celeste as Hortense, Mrs. W. Clifford as Mme. Dindon.

VICTOR DURAND// D 4a// H. G. Carleton// **Prince's**, Dec. 1884.

VICTOR VANQUISHED, THE// C 1a// Charles Dance// **Princess's**, Mar. 1856, with Frank Matthews as Charles XII of Sweden, John Pritt Harley as Baron de Gortz, Carlotta Leclercq as Ikla.

VICTORIA CROSS, THE// D 5a// J. W. Whitbread// **Pavilion**, July 1897.

VICTORINE; OR, "I'LL SLEEP ON IT"// D// J. B. Buckstone// **Adelphi**, Apr. 1841, with Frederick Yates, Mr. Lyon, Mrs. Yates, Mrs. Keeley, Mrs. Nailer, Paul Bedford, John Sanders, Mrs. Fosbroke.

VIDA// D 4a// Ina Cassilis & Charles Lander// **POW**, Mar. 1892.

VIDENA// D// J. A. Heraud// **Marylebone**, 1854.

VILLAGE BLACKSMITH, THE// n.a.// **Surrey**, June 1857.

VILLAGE DOCTOR, THE// D 2a// J. C. Cross// **Haymarket**, July 1839, with William Farren as Boncoeur, Benjamin Webster as Baron de la Fadaise, Walter Lacy as Ferdinand, T. F. Mathews as Coco, Mrs. W. Clifford as Marchioness de Viellecour, Miss Travers as Baroness de la Fadaise, Mrs. Walter Lacy (Miss Taylor) as Louise.

VILLAGE FORGE, THE// D 5a// George Conquest & Tom Craven// **Surrey**, Sept. 1890.

VILLAGE LAWYER, THE// F 1a// William Macready// **Victoria**, Jan. 1838, with Benjamin Wrench as Scout, W. H. Oxberry as Sheepface, William Davidge as Mittmus, Mr. Harwood as Charles, Mrs. Frank Matthews as Mrs. Scout, Miss Wilson as Kate/ **Olympic**, Jan. 1847, with Mr. Wilkenson, Robert Romer, J. Cowell, Mrs. Griffiths.

VILLAGE LIFE IN FRANCE; OR, THE VINE-DRESSER'S DAUGHTER// D// n.a.// **Sad. Wells**, Jan. 1837, with Mr. Campbell as Bazil, Mr. Burton as Marquis de Bronville, C. H. Pitt as Count de Clance, Mr. Ray as Theodore, Mr. Gay as Martin, Mr. Rogers as Botch, Mr. Ennis as Jaques, Miss Williams as Lauretta.

VILLAGE ORPHAN, THE; OR, THE FOSTER SISTERS// D 2a// n.a.// **Grecian**, Mar. 1862, with Alfred Rayner as Count D'Avigny, William James as Eugene, R. H. Lingham as Jules, F. Smithson as Francois, Ellen Hale as Camille, Harriet Coveney as Annette, Mrs. Charles Dillon as Noemi.

VILLAGE PRIEST, A// Play 5a// Adap. by Sidney Grundy fr F of William Busnach & M. Cauvius, Le Secret de la Terreuse// **Haymarket**, Apr. 1890, with Herbert Beerbohm Tree as Dubois, James Fernandez as Torquenie, Fred Terry as D'Arçay, Charles Allan as Captain, Mrs. Gaston Murray as Mme. D'Arçay, Rose Leclercq as Comtess de Trémeillan, Miss Norreys as Jeanne, Mrs. E. H. Brooke as Madeleine/ Scenery by Walter Hann & Walter Johnstone.

VILLAGE TALE, A// A. Younge// **Sad. Wells**, Apr. 1850, with Frank Graham as Foster, Henry Nye as Bloomfield, G. K. Dickinson as Philip, Teresa Bassano as Emma, Miss A. Brown as Bessy.

VILLAINOUS SQUIRE AND THE VILLAGE ROSE, THE// Play 1a// H. J. Byron// **Toole's**, June 1882.

VILLIKINS AND HIS DINAH// F// James Bruton// **Grecian**, Mar. 1854, with Charles Rice as Villikins, Charles Horn as Bosky, Eaton O'Donnell as Capt. Cockleschell, Henry Grant as Frimbly, Harriet Coveney as Dinah, Miss Johnstone as Mrs. Cockleschell.

VILLON, POET AND CUT-THROAT// T 1a// S. C. Courte// **Royalty**, June 1894.

VINE DRESSER OF THE RHINE, THE// D// n.a.// **Victoria**, July 1846, with F. Wilton as Prince Leopold, Mr. Green as Baron Leibheim, Mr. Randall as Count Hartenstein, E. Edwards as Maurice, William Seaman as Hans, J. Howard as Starrkopf, Mr. Coreno as Lynx, Julia Seaman as Fritz, Mrs. George Lee as Marie.

VIOLET, THE// D// n.a.// **Princess's**, Nov. 1845, with Mr. Wallack as André, Mr. Granby as Trenquet, Leigh Murray as Armand, Mrs. Fosbroke as Marchioness D'Orville, "A Young Lady" as Blanche, Mrs. Stirling as Blanchette/ Scenery by Mr. Nicholls.

VIOLET; OR, THE LIFE OF AN ACTRESS// D 3a// Dion Boucicault// **Grecian**, May. 1870, with George Conquest as Grimaldi, William James as Lord Arthur, G. H. MacDermott as Maltravers, John Manning as Wopshot, George Gillett as Dawdle, Lizzie Mandelbert as Violet, Alice Denvil as Julia.

VIOLET, THE// D 3a// J. M. Maddox// **Princess's**, Nov. 1845.

VIOLETTE LE GRANDE; OR, THE LIFE OF AN ACTRESS// D 3a// W. E. Suter// **Grecian**, Nov. 1853, with Basil Potter as Count D'Armandier, Richard Phillips as Victor, Charles Horn as de Courville, Edwin Dixon as Bonceur, Henry Power as Anatole, Charles Rice as Jaques, Jane Coveney as Violette, Harriet Coveney as Eloise.

VIOLIN MAKER OF CREMONA, THE// C 1a// Adap. by Henry Neville fr F of François Coppée, Le Luthier de Crèmone// **Olympic**, July 1877.

VIOLIN PLAYERS, THE// Play 1a// Adap. by Alfred Berlyn fr F of François Coppée, Le Luthier de Crèmone// **Shaftesbury**, Apr. 1890.

VIPER ON THE HEARTH, THE// D 1a// J. M. Campbell// **Criterion**, May 1888.

VIRGINIA; OR, THE SOLDIER'S DAUGHTER// T 5a// Adap. by E. F. Cole fr F of Latour de Saint y Bars// **Globe**, June 1889.

VIRGINIA; OR, THE SOLDIER'S DAUGHTER// T 5a// Adap. by John Oxenford fr F of Latour de Saint y Bars// **Marylebone**, May 1948, with Anna Cora Mowatt.

VIRGINIAN, THE// D 5a// Bartley Campbell// **St. James's**, Nov. 1876, with S. Piercy as Vernon, Clifford Cooper as Calvert, R. Markby as Richard, Mr. Bauer as Pennington, George Darrell as Jack, George Honey as Gingle, Lydia Foote as Kate, Miss Telbin as Miss Jenkins, Carrie Coote as Little Hattie, Mrs. John Wood as Loo Manning/ Scenery by Mr. Lloyds.

VIRGINIAN MUMMY, THE// F// n.a.// **Cov. Garden**, Mar. 1837, with Mr. Tilbury as Galen, John Pritchard as Capt. Rifle, John Webster as Charles, T. D. Rice as Ginger, Mr. Thompson as O'Leary, Charles Bender as Patient, Miss Lee as Lucy, Miss Nicholson as Susan/ **Sad. Wells**, Aug. 1839, with W. D. Broadfoot as Dr. Galen, Mr. Elvin as Capt. Rifle, Mr. Aldridge as Charles, T. D. Rice as Ginger Blue, J. W. Collier as O'Leary, Miss Norman as Lucy, Miss Cooke as Susan; May 1863, with Dan Leeson as Ginger Blue, Mr. Warren as Dr. Galen, Charles Harcourt as Capt. Rifle, F. Shepherd as Charles, H. Josephs as O'Leary, Charles Bender as Schoolmaster, Clara Dowton as Mary, Miss Austin as Lucy.

VIRGINIUS; OR, THE ROMAN FATHER// T// J. Sheridan Knowles// **Cov. Garden**, Jan. 1837, with George Bennett as Claudius, Henry Wallack as Denatus, W. C. Macready as Virginius, Mr. Thompson as Numitorius, John Pritchard as Icilius, John Webster as Lucius, Charles Bender as Titus, Eliza Vincent as Virginia, Mrs. W. West as Servia/ **Drury Lane**, Feb. 1837, with Mr. Mathews as Appius, A. Brindal as Caius, Edwin Forrest as Virginius, Mr. Cooper as Icilius, Mr. Warde as Denatus, Frederick Cooke as Marcus, Charles Diddear as Numitorius, Mr. Baker as Lucius, Robert Honner as Publius, Mr. Henry as Titus, Mr. Shuter as Servius, Miss Taylor as Virginia, Mrs. W. Clifford as Servia; Mar. 1843, with W. C. Macready, James Anderson, Helen Faucit, Samuel Phelps; Oct. 1853, with James Johnstone as Appius, Mr. Morgan as Caius, George Burt as Marcus, A. Younge as Denatus, G. V. Brooke as Virginius, Mr. Halford as Numitorius, William Belton as Icilius, Mr. Moorhouse as Lucius, Miss Anderton as Virginia, Mrs. Vickery as Servia; Apr. 1881, with John McCullough as Virginius, John Ryder as Denatus, J. H. Barnes as Appius, J. R. Gibson as Numitorius, G. Andrews as Lucius, P. C. Beverley as Marcus, Augustus Harris as Icilius, Lydia Cowell as Virginia, Mrs. Arthur Stirling as Servia/ Scenery by Julian Hicks & Henry Emden/ **Sad. Wells**, Dec. 1837, with Mr. Wilkins as Appius Claudius, F. Ede as Caius Claudius, Mr. Campbell as Denatus, C. H. Pitt as Icilius, David Osbaldiston as Virginius, Mr. King as Numitorius, Mr. George as Lucius, Lavinia Melville as Virginia, Miss Williams as Servia; Mar. 1843 (with subt. The Liberation of Rome), with C. J. Bird as Appius Claudius, Mr. Williams as Caius, Henry Marston as Virginius, Henry Howe as Icilius, Mr. Dry as Denatus, Mr. Richardson as Titus, Charles Fenton as Servius, Mr. Aldridge as Numitorius, Caroline Rankley as Virginia, Mrs. Henry Marston as Servia; July 1844, with T. H. Lacy as Appius Claudius, Henry Marston as Denatus, Samuel Phelps as Virginius, Charles Hudson as Icilius, Mr. Williams as Numitorius, Mr.

Coreno as Titus, Charles Morelli as Servius, Miss Cooper as Virginia, Mrs. Henry Marston as Servia; Dec. 1862, with E. F. Edgar as Appius Claudius, Alfred Montague as Caius Claudius, James Johnstone as Denatus, William Creswick as Virginius, Henry Forrester as Icilius, Sophie Miles as Virginia, Mrs. Davenport as Servia; Feb. 1868, with Charles Dillon as Virginius, R. Norman as Claudius, Mr. White as Appius, Mr. Howard as Vibulanus, C. W. Barry as Denatus, Mr. Hamilton as Numitorius, J. L. Warner as Icilius, Walter Searle as Titus, Miss Leigh as Virginia, Mrs. Walton as Servia/ **Haymarket**, Aug. 1840, with Henry Wallack as Appius, Mr. Becket as Spurius, J. Worrell as Vibulanus, Henry Howe as Caius, Mr. Caulfield as Marcus, Robert Strickland as Denatus, W. C. Macready as Virginius, George Bennett as Numitorius, Mr. Wallack as Icilius, John Webster as Lucius, Helen Faucit as Virginia, Mrs. W. Clifford as Servia; Nov. 1850, with Henry Howe as Appius, Thomas Coe as Spurius, George Braid as Vibulanus, John Parselle as Caius, Mr. Woolgar as Marcus, Mr. Stuart as Denatus, W. C. Macready as Virginius, Mr. Rogers as Numitorius, E. L. Davenport as Icilin, Miss Reynolds as Virginia, Mrs. Mary Warner as Servia/ **Princess's**, Apr. 1846, with John Ryder as Appius, Mr. Walton as Vibulanus, Mr. Mucklow as Spurius, Mr. Wynn as Caius, Augustus Harris as Marcus, Mr. Cooper as Denatus, W. C. Macready as Virginius, Charles Fisher as Numitorius, Leigh Murray as Icilius, James Vining as Lucius, Miss May as Virginia, Mrs. Ternan (late Miss Jarman) as Servia/ **Victoria**, Sept. 1846, with Mr. Archer as Claudius, Mr. Willis as Oppius, James Ranoe as Caius Claudius, Mr. Thomas as Mareus, Walter Searle as Denatus, David Osbaldiston as Virginius, F. Wilton as Numitorius, J. C. Bird as Icilius, Alfred Raymond as Lucius, Annette Vincent as Virginia, Mrs. Henry Vining as Servia/ **Olympic**, Mar. 1848, with George Maynard as Appius Claudius, Mr. Harcourt as Oppius, Mr. Wilson as Valerius, Mr. Butler as Vibulanus, Mr. Lawrence as Honorius, H. Lee as Caius Claudius, John Kinloch as Marcus, William Davidge as Denatus, G. V. Brooke as Virginius, H. J. Turner as Numitorius, Henry Holl as Icilius, Miss May as Virginia, Mrs. Brougham as Servia/ **Grecian**, Apr. 1854, with Henry Grant as Apius, T. Roberts as Claudius, Mr. Hamilton as Marcus, Basil Potter as Virginius, Eaton O'Donnell as Donatus, Richard Phillips as Icilius, Henry Power as Titus, Jane Coveney as Virginia; Sept. 1856 with Charles Dillon as Virginius, Richard Phillips as Icilius, Mr. Barrett as Denatus, Basil Potter as Appius, Mr. Hustleby as Caius, F. Charles as Lucius, John Manning as Titus, Mrs. Charles Dillon as Virginia, Jane Coveney as Servia/ **Surrey**, Oct. 1880, with William Creswick, J. A. Arnold, Lydia Cowell/ **Lyric**, May 1897.

VISITING CARD, THE// C // Tom Craven// **Britannia**, May 1887.

VIVANNE; OR, THE ROMANCE OF A FRENCH MARRIAGE// D 3a// G. Channinge// **Olympic**, July 1878.

VIVE LA LIBERTÉ; OR, THE FRENCH REVOLUTION// D 2a// D. W. Osbaldiston// **Victoria**, Mar. 1848, with N. T. Hicks as de Florville, Walter Searle as Laborde, Charles Morelli as Martois, J. Howard as Arnaud, John Dale as Darbois, F. H. Henry as Francois, Mr. Henderson as Courville, Mrs. George Lee as Jacqueline, Miss Burroughcliffe as Mathilde, Miss Young as Mariette, Miss Edgar as Lucille, Mrs. Andrews as Ursula.

VOICE FROM THE BOTTLE, A// F// J. P. Webster// **Princess's**, Mar. 1888, with Forbes Dawson as Tomkins, A. R. Hodgson as McTavish, Kate Melbourne as Mrs. Tomkins, Alice Chandos as Mrs. Growler.

VOLCANO, THE// F 3a// R. R. Lumley// **Court**, Mar. 1891.

VOLUNTEERS, THE; OR THE LADIES' RIFLE BRIGADE// F 1a// n.a.// **Astley's**, June 1859, with F. R. Herbert as Emperor Maximilian, J. W. Anson as Blunderbuski, C. Stanton as Duke of Weinsberg, W. Worboys as Bumpledorf, J. T. Anderson as Carlowitz, Kate Rivers as Matilda, Miss Dowton as Lelia.

VOTE FOR GIGGS// F 3a// Adap. fr F of Albin Valabrègué, L'Homme de Paille// **Vaudeville**, May 1892.

VOW OF SECRECY, THE; OR, THE PORTRAIT, THE MASK, AND THE EXILE// D 3a// n.a.// **Grecian**, June 1855, with Richard Phillips as Count de Chalais, Eaton O'Donnell as Aubrey, Basil Potter as Chevreuse, F. Charles as de Retz, Henry Grant as the Nameless One, T. Roberts as De Fiesque, Jane Coveney as Marie.

VOW OF SILENCE, THE; OR, THE OLD BLACKSMITH'S HOVEL// D 2a// Adap. fr F// **Victoria**, May 1854, with Alfred Saville as Baron von Griffenhausen, Mr. Henderson as Rodolph, T. E. Mills as Schwarzwald, John Hudspeth as O'Quake, J. Howard as Schwill, Mrs. Henry Vining as Bertha, Miss Dansor as Ravenga, Miss Laporte as Edith.

*

WAGER, THE; OR, THE LAST LINK IN THE CHAIN// D 3a// n.a.// **Sad. Wells**, July 1840, with Mr. Elvin as Walters, Henry Marston as Falconer, Robert Honner as O'Shanaughsey, Mr. Aldridge as Troop, Mr. Williams as Sir Marmaduke, Henry Hall as Triggertouch, Mrs. Robert Honner as Viola, Mrs. Richard Barnett as Mary, Miss Cooke as Mrs. Socrates/ Scenery by F. Fenton/ Music by Isaac Collins/ Machines by B. Sloman/ Prod. by R. Honner.

WAGES OF SIN, THE// D 5a// Frank Harvey// **Olympic**, July 1883, with C. M. York as Deane, H. Bennett as Wentworth, Frank Harvey as George Brand, J. Carter-Edwards as Marler, T. W. Benson as Drummond, H. Andrews as Judson, A. Lingham as Blunt, Annie Baldwin as Ruth, Polly Hunter as Rose, Charlotte Saunders as Jemima, Eyre Robson as Juliana, Nelly Lingham as Barbara, Katie West as Jenny.

WAGGONER OF WESTMORELAND, THE; OR, THE MARTINDALE MYSTERY// D 2a// W. T. Moncrief// **Grecian**, Nov. 1856, with Richard Phillips as Wheeler, C. Kelsey as Delamore, Mr. Hustleby as Thornton, John Manning as Frank, Henry Grant as Wordsworth, William Shuter as Simon, Ellen Crisp as Mrs. Delamore, Jane Coveney as Mabel.

WAIF, THE// D 1a// Adap. by Cotsford Dick fr F, Le Passant// **Haymarket**, Apr. 1892, with Mrs. Beerbohm Tree as Zanetto, Maud Milton as Silvia.

WAIF, THE; OR, SPRUNG FROM THE STREETS// D// Adap. by Felix Pyat fr F, La Chiffonier de Paris// **Holborn**, 1873.

WAIF OF THE STREETS, THE// D// n.a.// **Pavilion**, Apr. 1877.

WAIFS OF NEW YORK// D// O. B. Collins// **Albion**, May 1878.

WAIT AND HOPE// D 3a// H. J. Byron// **Gaiety**, Mar. 1871.

WAIT AND HOPE; OR, THE STAIN UPON THE HAND// D 3a// Lewis Nanton// **East London**, May 1869.

WAIT FOR AN ANSWER// F// Harry Lemon// **Holborn**, Sept. 1869.

WAIT 'TILL I'M A MAN; OR, THE PLAY-GROUND AND THE BATTLEFIELD// D 3a// C. H. Hazlewood// **Britannia**, Apr. 1868.

WAITER AT THE EAGLE, THE// F 1a// W. E. Suter// **Grecian**, Nov. 1863, with J. Jackson as Muddlebank, George Gillett as Johnstone, George Conquest as Jenkins, Marie Brewer as Mrs. Muddlebank.

WAITING CONSENT// C 1a// Mrs. R. Fairbairn ("May Holt")// **Folly**, June 1881, with W. Elmore, E. D. Ward, Miss Roland Phillips/ **Toole's**, Jan. 1890, with Frank Arlton as Hartley, C. M. Lowne as Aylmer, George Shelton as Scorcher, Irene Vanbrugh as Grace.

WAITING FOR AN OMNIBUS IN THE LOWTHER ARCADE ON A RAINY DAY// F 1a// J. Maddison Morton// **Adelphi**, June 1854, with Leigh Murray as Horatio, Paul Bedford as Barbican, Emma Harding as Fanny, Fanny Maskell as Patty.

WAITING FOR DEATH; OR, THE IRON GRAVE// D 4a// Maurice Comerford & Lionel Robertson// **Elephant & Castle**, Feb. 1878.

WAITING FOR THE TRAIN// C// A. A. Wilmot// **Novelty**, Feb. 1891.

WAITING FOR THE UNDERGRAD// n.a.// **Strand**, Aug. 1866.

WAITING FOR THE VERDICT; OR, FALSELY ACCUSED// D 3a// C. H. Hazlewood// **City of London**, Jan. 1859/ **Grecian**, Nov. 1866, with W. Shirley as Earl of Milford, Mr. Howard as Viscount Elmore, Charles Mortimer as Lt. Florville, Henry Grant as Rigson, John Manning as Brown, J. Jackson as Hundle, Mr. Hamilton as Sir Henry, Alfred Rayner as Jonathan Roseblade, William James as Jasper Roseblade, Lizzie Mandelbert as Martha, Mary A. Victor as Sarah, Mrs. Atkinson as Mrs. Burnley.

WALKER, LONDON// C 3a// J. M. Barrie// **Toole's**, Feb. 1892.

WALL OF CHINA, THE// F// Arthur Matthison// **Criterion**, Apr. 1876.

WALLACE, THE HERO OF SCOTLAND// D// W. Barrymore// **Sad. Wells**, Apr. 1837, with John Ayliffe as Ramsey, C. H. Pitt as Monteith, Mr. Hicks as Kirkpatrick, Mr. Williams as Earl Muir, Mr. King as Cressingham, Mr. Cobham Jr. as Wallace, Miss Pitt as Oswald, Miss Beresford as Marian, Miss Williams as Helen, Mrs. Harris as Madeline, Miss Young as Isabel; Dec. 1842, with Henry Marston as Wallace, C. J. Bird as Kirkpatrick, Mr. Franks as Marr, Mr. Dry as Monteith, Mr. Jones as Athlyn, Mr. Lambe as Cressingham, Mr. Aldridge as Saulis, Charles Fenton as Hamilton, P. Williams as Gerald, Miss Melville as Donald, Caroline Rankley as Lady Marian, Mrs. Richard Barnett as Helen, Mrs. Henry Marston as Madeline, Fanny Morelli as Isabel.

WALSTEINBERG THE ROVER; OR, THE CURSE OF THE ISLAND SEER// D// n.a.// **Sad. Wells**, May 1837, with Mr. Cobham Jr. as Walsteinberg, Mr. Hicks as Ruthwold, Mr. Scarbrow as Hermanoff, H. George as Plotsden, Mr. Campbell as Croesus, John Ayliffe as Jacobus, C. H. Pitt as Frederick, Mr. King as the Seer, C. J. Smith as Landshark, Miss Beresford as Geraldine, Miss Williams as Agatha, Lavinia Melville as Paulina.

WALTER BRAND; OR, THE ABBEY DUEL IN THE MIST// D 3a// Edward Fitzball// **Victoria**, Aug. 1854, with E. F. Saville as Sir Valentine, T. E. Mills as Verney, Mr. Henderson as Sternford, N. T. Hicks as Brand, Charles Rice as Buddie, Alfred Saville as Thrift, Mr. Morrison as Old Pritchard, Mrs. Henry Vining as Una, Miss Edgar as Alice, Mrs. Manders as Mrs. Silvertongue, Miss Laporte as Margery.

WALTER TYRREL// D// Edward Fitzball// **Cov. Garden**, May 1837, with John Dale as William II, John Webster as Prince Henry, Mr. Tilbury as Rivet, E. W. Elton as Tyrrel, John Pritchard as Robert, Mr. Harris as Paul, Benjamin Webster as Tassel, Helen Faucit as Editha, Eliza Vincent as Margaret.

WALTON, THE MECHANIC; OR, THE VICTIM

OF CIRCUMSTANTIAL EVIDENCE// D 3a// John Courtney// **Victoria**, Mar. 1854, with John Bradshaw as Wheatfield, T. E. Mills as Hawk, Mr. Henderson as Shye, J. Howard as Stone, N. T. Hicks as Walton, John Hudspeth as Poodle, Mr. Hitchinson as Whinston, Mr. Morrison as Nabbs, F. H. Henry as Philcox, Mrs. Henry Vining as Rose, Miss Dansor as Marian, Miss Laporte as Polly, Mrs. Manders as Mrs. Walton, Georgiana Lebatt as Betty.

WALTZ BY ARDITI, A// F 1a// John Oxenford// **Adelphi**, Mar. 1874, with Brittain Wright as Quaver, Howard Russell as Miner, Augustus Glover as Cartouche, Miss Hudspeth as Mrs. Quaver, Maud Howard as Angelique, Miss E. Phillips as Bridget.

WANDERERS, THE; OR, A GLEAM OF SUNSHINE// D 3a// William Travers// **Grecian**, Oct. 1869, with Charles Mortimer as Ledger, Mr. Dearlove as Red Tape, Mr. Goodin as Scalpel, Samuel Perfitt as Flasher, Thomas Mead as Winter, John Manning as Jack Drummer, Mr. Shirley as Caleb Drummer, Henry Power as Augustus, Lizzie Mandelbert as Ruth, Mary A. Victor as Nancy, Mrs. Atkinson as Mrs. Drummer/ Scenery by Messender & Soames.

WANDERING BOYS, THE; OR, THE CASTLE OF OLIVAL// D 3a// John Kerr// **Grecian**, Oct. 1857, with Richard Phillips as de Croissy, Henry Grant as Roland, William Shuter as Squire, Eaton O'Donnell as Hubert, Harriet Coveney & Ellen Hale as Wandering Boys, Jane Coveney as Baroness, Miss Johnstone as Marceline; Aug. 1867, with J. Jackson as Count de Croissy, Henry Power as Gregoire, Mary A. Victor & Miss De Lacie as the Wandering Boys, Henry Grant as Rowland, W. Shirley as Hubert, Mrs. Atkinson as the Baroness, Alice Denvil as Louisa, Mrs. Dearlove as Madeline.

WANDERING HEIR, THE// D 5a// Charles Reade// **Queen's**, Nov. 1873/ **St. James's**, Apr. 1877, with Mr. Allen as Lord Altham, Mr. Harrison as Richard Annesley, Edmund Leathes as James Annesley, J. D. Beveridge as Rowley, W. Hamilton as Purcell, C. Winstanley as Hanway, C. Herberte as Hanway, Charles Cooper as Parson, Clifford Cooper as Surefoot, Frank Hall as Jip, Mrs. John Wood as Philippa, Kate Pattison as Miss Gregory, Maude Milton as Maria, Maria Daly as Betty.

WANDERING JEW, THE// D 4a// Adap. by Leopold Lewis fr novel of Eugène Sue// **Adelphi**, Apr. 1873, with Benjamin Webster as Rodin, James Fernandez as Dagobert, William McIntyre as Morok, Brittain Wright as Goliath, Augustus Glover as D'Aigrigny, J. G. Shore as Jacques, F. Charles as Agricol, A. C. Lilly as Gabriel, Robert Romer as Loriot, C. J. Smith as Burgomaster, Mrs. Alfred Mellon as Francoise, Alma Murray as Rose, Miss E. Phillips as Blanche, Miss Hudspeth as Cephise, Maud Howard as Florine/ Scenery by F. Lloyds/ Music by Edwin Ellis/ Machines by Mr. Charker.

WANDERING JEW, THE// D// G. L. Whiting// **Britannia**, June 1873.

WANDERING JEW, THE// D 3a// T. G. Paulton// **Marylebone**, July 1873.

WANDERING MINSTREL, THE// F 1a// Henry Mayhew// **Sad. Wells**, Mar. 1848, with Mr. Williams as Crincum, Julia St. George as Carol, Charles Fenton as Tweedle, Henry Scharf as Jem Baggs, Mrs. W. Watson as Mrs. Crincum, Miss Marsh as Julia, Miss Newcombe as Peggy/ **Olympic**, June 1853, with Charles Bender as Crincum, F. Charles as Carol, Mr. Clifton as Tweedle, Frederick Robson as Jem Bags, Mrs. B. Bartlett as Mrs. Crincum, Harriet Gordon as Julia, Ellen Turner as Peggy.

WANTED// F// H. W. Williamson// **Gaiety**, Apr. 1884.

WANTED, A BRAVO; OR, THE ORIGIN OF HAIR POWDER// F// C. Webb// **Sad. Wells**, Sept. 1846, with Henry Mellon as Grand Duke, Henry Scharfe as Gagliamente, Mr. Branson as Gullelme, Mrs. Leigh Murray as The Duchess, Miss St. George as Loretta.

WANTED, A HUSBAND// n.a.// **Olympic**, Jan. 1850.

WANTED, 1000 SPIRITED YOUNG MILLINERS FOR THE GOLD DIGGINGS (Alt. title, Wanted, 1000 Milliners)// F 1a// J. Stirling Coyne// **Olympic**, Oct. 1852, with Charles Bender as Singleton, William Hoskins as Baggs, Henry Compton as Tipton, Ellen Turner as Selina, Lucy Rafter as Sophy, Isabel Adams as Caroline, Miss Shalders as Charlotte, Mrs. B. Bartlett as Angelica/ **Princess's**, Sept. 1870, with John Vollaire as Singleton, John Rouse as Baggs, J. Murray as Tipton, Marion Hill as Selina, Miss L. Morgan as Sophy, Miss J. Lovell as Charlotte, Miss Harrington as Caroline, Miss Hubert as Bella, Miss Heather as Jemima, Mrs. Stephens as Angelica/ **Adelphi**, Oct. 1880, with Mr. Cooper as Singleton, Harry Proctor as Tipton, J. G. Taylor as Joe Baggs, Clara Jecks as Selina Smith, Mrs. Alfred Mellon as Angelica.

WANTED, A WIFE// F 3a// J. H. Darnley// **Terry's**, May 1890.

WAPPING OLD STAIRS// D// T. G. Blake// **Sad. Wells**, Mar. 1839, with Mr. Harwood as Lt. Willoughby, Dibdin Pitt as Sq. Craverly, Mr. Elvin as George, Mr. Dry as Robson, E. F. Saville as Tom, John Dale as Old Adams, Mr. Conquest as Shallow, W. D. Broadfoot as Clark, W. Smith as Jack, Miss Richardson as Molly, Miss Martin as Sally.

WAPPING OLD STAIRS; OR, THE ROVER'S CHILD// D// n.a.// **Haymarket**, Nov. 1837, with J. W. Gough as Harden, T. P. Cooke as Garland, J. T. Haines as Capt. Spanish, Robert Strickland as Bunch, J. B. Buckstone as Phoenix, Mrs. Waylett as Mary, Mrs. Humby as Nanny.

WAR// D 3a// T. W. Robertson// **St. James's**, Jan. 1871.

WAR BALLOON, THE; OR, THE CRIME IN

THE CLOUDS// D// W. Lovegrove// **Victoria**, May 1871.

WAR CORRESPONDENT// D// n.a.// **Surrey**, Nov. 1898.

WAR IN ABYSSINIA, THE// D// n.a.// **Marylebone**, May 1868.

WAR IN TURKEY// D// n.a.// **Britannia**, May 1854.

WAR OF WEALTH, THE// D 4a// C. J. Dazey & Sutton Vane// **Surrey**, Oct. 1898.

WAR SPECIAL, THE// Play 1a// Fred Wright Jr.// **Criterion**, Apr. 1901.

WAR TO THE KNIFE// C 3a// H. J. Byron// **POW**, June 1865.

WAR WITH CHINA, THE; OR, BRITONS RULE THE WAVES// D 1a// J. P. Taylor// **Sad. Wells**, Feb. 1842, with Mr. Archer as Amd. Elliott, Mr. Dore as Capt. Elton, Mr. Jefferini as Breeze, John Herbert as Spriggs, Mr. Dry as Ichien-Long, Mr. Aldridge as Pow-Chong, J. W. Collier as Con Fu, Miss Richardson as Zara, Mrs. Richard Barnett as Albe.

WARLOCK OF THE GLEN, THE (also titled The Fisherman of the Ferry)// D 2a// n.a.// **Sad. Wells**, May 1837, with Mr. King as Clanronald, Mr. Hicks as Matthew, Mr. Campbell as Andrew, J. Dunn as Sandy, Mr. George as Donald, C. J. Smith as Ruthven, Mr. Scarbrow as Murdock, Miss Rogers as Adelbert, Miss Williams as Lady Adela, Mrs. Rogers as Marian, Mrs. Harris as Maude.

WARM MEMBER, A// C 1a// Pryce Seaton// **Terry's**, Apr. 1898.

WARM RECEPTION A// F// G. S. Hodgson// **Surrey**, Oct. 1872.

WARNING OF FATE, THE; OR, THE LOVERS OF MOSSDALE// D 3a// John Courtney// **Victoria**, Apr. 1850, with Mr. Leake as Tremayne, Mr. Henderson as Bestow, John Bradshaw as Marston, J. T. Johnson as Homestead, John Hudspeth as Boodle, Mr. Hitcihinson as Joskins, Mr. Humphreys as Tusselwig, Mrs. Humphreys as Lady Mariton, Miss Edgar as Julia,, Annette Vincent as Amy, Miss Barrowcliffe as Araminta, Mrs. Cooke as Dame Marston, Miss Mildenhall as Biddy.

WARNING TO BACHELORS, A// C 1a// James Mortimer// **Vaudeville**, Dec. 1871.

WARNING TO PARENTS, A// F// George Roberts// **Albion**, Mar. 1877.

WARNING TO WIVES// C// n.a.// **Sad. Wells**, Oct. 1847, with A. Younge as Capt. Bouverie, William Hoskins as Mortimer, Miss Cooper as Emily, Mrs. Henry Marston as Lady Loughborough, Julia St. George as Mary.

WARNING VOICE, A// D// n.a.// **City of London**, Apr. 1864.

WASLHA; OR, THE REVOLT OF THE SLAVES// D 3a// n.a.// **Victoria**, Nov. 1837, with William Davidge as King Premislas, John Parry as Prince Ludger, Mr. Roland as Count Melnich, Mr. Green as Graaf, Mr. Loveday as Baron Turendorff, Mr. Harwood as Edgard, Mr. Salter as Bolbec, Miss Richardson as Waslha, Mrs. Griffith as Regan, Mrs. Frank Matthews as Mina, Mrs. Loveday as Keby/ Scenery by C. J. James/ Music by L. Smith.

WASTREL, THE// D 4a// Henry Byatt & Hugh Moss// **Royalty**, Aug. 1894.

WATCH AND WAIT// D 3a// T. H. Higgie & R. Shepherd// **Surrey**, Sept. 1871.

WATCH BOY, THE// D// n.a.// **Lyceum**, Nov. 1865.

WATCH-CRY, THE// D 3a// Adap. by J. Palgrave Simpson// **Lyceum**, Nov. 1865, with Charles Horsman as Cosimo di Medici, Samuel Emery as Judael, Henry Widdicomb as Mosca, Mr. Raymond as Spoleti, Mr. Clifford as Salviati, Charles Fechter as Leone Salviati, Miss Elsworthy as Blanche/ Music by W. H. Montgomery.

WATCH DOG, THE; OR, THE LOST CASKET// D// n.a.// **Victoria**, May 1854, with N. T. Hicks as Le Bras, Mr. Henderson as D'Anney, Edwin Blanchard as Le Gros, John Hudspeth as Popinet, J. Howard as Peter, Miss Laporte as Therese, Miss Dansor as Marguerite.

WATCH DOG OF THE WALSINGHAMS, THE// D 5a// J. Palgrave Simpson// **Surrey**, Oct. 1869.

WATCHING AND WAITING// C 3a// Agatha & Archibald Hodgson// **Terry's**, June 1891.

WATCHMAKER OF CLERKENWELL, THE; OR, A DRUM OF THE OLDEN TIME// D// T. E. Wilks// **Sad. Wells**, Oct. 1843, with Mr. Morton as Audrey, Mr. Williams as Everin, J. B. Hill as Wharncliffe, W. H. Williams as Hands, Henry Marston as Jones, Mr. Coreno as Brown, C. J. Smith as Norton, C. J. Bird as Edward, R. H. Lingham as Scraps, Miss Cooke as Clara, Mrs. J. B. Hill as Ellen, Caroline Rankley as Mary, Miss Stephens as Epsibah/ Scenery by F. Fenton/ Music by W. Montgomery.

WATCHMAN OF NEW YORK, THE; OR, THE ORPHAN OF FIVE POINTS// D// n.a.// **Victoria**, Aug. 1857, with E. Sawford as Murray, Mr. Cohen as Capt. Simms, Mr. Morrison as Slocombe, J. H. Rickards as Carter, Miss Vaul as Henry Selby as child, W. H. Pitt as Henry Selby as adult, Mr. Hitchinson as Moody, Henry Dudley as Jenkins, John Dale as Quid, George Pearce as Mark, Mr. Henderson as Snawley, Charles Rice as Truncheon, Mrs. Robert Honner as Ada, Julia Seaman as Mrs. Carter, Phoebe Towers as Ellen, Miss Bailey as Emma, Miss Laporte as Sally.

WATER PARTY, THE// C 2a// Charles Dance// **Lyceum**, Mar. 1849, with Frank Matthews as Deputy Butts, Frederick Cooke as Deputy Figgins, Robert Roxby as Amulet, Mr. Granby as Easy, Drinkwater Meadows as Littlejohn, John Pritt Harley as Fluid, Mrs. Yates as Mrs. Butts, Mrs. Macnamara as Mrs. Figgins, Louisa Howard as Leonora, Miss Marshall as Amelia.

WATER WITCHES// F 1a// J. Stirling Coyne// **Eng. Opera House** (Lyceum), June 1842/ **Haymarket**, June 1859, with William Farren as Townsend, Edwin Villiers as Chester, George Braid as Weston, Mr. Weathersby as Harland, William Clark as Smith, Maria Ternan as Fanny, Fanny Wright as Caroline, Miss Henrade as Clara, Eliza Weekes as Maria, Mrs. Edward Fitzwilliam as Polly/ **Globe**, May 1871.

WATERCRESS GIRL, THE// n.a.// **City of London**, Oct. 1865.

WAVE OF WAR, THE// D 4a// F. Chesterley & H. Piffard// **Terry's**, Dec. 1887.

WAXWORK MAN, THE// D 3a// C. A. Clarke// **Victoria**, June 1871.

WAY OF THE WIND, THE// F// Wallace Mackay// **Globe**, Sept. 1876.

WAY OF THE WORLD, THE// C 5a// William Congreve// **Haymarket**, 1844.

WAY OF THE WORLD, THE// D 5a// W. B. Payne// **Britannia**, Sept. 1886.

WAY OF THE WORLD, THE// D 5a// H. E. Fielding// **West London**, July 1900.

WAY TO KEEP HIM, THE// C 3a// A. Murphy// **Haymarket**, June 1839, with William Farren as Sir Bashful, Walter Lacy as Sir Brilliant, Mr. Cooper as Lovemore, William Clark as William, J. Worrell as Sideboard, Miss Taylor as Widow Belmour, Miss Maywood as Mrs. Lovemore, Miss Travers as Lady Constant, Miss Gallot as Mignionette, Miss Grove as Furnish; Oct. 1845, with William Farren as Constant, Charles Hudson as Fashion, Henry Holl as Lovemore, William Clark as William, A. Brindal as Sideboard, Priscilla Horton as Lady Constant, Miss Fortescue as Mrs. Belmour, Mrs. Seymour as Mrs. Lovemore, Mrs. Humby as Muslin, Miss Woulds as Furnish; July 1858, with Henry Howe as Lovemore, J. B. Buckstone as Sir Bashful, William Farren as Sir Brilliant, William Clark as William, Thomas Coe as Sideboard, Mrs. Charles Young as Widow Bellmour, Miss Reynolds as Mrs. Lovemore, Mrs. Buckingham White as Lady Constant, Mrs. Edward Fitzwilliam as Muslin, Fanny Wright as Mignionette/ **Sad. Wells**, Apr. 1848, with A. Younge as Sir Bashful, William Hoskins as Sir Brilliant, Henry Marston as Lovemore, J. T. Johnson as William, Laura Addison as Widow Belmour, Miss Marsh as Lady Constant, Miss Edmonds as Mrs. Lovemore, Julia St. George as Mignionet, Miss Newcombe as Furnish, Mrs. W. Watson as Muslin.

WAYFARERS// Play 1a// Herbert Swears// **Matinée**, May 1898.

WAYS AND MEANS; OR, A TRIP TO DOVER// C// George Colman the younger// **Drury Lane**, May 1837, with George Bartley as Sir David, Mr. Cooper as Random, A. Brindal as Scruple, Drinkwater Meadows as Tiptoe, Mr. Shuter as Peery, Mrs. Charles Jones as Lady Dunder, Miss Lee as Harriet, Mrs. Humby as Kitty/ **Haymarket**, Sept. 1837, with William Dowton as Sir David, Frederick Vining as Random, Charles Selby as Scruple, Benjamin Webster as Tiptoe, Mrs. Julia Glover as Lady Dunder, Miss E. Phillips as Harriet, Miss Allison as Kitty/ **Sad. Wells**, Aug. 1845, with A. Younge as Sir David, Samuel Buckingham as Random, Mr. Morton as Scruple, Frank Graham as Peery, Henry Scharf as Tiptoe, Mrs. Henry Marston as Lady Dunder, Georgiana Lebatt as Kitty, Miss Huddart as Harriet; Mar. 1862, with Mr. Williams as Sir David, Frederick Villiers as Random, W. Mowbray as Scruple, Lewis Ball as Tiptoe, Mrs. Barrett as Lady Dunder, Ada Dyas as Harriet, Miss Hudspeth as Kitty.

WE ALL HAVE OUR LITTLE FAULTS// F 1a// W. E. Suter// **Grecian**, Oct. 1864, with William James as Rollick, John Manning as Gingernutt, George Conquest as Goosey, Mary A. Victor as Mrs. Rollick, Laura Conquest as Louisa.

WEAK POINTS// F 2a// J. B. Buckstone// **Haymarket**, Apr. 1838, with Benjamin Webster as Docker, Robert Strickland as Jolly, J. B. Buckstone as Wheedle, Mr. Hemming as Vernon, T. F. Mathews as Huxter, Mrs. Julia Glover as Penelope, Miss Cooper as Agnes, Mrs. Fitzwilliam as Sally, Mme. Sala as Mrs. Docker, Mrs. Gallot as Mrs. Huxter.

WEAK WOMAN// C 3a// H. J. Byron// **Strand**, May 1875, with Edward Terry, Marion Terry.

WEAKER SEX, THE// C 3a// Arthur Wing Pinero// **Court**, Mar. 1889.

WEALTH// C 2a// M. R. Lacy// **Royalty**, Oct. 1870.

WEALTH// D 4a// Henry Arthur Jones// **Haymarket**, Mar. 1889, with Herbert Beerbohm Tree as Matthew Ruddock, F. H. Macklin as Davoren, Charles Brookfield as John Ruddock, Henry Kemble as Dr. Driscoll, Edmund Maurice as Dashwood, Charles Allan as Cheeseley, Mr. Hargreaves as Buckmaster, Stewart Dawson as Palfreyman, Weedon Grossmith as Percy, Rose Leclercq as Mrs. Palfreyman, Miss Norreys as Madge, Miss Ayrtoun as Mrs. Cheeseley, Mrs. Beerbohm Tree as Edith.

WEALTH AND WANT; OR, THE VILLAGE POLITICIANS// D// W. L. Rede// **Sad. Wells**, Oct. 1838, with Mr. Mellor as Squire Deerham, Mr. Cathcart as Luttrell, Mr. Conquest as Beetle, Robert Honner as Snarkie, W. D. Broadfoot as Jobson, Dibdin Pitt as Farrow, Mr. Dry as Sandon, J. W. Collier as Rookem, Miss Richardson as Jane, Miss Cooke as Widow Franklin, Miss Hill as Fanny, Mrs. J. F. Saville as Sukey.

WEALTH GOT AND LOST// D 3a// C. H. Hazlewood// **Britannia**, Dec. 1870.

WEARING OF THE GREEN; OR, THE LOVER'S LEAP// D 3a// L. T. Downey// **Victoria**, Oct. 1877.

WEATHER PERMITTING// C 1a// W. R. Snow// **Globe**, Nov. 1872, with Carlotta Addison as Pamela Popinjay, Charles Neville as Frank Flutterby.

WEATHER-HEN, THE// C 4a// Brandon Thomas & Granville Barker// **Terry's**, June 1899/ **Comedy**, July 1899.

WEATHERCOCK, THE// F 1a// J. T. Allingham// **Olympic**, May 1841, with Mr. Turnour as Briefwit, Mr. Brookes as Old Fickle, Mr. Mulford as Sneer, Miss Fortesque as Variella, Miss Dawes as Ready.

WEAVER OF LYONS, THE; OR, THE THREE CONSCRIPTS// F 1a// James Barber// **Astley's**, Nov. 1844; Oct. 1849, with S. Smith as Francis, Mr. Plunket as Augustus, Mr. Adrian as Blouquet, Mr. Crowther as Chopin, Mr. Johnson as Captain, Mrs. Beacham as Adele.

WEAVER'S DAUGHTER, THE// D// W. Darlington// **Sad. Wells**, Mar. 1883.

WEB OF FATE, THE// D 4a// Augusta Tullock// **Elephant & Castle**, July 1900.

WEBSTER'S ROYAL RED BOOK// C 3a// Benjamin Webster// **Adelphi**, July 1849, with Paul Bedford as Bartholomew Briggs, Edward Wright as Tadcaster, J. Worrell as Canvas, Mr. Wayne as Barnaby Briggs, Mrs. Laws as Lucretia, Mrs. Frank Matthews as Mrs. Bartholomew Briggs/ Scenery by Pitt & Johnstone/ Machinery by Mr. Cooper.

WEDDED AND LOST; OR, THE PERILS OF A BRIDE// D// William Travers// **Britannia**, Sept. 1868.

WEDDED BLISS// C 1a// Adap. by Henry Paulton fr F// **Avenue**, Oct. 1882.

WEDDED TO CRIME// D 4a// Fred Jarman & Wilford Selwyn// **Sad. Wells**, May 1891.

WEDDING BELLS// D 3a// Clifford Merton// **Britannia**, Oct. 1876.

WEDDING BREAKFAST, THE// F// J. Maddison Morton// **Haymarket**, Aug. 1843, with William Farren as Dr. Gadabout, Henry Holl as Capt. Storks, Mrs. Stanley as Mrs. Matchem, Mrs. W. Clifford as Mrs. Yellowboy, Julia Bennett as Julia.

WEDDING DAY, THE// F 1a// Mrs. Inchbald// **Princess's**, May 1845, with Mr. Granby as Sir Adam, Mr. Hield as Contest, Leigh Murray as Lord Rakeland, Mr. Franks as John, Mr. Henry as William, "A Young Lady" as Lady Conest, Mrs. Fosbroke as Mrs. Hamford, Miss Mott as Hannah/ **Olympic**, Nov. 1845, with Charles Boyce as Lord Rakeland, Mr. Binge as Contest, James Browne as Sir Adam, Mrs. Walter Lacy as Lady Contest, Mrs. Griffith as Mrs. Hamford, Miss Martineau as Hannah; Jan. 1849, with H. J. Turner as Sir Adam, Mr. Norton as Contest, John Kinloch as Lord Rakeland, Mr. Lawrence as Milden, Miss Gray as Lady Contest, Mrs. England Young as Mrs. Hamford, Miss Adams as Hannah/ **Sad. Wells**, Dec. 1846, with A. Younge as Sir Adam, Mr. Morton as Lord Rakeland, Mr. Branson as Contest, Frank Graham as Minden, Miss Cooper as Lady Conest, Miss Stephens as Mrs. Hamford, Fanny Morelli as Hannah/ **Haymarket**, June 1848, with Mr. Ranger as Sir Adam, Henry Vandenhoff as Lord Rakeland, George Braid as Contest, Julia Bennett as Lady Contest, Mrs. Stanley as Mrs. Bamford, Miss Woulds as Hannah.

WEDDING EVE, THE// D 3a// J. B. Howe// **Britannia**, Apr. 1867.

WEDDING GOWN, THE// C// Douglas Jerrold// **Drury Lane**, June 1837, with Mr. Cooper as Lubeski, Mr. Hooper as Effingham, A. Brindal as Clarendon, Mr. Hughes as Creamly, Mr. Baker as Valise, George Bartley as Beeswing, Drinkwater Meadows as Junket, Miss Huddart as Augusta, Miss Taylor as Margaret, Mrs. W. Clifford as Lady Aubrey, Miss Somerville as Mrs. Fossil/ **Grecian**, Oct. 1856, with Richard Phillips, C. Kelsey, William Shuter, Eaton O'Donnell, Henry Power, John Manning, Jane Coveney, Miss Johnstone, Ellen Crisp, Harriet Coveney.

WEDDING GUEST, THE// Play 3a// J. M. Barrie// **Garrick**, Sept. 1900, with H. B. Irving.

WEDDING MARCH, THE// C 3a// F. L. Tomline// **Court**, Nov. 1873.

WEDDING PRESENT, A// F. Alfred Arthur// **St. Geo. Hall**, Nov. 1868.

WEEDS AND FLOWERS; OR, THE GARDEN OF LIFE// D 3a// W. H. Abel// **East London**, July 1870.

WEEDS AND FLOWERS OF ERIN, THE// D 3a// G. H. Macdermott// **Grecian**, Aug. 1870, with G. H. MacDermott as Big Ben Brady, W. Donne as Tim Higgins, J. Jackson as Barney Regan, Samuel Perfitt as Mr. Kindly, George Gillett as Archie Kindly, John Manning as Findon Fortescue, Walter Holland as Fanshaw Fortescue, William James as James Byrne, Alice Denvil as Noddle Duggins, Lizzie Mandelbert as Kate Kindly.

WEIRD WOMAN OF THE WRECK; OR, THE FLOATING BEACON// D// n.a.// **Sad. Wells**, Aug. 1840, with Robert Honner as Jack Junk, Mr. Dry as Augerstoff, Mr. Elvin as Frederick, Mr. Williams as Weignstadt, Mr. Aldridge as Maurice, Mr. Stilt as Ormoloff, Miss Richardson as Mariette, Mrs. Richard Barnett as Christine.

WELCOME HOME// C 1a// T. E. Wilks// **Sad. Wells**, Nov. 1842, with P. Williams as Sir William, Mr. Lambe as William, Mr. Dry as Mark Merton, Robert Honner as Mat Merton, C. J. Bird as

Adderly, Charles Fenton as Robson, Mrs. Richard Barnett as Louisa, Mrs. Andrews as Betsy.

WELCOME LITTLE STRANGER// n.a.// **Adelphi**, Mar. 1857.

WELCOME LITTLE STRANGER// C 3a// Adap. by James Albery fr F of MM. Crisafulli & V. Bernard, Le Petit Ludovic// **Criterion**, Aug. 1890.

WELL MATCHED// C// Philip Havard// **St. James's**, May 1889.

WELSH GIRL, THE// C// Mrs. J. R. Planché// **Haymarket**, Nov. 1842, with Robert Strickland as Sir Owen, Mr. Caulfield as Alfred, Mr. Tilbury as David, Mme. Vestris as Julia, Mrs. Frank Matthews as Dora/ **Princess's**, June 1846, with Mr. Granby as Sir Owen, Mr. Walton as David, Charles Fisher as Alfred, Mrs. Fosbroke as Dora, Mme. Vestris as Julia.

WELSH HEIRESS, A// C 1a// W. T. Cullum// **Comedy**, Jan. 1893.

WELSH RABBITS// C 1a// Robert Reece & Knight Summers// **Folly**, May 1881, with J. L. Toole, Emily Thorne.

WEP-TON-NO-MAH, THE INDIAN MAIL-CARRIER// D 5a// n.a.// **Elephant & Castle**, Sept. 1893.

WEPT OF THE WISH-TON-WISH, THE// D// W. Bayle Bernard// **Adelphi**, June 1850, with Henry Hughes as Maj. Gough, William Cullenford as Capt. Heathcote, J. Worrell as Content, Edward Wright as Skunk, O. Smith as Conanchet, C. J. Smith as Uneas, Mme. Celeste as Nazzamattah, Sarah Woolgar as Faith, Mrs. Laws as Abundance.

WERE WOLF, THE// D 1a// Lilian Mowbray & W. H. Pollock// **Avenue**, Feb. 1898.

WERNER; OR, THE INHERITANCE// D 5a// Lord Byron// **Cov. Garden**, Oct, 1837, with W. C. Macready as Werner, James Anderson as Ulric, George Bennett as Gabor, Charles Diddear as Baron Stralenheim, Drinkwater Meadows as Idenstein, Mr. Roberts as Fritz, Mr. Tilbury as Henric, Edwin Yarnold as Eric, W. H. Payne as Ludwig, Miss Huddart as Josephine, Eliza Vincent as Ida/ **Haymarket**, Nov. 1840, with W. C. Macready as Werner, James Wallack as Ulric, Samuel Phelps as Gabor, Robert Strickland as Idenstein, George Bennett as Stralenheim, Henry Howe as Fritz, T. F. Mathews as Henrick, Mr. Caulfield as Rodolph, J. Worrell as Eric, Mrs. Mary Warner as Josephine, Miss Charles as Ida; Nov. 1850, with W. C. Macready as Werner, E. L. Davenport as Ulric, Mr. Stuart as Gabor, Mr. Lambert as Idenstein, Henry Howe as Baron Stralenheim, John Parselle as Fritz, James Bland as Henric, Mrs. Mary Warner as Josephine, Miss Reynolds as Ida/ **Sad. Wells**, July 1844 (with subt., The Inheritance), with Mr. Morton as Count Strahlenheim, Samuel Phelps as Werner, Henry Marston as Gabor, Charles Hudson as Ulric, Mr. Williams as Idenstein, Mr. Sharpe as Fritz, Mr. Coreno as Henrick/ **Princess's**, June 1847, with Charles Fisher as Baron Stralenheim, Robert Honner as Count Rodolph, W. C. Macready as Werner, William Creswick as Ulric, John Ryder as Gabor, Mr. Granby as Idenstein, Mr. Wynn as Fritz, Mr. Walton as Henric, Augustus Harris as Eric, Mrs. Mary Warner as Josephine, Mrs. Henry Hughes as Ida; Jule, 1861, with Samuel Phelps as Werner, Edmund Phelps as Ulric, Mr. Raymond as Stralenheim, Drinkwater Meadows as Idenstein, John Ryder as Gabor, Robert Cathcart as Fritz, Edmund Garden as Henrick, Miss Atkinson as Josephine, Rose Leclercq as Ida/ **Grecian**, Nov. 1854, with T. Roberts as Stralenheim, Henry Grant as Gabor, Eaton O'Donnell as Idenstein, Basil Potter as Werner, Richard Phillips as Ulric, Ellen Crisp as Josephine, Jane Coveney as Ida/ **Lyceum**, June 1887, with Henry Irving, George Alexander, Ellen Terry, Winifred Emery.

WEST INDIAN, THE// C// Richard Cumberland// **Haymarket**, Apr. 1842, with Henry Holl as Belcour, Henry Wallack as Stockwell, J. W. Gough as Capt. Dudley, Malone Raymond as Maj. O'Flaherty, Henry Howe as Dudley, Mr. Tilbury as Fulmer, Robert Strickland as Varland, J. Worrell as Stukeley, Mrs. W. Clifford as Lady Rusport, Miss Charles as Charlotte, Mrs. Edwin Yarnold as Louisa, Mrs. Stanley as Mrs. Fulmer/ **Sad. Wells**, Apr. 1852, with George Bennett as Stockwell, Henry Marston as Belcour, Henry Mellon as Maj. O'Flaherty, Mr. Wilkins as Capt. Dudley, J. W. Ray as Varland, William Belford as Charles, Mr. Harris as Stukely, Mr. Williams as Fulmer, Mrs. Henry Marston as Lady Rusport, Miss Goddard as Charlotte, Miss E. Feist as Louisa, Miss Stephens as Mrs. Fulmer, Eliza Travers as Lucy.

WET DAY, A// F 3a// G. W. Browne// **Vaudeville**, Aug. 1884.

WET NURSE, THE// F 1a// n.a.// **Victoria**, Feb. 1850, with J. Neville as Grubb, John Hudspeth as Chip, J. Howard as Pry, Mrs. George Lee as Mrs. Grubb, Miss Barrowcliffe as Kitty.

WHALERS, THE// D// n.a.// **Victoria**, Dec. 1863.

WHAT! ANOTHER!// F// J. M. East & Brian Daley// **West London**, June 1901.

WHAT HAPPENED TO JONES?// F 3a// G. H. Broadhurst// **Vaudeville**, Aug. 1897/ **Strand**, July 1898/ **Terry's**, Jan. 1900.

WHAT HAVE I DONE?// C 1a// John Oxenford// **Olympic**, Mar. 1838, with Robert Keeley as Bounceable, Charles Selby as Wentworth, W. Vining as Col. Sternly, Mr. Stoker as Ens. Perkins, William Farren as Peter Perkins, Mrs. Macnamara as Mrs. Sternly, Miss Murray as Julia.

WHAT MIGHT HAVE BEEN// D// Russell Vaun// **Wyndham's**, Dec. 1900.

WHAT! MORE TROUBLE!// F 3a// W. T.

McCellan// **POW**, July 1899.

WHAT NEXT?// F// T. J. Dibdin// **Sad. Wells**, Aug. 1845, with A. Younge as Col. Touchwood, Samuel Buckingham as Maj. Touchwood, Henry Scharf as Sharp, Mr. Morton as Col. Clifford, R. H. Lingham as Mordaunt, Frank Graham as Brief, Mr. Williams as Snaggs, Mrs. Henry Marston as Mrs. Prudence, Miss Huddart as Clarissa, Miss Stephens as Sophia, Fanny Morelli as Sally.

WHAT TO EAT, DRINK, AND AVOID// F 1a// n.a.// **Olympic**, Sept. 1848, with Henry Compton as Wry, Samuel Emery as Topple, H. J. Turner as Blight, Samuel Cowell as Potts, Mrs. H. J. Turner as Mrs. Topple, Miss St. George as Jemima, Mrs. C. A. Tellet as Betsy Jane.

WHAT WILL BECOME OF HIM? OR, LIFE IN LONDON AS IT WAS AND IS// D Pro & 3a// Frederick Marchant// **Britannia**, May 1872/ **Marylebone**, Sept. 1874.

WHAT WILL MY AUNT SAY?; OR, FORBIDDEN FRUIT// C 1a// n.a.// **Princess's**, May 1850, with H. T. Craven as Sir John, Louisa Howard as Lady Louisa.

WHAT WILL THE NEIGHBORS SAY?// F// J. T. Douglass// **Standard**, Sept. 1873.

WHAT WILL THE WORLD SAY?// C 5a// Mark Lemon// **Cov. Garden**, Sept. 1841, with Charles Diddear as Lord Norwold, James Vining as Charles, C. J. Mathews as Hilary, George Bartley as Warner, William Farren as Capt. Tarradiddle, Mr. Granby as Grub, A. Brindal as Nibble, Mrs. Julia Glover as Lady Norwold, Mrs. Walter Lacy as Marian, Miss Cooper as Miss De Vere, Mrs. Orger as Tattle, Mrs. Humby as Mrs. Tarradiddle, Mrs. Tayleure as Mrs. Dearpoint/ Scenery by Grieve, T. Grieve & W. Grieve.

WHAT WILL THEY SAY AT BROMPTON?// C 1a// J. Stirling Coyne// **Olympic**, Nov. 1857, with Frederick Robson as Todd and Toddini, George Cooke as Croker, Miss Wyndham as Mrs. Todd, Miss Bromley as Perks, Mr. Addison as Terreboli, Harwood Cooper as Grimaldi, Miss Marston as Marietta.

WHAT'S YOUR GAME?// n.a.// **Surrey**, Sept. 1858.

WHEEL OF FORTUNE, THE// C// Richard Cumberland// **Drury Lane**, Mar. 1850, with W. H. Angel as Sir David, Basil Baker as Gov. Tempest, Charles Diddear as Woodville, Mr. Cooper as Sydenham, Mr. Vandenhoff as Penruddock, William Montague as Capt. Woodville, William Davidge as Weazle, Mr. Manderson as Trueman, Miss Phillips as Mrs. Woodville, Laura Addison as Emily, Mrs. Griffith as Dame Dunckly.

WHEEL OF FORTUNE, THE// D Pro & 4a// W. H. Poole// **Sad. Wells**, Jan. 1891.

WHEELS WITHIN WHEELS// C 3a// R. C. Carton// **Court**, May 1899/ **Criterion**, May 1901.

WHEN A MAN'S IN LOVE// C 3a// Anthony Hope & Edward Rose// **Court**, Oct. 1898.

WHEN GEORGE THE FOURTH WAS KING// Play 1a// F. W. Moore// **Grand**, Oct. 1896/ **Lyceum**, Oct. 1896, with Charles Groves as William Garden, Gilbert Hare as Joshua Dade, Frank Gillmore as Harry Joliffe, Mona Oram as Mary Lewis/ Scenery by W. Harford.

WHEN GREEK MEETS GREEK// D 4a// Dram. by Joseph Hatton fr his own novel// **Surrey**, June 1896.

WHEN THE CLOCK STRIKES NINE// D 3a// C. H. Hazlewood// **Britannia**, Mar. 1860.

WHEN THE LAMPS ARE LIGHTED// D 4a// G. R. Sims & Leo Merrick// **Grand**, Nov. 1897.

WHEN WE WERE TWENTY-ONE// Play 4a// H. V. Esmond// **Comedy**, Sept. 1901.

WHERE SHALL I DINE?// F// G. H. Rodwell// **Sad. Wells**, June 1844, with Charles Hudson as Sponge, Mr. Williams as Grumpy, Mr. Binge as Discount, Mr. Sharpe as Flint, Mr. Evain as Homely, G. F. Forman as Diggory, Mrs. Henry Marston as Mrs. Grumpy, Miss Lebatt as Dorothea, Emma Harding as Mrs. Discount, Fanny Morelli as Deborah.

WHERE THERE'S A WILL THERE'S A WAY// C 1a// J. Maddison Morton// **Olympic**, Nov. 1850, with Leigh Murray as Don Manuel, Henry Compton as Don Scipio, William Farren Jr. as Don Lopez, Mrs. Stirling as Dona Francesca, Miss Adams as Dona Blanche/ **Haymarket**, July 1855, with Leigh Murray as Don Manuel, Henry Compton as Don Scipio, Edwin Villiers as Don Lopez, Mrs. Stirling as Donna Francisca, Ada Swanborough as Donna Blanche/ **Sad. Wells**, Nov. 1856, with Frederic Robinson as Don Manuel, Lewis Ball as Don Scipio, William Belford as Don Lopez, Mr. Lacy as Secretary, Jenny Marston as Donna Francesca, Caroline Parkes as Donna Blanche/ **Princess's**, Oct. 1862, with George Vining as Don Manuel, George Belmore as Don Scipio, Robert Cathcart as Don Lopez, Miss M. Oliver as Donna Francesca, Marian Jones as Donna Blanche.

WHERE'S THE CAT?// C 3a// Adap. by James Albery fr G// **Criterion**, Nov. 1880, with Charles Wyndham, Herbert Beerbohm Tree, Mrs. John Wood, Mary Rorke, Edith Bruce.

WHERE'S YOUR WIFE?// F// J. V. Bridgman// **Strand**, Sept. 1863.

WHICH?// F 2a// A. G. Bagot// **Gaiety**, Feb. 1886.

WHICH CAN BE MY HUSBAND? (see Who's My Husband)

WHICH IS MY HUSBAND? (see Who's My Husband)

WHICH IS THE THIEF?// D// James Barber// **Princess's**, Aug. 1845, with Leigh Murray as Marquis de Solanges, Walter Lacy as de Beauvais, W. H. Oxberry as Gibalin, Emma Stanley as Adeline.

WHICH IS WHICH?// F 1a// n.a.// **Olympic**, Nov. 1842, with Mr. Brookes as Gen. Thornwell, Mr. Halford as Capt. Daring, Mr. Ross as Snell, Walter Searle as Halbert, Mr. Turnour as Tunley, Miss Lebatt as Emily, Miss Hamilton as Fanny, Miss Bartlett as Mary.

WHICH IS WHICH?// C 1a// S. Theyre Smith// **Court**, July 1871, with John Clayton, Louisa Moore/ **Gaiety**, Oct. 1873/ **Olympic**, Oct. 1880, with Arthur Dacre as Capper, Mr. Graeme as Gargle, Mr. Taylor as Paddles, Fanny Thorne as Bertha, Julia Roselle as Annie, Miss Dalby as Mrs. Mills.

WHICH MR. SMITH?// C 2a// A. B. Reach// **Lyceum**, Oct. 1846, with Frank Matthews as John Smith, Samuel Emery as Sludge, Henry Butler as Maylie, Frederick Vining as O'Gorman, J. W. Collier as Bob, Mr. Bellingham as Wimbledon, Mrs. Woollidge as Mrs. Smith, Miss Grove as Emma, Miss Turner as Susan.

WHICH WINS?// C 4a// J. W. Pigott// **Terry's**, June 1889.

WHILE IT'S TO BE HAD// F// Charles Collette// **Mirror**, Dec. 1874.

WHILE THERE'S LIFE THERE'S HOPE// n.a.// **Strand**, July 1863.

WHIPPING POST; OR, LIFE IN THE RANKS// D 4a// Edwin France// **Standard**, Aug. 1884.

WHIPS OF STEEL// C 4a// J. J. Delley & Mary Rowsell// **St. Geo. Hall**, May 1889.

WHIRLWIND, THE// C 4a// Sidney Rosenfeld// **Elephant & Castle**, Sept. 1890.

WHISKEY DEMON, THE; OR, THE DREAM OF THE REVELLER// D 5a// n.a.// **Pavilion**, Nov. 1867.

WHITE BOUQUET, THE// F 1a// Adap. fr F// **Globe**, Aug. 1875, with T. N. Wenman as Frederick Fastboy, Bessie Edwards as Mrs. Fastboy, H. Andrews as Spoffles, Kate Elliston as Susan.

WHITE BOY, THE// D// Tom Taylor// **Olympic**, Oct. 1866.

WHITE BOY OF DEVIL'S CRAIG, THE; OR, THE EXILE OF ERIN// D// n.a.// **Sad. Wells**, July 1837, with Mr. King as Fitzgerald, Mr. Campbell as Bernard, Mr. Griffiths as Connor, C. H. Pitt as Sullivan, Thomas Lee as Faherty, Mr. Hicks as Redmond, J. Dunn as Brass, Miss Williams as Honoria, Lavinia Melville as Letty, Mrs. Harris as Biddy.

WHITE BOYS// D// Edward Towers// **Surrey**, Jan. 1862/ **Grecian**, Apr. 1864, with Henry Grant as Gen. Darville, William James as Capt. Blakely, J. Jackson as Corp. Dickey, George Gillett as Lt. Somers, John Manning as Tape, George Conquest as Squall, Thomas Mead as O'Brien, J. B. Steele as O'Donnell, Jane Dawson as Norah, Marie Brewer as Kathleen.

WHITE BOYS, THE; OR, THE REBEL CHIEF (see White Boys)

WHITE BOYS, NA' BOUCHALEEN BAWN; OR, IRELAND IN '98// D 2a// Adap. by Edward and J. Towers fr F, Les Enfants Blanc// **Victoria**, Feb. 1862, with Walter Fredericks as Sir Hubert, J. H. Rickards as Capt. Brady, J. W. Ennis as O'Neil, W. Harmer as O'Hara, George Pearce as Flynn, George Yarnold as Corp. Mims, J. Howard as Corp. Skinner, W. H. Pitt as Finnagan, Topsy Lloyd as Phelim, Nelly Wood as Norah, Helen Love as Lady Trelawnly, Mrs. F. Lauri as Alice/ Scenery by Julian Hicks.

WHITE CHATEAU, THE; OR, PAST, PRESENT, AND FUTURE// D 4a// George Conquest// **Grecian**, Oct. 1861, with F. Smithson as Count d'Outreville, George Gillett as King of France, Henry Grant as Beautern, Henry Power as Carleu, William James as Octave, Thomas Mead as Pierre, George Conquest as Choler, Walter Holland as Capt. Noirier, Alfred Rayner as Durand, Jane Dawson as Louise, Mrs. Charles Dillon as Rosine, Mary A. Victor as Blanchette.

WHITE CHIEF, THE; OR, THE BUFFALO HUNTER OF THE DEATH PRAIRIE// D// Dram. by Thompson Townsend fr novel of Mayne Reid// **Pavilion**, Nov. 1866/ **Grecian**, Dec. 1866, with Henry Grant as Vicarran, Mr. Mathew as Roblade, Henry Powell as Carlos, Mr. Donn as Juan, J. Jackson as Dr. Camomile, John Manning as Muggins, W. Shirley as Don Antonio, Henry Power as Manuel, Alice Denvil as Postia, Mrs. Atkinson as Juanita, Lizzie Mandelbert as Cataline, Mary A. Victor as Betty.

WHITE ELEPHANT, THE// F// Henry Hayman// **Elephant & Castle**, Nov. 1875.

WHITE ELEPHANT, A// F 3a// R. C. Carton// **Comedy**, Nov. 1896.

WHITE FARM, THE; OR, THE WIDOW'S VISION// D 2a// W. J. Lucas// **Queen's**, 1856.

WHITE HAT, THE// F 1a// n.a.// **Adelphi**, Apr. 1873, with Frederick Moreland as Fuddle, A. C. Lilly as Penfold, Brittain Wright as Puddle, Miss Wilmot as Mary Maydew, Miss Hudspeth as Mary Muddle/ **Drury Lane**, Sept. 1875, with J. R. Jackson, Brittain Wright, W. Holman, Clara Jecks, Mrs. J. Carter, Miss Macdonald/ **Princess's**, Mar. 1876, with E. Shepherd as Fuddle, Brittain Wright as Puddle, A. C. Lilly as Penfold, Mabel Hayes as Mary, Lilian Adair as Mrs. Fuddle, Miss Macdonald as Mary Muddle.

WHITE HEATHER, THE// D 4a// Cecil Raleigh & Henry Hamilton// **Drury Lane**, May 1897, with Mrs. John Wood as Lady Janet, Kate Rorke as Marion, Pattie Browne as Lady Molly, Beatrice Lamb as Lady Hermione, Lillian Menelly as Blanche, Mary Brough as Lady

Lumley, Margaret Brough as Lady Delroy, Henry Neville as Lord Angus, H. De Lange as Trefusis, Dawson Milward as Capt. Maclintock, Robert Loraine as Beach, J. Rosier as Duke of Shetland/ Scenery by Joseph Harker, W. Perkins, Mr. Cleery, Bruce Smith & Robert Caney/ Music by J. M. Glover/ prod. by Arthur Collins.

WHITE HOOD, THE// D 2a// J. R. Planché// **Lyceum**, Nov. 1850, with George Vining as Louis de Vale, Henry Horncastle as de Grossenhayne, Basil Baker as Vanbloos, C. J. Mathews as Peter Pestlework, Mr. Bellingham as Heynes, Mr. Harcourt as Prunel, Mrs. Macnamara as Dame Judith, Fanny Baker as Marguerite/ Scenery by W. Beverly & Mr. Meadows.

WHITE HOODS, THE; OR, THE REVOLT OF FLANDERS// D// Edward Stirling// **Victoria**, Feb. 1852, with Mr. Raymond as Lewis de Male, J. T. Johnson as von Artavald, Mr. Richards as Lyon, F. H. Henry as Gilbert Mathew, Watty Brunton as Arnold Mathew, T. E. Mills as du Bois, J. Howard as de Bete, G. F. Forman as Von Dregger, Mr. Morrison as Moulder, JohnBradshaw as Vanderblast, Miss Fielding as Anne, Mrs. George Lee as Bianca, Georgiana Lebatt as Frauline Jeddart, Miss Edgar as Countess of Artois, Mrs. Manders as Ursula/ Scenery by Mr. Hawthorn/ Machines by Wood, Foster, & Boulanger/ Prod. by T. H. Higgie.

WHITE HORSE OF THE PEPPERS, THE// D 2a// Samuel Lover// **Haymarket**, May 1838, with Tyrone Power as Pepper, Charles Perkins as Col. Chesham, Benjamin Webster as Maj. Mansfelt, Robert Strickland as Donoghue, D. W. King as Phelim, Mrs. Fitzwilliam as Magdelene, Miss Cooper as Aggy/ Scenery by George Morris/ Music by W. Forde; June. 1851, with Charles Hudson as Gerald, John Parselle as Col. Chesham, Charles Selby as Maj. Mansfelt, Mr. Caulfield as Phelim, Mr. Lambert as Donoghue, Mrs. L. S. Buckingham as Magdelene, Mrs. Caulfield as Aggy; Oct. 1854, with Edwin Villiers as Chesham, Mr. Rogers as Mansfeldt, William Cullenford as Portreeve, Charles Hudson as Pepper, George Braid as Donoghue, Miss Schott as Phelim, Amelia Vining as Magdalene, Miss Lavine as Agatha/ **Adelphi**, Oct. 1848, with Charles Hudson as Gerald Pepper, J. Worrell as Col. Chesham, Paul Bedford as Maj. Mansfelt, William Cullenford as Darby Donoghue, John Sanders as Rafferty, Emma Harding as Magdelene, Sarah Woolgar as Aggy/ Scenery by Pitt & Johnstone/ Music by W. Forde/ Machinery by Mr. Cooper.

WHITE KNIGHT, THE// C 3a// Stuart Ogilvie// **Terry's**, Feb. 1898.

WHITE LIE, A// Ca.// Adap. by James Mortimer fr F of Henri Meilhac, L'Étè de St. Martin// **Novelty**, Nov. 1888.

WHITE LIE, A// D 3a// Sidney Grundy// **Court**, May 1889/ **Avenue**, Jan, 1893 in rev. vers.

WHITE MILLINER, THE// C 2a// Douglas Jerrold// **Cov. Garden**, Feb. 1841, with C. J. Mathews as Lord Ortolan, William Farren as Twilight, James Vining as Conway, Robert Keeley as Sneezum, Frank Matthews as Doddles, W. H. Payne as Muff, Miss Cooper as Lady Ortolan, Mme. Vestris as Albina, Mrs. Orger as Mrs. Mellowpear, Mrs. Humby as Betty/ Scenery by Grieve, T. Grieve & W. Grieve/ **Grecian**, June 1856, with Richard Phillips as Lord Ortolan, Eaton O'Donnell as Justice Twilight, F. Charles as Conway, John Manning as Sneezum, Jane Coveney as Albina, Ellen Hale as Lady Ortolan, Miss Johnstone as Mrs. Mellowpear, Harriet Coveney as Betty.

WHITE PASSPORT, THE// D 3a// n.a.// **Pavilion**, Mar. 1869.

WHITE PHANTOM, THE// D 2a// Cecil Pitt// **Marylebone**, Oct. 1867.

WHITE PILGRIM, THE// D 3a// Herman Merivale// **Court**, Feb. 1874, with George Rignold, Hermann Vezin, Miss Moodie, Mr. Bruce.

WHITE QUEEN, THE// D// J. W. Boulding// **Sad. Wells**, Oct. 1883/ **Grand**, July 1899 in rev. vers.

WHITE ROSE, THE// D 4a// Dram. by G. R. Sims & Robert Buchanan fr novel of Sir Walter Scott, Woodstock// **Adelphi**, Apr. 1892, with Leonard Boyne as Col. Everard, Charles Cartwright as Oliver Cromwell, George Cockburn as Col. Yarborough, Howard Russell as Capt. Pearson, Charles Collette as Tomkins, Mrs. Patrick Campbell as Elizabeth, Fuller Mellish as Charles Stuart, J. D. Beveridge as Sir Harry Lee, Mathew Brodie as Albert, Charles Dalton as Wildrake, Lionel Rignold as Holdfast, Evelyn Millard as Alice, Clara Jecks as Phoebe/ Scenery by Bruce Smith, W. Perkins, & Walter Hann/ Music by Henry Sprake/ Machines by H. Loftin.

WHITE SCARF, THE// n.a.// **Standard**, Jan. 1864.

WHITE SERGEANTS// n.a.// **Adelphi**, May 1850.

WHITE SLAVE, THE// D 5a// Bartley Campbell// **Grand**, Aug. 1884.

WHITE SLAVE, THE; OR, THE FLAG OF FREEDOM// D 2a// Edward Stirling// **Victoria**, Jan. 1850, with Mr. Henderson as Rebeliere, J. T. Johnson as Donation, Henry Dudley as Palerme, John Bradshaw as Bullseye, John Hudspeth as Whirligig, J. Howard as Holdfast, F. H. Henry as Mathieu, Mr. Hitchinson as Michael, Mrs. George Lee as Ellonorede, Mrs. Cooke as Madame Herbert, Miss Barrowcliffe as Jenny, Miss E. Morden as Negombo.

WHITE STOCKING, A// C 1a// Edward Ferris & Arthur Stewart// **Comedy**, Oct. 1896.

WHITE WOODS// n.a.// **Victoria**, Feb. 1852.

WHITEBAIT AT GREENWICH// F 1a// J. Maddison Morton// **Adelphi**, Nov. 1853/ **Olympic**, Aug. 1863, with Horace Wigan as Buzzard, Robert Soutar as Glimmer, Mr. Atkins as Small, Mrs. Leigh Murray as Mrs. Buzzard, Mrs. W. S. Emden as Sally.

WHITEFRIARS; OR, THE DAYS OF CLAUDE DUVAL// D pro & 3a// W. T. Townsend// **Grecian**, Sept. 1861, with George Gillett as Aumerle, R. H. Lingham as Charles II, Henry Grant as Titus Oates, Alfred Rayner as Col. Blood, William James as Mervyn, John Manning as Prance, Thomas Mead as Duval, Henry Power as Bradley, Jane Dawson as Lady Howard, Mary A. Victor as Patience, Miss Johnstone as Temperence, Ellen Hale as Aurora.

WHITER THAN SNOW// D 5a// Kenneth Lee// **Opera Comique**, June 1885.

WHO DID IT; OR, THE TRACK OF CRIME// D// n.a.// **Britannia**, Dec. 1867.

WHO IS SHE?// C 2a// Edward Stirling// **Olympic**, Nov. 1845, with Mr. Binge as Richelieu, Charles Boyce as Marquis de Javannes, James Browne as Antoine, Mr. Cockrill as Leopold, Mrs. Walter Lacy as Countess D'Egmont, Miss Treble as Baroness de Brion, Miss Mansfield as Du Barry.

WHO IS SYLVIA?// C 1a// Austin Fryers// **Opera Comique**, Nov. 1892.

WHO KILLED COCK ROBIN?// F 2a// Charles Mathews// **Haymarket**, Nov. 1865, with W. H. Chippendale as Tinkle, C. J. Mathews as Raggett, Mrs. C. J. Mathews as Satanella, Mrs. Edward Fitzwilliam as Hannah.

WHO SPEAKS FIRST?// C 1a// Charles Dance// **Lyceum**, Jan. 1849; Sept 1873, with F. Charles as Capt. Charles, E. F. Edgar as Militant, Georgina Pauncefort as Mrs. Militant, Miss Seymour as Smart/ **Sad. Wells**, Nov. 1852, with Henry Marston as Capt. Charles, William Belford as Militant, Mr. Williams as Potter, Mrs. Henry Marston as Mrs. Militant, Eliza Travers as Smart/ **Victoria**, Sept. 1871, with Walter Joyce as Capt. Charles, Henry Arnold as Millitant, Rose Cullen as Mrs. Millitant, Jenny Lee as Smart/ **Adelphi**, Feb. 1878, with Lydia Foote as Mrs. Militant, Clara Jecks as Smart, Robert Pateman as Capt. Charles, E. J. George as Ernest, E. J. George as Potter.

WHO STOLE THE POCKET-BOOK; OR, A DINNER FOR SIX// F 1a// J. Maddison Morton// **Adelphi**, Mar. 1852.

WHO WANTS A GUINEA?// C 5a// George Colman the younger// **Haymarket**, July 1867 (in 3a), with Mr. Rogers as Torrent, George Braid as Heartley, P. White as Hogmore, J. B. Buckstone as Gundy, Henry Howe as Barford, W. H. Chippendale as Oldskirt, W. H. Kendal as Sir Larry, Henry Compton as Bang, Mr. Clark as Carrydot, Walter Gordon as Henry, Ione Burke as Fanny, Mrs. Laws as Mrs. Glastonbury.

WHO'S A TRAVELLER?// F 1a// J. Howard & F. F. Cooper// **Grecian**, Mar. 1855, with Richard Phillips as Barker, John Manning as Dobbs, F. Charles as Parker, Eaton O'Donnell as Colly Wobble, Miss Johnstone as Mrs. Philpot, Maria Simpson as Miss Jones, Harriet Coveney as Mopps.

WHO'S MY HUSBAND?// F 1a// J. Maddison Morton// **Haymarket**, Oct. 1847; Dec. 1849, with Mr. Tilbury as Dr. Mull, Henry Howe as Capt. Jones, Robert Keeley as Tootles, Mrs. W. Clifford as Mrs. Thompson, Mrs. L. S. Buckingham as Sophonisba/ **Princess's**, Dec. 1847, with Mr. Tilbury as Dr. Mull, Henry Howe as Capt. Jones, Robert Keeley as Tootles, Mrs. W. Clifford as Mrs. Thompson, Mrs. L. S. Buckingham as Sophonisba, Mrs. Humby as Sally/ **Sad Wells**, Nov. 1861, with Miss Murray as Sir Harry, Ada Dyas as Sir Geoffrey, Mrs. Lingard as Lady Wentworth, Miss Hudspeth as Lady Alice, Mrs. Barrett as Dame Bridget.

WHO'S THE COMPOSER?// C 2a// J. Maddison Morton// **Haymarket**, Oct. 1845, with Mr. Tilbury as Marquis di Pompolo, Henry Holl as Count Fiesco, J. B. Buckstone as Cafarini, Charles Hudson as Filippo, Miss Fortescue as Dorothea, Julia Bennett as Carina.

WHO'S THE PAPA?// F 1a// n.a.// **Princess's**, Apr. 1845, with Henry Compton as Bottle, Mr. Hield as Gayton, Mr. Granby as Bernard, James Ranoe as Merton, F. C. Courtney as Eaton, Mrs. Brougham as Mrs. Bernard, Miss E. Honner as Charlotte, Mrs. Bosbroke as Mrs. Grubworm, Miss Somers as Hope.

WHO'S TO WIN; OR, THE POOL OF THE FOUR WILLOWS// n.a.// **Marylebone**, June 1877.

WHO'S TO WIN HIM// C 1a// T. J. Williams// **Lyceum**, Jan. 1868, with Minnie Sidney as Rose, Miss Goodall as Sylvia, Miss Armstrong as Minuetta, Miss L. Laidlaw as Musidora, Nellie Burton as Arabella, J. Nelson as Cyril, H. Thompson as Primrose, J. Francis as Squire Brushleigh.

WHO'S YOUR FRIEND? OR, THE QUEENSBURY FETE// C 2a// J. R. Planché// **Haymarket**, Aug. 1843, with Mr. Strickland as Viscount Leatherhead, Henry Holl as Sir Felix, C. J. Mathews as Fairland, J. Worrell as Thomas, Mme. Vestris as Countess of Rosedale, Mrs. Julia Glover as Lady Bab, Miss Carre as Mittens/ Scenery by George Morris/ **Sad. Wells**, May 1855, with Benjamin Webster as Fairland, George Cooke as Viscount Leatherhead, Frederick Moreland as Sir Felix, Robert Soutar as Thomas, Mme. Celeste as Countess of Rosedale, Mrs. Leman Rede as Lady Bab, Miss Robertson as Mittens.

WHO'S YOUR HATTER?// F 1a// n.a.// **Grecian**, Nov. 1855, with Eaton O'Donnell as Felt, John Manning as Gigle, F. Charles as Harry, Henry Power as Timothy, Miss Johnstone as Selina, Ellen Hale as Flora, Harriet Coveney as Patty.

WHO TOLD YOU SO? MILES' BOY!// F 1a// n.a.// **Victoria**, Apr. 1842, with Mr. James as Dr. Coates, William Seaman as Henry, Mr. Howard as Job, C. Williams as Reubin, Mr. Pilgrim as Miles, Mrs. Griffith as Mrs. Fidget, Helen Usher as Jane.

WHOM DO THEY TAKE ME FOR?// F// J. Maddison Morton// **Haymarket**, June 1847.

WHY DID YOU DIE?// F// C. J. Mathews// **Olympic**, Nov. 1837, with William Farren as Sir Andrew, C. J. Mathews as Frederick, John Brougham as Joseph, Miss Murray as Lady Caroline, Mrs. Keeley as Jenny; Aug. 1859, with Mr. Addison as Sir Andrew, George Vining as Stanley, Horace Wigan as Joseph, Mrs. Leigh Murray as Lady Caroline, Miss Cottrell as Emily, Mrs. W. S. Emden as Jenny/ **Cov. Garden**, Nov. 1839, with William Farren as Sir Andrew, C. J. Mathews as Stanly, John Brougham as Joseph, Miss Charles as Lady Caroline, Miss Lee as Emily, Mrs. Humby as Jenny.

WHY DON'T YOU MARRY? (a vers. of Why Don't She Marry)// T. H. Bayly// **Olympic**, Oct. 1837, with Robert Keeley as Tieck, James Bland as Corp. Max, Mme. Vestris as Lisette/ **Haymarket**, June 1838, with J. B. Buckstone as Tieck, Benjamin Webster as Corp. Max, Mme. Vestris as Lisette, Miss Gallot as Louise, Miss Holmes as Janet/ **Cov. Garden**, Oct. 1839, with Robert Keeley as Tieck, James Bland as Corp. Max, Mme. Vestris as Lisette, Miss Jackson as Louise, Miss Lane as Janet.

WHY SMITH LEFT HOME// F 3a// George Broadhurst// **Strand**, May 1899.

WHY WOMAN SINS// D// W. P. Sheen & Fred Jennings// **Terry's**, Jan. 1901.

WHY WOMEN WEEP// C 1a// F. W. Broughton// **Criterion**, Jan. 1888.

WICKED WIFE, A// D 1a// J. Courtney// **Haymarket**, Feb. 1857, with Henry Howe as De Langeais, Mr. Rogers as Rozaire, Henry Compton as Finot, Miss Reynolds as Julia, Julia Edouin as Jeanne, Mrs. Poynter as Mme. de Langeais, Ellen Sabine as Hilarine.

WICKED WORLD, THE// C 3a// W. S. Gilbert// **Haymarket**, Jan. 1873, with W. H. Kendal as Ethais, Edward Arnott as Phylion, J. B. Buckstone as Lutin, Madge Robertson (Mrs. Kendal) as Selenè, Amy Roselle as Dorine, Miss M. Lypton as Zayda, Blanche Henri as Neodie, Miss Francis as Locrine, Miss E. Harrison as Leila/ Scenery by John O'Conner/ Music by Mr. Hermann.

WIDOW BARNABY, THE// F 2a// Dram by T. H. Reynoldson fr novel of Mrs. Trollope// **Haymarket**, Jan. 1841, with J. W. Gough as Lord Mucklebury, J. Worrell as Singleton, J. Waldron as Sir John, John Webster as Col. Hubert, Frederick Vining as Maj. Allen, Henry Howe as Capt. Maintry, Mr. Caulfield as Templebrief, Benjamin Wrench as Snipe, Mrs. Julia Glover as Widow Barnaby, Miss Charles as Agnes, Mrs. Stanley as Mrs. Morton, Mrs. Frank Matthews as Betty.

WIDOW BEWITCHED, THE// C 1a// n.a.// Adap. fr F// **Princess's**, Dec. 1844, with Walter Lacy as Furnival, Mr. Granby as Lorimer, Mr. Henry as Joseph, Mrs. Stirling as Mrs. Lorimer, Miss E. Honner as Arabel, Miss Somers as Ellen.

WIDOW HUNT, A// n.a.// **St. James's**, Oct. 1867, with Henry Irving as Featherley, G. W. Blake as Icebrook, J. S. Clarke as Wellington de Boots, Arthur Brown as Trap, Ada Cavendish as Mrs. Featherley, Eleanor Bufton as Mrs. Swandown, Sophie Larkin as Mrs. de Boots, Kate Kearney as Fanny/ Scenery by Frederick Fenton/ **Strand**, Nov. 1868/ **Haymarket**, Sept. 1873, with Harry Crough as Featherly, Walter Joyce as Icebrooke, Mr. Barrier as Trap, Eleanor Bufton as Mrs. Swansdown, Linda Dietz as Mrs. Featherly, Emily Thorne as Mrs. De Boots, Fanny Morelli as Fanny.

WIDOW OF PALERMO; OR, THE LADY AND THE DEVIL// D 2a// n.a.// **Sad. Wells**, Dec. 1837, with Mr. Forrester as Wildlove, Mr. Nunn as Claudian, Mr. James as Raphael, Mr. Rogers as Jeremy, Miss Chartley as Negombo, Eliza Vincent as Zephyrina/ **Victoria**, May 1838, with Mr. Forester as Wildlove, Mr. Harwood as Clandian, William Davidge as Raphael, Mr. Vale as Jeremy, Mrs. John Parry as Zephyrina, Mrs. Corry as Negombo/ **Eng. Opera House** (Lyceum), Apr. 1843, with J. S. Balls as Col. Wildlove, Mr. Young as Claudian, Mr. Griffith as Rafael, J. Courtney as Jeremy, Mrs. Waylett as Zephyrina.

WIDOW WINSOME, THE// Alfred Colmore// **Criterion**, Oct. 1888.

WIDOWS BEWITCHED// n.a.// **Britannia**, Dec. 1854.

WIDOW'S VICTIM, THE// F// Charles Selby// **Grecian**, July 1856, with F. Charles as Twitter, John Manning as Tremain, Richard Phillips as Jeremiah Clipp, Tinsel John, Moustache, and as Strappado, Jane Coveney as Mrs. Rattleton, Ellen Hale as Mrs. Twitter, Harriet Coveney as Mme. Chatterly.

WIDOW'S WEEDS// C 1a// John Oxenford & Horace Wigan// **Strand**, Mar. 1870.

WIDOWER'S HOUSES// Play 3a// George Bernard Shaw// **Royalty**, Dec. 1892, with W. J. Robertson as Trench, Arthur Whittaker as Cokane, T. W. Percyval as Sartorius, James Welch as Lickcheese, Florence Farr as Blanche, N. de Silva as Annie.

WIFE, THE: A TALE OF MANTUA// D 5a// J. Sheridan Knowles// **Haymarket**, May 1838, with Edmund Glover as Leonardo Gonzaga, Charles Perkins as Ferrardo Gonzaga, Willis Jones as St. Pierre, Sheridal Knowles as Antonio, Mr. Hemming as Lorenzo, Mr. Hutchings as Count Florio, Mr. Santer as Hugo, Robert Strickland as Bartolo, T. F. Mathews as Bernardo, Miss Elphinstone as Mariana, Miss Gallot as Floribel; Mar. 1851, with E. L. Davenport as Leonardo, Henry Howe as Ferrardo, Charles Selby as Florio, James Wallack as

St. Pierre, Mr. Stuart as Antonio, John Parselle as Lorenzo, Mr. Hastings as Hugo, Henry Bedford as Bernardo, Laura Addison as Mariana, Mrs. L. S. Buckingham as Floribel/ **Sad. Wells,** May 1840, with Mr. Elvin as Leonardo Gonzago, Mr. Dry as Ferraro Gonzago, J. B. Hill as Count Florio, Mr. Williams as Antonio, Henry Marston as St. Pierre, Mr. Aldridge as Lorenzo, Mr. Thompson as Hugo, J. W. Collier as Bartolo, Mr. Richardson as Carlo, Charles Fenton as Mareo, Mrs. Robert Honner as Mariana, Mrs. J. F. Saville as Floribel; Nov. 1855, with Frederic Robinson as Leonardo Gonzago, Mr. Lunt as Ferrerdo Gonzago, Mr. Haywell as Count Florio, Henry Marston as St. Pierre, Mr. Barrett as Antonio, William Belford as Lorenzo, Mr. Lacy as Hugo, Lewis Ball as Bartolo, Margaret Eburne as Mariana, Caroline Parkes as Floribel/ **Princess's,** June 1845, with Leigh Murray as Leonardo Gonzaga, Mr. Lynne as Ferrardo Gonzaga, Charles Horn Jr. as Count Florio, William Wallack as St. Pierre, Mr. Archer as Antonio, W. H. Oxberry as Bartolo, Charlotte Cushman as Mariana, Miss E. Honner as Floribel; May 1847, with John Webster as Leonardo Gonzaga, John Ryder as Ferrardo Gonzaga, Augustus Harris as Count Florio, William Creswick as St. Pierre, Henry Hughes as Antonio, Charles Fisher as Lorenzo, S. Smith as Hugo, Samuel Cowell as Bartolo, Mrs. Butler (Fanny Kemble) as Mariana, Miss E. Honner as Floribel/ **Drury Lane,** Jan. 1851, with Mr. Cathcart as Leonardo Gonzago, Mr. Cooper as Ferardo Gonzago, Henry Butler as Count Florio, J. Neville as Antonio, James Anderson as St. Pierre, H. T. Craven as Lorenzo, Stephen Artaud as Bartolo, Robert Romer as Hugo, Fanny Vining as Mariana, Mrs. Barratt [sic] as Floribel/ **Grecian,** Oct. 1861, with Alfred Rayner, William James, Mr. Jackson, George Gillett, Henry Marston, R. H. Lingham, Mr. Costello, Jane Dawson, Lucrezia Hill/ **Astley's,** Oct. 1866, with Henry Vandenhoff as Leonardo, Basil Potter as Ferardo, Walter Ryder as Count Florio, Walter Joyce as Lorenzo, Mr. Dugarde as Antonio, W. Arthur as Bartolo, George Webster as Cosmo, Sophie Young as Mariana, Miss White as Floribel/ **Olympic,** May 1876, with Mrs. Rousby as Mariana, Miss Beaumont as Floribel, W. H. Fisher as Leonardo, Mr. Haywell as Ferrardo, Mr. Hallows as Count Florio, Henry Neville as St. Pierre, John Vollaire as Antonio, Lytton Sothern as Lorenzo, W. J. Hill as Bartolo.

WIFE, THE; OR, THE ONE WITNESS// D 2a// C. Z Barnett// **Victoria,** June 1846, with Roberts Tindell as Leyton, T. Fredericks as Bartram, E. F. Saville as Challoner, Walter Searle as Robert, Mr. Wilton as Ned, E. G. Burton as Swivel, Annette Vincent as Grace, Miss Backhous as Ruth, Eliza Terrey as Bell.

WIFE! CHILDREN! AND FRIENDS!; OR, THE SWEETS AND BITTERS OF LIFE// D 3a// n.a.// **Victoria,** Mar. 1843, with Mr. James as Capt. Hallington, Mr. Wilton as Lt. Murray, E. F. Saville as Melrose and as Abdallah, C. Williams as Hamed, John Gardner as Phelps, J. Howard as Goldberry, William Seaman as Edwin, John Dale as Barossa, Miss Martin as Ziska, Mrs. George Lee as Adelaide, Miss Wilton as Matilda, Miss Saddler as Mrs. Beauville/ Scenery by Morelli, Hawthorn & Mildenhall/ Music by W. J. Hill.

WIFE FOR A DAY, A// F 1a// W. Bayle Bernard// **Haymarket,** Mar. 1839, with Robert Strickland as Tucker, Walter Lacy as Montaguacker, Mr. Hill as Nathan, J. W. Gough as Willard, J. Worrell as Morton, Mrs. W. Clifford as Mrs. Tucker, Mrs. Frank Matthews as Angelique, Miss Gallot as Kezy.

WIFE FOR AN HOUR, A// C 1a// E. L. Blanchard// **Princess's,** May 1847, with Mr. Walton as Dumps, Mr. Granby as Quantum, James Vining as Collington, Samuel Cowell as Popps, Henry Compton as Gaiter, Mrs. Henry Hughes as Clara, Emma Stanley as Patty/ **Victoria,** May 1848, with J. Howard as Quantum, T. H. Higgie as Collington, Walter Searle as Popps, Mr. Hawkins as Dumps, Mrs. George Lee as Clara, Miss Burroughcliffe as Patty.

WIFE OF DIVES, THE// C 3a// S. X. Courte// **Opera Comique,** Nov. 1894.

WIFE OF SEVEN HUSBANDS, THE; OR, THE PEDLAR'S DREAM// D// George Almar// **Sad. Wells,** Apr. 1840, with Henry Marston as Lessarmour, Mr. Elvin as Laidlaw, Henry Hall as Gander, Mr. Dry as de Valence, Mrs. J. F. Saville as Gossamer, Charles Fenton as Saunders, George Burt as Shard, Mr. Aldridge as Langton, J. B. Hill as George, Miss Richardson as Margaret, Mrs. Morgan as Amy, Mrs. Richard Barnett as Patience.

WIFE OR NO WIFE// D 5a// John Heraud// **Haymarket,** July 1855, with William Cullenford as Earl Brookland, Mr. Rogers as Earl Norcliffe, Barry Sullivan as Lord Ormond, Henry Howe as Pierrepoint, William Farren as Sir Frank, Edwin Villiers as Urban, W. H. Chippendale as Lovegrove, Edith Heraud as Olympia, Miss Swanborough as Charissa, Ellen Chaplin as Dorié, Mrs. Poynter as Mary/ Scenery by George Morris & John O'Conner/ Machines by Oliver Wales.

WIFE, OR WIDOW?// F 1a// C. Long// **Grecian,** Apr. 1846, with Edwin Dixon as Capt. Impeton, T. W. Edmonds as Frederick, Frederick Robson as Dumbitton, Mr. Melvin as Crosser, Miss M. A. Crisp as Maude, Miss Johnstone as Constance.

WIFE OR WIDOW?// D 4a// Clifton Tayleure// **Grand,** Feb. 1886.

WIFE WELL WON, A// D 3a// Edmund Falconer// **Haymarket,** Dec. 1867, with E. A. Sothern as Bressange, J. B. Buckstone as Alexandre, P. White as Lavalle, Mr. Rogers as Goulard, George Braid as Latour, Madge Robertson as Marguerite de Launay, W. H. Kendal as Marquis de Chamont, Henry Howe as Count de Launay/ Scenery by John O'Conner, Parraud, & Maltby/ Machines by Oliver Wales/ Gas by F. Hope.

WIFE'S DEVOTION, A// D Pro & 3a// J. H. Darnley & G. M. Fenn// **West London,** Apr.

1896.

WIFE'S EVIDENCE, THE// D// C. H. Hazlewood// **Britannia**, May 1872.

WIFE'S FIRST LESSON, A (a vers. of Day after the Wedding)// F 1a// n.a.// **Sad. Wells**, Oct. 1862, with Henry Forrester as Col. Freelove, Alfred Montague as Lord Rivers, Charles Crook as James, Catherine Lucette as Lady Elizabeth/ **St. James's**, Jan. 1877, with F. H. Macklin as Col. Freelove, C. Stanford as Lord Rivers, E. Edmonds as Davies, Edith Challis as Lady Freelove, Maria Daly as Mrs. Davies.

WIFE'S JOURNAL, A// C 1a// T. W. Robertson// **Olympic**, Feb. 1855, with Samuel Emery as Brown, Henry Leslie as Harcourt, Miss Marston as Mrs. Brown.

WIFE'S PORTRAIT, THE// Adap. by Westland Marston fr G// **Haymarket**, Jan. 1862, with Henry Howe as Lindsay, William Farren as Dexter, Edwin Villiers as Capt. Morton, Mrs. Wilkins as Miss Lindsay, Mrs. Charles Young as Clara, Eliza Weekes as Mrs. Morton, Miss Stoneham as Janet, Miss Lovell as Ann/ **Sad. Wells**, Apr. 1863, with Hermann Vezin as Lindsay, Charles Maynard as Dexter, Mr. Britten as Capt. Morton, Mrs. Charles Young as Clara, Miss Rawlings as Miss Lindsay, Miss Russelle as Mrs. Morton/ **Princess's**, 1864.

WIFE'S REVENGE, A// D// n.a.// **Surrey**, Nov. 1857.

WIFE'S SACRIFICE, A// D 5a// Adap. by Sidney Grundy & Sutherland Edwards fr F of A. P. Dennery & Edmond Tarbé, Martyre// **St. James's**, May 1886, with W. H. Kendal as Julien, Clifford Cooper as Adm. de Marche, John Hare as Drake, Charles Brookfield as Palmieri, Herbert Waring as Burel, Robert Cathcart as Maltar, Mrs. W. H. Kendal as Isabelle, Georgina Pauncefort as Mme. de la Marche, Miss Vane as Mlle. Palmieri, Miss Webster as Pauline/ Scenery by W. Harford.

WIFE'S SECRET, THE// D 5a// George Lovell// **Haymarket**, Jan. 1848, with Henry Howe as Lord Arden, Charles Kean as Sir Walter, Benjamin Webster as Sneed, A. Brindal as Harrington, Mr. Rogers as Brouillard, Miss Reynolds as Neville, Mrs. Charles Kean as Lady Eveline, Mrs. Keeley as Maud/ Scenery by P. Phillips & George Morris/ **Princess's**, Oct. 1850, with Frederick Belton as Lord Arden, Charles Kean as Sir Walter, Mr. Addison as Sneed, Frederick Cooke as Harrington, Alfred Wigan as Brouillard, Miss Robertson as Neville, John Cathcart as Harry, Mrs. Charles Kean as Lady Eveline, Mrs. Keeley as Maud/ **Drury Lane**, Feb. 1861, with George Everett as Lord Arden, Charles Kean as Sir Walter, J. F. Cathcart as Sneed, Frank Barsby as Harrington, William Belford as Brouillard, Miss Chapman as Neville, Mrs. Charles Kean as Lady Eveline, Miss N. Chapman as Maud/ **Surrey**, Nov. 1868/ **Olympic**, Mar. 1877, with Mr. Avondale as Lord Arden, Henry Neville as Sir Walter, Robert Pateman as Sneed, Mr. Sartaud [Stephen Artaud?] as Etheridge, Dibdin Culver as Baroque, John Vollaire as Peter, Patty Chapman as Keppel, T. G. Warren as Robert, Bella Pateman as Lady Eveline, Camille Dubois as Maud/ **St. James's**, Apr. 1888, with Lewis Waller as Lord Arden, W. H. Kendal as Sir Walter, Mr. Mackintosh as Sneed, Mr. Bedford as Etheridge, E. Hendrie as Baroque, W. L. Branscombe as Peter, Charles Burleigh as Keppel, Mrs. W. H. Kendal as Lady Eveline, Fanny Brough as Maud/ Scenery by W. Harford/ Music by F. Schoening/ Prod. by John Hare.

WIFE'S TRAGEDY, THE// D 5a// Mrs. Edward Thomas// **Standard**, Dec. 1870.

WIFE'S TRIALS, A; OR, FIVE YEARS OF A MURDERER'S LIFE// D 3a// J. Rigday// **Sad. Wells**, Dec. 1837, with Mr. James as Foster, Mr. Rumball of Yeddort, Mr. Campbell as Levi, Mr. Rogers as Trap, Mr. Scarbrow as Isaac, S. Smith as Wat, Mr. Nunn as Mayflower, Mr. Gay as Burton, Miss Watkins as Margaret, Miss Chartley as Mary, Miss Pitt as Nancy/ Scenery by Mr. Battie/ Music by W. Montgomery.

WIFEY// C 3a// Adap. by James Mortimer fr F// **Strand**, Nov. 1885.

WIG AND GOWN// D 3a// James Albery// **Globe**, Apr. 1874, with Mr. Robinson as James Strickett, Lionel Brough as Sonbyson Sicl, J. L. Toole as Hammond Coote, Miss Glover as Albert Coote, Arthur Cecil as Justice Jones, Maria Daly as Miss Kenreutie, Carlotta Addison as Victoria Coote, Maria Harris as Susan.

WILD BOY, THE// D// M. Leclercq// **Olympic**, Jan. 1846, with M. Leclercq as the Wild Boy, J. Waldron as Baron Leitzmar, Spencer Forde as Czartoritski, Mr. Johnson as Cratmiaw, Mr. Cockrill as Carl, Robert Romer as Gawinski, Mr. Turnour as the Hermit, Mr. Darcie as Pletzke, Miss Hamilton as the Countess, Mrs. Griffith as Mrs. Gawinski, Miss Leclercq as Marriette, Miss Ward as Jejowski.

WILD BOY OF BOHEMIA, THE// D// John Walker// **Sad. Wells**, Oct. 1842, with Mr. Dry as Baron Leitzimer, C. J. Bird as Cratzlaw, Mr. Lambe as Czartoryski, Mr. Richardson as Plotzko, Mr. Aldridge as Alberto, P. Williams as Gawinski, John Herbert as Carl, Charles Fenton as Orloff, J. W. Collier as Wild Boy, Fanny Morelli as Countess Czartoryski, Mrs. Andrews as Jejouski, Mrs. J. W. Collier as Marinette, Mrs. Henry Marston as Mme. Gawinski/ Scenery by F. Fenton/ Machines by Mr. Cawdery/ Music by Isaac Collins.

WILD CHARLEY// D 2a// C. H. Hazlewood// **Britannia**, Oct. 1867.

WILD DUCK, THE// Play 5a// Adap. by William Archer fr Norw. of Henrik Ibsen// **Royalty**, May 1894/ **Globe**, [in trans. by Mrs. Archer] May 1897, with Leonard Outram as Werle, Courtenay Thorpe as Gregers Werle, James Welch as Old Ekdal, Laurence Irving as Hialmar Ekdal, Kate Phillips as Gina, Winifred Fraser as Hedvig, Charles Charrington as Relling, Leonard Calvert as Molvik.

WILD DUCKS// F 1a// Edward Stirling// **Marylebone**, Jan. 1850.

WILD FLOWER OF THE PRAIRIE, THE; OR, A FATHER'S LEGACY// D 2a// Frank Fuller & Harry Richardson// **Elephant & Castle**, Sept. 1877.

WILD GOOSE, A// D 5a// Edit. by Dion Boucicault fr orig. of J. Lester Wallack// **Haymarket**, Apr. 1867, with E. A. Sothern as Devlin, J. B. Buckstone as Bubb, Mrs. Chippendale as Lady Frances, Caroline Hill as Lady Merivale, Henry Howe as Col. Ferrers, Walter Gordon as Fane, Ione Burke as Aurelia, Fanny Wright as Pettifer, Mr. Rogers as Walsh, Mrs. Laws as Mrs. Pennycuick/ Scenery by John O'Conner & George Morris/ Machines by Oliver Wales/ Gas by J. Hope/ Music by Mr. Wallerstein.

WILD HORSE OF SAVOY, THE; OR, POVERTY AND CRIME// D 2a// n.a.// **Sad. Wells**, May 1854, with George Vining as Felix, James Worrell as Rosalvi, Edwin Yarnold as Jeronymo, Mr. Judd as Baptista, Mrs. Barrett as Melina, Miss Lavine as Genevieve, Miss Macarthy as Claudine, Miss Woolf as Ninette.

WILD IRISH GIRL, THE// D// G. D. Pitt// **Victoria**, Sept. 1842, with Mr. Howard as Squire Lincott, C. Williams as Lt. Sinclair, William Seaman as as Maj. Meerrcham, John Gardner as Addlepate, Mrs. George Lee as Ellen, Mrs. Griffiths as Lady Lincott, Eliza Vincent as Shelah/ Music by W. J. Hill.

WILD OATS; OR, THE STROLLING GENTLEMAN// C// John O'Keefe// **Haymarket**, Nov. 1837, with E. W. Elton as Rover, Robert Strickland as Sir George, T. P. Cooke as Dory, J. B. Buckstone as Sim, Benjamin Webster as Smooth, Mr. Hemming as Harry, T. F. Mathews as Lamp, J. Worrell as Trap, Mrs. Nisbett as Lady Amaranth, Mrs. Tayleure as Amelia, Mrs. Humby as Jane; Apr. 1841, with James Wallack as Rover, Robert Strickland as Sir George, Henry Howe as Harry, Henry Wallack as Dory, Mr. Gallot as Gammon, Benjamin Webster as Smooth, W. H. Oxberry as Sim, George Bennett as Banks, T. F. Mathews as Lamp, Mr. Bishop as Trap, Mrs. Stirling as Lady Amaranth, Mrs. Stanley as Amelia, Priscilla Horton as Jane; Mar. 1851, with James Wallack as Rover, John Parselle as Harry, Mr. Lambert as Sir George, James Bland as Dory, Henry Bedford as Smooth, J. B. Buckstone as Sim, Mr. Woolgar as Gammon, Mr. Caulfield as Lamp, Miss Reynolds as Lady Amaranth, Priscilla Horton as Jane, Mrs. Stanley as Amelia; Oct. 1856, with W. H. Chippendale as Sir George, James Murdoch as Rover, Mr. Rogers as Dory, Edwin Villiers as Harry, Henry Compton as Smooth, J. B. Buckstone as Sim, George Braid as Banks, William Cullenford as Gammon, Miss Talbot as Lady Amaranth, Mrs. Griffiths as Amelia, Bella Copeland as Jane; Oct. 1873 (in 3a), with W. H. Stephens as Sir George, W. H. Vernon as Rover, F. Charles as Harry, S. Hargreaves as Dorey, T. Thorne as Smooth, Edward Terry as Lamp, H. Cox as Trap, George Belmore as Gammon, Eleanor Bufton as Lady Amaranth, Emily Thorne as Amelia, Bella Goodall as Jane/ **Drury Lane**, Feb. 1840, with William Dowton as Sir George, John Lee as Harry, Mr. Waldron as Banks, Mr. Vining as Rover, W. Bennett as Dory, J. W. Ray as Gammon, Henry Compton as Smooth, W. H. Oxberry as Lamp, Mr. Attwood as Trap, Edwin Yarnold as Twitch, W. J. Hammond as Sim, Jane Mordaunt as Lady Amaranth, Miss Daly as Jane, Mrs. W. West as Amelia/ **Princess's**, Dec. 1844, with James Wallack as Rover, Mr. Fitzjames as Harry, Mr. Granby as Sir George, Henry Wallack as John, W. H. Oxberry as Sim, Mr. Walton as Gammon, Robert Honner as Lamp, Henry Compton as Ephraim, Mrs. Stirling as Lady Amaranth, Mrs. Brougham as Jane, Mrs. Fosbroke as Amelia/ **Sad. Wells**, Mar. 1845, with A. Younge as Sir George, Mr. Morton as Harry, Samuel Phelps as Rover, George Bennett as Zanka, Henry Marston as John, Mr. Williams as Gammon, Mr. Coreno as Pim, G. F. Forman as Smooth, Mr. Sharp as Lamp, Charles Fenton as Zachariah, Mrs. Mary Warner as Lady Amaranth, Mrs. Henry Marston as Amelia, Miss Lebatt as Jane/ **Criterion**, May 1891.

WILD PRIMROSE, THE// C 4a// n.a.// **Novelty**, Feb. 1891.

WILD RABBIT, THE// F 3a// George Arliss// **Criterion**, July 1899.

WILDERNESS, THE// C 3a// H. V. Esmond// **St. James's**, Apr. 1901.

WILDFIRE DICK// C// n.a.// **Sad. Wells**, Nov. 1837, with S. Palmer as Dick, Mr. Rogers as Drill, Thomas Lee as Spark, Mr. Scarbrow as Jones, Mr. Pateman as Ned, Lavinia Melville as Fanny, Miss Williams as Widow Belmont, Miss Vernon as Lucy.

WILDFIRE NED// n.a.// **Britannia**, Dec. 1866.

WILFUL MURDERS// F 1a// Thomas Higgie// **Princess's**, July 1847.

WILFUL WARD, THE// C 1a// J. P. Wooler// **Strand**, Nov. 1864.

WILL, THE// C 3a// Frederic Reynolds// **Cov. Garden**, June 1838, with George Bartley as Sir Solomon, George Bennett as Mandeville, Mr. Vining as Howard, Drinkwater Meadows as Veritas, Mr. Tilbury as Realize, John Ayliffe as Old Copsley, Miss Taylor as Albina, Mrs. W. Clifford as Mrs. Rigid, Miss E. Phillips as Cicely, Miss Garrick as Deborah/ **Sad. Wells**, May 1849, with A. Younge as Sir Solomon, Henry Mellon as Mandeville, Henry Marston as Howard, William Hoskins as Veritas, Mr. Williams as Realize, Miss Cooper as Albina, Mrs. Henry Marston as Mrs. Rigid, Julia St. George as Cicely, Miss Stephens as Deborah.

WILL AND THE WAY, THE// C 1a// J. H. McCarthy// **Avenue**, May 1890.

WILL HE COME HOME AGAIN?// C// Mrs. Bernard Whislaw// **Avenue**, Mar. 1891/ **Princess's**, May 1892.

WILLIAM AND SUSAN// C 3a// Adap. fr Douglas Jerrold's Black-Eyed Susan// **Drury Lane**, Mar. 1859.

WILLIAM AND SUSAN// D 3a// Adap. by W. G. Wills fr Douglas Jerrold's Black-Eyed Susan// **St. James's**, Oct. 1880, with John Hare as The Admiral, J. H. Barnes as Capt. Crosstree, Mr. Draycott as Lt. Pearce, W. H. Kendal as William, Robert Cathcart as White, T. N. Wenman as Truck, Mr. Mackintosh as Robert Mrs. W. H. Kendal as Susan, Kate Phillips as Polly/ Scenery by Gordon & Harford/ Music by Mr. Schoening.

WILLIAM SIMPSON, THE// C 1a// Percy Fitzgerald// **Olympic**, Dec. 1872, with Arthur Wood as Gaychicken, C. W. Garthorne as Jones, A. Knight as Younghusband, Miss J. Baber as Mrs. Mildman, Miss N. Bromley as Fanny, Miss N. Phillips as Georgina.

WILLIAM TELL; OR, THE HERO OF SWITZERLAND// D 4a// Adap. by Sheridan Knowles fr G of Friedrich Schiller// **Cov. Garden**, Apr. 1837, with George Bennett as Gesler, Mr. Harris as Sarnem, Mr. Tilbury as Struth, Benjamin Webster as Braun, Mr. Ray as Rodolph, John Collett as Lutold, Mr. Dubouchet as Gerard, Miss Lee as Anneli, Miss Nicholson as Agnes, Sheridan Knowles as William Tell, Miss Lane as Albert, Mr. Thompson as Melchtal, Mr. Beckett as Pierre, John Pritchard as Michael, Mrs. W. West as Emma/ **Sad. Wells**, June 1837, with Mr. Hicks as Gesler, J. Dunn as Sarnem, Mr. Tilbury as Struth, Mr. Conquest as Braun, Mr. Scarbrow as Rodolph, Mrs. Harris as Annelli, Miss Melville as Agnes, John Dale as William Tell, Master Melville as Albert, John Pritchard as Michael, Mrs. W. West as Anna; Mar. 1840, with Mr. Dry as Gesler, Mr. Aldridge as Sarnem, W. D. Broadfoot as Struth, J. W. Collier as Braun, Mrs. J. F. Saville as Anneli, Miss Pincott as Agnes, Henry Marston as William Tell, Miss Hicks as Albert, Miss Richardson as Emma; Jan. 1846, with George Bennett as Gesler, A. Younge as Struth, Mr. Morton as Sarnem, HenryScharf as Braun, Henry Marston as Michael, Mr. Williams as Waldman, Miss Huddart as Annette, Miss Lebatt as Agnes, Samuel Phelps as William Tell, Henry Mellon as Melchtal, Miss Stephens as Albert, Mrs. Mary Warner as Emma/ **Haymarket**, Aug. 1840, with Henry Wallack as Geiser, J. W. Gough as Sarnem, Robert Strickland as Struth, David Rees as Braun, Priscilla Horton as Anneli, Mrs. Stirling as Agnes, W. C. Macready as Tell, George Bennett as Melchtal, J. Worrell as Erni, T. F. Mathews as Waldman, John Webster as Michael, Henry Howe as Jagheli, Mrs. W. Clifford as Emma/ **Victoria**, Oct. 1846, with Mr. Archer as Gesler, F. C. Courtney as Sarnem, J. Howard as Struth, G. F. Forman as Braun, Annette Vincent as Agnes, Miss Fielding as Annelli, David Osbaldiston as William Tell, Miss Backhous as Albert, E. G. Burton as Waldemar, J. C. Bird as Michael, Mrs. Henry Vining as Emma/ **Surrey**, Feb. 1847, with Henry West Betty/ **Lyceum**, Jan. 1857, with Mr. McLien as Gesler, G. H. Burt as Sarnem, Mr. Fredericks as Rodolph, Charles Dillon as William Tell, Maria Wilton as Albert, Mr. Clifton as Erni, J. G. Shore as Michael, Mrs. Buckingham White as Emma.

WILLIAM TELL// D 5a// Adap. by Sheridan Knowles fr G of Schiller// **Olympic**, Feb. 1852, with Charles Diddear as Gesler, Charles Bender as Sarnem, Mr. Clifton as Struth, W. Shalders as Braun, Miss Adams as Anneli, Mrs. Julia Glover as Agnes, Henry Farren as William Tell, Louisa Howard as Albert, George Cooke as Melchtal, Mr. Sanger as Waldman, William Hoskins as Michael, Mrs. Barrett as Emma, Isabel Adams as Annette, Miss Wyndham as Julie/ Music by J. Barnard/ **Drury Lane**, Feb. 1860 (in 3a), with Charles Dillon as William Tell, Samuel Emery as Gesler, Miss Thirlwall as Albert, Mr. Mellon as Melchtal, Mr. Peel as Erni, Mr. Delafield as Michael, Miss Page as Emma.

WILLIE THE WANDERER// n.a.// **Marylebone**, Aug. 1866.

WILLIE REILLY AND HIS OWN DEAR COLLEEN BAWN// n.a.// **Marylebone**, May 1861.

WILLIKIN AND HIS DINAH// T 3a// J. Stirling Coyne// **Haymarket**, Mar. 1854.

WILLIS, MRS// F 3a// H. Malyon-Hesford// **Strand**, Mar 1900.

WILLOW COPSE, THE// D 5a// Dion Boucicault// **Adelphi**, Dec. 1849, with William Cullenford as Sir Richard, Henry Hughes as Luke, J. Worrell as Arthur, Edward Wright as Augustus, O. Smith as Hulks, Paul Bedford as Staggers, Mme. Celeste as Rose, Ellen Chaplin as Lucy, Sarah Woolgar as Meg; Oct. 1859, with Benjamin Webster, Sarah Woolgar, David Fisher/ **Haymarket**, Aug. 1850, with same cast/ **Princess's**, Nov. 1869.

WILLOW MARSH, THE// D 3a// Adolphe Faucquez// **Sad. Wells**, Oct. 1862, with James Johnstone as Marquis de Foix, E. F. Edgar as Eugene, Henry Forrester as Roux, W. H. Stephens as Count de Briancourt, Mr. Mowbray as Julian, Lewis Ball as Monaco, Charles Bender as Pierre, Sophie Miles as Marchioness de Foix, Miss Clements as Adele, Fanny Rivers as Julie.

WILLOW POOL, THE; OR, THE SHADOW OF DEATH// D 2a// n.a.// **Grecian**, Nov. 1870.

WINDMILL, THE// F 1a// Edward Morton// **Drury Lane**, Jan. 1842, with Morris Barnett as Marquis de Roueville, Robert Keeley as Low, Edwin Yarnold as Peter, Mrs. Selby as Marchioness de Roueville, Mrs. Keeley as Marian, Miss Sidney as Nancy/ **Sad. Wells**, Aug. 1847, with Henry Horncastle as Marquis Roueville, J. W. Collier as Low, Charles Fenton as Peter, Miss Newcombe as Marian, Miss Webb as Nancy/ **Olympic**, June 1858, with George Cooke as Marquis of Roueville, Lewis Ball as Low, J. H. White as Peter, Miss Castleton as Marchioness of Roueville, Mrs. W. S. Emden as Marian; Jan. 1866, with Frederick Younge as Low,

W. H. Stephens as Marquis of Roueville, Mrs. Stephens as Marchioness of Roueville, Lydia Foote as Marian.

WINDMILLS// C 3a// W. K. Tarpey// **Comedy**, June 1901.

WINDSOR CASTLE// D Pro & 3a// Frederick Marchant// **East London**, Feb. 1873.

WINE DOES WONDERS// C// J. Cobb// **Sad. Wells**, Nov. 1845, with Henry Marston as Young Mirable, A. Younge as Old Mirable, Samuel Buckingham as Duretete, Henry Scharf as Patit, R. H. Lingham as Dugard, Miss Cooper as Bissare, Miss Huddart as Oriana.

WINE HOUSE OF THE VALLEY, THE; OR, THE SOLDIER'S CURSE// D// J. P. Taylor// **Sad. Wells**, Nov. 1839, with Mr. Aldridge as Col. Churchill, Mr. Dry as Morley, Mr. Cathcart as Frank, Mr. Stilt as Seldin, Charles Montgomery as Oliver, Mr. Morgan as Lisle, Henry Hall as Pedrosa, Mr. Williams as Balthazar, Mrs. Robert Honner as Marie, Miss Pincott as Jacintha, Miss Cooke as Deborah.

WINGS OF THE STORM// D Pro & 3a// R. J. Barlow & William North// **Globe**, Oct. 1891.

WINIFRED'S VOW// C 3a// John Douglas// **Novelty**, Mar. 1892.

WINKHOPPER'S PLOT// F// V. C. Rolfe// **Novelty**, June 1897.

WINNING CARD, THE// C// Adap. by Arthur Wood fr F// **Haymarket**, Oct. 1867, with Mr. Rogers as Baron de Rocombole, P. White as Mendheim, Walter Gordon as Florian, Henry Compton as Pepin, Miss Dalton as Cecile, Mrs. Laws as Euphemia, Mrs. Edward Fitzwilliam as Jacqueline.

WINNING DEFEAT// D 4a// Duncan Campbell & Marcus Quaire// **Novelty**, May 1891.

WINNING HAND, THE// D 5a// George Conquest & St. Aubyn Miller// **Surrey**, Sept. 1895.

WINNING HAZARD, A// C 1a// J. P. Wooler// **POW**, Apr. 1865.

WINNING SUIT, THE// D 4a// Lewis Filmore// **Princess's**, Feb. 1863, with W. H. Stephens as King Alphonso, Hermann Vezin as Roderic, Henry Marston as Pedro, A. Wallace as Villa Nova, Amy Sedgwick as Orelia, Mrs. Henry Marston as Hostess, Miss Murray as Francesca.

WINTER IN LONDON; OR, A DEVILISH GOOD FRIEND// D 3a// W. E. Suter// **Grecian**, Apr. 1854, with Richard Phillips as Gabriel Wenworth, Charles Horn as Harry Dashfield, T. Roberts as Winford, Charles Rice as Stubble, Jane Coveney as _____, Eaton O'Donnell as Count Shikery, Harriet Coveney as Adeline, Agnes De Warde as Ellen, Jane Coveney as Marian/ Scenery by Mr. Jones/ Music by T. Berry/ Machines by Mr. Smith/ Prod. by R. Phillips.

WINTER'S TALE, THE// TC// William Shakespeare// **Cov. Garden**, May 1837, with W. C. Macready as Leontes, John Pritchard as Camillo, George Bennett as Antigonus, Mr. Harris as Cleomenes, John Dale as Polixines, William Farren as Autolycus, Benjamin Webster as Clown, E. W. Elton as Florizel, Helen Faucit as Hermione, Eliza Vincent as Perdita, Mrs. Julia Glover as Paulina, Mrs. W. West as Emilia, Mrs. Sarah Garrick as Hero; Sept. 1837, with same cast, except W. H. Payne as Dion, James Anderson as Florizel, Charles Diddear as Polixenes/ **Sad. Wells**, Nov. 1845, with Samuel Phelps as Leontes, Frank Graham as Camillo, George Bennett as Antigonus, Mr. Morton as Cleomenes, Mr. Warde as Dion, Edward Knight as Phocion, Charles Fenton as Thasius, Henry Mellon as Polixenes, Henry Marston as Florizel, R. H. Lingham as Archidamus, Mr. Williams as Shepherd, Henry Scharf as Clown, A. Younge as Autolycus, Mrs. Mary Warner as Hermione, Miss Cooper as Perdita, Mrs. Henry Marston as Paulina; July 1863, with Frederic Robinson as Leontes, Samuel Perfitt as Camilio, Henry Bradford as Antigonus, C. Alden as Cleomenes, W. Mowbray as Dion, J. Robins as Polixenes, Walter Joyce as Florizel, Mr. Tapping as Archidamus, Charles Fenton as Clown, Mr. Barrett as Autolycus, Miss Atkinson as Hermione, Marion Jones as Perdita, Mrs. Barrett as Paulina, Bessie Heath as Emilia/ **Marylebone**, Aug. 1847, with Mrs. Mary Warner, Frank Graham, James Johnstone, George Vining/ **Princess's**, Apr. 1856, with Charles Kean as Leontes, Ellen Terry as Mamillius, Frank Graham as Camillo, Mr. Cooper as Antigonus, Mr. Cathcart as Cleomenes, George Everett as Dion, John Ryder as Polixenes, Caroline Heath as Florizel, Henry Mellon as Archidamus, Kate Terry as Shepherd's servant, John Pritt Harley as Autolycus, Frederick Cooke as Time, Mrs. Charles Kean as Hermione, Carlotta Leclercq as Perdita, Mrs. Ternan as Paulina, Miss Clifford as Emilia/ Scenery by Grieve, Walter Gordon, F. Lloyds, Cuthbert, Dayes, Morgan, & G. Gordon/ Music by J. L. Hatton/ Machines by G. Hodsdon/ **Drury Lane**, Oct. 1878, with Agnes Robertson, John Ryder/ **Lyceum**, Sept. 1887, with Johnston Forbes Robertson as Leontes, John Maclean as Camillo, George Warde as Antigonus, Arthur Lewis as Cleomenes, F. H. Macklin as Polixines, Fuller Mellish as Florizel, W. H. Stevens as Old Shepherd, J. Anderson as Clown, Charles Collette as Autolycus, Sophie Eyre as Paulina, Helen Dacre as Emilia, Mary Anderson as Hermione and Perdita.

WINTERBOTTOMS, THE// F 1a// W. T. Moncrief// **Victoria**, Dec. 1838, with Mr. Johnstone as Gotobed, Mr. Forester as Jekylle, W. J. Hammond as Jeffrey, John Parry as Dobson, Miss Darion as Lady Winterbottom, Mrs. J. B. Hill as Celestine/ **St. James's**, Dec. 1859, with A. Denial as Gotobed, Charles Young as Jeffrey, C. H. Wilkenson as Jeykell, J. Francis as Dobson, Henry Reeves as Sgt. Crank, Nelly Moore as Celestina, Mrs. Manders as Lady Winterbottom.

WISDOM OF THE WISE, THE// C 3a// "J. O. Hobbes" (Mrs. P. M. Craigie)// **St. James's**, Nov. 1900, with George Alexander as Duke of St. Asaph, H. B. Irving as Lord Appleford, Wilfred Draycott as Bistern, Arthur Elwood as Wuthering, H. H. Vincent as Bradgers, A. E. Matthews as Romney, Fay Davis as Duchess of St. Asaph, Miss Granville as Mrs. Wuthering, Margaret Halstan as Mrs. Bistern, Julie Opp as Amabel, Henrietta Cowen as Mrs. Lynton/ Scenery by Walter Hann.

WISHING GLEN// n.a.// **Britannia**, June 1863.

WITCH, THE// D// Adap. by C. M. Rae fr G of Arthur Fitger, Die Hexe// **Princess's**, Oct. 1887 (in 4a vers.), with Edmund Gurney as Sir Rupert, John Beauchamp as Simeon, F. Grove as Xaver, Forbes Dawson as Folko, F. Dowse as Fr. Mathias, E. W. Thomas as Eilhart, Henry De Solla as Wolfram, T. C. Dwyer as Friedrich, Mrs. C. M. Rae as Lady Alma, Miss Beckett as Gela, Gertrude Warden as Thecla, Miss Lyndhurst as Olga, Florence Leslie as Adda, Jenny Lee as Elsa, Sophie Eyre as Lady Thalea/ **St. James's**, Nov. 1887 (in 5a vers.), with Henry Neville as Sir Rupert, A. Beaumont as Simeon, R. De Cordova as Xaver, Forbes Dawson as Folko, Mr. Staveley as Father Mathias, E. W. Thomas as Eilhart, S. Charteris as Wolfram, A. E. Aynesworth as Friedrich, Mrs. C. Marsham Rae as Lady Alma, Grace Arnold as Gela, Maud Cathcart as Thecla, Miss K. Lyndhurst as Olga, Sophie Eyre as Lady Thalea/ Music by Mr. Schoening, Prod. by Herbert Cathcart.

WITCH FINDER, THE: A CHRONICLE OF ANCIENT SALEM// D 3a// Robert Buchanan// **Sad. Wells**, Oct. 1864, with Alice Marriott as Elijah, George Melville as Holt, Charles Horsman as Vane, W. S. Foote as Flaxmore, W. H. Drayton as Jones, William Artaud as Heywood, John Mordaunt as Purvis, W. H. Courtley as Clown, Ellen Beaufort as Ruth, Lizzie Harrison as Hester, Mrs. Stevenson as Mistress Brogden/ Scenery by W. Broadfoot/ Machines by Henry Ellis.

WITCH OF DERNCLEUGH, THE// Dram. by J. R. Planché fr novel of Sir Walter Scott, Guy Mannering// **Eng. Opera House** (Lyceum), July 1838, with A. Brindal as Col. Mannering, Mr. Burnett as Hazlewood, Mr. Frazer as Henry Bertram, Mr. Baker as Dinmont, R. McIan as Dirk, Mr. Turnour as Dirkman, W. Bennett as Glossin, Henry Compton as Sampson, S. Jones as Gabriel, Lavinia Melville as Julia, Mme. Simon as Meg Merrilies.

WITCH OF WINDERMERE, THE// C 1a// Charles Selby// **Marylebone**, Dec. 1848.

WITCHES' WEEDS, THE; OR, PRIDE AND PATIENCE// D 3a// n.a.// **Pavilion**, Sept. 1868.

WITH FLYING COLOURS// D 5a// Seymore Hicks & Fred Latham// **Adelphi**, Aug. 1899, with Henry Vibart as Sir John, Aubrey Mallalieu as Wilfred, Robert Pateman as Hackett, W. L. Abingdon as Strangeways, Harry Nicholls as Belt, H. J. Carvill as Welldon, Charles Thursby as Lt. Andover, Suzanne Sheldon as Mary, Florence Lloyd as Polly, Mrs. Henry Leigh as Martha/ Scenery by W. Harford, E Banks, F. Tyars, & W. Hemsley/ Music by George Lewis.

WITH THE COLOURS// D 5a// Elliot Galer & James Mew// **Grand**, Aug. 1886.

WITHERED LEAVES// C 1a// Fred Broughton// **Terry's**, Oct. 1892.

WITHOUT INCUMBRANCES// F 1a// J. Palgrave Simpson// **Strand**, Aug. 1850/ **Olympic**, Sept. 1850, with Henry Compton as Pitapat, W. Shalders as Stagg, George Cooke as Sniffe, William Farren Jr. as Buckram, Mrs. B. Bartlett as Lady Buckram, Isabel Adams as Mrs. Stagg, Miss Adams as Frances, Mrs. Alfred Phillips as Patty.

WITHOUT LOVE// D 4a// Edmund Yates & A. W. Dubourg// **Olympic**, Dec. 1872, with William Rignold as Campero, C. H. Peveril as Baron von Derendorff, C. Parry as Tolosanne, A. Knight as Longages, H. B. Conway as Bernard, G. Canninge as Armande, Mr. Richardson as Cabanel, Ada Cavendish as Mme. Campero, Kate Rivers as Madelon, Miss D. Robins as Fifine.

WITNESS OF THE WAVE, THE; OR, THE MIDNIGHT MURDER ON THE CLIFF// D// J. B. Johnstone// **Victoria**, May 1850, with J. Neville as Sir Launcelot, Mr. Henderson as Danton, Mr. Humphreys as Blight, J. T. Johnson as Anster, Mr. Leake as Littlenut, John Hudspeth as Simon, J. Howard as Tittlebat, Mr. Hitchinson as Garnet, John Bradshaw as Jack, Mrs. George Lee as Maud, Mrs. Humpreys as Mrs. Spifflebustle, Miss Mildenhall as Esther, Mrs. Cooke as Dame Allerton, Miss Barrowcliffe as Sicely.

WIVES// C 3a// A. C. Calmour// **Vaudeville**, Mar. 1883.

WIVES AS THEY WERE AND MAIDS AS THEY ARE// C 5a// Mrs. Inchbald// **Cov. Garden**, Jan. 1842, with William Farren as Lord Priory, Mr. Cooper as Sir William, George Vandenhoff as Sir George, C. J. Mathews as Bronzely, Charles Diddear as Norberry, Drinkwater Meadows as Oliver, Helen Faucit as Lady Priory, Mrs. Julia Glover as Lady Mary, Louisa Nisbett as Miss Dorrillon/ **Haymarket**, June 1844, with William Farren as Lord Priory, Mr. Stuart as Sir William, C. J. Mathews as Bronzely, Henry Howe as Sir George, Mr. Tilbury as Norberry, William Strickland as Oliver, J. Worrell as Nabson, Mrs. Nisbett as Lady Priory, Mrs. Julia Glover as Lady Mary, Henel Faucit as Miss Dorrillon/ **Olympic**, Nov. 1856, with Mr. Addison as Lord Priory, Frederick Vining as Sir William, Gaston Murray as Sir George, George Vining as Bronzely, George Cooke as Norberry, J. H. White as Oliver, Mrs. Stirling as Miss Dorrillon, Mrs. Melfort as Lady Raffle, Miss Swanborough/ **Haymarket**, Sept. 1859, with Amy Sedgwick.

WIZARD OF THE WAVES, THE; OR, THE SHIP OF THE AVENGER// D 3a// J. T. Haines// **Victoria**, May 1843, with John Dale as Don

Jose, Charles Morelli as Ferrayez, Mr. Elliotson as Altaza, Mr. Paul as Domingo, Charles Maynard as Capt. Falkner, William Seaman as Belford, John Gardner as Treacle, E. F. Saville as Truck, J. W. Collier as Raddle, Mr. Gindon as Cutbody, Mrs. George Lee as Donna Isabinda, Miss Saddler as Donna Capella, Miss King as Dianez.

WIZARD OF THE WILDERNESS, THE// F// n.a.// **Gaiety**, Mar. 1873.

WOGGLE'S WAXWORKS// F// George Capel// **Surrey**, June 1879.

WOLF AND THE LAMB, THE// C// C. J. Mathews// **Haymarket**, Oct. 1861, with W. H. Chippendale as Gen. Dragonfell, Henry Howe as Col. Bronze, William Farren as Honeycomb, Miss M. Oliver as Mrs. Bellenden, Henrietta Lindley as Henrietta, Miss Weekes as Mary.

WOLF OF THE PYRENEES, THE// D 3a// William Travers// **Britannia**, Apr. 1868.

WOMAN// D// Dion Boucicault// **Cov. Garden**, Oct. 1843, with James Anderson as Doria, Samuel Phelps as Gaston de Foix, Walter Lacy as Cola de Foix, George Vandenhoff as Benoni, Charles Diddear as Giotto, Charlotte Vandenhoff as Inez, Louisa Nisbett as Lina, Miss Cooper as Ruth.

WOMAN ADRIFT, A// D Pro & 3a// W. T. McCellan// **Standard**, July 1901.

WOMAN AGAINST WOMAN// D 5a// Adap. by Frank Harvey fr F// **Grand**, Mar. 1886.

WOMAN AND HER MASTER; OR, THE PEER, THE POISONER & THE MANIAC// D 3a// H. Young// **Victoria**, Oct. 1854, with E. F. Saville as Earl of Moretown, Watty Brunton as Earl of Ayrtoun, Mr. Gates as Capt. Vernon, Alfred Saville as Brindsley, Mr. Morrison as Arden, W. H. Pitt as Digby Moretown, N. T. Hicks as Obie, J. Howard as Briard, Charles Rice as Debel, Phoebe Johnson as Godfrey, Mrs. Henry Vining as Alice, Miss Edgar as Lady Ayrtoun, Miss Laporte as Mrs. Brooks, Mrs. Manders as Mrs. Bantum/ Prod. by J. T. Johnson.

WOMAN AND WINE// D 4a// Arthur Shirley & Benjamin Landeck// **Pavilion**, Oct. 1897/ **Princes, Mar. 1899.**

WOMAN HATER, THE// F 3a// Adap. by Edward Terry fr orig. by David Lloyd// **Terry's**, Dec. 1887.

WOMAN HATER, THE// C 1a// W. Bayle Bernard// **Haymarket**, Feb. 1842, with Benjamin Webster as Baron Ravenspurg, Mr. Vining as Frederick, Henry Wallack as Stork, Miss Charles as Leila/ Scenery by George Morris.

WOMAN HATER, THE; OR, THE HUNGRY COURTIER// C 3a// Adap. by Henry Spicer fr orig. of Fletcher// **Olympic**, Mar. 1849, with Mr. Norton as Duke of Milan, Leigh Murray as Count Valore, Henry Compton as Lazarillo, John Kinloch as Arrigo, H. J. Turner as Lucio, Edward Stirling as Pandaro, Mrs. Stirling as Oriana, Miss Acosta as Julia.

WOMAN HATER, THE// C 1a// W. Bayle Bernard// **Sad. Wells**, July 1858, with Benjamin Webster as Baron Ravenspurg, W. Vernon as Frederick, Robert Romer as Stork, Miss Arden as Leila/ **Princess's**, Mar. 1863, with Benjamin Webster as Baron Ravenspurg, John Billington as Frederick, Robert Romer as Stork, Henrietta Sims as Lelia.

WOMAN HE LOVED AND THE WOMAN THAT LOVED HIM, THE// D 3a// Charles Daly// **Grecian**, July 1872.

WOMAN; HER RISE AND FALL IN LIFE// D// W. H. Pitt// **Britannia**, Nov. 1871.

WOMAN I ADORE, THE// F 1a// J. Maddison Morton// **Haymarket**, Oct. 1852, with J. B. Buckstone as Green, Mr. Clark as Piper, Mr. Caulfield as Judkins, Thomas Coe as Jackson, Mrs. L. S. Buckingham as Countess of Tiverton, Mrs. Selby as as Mrs. Smiler, Mrs. Caulfield as Patty.

WOMAN IN BLACK, THE; OR, HAUNTED LIVES// Rev. vers. of Haunted Lives, by Wilton Jones// **Olympic**, May 1884/ **Standard**, Dec. 1895.

WOMAN IN MAUVE, THE// D// Watts Phillips// **Haymarket**, Mar. 1865, with E. A. Sothern as Jocelyn, William Farren as The Count, Henry Howe as Harvey, Mr. Weathersby as Peters, Henry Compton as Beetles, P. White as Grumphz, Mr. Butler as Lt. Ferville, Edith Stuart as The Countess, Miss Lovell as Lucy, J. B. Buckstone as Mrs. Beetles/ Scenery by John O'Conner & George Morris/ Machines by Oliver Wales.

WOMAN IN RED, THE// D// n.a.// **Victoria**, Mar. 1864.

WOMAN IN RED, THE// D Pro & 3a// Adap. by J. Stirling Coyne fr F, La Tireuse de Cartes// **St. James's**, Apr. 1868, with Henry Crouch as Count Claudio, William Farren Jr. as Sanson, Basil Potter as Malliset, Thomas Bridgeford as Twitti, Mr. Allen as Spada, Mr. Evans as Reuben, Miss Potter as Claude, Miss Elsworthy as Countess Donati, Miss Love as Francesca, Mme. Celeste as Miriam, Miss Marion as Marguerite, Miss N. Nisbett as Ninon/ Scenery by Frederick Fenton/ Prod. by Mme. Celeste/ **Standard**, June 1869.

WOMAN IN THE CASE, A// C 3a// G. R. Sims & Leonard Merrick// **Court**, May 1901.

WOMAN IN WHITE, THE// D// n.a.// **Surrey**, Nov. 1860.

WOMAN IN WHITE, THE// D Pro & 4a// Wilkie Collins// **Olympic**, Oct. 1871, with John Billington as Sir Percival, Wybert Reeve as Hartright, Frederick Robson as Prof. Pesca, Marie Henderson as Mrs. Catherick, Ada Dyas as Anne and as Laura, Frederick Vining as Count Fosco, Edmund Garden as Kyrle, Mrs. Charles Viner as Marian, Maria Daly as Countess Fosco/ Scenery by Walter Hann/ Machines by Mr. Hoby/ Music by Mr. Richardson/ Prod. by Wilkie Collins & Mr. Vining.

WOMAN NEVER VEXT, A; OR, THE WIDOW OF CORNHILL// C 5a// J. R. Planché// **Sad. Wells**, Oct. 1852, with William Belford as Henry VI, George Bennett as Foster, Henry Marston as Stephen, Henry Mellon as Brown, Frederic Robinson as Robert, Mr. Barrett as Sir Godfrey, Charles Fenton as Lambskin, Lewis Ball as Clown, Mrs. Ternan as Agnes, Mrs. Barrett as Mrs. Foster, Teresa Bassano as Jane.

WOMAN OF BUSINESS// n.a.// **Adelphi**, Aug. 1864.

WOMAN OF COLOUR; OR, SLAVERY IN FREEDOM// D// n.a.// **Surrey**, Nov. 1853.

WOMAN OF NO IMPORTANCE, A// Play 5a// Oscar Wilde// **Haymarket**, Apr. 1893, with Herbert Beerbohm Tree as Lord Illingworth, Holman Clark as Sir John, Mr. Lawford as Lord Alfred, Charles Allan as Kelvil, Henry Kemble as Daubeney, Fred Terry as Arbuthnot, Rose Leclercq as Lady Hunstanton, Roma Le Thière as Lady Caroline, Blanche Horlock as Lady Stutfield, Mrs. Beerbohm Tree as Mrs. Allonby, Julia Neilson as Hester, Mrs. Bernard Beere as Mrs. Arbuthnot/ Scenery by Walter Hann & Walter Johnstone.

WOMAN OF THE PEOPLE, THE// D 4a// Trans. by Benjamin Webster fr F of A. P. Dennery & Julien Mallian// **Olympic**, Aug. 1878, with Frank Harvey as Bertrand, T. B. Appleby as Remy, John Morgan as Count de Bussiere, J. A. Rosier as Theobald, James Carter-Edwards as Appiani, George Warde as Dr. Leblanc, H. Bennett as Guillaume, H. Andrews as Grosmenu, Mlle. Beatrice as Marie, Emma Robberds as Sophie, Charlotte Saunders as Catherine, Fanny Wallis as Marguerite, Polly Hunter as Berlinguette/ Mise-en-Scène from the Theatre Porte St. Martin/ Music by M. Pilati/ Scenery by W. Hann & R. Messeder.

WOMAN OF THE WORLD, A// C 3a// n.a.// **Surrey**, Nov. 1858.

WOMAN OF THE WORLD, A// C 3a// J. Stirling Coyne// **Olympic**, Feb. 1868, with Horace Wigan as Goldenbird, Mr. Addison as Moleborough, C. J. Mathews as Merriton, Robert Soutar as Jones, Henry Ashley as Morden, George Vincent as Grouse, Mrs. Stirling as Mrs. Eddystone, Louisa Moore as Alice, Mrs. Caulfield as Lady Penfeather, Ellen Farren as Priscilla.

WOMAN OF THE WORLD, A// C 3a// Adap. by B. C. Stephenson fr G of Oscar Blumenthal, Der Probepfeil// **Haymarket**, Feb. 1886, with Helen Barry, Helen Forsyth, Maud Merrill, Gertrude Tempest, Herbert Beerbohm Tree, Charles Brookfield, Henry Kemble.

WOMAN OF THE WORLD, THE// D 2a// Dram. by Clara Cavendish// **Queen's**, Nov. 1858.

WOMAN OF THE WORLD, THE; OR, THE POISONER AND HIS VICTIM// D 2a// W. E. Suter// **Grecian**, June 1866, with George Gillett as Duke of Endell, J. Jackson as Sir John, W. Shirley as Dr. Meadows, William James as Stanmore, Charles Mortimer as Monti, Henry Power as Croker, Henry Grant as Maj. Edmonds, John Manning as Butts, Lizzie Mandlebert as Liza, Harriet Western as Joanna, Miss Dearlove as Mme. Arundelli, Mary A. Victor as Susan.

WOMAN; OR, LOVE AGAINST THE WORLD// C// Edmund Falconer// **Lyceum**, Sept. 1861, with Edmund Falconer, Mrs. Charles Young, Walter Lacy, Hermann Vezin.

WOMAN OUTWITTED, A// D 3a// D. M. Henry & Edwin Drew// **Novelty**, Nov. 1886.

WOMAN'S CAPRICE, A// C 1a// Adap. by H. M. Lewis// **POW**, Apr. 1895.

WOMAN'S FAITH, A// D 3a// n.a.// **Lyceum**, Nov. 1855.

WOMAN'S GUILT, A// D 3a// Bernard Copping// **Novelty**, Oct. 1896.

WOMAN'S HEART// Play 5a// Miss Vandenhoff// **Haymarket**, Feb. 1852, with Henry Howe as The Prince, Mr. Vandenhoff as Marquis Albrizzi, Mr. Stuart as Count Zellamino, John Parselle as Count Zerbino, Barry Sullivan as Angiolo, George Braid as Lorenzo, Amelia Vining as Lady Giulia, Miss Vandenhoff as Isolina, Miss Edgar as Metella/ Scenery by George Morris & John O'Conner/ Machines by F. Heselton.

WOMAN'S HEART, A// Play 1a// R. S. Bell// **Surrey**, Dec. 1897.

WOMAN'S LOVE; OR, KATE WYNSLEY THE COTTAGE GIRL// D// T. E. Wilks// **Victoria**, Apr. 1841, with Mr. James as Wynsley, Mr. Paul as Baldwin, E. F. Saville as Clitheroe, William Seaman as Scaresbrook, John Gardner as Hollyhock, Mr. Howard as O'Wells, Mr. Hitchinson as Hawkset, Eliza Vincent as Kate, Mrs. George Lee as Lady Adeline, Miss Wilton as Jessie, Miss Warde as Chloe, Miss Martin as Polly/ Scenery by Telbin & Hawthorn/ Prod. by Mr. Osbaliston/ **Sad. Wells**, July 1843, with Mr. Williams as Wynsley, R. H. Lingham as Baldwin, Henry Marston as Clotheroe, Mr. Bird as Scaresbrook, Mr. Coreno as Hollyhock, Caroline Rankley as Kate, Miss Stephens as Chloe, Mrs. Richard Barnett as Polly Pry, Henry Marston as Wilfred, C. J. Smith as O'Wells, Mr. Lambe as Old Martin, Miss Lane as Lady Adeline/ **Grecian**, July 1862, with Mr. Jackson as Winsley, Mr. Granville as Baldwin, R. H. Power as O'Wells, Thomas Mead as Wilford, Charles Warner as Scaresbrook, John Manning as Hollyhock, Miss Clarence Lindon as Kate, Ellen Hale as Adeline, Amalie Conquest as Polly Pry.

WOMAN'S LOVE, A// D 1a// Henry Woodville// **Vaudeville**, Mar. 1899.

WOMAN'S LOVE, A; OR, KATE WYNSLEY, THE COTTAGE GIRL// D 2a// T. E. Wilks// **Victoria,** Apr. 1841.

WOMAN'S LOVE; OR, THE GIPSY'S VEN GEANCE// D// Henry Cleveland// **Elephant & Castle,** May 1875.

WOMAN'S PERIL, A; OR, SAVED FROM DEATH// D 3a// W. E. Suter & A. Crofte// **Victoria,** July 1877.

WOMAN'S REASON, A// C 3a// Charles Brookfield & F. C. Philips// **Shaftesbury,** Dec. 1895, with Charles Brookfield, Charles Coghlan, Lewis Waller, Carlotta Addison, Florence West, Mrs. Herbert Beerbohm Tree.

WOMAN'S REVENGE// C 1a// John Howard Payne// **Haymarket,** Dec. 1837, with J. T. Haines as Maj. Denville, Mr. Hemming as Merton, Robert Strickland as Gregory, Mr. Gallot as Dobbins, Mr. Ray as John, Benjamin Webster as Fag, Mrs. Tayleure as Mrs. Simper, "a young lady" as Sophia, Mrs. Julia Glover as Miss Flashington.

WOMAN'S REVENGE, A// D 4a// Henry Pettitt// **Adelphi,** July 1893, with Charles Warner as Drummond, Charles Cartwright as Grimwade, E. W. Gardiner as Chilton, John Carter as John Overstone, Herbert Flemming as Robert Overstone, Rudge Harding as Sir John, Howard Russell as Justice Earle, Elizabeth Robins as Mary Lonsdale, Fanny Brough as Lottie, Gertrude Kingston as Mabel/ Scenery by Bruce Smith/ Music by Henry Sprake.

WOMAN'S SACRIFICE, A// D 4a// Adap. by Alice Chaplin fr F of Victor Hugo// **St. Geo. Hall,** June 1899.

WOMAN'S SECRET, A; OR, RICHELIEU'S WAGER// C// George Conquest// **Grecian,** Oct. 1853, with Basil Potter as Richelieu, Edwin Dixon as Duke d'Aumont, Richard Phillips as d'Aubigny, Charles Horn as d'Auray, Harriet Coveney as Marquise de Prie, Jane Coveney as Mlle. de Belle Isle, Ellen Crisp as Mariette.

WOMAN'S SIN, A; OR, ON THE VERGE// C Pro & 3a// Edwin France & Fred Dobell// **Sad. Wells,** July 1888.

WOMAN'S TEARS, A// D// Adap. by Arthur Bourchier fr F// **Comedy,** June 1890.

WOMAN'S THE DEVIL// F 1a// Edward Stirling// **Sad. Wells,** Feb. 1843, with Mr. Williams as Brilliant, Henry Howe as Arlington, Mrs. George Honey in 3 char. parts, Mrs. Richard Barnett as Tippet.

WOMAN'S TRIALS, A// D 3a// n.a.// **Drury Lane,** Nov. 1839.

WOMAN'S TRUST// D// Edward Towers// **Pavilion,** Sept. 1872.

WOMAN'S TRUTH, A// D 5a// Walter Reynolds// **Standard,** July 1887.

WOMAN'S VENGEANCE, A// D 5a// Adap. by Frank Harvey fr F// **Standard,** May 1888.

WOMAN'S VICTORY, A// C// Robert Dodson// **Comedy,** July 1885.

WOMAN'S VICTORY, A// D 5a// W. A. Brabner// **Pavilion,** Aug. 1895.

WOMAN'S WHIM, A// D Pro & 3a// Walter Stephens// **St. Geo. Hall,** Dec. 1867.

WOMAN'S WHIMS; OR, WHO'S TO WIN HER?// C// n.a.// **Sad. Wells,** Aug. 1837, with C. H. Pitt as Lavington, C. J. Smith as Avonmore, Mr. Spilling as Capt. Dunleary, Mr. Rogers as Simon, Thomas Lee as Thady, Mr. Ennis as Belgrave, Mr. George as Stokes, Mrs. Rogers as Mrs. Philpotts, Mrs. Harris as Matty, Miss Williams as Mrs. Dunleary, Lavinia Melville as Idonea.

WOMAN'S WIT; OR, LOVE'S DISGUISES// D 5a// J. Sheridan Knowles// **Cov. Garden,** May 1838, with Mr. Warde as Lord Athunree, George Bartley as Sir William, James Anderson as Sir Valentine, W. C. Macready as Walsingham, J. Waldron as Bradford, John Pritchard as Felton, Mr. Tilbury as de l'Epee, Charles Diddear as Lewson, Miss Taylor as Eustace, John Pritt Harley as Clever, Helen Faucit as Hero, Mrs. Serle as Emily.

WOMAN'S WON'T, A// F 1a// n.a.// **Lyceum,** Aug. 1890, with James Lewis as Father-in-Law, Mrs. G. H. Gilbert as Mother-in-Law, George Clarke as Husband, Isabel Irving as Wife.

WOMAN'S WORLD// C 3a// J. P. Hurst// **Court,** Dec. 1896.

WOMAN'S WRONGS; OR, THE FELON SON// D 3a// John Courtney// **Victoria** Sept. 1848, with E. Edwards as de Vervey, J. Howard as de Passey, T. H. Higgie as Eugene, J. T. Johnson as de Brien, G. F. Forman as Jambonneau, John Bradshaw as Brochette, Mr. Hawkins as Trompeau, F. H. Henry as Battisse, Annette Vincent as Pauline, Mrs. George Lee as Hewnriette, Mrs. Cooke as Mme. Rosier, Miss Burroughcliffe as Madelon, Miss Sharpe as Mme. Graffe.

WOMAN'S WRONGS// C 1a// A. M. Heathcote// **Toole's,** Sept. 1887.

WOMEN ARE SO SERIOUS// C 3a// Adap. by Brandon Thomas fr F of Pierre Wolff, Celles qu'on Respecte// **Court,** May 1901.

WON BY A HEAD// C 3a// Tom Taylor// **Queen's,** Mar. 1869.

WON BY HONOURS// C 4a// Annie Brunton ("L. S. Dee")// **Comedy,** July 1882, with E. S. Willard, George Alexander, T. W. Robertson, Mrs. E. S. Willard, Effie Liston, Fanny Robertson.

WONDER, THE: A WOMAN KEEPS A SECRET// C 3a// Susannah Centlivre// **Sad. Wells,** July

1837, with John Pritchard as Don Felix, Thomas Lee as Lissardo, Mr. Hicks as Col. Briton, Mr. King as Frederick, F. Ede as Don Lopez, Mr. Griffiths as Don Pedro, Mr. Ennis as Alguazil, Mrs. W. West as Donna Violante, Miss Williams as Isabella, Lavinia Melville as Flora, Mrs. Harris as Inis/ **Cov. Garden**, Jan. 1838, with Robert Strickland as Don Pedro, W. C. Macready as Don Felix, Drinkwater Meadows as Don Lopez, Mr. Vining as Col. Briton, Charles Diddear as Frederick, George Bartley as Gibby, Edwin Yarnold as Vasquez, Helen Faucit as Donna Violante, Ellen Clifford as Donna Isabella, Mrs. Julia Glover as Flora, Mrs. Humby as Inis/ **Haymarket**, Aug. 1840, with James Wallack as Don Felix, John Webster as Col. Briton, Robert Strickland as Don Pedro, J. W. Gough as Don Lopez, Henry Howe as Frederick, Benjamin Webster as Lissardo, T. F. Mathews as Alguazil, Helen Faucit as Donna Violante, Miss Travers as Donna Isabella, Miss Mattley as Inis, Miss Charles as Flora; Dec. 1849, with Mr. Tilbury as Don Pedro, James Bland as Don Lopez, Charles Kean as Don Felix, Henry Howe as Col. Briton, Henry Vandenhoff as Frederick, Benjamin Webster as Lisardo, Mrs. Charles Kean as Donna Violante, Mrs. L. S. Buckingham as Donna Isabella, Mrs. Keeley as Flora, Mrs. Caulfield as Inis; Oct. 1857, with Henry Sedley as Don Felix, W. H. Chippendale as Don Pedro, Henry Howe as Col. Briton, Henry Compton as Lissardo, Mr. Rogers as Gibby, Catherine Sinclair as Violante, Miss M. Oliver as Isabella, Mrs. Edward Fitzwilliam as Flora, Miss Lavine as Inis/ **Victoria**, Dec. 1841, with David Osbaldiston as Don Felix, Mr. James as Don Lopez, Mr. Howard as di Mendoza, C. Williams as Frederick, William Seaman as Col. Briton, Mr. Hitchinson as Vasquez, Eliza Vincent as Donna Violante, Mrs. George Lee as Isabella, Mrs. Howard as Flora/ **Princess's**, June 1846, with Mr. Wallack as Don Felix, Mr. Wynn as Don Lopez, Charles Fisher as Frederick, James Vining as Col. Briton, Mr. Granby as Don Pedro, Henry Compton as Lissardo, Mrs. Stirling as Donna Violante, Miss May as Donna Isabella, Miss Somers as Inis, Emma Stanley as Flora; Dec. 1850, with Mr. Wynn as Don Lopez, Mr. Addison as Don Pedro, Charles Kean as Don Felix, Frederick Cooke as Don Frederic, James Vining as Col. Briton, John Pritt Harley as Lizzardo, Mrs. Charles Kean as Donna Volante, Miss Murray as Donna Isabelle, Miss Vivash as Inez/ **Marylebone**, June 1848, with Fanny Vining/ **Drury Lane**, Feb. 1851, with J. W. Ray as Don Lopez, Henry Butler as Frederick, James Anderson as Don Felix, H. T. Craven as Col. Briton, Mr. Barrett as Don pedro, Louisa Nisbett as Donna Violante, Mrs. Barrett as Donna Isabella, Mrs. Bisson as Inis, Mrs. Walter Lacy as Flora; Mar. 1868, with Barry Sullivan as Don Felix, James Johnstone as Don Lopez, Mr. Barrett as Don Pedro, Henry Sinclair as Col. Briton, Charles Warner as Frederick, Mrs. Hermann Vezin as Donna Violante, Edith Stuart as Donna Isabella, Mrs. Harcourt as Inis, Kate Harfleur as Flora/ **Grecian**, Aug. 1856, with Richard Phillips, Henry Grant, William Shuter, Mr. Hustleby, Henry Power, Eaton O'Donnell, F. Charles, Jane Coveney, Ellen Hale, Ellen Crisp, Harriet Coveney.

WONDERFUL WOMAN, A; OR, THE MARQUIS AND THE COBBLER// C 2a// Charles Dance// **Lyceum**, May 1849/ **Sad. Wells**, Feb. 1852, with Frederic Robinson as Marquis de Frontignac, Henry Mellon as Viscount de Millefleurs, J. W. Ray as Crepin/ **Princess's**, Nov. 1855, with David Fisher as Marquis de Frontignac, George Everett as Viscount de Millefleurs, Mr. Cathcart as Rodolphe, Frank Matthews as Crepin, Caroline Heath as Mme. Bertrand, Maria Ternan as Cecile; Nov. 1859, with Augustus Harris as Marquis de Frontignac, J. G. Shore as Viscount de Millefleurs, Henry Irving as Rodolphe, Frank Matthews as Crepin, Carlotta Leclercq as Hortense, Rose Leclercq as Cecile; May 1881, with Henry Neville as Marquis de Frontingenac, F. Charles as Viscomte de Milifleurs, H. C. Sydney as Rodolphe, Harry Jackson as Crepin, Louisa Payne as Hortense, Carrie Hope as Cecile/ **St. James's**, Jan. 1862, with George Vining as Marquis de Frontignac, Frank Matthews as Crepin, Henry Ashley as Viscount de Millefleurs, F. Charles as Rodolph, Isabel Adams as Mme. Hortense, Nelly Moore as Cecil/ **Astley's**, Dec. 1863, with C. W. Chamberlaine as Marquis de Frontignac, Mr. Frazer as Viscount de Millefleurs, Frank Matthews as Crepin, Miss Desborough as Mme. Bertrand, Miss Nisbett as Cecile.

WOOD DEMON, THE// n.a.// **Grecian**, Dec. 1873.

WOOD WOLF OF THE BLACK MOUNTAINS, THE; OR, THE MILO OF BRITTANY// D// W. T. Moncreieff// **Sad. Wells**, Nov. 1842, with Mr. Aldridge as Charlemagne, Mr. Dry as Count Galtier, Mr. Bird as Sir Amedée, Gustave Noel as Lionard, Mr. Starmer as Coquelane, John Herbert as Gilles, Miss Melville as Alphonse, Caroline Rankley as Princess Isabeau, Fanny Morelli as Clotilde, Miss Andrews as Dame Ursula.

WOODBARROW FARM// C 3a// Jerome K. Jerome// **Comedy**, June 1888/ **Vaudeville**, Jan. 1891.

WOODCOCK'S LITTLE GAME// F 2a// J. Maddison Morton// **St. James's**, Oct. 1864, with C. J. Mathews, H. J. Montague, Mrs. Frank Matthews/ **St. James's** Nov. 1864, with C. J. Mathews as Woodcock, H. J. Montague as Larkings, James Johnstone as Swansdown, Walton Chamberlaine as David, Mrs. Frank Matthews as Mrs. Carver, Fanny Hunt as Mrs. Woodcock, Miss Wentworth as Mrs. Larkings/ **Olympic**, June 1867, with C. J. Mathews as Woodcock, H. J. Montague as Larkings, John Clayton as Swansdown, Harwood Cooper as David, Mrs. Frank Matthews as Mrs. Carver, Maria Harris as Mrs. Woodcock, Mrs. Charles Mathews as Mrs. Larkings/ **Gaiety**, July 1880, with Alfred Thompson, Charles Young, W. S. Gilbert, Sophie Larkin, Kate Bishop.

WOODMAN AND HIS DOGS, HECTOR AND BRUIN, THE// D// n.a.// **Victoria**, May 1859, with Mr. Henderson as Sinclair, W. Harmer as Fernly, J. Mathews as Moore, J. Chappell as Shorrock, F. H. Henry as Const. Dobson, Mr. Carter as Welford, John Bradshaw as

Rathbone, J. Howard as Spriggins, Mrs. E. F. Saville as Maria, Miss Laporte as Polly, Miss Barrowcliffe as Margaret.

WOODMAN'S HUT, THE; OR, THE BURNING FOREST// D 3a// S. J. Arnold// **Cov. Garden,** May 1837, with John Webster as Count Conenburg, J. Worrell as Worther, John Pritchard as Wolfender, George Bennett as Kaunitz, Charles Bender as Dangerfeldt, Mr. Ransford as Schampt, Benjamin Webster as Moritz, Mr. Tilbury as Bruhl, Eliza Vincent as Amelia, Miss Lee as Maria, Miss Nicholson as Laura/ **Sad. Wells,** Dec. 1843, with Mr. Bird as Count Ferdinand, Mr. Lamb as Count Werther, Mr. Dry as Wolfender, Mr. Williams as Kaunitz, Robert Romer as Schampt, Mr. Franks as Dangerfeldt, Charles Fenton as Bruhl, Mr. Coreno as Moritz, Caroline Rankley as as Amelia, Miss Melville as Maria, Mrs. Richard Barnett as Laura.

WOOING IN JEST AND LOVING IN EARNEST// D 1a// A. C. Troughton// **Strand,** Nov. 1858.

WOOING ONE'S WIFE// F 1a// J. Maddison Morton// **Olympic,** Oct. 1861, with Henry Neville as Maj. von Walstein, Gaston Murray as Muldorf, Horace Wigan as Muffenhausen, Mrs. Leigh Murray as Baroness Muldorf, Miss Hughes as Gertrude.

WOOL-GATHERING// C// Adap. by A. Longridge fr G of Kotzebue, Die Zerstreuten// **St. Geo. Hall,** June 1888.

WORD OF HONOUR, THE; A JERSEY LOVE STORY// D 3a// Paul Meritt// **Grecian,** Oct. 1874.

WORK AND WAGES// D 5a// William Bourne// **Pavilion,** June 1890.

WORK GIRL, THE// D Pro & 4a// Arthur Shirley & George Conquest// **Surrey,** Apr. 1895.

WORKHOUSE, THE PALACE, AND THE GRAVE, THE// n.a.// **Britannia,** Dec. 1858.

WORKMAN, THE// D 3a// Edward Towers// **Pavilion,** Oct. 1880.

WORKMAN, THE; OR, THE SHADOW ON THE HEARTH// D 5a// Frank Harvey// **Olympic,** July 1881, with Frank Harvey as John Tressider, T. B. Appleby as Phil Tressider, J. Carter-Edwards as Sir Henry, David Gaunt as Craven, H. Bennett as Crank, S. Grant as Jackson, A. Lingham as Melton, Charlotte Saunders as Debora, Lizzie Baldwin as Miriam, Emmeline Falconer as Bessie, Eyre Robson as Rachel, Ida Courtney as Mary, Polly Hunter as Milly/ Music by T. H. Wright/ Prod. by Frank Harvey.

WORKMEN OF PARIS, THE; OR, THE DRAMAS OF THE WINE SHOP// n.a.// **Adelphi,** Dec. 1864, with Benjamin Webster as as Van Gratz, John Billington as Albert, C. H. Stephenson as McMahon, Richard Phillips as Danbry, Robert Romer as Cabechan, C. J. Smith as Patois, W. H. Eburne as Jacques, Henrietta Simms as Josépha, Mrs. Billington as Countess de Marsan, Mrs. Stirling as Marguerite, Mrs. Alfred Mellon (Sarah Woolgar) as Blanche, Mrs. A. Seaman as Rosette/ Scenery by Gates & Thompson/ Music by M. Artus/ Machines by Mr. Charker.

WORLD, THE// D 5a// Paul Meritt, Henry Pettitt & Augustus Harris// **Drury Lane,** July 1880, with William Rignold as Sir Clement, Augustus Harris as Harry, T. W. Ford as Blackstone, Charles Harcourt as Bashford, Harry Jackson as Jewell, J. R. Gibson as Lumley, R. S. Boleyn as Pearson, Augustus Glover as Locksey, Arthur Matthison as Owen, A. C. Lilly as Hawkins, Philip Beck as Wyndham, Helen Barry as Mabel, Fanny Josephs as Mary, Fanny Brough as Ned, Annie Lambert as Alice, Miss Macnamara as Miss McTab/ **Princess's,** Feb. 1884.

WORLD AGAINST HER, THE// D 5a// Frank Harvey// **Grand,** Aug. 1887/ **Surrey,** July 1888.

WORLD AND THE STAGE, THE// D 3a// Adap. by J. Palgrave Simpson fr F// **Haymarket,** Mar. 1859, with Mr. Rogers as Sir Norman, William Farren as Malpas, Henry Howe as Ashton, Henry Compton as Buzzard, J. B. Buckstone as Dewlap, J. Worrell as Col. Gabble, Ellen Ternan as Lady Castlecrag, Amy Sedgwick as Kate, Mrs. Poynter as Miss Lipgine, Eliza Weekes as Hepzibah, Mrs. Griffiths as Lady Fanny, Fanny Wright as Mme. Moreau/ Scenery by John O'Conner & George Morris/ Machines by Oliver Wales.

WORLD OF FASHION, THE// C 3a// Adap. by John Oxenford fr F// **Olympic,** Apr. 1862, with Gaston Murray as Duke d'Anjeau, Frederick Vining as Count de Vieux Chateau, Walter Gordon as Adolphe, Henry Neville as de Pontcalec, Mrs. Leigh Murray as Countess de Vieux Chateau, Miss Marston as Marchioness de Bellerose, Miss Cottrell as Mme. Dubois, Miss Hughes as Isabelle, Amy Sedgwick as Marie.

WORLD OF SIN, THE// D 4a// Walter Melville// **Standard,** Nov. 1900.

WORLD, THE FLESH, AND THE DEVIL, THE// D 4a// Arthur Shirley, Robert Castleton, & F. Vancrossan// **Surrey,** June 1901.

WORLD'S WAR; OR, THE TURKS' FAITH AND THE CHRISTIANS' VALOUR// D 3a// H. Young// **Victoria,** Apr. 1854, with T. E. Mills as Richard I, Mr. Hitchinson as Philip Augustus, Mr. Henderson as Earl of Lusignan, Mr. Green as Montmorency, R. H. Kitchen as Marquis of Montserrat, Mr. Laurence as King Leopold, Mr. Carter as Emperor Frederick, Mr. Brunton as Sir Eustace, J. Howard as de Marigny, Alfred Saville as Archbishop William, Georgiana Lebatt as Queen Berengaria, Mrs. Henry Vining as Mathilde, Miss Laporte as Hermenia, Mr. Morrison as Saladin, N. T. Hicks as Abhel, Miss Sutton as Agnese, Mrs. Andrews as Zema, Annie Merriton as Zerayda, Phoebe Johnson as Leida, Miss Dansor as Akrouya/ Scenery by Hawthorn, Hicks & Lawrence/

Machines by Wood and Foster/ Music by Mr. Mingaye/ Prod. by J. T. Johnson.

WORRYBURY'S WHIMS// F// Charles Rose & Dominic Murray// **Alexandra**, May 1865.

WORSHIP OF BACCHUS, THE// D 5a// Paul Meritt & Henry Pettitt// **Olympic**, July 1879, with W. H. Vernon as Brayton, E. H. Brooke as Luard, Arthur Williams as Croton, Edward Righton as Needham, Luigi Lablache as Waverley, C. Strick as Viscount St. Loo, J. Stephens as Masham, as Dr. Belton, Louise Moody as Mary, Katie Brown as Mattie, Maria Davis as Ambrosia, Edith Bruce as Miss Tudor, Fanny Josephs as Amy/ Scenery by Henry Emden/ Music by Edward Solomon/ Machines by Mr. Collins/ Gas by Mr. Hinkley/ Prod. by Edward Righten with the authors.

WORST WOMAN IN LONDON, THE// D 4a// Walter Melville// **Standard**, Oct. 1899.

WRANGLING LOVERS, THE; OR, LIKE MASTER LIKE MAN// C 1a// W. Lyon// **Sad. Wells**, May 1837, with C. H. Pitt as Don Carlos, Thomas Lee as Lopez, Mr. Rogers as Sancho, Miss Melville as Jacintha.

WRATH; OR, A MESSAGE OF THE DEAD// D 3a// Dram. by C. H. Stephenson fr novel of Ouida// **Standard**, Dec. 1882.

WRECK, THE; OR, THE BUCCANEER'S BRIDAL// D 2a// n.a.// **Sad. Wells**, Aug. 1840, with Henry Marston as Glennon, Mr. Dry as Brinkley, J. B. Hill as Wheatly, Mr. Aldridge as Fallowfield, Mr. Richardson as Coulter, Mr. Priorson as Plumsley, J. W. Collier as Gogmagog, Miss Cooke as Dame Fallowfield, Mrs. J. F. Saville as Jane, Miss Louise as Kate, Mrs. Richard Barnett as Bella.

WRECK AND RESCUE; OR, THE LABYRINTH OF DEATH// D 4a// Thomas Mead// **Grecian**, Apr. 1863, with Thomas Mead as Denis Tregorn, J. Jackson as Bertram Tregorn, Alfred Rayner as Marcus, William James as Alan, John Manning as Chau, Jane Dawson as Marion, Miss Shirley as Jean/ Scenery by C. Smithers/ Machines by Mr. Smithers Sr./ Music by Mr. Edroff.

WRECK ASHORE, THE; OR, THE BRIDEGROOM OF THE SEA// D 2a// J. B. Buckstone// **Sad. Wells**, July 1837, with Mr. King as Bertram, C. H. Pitt as Barnard, Mr. Hicks as Capt. Grampus, J. Dunn as Magog, Thomas Lee as Starling, Mr. Ennis as William, Mrs. W. West as Alice, Lavinia Melville as Bella, Mrs. Harris as Dame Barnard, C. J. Smith as Blackadder, Miss Young as Lucy, Mrs. Andrews as Mrs. Starling; July 1864, with Edmund Phelps as Bertram, T. W. Neale as Capt. Grampus, G. Clementson as Barnard, F. Francis as Starling, T. B. Bennett as Magog, Charles Mowbray as Blackadder, F. Warboys [Worboys?] as Barbelot, Kate Stonor as Alice, Minnie Davis as Bella/ **Adelphi**, Apr. 1842, with Mr. Lyon as Miles Bertram, Mr. Hemming as Walter Bernard, O. Smith as Captain Grampus, Paul Bedford as Marmaduke Magog, Edward Wright as Jemmy Starling, Mrs. Yates as Alice, Mrs. Keeley as Bella, Mrs. Hicks as Lucy, Miss O'Neill as Mrs. Starling; July 1880, with E. H. Brooke as Miles Bertram, E. B. Norman as Walter Bernard, James Fernandez as Capt. Grampus, J. G. Taylor as Magog, Robert Pateman as Jemmy Starling, Bella Pateman as Alice, Clara Jecks as Bella, Harriet Coveney as Dame Barnard/ Scenery by Julian Hicks/ **Haymarket**, Sept. 1848, with Charles Boyce as Bertram, J. Worrell as Bernard, O. Smith as Grampus, Charles Munyard as Starling, Edward Wright as Magog, Mrs. Yates as Alice, Sarah Woolgar as Bella, Mrs. Laws as Dame Bernard.

WRECK OF HOME, THE; OR, THE BRIDE, THE CULPRIT WIFE, AND THE PENITENT// D 3a// T. E. Wilks// **Victoria**, Sept. 1843, with John Dale as Adm. Thornley, Mr. Wilton as Manson, C. Williams as Lt. Sullivan, David Osbaldiston as Capt. Brillian, William Seaman as Crayford, William James as Roper, John Gardner as Gaff, Mr. Paul as O'Garraty, Charles Morelli as Brightly, Annette Vincent as Inez, Mrs. Atkinson as Ellen, Miss Ridgeway as Mrs. Cormack, Miss Wilton as Florence, Mrs. Wilton as Mrs. Amwell.

WRECK OF THE GOLDEN MARY// D 3a// Dram. fr story of Charles Dickens// **Victoria**, Jan. 1857/ **Grecian**, Jan. 1857, with H. Campbell as Joe Fenton, Mr. Hustleby as Whichelo, Richard Phillips as Brandsman, C. Kelsey as Ned Temple, Henry Grant as Tarrant, Miss Chapman as Amy, Jane Coveney as Mary, Harriet Coveney as Suke, Eaton O'Donnell as Capt. Ravender, William Shuter as Steadiman, Miss Taylor as Lucy.

WRECK OF THE HEART, THE; OR, THE STORY OF AGNES PRIMROSE// D 3a// G. D. Pitt// **Victoria**, Nov. 1841, with Mr. James as Norwynne, C. Williams as Henry (son), John Dale as William, William Seaman as Henry (nephew), Mr. Collen [Cullen?] as Old Primrose, John Gardner as Muffinface, Mrs. George Lee as Rebecca, Miss Sadler as Caroline, Mrs. Howard as Mrs. Muffinface, Miss Wilton as Little William, Mrs. Garthwaite as Irish Sal, Mrs. Seaman as Bet.

WRECK OF TWENTY YEARS, THE// D 2a// Thomas Blake// **Sad. Wells**, July 1838, with John Webster as Squire Granville and Edmund, Dibdin Pitt as Cringe, Mr. Phillipson as George, Mr. Cathcart as Thornton, Mr. Conquest as Dumps, Mr. Mellor as Holmes, Mrs. Robert Honner as Esther and Fanny, Mrs. J. F. Saville as Sally, Miss Richardson as Mause/ Scenery by Mr. Telbin.

WRECKED, BUT NOT LOST// D// C. H. Stephenson// **City of London**, Nov. 1867.

WRECKED IN LONDON// D 4a// George Roberts// **Elephant & Castle**, Aug. 1887.

WRECKER, THE// D// Frederick Marchant & C. I. Pitt// **Britannia**, July 1878.

WRECKER'S DAUGHTER, THE// D 5a// J. Sheridan Knowles// **Drury Lane**, June 1837, with Sheridan Knowles as Norris, Mr. Evans as Robert, Mr. Cooper as Edward, Charles Diddear as Wolf, Mr. Baker as Clergyman, Mr. Hooper as Philip, A. Brindal as Stephen, Miss Huddart as Marian/ **Sad. Wells**, Feb. 1844, with Henry Marston as Robert, Henry Hall as Norris, C. J. Smith as Wolf, Mr. Bird as Edward, Mr. Williams as Philip, Charles Fenton as Ambrose, Caroline Rankley as Marian/ **Marylebone**, Feb. 1848, with Mrs. Mary [?] Warner.

WRECKER'S SON, THE// D// n.a.// **Sad. Wells**, Oct. 1837, with Mr. Wilkins as Colvins, Mr. King as Luke Trelawny, C. H. Pitt as Joseph Trelawny, Mr. Campbell as Spiritsail, Mr. George as Philip, Mr. Griffith as Old Stupid, Thomas Lee as Young Stupid, Miss Williams as Ellen, Miss Vernon as Widow Gurnet, Mrs. Rogers as Polly.

WREN BOYS; OR, THE MOMENT OF PERIL// D 2a// T. E. Wilks// **City of London**, Oct. 1838/ **Victoria**, Mar. 1842, with E. F. Saville as Hamond, William Seaman as Fitzroy, Mr. Paul as O'Donnel, John Gardner as Wildgoose, John Dale as O'Conner, Eliza Vincent as Emily, Mrs. George Lee as Catherine, Miss Collett as Rose.

WRINKLES; A TALE OF TIME// D 3a// H. J. Byron// **POW**, Apr. 1876.

WRITING ON THE SHUTTERS// F// n.a.// **Drury Lane**, Feb. 1855.

WRITING ON THE WALL, THE; OR, THE MODEL FARM// D 3a// Thomas and J. Maddison Morton// **Haymarket**, Aug. 1852, with J. Worrell as Sir Philip, John Parselle as Harlow, Edward Wright as Trotter, O. Smith as Tobias, Samuel Emery as Oliver, William Cullenford as Harrowell, Mr. Lindon as Jacky, Paul Bedford as Smithers, George Honey as Walker, C. J. Smith as Gammon, Mrs. Leigh Murray as Lady Elton, Ellen Chaplin as Margarette,, Sarah Woolgar as Carlotta, Miss Turner as Nancy/ Scenery by T. Pitt & Mr. Turner/ Machines by T. Ireland/ **Adelphi**, Aug. 1855, with G. Lee as Sir Philip, John Parselle as Harlowe, Edward Wright as Fergusson Trotter, Charles Selby as Tobias, Paul Bedford as Smithers, Mr. Woolgar as Walker, C. J. Smith as Gammon, Mrs. Leigh Murray as Lady Elton, Miss Wyndham as Margaret, Sarah Woolgar as Carlotta.

WRITTEN ON SAND// C 1a// F. W. Broughton// **Olympic**, Aug. 1884.

WRONG BABY, THE// F 1a// George Conquest// **Grecian**, Feb. 1857, with Henry Grant as Solus, John Manning as Hubby, C. Kelsey as Holdoise, Miss Johnstone as Mrs. Comfort, Miss Poynter as Mrs. Clack, Harriet Coveney as Mrs. Chatter, Ellen Crisp as Mrs. Cuddle.

WRONG BOX, THE// C 2a// n.a.// **Olympic**, Mar. 1854, with Priscilla Horton (Mrs. T. G. Reed) as Hercules III, Alfred Wigan as Count de Candolle, Mr. Robinson as Rene, Miss Wyndham as Helene, Ellen Turner as Carlotta/ Music by T. G. Reed.

WRONG DOOR, THE// F 3a// Ina Cassilis// **Comedy**, Apr. 1890.

WRONG ENVELOPE, THE// C// Edith Cuthell// **Novelty**, June 1888.

WRONG GIRL, THE// F 3a// H. A. Kennedy// **Strand**, Nov. 1894.

WRONG MAN, THE// F 2a// J. Maddison Morton// **Cov. Garden**, Nov. 1841, with George Bartley as Sir Bryan, C. J. Mathews as Beechwood, John Pritt Harley as Tack, J. M. Ridgway as Joseph, John Ayliffe as Ralph, Mrs. Tayleure as Tomasina, Miss Cooper as Alice, Mrs. Humby as Patty.

WRONG MAN IN THE RIGHT PLACE, THE// F// J. Maddison Morton// **Princess's**, Apr. 1871.

WRONG MR. WRIGHT, THE// F 3a// G. H. Broadhurst// **Strand**, Nov. 1899.

WRONGED// D 3a// William Travers// **Sad. Wells**, Nov. 1869, with Edgar Newbound as Beresford, Mr. Goodwin as Revel, Richard Edgar as Picco, G. Weston as Uppers, Edmund Phelps as Le Cour, T. W. Ford as Griffenean, Mr. Howard as Maxwell, Mrs. E. F. Edgar as Mme. Lemoineau, Eliza Clayton as Eugenie, Glorence Gerald as Rose, Julia Summers as Maria, Miss Bennett as Alice.

WRONGS OF POLAND, THE// n.a.// **Victoria**, Feb. 1865.

WYLLARD'S WEIRD// C Pro & 3a// Dram. by Harry Lobb fr novel of Miss Braddon// **Criterion**, Dec. 1887.

*

YANKEE HOUSEKEEPER, THE// C 1a// n.a.// **Drury Lane**, Apr. 1856, with Mrs. W. J. Florence as Pegg Ann, W. J. Florence as O'Conner, Mr. Tilbury as Maj. Skinner, J. Halford as Post, C. W. Bernard as Somers, Emma Wadham as Fenella, Mrs. Barratt as Mrs. Skinner/ **Princess's**, Feb. 1862, with W. J. Florence as O'Conner, Edmund Garden as Maj. Skimmer, Robert Cathcart as Somers, Frederick Moreland as Post, Mr. Collett as Stave, Mrs. W. J. Florence as Peg, Mrs. Weston as Mrs. Skimmer, Marie Henderson as Fennella.

YANKEE PEDLER, THE; OR, OLD TIMES IN VIRGINIA// C 1a// W. Bayle Bernard// **Olympic**, Jan. 1837, with Frank Matthews as Col. Bantam, Mr. Brougham as Morland, Mr. Wyman as Cowpens, Mr. Collier as Sam

Slanch, Mr. Hill as Hiram Dodge, Mrs. Fitzwaller as Nancy/ **Haymarket**, July 1838, with William Strickland as Col. Bantam, Mr. Hutchings as Morland, J. Worrell as Slingsby, Mr. Hill as Hiram Dodge, T. F. Mathews as Slaunch, Mr. Green as Old Pomp, Miss Gallot as Nancy, Miss Patridge as Miriam/ **Adelphi**, Jan. 1852, with Samuel Emery as Col. Bantam, William Cullenford as Cowpens, J. Worrell as Morland, C. J. Smith as Slingsby, Josh Silsbee as Hiram Dodge.

YAROMEER THE YAGER; OR, THE HUNGARIAN WILLIAM TELL// D// n.a.// **Sad. Wells**, Nov. 1837, with Mr. King as Count Falconhertz, Mr. Ennis as Spatz, Mr. George as Count Ivenfort, Mr. Ede as Edmund, C. H. Pitt as Count Flittergold, Mr. Campbell as Yaromeer, Mr. Rogers as Nibble, Miss Williams as Zuleka, Miss Pitt as Blonda, Miss Vernon as Cretta.

YE LEGENDE; OR, THE FOUR PHANTOMS// C 3a// H. P. Grattan// **Imperial**, Sept. 1883.

YE WYNWYNWN; OR, THE WELSH CHORISTER// F 1a// J. F. McArdle// **Olympic**, Nov. 1875, with G. W. Anson as Jones, Mr. Crichton as Gawkins, Alfred Nelson as Flunker, Mrs. Stephens as Mrs. Fritzgig, Annie Taylor as Jennie.

YELLOW ADMIRAL, THE; OR, THE PERILS OF THE BATTLE AND THE BREEZE// D 3a// n.a.// **Victoria**, May 1845, with Ersser Jones as Grimville, Mr. Edgar as Capt. Dixon, J. T. Johnson as Lt. Brightwell, William Seaman as Layton, Henry Howard as Block, John Dale as Hernshaw, Mr. Cooke as Saunders, Mr. Hitchinson as Hayleg and as Mustapha, Walter Searle as Von Dundersclush, T. H. Higgie as Shunk, Annette Vincent as as Eliza, Miss Jefferson as Patience, Eliza Terrey as Lucy, Mrs. Seaman as Odalisque.

YELLOW HUSBAND, THE// F// Mark Lemon// **Haymarket**, May 1843, with J. B. Buckstone as Peewit, J. W. Gough as Briggs, T. F. Mathews as Halfbound, Henry Howe as Jackson, James Bland as Phibbs, Mrs. Humby as Mrs. Peewit, Miss C. Conner as Susan.

YELLOW PASSPORT, THE// D Pro & 4a// Dram. by Henry Neville fr F of Victor Hugo, Les Misérables// **Olympic**, Dec. 1868, with Mr. Neville as Bishop Myriel, George Vincent as Thenardier, Henry Neville as Jean Valjean, Harwood Cooper as Verbois, Teresa Furtado as Fantine, Miss Schavey as Magloire, Mrs. Caulfield as Mme. Thenardier, Horace Wigan as Javert, J. G. Taylor as Gillenormand, E. Atkins as Champmathieu, H. Vaughan as Marius/ Scenery by Mr. Hicks/ Machines by T. Staines/ Music by Edwin Ellis/ Prod. by Horace Wigan.

YELLOW PERIL, THE// Play 1a// Edward Ferris & Paul Heriot// **Vaudeville**, Sept. 1900.

YEOMAN'S SERVICE// C 1a// T. E. Pemberton// **Novelty**, Sept. 1885.

YES OR NO// C 3a// Emily Beauchamp// **Strand**, Dec. 1897.

YEW TREE RUINS, THE; OR, THE WRECK, THE MISER AND THE MURDERER// D// J. T. Haines// **Victoria**, Feb. 1841, with Mr. Blanchard as Lord Aveline, John Dale as Sir Wilfred, Charles Bender as Wardle, Mr. Attwood as Pelican, Mr. Hicks as Trevalyon, J. T. Haines as Kynon, F. C. Courtney as Fielder, Walter Searle as Tares, Miss E. Montague as Beatrice, Mrs. Hicks as Rose, Miss Warde as Margaret, Miss B. Kemble as Dame Elvey, Miss Pettifer as Nancy/ **Grecian**, Aug. 1861, with Mr. Smithson as Lord Aveline, R. H. Lingham as Sir Wilfred, J. Jackson as Maurice, John Manning as Pelican, Henry Grant as Fielder, George Gillett as Trevalyon, Alfred Rayner as Rynon, Jane Coveney as Beatrice, Lucreza Hill as Nancy, Ellen Hale as Rose, Miss Johnston as Dame Elvy.

YORICK'S LOVE// T 3a// Adap. by W. D. Howells fr Span// **Lyceum**, Apr. 1884, with Lawrence Barrett as Yorick, Louis James as Heywood, James Fernandez as Walton, Mark Quinton as Edmund, Philip Ben Greet as Woodford, F. W. Irish as Gregory, Marie Wainwright as Alice, Annie Rose as Dorothy/ Scenery by Hawes Craven & W. G. Cuthbert/ Music by Andrew Levey/ Machines by Mr. Knight.

YORKSHIRE LASS, A// D 4a// J. W. Jones// **Olympic**, Feb. 1891.

YOU CAN'T MARRY YOUR GRANDMOTHER// C 2a// T. H. Bayly// **Olympic**, Mar. 1838, with William Farren as Bloomly, C. J. Mathews as Algernon, Robert Keeley as Tom Small, James Vining as Ready, Mrs. Orger as Mrs. Trim, Miss Goward as Mrs. Pickle, Mme. Vestris as Emma/ **Haymarket**, June 1838, with William Strickland as Sir Rose, C. J. Mathews as Algernon, J. B. Buckstone as Tom Small, Mr. Hutchings as Ready, Mme. Vestris as Emma, Mrs. Orger as Susan, Mrs. Gallot as Mrs. Pickle/ **Cov. Garden**, Oct. 1839, with William Farren as Bloomly, C. J. Mathews as Algernon, Robert Keeley as Small, James Vining as Ready, Mrs. Orger as Mrs. Trim, Miss Goward as Mrs. Pickle, Mme. Vestris as Emma/ **Sad. Wells**, Oct. 1846, with A. Younge as Sir Rose, William Hoskins as Algernon, Mr. Morton as Ready, Henry Scharf as Small, Miss Cooper as Emma, Mrs. Henry Marston as Susan, Mrs. Francis as Mrs. Pickle/ **Olympic**, Feb. 1858, with Mr. Addison as Sir Rose, Walter Gordon as Algernon, Henry Leslie as Ready, Horace Wigan as Tom Small, Miss Wyndham as Emma, Mrs. Stephens as Mrs. Pickle, Mrs. W. S. Emden (Miss Somers) as Susan.

YOU MUSTN'T LAUGH// F 3a// Trans. fr Rus. by G. A. Lubinoff// **Opera Comique**, Nov. 1892.

YOU NEVER CAN TELL// C 3a// George Bernard Shaw// **Royalty**, Nov. 1899, with Yorke Stephens as Valentine, Roland Bottomley as Clandon, Hermann Vezin as Crampton, James Welch as Waiter, Sydney Warden as McComas, Charles Charrington as Bohun, Edward Knoblauch as Jo, Winifred Fraser as Dolly, Margaret Halstan as Gloria, Elsie Chester as Mrs. Clandon, Mabel Hardinge as Maid.

YOU NEVER KNOW// F 3a// G. Dale// **Gaiety**, Nov. 1899.

YOUNG ACTRESS, THE// Dion Boucicault// **Drury Lane**, May 1856.

YOUNG APPRENTICE, THE; OR, THE WATCH-WORDS OF OLD LONDON// D 3a// C. H. Hazlewood// **Britannia**, Mar. 1868.

YOUNG COUPLE, THE// C// n.a.// **Drury Lane**, Dec. 1851, with Kate Bateman as Henrietta, Ellen Bateman as Charles.

YOUNG COUPLES// C 2a// J. H. Johnstone// **Gaiety**, Feb. 1884.

YOUNG ENGLAND// F// J. Maddison Morton// **Haymarket**, Dec. 1844, with William Strickland as Maj. Martinet, Henry Holl as Capt. Dashalong, J. B. Buckstone as Pooley, Mr. Tilbury as Pounce, Mrs. L. S. Buckingham as Mrs. Dashalong, Mrs. Humby as Mrs. Pooley, Mrs. Stanley as Mrs. Smiler.

YOUNG FOLKS' WAYS// C 4a// Mrs. Francis Hodgson Burnett & William Gillette// **St. James's**, Oct. 1883, with Brian Darley as The Marquis, John Maclean as Desmond, W. H. Kendal as Estabrook, John Hare as Old Rogers, George Alexander as Hardy, Herbert Waring as Drew, Mrs. W. H. Kendal as Nora Desmond, Linda Dietz as Kate, Mrs. Hermann Vezin as Mrs. Rogers/ Scenery by W. Harford.

YOUNG HUSBANDS// C 2a// John Besemeres ("John Daly")// **Sad. Wells**, Aug. 1852, with Mrs. Henry Marston as Mrs. Carey, Lewis Ball as Fagg, Frederic Robinson as Spooner, Mr. Wallis as Vacil, Mr. Barrett as Gadbury, Eliza Travers as Mrs. Fagg, Miss Stephens as Mrs. Spooner, Teresa Bassano as Anna.

YOUNG KING, THE// D 2a// n.a.// **Haymarket**, July 1837, with Mrs. Nisbett as Duke Philip, William Farren as Putzi, J. T. Haines as Montero, Robert Strickland as Ereté, Mr. Collins as Moreau, Miss Taylor as Aloyse, Mrs. Julia Glover as Mme. Ramylye, Miss E. Honner as Lisette/ Scenery by George Morris/ Music by T. German Reed.

YOUNG LAD FROM THE COUNTRY, A// F 1a// John Oxenford// **Drury Lane**, Nov. 1864, with Mr. Fitzjames as Parkinson, G. F. Neville as Podmore, George Spencer as Jones, Garston Belmore as Dobbs, Rose Leclercq as Lucy, Helen Howard as Jemima.

YOUNG MAN IN GREEN, THE; OR, THE VOL-UNTEER REVIEW// F// T. J. Williams// **Lyceum**, Feb. 1869.

YOUNG MAN OF THE PERIOD, THE// F// J. T. Douglass// **Standard**, July 1869.

YOUNG MR. YARDE// F 3a// Harold Ellis & Paul Rubens// **Royalty**, Nov. 1898.

YOUNG MRS. WINTHROP// C 4a// Bronson Howard// **Marylebone**, Sept. 1882, with Duncan Campbell, George Delaforce, Mrs. Brunton, Jennie Gwynne/ **Court**, Nov. 1884, with H. B. Conway, Arthur Cecil, Marion Terry, Lydia Foote, Mrs. John Wood.

YOUNG MOTHER, THE// C 1a// Charles Selby// **Haymarket**, Feb. 1859, with J. B. Buckstone, William Farren.

YOUNG PRETENDER, A// C 3a// Barton White// **Opera Comique**, Dec. 1891.

YOUNG QUAKER, THE// C// John O'Keefe// **Haymarket**, Nov. 1850, with Mr. Rogers as Old Sadboy, Mr. Lambert as Chronicle, Benjamin Webster as Young Sadboy, John Parselle as Capt. Ambush, Charles Selby as Shadrach, Henry Bedford as Spatterdash, J. B. Buckstone as Clod, Priscilla Horton as Araminta, Miss Reynolds as Dinah, Mrs. Young as Mrs. Millefleur, Miss E. Woulds as Judith, Mrs. Fitzwilliam as Pink/ Scenery by George Morris/ Machines by F. Neselton.

YOUNG RECRUIT, THE// n.a.// **Pavilion**, Nov. 1860.

YOUNG SCAMP, THE; OR, MY GRAND-MOTHER'S PET// C 1a// Edward Stirling// **Princess's**, Mar. 1844, with Mr. Fitzjames as Arthur, Mr. Granby as Gen. Beauvoir, Mrs. Keeley as Joseph, Robert Keeley as Mildew, Mme. Sala as Mrs. Manly, Miss Noel as Mrs. Swansdown, Miss E. Honner as Eliza.

YOUNG SCULPTOR, THE// D// Henry Mayhew// **St. James's**, Feb. 1839, with Mrs. Hooper as Juan, Jane Mordaunt as Henrice, Mr. Hooper as Michaelangelo, Alfred Wigan as Marquis Appiani, F. Carlton as Beppo, E. Pitt as Roderigo, Mr. Canning as Guido, Miss Stanley as Leonora, Miss Laylor as Anna.

YOUNG WIDOW, THE// F 1a// J. T. Rodwell// **Sad. Wells**, June 1837, with C. H. Pitt as Mandeville, Mr. Conquest as Splash, Lavinia Melville as Aurelia, Mrs. Harris as Lucy; July 1845, with Mr. Morton as Mandeville, S. Buckingham as Splash, Miss Cooper as Aurelia, Miss Lebatt as Lucy/ **Victoria**, Nov. 1837, with Benjamin Wrench as Splash, Edward Hooper as Mandeville, Mrs. Hooper as Aurielia, Mrs. Frank Matthews as Lucy/ **St. James's**, Jan. 1868, with Mr. Stretton as Mandeville, Thomas Bridgeford as Splash, Ada Cavendish as Amelia, Kate Kearney as Lucy.

YOUNG WIFE, A// C 4a// A. Lubimoff// **Vaudeville**, July 1884.

YOUNG WIVES AND OLD HUSBANDS// C 3a// Richard Harris// **Opera Comique**, Dec. 1876.

YOUNGER SON, THE// C 4a// R. S. Sievier// **Gaiety**, June 1893.

YOUR HEAD'S IN PERIL// F// Charles Webb// **Sad. Wells**, Feb. 1851, with Mr. Williams as Mofph, A. Younge as Mulhl, William Hoskins as Tipper, Mrs. Archbold as Mme. Mulph, Eliza Travers as Bertha, Lucy Rafter as Baroness Doubelhoff.

YOUR LIFE'S IN DANGER// F 1a// J. Maddison Morton// **Haymarket**, Dec. 1848, with Robert Keeley as Strong, Mr. Tilbury as Schoonenberg, Mr. Rogers as Krakwitz, Mrs. W. Clifford as Mme. Schoonenberg, Miss Reynolds as Countess Landsorff, Mrs. Humby as Jenny/ **Sad. Wells**, Apr. 1857, with Charles Fenton as Schpoonenburg, Mr. Lingham as Krakwitz, Robert Keeley as Strong, Miss Jackson as Countess, Miss Weston as Jenny, Mrs. Weston as Mme. Schpoonenburg/ **Princess's**, Mar. 1870, with John Vollaire as Schpoonenberg, Dan Leeson as Krakwitz, Edmund Coles as Strong, Emma Barnett as Countess Landsdorf, Mrs. Caulfield as Mme. Schpoonenberg, Miss Lennox Grey as Jenny.

YOUR VOTE AND INTEREST// F// Alfred Maltby// **Court**, Feb. 1874.

YOUR WIFE// F 3a// Adap. by J. H. McCarthy fr F, Prète moi ta Femme// **St. James's**, June 1890, with Arthur Bourchier as Daryl, Ernest Lawford as Verity, Mr. Everill as Crabbe, H. De Lange as Pappenberg, Edith Chester as Amy, Annie Irish as Lucy, Adrienne Dairoilles as Josephine/ Scenery by P. W. Goatcher.

YOU'RE ANOTHER// C// L. S. Buckingham// **Drury Lane**, Oct. 1860, with Mr. Tilbury as Codger, C. J. Mathews as Meddler, Robert Roxby as Twitter, Miss H. Howard as Clara, Mrs. Dowton as Sally.

YOURS TILL DEATH// D 4a// Mortimer Murdock// **Pavilion**, Nov. 1878.

YOUTH// D 8a// Paul Meritt & Augustus Harris// **Drury Lane**, June 1881, with John Ryder as Darlington, Augustus Harris as Frank, Arthur Matthison as Col. Dalton, W. H. Vernon as Maj. Reckley, H. Kelcey as Capt. Loverton, F. Charles as Capt. Lavender, Caroline Hill as Spratley, Harry Jackson as O'Pheysey, Harry Nicholls as Gardham, Louise Willes as Mrs. Walsingham, Mrs. Billington as Mrs. Darlington, Marie Litton as Eve, Maude de Vere as Kitty, Helen Cresswell as Alice, Miss Macnamara as Miss Jones, Amy Coleridge as Bessie.

YOUTH, LOVE, AND FOLLY// F 1a// William Dimond// **Sad. Wells**, Sept. 1844, with T. H. Higgie as Florimond, Mr. Morton as de Linval, A. Younge as Baron de Briancourt, Mr. Coreno as Antoine, Miss Lebatt as Arinette, Miss Huddart as Clotilda, Georgiana Lebatt as Bona/ **Drury Lane**, Mar. 1855.

YOUTH WHO NEVER SAW A WOMAN, THE// F 1a// n.a.// **Grecian**, Sept. 1868, with Samuel Perfitt as Philippe, Henry Grant as Anselme, Mary A. Victor as Lubin, Rose Belmore as Eliza, Mrs. Atkinson as Gertrude.

YOUTHFUL QUEEN, THE (also subt. Christine of Sweden)// C// Charles Shannon// **Haymarket**, June 1837, with Robert Strickland as Oxensteirn, Frederick Vining as Bury, John Webster as Steinberg, Miss Taylor as Queen Christine, Miss E. Phillips as Emma; Sept. 1839, with Robert Strickland as Count Oxensteirn, Mr. Cooper as Frederick, Walter Lacy as Steinberg, Ellen Tree as Christine, Miss Travers as Emma/ **Sad. Wells**, July 1837, with C. H. Pitt as Bury, John Pritchard as Steinberg, Mr. Griffiths as Count Oxensteirn, Miss E. Melville as Queen Christina, Miss Young as Emma/ **Drury Lane**, June 1838, with F. Cooke as Count Oxensteirn, Mr. Cooper as Bury, J. S. Balls as Steinberg, Mrs. Ternan as Christine, Miss Fitzwalter as Emma/ **Cov. Garden**, May 1840, with Frank Matthews as Count D'Oxensteirn, James Vining as Bury, C. J. Mathews as Steinberg, Ellen Tree as Christine, Miss Lee as Emma/ **Olympic**, May 1842, with Mr. Brookes as Count Oxensteirn, Mr. Halford as Capt. De Bory, Mr. Fitzjames as Chev. Steinberg, Miss Mitchell as Queen Chrstine, Miss Arden as Emma.

YULE LOG, THE// F 1a// Benjamin Webster Jr.// **Adelphi**, Feb. 1873.

*

ZANA; OR, THE PRIDE OF THE ALHAMBRA// D 3a// n.a.// **Britannia**, Sept. 1870.

ZANGA// D// n.a.// **Victoria**, Aug. 1877.

ZARAH// D// George Soane// **Sad. Wells**, June 1838, with Dibdin Pitt as Sir Hugh, John Webster as Ormiston, J. W. Collier as Pedlar, Mr. Hitchinson as Launce, Mr. Harwood as Showman, Mr. Phillips as Mug, Mr. Wilkins as Jack, C. J. Smith as Maugraby, Mr. Dry as Zamet, Mrs. J. F. Saville as Amy, Miss Pitt as Peggy, Miss Norman as Lucy, Mrs. Cooke as Zilpah, Mrs. Harwood as Marathon, Mrs. Robert Honner as Zarah.

ZAZA// Play 5a// Adap. by David Belasco fr F of Pierre Barton & Charles Simon// **Garrick**, Apr. 1900.

ZELMA; OR, AN INDIAN'S LOVE// D 1a// Edgar Newbound// **Britannia**, Dec. 1876.

ZEPHYR// C 4a// Mrs. Bernard Wishaw// **Avenue**, Mar. 1891.

ZILLAH// D 5a// J. Palgrave Simpson & Claude Templar// **Lyceum**, Aug. 1879, with Genevieve Ward, J. H. Barnes, Johnston Forbes Robertson.

ZILLAH; A TALE OF WASHINGTON// D// John Courtney// **Victoria**, Aug. 1848, with E. Edwards as Gen. Washington, John Bradshaw as Rugsdale, Mr. Henderson as Lt. Lethridge, Mr. Hitchinson as Capt. Carson, F. H. Henry as Capt. Clavers, Mr. Hawkins as Sly, Miss

Richardson as Zillah, Mrs. George Lee as Caroline, Miss Young as Rose, Miss Sharpe as Miami, Miss Edgar as Fleetanella/ Music by Mr. Burroughcliffe/ Prod. by T. H. Higgie.

ZOHRAB THE HOSTAGE; OR, THE FORTRESS OF MEZANDERAN// D// n.a.// **Cov. Garden,** Feb. 1837, with John Pritchard as Mohamed, George Bennett as Zaul Khan, Mr. Collins as Zohrab, John Webster as Sadek, Benjamin Webster as Bacha-Humpho, Miss Turpin as Amina, Eliza Vincent as Mariam, Mme. Vedy as Ismena.

INDEX OF PLAYWRIGHTS, ADAPTORS, AND TRANSLATORS

ABOUT THE COMPILER

DONALD MULLIN is Professor of Drama in the Department of Drama, University of Guelph, Ontario, Canada. His books include *The Development of the Playhouse: Theatre Architecture from the Renaissance to the Present*, and *Victorian Actors and Actresses in Review*, and he has contributed articles to *Theatre Notebook*, *Theatre Survey*, and *Theatre Journal*.